explotio

Think
Spring

tulip

pansey

The Marriage
and
Family Experience

F I F T H   E D I T I O N

The Marriage
and
Family Experience

F I F T H   E D I T I O N

Bryan Strong
UNIVERSITY OF CALIFORNIA, SANTA CRUZ

Christine DeVault

West Publishing Company
ST. PAUL   ◆   NEW YORK   ◆   LOS ANGELES   ◆   SAN FRANCISCO

Copyediting:	Judith Lary, Naples Editorial Service
Composition:	Parkwood Composition
Artwork:	John and Jean Foster (graphic illustrations)
	Cyndie Clark-Huegel, Darwin and Valley Hennings (two-and four-color anatomical illustrations)
	Ben Turner Graphics (graphic illustrations)
Cover and Interior Design:	K. M. Weber
Cover Quilt:	*To Live in Peace and Liberty*, by Karin Schoch, Stein am Rhein, Switzerland

Quiltmaker's Statement: We all, regardless of origin, color, or descent, should try with all our might, our spirit, and our heart to live together in peace and to take care of our earth, now and in the future. For the earth does not belong to the people, but the people belong to the earth. This is my vision or dream of the future, and I hope this dream will become a reality and a circle will be closed.

A STUDENT STUDY GUIDE

A study guide has been developed to assist students in mastering the concepts presented in this text. It reinforces chapter material presenting it in a concise format with review questions. An examination copy is available to instructors by contacting West Publishing Company. Students can purchase the study guide from the local bookstore under the title *Study Guide to Accompany The Marriage and Family Experience, Fifth Edition*, prepared by Suzanne Cobb Platt and Linda Green, Normandale Community College.

Library of Congress Cataloging-in-Publication Data

Strong, Bryan.
    The marriage and family experience / Bryan Strong, Christine DeVault. — 5th ed.
    p. cm.
Includes bibliographical references and index
ISBN 0-314-88136-0(hard)
 1. Marriage. 2. Family. I. DeVault, Christine. II. Title.
HQ734.S9738 1992
306.8—dc20   91-2821
                CIP ∞

Acknowledgements and Photo Credits appear following the index.

This book is dedicated to the memory
of our dear friend Gilbert Moreno
who brought music and laughter and
love into so many lives.

May you live every day of your life.
Jonathan Swift
(1667–1745)

Contents
in Brief

Contents

Preface

A S WE REVIEWED *THE MARRIAGE AND FAMILY EXPERIENCE* FOR THE FIFTH EDITION, we were struck by the multiplicity of changes American marriages and families have undergone since we first published our textbook in the 1970s: the rise of single-parent families; dual-worker families and stepfamilies; the emergence of family violence as an issue; the increasing recognition of ethnic diversity; concern over poverty and families; and heightened awareness of family/workplace conflicts, to name but a few. We have chronicled these changes in our various editions, hoping that students might better understand their lives and relationships as a result.

While there is change around us, what does not change is the authors' enduring belief that our families, whatever their form, are the crucibles in which our humanity is born, nurtured and fulfilled. They are what make us human, and they need to be cherished, honored, and supported. This belief provides the underlying theme of our textbook.

We have attempted to present the study of marriage and the family in a manner that enlarges both our personal and intellectual understanding. A functional approach does not exclude an academic approach; nor does an academic approach exclude a functional one. We have tried, in fact, to combine the virtues of both. Ideas allow us to see beyond our own limited experience, and our personal experience breathes life into ideas. We believe that good scholarship encourages individual understanding and that personal exploration encourages intellectual growth. *The Marriage and Family Experience* reflects a singular attempt to unify functionally-oriented and academically-oriented approaches into a single textbook.

We have continued our interdisciplinary approach, since the perspective of a single discipline, such as sociology or psychology, creates only a partial picture of marriage and the family. We have incorporated work from not only sociology and psychology, but also history, economics, communication, folklore, literature, and ethnic studies. To limit ourselves to but one branch of knowledge would leave us much like the blind men who tried to describe the nature of the elephant: each mistook a part for the whole and, while they argued among themselves, the elephant walked away.

❖ FEATURES

We have meticulously revised our textbook, line by line, to reflect the most current research available. The most significant changes in this edition include:

◆ Incorporation of America's diverse family systems—both in terms of structure and ethnicity—as an organizing principle throughout the textbook.

◆ Significant expansion of Chapter 12, "The Family, Work, and Economics," to reflect economic and workplace issues, such as poverty and the family and family/workplace conflicts, that are increasingly important for contemporary families.

◆ A new chapter on the sociological and psychological aspects of health, Chapter 13, "Health and the Family." It includes the health care crisis, health and marital status, stress and the family, elder care, care of the chronically ill, and death and dying.

◆ New or expanded topics include:

–African-American, Latino, Asian-American, and Native American families
–poverty and the family
–dispelling nuclear family stereotypes
–rediscovering the extended family
–new social science of love
–gender roles and ethnicity
–workplace/family links
–gender theory
–family policy
–models of family violence
–family traditions and rituals
–AIDS and families
–abortion controversy
–raising children to be prejudice free

In researching this edition, we used computerized library and reference services to supplement our traditional bibliographic research. By utilizing Melvyl, the University of California's on-line catalog (which accesses over 10 million books and periodicals), MEDLINE (the on-line version of *Index Medicus*), and PsycLit and SocioFile CD-ROM databases, we were able to compile extensive bibliographies of the latest and most important research in marriage and the family. As a result, the fifth edition of *The Marriage and Family Experience* continues to be one of the most comprehensively-researched textbooks in the field.

❖ PEDAGOGY

Over the years we have developed a number of pedagogical features to engage students in exploring the chapters from both an intellectual and a personal perspective. Each chapter includes the following learning tools:

Previews

"Previews" open each chapter with self-quizzes that challenge students' preconceptions about marriage and the family.

Chapter Outline

Chapter outlines at the beginning of each chapter facilitate student comprehension.

Understanding Yourself

"Understanding Yourself" uses research topics and methods as starting points for students to examine their own lives. We have found that integrating research, methodology, and self-examination brings to life what could be burdensome abstractions devoid of personal meaning. In Chapter 4, for example, we explore the concept of androgyny by having students complete a gender role inventory patterned after Bem's Sex Role Inventory. In Chapter 6, we use a computer dating questionnaire to personalize the concept of homogamy in mate selection. In Chapter 10, we ask students to examine the concept of marital satisfaction by completing Graham Spanier's Dyadic Adjustment Scale, one of the most widely used research instruments in the field.

Perspectives

"Perspectives" focus on high-interest topics, such as sexual addiction, family stereotypes, rearing children to be prejudice free, and the relationship between love and sexuality.

Reflections

"Reflections" are found within the running text. They ask students to reflect on how the ideas discussed in the previous section may provide insights into their own lives, families, and relationships. Students are asked, for example, to look at the pluses and minuses of a relationship to illustrate exchange theory, to examine how their own families meet their intimacy needs, and to think about the kinds of rituals their families practice.

Chapter Summary

At the end of each chapter, the main ideas are summarized to assist students in reviewing the chapter material. Key terms are italicized.

Suggested Readings

At the end of each chapter, an annotated suggested readings list provides material of interest or for further research. A suggested film section lists classic and contemporary films that may provoke interest or controversy available on video.

Margin Quotes

Quotes in the margins offer unusual, thoughtful, humorous, or provocative insights. A single quotation may spark an intense class discussion or lead a person to reexamine long-held beliefs. Instructors and students alike have remarked that the margin quotes are almost like having a second book.

Readings

Readings at the end of each chapter offer different perspectives on the material covered within the body of the chapter. They include essays, articles, and excerpts from books, journals, magazines, and newspapers. These readings were carefully chosen to present ideas, information, and points of view at a level appropriate for most undergraduate students. They allow professors to dispense with supplemental readings and provide students with a change of pace. Many students view the readings as their reward at the end of the chapter. About half of the readings are new to the fifth edition.

Glossary

A glossary of key terms is included at the back of the textbook to assist students in their understanding and comprehension. Most of the glossary terms appear in bold face in the text and in italics in chapter summaries.

Resource Center

A resource center at the end of the textbook contains a self-help directory and practical information on finances and budgeting, personal health, birth control, sexually transmitted diseases and other topics relating to individual and family well-being. In addition, it contains study guides for marriage and family studies, and African-American, Latino, Asian-American, Native American, and ethnic studies to assist students in their research.

Study Guide

A revised study guide prepared by Suzanne Cobb Platt and Linda Green, both of Normandale Community College, contains chapter goals, review and study questions, key terms, values-clarification exercises, and detailed chapter outlines to expand student learning.

❖ SUPPLEMENTAL PACKAGE

Instructor's Manual

Christine DeVault and Bryan Strong have written an entirely new instructor's manual, including a new test bank (with page references), chapter summaries, key terms and ideas, discussion questions and activities, and suggestions for guest lecturers, panels, films, and videos. Appendices include tables of demographic data on aspects of American family life, including African-American and Latino families.

Video Library

Professionally produced videos on various marriage and family subjects are available to qualified adopters.

Transparencies

Transparency masters and acetates, some from the text and some newly-created, enhance the presentation of lectures.

Computerized Text Bank

WESTEST 2.0 computerized test bank is available for IBM PCs, IBM compatibles, and Macintosh computers.

❖ ACKNOWLEDGEMENTS

We would like to acknowledge the assistance of many people in writing this new edition. In doing our research, we were kindly assisted by the reference staff of the

Dean McHenry Library at the University of California, Santa Cruz. We would like to thank reference librarians Alan Ritch, Deborah Murphy, Judy Steen, Paul Machlis, and Jaquelyn Maria for their assistance in compiling bibliographies, answering reference questions, verifying citations, obtaining books and journals through interlibrary loan, and assisting us in the use of on-line and CD-ROM bibliographic systems. Jeanie Jordan at Government Documents assisted us in finding census data and researching government publications on Silver Platter's GPO database. We are grateful to Lars Johanson of the U.S. Bureau of the Census for pre-releasing census data about marriages and family. He was most gracious and helpful.

We would like to thank Professor Stephen Ciafullo for inviting the senior author to present the keynote address at Family Forum VI, sponsored by Central Missouri State University at Warrensburg, Missouri. Professor Ciafullo, Professor Gregory Kennedy, and their families extended to us the greatest hospitality and warmth.

Ruth Gunn Mota, Director of Education, Santa Cruz AIDS Project, provided valuable information about HIV and AIDS. She, the SCAP staff, and a number of people with AIDS in our community are deeply committed to increasing AIDS awareness among students and the community, we applaud their work.

At West Publishing Company, we would like to thank Carole Grumney, our editor for the last ten years, who has been the soul of patience, as always. We also thank Carole Balach in West's production department, with whom we have been in almost daily contact for months, for her dedication and steadfast optimism. Charlotte Davis was also gracious and cheerful when we called. Thanks also to Kristen Weber—our favorite designer—who has designed the last three editions of the book. We are indebted to Judy Lary, our meticulous copyeditor, who labored long and hard and didn't miss a missing comma.

Our friend and colleague Art Aron, one of the leading researchers in the social psychology of love, assisted us in revising our love chapter. Terrence Crowley, professor of library science at San Jose State University, continues to assist us in difficult research questions. Fran Bussard, formerly of Chico State University, remains a rich source of insight into personal relationships and communication, not to mention homemade fettucine and peach pie.

We also wish to thank Zoe Sodja, Cheryl VanDeVeer, Judy Burton, Joan Tannheimer, Valerie Wells, and Rebekah Levy for their time and cheerful help inputting the text.

Finally, the authors thank their children—Gabe, Willy, Maria, and Kristin—who over the years have provided hands-on experience in family studies and who continue to challenge and delight as they move us through the stages of the family life cycle. And once again we would like to thank each other for the support, good humor (the occasional growl notwithstanding), and love given freely in the daily living of life.

❖ REVIEWERS

Each edition has benefited from the insightful comments and thoughtful suggestions of our many reviewers. They have been exceptionally aware of the dual requirements of a good textbook—academic integrity and student interest—and have helped us maintain our commitment to both. We would like to thank Patt Takeuchi for her insights on Asian-American families, notably Japanese-American families. The professors and consultants who assisted us in this edition are listed below in alphabetical order. We are greatly indebted to them all. Special thanks to Richard Gelles who painstakingly reviewed our family violence chapter.

Rebecca Adams
Purdue University

Lois Bryant
University of Missouri, Columbia

Sandra Caron
University of Oregon

Ann Engin
University of South Dakota

Richard Gelles
University of Rhode Island

Jan Hare
University of Maine

Ana Matiella
ETR Associates

Violet Moore
Western Kentucky University

◆ Bryan Strong

◆ Christine DeVault

September, 1991
Felton, California

About the Authors

Bryan Strong and Christine DeVault are married to each other and have coauthored numerous books and articles together. Mr. Strong received his doctorate from Stanford University and teaches at the University of California—Santa Cruz. His fields of expertise include marriage and the family, human sexuality, and American social history. Ms. DeVault, an educational writer and consultant in family life education, received her degree in sociology from the University of California—Berkeley. A fluent Spanish speaker, she has taught English as a second language in addition to sociology and history. The authors have four children; the family, together with their large dog, two cats, and a canary, live in Felton, California.

PART ONE

Perspectives

The Meaning of Marriage and the Family

P R E V I E W

To gain a sense of what you already know about the material covered in this chapter, answer "true" or "false" to the statements below. You will find the answers on page 21.

1. The majority of American families are traditional nuclear families in which the husband works and the wife stays at home caring for the children. True or false?
2. The traditional nuclear family is the healthiest form of the family. True or false?
3. Because of technological advances, the family is no longer the sole agent of reproduction. True or false?
4. All cultures traditionally divide at least some work into male and female work. True or false?
5. As a result of industrialization, the family is no longer an important productive unit. True or false?
6. If women were paid for their household and homemaking responsibilities, they would make over $50,000 a year. True or false?
7. The majority of cultures throughout the world prefer polygyny (the practice of having several wives). True or false?
8. Never-married individuals tend to live longer than married persons. True or false?
9. Intimacy is a primary human need. True or false?
10. Homemakers produce valuable services that are often overlooked because women are not paid for such work. True or false?

Marriage is a great institution, but I'm not ready for an institution yet.

Mae West

Toward the end of the eighteenth century, three sportsmen hunting in the woods of Caune, France, were startled by the sight of a young boy gathering roots and acorns. The boy hunched over the ground like a wild animal, naked but for a tattered shirt. As soon as the boy sighted the hunters, he fled and attempted to climb a tree to hide. The hunters quickly captured him and brought him to a neighboring village. He remained in the village a week and then escaped. A few months later he sought refuge in a peasant's dwelling; he was retained and later was taken to Paris.

The boy, who apparently had been abandoned in the woods at an early age, became known as "the Young Savage of Aveyron." He had lived alone from the time he was abandoned, sleeping in the fields and foraging for food. Without human contact, his mental development was little more than that of a one-year-old child. A contemporary (quoted in Itard, 1801 [1972]) described the boy as:

incapable of attention . . . and consequently of all the operations of the mind which depended upon it; destitute of memory, of judgment, even of a disposition to imitation; and so bounded were his ideas, even those which related to his immediate wants, that he could not even open a door, nor get on a chair to obtain the food which was put out of the reach of his hand; in short, destitute of every means of communication . . . his pleasure, and agreeable sensation of the organs of taste, his intelligence, a susceptibility of producing incoherent ideas, connected with his physical wants; in a word, his whole existence was a life purely animal.

When the boy, now named Victor, was brought to Paris, he was put under the tutelage of a young physician named Jean Itard (Malson, 1972). Itard painstakingly undertook to educate the boy in human speech. He taught him to walk and sit, groom himself, open doors, and use instruments and tools. Over the years, he taught the boy how to think conceptually and to express his simplest needs in writing.

The story of Victor and Itard is a remainder of what we tend to take for granted: that the family is the nursery of our humanity. The traits that make us human are not given to us full-blown; rather, they exist potentially in us and are first developed within the family or its surrogate. When Itard took in Victor, he began to undertake the task of socialization, of making him human, one of the basic tasks of the family. If it were not for families that socialize and educate us, we, too, would be like the wild boy of Aveyron. We would not know how to speak, how to walk, how to interact with others, how to love.

❖ CONTEMPORARY AMERICAN MARRIAGES AND FAMILIES

Definitions and Incidences

Before we begin examining marriages and families in any detail, it is important to define some of the terms we will be using. Some are so common that they hardly need definition. But as you will see, some terms, such as *family,* are more complex than we usually believe.

COHABITATION. **Cohabitation** technically refers to individuals sharing living arrangements in an intimate relationship, whether these individuals are married or unmarried. Most commonly, however, it refers to "living together" relationships in which unmarried individuals share living quarters and are sexually involved. A cohabiting relationship may be similar to marriage in many of its functions and roles, but it does not have equivalent legal sanctions or rights. In 1990, there were 2.9 million heterosexual couples living together (there were also 1.5 million gay or lesbian couples living together in 1987.) (U.S. Bureau of the Census, 1988 and 1991). About a third of the heterosexual couples have children living with them. Over ninety thousand gay and lesbian couples have children living with them.

MARRIAGE. **Marriage** is a union between a man and a woman: the two individuals perform a public ritual (which means that their union is socially recognized), they are united sexually, and they cooperate in economic matters. The union is assumed to be more or less permanent. If the married couple has children, the children will have certain legal rights. Although gay and lesbian couples may consider themselves married, their marriages are not recognized legally. Recently, San Francisco joined several other critics in recognizing the significance of cohabiting heterosexual relationships and gay and lesbian relationships in its 1991 "domestic partners act."

The incidence of marriage differs according to race and ethnicity (U.S. Bureau of the Census, 1990). In 1988, 111.3 million Americans over eighteen years of age were married. This represents 62.7 percent of the adult population. An additional 13.5 million (7 percent) were widowed. Among whites, 64.6 percent were married and 7.7 percent were widowed. Among African Americans, 46.7 percent were married and 9 percent were widowed. Among Latinos, 61.5 percent were married and 4.3 percent were widowed. In 1980, the latest date for which figures are available, 85.1 percent of Asian Americans, 75.4 percent of Pacific Islanders, and 71.9 percent of native Americans were married (U.S. Bureau of the Census, 1990).

SEPARATION AND DIVORCE. **Separation** refers to the *physical* separation of two married people. It may or may not lead to divorce. Many more people separate than divorce. **Divorce** is the legal dissolution of a marriage. Over the last twenty years, divorce has changed the face of marriage and the family in America. The divorce rate is two to three times what it was for our parents and grandparents. About half of all those who currently marry divorce within seven years. Among all Americans, 13.9 million (8.2 percent) are divorced. Among African-Americans, 10 percent are divorced; among Latinos, 7.4 percent are divorced.

Divorce has become so widespread that many scholars are beginning to view it as part of the normal life course of American marriages (Raschke, 1987). The high divorce rate does not indicate that Americans devalue marriage, however. Paradoxically, Americans divorce because they value marriage so highly: If a marriage does not meet their standards, they divorce to marry again. They hope that their second marriages will fulfill the expectations that their first marriages failed to meet (Furstenberg and Spanier, 1987).

Contemporary divorce patterns create three common experiences for American marriages and families: single-parent families, remarriage, and stepfamilies. Because of their widespread incidence, these variations are becoming part of our normal marriage and family patterns. They no longer represent deviations or failures as they did for our parents or grandparents; instead they represent part of the normal life course for contemporary Americans. The majority of young Americans will probably have some experience of single-parent families, remarriage, or stepfamilies as either children or adults.

REMARRIAGE. Half of all recent marriages are remarriages for at least one partner (Bumpass, Sweet, and Martin, 1990). Although remarriages are increasing at a faster rate than first marriages, remarriage rates are dramatically affected by race and ethnicity. Remarriage rates for African-Americans have been dropping disproportionately during the last twenty years; African-Americans remarry at about one-quarter the rate of whites. Latinos remarry at about half the rate of Anglos.

If anyone means to deliberate successfully about anything, there is one thing he must do from the outset. He must know what it is he is deliberating about; otherwise he is bound to go utterly astray. Now most people fail to realize that they don't know what this or that really is; consequently when they start discussing something, they dispense with any agreed definition, assuming that they know the thing; then later on they naturally find, to their cost, that they agree neither with each other or with themselves.

Plato, Phaedrus

As to marriage or celibacy, let a man take which course he will, he will be sure to repent it.

Socrates (4th century B.C.)

Those who remarry are older, have more experience in both life and work, and have different expectations than those who marry for the first time. About one-third of all children are born to remarried families. Ironically, despite the hopes and experience of those who remarry, their divorce rate is about the same as for those who marry for the first time. Remarriage can also create a stepfamily. When remarriages include children, a person may become not only a husband or wife but also a stepfather or stepmother.

The family is a society limited in numbers, but nevertheless a true society, anterior to every state or nation, with rights and duties of its own, wholly independent of the commonwealth.

Pope Leo XIII (1810–1903)

FAMILY. In Western culture, the **family** traditionally has been defined as a married couple or group of adult kin with children who cooperate and divide labor along gender lines, rear children, and share a common dwelling place. During the twentieth century, Americans have tended to identify the nuclear family as *the* family. But the older (and wider) definition of family also includes other kin, especially in-laws, grandparents, aunts and uncles, and cousins. To distinguish it from the nuclear family, this wider family is known as the extended family.

Until recently, American researchers have focused on the traditional nuclear family, composed of a married couple and their biological children; in this family, the husband is employed outside the home while the wife remains at home performing housework and child-care tasks. The emphasis on the traditional nuclear family as *the* American family has ignored a simple reality: The traditional nuclear family is a minority family form. Today, fewer than 13 percent of contemporary American families fit this model! As such, there is no typical American family. Instead, we have

The traditional nuclear family is a powerful cultural symbol that fails to reflect the diversity of family forms in contemporary America. As a reflection of reality, the traditonal nuclear family is a minority family in America.

single-parent families, stepfamilies, cohabiting families, dual-earner families, families without children, gay and lesbian families, and so on. The majority of Americans are members of one of these other family forms, not the traditional nuclear family.

The most widespread family forms in contemporary America are intact two-parent families, stepfamilies, and single-parent families. By the year 2000 there will be more stepfamilies than any other family form (Pill, 1990). Since 1970, single-parent families have been increasing at four to five times the rate of two-parent families. In 1989, there were 51.8 million two-parent families (including both intact families and stepfamilies) with children under eighteen years. Intact two-parent families represent 47 percent of all families. In 1989, there were 6 million single-parent families. Of our families, 58.1 percent are intact, two-parent families, 15.8 percent are stepfamilies, 21 percent are mother/child families, 2.5 percent are father/child families, and 2.7 percent are other family forms, such as cohabiting or gay or lesbian families (Saluter, 1989).

To include these diverse forms, the definition of family needs to be revised. A more contemporary definition defines the family as one or more adults related by blood, marriage, or affiliation who cooperate economically, who may share a common dwelling place, and who *may* rear children. Such a definition more accurately reflects the diversity of contemporary American families.

❖ FORMS AND FUNCTIONS OF THE FAMILY

Forms of Marriage and Family

NUCLEAR AND EXTENDED FAMILIES. Society "created" the family to undertake the task of making us human. According to some anthropologists, the **nuclear family,** consisting of the father/mother/child triad, is universal, either in its basic form or as the building block for other family forms (Murdock, 1967). Other anthropologists disagree that the father is necessary, arguing that the basic family unit is the mother and child dyad (Collier, Rosaldo, and Yanagisako, 1982). The use of artificial insemi-nation and new reproductive technologies, as well as the rise of single-parent families headed by women, are cited in support of the mother/child dyad.

But whatever its most basic form, the nuclear family is imbedded within a larger family, the **extended family,** which consists not only of the married couple and their children but also of other relatives, especially in-laws, grandparents, aunts and uncles, and cousins. In the majority of non-European countries, the extended family is often regarded as the basic family unit (Murdock, 1967). For many Americans, especially African-Americans, Latinos, and Asian-Americans, the extended family takes on great importance.

MONOGAMY AND POLYGAMY. Within Western cultures, such as that in the United States, the preferred form of marriage is **monogamy,** in which there are only two spouses, the husband and wife. But monogamy is a minority preference among world cultures, practiced by only 24 percent of the known cultures (Murdock, 1967). The preferred marital arrangement is **polygamy,** the practice of having more than one wife or husband. One study of cultures throughout the world found that 75 percent of these cultures (representing, nevertheless, a minority of the world's population) preferred *polygyny,* the practice of having two or more wives, and 1 percent preferred *polyandry,* the practice of having two or more husbands (Murdock,

The traditional nuclear family of the 1940s and 1950s began to be replaced in the 1960s by more diverse family forms, such as single-parent families, stepfamilies and dual-worker families.

1967). Within polygamous societies, however, plural marriages are in the minority, primarily for simple economic reasons: they are a sign of status that relatively few people can afford. Although problems of jealousy may arise in plural marriages—the

FIGURE 1.1

A Model Genogram

This figure represents a sample genogram for a woman named Jenny, a college senior. She and her boyfriend Robert, a musician, are planning to marry, but their relationship is marked by conflict. As soon as one problem gets resolved (or ignored), another

seems to crop up. They go back and forth between wanting to marry or break up. The genogram indicates that Jenny's family relationships are marked by closeness and conflict. Her parents and grandparents tended to be noncommunicative; the only way they

could open up was through fighting. Their conflicts broke down barriers against intimacy. By contrast, Robert's family was communicative with little conflict. The style in his family was to be open; conflict was not used as a means of achieving intimacy.

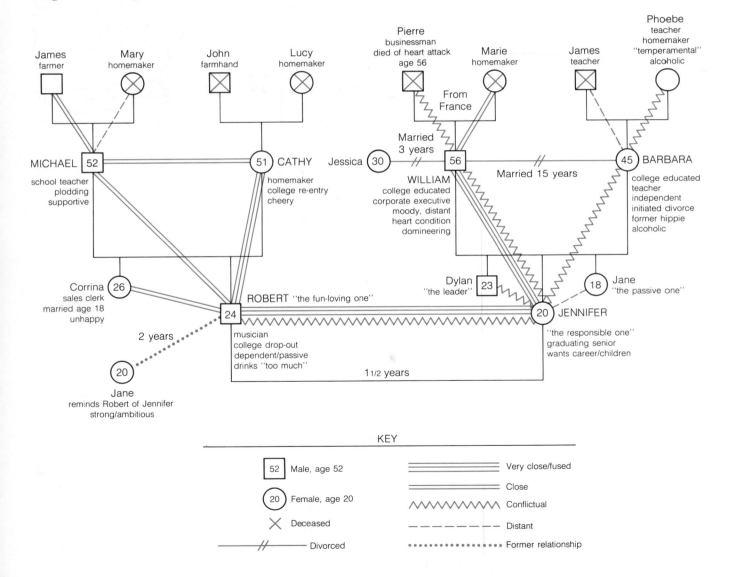

Mapping Family Relationships: The Genogram

While we can easily identify family structure in terms of parents, children, grandparents, aunts and uncles, and so on, it is more difficult to discern the emotional structure of families. These emotional structures are especially important, as our families are among the most important influences in our lives. Many of our patterns of interactions, deepest feelings, relationship expectations, and personal standards reflect our family of orientation.

In recent years, family therapists have been using a device called a *genogram* to look at family relationships. A genogram is a diagram of the emotional relationships of a family through several generations. It is something like a family tree of family interactions. If we can understand the ingrained patterns in our family relationships we can often understand the nature of our present relationships (Bahr, 1990).

If the marital relationships of our parents and grandparents are marked by conflict, for example, we may unconsciously model our own relationships after theirs. We may experience connection with others through conflict. If their relationships are marked by emotional distance, we may find ourselves distant in our "close" relationships. If their relationships, however, are characterized by warmth and sharing, we may choose similar relationships.

Using the genogram in Figure 1.1 as a model, draw a genogram of your own family relationships on a large sheet of paper. Use the symbols in the example to indicate relationships. Your genogram should include the following information about you, your parents, and your grandparents:

◆ Name and date of birth. If deceased, year and cause of death.
◆ Education and occupation.
◆ Siblings in each generation.
◆ Marital history, including years of marriage, divorces, years of singlehood (including single parenting), and date of remarriage.

Fula in Africa, for example, call the second wife "the jealous one"—there are usually built-in control mechanisms to ease the problem. The wives may be related, especially as sisters; if they are unrelated, they usually have separate dwellings. Women in these societies often prefer that there be several wives: plural wives are a sign of status and, more important, ease the workload of individual wives. This last fact is apparent even in our culture; it is not uncommon to hear overworked American homemakers exclaim, "I want a wife."

Although polygamy sounds strange or exotic, it may not really seem so strange if we look at American marital practices. Considering the high divorce rate in this country, monogamy may no longer be the best way of describing our marriage forms. Our marriage system might be called serial monogamy or modified polygamy, because one person may have several spouses over his or her lifetime. In our nation's past, African slaves tried unsuccessfully to continue their traditional polygamous practices when they first arrived in America; these attempts, however, were rigorously suppressed by their masters (Guttman, 1976). Mormons also practiced polygamy until the late nineteenth century. Even today, an estimated three thousand to ten thousand fundamentalist Mormons continue to practice polygamy despite its prohibition by the church. And one scholar suggests that housekeepers, usually women, perform many of the functions of junior wives for American families (Hochschild, 1989).

Family Functions

Whether it is the father/mother/child nuclear family, a married couple with no children, a single-parent family, a stepfamily, a dual-worker family, or a cohabiting family, the family generally performs four important functions. First, it provides a source of intimate relationships. Second, it acts as a unit of economic cooperation. Third, it may produce and socialize children. Fourth, it assigns status and social roles to individuals. Although these are the basic functions that families are "supposed" to fulfill, families do not necessary have to fulfill them all—as in families without children—nor do they always fulfill them well—as in abusive families.

INTIMATE RELATIONSHIPS. Intimacy is a primary human need. As the ancient philosopher Aristotle wrote, "Only an animal or a god can live alone." He appears to have been right. Human companionship strongly influences rates of cancer, tuberculosis, suicide, accidents, and mental illness. Studies consistently show that married couples and adults living with others are generally healthier and have a lower mortality rate than divorced, separated, and never-married individuals (Ross, Mirowsky, and Goldsteen, 1991). This holds true for both whites and African-Americans (Broman, 1988).

Marriage and the family furnish emotional security and support. This has probably been true from earliest times. The book of Ecclesiastes, written thousands of years ago, suggests the importance of companionship:

Two are better than one, because they have a good reward for their toil. For if they fall, one will lift up his fellow; but woe to him who is alone when he falls and has not another to lift him up. Again if two lie together, they are warm; but how can one be warm alone? And though a man might prevail against one, two will withstand him. A three-fold cord is not quickly broken.   Ecclesiastes 4:9–12

In our families we find our strongest bonds. These bonds can be forged from love, attachment, loyalty, or guilt. The need for intimate relationships, whether they are satisfactory or not, may hold unhappy marriages together indefinitely. Loneliness may be a terrible specter. Among the newly divorced, it may be one of the worst aspects of the marital breakup.

Since the nineteenth century, marriage and the family have become important as the source of companionship and intimacy. They have become a "haven in a heart-

The word "ordinary" in the dictionary . . . says "familiar; unexceptional; common." Given that set of definitions, it's one of the biggest words in the English language, since life, death, childbirth, love, hate, age, and sex are all familiar, unexceptional and common.

Mary Cantwell

Fidelity is part of every human relationship. It is the strain toward permanence and toward public commitment to permanence that is involved in any relationship beyond the most superficial. Fidelity is a longing for love that does not end.

Andrew Greeley

Marriage unites not only two individuals but also two families.

less world" (Lasch, 1978). As society has become more industrialized and bureaucratic, it is increasingly within the family that we expect to find intimacy and companionship. In the larger world around us, we are generally perceived in terms of our roles. A professor sees us primarily as a student; a used-car salesperson relates to us as a potential buyer; a politician views us as a voter. Only among our intimates are we seen on a personal level as David or Maria. Before marriage, our friends are our intimates. After marriage, our partner is expected to be the one with whom we are most intimate. With our partner we disclose ourselves most completely, share our hopes, rear our children, grow old.

The need for intimacy is so powerful that we may rely upon animals if our intimacy needs are not met by humans. Studies on the role of pets in human relationships suggest that the most prized aspects of pets, especially dogs and cats, is their attentiveness to their owners, their welcoming and greeting behaviors, and their role as confidants—qualities valued in our intimate relationships with humans as well. In fact, one study (Albert and Bulcroft, 1988) found that 87 percent of those who owned pets considered them "family members." One study found that 98 percent of dog owners spent time talking to their pets, 75 percent thought that their dogs were sensitive to their moods and feelings, and 28 percent even confided in their pets (Arehart-Treichel, 1982). Pets give children an opportunity to nurture, and provide a best friend, someone to love. For adults, especially men, they are an outlet for touching; they act as companions and as social catalysts. Dog owners are more likely to interact with strangers when they are with their dogs than when they are without them.

ECONOMIC COOPERATION. The family is also a unit of economic cooperation that traditionally divides its labor along gender lines, that is, between males and females (Ferree, 1991; Thompson and Walker, 1989; Voydanoff, 1987). Although the division of labor by gender is characteristic of virtually all cultures, the work males and females perform (apart from childbearing) varies from culture to culture. Among the Nambikwara in Africa, for example, the fathers take care of the babies and clean them when they soil themselves; the concubines of the chief prefer hunting over domestic activities. In American society, from the last century until recently, men were expected to work away from home while women remained at home caring for the children and house. There is no reason, however, why these roles cannot be reversed. Such tasks are assigned by culture, not biology. Only a woman's ability to give birth is biologically determined. And some cultures practice *couvade*, ritualized childbirth in which a male gives birth to the child's spirit while his partner gives physical birth; in some of these cultures, because the male gives birth to the spirit, his role is considered more important than the female's (Gregor, 1985).

Regardless of what activities men and women do, work traditionally has been divided into "man's work" and "woman's work." This makes the sexes interdependent, cementing their need for each other (Lévi-Strauss, 1956). In tribal societies, where the extended family is the basic producing unit, it is impossible for men and women to survive without each other. In contemporary America, however, interdependence between the sexes has greatly lessened. In earlier times, a man needed a wife to cook his food; today he can make his own dinner or eat out. A woman once needed a husband for economic support; today she can support herself (although most women have difficulty supporting children single-handedly). One result of reduced female dependence on males it that women who work are more likely to divorce than those who remain at home full-time (Spitze, 1991).

We commonly think of the family as a consuming unit, but it also continues to be an important producing unit, although its productive activities are less apparent than formerly. Modern families no longer raise much of their own food, weave their own cloth, or spin their own yarn. We usually do not view the family as a productive unit because of its relative unimportance in the money economy as a whole. The family, for example, pays no wages for its work, nor does it call its members employees. The husband does not get paid for building a shelf or attending to the children; the wife is not paid for fixing the leaky faucet or cooking. Although children contribute to the household economy by helping around the house, they generally are not paid for such things as cooking, cleaning their rooms, or watching their younger brothers or sisters (Coggle and Tasker, 1982; Gecas and Seff, 1991). Yet they are all engaged in productive labor (Zick and Bryant, 1990).

Recently, economists have begun to reexamine the family as a productive unit (Ferree, 1991). If men and women were compensated monetarily for the work done in their households, the total would be equal to the entire amount paid out in wages by every corporation in the United States. Unpaid household work by women in 1990 was worth well over $1 trillion; such work by men was worth $610 billion. Similarly, household assets—homes, cars, appliances, lawnmowers, tools, and so on—produce an annual return equal to the net profits of all U.S. corporations. The household as a productive unit is very much alive. During recessionary periods, for example, family members produce more goods—such as clothes or food—at home (Voydanoff, 1991). About 34 percent of the nation's families have a garden, and gardening is the fifth most popular hobby in America. Gardening is rarely seen as one of the family's productive activities because most families don't produce a cash crop, even though families produce over $16 billion worth of vegetables and fruits from their home gardens yearly (Adler et al., 1982).

As a service unit, the family is dominated by women. Because women's work at home is unpaid, the productive contributions of homemakers have been overlooked (Ciancanelli and Berch, 1987; Walker, 1991). Yet women's household work is equal to about 44 percent of the gross national product (GNP), and the value of such work is double the reported earnings of women. Burns (1972) wrote:

> The invisible household economy might also be called the matriarchal economy, because it is dominated by women. They perform most of the labor, make most of the household decisions, and are employed as managers for the labor and assets of the household. More than a few observers have noted that the household economy is invisible precisely because it is controlled by women and that present accounting conventions have the effect of demeaning the work and value of women.

If a woman were paid wages for her labor as mother and homemaker according to the wage scale for chauffeurs, nurses, baby-sitters, cooks, therapists, and so on, her services today would be worth more than $50,000 a year. Many women would make more for their work in the home than men do for their jobs outside the home. Because family power is partly a function of who earns the money, paying women for their household work might have a significant impact on husband-wife relations.

REPRODUCTION AND SOCIALIZATION. The family makes society possible by producing and rearing children to replace the older members of society as they die off. Traditionally, reproduction has been a unique function of the family. Yet even this domain has not remained immune to technological change. Developments in artificial insemination and in vitro fertilization have separated reproduction from sexual intercourse. In addition to permitting infertile couples to give birth, such techniques have also made it possible for lesbian couples to become parents.

As always, the most automated appliance in the household is the mother.

Beverly Jones

Children . . . have no choice about being born into a system; nor do parents have a choice, once children are born, as to the existence of the responsibilities of parenthood . . . . In fact, no family relationships except marriage are entered into by choice.

Monica McGoldrick and Elizabeth Carter

The family traditionally has been responsible for socialization. Children are help-less and dependent for years following birth. They must learn how to walk and talk, how to take care of themselves, how to act, how to love, how to touch and be touched. Teaching the child how to be human and how to fit into his or her particular culture is one of the family's most important tasks. Without such socialization, we would be like the wild child of Aveyron.

This socialization function, however, is dramatically shifting away from the family. One researcher (Guidubaldi, 1980) believes that the increasing lack of parental commitment to childrearing may be one of the most significant societal changes in our lifetime. With the rise of compulsory education, the state has become responsible for a large part of the socialization of children older than five. The increase in working mothers has placed many infants, toddlers, and small children in day-care, reducing the family's role in socialization. By 1995, scholars estimate that the mothers of two-thirds of all preschool children and three-fourths of all school-age children will be in the work force (Hofferth and Phillips, 1987). Even while children are at home, television rather than family members may be rearing them (Dorr, Kovaric, and Doubleday, 1989).

The Simpsons are a misunderstood and underrated family.

Homer Simpson

ASSIGNMENT OF SOCIAL ROLES AND STATUS. We fulfill various *social roles* as family members, and these roles provide us with much of our identity. During our life-times, most of us will belong to two families: the family of orientation and the family of marriage. The **family of orientation** (sometimes called the *family of origin*) is the family in which we grow up, the family that orients us to the world. The family of orientation may change over time if the marital status of the child's parents changes. The family of orientation originally may be an intact nuclear family or a single-parent family; later it may become a stepfamily. The **family of marriage** is the family we form through marriage. (This family had traditionally been referred to as the *family of procreation,* but as many families do not have children or have stepchildren, this older term is no longer an adequate description.) Most Americans will form families of marriage sometime in their lives. Much of our identity is formed in the crucibles of these two families.

In our family of orientation, we are given the roles of child, son or daughter, brother or sister, stepson or stepdaughter. We internalize these roles until they become a part of our being. In each of these roles we are expected to act in certain ways. For example, children obey their parents, sons roughhouse with their fathers, daughters imitate their mothers, siblings help each other. Sometimes our feelings fit the expectations of our roles; other times they do not.

The family roles of offspring and siblings are most important when we are living with our parents, brothers, and sisters in our family of orientation. After we leave home, they gradually diminish in everyday significance, although they continue throughout our lives. In relation to our parents, we never cease being children; in relation to our siblings, we never cease being brothers and sisters. The roles change as we grow older. They begin the moment we are born and end only when we die.

As we leave our family of orientation, we usually are also leaving adolescence and entering adulthood. Being an adult in our society is defined in part by entering new family roles—those of husband or wife, father or mother. These roles are given to us by our family of marriage, and they take priority over the roles we had in our family of orientation. When we marry, we transfer our primary loyalties from our parents and siblings to our husbands or wives. Later, if we have children, we form additional bonds with them. When we assume the role of husband or wife, we assume an entire new social identity linked with responsibility, work, and parenting. In earlier times such roles were considered to be lifelong in duration. Because of divorce, however, these roles may last for considerably less time.

The status or place we are given in society is acquired in large part through our families. Our families place us in a certain socioeconomic class, such as blue collar (working class), middle class, or upper class. We learn the ways of our class through identifying with our families. Different classes see the world through different eyes. In blue-collar families, for example, work may be viewed as a means of earning a living. Work does not necessarily bring fulfillment; rather, it is drudgery undertaken for the sake of the family. Family is an escape from work. In middle-class families, by contrast, work is often seen as something that gives a person a sense of success or failure as an individual; it is a source of pleasure and fulfillment. Work and family may compete for loyalties.

Our families also give us our racial or ethnic identities as white (or Anglo), African American, Latino, Jewish, Irish American, Asian American and so forth. Families also provide us with a religious tradition as Protestant, Catholic, Jewish, Greek Orthodox, Islamic, agnostic, atheist, and so on. These identities help form our cultural values and expectations.

✍ Why Live in Families?

As we look at the different functions of the family, we can see theoretically that most of them can be fulfilled outside the family. In terms of reproduction, for example, artificial insemination permits a woman to be impregnated by an anonymous donor, while embryonic transplants allow one woman to carry another's embryo. Children can be raised communally, cared for by foster families or childcare workers, or sent to boarding schools. Most of our domestic needs can be satisfied by eating frozen foods or going to restaurants, sending our clothes to the laundry, and hiring help to wash the mountains of dishes accumulating (or growing new life forms) in the kitchen and to clean the bathroom. Friends can provide us with emotional intimacy, therapists can listen to our problems, and sexual partners can be found outside of

Nicole Hollander

Bob and Carol and Mike and Alice

Two astronauts marooned in space, Bob and Debbie, discover that they both watched "The Brady Bunch" as children. Here, they discuss the show.

Debbie: I often wonder how the Bradys got together. Mike had three boys and Carol had three girls — all with lovely hair of gold, like their mother — so each of them had to have been married previously. What happened to their spouses?

Bob: Well, actually, Mike Brady dumped his wife for Carol the afternoon he met her at the auto show, which, as you can imagine, put his wife's nose out of joint. So one day she just showed up with the three boys and dropped them off in front of the split level. As far as I know, Carol was never married to any of the girls' fathers.

Debbie: And Alice, the housekeeper?

Bob: Defrocked priest? Transsexual psychic healer? The series has never been clear on that. My own theory is that she was robotic. Mike designed her. He was an archi-tect, you know. He designed the house that the Brady bunch lived in.

Debbie: I loved that house, especially the kitchen. I've always been fond of avocado appliances and bright orange walls. It's amazing how clean that kitchen was with six kids around — and those kids! They'd come home from school, head straight for that avocado refrigerator and take out a piece of fruit. No Ho-Ho's for those cuties.

Bob: Watching too many episodes of "The Brady Bunch" turned me into a soft-centered zombie. I lay on the couch in a state of altered consciousness and let the images of the perfectly thin, perfectly caring Bradys wash away the images of my real family.

Debbie: I wonder what it would take to make the Bradys lose control, to blow the tops of their heads off. I'd like to try. I'd like to stand very close to Mr. and Mrs. Brady and scream, "Get real," to see the veins in Carol's neck stick out (and you know they would). At the same time I always felt a dreamlike state of pleasure staring at their perfect family life.
　　　　　　　　　　　　　　　　　　　　　　　　— N.H.

marriage. With all the limitations and stresses of family life, why bother living in families?

Sociologist William Goode (1982) suggests that there are several advantages to living in families. First, families offer continuity as a result of emotional attachments, rights, and obligations. Once we choose a partner or have children, we do not have to continually search for new partners or family members who can perform a family task or function better, such as cook, paint the kitchen, provide companionship, or bring home a paycheck. We expect our family members—whether partner, child, parent, or sibling—to participate in family tasks over their lifetimes. If at one time we need to give more emotional support or attention to a partner or child than we receive, we expect the other person to reciprocate at another time. Or if we ourselves are down, we expect our family to help. We further expect that we can enjoy the fruits of our labors together. We count on our family to be there for us in multiple ways. We rarely have the same extensive expectations of friends.

Second, families offer close proximity. We do not need to travel crosstown or cross-country for conversation or help. With families, we do not even need to go out of the house; a husband or wife, parent or child, brother or sister, is often right at hand (or underfoot, in the case of children). This close proximity facilitates cooperation and communication.

Third, families offer us an abiding familiarity with others. Few people know us as well as our family members, for they have seen us in the most intimate circumstances throughout much of our lives. They have seen us at our best and our worst, when we are kind or selfish, understanding or intolerant. This familiarity and close contact require us to make adjustments in living with others. As we do so, we also expand our own knowledge of ourselves and others.

Fourth, families provide us with many economic benefits. They offer us economies of scale. Various activities, such as laundry, cooking, shopping, and cleaning, can be done almost as easily for several people as for one. It is almost as easy to prepare a meal for three people as it is for one, and the average cost per person in both time and money is usually less. As an economic unit, a family can cooperate to achieve what a single individual could not. It is easier for a working couple to purchase a house than a single individual, for example, because the couple can pool their resources.

Because most domestic tasks do not take great skill (a corporate lawyer can mop the floor as easily as anyone else), most family members can learn to do them. As a result, members do not need to go outside the family to hire experts. In fact, for many family tasks, ranging from embracing a partner to bandaging a child's small cut or playing peek-a-boo with a baby, there are no experts to compete with family members—they tend to be the best.

These are only some of the theoretical advantages families offer to their members. Of course, not all families perform all these tasks or perform them well. But families, based on mutual ties of feeling and obligation, offer us greater potential for fulfilling our needs than organizations based on profit (such as corporations) or compulsion (such as governments).

❖ REFLECTIONS   *As you review the functions of the family—intimacy, economic cooperation, reproduction and socialization, and assignment of social roles and status—examine your own family. How does it fulfill these functions? How does your family structure, such as intact nuclear family, single-parent family, or stepfamily, affect how your family fulfills these functions?*

Home—the place where, when you have to go there, they have to let you in.

Robert Frost (1874–1963)

PERSPECTIVE

Stereotyping Families

Each day we are presented with a vast amount of information that we need to organize and make sense of. One of the ways we manage this information is by categorizing it. A **stereotype** is a special kind of category: it is a set of beliefs about the personal characteristics of a group of people. Stereotypes are highly simplified, over-generalized, and widely-held beliefs about people. Most of us are probably aware of stereotypes about ethnicity and gender. But there are also numerous stereotypes centering around family (Ganong, Coleman, and Mapes, 1990; for family stereotypes on television, see Taylor, 1989a and 1989b, and Fabes, Wilson, and Christopher, 1989).

Probably the most far-ranging family stereotype is that the traditional nuclear family is the only healthy or normal family structure. As a description of American family life, the nuclear family exists more as a cultural symbol or norm than as a reality, yet it has a powerful effect on us. There are numerous consequences.

◆ *The nuclear family stereotype makes other family forms and life-styles appear deviant or suspect.* Studies indicate that married men and women are generally rated more positively than single individuals. Married persons are perceived as being more mature, more responsible, and better citizens. Similarly, mothers and fathers are viewed more positively than adults who are voluntarily childless. Even the perception of children is affected by whether they are from two-parent or single-parent families: The personalities and behaviors of children from two-parent families were rated higher. Single-parent families are seen as "broken" and stepfamilies as "unhappy." Those who live together are regarded as "immoral," and gay and lesbian relationships are called "perverse." Although family forms and relationships have become increasingly diverse in recent years, cultural stereotypes have remained unchanged (Ganong et al., 1990).

◆ *Nuclear family stereotypes intermingle with stereotypes about ethnicity, affecting our perceptions of African-American, Latino, and other ethnic families.* Such stereotypes are potentially harmful, observed Lois Bryant and her colleagues (Bryant, Coleman, and Ganong, 1988): "When stereotypes are distorted and overgeneralizations are made, the result can be ethnocentrism or prejudice." Ethnic differences from the nuclear family model are viewed as deviant rather than as expressions of cultural pluralism (Billingsley, 1968; Mirandé, 1985). Common stereotypes depict the African-American family as "unstable, disorganized, and unable to provide its members with the social and psychological support and development needed to assimilate fully into American society" (Dodson, 1988). Stereotypes about Latino families view them as rigid and authoritarian, dominated by macho fathers (Mirandé, 1985). Until recently, these stereotypes have affected much scholarly research (Demos, 1990; Mirandé, 1985). Such stereotypes seriously distort our understanding of families from different ethnic groups.

◆ *The emphasis on family structure tends to distract us from examining what actually goes on within a particular family.* We tend

❖ EXTENDED FAMILIES AND KINSHIP

Extended Families

Most people throughout the world live in some form of extended family. Parents and children, the core of the nuclear family, combine with other kin and nuclear families to form extended families. The kinship system is based on the reciprocal rights and obligations of the different family members, such as those between grandparents and grandchildren and mothers-in-law and sons-in-law.

Although American families often exist as some form of extended family, we sometimes don't recognize the fact because we uncritically accept the nuclear family model as our definition. We may even be blind to the reality of our own family structure. When someone asks us to name the members of our family, if we are unmarried we will probably name our parents, brothers, and sisters. If we are married, we will probably name our husband or wife and children. Only if questioned further may we include our grandparents, aunts or uncles, cousins, even friends or

PERSPECTIVE

to assume that a family is happy simply because it is intact. But a nuclear family is not necessarily a happy family. Nuclear families may engage in small-scale nuclear warfare. Although they fit the structural norm on the outside, they may be hiding extensive conflict, alcoholism, incest, abuse, and hatred beneath the surface. We must look beneath a family's structure to see whether it is performing its functions. Is it socializing its children in a healthy way? Is it providing intimacy for its members? A stepfamily or single-parent family may perform the family functions far better than an unhappy but intact nuclear family.

◆ *We may misinterpret the behavior of individuals according to our stereotypes.* We may mistakenly attribute an adolescent's rebelliousness at school to being reared in a "broken home" instead of correctly attributing it to, say, rigid school rules. Or we may ignore behavior that does not fit our stereotypes. If we believe stepmothers are uncaring, we may not notice a stepmother's tenderness or may even interpret it as self-serving.

◆ *Family stereotypes influence how different families perceive and value themselves.* An unhappy traditional family may convince itself that it is a happy family because it fulfills our society's family norms. A happy stepfamily may feel deviant because it is not a biological family. These stereotypes lead single persons, divorced men and women, and members of stepfamilies to devalue themselves (Cargan, 1986; Coleman and Ganong, 1987; Gerstel, 1987).

◆ *Because we believe that the nuclear family is the family, we ignore the potentially rich family ties offered by our extended family.* We act as if relying on friendship and support from our kin is a sign of dependence and weakness instead of strength and vitality. Scholars also fail to examine the nature of extended family relationships because they focus their research on nuclear families. Those families that do participate in extended family networks, especially African-Americans and Latinos, are viewed as somehow deficient for not being self-sufficient (Ellison, 1990; Goetting, 1990; Mirandé, 1985).

◆ *Family stereotypes prevent us from dealing with the changing nature of America's families.* We attribute the problems faced by nontraditional families to their divergence from the traditional nuclear family. Yet many of the problems and stresses experienced by these families are the result of society's failure to give them sup-

port and encouragement. A dual-earner marriage, for example, tends to have increased stress because the woman, besides being wife and mother, has the additional role of worker to fulfill. Society (and often her husband) expects her to continue her primary responsibility for housework and child care. The workplace makes no provision for the special needs of parents, such as child care, paid leave to care for sick children, and so on. Federal policies fail to support child-care initiatives because conservative "pro-family" groups believe such policies would undermine the traditional family by encouraging mothers to work. Single-parent families may be stressful for a mother, not because of the father's absence per se but because of the poverty in which she and her children are trapped.

As long as the traditional nuclear family is upheld as our only ideal family, other family forms will continue to suffer. A first step in eliminating these harmful stereotypes is recognizing that there is no single type of normal American family. We need a new family model that recognizes the diversity of family forms. We need to realize that there are many types of normal American families, embracing different family structures with ethnic variations.

neighbors who are "like family." We may not name all our blood relatives, but we will probably name the ones with whom we feel emotionally close.

Kinship System

CONJUGAL AND CONSANGUINEOUS RELATIONSHIPS. Family relationships are generally created in two ways: through marriage and through birth. Extended family relationships created through marriage are known as **conjugal relationships.** [The word ~~marriage~~ "conjugal" is derived from the Latin *conjungere,* meaning "to join together."] In-laws, such as mothers-in-law, fathers-in-law, sons-in-law, and daughters-in-law, are created by law—that is, through marriage. **Consanguineous relationships** are created ~~Birth; blood~~ through blood ties—that is, birth. [The word "consanguineous" is derived from the Latin *com-,* "joint," + *sanguineus,* "blood."] Parents, children, grandparents, and grandchildren, for example, have consanguineous relationships. Aunts and uncles may be either consanguineous or conjugal. Our families of orientation and marriage provide us with some of the most important roles we will assume in life. These nuclear family roles, such as parent/child, husband/wife, and sibling, combine with extended family roles, such as grandparent, aunt/uncle, cousin, and in-law, to form the **kinship system.** The kinship system is the social organization of the family.

KIN RIGHTS AND OBLIGATIONS. In some societies, mostly non-Western or non-industrialized cultures, kinship obligations may be very extensive. In cultures that emphasize kin groups, close emotional ties between a husband and wife are viewed as a threat to the extended family. An extreme form of precedence of the kin group over the married couple is the institution of spirit marriage, which continues in China today. In a spirit marriage, according to anthropologist Janice Stockard (1989), a marriage is arranged by families whose son and daughter died unmarried. After the dead couple is "married," the two families adopt an orphaned boy and raise him as the deceased couple's son to provide family continuity. In another Cantonese marriage form, women did not live with their husbands until at least three years after marriage, as their primary obligation remained with their own extended family. Among the Nayar of India, men have a number of clearly defined obligations toward the children of their sisters and female cousins, although they have few obligations toward their own children (Gough, 1968).

In American society the basic kinship system consists of parents and children, but it may include other relatives as well. Each person in this system has certain rights and obligations as a result of his or her position in the family structure. Furthermore, a person may occupy several positions at the same time. For example, an eighteen-year-old female may simultaneously be a daughter, a sister, a cousin, an aunt, and a granddaughter. Each role entails different rights and obligations. As a daughter, the young woman may have to defer to certain decisions of her parents; as a sister, to share her bedroom; as a cousin, to attend a wedding; as a granddaughter, to send a Christmas card.

In our own culture, the nuclear family has many norms regulating behavior, such as parental support of children and sexual fidelity between spouses, but the rights and obligations of relatives outside the basic kinship system are less strong and less clearly articulated. Because there are neither culturally-binding nor legally enforceable norms regarding the extended family, some researchers suggest that such kinship ties have become more or less voluntary. We are free to define our kinship relations much as we wish. Like friendship, they may be allowed to wane (Goetting, 1990).

While extended families have declined in significance for white middle-class Americans, they continue to be especially important to African-American, Latino, and Asian-American families. Among African Americans, for example, extended families provide reciprocal aid and assistance, help with child care, facilitate household cooperation, and give care to aging parents and grandparents (Taylor, 1986 and 1990). They also provide foster care for children whose parents are unable to care for them (Resnick, 1990; Shimkin, Shimkin, and Frate, 1978). Among Latinos **la familia** embraces not only the nuclear but also the extended family. In *la familia*, **abuelos** (grandparents) are especially influential as warm and affectionate figures to their grandchildren (Mirandé, 1985). Among Japanese-Americans, despite acculturation and intermarriage, some families attempt to preserve the traditional concept of the **ie** [pronounced *ee-eh*], that is, the family that encompasses not only members of the present extended family but also deceased and yet-to-be born family members (Kikumura and Kitano, 1988). Among Chinese-Americans, elders continue to influence younger family members (Huang, 1988).

Despite the increasingly voluntary nature of kin relations, our kin create a rich social network for us. Studies suggest that most people have a large number of kin living in their area (Mancini and Blieszner, 1989). Adult children and parents often live close to each other, make regular visits, and help each other with child care, housework, maintenance, repairs, loans, and gifts. The relations between siblings are often strong throughout the life cycle (Lee, Mancini, and Maxwell, 1990).

We generally assume kinship to be lifelong. In the past, if a marriage was disrupted by death, in-laws generally continued to be thought of as kin. They rallied around the surviving widow or widower, providing assistance and support. The rise of divorce, however, has created a unique phenomenon: ex-kin. When a marriage ends through divorce, what is the role of former in-laws? What kinship ties or responsibilities do former mothers-in-law or fathers-in-law continue to have toward their son's or daughter's former spouse? If there are no children involved, the answer seems to be none. But if the in-law is also a grandparent, the issue becomes more complicated. While relating to their grandchild, how do grandparents relate to their former son- or daughter-in-law—as a relative, friend, acquaintance, stranger, or an enemy? Family loyalties may call for them to align themselves against their child's former spouse, but what if a close relationship was formed between the ex-inlaws

Extended families are important sources of strength. Family rituals, such as tamale-making in this Latino family, help maintain kinship bonds.

and the ex-spouse? What if the former spouse needs assistance in child care? In another time, when divorce was considered deviant, shunning the former spouse may have seemed appropriate. But today, divorce is as much a part of the American family system as marriage. Although shunning the ex-spouse may no longer be appropriate (or polite), no new guidelines on how to behave have been developed. The ex-kin role is a **roleless role**; that is, it is a role with no clearly defined rules.

FICTIVE KIN. Blood relationships do not define the type of feelings that a person will have. Instead, they provide a framework to encourage brotherly feelings toward a brother, motherly feelings toward a child, and so on. The strength of kinship ties ultimately depends more on feeling than on biology. A brother or sister can seem like a stranger; a grandmother can be more of a mother than one's biological mother; a parent can be like a brother or sister. The names we call our relatives or friends reflect degrees of feelings (Schneider, 1980).

Feelings of kinship can extend beyond traditional kin (see Chapter 18). We form **fictive kin** (or *pseudokin*) by transforming friends and neighbors into kin: "He is like a brother to me," "We are like cousins." In Latino culture, **compadres** and **comadres** (the godparents of one's children) are important figures in the family. Because divorce and geographic mobility are breaking down our ability to interact with in-laws and biological kin, we are beginning to form new kinds of kin (Kempler, 1976; Lindsey, 1982). Single persons may attempt to create families from friends by sharing time, problems, meals, and houses with each other (Lindsey, 1982). They may also create cooperative or communal living arrangements with each other. Single parents may form networks with other single parents for emotional support and exchange of child care (McLanahan et al., 1981). Family networks may be formed in which three or four families from the same neighborhood share problems, exchange services, and enjoy leisure together. An **affiliated family** is a family in which unrelated individuals are treated as family members. In this situation, another person, usually an older widow, widower, or single person, spends time with the family in a role similar to that of an aunt, uncle, or grandparent, joining in family activities, child care, work, meals, housework, or recreation. Often he or she is called by some family name, such as "Auntie," "Gramps," or "Pop" (Kempler, 1976).

❖ R E F L E C T I O N S   *What are the different kinship roles—such as nephew or niece, aunt or uncle, in-law, grandson or granddaughter—that you play as a result of being a member of your extended family? What rights and obligations does each of these roles entail in your family?*

◆ As you begin studying marriage and the family, you can see that such study is both abstract and personal. It is abstract insofar as you learn about the general structure, processes, and meanings associated with marriage and the family. But the study of marriage and the family is also personal: it is *your* present, *your* past, and *your* future that you are studying. It is the family from which you came, the family in which you are now living, and the family that you will create. What R. D. Laing (1972) wrote some years ago may ring true for you today:

The first family to interest me was my own. I still know less about it than I know about many other families. This is typical. Children are the last to be told what was really going on.

As you continue your study of marriage and the family, much of what was unknown in your own family may become known. You may discover new understanding, strength, complexity, and love.

❖ SUMMARY

◆ The *nuclear family* consists of the mother/father/child triad. The *extended family* consists of the nuclear family *and* other relatives. *Monogamy* refers to the marital form in which there are two spouses, husband and wife. *Polygamy* refers to the practice of having more than one husband or wife.

◆ *Marriage* is a socially recognized union between a woman and a man. Its main characteristics are (1) the performance of a public ritual to sanction the union; (2) sexual unification; and (3) economic cooperation. *Divorce* is the legal dissolution of marriage following *separation*. High divorce rates have made single-parent families and stepfamilies important family forms in contemporary America. Divorce, remarriage, single-parent families, and stepfamilies are normal aspects of the contemporary American marriage system. *Cohabitation*, in which an unmarried couple lives together and is sexually involved, has become so common that some regard it as part of the family life cycle.

◆ A *family* may be defined as one or more adults who cooperate and divide labor, share a common dwelling, and may be raising children. The four important family functions are (1) provision of intimacy; (2) formation of a cooperative economic unit; (3) reproduction and socialization; and (4) assignment of status and social roles, which are acquired both in our *family of orientation* (in which we grow up) and our *family of marriage* (which we form by marrying).

◆ Advantages to living in families include: (1) continuity of emotional attachments; (2) close proximity; (3) familiarity with family members; and (4) economic benefits.

◆ *Stereotypes* are highly simplified, over-generalized beliefs. The strongest family stereotype is that the traditional nuclear family is the norm against which all other families are measured. The consequences of this stereotype include the following: (1) other family forms and life-styles, such as single-parent families and stepfamilies, are misperceived as deviant; (2) ethnic family differences are misinterpreted as deviant; (3) behavior may be misconstrued according to stereotypes; (4) those in nontraditional families and life-styles may devalue themselves; (5) the focus on formal structure discourages us from examining whether a family—regardless of its form—fulfills its functions; and (6) society fails to support other family forms.

◆ The extended family consists of grandparents, aunts, uncles, cousins, and in-laws. It may be formed *conjugally*, through marriage, creating in-laws and step-kin, or *consanguineously*, by birth, through blood relationships. Extended families are especially important for African-American, Latino, and Asian-American families. The Latino *familia* is an extended family including *abuelos* (grandparents) and *compadres* (godparents).

◆ The *kinship system* is the social organization of the family. In the nuclear family it generally consists of parents and children, but it may also include members of the extended family, especially grandparents, aunts, uncles, and cousins. Kin can be *fictive*: a nonrelated person can be *as* kin or a relative may fulfill a different kin role, such as a grandmother taking the role of a child's mother. The *affiliated family* consists of related family members and fictive kin. Traditionally, kinship was assumed to be lifelong, but with divorce and remarriage on the rise, kin formed through marriage may change.

Answers to Preview Questions

The answers to the preview questions at the beginning of the chapter are listed below. As you check your answers, whether you were correct or not, think about your reasons for each response. What were they? What was their source? How valid is the source? As you read the chapter, you will find the questions discussed in greater depth.

1. F	6. T
2. F	7. T
3. T	8. F
4. T	9. T
5. F	10. T

❖ SUGGESTED READINGS

To assist you in doing research on finding more information on topics that interest you, see "Reference Guides" in the Resource Center. Reference guides include those for studying marriage and the family as well as guides for African-American, Latino, Asian-American, Native American, and women's studies. The reference guides also contain a list of the most important journals and databases for studying marriage and the family.

The books below may interest you if you wish to explore some of the ideas or topics raised in this chapter.

Goode, William. *The Family*, 2d ed. Englewood Cliffs, N.J.: Prentice-Hall, 1981. A brief theoretical overview of the family from a sociological perspective.

Hutter, Mark. *The Changing Family: Comparative Perspectives*. New York: Macmillan, 1988. A cross-cultural comparison of developing nations and American family systems (including African-American, Latino, and Japanese-American families).

Malson, Lucien. *Wolf Children and the Problem of Human Nature*. New York: Monthly Review Press, 1972. A study concerning wild children, which also reprints Jean Itard's studies of Victor.

McGoldrick, Monica, and Randy Gerson. *Genograms in Family Assessment*. New York: Norton, 1985. The use of genograms in diagramming family relationships; includes genograms of famous historical personages.

Queen, Stuart A., et al. *The Family in Various Cultures,* 5th ed. New York: Harper and Row, 1985. A classic cross-cultural textbook; well-rounded sociological perspective.

Schneider, David M. *American Kinship: A Cultural Account,* 2d ed. Chicago: University of Chicago Press, 1980. A short examination of the American family in terms of kinship.

Stack, Carol B. *All Our Kin: Strategies for Survival in a Black Community.* New York: Harper & Row, 1974 (paperback). A classic study of kin relations that demonstrates their elasticity and significance in an African-American community.

Tremblay, Hèléne. *Families of the World: Family Life at the End of the 20th Century.* 2 vols. Vol. 1, *The Americas and the Caribbean* (1988); Vol 2, *Asia and the Pacific Islands* (1990). Engaging color photographs and stories of families around the world.

Suggested Films

The suggested films in this and subsequent chapters are generally available on videotape. They have been selected to provide addi-

tional insight to the topics discussed in each chapter. Some are comic, others dramatic, and still others tragic. Some are classics, others are more contemporary. View them critically, utilizing what you have learned in the textbook and class.

Most of the films are readily available for rental at better video stores. Some classics may be found at your public library or university library. Many of the Public Broadcasting System's (PBS) performances or TV movies may be found in good public libraries (or watch for reruns on television).

Quest for Fire (1981). An imaginative look at tribal and family life as it might have been 80,000 years ago. A special language of words and gestures was created for the film by Anthony Burgess and Desmond Morris.

The Wild Child (1969). The classic film by Francois Truffaut, the great French director, of the relationship between Victor, "the young savage of Aveyron," and Jean Itard, the doctor who tried to "civilize" him.

READINGS

THE AMERICAN FAMILY OF THE 1990s

Jerrold Footlick

American families are changing. How are they changing according to this essay? Do you agree or disagree with the description of change? What evidence can you gather from Chapter 1 to support or contest the main ideas?

The upheaval is evident everywhere in our culture. Babies have babies, kids refuse to grow up and leave home, affluent Yuppies prize their BMWs more than children, rich and poor children alike blot their minds with drugs, people casually move in with each other and out again. The divorce rate has doubled since 1965, and demographers project that half of all first marriages made today will end in divorce. Six out of 10 second marriages will probably collapse. One third of all children born in the past decade will probably live in a stepfamily before they are 18. One out of every four children today is being raised by a single parent. About 22 percent of children today were born out of wedlock; of those, about a third were born to a teenage mother. One out of every five children lives in poverty; the rate is twice as high among blacks and Hispanics.

Most of us are still reeling from the shock of such turmoil. Americans—in their living rooms, in their boardrooms and in the halls of Congress—are struggling to understand what has gone wrong. We find family life worse than it was a decade ago, according to a *Newsweek* Poll, and we are not sanguine about the next decade. For instance, two thirds of those polled think a family should be prepared to make "financial sacrifices so that one parent can stay home to raise the children." But that isn't likely to happen. An astonishing two thirds of all mothers are in the labor force, roughly double the rate in 1955, and more than half of all mothers of infants are in the work force.

Parents feel torn between work and family obligations. Marriage is a fragile institution—not something anyone can count on. Children seem to be paying the price for their elders' confusion. "There is an increasing understanding of the emotional cost of having children," says Larry L. Bumpass, a University of Wisconsin demographer. "People once thought parenting ended when their children were 18. Now they know it stretches into the 20s and beyond." Divorce has left a devastated generation in its wake, and for many youngsters, the pain is compounded by poverty and neglect. While politicians and psychologists debate cause and solution, everyone suffers. Even the most traditional of families feel an uneasy sense of emotional dislocation. Three decades ago the mother who keep the house spotless and cooked dinner for her husband and children each evening could be confident and secure in her role. Today, although her num-

READINGS

bers are still strong—a third of mothers whose children are under 18 stay home—the woman who opts out of a paycheck may well feel defensive, undervalued, as though she were too incompetent to get "a real job." And yet the traditional family retains a profound hold on the American imagination.

Now the tradition survives, in a way, precisely because of Ozzie and Harriet. The television programs of the '50s and '60s validated a family style during a period in which today's leaders—congressmen, corporate executives, university professors, magazine editors—were growing up or beginning to establish their own families. (The impact of the idealized family was further magnified by the very size of the postwar generation.) "The traditional model reaches back as far as personal memory goes for most of those who [currently] teach and write and philosophize," says Yale University historian John Demos.. "And in a time when parents seem to feel a great deal of change in family experience, that image is comfortingly solid and secure, a counterpoint to what we think is threatening for the future."

We *do* feel uneasy about the future. We have just begun to admit that exchanging old-fashioned family values for independence and self-expression may exact a price. "This is an incendiary issue," says Arlie Hochschild, a sociologist at the University of California, Berkeley, and author of the controversial book *The Second Shift.* "Husbands, wives, children are not getting enough family life. Nobody is. People are hurting." A mother may go to work because her family needs the money, or to afford luxuries, or because she is educated for a career or because she wants to; she will be more independent but she will probably see less of her children. And her husband, if she has a husband, is not likely to make up the difference with the children. We want it both ways. We're glad we live in a society that is more comfortable living with gay couples, working women, divorced men and stepparents and single mothers—people who are reaching in some fashion for self-fulfillment. But we also understand the value of a family life that will provide a stable and nurturing environment in which to raise children—in other words, an environment in which personal goals have to be sacrificed. How do we reconcile the two?

The answer lies in some hard thinking abut what a family is for. What do we think about when we think about family? Many of us have an emotional reaction to that question. Thinking about family reminds us of the way we were, and the way we dreamed we might be. We remember trips in the car, eager to find out whose side the road would have more cows and horses to count. We remember raking leaves and the sound of a marching band at the high-school football game. We remember doing homework and wondering what college might be like. It was not all fun and games, of course. There were angry words spoken, and parents and grandparents who somehow are no longer around, and for some of us not enough to eat or clothes not warm enough or nice enough. Then we grow up and marvel at what we can accomplish, and the human beings we can produce, and we sometimes doubt our ability to do the things we want to do—have to do—for our children. And live our own lives besides.

Practical considerations require us to pin down what the family is all about. Tax bills, welfare and insurance payments, adoption rights and the other real-life events can turn on what constitutes a family. Our expectations of what a family ought to be will also shape the kinds of social policies we want. Webster's offers 22 definitions. The Census Bureau has settled on "two or more persons related by birth, marriage or adoption who reside in the same household." New York state's highest court stretched the definition last summer: it held that the survivor of a gay couple retained the legal rights to an apartment they had long shared, just as a surviving husband or wife could. Looking to the "totality of the relationship," the court set four standards for a family: (1) the "exclusivity and longevity of a relationship"; (2) the "level of emotional and financial commitment"; (3) how the couple "conducted their everyday lives and held themselves out to society"; (4) the "reliance placed upon one another for daily services." That approach incenses social critic Midge Decter. "You can call homosexual households 'families,' and you can define 'family' any way you want to, but you can't fool Mother Nature," says Decter. "A family is a mommy and a daddy and their children."

A State of California task force on the future of the family came up with still another conclusion. It decided a family could be measured by the things it should do for its members, which it called "functions": maintain the physical health and safety of its members; help shape a belief system of goals and values; teach social skills, and create a place for recuperation from external stresses. In a recent "family values" survey conducted for the Massachusetts Mutual Insurance Co., respondents were given several choices of family definitions; three quarters of them chose "a group who love and care for each other." Ultimately, to appropriate U.S. Supreme Court Justice Potter Stewart's memorable dictum, we may not be able to define a family, but we know one when we see it.

We enter the 21st century with a heightened sensitivity to family issues. Helping parents and children is a bottom-line concern, no longer a matter of debate. Economists say the smaller labor force of the future means that every skilled employee will be an increasingly valuable asset; we won't be able to afford to waste human resources. Even now companies cannot ignore the needs of working parents. Support systems like day care are becoming a necessity. High rates of child poverty and child abuse are everybody's problem, as is declining school performance and anything else that threatens our global competitiveness. "By the end of the century," says Columbia University sociologist Sheila B. Kamerman, "it will be conventional wisdom to invest in our children."

READINGS

Those are the familiar demographic forces. But there are other potential tremors just below the surface. By 2020, one in three children will come from a minority group—Hispanic-Americans, African-Americans, Asian-Americans and others. Their parents will command unprecedented political clout. Minorities and women together will make up the majority of new entrants into the work force. Minority children are usually the neediest among us, and they will want government support, especially in the schools. At about the same time, many baby boomers will be retired, and they will want help from Washington as well. Billions of dollars are at stake, and the country's priorities in handing out those dollars are not yet clear. After all, children and the elderly are both part of our families. How should the government spend taxpayers' dollars—on long-term nursing care or better day care?

THE AMERICAN FAMILY: A POEM

Marilyn Ihinger-Tallman

How does the author define family? For the author, which is more important: the family's structure or the interactions of its members? Do you agree? Is the poem optimistic, pessimistic, or realistic in its description of families?

THE ASSIGNMENT: Write a short piece on the state of the American family.

The state . . .
> A set of circumstances or
> attributes characterizing . . . a thing
> at a given time . . .

of the American . . .
> America . . .
> God shed Grace
> crown thy good . . . brotherhood
> from sea to sea
> she gets your teeming masses

family . . .
> Fellowship . . .
> a group of individuals living under
> one roof . . .
> the basic unit in society. . . .

The state of the family—

Which family?
> The teenage mother?
> who finds her life

irreversibly changed
with the cry of her newborn

They are increasing in number . . .

Which family?
> The yuppie couple?
> who give away
> their child's toys to make room for more.
> The dual-career couple?
> who learn Lamaze
> and breathe together
> as they bring their to-be-privileged
> preciously conceived
> one-of-a-kind
> child into the world

They are increasing in number . . .

Which family?
> The cohabiting couple?
> who live with her young child
> and include his on weekends
> if his ex doesn't give him grief
> and spoil their plans

They are increasing in number . . .

Which family?
> The elderly couple?
> Who live a mile
> from their married daughter and her kids
> and son-in-law
> they help out as much as they can
> babysitting, things like that
> for they love them so

But what scares them most
is that son
got divorced last year
and now ex-daughter-in-law
remarries next month
and is taking grandson Zack away
Zack, who looks just like gran'pa
Oh Zack
are you lost forever?

They are increasing in number . . .

Which family?
> those in the working class?
> the super rich?

the underclass?
what happened to the middle class?

They are decreasing in number . . .

Which family?
    The dual-career couple?
    who live apart for now
    because she got a terrific promotion
    but had to move to Cleveland
    will they ever have those children
    they planned?

Which family?
    The one that lives
    in the cute house behind the white picket fence
    with the apricot and apple tree in the side yard
    in suburbia
    the one with the stay-at-home mom
    and hard-working dad
    and 2.3 kids and a dog named Arnie

They are decreasing in number . . .

Which family?
    The abusive family?
    what about those families
    in which fathers
    drunk or sober

creep up stairs in the dark
to fondle the small beasts and
feel the private parts
of daughter
frightened. scared to breathe.
while mothers
absent, or too dependent, or too passive
turn their heads

and mothers, fathers, frustrated
scream
push
hit
the children
then children hit children
and later, husbands and wives and children

Can they be increasing in number . . .

The state of the family
changing
in the land of abundance
and resources
teeming masses living in families

families in different sets of circumstances
possessing different attributes
all in America
God shed grace on thee

CHAPTER 2

American Marriages and Families: Past and Present

PREVIEW

To gain a sense of what you already know about the material covered in this chapter, answer "true" or "false" to the statements below. You will find the answers on page 54.

1. Today there is greater diversity in American families than at any previous time. True or false?
2. During the colonial period, women commonly had their last child around the same time their first grandchild was born. True or false?
3. The Puritans believed that children were born innocent but were corrupted by an evil world. True or false?
4. The housewife who remains at home caring for her husband and children while her husband works outside the home has always been a natural part of family structure. True or false?
5. Under slavery, laws prohibited masters from selling their slaves' children except when the children refused to work. True or false?
6. For immigrant families, family goals generally took precedence over individual goals. True or false?
7. Latinos are the fastest growing American ethnic group. True or false?
8. The belief that men and women should share household decision making and childrearing is a twentieth-century phenomenon. True or false?
9. The 1950s "golden age of the traditional family" was an exception to the general family trends of the last seventy years. True or false?
10. After decades of significant change, attitudes toward marriage and the family have stabilized except for increasing support of egalitarian gender roles. True or false?

*Those who do not remember the past are
condemned to repeat it.*

George Santayana (1863–1952)

*A people without history is like wind on the
buffalo grass.*

Teton Sioux proverb

AMERICAN MARRIAGES AND FAMILIES have undergone fundamental changes within the last generation (Mintz and Kellogg, 1988). Contemporary American families are characterized by diversity in family forms and styles and in ethnic groupings. The traditional nuclear family (itself a nineteenth-century invention) in which the husband works outside the home for wages while the wife works within the home and cares for children accounts for a small minority of American families today. We have a multiplicity of family forms: single-parent families (the fastest-growing family form), dual-worker families, stepfamilies (also known as blended or reconstituted families), and traditional families. The institution of marriage has been altered substantially with the rise of divorce and remarriage. "Till death do you part" is becoming increasingly, "Till divorce do you part." These changes in marriage and the family first emerged on a large scale in the early 1970s. Probably the majority of those reading this textbook have experienced these changes as either husbands, wives, parents, or children. In this chapter, we will examine what marriages and families once were in this country and what they are now.

Divorce, remarriage, and diverse family forms are not new. There have always been dual-worker families, single-parent families, and stepfamilies. Throughout history, most families have been dual-worker families insofar as husbands and wives worked the fields, tended gardens, spun and wove cloth, preserved and prepared food, and so on. In fact, for families of the past, *dual-worker family* may be a misnomer; *total-worker family* would be more accurate. Historically, most members of the family—from the small child who weeded or tended animals to the aged adult who supervised children, taught them skills, and told stories—were productive. Only with the rise of industrialization in the nineteenth century did women and children, at least in the middle class, become significantly less involved in the production of goods. At the turn of the century, however, large numbers of women—around one out of five—were working outside the home as factory workers, clerks, agricultural workers, or domestics. There have always been large numbers of single-parent families and stepfamilies. What makes contemporary single-parent families and stepfamilies different from those of the past is that historically these families were most often created by death rather than divorce (Kain, 1990).

❖ THE COLONIAL ERA

Native American Families

The greatest diversity in American family life probably existed during our country's earliest years, when two million Native Americans inhabited what is now the United States and Canada. There were over 240 groups with their own distinct family and kinship patterns. Many groups were **patrilineal**: rights and property flowed from the father. Others, like the Zuni and Hopi in the southwest and the Iroquois in the northeast, were **matrilineal**; rights and property descended from the mother.

Native American families tended to share certain characteristics, although it is easy to overgeneralize (Mintz and Kellogg, 1988). Most families were small. There was a high child mortality rate, and mothers breastfed their infants; during breastfeeding, mothers abstained from sexual intercourse. Children were often born in special birth huts. As they grew older, the young were rarely physically disciplined. Instead, they were taught by example. Their families praised them when they were good and publicly shamed them when they were bad. Children began working at an early age. Their play, such as hunting or playing with dolls, was modeled on adult activities. Ceremonies and rituals marked transitions into adulthood. Girls

PERSPECTIVE

The Ohlone: Native American Marriage and Family Ways

In many ways, the Ohlone of the San Francisco and Monterey Bay region in present-day California reflected many basic characteristics of Native American groups (Margolin, 1978). When an Ohlone boy sought marriage, for example, he presented his request to his parents. He and his prospective bride knew and liked each other, but custom called for the marriage to be arranged by both parents. His parents conferred with other important relatives; the family as a whole decided whether the match was good. A relative informally approached the girl's parents to sound out their feelings. Her family called in other members to discuss the proposal. If the proposal was accepted, the boy's family made a formal visit. At this visit, baskets, beads, feathers, furs, and other valuable gifts were brought. Valuable gifts conferred status on the girl and her family, because they indicated the family's high standing in the village.

If the marriage proposal was accepted, the girl's family prepared a wedding feast that lasted for several days. Following the feast, the newly married couple wandered outside the village to a thicket of willows, where they consummated their marriage. After a while they returned, with the groom's face scratched and clawed. The marks were a sign that the marriage had been consummated; they showed that the bride was modest. After the marriage, the youth stayed with his wife's family for a few months. Then, if the girl's parents approved of their son-in-law, she left to live with her husband.

Sometimes men had two wives, often in separate villages. Within the village the wives were often sisters, as they preferred sharing husband and housework with a family member. In marriage, fidelity was expected and divorce was discouraged. If divorce was necessary, however, the man or woman simply moved out of the family dwelling. They could then remarry.

The Ohlone restricted their sexual activities because they believed sexuality interfered with their relationship with the spirit world; it weakened their powers.

Men were sometimes overcome by desire, however, and ignored the various taboos surrounding sexuality, such as sexual restrictions during menstruation and breastfeeding (which lasted about two years). If a man or woman violated these taboos and later fell ill or had bad luck, it was said that they were being punished for their weakness.

Although the Ohlone restricted their sexuality, they accepted same-sex relationships. If a boy began imitating women and wearing women's clothes as he grew older, he was allowed to marry another man. Sometimes he became the second "wife" of a wealthy man whose other wives were women. Women attracted to other women were also accepted, but they were not allowed to adopt male roles; their same-sex orientation was restricted to sexual activities.

When a woman became pregnant, both she and her husband followed prescribed rituals. They abstained from sex and both were careful to avoid meat, fish, and salt, fearing that these would cause a difficult birth. The husband curbed his anger for fear of injuring the baby by disturbing the harmony of nature. He hunted little because it was bad to hurt living things during pregnancy. When the woman went into labor, she went to her hut and was attended by the old women, who caressed, massaged, and encouraged her. Following birth, the mother was led to a stream, where she splashed cold water on

herself and the baby. A few days later, she began breastfeeding. From then on, until she weaned her child two years later, both she and her husband refrained from physical contact.

As the Ohlone raised their children, they sought to strengthen the bonds that linked the child to his or her family, clan, and tribe. The child's identity, strength, and fulfillment were found in belonging to family and clan. Selfishness and extreme individualism were discouraged because they weakened the bonds on which the family and community depended.

The child was watched over by the immediate and extended family. Children were not physically punished; instead, good behavior was taught by example. By age five, children were expected to engage in useful work, such as gathering berries and carrying wood. At age eight, boys and girls entered separate worlds. Boys began hunting, working rope and nets, and attending rituals in the sacred sweat-house, where sauna-like heat purified their bodies and spirits. During puberty, the boys passed into manhood through a series of ceremonies.

As girls grew older, they helped to grind acorns and gather roots and herbs; they also learned to weave intricate baskets. A girl's passage into womanhood was marked by *menarche*, her first menstrual bleeding. Menarche was one of the most important events for the Ohlone girl, marking the beginning of her spiritual power. At menarche, she retired to a menstrual hut and began fasting in order to gather her spiritual power. The village women visited her and shared their secrets of female power. In the night, both male and female members of her family performed sacred menstrual dances. From then on, whenever she menstruated, she withdrew to her menstrual hut, where she communed with the spirit world through dreams and fasting.

continued on next page

PERSPECTIVE

The Ohlone flourished until the late eighteenth century and the arrival of the Catholic missionaries led by Junipero Serra (who was beatified in 1988 in preparation for sainthood). The padres, seeking to convert and "civilize" the Ohlones, uprooted and herded them into missions and destroyed their culture. After reducing the Ohlones to servitude, the padres became their "defenders" against the demands of Spanish and Mexican settlers and soldiers. Under the mission system, an estimated 100,000 native Californians–half the population–died (Fogel, 1988). Another quarter perished within ten years of the arrival of the Forty-Niners during the California gold rush.

underwent puberty ceremonies at first menstruation. For boys, events such as getting the first tooth and killing the first large animal when hunting signified stages of growing up. A vision quest often marked the transition to manhood.

Marriage took place early for girls, usually between the age of twelve and fifteen years; for boys, it took place between the age of fifteen and twenty years. Some tribes arranged marriages; others permitted young men and women to choose their own partners. Most groups were monogamous, although some allowed two wives. Some tribes permitted men to have sexual relations outside of marriage when their wives were pregnant or breastfeeding.

Colonial Families

If we could go back and live again in all of our two hundred and fifty million arithmetical ancestors of the eleventh century, we should find ourselves doing many surprising things, but among the rest we should certainly be ploughing most of the fields of the Contentin and Calvados, going to mass in every parish church in Normandy [France]; rendering military service to every lord, spiritual or temporal, in all this region; and helping to build the Abbey church at Mont-Saint-Michel.

Henry Adams (1838–1918)

From earliest colonial times, America has been an ethnically diverse country. In the houses of Boston, the mansions and slave quarters of Charleston, the *maisons* of New Orleans, the *haciendas* of Santa Fe, and the Hopi dwellings of Oraibi (the oldest continuously inhabited place in the United States, dating back to 1150 A.D.), American families have provided emotional and economic support for their members. With different languages, family roles, customs, and traditions, these families were the original crucible from which our contemporary families were formed.

FIRST ARRIVALS. Colonial America was initially settled by waves of explorers, soldiers, traders, pilgrims, servants, prisoners, immigrants, and slaves. In 1565, at St. Augustine, Florida, the Spanish established the first permanent European settlement in what is now the United States. But the members of these first groups came as single men–as explorers, soldiers, and exploiters.

In 1620, the leaders of the Jamestown colony in Virginia, hoping to promote greater stability, began importing English women to be sold in marriage. The company reasoned (quoted in Miller, 1966):

We are tomorrow's past.

Mary Webb

. . . The Plantation can never flourish till families be planted and the respect of wives and children fix the people to the soyle [soil], therefore have given this faire beginninge for the reimbursinge of whose charges, it is ordered that every man that marries them give 120 lb waight of best leafe Tobacco for each of them. . . .

In colonial America, families were the center of daily life. The family, said Plymouth's William Bradford, was "a little commonwealth." This was hardly an exaggeration, as the well-being of the community depended on the well-being of the family. The family was the cornerstone of colonial society; it was required for survival.

THE FAMILY AS THE BASIC ECONOMIC AND SOCIAL UNIT. The European colonists who came to America attempted to replicate their familiar family system. This system, strongly influenced by Christianity, emphasized **patriarchy** (rule by father or eldest male), the subordination of women, sexual restraint, and family-centered production. The family was basically an economic and social institution, the primary unit for producing most goods and caring for the needs of its members. The family planted and harvested food, made clothes, provided shelter, and cared for the necessities of life. Each member was expected to contribute economically to the welfare of the family. Husbands plowed, planted, and harvested crops. Wives supervised apprentices and servants, kept records, cultivated the family garden, assisted in the farming, and marketed surplus crops or goods, such as grain, chickens, candles, and soap. Older children helped their parents and, in doing so, learned the skills necessary for later life.

As a social unit, the family reared children and cared for the sick, infirm, and aged. Its responsibilities included teaching reading, writing, and arithmetic, because there were few schools. The family was also responsible for religious instruction: it was to join in prayer, read scripture, and teach the principles of religion.

Because of the family's importance, New England towns appointed tithingmen to observe groups of ten families. The tithingmen were to report how well each family performed its functions and enforced morality. These observers reported the children's behavior and the kind of education they received; they noted how husband and wife behaved toward each other; they determined whether the family attended church. If a couple fought excessively, the husband and wife were brought to court, where they were ordered to end their arguing or face fines, whipping, or the stocks (Miller, 1975).

Unlike New Englanders, the planter aristocracy that came to dominate the Southern colonies did not give high priority to family life; hunting, entertaining, and politics provided the greatest pleasure. However, while the planters attempted to imitate the English gentry, the majority of Southern white families more closely resembled the New England family. By the beginning of the nineteenth century, these families shared common ideals and values. The planter aristocracy continued to idealize gentry ways, until the Civil War destroyed the slave system upon which the planters based their wealth.

MARITAL CHOICE. Romantic love was not a factor in choosing a partner; one practical seventeenth-century marriage manual advised women that "this boiling affection is seldom worth anything . . ." (Fraser, 1984). Since marriage had profound economic and social consequences, parents often selected their children's mates. Such choices, however, were not as arbitrary as it may seem. Parents tried to choose partners whom their children already knew and with whom they seemed compatible. Children were expected to accept the parents' choices. One father wrote in his will that if his daughters did not accept the choices of the executor, "but of their own fantastical brain bestow themselves upon a light person," their inheritance would be cut in half (Miller, 1975).

Love came after marriage. In fact, it was a person's duty to love his or her spouse (Leites, 1982). The inability to desire and love a marriage partner was considered a defect of character. Each was obliged to be kind and loving to the other, to treat the other with understanding and affection. For colonial Americans, love was respectful and considerate, not romantic.

Although the Puritans prohibited premarital intercourse, they were not entirely successful. **Bundling,** the New England custom in which a young man and woman

God's universal law gave to man despotic power
Over his female in due awe.

John Milton (1608–1674)

spent the night in bed together, separated by a wooden bundling board, was a consequence of harsh winters, the lack of fuel, and the difficulty of traveling, all of which made it difficult for the man to return home after an evening of courting. It provided a courting couple with privacy; it did not, however, encourage restraint. An estimated one-third of all marriages in the eighteenth century took place with the bride pregnant (Smith and Hindus, 1975). Some historians believe that premarital pregnancy was a means by which the young exerted control over their marital choice by presenting their parents with a *fait accompli* (D'Emilio and Freedman, 1988).

The Governor of Hartford upon Connecticut came to Boston, and brought his wife with him (a godly young woman and of special parts) who was fallen into a sad infirmity, the loss of her understanding and reason which had been growing upon her divers years by occasion of her giving herself wholly to reading and writing, and had written many books. Her husband being very loving and tender of her, was loath to grieve her; but he saw his error when it was too late. For if she had attended her household affairs, and such things as belong to women, and not gone out of her way and calling to meddle in such things as are proper for men, whose minds are stronger, etc., she had kept her wits, and might have improved them usefully and honorably in the place God had set her.

John Winthrop

FAMILY LIFE. The colonial family was strictly patriarchal. The authority of the husband/father rested in his control of land and property, because in an agrarian society like colonial America, land was the most precious resource. The manner in which the father decided to dispose of his land affected his relationships with his children. In many cases, children were given land adjacent to the father's farm, but the title did not pass into their hands until the father died. Sometimes the father deeded land to his children when they reached adulthood or married but carefully stipulated that his children would provide lifetime support. As one historian (Fischer, 1978) noted, "Land was an instrument of generation politics—a way of preserving both the power and authority of the elderly. Sons were bound to their fathers by ties of economic dependency; youth was the hostage of age." This power also gave fathers control over their children's marital choices as well as keeping them geographically close.

This strongly rooted patriarchy called for wives to submit to their husbands. The wife was not an equal, but a "helpmate." This subordination was reinforced by traditional religious doctrine, especially the teachings of Paul of Tarsus. Like her children, the colonial wife was economically dependent on her husband. Upon marriage, she transferred many of the rights she had held as a single woman to her husband, such as the right to inherit or sell property, to conduct business, and to attend court.

For women, marriage marked the beginning of a constant cycle of childbearing and childrearing. On the average, colonial women had six children and were consistently bearing children until around age forty. Women often became grandmothers while they were bearing their last children. As a result, most women were involved in childbearing or childrearing activities until their deaths. A woman without children under her care—whether her own, her grandchildren, or nieces and nephews—was a rarity.

CHILDHOOD. The colonial conception of childhood was radically different from ours. First, children, were believed to be evil by nature. The community accepted the traditional Christian doctrine that children were conceived and born in sin. Jonathan Edwards, the leading evangelist in colonial America, described unrepentant children as "young vipers and infinitely more hateful than vipers" (quoted in Wishy, 1968). Parents saw the child's spontaneity not as a delight but as a sign of rebelliousness. This view of the child supported the stern authoritarianism that characterized childrearing during this time.

Second, childhood did not represent a period of life radically different from adulthood. Such a conception is distinctly modern (Aries, 1962; Meckel, 1984; Vann, 1982). In colonial times, a child was regarded as a small adult. When children were six or seven, childhood ended for them. From that time on, they began to be part of the adult world, participating in adult work and play. Since children were treated similarly to adults after about six years of age, there was no sudden change in their status during adolescence. They were never protected from the world because they participated in it. As such, children's lives were marked by continuity rather than discontinuity. Such continuity protected them from the identity crises that arise when individuals abruptly change their roles or status.

Third, when children reached the age of ten, they were often "bound out" for several years as apprentices or domestic servants. They lived in the home of a relative or stranger, where they learned a trade or skill, were educated, and were properly disciplined (Morgan, 1966). By putting their children out, Puritan families avoided the conflict between independence and dependence as their children reached maturity.

African-American Families

In 1619, a Dutch man-of-war docked at Jamestown in need of supplies. As part of its cargo were twenty Africans who had been captured from a Portuguese slaver. The captain quickly sold his captives as indentured servants. Among these Africans was a woman known by the English as Isabella and a man known as Antony; their African names are lost. In Jamestown, Antony and Isabella married. After several years, Isabella gave birth to William Tucker, the first African-American child born in what is today the United States. William's birth marked the beginning of the African-American family, a unique family system that grew out of the African adjustment to slavery in America.

During the eighteenth century and later, West African family systems were severely repressed throughout the New World (Guttman, 1976). At first, some slaves tried unsuccessfully to continue polygamy, which was strongly rooted in many African cultures. The slaves were more successful in continuing the traditional African emphasis on the extended family, in which aunts, uncles, cousins, and grandparents played important roles. Although slaves were legally prohibited from marrying, they created their own marriages. Despite the hardships placed on them, they developed strong emotional bonds and family ties. Slave culture discouraged casual sexual relationships and placed a high value on marital stability. On the large plantations, most slaves lived in two-parent families with their children. To maintain family identity, parents named their children after themselves or other relatives or gave them African names. As time went on, the developing African-American family blended West African and English family traditions (Guttman, 1976). In the harsh slave system, the family provided strong support against the daily indignities of servitude.

❖ NINETEENTH-CENTURY MARRIAGES AND FAMILIES

The colonial family could trace its roots back thousands of years to the beginning of settled agricultural life. But in the nineteenth century, the traditional colonial family form gradually vanished and was replaced by the modern family. This new family was radically different from any family system seen before in the world. It was created as a result of industrialization. Ironically, it is this historically radical nineteenth-century family form that we tend to think of as the "traditional" American family, even though the colonial family followed the true traditional form.

To study the history of the American family is to conduct a rescue mission into the dreamland of our national self-concept. No subject is more closely bound up with our sense of a difficult present—and our nostalgia for a happier past.

John Demos

Industrialization Shatters the Old Family

In the nineteenth century, industrialization transformed the face of America. It also transformed American families from self-sufficient farm families to wage-earning urban families. As factories began producing gigantic harvesters, combines, and tractors, significantly fewer farm workers were needed. Looking for employment, workers migrated to the cities, where they found employment in the ever-expanding factories and businesses. Families no longer worked together in the fields or the home producing food, clothing, and other necessities; instead these were produced by large-scale farms and factories. Food and other goods were purchased with wages earned in factories and stores. Because goods were now bought rather than made in the home, the family began its shift from being primarily a production unit to being a consumer and service-oriented unit. With this shift, a radically new division of labor arose in the family. Men began working outside the home in factories or offices for wages to purchase the family's necessities and other goods. Men became identified as the family's sole provider or "breadwinner." Their work was given higher status than women's work because it was paid in wages. Men's work began to be identified as "real" work.

At the same time industrialization made husbands the breadwinner in the family, it also undercut much of their power over their children as fathers. Previously, fathers could control their children by withholding land and property. With the rise of factories, farming decreased in importance, and children were able to find employment in towns and cities. They were no longer dependent on their fathers.

Industrialization also created the housewife, the woman who remained at home attending to household duties and caring for children. Previously, men and women were interdependent within the family unit, because women produced many of the family's necessities. Now, however, goods were purchased with money earned by husbands. Because much of what the family needed had to be purchased with the husband's earnings, the wife's contribution in terms of *unpaid* work and services went unrecognized, much as it continues today.

Marriage and Families Transformed

Without its central importance as a work unit, the family became the focus and abode of feelings. In earlier times, the necessities of family-centered work gave marriage and family a strong center based on economic need. The emotional qualities of a marriage mattered little as long as the marriage produced an effective working partnership. Without its productive center, however, the family focused on the relationships between husband/wife and parent/child. Affection, love, and emotion became the defining qualities of a good marriage.

THE POWER OF LOVE. This new affectionate foundation of marriage brought love to the foreground. Men and women chose their partners on the basis of love, and love was supposed to bring personal happiness. Love as the basis of marriage represented the triumph of individual preference over family, social, or group considerations. Parents had little power in selecting their children's partners, and their children were no longer as economically dependent on them. Women now had a new degree of power; they were able to choose whom they would marry. As historian Carl Degler (1980) observed:

Simply because affection was a chief basis for marital choices, courtship in the 19th century was an important stage in family formation. At perhaps no other point in the course of a marriage was a woman's autonomy greater or more individualistically exercised.

Women could rule out undesirable partners during courtship; they could choose mates with whom they believed they would be compatible.

Many a family tree needs trimming.

Kin Hubbard (1868–1930)

Because of the affectionate bond, women had more power in influencing the marital relationship. A husband was expected to act out of love toward his wife; he was expected to be considerate of her feelings. Love created a mutuality and a kind of emotional equality that had been absent earlier in marriages. Mutual esteem, friendship, and confidence became guiding ideals. Without love, marriages were considered empty shells.

CHANGING ROLES FOR WOMEN. The two most important family roles for middle-class women in the nineteenth century were the housewife and mother roles. As there was a growing emphasis on domesticity in family life, the role of the housewife increased in significance and status. There was no such thing as "just" a housewife in the nineteenth century; indeed, the roles of housewife and mother were idealized as among the most important in society. Home was the center of life, and the housewife was responsible for making family life a source of fulfillment for everyone. She tended to the needs of her husband and responded to his complaints of the outside world; she nurtured her children. New family celebrations appeared that the housewife was responsible for orchestrating: birthday parties with birthday cakes; Christmas, with presents and caroling; Thanksgiving, with turkey stuffed with dressing.

Women also increasingly focused their identities on motherhood. The nineteenth century witnessed the most dramatic decline in fertility in American history. Between 1800 and 1900, fertility dropped by 50 percent, falling from an average of 7 to about 3.5 children per women. Women reduced their childbearing by insisting that they, not men, control the frequency of intercourse. Childrearing rather than childbearing became one of the most important aspects of a woman's life. Having fewer children allowed more time to concentrate on mothering. Although women were no longer responsible for educating their children, they were responsible for making the children feel loved, developing their unique potential, and forming a special mother/child bond.

Having fewer children also opened the door to greater participation in the world outside the family. This outside participation manifested itself in women's heavy involvement in the abolition, prohibition, and women's emancipation movements. Women participated in these movements as a means of protecting the home and family. Because women were viewed as especially selfless and moral, their uplifting influence in politics and reform was thought to counteract the destructive forces of self-interest, corruption, and commercialism.

CHILDHOOD AND ADOLESCENECE. A strong emphasis was placed on children as part of the new family. The belief in childhood innocence replaced the idea of childhood corruption (Aries, 1982). A new sentimentality surrounded the child, who was now viewed as born in total innocence. William Wordsworth's poem "Ode: Intimations of Immortality from Recollections of Early Childhood" summed up the new view of the child (see marginalia). The child had come from the bosom of God and possessed angelic qualities. It was only through contact with the world that this original goodness was corrupted. Protecting children from experiencing or even knowing about the evils of the world became a major part of childrearing.

The nineteenth century also witnessed the beginning of adolescence (Kett, 1977). Society had defined a new stage in life, characterized by immaturity, inexperience, and emotional turmoil. Adolescence was an outgrowth of nineteenth-century childhood, during which parents sheltered their children by protecting them from worldly knowledge. In contrast to colonial youths, who participated in the adult world of

---

What is morality at any given time or place? It is what the majority then and there happen to like and immorality is what they dislike.

Alfred North Whitehead (1861–1947)

Ode: Intimations of Immortality from Recollections of Early Childhood

Our birth is but a sleep and a forgetting:
The soul that rises with us, our life's star,
Hath had elsewhere its setting,
And cometh from afar;
Not in entire forgetfulness,
And not in utter nakedness,
But trailing clouds of glory do we come
From God, who is our home.
Heaven lies about us in our infancy;
Shades of the prison-house begin to close
Upon the growing boy,
But he beholds the light, and whence it
* flows.*
He sees it in his joy;
The youth, who daily farther from the east
Must travel, still is Nature's priest,
And by the vision splendid
Is on his way attended;
At length the man perceives it die away,
And fade into the light of common day.

William Wordsworth (1770–1850)

work and other activities, nineteenth-century adolescents were kept economically dependent and separate from adult activities. Feminist Charlotte Perkins Gilman (quoted in Kennedy, 1970) said it was the family's duty to ensure children "an even longer period of immaturity." Because they were kept separate from the adult world, children often felt apprehensive when they did enter it. This apprehension sometimes led to the emotional conflicts associated with adolescent identity crises.

Education also changed as schools, rather than families, became responsible for teaching reading, writing, and arithmetic. But the school did more than educate children; it socialized them as well, encroaching on still another traditional function of the family. Ideas and values were now transmitted by an impersonal institution over which the family had little control. Conflicts between the beliefs of the family and those of the school were inevitable. At school, the child's peer group increased in importance.

The African-American Family: Slavery and Freedom

Although there were large numbers of free African Americans—100,000 in the North and Midwest and 150,000 in the South—most of what we know about the African-American family prior to the Civil War is limited to the slave family.

THE SLAVE FAMILY. By the nineteenth century, the slave family had already lost much of its African heritage. Under slavery, the African-American family lacked two key factors that helped give free African-American and white families stability. First, the enslaved African-American family lacked autonomy. Slave marriages were not recognized as legal. Final authority rested with the owner in all decisions about the lives of slaves. If the owner decided to break up a family by selling a husband, wife, or

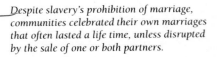

Despite slavery's prohibition of marriage, communities celebrated their own marriages that often lasted a life time, unless disrupted by the sale of one or both partners.

children, laws granted him that right. In the upper South, slave breeding was an important source of income for planters. The separation of families was a common occurrence, spreading grief and despair among thousands of slaves. One former slave (quoted in Botkin, 1945) remembered:

My mother told me that he [her master] owned a woman who was the mother of several children, and when her babies would get about a year or two of age he'd sell them, and it would break her heart. She never got to keep them. When her fourth baby was born and was about two years old, she just studied all the time about how she would have to give it up, and one day she said, "I just decided I'm not going to let Old Master sell this baby; he just ain't going to do it." She got up and give it something out of a bottle and pretty soon it was dead.

The slave owners used the slaves' affection for their families to ensure control. One slaveholder (quoted in Genovese, 1976) wrote, "It is necessary that Negroes have wives, and you ought to know that nothing attaches them so much to a plantation as children." Although some slaveholders went to great lengths to hold families together, the majority were willing to sacrifice the slaves' families when profits were at stake. Frederick Douglass (quoted in Stampp, 1956) referred to slaveholder control over the enslaved African-American family as "that painful uncertainty which in one form or another was ever obtruding itself in the pathway of the slave." (See the reading by Frederick Douglass, "A Slave Childhood," for a description of a slave child's life.)

Second, the slave family had little economic importance as a unit. Slave families worked for their masters, not themselves. It was impossible for the slave husband/father to become the provider for his family. Yet he did provide an important part of their sustenance by hunting and trapping. If plantation food allowances had been the only source of nourishment for slave families, malnutrition would have been much more widespread. One slave (quoted in Genovese, 1976) recalled, "My dear old daddy partly raised his children on game. He caught rabbits, coon an' possums. He would work all day and hunt at night."

The slave women worked in the fields beside the men. When they returned home to their cabins, the women worked their gardens to supplement the family's food supply. Then, working into the night, they prepared meals for their family and tended to other household tasks. In this limited way, the family worked as a productive unit. But its roles and functions were radically different from white middle-class families.

When a slave was pregnant, her owner determined her care during pregnancy and her relation to her infant after birth. During pregnancy a field slave continued her work; only in the last few weeks before birth were her duties relaxed. After birth she was generally given a few days off (or weeks, in some cases). The new mother usually carried her baby to the fields with her or left it in the care of an elderly slave. The planters desire to maximize a woman slave's productivity, despite her pregnancy, led to a decline in slave fertility and an increase in miscarriages during the final decades of slavery (G. Jones, 1985).

The age at which children recognized themselves as slaves depended on whether they were children of field or house slaves. If their parents were field slaves, they would be subject to slave discipline from the beginning. One former slave (quoted in Blassingame, 1972) recalled: "I was born a slave. . . . I was made to feel, in my boyhood's first experience, that I was inferior and degraded and that I must pass through life in a dependent and suffering condition." But if the children were offspring of house slaves (or the slave owner), they were often playmates of their master's children. They would play games, hunt, and fish together, and sometimes

The man over there says women need to be helped into carriages and lifted over ditches, and to have the best place everywhere. Nobody ever helps me into carriages and over puddles, or gives me the best place—and ain't I a woman? Look at my arm! I have ploughed and planted and gathered into barns, and no man could head me—and ain't I a woman? I could work as much and eat as much as a man . . .and bear the lash as well! And ain't I a woman? I have born thirteen children, and seen most of 'em sold into slavery, and when I cried out with my mother's grief, none but Jesus heard me—and ain't I a woman?

Sojourner Truth (1797?–1883)

Bye baby buntin'
Daddy's gone a–huntin'
Ter fetcha little rabbit skin
Ter wrap de baby buntin' in.

Slave lullaby

(although it was illegal) learn to read together. Only gradually would they learn that they were slaves. But the day would come when such a child would know that he or she was a slave, and that time would be filled with grieving, anger, and humiliation. The knowledge created a deep crisis in the child's concept of self.

AFTER FREEDOM. When freedom came, the formerly enslaved African-American family had strong emotional ties and traditions forged from slavery and from their West African heritage (Guttman, 1976; Lantz, 1980). Because they were now legally able to marry, thousands of former slaves who had "jumped the broomstick" in slave marriage now formally renewed their vows. The first year or so after freedom was marked by what was called "the traveling time," in which African Americans traveled up and down the South looking for lost family members who had been sold. Relatively few families were reunited, although many continued the search well into the 1880s (Litwack, 1979).

African-American families remained poor, tied to the land by the sharecrop system, which kept them in a state of semislavery, and by segregation, which kept them subordinate. Despite poverty and continued exploitation, the Southern African-American family usually consisted of both parents and their children. Extended kin continued to be important: aunts, uncles, grandparents, cousins, and in-laws provided a rich source of affection and kindly assistance through thick and thin.

Immigration: The Great Transformation

THE OLD AND NEW IMMIGRANTS. In the nineteenth and early twentieth centuries, great waves of immigration swept over America. Between 1820 and 1920, 38 million immigrants came to the United States. Historians commonly divided them into "old" immigrants and "new" immigrants. The old immigrants, who came between 1830 and 1890, were mostly from western and northern Europe; they generally arrived in northern ports, such as Boston and New York. These immigrants were Irish, German, Scandinavian, and English peasants and laborers. During this period, Chinese also immigrated in large numbers to the West Coast, where they formed settlements in San Francisco and Vancouver, British Columbia. The new immigrants began to arrive in great numbers between 1890 and 1914 (when World War I virtually stopped all immigration). They came from eastern and southern Europe, mainly from Italy, Russia, Austria-Hungary, Greece, and Poland. Japanese also immigrated to the West Coast and Hawaii during this time. Today, Americans can trace our roots to numerous ethnic groups.

Although in the nineteenth century, most ethnic groups immigrated to the United States, others were "incorporated" as a result of American expansionism. As the United States expanded its frontiers, surviving Native Americans were incorporated. The United States acquired its first Latino population when it annexed Texas, California, New Mexico, and part of Arizona after its victory over Mexico in 1848. More than 80,000 former inhabitants of Mexico became Americans and provided the foundation for Latino culture in California and the Southwest. The Spanish-American War (1898) brought the Philippines (granted independence in 1946), Puerto Rico, and Guam under American control as U.S. territories. After the United States annexed Hawaii in 1900, Hawaiians (and the Japanese and Chinese living there) found themselves under American territorial rule.

THE IMMIGRANT EXPERIENCE. Most immigrants were uprooted; they left only when life in the old country became intolerable (Handlin, 1979). The decision to leave

---

The struggle of man against power is the struggle of memory against forgetting.

Milan Kundera

Except for Native Americans, most of us have ancestors who came to America voluntarily or involuntarily. Between 1820 and 1920, more than 38 million immigrants came to the United States.

their homeland was never easy. It meant leaving behind ancient ties, traditional customs, and familiar ways. Often it was a choice between life or death, when beyond the specter of poverty loomed famine, riots, and revolution.

Most immigrants arrived in America without skills. Although most came from small villages, they soon found themselves in the concrete cities of America. But because families and friends kept in close contact even when separated by vast oceans, immigrants seldom left their native countries without knowing where they were going—to the ethnic neighborhoods of New York, Chicago, Boston, San Francisco, Vancouver, and other cities. There they spoke their own tongues, practiced their own religions, and ate their customary foods. (See the reading, "A Russian Jew Discovers America.")

The immigrants transformed American cities. By 1910, almost ten million city dwellers were foreign born. Neighborhoods became Little Italys, Chinatowns, East European ghettoes, and Irish shantytowns, where outsiders had the sense of stumbling into a foreign land. Unfamiliar smells, accents, voices, and sights greeted strangers. In these cities, immigrants created great economic wealth for America by providing cheap labor to fuel growing industries.

In America, kinship groups were central to the immigrants' experience and survival (Bodnar, 1985). Parents, brothers and sisters, and aunts and uncles in America sent passage money to their relatives at home. They sent information about where to live and find work. Families and relatives clustered close together in ethnic neighborhoods. Informal networks exchanged information about employment locally and in other areas.

The family economy, critical to immigrant survival, was based on cooperation among family members. All family members, including the children, worked in order for the family to survive. When children worked, their income went to the family resource pool. As one scholar noted (Bodnar, 1985):

Essentially, family goals came to supercede individual goals, and parents and children both worked vigorously to contribute to familial welfare. Immigrant parents were often able to direct the career paths of their progeny because . . . . [they were] able to provide access to industrial jobs or housing in crowded cities. Boys and girls were frequently asked to leave school early and start work either in a mill or in a family business. Girls were often kept at home caring for younger brothers and sisters or performing household chores. . . . Boys were urged to learn a job skill or a business rather than pursue a formal education. . . . Often they received such training on the job from fathers or other kin.

For most immigrant families, as for African-American families, the middle-class idealization of motherhood and childhood was a far cry from reality. Because of low industrial wages, many immigrant families could survive only by pooling their resources and sending mothers and children to work in the mills and factories. Among Irish millhands in the 1860s, most fathers could earn only half of what was needed to support a family at subsistence levels. In Chicago fifty years later, a Polish meatpacker earned about 38 percent of what was needed for his family. Working mothers and children became major contributors to the family. Irish children, for example, contributed from one-third to one-half of the family income. The proportion of mothers working varied by region and ethnic group (Bodnar, 1985).

Most groups experienced hostility. "No Irish need apply" signs were prominently displayed in Boston during the 1840s. Asians were placed in segregated schools in San Francisco, and, during World War II, Japanese Americans and Japanese Canadians were interred in "relocation" camps. Crime, vice, and immortality were attributed to the newly arrived ethnic groups; ethnic slurs became part of everyday parlance.

The New Colossus

Not like the brazen giant of Greek fame,
With conquering limbs astride from land to
*   land,*
Here at our sea-washed, sunset gates shall
*   stand*
A mighty woman with a torch, whose
*   flame*
Is the imprisoned lightning, and her
*   name*
Mother of Exiles. From her beacon–hand
Glows world-wide welcome; her mild eyes
*   command*
The air-bridged harbor that twin cities
*   frame.*
"Keep, ancient lands, your storied pomp!"
*   cries she*
With silent lips. "Give me your tired, your
*   poor,*
Your huddled masses yearning to breathe
*   free,*
The wretched refuse of your teeming shore.
Send these, the homeless, tempest-tossed to
*   me,*
I lift my lamp beside the golden door."

Emma Lazarus (1849–1887)

Probe the earth and see where your main roots run.

Henry David Thoreau

Discovering Your Family Past

We are descendants of the past, yet our knowledge of our own family's past is often dim or nonexistent. But our parents, grandparents, and great-grandparents—and their parents and grandparents—all have a story, and their stories are our families history. "Each of us is all the sums he has not counted: subtract us into nakedness and night again, and you shall see begin in Crete four thousand years ago the love that ended yesterday in Texas. . . . before." Thomas Wolfe wrote in *Look Homeward, Angel.* "Every moment is a window on all time." The history of our own family is part of the history of the family as well as humankind's.

The past is not so distant or abstract when we understand that its facts are the flesh from which we were born. What do you know of your family's history? How did your parents meet? From where did their parents and their parents' parents come? Were they immigrants, slaves, Native Americans? You only need to go back a few generations to reach into the nineteenth century, when life was radically different from today.

You can explore your own family history through photographs and family trees. Photographs are often used by psychologists as maps of family feelings and relationships. Gather together family photographs of your immediate family and your forebears—grandparents, great-grandparents, and so on. Identify who is in these pictures. If you don't know, find out from someone who does. Look at the faces of these people, the body language, the positions of the family members relative to one another. Are family members clustered closely together or far apart? Is someone standing off from the others? Is someone looking gloomy amidst others who are smiling? What family resemblances do you see? Do you look like a great-great-grandparent, for example?

On separate sheets of paper, gather information about each of your pictured relatives. Then, after you read this chapter, find out what aspects of the family that we have discussed apply to your family members. Was a great-grandfather a child laborer? Was a great-great-grandmother a slave? How did your relatives go about their daily tasks in the household? Did they make their bread or buy it?

On page 42 there are examples of two types of family trees and a "family wheel." Depending on your family's form (nuclear, step, or adoptive, for example), one of these ways of depicting family history may be appropriate for you. Or you may want to create a unique way of showing your family's inter-connections, such as the "family web" described by Jennifer Meyer on page 356. If you don't have information that you need to create your family tree (or other depiction of family history), ask someone in your family who might know. After you fill out the names and dates, try to find out stories about the oldest family members. Where did they come from? What important historical events occurred during their lifetimes? In which events did they actually participate? What were their own experiences of joy and sorrow? What did they pass down—love of learning, ambition, money, pride?

After you gather information about your relatives and fill in your family tree, go back to the genogram you completed in the previous chapter. Your genogram and family history are complementary: each will help illuminate the other (Bahr, 1990; Friedman, Rohrbaugh, and Krakauer, 1988). Does the new information you gathered shed additional light on your genogram? Does your genogram help you understand your family history?

As you think about your family history, remember that you too will probably leave direct or indirect descendants. You are both a repository and creator of your own family history. Even now you have stories to tell your present or future children, grandchildren, or other descendants—stories about the times in which you lived, the people you loved, the dreams you lost and found, your triumphs and your sorrows. What values, traits, or memories do you wish to pass on to your descendants? What are the stories you will tell your grandchildren?

Strong activist groups arose to prohibit immigration and promote "Americanism." Literacy tests required immigrants to be able to read at least thirty words in English. In the early 1920s, severe quotas were enacted that slowed immigration to a trickle.

❖ TWENTIETH-CENTURY MARRIAGES AND FAMILIES

The Rise of Companionate Marriages: 1900–1960

The past is never dead; it is not even past.

William Faulkner (1897–1962)

By the beginning of the twentieth century, the functions of American middle-class families had been dramatically altered from earlier times. Families had lost many of their traditional economic, educational, and welfare functions. Food and goods were produced outside the family, children were educated in public schools, and the poor, aged, and infirm were increasingly cared for by public agencies and hospitals. The primary focus of the family was becoming even more centered on meeting the emotional needs of its members.

THE NEW COMPANIONATE FAMILY. Beginning in the 1920s, a new ideal family form was beginning to emerge that rejected the "old" family based on male authority and sexual repression. This new family form was based on the **companionate marriage**. There were four major features of this companionate family (Mintz and Kellogg, 1988). First, men and women were to share household decisionmaking and tasks. The husband was no longer the sole decision maker, nor was the wife the sole person responsible for household tasks and child care. Second, marriages were expected to provide romance, sexual fulfillment, and emotional growth. Third, wives were no longer expected to be guardians of virtue and sexual restraint. Instead, they were to be sexually alluring and responsive to their husbands. Fourth, children were no longer to be protected from the world but were to be given greater freedom to explore and experience the world; they were to be treated more democratically and encouraged to express their feelings. The heyday of this family was the 1950s.

"LEAVE IT TO BEAVER": THE GOLDEN AGE OF THE FIFTIES. Many of us look back on the fifties as a kind of golden age of the family. The family of television's Beaver Cleaver was typical of the 1950s, when the father was the breadwinner and the mother was the housewife in over 70 percent of all families. Marriage and family seemed to be central to American lives. It was a time of youthful marriages, increased birthrates, and a stable divorce rate. But the decade was also an exception to the general trends of delayed marriages, decreasing birth rates, and rising divorces. The fifties was an aberration.

Perhaps one of the things that makes the fifties so appealing to many in retrospect was the general and uncritical acceptance of traditional gender and marital roles. Man's place was in the world and woman's place was in the home. Women were expected to place motherhood first; they were to be "properly" flattering of men; they were not to excel. (There were even debates as to whether men should be given preference over women in college admissions.) Women who sought careers or advanced degrees were described as being neurotic or suffering from "penis envy."

The fifties were also a time of unprecedented prosperity. Real income had risen 20 percent in the fifteen years following World War II. (By contrast, it has fallen almost that same amount since the early 1970s.) This prosperity fueled the movement to the suburbs, where families readily purchased look-alike homes at affordable prices. By 1960, half the population lived in suburbs.

Suburbanization profoundly affected family life. Most residents were young couples and their children. Few suburban housewives were employed outside the home. Indeed, children seemed to dominate the suburban landscape. Mothers were transformed into chauffeurs, transporting their children to lessons, games, and parties. To the degree that mothers subordinated themselves to their children, they found themselves isolated from other interests and people. This isolation, coupled with a transient life-style occasioned by company moves, made loneliness one of suburbia's compelling problems.

Aspects of Contemporary American Marriages and Families: 1970 to the Present

Today, despite television reruns of "Leave It to Beaver," less than a fifth of American families resemble the Beaver's. In the 1990s, Beaver's family seems gone forever (see Table 2.1).

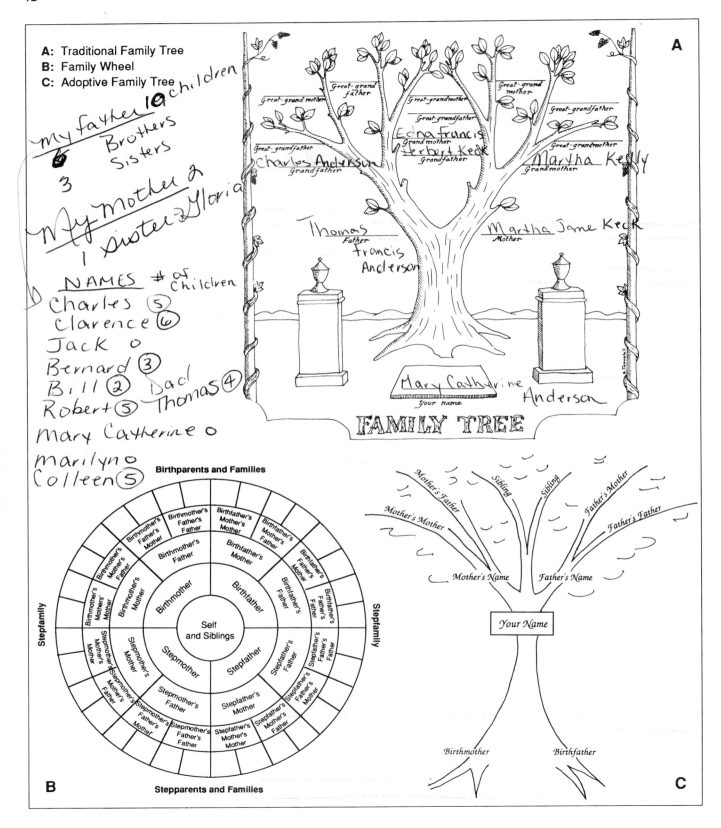

A: Traditional Family Tree
B: Family Wheel
C: Adoptive Family Tree

My father 10 children
6 Brothers
3 Sisters

My mother 2
1 sister Gloria

NAMES # of Children
Charles ⑤
Clarence ⑥
Jack 0
Bernard ③
Bill ② Dad
Robert ⑤ Thomas ④
Mary Catherine 0
Marilyn 0
Colleen ⑤

Great-grand father
Great-grand mother
Great-grandmother
Great-grand mother
Great-grandfather
Great-grandfather
Great-grandmother
Edna Francis Grandmother
Herbert Keck Grandfather
Charles Anderson Grandfather
Martha Kelly Grandmother

Thomas Father
Francis Anderson
Martha Jane Keck Mother

Mary Catherine Anderson
Your name

FAMILY TREE

Birthparents and Families

Self and Siblings

Birthmother
Birthfather
Birthmother's Mother
Birthmother's Father
Birthfather's Mother
Birthfather's Father
Birthmother's Mother's Mother
Birthmother's Mother's Father
Birthmother's Father's Mother
Birthmother's Father's Father
Birthfather's Mother's Mother
Birthfather's Mother's Father
Birthfather's Father's Mother
Birthfather's Father's Father

Stepfamily
Stepfamily

Stepmother
Stepfather
Stepmother's Mother
Stepmother's Father
Stepfather's Mother
Stepfather's Father
Stepmother's Mother's Mother
Stepmother's Mother's Father
Stepmother's Father's Mother
Stepmother's Father's Father
Stepfather's Mother's Mother
Stepfather's Mother's Father
Stepfather's Father's Mother
Stepfather's Father's Father

Stepparents and Families

B

Mother's Mother
Mother's Father
Sibling
Sibling
Father's Mother
Father's Father

Mother's Name
Father's Name

Your Name

Birthmother
Birthfather

C

TABLE 2.1	How Families Have Changed, 1970–1988				
	1970	1980	1988	PERCENT CHANGE 1970–1988	
Population	205,100,000	227,700,000	246,100,000	Up	20
Marriages performed	2,159,000	2,413,000	2,389,000	Up	11
Divorces granted	708,000	1,182,000	1,183,000	Up	67
Married couples	44,728,000	48,643,000	51,809,000	Up	16
Married couples with children	25,541,000	24,501,000	24,600,000	Down	3
Unmarried couples with children present	196,000	424,000	891,000	Up	355
Single-parent families	4,560,000	6,051,000	7,320,000	Up	61
Unmarried couples	523,000	1,600,000	2,200,000	Up	446
Births	3,731,000	3,598,000	3,913,000	Up	5
Births to unmarried women	398,000	600,000	933,000	Up	134

SOURCE: Bureau of the Census. *U.S. Statistical Abstract, 1990.* Washington, DC: Government Printing Office, 1990. U.S. Bureau of Census. Population Reports. P-20. *Marital Status and Living Arrangements, March, 1990.* Washington, D.C., 1991.

DIVERSITY OF FAMILY FORMS. One of the most striking features of contemporary American families is their diversity. The traditional nuclear family is a minority today. There is no dominant family form as there was in the past. Instead, we have a number of family forms, some of which may overlap:

◆ *Marriage without children,* in which husband and wife defer childbearing, are infertile, or choose not to have children.
◆ *Two-parent family,* in which both husband and wife are present.
◆ *Dual-worker family,* in which both husband and wife are employed. There may or may not be children.
◆ *Single-parent family,* in which only one parent is present. This family is created through divorce, births to unmarried women, or death.
◆ *Extended family,* a three-generational family including kin and fictive kin. This family form is especially important to African Americans, Latinos, Asian Americans, Native Americans, and various other ethnic groups.
◆ *Stepfamily,* in which at least one parent is not the child's biological parent.
◆ *Binuclear family,* in which two families—the custodial family and the noncustodial family—interact with each other in rearing children born in the original marriage or relationship.
◆ *Cohabitation,* in which a heterosexual, gay, or lesbian couple lives together without marriage. Unlike other family forms, cohabitation is not recognized by society as a family institution.
◆ *Gay or lesbian family,* in which children are reared in a gay single-parent or dual-parent (two "moms" or two "dads") family.

These family forms are largely the product of a rising divorce rate, a higher percentage of births to single women, economic changes, and changing gender roles.

The growing numbers of single-parent families and stepfamilies reflect the fact that over half of all recent marriages end in divorce and about 25 percent of all births are to single women. Almost 90 percent of single-parent families are headed by women. Yet single parenthood is a transitional state; most single parents eventually marry or remarry. Their marriages form the basis for stepfamilies. The chances are about fifty-

fifty that children born today will spend at least part of their lives in a single-parent family. The chances are somewhat smaller that they will also live in a stepfamily.

Economics has played a major role in transforming the traditional family into the dual-worker family. For generations, African-American families were affected by low wages, forcing both spouses to work. Later, beginning in the 1970s, middle-class families were pummelled by inflation, forcing women into the work force to maintain their families' standard of living. The expanding economy, especially in service, sales, and clerical work, provided additional opportunities (at low pay), especially for women. At the same time, female employment barriers began to fall; women began moving into management positions and the professions.

It is difficult to overestimate the consequences of female employment. A wife's employment severs the bonds of economic dependency on her husband. Women's greater economic independence helps equalize the husband/wife power equation in marriage. Because a woman earns income, she gains status; she also gains the economic ability to leave an unsatisfactory marriage. Work also changes the nature of childhood for the children of employed mothers (Spitze, 1991).

CHANGING ATTITUDES TOWARD FAMILY ISSUES. During the 1960s and 1970s, there were dramatic changes in norms and values concerning marriage, divorce, gender roles, and childbearing. These changes stabilized in the 1980s, however, and there have been few significant changes since then except for attitudes toward gender roles, which continued to become more egalitarian (Thornton, 1989).

During the 1960s and 1970s, negative attitudes toward remaining single declined substantially. Nevertheless, there was no strong movement toward Americans wanting to remain single. During the 1980s, there were more positive attitudes toward marriage. In the early 1960s, 85 percent of the mothers in Arland Thornton's study (1989) believed all married couples should have children; by the 1980s, the number had fallen to 43 percent. Acceptance of divorce increased rapidly through the mid-1970s but has remained stable since then. In 1962, 51 percent of female respondents believed it was wrong to "stay together for the sake of the children"; by 1977, the number had increased to 80 percent.

Dramatic changes also took place in attitudes regarding sexuality and cohabitation. In 1965, 69 percent of the young women and 65 percent of the young men said that premarital sex was always or almost always wrong. Twenty years later, only 22 percent of the young women and 34 percent of the young men held similar beliefs. Attitudes toward extramarital sex, however, remain unchanged. In 1965, over 80 percent viewed an extramarital affair as always wrong; in 1985, 84 percent of the women and 88 percent of the men considered extramarital sex wrong. There continued to be growing acceptance of cohabitation without marriage, although only about one-third of all respondents approve of it.

Reviewing these trends, Thornton (1989) believes that our norms and values may have changed significantly. Marriage is less important in structuring our intimate relationships because premarital sex and cohabitation are increasingly accepted. Fidelity within a relationship has become more important, however. As a society we have become increasingly tolerant of diversity; we have enlarged the realm of privacy and accepted the primacy of individual choice over social rules. At the same time, we have not increasingly endorsed remaining single, getting divorced, and having childless marriages. Thornton (1988) noted that "what has changed in these areas of family life has been an increased tolerance for behavior not previously accepted . . . not an increase in an active embracement of such behavior."

Cultural Diversity

Americans come from diverse roots. According to the 1990 census, in identifying their ancestry, Americans cited over 130 ethnic groups. Over 16 million Americans speak non-English languages at home. In 1990, immigration laws were reformed to permit a 45 percent increase in immigration between 1992–1994 and a 35 percent increase in subsequent years. Between 1992 and 1994, 700,000 immigrants will be granted visas yearly; afterward, 675,000 immigrants will be admitted each year. As a result, continued Latino and Asian immigration promises to make ethnicity a major factor in American life well into the next century.

The descendants of nineteenth-century immigrants, however, are finding their ethnic identities declining in significance as they leave their ethnic neighborhoods for the suburbs, increase their economic status, and marry outside their group. A major study (Lieberson and Waters, 1988) on contemporary ethnic groups in America concluded:

White ethnics, while different from one another on a variety of measures, are still much more similar to each other than they are to blacks, Hispanics, American Indians, and Asians. . . . For whatever cause(s), a European–non-European distinction remains a central division in the society.

As new immigrants arrive, primarily from Latin America and Asia, they find their ethnic identities major factors in organizing their lives. According to the latest data available, there are at least 16 to 18 million foreign-born Americans. Europeans accounted for 5.3 million, Asians represented 3.8 million (mostly, in numerical order, from the Philippines, Korea, China, Vietnam, and Japan), and Caribbeans totaled 1.8 million (U.S. Bureau of the Census, 1988). Because of the large numbers of undocumented aliens from Latin America, precise numbers of foreign-born Latinos are unknown, although the number may run as high as 7 million. There has been relatively little immigration from black Africa in the twentieth century.

Families from ethnic groups such as African Americans, Latinos, and Asians often face prejudice and discrimination. Such discrimination has often limited educational and work opportunities for these people. As a result, families from these different ethnic groups often face hardships and challenges that white middle-class families do not.

AFRICAN-AMERICAN FAMILIES. The largest ethnic group in the United States is African American. The African-American family, as we have seen, can trace its roots back to the beginnings of the earliest European settlements. Between 1980 and 1990, the African-American population increased by approximately 16 percent. In 1990, there were over 31 million African Americans in the United States. Between 1990 and 2000, the African-American population will increase by 12.8 percent, to 35.2 million (U.S. Bureau of the Census, 1988 and 1990).

In the twentieth century, especially after World War II, there was a movement of African Americans from the South to other parts of the country, especially to urban areas (Lemann, 1991). Robert Staples (1991) noted:

Unlike the European immigrants before them, African Americans were disadvantaged by the hard lines of northern segregation along racial lines. Furthermore, families in cities are more vulnerable to disruptions from the traumatizing experience of urbanization, the reduction of family functions, and the loss of extended family support.

In the cities, African Americans were especially vulnerable to economic forces. The postwar technological revolution diminished the need for industrial workers, the backbone of the working-class African-American family. After the mid-1950s, the unemployment rate for African Americans surged to two to three times the rate for whites. As a result, the gradual increase of the African-American middle class has been more than counterbalanced by the demise of the African-American working class, replaced by the underclass (Billingsley, 1988).

We boast of being immigrants . . .when we are no longer subject to the immigrants' ordeal, after we have become certifiable natives and, often, at a time when we and our kind are busily closing the door to others.

Meg Greenfield

We are increasingly becoming a world of migrants, made up of bits and fragments from here, there. We are here. And we have not really left anywhere we have been.

Salman Rushdie

I am the dream and hope of the slave.

Maya Angelou

The tree of love gives shade to all.

African–American proverb

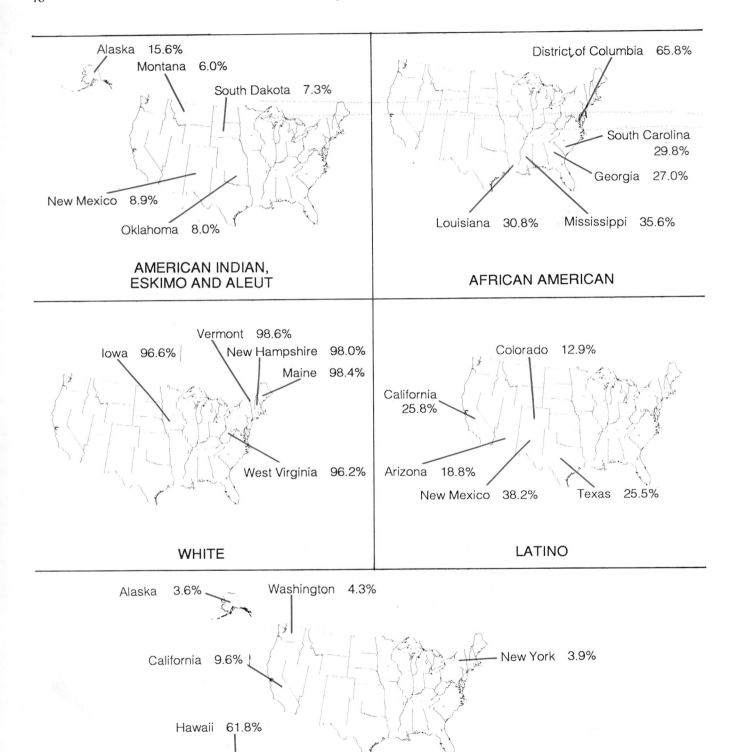

AMERICAN INDIAN,
ESKIMO AND ALEUT

AFRICAN AMERICAN

WHITE

LATINO

ASIAN OR
PACIFIC ISLANDER

The geographical movement out of the South led to a pursuit of individual rather than family goals. The strong tradition of familialism continues, however, as intergenerational ties are emphasized in the African-American family. Kinship bonds are especially important, for they provide economic assistance and emotional support in times of need (Taylor et al., 1991). Women, as well as men, have an important economic role. African-American families, in contrast to white families, have often been dual-earner families as a result of economic need.

As we examine African-American families, much of what they experience, such as high divorce rates or high rates of birth to single women, turn out to be associated with poverty rather than anything inherent in African-American families themselves. Although there seems to be greater marital instability in African-American families than in white families, for example, when divorce rates are adjusted according to socioeconomic status, the differences become minimal. Poor African Americans have divorce rates similar to poor whites, and middle-class African Americans have divorce rates similar to middle-class whites (Raschke, 1987). Thus, understanding socioeconomic status, especially poverty, is critical in examining African-American family life (Bryant and Coleman, 1988; Staples and Mirandé, 1980).

LATINO FAMILIES. Latinos are the fastest growing and second largest ethnic group in the United States. Between 1980 and 1990, Latino population increased by approximately 35 percent. Most of this increase resulted from immigration from Mexico (Vega, 1991). Between 1990 and 2000, Latinos are expected to increase another 27 percent and number 25.2 million (U.S. Bureau of the Census, 1988). In 1988, there were approximately 19.4 million Latinos in the United States; 12 million were of Mexican descent. Latinos account for 22 percent of the Texas population, 16 percent of the California and Arizona populations, and 14 percent of the New Mexico population. Puerto Ricans are concentrated in the Northeast, especially New York. The greatest concentration of Cubans is found in Florida.

It is important to remember that there is considerable diversity among Latinos, between those of Mexican, Cuban, Puerto Rican, and other heritages. For example,

FIGURE 2.1

Geographic Distribution of Ethnic Groups by Population Density According to 1990 Census (opposite page)

These maps indicate the highest concentrations by state of specific ethnic or racial groups and the proportion they form of a state's population. In 1985, 27 percent of all new immigrants settled in California, which has the greatest ethnic diversity of any state. It has the most people of English, German, Irish, Latino, Swedish, Portuguese, and Iranian descent. New York has the most of Polish, Italian, and African descent.

Out of poverty, poetry
Out of suffering, song.

Mexican proverb

For Latinos, la familia is a central part of their lives. Children are especially valued.

Frijoles, tortillas, y chile are more American than the hamburger.

Luis Valdez

40 percent of Cuban Americans earn over $35,000 annually, while only 15 percent of Puerto Ricans and 23 percent of Mexican Americans earn as much. Furthermore, there are 2.5 times as many single-parent families among Puerto Ricans as there are among Mexican Americans. (For an overview of Mexican American families, see Becerra, 1988; for Cuban American families, see Szapoznik and Hernandez, 1988; for Puerto Rican families, see Sánchez-Ayéndez, 1988.)

Spanish and Mexican settlements date back to the early seventeenth century in the Southwest. Because these areas bordered Mexico and had indigenous Latino cultures, they provided a magnet for Mexican and other Latino immigrants. Latino immigration was very small, however, until the turn of the century (Griswold Del Castillo, 1984). The massive influx of Mexican and other Latino immigrants began after 1945. Attracted by the American demand for workers and uprooted by poverty at home, twice as many Latinos immigrated between 1945 and 1965 as had come to the United States in the previous hundred years. Hope, combined with civil wars, revolutions, repression, poverty, and hunger drove hundreds of thousands from Guatemala, El Salvador, Cuba, Haiti, and other Latin American and Caribbean countries.

As with the European immigrants who preceded them, family networks help sustain the Latino immigrants. Three-fourths of Cuban and half of Mexican immigrants reported assistance from relatives residing in the United States. In fact, Mexican American family networks provide significant community and family links between the United States and Mexico (Vega, 1991). Although *la familia* is centered around the nuclear family, it also includes the extended family of grandparents, aunts, uncles, and cousins who tend to live close by, often in the same block or neighborhood. There is close kin cooperation and mutual assistance, especially in times of need, when the family bands together. Children are especially important; over one-third of Latino families have five or more children. Because Spanish is important in maintaining ethnic identity, many Latinos as well as educators support bilingualism in schools and government. Catholicism is also an important factor in Latino family life. Although there is a tradition of male dominance, day-to-day living patterns suggest that women have considerable power and influence in the family (Griswold Del Castillo, 1984).

It's not a "melting pot" anymore. . . . (It's) a fusion chamber. We are creating American culture daily.

Bharati Mukherjee

ASIAN-AMERICAN FAMILIES.   In 1990 there were approximately 6 million Asian Americans living in the United States; they comprise ten percent of the California population. By 2000, the Asian-American population will increase to 10 million (Lev, 1991). They are an especially diverse group, comprising Chinese, Japanese, Filipino, Vietnamese, Cambodian, Hmong, and other groups. The two largest and oldest groups are the Chinese Americans and Japanese Americans. Other groups, such as Vietnamese, Cambodians, Laotians, and Hmong, are more recent arrivals, first coming to this country in the 1970s as refugees from the upheavals resulting from the Vietnam war. In the 1980s, Koreans and Filipinos began immigrating in larger numbers. Because of their cultural diversity and degree of assimilation, generalizations about Asian Americans are risky. In addition, there has been very little research on Asian-American family relationships (see Chapter 3). (For an overview of Korean-American families, see Min, 1988; for Vietnamese-American families, see Tran, 1988; for Hmong families, see Hendricks, Downing, and Deinard, 1986).

Chinese Americans trace their ancestry in the United States to the mid-nineteenth century, when they came as laborers in the gold camps and railroads. (The Chinese word for laborer, *ku-li,* translates as "bitter strength.") Almost all the immigrants were men who had come alone to the "Golden Mountain," sending money home to their wives, who lived with their husbands' parents. Beginning in 1882, anti-Chinese sentiment led to the Exclusion Acts, which restricted Asian immigration. These acts virtually prohibited Chinese women from entering the United States until 1943, resulting in most Chinese men living without intimate marital ties in the United States. By 1930, there were four Chinese men for every Chinese woman in this country; today, the ratio is about equal. More recent immigrants tend to be from Taiwan or Hong Kong rather than mainland China itself.

Contemporary Chinese-American families continue to emphasize familialism, although filial piety and strict obedience to parental authority have become less strong. Chinese Americans tend to be better educated, have higher incomes, and have lower rates of unemployment than the general population. Their sexual values and attitudes toward gender roles tend to be more conservative; they tend to have a strong sense of family.

The second-largest group of Asian Americans is Japanese Americans. First-generation Japanese, called *Issei,* arrived in Hawaii and on the West Coast toward the end of the nineteenth century, where they engaged mostly in agriculture and domestic work. Like the Chinese, they suffered discrimination. In 1924 the Chinese Exclusion Acts were extended to forbid Japanese immigration. *Issei* were prohibited from becoming citizens, and in California, laws were passed to prevent them from owning or leasing farm land. American-born children of *Issei,* called *Nisei,* were granted citizenship, however. When the Japanese attacked the United States in World War II, Japanese Americans were incarcerated in so-called "relocation" camps and their property confiscated. (Only recently—almost fifty years later—did the federal government acknowledge its error and begin making small compensatory payments to the camp survivors.)

Sansei, third-generation Japanese Americans, have experienced more **acculturation** than other Asian-American groups. Almost half of all Japanese Americans, especially women, marry non-Japanese. *Sansei* emphasize *ie* (the Japanese extended family of past, present, and future generations), have high levels of education, and value achievement, diligence, and loyalty. In contrast to their elders, *Sansei* are more independent and individualistic, which sometimes causes cultural tension between the generations. Over a third of their children, *Yonsei,* who are mostly school-age or adolescent, are of mixed marriages, though they often continue to identify themselves as Japanese Americans.

NATIVE AMERICAN FAMILIES. From the beginning of European contact, Native Americans were decimated by invasion, war, famine, and disease. The unique family structures of each surviving tribe were deliberately undermined by the federal government's program of forced enculturation (1870–1930). Missionaries and government agents worked hand in hand to destroy traditional Indian family forms and replace them with the structure and norms of the conventional white nuclear family. As scholar John Price (1981) noted, "Christian missionaries usually tried to eliminate plural marriages and matrilineal customs without understanding the crucial roles these practices had in the normal functioning of native societies." Communal land was turned into private property, regulations were introduced making the man head of the family, and leaders no longer came from the clans (extended kin) but were elected. Church activities replaced traditional religious rituals.

Approximately 1.5 million Americans identify themselves as being of native descent. Those who continue to be deeply involved with their own traditional culture give themselves a tribal identity, such as Hopi, Navajo, or Sioux. Those who are more

Question: What is cultural deprivation? Answer: Living in a split level house in suburbia with a color TV.

Native American riddle

Powwows are an important mechanism for the development of Native American cultural identity as well as tribal identity.

acculturated, such as urban dwellers, tend to give themselves an ethnic identity as American Indians. Most Americans of native descent consider themselves members of a tribal group rather than an ethnic group. And, observed Price (1981), "Specific tribal identities are almost universally stronger and more important than identity as a Native American."

Because of the marked poverty on reservations and pressures toward acculturation, there has been a considerable migration of Native Americans to urban areas since World War II. Today, about half of Americans of native descent live in cities. In the cities, Indians are separated from their traditional tribal cultures and experience great cultural conflict as they attempt to maintain traditional values. Not surprisingly, those in the cities are more acculturated than those remaining on the reservations. Urban Native Americans may attend **powwows,** intertribal social gatherings centering around drumming, singing, and traditional dances. Powwows are important mechanisms in the development of the Native American ethnic identity in contrast to the tribal identity. Urban Native Americans, however, may visit the reservations regularly; in fact, these visits are sometimes described as a specialized form of commuting.

Because of the importance of tribal identities and practices, there is no single type of Native American family. Perhaps the most important factor affecting tribal identities is the degree of acculturation. A study (Miller, 1979) of a group of urban Native American families found that 39 percent were transitional, adopting white values; 22 percent were traditional, maintaining Indian values; 23 percent were bicultural, holding both Indian and white values; and 16 percent were marginal, failing to sustain Indian values or incorporate white ones.

❖ SOURCES OF FAMILY CHANGE

Marriages and families are sensitive to the different forces in society. As we saw when examining our history, the family has responded to different forces in American life. The most important sources of change are economic, demographic, and gender role changes (Mintz and Kellogg, 1988).

If history repeats itself, and the unexpected always happens, how incapable must man be of learning from experience.

George Bernard Shaw

Economic Changes

The family was once the primary economic unit in society, meeting most of the needs of its members: it provided food, clothing, household goods, and occasionally surplus crops, which it bartered or marketed. Today, the family has moved from being primarily an economic producing unit to a consuming, service-oriented unit. It no longer makes its clothing but buys it; it no longer grows its food but shops for it—or eats out at fast-food restaurants.

Inflation, economic hardship, and an expanding economy have led to married women entering the work force in unprecedented numbers. As a result, the dual-worker marriage and the employed mother have become prominent features of contemporary families. As women have increased their participation in the work force, they have decreased their economic dependency on men. Because working in the labor force provides both income and alternative roles for women, women have been able to increase their marital power.

Demographic Changes

The family has also changed demographically—that is, in terms of the characteristics of its members, such as age, number of children, sex ratio, divorce and death rate (Glick, 1988; Watkins and Menkin, 1987). Four of the most important demographic changes affecting the family have been (1) declining fertility (that is, the number of children a woman bears), (2) increased divorce rate, (3) the gradual aging of the population, and (4) race and ethnicity.

◆ *Declining Fertility.* As women bear fewer children, they have fewer years of child-rearing responsibility. With fewer children, partners are able to devote more time to each other. Parents are able to expend greater energy on each child. And women have greater opportunity for entering the work force.

◆ *Increased Divorce Rate.* The increased divorce rate, beginning in the late nineteenth century (as early as 1900, the United States had the highest divorce rate in the world), has led to the rise of single-parent families and stepfamilies.

◆ *Increased Longevity.* As men and women live longer, they are experiencing aspects of family life that few experienced before. In colonial times, because of a relatively short life expectancy, a husband and wife could expect a marriage to last up to twenty-five years. With today's much longer life expectancy, a couple can remain married for fifty to sixty years. Today's couples can also expect to live many years without children at home; they can expect to become grandparents and as many as one-fourth may become great-grandparents. American women can also expect a prolonged period of widowhood following the death of their husbands. Since men tend to marry women younger than themselves and there are more women than men, most widows will not remarry.

◆ *Race and Ethnicity.* Americans have always had diverse family systems, including the original Native American family systems, the dominant American family system

(based on the white English/European heritage), and the African-American family system. To these family systems were added nineteenth- and twentieth-century immigrant family systems. Immigration transformed America from a mainly Protestant country to one of religious pluralism.

Gender Role Changes

A third basic force altering American marriages and families is changing gender roles, especially women's roles. In colonial times, men were primarily responsible for tilling fields, harvesting crops, and manufacturing work implements. Women were the primary producers of family goods and necessities. If there was a surplus of crops or goods, women marketed or bartered them. But as production of clothing, household goods, tools, and food was transferred to factories and large-scale farms, men and women developed new roles. In the nineteenth century, men increasingly worked in factories and offices. As a result, families were no longer self-sufficient. Instead, they relied on wages brought home by the husband and, in working-class families, by the children. At the same time, women concentrated on mothering and household management. Women were now expected to be responsible for shaping their children's character and tending to the needs of their husbands. These changes led to the "invention" of the male breadwinner and the female housewife.

The emphasis on childrearing and housework as the proper duties of women continued unchallenged until the 1940s. During World War II, however, a massive influx of married women poured into factories and stores to replace men who were fighting. Thus began a trend in which women increasingly entered the labor force. By being less economically dependent on men, women gained greater power in marriage.

The feminist movement of the 1960s and 1970s caused women (whether they identified themselves as feminists or not) to reexamine their traditional assumptions about women's roles. Betty Friedan's *The Feminine Mystique,* published in 1963, became a national sensation. It attacked the traditionalist assumption that women found their greatest fulfillment in being mothers and housewives. The book tapped into fundamental discontent that many women were experiencing in suburbia. These women did everything they were supposed to do—were married, had three children, baked, cleaned, and joined clubs—but many were still dissatisfied. The women's movement challenged the female roles of housewife, helpmate, and mother. Practically, the dual-worker marriage made the traditional division of roles an important question for *all* women. Today, contemporary women have dramatically different expectations of male/female roles in marriage, childrearing, household work, and the workplace than did their grandmothers or even their mothers.

History is the ship carrying living memories to the future.

Stephen Spender

As we near the end of the twentieth century, we see that American families have changed radically during our history as a nation. The most radical change came about in the nineteenth century as we changed from a farming society to an industrial one. Within our own lifetime, families have been undergoing the most significant changes of the twentieth century as the once-dominant traditional white nuclear family has been supplanted by more diverse forms: the single-parent family, the stepfamily, the dual-worker family, and ethnic extended families. Our task as a society is not to decry the "decline" of the traditional family; rather, it is to support and strengthen the contemporary family as it is evolving in today's world.

❖ SUMMARY

◆ In the early years of colonization, there were two million Native Americans in what is now called the United States. Many of the families were *patrilineal;* rights and property flowed from the father; some other tribal groups were *matrilineal.* Most families were small. Native American children were rarely physically disciplined; they began working at an early age. Rituals marked transitions into adulthood. Most groups were monogamous.

◆ Diverse groups settled America, including English, Germans, and Africans. In colonial America, marriages were arranged. Marriage was an economic institution and the marriage relationship was *patriarchal* and companionate. The family was self-sufficient. Women's economic contributions were recognized. Children were also economically important, and from the age of about six or seven, they were regarded as small adults.

◆ African-American families began in the United States in the early seventeenth century. They continued the African tradition that emphasized kin relations. Most slaves lived in two-parent families that valued marital stability.

◆ In the nineteenth century, industrialization revolutionized the family's structure. The family was no longer economically self-sufficient. Men became wage earners, and women, once they married, became housewives. Childhood was sentimentalized, and adolescence was invented. Marriage was increasingly based on emotional bonds. Courtship was based on romance, and marriages were supposed to be havens from the harsh world. Women were expected to be sexually restrained, even in marriage, which may have contributed to the declining birthrate.

◆ The stability of the African-American slave family suffered because it lacked autonomy and had little economic importance. Slave families were broken up by slaveholders, and marriage between slaves was not legally recognized. African-American families formed solid bonds nevertheless. Parents' relations with their children were influenced by the slaveholder. The children of field hands learned early on that they were slaves; the children of house slaves often did not realize that they were slaves until they reached middle childhood.

◆ Thirty-eight million people immigrated to the United States between 1820 and 1920. Most immigrants were uprooted and experienced hostility. Kinship groups were important for survival. The family economy focused on family survival rather than individual success.

◆ Beginning in the twentieth century, *companionate marriage* became an ideal. Men and women shared household decision making and tasks, marriages were expected to be romantic, wives were expected to be sexually active, and children were to be treated more democratically.

◆ The 1950s, the golden age of the companionate marriage, was an aberration. It was an exception to the general trend of rising divorce and nontraditional gender roles. Prosperity was unusually high; suburbanization led to increased isolation.

◆ Contemporary American families are characterized by diversity of family forms, including two-parent families, single-parent families, extended families, stepfamilies, binuclear families, gay and lesbian families, and cohabiting families. These families have arisen as a result of several trends, including a high divorce rate, increased rate of births to single women, economic changes, and changing gender roles.

◆ During the 1960s and 1970s, there were dramatic changes in attitudes toward single status, marriage, divorce, gender roles, and childbearing. Since the mid-1970s, the changes have stabilized, except for attitudes about gender roles, which are becoming increasingly egalitarian.

◆ Contemporary families are culturally diverse; there are over 130 ethnic groups in America. African Americans and Latinos are the largest ethnic groups, and extended family ties are especially important to these groups.

◆ Since the 1950s, technological changes have decimated the African-American working class, giving rise to the underclass. Many of the problems African-American families experience are the result of low socioeconomic status rather than family structure.

◆ Latinos, who are the fastest-growing ethnic group, emphasize extended kin relationships, cooperation, and mutual assistance. *La familia* includes not only the nuclear family but also the extended family. Catholicism exerts a strong influence on Latino families. Bilingualism helps maintain ethnicity.

◆ Among Asian Americans, Chinese Americans and Japanese Americans have been in the United States the longest. Both groups have experienced great discrimination. Chinese Americans continue to emphasize familialism. Japanese Americans, the most *acculturated* of Asian Americans, continue to emphasize the *ie,* the extended family that includes past, present, and future members. Native Americans endured forced enculturation for 60 years as the government and Christian missionaries attempted to assimilate them into mainstream white culture. Tribal identity is their key identity. Poverty forced many off reservations to cities. *Powwows* are social gatherings centering around drumming, singing, and dancing.

◆ Throughout American history, economic, demographic, and gender role changes have significantly affected the family. Economically, the family has moved from being primarily a producing unit to a consuming unit. Demographic effects include declining fertility, increased divorce, increased longevity, and changing ethnic composition. Changing gender roles are reshaping the family as women become more equal in the workplace and at home.

Answers to Preview Questions

The answers to the preview questions at the beginning of the chapter are listed below. As you check your answers, whether you were correct or not, think about your reasons for each response. What were they? What was their source? How valid is the source? As you read the chapter, you will find the questions discussed in greater depth.

1. F	6. T
2. T	7. T
3. F	8. T
4. F	9. T
5. F	10. T

❖ SUGGESTED READINGS

American Family History: A Historical Bibliography. Santa Barbara, Calif.: ABC-Clio Information Services, 1984. Abstracts of books and articles on family history in the United States and Canada.

Bellah, Richard, et al. *Habits of the Heart: Individualism and Commitment in American Life.* New York: Perennial Library, 1986 (paperback). A provocative interpretation of the contemporary American psyche and the conflict between individualism and commitment. Uses a rich historical perspective.

√ Degler, Carl. *At Odds: Women and the Family from the Revolution to the Present.* New York: Oxford University Press, 1980 (paperback). An important work on women in the nineteenth and early twentieth centuries by a major American historian.

Davis, Marilyn. *Mexican Voices/American Dreams: An Oral History of Mexican Immigration.* New York: Henry Holt, 1990. Recent immigrants from Mexico tell their stories in a moving manner.

D'Emilio, John, and Estelle Freedman. *Intimate Matters: A History of Sexuality in America.* New York: Harper and Row, 1988. An interpretative history of sexuality from the seventeenth century to the present. Especially strong in its exploration of sexual issues and politics and the sexuality of women, African Americans, gay men and lesbians.

Dinnerstein, Leonard, and David Reimers. *Ethnic Americans: A History of Immigration,* 3d ed. New York: Harper and Row, 1988. An excellent history of immigration, assimilation, and family life from colonial times to the mid-1980s; especially strong on post-World War II and current immigration.

Eichler, Margrit. *Families in Canada Today.* Toronto: Gage, 1983. An examination of recent changes in the Canadian family.

Griswold Del Castillo, Richard. *La Familia: Chicano Families in the Urban Southwest, 1848 to the Present.* Notre Dame, Ind.: University of Notre Dame, 1984. The transformations undergone by Latino families in Los Angeles, Tucson, Santa Fe, and San Antonio from the mid-nineteenth century to the beginning of the 1980s.

Guttman, Herbert. *The Black Family: From Slavery to Freedom.* New York: Pantheon Books, 1976 (paperback). The definitive study of the African-American family through the end of the 1920s.

Herskovitz, Melville J. *Dahomey: An Ancient West African Kingdom.* 2 vols. Evanston, Ill.: Northwestern University Press, 1967; reprint of 1938 edition. The classic work on the West African society from where large numbers of American slaves originated.

Jackson, James S., ed. *Life in Black America: Findings from a National Survey.* Newbury Park, Calif.: Sage Publications, 1991 (paperback). Based on the National Survey of Black Americans, this is the first study of a truly representative cross-section of African Americans. Includes essays on family life, males and females, neighborhoods, and racial identity.

Kain, Edward. *The Myth of Family Decline: Understanding Families in a World of Rapid Social Change.* Lexington, Mass.: Lexington Books, 1990. A challenging book viewing contemporary changes as evolutionary rather than revolutionary.

Lavrin, Asunción, ed. *Sexuality and Marriage in Colonial Latin America.* Lincoln, Nebr.: University of Nebraska Press, 1989. A collection of scholarly essays on the creation and early development of New World family systems resulting from the subjugation of the Aztecs and other native peoples by Spanish conquistadors and missionaries.

Lemann, Nicolas. *The Promised Land: The Great Black Migration and How It Changed America.* New York: Alfred A. Knopf, 1990. An engagingly written description of the movement of African Americans from the South to the Midwest and North, much of it seen through the eyes of a woman whose life is followed from the sharecropper society of the Missippi Delta in 1941 to present-day Chicago.

Margolin, Malcolm. *The Ohlone Way: Indian Life in the San Francisco and Monterey Bay Area.* Berkeley, Calif.: Heyday Books, 1978 (paperback). An outstanding telling of California Indian life and family ways.

McAdoo, Harriet, ed. *Black Families.* Second edition. Beverly Hills, Calif.: Sage Publications, 1988 (paperback). Examines conceptual, historical, demographic, and economic aspects of African-American family systems, male/female relationships and socialization.

Mindel, Charles, Robert Habenstein, and Roosevelt Wright, Jr., eds. *Ethnic Families in America: Patterns and Variations,* 3d ed. New York: Elsevier North Holland, Inc., 1988. A collection of essays on different ethnic groups; historical background and contemporary status.

Mintz, Steven, and Susan Kellogg. *Domestic Revolutions: A Social History of American Family Life.* New York: The Free Press, 1988. A brief, well-written history of American marriage and family.

Parr, Jay. *Childhood and Family in Canadian History.* Toronto: McClelland and Stewart, 1982. A useful history of Canadian families.

Rothman, Ellen. *Hands and Hearts: A History of Courtship in America.* New York: Basic Books, 1984. A history of courtship from colonial times.

Salmoral, Manuel Lucena. *America 1492.* New York: Facts of File, 1990. A beautifully illustrated depiction of Native American family, cultural, and political life in the Americas on the eve of Columbus's encounter with the New World.

Solomon, Barbara, ed. *American Families: Twenty-eight Short Stories.* New York: New American Library, 1989 (paperback). A history of 20th century American family life told through short stories.

Staples, Robert, ed. *The Black Family: Essays and Studies.* Fourth edition. Belmont, Calif.: Wadsworth Publishing Co., 1991 (paperback). A valuable collection of essays.

Wishy, Bernard. *The Child and the Republic.* Philadelphia: University of Pennsylvania Press, 1968. An excellent study of changing attitudes toward children and childrearing in the nineteenth century.

Suggested Films

The Autobiography of Miss Jane Pittman (1974). Slavery and freedom seen through the eyes of a hundred-year-old woman.

The Colored Museum (PBS Great Performances, 1989). Playright George Wolfe's satirical sketches of African American stereotypes.

Eat a Bowl of Tea (1989). Brilliant comedy of a young Chinese American who goes to China for an arranged marriage and his bride's subsequent, and scandalous, adjustment to postwar American life.

El Norte (1984). Peasants flee war-torn Guatemala to the United States, searching for safety and freedom.

Farewell to Manzanar (1976). The moving story of a Japanese-American family interned in World War II relocation camp.

Hester Street (1975). Poignant, simple story of young Jewish immigrant who joins her husband in New York City at turn of the century, only to discover that he has rejected the old ways and expects her to do likewise.

Powwow Highway (1989). The comic odyssey of a young Cheyenne who decides to follow the sacred path in an old junkyard Buick; quietly camouflages its concerns about contemporary Native American life in its comedy.

A Raisin in the Sun (1961; also PBS Great Performances, 1990). Chicago African-American family tries to make sense of their constrained lives.

Zoot Suit (1981). Luis Valdez's stylized "musical" of the railroading of Los Angeles Latinos into prison during World War II.

READINGS

❖

A SLAVE CHILDHOOD

Frederick Douglass. Excerpt from
Life and Times of Frederick Douglass.

Frederick Douglass, one of the leading black abolitionists, describes his early childhood in this excerpt from his autobiography. In what significant ways did the slave family differ from the nonslave family in the nineteenth century?

Whether because [my grandmother] was too old for field service, or because she had so faithfully discharged the duties of her station in early life, I know not, but she enjoyed the high privilege of living in a cabin separate from the quarters, having imposed upon her only the charge of the young children and the burden of her own support. She esteemed it great good fortune to live so, and took much comfort in having the children. The practice of separating mothers from their children and hiring them out at distances too great to admit of their meeting, save at long intervals, was a marked feature of the cruelty and barbarity of the slave system; but it was in harmony with the grand aim of that system, which always and everywhere sought to reduce man to a level with the brute. It had no interest in recognizing or preserving any of the ties that bind families together or to their homes.

My grandmother's five daughters were hired out in this way, and my only recollections of my own mother are a few hasty visits made in the night on foot, after the daily tasks were over, and when she was under the necessity of returning in time to respond to the driver's call to the field in the early morning. These little glimpses of my mother, obtained under such circumstances and against such odds, meager as they were, are ineffaceably stamped upon my memory. She was tall and finely proportioned, of dark, glossy complexion, with regular features, and amongst the slaves was remarkably sedate and dignified.

Of my father I know nothing. Slavery had no recognition of fathers, as none of families. That the mother was a slave was enough for its deadly purpose. By its law the child followed the condition of its mother. The father might be a freeman and the child a slave. The father might be a white man, glorying in the purity of his Anglo-Saxon blood, and the child ranked with the blackest slaves. Father he might be, and not be husband, and could sell his own child without incurring reproach, if in its veins coursed one drop of African blood.

continued on next page

Living thus with my grandmother, whose kindness and love stood in place of my mother's, it was some time before I knew myself to be a slave. I knew many others things before I knew that. Her little cabin had to me the attractions of a palace. Its fence-railed floor—which was equally floor and bedstead—upstairs, and its clay floor downstairs, its dirt and straw chimney, and windowless sides, and that most curious piece of workmanship, the ladder stairway, and the hole so strangely dug in front of the fireplace, beneath which grandmamma placed her sweet potatoes, to keep them from frost in winter, were full of interest to my childish observation. The squirrels, as they skipped the fences, climbed the trees, or gathered their nuts, were an unceasing delight to me. There, too, right at the side of the hut, stood the old well, with its stately and skyward-pointing beam, so aptly placed between the limbs of what had once been a tree, and so nicely balanced, that I could move it up and down with only one hand, and could get a drink myself without calling for help. Nor were these all the attractions of the place. At a little distance stood Mr. Lee's mill, where the people came in large numbers to get their corn ground. I can never tell the many things thought and felt, as I sat on the bank and watched that mill and the turning of its ponderous wheel. The millpond, too, had its charms, and with my pin-hook and threadline, I could get amusing nibbles if I could catch no fish.

It was not long, however, before I began to learn the sad fact that this house of my childhood belonged not to my dear old grandmother, but to some one I had never seen, and who lived a great distance off. I learned, too, the sadder fact, that not only the home and lot, but that grandmother herself and all the little children around her belonged to a mysterious personage, called by grandmother, with every mark of reverence, "Old Master." Thus early did clouds and shadows begin to fall upon my path.

I learned that this old master, whose name seemed ever to be mentioned with fear and shuddering, only allowed the little children to live with grandmother for a limited time, and that as soon as they were big enough they were promptly taken away to live with the said old master. These were distressing revelations, indeed. My grandmother was all the world to me, and the thought of being separated from her was a most unwelcome suggestion to my affections and hopes.

I wished that it was possible for me to remain small all my life, knowing that the sooner I grew large the shorter would be my time to remain with them. Everything about the cabin became doubly dear and I was sure that there could be no other spot on earth equal to it. But the time came when I must go, and my grandmother, knowing my fears, and in pity for them, kindly kept me ignorant of the dreaded moment up to the morning (a beautiful summer morning) when we were to start; and, indeed, during the whole journey, which, child as I was, I remember as well as if it were yesterday, she kept the unwelcome truth hidden from me.

The distance from Tuckahoe to Colonel Lloyd's, where my old master lived, was full twelve miles, and the walk was quite a severe test of the endurance of my young legs. The journey would have proved too severe for me, but that my dear old grandmother (blessings on her memory) afforded occasional relief by "toting" me on her shoulder. Advanced in years as she was, as was evident from the more than one gray hair which peeped from between the ample and graceful folds of her newly and smoothly ironed bandanna turban, grandmother was yet a woman of power and spirit. She was remarkably straight in figure, and elastic and muscular in movement. I seemed hardly to be a burden to her. She would have "toted" me farther, but I felt myself too much of a man to allow it. Yet while I walked I was not independent of her. She often found me holding her skirts lest something should come out of the woods and eat me up. Several old logs and stumps imposed upon me, and got themselves taken for enormous animals. I could plainly see their legs, eyes, ears, and teeth, till I got close enough to see that the eyes were knots, washed white with rain, and the legs were broken limbs, and the ears and teeth only such because of the point from which they were seen.

As the day advanced the heat increased, and it was not until the afternoon that we reached the much-dreaded end of the journey. Here I found myself in the midst of a group of children of all sizes and of many colors—black, brown, copper-colored, and nearly white. I had not before seen so many children. As a newcomer I was an object of special interest. After laughing and yelling around me and playing all sorts of wild tricks, they asked me to go out and play with them. This I refused to do. Grandmamma looked sad, and I could not help feeling that our being there boded no good for me. She was soon to lose another object of affection, as she had lost many before. Affectionately patting me on the head, she told me to be a good boy and go out to play with the children. They are "kin to you," she said, "go and play with them." She pointed out to me my brother Perry, and my sisters, Sarah and Eliza. I had never seen them before, and though I had sometimes heard of them and felt a curious interest in them, I really did not understand what they were to me or I to them. Brothers and sisters we were by blood, but slavery had made us strangers. They were already initiated into the mysteries of old master's domicile, and they seemed to look upon me with a certain degree of compassion. I really wanted to play with them, but they were strangers to me, and I was full of fear that my grandmother might leave for home without taking me with her. Entreated to do so, however, and that, too, by my dear grandmother, I went to the back part of the house to play with them and the other children. Play, however, I did not, but stood with my back against the wall witnessing the playing of the others. At last, while standing there, one of the children, who had been in the kitchen, ran up to me in a sort of roguish glee, exclaiming, "Fed, Fed, grandmamma gone!" I could not believe it. Yet, fearing the worst, I ran into the kitchen to see for myself, and lo! she was indeed gone, and was now far away, and "clean" out of sight. I need not tell all that happened now. Almost heartbroken at the discovery, I fell upon the ground and wept a boy's bitter tears, refusing to be comforted. My brother gave me peaches and pears to quiet me, but I promptly threw them on the ground. I had never been deceived before and something of resentment mingled with my grief at parting with my grandmother.

It was now late in the afternoon. The day had been an exciting and wearisome one, and I know not where, but I suppose I sobbed myself to sleep, and its balm was never more welcome to any wounded soul than to mine. The reader may be surprised that I relate so minutely an incident apparently so trivial, and which must have occurred when I was less than seven years old, but, as I wish to give a faithful history of my experience in slavery, I cannot withhold a circumstance which at the time affected me so deeply, and which I still remember so vividly. Besides, this was my first introduction to the realities of the slave system.

❖

A RUSSIAN JEW DISCOVERS AMERICA

Abraham Cahan. Excerpt from *The Rise of David Levinsky.*

The Rise of David Levinsky was the first important Jewish novel written in America. It describes the early Russian childhood of David Levinsky, his arrival in America near the turn of the century, and his rise to wealth, prominence—and loneliness. A Talmudic scholar tells David, a newly arrived "green one," that "America is a topsy-turvy country." What does the scholar mean? What adjustment did the scholar have to make?

. . . When it grew dark and I was much in need of rest I had a street peddler direct me to a synagogue. I expected to spend the night there. What could have been more natural?

At the house of God I found a handful of men in prayer. It was a large, spacious room and the smallness of their number gave it an air of desolation. I joined in the devotions with great fervor. My soul was sobbing to Heaven to take care of me in the strange country.

The service over, several of the worshipers took up some Talmud folio or other holy book and proceeded to read them aloud in the familiar singsong. The strange surroundings suddenly began to look like home to me.

One of the readers, an elderly man with a pinched face and forked little beard, paused to look me over.

"A green one?" he asked, genially.

He told me that the synagogue was crowded on Saturdays, while on weekdays people in America had no time to say their prayers at home, much less to visit a house of worship.

When he heard that I intended to stay at the synagogue overnight he smiled ruefully.

"One does not sleep in an American synagogue," he said. "It is not Russia." Then, scanning me once more, he added, with an air of compassionate perplexity: "Where will you sleep, poor child? I wish I could take you to my house, but—well, America is not Russia. There is no pity here, no hospitality. My wife would raise a rumpus if I brought you along. I should never hear the last of it."

With a deep sigh and nodding his head plaintively he returned to his book, swaying back and forth. But he was apparently more interested in the subject he had broached. "When we were at home," he resumed, "she, too, was a different woman. She did not make life a burden to me as she does here. Have you no money at all?"

I showed him the quarter I had received from the cloak contractor.

"Poor fellow! Is that all you have? There are places where you can get a night's lodging for fifteen cents, but what are you going to do afterward? I am simply ashamed of myself."

" 'Hospitality,' " he quoted from the Talmud, " 'is one of the things which the giver enjoys in this world and the fruit of which he relishes in the world to come.' To think that I cannot offer a Talmudic scholar a night's rest! Alas! America has turned me into a mound of ashes."

"You were well off in Russia, weren't you?" I inquired, in astonishment. For, indeed, I had never heard of any but poor people emigrating to America.

"I used to spend my time reading Talmud at the synagogue," was his reply.

Many of his answers seemed to fit, not the question asked, but one which was expected to follow it. You might have thought him anxious to forestall your next query in order to save time and words, had it not been so difficult for him to keep his mouth shut.

"She," he said, referring to his wife, "had a nice little business. She sold feed for horses and she rejoiced in the thought that she was married to a man of learning. True, she has a tongue. That she always had, but over there it was not so bad. She has become a different woman here. Alas! America is a topsy-turvy country."

He went on to show how the New World turned things upside down, transforming an immigrant shoemaker into a man of substance, while a former man of leisure was forced to work in a factory here. In like manner, his wife had changed for the worse, for, lo and behold! instead of supporting him while he read Talmud, as she used to do at home, she persisted in

continued on next page

sending him out to peddle. "America is not Russia," she said. "A man must make a living here." But, alas! it was too late to begin now! He had spent the better part of his life at his holy books and was fit for nothing else now. His wife, however, would take no excuse. He must peddle or be nagged to death. And if he ventured to slip into some synagogue for an afternoon and read a page or two he would be in danger of being caught redhanded, so to say, for, indeed, she often shadowed him to make sure that he did not play truant. Alas! America was not Russia. . . .

AN ASIAN-AMERICAN IMMIGRANT FAMILY

James M. Freeman and Usha Welaratna

Immigration has transformed American life during the last decade. Although Latinos have accounted for the greatest increase, Asian-American immigrants have also made a substantial contribution to population growth. Asian Americans comprised 3 percent of the U.S. population in 1991, but they outnumber African Americans in ten states and Latinos in three states.

Immigrants leave their native lands for many reasons, usually personal or economic; refugees are immigrants who flee their countries because of war, oppression, or persecution, seeking "refuge." Whether an immigrant is a refugee or not significantly affects his or her adjustment because of possible past trauma. The adjustment of Southeast Asian refugees is often painful, as this essay suggests. What are some of the problems they confront? What kinds of adjustments must they make? How could American society be more sensitive to the needs of refugees? Of immigrants in general? How do you think the adjustment problems of Southeast Asian refugees might be similar to or different from those of refugees from Guatemala or El Salvador? From countries at peace, such as European countries, the Soviet Union, or Mexico?

Mr. Ngon is an 80-year-old former civil servant from South Vietnam. In 1975, he and his family fled to America as refugees; they were unable to bring with them anything other than the clothes they wore. In a few short years, Mr. Ngon's family has come a long way toward achieving the American dream. Mr. Ngon and his wife live in a spacious new house. All of their sons are highly educated and successful in the health professions and the electronics industry.

To the outside world, Mr. Ngon's family represents a stunning success story, an example of the Asian "model minority." But beneath the outer appearance of economic success lies sorrow, family separation, conflict and unanticipated change; loneliness and the feeling of being ill-at-ease in the United States. Mr.

Ngon and his wife view themselves as having failed because members of their family have grown apart, and their children and grandchildren do not obey them. In contrast, their sons view them as old-fashioned disciplinarians who meddle excessively in their lives.

Since 1975, more than 950,000 Indochinese refugees and immigrants from Vietnam, Laos, and Cambodia have sought and been granted refuge or admission in the United States. According to the Refugee Act of 1980, the primary goal in the resettlement of these refugees is "the achievement of self-sufficiency as quickly as possible." This is demonstrated by having regular employment and often by the prestige and income of the jobs held.

According to many studies about refugees, and many federally funded projects that purport to assist them, success in employment is the primary indicator of the success of refugees in adapting to American culture. Based on this view, Vietnamese refugees and immigrants, such as Mr. Ngon's family, typically are described as successful in adjusting to the United States, while Cambodians are often cited as a group that is less successful.

Overlooked in these conclusions is how Vietnamese and Cambodians themselves describe their own adjustments.

"In America," Mr. Ngon says, "there is nothing to hold our family together. In this city, my family numbers some 16 people spanning three generations; we live in several different locations in the city. Even so, we have nothing to look forward to. If I returned to Vietnam, the Communists would put me in a re-education camp, which would kill me. But here in America, my wife and I will die a lonely death, abandoned by our children."

Faced with death or divorce, Americans also experience the pain of family separation and break-up. They have learned to find support groups to help them through their crises that often include individuals who are not relatives. This contrasts with Vietnamese and Cambodian refugees, who depend primarily on families or relatives, and often don't know how to deal with outsiders for emotional support. But now their families have been shattered because of war and flight from oppression.

Of course, many Vietnamese families succeed both economically and socially. This occurs where the children are given more freedom than they would have had in Vietnam, but are still under firm, disciplined parental control and direction over education, career preparation and social behavior. For these families, maintenance of family bonds is an integral part of their educational, economic and occupational successes.

The problems of Cambodian families are often assumed to be quite different from those of the Vietnamese. Some social scientists and refugee service providers assert that Cambodians have not gained economically as fast as the Vietnamese because they do not look for technologically advanced "high status" jobs and that even refugee children who were educated in America tend to choose "low status" jobs entailing human services, such as nursing, catering, and small repair businesses.

Such a view blurs the important distinction between Cambodian and American points of view. For Cambodians, service jobs are not low status. In Cambodia, it was an individual's good conduct and cooperation with others rather than his wealth that brought him recognition. What American researchers perceive as low-status jobs entailing human services are the high-status jobs from the Cambodian perspective. For example, one 16-year-old refugee said, "I think it is important to help people. My religion (Buddhism) says to do good things, kind things to people."

Even those who have the opportunity to meet the American model of success often do not choose to make use of it. Examples are a 22-year-old woman who holds a well-paying job, and a 16-year-old who started her first job a few months earlier. Both are survivors of the "Killing Fields" holocaust of Pol Pot, in which between one and three million Cambodians were killed or died due to starvation or sickness. Both give their money to their mothers and do not believe that their economic independence gives them the right to assert individual independence. The 22-year-old says, "To me, money is no big deal. Of course it is something you need to live, but it's not the main thing. I am not like the Americans. I don't take what I have for granted. There's more to life, more to families than money and stuff. To me, to have a pretty close family is more important."

Cambodian social values, reinforced by Theravada Buddhist values, and now the Pol Pot tragedy, impart to Cambodian refugees a deep moral obligation to do their duty to their people. From a Cambodian point of view, economic success, while important, is not enough; holding the highest paying job is not the primary consideration. If a person holds a job, but that person's family is falling apart and the people are disturbed, then by Cambodian standards that cannot be called "successful adjustment." Many people in the Cambodian community are not making a lot of money, but they are self-sufficient and they are living a life that they find fulfilling. A refugee from a peasant background said she would like to grow vegetables for a living. When told that this activity involved hard work, she replied, "Growing vegetables is hard work, but I will feel happy. So it is not hard work." The 22-year-old woman commented, "Money comes and goes. To me, the main thing is happiness. It is what is within you that really counts.

Clearly, the criteria for what constitutes a good life differ from Cambodian and American perspectives. Cambodians prefer a cooperative, harmonious, non-aggressive environment in family and society to a more remunerative, aggressive, non-harmonious lifestyle that is valued in America. Cambodians themselves are quite clear and articulate about this distinction.

Most Cambodian refugees in America have survived the Pol Pot holocaust. Despite this, and the difficulties they have encountered in America, many are, from their view, making good adjustments in America.

There are many views of "success" and "successful" refugee adjustment in America. For refugees, economic self-sufficiency by itself does not signify successful adjustment to America if it comes at the expense of disruption of the family, often the only institution that provides any meaningful long-term economic and emotional support for newly arrived refugees and immigrants. Neither Vietnamese nor Cambodians live for houses, cars, and gadgets alone, though they may value these, along with economic self-sufficiency.

CHAPTER 3

Studying Marriage and the Family

PREVIEW

To gain a sense of what you already know about the material covered in this chapter, answer "true" or "false" to the statements below. You will find the answers on page 82.

1. Many researchers believe that love and conflict can coexist. True or false?
2. Research in marriage and the family has little effect on how we understand the day-to-day interactions of our own and other families. True or false?
3. Families have a tendency to resist change. True or false?
4. Research refutes the stereotype that African-American families are inherently dysfunctional. True or false?
5. In day-to-day living, women in Latino families tend to have substantial power. True or false?
6. Loving relationships are always characterized by unselfish behavior. True or false?
7. As a branch of social science, most marriage and family research is experimental. True or false?
8. Most knowledge we have about families comes from clinical sources in which therapists intervene in family problems. True or false?
9. According to some scholars, in love relationships we tend to weigh the costs against the benefits of the relationship. True or false?
10. When we interact with people, we *interpret* words or actions. True or false?

*A great many people think they are
thinking when they are merely rearranging
their prejudices.*

William James (1842–1910)

*Knowledge rests not upon truth alone, but
on error also.*

Carl Jung

❖ THE VALUE OF RESEARCH

IN ST. PAUL, MINNESOTA, A RECENT QUESTIONNAIRE ON MARITAL ATTITUDES asked a group of Americans to agree or disagree with the following statements (Meredith and Rowe, 1986).

◆ "It is proper for a man to pay a bride price for his wife." Fifty-eight percent agreed, 21 percent disagreed, and 21 percent were not sure.
◆ "Marrying for greater family power is a good reason for marriage." Seventy-nine percent agreed, 5 percent disagreed, and 16 percent were not sure.
◆ "It is best to have go-betweens arrange the marriage, rather than the boy and girl themselves." Sixty-seven percent agreed, 18 percent disagreed, and 15 percent weren't sure.
◆ "If the father dies, the father's family should decide what happens to the children." Fifty-two percent agreed, 21 percent disagreed, and 27 percent weren't sure.

These Americans were immigrant Hmong (pronounced *mong*) who had fled Southeast Asia after the collapse of Laos in 1975. The questions were designed to determine the degree to which they were maintaining traditional Hmong values or assimilating mainstream American ones. Questions such as these reveal the diversity of research issues that family scholars address. And the responses are a reminder of the diversity within American family life.

Researchers in marriage and the family have had an immense impact on our awareness of how families work and don't work. Their research affects us both personally and socially. As you study research findings, you'll discover yourself reflecting on your own relationships, marriages, or families, because the questions researchers ask often touch on intensely personal issues in your own life. In part, this is because many of the questions researchers ask are of direct personal concern to themselves. Their research often helps them understand their own personal lives. For example, for fifteen years, Philip Cowan and Carolyn Cowan have been researching the effect of the first child on marriages. They explained how they became interested in the topic (Cowan and Cowan, 1990):

We were just beginning to come up for air from an enormously stressful period for a decade-old marriage with three young children and two budding careers. We loved the parenting part, . . . but the toll these years had taken on our relationship as a couple had been totally unexpected. The dangers of serious marital strain were becoming apparent to us as our friends and neighbors began separating and divorcing at a frightening rate. . . . As we tried to make sense of our lives and those of our friends, we began to think of the transition to parenthood as a vulnerable time for couple relationships.

Recognizing the significance of the experience not only for themselves but for others, they developed the "Becoming a Family" research project to assist couples in the transition to parenthood. Their work gave them valuable insights into their own lives and provided tools for assisting others during their transition periods.

Researchers' questions and findings may also give you new perspectives and insights into your relationships. As you study how people communicate, for example, you will be able to use research findings to evaluate your own communication patterns, pinpoint difficulties, and discover possible solutions to them.

Understanding Changes in Marriage and the Family

Family scholars are responding to the changing family and are attempting to understand it (Berardo and Sheehan, 1984). In doing so, they are teaching us how to understand what is happening to families in today's society. Their research arises out of major concerns and trends, as well as the researchers' own personal experiences and their interactions with teachers, social workers, lawyers, nurses, physicians, and other professionals involved in family matters. Reviewing the scholarship of the 1980s, Felix Berardo (1991) observed

what was evident in the 1980s was a renewed and growing concern, perhaps even a greater sense of urgency, that our marriage and family institutions were being severely weakened and threatened under the press of accelerated and pervasive social change.

In the last few decades, with the rise of cohabitation, divorce, dual-earner families, single-parent families, and stepfamilies, the once-dominant nuclear family has declined in importance. To many Americans, this decline represents the decline of the family itself. Family scholars, however, offer a different perspective. They look at contemporary families in terms of change rather than decline. This slight shift in perspective allows researchers to achieve fresh insights into contemporary marriages and families. For example, researchers are beginning to view divorce as an emerging norm in the contemporary American marriage and family system. Divorce no longer represents social or personal aberration. Instead, it is a socially acceptable (albeit painful) path that married partners may take (Raschke, 1987). Divorce is a process involving reorganization and redefinition of the family instead of its destruction. What emerges from divorce are different family forms—the single-parent family and the stepfamily. Both represent family adjustments in response to divorce.

Researchers are pointing out the differences between these emerging family forms and traditional nuclear families. The single-parent family and stepfamily carry on the traditional function of socializing children but do it differently because their structures are different. By pointing out how the stepchild/stepparent relationship differs from the biological child/biological parent relationship, for example, researchers and therapists are able to help members of stepfamilies adjust to one another.

Family researchers are also reexamining African-American families, looking at their strengths and values and rejecting the old stereotype of African-American families as dysfunctional. In addition, they are reexamining ethnic families from a pluralistic perspective. Rather than judging ethnic families from the traditional Anglo-Saxon Protestant point of view, researchers are increasingly looking at the unique strengths of these families. These reevaluations reinforce the traditional American commitment to pluralism, finding health in diversity. This new research also assists America's diverse racial and ethnic groups in building on their particular family strengths, such as the importance of their extended families.

Research and Social Issues

Family researchers also pay an important role in the development of social issues and the formulation of public policy. Family scholars, for example, have documented the widespread incidence of violence and abuse in the family. National survey data analyzed by researchers reveal that violence is widespread in all social classes, not just occasionally among poor or psychologically disabled individuals, as was formerly believed. By making surveys and examining statistics, scholars found that two million wives are assaulted each year in this country. Between two and six million children are abused or neglected each year. As many as one-third of college students may experience violence in dating.

Feminists scholarship is also reexamining the family, using three basic tenets of feminism: (1) a belief that women are exploited and devalued, (2) a commitment to

Have no respect whatsover for authority; forget who said it and instead look at what he starts with, where he ends up, and ask yourself, "Is it reasonable?"

Richard Feynman

. . .men do not seek the truth. It is the truth that pursues men who run away and will not look around.

Lincoln Steffens

Nothing is so firmly believed as that which is least known.

Michel de Montaigne (1533–1592)

PERSPECTIVE

Race and Ethnicity in Studying Marriage and Family

Until the last fifteen years, most research about American marriages and families was limited to the white, middle-class family. The traditional nuclear family was the norm against which all other families were evaluated. As we saw in previous chapters, such a perspective distorted our understanding of other family forms, such as single-parent families and stepfamilies. These family forms were often viewed as pathological because they differed from the traditional norm. A similar distortion also has influenced our understanding of African-American, Latino, Asian-American, and Native American families. Instead of recognizing the strengths of diverse racial and ethnic family systems, these families were viewed as "tangles of pathology" for failing to meet the model of the traditional white nuclear family.

Dual-worker marriages, employed mothers, divorce, and single-parent families, for example, were singled out by earlier researchers as examples of the "dysfunctional" African-American family. But with female employment and divorce rates accelerating among whites, note two researchers (White and Parham, 1990), social scientists now have legitimized family structures that earlier were considered examples of African-American family pathology. A substantial number of changes over the last two decades have affected all American families, but they first occurred primarily among African-American families. "Many changes that have occurred have meant that white families are becoming more like African-American families," observed Harriet Pipes McAdoo (1988).

Part of this distortion is a result of how little researchers know of families from African-American, Latino, and other ethnic groups. First, there are relatively few studies on such groups. Out of 22,500 articles published on marriage and the family between 1974 and 1990 in sociology and psychology, only 3 percent focused on African-Americans and 1 percent on Latinos. For Asian-Americans this gap is even more dramatic: .007 percent of studies were on Chinese-Americans, .01 percent on Japanese-Americans, and .01 percent on Vietnamese-Americans. There is virtually no sociological or psychological research on Native Americans families, although some research may be found in anthropology journals.

Furthermore, many of the earlier studies were flawed or distorted by focusing on problems rather than strengths, giving the impression that all families from a particular racial or ethnic group were riddled by troubles and pathologies (Dilworth-Anderson and McAdoo, 1988; Taylor, Chatters, Tucker, and Lewis, 1991). Two of the most prominent examples are the "culture of poverty" approach to studying African-American families and the "machismo syndrome" used in studying Latino families (Demos, 1990; Mirandé, 1985).

changing the condition of women, and (3) a critique of the traditional social sciences as inherently biased against women (Komarovsky, 1988; Walker and Thompson, 1984). Feminist scholars are attempting to integrate their work into the general field of marriage and family studies. Their work in family programs emphasizes certain principles (Walker et al., 1988):

◆ *Recognition of cultural context,* in which personal problems are seen as rooted in the social, political, and economic structure. Feminists avoid blaming, for example, the victims of poverty, gender inequality, and racial discrimination.
◆ *Responsiveness to the vulnerable,* in which women, the poor, minorities, the disabled, the young and aged, and gay men and lesbians are viewed as being vulnerable.
◆ *Participation and equality,* in which all are encouraged to participate equally in activities affecting them, such as health care.
◆ *Celebration of diversity,* in which different family forms and relationships, lifestyles, and minority or ethnic values and customs are viewed as sources of strength.

PERSPECTIVE

The culture of poverty approach views African-American families as being deeply enmeshed in illegitimacy, poverty, and welfare as a result of their slave heritage. As one scholar (Demos, 1990) noted, the culture of poverty approach "views black families from a white middle-class vantage point and results in a perjorative analysis of black family life." It ignores the majority of families that are intact or middle class. It also fails to see African-American family strengths such as strong kinship bonds, role flexibility, love of children, commitment to education, and care for the elderly.

Over the last decade, however, there has been a trend toward the cultural equivalent perspective, especially in African-American studies. This perspective sees white and African-American families as sharing the same cultural values (L. Johnson, 1988). If there are differences between the two, such as a higher birthrate to single African-American women, these differences are attributed to continued social and economic discrimination. The cultural equivalent perspective rejects the view that the heritage of slavery or inherent personality defects and deviant values are to blame for family instability, poverty,

or community problems.

Studies of Latino families have been distorted by the view that they are authoritarian, dominated by a cold and distant father. According to this view, the father's **machismo,** a man's sense of strength, forcefulness, or vigor, demands deference, respect, and absolute obedience from both wife and children, making them dependent and subordinate. As William Madsen (1973) wrote: "Ideally the Latin male acknowledges only the authority of his father and God. In case of conflict between these two sources, he should side with his father." Such studies perpetuate erroneous stereotypes. They rely on pathological models that caricaturize *machismo,* making it the root of all problems experienced by Latino families (Mirandé, 1985). More recent research indicates that within the cultural context, *machismo* is characterized by courage, generosity, and respect for others. As Rosina Becerra (1988) writes, "The machismo role encourages protection of and provision for family members, the use of fair and just authority, and respect for the role of wife and children." While the ideology of patriarchy continues to exist, in the day-to-day world Latinas are

not necessarily subservient; instead, they exert considerable influence and power in the family (Becerra, 1988, Griswold del Castillo, 1984). Contemporary research focuses on social adaptation of newer immigrants, gender role flexibility, especially among employed women, and general acculturation (Vega, 1991).

In America's pluralistic society, it is important that students and researchers alike reexamine diversity among our different racial and ethnic groups as possible sources of strength rather than pathology. Differences may not necessarily be problems but solutions to problems; they may be signs of adaptation rather than weakness. One groups's problem may be another's solution (Adams, 1985). As two family scholars (Dilworth-Anderson and McAdoo, 1988) pointed out, "Whether a phenomenon is viewed as a problem or a solution may not be objective reality at all but may be determined by the observer's values." This is especially important to remember as we study America's diverse racial and ethnic family systems.

The Search for Objectivity

What most of us know about marriage and the family comes from our personal experiences and observations (of our own families, other families, media descriptions, and so on). To these perceptions are added religious and social **norms**—that is, standards of expectations about marriage and the family. As a result, when we describe marriage, for example, our descriptions are often mixtures of our own experiences, media images, and feelings of what marriage *ought* to be. Such descriptions tend to be very subjective; they may be valid for ourselves but not for others. Yet we often act as if our subjective experiences are universally true. Although our personal experiences and values are limited, they often become the standards by which we evaluate others. If we grew up in a family that was very religious (or agnostic), we may believe that all families should be religious (or agnostic). Whether we are right or wrong, we are making subjective value judgments.

Family scholars and researchers attempt to step outside their personal roles and values to objectively describe marriages and families. They seek to describe them as

He who knows nothing doubts nothing.

French proverb

What Do Surveys Tell You about Yourself?

Survey questionnaires are the leading source of information about marriage and the family. The questionnaire below, called "The Marriage and Family Life Attitude Survey," was developed by Don Martin to gain information about attitudes toward marriage and the family. (The survey instrument formed the basis for a study of college-student attitudes [Martin and Martin, 1984] toward marriage and the family that is reprinted as a reading at the end of this chapter.) On a scale of one to five, indicate for each statement below whether you strongly agree (1), slightly agree (2), neither agree nor disagree (3), slightly disagree (4), or strongly disagree (5).

1	2	3	4	5
STRONGLY AGREE	SLIGHTLY AGREE	NEITHER AGREE NOR DISAGREE	SLIGHTLY DISAGREE	STRONGLY DISAGREE

I. *Cohabitation and Premarital Sexual Relations*
1. I have or would engage in sexual intercourse before marriage.
2. I believe it is acceptable to experience sexual intercourse without loving one's partner.
3. I want to live with someone before I marry him/her.
4. If I lived intimately with a member of the opposite sex, I would tell my parents.

II. *Marriage and Divorce*
1. I believe marriage is a lifelong commitment.
2. I believe divorce is acceptable except when children are involved.
3. I view my parents' marriage as happy.
4. I believe I have the necessary skills to make a good marriage.

III. *Childhood and Child Rearing*
1. I view my childhood as a happy experience.
2. If both my spouse and I work, I would leave my child in a daycare center while at work.
3. If I have a child, I feel only one parent should work so the other can take care of the child.
4. The responsibility for raising a child is divided between both spouses.
5. I believe I have the knowledge necessary to raise a child properly.
6. I believe children are not necessary in a marriage.
7. I believe two or more children are desirable for a married couple.

IV. *Division of Household Labor and Professional Employment*
1. I believe household chores and tasks should be equally shared between marital partners.
2. I believe there are household chores that are specifically suited for men and others for women.
3. I believe women are entitled to careers as equal to those of men.
4. If my spouse is offered a job in a different locality, I will move with my spouse.

In all matters of opinion, our adversaries are insane.

Mark Twain

they are, not as they *should* be or as they themselves have personally experienced them. Scholars studying premarital intercourse, for example, seek to find its incidence, the characteristics of those who engage in it, and its relationship to marital stability. They do not ask whether it is right or wrong or whether people *should* or *should not* engage in it. Such questions are **normative**; that is, they deal with norms. They are best answered within the domain of ethics and religion rather than social science.

In order to explore marriage and the family objectively, researchers develop hypotheses—that is, unproven ideas, theories, or propositions. They next develop a research plan, collect data, and then analyze and interpret the data to determine whether their hypotheses are valid. The various research methods they use to collect their data each have inherent advantages and disadvantages. The methods described in the following sections are the most important ones used in marriage and family research. (For a discussion of value judgments and social science, see, Pollis, 1988 and Reis, 1980.)

UNDERSTANDING YOURSELF

V. *Marital and Extramarital Sexual Relations*
1. I believe sexual relations are an important component of a marriage.
2. I believe the male should be the one to initiate sexual advances in a marriage.
3. I do not believe extramarital sex is wrong for me.

VI. *Privacy Rights and Social Needs*
1. I believe friendships outside of marriage with the opposite sex are important in a marriage.
2. I believe the major social functioning in a marriage should be with other couples.
3. I believe married couples should not argue in front of other people.
4. I want to marry someone who has the same social needs as I have.

VII. *Religious Needs*
1. I believe religious practices are important in a marriage.
2. I believe children should be made to attend church.
3. I would not marry a person of a different religious background.

VIII. *Communication Expectations*
1. When I have a disagreement in an intimate relationship, I talk to the other person about it.
2. I have trouble expressing what I feel towards the other person in an intimate relationship.
3. When I argue with a person in an intimate relationship, I withdraw from that person.
4. I would like to learn better ways to express myself in a relationship.

IX. *Parental Relationships*
1. I would not marry if I did not get along with the other person's parents.
2. If I do not like my spouse's parents, I should not be obligated to visit them.
3. I believe each spouse's parents should be seen an equal amount of time.
4. I feel parents should not intervene in any matters pertaining to my marriage.
5. If my parents did not like my choice of a marriage partner, I would not marry this person.

X. *Professional Counseling Services*
1. I would seek premarital counseling before I got married.
2. I would like to attend marriage enrichment workshops.
3. I will seek education and/or counseling in order to learn about parenting.
4. I feel I need more education of what to expect from marriage.
5. I believe counseling is only for those couples in trouble.

After you have completed this questionnaire, ask yourself the questions below:

◆ Were the questions correctly posed so that your responses adequately portrayed your attitudes.
◆ Were questions omitted that are important for you regarding marriage and the family? If so, what were they?
◆ Do your attitudes reflect your actual behavior?

❖ RESEARCH METHODS

An enormous amount of research on marriage and the family is undertaken each year. Sociology and psychology journals published over 22,500 articles on the family between 1974 and 1990. The Family Resources Database (which we used extensively in the research for this textbook) adds 3,000 journal articles annually to its computerized database of family studies. The database includes 1,200 journals, books, government documents, directories, and audiovisual materials. Of the journals, fifty are major publications in the general area of marriage and the family.

What researchers know about marriage and the family comes from four basic sources: (1) surveys, (2) clinical studies, (3) direct observation, and (4) experimental research. There is continual debate as to which method is best for studying marriage and the family. But such argument may miss an important point: Each method may provide important and unique information that another method may not (Cowan and Cowan, 1990).

It is a capital mistake to theorize before one has data.

Sherlock Holmes

Knowledge is of two kinds. We know a subject ourselves, or we know where we can find information upon it.

John Boswell, *Life of Johnson*

The fact will one day flower into a truth.

Henry Thoreau (1817–1862)

Facts do not cease to exist because they are ignored.

Aldous Huxley

Surveys

The survey method, using questionnaires or interviews, is the most popular data-gathering technique in marriage and family studies. In recent years, well over half of all research studies on marriage and the family relied *exclusively* on survey methods (Galligan, 1982). Because of funding difficulties, studies have been relying increasingly on the interpretation of secondary data, mainly large government surveys and census data in which the material has been made public. In 1977, for example, secondary data sources accounted for about 43 percent of research articles, while in 1987, these sources amounted to 53 percent (Nye, 1988). As a result of this quantification, demographic issues, such as divorce rates, are receiving increasingly more attention than qualitative issues, such as the causes of divorce.

Surveys may be conducted in person, over the telephone, or by written questionnaire. The purpose of a survey is to gather information from a small, representative group of people and to infer conclusions that are valid for a larger population. Questionnaires offer anonymity, may be completed fairly quickly, and are relatively inexpensive to administer. Questionnaires usually do not allow for an in-depth response, however; a person must respond with a short answer, a yes, a no, or a choice on a scale of one to ten. Unfortunately, marriage and family issues are generally too complicated for questionnaires to explore in depth.

Interview techniques avoid some of the shortcomings of questionnaires, because interviewers are able to probe in greater depth and follow paths suggested by the interviewee. Interviewers, however, may allow their own preconceptions to bias their interpretation of responses as well as the way in which they frame questions.

Whether done by questionnaires or interviews, surveys have certain inherent problems. First, how representative is the sample that volunteered to take the survey? Self-selection tends to bias a sample. Second, how well do people understand their own behavior? Third, are people underreporting undesirable or unacceptable

Family researchers are concerned about the family's well being in practice as well as theory. Here, Richard Gelles, one of the leading scholars in family violence, weilds a mop in the kitchen.

behavior? They may be reluctant to admit that they have extramarital affairs or that they are alcoholics, for example.

Surveys are well suited for determining the incidence of certain behaviors or for discovering traits and trends. Surveys are more commonly used by sociologists than by psychologists because they tend to deal on a general or societal level rather than on a personal or small-group level. But surveys are not able to measure very well how people interact with each other. For researchers and therapists interested in studying the dynamic flow of relationships, surveys are not as useful as clinical, experimental, and observational studies.

Lies, damned lies and statistics.

Benjamin Disraeli

Clinical Studies

Clinical studies or case studies are in-depth examinations of a person or small group of people who come to a psychiatrist, psychologist, or social worker with psychological or relationship problems. The people are interviewed individually. The case-study method is the traditional approach of all clinical research; with few exceptions it was the sole method of clinical investigation through the first half of the twentieth century (Runyan, 1982). The advantage of clinical approaches is that they offer long-term, in-depth study of various aspects of marriage and family life. The primary disadvantage is that we cannot necessarily make inferences about the general population. People who enter psychotherapy are not a representative sample. They may be more motivated to solve their problems or have more intense problems than the general population.

Clinical studies, however, have been very fruitful in developing insight into family processes. Such studies have been instrumental in the development of family systems theory, discussed later in this chapter. By analyzing individuals and families in therapy, psychiatrists, psychologists, and therapists such as R. D. Laing, Salvador Minuchin, and Virginia Satir have been able to understand how families create roles, patterns, and rules that family members follow without being aware of them. A typical rule that a family may have, for example, is not to be aware that it has rules, such as rules against discussing or expressing certain types of feelings (anger, love, aggression, and so on).

We should be careful to get out of an experience only the wisdom that is in it— and stop there; lest we be like that cat that sits down on a hot stove-lid. She will never sit down on a hot stove-lid again—and that is well; but also she will never sit down on a cold one anymore.

Mark Twain

Direct Observation

Direct observation and experimental studies (discussed in the next section) account for less than 5 percent of recent research articles (Nye, 1988). Researchers attempt to study behavior systematically through direct observation while remaining as unobtrusive as possible. To measure power in a relationship, for example, an observer-researcher may sit in a home and note exchanges between a husband and wife. The obvious disadvantage of this method is that the couple may hide unacceptable ways of dealing with decisions, such as by threats of violence, while the observer is present.

Another problem with observational studies is that a low correlation often exists between what observers see and what the people observed report about themselves. This is especially true in observational studies of power (Cromwell and Olson, 1975). Interestingly, when there is a discrepancy, psychologists tend to distrust self-reports and sociologists tend to trust them too much, according to one researcher (Gottman, 1979). Another researcher (Olson, 1977) has suggested that self-reports and observations really measure two different views of the same thing: a self-report is an insider's view, whereas an observer's report is an outsider's view.

Seeing is believing. I wouldn't have seen it if I hadn't believed it.

Ashleigh Brilliant

Discovery consists of seeing what everybody has seen and thinking what nobody has thought.

Albert Szent–Gyorgyi

What really teaches a man is not experience but observation.

H. L. Mencken

Experimental Research

Little experimental research is done on marriage and the family. Experimental findings can be very powerful, because such research gives investigators control over many factors and enables them to isolate variables, that is, aspects of the experiment that can be manipulated. Researchers believing that single adults are stigmatized, for example, tested their hypothesis experimentally. Two scholars (Etaugh and Malstrom, 1981) devised a simple experiment in which subjects were asked to evaluate twenty traits of a person described in a short paragraph. The person was variously identified as married, widowed, divorced, or never married. When identified as married the individual was rated more favorably than when identified as single (whether widowed, divorced, or never married). Widowed persons were rated higher than divorced or never married. Divorced individuals were rated the lowest. This pencil-and-paper experiment confirmed the researchers' belief that single individuals are stigmatized.

The obvious problem with such studies is that we respond differently to people in real life than we do in controlled situations, especially in paper-and-pencil situations. We may not stigmatize a divorced person at all in real life. Experimental situations are usually faint shadows of the complex and varied situations we experience in the real world.

❖ THEORIES OF MARRIAGE AND THE FAMILY

We use surveys, clinical studies, observations, and experiments to gather data on marriages and families. We use theory to provide general principles for explaining the data (Miller, 1986). Theories also suggest directions for research because of the questions they raise.

The theories we discuss in this section, are symbolic interaction, social exchange theory, conflict theory, gender theory, and family systems theory. These theories are currently among the most influential ones used by sociologists and psychologists.

As you study these different theories, notice how the choice of a theoretical perspective influences the way data are interpreted. As you read this textbook, ask yourself how a different theoretical perspective would lead to different conclusions about the same material.

Symbolic Interaction Theory

Symbolic interactionists, like the rest of us, are concerned with relationships. When we complain that we can't relate to our spouse, that our partner doesn't understand us, that we can't communicate, we are complaining about matters that are at the heart of symbolic interaction.

INTERPRETING MEANINGS. **Symbolic interaction** is a theory that looks at how people interact. The key factor in these interactions is communication. We communicate with each other with more than words. We communicate through symbols, which include not only words but also intonations, gestures, movements, and so on. When we interact with people, we do more than simply react to them. We interpret or define their actions.

If someone we meet asks us to go to the movies, we interpret what he or she means. On one level, the invitation is simply a suggestion to share an entertainment, but the invitation also conveys symbolic meaning. In our culture, an invitation to the

The family is a "unity" of interacting personalities according to symbolic interaction theory. How family members interact with each other is partly determined by their social roles. What social roles are being enacted in this photograph?

movies by someone we have just met is a "date"—and a date is a means by which people get to know each other; it is a part of American courtship. We react by being flattered or flustered, depending on whether we are unattached, whether we think it would be fun to spend time with the person, and other factors.

In a relationship, it is not always clear what words or actions mean. If we like the person with whom we went to the movies and we continue to see that person, what does this mean? Individuals often need to clarify a relationship. The way they do this is through communication. If they have good communication, they can generally discover what each thinks or feels. If they have poor communication, they are left to guess what a particular symbolic act means. Does this continual dating mean love? Does it mean commitment? To find out, they may have to ask, and to ask is to initiate communication.

THE FAMILY AS A UNITY OF INTERACTING PERSONALITIES. In the 1920s, Ernest Burgess (1926) defined the family as a "unity of interacting personalities." This definition has been critical to symbolic interaction theory and in the development of marriage and family studies. Marriages and families consist of individuals who interact with one another over a period of time. The way each person interacts with others is partly defined by his or her social roles. A social role is an established pattern of behavior that exists independently of a person. For example, the role of a husband or wife exists independently of any particular husband or wife, just as your role as a student exists independently of you.

The most instructive experiences are those of everyday life.

Friedrich Nietzschke

Each member in a marriage or family has one or more roles—such as husband, wife, mother, father, child, or sibling. Three important processes in this world of social roles include role taking, role playing, and role making. *Role taking* refers to our tendency to take on roles in different social situations and to modify our actions accordingly. When you enter school, you take on a student role; when you enter marriage, you take on a husband or wife role; and so on. If you feel you don't know how to act in a certain situation, if often means that you don't know the appropriate role to take. It is fairly common for people to ask what role they are expected to play in a meeting, organization, or relationship. *Role playing* refers to our changing roles in response to the roles of others. One moment we may be acting as a son or daughter in response to our parents. Another moment we may take on the role of a husband or wife in response to our partner. In a third moment we may play the role of a parent in response to the crying of an infant. *Role making* refers to our creation or modification of existing roles. Role making is particularly critical, because the social roles we are given do not necessarily fit us particularly well. The male role, for example, typically calls for an aggressive personality and the pursuit of worldly success, but a man may instead be cooperative and interested more in family life than in power or fame. Similarly, a female role traditionally calls for conciliatory behavior and family orientation, but a woman's temperament may lead her to politics. In both instances, the man and woman must modify their roles to fit their temperaments.

There is a constant interplay of roles, communication, and symbols as we play different roles and modify them according to the expectations of others, the situation, and our own needs.

Symbolic interaction has been used extensively in analyzing marital adjustment, dating, and mate selection. It has had a notable impact not only on researchers but also on those interested in process and change—clinical psychologists, social workers, counselors, and therapists.

CRITIQUE. Although symbolic interaction shifts the focus to the daily workings of the family, it suffers from several drawbacks. First, the theory tends to minimize the role of power in relationships. If a conflict exists, it may take more than simply communicating to resolve it. If one partner strongly wants to pursue his career in Los Angeles and the other just as strongly wants to pursue hers in Boston, no amount of communication and role adjustment may not be sufficient to resolve the conflict. Ultimately, the partner with the greater power in the relationship may prevail.

Second, symbolic interaction doesn't fully account for the emotional aspects of human life, especially for unconscious processes. It sees us only as the sum of our roles. It neglects the "I"—the "self" or the "soul"—that exists independently of our roles. Limiting us to the sum of our parts limits our uniqueness as human beings.

Third, the theory emphasizes individualism. It encourages competence in interpersonal relationships and values individual happiness and fulfillment over stability, duty, responsibility, and other familial values. As Jay Schvaneveldt (1981) observed, "The welfare and happiness of marital partners are held above the belief that the marital union or family union should stay intact. The happiness of the individual family members appears to be the dominant value."

Fourth, the theory does not place marriage or family within a larger social context and thereby disregards or minimizes the forces working on families from the outside, such as economic discrimination against minorities and women.

❖ REFLECTIONS *Using symbolic interaction theory, examine the different roles you play in your relationship, marriage, or family. How do you feel about these roles? How do you go about changing the contents of these roles? What encourages or discourages such changes?*

Social Exchange Theory

According to **social exchange theory,** we measure our actions and relationships on a cost-benefit basis. In relationships, we try to maximize our benefits and minimize our costs to obtain the most advantageous result. At first glance, exchange theory may be the least attractive theory we use to study marriage and the family. It seems more appropriate for accountants than lovers. But all of us use a cost-benefit analysis to some degree to measure our actions and relationships.

There is no truth that a blockhead could not turn into an error.

Luc de Vauvenargues

HOW EXCHANGE THEORY WORKS. One reason we don't recognize our use of this interpersonal accounting is that we do much of it unconsciously. If a friend is unhappy with a partner, you may ask "What are you getting out of the relationship?" Your friend will start listing pluses and minuses: "On the plus side, I get company and a certain amount of security; on the minus side, I don't get someone who *really* understands me." When the emotional costs outweigh the benefits of the relationship, your friend will probably end it. This weighing of costs and benefits is exchange theory at work.

The fundamental ideas of exchange theory go back to the ancient Greek philosopher Epicurus, who founded the Epicurean or hedonic (from which the word "hedonism" is derived) school of philosophy. The basis of Epicurean thought is that people seek pleasure and avoid pain. The Epicureans developed a "hedonic calculus" by which people could determine whether an action was worthwhile based on the amount of pleasure minus the pain it brought. Exchange theorists are the heirs to ancient hedonic thought. According to exchange theorists, people maximize their rewards and minimize their costs by employing their resources to gain the most favorable outcome. An outcome is basically figured by the equation *Reward − Cost = Outcome.*

One problem many of us have in recognizing our own exchange activities is that we think of rewards and costs as tangible objects, like money. In personal relationships, however, resources, rewards, and costs are more likely to be things such as love, companionship, status, power, fear, longing, and so on. As people enter into relationships, they have certain resources—either tangible or intangible—that others consider valuable, such as intelligence, warmth, good looks, or high social status. People consciously or unconsciously use their various resources to obtain what they want, as when they "turn on" the charm, for example.

Traditionally, a woman trades her career for a family, but a man might also quit his job to stay at home. Most of us have had friends whose relationships are a mystery to us. For example, we may not understand what our friend sees in his or her partner; our friend is so much better looking and more intelligent than the partner. (Attractiveness and intelligence are typical resources in our society.) But it turns out that the partner has a good sense of humor, is considerate, and is an accomplished flutist, all of which our friend values highly.

EQUITY. A corollary to exchange is **equity:** exchanges that occur between people have to be fair, to balance out. In the everyday world, we are always exchanging favors—you do the dishes tonight and I'll take care of the kids. Often we don't even articulate these exchanges; we have a general sense that ultimately they will be recip-rocated. If in the end we feel that the exchange wasn't fair, we are likely to be resentful and angry. As Gerald Patterson (1971) observed:

> There is an odd kind of equity which holds when people interact with each other. In effect, we get what we give, both in amount and in kind. Each of us seems to have his own bookkeeping system for love and for pain. Over time, the books are balanced.

Some researchers suggest that people are most happy when they get what they feel they deserve in a relationship (Hatfield and Walster, 1981). Oddly enough, both partners feel uneasy in an inequitable relationship:

> While it's not surprising that deprived partners (who are, after all, getting less than they deserve) should feel resentful and angry about their inequitable treatment, it's perhaps not so obvious why their *over*benefited mates (who are getting more than they deserve) feel uneasy too. But they do. They feel guilty and fearful of losing their favored position.

When partners recognize that they are in an inequitable relationship, they generally feel uncomfortable, angry, or distressed. They try to restore equity in one of three ways:

◆ They attempt to restore *actual* equity in the relationship.
◆ They attempt to restore *psychological* equity by trying to convince themselves and others that an obviously inequitable relationship is actually equitable.
◆ They decide to end the relationship.

Society regards marriage as a permanent commitment (even if reality seems to contradict the assumption). Because marriages are expected to endure, exchanges take on a long-term character. Instead of being calculated on a day-to-day basis, outcomes are judged over time.

An important ingredient in these exchanges is whether the relationship is fundamentally cooperative or competitive. In cooperative exchanges, both husbands and wives try to maximize their "joint profit" (Scanzoni, 1979). These exchanges are characterized by mutual trust and commitment. Thus a husband might choose to work part-time and also care for the couple's infant so that his wife may pursue her education. In a competitive relationship, however, each is trying to maximize his or her own individual profit. If both spouses want the freedom to go out whenever or with whomever each wishes, despite opposition from the other, the relationship is likely to be unstable.

Exchange theory assumes that individuals are rational, calculating animals, weighing the costs and rewards of their relationships. Sometimes we are rational, sometimes we are not. Sometimes we act altruistically without expecting any reward. This is often true of love relationships and parent-child interaction.

Exchange theory also has difficulty ascertaining the value of costs, rewards, and resources. If you want to buy eggs, you know they are $1.15 a dozen and you can compare buying a dozen eggs with spending the same amount on a notebook. But how does the value of an outgoing personality compare with the value of a compassionate personality? Is a pound of compassion equal to ten pounds of enthusiasm? Compassion may be the trait most valued by one person but may not be important to another. The values that we assign to costs, rewards, and resources are highly individualistic.

❖ REFLECTIONS   *Think about what benefits you are receiving from your current (or past) intimate, marital, or family relationships. What are the benefits and costs?*

Make a list to compare the benefits and the costs. Assign a value from one to ten for the various items on your list, ten being the highest value and one being the lowest. Based on the equation Reward − Cost = Outcome, how would you predict the ultimate outcome? Think about the last time you made a trade-off in a relationship. Was it fair? If it wasn't, how did you feel? How did the other person feel?

Conflict Theory

Conflict theorists believe that life involves discord. According to **conflict theory,** society is not viewed as basically cooperative but as divided, with individuals and groups in conflict with each other. Conflict theorists try to identify the competing forces.

We never really understand things. We just get used to them.

John Von Neuman

We are familiar with the analysis of society in terms of competing interests: Republicans versus Democrats, rich versus poor, environmentalists versus developers, and so on. In these analyses, power is a critical element. The group with the most power wins.

But how can we analyze marriages and families in terms of conflict and power? Marriage and family relationships are based on love and affection, aren't they? Conflict theorists would agree that love and affection are important elements in marriages and families, but they believe that conflict and power are also fundamental. Marriages and families are composed of individuals with different personalities, ideas, values, tastes, and goals. Each person is not always in harmony with every other person in the family. Imagine that you are living at home and want to do something your parents don't want you to do, such as spend the weekend with a friend they don't like. They forbid you to carry out your plan. "As long as you live in this house, you'll have to do what we say." You argue with them, but in the end you stay home. Why did your parents win the disagreement? They did so because they had greater power, according to conflict analysts.

SOURCES OF CONFLICT. Conflict theorists do not believe that conflict is bad; instead, they think it is a natural part of family life. Families always have disagreements, from small ones, like what movie to see, to major ones, such as how to rear children. Families differ in the number of underlying conflicts of interest, the degree of underlying hostility, and the nature and extent of the expression of conflict. Conflict can take the form of competing goals, such as a husband wanting to buy a new CD player and a wife wanting to pay off credit cards. Conflict can also occur because of different role expectations: an employed mother wants to divide housework fifty-fifty, but her husband insists that household chores are "women's work."

SOURCES OF POWER. When conflict occurs, who wins? Family members have different resources and amounts of power. Four important sources of power are legitimacy, money, physical coercion, and love. When arguments arise in a family, a man may want his way "because I'm the head of the house" or a parent "because I'm your mother." These appeals are based on legitimacy—that is, the belief that the person is entitled to prevail by right. Money is a powerful resource in marriages and families. "As long as you live in this house . . ." is a directive based on economics. Because men tend to earn more than women, they have greater economic power; this economic power translates to marital power. Physical coercion is another important source of power. "If you don't do as I tell you, you'll get a spanking" is one of the most common forms of coercion of children. But physical abuse of a spouse is also common, as we will see in Chapter 15. Finally, there is the power of love. Love can be used to coerce someone emotionally, as in "If you really loved me, you'd do what I ask," or love can be a freely given gift, as in the case of a person giving up something important, such as a plan, desire, or career, to enhance a relationship.

Everyone in the family has power, although the power may be different and unequal. Adolescent children, for example, have few economic resources, so they must depend on their parents. This dependency gives the parents power. But adolescents also have power through the exercise of personal charm, ingratiating habits, temper tantrums, wheedling, and so on.

Families cannot live comfortably with much open conflict. The problem for families, as for any group, is how to encourage cooperation while allowing for differences. Because conflict is seen as normal, conflict theory seeks to channel it and to seek solutions through communication, bargaining, and negotiations. We return to these items in Chapter 14, "Communication and Conflict Resolution."

CRITIQUE. A number of difficulties arise in conflict theory. First, conflict theory derives from politics, in which self-interest, egotism, and competition are dominant elements. Yet is such a harsh judgment of human nature justified? People's behavior is also characterized by self-sacrifice and cooperation. Love is an important quality in relationships. Conflict theorists don't often talk about the power of love or bonding, yet the presence of love and bonding may distinguish the family from all other groups in society. We often will make sacrifices for the sake of those we love. We will defer our own wishes to another's desires; we may even sacrifice our lives for a loved one.

Second, conflict theorists assume that differences lead to conflict. Differences can also be accepted, tolerated, or appreciated. Differences do not necessarily imply conflict.

Third, conflict in families is not easily measured or evaluated. Families live much of their lives privately, and outsiders are not always aware of whatever conflict exists or how pervasive it is. Also, much overt conflict is avoided because it is regulated through family and societal rules. Most children obey their parents, and most spouses, although they may argue heatedly, do not employ violence.

❖ REFLECTIONS   *Using conflict theory, examine the recurring conflicts in your relationship, marriage or family. Who wins these various conflicts? What resources do the winners have? The losers? Do they differ according to the type of conflict? What are your resources in relationships? How do you use them?.*

Gender Theory

Since the 1960s, feminist scholars have been developing alternative approaches to studying society. Feminists begin with two assumptions: first, that male/female relationships are characterized by power issues; and second, that society is constructed in such a way that males dominate females. Feminists argue that male/female relationships—whether personal, familial, or societal—reflect and encourage male dominance, putting females at a disadvantage. Male dominance is neither natural nor inevitable, however. Instead, it is created by social institutions, such as religious groups, government, and the family (Ferree, 1991). The question for feminists is how is male/female inequality created?

SOCIAL CONSTRUCTION OF GENDER. In the 1980s, gender theory emerged as the most important feminist model explaining inequality. **Gender theory** asserts that society may be best understood by how it is organized according to gender. Gender is viewed as a basic element in social relationships based on the *socially perceived* differences between the sexes that justify unequal power relationships (Scott, 1986). Imagine, for example, an infant crying in the night. In the mother/father parenting relationship, which parent gets up to take care of the baby? In most cases, the mother does because (1) women are socially perceived to be nurturing and (2) it's the woman's "responsibility" as mother (even if she hasn't fully slept in four nights and is employed full-time).

Gender theory focuses on (1) how specific behaviors (such as nurturing or aggression) or roles (such as childrearer, truck driver, or secretary) are defined as male or female; (2) how labor is divided into man's work and woman's work both at home and in the workplace; and (3) how different institutions bestow advantages on males (such as male-only clergy in many religious denominations or women receiving less pay than men for the same work).

The key to the creation of gender inequality lies in the belief that men and women are, indeed, "opposite" sexes—that they are opposite each other in personalities, abilities, skills, and traits. Furthermore, the differences between the sexes are unequally valued: reason and aggression (defined as male traits) are considered to be more valuable than emotion and passivity (defined as female traits). In reality, however, males and females are more like each other than they are different. Both sexes are reasonable and emotional, aggressive and passive (Ferree, 1991).

Gender is socially constructed. In other words, it is neither innate nor instinctive; it is the result of the exercise of social power. Making the sexes appear to be opposite and of unequal value requires the suppression of natural similarities by the use of social power. The exercise of social power might take the form of greater societal value being placed on looks over achievement for women, sexual harassment of women in the workplace or university, patronizing attitudes toward women, and so on.

GENDER THEORY AND THE FAMILY. In applying gender theory to the family, feminists perceive families as being intimately tied to the larger society, rather than being a refuge from it. Power relationships exist not only within society but within the family as well. The issue of who does housework or who cares for the children, feminists argue, is primarily an issue of power. Why should women employed full-time continue to bear prime responsibility for these tasks? And why is women's unpaid household work devalued as being worth less than men's paid work?

Feminists also question whether the family can be viewed as a single, unitary whole with each member sharing the same set of interests. Individual interests may actually be in conflict, such as whose job or career takes precedence. The most extreme example of such conflict is in violent relationships, whether they involve child or spousal abuse.

CRITIQUE. Gender theory derives many of its ideas and assumptions from conflict theory. It reduces interactions to issues of power and dominance, which, on the abstract level, may appear to be correct. But when applied to any specific male/female relationship, such a description may not be accurate. Furthermore, gender theory underestimates altruism, love as an antidote to power, and the actual amount of cooperation between the sexes in day-to-day interactions.

TABLE 3.1   Social and Economic Characteristics of White, African-American, Latino, Asian-American, Pacific-Islander, and Native American Households, 1988. Numbers in 1000s.

	Total	White	African American	Latino[1]	Asian[2] American	Pacific[2] Islanders	Native America
Total Persons	241,155	203,869	29,333	19,431	3467	260 1479	
Marital Status (persons)							
Total	177,700	152,600	19,500	12,600	X	X	X
Single	38,900	30,800	6,700	3,400	X	X	X
Married	111,300	98,600	9,100	7,700	170	151	144
Divorced	13,900	11,700	2,000	900	N/A	N/A	X
Widowed	13,500	11,500	1,800	500	X	X	X
Family Type							
Married couple	51,809	46,644	3,682	3,204	651	40	238
w/own children	24,600	21,699	2,016	2,123	X	X	X
Female head no spouse present	10,608	7,235	3,074	754	78	10.3	75.1
Male head no spouse present	2,715	2,165	421	114	36	2.8	17.9
Economic Characteristics							
Median income	30,853	32,274	18,098	20,306	23,095	17,984	13,678
Persons below poverty level	32,546	21,409	9,683	5,470	X	X	380
Unemployed	6,701	4,944	1,547	732	357	42	351

SOURCE: U.S. Bureau of Census, *Statistics Abstract of the United States, 1990* (110th edition). Washngton, D.C. 1990. Tables 43, 44, 45 and 50.

1 May be of any race.
2 1980 census Figures

Researchers analyze demographic data to further our understanding of marriage and the family. As you examine Tables 3.1 and 3.2, note that race and ethnicity are significant variables. How do you account for the differences?

Gender theory is valuable in describing the social construction of gender, an idea that is widely accepted by sociologists. It also has pointed out areas of family life that need to be explored further, such as the division of household labor and parenting responsibilities (Thompson and Walker, 1989).

❖ REFLECTIONS   *Using gender theory, examine the division of labor in your family. How is housework divided? How is unpaid household work valued in comparison to paid work in the workplace?*

Family Systems Theory

Family systems theory is a relatively new approach but an increasingly important one for studying the family. It is especially significant in clinical and social work. It is the dominant approach in understanding substance abuse, such as alcoholism; it is

Every truth is true only up to a point. Beyond that, by way of counterpoint, it becomes untruth.

Soren Kierkegaard (1813–1855)

TABLE 3.2 Social and Economic Characteristics of White, African-American, Latino, Asian-American, Pacific-Islander, and Native American Households, 1988. Percent Distribution.

	Total	White	African American	Latino[1]	Asian[2] American	Pacific[2] Islanders	Native American
Marital Status							
Total	100	100	100	100	X	X	X
Single	21.9	20.2	34.3	26.9	X	X	X
Married	62.7	64.6	46.7	61.5	X	X	X
Divorced	7.8	7.7	10.0	7.4	X	X	X
Widowed	7.6	7.5	9.0	4.3	X	X	X
Family Type							
Married couple	79.5	83.2	51.3	69.8	85.1	75.4	71.9
w/own children	37.8	38.7	28.1	46.3	X	X	X
Female single parent	9.6	7.7	28.1	16.4	10.2	19.4	22.7
Male single parent	1.6	1.5	2.2	2.5	4.7	5.2	5.4
Economic Characteristics							
Median income[3]	—	—	—	—	—	—	—
Persons below poverty level	13.5	10.5	33.1	28.2	10.3	16.1	23.7
Unemployed	5.5	4.7	11.7	8.2	4.6	7.3	13

SOURCE: U.S. Bureau of Census, *Statistics Abstract of the United States, 1990* (110th edition). Washngton, D.C. 1990. Tables 43, 44, 45 and 50.

1 May be of any race.
2 1980 census Figures
3 Not applicable

also widely used is discerning the dynamics of incest. Compared to symbolic interaction, from which it takes many of its ideas, systems theory is still in its infancy.

STRUCTURE AND PATTERNS OF INTERACTION. Systems theory views the family as a structure of related parts or subsystems. Each part carries out certain functions. These parts include the spousal subsystem, the parent/child subsystem, the parental subsystem (husband and wife relating to each other as parents), and the personal subsystem (the individual and his or her relationships). One of these subsystems' important tasks is maintaining their boundaries. For the family to function well, the subsystems must be kept separate (Minuchin, 1981). Husbands and wives, for example, should prevent their conflicts from spilling over into the parent/child subsystem. Sometimes a parent will turn to the child for the affection that he or she ordinarily receives from a spouse. When the boundaries of the separate subsystems blur, as in incest, the family becomes dysfunctional.

As in symbolic interaction, interaction is important in systems theory. A family system consists of more than simply its members. It also consists of the *pattern* of interactions of family members: their communication, roles, beliefs, and rules. Marriage is more than a husband and wife; it is also their pattern of interactions. The structure of marriage is determined by how the spouses act in relation to each other over time (Lederer and Jackson, 1968). Each partner influences and, in turn, is influenced by the partner. And each interaction is determined in part by the previous interactions. This emphasis on the pattern of interactions within the family is a distinctive feature of the systems approach.

The universe is like a safe to which there is a combination. But the combination is locked up in the safe.

Peter DeVries

THE FAMILY SYSTEM AS A MOBILE. Virginia Satir (1988) compared the family system to a hanging mobile. In a mobile all the pieces, regardless of size and shape, can be grouped together and balanced by changing the relative distance between the parts. The family members, like parts of the mobile, require certain distances between each other to maintain their balance. Any change in the family mobile—such as a child leaving the family, family members forming new alliances, hostility distancing the mother from the father—affects the stability of the mobile. This disequilibrium often manifests itself in emotional turmoil and stress. The family may try to restore the old equilibrium by forcing its "errant" member to return to his or her former position. Or it may adapt and create a new equilibrium with its members in changed relation to each other.

ASSUMPTIONS OF THE FAMILY SYSTEM APPROACH. In looking at the family as a system, researchers and therapists make the following assumptions:

◆ Interactions must be studied in the context of the family system. Each action affects every other person in the family. The family exerts a powerful influence on our behaviors and feelings, just as we influence the behaviors and feelings of other family members. On the simplest level, an angry outburst by a family member can put everyone in a bad mood. If the anger is constant, it will have long-term effects on each member of the family, who will cope with it by avoidance, hostility, depression, and so on.

◆ The family has a structure that can only be seen in its interactions. Each family has certain preferred patterns of transactions that ordinarily work in response to day-to-day demands. These patterns become strongly ingrained "habits" of interactions that make change difficult. A warring couple, for example, may decide to change their ways and resolve their conflicts peacefully. They may succeed for a while, but soon they fall back into their old ways. Lasting change requires more than changing a single behavior; it requires changing a pattern of relating.

◆ The family is a purposeful system; it has a goal. In most instances, its goal is to remain intact as a family. It seeks **homeostasis** (that is, stability). This goal of homeostasis makes change difficult, for change threatens the old patterns and habits to which the family has become accustomed.

◆ Despite its resistance to change, each family system is transformed over time. A well-functioning family system constantly changes and adapts to maintain itself in response to its members and the environment. The system changes through the family life cycle, for example, as partners age and as children are born, grow older, and leave home. The parent must allow the parent/child relationship to change. A parent must adapt to an adolescent's increasing independence by relinquishing some parental control. The family system adapts to stresses to maintain family continuity while making restructuring possible. If the primary wage earner loses his or her job, the family adapts to the loss in income; the children may seek work, recreation is cut, the family may be forced to move.

Better to doubt what is obscure than argue about uncertainties.

Augustine, Bishop of Hippo

CRITIQUE. It is difficult for researchers to agree on exactly what family systems theory is. Many of the basic concepts are still in dispute even among the theory's adherents (Melito, 1985). Some argue that there is no such thing as a coherent family systems theory. As a result, family systems is really more of an approach than a theory. It is "a loosely connected series of concepts" (Papp, 1983).

Family systems theory originated in clinical settings in which psychiatrists, clinical psychologists, and therapists tried to explain the dynamics of dysfunctional families.

While its use has spread beyond clinicians, its greatest success has been found in the analysis and treatment of dysfunctional families. As with clinical research, however, the basic question is whether its insights apply to healthy families as well as to dysfunctional ones. Do healthy families, for example, seek homeostasis as their goal, or do they seek individual and family well-being?

❖ REFLECTIONS   *How does your family deal with change? Does it accept or resist change? How does its reaction to change affect you? To get a visual sense of your family's response to change, draw a picture of your family as a mobile. Imagine a current or impending change, and redraw the mobile to reflect how your family deals with the change. Does your family try to maintain the old equilibrium or does it adjust to form a new one?*

◆ As you look over these various theories, which one makes the most sense to you for understanding your own relationships and families? Why? What are the problems with the other theories?

The methodologies and theories we use allow us to objectively examine marriage and the family. They allow us to step outside our own individual experiences to view marriage and family from a broader perspective. At the same time, such study enhances our understanding of our own relationships by allowing us to view them within a larger context. Thus the study of marriage and the family is not an abstract exercise; it is an excursion into the very heart of our relationships and experiences.

Discovery comes from dialogue that starts with the sharing of ignorance.

Marshall McLuhan

❖ SUMMARY

◆ Studying marriage and the family permits us to reflect on our own relationships, because their functions, processes, and issues are often the same ones that researchers are exploring. Our personal understanding is often subjective, affected by societal *norms* and the desire to seek *normative* standards. Researchers seek to study marriages and families objectively.

◆ Research affects how we understand marriage and the family in society. Studies suggest that the family is not declining but is changing. Research helps to break down stereotypes of African-American and other ethnic families, examining their strengths from a pluralistic perspective. It also has an important role in the development of social issues and the formulation of public policy, such as calling attention to the issue of family violence.

◆ Research data come from surveys, clinical studies, direct observation, and experiments.

◆ *Surveys* are the most important source of data. Their purpose is to gather information from a small, representative sample of the population and to infer from this sample conclusions that are valid for a larger group. Surveys are most useful for dealing with societal or general issues rather than personal or small-group issues. Surveys use questionnaires and interviews. Inherent problems with the survey method include (1) volunteer bias or an unrepresentative sample,

(2) individuals' lack of self-knowledge, and (3) underreporting of undesirable or unconventional behavior.

◆ *Clinical studies* are in-depth examinations of individuals or small groups who have entered a clinical setting for the treatment of psychological or relationship problems. The primary advantage of clinical studies is that they allow in-depth study; their primary disadvantage is that the people coming into a clinic are not representative of the general population.

◆ *Direct observation* refers to studies in which interpersonal behavior is studied in a natural setting, such as the home, by an unobtrusive observer.

◆ *In experimental studies* the researcher manipulates the variables. They are of limited use in marriage and family research because of the difficulty of controlling behavior and duplicating real-life conditions.

◆ Theories attempt to provide frames of reference for the interpretation of data. Theories studied in this chapter are (1) symbolic interaction, (2) social exchange theory, (3) conflict theory, (4) gender theory, and (5) family systems theory.

◆ *Symbolic interaction* examines how people interact and how we interpret or define others' actions through the symbols they communicate—their words, gestures, and actions. Within the family, each person is given various social roles: husband/father, wife/mother, son/brother, daughter/sister, and so on. Three important role processes include role taking, role playing, and role making. The drawbacks to the symbolic interaction approach include (1) a tendency to minimize the role of power in relationships, (2) failure to fully account for the emotional aspects of human life, (3) emphasis on individualism and personal fulfillment at the expense of the marital or family unit, and (4) inadequate attention to the social context.

◆ *Social exchange theory* suggests that we measure our actions and relationships on a cost-benefit basis. People seek to maximize their rewards and minimize their costs to gain the most favorable outcome. People have resources that others consider valuable; they use these resources in making exchanges with others. A corollary to exchange is *equity*: exchanges must balance out, or hard feelings are likely to ensue. Exchanges in marriage can be either cooperative or competitive. In cooperative exchanges, both partners try to maximize their *joint* profit; in competitive exchanges, each tries to maximize his or her own *individual* profit. Criticism of exchange theory includes (1) its assumption that individuals are rational and calculating in relationships and (2) the belief that the value of costs, rewards, and resources can be gauged.

◆ *Conflict theory* assumes that individuals in marriages and families are in conflict with each other. Power is often used to resolve the conflict. Four important sources of power include legitimacy, money, physical coercion, and love. Criticism of conflict theory includes (1) its politically based view of human nature, (2) its assumption that differences lead to conflict, and (3) difficulty in measuring and evaluating conflict.

◆ According to *gender theory,* gender is viewed as a basic element in social relationships based on the socially perceived differences between the sexes that justify unusual power relationships. Gender theory focuses on how specific behaviors and roles are defined as male or female, how labor is divided into male and female work, and how institutions bestow advantages on males. The key to creating gender inequality lies in believing that men and women are opposite in personalities, abilities, skills, and traits. Furthermore, the differences between the sexes are unequally valued in society. One problem with gender theory is that it reduces male/female relations to power and dominance issues, underestimating the role of love and altruism in such relationships.

◆ *Family systems theory* approaches the family in terms of its structure and pattern of interactions. Systems analysts believe that (1) interactions must be studied in the context of the family, (2) family structure can be seen only in the family's interactions, (3) the family is a purposeful system seeking homeostasis, and (4) family systems are transformed over time. Family systems theory is not a coherent, system-

atic theory, and it has been criticized because it is based on clinical studies of nonrepresentative families.

Answers to Preview Questions

The answers to the preview questions at the beginning of the chapter are listed below. As you check your answers, whether you were correct or not, think about your reasons for each response What were they? What was their source? How valid is the source? As you read the chapter, you will find the questions discussed in greater depth.

1. T	6. F
2. F	7. F
3. T	8. F
4. T	9. T
5. T	10. T

For a list of useful journals, bibliographies, periodical indexes, and databases for writing papers or for doing additional research in areas that interest you, see Resource Center.

Booth, Alan ed. *Contemporary Families: Looking Forward, Looking Back.* St. Paul, Minn.: National Council on Family Relations, 1991. The definitive review of family research in the 1980s. Invaluable.

Burr, Wesley, et al., eds. *Contemporary Theories about the Family.* 2 vols. New York: Macmillan, 1979. A comprehensive and highly technical discussion of major family theories by leading scholars.

Copeland, Ann, and Kathleen White. *Studying Families.* Newbury Park, Calif.: Sage Publications, 1991 (paperback). Research issues in studying diverse families, such as cohabiting parents, gay and lesbian families, and childless marriages.

Engram, Eleanor. *Science, Myth, Reality: The Black Family in One-half Century of Research.* Westport, Conn.: Greenwood Press, 1982. Misperceptions, biases, and half-truths affecting our understanding of African-American families.

Hess, Beth, and Myra Marx Ferree eds. *Analyzing Gender.* Newbury Park, Calif.: Sage Publications, 1987. A valuable collection of feminist essays on gender theory.

Marin, Gerardo, and Barbara Marin. *Research with Hispanic Populations.* Newbury Park, Calif.: Sage Publications, 1991 (paperback). Examines problems of using research approaches designed for the Anglo population with Latinos; suggests ways of overcoming limitations and developing appropriate methods and techniques.

Miller, Brent. *Family Research Methods.* Newbury Park, Calif.: Sage Publications, 1986. A succinct description of basic research methodology and issues in marriage and the family.

Nye, F. Ivan, and Felix Berardo, eds. *Emerging Conceptual Frameworks in Family Analysis,* rev. ed. New York: Praeger,

1981 (paperback). A classic overview of different conceptual approaches to studying families, including anthropological, economic, interactional, developmental, and structural-functional approaches.

Statistics Canada. *Canada Yearbook.* Ottawa: Supply and Services (published annually). Includes current statistics regarding Canadian marriages.

Sigel, Irving, and Gene Brody, eds. *Methods of Family Research: Biographies of Research Projects.* 2 vols. Hillsdale, N.J.: Lawrence Erlbaum Associates, Publishers, 1990. Essays by leading researchers discussing how they went about creating their studies.

Sussman, Marvin, and Suzanne Steinmetz, eds. *Handbook of Marriage and the Family.* New York: Plenum Press, 1987. The definitive reference book on marriage and the family. Thirty chapters by leading scholars cover the major areas and issues in family research, including theory, demography, law, gender roles, violence, the family life cycle, single-parent families, parent/child socialization, remarriage, and ethnicity.

Thorne, Barrie, with Marilyn Yalom. *Rethinking the Family: Some Feminist Questions.* New York: Longman, 1982 (paperback). An important feminist work critiquing traditional interpretations of the family.

U.S. Bureau of the Census. *Statistical Abstract of the United States.* Washington, D.C.: Government Printing Office. Published annually, the *Statistical Abstract* is a compilation of the latest statistics relating to various aspects of American life and commerce, including several sections pertinent to the study of marriage and the family.

READINGS

❖

SELECTED ATTITUDES TOWARD MARRIAGE AND FAMILY LIFE AMONG COLLEGE STUDENTS

Don Martin and Maggie Martin*

This study first appeared in Family Relations, a scholarly journal. (The questionnaire on which the study based its research is the one you completed in "Understanding Yourself" on pp. 66–67.) The article gives you a sense of the nature of scholarly articles in the field of marriage and the family. It follows the standard scholarly format of Introduction, Method, Results, and Discussion. What are the study's strengths? Weaknesses?

ABSTRACT: *This paper discusses the results of an extensive research study that analyzed the attitude of college students in several universities in the United States. Ten attitude areas are identified and outlined including cohabitation, premarital sexual relations, marriage and divorce, child rearing, division of labor, marital and extramarital sexual relations, social needs, communication, parental relationships and counseling services. Implications for premarital counseling and future research are discussed.*

* Don Martin is an Assistant Professor, Counseling and Educational Psychology, New Mexico State University, Las Cruces, NM 88003. Maggie Martin is an Assistant Professor in the Speech and Communications Department, El Paso Community College, El Paso, TX.

Key Concepts: attitudes, family life, marriage, premarital counseling.

(*Family Relations*, 1984, **33**, 293–300.)

Marriage and family life in America have been considerably altered since the onset of the Industrial Revolution. Variations and modifications in family structure, values and socialization patterns suggest a realization among educators, human service professionals and the general public that the family is experiencing a new definition of its future status in American society (Cornish, 1979; Medora & Burton, 1980; Olson, 1972; Thamm, 1975).

Young adults have experienced many of the changes associated with the alteration of the definition of the family. These include but are not limited to the rising divorce rate, the increasing number of single parent families and the mobilization or "splitting apart" of siblings and relatives (Thamm, 1975). These young adults are developing and defining the concepts of future marriage and family life in America as they assume the roles of spouses and parents.

Among the apparent contributing factors to current trends in marriage and family life are the change from the traditional extended family model, the development of the nuclear family model, and the increasing frequency of marriage dissolution. The lack of preparation among young adults for marriage, searches for alternative dating patterns and cohabitation among college students and premarital sexual behavior which affect sex role development and views toward the family also contribute to the current trends.

While these trends may indicate dramatic changes in the American family structure, identifying and documenting these changes has been difficult. Several educators and human service professionals have anticipated the demise of the traditional American family (Bernard, 1970; Johnson, 1977). Others anticipate even more changes in the family in the years ahead (Cornish, 1979; Olson, 1972).

continued on next page

READINGS

One factor that appears to contribute to marital problems and divorce among young adults is lack of preparation for the commitment of marriage. Few guidelines are available and young adults are questioning whether marriages can meet their expectations and desires (Olson, 1972). Several authors suggest that societal pressures can coerce people into marriage before they are prepared (Knox, 1980; Ryder, Kafka, & Olson, 1971).

In an effort to establish more meaningful relationships in life and yet not commit to legalities of marriage, college students are exploring alternative lifestyles such as cohabitation (Macklin, 1972). Increasing numbers of couples are living together or cohabitating in order to learn to cope adequately with differences, conflict and the concept of commitment in a relationship (Glick & Spanier, 1980; Macklin, 1972).

Young adults may believe these cohabitating relationships provide both the happiness and freedom that are necessary as learning experiences before a couple enters marriage (Bower & Christopherson, 1977). Olson (1972) concluded that merely living together would not be a sufficient preparation for marriage.

The increase of premarital sexual behavior among college students and its relationship to marriage has also been an area of interest to marital researchers (Christensen & Gregg, 1970). In examining these sexual behaviors, investigators have found that college students report more sexual contact with one's future spouse than with other previous sexual partners (Bell & Chaskes, 1970). There are also indications of a strong trend among young adults toward exploring sexual experiences in addition to relationships with some type of mutual commitment (Medora & Burton, 1980; Mosher & Cross, 1971). Olson (1972) concluded that current increases in premarital sexual behavior were primarily an outgrowth of the women's rights movement of the 1960s.

Other important attitudes toward marriage and family life that appear to be undergoing change are expectations regarding appropriate role relationships between a husband and wife (Keller, Maxwell, & Ritzert, 1978). Today, many couples are experiencing role conflicts in regard to areas such as division of labor and professional employment in a relationship (Parelius, 1975). Otto (1970) contended that sex roles are changing dramatically and that individuals must examine these sex roles within their relationships or the institution of marriage will not last. How these attitudes may affect future marital relationships has not been fully researched (Parelius, 1975).

Thus, it appears from the literature that college undergraduates' perceptions of marriage and family are only partially understood by researchers and educators. In an attempt to better understand the beliefs of students of the 1980's, the present study examined the attitudes of contemporary students toward marriage and family life.

METHOD

Subjects

The subjects were 5,237 students in four universities from the states of Arkansas, Louisiana, Oklahoma and Texas. These states were chosen since the authors wanted a representative sample of student attitudes in the Southwestern United States. These universities were sampled since they were more likely to enroll students with varied socioeconomic and living environments. Students were selected from both residence hall populations and general education classes at each university. Each of the schools is a medium-sized university enrolling between 10,000 and 25,000 students. Females comprised 57% of the population survey with males comprising the remaining 43%. Subjects ranged in age from 16 to 36 years. Ninety-five percent were between the ages of 17 and 25 years. . . .

Instrument

The Marriage and Family Life Attitude Survey (Martin, 1982) was the instrument used specifically in this research [reprinted on pp. 66–67 in this textbook]. It contains 43 items or attitude statements that elicit specific information regarding perceptions about marriage and family life. It is based on prominent literature in marriage and family therapy and the pioneering work of Sager (1976). Martin (1982) reported an internal reliability coefficient of .81 and a test rates and reliability coefficient of .79 for the instrument.

Each item was submitted for review and recommendation to a panel of 10 experts in the field of marriage and family counseling. Each panel member was a licensed psychologist and an approved supervisor in the American Association for Marriage and Family Therapy. A pilot study using 100 college students was also conducted with all the items to determine face validity, item skew, readability and other validation requirements.

In answering attitude statements, respondents were instructed to rate each of the attitudes on a one to five point Likert type scale ranging from strongly agree to strongly disagree. Seventy-four percent of the questionnaires were returned completed. Although this was a modest return, it compares favorably with survey research criteria when participants are not paid or compensated for their completion of the task (Wright, 1983).

Data Analysis

Analysis of data focused on the following attitudinal areas: cohabitation and premarital sexual relations, marriage and divorce, childhood and child rearing, division of household labor and professional development, marital and extramarital sexual relations, privacy rights and social needs, religious needs, communication expectations, parental relationships and professional counseling services. Quantitative data were analyzed through descriptive statistics reporting agreement or disagreement responses. Residual neutral responses are generally not discussed.

Results

The attitude statements were grouped within the 10 topic areas. The following are the results for each topic area:

1. Cohabitation and Premarital Sexual Relations. Respondents were divided as to whether it is wrong to engage in sexual intercourse before marriage. A majority indicated they have or would engage in this action at the present time. Seventy-two percent indicated that it is not acceptable to experience sexual intercourse without love of one's partner. Sixty-four percent believe they would not cohabit before marriage; if they did, the majority would inform their parents.

2. Marriage and Divorce. Seventy-five percent of the respondents viewed their parents' marriage as happy. Over 90% saw marriage as a lifelong commitment. The majority of respondents did not believe divorce was acceptable with or without children. While close to 80% believed they had the skills necessary for a good marriage, the respondents were evenly divided as to whether or not they were prepared for marriage.

3. Childhood and Child Rearing. Eighty-eight percent view childhood as a happy experience. The majority of respondents would leave their children with a relative or in a daycare center if they worked. Respondents were divided as to whether a parent should stay home to rear children, but strongly believed the responsibility of child-rearing should be equally divided between both parents, and that they, personally, had the knowledge necessary for such an undertaking. While respondents were divided as to whether children were necessary in a marriage, approximately 76% believed two or more children were desirable for a married couple.

4. Division of Household Labor and Professional Employment. The majority indicated that household chores should be divided equally, but that they are sex specific. Results indicated that equal careers were agreeable but it was not necessary that both spouses work. Approximately 64% would move with a spouse because of a job offer in a different locality.

5. Marital and Extramarital Sexual Relations. Sexual relations were important in a marriage and sexual advances should be initiated by either partner. Extramarital sex was not acceptable under any conditions.

6. Privacy Rights and Social Needs. Although friendships with the opposite sex outside of marriage were important, more

respondents indicated that major social functioning should be with other couples. Partners do need time away from the spouse but social needs should be compatible. Over 70% believed that arguments should not be voiced in the company of other people.

7. Religious Needs. Over 80% agreed that religious practices are important in a marriage but there was a division as to whether children should be made to attend church. Approximately 75% would marry a person of a different religious background.

8. Communications Expectations. A large majority of respondents indicated that couple disagreements and feelings were discussed. Over 60% would not withdraw from their partner when they argued, but over 75% would like to learn better ways to communicate.

9. Parental Relationships. Approximately 75% of the respondents indicated that they would marry someone regardless of the partner's parental disapproval. If a spouse's parents were disliked, a majority would still visit them. They also felt that each spouse's parents should be seen an equal amount of time. However, 60% indicated that parents were not to intervene in matters pertaining to the couple's marriage. Seventy-five percent designated that their parents wanted them to be married.

10. Professional Counseling Services. Over 75% of the respondents would like more knowledge about parenting skills and professional help to be available for child and marriage difficulties. Approximately 50% would seek premarital counseling and marriage enrichment workshops. Over 60% did not believe that counseling should be limited to couples with troubles, and more than half of the subjects wanted more education on what to expect from marriage.

DISCUSSION

Numerous attitudinal areas were revealed by the *Marriage and Family Life Attitude Survey* (Martin, 1982) which may prove useful for human service professionals in helping young adults become better prepared for their future marriages and family life. The possible lack of dating experience on college campuses may provide a valuable clue to the misunderstandings that may occur in relationship interactions. It would appear that young adults may need communication skills training in appropriate methods of meeting potential partners of the opposite sex and in methods of maintaining these relationships (Knox & Wilson, 1981). Clearer understandings of the needs of persons in a relationship might also be necessary. Since appropriate role models for adults may be lacking, more couple's group programs with opposite sex co-facilitators may prove valuable (Martin, 1982).

Since divorce has become quite common in the United States, a better understanding of the ramifications of the process might be helpful. Students in this study strongly disagreed with divorce and viewed marriage as a lifelong process. Present statis-

continued on next page

READINGS

tics indicate a discrepancy between these attitudes and the reality of what is presently occurring in American society. Perhaps a clearer presentation of the marriage relationship by human service professionals might help young adults prepare for this challenging interactive process.

Attitudes toward equality of relationships in regard to child rearing, domestic responsibilities and professional employment may have an even greater impact on family life than is currently observed. Human service professionals need to help couples understand the total implications of "equal" relationships and dual-career marriages in a society that is still contending with sex-role stereotyping. Supplementary data indicate that males and females of this study will maintain some traditional values. Whether these are expected or desired is not clearly understood (Gilbert, Holohan & Manning, 1981).

Premarital sexual intercourse is relatively acceptable but has social and moral ramifications. Recent literature has related premarital sexual guilt with the lack of contraceptive use by females (Herold & Goodwin, 1981). An exploration of this area and the apparent sexual "double standard" for males and females may be a fruitful encounter for human service professionals. With approximately half of these students approving of sexual intercourse before marriage, it appears appropriate to develop workshops for young adults in topic areas such as birth control, sexuality and love relationships.

Family life education in child care and child rearing, parental and in-law relationships, and daycare facilities may prove valuable for young adults. At the present time much of this training is developed for married couples already placed in problem situations rather than developing preventive programs which may help avoid some of these dilemmas.

On a concluding note, it appears that professional counseling services are becoming more acceptable to young adults as they view their present status and their future marriage and family life. Educational workshops on parenting skills, marriage enrichment and marriage counseling are desired. There is a need for premarital counseling and couple communication programs for young adults as they seek to improve relationships. If difficulties do occur in a marriage relationship, most would approve of seeking help from a human service professional.

REFERENCES

Bell, R. R., & Chaskes, J. B. (1970). Premarital sexual experience among coeds, 1958 to 1968. *Journal of Marriage and the Family, 32,* 81–84.

Bernard, J. (1970). Woman, marriage, and the future. *Futurist, 4,* 41–43.

Bower, D. W., & Christopherson, H. (1977). University student cohabitation: A regional comparison of selected attitudes and behavior. *Journal of Marriage and the Family, 39,* 447–452.

Christensen, H. T., & Gregg, C. F. (1970). Changing sex norms in America and Scandinavia. *Journal of Marriage and the Family, 32,* 616–627.

Cornish, E. (1979). The future of the family: Intimacy in an age of loneliness. *Futurist, 13* (1), 45–49.

Gilbert, L., Holohan, C., & Manning, L. (1981). Coping with conflict between professional and marital roles. *Family Relations, 30,* 419–426.

Glick, P. C., & Spanier, G. B. (1980). Married and unmarried cohabitation in the United States. *Journal of Marriage and the Family, 42,* 19–30.

Herold, E., & Goodwin, M. (1981). Premarital sexual guilt and contraceptive attitudes and behavior. *Family Relations, 30,* 247–258.

Johnson, W. D. (1977). Establishing a national center for the study of divorce. *The Family Coordinator, 26,* 331–336.

Keller, J. F., Maxwell, J. W., & Ritzert, J. Y. (1978). Marriage role expectations: A comparison of freshmen and senior college students. *International Journal of Sociology of the Family, 8,* 81–87.

Knox, D. (1980). Trends in marriage and the family—the 1980's. *Family Relations, 30,* 255–263.

Macklin, E. D. (1977). Heterosexual cohabitation among unmarried college students. *The Family Coordinator, 21,* 463–472.

Martin, D. (1982). Premarital group counseling. *Journal for Specialists in Group Work, 2,* 96–105.

Medora, N. P., & Burton, M. M. (1980). Premarital sexual norms of an undergraduate student population at a southern university. *Family Perspective, 14,* 15–20.

Mosher, D. L., & Cross, H. J. (1971). Sex guilt and premarital sexual experience of college students. *Journal of Consulting and Clinical Psychology, 33,* 27–32.

Olson, D. H. (1972). Marriage of the future: Revolutionary or evolutionary change? *The Family Coordinator, 21,* 383–394.

Otto, H. A. (Ed.) (1970). *The family in search of a future.* New York: Appleton, Century and Crofts.

Parelius, A. (1975). Emerging sex role attitudes, expectations, and strains among college women. *Journal of Marriage and the Family, 37,* 146–154.

Ryder, R. G., Kafka, J. S., & Olson, D. H. (1971). Separating and joining influences in courtship and early marriage. *American Journal of Orthopsychiatry, 41,* 450–464.

Sager, C. (1976). *Marriage contracts and couple therapy.* New York: Brunner/Mazel.

Thamm, R. (1975). *Beyond marriage and the nuclear family.* San Francisco: Canfield Press.

Wright, H. N. (1983). *Premarital counseling.* Chicago: Moody.

READINGS

BLACK FAMILIES IN WHITE AMERICA

Andrew Billingsley

In this classic study written almost a quarter century ago, Andrew Billingsley critiques Daniel Moynihan's The Negro Family (popularly known as "The Moynihan Report"), which ascribed problems in African-American families to a "tangle of pathology." What is his critique of the Moynihan Report? Do you believe that his points continue to remain valid? Why?

There are a number of methodological and substantive problems with the Moynihan report. A major distortion was his singling out instability in the Negro family as the causal factor for the difficulties Negroes face in the white society. It is quite the other way round. But coming just at the time the nation was trying to find a single cause of the Watts riots, Moynihan's thesis struck a responsive chord in the collective American breast. ". . . At the center of the tangle of pathology," he concluded,

is the weakness of the family structure. Once or twice removed, it will be found to be the principal source of most of the aberrant, inadequate, or antisocial behavior that did not establish, but now serves to perpetuate, the cycle of poverty and deprivation.

He could come to such faulty and inverse conclusions in part because he had no theoretical framework to guide him in the analysis of his statistical data, and in part because his data were limited.

Another serious shortcoming of the whole report was the tendency, common among liberal social scientists, to compare Negroes with whites on standardized objective measures which have been demonstrated to have meaning only in the white, European subculture. Many statistical studies which compare Negroes and whites fall into the almost inevitable position of characterizing the Negro group as deviant. If all a study can describe about Negro family life is what it simultaneously describes about white families, it cannot tell us very much about Negro family life. Moynihan compounded this error, however, by his failure to take into account two very important aspects of the Negro experience: social class and social caste.

Simple white-Negro comparisons on almost any set of standardized variables will necessarily produce distortions, for they ignore the important dimension of social class. The white sample will contain large numbers of middle and upper income families and the Negro sample will be dominated by low income

families. Using statistics for the same year Moynihan found that 25 per cent of Negro families were broken, Lee Rainwater has shown that if one considers only Negro families with family incomes of $3,000 or above, this proportion dropped from 25 per cent to 7 per cent, while for Negroes earning less than $3,000, it rose to 36 per cent. But while income level explains a great deal of the original racial differential, it does not explain it all. For at all income levels, the rate of broken families is higher among Negroes. Thus among white families earning $3,000 or under, the rate is 22 per cent—considerably less than the 36 per cent for Negro families. And among white families earning $3,000 and over, it drops to 3 per cent, less than half the Negro rate.

This brings us, then, to the second major variable overlooked by Moynihan, despite his own analysis of this factor elsewhere in his report. We refer to the importance to the Negro experience in America of the caste-like barriers which exclude Negro families from so many of the resources of the society. Even when the income *levels* are similar for the white and the Negro samples, the two groups are not comparable. For we know that even in the low income category of under $3,000, the mean incomes for white families falls considerably toward the top of that range, while the mean income of Negro families is considerably lower. A white family with an income of $2,750 and a Negro family with the income of $1,500 are both under $3,000 and both undoubtedly lower class, but they do not have the same resources and options available to them. Even if two groups of white and Negro families were matched with exactly the same income, education, and occupation, they would still not be comparable. For the Negro group must reflect its experience with the caste barrier as well as its distinctive history, both of which set the conditions for growing up black in white America. Thus, white-Negro comparative studies may be very important for certain purposes, but they are wholly inadequate for understanding processes of causation and other dynamics of Negro family life, particularly if they are conducted without a general theoretical framework.

The low income Negro family faces three insidious problems. One is poverty, the other is prejudice, and the third is historical subjugation in his own country because of his race. The low income white family faces only one of these problems, and in this respect is better off than even the middle class Negro family—contrary to the implications of the Moynihan report. For the middle class Negro makes considerably less money than the middle class white, and in addition, must face the color bar in ways unknown to the experience of his white counterpart. However powerful the variable of social class, it does not obliterate and, indeed, was not invented to account for the racial factor.

PART TWO

Getting Together

CHAPTER 4

Contemporary Gender Roles

To gain a sense of what you already know about the material covered in this chapter, answer "true" or "false" to the statements below. You will find the answers on page 116.

1. Gender roles generally reflect the instinctive nature of males and females. True or false?
2. Gender-role content is influenced by ethnicity. True or false?
3. Psychologists believe that the increasing similarity of male and female gender roles represents a decline in mental health. True or false?
4. Among immigrants, men generally experience greater gender-role stress than women. True or false?
5. Is it often possible to tell the sex of an infant based on its level of activity. True or false?
6. Peers are the most important influence on gender-role development from adolescence through old age. True or false?
7. For African Americans, the traditional female gender role includes work *and* motherhood. True or false?
8. The traditional female gender role discourages self-confidence in women. True or false?
9. It is relatively easy to change gender-role behaviors if one wants to change. True or false?
10. The double standard of aging means that men gain and women lose status as they age. True or false?

*The great question ... which I have not
been able to answer, despite my thirty
years of research into the feminine soul, is
"What does a woman want?"*

Sigmund Freud (1856–1939)

L ET US BEGIN WITH A STORY AND A QUESTION. Jason and his father were driving on
the highway when suddenly another car veered into their path. The oncoming
car struck with such force that Jason's father was killed instantly, and Jason suffered
severe head injuries. An ambulance rushed the bleeding boy to the hospital where,
fortunately, one of the country's leading neurosurgeons was in residence. Because it
was late at night and there was nothing to do, the surgeon was engaged in a friendly
poker game with several other physicians. Upon being paged to the operating room,
the surgeon cursed and sprinted down the corridor. Entering the operating room,
the surgeon exclaimed, "My God! I can't operate on this boy. He's my son." The
question is, who was the surgeon?

If you can't figure out the answer, you are probably not alone. The surgeon is
Jason's mother. The trick of the story is based on the use of gender-role stereotypes
in describing the surgeon. According to traditional female stereotypes, women aren't
neurosurgeons, don't play poker, don't curse or sprint down halls. Fortunately,
more people each year are able to answer the question correctly as we become
increasingly aware of gender-role stereotypes. But you might try the story on friends
or classmates to see how well they do.

Our gender roles have a tremendous impact on our lives. They influence our self-
image, our dating and marital relationships, our achievement in school and careers,
and many other aspects of our lives. In this chapter we look at gender roles, how
they are formed, and how they affect us.

❖ STUDYING GENDER ROLES

Until the rise of the women's movement in the 1960s, little interest was expressed in
gender roles, and that small interest reinforced traditional notions that woman's
place was in the home and man's place was everywhere else (Spence et al., 1985). As
a result of the women's movement, however, both the public and researchers began
reexamining traditional gender ideas. "In the span of a few years," writes Janet
Spence and her colleagues (1985), "inquiries into these matters have grown from a
trickle to a torrent."

Initially, this torrent of research focused on women's roles; more recently, this
examination has expanded to include male roles, especially male family roles (Losh-
Hesselbart, 1987). Previously, researchers showed little interest in male family roles
because gender-role stereotypes about men blinded researchers to the actual roles
that men play in the day-to-day activities of home life. Researchers assumed that the
male role in the family was limited to that of provider.

Most gender-role studies have focused on the white middle class. Very little is
known about gender roles among African Americans, Latinos, Asian Americans, and
other ethnic groups (Binion, 1990; Reid and Comas-Diaz, 1990; True, 1990; see *Sex
Roles* 22: 7–8 [April 1990] for a special issue on gender roles and ethnicity). Students and researchers must be careful not to project gender-role concepts or aspirations based on white middle-class values onto other groups. Too often such projections can lead to distortions or moral judgments. There is evidence, for example,
that the traditional woman's role of dependent homemaker has not been an important one for African-American women; instead, African Americans emphasized the
"strong" woman who both raised a family and worked outside the home (Gump,
1980; E. Smith, 1982). Similarly, *machismo* has a positive meaning among Latinos,
but Anglos often use the term in a derogatory sense.

Before we continue further, we need to define several key terms, because lack of
agreement sometimes causes confusion when studying gender roles. These key

terms include *gender, role, gender role, gender-role stereotype, gender-role attitudes,* and *gender-role behavior.* **Gender** refers to male or female. **Role** refers to the culturally defined expectations that an individual is expected to fulfill in a given situation in a particular culture. **Gender roles,** are the roles that a person is expected to perform as a result of being male or female in a particular culture. (The term *gender role* is gradually replacing the traditional term *sex role*). A **gender-role stereotype** is a rigidly held and oversimplified belief that all males and females, as a result of their sex, possess distinct psychological and behavioral traits. Stereotypes tend to be false not only for the group as a whole (all men are aggressive) but for any individual member of the group (Michael may not be aggressive). Even if the generalization is statistically valid in describing a group average (males are taller than females), such generalizations do not necessarily predict whether Jason will be taller than Tanya. **Gender-role attitudes** refer to the beliefs we have of ourselves and others regarding appropriate male and female personality traits and activities. **Gender-role behaviors** refer to the actual activities or behaviors we engage in as males and females. When we discuss gender roles, it is important not to confuse stereotypes with reality and attitudes with behavior.

❖ SOCIALIZATION THEORIES

Gender and Gender Roles

At birth, we are identified as either male or female. This identity, based on genitalia, is called **gender identity,** and we learn it at a very young age. It is perhaps the deepest concept we hold of ourselves. The psychology of insults suggests this depth, for few things offend a person so much as to be tauntingly characterized as a member of the "opposite" sex. Gender identity determines many of the directions our lives will take—for example, whether we will fulfill the role of husband or wife, father or mother. When the scripts are handed out in life, the one you receive depends largely on your gender identity.

Each culture determines the content of gender roles in its own way. Among the Arapesh of New Guinea, both sexes possessed what we consider feminine traits. Men and women alike tended to be passive, cooperative, peaceful, and nurturing. The father was said to "bear a child" as well as the mother; only the father's continual care could make a child grow healthily, both in the womb and in childhood. Eighty miles away, the Mundugumor lived in remarkable contrast to the peaceful Arapesh. "Both men and women," Margaret Mead (1975) observed, "are expected to be violent, competitive, aggressively sexed, jealous, and ready to see and avenge insult, delighting in display, in action, in fighting." She concluded, "Many, if not all of the personality traits which we have called masculine or feminine are as lightly linked to sex as are the clothing, the manners, and the form of head-dress that a society at a given period assigned to either sex. . . . The evidence is overwhelmingly in favor of social conditioning." Biology creates males and females, but culture creates masculinity and femininity.

Although there are a number of ways of examining how we acquire our gender roles, two of the most prominent are social learning theory and cognitive development theory.

Throughout history the more complex activities have been defined and redefined, now as male, now as female—sometimes as drawing equally on the gifts of both sexes. When an activity to which each sex could have contributed is limited to one sex, a rich, differentiated quality is lost from the activity itself.

Margaret Mead (1901–1978)

If you want anything said, ask a man. If you want anything done, ask a woman.

Margaret Thatcher

❖ REFLECTIONS   *To get a sense of the significance of gender roles, would you be a similiar person if you were the other sex? Would your plans be different? Your activities, feelings, goals?*

Cognitive Social Learning Theory

Cognitive social learning theory is derived from behaviorist psychology. In explaining our actions, behaviorists emphasize observable events and their consequences rather than internal feelings and drives. According to behaviorists, we learn attitudes and behaviors as a result of social interactions with others (hence the term *social learning*).

The cornerstone of cognitive social learning theory is the belief that consequences control behavior. Acts that are regularly followed by a reward, or *positive* reinforcement, are likely to occur again; acts that are regularly followed by a punishment, or *negative* reinforcement, are less likely to reoccur. Girls are rewarded for playing with dolls ("What a nice mommy!"), but boys are not ("What a sissy!").

This behaviorist approach has been modified recently to include **cognition**—that is, mental processes that intervene between stimulus and response, such as evaluation and reflection. The cognitive processes involved in social learning include our ability to (1) use language, (2) anticipate consequences, and (3) make observations. By using language, we can tell our daughter that we like it when she does well in school and that we don't like it when she hits someone. A person's ability to anticipate consequences affects behavior. A boy doesn't need to wear lace stockings in public to know that such dressing will lead to negative consequences. Finally, children observe what others do. A girl may learn that she "shouldn't" play video games by seeing that the players in video arcades are mostly boys.

We also learn gender roles by imitation. Learning through imitation is called **modeling.** Most of us are not even aware of the many subtle behaviors that make up gender roles—the ways in which men and women use different mannerisms and gestures, speak differently, use different body language, and so on. We don't "teach" these behaviors by reinforcement. Children tend to model friendly, warm, and nurturing adults; they also tend to imitate adults who are powerful in their eyes—that is, adults who control access to food, toys, or privileges. Initially, the most powerful models that children have are their parents. As children grow older and their social world expands, so do the number of people who may act as their role models: siblings, friends, teachers, media figures. Children sift through the various demands and expectations associated with the different models to create their own unique selves.

Cognitive Development Theory

In contrast to social learning theory, cognitive development theory focuses on the child's active interpretation of the messages he or she receives from the environment. Whereas social learning assumes that children and adults learn in fundamentally the same way, cognitive development theory stresses that we learn differently depending on our age. Swiss psychologist Jean Piaget showed that children's ability to reason and understand changes as they grow older (Santrock, 1983). Lawrence Kohlberg (1969) took Piaget's findings and applied them to how children assimilate gender-role information at different ages. At age two, children can correctly identify themselves and others as boys or girls, but they tend to base this identification on superficial features such as hair and clothing. Girls have long hair and wear dresses; boys have short hair and never wear dresses. Some children even believe they can change their gender by changing their clothes or hair length. They don't identify gender in terms of gentalia, as older children and adults do. No amount of reinforcement will alter their view because their ideas are limited by their developmental stage.

When children are six or seven, they begin to understand that gender is permanent; it is not something you can change as you can your clothes. They acquire this understanding because they are capable of grasping the idea that basic characteristics do not change. A woman can be a woman even if she has short hair and wears pants. Oddly enough, although children can understand the permanence of gender, they tend to insist on rigid adherence to gender-role stereotypes. Even though boys can play with dolls, children believe they shouldn't because dolls are for girls. Researchers speculate that children exaggerate gender roles to make the roles "cognitively clear."

According to cognitive social learning theory, boys and girls learn appropriate gender-role behavior through reinforcement and modeling. But according to cognitive development theory, once children learn that gender is permanent, they independently strive to act like "proper" girls or boys. They do this on their own because of an internal need for congruence, the agreement between what they know and how they act. Also, children find performing the appropriate gender-role activities rewarding in itself. Models and reinforcement help show them how well they are doing, but the primary motivation is internal.

❖ LEARNING GENDER ROLES

Gender-Role Learning in Childhood and Adolescence

It is difficult to analyze the relationship between biology and personality, for learning begins at birth. Evidence shows, for example, that infant females are more sensitive than infant males to pain and to sudden changes of environment. Such responses may be encouraged by learning that begins immediately after birth.

In our culture, infant girls are usually held more gently and treated more tenderly than boys, who are ordinarily subjected to rougher forms of play. The first day after birth, parents rate their daughters as soft, fine featured, and small, and their sons as hard, large featured, big, and attentive. Fathers tend to stereotype their sons more extremely than mothers do (Fagot and Leinbach, 1987; Rubin et al., 1974). Although it is impossible for strangers to know the sex of a diapered baby, once they learn the baby's sex, they respond accordingly. In one well-known experiment, three groups played with Baby X (Condry and Condry, 1976). The first group was told that the baby was a girl, the second group was told that the baby was a boy, and the third group was not told what sex the baby was. The group that did not know what sex Baby X was felt extremely uncomfortable, but the group participants then made a decision based on whether the baby was "strong" or "soft." When the baby was labeled a boy, its fussing behavior was called "angry"; if the baby was labeled a girl, the same behavior was called "frustrated." The study was replicated numerous times with the same general results.

PARENTS AS SOCIALIZING AGENTS. During infancy and early childhood, a child's most important source of learning is the primary caretaker, whether the mother, father, grandmother, or someone else. Most parents are not aware that their words and actions contribute to their children's gender-role socialization (Culp et al., 1983). Nor are they aware that they treat their sons and daughters differently because of their gender. Although parents may recognize that they respond differently to sons than to daughters, they usually have a ready explanation—the "natural" differences in the temperament and behavior of girls and boys. Parents may also believe they adjust their responses to each particular child's personality. In an everyday living sit-

What are little girls made of?
Sugar and spice
And everything nice.
That's what little girls are made of.

What are little boys made of?
Snips and snails and puppy dogs' tails.
That's what little boys are made of.

Nursery rhyme

If I had knowledge only of the anatomy and cultural capacities of men and women, I would predict that women rather than men would be more likely to gain control over the technology of defense and aggression, and that if one sex were going to subordinate the other, it would be female over male. While I would be impressed with the physical dimorphism—the greater height, weight, and strength of the males— I would be even more impressed by something which the females have and which the males cannot get—namely, control over the birth, care and feeding of babies. Women, in other words, control the nursery, and because they control the nursery, they can potentially modify any lifestyle that threatens them.

Marvin Harris, Cows, Pigs, Wars, and Witches

Gender-role stereotypes may be reinforced by schools, religious, and other institutions. This girl was prohibited from playing on her school's basketball team until the courts intervened.

uation that involves changing diapers, feeding babies, stopping fights, and providing entertainment, it is difficult for harassed parents to recognize that their own actions may be largely responsible for the differences they attribute to nature.

Children are socialized in gender roles through four very subtle processes: manipulation, channeling, verbal appellation, and activity exposure (Oakley, 1985).

◆ *Manipulation:* Parents manipulate their children from infancy onward. They treat a daughter gently, tell her she is pretty, and advise her that nice girls do not fight. They treat a son roughly, tell him he is strong, and advise him that big boys do not cry. Eventually, children incorporate their parents' views in such matters as integral parts of their personalities.

◆ *Channeling:* Children are channeled by directing their attention to specific objects. Toys, for example, are differentiated by sex. Dolls are considered appropriate for girls, cars for boys.

◆ *Verbal Appellation:* Parents use different words with boys and girls to describe the same behavior. A boy who pushes others may be described as "active," whereas a girl who does the same is usually called "aggressive."

◆ *Activity Exposure:* The activity exposure of boys and girls differs markedly. Although both are usually exposed to feminine activities early in life, boys are discouraged from imitating their mothers, whereas girls are encouraged to be "mother's little helpers." Even the chores children do are categorized by gender. Girls may wash dishes, make beds, and set the table; boys are assigned to carry out trash, rake the yard, and sweep the walk. The boy' domestic chores take him outside the house, whereas the girl's keep her in it—another rehearsal for traditional adult life.

It is generally accepted that parents socialize their children differently according to gender (Block, 1983; Fagot and Leinbach, 1987). Fathers more than others pressure their children to behave in gender-appropriate ways. Fathers set higher standards of achievement for their sons than for their daughters; for their daughters, fathers emphasize the interpersonal aspect of their relationship. But mothers also reinforce the interpersonal aspect of their parent/daughter relationship (Block, 1983).

By adolescence, both parents and their teenage children believe that parents treat boys and girls differently. It is not clear, however, whether parents are reacting to differences or creating them (Fagot and Leinbach, 1987). It is probably both, although by that age, gender differences are fairly well-established in the minds of adolescents. Although awareness of differences may be related to parents and adolescents both recognizing the visible changes accompanying puberty—the development of breasts among girls and change in musculature among boys—for parents most of the change is probably cumulative. That is, interactions with their children reflect long-held traditional beliefs about the differences between males and females. One researcher concluded that parental gender-role attitudes for their four-year-old children predicted their attitudes toward their children when they were fifteen years old (Block, 1983).

Various studies have indicated that ethnicity and class are important in influencing gender roles (Zinn, 1990; see Wilkinson, Chow, and Zinn, 1992, for new scholarship on the intersection of ethnicity, class, and gender). More than middle-class families, working-class families tend to differentiate more sharply between boys and girls in terms of appropriate behavior; they tend to place more restrictions on girls. There is evidence that African-American families, more than white families, socialize their daughters to be more independent (Gump, 1980; E. Smith, 1982). Indeed, among African Americans, the "traditional" female role model may never have existed. The African-American female role model in which the woman is both wage earner and homemaker is more typical and more accurately reflects African-American experience (Basow, 1986).

As children grow older, their social world expands and so do their sources of learning. Around the time children enter day-care or kindergarten, teachers and peers become important influences.

TEACHERS AS SOCIALIZING AGENTS. Day-care centers, nursery schools, and kinder-gartens are often the child's first experience in the wider world outside the family. Teachers become important role models for their students. Because most day-care, kindergarten, and elementary school teachers are women, children tend to think of child/adult interactions as primarily the province of women. In this sense, schools reinforce the idea that women are concerned with children whereas men are not (Koblinsky and Sugawara, 1984).

Teachers tend to be conventional in the gender-role messages they convey to chil-dren (Wynn and Fletcher, 1987). They encourage different activities and abilities in boys and girls. They give children messages about appropriate activities, such as con-tact sports for boys and gymnastics for girls. Academically, teachers tend to encourage boys more than girls in math and science and girls more than boys in language skills.

Although schools tend to reinforce traditional gender roles, they can also change them. Among schools that have developed nonsexist curricula, there is significantly less gender-role stereotyping (Koblinsky and Sugawara, 1984; Wynn and Fletcher, 1987). As Tavris and Wade (1984) point out:

Nothing about children's classroom behavior is impervious to change. Using praise and atten-tion as rewards, preschool teachers can get girls to be more independent and both sexes to play more with each other and select both boys' and girls' toys. The effects are surprisingly rapid; simply by moving in a particular area and giving attention to a particular type of play, a teacher, within minutes, can eliminate sex differences in play patterns that were "obvious" all semester. When the teacher withdraws attention or praise, children tend to revert rapidly to their previous sex-typed behavior. Still, the fact that such behavior can be eliminated quickly shows the enormous impact of the environment—including the teacher—on children's day-to-day conformity to sex roles.

PEERS AS SOCIALIZING AGENTS. Peers—the child's age-mates—become especially important when children enter school. By granting or withholding approval, friends and playmates influence what games children play, what they wear, what music they listen to, what television programs they watch, and even what cereal they eat. Peer influence is so pervasive that it is hardly an exaggeration to say that in some cases children's peers tell them what to think, feel, and do. Peers provide standards for gender-role behavior in several ways (Carter, 1987b):

1. *Peers provide information about gender-role norms through play activities and toys.* Girls plays with dolls that cry and wet or glamorous dolls with well-developed fig-ures and expensive tastes. Boys play with dolls known as "action figures," such as GI-Joe and Ninja Turtles, with guns, numchuks, and bigger-than-life biceps.
2. *Peers react with approval or disapproval to other's behavior.* Smiles encourage a girl to play with makeup or a boy to play with a football.
3. *Peers influence the adoption of gender-role norms through verbal approval or disap-proval.* "That's for boys!" or "Only girls do that!" is severe negative reinforcement when a girl plays with a football or a boy wears an earring.
4. *Children's perceptions of their friends' gender-role attitudes, behaviors, and beliefs encourage them to adopt similar ones in order to be accepted.* If a girl's friends play

Treat people as if they were what they ought to be and you help them become what they are capable of being.

Johann Goethe (1749-1832)

TABLE 4.1	Stereotypic Sex Role Differences Compared to Research Findings
STEREOTYPE	**FINDINGS**
Aggression Males are more aggressive. Females are less aggressive.	Strong consistent differences in physical aggression. Inconsistent finding with indirect aggression.
Dependency Females are more submissive and dependent. Males are more assertive and independent.	Weak differences that are more consistent for adults than for children.
Emotionality Females are more emotional and excitable. Males are more controlled and less expressive.	Moderate differences on some measures. Overall, findings inconclusive.
Verbal Skills Females excel in all verbal areas including reading. Males are less verbal and have more problems learning to read.	Moderate differences, especially for children. Moderate differences, especially for children.
Math Skills Males are better in mathematical skills. Females are less interested and do less well in mathematics.	Moderate differences on problem-solving tests, especially after adolescence.

SOURCE: From Frank Cox, *Human Intimacy* (St. Paul, Minn.: West), 1984.

soccer, she is more likely to play soccer. If a boy's same-sex friends display feelings, he is more likely to display feelings.

During adolescence, peers continue to have a strong influence, but current research indicates that parents are more influential than peers (Gecas and Seff, 1991). Older research viewed peer groups as the family's "enemy" in socializing children for their transition to adulthood. But today, youth culture appears to be adult culture writ small. Youth culture generally reflects the values of adult culture, such as its individualism, consumerism, gender-role attitudes, and so on.

Parental influence is especially strong on their adolescent's educational goals and plans for the future. Peer influence is stronger on peripheral issues, such as clothing and hair styles, taste in music, television and films, and recreational activities, such as hanging out, partying, and camping. Parents influence their adolescent's behavior primarily by establishing norms, whereas peers influence them through modeling behavior.

Even though parents tend to fear the worst from peers, peers provide important positive influences. It is within their peer groups, for example, that adolescents learn to develop intimate relationships (Gecas and Seff, 1991). And adolescents in peer groups tend to be more egalitarian in gender roles than parents, especially fathers (Thornton, 1989).

❖ REFLECTIONS   *How did your parents influence the development of your gender role? In what ways did you model yourself after your same-sex parent? In what ways are your conceptions of the appropriate gender role similar to or different from those of your parents?*

Gender-Role Learning in Adulthood

Researchers have generally neglected gender-role learning in adulthood (Losh-Hesselbart, 1987; Sinnott, 1986). Several scholars, however, have formulated a life-span perspective to gender-role development known as role transcendence (Hefner, Rebecca, and Oleshansky, 1975).

The role transcendence approach argues that there are three stages an individual goes through in developing his or her gender-role identity: (1) undifferentiated, (2) polarized, and (3) transcendent stages. Young children have not clearly differentiated their activities into those considered appropriate for males or females. As the children enter school, however, they begin to identify behaviors as masculine and feminine. They tend to polarize masculinity and femininity as they test the appropriate roles for themselves. As they enter young adulthood, they begin slowly to shed the rigid male/female polarization as they are confronted with the realities of relationships. As they mature and grow older, men and women transcend traditional masculinity and femininity. They combine masculinity/femininity into a more complex transcendent role, a role similar to androgyny (see pages 111–113).

For adults, gender-role development takes place in contexts outside of the family of orientation. In adulthood, college, marriage, parenthood, and the workplace provide new or different sources of gender-role learning.

We forfeit three-fourths of ourselves to be like other people.

Arthur Schopenhauer (1788-1860)

COLLEGE. The college and university environment, emphasizing critical thought and independent behavior, contrasts markedly with the high school setting, which emphasizes social conformity through dress codes and chaperoned dances and intellectual conformity through noncontroversial, watered-down subject matter. In the college setting, many young adults learn to think critically, to exchange ideas, to discover the basis for their actions. In particular, in the college environment, many young adults first encounter alternatives to traditional gender roles, either in their personal relationships or in their courses. This is especially true for students enrolled in women's studies classes (Losh-Hesselbart, 1987).

MARRIAGE. Marriage is an important source of gender-role learning, for it creates the roles of husband and wife. For many individuals, no one is more important than their partner for shaping gender-role behaviors through interaction. Our partner has expectations of how we should act as a male or female, and these expectations are important in shaping behavior.

Husbands tend to believe in innate gender roles more than wives. This should not be especially surprising, because men tend to be more traditional and less egalitarian about gender roles (Thornton et al., 1983). Husbands stand to gain more in marriage by believing that women are "naturally" better at cooking, cleaning, shopping, and caring for children. But husband and wife influence each other. One study (Mirowsky and Ross, 1987) found that when husband and wife disagree about innate gender roles, both tend to modify their position in the direction of the other. The more one partner believes in the innateness of gender roles, however, the more the other one also does. The mutual influence of husband and wife on each other, the researchers estimate, reduces the disagreement by almost a third in contrast to an unmarried pair.

PARENTHOOD. For most men and women, motherhood alters women's lives more significantly than fatherhood alters men's lives. For men, much of fatherhood means

Contemporary fatherhood entails more than merely the provider role. It includes care and nurturing as well.

providing for their children. As a consequence, fatherhood does not create the same work/family conflict as motherhood does for women. Men's work role allows them to fulfill much of their perceived parental obligation.

Yet contemporary fatherhood has become more complex. Traditional fatherhood has been tied to marriage. With almost a quarter of all current births occurring to unmarried women and half of all current marriages ending in divorce, what is the father's role for men not married to their children's mother? What are their role obligations as single fathers as distinguished from those of married fathers? For many men, it is painfully unclear, as evidenced by the low rates of contact between unmarried or divorced fathers and their children.

Although women today have greater latitude as wives (it is acceptable to work outside the home), they are still under considerable pressure to become mothers. Once a woman becomes a mother, especially if she is white, she is likely to leave the work force for at least a few months. Even young girls recognize this pressure and accept the notion of working until the arrival of the first child, then combining work and motherhood as the children get older (Archer, 1985). When children are born, roles tend to become more traditional, even in nontraditional marriages. The wife remains at home, at least for a time, and the husband continues full-time work outside the home. The woman must then balance her roles as wife and mother against her own needs and those of her family. Her husband may want her role as wife to take precedence over that of mother, while the children, insistently tugging at her for attention, demand that they be given first priority.

Workplaces have their own cultures that influence the way workers and managers feel about themselves as men and women.

It is fairly well established that men and women are psychologically affected by their occupations (Menaghan and Parcel, 1991; Schooler, 1987; Tavris and Wade, 1984). Work that encourages self-direction, for example, makes people more active, flexible, open, and democratic; restrictive jobs tend to lower self-esteem and make people more rigid and less tolerant. If we realize that female occupations are usually low status with little room for self-direction, we can understand why women are not as achievement-oriented as men. Because men and women have different opportunities for promotion, they have different attitudes toward achievement. Women typically downplay any desire for promotion, suggesting that promotions would interfere with their family responsibilities. But this may be related to a need to protect themselves from frustration, since most women are in dead-end jobs in which promotion to management positions is unlikely.

Household work affects women psychologically in many of the same ways that paid work does in female-dominated occupations such as clerical and service jobs (Schooler, 1987). Women in both situations feel greater levels of frustration owing to the repetitive nature of the work, time pressures, and being held responsible for things outside their control. Such circumstances do not encourage self-esteem, creativity, or a desire to achieve.

❖ REFLECTIONS   *During high school, what influence did your peers have on your gender-role development? How important were your boyfriends/girlfriends in developing your sense of yourself as a woman or man? Is college different? If so, how? Who are the people that most influence your gender-role concepts today?*

❖ CHANGING GENDER ROLES

Within the past generation, there has been a significant shift from traditional toward more egalitarian gender roles. While women have changed more than men, men also are changing. These changes seem to affect all classes. Those from conservative religious groups, such as Mormons, Catholics, and fundamentalist and evangelical Protestants, adhere most strongly to traditional gender roles (Spence et al., 1985).

The greatest change in gender-role attitudes appears to have occurred in the 1970s. These roles are continuing to change and become more egalitarian, but at a lesser pace. Between the late 1970s and mid-1980s, support for traditional gender roles for wives has decreased, especially among women. There is still considerable disagreement about the ideal roles for wives and mothers, however. This is especially true for men, who believe maternal employment is harmful to children or to the mother/child relationship (Mason and Lu, 1988).

Despite the continuing disagreement, it is likely that the egalitarian trend will continue (Mason and Lu, 1988; Thornton, 1989). Using an exchange model, researchers Carolyn Morgan and Alexis Walker (1983) suggest that as women increase their participation in the work force, the divorce rate continues to be high, and couples have fewer children, the costs will outweigh the benefits for women maintaining traditional gender roles. Because men benefit from women's increased income, they are more likely to support gender equality.

According to the exchange model, women are more likely than men to support egalitarian gender roles, because women have more to gain and men have more to lose. Men's support for gender equality has increased, but not as much as women's.

Everybody wants to be somebody; nobody wants to grow.

Johann Goethe

The things we admire in men, kindness and generosity, openness, honesty, understanding and feeling are the concomitants of failure in our system. And those traits we detest, sharpness, greed, acquisitiveness, meanness, egotism and self-interest are the traits of success.

John Steinbeck, Cannery Row

The cost/benefit ratio of maintaining traditional gender roles continues to favor men in many ways. Employed women desire greater male participation in housework, for example, but as most women know, men display little enthusiasm for such work. Men continue to benefit from their partners' scrubbing the floors, doing the dishes, cleaning the bathrooms, cooking the meals, doing the shopping, changing the diapers, and washing the clothes while they themselves watch television, read the newspaper, or occasionally take out the trash. As long as their partners are willing to do the housework *and* work outside the home, men appear to have little to gain by adopting egalitarian gender roles. Therefore, they are less supportive than women in changing traditional housework responsibilities. Only when the cost becomes too great—involving frustration, fights, guilt—are men likely to accept a more egalitarian or equitable division of household labor.

Traditional Gender Roles

According to traditional gender-role stereotypes, many of the traits ascribed to one sex are not ascribed to the other. Men show instrumental traits—that is, goal-oriented, self-directing traits such as logic and aggression. Women display expressive traits— that is, interpersonal, emotive traits such as compassion and nurturing (Hort, Fagot, and Leinbach, 1990). These personality traits theoretically complemented their traditional roles in the family. Because of this basic difference, men were expected to participate in the world of work and politics. Their central male role was worker; in the family, this role translated to breadwinner. Because women were thought to be primarily expressive, they were expected to remain in the home as wives and mothers.

TRADITIONAL MALE GENDER ROLE.   What is it to be a "real" man in America? Bruce Feirstein parodied him in *Real Men Don't Eat Quiche* (1982):

QUESTION: How many Real Men does it take to change a light bulb?
ANSWER: None. Real Men aren't afraid of the dark.

QUESTION: Why did the Real Man cross the road?
ANSWER: It's none of your damn business.

This humor contains something both familiar and chilling. Being a male in America carries a certain uneasiness. Men often feel they need advice about how to act out their male roles; they are unsure of what it means to be masculine.

Central features of the traditional male role, whether white, African-American, Latino, or Asian-American, include dominance and work. Both have consequences for family relationships. Males are generally regarded as being more power-oriented than females. Men demonstrate higher degrees of aggression, especially violent aggression (such as assault, homicide, and rape), seek to dominate and lead, and show greater competitiveness. While aggressive traits may be useful in the corporate world, politics, and the military (or in hunting sabre-toothed tigers), such characteristics, are rarely helpful to a man in fulfilling marital and family roles requiring understanding, cooperation, communication, and nurturing.

The centrality of men's work identity affects their family roles as husbands and fathers. Traditional men see their primary family function as that of provider, which takes precedence over all other family functions, such as nurturing and caring for children, doing housework, preparing meals, and being intimate. Because of this focus, traditional men are often confused by their spouses' expectations of intimacy; they believe that they are good husbands simply because they are good providers (Rubin, 1983).

One's only real life is the life one never leads.

Oscar Wilde (1854-1900)

Femininity expresses the idea that there are things worth living for. Masculinity expresses the idea that there are things worth dying for.

John Wheeler, Touched with Fire

Rabbi Zusya said that on the Day of Judgment, God would ask him, not why he had not been Moses, but why he had not been Zusya.

Walter Kaufmann

Youth culture generally reflects the values of adult culture. Through their play activities peers reinforce gender-role norms. What are these boys learning about the male role?

TRADITIONAL FEMALE GENDER ROLE. Although the main features of traditional male gender roles do not appear to have significant ethnic variation, there are striking ethnic differences in female roles.

The tendency to identify manhood with a capacity for physical violence has a long history in America.

Marshall Fishwick

Whites. Traditional white female gender roles center around women's roles as wives and mothers. When a woman leaves adolescence, she is expected to get married and have children. Although a traditional woman may work prior to marriage, she is not expected to defer marriage for work goals. And soon after marriage, she is expected to be "expecting." Once married, she is expected to devote her energies to her husband and family and to find her meaning as a woman by fulfilling her roles as wife and mother. Within the household, she is expected to subordinate herself to her husband. Often this subordination is sanctioned by religious teachings. In the New Testament, for example, Paul of Tarsus declared, "Wives, submit yourselves to your husbands as unto the Lord. For the husband is the head of the wife, even as Christ is the head of the Church" (Ephesians 5: 22–23).

African Americans. The traditional female gender role did not extend to African-American women. This may be attributed to a combination of the African heritage, slavery (which subjugated women to the same labor and hardships as men), and economic discrimination that forced women into the labor force. Karen Drugger (1988) notes:

A primary cleavage in the life experiences of Black and White women is their past and present relationship to the labor process. In consequence, Black women's conceptions of womanhood emphasize self-reliance, strength, resourcefulness, autonomy, and the responsibility of providing for the material as well as emotional needs of family members. Black women do not see labor-force participation and being a wife and mother as mutually exclusive; rather, in Black culture, employment is an integral, normative, and traditional component of the roles of wife and mother.

African-American men are generally more supportive than white or Latino men of more egalitarian gender roles.

Latinas. In traditional Latina gender roles, women subordinate themselves to males (Vasquez-Nuthall, Romero-Garcia, and De Leon, 1987). But this subordination is based more on respect for the male's role as provider than on dominance (Becerra, 1988). Unlike Anglo culture, gender roles are strongly affected by age roles in which the young subordinate themselves to the old. In this dual arrangement, notes Becerra (1988), "females are viewed as submissive, naive, and somewhat childlike. Elders are viewed as wise, knowledgeable, and deserving of respect." As a result of this intersection of gender and age roles, older women are treated with greater deference than younger women.

GENDER ROLES IN TRANSITION: IMMIGRANT EXPERIENCES. The enormous rise in immigration beginning in the 1980s brought great numbers of Latinos and Asians to the United States. By 1991, over 20 million Americans were foreign born; today, more than 750,000 immigrants are arriving in the United States annually. The process of adaptation to a new environment, culture, and language places individuals under considerable stress. In adjusting to life in the United States, women tend to experience greater stress than men. Mental health workers attribute women's greater stress to conflicting gender-role expectations and family roles (Aneshensel and Pearlin, 1987).

As Latinas become more acculturated, they adopt more egalitarian gender roles (Vasquez-Nuthall, Romero-Garcia, and De Leon, 1987). First-generation Latinas have held significantly more traditional gender-role attitudes than second- and third-generation Latinas. This traditionalism is reflected in part by the reluctance of first-generation Latinas to work outside the home (Ortiz and Cooney, 1984). Researchers found that for immigrant Latinas, the shift from a culture emphasizing definite male/female gender roles to one with greater freedom has affected their self-identity (Salgado de Snyder, Cervantes, and Padilla, 1990). This shift has been a potential source of both personal and family conflict. As a Latina has demanded greater input in making decisions or has asked her partner's assistance in child care—behavior more typical among Anglos—she has been likely to both encounter resistance from her husband and to feel guilty for violating traditional Latino norms. Asian women, noted Reiko True (1990), struggling to establish themselves in American society, "often find themselves trapped within restrictive roles and identities as defined by Asian cultures or by general American stereotypes."

Although immigrant males also experience stress resulting from changed male/female relationships, their greatest stress tends to be occupational. This difference results from the priority of work roles over family roles for males. Latino males have experienced occupational stress, for example, reflecting their difficulty in finding good jobs or job advancement as a result of language differences, education, or discrimination (Salgado de Snyder, Cervantes, and Padilla, 1990). Although many Asian male immigrants tend to be from white-collar backgrounds, they also experience occupational stress resulting from discrimination and language difficulties.

Gender-role stress increases for both men and women as their children adopt more typically American gender roles. Parents and children may come into conflict about appropriate gender-related behavior because parents tend to be more culturally traditional and their children tend to be more Americanized.

Contemporary Gender Roles

Until recently, most Americans tended to look at men and women as if they were almost distinct species who shared few traits, behaviors, and attitudes. Males traditionally suppressed "feminine" traits in themselves and females suppressed "masculine" traits. What is apparently happening today, especially among women, is that gender roles are becoming more *androgynous*—that is, incorporating both masculine and feminine traits. There is a considerable body of evidence suggesting that androgynous gender roles help us have more flexible and fulfilling relationships and lives.

Contemporary gender roles are evolving from traditional hierarchical gender roles (in which one sex is subordinate to the other) to more egalitarian roles (in which both sexes are treated equally) and androgynous roles (in which both sexes display the instrumental and expressive traits previously associated with one sex). Thus, contemporary gender roles often display traditional elements as well as egalitarian and androgynous ones.

Within the family, attitudes toward gender roles have become more liberal; in practice, however, gender roles continue to favor men, especially in terms of housekeeping and child-care activities (Atkinson, 1987). Some of the most important changes affecting contemporary gender roles in the family are briefly described in the following sections.

WOMEN AS WORKERS AND PROFESSIONALS. Even though the traditional roles for women have typically been those of wife and mother, in recent years (especially among whites) an additional role has been added: employed worker or professional. It is now generally expected that most women will be gainfully employed at various times in their lives. For most women, entrance into work or a career does not

cathy®   **by Cathy Guisewite**

Cathy © 1989 Cathy Guisewite. Reprinted with permission of Universal Press Syndicate.

exclude their more traditional roles as wives and mothers. Such work, however, may radically conflict with their family roles. Their work role, for example, requires them to be at the office or factory. Their traditional family roles require them to be at home caring for the husband, house, and children. At some point, unlike most men, women have to make choices. Do their work roles take precedence over their family roles? Women generally attempt to reduce the conflict between work and family roles by giving family roles precedence. As a result, they tend to work outside the home before and after marriage and until the arrival of the first child. Even if a woman is working full time, however, she continues to remain responsible for housework and child care. When a woman's first child arrives, the role of mother is expected to take priority over the role of worker. This expectation continues until the youngest child reaches school age, although half of today's working mothers return to the work force within a year of the birth of their youngest child (Hofferth and Phillips, 1987).

QUESTIONING MOTHERHOOD. Record numbers of women are rejecting motherhood because of the conflicts it creates. It is estimated that between 20 to 25 percent of female "baby boomers" are choosing to remain childless to maximize work opportunities and time with their husbands (Nock, 1987). (This is in contrast to about a 10 percent childlessness rate of the previous generation.) Similarly, women are having fewer children than ever before. Stephen Nock (1987) suggests that women are limiting their fertility or remaining childless because childbearing symbolizes the acceptance and limitations of traditional gender roles.

Women from ethnic and minority status groups, however, are less likely to view motherhood as an impediment. African-American women and Latinas tend to place greater value on motherhood than the white or Anglo majority. For African Americans, the tradition has generally combined work and motherhood; the two are not viewed as necessarily antithetical (Basow, 1986). For Latinas, the cultural and religious emphasis on family, the higher status conferred on motherhood, and their own familial attitudes have contributed to high fertility rates (Jorgensen and Adams, 1988).

GREATER EQUALITY IN MARITAL POWER. Although husbands were once the final authority, wives have greatly increased their power in decision making. They are no longer expected to be submissive but to have significant, if not equal, input in marital decision making. This trend toward equality is limited in practice by an unspoken rule of marital equality: "Husbands and wives are equal, but husbands are more equal." In actual practice, husbands continue to have greater power than wives. Husbands have become what sociologist John Scanzoni (1982) describes as the "senior partner" of that marriage.

The perpetual obstacle to human advancement is custom.

John Stuart Mill (1806–1873)

BREAKDOWN OF INSTRUMENTAL/EXPRESSIVE DICHOTOMY. The identification of masculinity with instrumentality and femininity with expressiveness appears to be breaking down. In part, this is because the instrumental/expressive dichotomy was a false dichotomy to begin with. This division of traits, developed by sociologist Talcott Parsons (1955), was more theoretical than real. Parsons believed that the more an individual was instrumental, the less he or she was expressive, and vice versa. In reality, instrumentality and expressiveness exist independently of each other (Spence et al., 1985).

While men and women may identify themselves as masculine or feminine, they generally view themselves as possessing both instrumental and expressive traits. As a group, however, men perceive themselves to be more instrumental than do women, and women perceive themselves as being more expressive than do men. A substantial minority of both sexes is relatively high in both instrumentality *and* expressiveness or low in both. Interestingly, the instrumental/expressiveness ratings men and women give each other have very little to do with how they rate themselves as masculine or feminine (Pedhazur and Tetenbaum, 1979; Spence and Sawin, 1985).

EXPANSION OF MEN'S FAMILY ROLES. The key assumption about male gender roles has been the centrality of work and success to a man's sense of self. This assumption has led many researchers to believe that men's primary family role has been that of provider. As a result, until recently there has been little research into men's participation in family life. Unlike research into female role conflicts, the idea that men's work may conflict with family roles has rarely been explored. Although both the public and researchers have expressed concern about the impact of working mothers on the family, few have expressed similar concern about working fathers. In fact, the term *working father* seems redundant, since work is what is expected of fathers (Cohen, 1987).

New research indicates that men consider their family role to be much greater than that of the family breadwinner. As researchers have long pointed out, economic responsibilities are only one small part of men's family lives (Bohannan, 1971; Goetting, 1982). Other dimensions include emotional, psychological, community, and legal dimensions; they also include housework and child-care activities. One study (Cohen, 1987) confirmed the emerging picture of men in families: being a husband and father goes far beyond simple breadwinning. Men indicated that the expressive friendship roles in marriage and nurturant roles in fatherhood were the central elements of their family roles. In fact, only about half of the respondents indicated that "breadwinning" was a husband's major responsibility.

Fathers are increasing their child-care and nurturing activities. More men feel competent in infant care, such as giving bottles, changing diapers, and soothing a crying baby. They spend greater time interacting with their children. But the man's role continues to be "secondary caretaker," and he is more likely to obtain relief from his duties than the mother.

Housework remains a central area of dispute (Atkinson, 1987; Cohen, 1987). While some studies suggest that men are spending more time on housework, rarely is housework divided fifty-fifty. More often than not, women continue to be primarily responsible for cooking, cleaning, shopping, and the like. Men's household work tends to center around automobile maintenance, repairs, and outdoor responsibilities, such as gardening and mowing the lawn (Spence et al., 1985). (But, as one woman asked, how often do you have to repair the toaster or paint the house?)

❖ CONSTRAINTS OF CONTEMPORARY GENDER ROLES

Even though there is substantially more flexibility offered men and women today, contemporary gender roles and expectations continue to limit our potential. Indeed, there is considerable evidence that stereotypes about gender traits have not changed very much over the last twenty years. In the 1960s a classic study of gender-related stereotypes found that college students rated "typical" adult men and women differently. Men were considered to be more instrumental and women were rated as being more expressive (Rosenkrantz et al., 1968). Studies over the years have confirmed that these stereotypes remain strong. Males are perceived as having

The wimp is the man who has a social conscience, who can understand the oppression of women, who is warm and caring, who fixes the family's meals after a rough day at the office. Women don't view such men as wimps; only other men see them that way.

Lucia Gilbert

Life shrinks or expands in proportion to one's courage.

Anaïs Nin

more undesirable self-oriented traits (such as being arrogant, self-centered, and domineering) than females. Females are viewed as having more traits reflecting a lack of a healthy sense of self (such as being servile and spineless) than males. Only "intellectual" seems to be applied to women more than in the past (Spence et al., 1985).

These limitations are particularly important, as studies suggest that couples who are most traditional in their gender-role attitudes also express the least martial satisfaction (Spence et al., 1985).

Limitations on Men

Men are required to work and to support their families. The male as provider is one of men's central roles in marriage; the provider role is *not* central for women. As a result, men do not have the same role freedom to *choose* to work as women have. Therefore, when the man's roles of worker and father come into conflict, usually it is the father role that suffers (Cohen, 1987; Weiss, 1985). A factory worker may want to spend time with his children to lighten his wife's burdens, but his job does not allow flexibility. Because he must provide income for his family, he will not be able to be more involved in parenting. In a familiar scene, a little boy comes into the father's study to play and the father says, "Not now. I'm busy working. I'll play with you later." When the boy returns, the "not-now-I'm-busy" phrase is repeated. The scene recurs as the boy grows up until one day, as his son leaves home, the father realizes that he never got to know him.

Men continue to have greater difficulty expressing their feelings than women. Men cry less and show love, happiness, and sadness less (Balswick, 1980; Lombardo et al., 1983). When men do express their feelings, they are more forceful, domineering, and boastful; women, in contrast, tend to express their feelings more gently and quietly. When a woman asks a man how he feels, a common response is "I don't know," or "Nothing." Such men have lost touch with their inner lives because they have repressed feelings that they have learned are inappropriate.

Male inexpressiveness often makes men strangers to both themselves and their partners. A major complaint of married women is that their husbands do not show them enough affection or attention (Rubin, 1983). Married couples who rate themselves as poorly adjusted tend to be ones in which the husband has poor communication skills (Noller, 1984).

Men continue to expect to be the dominant member in a relationship. Unfortunately, the male sense of power and command does not facilitate personal relationships. Men who are unable to achieve power in their work relationships may seek power and status at home, putting their displaced frustration and anger into their marital relationships. But under such circumstances—without mutual respect and equality—genuine intimacy is difficult to achieve. One cannot control another person and at the same time be intimate with that person. Middle-class men often talk about egalitarian marriages but allow their partners relatively less power in the relationship. A tension exists between ideology and reality.

Limitations on Women

There is considerable evidence that the traditional female gender role does not facilitate self-confidence or mental health. Both men and women tend to see women as being less competent than men. One study found that women generally predicted they would not do as well on a test as the men taking the same test (Erkut, 1983). Another study of 1,850 men and women found that women had significantly lower self-esteem (Hoelter, 1983). A recent study by Carole Gilligan, discussed at greater length in Chapter 11, revealed that the self-esteem of adolescent girls plummetted between the age of nine and the time they started high school (Daley, 1991). Traditional women married to traditional men experience the most symptoms of stress (feeling tired, depressed, or worthless) and express the most dissatisfaction about life as a whole (Spence et al., 1985). The combination of gender-role stereotypes and racial/ethnic discrimination tends to encourage feelings of both inadequacy and lack of physical attractiveness among African-American women, Latinas, and Asian-American women (Basow, 1986).

Because of difference in gender roles, Bernard (1972) has suggested that each sex experiences marriage differently. There is, she argued, a "his" and "her" marriage. Men appear to be more satisfied in marriage than women (Rettig and Bubolz, 1983). More wives than husbands report frustration, dissatisfaction, marital problems, and desire for divorce. More wives than husbands experience anxiety or feel they are on the edge of a nervous breakdown; more wives blame themselves for their poor adjustment than do husbands (Mugford and Lally, 1981; Rubenstein, 1982). Unmarried women, Bernard suggested, tend to be happier and better adjusted than married women. (For a critique of "his" or "her" marriages, see Schumm, 1985.)

Finally, femininity is intimately tied to youth and beauty. As women get older, they tend to be regarded as more masculine. A young woman, for example, is "beautiful" but an older woman is "handsome." Also, culture treats aging in men and women differently: as men age, they become distinguished; as women age, they simply get older. (See Perspective, "The Double Standard of Aging.")

Resistance to Change

We may think that we want change, but both men and women reinforce traditional gender-role stereotypes among themselves *and* the other sex (Hort, Fagot, and Leinback, 1990). Both sexes react more negatively to men displaying so-called female traits—such as crying easily or needing security—than do women displaying male traits—such as assertiveness or worldliness. And both define male gender-role stereotypes more rigidly than they do female stereotypes. Interestingly, men do not define women as rigidly as women do men: both men and women describe their ideal female in very androgynous terms (Hort, Fagot, and Leinback, 1990).

Despite the limitations that traditional gender roles place on us, changing these roles is not easy. Gender roles are closely linked to self-evaluation. Our sense of adequacy depends on gender-role performance as defined by parents and peers in childhood ("You're a good boy/girl"). Because gender roles often seem to be an intrinsic part of our personality and temperament, we may defend these roles as being natural even if they are destructive to a relationship or to ourselves. To threaten an individual's gender role is to threaten his or her gender identity as male or female, because people do not generally make the distinction between gender role and gender identity. Such threats are an important psychological mechanism that keeps people in traditional but dysfunctional gender roles.

Lillian Rubin (1983), a prominent psychologist, described her own difficulty in changing roles when her husband changed careers to become a writer and she assumed the primary provider role in the family. At first her husband was relieved to be freed from the financial responsibilities he had assumed for so many years. Then he fell into a six-month depression. Although Rubin was already a successful therapist, writer, and researcher, something in her life "had been altered profoundly." She grew angry. Her work was no longer voluntary. It was necessary to support

Women have served all these centuries, as looking glasses possessing the magic and delicious power of reflecting the figure of man at twice its natural size.

Virginia Woolf, A Room of One's Own

All males, without exception, whatever their age, suffer from penis rivalry . . . This trait has now become a threat to the future existence of the human race. . . . Today our phallic toys have become too dangerous to be tolerated. I see little hope for a peaceful world until men are excluded from the realm of foreign policy altogether and all decisions concerning international relations are reserved for women, preferably married ones.

W. H. Auden (1907–1973)

PERSPECTIVE

The Double Standard of Aging

The double standard of aging (like the double standard of sex) shortchanges women. Society is more tolerant of men who deviate from its standards than of women who do so. Masculinity is associated with independence, assertiveness, self-control and physical ability; with the exception of physical ability, none of these traits necessarily decreases with age. For the most part they intensify as one gains more experience in the world. But femininity is closely associated with attractiveness. Susan Brownmiller (1983) pointed out in her book, *Femininity*:

Feminity is not something that improves with age, for girlishness, with its innocent modesty, its unthreatening inpudence, and its promise of ripe sexuality in the rosy future, typifies the feminine principle at its best. Women who rely on a feminine strategy as their chief means of survival can do little to stop the roaring tide of maturity as they watch their advantage slip by.

When Americans marry, a man is likely to marry a woman his same age or younger (in 85 percent of marriages, this is the case; in 75 percent of marriages, the wife is less than five years younger than the husband). The explanation for women marrying older men is related to gender roles. Traditionally, a woman's social status had depended on her husband's; he works and achieves status that reflects on her. Many women have therefore preferred to marry older men, who have probably worked longer and acquired greater status than younger men. Men have traditionally favored younger women because physical attractiveness is an important aspect of the male mate selection process and because our society links the attractiveness of women to their youth.

This arrangement places women at a disadvantage. If a woman marries a man older than herself, she is more likely to become a widow with many years left in her own life. In itself, the loneliness of widowhood can be a burden; but beyond that, it is more difficult for a widow than a widower to find a new partner. As women get older, they become less eligible for marriage because they are considered to have lost their attractiveness and because they have fewer potential partners. An older woman's pool of eligible partners is limited to those of her own age or older. If she were a man, however, she could choose not only from those of her own age group but also from those who are younger.

Man's love is of man's life a part; it is woman's whole existence.

Lord Byron (1788–1824)

the family, and she began to hate it. Rubin was stunned by her reaction. She and her husband had planned and agreed on the change; both thought he should be free to pursue his own interests. She wrote:

But speaking the words and living the results are two different things. Suddenly we found ourselves face to face with our inner sense of the way things *ought* to be. Suddenly, we had to confront the realization that we were still dominated by the stereotypic images of male and female roles—images we would have sworn we had, by then, routed from our consciousness.

He struggled with his sense of failure, with the fear that somehow his very manhood had been damaged. I—the liberated, professional woman—was outraged and enraged that he wasn't taking care of me any longer. I felt as if he had violated some basic contract with which we had lived, as if he had failed in his most fundamental task in life—to keep me safe and cared for, to protect and support me.

People can accept minor changes, Rubin found, but deep ones are more difficult.

Smaller changes may be tolerated quite easily. But one that puts a woman in a position of economic superiority and a man in the dependent female role is quite another matter. Most men still can't cope with not being able to support the family, and most women still have difficulty in accepting the need to support themselves.

Finally, the social structure itself works to reinforce traditional gender norms and behaviors. Some religious groups, for example, strongly support traditional gender roles. The Catholic church, conservative Protestantism, orthodox Judaism, and the

Wives, submit yourselves unto your own husbands, as unto the Lord.

Paul of Tarsus (Ephesians 5:22)

Mormons, for example, view traditional roles as being divinely ordained. Accordingly, to violate these norms is to violate God's will. The marketplace also helps enforce traditional gender roles. The wage disparity between men and women (women earn about 70 percent of what men earn) is a case in point. Such a significant difference in income makes it "rational" that the man's work role take precedence over the woman's work role. If a man or woman needs to remain at home to care for the children or an elderly relative, for example, it makes economic sense for the woman to quit her job, because her male partner probably earns more money.

Instead of seeking to blame one sex for the victimization of the other, we should try to understand the constraints placed on both sexes by rigid gender-role stereotyping.

❖ REFLECTIONS *Do gender roles, either traditional or contemporary, help us fulfill our potential as human beings? Do they help us to love? To rear children well? If you were to decide, what would gender roles be like?*

Why is it men are permitted to be obsessed about their work, but women are only permitted to be obsessed about men?

Barbra Streisand

❖ CHANGING CONCEPTS OF GENDER ROLES

Bipolar Gender Roles

The traditional view of masculinity and femininity is bipolar: masculinity and femininity are opposite, or mirror images, of each other. Our popular terminology reflects this. When people speak of the "opposite" sex, they suggest that each sex has little in common with the other. Our gender-role stereotypes fit this bipolar pattern, as we have seen: men, aggressive; women, passive; men, instrumental; women, expressive; and so on. According to this view of gender roles, a *real* man possesses exclusively masculine traits and behaviors and a *real* woman possesses exclusively feminine traits and behaviors. Because the sexes have little in common, a "war of the sexes" is the norm.

This older conception does not account for many people having traits ascribed to both sexes and still feeling profoundly masculine or feminine (Heilbrun, 1982). When people believe that individuals should not have attributes of the other sex, males suppress their expressive traits and females suppress their instrumental traits. As a result, the range of human behaviors is limited by a person's gender role. Sandra Bem (1975) has argued that "our current system of sex role differentiation has long since outlived its usefulness, and . . . now serves only to prevent both men and women from developing as full and complete human beings."

Are men and women as different as traditional gender-role stereotypes portray us? Certainly, we are different biologically and anatomically. Men impregnate and women gestate; men have penises and women have vulvas. But if we reflect on our own lives, whether we are male or female, we will see that men and women have much in common. Men seek intimacy as well as achievement, and women seek achievement as well as intimacy. Each of us contains both instrumental and expressive traits.

Today our ideas of what it means to be male and female are changing. For many, the older gender roles seem archaic, limiting, inappropriate, even dehumanizing. Confusion abounds. What is the new vision of being male and female in America?

The war between the sexes is the only one in which both sides regularly sleep with the enemy.

Quentin Crisp

Androgynous Gender Roles

Some scholars have challenged the traditional masculine/feminine gender-role dichotomy, arguing that such models are unhealthy and fail to reflect the real world.

When man lives he is soft and tender; when he is dead he is hard and tough. All living plants and animals are tender and fragile; when dead they become withered and dry. Thus it is said: The hard and tough are parts of death; the soft and tender are parts of life. This is the reason why soldiers when they are too tough cannot carry the day; when the tree is too tough it will break. The position of the strong and great is low, but the position of the weak and tender is high.

Lao-Tse (7th century B.C.)

Because we see characteristics in God that our society identifies as "feminine" as well as those deemed "masculine," it is important to acknowledge the "androgyny" of God. We speak of God's loving-kindness, of tender and nurturing qualities. We hear Isaiah describe God as being like a woman in childbirth, who suffers through the creativity of birth while anticipating the promise that she knows to be present in her child . . . .

Task Force on Human Sexuality and Family Life."Sexuality: A Divine Gift.," Episcopal Church Center

If we do not redefine manhood, war is inevitable.

Paul Fussell

Instead of looking at gender roles in terms of the bipolar model, they suggest examining them in terms of **androgyny** (Roopnarine and Mounts, 1987). Androgyny is derived from the Greek *andros,* meaning "man," and *gyne,* meaning "woman." It refers to flexibility in gender roles and the unique combination of instrumental and expressive traits as influenced by individual differences, situations, and stages in the life cycle (Bem, 1976; Kaplan, 1979: Kaplan and Bean, 1976). An *androgynous* person combines both the instrumental traits previously associated with masculinity and the expressive traits associated with traditional femininity. An androgynous lifestyle allows men and women to choose from the full range of emotions and behaviors, according to their temperament, situation, and common humanity, rather than their sex. Males may be expressive. They are permitted to cry and display tenderness; they can touch, feel, and nurture without being called "effeminate." Women can express the instrumental aspects of their personalities without fear of disapproval. They can be aggressive or career-oriented; they can seek leadership, be mechanical or physical.

Flexibility and integration are important aspects of androgyny. Individuals who are rigidly both instrumental and expressive, despite the situation, are not considered androgynous. A woman who is always aggressive at work and passive at home, for example, would not be considered androgynous, as work may call for compassion and home life for assertion.

There is considerable evidence that androgynous individuals and couples have greater ability to form and sustain intimate relationships and adopt a wider range of behaviors and values. Androgynous college students and older individuals tend to have greater confidence in social situations than sex-typed individuals (Puglisi and Jackson, 1981; Spence et al., 1975). Androgynous individuals have shown greater resilience to stress (Roos and Cohen, 1987). They are more aware of love feelings and more expressive of them (Ganong and Coleman, 1987). Also, androgynous couples may have greater satisfaction in their relationships than sex-typed couples. One study found that androgynous couples felt more commitment and satisfaction in their relationships than sex-typical couples (Stephen and Harrison, 1985). Another study found that androgynous couples expressed greater sexual satisfaction than couples with stereotypic sex roles (Rozenweig and Dailey, 1989). Even those couples who generally believed themselves to be stereotypical experienced more satisfaction if they considered their behavior "feminine" in sexual situations, such as being sexually responsive, expressive, and tender. Transcending traditional male and female behaviors and values, the androgynous couples were more flexible in their responses to each other and to the environment.

It is not clear what proportion of individuals may be identified as androgynous or traditional. Although it has been suggested that androgyny is a white middle-class concept, one study (Binion, 1990) of African-American women indicated that 37 percent identified themselves as androgynous, 18 percent as feminine, and 24 percent as masculine. The remaining were undifferentiated. That such a large percentage were androgynous or masculine, the study argues, is not surprising, given the demanding family responsibilities and cultural expectations that require instrumental and active traits. Another study of college students from India indicated a high degree of androgyny, suggesting cross-cultural validity (Ravinder, 1987).

As Sandra Bem (1974) observed in her pioneering study on androgyny, "In a society where rigid sex role differentiation has already outlived its utility, perhaps the androgynous person will come to define a more human standard of psychological health."

UNDERSTANDING YOURSELF

Masculinity, Femininity and Androgyny

17. Warm
18. Unpredictable
19. Independent-minded
20. Compassionate
21. Reliable

Increased interest in androgynous gender roles has led to the development of a number of instruments to measure masculinity, femininity, and androgyny in individuals. The one below is patterned after the Bem Sex Role Inventory (BSRI), which is one of the most widely used tests (Bem, 1974, 1981).

To get a rough idea of how androgynous you are, examine the twenty-one personality traits below. Use a scale of 1 to 5 to indicate how well a personality trait describes yourself.

1	2	3	4	5
NOT AT ALL	SLIGHTLY	SOMEWHAT	QUITE A BIT	VERY MUCH

1. Aggressive
2. Understanding
3. Helpful
4. Decisive
5. Nurturing
6. Happy
7. Risk-taker
8. Shy
9. Unsystematic
10. Strong
11. Affectionate
12. Cordial
13. Assertive
14. Tender
15. Moody
16. Dominating

Scoring Sex Role Inventory

Your masculinity, femininity, and androgyny scores may be determined as follows:

1. To determine your masculinity score, add up your answers for numbers 1, 4, 7, 10, 13, 16 and 19, divide the sum by seven.
2. To determine your femininity score, add up your answers for numbers 2, 5, 8, 11, 14, 17 and 20, divide the sum by seven.
3. To determine your androgyny score subtract the feminity score from the masculinity score.

The closer your score is to zero, the more androgynous you are. A high positive score indicates masculinity; a high negative score indicates femininity. A high masculine score not only indicates masculine attributes but also a rejection of feminine attributes. Similarly, a high feminine score indicates not only feminine characteristics, but a rejection of masculine attributes.

Not all researchers are convinced, however, that androgyny necessarily leads to greater psychological health and happiness. Some have hypothesized that instrumental traits in general, rather than androgyny, may lead to higher self-esteem for both men and women (Orlofsky and O'Heron, 1987). It is not always clear-cut whether androgyny or instrumentality is the most important factor accounting for higher rates of self-esteem, adjustment, and flexibility (Basow, 1985). There is evidence, in fact, that femininity is associated with depression among the elderly (Krames, England, and Flett, 1988). It will probably be some time before these factors can be tested to everyone's satisfaction.

Androgyny, like other personality theories, assumes that masculinity and femininity are basic aspects of an individual's personality. It assumes that when we are active, we are expressing our masculine side and when we are sensitive, we are expressing the feminine side of our personality. Living up to an androgynous gender role may be just as stultifying to an individual as trying to be traditionally masculine or feminine. In advocating the expression of both masculine and feminine traits, perhaps we are imposing a new form of gender role rigidity on ourselves. Bem, who was one of the leading proponents of androgyny, has become increasingly critical of the idea. She believes now that androgyny replaces "a prescription to be masculine or feminine with the doubly incarcerating prescription to be masculine and feminine. The individual now has not one but two potential sources of inadequacy to contend with" (Bem, 1983).

Gender Schema

Although actual differences between males and females are minimal or nonexistent except in levels of aggression, verbal skills, and visual/spatial skills, culture creates or exaggerates these differences (Carter, 1987c). Why does it create or magnify differences where they do not seem to exist in nature?

Sandra Bem (1983) notes that although gender is not inherent in inanimate objects or in behaviors, we treat both objects and behaviors as if they were masculine or feminine or in some way related to gender. These gender divisions form a complex structure of associations that affect our perceptions of reality. Bem referred to this cognitive organization of the world by gender as **gender schema.**

A *schema* is a set of interrelated ideas that helps us process information by categorizing it in ways that are useful for us. We may or may not have schemas for categorizing people by age, ethnicity, nationality, physical characteristics, and so on. Gender is one such way of categorizing. Those who have strong gender schemata quickly categorize people's behavior, personality characteristics, objects and so on into masculine/feminine categories. They disregard information that does not fit their gender schema. Such gender schemata view the earth, for example, as feminine, as "Mother Earth"; humanity is collectively known as "man," although there are more females than males. Some languages divide nouns into masculine and feminine. Dogs are regarded as masculine, cats as feminine.

Processing information by gender is important in cultures such as ours. First, gender-schema cultures make multiple associations between gender and other non–sex-linked qualities, such as affection and strength. Our culture regards affection as a feminine trait and strength as a masculine one. Second, such cultures make gender distinctions important, using them as a basis for norms, status, taboos, and privileges (see gender theory, pp. 77–78). Men are assigned leadership positions, for example, while women are placed in the rank and file (if not kept in the home); men who work outside the home receive higher status as providers than women who work within the home as homemakers. "Gender has come to have cognitive primacy over many other social categories," wrote Bem (1985), "because the culture has made it so." Also, children are taught that "the dichotomy between male and female has intensive and extensive relevance to virtually every domain of human experience" (Bem, 1985). Thus children learn very early that it is important whether someone is male or female. They also learn that an activity (nurturing, fighting), feeling (compassion, anger), behavior (playing with dolls or hammers), clothing (dresses or pants) or even color, (pink or blue) is appropriate for one sex but not the other.

Bem believes that those who use gender schema in processing information tend to follow traditional bipolar gender roles. She argues that the degree of reliance on gender schema depends on how much gender was emphasized during childhood socialization.

Some leading researchers believe that Bem's approach may replace androgyny as the most important way of examining gender difference (Carter, 1987c). In the last few years, almost fifty studies have been conducted to test the gender schema hypothesis, with interesting results. One study, for example, supports Bem's hypothesis that those advocating bipolar gender roles tend to think more gender-schematically than those who are androgynous (Schmitt and Millard, 1988).

Bem suggests doing away with the concept of masculine and feminine altogether. The gender schema, she argues, is not inevitable. In many cultures the masculine/feminine division is not as important as it is in ours. Bem (1985) makes her point by telling of her four-year-old son's experience when he went to nursery school wearing a barrette:

All are but parts of one stupendous whole Whose body nature is, and God the soul.

Alexander Pope (1688 - 1744)

We unwittingly set the stage for feelings of inadequacy and inferiority. The more rigidly we define ourselves the less likely we are able to cope with the infinite variety of life.

Ernest Rossi

He who knows the masculine but keeps to the feminine will be in the whole world's channel.

Taoist aphorism

Several times that day, another little boy told Jeremy that he, Jeremy, must be a girl because "only girls wear barrettes." After trying to explain to this child that "wearing barrettes doesn't matter" and that "being a boy means having a penis and testicles," Jeremy finally pulled down his pants as a way of making his point more convincingly. The other child was not impressed. He simply said, "Everybody has a penis; only girls wear barrettes."

One child had acquired a superficial understanding of gender, while Jeremy had understood that anatomy was the only relevant distinction between boys and girls.

❖ REFLECTIONS *Think about your gender role. Would you describe yourself as masculine, feminine, or androgynous? Why? Do you have traits associated with the other sex? What are they? How do you feel about them?*

◆ Contemporary gender roles are still in flux. Few of us are entirely egalitarian or traditional. Those who are androgynous or who have egalitarian attitudes, especially males, may be more traditional in their behaviors than they imagine. Few with egalitarian or androgynous attitudes, for example, divide *all* labor along lines of ability, interest, or necessity rather than gender. And those who are traditional in their outlook rarely find that wives submit to their husbands in *all* things. Among contemporary men and women, women find that their increasing access to employment puts them at odds with their traditional (and personally valued) role as mother. Women continue to feel conflict between their emerging equality in the workplace and their continued responsibilities at home. Within marriages and families, the greatest areas of gender inequality continue to be the division of housework and child care. But change continues to occur in the direction of greater gender equality. And this equality promises greater intimacy and satisfaction for both men and women in their relationships.

If you would marry suitably, marry your equal.

Ovid (43 B.C–18 A.D.)

Whatever you can do or dream you can, begin it. Boldness has genius, power, and magic in it. Begin it now.

Johann Goethe (1749–1832)

❖ SUMMARY

◆ *Gender identity* refers to being male or female. *Gender role* refers to the role a person is expected to perform as a result of being male or female in a particular culture. Gender roles are culturally relative, whereas gender identity is not. *Gender-role stereotypes* refer to rigidly held and oversimplified beliefs that males and females, as a result of their sex, possess distinct psychological and behavioral traits. *Gender-role attitudes* are beliefs that we have about ourselves and others regarding appropriate male and female personality traits and activities. *Gender-role behaviors* are the actual activities or behaviors that we or others engage in as males and females.

◆ The two most important socialization theories are *cognitive social learning theory* and *cognitive development theory*. Cognitive social learning theory emphasizes learning behaviors from others through positive and negative *reinforcement* and modeling. Reinforcement is modified through cognitive processes, such as the use of symbols, anticipation of consequences, and observation. *Modeling* is the imitation of the behavior of powerful figures.

◆ Cognitive development theory asserts that once children learn that gender is permanent, they independently strive to act like "proper" boys or girls because of an internal need for congruence.

◆ Children learn their gender roles through *manipulation, channeling, verbal appellation,* and *activity exposure*. Parents, teachers, and peers, are important agents of socialization during childhood and adolescence. Ethnicity and social class influence gender roles. Among African Americans, strong women are important female role models.

◆ During adolescence, parents are more important influences than peers. Peers, however, have more egalitarian gender-role attitudes than adults. For students, colleges and universities are important sources for gender-role learning, especially for nontraditional roles. Marriage, parenthood, and the workplace also influence the development of adult gender roles.

◆ Traditional male roles, whether white, African American, Latino, or Asian American, emphasize dominance and work. A man's central family role has been viewed as being the provider. For women there is greater role diversity according to ethnicity. Traditional female roles among middle-class whites emphasize passivity, compliance, physical attractiveness, and being a wife and mother. Work outside the home is acceptable as long as it does not interfere with other traditional role components. Among African Americans, women are expected to be instrumental; there is no conflict between work and motherhood. Among Latinos, women are deferential to men generally from respect rather than subservience; elders, regardless of gender, are afforded respect. Immigrants face gender-role stress, especially women, as they adapt to American standards.

◆ Contemporary gender roles are more egalitarian. Important changes affecting contemporary gender roles include (1) acceptance of women as workers and professionals, (2) increasing questioning, especially among white women, of motherhood as a core female identity, (3) greater equality in marital power, (4) breakdown of instrumental/expressive dichotomy, and (5) expansion of male family roles.

◆ Research indicates that gender-role stereotypes have changed little over the last few decades. Limitations of contemporary gender roles on men include the primacy of the provider role, which limits men's father and husband roles; difficulty in expressing feelings; and a sense of dominance that precludes intimacy. Limitations for women include diminished self-confidence and mental health and the association of femininity with youth and beauty, which creates a disadvantage as women age. Ethnic women may suffer both racial discrimination and gender-role stereotyping, which compound each other.

◆ Changing gender-role behavior is often difficult because (1) each sex reinforces the traditional roles of its own and the other sex, (2) we evaluate ourselves in terms of fulfilling gender-role concepts, (3) we have internalized our roles, and (4) the social structure reinforces traditional roles.

◆ *Androgyny* combines traditional male and female characteristics into a more flexible pattern of behavior, rather than seeing the sexes as bipolar opposites. Evidence suggests that androgyny contributes to psychological and emotional health. Some researchers, however, believe that androgyny may impose a double burden of expectation on people. An alternative is to discard the idea that instrumental traits are masculine and expressive traits feminine and think of them as human traits. *Gender schema* refers to the tendency to divide objects, activities, and behaviors into masculine and feminine categories.

Answers to Preview Questions

The answers to the preview questions at the beginning of the chapter are listed below. As you check your answers, whether you were correct or not, think about your reasons for each response. What were they? What was their source? How valid is the source? As you read the chapter, you will find the questions discussed in greater depth.

1.	F	6.	F
2.	T	7.	T
3.	F	8.	T
4.	F	9.	F
5.	F	10.	T

❖ SUGGESTED READINGS

Bernard, Jessie. *The Future of Marriage,* 2d ed. New Haven, Conn. Yale University Press, 1982. A provocative examination of contemporary American marriages. Bernard argues that within the same marriage there are actually two marriages, "his" and "her" marriages, resulting from gender roles.

Bly, Robert. *Iron John: A Book about Men.* Reading, Mass. Addison-Wesley, 1990. The controversial "wildman," founder of the mythopoetic men's movement, describes men's losses and their need to reconnect emotionally with other men through myth and ritual.

Kimmel, Michael, and Michael Messner, eds. *Men's Lives.* New York: Macmillan, 1989 (paperback). A collection of reflections, stories, and articles about growing up, sports, intimacy, war, families, masculinity, sexuality, and power.

Carter, D. Bruce. *Current Conceptions of Sex Roles and Sex Typing.* New York: Praeger, 1987. A scholarly overview of contemporary research and theory on gender roles.

Ehrenreich, Barbara. *The Hearts of Men: American Dreams and the Flight from Commitment.* Garden City, N.Y.: Anchor/ Doubleday, 1984 (paperback). A provocative analysis of contemporary male/female relationships in which the author finds men rejecting commitment because it forces them into stifling traditional male roles of breadwinner and successmonger.

Fisher, Dexter. *The Third Woman: Minority Women Writers in the United States.* Boston: Houghton-Mifflin, 1990 (paperback). A collection of fine writings by women of African-American, Latino, Asian-American, or Native American heritage.

Gary, Lawrence, ed. *Black Men.* Newbury Park, Calif.: Sage Publications, 1981 (paperback). An interdisciplinary examination of black males, including gender roles.

Gilligan, Carole. *In a Different Voice: Psychological Theory and Women's Development.* Cambridge, Mass.: Harvard University Press, 1982 (paperback). A challenge to traditional developmental theories that view women's commitments to relationships and connectedness as somehow being inferior to male commitments to abstract principles and logic.

LeGuin, Ursula. *The Left Hand of Darkness.* New York: Ace Books, 1969 (paperback). A classic science fiction novel about a utopian society in which the division of people into males and females is meaningless except in terms of impregnation, gestation, and birth.

Mead, Margaret. *Male and Female.* New York: William Morrow, 1975 (paperback). The renowned anthropological study of what it means to be male and female in different cultures.

Rodgers-Rose, La Frances. *The Black Woman.* Newbury Park, Calif.: Sage Publications, 1980 (paperback). A collection of essays on various aspects of black women, including gender and family roles.

Sanford, Linda, and Mary Ellen Donovan. *Women and Self-Esteem.* New York: Penguin Books, 1985 (paperback). A sensitive examination of the problem of low self-esteem in women and how to overcome it.

Tavris, Carol, and Carole Wade. *The Longest War: Sex Differences in Perspective,* 2d ed. New York: Harcourt Brace Jovanovich, 1984 (paperback). An outstanding overview of current research and thought on gender roles and sex differences.

Suggested Films

The Great Santini (1979). Robert Duvall's fine character study of the conflict between a Marine officer and his son: two different visions of manhood.

Rambo (1983). The archetypal "real" man.

A Room of One's Own (PBS Masterpiece Theatre, 1990). Renowned British actress Maggie Smith in a one-woman show based on Virginia Woolf's lectures about women's rights: witty, moving, and powerful.

Thelma and Louise (1991). Susan Sarandon and Geena Davis hit the road in a controversial interpretation of the traditional men's "buddy movie."

READINGS

THE MALE MYSTIQUE

Andrew Kimbrell

While attention has usually been focused on the emotional costs of traditional female gender roles, the costs of traditional male gender roles have largely been ignored. According to Kimbrell, who represents many of the views of the new men's movement, what are the costs of being male in our society? What are their sources? Do you agree? Why?

Men are hurting—badly. Despite rumors to the contrary, men as a gender are being devastated physically and psychically by our socioeconomic system. As American society continues to empower a small percentage of men and a smaller but increasing percentage of women, it is causing significant confusion and anguish for the majority of men.

In recent years, there have been many impressive analyses documenting the exploitation of women in our culture. Unfortunately, little attention has been given to the massive disruption and destruction that our economic and political institutions have wrought on men. Far too often, men as a gender have been thought of as synonymous with the power elite.

But thinking on this subject is beginning to change. Over the last decade, men have begun to realize that we cannot properly relate to one another, or understand how some of us in turn exploit others, until we have begun to appreciate the extent and nature of our dispossessed predicament. In a variety of ways, men across the country are beginning to mourn their losses and seek solutions. This new sense of loss among men comes from the deterioration of men's traditional roles as protectors of family and the earth (although not the sole protectors). And much of

this mourning also focuses on how men's energy is often channeled in the direction of destruction—both of the earth and its inhabitants. The mission of many men today—both those involved in the men's movement and others outside it—is to find new ways that allow men to celebrate their generative potential and reverse the cycle of destruction that characterizes men's collective behavior today. These calls to action are not abstract or hypothetical. The oppression of men, especially in the last several decades, can be easily seen in a disturbing upward spiral of male self-destruction, addiction, hopelessness and homelessness.

While suicide rates for women have been stable over the last 20 years, among men—especially white male teen-agers—they have increased rapidly. Male teen-agers are five times more likely to take their own lives than females. Overall men are committing suicide at four times the rate of women. America's young men are also being ravaged by alcohol and drug abuse. Men between the ages of 18 and 29 suffer alcohol dependency at three times the rate of women of the same age group. More than two-thirds of all alcoholics are men, and 50 percent more men are regular users of illicit drugs than women. Men account for more than 90 percent of arrests for alcohol and drug abuse violations.

A sense of hopelessness among America's young men is not surprising. Real wages for men under 25 have actually declined over the last 20 years, and 60 percent of all high school dropouts are males. These statistics account in part for the increasing rate of unemployment among men and for the fact that more than 80 percent of America's homeless are men.

The stress on men is taking its toll. Men's life expectancy is 10 percent shorter than women's, and the incidence of stress-relat-

continued on next page

ed illnesses such as heart disease and certain cancers remains inordinately high among men.

And the situation for minority men is even worse.

Men are also a large part of the growing crisis in the American family. Studies report that parents today spend 40 percent less time with their children than did parents in 1965, and men are increasingly isolated from their families by the pressures of work and the circumstances of divorce.

The current crisis for men, which goes far beyond statistics, is nothing new. We have faced a legacy of loss, especially since the start of the mechanical age. From the Enclosure Acts, which forced families off the land in Tudor England, to the ongoing destruction of indigenous communities throughout the Third World, the demands of the industrial era have forced men off the land, out of the family and community, and into the factory and office. The male as steward of family and soil, craftsman, woodsman, native hunter, and fisherman has all but vanished.

As men became the primary cog in industrial production, they lost touch with the earth and the parts of themselves that needed the earth to survive. Men by the millions—who long prided themselves on their husbandry of family, community and land—were forced into a system whose ultimate goal was to turn one man against another in the competitive "jungle" of industrialized society.

The factory wrenched the father from the home, and he often became a virtual nonentity in the household. By separating a man's work from his family, industrial society caused the permanent alienation of father from son. Even when the modern father returns to the house, he is often too tired and too irritable from the tensions and tedium of work in the factory or corporation to pay close attention to his children.

While the loss of fathers is now beginning to be discussed, men have yet to fully come to terms with the terrible loss of sons during the mechanized wars of this century. World War I, World War II, Korea and Vietnam were what the poet Robert Graves called "holocausts of young men." In the battlefields of this century, hundreds of millions of men were killed or injured. In World Wars I and II—in which more than 100 million soldiers were casualties—most of the victims were teen-age boys, the average age being 18.5 years.

Instead of grieving over and acting on our loss of independence and generativity, modern men have often engaged in denial—a denial that is linked to the existence of a "male mystique." This defective mythology of the modern age has created a "new man." The male mystique recasts what anthropologists have identified as the traditional male role throughout history—a man, whether hunter-gatherer or farmer, who is steeped in a creative and sustaining relationship with his extended family and the earth household. In the place of this long-enduring, rooted masculine role, the male mystique has fostered a new image of men: autonomous, efficient, intensely self-interested, and disconnected from community and the earth.

Ironically, men's own sense of loss has fed the male mystique. As men become more and more powerless in their own lives, they are given more and more media images of excessive, caricatured masculinity with which to identify.

The primary symbols of the male mystique are almost never caring fathers, stewards of the land or community organizers. Instead, over several decades these aggressively masculine figures have evolved from the Western independent man (John Wayne, Gary Cooper) to the blue-collar macho man (Sly Stallone and Robert DeNiro) and finally to a variety of military and police figures concluding with the violent revelry of "Robocop."

Modern men are entranced by this simulated masculinity—they experience danger, independence, success, sexuality, idealism and adventure as voyeurs. Meanwhile, in real life most men lead powerless, subservient lives in the factory or office—frightened of losing their jobs, mortgaged to the gills and still feeling responsible for supporting their families. Their lauded independence disappears the minute they report for work. The disparity between their real lives and the macho images of masculinity perpetrated by the media confuses and confounds many men.

Men can no longer afford to lose themselves in denial. We need to experience grief and anger over our losses and not buy into the pseudo-male stereotypes propagated by the male mystique. We are not what we are told we are.

The current generation of men faces a unique moment in history. Will we choose to remain subservient tools of social and environmental destruction or to fight for rediscovery of the male as a full partner and participant in family, community and the earth?

There is a world to gain. The male mystique, in which many of today's men are trapped, is threatening the family and the planet with irreversible destruction.

A men's movement based on the recovery of masculinity could renew much of the world we have lost. By changing types of work and work hours, we could break our subordination to corporate managers and return much of our work and lives to the household. We could once again be teaching, nurturing presences to our children. By devoting ourselves to meaningful work with appropriate technology, we could recover independence in our work and our spirit. By caring for each other, we could recover the dignity of our gender and heal the wounds of addiction and self-destruction. By becoming husbands to the earth, we could protect the wild and recover our creative connections with the forces and rhythms of nature.

Ultimately we must help fashion a world without the daily frustration and sorrow of having to view each other as a collection of competitors instead of a community of friends.

Shortly after World War I, Ford Madox Ford, one of this century's greatest writers, depicted 20th century men as continually pinned down in their trenches, unable to stand up for fear of annihilation. As the century closes, men remain pinned down by an economic and political system that daily forces millions of us into meaningless work, powerless lives, and self-destruction. The time has come for men to stand up.

MEDIA STEREOTYPES OF WOMEN

Linda Sanford and Mary Donovan.
Excerpt from *Women and Self-Esteem*.

As you examine media stereotypes of women, ask yourself if there are other female stereotypes. Do female stereotypes differ according to race and ethnicity? Do you believe men's stereotypes of women differ from women's stereotypes of women. Are there comparable stereotypes of men?

The proliferation of stereotypes that modern technology has made possible has given us a culture in which no group has been spared stereotyping. Stop people on the street and ask them what the stereotyped image of Southerners is, and one response probably will be "Southerners are racist." And so it goes with other groups. Asians are inscrutable. New Englanders are thrifty and taciturn. Californians are flaky. Black men are either athletes or shiftless bums emasculated by "their" women. Feminists are ugly man-haters. Telephone operators are rude. New Yorkers are tough. Jews are greedy. Gay men are effeminate. Lesbians are butchy. Easterners are snobs. Hispanics are hot-blooded. Black women are maids or prostitutes or on welfare. WASPs are up-tight. Older women are "biddies." All working-class and poor people have totally miserable lives. Blondes are dumb. These are just some of the more common stereotypes that abound in our culture today. The list could go on.

Not all stereotypes are clearly negative, but upon closer examination we can see their limiting nature as they strip away our individuality and render us a "type." Elaine Kanzaki Wong writes specifically of effects of stereotypes on Asian women:

Occasionally, Asian women meet men who are what I dub "Orientalphiles." These men claim to be enamored of everything Oriental, i.e., the artwork, classic paintings, pottery, enamelware, clothing and various artificial artifacts. In short, they admire everything about the culture and, of course, that includes Oriental women. Because so much is presented as negative in the stereotypes about Asians, the Asian woman finds herself distinctly vulnerable in this positive stereotype situation and might respond positively when she might be better responding negatively. Is she not, after all, being regarded as another Oriental *objet d'art?*

Women are one of the most stereotyped groups in our society. Here's a sampling of the more popular stereotypes of women that abound in American culture today:

◆ *Women as Evil:* The image of women as evil temptresses with diabolical plans to do harm to men is a common theme in pop music lyrics ("Witchy Woman," "Evil Woman" and "Maneater"), in television programming today ("Dynasty," "Knots Landing," "Falcon Crest" and every soap opera), and in feature films (*Body Heat, An Officer and a Gentleman, In the Still of the Night*). Women with teeth in their vaginas or who are hiding other deadly weapons with the intent of killing their unsuspecting lovers are prevalent images in pornography as well.

◆ *Woman as Sex Object:* In every medium, women are depicted as sex-kittenish playthings for men, useful only for men's sexual gratification. Moreover, women's sexuality is used to sell everything from blue jeans to scotch to automobiles to industrial machinery. Given a moment to think or to look around our environs, each of us could come up with scores of examples.

◆ *Woman as Victim:* Again in every medium, women are frequently portrayed as victims in need of rescue by males (most police programs, with the exception of "Hill Street Blues" and "Cagney and Lacey"), victims who bring on their own victimization through gross stupidity, or victims who are being justifiably punished for evil or sexual behavior (*Looking for Mr. Goodbar, Straw Dogs, Dressed to Kill*). The helplessness of the female victim is often glorified (songs like "Love Has No Pride," and the "I'm Black and Blue and I Love It" Rolling Stones advertising campaign).

◆ *Woman as Madonna:* Many of us were raised seeing an endless parade of perfect mothers in the characters of Mrs. Cleaver, Mrs. Nelson, Mrs. "Father Knows Best" and Donna Reed. The all-giving, one-dimensional mother is still alive and well on every soap opera and in commercials (the Italian mother or the mother of a child with a common cold). This image is not only narrow and unrealistic, it has become a tyrannical ideal against which we often unfairly measure our mothers and our performance as mothers.

◆ *Woman as Destructive Mother:* Media portrayals of violent criminals often make the point that the poor boys had mothers who were so castrating and malevolent that their sons had no other choice than to become antisocial. This is particularly true in dramas about rapists: He is not responsible for his hatred of women, his mother is (*Rage*). Short of turning men into criminals and psychopaths, mothers make their children miserable (*Portnoy's Complaint, Psycho, Frances, Kramer vs. Kramer, Ordinary People*). This extends to a preponderance of negative stereotypes about mothers-in-law, stepmothers and foster mothers.

◆ *Woman as Mentally Ill:* The entertainment media seem most interested in exploring the lives of women who can be portrayed as mentally ill. Rarely do we hear about women who—like most of us—have problems and cope with them without going crazy or becoming bizarre. But we hear plenty about women who are neurotic and incapable of figuring anything out without the help

continued on next page

of an expensive psychiatrist (*An Unmarried Woman, Fear of Flying,* the women friends of the star on "Family Tree"), and we hear even more about women who are either suicidal or just plain insane (*Edie,* the myriad articles and books about Sylvia Plath, movies such as *The Three Faces of Eve* and *Frances,* the women in Tennessee Williams plays). Not only are mentally ill women commonly portrayed, but they are portrayed as if they were their mental illnesses—nothing more. When the life of Billie Holiday is made into a movie (*Lady Sings the Blues*) or the life of Edith Piaf is made into a play (*Piaf*), their problems are emphasized at the expense of a more total understanding of them. And although we do hear and see stories of women alcoholics, mental patients, drug addicts, etc., who overcome their problems and become "good" women, they are still defined by their problems.

◆ *Woman as Moron:* We see her most often in advertising: She is so obsessed with ridding her environs of dirt that she spends all her time and energy getting "caked-on grime" out of corners, gunning down germs with an arsenal of wonder products, talking to a little man in a little boat in her toilet bowl, and fretting about dirty shirt collars of her slovenly husband who won't wash his neck. On television and in films, working-class and rural women in particular are often portrayed as dolts ("The Beverly Hillbillies," "Petticoat Junction," Edith Bunker, "Laverne and Shirley," the women in "The Honeymooners"). However, this image of woman as idiot cuts across class lines. "I Love Lucy," Phyllis Diller and "Gidget" also are examples.

◆ *Woman as Obstacle to Other Women's Happiness:* This is the stuff of soap operas, pop music ("Nobody"), films (*All About Eve*) and television shows in which women fight with each other over men, money or recognition. We also see it in advertising ("Mother, I'd rather do it myself!" and commercials where women competitively compare their laundry or the well-being of their children).

◆ *Woman as Superwoman:* This is a standard image in newspaper feature columns about career women. Slick providers of simplistic advice tell us we can "have it all." Enjoli assures us that if we wear their perfume we can be a supermom, high-paid executive, gourmet cook and cosmic lover to our husbands simultaneously, and then Geritol takes the credit for it. The superwoman image is fast becoming an ideal just as prevalent and oppressive as Woman as Sex Object or Woman as Madonna.

Compounding the problem of stereotyping in the mass media is the problem of unequal representation. The number of images of women we see is relatively small compared to the number of men. In prime-time TV, for example, male characters outnumber females by a margin of three to one, and on children's TV only 16 percent of the major characters are female. In the movies a similar situation prevails, with the leading female roles in the last decade being so few in number that all but a handful

of female superstars like Jane Fonda and Meryl Streep go for long periods without work.

To further compound the problems of stereotyping, the mass media are not just dominated by men, they're dominated by white men. On prime-time TV, a full 62 percent of the characters were white males in 1980 (compared to 68 percent in 1968); and in network children's TV only 3.7 percent of the characters in 1982 were black, 3.1 percent Hispanic and 0.8 percent Asian. Native Americans were represented solely by Tonto on "The Lone Ranger Adventure Hour." Perhaps the medium where white males dominate the most is film. According to the NAACP, only 12 of the 240 feature films released by American studios in 1981 had black males in leading or supporting roles, and only one black female had a leading role (Cicely Tyson in *Bustin' Loose*). As for Asians, Native Americans, and Hispanics, almost never do they appear in studio films, and where they do appear, it's only in the most stereotyped roles—as evil Japs and seductive lotus blossoms in World War II movies, scalping savages and stupid squaws in Westerns, and moronic and seedy señors and señoritas in B movies. This insults ethnic group viewers, and also hurts minority group members who have worked in the entertainment industry. Rita Moreno, for years confined by type-casting to play flamenco dancers, Indian maidens, and sexy, dumb and barefoot señoritas, explains:

I wasn't conscious of the casting stereotypes in those days—not that they've completely changed now. If you were a Latina, you played poor, brown-skinned princesses: Mexican, Spanish, Indian; we all looked alike. Or so they seemed to think. . . . The more I played those dusky innocents, the worse I felt inside. Once I was an Indian maiden in *Jivaro,* with Rhoda Fleming. There she was, in frills, all pink and blonde and big-breasted. Right next to her, I had an ugly wig on, brown-shoe-polish makeup, and wore a tattered leopard skin. I felt ugly and stupid, and every time I looked down at my bare feet I grew more ashamed. . . . A little later I was doing a film with Richard Egan. Near the end, when I got jilted, I asked him, "Why joo no luv Oola no more?" When he told me, I took two steps back and fell over a hundred-foot cliff. I call it the Yonkee Peeg school of acting.

Most grown women are not dummies who are indoctrinated into believing that because women are depicted in the mass media in a certain way then that's what we as individuals must be like. But regardless of how we women perceive ourselves, the way others perceive us and thus treat us is usually shaped to a large extent by media stereotypes. Virtually every woman we interviewed, regardless of color, has had the experience of being seen and treated as an inferior by women and men alike simply because she is female. And women of color, lesbians, older women, and women with disabilities have had the experience of being viewed as doubly inferior because of the stereotypes about

READINGS

both women and their particular group. For example, Anita Neilsen and Linda Jeffers, Wampanoag Indians who give tours to the public at the Wampanoag Indian Program at Plymouth Plantation in Massachusetts, report that many of the people who come to the site believe, first of all, that "all the Indians are dead." Then when they are told that this is not so, they presume that the Indians practiced scalping, that Indian women are all drudges and slaves to men, and that the Indians encroached upon the white settlers' lands rather than the other way around. (Many visitors ask Neilsen and Jeffers sincerely, "How did you happen to move near the Pilgrims?" as if the Pilgrims had been in Massachusetts first.)

Love, Commitment, and Intimacy

To gain a sense of what you already know about the material covered in this chapter, answer "true" or "false" to the following statements. You will find the answers on page 142.

1. Researchers tend to believe that whatever form of love they value most is "true" love. True or false?
2. People tend to think that love and commitment overlap in important aspects. True or false?
3. Everyone has experienced unrequited (unreturned) love. True or false?
4. In romantic relationships, caring is less important than physical attraction. True or false?
5. Males and females, whites, African Americans, Latinos, and Asians, heterosexuals, gay men and lesbians, old and young are equally as likely to fall in love. True or false?
6. In many ways, love is like the attachment an infant experiences for his or her caregiver. True or false?
7. You always hurt the one you love. True or false?
8. Infatuation is usually equally intense for both parties. True or false?
9. Not telling the person you like that you like him or her is important in getting that person to fall in love with you. True or false?
10. Partners with different styles of loving are likely to have more satisfying relationships. True or false?

We are shaped and fashioned by what we love.

Johann Goethe

The head is always the dupe of the heart.

François de La Rochefoucauld

Was it not by loving that I learned to love? Was it not by living that I learned to live?

Jorge Amado

LOVE IS ESSENTIAL TO OUR LIVES. Love binds us together as men and women, parents and children, friends and neighbors. Its importance can hardly be overrated, for we make major life decisions, such as marrying, based on love (Simpson et al., 1986). Love creates bonds that endure the greatest hardships, suffer the severest cruelty, overcome any distance. Because of its significance, we may torment ourselves with the question, "Is it *really* love?" Many of us have gone through frustrating scenes such as the following (Greenberg and Jacobs, 1966):

YOU: "Do you love me?"
MATE: "Yes, of course I love you."
YOU: "Do you *really* love me?"
MATE: "Yes, I really love you."
YOU: "You are *sure* you love me—you are absolutely sure?"
MATE: "Yes, I'm absolutely sure."
YOU: "Do you know the meaning of love?"
MATE: "I don't know."
YOU: "Then how can you be sure you love me?"
MATE: "I don't know. Perhaps I can't."
YOU: "You can't, eh? I see. Well, since you can't even be sure you love me, I can't really see much point in our remaining together. Can you?"
MATE: "I don't know. Perhaps not."
YOU: "You've been leading up to this for a pretty long time, haven't you?"

Love is both a feeling and an activity. A person feels love for someone and acts in a loving manner. But we can also be angry with the person we love, frustrated, bored, or indifferent. This is the paradox of love: it encompasses opposites. Love includes affection and anger, excitement and boredom, stability and change, bonds and freedom. Its paradoxical quality makes some ask whether they are *really* in love when they are not feeling "perfectly" in love or when their relationship is not going smoothly. Love does not give us perfection, however; it gives us meaning. In fact, as sociologist Ira Reiss (1980) suggested, a more important question to ask is not if one is feeling love but, "Is the love I feel the kind of love on which I can build a lasting relationship or marriage?"

We can look at love in many ways besides through the eyes of lovers, although other ways may not be as entertaining. Whereas love was once the province of lovers, madmen, poets, and philosophers, social scientists have begun to appear on the scene. They have bravely disregarded William Blake's warning:

He who binds to himself a Joy
Doth the winged life destroy;
But he who kisses the Joy as it flies
Lives in eternity's sunrise.

Studying love is no guarantee of finding it. As John A. Lee (1988), a major researcher, explained, "I have studied love because it is my life's most difficult problem. Although I have made much progress, the 'impossible dream' of a truly fulfilling mutual love remains one I have yet to achieve." The study of romantic love is still in its infancy. In the thirty-four years between 1949 and 1983, only twenty-seven articles on love appeared in sociology and psychology journals (Baron, 1983). But now, because the interest in love research is growing at such a pace, one researcher suggests that if Elizabeth Barrett Browning wrote her poem today, she would respond to "How do I love thee?" with "Let me count the articles" (Rubin, 1988). Until recently, researchers failed to investigate love for several reasons (Berscheid and Walster, 1978). First, they did not believe that the phenomenon of love could be subject to scientific examination and prediction. Second, the study of romantic love was taboo; putting love under scientific scrutiny would destroy its mystery. Third, the researchers weren't exactly sure how to study love; they could not envision an appropriate methodology for examining such phenomena as "love at first sight," sexual attraction, and so on.

Love research is also complicated by the kinds of love that different researchers prefer. As John Lee (1988) noted, "The kind of love the researchers like best is the only 'true' love." Because the study of love is still in its infancy, there is still no common vocabulary: what one researcher calls romantic love is infatuation to another (Rubin, 1988).

❖ THIS THING CALLED LOVE: THE PHENOMENA OF LOVE AND COMMITMENT

Love and commitment are closely linked in our intimate relationships; they help to create and sustain each other. Love reflects the positive factors—such as caring—that draw people together and sustain them in a relationship. Commitment reflects the stable factors—including love but also obligations and social pressure—that help maintain the relationship "for better or for worse." Although the two are related, they are not necessarily connected. One can exist without the other. It is possible to love someone without being committed. It is also possible to be committed to someone without loving him or her. Yet, when all is said and done, most of us long for a love that includes commitment and a commitment that encompasses love.

Prototypes of Love and Commitment

Despite centuries of discussion, debate, and complaint by philosophers and lovers, no one has succeeded in finding definitions of love and commitment on which all can agree. Ironically, such discussions seem to engender conflict and disagreement rather than love and harmony.

Because of the unending confusion surrounding definitions of love, some researchers wonder whether such definitions are even possible (Fehr, 1988; Kelley, 1983). In the everyday world, however, we do seem to have something in mind when we tell someone we love him or her. We may not have formal definitions of love, but we do have prototypes (that is, models) of what we mean by love stored in the backs of our minds. Researchers suggest that instead of looking for formal definitions of love and commitment, we examine people's prototypes; in some ways these prototypes may be more important than formal definitions. For example, when we say "I love you," we are referring to our prototype of love rather than its definition. By thinking in terms of prototypes, we can study how people actually use the words *love* and *commitment* in real life and how their meanings of love and commitment help define the progress of their intimate relationships.

To discover people's prototypes, researcher Beverly Fehr (1988) asked 172 respondents to rate the central features of love and commitment. The twelve central attributes of love they listed are given in order:

◆ Trust
◆ Caring
◆ Honesty
◆ Friendship
◆ Respect
◆ Concern for the other's well-being

◆ Loyalty
◆ Commitment
◆ Acceptance of the other the way s/he is
◆ Supportiveness
◆ Wanting to be with the other
◆ Interest in the other

*Love looks not with the eyes,
But with the mind.*

William Shakespeare, A Midsummer Night's Dream

Only love with its science makes us so innocent.

Violeta Parra

The twelve central attributes of commitment, listed in order, were as follows:

◆ Loyalty
◆ Responsibility
◆ Living up to your word
◆ Faithfulness
◆ Trust
◆ Being there for the other in good and bad times

◆ Devotion
◆ Reliability
◆ Giving your best effort
◆ Supportiveness
◆ Perseverance
◆ Concern about the other's well being

There are many other characteristics identified as features of love (euphoria, thinking about the other all the time, butterflies in the stomach) or commitment (putting the other first, contentment). These, however, tend to be peripheral. As relationships progress, the central aspects of love and commitment become more characteristic of the relationship than the peripheral ones. The central features, observed Fehr (1988), "act as true barometers of a move toward increased love or commitment in a relationship." Similarly, violations of central features of love and commitment were considered to be more serious than violations of peripheral ones. A loss of caring, trust, honesty, or respect threatens love, while the disappearance of butterflies in the stomach does not. Similarly, lack of responsibility or faithfulness endangers commitment, whereas discontent is not perceived as threatening. Researchers have found that love *and* commitment were correlated to satisfaction in romantic relationships (Hendrick and Hendrick, 1988b).

A review of the research finds a number of attitudes, feelings, and behaviors associated with love (Kelley, 1983).

In terms of attitudes and feelings, positive attitudes and feelings toward the other bring people together. Zick Rubin (1970, 1973) found that there were four feelings

The physical expression of love through touching, hugging, kissing, and sexuality is an important aspect of love.

identifying love. These ideas, which correspond fairly well to the prototypical characteristics identified with love, were:

◆ *Caring* for the other, wanting to help him or her; MOST IMP
◆ *Needing* the other, having a strong desire to be in the other's presence and to have the other care for you;
◆ *Trusting* the other, mutually exchanging confidences;
◆ *Tolerating* the other, including his or her faults.

Of these, caring appears to be the most important, followed by needing, trusting, and tolerating (Steck, Levitan, McLane, and Kelley, 1982). Davitz (1969) identified similar feelings associated with love but noted in addition that respondents reported feeling an inner glow, optimism, and cheerfulness. They felt harmony and unity with the person they loved. They were intensely aware of the other person, feeling that they were fully concentrated on him or her.

Love is also expressed in certain behaviors. One study (Swensen, 1972) found that romantic love was expressed in several ways. Notice that the expression of love often overlaps thoughts of love.

◆ *Verbally expressing affection*, such as saying "I love you";
◆ *Self–disclosing*, such as revealing intimate facts about yourself;
◆ *Giving nonmaterial evidence*, such as emotional and moral support in times of need, and respecting the other's opinion;
◆ *Expressing nonverbal feelings*, such as feeling happier, more content, more secure when the other is present;
◆ *Giving material evidence*, such as gifts, flowers, or small favors, or doing more than your share of something;
◆ *Physically expressing love*, such as hugging, kissing, making love; most import
◆ *Tolerating the other*, such as accepting his or her idiosyncracies, peculiar routines, or forgetfulness about putting the cap on the toothpaste.

These behavioral expressions of love are consistent with the prototypical characteristics of love. In addition, recent research supports the belief that people "walk on air" when they are in love. Researchers have found that those in love view the world more positively than those who are not in love (Hendrick and Hendrick, 1988a).

Factors Affecting Commitment

Although we generally make commitments because we love someone, love alone is not sufficient to make a commitment last. Our commitments seem to be affected by several factors that can strengthen or weaken the relationship. Ira Reiss (1980) believes that there are three important factors: (1) the balance of costs to benefits, (2) normative inputs, and (3) structural constraints.

1. *The Balance of Costs to Benefits*. Whether we like it or not, human beings have a tendency to look at romantic and marital relationships from a cost-benefit perspective. Most of the time, when we are satisfied, we are unaware that we may judge our relationships in this manner. But when there is stress or conflict, we often ask ourselves, "What am I getting out of this relationship?" Then we add up the pluses and minuses. If the result is on the plus side, we are encouraged to continue the relationship; if the result is negative, we are more likely to discontinue it.

2. *Normative Inputs*. Normative inputs for relationships are the values that you and your partner hold about love, relationships, marriage, and family. These values can

Love cannot save life from death, but it can fulfill life's purpose.

Arnold Toynbee (1889–1975)

*Upon my bed by night
I sought him, but found him not;
I called him, but he gave no answer.
In the streets and in the squares,
  I will seek him whom my soul loves.
The watchmen found me as they went
  about in the city.
"Have you seen him whom my soul loves?"
Scarcely had I passed them,
When I found him whom my soul loves.
I held him, and would not let him go
  until I had brought him into my
    mother's house,
  and into the chamber of her that
    conceived me.
I adjure you, O daughters of Jerusalem,
  by the gazelles or the hinds of the field,
  that you stir not up nor awaken love
    until it pleases.*

Song of Solomon

Add plus & minuses
side you continue
relationship
mutual gain theory

either sustain or detract from a commitment. How do you feel about a love commitment? A marital commitment? Do you believe that marriage is for life? Does the presence of children affect your beliefs about commitment? What are the values that your friends, family, and religion hold regarding your type of relationship?

3. *Structural Constraints*. The structure of a relationship will add to or detract from commitment. Depending on the type of relationship—whether it is dating, living together, or marriage—different roles and expectations are structured in. In marital relationships, there are partner roles (husband/wife) and economic roles (employed worker/homemaker). There may also be parental roles (mother/father).

These different factors interact to increase or decrease individuals' commitment to each other. Commitments are more likely to endure in marriage than in cohabiting or dating relationships, which tend to be relatively short-lived. They are more likely to last in heterosexual relationships than in gay or lesbian relationships (Testa et al., 1987). The reason commitments tend to endure in marriage may or may not have anything to do with a couple being happy. Marital commitments tend to last because of norms, and structural constraints may compensate for the lack of personal satisfaction.

For most people, love seems to include commitment and commitment includes love. The two seem to overlap considerably. As we saw, Fehr (1988) found that if a person violated a central attribute of love, such as caring, that person was also seen as violating his or her commitment. And if a person violated a central attribute of commitment, such as loyalty, it called love into question.

Because of the overlap between love and commitment, we can mistakenly assume that if someone loves us, he or she is also committed to us. As one researcher (Kelley, 1983) pointed out, "Expressions of love can easily be confused with expressions of commitment. . . . Misunderstandings about a person's love versus commitment can be based on honest errors of communication, on failures of self-understanding." Or a person can intentionally mislead his or her partner to believe that there is a greater commitment than there actually is. Even if a person is committed, it is not always clear what the commitment means: Is it a commitment to the person or to the relationship, for a short time or for a long time? Is it for better and for worse?

❖ REFLECTIONS   *What are the ideas you associate with love? Committment? Do they overlap? Have you ever mistaken love for committment? Why?*

❖ HOW DO I LOVE THEE? APPROACHES TO THE STUDY OF LOVE

Researchers have developed a number of ways to study love (Hendrick and Hendrick, 1987). Some of these ways are discussed in this section.

Styles of Love   *Know*

"How do I love thee?" asked Elizabeth Barrett Browning in one of her poems. She went on to answer her own question:

I love thee to the depth and breadth and height
My soul can reach, when feeling out of sight
For the ends of Being and ideal Grace.
I love thee to the level of every day's
Most quiet need, by sun and candle-light.

The meeting of two personalities is like the contact of two chemical substances; if there is any reaction, both are transformed

Carl Jung (1875–1971)

Lovers and madmen have such seething brains,
Such shaping fantasies, that apprehend
More than cool reason ever comprehends.
The lunatic, the lover and the poet
Are of imagination all compact. . . .

William Shakespeare, A Midsummer Night's Dream

I love thee freely, as men strive for right.
I love thee purely, as they turn from praise.
I love thee with the passion put to use
In my old griefs, and with my childhood's faith.

Sociologist John Lee has counted the ways differently. "I love thee erotically, madly, playfully, companionately, altruistically, pragmatically," he might say. Lee (1973, 1988) described six basic styles of loving:

- ◆ **Eros:** love of beauty
- ◆ **Mania:** obsessive love
- ◆ **Ludis:** playful love
- ◆ **Storge:** companionate love
- ◆ **Agape:** altruistic love
- ◆ **Pragma:** practical love

[handwritten annotation: remember this know (was on test)]

In addition to these pure forms there are mixtures of the basic types: Storgic-Eros, Ludic-Eros, and Storgic-Ludis. The six basic types can be described as follows:

Eros. Erotic lovers delight in the tactile, the sensual, the immediate; they are attracted to beauty (though beauty may be in the eye of the beholder). They love the lines of the body, its feel and touch. They are fascinated by every detail of their beloved. Their love burns brightly but soon flickers and dies.

Mania. The word *mania* comes from the Greek word for madness. The Russian poet Lermontov aptly described a manic lover:

He in his madness prays for storms,
And dreams that storms will bring him peace.

For manic lovers, nights are marked by sleeplessness and days by pain and anxiety. The slightest sign of affection brings ecstasy for a short while, only to disappear. Satisfactions last but a moment before they must be renewed. Manic love is roller-coaster love. The French ballad "Plaisir d'Amour" is the manic lover's anthem:

The pleasures of love are but a moment long
But the pain of love endures the whole life through.

Ludis. For ludic lovers, love is a game, something to play at rather than to become deeply involved in. Love is ultimately ludicrous. Love is for fun; encounters are casual, carefree, and often careless. "Nothing serious" is the motto of ludic lovers.

The patron saint of ludic lovers is the poet Sir John Suckling (1609–1642), a favorite of the English court (and the inventor of cribbage), who, when banished, committed suicide. His poem "The Constant Lover" sums up the philosophy of the ludic lover.

Out upon it, I have loved
Three whole days together!
And am like to love three more,
If it prove fair weather.

Storge. Storge (pronounced *stor*-gay) is the love between companions. It is, wrote Lee, "love without fever, tumult, or folly, a peaceful and enchanting affection." It begins usually as friendship and then gradually deepens into love. If the love ends, it also occurs gradually, and the couple often become friends

*It lies not in our power to love or hate,
For will in us is over-ruled by fate.*

Christopher Marlowe, Hero and Leander

If you start with the belief that love is the pleasure of a moment, is it really surprising that it yields only a momentary pleasure?

Walter Lippmann, A Preface to Morals

There is more self-love than love in jealousy.

François de La Rochefoucauld

once again. Of such love Theophile Gautier wrote, "To love is to admire with the heart; to admire is to love with the mind."

Agape. Agape (pronounced *ah*-ga-pay) is the traditional Christian love that is chaste, patient, and undemanding; it does not expect to be reciprocated. It is the love of saints and martyrs. Agape is more abstract and ideal than concrete and real. It is easier to love all of humankind in such a way than an individual.

altruistic

Pragma. Pragmatic lovers are, first and foremost, logical in their approach toward looking for someone who meets their needs. They look for a partner who has the background, education, personality, religion, and interests that are compatible with their own. If they meet a person who meets their criteria, erotic or manic feelings may develop. But, as Samuel Butler warned, "Logic is like the sword—those who appeal to it shall perish by it."

practical

Lee believes that to have a mutually satisfying love affair, a person has to find a partner who shares the same style and definition of love. The more different two people are in their styles of loving, the less likely it is that they will understand each other's love. Research confirms that love styles are also linked to gender and ethnicity (Hendrick and Hendrick, 1986).

Two researchers (Hendrick and Hendrick, 1988a) found that college students in love were more erotic and agapic and less ludic than those not in love. In another study, researchers found that heterosexual and gay men have similar attitudes toward eros, ludis, storge, and mania. The research also confirmed that gay male relationships have multiple emotional dimensions and are not based solely on sex (Adler, Hendrick, and Hendrick, 1989).

Romantic Love and Adrenaline: The Two-Component Theory

Love brings great pleasure. Christina Rossetti wrote:

My heart is like a singing bird
  Whose nest is in a watered shoot;
My heart is like an apple-tree
  Whose boughs are bent with thick-set fruit;
My heart is like a rainbow shell
  That paddles in a halcyon sea;
My heart is gladder than all these
  Because my love is come to me.

But love can also be torture, as the Roman poet Catullus complained in the first century B.C.:

I hate and I love.
You ask how that can be.
Yet I do not know.
But I feel it and I am tormented.

The contradictory nature of romantic love has confused lovers (and those who theorize about love) for centuries. Is passionate love pleasure or pain—or is it both?

The scientific explanation of romantic love was given a boost by Stanley Schachter's *two-component theory* of human emotions. According to his theory, for a person to experience an emotion, two factors must be present: (1) physiological arousal, and (2) an appropriate emotional explanation for the arousal. By recognizing that love is accompanied by physiological arousal, psychologists are able to explain why both intensely positive and intensely negative experiences can lead to

---

Love gives itself; it is not bought.

Henry Longfellow (1807 - 1882)

According to the two-component theory of emotions, for a person to experience an emotion there must be (1) physiological arousal and (2) an appropriate emotional explanation for the arousal. What emotions might the couple here be experiencing? Why?

◆ UNDERSTANDING YOURSELF ◆

Your Style of Love

John Lee, who developed the idea of styles of love, also developed a questionnaire that allows men and women to identify their style of love. Complete the questionnaire to identify your style of love. Then ask yourself to which style of love you find yourself drawn in others. Is it the same or different?

Graph Your Own Style of Loving

Consider each characteristic as it applies to a current relationship that you define as love, or to a previous one if that is more applicable. For each, note whether the trait is *almost always* true (AA), *usually* true (U), *rarely* true (R), or *almost never* true (AN).

	Eros	Ludis	Storge	Mania	Ludic Eros	Storgic Eros	Storgic Ludis	Pragma
1. You consider your childhood less happy than the average of peers.	R		AN	U				
2. You were discontented with life (work, etc.) at time your encounter began.	R		AN	U	R			
3. You have never been in love before this relationship.				U	R	AN	R	
4. You want to be in love or have love as security.	R	AN		AA		AN	AN	U
5. You have a clearly defined ideal image of your desired partner.	AA	AN	AN	AN	U	AN	R	AA
6. You felt a strong gut attraction to your beloved on the first encounter.	AA	R	AN	R		AN		
7. You are preoccupied with thoughts about the beloved.	AA	AN	AN	AA			R	
8. You believe your partner's interest is at least as great as yours.		U	R	AN			R	U
9. You are eager to see your beloved almost every day; this was true from the beginning.	AA	AN	R	AA		R	AN	R
10. You soon believed this could become a permanent relationship.	AA	AN	R	AN	R	AA	AN	U
11. You see "warning signs" of trouble but ignore them.	R	R		AA		AN	R	R
12. You deliberately restrain frequency of contact with partner.	AN	AA	R	R	R	R	U	
13. You restrict discussion of your feelings with beloved.	R	AA	U	U	R		U	U
14. You restrict display of your feelings with beloved.	R	AA	R	U	R		U	U
15. You discuss future plans with beloved.	AA	R	R				AN	AA
16. You discuss wide range of topics, experiences with partner.	AA	R				U	R	AA
17. You try to control relationship, but feel you've lost control.	AN	AN	AN	AA	AN	AN		
18. You lose ability to be first to terminate relationship.	AN	AN		AA	R	U	R	R
19. You try to force beloved to show more feeling, commitment.	AN	AN		AA		AN	R	
20. You analyze the relationship, weigh it in your mind.			AN	U		R	R	AA
21. You believe in the sincerity of your partner.	AA			U	R	U	AA	
22. You blame partner for difficulties of your relationship.	R	U	R	U	R	AN		
23. You are jealous and possessive but not to the point of angry conflict.	U	AN	R		R	AN		
24. You are jealous to the point of conflict, scenes, threats, etc.	AN	AN	AN	AA	R	AN	AN	AN
25. Tactile, sensual contact is very important to you.	AA		AN		U	AN		R
26. Sexual intimacy was achieved early, rapidly in the relationship.	AA		AN	AN	U	R	U	
27. You take the quality of sexual rapport as a test of love.	AA	U	AN		U	AN	U	R
28. You are willing to work out sex problems, improve technique.	U	R		R	U		R	U
29. You have a continued high rate of sex, tactile contact throughout the relationship.	U		R	R	U	R		R
30. You declare your love first, well ahead of partner.		AN	R	AA		AA		
31. You consider love life your most important activity, even essential.	AA	AN	R	AA		AA	R	R
32. You are prepared to "give all" for love once under way.	U	AN	U	AA	R	AA	R	R
33. You are willing to suffer abuse, even ridicule from partner.		AN	R	AA			R	AN
34. Your relationship is marked by frequent differences of opinion, anxiety.	R	AA	R	AA	R	R		R
35. The relationship ends with lasting bitterness, trauma for you.	AN	R	R	AA	R	AN	R	R

To diagnose your style of love, look for patterns across characteristics. If you consider your childhood less happy than that of your friends, were discontent with life when you fell in love, and very much want to be in love, you have "symptoms" that are rarely typical of eros and almost never true of storge, but which do suggest mania. Where a trait did not especially apply to a type of love, the space in that column is blank. Storge, for instance, is not the *presence* of many symptoms of love, but precisely their absence; it is cool, abiding affection rather than *Sturm und Drang*.

SOURCE: From J. A. Lee, "The Styles of Love," *Psychology Today*, 1974. Reprinted by permission.

Why so pale and wan, fond lover?
  Prithee, why so pale?
Will, when looking well can't move her,
  Looking ill prevail?
  Prithee, why so pale?
Why so dull and mute, young sinner?
  Prithee, why so mute?
Will when speaking well can't win her,
  Saying nothing do't?
  Prithee, why so mute?
Quit, quit for shame! This will not move;
  This cannot take her.
If of herself she will not love,
  Nothing can make her.
  The devil take her!

John Suckling (1609–1642)

Beauty stands
In the admiration of weak minds
Led captive

John Milton (1608–1674)

The physical responses and sensations
accompanying sexual arousal are often labeled as
feelings of love.

I am not one of those who do not believe in
love at first sight, but I do believe in taking
a second look.

Henry Vincent (1813–1878)

love. Stimuli that generate attraction, sexual arousal, jealousy, loneliness, rejection, relief, confusion, and gratitude, for example, can all produce intense physiological arousal. "Thus, these positive *and* negative experiences may all have the potential for deepening an individual's passion for another" (Berscheid and Walster, 1974).

The way people label their physiological responses is important in determining the way they feel. In a situation in which those feelings may reasonably be labeled "love," the person may indeed experience love. We learn to label our physiological responses as we grow up. The adolescent girl may ask, "When I see Willy come into English class, my heart leaps. Does that mean I am in love?" The response is crucial. If the answer is yes, she is going to identify the feeling with love. If a boy gets nervous every time he talks to a particular girl, he may label the nervousness "love" and fall in love; if he labels the nervousness "fear" he will not fall in love with the girl and may even avoid her.

A number of unpleasant situations may generate physiological arousal, including fear, rejection, frustration, and challenge. Similarly, pleasant experiences—attraction, sexual arousal, satisfaction of needs, excitement—may facilitate passion. There are few of us who have not fallen in love or had infatuations as a result of these strange, mysterious, and wonderful physiological arousal mechanisms.

We can turn to Shakespeare (as a social psychologist) for an illustration of the two-component theory. In *A Midsummer Night's Dream,* Titania, Queen of the Fairies, is given a potion that will make her fall in love with the first being she sees when she awakens from her sleep. The love potion is a stimulant that, like certain drugs, induces intense physiological responses. This stimulation is the basis for all love potions and spells, real or imagined. In this aroused state, Titania awakens and her eyes fall on Bottom, who has just been transformed into a donkey:

TITANIA: What angel wakes me from my flowery bed? . . .
Thy fair virtue's force perforce doth move
On the first view to say, to swear, I love thee.
BOTTOM: Methinks, mistress, you should have little reason for that: and yet to say
the truth, reason and love keep little company together now-a-days

Of course, Bottom is neither wise nor beautiful; he is a donkey. But love aroused keeps no company with reason—although in a comedy about love, it is reasonable that Titania believes she is in love with a donkey. (We all may make that mistake sometimes!) When the spell induced by the potion is broken (that is, when the physiological stimuli stop), Titania comes to see Bottom as the donkey he truly is. So it is with all romantic love, according to Schacter's theory. It does not endure; indeed, it cannot endure. People cannot sustain the high degree of physiological stimulation. J.K. Folsom (quoted in Hatfield and Walter, 1981) wrote:

Love grows less exciting with time for the same biological reasons that the second run on a fast toboggan slide is less exciting than the first. The diminished excitement, however, may increase the real pleasure. Extreme excitement is practically the same as fear, and is unpleasant. After the excitement has diminished below a certain point, however, pleasure will again diminish, unless new kinds of pleasure have meanwhile arisen.

Because of the physiological arousal that accompanies sexual arousal, we can mistake sexual attraction for love, especially since we are expected to be sexually attracted to those we love. As Erich Fromm (1974) pointed out:

Because sexual desire is in the minds of most people coupled with the idea of love, they are easily misled to conclude that they love each other when they want each other physically. . . . Sexual attraction creates, for the moment, the illusion of union.

Without love, however, the illusion of oneness soon disappears and people are left as far apart as before. In some ways, remarked Fromm (1974), they become even more distant, "because when the illusion has gone they feel their estrangement even more markedly than before."

Love as Attachment

Attachment theory, the most prominent new approach to the study of love, examines love as a form of attachment that finds its roots in infancy (Hazan and Shaver, 1987; Shaver et al., 1984, 1988). Research suggests that romantic love and infant/caregiver attachment have similar emotional dynamics. Phillip Shaver and his associates (1988) suggest that "all important love relationships—especially the first ones with parents and later ones with lovers and spouses—are attachments. . . ." Based on infant/caregiver work by John Bowlby (1969, 1973, 1980), some love researchers suggest numerous similarities between attachment and romantic love (Shaver et al., 1988). These include the following:

ATTACHMENT	ROMANTIC LOVE
Attachment bond's formation and quality depends on attachment object's (AO) responsiveness and sensitivity.	Feelings of love are related to lover's interest and reciprocation.
When AO is present, infant is happier.	When lover is present, person feels happier.
Infant shares toys, discoveries, objects with AO.	Lovers share experience and goods, give gifts.
Infant coos, talks baby talk, "sings."	Lovers coo, sing, and talk baby talk.
Feelings of oneness with AO.	Feelings of oneness with lover.

Studies conducted by Mary Ainsworth and colleagues (1978, cited in Shaver et al., 1988) indicate that there are three styles of infant attachment: secure, anxious/ambivalent, and avoidant. In *secure* attachment, the infant feels secure when the mother is out of sight. He or she is confident that the mother will offer protection and care. In *anxious/ambivalent* attachment, the infant shows separation anxiety when the mother leaves. He or she feels insecure when the mother is not present. In *avoidant* attachment, the infant senses the mother's detachment and rejection when he or she desires close bodily contact. The infant shows avoidance behaviors with the mother as a means of defense. Sixty-six percent of the infants in the study were secure, 19 percent were anxious/ambivalent, and 21 percent were avoidant.

Shaver and his associates (1988) hypothesized that the styles of attachment developed during infancy continue through adulthood. They conducted several surveys with adults, which revealed similar styles of attachment.

◆ *Secure Adults.* Secure adults found it relatively easy to get close to others. They felt comfortable depending on others and having others depend on them. They didn't frequently worry about being abandoned or having someone get too close to them. More than avoidant and anxious/ambivalent adults, they felt that others generally liked them; they believed that people were generally well-intentioned and good hearted. In contrast to the other styles, secure adults were less likely to believe in media images of love and believe that romantic love can last. Their love experiences

Never seek to tell thy love
  Love that never told can be;
For the gentle wind does move
  Silently, invisibly.
I told my love, I told my love,
  I told her all my heart;
Trembling, cold, in ghastly fears,
  Ah! She did depart!
Soon as she was gone from me,
  A traveler came by,
Silently, invisibly,
  He took her with a sigh.

William Blake (1757–1827)

Love reckons hours for months, and days for years; and every little absence is an age.

John Dryden (1631–1700)

It is easier to stay out than get out.

Mark Twain

Tend to fall in Love easily - they also think sex is the ultimate bond.

tended to be happy, friendly, and trusting. They accepted and supported their partners. On the average, their relationships lasted ten years. About 56 percent of the adults in the study were secure.

◆ *Anxious/Ambivalent Adults.* Anxious/ambivalent adults felt that others did not get as close as they themselves wanted. They worried that their partners didn't really love them or would leave them. They also wanted to merge completely with another, which sometimes scared others away. More than others, they felt that it is easy to fall in love. Their experiences in love were often obsessive and marked by desire for union, high degrees of sexual attraction and jealousy, and emotional highs and lows. Their love relationships lasted an average of five years. Between 19 and 20 percent of the adults were identified as anxious/ambivalent.

◆ *Avoidant Adults.* Avoidant adults felt discomfort in being close to others; they were distrustful and fearful of becoming dependent. More than others, they believed that romance seldom lasted but that at times it could be as intense as it was at the beginning. Their partners wanted more closeness than they did. Avoidant lovers feared intimacy and experienced emotional highs and lows and jealousy. Their relationships lasted six years on the average. Between 23 and 25 percent of the adults in the study were avoidant.

In adulthood, the attachments styles developed in infancy combined with sexual desire and caring behaviors to give rise to romantic love.

❖ REFLECTIONS   *What is your attachment style in adulthood? From what you know about your infancy, is it the same or different? Do you find yourself attracted to those with similar or different attachment styles?*

❖ ASPECTS OF LOVE: FALLING IN LOVE AND UNREQUITED LOVE

Even though love has become an increasingly prominent research topic during the last decade, little research has been devoted to two common aspects of love: falling in love and unrequited love. About 90 percent of college students report having fallen in love and 75 percent have experienced unrequited love (Aron et al., 1989; Aron, Aron, and Allen, 1989).

Falling in Love

Love is such a tissue of paradoxes, and exists in such an endless variety of forms and shades that you may say almost anything about it that you please, and it is likely to be correct.

Henry Fink, Romantic Love and Personal Beauty

In the United States, everyone seems equally likely to fall in love: males and females, young children and the elderly, heterosexuals, gay men and lesbians, whites, African Americans, Latinos, and Asian Americans (Aron, Aron, Paris et al., 1989). Only recent immigrants from areas without the romantic love ethic appear exempt; and even among these immigrants, such as the Hmong, the younger generation is rapidly assimilating romantic love ideals (Meredith and Rowe, 1986). In fact, throughout the world, romantic love is increasingly displacing other forms of love, such as companionate love, as the most valued form of love (Goode, 1963). As such, falling in love—the transition from not being in love to being in love—is critical in the development of intimate relationships.

WHO FALLS IN LOVE? According to the latest research findings, there is little gender difference in overall romanticism. Those who are more expressive—whether they are male or female—tend to be more romantic (Hatfield and Rapson, 1987). More males than females, however, reported never having been in love. And more females than males—64 percent versus 46 percent—reported currently being in love (Hendrick and Hendrick, 1986).

Age seems to have little effect on falling in love. A study of romantic relationships with respondents from the ages of four through eighteen years found little difference in intensity of love between very young children and late adolescents. Males and females experienced the same high emotional levels except at ages ten through twelve years, when the intensity fell dramatically for boys (Hatfield and Rapson, 1987). Among middle-aged men and women, passionate love appears to be as frequent as for younger adults. It is reasonable to suppose that the elderly also may fall in love, although there are no studies of love among the elderly.

Personality traits appear to have a strong influence on falling in love. Attachment styles seem to affect whether one falls in love. In one study (Hazan and Shaver, 1987), the researchers found that almost no avoidants and only 9 to 15 percent of securely attached men and women reported that it was easy for them to fall in love. Twenty to thirty percent of anxious/ambivalents, however, indicated that falling in love was easy. Other researchers used Lee's six styles of love to determine the relationship between falling in love and style of loving. They found that those who had been in love or were currently in love scored higher on ludic (playful) love and lower on eros (romantic/passionate love) and agape (selfless love) compared to those who had not been or were not currently in love (Hendrick and Hendrick, 1986).

Individuals also appear to have a "readiness" to fall in love. Men and women are more likely to fall in love when they have temporarily lowered self-esteem, such as following a breakup, when they are looking for adventure, or when they are desiring to have a close relationship.

WHERE DO PEOPLE FALL IN LOVE? The setting *where* people fall in love appears to be important. Fifty-eight percent of the respondents in one study (Aron, Dutton, Aron, and Iverson, 1989) indicated that the circumstances in which they met were "unusual," and 34 percent said that they felt isolated or special in relation to the people around them. Romantic settings—such as a party, a candlelit dinner, or a deserted beach—give cues that romantic feelings are appropriate. In keeping with the two-component theory of love, one aspect of unusual circumstances is the generation of strong emotion or physiological arousal, which increases the likelihood of attraction.

SELF-DISCLOSURE AND RECIPROCITY. Revealing oneself is important in falling in love, but the mere disclosure of feelings is not the key element. Self-disclosure is most meaningful if you reveal to the other person that you like him or her. Being liked by the other person, whether it is revealed through words, eye contact, or physical contact, is a powerful force to induce you to like someone. In fact, it may be *the* most important factor.

Paradoxically, not *being* liked can also encourage falling in love. Some men and women respond to the challenge of overcoming another's resistance. In fact, some studies suggest that we like those better who initially disliked or refused us than those who liked us all along.

Unrequited Love

As most of us know from painful experience, love is not always returned. We may reassure ourselves that, as Tennyson wrote 150 years ago, "'Tis better to have loved and lost/Than never to have loved at all." Too often, however, such words sound like

I will reveal to you a love potion, without medicine, without herbs, without any witch's magic. If you want to be loved, then you must love.

Hecaton of Rhodes

The heart is wild. It spins through nebulae that burn like mercury. And it is not vanquished by the darkness it traverses. Love—or even its possibility—requires that we live fantastically.

Earl Jackson, Jr.

No disguise can long conceal love where it exists, nor long feign it where it is lacking.

François de La Rochefoucauld

*'Tis better to have loved and lost
Than never to have loved at all.*

Alfred, Lord Tennyson (1809–1892)

*My love is like to ice, and I to fire:
How comes it then that this her cold so
    great
Is not dissolved through my so hot desire,
But harder grows the more I her entreat?
Or how come it that my exceeding heat
Is not allayed by her heart-frozen cold,
But that I burn much more in boiling
    sweat,
And feel my flames augmented manifold?
What more miraculous thing may be
    told
That fire, which all things melts, should
    harden ice,
And ice, which is congeal'd with senseless
    cold,
Should kindle fire by wonderful device?
Such is the power of love in gentle
    mind,
That it can alter all the course of kind.*

Edmund Spenser (16th Century)

*Absence makes the heart grow fonder; then
you forget.*

Floyd Zimmerman

*Love is a flickering flame between two
darknesses . . . . Whence does it
come? . . . From sparks incredibly
small. . . . How does it end? . . . In
nothingness equally incredible . . . The
more raging the flame, the sooner it is
burnt out.*

Heinrich Heine (1797–1856)

rationalizations. Who among us does not sometimes think, "'Tis better never to have loved at all"? Unrequited love is a common experience; a recent study found that about 75 percent of its respondents had experienced it and about 20 percent were currently experiencing it (Aron, Aron, and Allen, 1989). Many people find their lives—and sleep—disrupted by unrequited love.

Unrequited love presents a paradox: If the goal of loving someone is an intimate relationship, why should we continue to love a person with whom we could not have such a relationship? Arthur Aron and his colleages addressed this question in a study of almost 500 college students (Aron et al., 1989). The researchers found three different motivations underlying the experience of unrequited love.

◆ *The Cyrano style*—the desire to have a romantic relationship, with a specific person regardless of how hopeless the love is. In this style, the benefits of loving someone are so great that it does not matter how likely the love is to be returned. Being in the same room with the beloved—because he or she is *so* wonderful—may be sufficient reason for loving someone who does not reciprocate. This style is named after Cyrano de Bergerac, whose love for Roxanne was so great it was irrelevant that she loved someone else.

◆ *The Giselle style*—the misperception that a relationship is more likely to develop than it actually is. This might occur if one misreads the other's cues, such as mistakenly believing that friendliness is a sign of love. This style is named after Giselle, the tragic ballet heroine who was misled by Count Albrecht to believe that her love was reciprocated.

◆ *The Don Quixote style*—the general desire to be in love, regardless of whom one loves. In this style, the benefits of being in love—such as being viewed as a romantic or the excitement of extreme emotions—are more important than actually being in a relationship. This style is named after Don Quixote, whose love for the common Dulcinea was motivated by his need to dedicate knightly deeds to a lady love. "It is as right and proper for a knight errant to be in love as for the sky to have stars," Don Quixote explained.

Using styles-of-attachment theory, the researchers found that some people were predisposed to be Cyranos, other Giselles, and still others Don Quixotes. Anxious/ambivalents tended to be Cyranos, avoidants were Don Quixotes, and secures were Giselles. Those with anxious/ambivalent attachment styles were most likely to experience unrequited love; those with secure attachment styles were least likely to experience such love. Avoidants experienced the greatest desire to be in love in general, yet they had the least probability of being in a specific relationship. Anxious/ambivalents showed the greatest desire for a specific relationship; they also had the least desire to be in love in general.

❖ THE TRANSFORMATION OF LOVE: FROM PASSION TO INTIMACY

The Instability of Passionate Love

Ultimately, romantic love may be transformed or replaced by a quieter, more lasting love. Otherwise, the relationship will likely break up and each person will search for another who will once again ignite his or her passion.

THE PASSAGE OF TIME: CHANGES IN INTIMACY, PASSION, AND COMMITMENT. According to researcher Robert Sternberg (1988), time affects our levels of intimacy, passion and commitment.

Intimacy over Time. When we first meet someone, intimacy increases rapidly as we make critical discoveries about each other, ranging from our innermost thoughts about life and death to our preference for strawberry or chocolate ice cream. As the relationship continues, the rate of growth decreases and then levels off. After the growth levels off, the couple no longer "consciously" feels as close to each other. This may be because they actually are beginning to drift apart, or it may be because they are continuing to grow intimate at a different, less conscious, but deeper level. It is the kind of intimacy that is not easily observed. Instead, it is a latent intimacy that nevertheless is forging stronger, more enduring bonds between them.

Passion over Time. Passion is subject to habituation: what was once thrilling, whether it be love, sex, or roller coasters, becomes less so the more we get used to it. Once we become habituated, more time with a person (or more sex or more roller coaster rides) does not increase our arousal or satisfaction.

If the person leaves, however, we experience withdrawal symptoms (fatigue, depression, anxiety), just as if we were addicted. In becoming habituated, we have also become dependent. We fall beneath the emotional baseline we were at when we met our partner. Over time, however, we begin to return to that original level.

Commitment over Time. Unlike intimacy and passion, time does not necessarily diminish, erode, or alter commitments. Our commitments are most affected by how successful our relationship is. Initially, commitment grows more slowly than intimacy or passion. As the relationship becomes long-term, commitment growth levels off. Our commitment will remain high as long as we judge the relationship to be successful. If the relationship begins to deteriorate, after a time the commitment will probably decrease. Eventually it may disappear and an alternative relationship may be sought.

DISAPPEARANCE OF ROMANCE AS CRISIS. The disappearance (or transformation) of passionate love is often experienced as a crisis in a relationship. A study of college students (Berscheid, 1983) found that half would seek divorce if passion disappeared from their marriage. But intensity of feeling does not necessarily measure depth of love. Intensity, like the excitement of toboggan runs, diminishes over time. It is then that we begin to discover if the love we experience for each other is one that will endure.

Our search for enduring love is complicated by our contradictory needs. Elaine Hatfield and William Walster (1981) wrote:

What we really want is the impossible—a perfect mixture of security and danger. We want someone who understands and cares for us, someone who will be around through thick and thin, until we are old. At the same time, we long for sexual excitement, novelty, and danger. The individual who offers just the right combination of both ultimately wins our love. The problem, of course, is that, in time, we get more and more security—and less and less excitement—than we bargained for.

The disappearance of passionate love, however, enables individuals to refocus their relationship. They are given the opportunity to move from an intense one-on-one togetherness that excludes others to one that includes family, friends, and external goals and projects. They can look outward on the world together.

THE REEMERGENCE OF ROMANTIC LOVE. Contrary to what pessimists believe, many people find that they can have both love and romance and that the rewards of intimacy include romance. One researcher (Knox, 1970), in a study of dating high

---

Love is patient and kind; love is not jealous or boastful; it is not arrogant or rude. Love does not insist on its own way; it is not irritable or resentful; it does not rejoice at wrong, but rejoices in the right. Love bears all things, believes all things, hopes all things, endures all things.

I Corinthians 13: 4–7

if your relationship is only passion you will never have love. It will END you will recover over time

Love and you shall be loved. All love is mathematically just, as much as two sides of an algebraic equation.

Ralph Waldo Emerson (1803–1882)

Love is unjust; justice loveless.

Delmore Schwartz

It is only with the heart that one can see rightly; what is essential is invisible to the eye.

Antoine de Saint-Exupery, The Little Prince

PERSPECTIVE

Love and Sexuality

Love and sexuality are intimately connected in our culture (Aron and Aron, 1991). We can see this if we look at some of the words we use to describe sexual intercourse. When we say that we "make love" or are "intimate" with someone, we generally mean that we are sexually involved. But this sexual involvement carries overtones of relationship, caring, or love; it possesses potential richness of meaning. Such meanings are absent in the more technical terms *sexual intercourse* and *coitus* or the obscene *fuck* or *screw*.

Although love and sexuality are connected, researchers have been unable to agree on the nature of that connection (see Aron and Aron, 1991, for a literature review). In the sociobiological perspective, males, who are constantly fertile from early adolescence on, seek to impregnate as many females as possible to insure the continuation of their genes. For males, sex is important. Females ovulate only once a month, however; a single act of intercourse can result in pregnancy, childbirth, and years of childrearing. For women, it is important to be selective about choosing a partner with whom to pass on their genes. Women want partners on whom they can rely for childrearing and support. As a result, love is important for females. Love is their guarantee that males will remain with them to share childrearing tasks. Females trade sex for love, and males trade love for sex.

By contrast, sociologist Ira Reiss (1986) argues that reproduction is secondary to sex. Instead, the essential aspects of sex are pleasure and self-disclosure. The altered consciousness involved in sexual arousal permits a unique "psychic release." In this, the "elemental physical and emotional disclosures of sexuality can further

and deepen psychic disclosures." These deep disclosures help promote and sustain love.

Exchange theorists give sex and love about equal weight in close relationships. Both are interpersonal resources that are exchanged by partners and influence the relationship (Safilios-Rothschild, 1976). Researchers (Rettig and Bulbolz, 1983) found that among married men and women, there was a high correlation between the degree of love and the quality of sex. The greater the love, the better the sex.

Other researchers emphasize love, making sexuality less important in relationships. Hatfield and Walster (1978) view sexuality as somewhat important in romantic love and of little significance in companionate love. And, using Lee's styles of loving, Hendrick and Hendrick (1987) found sex to be related to the love style: erotic lovers were "intense" about their sexuality, whereas pragmatic lovers were "practical." They concluded that "love and sexuality were strongly linked to each other and to both the physical and spiritual aspects of the human condition."

Sex is most highly valued in our culture when it is linked with love. In fact, sex with affection rivals marriage as the accepted moral standard of sexual inter-

course. With the "sex with affection" standard of premarital intercourse, we use individualistic rather than social norms to legitimize sexual relations. Our sexual standards are now personal rather than institutional. Researchers report that those in love tend to be less permissive in their sexual attitudes than those not in love. Lovers are also less instrumental in their views about sexuality than those not in love. For lovers, sex is more an expression of intimacy than an exchange of pleasures (Hendrick and Hendrick, 1988).

Relationships change, sometimes dramatically, after an individual first engages in sexual intercourse with a new partner. A person with whom someone has intercourse, even if he or she is a stranger, is no longer like any other person. "After coitus," wrote Gagnon (1977), "the couple will change, with reference to themselves, to each other, and to their surrounding social world." Sexual intercourse represents a new or different degree of intimacy. Each person consciously or unconsciously evaluates what the sexual act means. Does it mean that intimacy has been increased or that boundaries have been violated? Is it a call for greater commitment or for distancing? Is it a sign of love or indifference?

Men, Sex, and Love

Men and women who are not in an established relationship have different expectations. Men are more likely than women to separate sex from affection. Studies consistently demonstrate that for the majority of men, sex and love are not intimately connected (Blumstein and Schwartz, 1983; Carroll et al., 1985).

Although men are more likely than women to separate sex and love, Levine and

school seniors, couples married for less than five years, and couples married for more than twenty years, found that romantic love did not die. Instead, its conceptualization changed to include more realistic elements. Intimacy was added to feelings of love. In fact, romantic love was strongest among dating couples and those married more than twenty years.

male will think the woman is worth something. They will remember the friendship.

Chapter 5 ◆ Love, Commitment, and Intimacy   139

PERSPECTIVE

Barbach (1985) found in their interviews that men indicated that their most erotic sexual experiences took place in a relational context. The researchers quoted one man:

Emotions are everything when it comes to sex. There's no greater feeling than having an emotional attachment with the person you're making love to. If those emotions are there, it's going to be fabulous. . . . They don't call it "making love" for nothing.

Most men in the study responded that it was primarily the emotional quality of the relationship that made their sexual experiences special.

Women, Sex, and Love

Women generally view sex from a relational perspective. In the decision to have sexual intercourse, the quality and degree of intimacy of a relationship were more important for women than men (Christopher and Cate, 1984). Women were more likely to report feelings of love if they were sexually involved with their partners than if they were not sexually involved (Peplau et al., 1977).

While women generally seek emotional relationships, some men initially seek physical relationships. This difference in intentions can place women in a bind. Carole Cassell (1984) suggests that today's women face a "damned if you do, damned if you don't" dilemma in their sexual relationships. If a woman has sexual intercourse with a man, he says goodbye; if she doesn't, he says he respects here *and* still says goodbye. A young woman Cassell interviewed related the following:

I really hate the idea that, because I'm having sex with a man whom I haven't known for a long, long time, he'll think I don't value myself. But it's hard to know what to do. If you meet a man and date him two or three times and don't have sex, he begins to feel you are either rejecting him or you have serious sex problems. . . . But I really dread feeling that I could turn into, in his eyes, an easy lay, a good-time girl. I want men to see me as a grown-up woman who has the same right as they do to make sexual choices.

Traditionally, women were labeled "good" or "bad" based on their sexual experience and values. "Good" women were virgins, sexually naive, or passive, whereas "bad" women were sexually experienced, independent, and passionate.

Sex without Love

Is love necessary for sex? We assume that it is, but that assumption is one of motives and values. It cannot be answered by reference to empirical or statistical data (Crosby, 1985). The question becomes a more fundamental one: Is sexual activity legitimate in itself, or does it require justification? John Crosby (1985) observed:

Our society and culture . . . have held, at least implicitly, that sexual expression must be justified before it is acceptable. This justification has assumed several forms, including procreation, the expression of marital privilege, and the expression of love and affection. . . . [S]exual pleasure is a value in itself and hence capable of being inherently meaningful and rewarding. The search for extrinsic justification and rationalization simply belies our reluctance to believe that sex is a pleasurable activity in and of itself.

To believe that sex does not require love as a justification, argues Crosby, does not deny the significance of love and affection in sexual relations. In fact, love and affection are important and desirable for enduring relationships. They are simply not necessary, Crosby believes, for affairs in which erotic pleasure is the central feature.

Albert Ellis (1958) similarly argued that, although love and affection are desirable, they are not necessary. People can have satisfying erotic involvement with friends, acquaintances, or strangers, he believed. He made several points in his argument. First, many individuals find great satisfaction in sexual relations without love. Second, the majority of people who find greater satisfaction in sex with love probably do not do so their entire lives. Especially in their youth, such people probably found sex without love satisfying. Third, many people who condemn sex without love have not thought out their views carefully; there are times when they probably would find sex without love very satisfying.

Over a person's lifetime, affectional sex is probably most rewarding, argued Ellis, because it connects people with each other's emotional and intellectual dimensions. "I can easily see, however, even the most intelligent and highly cultured individuals spending a *little* time with members of the other sex with whom they have common sex and cultural but no real love interests" (Ellis, 1958).

❖ REFLECTIONS *What is the relationship between love and sex for you? Do your actions always follow your beliefs?* In your own experience, do you believe men and women perceive the relationship between love and sex differently? Do you and your partner generally agree about the relationship between love and sex?

Romantic love may be highest during the early part of marriage and decline as stresses from childrearing and work intrude on the relationship. Most studies suggest that marital satisfaction proceeds along a U-shaped curve, with highest satisfactions in the early and late periods (see Chapter 10). Romantic love may be affected by the same stresses as general marital satisfaction. In fact, romantic love begins to increase as children leave home (Knox, 1970). In later life, romantic love may play an important role in alleviating the stresses of retirement and illness. Aging adults find that emotional security and loyalty are often more important than sexual intimacy or communication (Reedy et al., 1981).

Intimate Love: Commitment, Caring, and Self-Disclosure

Beware, my Lord, of jealousy. It is the green-eyed monster that mocks the meat it feeds on.

William Shakespeare, Othello

Although love is one of the most important elements of our humanity, it may come and go. Perhaps one of the most profound questions about love is, as novelist Tom Robbins (1980) wrote, how to make it last:

Albert Camus wrote that the only serious question is whether to kill yourself or not. Tom Robbins wrote that the only serious question is whether time has a beginning or end. Camus clearly got up on the wrong side of the bed, and Robbins must have forgotten to set his alarm. There is only one serious question. And that is, Who knows how to make love stay?

The kind of love that seems to stay is what we might call intimate love. In this love, each person knows he or she can count on the other. The excitement comes from the achievement of other goals—from creativity, from work, from childrearing, from friendships—as well as from the relationship. Hatfield and Walster (1981) wrote:

A husband and wife often enjoy being able to count on the fact that, while their friends must contend with one emotional upheaval after another, their lives drift on in a serene, unruffled flow. They enjoy the fact that they can share day-to-day pleasures and that, in old age, they'll be together to reminisce and savor their lives. This portrait is very alluring.

The key to making love stay does not seem to be in love's passionate intensity but in transforming it into intimate love. Intimate love is based on commitment, caring, and self-disclosure.

Being physically limited does not necessarily inhibit love and sexuality anymore than being able-bodied guarantees them.

COMMITMENT. Commitment is an important component of intimate love, for it is a "determination to continue" a relationship or marriage in the face of bad times as well as good (Reiss, 1980). It is based on conscious choice rather than on feelings, which, by their very nature, are transitory. Commitment is a promise of a shared future, a promise to be together come what may.

Commitment has become an important concept in recent years. We seem to be as much in search of commitment as we are in search of love or marriage. We speak of "making a commitment" to someone or to a relationship. (Among singles, commitment is sometimes referred to as "the C-word.") A "committed" relationship has become almost a stage of courtship, somewhere between dating and being engaged or living together.

CARING. Caring is the commitment to place another's needs before your own. As such, caring requires that you treat your partner as an end in himself or herself. It requires what the philosopher Martin Buber called an *I-Thou relationship*. Buber described two fundamental ways of relating to people: I-Thou and I-It. In an I-Thou relationship, each person is treated as a Thou—that is, as a person whose life is valued as an end in itself. In an I-It relationship, each person is treated as an It; the person has worth only as someone who can be used. When a person is treated as a Thou, his or her humanity and uniqueness are paramount.

SELF-DISCLOSURE. When we self-disclose, we reveal ourselves—our hopes, our fears, our everyday thoughts—to others. Self-disclosure deepens others' understanding of us. It also deepens our own understanding, for we discover unknown aspects as we open ourselves to others.

Without self-disclosure, we remain opaque and hidden. If others love us, such love leaves us with anxiety: are we loved for ourselves or for the image we present to the world?

Together, these elements help transform love. But in the final analysis, perhaps the most important means of sustaining love is our words and actions; caring words and deeds provide the setting for maintaining and expanding love (Byrne and Murnen, 1988).

◆ The study of love is only beginning, but it is already helping us to understand the various components that make up love. Although there is something to be said for the mystery of love, understanding how it works in the day-to-day world may help us keep our love vital and alive.

There is no love apart from the deeds of love; no potentiality of love than that which is manifested in loving. . . .

Jean-Paul Sartre, Existentialism as Humanism

She knew a great deal about pulleys and hoists but nothing about love. She went to the library to look up as she had looked up the mechanical advantages of pulleys. Surely great writers and great lovers of the past had written things worth reading. Here were some of the things great writers had written:

Love begets love
Love conquers all things
Love ends with hope
Love is a flame to burn out human ills
Love is all truth
Love is truth and truth is beauty
Love is blind
Love is the best
Love is heaven and heaven is love
Love is love's reward

"Oh my God," she said aloud in the library and smacked her head. "What does all that mean? These people are crazier than I am!"

Walker Percy, The Second Coming

❖ SUMMARY

◆ *Prototypes* of love and commitment are models of how people define these two ideas in everyday life. The central aspects of the love prototype include trust, caring, honesty, friendship, respect, and concern for the other; central aspects of the commitment prototype include loyalty, responsibility, living up to one's word, faithfulness, and trust.

◆ Attitudes and feelings associated with love include caring, needing, trusting, and tolerating. Behaviors associated with love include verbal, nonverbal, and physical expression of affection, self-disclosure, giving of nonmaterial and material evidence, and tolerance. *Commitment* is affected by the balance of costs to benefits, normative inputs, and structural constraints.

◆ According to John Lee, there are six basic styles of love: *eros, mania, ludis, storge, agape,* and *pragma.*

◆ The *two-component theory* of human emotions suggests that physiological arousal and an appropriate emotional explanation for the arousal must be present for love to occur.

◆ The *attachment theory* of love views love as being similar in nature to the attachments we form as infants. The attachment (love) styles of both infants and adults are *secure, anxious/ambivalent,* and *avoidant.*

◆ *Falling in love* is the transition from not being in love to being in love. There is little difference in levels of romanticism between men and women, young and old. Attachment style tends to influence falling in love: anxious/ambivalents fall in love most easily. People tend to fall in love in unusual situations or when they have felt isolated or special in relation to others. Disclosure of liking the other person is important in having love reciprocated.

◆ *Unrequited love* is a common experience. There are three styles of unrequited love: (1) the *Cyrano style,* the desire to have a relationship with another, regardless of how hopeless, (2) the *Giselle style,* the misperception that a relationship is more likely to develop than it is, and (3) the *Don Quixote style,* the general desire to be in love. Anxious/ambivalents are most likely to be Cyranos, avoidants to be Don Quixotes and secures to be Giselles.

◆ Time affects romantic relationships. The rapid growth of intimacy tends to level off, and we become habituated to passion. Commitment tends to increase, provided that the relationship is judged to be rewarding.

◆ Romantic love tends to diminish. It may either end or be replaced by intimate love. Many individuals experience the disappearance of romantic love as a crisis. Romantic love seems to be most prominent in adolescence and in early and later stages of marriage. Intimate love is based on commitment, caring, and self-disclosure.

Answers to Preview Questions

The answers to the preview questions at the beginning of the chapter are listed below. As you check your answers, whether you were correct or not, think about your reasons for each response. What were they? What was their source? How valid is the source? As you read the chapter, you will find the questions discussed in greater depth.

1. T		6. T	
2. T		7. F	
3. F		8. F	
4. F		9. F	
5. T		10. F	

❖ SUGGESTED READINGS

Aron, Arthur, and Elaine Aron. *Love and the Expansion of Self.* New York: Hemisphere Publishing Co., 1986. A theoretical exploration of love that integrates social psychology with Eastern thought.

Bellah, Robert. *Habits of the Heart: Individualism and Commitment in American Life.* Berkeley, Calif.: University of California Press, 1985 (paperback). A reflective book examining the traditional American conflict between individuality and community; in marriage and the family, this conflict leads to a tension between independence and commitment.

Buscaglia, Leo. *Loving Each Other.* New York: Ballantine Books, 1984 (paperback). America's most popular proponent of love in a series of thoughtful essays about relationships.

Hatfield, Elaine, and William Walster. *A New Look at Love.* Reading, Mass.: Addison-Wesley, 1981 (paperback). A breezy but serious examination of love from a sociological perspective.

Lawrence, D. H. *Women in Love.* New York: Penguin Books, 1976. One of the great novels of the twentieth century, which explores in shimmering prose the "sacred mysteries" of love and sexuality.

Peck, M. Scott. *The Road Less Traveled: A New Psychology of Love, Traditional Values, and Spiritual Growth.* New York: Simon and Schuster, 1978 (paperback). A psychological/spiritual approach to love that sees love's goal as spiritual growth.

Singer, Irving. *The Nature of Love.* 3 vols. Chicago: University of Chicago Press, 1987. A philosopher's examination of the history of love from the ancient Greek philosopher Plato to the twentieth-century French existential philosopher Jean-Paul Sartre.

Sternberg, Robert, and Michael Barnes, eds. *The Psychology of Love.* New Haven, Conn.: Yale University Press, 1988. An excellent collection of essays by some of the leading researchers into love.

White, Greg, and Paul Mullen. *Jealousy: A Clinical and Multidisciplinary Approach.* New York: Guilford, 1989. A comprehensive examination of what we know about jealousy (and its treatment).

Suggested Films

Beauty and the Beast (French; 1946). Jean Cocteau's surrealistic rendition of the popular fairy tale about the transforming power of love.

Cyrano de Bergerac (French; 1990). Cyrano is a swordsman and poet whose tragic love story makes him *the* unrequited lover; portrayed by Gérard Depardieu. An earlier, and even more romantic, version starred José Ferrer, who won an Oscar for his portrayal in 1951 (also on videocassette). Steve Martin's *Roxanne* was loosely based on Edmond Rostand's play; also on videocassete.

Romeo and Juliet (1967). Shakespeare's archetypal play of star-crossed lovers transformed into a powerful film. What happens, to use modern jargon, when families fail to be supportive of a relationship.

Sherman's March (1988). A filmmaker looks up old girlfriends to understand love in 20th century America in this wry documentary.

Torchsong Triology (1989). The comic, moving story of a female impersonator's search for love. Based on Tony-winning play.

MAKING LOVE WORK

Robert Sternberg. Excerpt from *Love the Way You Want It.*

The author is one of the leading researchers on love in this country. In this excerpt from his book, Sternberg tries to combine the results of social science research on love with a practical application. Sternberg believes that love requires ten qualities. Do you think that these qualities are the most important ones? Why? Would you include other qualities?

You Tolerate Ambiguity   Relationships are inherently ambiguous. Much of the time, it is hard to pinpoint exactly what is going on. Some people are willing to accept ambiguity as a given in a relationship and work to improve communication to reduce its negative consequences. But for others, ambiguity is a constant source of frustration and unhappiness.

In the first blush of love, we make promises, and mean them. We say, "I'll never leave you," "I'll never hurt you," "I'll always feel this way about you." We try, with our words and our wills, to pin down the future, in the same way that the Three Little Pigs sealed their house against the wolf's attack. But there is no way to be absolutely secure in life. People who are successful at love accept ambiguity. More than that, they are able to rejoice in the mysterious turns of life.

You See Obstacles as Challenges   Sooner or later, every relationship runs into obstacles. They might be financial, parental, career-related, sexual, or any number of things. People who thrive in relationships are those who are willing to accept obstacles as challenges rather than as signs of defeat.

Unless you accept obstacles as part of the challenge of a relationship, it is unlikely that you will be very successful. Moreover, your ability to overcome difficulties will be greatly enhanced if your partner feels the same way. It is much easier to get over the rough spots if both of you strive to do so, rather than if one of you carries all the burden. If one of you carries the burden, you may force change occasionally, but it probably won't work over the long term. When you both contribute, you can usually overcome your problems. Indeed, this is one of the cornerstones of a good relationship.

Viewing your problems as challenges is not a stoic posture. It doesn't mean "grin and bear it." Rather, it is having a deep curiosity about life, a tendency to ask, when problems arise, "What is this teaching me? How can I turn this problem into something of value?"

You Embrace the Future   "Nothing ventured, nothing gained," goes the old saying. People who succeed in relationships are those who are willing to try new things. They are not afraid to open themselves up to the possibilities that the future offers. If you remain stuck in the present, with an eye to the past, you may never get hurt—at least, not in the way you have learned to think about hurt. But you'll never be where the action in life is, either.

Embracing the future does not mean that you behave like a stuntman, crashing against life at every turn. Being a thrill-seeker won't help you achieve a mastery of love. The challenge is not to seek out risks, but rather to accept them when they present themselves.

You Seek Growth   Truly creative people are always growing. They understand that life is a dynamic process and that to stand still is to stagnate. The myth of living "happily ever after" denies the necessity of growth and change. Life is not like that, and neither are relationships. Relationships require ongoing renewal, and sometimes they change in major ways. Successful couples are not afraid to change and grow.

There is always the danger in a relationship that you might grow apart. When you first meet someone, you may find that you are compatible and that you get along well because you are at a point in your lives when your needs are closely matched. But it's possible that the person who attracts you now may not have attracted you at another time in your life when your mutual needs were not as similar. It is important to realize that the closeness you feel now may not continue or be easily maintained. The most difficult task in a relationship is often being able to grow together rather than apart. To accomplish this, you need to put as much communication, support, and sharing into your relationship as possible.

The willingness to grow and take responsibility for one's life is a fundamental quality of a successful relationship. Furthermore, this quality is essential to the ability to live productively. When we allow ourselves to be stuck in a negative self-story, we do not take advantage of the gift of life.

You Believe in Yourself   There will be many times, during the course of a relationship, when you will find yourself questioning your judgment, possibly even your sanity. There may be times when you begin to lose belief in yourself and begin to doubt that you have made the right decisions. Indeed, it is impossible to be involved in a close relationship without making mistakes. But one of the most important lessons about intelligence is that smart people are not people who never make mistakes; they are people who learn something of value from their mistakes. The ultimate test of Relationship Intelligence is how much you learn from your mistakes and how well you apply what you learn.

An important skill to develop is the ability to detach yourself from your mistakes and view them objectively. Ultimately, you are the person you are, not only because of your successes, but also because of your failures. But whether you succeed or fail, you need to keep the courage of your convictions and your

continued on next page

belief in yourself. If you don't believe in yourself, you can't expect anyone else to believe in you.

You Are Willing to Forgive   I know people who pride themselves on never forgetting or forgiving a slight. They possess photographic memories for what they perceive to be insults or wrongs, and they are willing to wait months, sometimes years, to get their revenge. Or they "get back" in more passive ways, reminding the person who hurt them of the past behavior. As a result, they continue, year after year, to throw hand grenades into the relationship.

If you find that you are struggling to forgive your partner for a past mistake, you should examine what your end goal is. Are you interested in finding a way to make your relationship better, or are you more interested in punishing your partner and making him or her suffer? Your answer to this question will determine whether you will be open to resolving your conflicts and growing in your relationship.

You Can Accept Others as They Are   Most people have at least some desire to exert control over others. We imagine what we would like other people to be, and then, consciously or unconsciously, we try to mold them into the image we have created. Some of the changes for which we work may be genuinely constructive. But too often we ask others to be what they are not. Sometimes people fall in love with an image, not the reality, and spend their relationships resenting that their partners cannot be what they never were.

You are never going to find anyone who is the perfect image of what you are looking for. So find someone whose perceived flaws are ones you can live with and accept them, just as you hope that person will accept your flaws. This is not to say that you should never try to help a person improve. But you must understand that improvement can't be forced from the outside; it must come from within.

Sometimes the thrill or romance can dazzle us to the point where we put off confronting the truth about a person. We avoid examining real issues, such as: Is this a person whose goals and life-style match what we want in life? A decision to commit to another person is also a decision to accept that person for what he or she is.

You Are Optimistic   A bottle half empty is also a bottle half full. How you describe it has to do with your inner sense of optimism. It is a lot easier, and generally more satisfying, to live with a person who sees the bottle half full than one who sees it half empty. Almost any turn of events can be construed in a way that is either more positive or more negative. If you turn every disagreement into a major crisis and every misfortune into a major disaster, or if you look for the downside of every happy event, you will succeed not only in making yourself miserable, but in doing the same for those around you.

Some people wait for happiness to come to them, expecting it to appear as a bolt out of the blue. They do not seek it out, nor do nor do they recognize it in the life they have. If you do not possess the quality of optimism, it will be hard for you to truly succeed in a relationship. Relationships constantly demand that we operate from our hopes not our fears. They challenge us to find the possibilities in every struggle. If you're predisposed to look on the gloomy side, even the everyday hassles of being in a relationship might feel overwhelming.

You Have Patience   When things aren't going our way, we often need patience to allow time for them to work themselves out. We do not live in an age when people are very good at delaying gratification. But sometimes we would be much happier if we were willing to wait for gratification, rather than insisting on having everything right away.

In matters of love, we are especially reluctant to let time take its course. We cannot stand to be without a mate and when we find someone we like, we want to rush into commitment. There is a sense of desperation underlying our search for love, a fear that we might miss out on it altogether and be lonely forever.

Successful relationships are not born from desperation. Nor do they happen overnight. It takes time to develop the bond of intimacy that is needed to make a relationship strong and enduring. The term "love at first sight" would be better phrased as "passion at first sight." And the urgency of passion is not a sufficient foundation for a lasting relationship.

Your Love Is Selfless   If I were asked the single most frequent cause of the destruction of relationships, and the single biggest contributor to "dumb love," I would say it is selfishness. We live in an age of narcissism and many people have never learned or have forgotten how to listen to the needs of others. The truth is, if you want to make just one change in yourself that will improve your relationship—literally, overnight—it would be to put your partner's interests on an equal footing with your own. Selflessness does not mean that you sacrifice your own wants and needs for another person's. Rather, it is the ability to achieve a balance in your relationship. You respect your partner and consider his or her needs as being just as important as yours. And you possess the quality of compassion—the ability to recognize and respond during those times when your partner needs more attention than you do.

Selfishness is usually based in a fear people have that, once they open the door, they will be swept away by a violent tide and soon lose all of their freedom and individuality. On the other hand, I have observed people who *always* put others' needs ahead of their own, claiming that their needs are not worthy of equal consideration. The concept of equality transcends both of these responses. The quality of selflessness allows two people to be everything they can be as individuals, while they grow as a couple.

READINGS

ON JEALOUSY

Leo Buscaglia. Excerpt from *Loving Each Other.*

What is Buscaglia's attitude toward jealousy? Are any of your feelings of jealousy similar to the ones he describes? Have you found that for yourself jealousy is "an all-consuming monster" or "a challenge for you to grow in self-respect and personal knowledge"? Why?

Since few of us who choose to form relationships with others will be totally free of jealousy, perhaps it would be best to look at better, more lasting ways to come to terms with the emotion. The great psychoanalyst/philosopher Theodore Reich has said, "Jealousy is a sign that something is wrong, not necessarily rotten, in the organism of love." Perhaps seeing jealousy as a warning of "something wrong" is the first positive step to its being corrected, since to fight or try to negate jealousy doesn't actually solve anything. The only real solution to jealousy seems to be to work it out. Feeling a strong emotion is necessary to making changes. Anthropologist Margaret Mead has suggested that jealousy is an emotion which is "a festering spot in every personality so affected, an ineffective, negativistic attitude which is more likely to lose than gain any goal." But, she admits that it may be of value for it may be responsible for the passion, the intensity, from which is born enterprise. In her anthropological studies of the people of Samoa she found no jealousy, but she also found few strong feelings, competition, or motivation.

We are responsible for our jealousy, no one else. Blaming others for what we feel, can lead nowhere. Change will only begin when we are willing to accept our jealousy as our responsibility, not necessarily bad unless negatively acted upon. Relieving others of our responsibility, we can then begin the productive processes necessary for finding out what can be done about it.

Rollo May, the famous analyst, has said:

Jealousy requires turning one's attention to one's self and asking why is my self-esteem so low in the first place? I quite understand that this question may be difficult to answer. But at least it turns your concern to an area you can do something about.

Persons who cling to jealousy destroy *themselves.* They use energies for dead-end feelings which could be channeled into creative solutions. Of course, no one chooses to be jealous, it simply happens. What is essential is to change the values and beliefs which created the response. Jealousy generates much feeling, but actually produces little action. It becomes an insidious process which keeps us from seeing accurately what there is. It nurtures only itself. It succeeds only in making us feel impotent. As such, jealousy is most often a product of our personal insecu-

rity and low self-esteem. It occurs because we see ourselves as having less to give than the object of our jealousy. It steals our rationality. We become unable to see our strengths and allow ourselves to be overcome by what we are convinced are weaknesses and inadequacies. We feel valueless. We lose our sense of dignity and worth. We become frenzied, paralyzed or afraid to act. We forget the simple fact that because someone does not elect to meet whatever conditions have been imposed in our relationship, our true inner value as a person is not diminished, nor is theirs. We forget that we cannot force anyone to meet our needs, to be what we want them to be, do what we want them to do, respond as we would have them respond or feel what we think they should feel. This is a human impossibility, an illusion, a fantasy. Even if the other person concedes to being "ours," at best that is only a figure of speech.

Perhaps we must finally accept the fact that we can never possess another human being. A decision to unite is an agreement between two separate units, which will always, in a sense, be separate. We must learn that loving others is to want them to be themselves—painful as it may be—with or without you. After all is said and done, what else can we do but wish them well? If a friend or loved one wants to go, even if we devise a hundred ways to try to hold on, we will never be successful. And how little we value ourselves when we manipulate someone in order to keep them, when they would rather be elsewhere. We are better without those individuals in our lives.

Jealousy diminishes only when we regain a feeling of worth and self-respect, stop internalizing the problem and begin to view it objectively as something stemming from our personal demands and needs. These may arise from our desire for status or loyalty. They may be due to our insecurity, our need to control, to possess, our need for exclusivity, or fear of loss of face.

Loyalty in a relationship is based upon trust and respect. It can only be offered, never demanded. It is based upon voluntary devotion. Relationships are continually changing. A mutual agreement to be loyal or honest will form the basis from which future trust will arise. Loyalty is, therefore, a pact. Fidelity is a pact. The earlier these qualities are discussed and agreed upon in a relationship, the more secure the future of the relationship. Of course, the decision must be mutual, and the decision must be binding. Any change in the expectations over time must be accepted, discussed, and new decisions formed.

The word "jealousy" stems from the Greek word "jeal." It suggests that a valued possession is in danger and that some action must be taken. It implies that what can be seen as a negative phenomenon can be changed to a positive one over time. As the relationship, and those involved in it, becomes stronger and more secure, so will jealousy be minimized. Learning to let go, since most of us believe that love is based on "holding on to," is

continued on next page

READINGS

very difficult. Perhaps the greatest love presupposes the greatest freedom. There is an old saying which suggests that love must be set free, and when it comes back to you, only then will you know real love.

When we have finally conquered extremes of jealousy, we will emerge better and stronger lovers. We will understand the joy and strength which comes from solving our own problems, meeting our own needs, and loving freely without demands. As always after having conquered something of a lower order, we will be lifted to new and greater heights.

Eleanor Roosevelt said:

Every time you meet a situation, although you think at the time it is an impossibility and you go through the tortures of the damned, once you have met it and lived through it, you find that forever after you are freer than you were before.

Don't be afraid of jealousy. It is a natural and normal emotion. Everyone who cares and loves feel jealous at one time or another. The essential decision is whether you will allow your jealousy to become an all-consuming monster, capable of destroying you and those you love, or become a challenge for you to grow in self-respect and personal knowledge. The challenge will rest with you.

CHAPTER 6

Pairing and Singlehood

PREVIEW

To gain a sense of what you already know about the material covered in this chapter, answer "true" or "false" to the following statements. You will find the answers on page 175.

1. Looking for a mate can be compared to shopping for goods in a market. True or false?
2. Generally, the most important factor in judging someone at the first meeting is how he or she looks. True or false?
3. Interfaith marriages have no higher divorce rates than same-faith marriages. True or false?
4. If a woman asks a man out on a first date, it is generally a sign that she wants to have sex with him. True or false?
5. Both men and women report feelings of pressure to have sexual intercourse on dates. True or false?
6. Singles, compared to their married peers, tend to be more dependent on their parents. True or false?
7. An important dating problem that men cite is their own shyness. True or false?
8. Cohabitation has become part of the courtship process among young adults. True or false?
9. Pooling money in cohabiting relationships indicates a high degree of commitment. True or false?
10. Cohabitors who have been previously married are more likely than never-married cohabitors to view their cohabitation as a test of their marital compatibility. True or false?

*A proposal of marriage in our society tends
to be a way in which a man sums up his
social attributes and suggests to a woman
that hers are not so much better as to
preclude a merger or partnership in these
matters.*

Erving Goffman

ALTHOUGH THEORETICALLY WE HAVE FREE CHOICE in selecting our partners, in reality our choices are somewhat limited by "rules" of mate selection. If we know what the rules are, we can make deductions about whom we will be likely to choose as dates or partners.

There is a game you can play if you understand some of the principles of male/female mate selection in our culture. Without ever having met a friend's new boyfriend or girlfriend, you can deduce many things about him or her, using basically the same method of deductive reasoning that Sherlock Holmes used to astound Dr. Watson. For example, if a female friend at college has a new boyfriend, it is safe to guess that he is about the same age or a little older, taller, and a college student; he is probably about as physically attractive as your friend (if not, they will probably break up within six months); his parents probably are of the same ethnicity and social class as hers; and most likely he is about as intelligent as your friend. If a male friend has a new girlfriend, many of the same things apply, except that she is probably the same age or younger and shorter than he is. After you have described your friend's new romantic interest, don't be surprised if he or she exclaims, "Good grief, Holmes, how did you know that?" Of course, not every characteristic may apply, but you will probably be correct in most instances. These are not so much guesses as deductions based on the principle of homogamy discussed in this chapter.

In this chapter we not only look at the general rules by which we choose partners but we also examine romantic relationships, the singles world, and living together. Over the last decade or two, many aspects of pairing, such as the legitimacy of premarital intercourse and cohabitation, have changed considerably, radically affecting marriage. Today large portions of American society accept and approve of both premarital sex and cohabitation. Marriage has lost its exclusiveness as the only legitimate institution in which people can have sex and share their everyday lives. As a result, it has lost some of its power as an institution.

Each year, more and more adult Americans are single. In 1990, 40.3 million adult Americans—29.9 percent of all men and 22.8 percent of all women—had never married (U.S. Bureau of Census, 1991). Rates of singlehood vary by ethnicity. Among whites, 20.2 percent of the men and 16.8 percent of the women had never married. Among African Americans, 34.3 of the men and 32.1 of the women were single. And among Latinos, 26.9 percent of the men and 21.8 of the women had not married (U.S. Bureau of Census, 1990).

❖ CHOOSING A PARTNER

How do we choose the people we date, live with, or marry? At first glance, it seems that we choose them on the basis of love, but other factors also influence us. These factors have to do with bargaining and exchange (as discussed in Chapter 3). We select our partners in what might be called a marriage marketplace.

The Marriage Marketplace

In the marriage marketplace, as in the commercial marketplace, people trade or exchange goods. Unlike a real marketplace, however, the marriage marketplace is not a place but a process. In the marriage marketplace, the goods that are exchanged are not tomatoes, waffle irons, or bales of cotton; *we* are the goods. Each of us has certain resources, such as social class, status, looks, and personality, that make up our marketability. We bargain with these resources. We size ourselves up and rank ourselves as a good deal, an average package, or something to be remaindered; we do the same with potential dates or mates.

The idea of exchange as a basis for choosing marital partners may not be romantic, but it is deeply rooted in marriage customs. In some cultures, for example, arranged marriages take place after extended bargaining between families. The woman is expected to bring a dowry in the form of property (such as pigs, goats, clothing, utensils, land) or money; or a woman's family may demand a brideprice if the culture places a premium on women's productivity. Traces of the exchange basis of marriage still exist in our culture in the traditional marriage ceremony when the bride's father pays the wedding costs and "gives away" his daughter.

The traditional marital exchange is related to gender roles. Traditionally, men have used their status, economic power, and role as protector in a trade-off for women's physical attractiveness and nurturing, childbearing, and housekeeping abilities; women, in return, have gained status and economic security in the exchange.

As women enter careers and become economically independent, the terms of bargaining change. When women achieve their own occupational status and economic independence, what do they ask from men in the marriage exchange? Constantine Safilios-Rothschild (1976) suggests that many women expect men to bring more expressive, affective, and companionable resources into marriage. Independent women do not have to settle for a man who brings little more to the relationship than a paycheck; they want a man who is a companion, not simply a provider.

But even today a woman's bargaining position is not as strong as a man's. In 1991 women earned only 70 percent of what men made (and this was a record high!). Women are still significantly underrepresented in the professions. Furthermore, many of the things that women traditionally used to bargain with in the marital exchange—child care, housekeeping services, sexuality—are today devalued or available elsewhere. Children are not the economic assets they once were. A man does not have to rely on a woman to cook for him, sex is often accessible in the singles world, and someone can be paid to do the laundry and clean the apartment.

Women are at a further disadvantage because of the double standard of aging. Physical attractiveness is a key bargaining element in the marital marketplace, but the older a woman gets, the less attractive she is considered. For women, youth and beauty are linked in most cultures. As women get older, their field of eligible partners declines because men tend to choose younger women as mates.

We tend to overlook the bargaining aspect of relationships because, as we said before, it doesn't seem very romantic. We bargain, nevertheless, but usually not openly or consciously. We exchange our social and personality characteristics. To get a sense of the complexity of bargaining in our culture, let's examine the role of physical attractiveness.

Physical Attractiveness

THE HALO EFFECT. Imagine yourself unattached at a party. You notice someone is standing next to you as you reach for some chips. He or she says hello. In that moment, you have to decide whether to engage him or her in conversation. On what basis do you make that decision? Is it looks, personality, style, sensitivity, intelligence, or something else?

If you're like most of us, you consciously or unconsciously base this decision on appearance. If you decide to talk to the person, you probably formed a positive opinion about his or her appearance. In other words, he or she looked "cute," like a

The beautiful bird gets caged.

Chinese proverb

Physical attractiveness is most important at first meeting. Afterwards it diminishes in importance as people get to know each other better.

I'm tired of all this nonsense about beauty being only skin-deep. That's deep enough. What do you want—an adorable pancreas?

Jean Kerr

"fun person," gave a "good first impression," or seemed "interesting." As Elaine Hatfield and Susan Sprecher (1986) point out:

Appearance is the sole characteristic apparent in every social interaction. Other information may be more meaningful but far harder to ferret out. People do not have their IQs tattooed on their foreheads, nor do they display their diplomas prominently about their persons. Their financial status is a private matter between themselves, their bankers, and the Internal Revenue Service.

Physical attractiveness is particularly important during the initial meeting and early stages of a relationship. If you don't know anything else about a person, you tend to judge him or her on appearance. (See Berscheid, 1985, for a review of the literature on interpersonal attraction.)

Most people would deny that they are attracted to others just because of their looks. We do so unconsciously, however, by *inferring* qualities based on looks. This inference is based on a **halo effect:** good-looking people are assumed to possess more desirable social characteristics than unattractive people. In one well-known experiment (Dion et al., 1972), students were shown pictures of attractive people and asked to describe what they thought these people were like. Attractive men and women were assumed to be more sensitive, kind, warm, sexually responsive, strong, poised, and outgoing than others; they were assumed to be more exciting and to have better characters than "ordinary" people. Research indicates that overall, the differences in perceptions between very attractive and average people are minimal. It is when attractive and average people are compared to those considered to be unattractive that there are pronounced differences, with those perceived as unattractive being rated more negatively (Hatfield and Sprecher, 1986).

A study (Tanke, 1982) of men from two universities found that among the various traits attributed to attractive women, the trait most affected by their appearance was their sexual behavior. Attractive women were viewed as more sexually warm, exciting, and permissive than unattractive ones. An unpublished study (cited in Hatfield and Sprecher, 1986) found that attractive men and women were believed to have a stronger sex drive, to be sexually permissive, to enjoy multiple sexual relationships, and to play a more dominant role in sexual activities.

THE RATING AND DATING GAME. In casual relationships, the physical attractiveness of a romantic partner is especially important. Hatfield and Sprecher (1986) suggest three reasons why people prefer attractive people over unattractive ones. First, there is an "aesthetic appeal," a simple preference for beauty. Second, there is the "glow of beauty," in which we assume that good-looking people are more sensitive, kind, warm, modest, self-confident, sexual, and so on. Third, we achieve status by dating attractive people. Sociologist Willard Waller (1937) described the process as the "rating and dating" complex. According to Waller, men and women rated potential dates on a scale of one to ten and tried to date the best. The men and women evaluated themselves and others in terms of how their dates ranked.

Several studies (cited in Hatfield and Sprecher, 1986) have demonstrated that good-looking companions increase our status. In one study, men were asked their first impressions of a man seen alone, arm-in-arm with a beautiful woman, and arm-in-arm with an unattractive woman. The man made the best impression with the beautiful woman. He ranked higher alone than with an unattractive woman. In contrast to men, women do not necessarily rank as high when seen with a handsome man. A study in which married couples were evaluated found that it made no difference to a woman's ranking if she was unattractive but had a strikingly handsome husband. If an unattractive man had a strikingly beautiful wife, it was assumed that he had something to offer other than looks, such as fame or fortune.

Taught from infancy that beauty is woman's sceptre, the mind shapes itself to the body, and roaming around its gilt cage, only seeks to adorn its prison.

Mary Wollstonecraft (1759–1797), A Vindication of the Rights of Women

TRADE-OFFS. People don't necessarily gravitate to the most attractive person in the room; they tend to gravitate to those who are about as attractive as themselves. Sizing up someone at a party or dance, a man may say, "I'd never have a chance with her; she's too good looking for me." Even if people are allowed to specify the qualities they want in a date, they are hesitant to select anyone notably different from themselves in social desirability. We tend to choose people who are our equals in terms of looks, intelligence, education, and so on (Hatfield and Walster, 1981). However, if two people are different in looks or intelligence, usually the individuals make a trade-off in which a lower-ranked trait is exchanged for a higher-ranked trait. A woman who values status, for example, may accept a lower level of physical attractiveness in a man if he is wealthy or powerful.

We may daydream of movie-star lovers, but in real life we are more practical. Hatfield and Walster (1981) wrote:

Although we prefer partners who are more desirable than ourselves, our actual choices are influenced by matching considerations. We all tend to end up with partners of approximately our own social value. Thus, our selection of a mate appears to be a delicate compromise between our desire to capture an ideal partner and our realization that we must eventually settle for what we deserve.

Who ever heard of an ugly or pretty man? The beauty of a man is not in his face, but in his character, in his social standing, in his money. Who ever heard of a rich man that was ugly?

Jorge Amado

ARE LOOKS IMPORTANT TO EVERYONE? For all of us ordinary-looking people, it's a relief to know that looks aren't everything. Looks are most important to certain types or groups of people and in certain situations or locations, such as classes, parties, and bars, where people do not interact with each other extensively on a day-to-day basis. Looks are less important to those in ongoing relationships and to those older than young adults. Looks are also less important if there are regular interactions between individuals who, for example, work together or commute in the same automobile (Hatfield and Sprecher, 1986). Looks tend to be especially important in adolescence and youth because of our need to conform. It is at this time that we are most vulnerable to pressure from our peers to go out with handsome men and beautiful women.

Men tend to care more about how their partners look than do women. This may be attributed to the disparity of economic and social power. Because men tend to have more assets (such as income and status) than women, they do not have to be concerned with their potential partner's assets. Therefore, they can choose partners in terms of their attractiveness. Because women lack the earning power and assets of men, they have to be more practical. They have to choose a partner who can offer security and status.

Most research on attractiveness has been done on first impressions or early dating. Researchers are finding, however, that attractiveness is important in established relationships as well as in beginning or casual ones. Most people expect looks to become less important as the relationship matures, but Philip Blumstein and Pepper Schwartz (1983) found that the happiest people in cohabiting and married relationships thought of their partners as attractive. People who found their partners attractive had the best sex life.

Physical attractiveness continues to be important throughout marriage. One study (Margolin and White, 1987) found that as husbands and wives aged, changes in the wife's physical appearance seemed to have greater impact on the quality of marital sexuality than changes in the husband's appearance. These changes led to greater sexual disinterest, a decline in sexual satisfaction, and, to a lesser extent, unfaithfulness, especially on the part of the husband.

❖ REFLECTIONS   *How important are looks to you? Have you ever mistakenly judged someone by his or her looks? How did you discover your error? Have you ever made trade-offs in a relationship? What did you and your partner trade?*

The Field of Eligibles

ENDOGAMY AND EXOGAMY.   The men and women we date, live with, or marry usually come from the *field of eligibles*—that is, the people of whom our cultures approves as potential partners. The field of eligibles is defined by two principles: **endogamy**, marriage within a particular group, and **exogamy**, marriage outside the group.

Endogamy.   People usually marry others from a large group such as the nationality, ethnic group, or social class with which they identify, because they share common assumptions, experiences, and understandings. Endogamy strengthens group structure. If people already have ties as friends, neighbors, work associates, or church members, a marriage between such acquaintances solidifies group ties. To take an extreme example, it is easier for two Americans to understand each other than it is for an American and a Fula tribesperson from Africa. Americans are monogamous and urban, whereas Fulanis are polygamous wandering herders. But another, darker force may lie beneath endogamy: this is the fear and distrust of outsiders, those who are different from ourselves. Both the need for commonality and the distrust of outsiders urge people to marry individuals like themselves.

Style is the physiognomy of the mind, and a safer index to character than the face.

Arthur Schopenhauer (1788–1860)

ENV IN (es in within)

PERSPECTIVE

The Marriage Squeeze

One of the facts of contemporary life is that more women than men are eligible for marriage. After World War II through the early 1960s, there was a significant increase in the birthrate, resulting in the "baby boom." Since women tend to marry men several years older than themselves, "baby-boom" women reached the average age for marriage two years earlier than men born the same year. The result was a "marriage squeeze" in which there were greater numbers of women than men looking for marriage partners.

The marriage squeeze has partly reversed itself in the 1990s as the smaller number of women born after the baby boom have more older men to choose from. In fact, that time has already arrived for white women under thirty, where there are as many as 25 percent more "suitable" men for every 100 "suitable" women. (Suitability is defined by educational level and age preference.) After age thirty, however, the marriage squeeze is in force again. As these women age, the marriage squeeze becomes even tighter.

The Marriage Gradient

"All the good ones are taken," is a common complaint of women in their thirties and beyond. (And for African-American women, it begins even earlier.) According to sociologist Jesse Bernard, their complaint may be right. Bernard (1982) wrote:

In our society, the husband is assigned a superior status. It helps if he actually *is*

Marriage: Squeeze and Gradient

superior in ways—in height, for example, or age or education or occupation—for such superiority, however slight, makes it easier for both partners to conform to the structural imperatives. The [woman] wants to be able to "look up" to her husband, and he, of course, wants her to. The result is a situation known sociologically as the marriage gradient.

Men and women, as we have seen, tend to marry those with the same class and cultural background. But within this general homogamy, men tend to marry women slightly below them in age, education, and so on. This tendency creates the marriage gradient. Bernard continues:

The result is that there is no one for the men at the bottom to marry, no one to look up to them. Conversely, there is no one for the women at the top to look up to; there are no men superior to them. . . .[The] never-married men . . . tend to be "bottom-of-the-barrel" and the women . . . "cream-of-the-crop."

Among college-educated men and women, the "cream-of-the-crop" by educational status, 93 percent of the men married but only 83 percent of the women were married. By educational status, college-educated men represented the highest proportion of males who married, while college-educated women represented the lowest proportion of females who married (Glick, 1984b).

African Americans have a lower marriage rate than whites. Comparing the rates between African Americans and whites, sociologist Robert Staples (1988) suggests that the differences can be understood best by examining them along class and gender lines. Staples argues:

Among lower-income Blacks, the structural constraints consist of the unavailability and undesirability of Black males in the eligible pool of potential mates. Due to the operational effects of institutional racism, large numbers of Black males are incarcerated, unemployed, narcotized, or fall prey to early death.

Among middle-class African Americans, significantly more women attend college than men, making it more difficult for women to find men with comparable educational backgrounds, an important element in homogamy. As a result, researchers have found that homogamy has been less important for African-American women in contrast to white women. Compared to white women, African-American women have tended to marry less educated men and men who have previously been married (Taylor et al., 1991).

Exogamy. The principle of exogamy requires us to marry outside certain groups—specifically, outside our own family (however defined) and outside our same sex. Exogamy is enforced by taboos that are deeply embedded within our psychological makeup. The violation of these taboos may cause a deep sense of guilt. A marriage between a man and his mother, sister, daughter, aunt, niece, grandmother, or granddaughter is considered incestuous; women are forbidden to marry their corresponding male relative. Beyond these blood relations, however, the definition of incestuous relations changes. One society defines marriages between cousins as incestuous, whereas another may encourage such marriages. Some states prohibit marriages between stepbrothers and stepsisters as well as cousins; others do not.

Heterogamy and Homogamy. Endogamy and exogamy interact to limit the field of eligibles. It is further limited by society's encouragement of homogamy. **Homogamy** refers to the tendency to choose a mate whose personal or group characteristics are similar to ours. **Heterogamy** refers to the tendency to choose a mate whose personal or group characteristics differ from our own. The strongest pressures are toward homogamy. As a result, those we choose for partners tend to follow certain patterns. As George Bernard Shaw wrote, "Fashionable ladies fall in love with acrobats and have to marry colonels. Shops assistants fall in love with countesses and are obliged to marry shop girls." These homogamous considerations generally apply to heterosexuals, gay men, and lesbians alike in their choice of partners.

Although there has been a growing tendency allowing individual choice of partners without state interference (in 1966, the U.S. Supreme Court, for example, declared unconstitutional laws prohibiting marriage between individuals of different races in a decision appropriately called *Loving* vs. *Virginia),* statutes continue to prohibit gay or lesbian marriages. The military also enforces its own particular form of homogamy, barring relationships and marriages between officers and enlisted personnel as "fraternizing."

The most important elements of homogamy include those listed below. These elements are strongest in first marriages and weaken in second and subsequent marriages (Glick, 1988).

Race and Ethnicity. Most marriages are between members of the same race. Between 1970 and 1986, the number of interracial marriages increased 2.5 times, from 310,000 to 827,000, or about 1.5 percent of all marriages. Only 22 percent of interracial marriages were between African Americans and whites (0.3 percent of all marriages). In 75 percent of African American/white marriages, African-American men marry white women. Most interracial marriages are between whites and African Americans, Asian Americans, or Native Americans (U.S. Bureau of the Census, 1990). It is not clear whether interracial marriages are as stable or less stable than nonmixed marriages, because the few published studies are contradictory (Heer, 1974; Monahan, 1970).

The degree of intermarriage is of concern to members of ethnic groups because it affects the assimilation rate and continued ethnic identity (Stevens and Schoen, 1988). Ethnic identity continues to be important for Latinos, who tend to marry others of their own ethnic group. Among Italians, Poles, Germans, and Irish, however, only one in four in this country marries within his or her ethnic group.

Related to racial and ethnic homogamy is linguistic homogamy, which is determined by the language spoken at home by native-born Americans (Steven and Schoen, 1988). Linguistic homogamy is especially important for Latinos. There are more than 11 million native-born Spanish speakers in the United States, as well as over a million each of German, French, Italian, and Polish speakers. (African-Americans lost their native languages as a result of forced assimilation during slavery.) Linguistic homogamy allows direct transmission of cultural characteristics across generations. Among European ethnic groups whose members speak a non-English language at home, language continues to be an important factor in mate selection, especially for those with lower levels of education.

Religion. Until the late 1960s, religion was a significant factor affecting marital choice. Today, however, approximately 15 to 20 percent of all marriages are interfaith (Glenn, 1982). Almost half of all Catholics marry outside their faith (Maloney, 1986). Almost 25 percent of Jews choose a non-Jewish partner, up from 6 percent in the early 1960s (Gruson, 1985).

Religious groups tend to discourage interfaith marriages, believing that they may weaken individual beliefs, lead to children being reared in a different faith, or secularize the family. Such fears, however, may be overstated. Among Catholics who marry Protestants, there seems to be little secularization by those who feel themselves to be religious (Petersen, 1986). Only a few studies have looked at the effect of interfaith marriage on marital stability. These show that although divorce rates vary according to religions and denominations, in general interfaith marriages tend to have about a 10 percent higher divorce rate than marriages within the same faith (Bumpass and Sweet, 1972; also see Glenn, 1982, on marital happiness). More recently, researchers studied the effects of three types of religious homogamy—denominational affiliation, church attendance, and belief in the Bible—on marital satisfaction and stability (Heaton and Pratt, 1990). They found that denominational homogamy was the most important factor contributing to marital success. Joint church attendance had a slight impact, and similar beliefs about the Bible had little effect.

Socioeconomic Class. Most people marry within their own socioeconomic class because of shared values, tastes, goals, occupations, and expectations. People tend to marry those who have the same educational background as themselves, reflecting the fact that educational attainment is related to class. Even if a person marries someone from a different race or ethnic group, religion, or age group, the couple will probably be from the same socioeconomic class. Women, more than men, sometimes marry below their class, possibly as a result of women's slightly lower status.

Age. People tend to marry others within their age group, although the man is usually slightly older than the woman. Age is important because we view ourselves as members of a generation, and each generation's experience of life leads to different values and expectations. Furthermore, different developmental and life tasks confront us at different ages. A twenty-year-old woman wants something different from marriage and from life than a sixty-year-old man does. By marrying people of similar ages, we ensure congruence for developmental tasks. (See Atkinson and Glass, 1985, for discussion of age in marriage.)

These factors in the choice of partner interact with one another. Race, ethnicity, and socioeconomic class, for example, are often closely related because of discrimination. Many African Americans and Latinos are working class and are not as well educated as whites. Whites generally tend to be better off economically and are usually better educated. Thus a marriage that is endogamous in terms of race is also likely to be endogamous in terms of education and social class.

More recently, social scientists have been studying marital homogamy in terms of personality characteristics (Antill, 1983; Buss, 1984; Kurdeck and Smith, 1987; Lesnick-Oberstein and Cohen, 1984). They have found that people tend to choose partners who share similar characteristics. Individuals who were impulsive, accurate reasoners, quarrelsome, or extroverted chose similar partners. The researchers hypothesized that choosing partners who share similar personality characteristics provides greater communication, empathy, and understanding.

Marriages that are homogamous tend to be more stable than heterogamous ones (Burr, 1973; but see Dean and Gurak, 1978). Three possible explanations have been given for this (Udry, 1974):

Fashionable ladies fall in love with acrobats and have to marry colonels. Shop assistants fall in love with countesses and are obliged to marry shop girls.

George Bernard Shaw

The man who marries for money earns it.

Yiddish proverb

FIGURE 6.1

Ratio of unmarried men to unmarried women in 1990.

SOURCE: U.S. Bureau of Census, *Marital Status and Living Arrangements: March, 1990*. Current Population Reports, 1991. Figure 9.

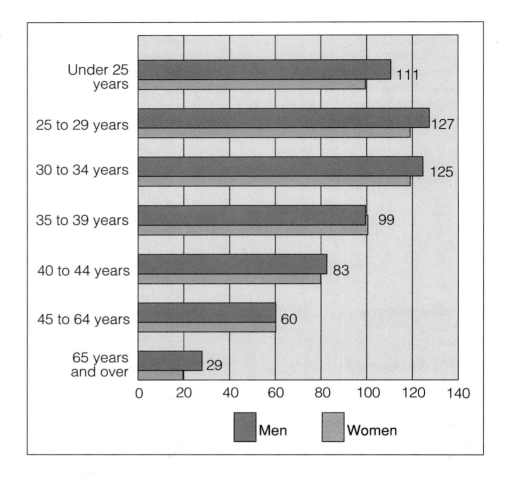

1. Heterogamous couples may have considerably different values, attitudes, and behaviors, which may create a lack of understanding and conflict.

2. Hetergamous marriages may lack approval from parents, relatives, and friends. Couples are then cut off from important sources of support during crises.

3. Heterogamous couples are probably less conventional and therefore less likely to continue an unhappy marriage for the sake of appearances.

❖ REFLECTIONS   *Think in terms of heterogamy and homogamy about those who are or have been your romantic or marital partners. In what respects have your partners shared the same racial, ethnic, religious, socioeconomic, age, and personal traits with you? In what respects have they not? Have shared or differing characteristics affected your relationships? How?*

The Stages of Mate Selection: Stimulus-Value-Role

Let us say that you meet someone who fits all the criteria of homogamy: same ethnic group, religion, educational level, and class background. Homogamically speaking, he is "Mr. Right," she is "Ms. Right," and your children would be "Little Rights." He or she is the person your parents dream of you marrying. And, of course, you can't stand each other. Homogamy by itself doesn't work. You need to start with "magic." Or, more precisely, according to Bernard Murstein (1976, 1987), you need to start with stimulus, the chemistry of attraction that *stimulates* you to want to have a relationship with another.

Murstein developed a three-stage theory—the stimulus-value-role theory—to explain the development of romantic relationships. This theory is based on exchange. Each partner evaluates the other; if the exchange seems more or less equitable, the two will progress to the next stage.

◆ Stimulus refers to each person being drawn or attracted to the other before actual interaction. This attraction can be physical, mental, or social; it can be based on a person's reputation or status. The stimulus stage is, according to Murstein, most prominent on the first encounter, when one has little information with which to evaluate the other person.

◆ Value refers to partners weighing each other's basic values, trying to determine if they are compatible. Each person tries to figure out the other's philosophy of life, politics, sexual values, religious beliefs, and so on. If both highly value rap music, it is a plus for the relationship. If they disagree on religion—one is a dedicated fundamentalist and the other a militant atheist—it is a minus for the relationship. Each person adds or subtracts the pluses and minuses along value lines. Based on the outcome, the couple will either disengage or go on to the next stage. Values are usually determined between the second and seventh meetings.

◆ Role refers to behaviors, or how each person fulfills his or her roles as lover, companion, friend, worker—and potential husband or wife, mother or father. Are their behaviors consistent with marital roles? Are they emotionally stable? This aspect is evaluated in the eighth and subsequent encounters.

In this theory, all couples go through these stages in a defined sequence. Although this theory has been one of the most prominent theories explaining relationship development, it has been criticized by some scholars. Most notably, scholars ask if men and women *really* test their degree of fit (Huston et al., 1981). For example, militant fundamentalists and atheists may sometimes believe that they are compatible. They may not discuss religion; instead they might focus on the "incredible" sexual intensity of their relationship. Or they may make errors in arithmetic: they may mistakenly believe that religion is not *that* important, only to discover after they are married that religion is *very* important.

apply info to notes

❖ ROMANTIC RELATIONSHIPS

As more and more people delay marriage, never marry, or seek to remarry after divorce or widowhood, romantic relationships, observes one scholar (Surra, 1991), "will take different shapes at different points in time, as they move in and out of marriage, friendship, romance, cohabitation, and so on." As a result, researchers are shifting from the traditional emphasis on mate selection toward the study of the formation and development of romantic relationships, such as the dynamics of heterosexual dating, cohabitation, post-divorce relationships, and gay and lesbian relationships. The field of personal relationships is developing broad focus (Kelley et al., 1983; Perlman and Duck, 1987).

Dating, going out, getting together—all such terms describe important rituals for pairing and, in many cases, for finding a marriage partner. In contemporary America, most individuals—whether they are single, divorced, widowed, or gay or lesbian—find romantic partners by some form of dating. They narrow the field through a process of getting to know the other person. Those potential partners who do not

Dreams are the touchstones of our character.

Henry David Thoreau

The physical expression of affection is an important aspect of relationships.

fit the general characteristics required by endogamy tend to be weeded out through peer pressure or parental veto.

The functions of dating vary with age and motivation. Initially, dating is for fun, for doing something with someone—going to the beach, having coffee, seeing a movie, going dancing, hanging out. Dating helps us learn to relate to another person. In high school or college, dating may become more involved; choosing a partner may be at stake. Is your date a potential mate? If so, will that person be a good partner? Will he or she be caring, loving, loyal, dependable, like children, work? And if one is a single parent, how will the other be as a stepparent? The rush of romantic feelings sometimes makes such considerations appear irrelevant; love will triumph over all, we like to think, as we hide our heads in the sand. Even if these issues are discussed, it may not be possible to predict how a partner will act in a marital or long-term relationship. There are some clues, however, which we will discuss later in this chapter.

On-Going Relationships

TRADITIONAL DATING. The traditional dating pattern is formal. Each person has a role to play. The man initiates the date; the woman waits to be called. The man is anxious lest he be turned down; he may feel his stomach churn while he tries to appear calm and calls the woman or "accidentally" runs into her (after weeks of planning). The woman's problems are complementary. Because she must wait to be called and must appear demure, she can only express her interest indirectly by glances, tone of voice, body language, or playing helpless (Larkin, 1979). She may be so indirect that the man doesn't catch on. Also, she might not even be called by the person with whom she wants to go out—someone else may call instead. It may be as difficult for a woman to turn down a man as it is for some men to ask out a woman. "I don't want to hurt his feelings" is a common reason expressed by women who find themselves going out on a date with someone they don't particularly like.

The woman on a formal date is supposed to be passive, expects to have her way paid, and tries to please the man without truly giving in to sexual pressure. In accordance with the traditional female stereotype, she is expected to display less sexual interest than the man and to curtail the sexual advances of her date (Allgeier and McCormick, 1982). The relationship is an exchange of favors. This type of dating is ultimately oriented toward mate selection.

GETTING TOGETHER. Over the last decade an alternative to the traditional dating pattern has emerged, both among high school and college students (Miller and Gordon, 1986). It is often referred to as "getting together." Egalitarian gender roles, probably more than any other factor, are responsible for this emerging pattern. Getting together is based on mutuality and sharing. Equality is an important value, and to symbolize equality, each person pays his or her own way. Therefore, the feelings of obligation that accompany one person spending money are absent. The man does not expect the woman to kiss him or go to bed with him in exchange for his showing her a good time. The woman does not feel that she owes the man anything. They go out together as equals.

Traditional gender roles are deemphasized. The woman may call up the man rather than wait for his call. Honesty and intimacy are highly valued, and self-disclosure is considered an important quality. Instead of being centered around an event, getting together emphasizes spontaneity. Males and females do not necessarily get together as couples but often meet in groups. They get together informally for pizza or hamburgers, for a picnic, or to study for a class. A man and a woman may begin to spend more time together as a result of these gatherings, but often it is within the group context. Neither person has the responsibility for asking the other out. Much of the anxiety of formal dating is avoided.

Sexuality moves from an exchange of favors to mutual involvement and satisfaction. Ideally, sexual involvement reflects true feelings and desires rather than the need to prove oneself or pay a debt. Friendship, respect, and common interests serve as the basis for decisions about whether to become sexually involved (Libby, 1976).

When people get together in this fashion, the pattern of mate selection may include the following sequence of steps: (1) getting together formally, (2) living together, and/or (3) marriage. When compared to dating, however, getting together is not as oriented toward eventual mate selection.

FRIENDSHIPS. Relations between men and women who are "just friends" generally differ from those in which men and women are dating or are romantically involved (Komarovsky, 1985). Among those who are just friends, women are more likely to share expenses, to take the initiative in calling male friends, and to self-disclose than they are in dating relationships. Because sex is not perceived as part of a friendship, many of the conflicts about sex are absent. Friendship offers many of the same advantages—such as acceptance, spontaneity, and understanding—as a romantic relationship (Davis, 1985).

Same-sex friendships tend to predominate, but male/female friendships are fairly common. In Keith Davis's (1985) study of 250 students and members of one community, 56 percent of the men and 44 percent of the women had close friends of the other sex. But close male/female friendships differed from same sex friendships. Same-sex friends tend to self-disclose more, offer practical help, have a greater sense of stability in the relationship, and show a greater willingness to give their utmost.

It is not uncommon for male/female friends to become romantically involved eventually. The development of both friendships and romantic relationships follows

UNDERSTANDING YOURSELF

Computer Dating and Homogamy

Compatibility Plus, a computer dating service, distributes this questionnaire to its clients. Complete the questionnaire and then examine it in terms of the social and personality characteristics you and your "ideal match" share. To what extent do you find homogamy operating? What do you think would be your chances of liking a person who was your "ideal match"? What other factors would be important?

❖ Questionnaire Instructions

Each question has two headings: "YOURSELF" and "IDEAL MATCH."

◆ For "YOURSELF" mark the box on the left that best describes you.
◆ Then, mark all the boxes on the right that best describe your "IDEAL MATCH."
◆ Please answer all the questions. If none of the choices is the exact answer you wish to give, then mark the answer that comes closest.

YOURSELF   IDEAL MATCH

1. Age **32** yrs.
2. Minimum age acceptable   **32** yrs.
   Maximum age acceptable   **55** yrs.
3. Height: **5** ft. **6** in.
4. Minimum height acceptable   **5 7** in.
5. Sex
   ☐ 1) Male .... ☑
   ☑ 2) Female .... ☐
6. Race
   ☑ 1) White .... ☑
   ☐ 2) Hispanic .... ☐
   ☐ 3) Oriental .... ☑
   ☐ 4) Black .... ☑
   ☐ 5) Other _____ ☐
                        (write in)

7. Body Build
   ☐ 1) Heavy .... ☐
   ☐ 2) Moderately heavy .... ☐
   ☐ 3) Average .... ☑
   ☑ 4) Moderately thin .... ☐
   ☐ 5) Other_____ ☐
                        (write in)
8. Religion
   ☑ 1) Catholic .... ☑
   ☐ 2) Protestant .... ☐
   ☐ 3) Jewish .... ☑
   ☐ 4) Eastern Mysticism .... ☐
   ☐ 5) Atheist or Agnostic .... ☐
   ☐ 6) Other_____ ☐
                        (write in)
9. Economic Bracket
   ☐ 1) Low income .... ☐
   ☐ 2) Average income .... ☐
   ☑ 3) Above average .... ☑
   ☐ 4) Much above average .... ☑
10. Furthest Education
   ☐ 1) Grade School.................................. ☐
   ☐ 2) High School .... ☐
   ☑ 3) Some College .... ☐
   ☐ 4) Graduated College .... ☑
   ☐ 5) Post-graduate study....................... ☑
11. Diet
   ☑ 1) No restrictions .... ☑
   ☐ 2) No red meat .... ☐
   ☐ 3) Kosher .... ☐
   ☐ 4) Macrobiotic .... ☐
   ☐ 5) Vegetarian .... ☐
12. Tobacco use
   ☑ 1) Non-smoker (only) .... ☑
   ☐ 2) Light smoker.................................. ☐
   ☐ 3) Regular smoker .... ☐
13. Children Living With You
   ☐ 1) None .... ☑
   ☐ 2) One .... ☑
   ☑ 3) Two.. ☑
   ☐ 4) Three or more .... ☑

some of the same patterns. As friends make the transition to romantic partners, they may perceive a danger: friends tend to stay friends, but lovers may part. Because they value the stability, friends who fall in love with each other may hesitate to change their relationship. Others, however, believe that their friendship gives them a strong basis for love.

UNDERSTANDING YOURSELF

14. Political Outlook
- ☐ 1) Liberal... ☐
- ☑ 2) Moderate... ☑
- ☐ 3) Conservative.. ☐
- ☐ 4) Progressive–Radical.. ☐
- ☐ 5) Other _____ ☐
  (write in)

15. Affection
- ☑ 1) Very affectionate... ☑
- ☐ 2) Moderately affectionate .... ☐
- ☐ 3) Mildly affectionate.. ☐
- ☐ 4) Non-demonstrative... ☐
- ☐ 5) Other _____ ☐
  (write in)

16. Sense of Humor
- ☑ 1) Very funny or witty .... ☑
- ☐ 2) Average .... ☐
- ☐ 3) Mild .... ☐

17. Assertiveness
- ☑ 1) Very assertive .... ☑
- ☐ 2) Moderately assertive...................................... ☐
- ☐ 3) Mildly assertive .... ☐
- ☐ 4) Non-assertive .... ☐

18. General Disposition
- ☑ 1) Easy going–flexible... ☑
- ☐ 2) Moderate.. ☐
- ☑ 3) Firm... ☑

19. Favorite Parties
- ☑ 1) Loud and lively .... ☑
- ☑ 2) Quiet and formal.. ☑
- ☑ 3) Small and intimate .... ☑
- ☐ 4) None–prefer one to one .... ☐

20. Dancing
- ☐ 1) Love it.. ☐
- ☑ 2) Like it... ☐
- ☐ 3) Mild interest.. ☑
- ☐ 4) Dislike it.. ☐

21. Sexual Activity
- ☑ 1) Very important... ☑
- ☐ 2) Moderately important .... ☐
- ☐ 3) Not essential .... ☐

22. Relationship Desired
- ☑ 1) Committed one to one ..... *meaning monogamous* .... ☑
- ☑ 2) Friends and lovers... ☑
- ☐ 3) Nonsexual friendship .... ☐
- ☐ 4) Just sexual .... ☐

23. Favorite Activities and Interests
(Check all you enjoy)
- ☑ swimming
- ☐ surfing
- ☐ sailing
- ☑ bicycling
- ☑ jogging
- ☑ hiking
- ☐ skiing
- ☐ tennis
- ☐ racquetball
- ☐ volleyball
- ☑ aerobics
- ☑ dancing *ballet*
- ☑ walking
- ☑ partying
- ☑ playing music
- ☑ listening to music
- ☑ concerts
- ☑ plays
- ☑ movies
- ☑ beach
- ☑ travelling
- ☑ golf
- ☐ yoga
- ☐ meditation
- ☐ astrology
- ☑ photography
- ☑ art
- ☑ cooking
- ☐ politics
- ☐ shopping
- ☑ reading
- ☐ bars
- ☐ television

23. Personality Traits
(Check all that describe you)
- ☑ sexy
- ☑ spontaneous
- ☑ romantic
- ☑ playful
- ☑ positive
- ☑ energetic
- ☑ inquisitive
- ☑ sociable
- ☑ athletic
- ☑ relaxed
- ☑ open
- ☑ intelligent
- ☑ considerate
- ☑ imaginative
- ☐ conventional
- ☑ patient
- ☑ talkative
- ☑ generous
- ☑ sincere
- ☑ tolerant
- ☑ loyal
- ☑ witty
- ☑ emotional
- ☐ possessive
- ☐ frugal
- ☑ polite
- ☑ decisive
- ☐ reserved
- ☐ moody
- ☐ serious
- ☐ anxious
- ☐ lazy
- ☐ demanding

25. Additional Remarks: *Always be kind*
_____

POWER IN DATING RELATIONSHIPS. Power doesn't seem to be a concern for most people in dating relationships. In fact, one study of dating couples found that both men and women thought that they had about equal power in their relationships (Sprecher, 1985).

Even though most dating couples may not think about power too much, that doesn't mean that power is a nonexistent issue in dating relationships (Grauerholz,

1987). If power does become a source of conflict, it may not become as intense an issue as in a marriage. Strong power conflicts can be avoided by dissolving the relationship in question.

In marriage, the person with the most economic resources usually has the most power. Generally, this means the man, because he is more likely to be employed and to earn more money than the woman. In dating relationships, however, economic resources do not appear to be as important a power resource for men as their ability to date other women (Sprecher, 1985). The easier men thought it would be for them to go out with other women, the more power they had in a dating relationship.

Controlling sex and the reciprocation of love is an important resource for women (Safilios-Rothschild, 1976, 1977). This seems to be true both in marriage and in dating relationships. As long as her partner is in love with her, the woman is able to use that love as a resource. One researcher (Sprecher, 1985) wrote:

> Women probably have traditionally had to become skilled at controlling their emotions in heterosexual relationships in order to acquire bargaining power. Indeed, evidence has been found that men are more romantic than women. . . . It has also been found that men are the first to fall in love . . . and the last to fall out of love. . . . The evidence suggests that men may value and need the love from women more than women value and need the love from men. Often unable to have access to other desirable resources (money, status), women have had to use the control of love as a means to gain some power in a relationship.

The more men and women contributed to the affective side of the relationship relative to their partners, the less power they felt they had. For women, in fact, the less they loved their partner, the more power they felt they had.

❖ REFLECTIONS   *Look at power in your romantic relationships. When a disagreement occurs, who generally wins? Does it depend on the issue? When one person wants to go to the movies and the other wants to go to the beach, where do you end up going? If one wants to engage in sexual activities and the other doesn't, what happens?*

Problems in Dating

Satisfaction in dating relationships appears to be related to whether one believes the other will make a good marital partner in the future, is approved by parents and peers, and provides sustained and positive experiences (Riffer and Chin, 1988). But dating, as we all know, whether it is a source of recreation or a means of selecting a partner, can cause problems and create stress.

DATING RITUALS IN FLUX.   Dating rituals are in flux (Komarovsky, 1985). Although nontraditional women believe that the male prerogative of initiating the first date is a patriarchal holdover, few dare violate this norm. After one or two dates and in established relationships, both men and women appear equally free to initiate dates (modified by power issues or personal involvement). Mirra Komarovsky wrote:

> The strongest sanction against violating the male prerogative of the first move was the male interpretation of such initiative as a sexual come-on. Men described such aggressive women as "sluts." Indignant as the women were to this inference, they hesitated to expose themselves to the risks, unless they were among the very few who did so with full knowledge of the implications.

Komarovsky recounted the experiences of one first-year college woman who was eager to share some of the new ideas she encountered in her classes:

There was this one guy in my philosophy class who was really bright. He used to make brilliant comments in class and I wanted to get to know him, so I could talk to him about philosophy. So I approached him and asked him whether he would like to go out for a cup of coffee. My intention was to talk about the lecture, but when we sat down, all he wanted to talk about was how I felt about sex, and when we could go out on a date. I kept telling him that sex wasn't the reason I asked him out. I was trying to be honest and straightforward with him, but he wouldn't believe it. He thought that the reason I asked him out for a cup of coffee was a sexual come-on. I never asked another guy out on a date.

Another problem is who pays when going out on a date. Some women in Komarovsky's study were fearful that male acquaintances would be put off if they offered to pay their share. Other women, whether traditional or egalitarian, who offered to pay found themselves mocked by their dates. Some men who allowed their dates to pay still insisted on choosing where they went, whether the women wanted to go there or not. Still others allowed their dates to pay but not publicly; instead, for example, the women secretly slipped money to their dates under the dinner table.

Divergent gender role conceptions also complicate dating in the initial stages (and sometimes beyond). Often when two people lack complementary gender role conceptions, the woman is more egalitarian and the man more traditional. The man may want the woman to be subordinate to his desires and wishes. She, however, may ask for an equal share in the decisionmaking. In such cases, the relationship is not likely to become mutually satisfying.

Finally, it is apparent that large numbers of both men and women have sexual involvements outside dating relationships that are considered exclusive. One study of college students (Hansen, 1987) indicated that over 60 percent of the men and 40 percent of the women had been involved in erotic kissing outside the relationship; 35 percent of the men and 11 percent of the women had had sexual intercourse with someone else. Of those who knew of their partner's affair, a large majority felt that it had hurt their own relationship. When both partners had engaged in affairs, each believed that their partner's affair had harmed the relationship more than their own had. Both men and women seem to be unable to acknowledge the negative impact of their own outside relationships. It is not known whether those who tend to have outside involvement in dating relationships are also more likely to have extramarital relationships after they marry.

PROBLEMS AMONG WOMEN. In a random study of 227 college women and 107 men, nearly 25 percent of the women said that they received unwanted pressure to engage in sex, usually before the establishment of an emotional bond between the couple (Knox and Wilson, cited in Knox, 1991). (For a discussion of acquaintance rape, see Chaper 15.) Komarovsky (1985) cited male sexual pressure as a major barrier between men and women. A woman who wanted to see a man again faced a dilemma: how to encourage him to ask her out again without engaging in more sexual activity than she wanted. Men whose sexual advances were rejected by their dates often salved their hurt egos by accusing the women of having sexual hang-ups or being lesbians. Women rated places to go (23 percent) and communication (22) almost as high on their list of dating problems as sexual pressure (Knox, 1985).

PROBLEMS AMONG MEN. For men, the number-one problem, cited by 35 percent, was communicating with their dates (Knox, 1985). Men often felt that they didn't know what to say, or they felt anxious about the conversation dragging. Communication may be a particularly critical problem for men, because traditional gender roles do

There are two tragedies in life. One is to lose your heart's desire. The other is to gain it.

George Bernard Shaw

not encourage the development of intimacy and communication skills among males. A second problem, shared by almost identical numbers of men and women, was where to go. A third problem, named by 20 percent of the men but not mentioned by women, was shyness. Although men can take the initiative to ask for a date, they also face the possibility of rejection. For shy men, the fear of rejection is especially acute. A final problem, again one not shared by women, was money, cited by 17 percent of the men. Men apparently accept the idea that they are the ones responsible for paying for a date.

The problems of shyness and money are related to traditional conceptions of dating in which the male initiates the first date and pays the woman's expenses. It seems that a common ground exists here for change, since women find themselves limited by not being able to initiate the first date and would often be happy to share expenses.

BREAKING UP. "Most passionate affairs end simply," Hatfield and Walster (1981) noted. "The lovers find someone they love more." Love cools; it changes to indifference or hostility. This may be a simple ending, but it is also painful, because few relationships end by mutual consent (Hill et al., 1976). In Hill and his colleagues' two-year study of 231 college couples, the average couple had been going out for eight months; three-fourths were dating each other exclusively. Generally, the men fell in love more rapidly and the women fell out of love more quickly. At the end of the study, only 128 couples were still together. Fifty-one percent of the break-ups were initiated by the women, 42 percent were initiated by the men, and 7 percent were mutual. (If the man initiated the breakup, the chance was greater that the couple remained friends.) For college students, breakups are more likely to occur during vacations or at the beginning or end of the school year. Such timing is related to changes in the person's daily living schedule and the greater likelihood of quickly meeting another potential partner.

Breaking up is rarely easy, whether you are initiating it or "receiving" it. Thinking about the following may help.

If you initiate the breakup:

◆ *Be sure that you want to break up:* If the relationship is unsatisfactory, it may be because conflicts or problems have been avoided or have been confronted in the wrong way. Instead of being a reason to break up, conflicts or problems may be a rich source of personal development if they are worked out. Sometimes people erroneously use the threat of breaking up as a way of saying, "I want the relationship to change."

◆ *Acknowledge that your partner will be hurt.* There is nothing you can do to erase the pain your partner will feel; it is only natural. Not breaking up because you don't want to hurt your partner may actually be an excuse for not wanting to be honest with him or her, or with yourself.

◆ *Once you end the relationship, do not continue seeing your former partner as "friends" until considerable time has passed.* Being friends may be a subterfuge for continuing the relationship on terms wholly advantageous to yourself. It will only be painful for your ex-partner, since he or she may be more involved in the relationship than you. It may be best to wait to become friends until your partner is involved with someone else (and by then he or she may not care).

◆ *Don't change your mind.* Ambivalence after ending a relationship is not a sign that you made a wrong decision; neither is loneliness. Both indicate that the relationship was valuable for you.

If your partner breaks up with you:

◆ *The pain and loneliness you feel are natural.* Despite their intensity, they will eventually pass. They are part of the grieving process that attends the loss of an important relationship, but they are not necessarily signs of love.

◆ *You are a worthwhile person, whether you are with a partner or not.* Spend time with your friends; share your feelings with them. They care. Do things that you like; be kind to yourself.

◆ *Repeat these clichés:* No one ever died of love. (Except me.) There are other fish in the ocean. (Who wants a fish?) In other words, keep a sense of humor, it may help ease the pain.

❖ R E F L E C T I O N S   *When you have broken up with someone, what coping strategies have you used? Which were effective? Ineffective? Why?*

❖ SINGLEHOOD

Almost 79 million adult Americans were unmarried in 1990. They represent a diverse group: never-married, divorced, young and old, single parents, gay men and lesbians, widows and widowers, and so on. And they live in diverse situations that affect how they experience their singleness. In 1989, almost 22 million Americans of all ages—representing 24 percent of the population—lived alone. Thirteen million unmarried adults between the ages of eighteen and twenty-four, over half that age group, lived with their parents. Almost 7.5 million adults are single parents. Over 5.6 million unmarried men and women cohabit; many hundreds of thousands more cohabit in gay and lesbian relationships (U.S. Bureau of the Census, 1991). Other men and women share housing as friends or roommates; the elderly live with their children, in senior apartments, or in rest homes; military men and women live in barracks; and so on.

As you can see, the varieties of unmarried life-styles in America are too complex to examine under any single category. Those who are regarded as singles, however, are generally young or middle-aged adults, heterosexual, not living with someone, and working rather than attending school or college. In this section, we will focus on never-married singles. Those who are not married because of the death of a spouse are generally studied in the context of widowhood; they usually do not participate in a singles life-style. Gay men and lesbians are generally studied within a context of the gay and lesbian world. For many gay men and lesbians, however, the only reason they remain unmarried is that society refuses to permit marriages between those of the same sex.

The number of single adults is rising as a result of several factors (Buunk and van Driel, 1989; Macklin, 1987):

◆ Delayed marriage, with a median age at marriage of 26 years for men and 23.8 years for women in 1990 (U.S. Bureau of Census, 1991). The longer one postpones marriage, the greater the likelihood of never marrying. It is estimated that between 8 and 9 percent of men and women now in their twenties will never marry.
◆ Expanded life-style and employment options currently open to women.
◆ Increased rates of divorce and decreased likelihood of remarriage, especially among African Americans. In 1988, 7.6 percent of the population was divorced.
◆ Increased number of women enrolled in colleges and universities.
◆ More liberal social and sexual standards, including the increasing acceptance of cohabitation.

The land of marriage has this peculiarity, that strangers are desirous of inhabiting it, whilst its natural inhabitants would willingly be banished from thence.

Michel de Montaigne

◆ Ratio of unmarried men to unmarried women. In 1990, the sex ratio for ages 18 to 24 years is 111 men per 100 women; for ages 25 to 29 years, it is 127 men per 100 women; for ages 30 to 34, it is 125 men per 100 women.

There are significant differences in rates of singlehood between whites, African Americans, and Latinos. Among whites, never-married men and women represent 20 percent of the population; among African Americans, they represent 30 percent of the population; among Latinos, never-married individuals represent 25 percent of the population.

The rise in the number of never-married African-American women has been particularly startling (Taylor et al, 1991). Between 1975 and 1985, the proportion of married African-American women declined from 80 percent to 65 percent (compared to an 89 percent to 82 percent drop for whites). Among African Americans born in 1954, about 86 percent of the men are expected to marry by the time they reach 45 years, but only 70 percent of the women are expected to marry. The reasons for the differences between white and African-American marriage patterns are discussed in this chapter's "Perspective."

Culture and the Individual versus Marriage

Despite the importance of intimate relationships for our development as human beings, our culture is ambivalent about marriage. Paul of Tarsus (I Cor. 7: 7–9) declared that it was best for people to remain chaste, as he himself had done. "But if

---

T A B L E   6.1   Pushes and Pulls Toward Marriage and Singlehood

Which of these pushes and pulls are true for you? Why?

TOWARD MARRIAGE

Pushes	Pulls
Cultural norms	Love and emotional security
Loneliness	Physical attraction and sex
Parental pressure	Desire for children
Economic pressure	Desire for extended family
Social stigma of singlehood	Economic security
Fear of independence	Peer example
Media images	Social status as "grown up"
Guilt over singlehood	Parental approval

TOWARD SINGLEHOOD

Pushes	Pulls
Fundamental problems in marriage	Freedom to grow
Stagnant relationship with spouse	Self-sufficiency
Feelings of isolation and loneliness	Expanded friendships
Poor communication with spouse	Mobility
Unrealistic expectations of marriage	Career opportunities
Sexual problems	Sexual exploration
Media images	

SOURCE: Adapted from Peter J. Stein. "Singlehood: An Alternative to Marriage." *The Family Coordinator* 24:4 (1975).

they cannot," he wrote, "let them marry: For it is better to marry than to burn." In contemporary culture we find two contradictory myths about marriage, which many people hold simultaneously. Richard Udry (1974) observed:

The first myth—"and they lived happily ever after"—portrays marriage as a continuous courtship. The second myth is the picture of the domestic grind: the husband sits behind the paper, the wife moves about in the morning disarray; the husband leaves for work, the wife spends the day among dishes, diapers, and dirty little children. Although, as with most myths, no one *really* believes either one of them, they continue to affect the behavior of most people.

A continuing tension exists between the alternatives of singlehood and marriage (Stein, 1976). The singles subculture is glorified in the mass media; the marriages portrayed on television are situation comedies or soap operas abounding in extra-marital affairs. Yet single persons are rarely fully satisfied with being single and may yearn for marriage. They are pulled toward the idea of marriage by their desires for intimacy, love, children, and sexual availability. They are also pushed toward marriage by parental pressure, loneliness, and fears of independence. Married persons, at the same time, are pushed toward singlehood by the limitations they feel in married life. They are attracted to singlehood by the possibility of creating a new self, having new experiences, and achieving independence. (For the pros and cons of singlehood, see Stein and Finguid, 1985, and Schumm, 1985.)

Types of Never-Married Singles

Much depends on whether a person is single by choice and whether he or she considers being single temporary or permanent (Shostak, 1987). If one is voluntarily single, his or her sense of well-being is likely to be better than that of a person who is involuntarily single. Arthur Shostak (1981, 1987) has divided singles into four types. Singles may shift from one type to another at different times.

◆ *Ambivalents.* Ambivalents are voluntarily single and consider their singleness temporary. They are not seeking marital partners, but they are open to the idea of marriage. These are usually younger men and women who are actively pursuing education, career goals, or "having a good time." Ambivalents may be included among those who are cohabiting.
◆ *Wishfuls.* Wishfuls are involuntarily and temporarily single. They are actively seeking marital partners but have been unsuccessful so far. They consciously want to be married.
◆ *Resolveds.* Resolved individuals regard themselves as permanently single. A small percentage are priests or nuns or single parents who prefer rearing their children alone. The largest number, however, are "hardcore" singles who simply prefer the state of singlehood. Their numbers increased at five times that of the population between 1970 and 1980.
◆ *Regretfuls.* Regretful singles would prefer to marry but are resigned to their "fate." A large number of these are well-educated, high-earning women over forty who find a shortage of similar men as a result of the marriage gradient.

All but the resolveds share an important characeristic: they want to move from a single status to a romantic couple status. "The vast majority of never-married adults," wrote Shostak (1987) "work at securing and enjoying romance." Never-married singles share with married Americans "the high value they place on achieving intimacy and sharing love with a special one" (Shostak, 1987).

A woman without a man is like a fish without a bicycle.

Gloria Steinem

❖ R E F L E C T I O N S   *For you, what are the pushes and pulls between singlehood and marriage? If you are unmarried, as what type of single would you classify yourself? Why?*

Singles: Myths and Realities

Cargan and Melko (1982), in a study of 400 households in Dayton, Ohio, examined various myths and realities about singlehood. They concluded the following:

MYTHS.

◆ *Singles are dependent on their parents.* Few differences exist between singles and marrieds in their perceptions of their parents and relatives. They do not differ in perceptions of parental warmth or openness and differ only slightly in the amount and nature of parental conflicts.
◆ *Singles are self-centered.* Singles value friends more than do married people. Singles are more involved in community service projects.
◆ *Singles have more money.* Fewer than half the singles interviewed made more than $10,000 a year. Married couples were better off economically than singles, in part because both partners worked.
◆ *Singles are happier.* Singles tend to believe that they are happier than marrieds, whereas marrieds believe that they are happier than singles. Single men, however, exhibited more signs of stress than single women. A national survey conducted by Robert Weiss (1981) found that 23 percent of the single men and 27 percent of the single women felt lonely; in contrast, only 6 percent of the married women and 10 percent of the married men reported feeling lonely.
◆ *Singles view singlehood as a lifetime alternative.* The majority of singles expected to be married within five years. They did not view singlehood as an alternative to marriage but as a transitional time in their lives.

REALITIES.

◆ *Singles don't easily fit into married society.* Singles tend to socialize with other singles. Married people think that if they invite singles to their home, they must match them up with an appropriate single member of the other sex. Married people tend to think in terms of couples.
◆ *Singles have more time.* Singles are more likely to go out twice a week and much more likely to go out three times a week compared with their married peers. Singles have more choices and more opportunities for leisure-time activities.
◆ *Singles have more fun.* Although singles tend to be less happy than marrieds, they have more "fun." Singles go out more often, engage more in sports and physical activities, and have more sexual partners than marrieds. Apparently fun and happiness are not equated.
◆ *Singles are lonely.* Singles tend to be more lonely than married people; the feeling of loneliness is more pervasive for the divorced than for the never-married.

Relationships in the Singles World

Although dating in the singles world is somewhat different from dating in high school and college, there are similarities. Like their counterparts in school, singles emphasize recreation and entertainment, sociability, and physical attractiveness. But singles have considerably more casual sexual involvements. There are few virgins in the singles

Heterosexuals, gays, and lesbians cohabit. A significant difference between heterosexual and gay cohabitation is that many gay men and lesbians who would marry are prohibited from doing so by current laws.

world. The casualness of sex may be a source of problems. Men often desire more casual sex and fewer commitments than women; women often want greater intimacy, commitment, and emotional involvement than men.

MEETING EACH OTHER. The problem of meeting other single people is very often the central problem of the singles world. In college, students meet each other in classes or dormitories, at school events, or through friends. There are many meeting places and large numbers of eligibles. Singles have less opportunity to meet available people. For one thing, there are fewer eligible persons. For another, singles who are not also in school or taking courses do not have access to an informal network such as school provides. As a result, a singles industry of bars, resorts, clubs, and housing makes billions of dollars by providing opportunities for singles to become doubles.

Because of this lack of structure, most singles have to rely on meeting someone through friends; the blind date and arranged dinner party are major devices for meeting others in the singles world. One single person (in Bradley et al., 1977) said:

I will never say no when a friend says, "Hey, I'd like you to meet someone." I want to be totally open and available for any type of new meeting or encounter. Even if I'm tired, not feeling too well, doubtful, dubious, whatever, I'll usually make the effort to meet someone and consider the possibility, "This could be someone important. This could be someone wonderful."

Other frequent means of meeting singles include hobbies, work, and talking to a stranger (Barkas, 1980). Singles bars, bars, social or community functions, health clubs, and placing or answering personal ads are used less frequently. The least frequent means are video dating services, singles resorts or clubs, or introduction services (Mullan, 1984). Among those who are willing to try nontraditional means of meeting a partner, there may be less emphasis on homogamy. In a study of students who were asked to create advertisements of themselves, respondents tended to be less traditional regarding careers, ethnicity, and religion (LaBeff et al., 1989).

Miss, n. A title with which we brand unmarried women to indicate that they are in the market. Miss, Missis (Mrs.) and Mister (Mr.) are the three most distinctly disagreeable words in the language, in sound and sense. Two are corruptions of Mistress, the other of Master. In the general abolition of social titles in this country they miraculously escaped to plague us. If we must have them, let us be consistent and give one to the unmarried man. I venture to suggest Mush, abbreviated to Mh.

Ambrose Bierce (1842–1914?)

RELATIONSHIPS. When people form relationships within the singles world, both the man and woman tend to remain highly independent (Gagnon and Greenblat, 1978). Singles work, and, as a result, the man and woman tend to be economically independent of each other. They may also be more emotionally independent, because much of their energy may already be heavily invested in their work or careers. The relationship that forms consequently tends to emphasize autonomy and egalitarian roles. The fact that single women work is especially important. Single women tend to be more involved in their work, either from choice or necessity, but the result is the same: they are accustomed to living on their own without being supported by a man.

The emphasis on independence and autonomy blends with an increasing emphasis on self-fulfillment, which, some critics argue, makes it difficult for some to make commitments. Commitment requires sacrifice and obligation, which may conflict with ideas of "being oneself." A person under obligation can't necessarily do what he or she "wants" to do; such a person may have to do what "ought" to be done (Bellah et al., 1985; Lasch, 1977).

According to Barbara Ehrenreich (1984), men are more likely to flee commitment because they need women less than women need men. They feel oppressed by their obligation to be the family breadwinner. In the marital exchange, argues Ehrenreich, men need women less because men make more money than women and can obtain many of the "services" provided by wives, such as cooking, cleaning, intimacy, and sex, outside marriage without being tied down by family demands and obligations. Thus, men may not have a strong incentive to commit, marry, or stay married.

❖ COHABITATION

The Rise of Cohabitation

In 1990, more than 2.9 million heterosexual couples (and 1.5 million gay and lesbian couples) were living together in the United States (U.S. Bureau of the Census, 1991). In contrast, only 523,000 heterosexual couples were cohabiting in 1970. (For census purposes, heterosexuals who cohabit are called POSSLQs [pronounced *possel-kews*]—persons of the opposite sex sharing living quarters.) Cohabitation appears to be becoming part of the courtship process (Macklin, 1987; Tanfer, 1987).

Concerning cohabitation, Paul Glick and Graham Spanier (1980) noted, "Rarely does social change occur with such rapidity. Indeed, there have been few developments relating to marriage and family life which have been as dramatic as the rapid rise in unmarried cohabitation." Cohabitation is increasingly accepted at almost every level of society. By age 30, about half of all men and women will have cohabited. Currently, 4 percent are cohabiting (Bumpass and Sweet, 1988). Some scholars, in fact, believe that cohabitation is becoming institutionalized as part of the normal mate selection process (Gwartney-Gibbs, 1986). Today the only difference between those who cohabit and those who do not lies not in social adjustment, family background, or social class but in degree of religiousness. Those who have a high degree of religiosity and regular church attendance tend not to live together before marriage. For the religious, living together is still often considered "living in sin" (Newcomb, 1979). (For a discussion of cohabitation in Canada, see White, 1987).

Living together has become more widespread and accepted in recent years for several reasons. (For the pros and cons, see Gaylin, 1985, and Atwater, 1985.)

◆ *The general climate regarding sexuality is more liberal than it was a generation ago.* Sexuality is more widely considered to be an important part of a person's life, whether or not he or she is married. The moral criterion for judging sexual intercourse has shifted; love rather than marriage is now widely regarded as making a sexual act moral.

◆ *The meaning of marriage is changing.* Because of the dramatic increase in divorce over the last two decades, marriage is no longer thought of necessarily as a permanent commitment. Permanence is increasingly replaced by serial monogamy—a succession of marriages. Since the average marriage now lasts only seven years, the difference between marriage and living together is losing its sharpness.

◆ *Men and women are delaying marriage longer.* As long as children are not desired, living together offers advantages for many couples. When the couple want children, however, they will usually marry so that the child will be "legitimate."

Cohabitation does not seem to threaten marriage. Eleanor Macklin (1987), one of the major researchers in the field, noted:

Nonmarital cohabitation in the United States serves primarily as a part of the courtship process and not as an alternative to marriage. The great majority of young persons plan to marry at some point in their lives . . . and most cohabiting relationships either terminate or move into legal marriage within a year or two.

The most notable social impact of cohabitation is that it delays the age of marriage for those who live together. As a consequence, cohabitation may actually encourage more stable marriages, because the older a person is at the time of marriage, the less likely he or she is to divorce. Furthermore, a later marriage is likely to produce fewer children. Those who cohabit before marriage tend to want few or no children (Newcomb, 1979).

Types of Cohabitation

There is no single type of cohabitation, just as there is no single type of person who cohabits. At least five different types of relationships can be described, according to Macklin (1978):

◆ *Temporary casual convenience.* Two people share the same living quarters because it is expedient and convenient to do so.

◆ *Affectionate dating or going together.* Two people live together because they enjoy being with each other; they will continue living together as long as it is mutually satisfying.

◆ *Trial marriage.* This includes persons who are "engaged to be engaged" as well as couples who are trying to discover if they want to marry each other.

◆ *Temporary alternative to marriage.* Two people are committed to each other but are waiting for a better time to marry.

◆ *Permanent alternative to marriage.* Two people live together essentially as husband and wife but reject the idea of marriage.

Most college students who live together identify their cohabiting relationship as strong, affectionate, and monogamous. They share a deep attachment to each other but have not reached the point of making a long-term commitment. It is not known what proportion of older cohabiting couples fall into the various types.

Living together takes on a different quality among those who have been previously married. In 1989, about 40 percent of cohabitating relationships had at least one previously married partner, and about 30 percent of all cohabiting couples had children from earlier relationships. As a result, the motivation in these relationships is often colored by painful marital memories and the presence of children (Bumpass and Sweet, 1990). In these cases, men and women tend to be more cautious about making their commitment. They use their cohabitation as a way of testing their compatibility in marriage (Buunk and van Driel, 1989).

Cohabitation and Marriage Compared

TRANSITORY NATURE OF LIVING TOGETHER. Living together tends to be more transitory than marriage (Teachman and Polonko, 1990). A study based on national census figures indicates that 63 percent of such couples maintain a cohabiting relationship less than two years (Glick and Spanier, 1980). Either the couple split up or they get married. Those who marry after they have lived together usually do so because they want to formalize their commitment, because they want to have children, or because of pressures from parents or employers. Although cohabitation usually does not last as long as marriage, such relationships are often extremely satisfactory. They often end not because the relationship itself is bad but because marriage satisfies new or different needs.

DIFFERENT COMMITMENTS. When a couple live together, their primary commitment is to each other. As long as they feel they love each other, they will stay together. In marriage, the couple make a commitment not only to each other but to their marriage as well. Marriage often seems to become a third party that enters the relationship between a man and a woman. Each partner will do things to save a marriage; they may give up dreams, work, ambitions, and extramarital relationships to make a marriage work. A man and a woman who are living together may not work as hard to save their relationship. Although society encourages married couples to make sacrifices to save their marriage, unmarried couples rarely receive the same support. Parents may even urge their "living together" children to split up rather than give up plans for work, school, or career. If the couple is beginning to encounter sexual difficulties, it is more likely that they will split up if they are cohabiting than if they are married. It may be easier to abandon a problematic relationship than to change it.

TABLE 6.2   Unmarried Couples, by Selected Characteristics, 1970 to 1986, and by Marital Status of Partners, 1990 (in thousands)

PRESENCE OF CHILDREN AND AGE OF HOUSEHOLDER	1970	1980	1990	MARITAL STATUS OF MALE	TOTAL	MARITAL STATUS OF FEMALE NEVER MARRIED	DIVORCED	WIDOWED	HUSBAND ABSENT
Unmarried couples	523	1,589	2,856	Total 1990	2,856	1,595	963	142	157
No. of children under 15 yr.[1]	327	1,159	1,966	Never married	1,584	1,178	311	30	65
Some children under 15 yr.[1]	196	431	891	Divorced	973	285	555	60	44
Under 25 yr. old	55	411	911	Widowed	95	27	3	34	3
25–44 yr. old	103	837	1,945	Married, wife absent	204	77	40	19	46

[1]Children in unmarried-couple households are under 14 years old.

SOURCE: U.S. Bureau of the Census. *Marital Status and Living Arrangements: March 1990.* Population Reports Series, p. 20, 1991.

FINANCES. A striking difference between cohabiting and married couples is the pooling of money as a symbol of commitment (Blumstein and Schwartz, 1983). People generally assume that in marriage the couple will pool their money. This arrangement suggests a basic trust or commitment to the relationship; the individual is willing to sacrifice his or her particular interests to the interests of the relationship. Among most cohabiting couples, money is not pooled. In fact, one of the reasons couples cohabit rather than marry is to maintain a sense of financial independence. One man said, "A strong factor in the success of the relationship is the fact that we're economically independent of each other. We make no decisions that involve joint finances and that simplifies life a great deal" (Blumstein and Schwartz, 1983). Only if the couple expect to be living together for a long time or to marry do they pool their income. As Blumstein and Schwartz point out:

> Since the majority of cohabitors do not favor pooling, these facts say important things about pooling and commitment. When couples begin to pool their finances, it usually means they see a future for themselves. The more a couple pools, the greater the incentive to organize future financial dealings in the same way. As a "corporate" sense of the couple emerges, it becomes more difficult for the partners to think of themselves as unattached individuals.

WORK. Traditional marital roles call for the husband to work; it is left to the discretion of the couple whether the woman works. The husband is basically responsible for supporting his wife and family. In cohabiting relationships, the man is not expected to support his partner (Blumstein and Schwartz, 1983). If the woman is not in school, she is expected to work. If she is in school, she is nevertheless expected to support herself. Married couples may fight about the wife going to work; such fights do not generally occur among cohabiting couples.

SOCIETAL SUPPORT. Compared to marriage, cohabitation receives less social support, except from peers. It may be considered an inferior or immoral relationship—inferior to marriage because it does not symbolize lifetime commitment and immoral because it involves sexual activity without the sanction of marriage.

This lack of social reinforcement is an important factor in the greater instability of living-together relationships. Parents usually do not support cohabitation with the same enthusiasm as they would marriage. (If they do not like their son's or daughter's partner, however, they may console themselves with the thought that "at least they are not married.") Young adults often must hide the fact that they are living together for fear of parental rejection, anger, or reprisals.

Unmarried couples often find the greatest amount of social support from their friends, especially other couples who are living together. They are able to share similar problems with fellow cohabitants, such as whether to tell parents, how to handle visiting home together, difficulties in obtaining housing, and so forth. Because unmarried couples tend to have similar values, commitments, and uncertainties, they are able to give each other support in the larger noncohabiting world.

Impact of Cohabitation on Marital Success

There is no consensus on whether cohabitation significantly increases or decreases later marital stability (Teachman and Polonko, 1990). Although couples who are living together often argue that cohabitaton helps prepare them for marriage, such couples are statistically as likely to divorce as those who do not live together before marriage. In one study (Newcomb and Bentler, 1980), researchers interviewed 159 couples applying for marriage licenses. About half were living together at the time; the other half had not lived together. Four years later, the researchers were able to interview seventy-seven of these couples. Thirty-one percent had divorced. Those who had lived together were no less likely to have divorced than those who had not lived together. Among those still married, each group expressed about the same degree of marital satisfaction. Those who had lived together before argued less but had more problems with alcohol, drugs, and extramarital affairs. The differences probably had less to do with the effect of premarital cohabitation than with different personality characteristics. People who live together before marriage tend to be more liberal, more sexually experienced, and more independent than people who do not live together before marriage. Other studies have found that those who had cohabited before marriage were no more or less satisfied with their marriages than other couples (Jacques and Chason, 1979; Watson, 1983).

One study, however, noted slightly less marital satisfaction among married couples who had cohabited than among married couples who had not (DeMaris and Leslie, 1984). The researchers suggest that either cohabiting couples expect more out of marriage and are disappointed or else they are less likely to adapt well to traditional marital roles. They concluded:

The evidence accumulated to date would indicate that, while living together before marriage is increasingly becoming a common phase of courtship, cohabitation has no particular advantage over traditional practices in assuring couple compatibility in marriage.

❖ REFLECTIONS   *Have you ever cohabited? It you have, what were the advantages and disadvantages compared to marriage? If you have not cohabited, would you consider it? For yourself, what would be the pros and cons?*

❖ SUMMARY

◆ The *marriage marketplace* refers to the selection activities of men and women when sizing someone up as a potential date or mate. In this marketplace, each person has resources, such as social class, status, age, and physical attractiveness. People tend to choose partners whose overall rating is about the same as their own.

◆ The *marital exchange* is based on gender roles. Traditionally, men offer status, economic resources, and protection; women offer nurturing, childbearing, homemaking skills, and physical attractiveness. Recent changes in women's economic status give women more bargaining power; the decline in the value of housekeeping and children and the increase of female sexual availability give men more bargaining power.

◆ Initial impressions are heavily influenced by physical attractiveness. A *halo effect* surrounds attractive people, from which we infer that they have certain traits, such as warmth, intelligence, sexiness, and strength.

◆ The *"rating and dating"* game refers to the evaluation of men and women by their appearance. Most people, however, choose equals in terms of looks, intelligence, and education. If there is an appreciable difference in looks, usually there is some kind of trade-off in which a lower-ranked trait is exchanged for a higher-ranked one.

◆ The *field of eligibles* consists of those whom our culture approves as potential partners. It is limited by the principles of *endogamy*, marriage within a particular group, and *exogamy*, marriage outside the group.

◆ The field of eligibles if further limited by *homogamy*, the tendency to choose a mate whose individual or group characteristics are similar to ours, and by *heterogamy*, the tendency to choose a mate whose individual or group characteristics are different from ours. Homogamy is especially powerful in our culture, particularly the factors of race, religion, socioeconomic class, and age.

◆ According to Murstein, romantic relationships go through a three-stage development process: *stimulus-value-role*. Stimulus is what brings people together; value refers to the compatability of each person's basic values; and role refers to behaviors in roles as lover, companion, and so on.

◆ Traditional dating emphasizes formality, traditional gender roles, male assertiveness, and female passivity. More recently, the idea of "getting together" has developed. Getting together emphasizes mutuality, spontaneity, and egalitarian gender roles. It is less oriented toward mate selection than traditional dating.

◆ Friendship offers some of the same benefits as romantic or dating relationships. In contrast to dating relationships, sex is usually not an issue in friendships. Friendships may sometimes develop into romantic relationships.

◆ Problems in dating include who initiates the first date, who pays, and complementary gender role conceptions. For women, problems include sexual pressure from men, communication, and where to go on the date. For men, problems include communication, where to go, shyness, and money.

◆ The singles world consists of men and women over the age of twenty-five who have never married or are divorced, who are working, and who do not have primary childrearing responsibilities. In the singles world, relationships tend to be casual. Meeting other unattached persons is a major difficulty for singles. Continual tension exists between the alternatives of singlehood and marriage.

◆ Singles may be classified into *ambivalents,* who are voluntarily and temporarily single; *wishfuls,* who are involuntarily and temporarily single; *resolveds,* who are permanently single by choice; and *regretfuls,* who are permanently and involuntarily single.

◆ Relationships in the singles world tend to stress independence and autonomy. The emphasis on individual self-fulfillment works against the making of commitments. The marital exchange favors men in the singles world and may also work against commitment.

◆ Cohabitation has become acceptable in society. At least five types of cohabitation have been noted: (1) temporary casual convenience, (2) affectionate dating or going together, (3) trial marriage, (4) temporary alternative to marriage, and (5) permanent alternative to marriage. Compared with marriage, cohabitation is more transitory, has different commitments, and lacks extensive social support. It does not seem to have much effect on eventual marital success. Cohabitation has become increasingly popular because of a more liberal sexual climate, the changed meaning of marriage, delayed marriage, and delayed childbearing.

Answers to Preview Questions

The answers to the preview questions at the beginning of the chapter are listed below. As you check your answers, whether you were correct or not, think about your reasons

for each response. What were they? What was their source? How valid is the source? As you read the chapter, you will find the questions discussed in greater depth.

1.	T	6.	F
2.	T	7.	T
3.	F	8.	T
4.	F	9.	T
5.	T	10.	T

❖ SUGGESTED READINGS

Cargan, Leonard, and Matthew Melko. *Singles: Myths and Realities.* Beverly Hills, Calif.: Sage Publications, 1982. One of the best studies of the singles life-style.

Hatfield, Elaine, and Susan Sprecher. *Mirror, Mirror: The Importance of Looks in Everyday Life.* Albany, N.Y.: State University of New York Press, 1986. A survey concerning the significance of looks in relationships and our daily lives.

Mullan, Bob. *The Mating Trade.* Boston: Routledge & Kegan Paul, 1984. An excellent study of traditional matchmakers (the Jewish *shadkhan* and the Japanese *nakado*), marriage bureaus (which arrange marriages), dating services, and more recent innovations, including computer and video dating, personal ads, and gay dating services.

Murstein, Bernard. *Paths to Marriage.* Beverly Hills, Calif.: Sage Publications, 1986. A comprehensive discussion of love, dating, courtship, and marital choice from a social science perspective.

Perlman, Dan, and Steve Duck, eds. *Intimate Relationships: Development, Dynamics, and Deterioration.* Beverly Hills, Calif.: Sage Publications, 1987. An important collection of scholarly essays in the developing field of personal relationships.

Staples, Robert. *The World of Black Singles: Changing Patterns of Male/Female Relations.* Westport, Conn.: Greenwood Press, 1981. An excellent, well-written study of contemporary African-American relationships.

Whyte, Martin K. *Dating, Mating, and Marriage.* N.Y.: Aldine de Gruyter, 1990. A three-generational study of change based on a 459-member sample of women in Detroit.

Suggested Films

When Harry Met Sally (1989). Friends become lovers . . . eventually.

Annie Hall (1977). Woody Allen's classic comedy about love and disappointment.

The Importance of Being Earnest (1952). One of the great comic masterpieces of the theatre, written in the 1890s by Oscar Wilde, beautifully brought to film.

THE STATUS OF SINGLEHOOD

Enid Nemy

According to several researchers, single men and women have diminished status in American society. Do you agree? Why? What are the factors that affect a single person's status?

They don't all say it in the same way.

David Richenthal, a Manhattan lawyer in his early 40's who is single and lives alone, defined it as a dichotomy—on one side, society's "superficial" perception of single people and, on the other, singles' view of themselves.

"I've always had the emotional perception that the world at large is created for couples," he said.

For Mary Pizzarelli, who is in her early 30's, single means "always defending yourself to others; it's like, 'Why do you exist?'"

Not everyone living alone—a group now approaching 10 percent of the population according to census figures—shares these beliefs, but few would deny that life for singles is on a different track than that of married couples or single people who live together. In this era, saturated with images of home, hearth and children, the family of one finds itself further from the norm than it has been in the recent past.

"As in most societies, singles in our society are relegated to a diminished status," said Dr. Lawrence Hatterer, a Manhattan psychoanalyst whose practice is, in good part, made up of single men and women. "This despite the fact that there is greater acceptance of singles today and there are significant and growing groups of people who live alone, function with self-satisfaction and are respected as total human beings."

Still, he said, "marriage is perceived as being part of the success ethic, of being a total person. Single is perceived as being a flawed aspect."

Single people have to fend for themselves more, said Dr. Carol J. Weiss, a psychiatrist associated with New York Hospital-Cornell Medical Center who also has a private practice. "When someone is single, it is used to some degree and in a subtle way as a judgment against them," she said.

Nevertheless, in the past 20 years the number of men and women living alone has grown by more than 112 percent. Census figures have gone from 10,850,000 in 1970 to 23 million today; 61 percent of these people are women.

People who live alone make up "one of the fastest-growing household typologies in the last 20 years," said Peter Francese, the publisher of *American Demographics* magazine. Of this group, 46 percent are between the ages of 30 and 64, 40 percent are over 64 and only 14 percent are under 30.

Most single men and women are well aware that attitudes about them, both society's and their family's, are based not on fact but on perception.

"Whenever I go to a family wedding, I'm put with second cousins in their teens and early 20's," said Teri Leve, a freelance artist in Manhattan who is 44. "They never seat me with couples. I'm put at the children's table because I'm single. It's extremely insulting."

Ms. Pizzarelli, director of membership renewals at the Metropolitan Opera, said: "If you're a woman over 30 and not married, people feel sorry for you rather than thinking you might have a fulfilling life. They think something must be wrong that you haven't married yet."

She and a great many women who have never been married believe that single men have a somewhat better time of it in the eyes of society and that they are looked upon less judgmentally. One of the principal differences, they say, is that it is assumed, even by some women, that a man is single by choice but that a woman is not necessarily so.

Dr. Hatterer, who is married and an associate professor of clinical psychiatry at Cornell Medical College, agreed. There is, he said, a certain status or hierarchy in the world of single men and women. It exists not among the singles themselves but in society's perception of them.

But there are exceptions, he said, just as there are in the matter of status in society at large. Prestigious jobs, fame and money change perceptions about everyone. Physical attractiveness and a winning personality can also be contributing factors in mentally placing someone on a specific rung of society's ladder.

According to a dozen singles interviewed last week, Dr. Hatterer's pecking order is fairly accurate.

At the top of the heap in the eyes of society, Dr. Hatterer said, are "single attractive men, functioning heterosexuals."

"They are the kingpins," he said.

Mr. Richenthal agreed that there is a demand for single men. "But unless you feel in demand from someone you're attracted to, what does it mean that society tells you you are a great catch?" he said.

In fact, he was not quite sure that at a certain age, an unmarried man was not looked on as having some disabilities or character defects. "Sometimes I think it might be better to be regarded as divorced," he said.

But it is widowers who are next on the list, Dr. Hatterer said, because they are perceived as not only heterosexual but as not having been promiscuous, an important attribute today because of AIDS. Widowers are also thought of as capable of a stable and lasting relationship, "which makes people feel safer," he said.

Widows follow, perceived as "less valuable than widowers," Dr. Hatterer said, because (a) there are more of them, (b) elements of age come into play to a greater degree and (c) there are considerations of whether they will carry their own weight financially.

continued on next page

The next rung consists of divorced men and women. Perceptions of them vary greatly, depending on how frequently the person has been divorced, how long the marriage or marriages lasted, the quality of the relationship, children, their ages and where they are, and the financial situation.

"We still have to deal with pockets of society who perceive divorce as a failure," he said. "But divorced men are thought of less in terms of failure than divorced women."

Women who have never been married do not perceive themselves as a notch below widows and divorced women, but many acknowledge that in society's eyes, they often are.

Dr. Weiss, however, believes that attractiveness and personality play a more important role in the perception of singles than does their sex. She places single men and women on a more equal basis in the hierarchy.

"I think that if it's an attractive woman who isn't married, there is usually an assumption that, like men, she could have been," she said.

Dr. Hatterer's view is that it also depends to some extent on how a woman perceives herself.

"If she perceives herself as not dependent, whether for nourishment, status or money, she generally fares better in the eyes of society, as do unmarried women who are employed," he said. "And single women with some power, money and accomplishment fare even better."

Homosexual men and women are considered to have the most difficulty when it comes to how they are perceived by others. But as with all categories of singles, talent, fame, affluence and personality elevate some of the top levels.

"Sexual preference is often overlooked if a gay man or woman is famous, powerful or rich," said Jeff Perrone, 37, a gay artist. "They may have a wider circle of friends, be invited to more dinner parties and be more in demand, but I don't know if they're more accepted."

"My reaction, and that of my friends, is that we basically won't be accepted anyway, so we say we don't care, and we don't," he said. "But I realize that there are gay people who do."

THE DILEMMA OF BLACK SINGLE WOMEN

Gloria Naylor

Black single women have to deal with the same problems as white single women as well as issues of racisim and assimilation. What is the author's assessment of the situation?

The Chinese restaurant is in a section of Pennsylvania Avenue in Washington where the table linen is changed after each meal, the Boston ferns are real, and the stir-fried string beans and ginger will cost you the down payment on a plot of land to grow your own. The young woman who comes in and sits alone could have stepped out of any Ebony Christmas ad for Courvoisier: her shoulder-length braids are impeccable, the honey-brown skin has red highlights around the cheekbones from either the chill wind or conservatively applied blush. She moves her manicured hands with the grace of someone who is accustomed to having them pampered each week. As she places her leather portfolio on the seat beside her and picks up the menu, her body language is indisputable: she is treating herself in celebration of some personal victory—a successful business meeting? A new promotion at work? bank approval of a condominium loan? Any of those could be plugged into this picture realistically, and what is all too real is the fact that she's celebrating alone.

Now, it's quite possible that young woman elected to be eating there by herself, or that she had a male counterpart waiting somewhere with yellow roses and a bottle of fairly decent wine to cap off her achievement, but the statistics and a random sampling of my friends tell me that it is not the likely case. I don't have to go to the census reports to find out that stable relationships between black men and women are quickly losing ground as the divorce rates, households headed by women and the numbers of never-married women proliferate; I can just start flipping through my telephone book. In the B's is a divorced friend who just decided to adopt a child alone, in the C's one in her early 40's who has never married, in the L's another divorced friend who went to St. Croix to find a new husband, in the M's three women raising a sum total of eight children single-handedly. Were I to ring them up, the personal histories and causes for their situations would vary, but their bewilderment would be consistent and echo my own. What exactly *is* the problem between us and our men today?

It is the same problem that is at the root of deteriorating relationships in all America, and then some. But it's the "then some" that compounds our predicament. While dealing with the pressures of modernization, along with the transitory nature of the nuclear family that all American couples must deal with, we must also battle the erosive factors that racism thrusts into the landscape of our personal relationships. One is a factor of numbers: we are a minority community overrepresented in the pools of the unemployed, the poorly educated and those subsisting below the poverty line, which will concomitantly insure overrepresentation in teenage pregnancy, drug abuse and the prison population. In short, there just aren't enough viable mates out there for black women and bleak prospects of a greater percentage being born.

continued on next page

And this shrinking pool of prospects means that a vicious cycle is setting in for the future: our women will marry later, if at all, thus having fewer children or none. True, smaller families are occurring in the white middle-class community as well; but the loss of numbers has deeper implications for a minority community whose majority is confined to an underclass.

The second factor raises a very painful subject: one of the high costs of assimilation for the few has been the erosion of a healthy ethnocentric identity. Black professionals have found the rewards are greater for those who can swim the fastest and easiest with the flow, which means superimposing an alien set of values upon a distinct racial personality. Assertive, self-directed women were traditionally looked upon as valuable assets in African and African-American families; it was a matter of common sense and survival in heavily agricultural existences and the subsequent low-paid urban ones. It gave rise to a breed of women who are conditioned to serve a functional rather than an ornamental role for their male counterparts. The concept is relatively new for us that a woman who insists on equal (or even superior) weight being given to her opinions, her salary and her decision-making ability in the home is "threatening" to black manhood.

Assimilation has not stopped with the adoption of a life-style by the leaders of the power structure; our men have adopted the upper-middle-class perceptions of an "ideal" balance between the sexes, too. Thus, professional black women find themselves having to juggle the pressure of their own careers with tense personal relationships because of expectations that they be something they simply are not—but more importantly, cannot be. It hurts to think that one of the impediments to stability with our men might be, at its most basic level, everything that is *us.*

I know that consolation cannot be found by going back to my phone book and ringing up my white female friends. They have their own horror stories to tell. They may be in a slightly larger boat, but it's still rocky.

I tend to look with a jaundiced eye upon the businesses that have grown out of this search for compatible partners: computer dating services, singles' travel clubs and newsletters. It is so typically American to find a way even to package loneliness—the construction of smaller apartments, the canning of soup for one. The "personal" columns, once confined to the back pages of smut magazines as the province of men who didn't have the courage to ask a woman to her face if she liked having hard-boiled eggs bounced on her navel, have found a new respectability and a new clientele.

Not surprisingly, ads, along with magazines like *Chocolate Singles,* are gaining popularity among upwardly mobile black women. They replace the personal networks once provided by church attendance and family and friends, now lost to individuals who are demographically and socially in transit. Such publications, composed of a few pages of newsprint with slick covers, attempt to disguise the fact that they are primarily a clearinghouse for personal ads. Tongue-in-cheek names like *Chocolate Singles* are emblematic of this subterfuge. Why not call it "Dark and Desperate," getting straight to the point? In the December issue the personals section bore out the living reality: the "Male Advertisers" took up three and a half columns, the "Female Advertisers" twice that many.

Professional black women using these ads suggest that an increasing number are finally deciding to broaden their options: the phrases "any nationality," "open to a variety of cultural experiences" and "race unimportant" appear. I happen to be in the camp that believes race and culture hold a great deal of importance in compatibility. Yet, while the natural inclination of human beings is like to like, the most unnatural thing in the world is to go through life without feeling appreciated and loved.

Unlike the alarmists, I don't see this as portending the demise of our ethnic uniqueness. I have only painted one side of the scenario: the statistics also bear out that for each black woman who is alone, there is one in a stable relationship. Among my acquaintances are many families who are a living counterpart (if a much less saccharine version) of "The Cosby Show." Depending upon how you look at it, the glass is either half-empty or half-full, but half either way is far from sufficient.

PART THREE

Sexuality

CHAPTER 7

Sexual Learning and Behavior

To gain a sense of what you already know about the material covered in this chapter, answer "true" or "false" to the following statements below. You will find the answers on page 209.

1. Unlike most behavior, sexual behavior is instinctive. True or false?
2. A woman's breasts are universally considered to be erotic. True or false?
3. It is fairly common to have erotic fantasies during sexual intercourse. True or false?
4. A significant number of women require manual or oral stimulation of the clitoris to experience orgasm. True or false?
5. The most important factor affecting a healthy aged person's sexual interaction is the availability of a partner. True or false?
6. Men are more likely to have multiple orgasms than women. True or false?
7. Many husbands and wives continue to masturbate after marriage. True or false?
8. The male sexual script equates sex with intercourse. True or false?
9. Women are more likely than men to sexually identify with media figures. True or false?
10. Oral-genital sex has become a widely accepted part of the American sexual repertoire. True or false?

The sexual act is in time what the tiger is in space.

Georges Bataille

The only unnatural sex act is one that can't be performed.

Alfred Kinsey

❖ LEARNING TO BE SEXUAL

I MAGINE YOURSELF SITTING ON THE BEACH, READING. You see a man or woman walk by and feel a flash of sexual attraction to him or her. What is it that attracts you? Often we ascribe our feelings to the other person, saying that he or she has sex appeal. Actually, this sex appeal resides more in us than in the person to whom we are attracted. Our culture defines what is "sexy." Through learning we incorporate our culture's ideas of what traits, looks, body features, and so on are sexually appealing.

Beneath the apparent instinctiveness of sexuality lies a profound amount of learning that begins in childhood. We learn to whom to be attracted, when to be attracted, what to do sexually, and how to feel about what we do. All of these factors are defined by culture and learned by each individual (Cook, 1981; Simon and Gagnon, 1984).

Cultures vary in what they consider sexually attractive and arousing (Dion, 1981; Rosenblatt and Anderson, 1981). The aspects of beauty that appear universal are health and youth, both of which are linked to the reproductive aspects of sexuality. The only cultural constants of a man's sexual attractiveness are his skills, prowess, strength, and health, not his appearance per se. In contrast, a woman's sexual attractiveness tends to be perceived more in terms of physical appearance. The specifics of attractiveness vary from culture to culture. Many cultures view a woman's breasts as nonsexual; in our culture, breasts are considered to be erotic. In Victorian America, a woman's ankles were seen as being erotic; today no one pays much attention to ankles. Obesity in men was valued in Polynesia; in the United States, fitness and a trim body are the ideal.

Although we are born with the potential to be sexual, we actually learn how to behave sexually. In this chapter we will examine how we learn to be sexual and how this differs for males and females. We will also examine the sexual response cycle, sexual behavior, sexuality and aging, and sexual dysfunctions.

The Role of Culture

Our sexual behaviors are the result of a complicated series of sexual decisions. These decisions, however, rarely reach our awareness. Over time they have become automatic. This is because we have repeated the decision many times before, and we have been given a ready-made cultural script that encourages us to act in certain ways. As John Gagnon (1977) wrote:

There is nothing in any particular event in itself which produces sexual arousal—the classification of a stimulus as sexual and a response as sexual is the outcome of a history of decisions made by an individual in a particular society and culture. It is usually difficult for us to recall our first making the decisions to label and connect stimulus and response, partly because we often merely accept the models provided us.

Think again about reading on the beach and seeing the attractive man or woman walking along the water's edge. This time, the person smiles at you in passing. You might smile back briefly, then resume your reading. Or you might encode or define the event as sexual, the smile as a flirtation or a sexual invitation. If you encode the event as sexual, what will you do? A typical response in our culture is to begin a sexual fantasy of meeting the person later on the beach, walking in the moonlight, and spending the rest of the evening kissing or making love next to a brightly burning fire. Once you decide to define the event as sexual, the fantasy begins to unfold without much more ado. What you are not aware of is that you have learned to define certain kinds of smiles as flirtatious or erotic and people dressed in bathing suits as erotic objects. Being at the beach is a legitimate place for erotic fantasies; it is culturally appropriate to have fantasies about strangers (but not to engage in real-life sexual behaviors with them). Typical erotic fantasies in our culture include romance, kissing, or making love, with each individual providing his or her own details.

When we are engaged in sexual activities, we experience love, guilt, tenderness, anxiety, hostility, security, and other feelings. We may believe that the feelings come from the physical acts, but they are feelings we have learned to associate with the acts. This learning can be explained by Stanley Schacter's two-component theory of emotion. As you recall from Chapter 5, Schacter argued that two factors must coexist for a person to experience an emotion. First, the person must be physiologically aroused. Second, it must be appropriate for the person to interpret the physiological arousal in emotional terms. Needless to say, sexual arousal and behaviors are strong physiological events; even the frustration caused by sexual inhibitions facilitates physiological responses. We have learned to associate these arousals with various emotions. Most of us learned in childhood and adolescence, for example, to associate masturbation with guilt. Our culture teaches us—especially females—to associate sexual intercourse with love. But love is no more a part of the physiological responses that make up sex than is guilt. We may even link hatred, jealousy, and pain to sexual arousal (Dutton and Aron, 1974).

The link between emotions and sexual activity can be confusing. When two people make love, they may associate quite different emotions with the act; one person may feel a great sense of intimacy, whereas the other may feel alienation. We may mislabel our feelings about someone because of our arousal. People often ask themselves if it is sexual attraction or love that they feel: "Am I in love or in lust?"

Sexual Scripts

Our gender roles are critical in learning sexuality. Gender roles tell us what behavior (including sexual behavior) is appropriate for each gender. Our sexual impulses are organized and directed through our sexual scripts, which we learn and act out. A script is like a road map or blueprint that gives general directions; it is more like a sketch than a detailed picture of how our culture expects us to act. But even though a script is generalized, it is often more important in guiding our actions than our own experiences. Over time, we may modify or change our scripts, but we will not throw them away.

The interpersonal script is the area of shared conventions that makes sexual behavior possible. People follow a sequence of steps to define a situation as sexual and to act on that definition. Inviting a person to study with you at the library defines the situation as nonsexual; inviting a person to study with you in your apartment when your roommate is gone may define the situation as potentially sexual. More clues are needed to clear up ambiguity. Signs or gestures—verbal or nonverbal—also define encounters as sexual or nonsexual. People try to make their sexual motives clear (or unclear) by the way they look at each other, by the tone of their voices, by the movement of their bodies, or by other culturally shared phenomena: proximity, touching, glances, words. Moving from the living room to the bedroom to study further defines the situation as erotic. Then the individuals must decide what sexual behaviors are going to take place: kissing, petting, oral sex, sexual intercourse, and so on. This decision depends on many factors. How much do I like or love this person? What are my moral values? Are condoms available? What if my roommate comes home? If I say no, what will be the consequences for our relationship?

Remember this

In our society, intimacy is more frightening than sex. This is somewhat more of a problem for men, but it is also true for women.

Helen Singer Kaplan

Because sexual desire is in the minds of most people coupled with the idea of love, they are easily misled to conclude that they love each other when they want each other physically. . . . Sexual attraction creates, for the moment, the illusion of union, yet without love this "union" leaves strangers as far apart as they were before.

Erich Fromm, The Art Of Loving

If the couple decide to have intercourse, they will probably follow the general cultural script for sexual intercourse, even though it may not fit the particular situation or individuals. Although the script calls for the male to caress his partner's breasts, she may be self-conscious about their size and may not respond to his touch. She may like having the light on; he may not. The man may prefer the woman-on-top position, although she may expect him to be on top. Partners may be concerned about the way their genitals appear, whether the penis is too small, whether the vagina has an unpleasant odor. The man may worry about becoming erect, the woman about being orgasmic. The couple must discover how to interact compatibly with their bodies, how to move arms and legs and pelvises, how to move the genitals to give pleasure to both partners. When it is over, the individuals must return to their nonsexual world—yet coitus has given new meaning to their interactions. What do they say to each other now? To others? Only after partners have had experience with each other will the integration of sexual and nonsexual roles become easier.

As a couple spend more time together, they are able to integrate sexual intimacy with emotional intimacy, trust, and comfort. This allows many couples to experience greater satisfaction and fulfillment in their sexual experiences. Linda Levine and Lonnie Barbach (1985), in a study of 120 men, observed:

Part of the reason sex was better in an emotionally involved relationship was that the caring and comfort facilitated a level of communication that enhanced the physical experience. With time came a sense of safety and security that enabled the partners to risk communicating specific sexual information that was often necessary in order for the sex to be especially fulfilling.

SCRIPT AMBIGUITIES. One of the major problems men and women have is how to interpret signals—gestures, mannerisms, and so on—as sexual or nonsexual. Was the smile given to us by the man or woman on the beach actually flirtatious or was it merely friendly? Men are more likely to interpret the smile as flirtatious, whereas women are more likely to find it friendly. Men tend to sexualize relationships more than females. For example, if a woman initiates the first date, men are likely to view that as a sign that the woman wants to have sex (Komarovsky, 1985).

Sources of Learning

The cultural scripts we are given for sexual behavior tend to be traditional. These scripts are most powerful during adolescence, when we are first learning to be sexual. Gradually, as we gain experience, we modify and change these sexual scripts. Initially we learn our sexual scripts primarily from our parents, peers, and the media. As we get older, interactions with our partners become increasingly important. In adolescence, both middle-class whites and middle-class African Americans appear to share similar values and attitudes about sex and male/female relationships (Howard, 1988).

PARENTS. Despite their best efforts, parents are usually not much help for adolescents trying to understand their emerging sexuality. Parents reveal little of their own sexual feelings while expecting to be privy to their child's sexual world. Such parents are in a dilemma. On the one hand, they are supposed to play a positive role in the development of their child's sexuality; on the other hand, almost no form of sexual behavior is approved by society before marriage. As a result, parents tend to limit their sexual teachings to prohibitions reflecting societal values. In fact, most of their

Pop culture saturates us with its erotic images. Music videos have the most sexual content of any medium, transforming Madonna into one of the leading erotic icons of the 1990s.

what A
PIG!!!

efforts are directed toward limiting sexual behaviors rather than guiding them. One mother who found erotica in her son's room wrote to "Dear Abby," describing how she handled such problems:

> When I find a girlie magazine in the room of any of our three teenage sons, I remove it and replace it with a 3 x 5 index card with a Bible verse covering that very subject. I've never had a complaint from any of them, as they know from the verses that they are to "abstain from fleshy lusts."

Needless to say, such acts, however well intentioned, only make it more difficult for adolescents to turn to their parents.

Parental norms and beliefs appear not to have a strong effect on an adolescent's decision to become sexually active. Peers seem to be the most important factor. But lack of rules and structure seem to be related to more permissive sexual attitudes and premarital sex (Forste and Heaton, 1988; Miller, McCoy, Olson, and Wallace, 1986). Parental communication does have considerable impact on whether an adolescent will use contraception (Baker, Thalberg, and Morrison, 1988). A study of African-American adolescents (Scott-Jones and Turner, 1988) found that the majority of parents not only gave their daughters information about sex but also instructed them about contraception. Mothers and grandmothers are especially important sources of sex information for African-American adolescents (Tucker, 1989). Although parents may seem to have little impact on their children's decision making, the strategy of advising, "Don't have sex, but if you do, use a condom," offers hope toward preventing adolescent pregnancies and sexually transmitted diseases. Sex educator Sol Gordon (1984) recommends this "double standard of sex education."

— lecture

lecture

Regardless of ethnicity, parents rarely advise their young or adolescent children of the erotic or pleasurable aspects of sexuality, perhaps for fear that such knowledge will encourage them to engage in sexual activities.

PEERS.   Peers, especially from ages twelve to sixteen, are a powerful source of sexual learning. (See the reading, "The Slumber Party," by Marilyn Hiller.) Unfortunately, because they lack experience and rely on the media for information, adolescent peers tend to reinforce sexual stereotypes. Adolescent males in particular camouflage their sexual ignorance, which leads to greater misinformation. Bill Cosby (1968) recalled early adolescence, with its pressures to have sexual intercourse, and his own ignorance. "But how do you find out how to do it without blowin' the fact that you don't know how to do it?" On his way to his first sexual encounter, he realized that he didn't have the faintest idea of what to do:

So now I'm walkin', and I'm trying to figure out what to do. And when I get there, the most embarrassing thing is gonna be when I have to take my pants down. See, right away, then, I'm buck naked . . . buck naked in front of this girl. Now, what happens then? Do . . . do you just . . . I don't even know what to do. . . . I'm gonna just stand there and she's gonna say, "You don't know how to do it." And I'm gonna say, "Yes I do but I *forgot*." I never thought of her showing me, because I'm a man and I don't want her to show me. I don't want *nobody* to show me, but I wish somebody would kinda slip me a note.

An adolescent's perception of peers' sexual behavior may be the single most important factor influencing his or her own sexual behavior. But such perceptions are often unreliable indicators of actual behavior. In keeping with traditional gender roles, boys tend to exaggerate their sexual experience and girls tend to understate it.

Premarital sexual intercourse appears to have a somewhat greater positive effect on subsequent sexual attitudes and behaviors for white adolescents than for African-American adolescents. Whites become more positive about sex; African Americans generally have been positive from the start. After premarital sex, whites tend to select friends from among other whites who are sexually experienced. Such peer influence supports their sexual values. All in all, the researchers believe that sexual experience does not create any overwhelming psychological or social changes in whites or African Americans (Billy, Landale, Grady, and Zimmerle, 1988).

Peer influence appears to have been responsible for two of the most notable changes in sexual scripts in the last twenty years: the legitimacy of premarital sex for women and oral-genital sex for both sexes (Gagnon and Simon, 1987; Reed and Weinberg, 1984). The initial support for these changes came from peers, who advocated them as part of the sexual revolution of the 1960s and 1970s. Peers emphasized the relational context of sexuality as opposed to its marital context, making female sexuality acceptable outside of marriage. Youth also rejected the reproductive model of sex that emphasized procreation as the sole goal of sexuality. Instead, they replaced it with a new model that viewed erotic pleasure as a legitimate end in itself. This contemporary model transformed oral sex from an immoral activity to a mutually satisfying one.

THE MEDIA.   The media has a profound impact on our sexual attitudes. Anthropologist Michael Moffatt (1989) noted that about a third of the students he studied at Rutgers University mentioned the impact of college and college friends on their sexual development and another third mentioned their parents and religious values. But he found that *the* major influence on their sexuality was contemporary American pop culture.

Our collective fantasies center on mayhem, cruelty, and violent death. Loving images of the human body—especially of bodies seeking pleasure or expressing love—inspire us with the urge to censor.

Barbara Ehrenreich

The direct sources of the students' sexual ideas were located almost entirely in mass consumer culture: the late-adolescent/young-adult exemplars displayed in movies, popular music, advertising, and on TV; Dr. Ruth and sex manuals; *Playboy, Penthouse, Cosmopolitan, Playgirl,* etc; Harlequins and other pulp romances (females only); the occasional piece of real literature; sex education and popular psychology as it had filtered through these sources, as well as through public schools, and as it continued to filter through the student-life infrastructure of the college; classic soft-core and hard-core pornographic movies; books; and (recently) home videocassettes.

PARTNERS. Parents, peers, and the media become less important in our sexual learning as we get older, to be replaced by our sexual partners. The experience of interpersonal sexuality is ultimately the most important source of modifying traditional sexual scripts. Describing the sources of men's sexual learning, Levine and Barbach (1985) noted:

Before their first sexual encounter, men could only rely on secondary sources for information about sex. But once they lost their virginity, women became their primary source of information. It was their continued sexual experience that ultimately expanded and enriched men's sexual repertoire. Their skill at the game of love evolved over time, through trial and error. Each experience left them with a clearer sense of themselves as sexual men. But until they acquired this self-confidence, many men were reluctant to drop their he-man facades and reveal to their partners that they were less than skilled lovers.

In relationships, men and women learn that the sexual scripts and models they learned from parents, peers, and the media do not necessarily work in the real world. They adjust their attitudes and behaviors in everyday interactions. If they are married, sexual expectations and interactions become important factors in their sexuality (see Chapter 8).

❖ REFLECTIONS *Think about what you learned about sex and sexuality from your parents, peers, the media, or your partners. What was their influence on your sexual attitudes and behavior? On your sexual morality or values? Do you view their contributions positively or negatively? Why?*

Traditional Sexual Scripts

Traditional sexual scripts are most powerful when we are young and inexperienced. These scripts vary according to gender. Male scripts tend to exaggerate sexuality, whereas female scripts tend to underrate it. *— Lecture*

MALE SEXUAL SCRIPTS. Bernie Zilbergeld (1979) calls the male sexual script the "fantasy model" of sex. He suggests that men hold a number of myths about sexuality, which include the following:

◆ *Men should not have (or at least should not express) certain feelings.* Men should not express doubts; they should be assertive, confident, and aggressive. Tenderness and compassion are not masculine feelings.
◆ *Performance is the thing that counts.* Sex is something to be achieved, to be a winner at. Feelings only get in the way of the job to be done. Sex is not for intimacy but for orgasm.
◆ *The man is in charge.* As in other things, the man is the leader, the person who knows what is best. The man initiates sex and gives the woman her orgasm. A real man doesn't need a woman to tell him what women like; he already knows.

To be a really good lover, then, one must be strong and yet tender.

How strong?

I suppose being able to lift fifty pounds should do it.

Woody Allen, Without Feathers

◆ *A man always wants sex and is ready for it*. It doesn't matter what is going on, a man wants sex; he is always able to become erect. He is a machine.

◆ *All physical contact leads to sex*. Since men are basically sexual machines, any physical contact is a sign for sex. Touching is seen as the first step toward sexual intercourse; it is not an end in itself. There is no physical pleasure except sexual pleasure.

◆ *Sex equals intercourse*. All erotic contact leads to sexual intercourse. Foreplay is just that: warming up, getting one's partner excited for penetration. Kissing, hugging, erotic touching, or oral sex are only preliminaries to intercourse.

◆ *Sexual intercourse leads to orgasm*. The orgasm is the proof of the pudding. The more orgasms, the better the sex. If a woman does not have an orgasm, she is not sexual. The man feels that he is a failure because he was not good enough to give her an orgasm. If a woman requires clitoral stimulation to have an orgasm, she has a problem.

Common to all these myths is a separation of sex from love (or any feelings). Sex is a performance.

FEMALE SEXUAL SCRIPTS. Whereas the traditional male sexual focuses on sex over feelings, the traditional female sexual script focuses on feelings over sex, on love over passion. The traditional female sexual scripts cited by Barbach (1982) include the following:

◆ *Sex is good and bad*. Women are taught that sex is both good and bad. What makes sex good? Marriage or a committed relationship. What makes sex bad? A casual or uncommitted relationship. Sex is good, so good that a woman needs to save it for her husband (or for someone with whom she is deeply in love). Sex is bad; if it is not sanctioned by love or marriage, she'll get a bad reputation.

◆ *Sex is for men*. Men want sex, women do not. Women are sexually passive, waiting to be aroused. As a result of this script, women do not feel comfortable about asserting their sexual needs and desires.

◆ *Men should know what women want*. This script tells women that men know what they want—even if women don't tell them. Women are supposed to remain pure and sexually innocent. It is up to the man to arouse the woman, even if he doesn't know what a particular woman finds arousing. To keep her image of sexual innocence, she does not tell him what she wants.

◆ *Women shouldn't talk about sex*. Many women cannot easily talk about sex. Our language does not have many good words to describe it. We only have scientific words ("sexual intercourse"), obscene words ("fuck"), and euphemisms ("make love"); the first seems cold, the second dirty, and the third coy. Not only does the lack of words inhibit communication but so does the reluctance to admit sexual feelings and the lack of sexual assertiveness. People sometimes feel that they don't know their partners well enough to communicate their needs. Ironically, they know their partners well enough to have sex but not well enough to talk about it.

◆ *Women should look like "Playmates."* The media present ideally attractive women as "Playmates," beautiful models with slender hips, large breasts, and long legs. They are always young, with not a pimple, wrinkle, or gray hair in sight. Ordinary women worry that they are too fat, too plain, too old. As a result of these cultural images, many women are self-conscious about their physical appearance. They often feel awkward without their clothes on to hide their imagined flaws.

◆ *Women are nurturers*. Women give, men receive. Women give themselves, their bodies, their pleasures to men. Everyone else's needs come first—his desire over hers, his orgasm over hers. If a woman always puts her partner's enjoyment first, she

Sex, depersonalized, allows us to avoid the challenge of using our whole self, our total energies and feelings, to present and communicate ourselves to another. Sex is the victim of the fear of love.

Rosemary Reuther

Sentiments are for the most part traditional; we feel them because they were felt by those who preceded us.

William Hazlitt (1778–1830)

may be depriving herself of her own enjoyment. As Barbach (1982) points out, "If our attention is so totally riveted on another person, or on external events rather than on ourselves, it is impossible to experience the full pleasure and sensation of the sexual event."

◆ *There is only one right way to have an orgasm.* Women often learn that there is only one "right" way to have an orgasm: during sexual intercourse as a result of penile stimulation. But there are many ways to have orgasm: through oral sex; manual stimulation before, during or after intercourse; masturbation with a vibrator; and so on. For women who rarely or never have orgasm during heterosexual intercourse to believe this is the only legitimate way to orgasm deprives them of expressing themselves sexually in other ways.

Contemporary Sexual Scripts

Traditional sexual scripts have been challenged by more liberal and egalitarian ones. Sexual attitudes and behaviors have become increasingly liberal for both white and African-American males and females; African-American attitudes and behaviors continue to be somewhat more liberal than those of whites (Belcastro, 1985; Gutherie, 1988; Peters and Wyatt, 1988; Weinberg and Wilson, 1988; Wilson, 1986). Many college-age women have made an explicit break with the more traditional scripts, especially the good girl/bad girl dichotomy and the older belief that "nice" girls don't enjoy sex (Moffatt, 1989). Older professional single women also appear to reject the old images (Davidson and Darling, 1988). We do not know how Latino sexuality and Asian-American sexuality have changed, as there is almost no research on their sexual scripts, values, and behavior.

Contemporary sexual scripts include the following elements for *both* genders (Gagnon and Simon, 1987; Reed and Weinberg, 1984; Rubin, 1990; Seidman, 1989; Strong and DeVault, 1988):

◆ Sexual expression is a positive good.
◆ Sexual activities are a mutual exchange of erotic pleasure.
◆ Sexuality is equally involving and both partners are equally responsible.
◆ Legitimate sexual activities are not limited to sexual intercourse but also include masturbation and oral-genital sex.
◆ Sexual activities may be initiated by either partner.
◆ Both partners have a right to experience orgasm, whether through intercourse, oral-genital sex, or manual stimulation.
◆ Nonmarital sex is acceptable within a relationship context.

These contemporary scripts give increasing recognition to female sexuality; they are increasingly relationship-centered rather than male-centered. Women, however, are still not granted full sexual equality with males (Williams and Jacoby, 1989).

The sources of these script changes may be traced to increasingly egalitarian gender roles; the replacement of the conservative sex-as-reproduction ideology with the liberal sex-as-pleasure ideology that emphasizes the pleasurable, bonding aspects of sexuality; and the recognition of female sexuality (Strong and De Vault, 1988).

❖ REFLECTIONS *What are the sexual scripts you have acquired as a man or woman? Have they enhanced, limited, or inhibited your sexuality? Why? Have they changed over time? Why?*

Your Sexual Scripts

Our sexual scripts tell us the *whos, whats, whens, wheres,* and *whys* of sexuality (Gagnon, 1977). They tell us with whom to be sexual, what to do sexually, when to be sexual, where to engage in sexual activities, and why we engage in these activities. These scripts change over time, depending on a person's age, sexual experience, and interactions with intimate partners and others. Let's examine them in relation to yourself.

Who   The factors of homogamy and heterogamy are almost as strong in selecting sexual partners as they are in choosing marital partners, in part because marital and sexual partners are often one and the same. Society tells us to have sex with people who are not closely related to us, who are around our age, and who are of the other sex (heterosexual). Less acceptable is having sex with oneself (that is, masturbation) and sex with members of the same sex (gay or lesbian sexuality).

Examine the *whos* in your sexual script. With whom do you engage in sexual behaviors? How do your choices reflect homogamy and heterogamy? What social factors influence your choice? Does your autoerotic behavior change if you are in a relationship? How? Why?

What   Society classifies sexual acts as good and bad, moral and immoral, appropriate and inappropriate. What sexual acts are part of your sexual script? How are they regarded by society? How important is the level of commitment in a relationship in determining your sexual behaviors? What level of commitment do you need for kissing? Petting? Sexual intercourse? What occurs when you and your partner have different sexual scripts for engaging in various sexual behaviors?

When   *When* refers to timing. You might make love when your parents are out of the house or, if a parent yourself, when your children are asleep. Usually, this type of *when* is related to privacy. But *whens* are also related to

age. At what age is it appropriate for a person to engage in sexual activities? When does a person's sexual activity end?

When are the times you engage in sexual activities? Are the times related to privacy? When did you experience your first erotic kiss? At what age did you experience your first intercourse? If you have not experienced sexual intercourse, at what age do you think it would be appropriate? How was (or will) the timing for first intercourse (be) determined? What influences (friends, parents, religion) are brought to bear on the age timing of sexual activities?

Where   Where does society approve of sexual activities occurring? In our society, it is usually in the bedroom, where a closed door signifies privacy. For adolescents it may also be in an automobile. Fields, beaches, motels, and drive-in theaters may be identified as locations for sex. Churches, classrooms, and front yards usually are not.

For yourself, where are the acceptable places to be sexual? What makes them acceptable for you? Have you ever had conflicts with partners about the wheres of sex? Why?

Why   The *whys* are the explanations we give ourselves and others about our sexual activities. There are many reasons for having sex: procreation, love, passion, revenge, intimacy, exploitation, fun, pleasure, relaxation, boredom, achievement, relief from loneliness, exertion of power, and on and on. Some of these explanations are approved, others are not; some we conceal, others we do not.

What are your reasons for sexual activities? Do you have different reasons for different activities, such as masturbation, oral sex, or sexual intercourse? Do the reasons change with different partners? With the same partner? Which reasons are societally approved, and which are disapproved? What reasons do you make known, and which do you conceal? Why?

❖ THE SEXUAL RESPONSE CYCLE: PSYCHOLOGICAL AND PHYSIOLOGICAL ASPECTS

Sexual scripts help us define what is sexual; when something is defined as sexual, we may respond to it sexually. When we respond sexually, we begin what is known as the sexual response cycle. Helen Singer Kaplan (1979) has developed a triphasic model to describe the sexual response cycle that has superceded the old four-stage model of Masters and Johnson. According to this model, the human sexual response cycle consists of three phases:

- ◆ Desire phase
- ◆ Excitement phase
- ◆ Orgasmic phase

The desire phase represents the psychological element of the sexual response cycle; the excitement and orgasmic phases represent its physiological aspects.

Sexual Desire

Desire can exist separately from overtly physical sexual responses. It is the psychological component that motivates sexual behavior. We can feel desire but not be aroused. It can suffuse our bodies without producing explicit sexual stirrings. According to Kaplan (1979), "Sexual desire is an appetite or drive which is produced by the activation of a specific neural system in the brain, while the excitement and orgasm phases involve the genital organs." We experience sexual desire as erotic sensations or feelings that motivate us to seek or to become receptive to sexual experiences. These sensations generally cease after orgasm.

What is it men in women do require?
The lineaments of Gratified Desire.

What is it women do in men require?
The lineaments of Gratified Desire.

William Blake (1757–1827)

Physiological Responses: Excitement and Orgasm

A person who is sexually excited experiences a number of bodily responses. Most of us are conscious of some of these responses: a rapidly beating heart, an erection or lubrication, orgasm. Many other responses may take place below the threshold of awareness, such as curling of the toes, the ascent of the testes, the withdrawal of the clitoris beneath its hood, and a flush across the upper body.

The physiological changes that take place during the sexual response cycle depend on two processes: vasocongestion and myotonia. **Vasocongestion** occurs when body tissues become engorged with blood. For example, blood fills the genital regions of both males and females, causing the penis and clitoris to enlarge. **Myotonia** refers to increased muscle tension as orgasm approaches. Upon orgasm, the body undergoes involuntary muscle contractions and then relaxes. (The word "orgasm" is derived from the ancient Sanskrit *urja* meaning "vigor" or "sap.")

EXCITEMENT PHASE. In women, the vagina becomes lubricated and the clitoris enlarges during this phase. The vaginal barrel expands, and the cervix and uterus elevate, a process called "tenting." The labia majora flatten and rise; the labia minora begin to protrude. The breasts may increase in size and the nipples may become erect. Vasocongestion causes the outer third of the vagina to swell, narrowing the vaginal opening. This swelling forms the **orgasmic platform**; during sexual intercourse, it increases the friction against the penis. The entire clitoris retracts but remains sensitive to touch.

In men, the penis becomes erect as a result of vasocongestion, and the testes begin to rise. The testes may enlarge up to 150 percent of their unaroused size.

ORGASMIC PHASE: **Orgasm** is the release of physical tensions after the build-up of sexual excitement; it is usually accompanied by ejaculation of semen in physically mature males. In women, the orgasmic phase is characterized by simultaneous rhythmic contractions of the uterus, orgasmic platform, and rectal sphincter. In men, muscle contractions occur in the vasa deferentia, seminal vesicles, prostate, and the urethral bulb, resulting in the ejaculation of semen. Ejaculation usually accompanies male orgasm, but ejaculation and orgasm are separate processes.

SEXUAL STRUCTURE

The Male Reproductive System

The Penis

Both urine and semen pass through the penis. Ordinarily, it hangs limp and may be used for the elimination of urine, since it is connected to the bladder by the urinary duct. The penis is usually between two-and-one-half to four inches in length. When a man is sexually aroused it grows to about five to eight inches in length, is hard, and becomes erect (hence the term *erection*). When the penis is erect, muscle contractions temporarily close off the urinary duct, allowing the ejaculation of semen.

The penis consists of three main parts: the root, the shaft, and glans penis. The *root* connects the penis to the pelvis. The *shaft*, which is the spongy body of the penis, hangs free. At the end of the shaft is the *glans penis*, the rounded tip of the penis. The opening at the tip of the glans is called the *urethral meatus*. The glans penis is especially important in sexual arousal because it contains a high concentration of nerve endings, making it erotically sensitive. The glans is covered by a thin sleeve of skin called the *foreskin*. Circumcision is the surgical removal of the foreskin.

When the penis is flaccid, blood circulates freely through its veins and arteries. But as it becomes erect, the circulation of blood changes dramatically. The arteries expand and increase the flow of blood into the penis. The spongelike tissue of the shaft becomes engorged and expands, compressing the veins within the penis so that the additional blood cannot leave it easily. As a result, the penis becomes larger, harder, and more erect.

FIGURE 7.A

External Male Genitalia

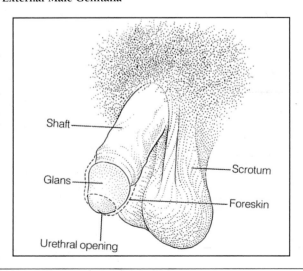

Shaft

Glans

Urethral opening

Scrotum

Foreskin

The Testes

Hanging behind the male's penis is his *scrotum,* a pouch of skin holding his two *testes* (singular *testis;* also called *testicles*). The testes are the male reproductive glands (also called *gonads*), which produce both sperm and the male hormone *testosterone.* The testes produce sperm through a process called *spermatogenesis.* Each testicle produces between one hundred million and five hundred million sperm daily. Once the sperm are produced, they move into the *epididymis,* where they are stored prior to ejaculation.

The Path of the Sperm

The epididymis merges into the tubular *vas deferens* (plural *vasa deferentia*). The vas deferens can be felt easily within the scrotal sac. Extending into the pelvic cavity, each vas deferens widens into a flasklike area called the *ampulla* (plural *ampullae*). Within the ampullae, the sperm mix with an activating fluid from the *seminal vesicles.* The ampullae connect to the *prostrate gland* through the *ejaculatory ducts.* Secretions from the prostate account for most of the milky, gelatinous liquid that makes up the *semen* in which the sperm are suspended. Inside the prostate, the ejaculatory ducts join to the urinary duct from the bladder to form the urethra, which extends to the tip of the penis. The two *Cowper's glands,* located below the prostate, secrete a clear sticky fluid into the urethra that appears as small droplets on the meatus during sexual excitement.

If the erect penis is stimulated sufficiently through friction, an ejaculation usually occurs. *Ejaculation* is the forceful expulsion of semen. The process involves rhythmic contractions of the vasa deferentia, seminal vesicles, prostate, and penis. The first few contractions occur at about one-second intervals and usually include the expulsion of semen. Within three or four seconds, however, the contractions taper off. Altogether, the expulsion of semen may last from three to fifteen seconds. The pleasurable sensations that accompany the contractions and expulsion are called *orgasm.* It is also possible to have an orgasm without the expulsion of semen.

The Female Reproductive System

External Genitals

The female's external genitals are known collectively as the *vulva,* which includes the mons veneris, labia, clitoris, urethra, and introitus. The *mons veneris* (literally "mountain of Venus") is a protuberance formed by the pelvic bone and covered by fatty tissue. During puberty, it begins to be covered with pubic hair. The *labia* are the vaginal lips surrounding the entrance to the vagina. The *labia majora* ("major lips") are two large folds of spongy flesh extending from the mons veneris along the midline between the legs. The outer edges of the labia majora are often darkly pigmented and are covered with pubic hair.

FIGURE 7.B

Cross Section of the Male Reproductive System

1. The testis produces sperm.
2. Sperm mature in the epididymis.
3. During ejaculation, sperm travel through the vas deferens. 4. The seminal vesicles and the prostate gland provide fluids. 5. Sperm mix with the fluids, making semen. 6. Semen leaves the penis by way of the urethra.

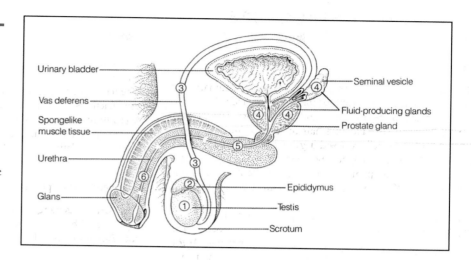

Usually the labia majora are close together, giving them a closed appearance. The *labia minora* ("minor lips") lie within the fold of the labia majora. The upper portion folds over the clitoris and is called the *clitoral hood*. During sexual excitement the labia minora become engorged with blood and double or triple in size. The labia minora contain numerous nerve endings that become increasingly sensitive during sexual excitement.

The *clitoris is the center of erotic arousal in the female*. It contains a high concentration of nerve endings and is highly sensitive to erotic stimulation. The clitoris becomes engorged with blood during sexual arousal and may increase greatly in size. Its tip, the *glans clitoridis*, is especially responsive to touch.

Between the folds of the labia minora are the urethral opening and the *introitus*. The introitus is the opening to the vagina; it is often partially covered by a thin membrane called the *hymen*, which may be broken accidentally or intentionally before or during first intercourse.

Internal Genitals

The *vagina* is an elastic canal extending from the vulva to the cervix. It envelops the penis during sexual intercourse and is the passage through which a baby is normally delivered. The vagina's first reaction to sexual arousal is "sweating," that is, the production of lubrication through the vaginal walls.

FIGURE 7.C

External Female Genitalia

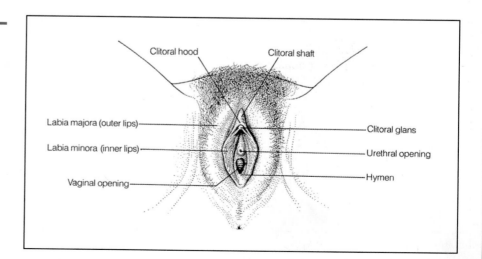

A few centimeters from the vaginal entrance, on the vagina's anterior front wall, there is, according to some researchers, an erotically sensitive spot that they have dubbed the "Grafenberg spot" or "G-spot" (Ladas et al., 1982; Whipple and Perry, 1981). It is a slight bump that may grow to twice its usual size as a result of stimulation; when it is stimulated it causes sensations similar to those of urination. The spot is associated with female ejaculation, the expulsion of clear fluid from the urethra, experienced by a small percentage of women.

A female has two *ovaries*, reproductive glands (gonads) that produce *ova* (eggs) and the female hormones *estrogen* and *progesterone*. At the time a female is born, she already has all the ova she will ever have, more than forty thousand of them. About four hundred will mature during her lifetime and be released during ovulation; ovulation begins in puberty and ends at menopause.

The Path of the Egg

The two *fallopian tubes* extend from the uterus up to, but not touching, the ovaries. When an egg is released from an ovary during the monthly *ovulation,* it drifts into a fallopian tube. If it is fertilized by sperm, fertilization usually takes place within the fallopian tube. The fertilized egg will move into the uterus.

The *uterus* is a hollow, muscular organ within the pelvic cavity. The pear-shaped uterus is normally about three inches long, three inches wide at the top, and an inch at the bottom. The narrow, lower part of the uterus projects into the vagina and is called the *cervix.* If an egg is fertilized, it will attach itself to the inner lining of the uterus, the *endometrium.* Inside the uterus it will develop into an embryo and then into a fetus. If an egg is not fertilized, the endometrial tissue that developed in anticipation of fertilization will be shed during *menstruation.* Both the unfertilized egg and inner lining of the uterus will be discharged in the menstrual flow.

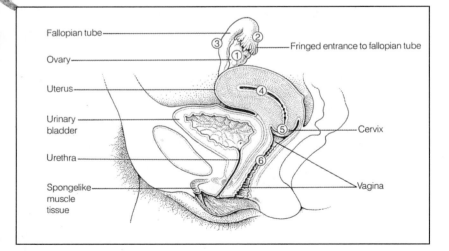

FIGURE 7.D

Cross Section of the Female Reproductive System

1. A follicle matures in the ovary and releases an ovum. 2. The fimbriae trap the ovum and move it into the fallopian tube. 3. The ovum travels through the fallopian tube to the uterus. 4. If the ovum is fertilized, the resulting blastocyst descends into the uterus. 5. If not fertilized, the ovum is discharged through the cervix into the vagina along with the shed uterine lining during the menstrual flow. 6. The vagina serves as a passageway to the body's exterior.

Following orgasm, one of the most striking differences between male and female sexual response occurs as males experience a **refractory period.** The refractory period denotes the time following orgasm during which male arousal levels return to prearousal or excitement levels. During the refractory period, additional orgasms are impossible. Females do not have any comparable period. As a result, they have greater potential for multiple orgasms—that is, having a series of orgasms. Although most women have the potential for multiple orgasms, only about 13 to 16 percent regularly experience them. For multiple orgasms, women generally require continued stimulation of the clitoris. Most women (or their partners), however, do not seek additional orgasms after the first one because our culture uses the first orgasm (usually the male's) as a marker to end sexual activities. If a woman desires additional orgasms, she needs continued stimulation by her partner or herself.

In sexual intercourse, orgasm has many functions. For men, it serves a reproductive function by causing ejaculation of semen into a woman's vagina. For both men and women, it is a source of erotic pleasure, whether it is in an autoerotic or relational context; it is intimately connected with our sense of well-being. We may measure both our sexuality and ourselves in terms of orgasm. Did I have one? Did my partner have one? When we measure our sexuality by orgasm, however, we discount activities that do not necessarily lead to orgasm, such as touching, caressing, and kissing. We discount erotic pleasure as an end in itself.

Men tend to be more consistently orgasmic than women, especially in sexual intercourse. If all women are potentially orgasmic, why do a smaller proportion of women have orgasms than men? An answer may be found in our dominant cultural model that calls for female orgasm to occur as a result of penile thrusting during heterosexual intercourse in the face-to-face, male-above position. This traditional American model calls for a "no-hands" approach. The woman is supposed to be orgasmic without manual or oral stimulation by her partner or herself. If she is orgasmic during masturbation or cunnilingus, such orgasms are usually discounted because they aren't considered "real" sex—that is, heterosexual intercourse.

The problem for women in sexual intercourse is that the clitoris frequently does not receive sufficient stimulation from penile thrusting alone to permit orgasm. In an influential study on female sexuality, Shere Hite (1976) found that only 30 percent of her 3,000 respondents experienced orgasm regularly through sexual intercourse "without more direct manual clitoral stimulation being provided at the time of orgasm." Hite concludes that many women need manual stimulation during intercourse to be orgasmic. They also need to be more assertive. She writes, "Orgasm is more likely to come when the woman takes over responsibility for and control of her own stimulation." There is no reason, Hite points out, why a woman cannot be manually stimulated by herself or her partner to orgasm before or after intercourse. But to do so, a woman has to assert her own sexual needs and move away from the idea that sex is centered around male orgasm. The sexual script has to be redefined. Recent research indicates that women who experience orgasm after their partners may be less satisfied emotionally and physiologically than women who experience orgasm before or during their partner's orgasm (Darling, Davidson, and Cox, 1991). The researchers suggest that increased awareness of orgasmic timing (and techniques) may lead to more satisfaction.

❖ SEXUAL BEHAVIOR

Sexual behavior is a complex activity, more than the simple release of tension through orgasm. Orgasm does not even have to be the goal of erotic activity. We may engage in erotic activity for its own sake, for the sheer pleasure of touch and arousal. But whether or not our erotic activities include orgasm, they involve deep feelings about ourselves and others, ranging from ecstatic delight and pleasure to guilt and shame, from love to contempt, from self-respect to self-degradation. Although our culture gives us certain meanings to associate with sex (for example, masturbation is bad, sex within marriage is sacrosanct), we ourselves are ultimately responsible for how we feel about our sexual behavior. Because we learn to be sexual, we can also unlearn those aspects of our sexuality—feelings, attitudes, or behaviors—that do not contribute to our functioning as healthy, happy human beings.

Autoeroticism

Autoeroticism refers to sexual activities that involve only the self. Autoeroticism is an intrapersonal activity rather than an interpersonal one. It may be the most diverse form of sexuality a person experiences, for it includes masturbation, sexual fantasies, and erotic dreams. Ironically, it is also the form of sexual behavior about which many people feel the greatest anxiety and guilt.

Two monks, Tanzan and Ekido, were travelling down the road in a heavy rain. As they turned a bend, they came upon a beautiful young woman in a silk kimono. She was unable to pass because the rain had turned the road to mud.

Tanzan said to her, "Come on," and lifted her in his arms and carried her across the mud. Then he put her down and the monks continued their journey.

The two monks did not speak again until they reached a temple in which to spend the night. Finally, Ekido could no longer hold back his thoughts and he reprimanded Tanzan. "It is not proper for monks to go near women," he said. "Especially young and beautiful ones. It is unwise. Why did you do it?"

"I left the woman behind," replied Tanzan. "Are you still carrying her?"

Zen tale

SEXUAL FANTASIES. "A fantasy is a map of desire, mastery, escape, and obscuration," wrote Nancy Friday (1980), "the navigational path we invent to steer ourselves between the reefs and shoals of anxiety, guilt, and inhibition." Erotic fantasy is probably the most universal of all sexual behaviors. Nearly everyone has experienced such fantasies, but because they may touch on feelings or desires considered personally or socially unacceptable, they are not widely discussed. Fantasies may interfere with an individual's self-image, causing confusion as well as a loss of self-esteem. No necessary relationship exists, however, between a person's sexual fantasies and what he or she does in real life. Nevertheless, people often feel guilty about having sexual fantasies, believing them to be deviant, obsessive, or a sign of sexual addiction (Davidson and Hoffman, 1986). African Americans tend to be more accepting of their fantasies than whites, who often feel guilty about them (Price and Miller, 1984).

There appear to be gender differences in fantasies (Strong and DeVault, 1988). Men's fantasies tend to be more visual, focusing on the physical characteristics of the partner. The partner may be anonymous. Women's tend to have greater relational content, although their fantasies may also be intensely physical. Some women have rape fantasies, which they find especially disturbing. But as Molly Haskell (1976) pointed out, although women may have rape fantasies, they do *not* secretly wish to be raped: "The world of difference between 'rape fantasy' and rape can be expressed in one word: control. The point of a fantasy is that a woman . . . orders the reality within it, ordains its terms, and censors it according to her needs. The point of rape is that a woman is violated against her will."

Sexual fantasies serve a number of important functions in maintaining our psychological equilibrium. First, fantasies help direct and define our erotic goals. They take our generalized sexual drives and give them concrete images and specific content. These goals are generally conservative insofar as they usually do not greatly exceed idealized models of the type of person we are attracted to; we fantasize about certain types of men or women and reinforce our attraction through fantasy involvement. Second, sexual fantasies allow us to plan or anticipate situations that may arise. They are a form of rehearsal in which we mentally practice how to act. Third, erotic fantasies provide an escape from a dull or oppressive environment. Fourth, even if our sexual lives are satisfactory, we may indulge in sexual fantasies to bring novelty and excitement into the relationship. Many people fantasize things they would not actually do in real life. Fantasy offers a safe outlet for sexual curiosity. One study (Davidson and Hoffman, 1986) found that fantasies appear to help many married women become sexually aroused and experience orgasm during sexual intercourse. Fifth, sexual fantasies have an expressive aspect in somewhat the same manner as dreams. Our sexual fantasies may offer a clue to our current interests, pleasures, anxieties, fears, or problems. Since fantasies take only a few details from the stream of reality, what we select is often meaningful, expressing feelings that lie beneath the surface of our consciousness (Sue, 1979).

It is fairly common to have sexual fantasies during sexual intercourse, transforming one partner into a Tom Cruise or Whitney Houston. Various studies report that between 60 to 90 percent of the respondents fantasize during sex, depending on gender and ethnicity (Knafo and Jaffe, 1984; Price and Miller, 1984; Sue, 1979;). African Americans are somewhat more likely to have experienced fantasies during intercourse (Price and Miller, 1984). One study (Cado and Leitenberg, 1990) found that 84 percent of its respondents reported having such fantasies. Those who felt guilty (about a quarter) reported significantly fewer fantasies than those who did not feel guilty. The respondents who felt guilty tended to believe that fantasies during intercourse were abnormal, immoral, and uncommon. They also believed that such fantasizing indicated that something was wrong with their relationship. "If something wasn't wrong with our relationship," they thought, "I wouldn't be having fantasies." The researchers suggest that guilty reactions to such fantasies inhibit sexual satisfaction and adjustment. If fantasizing during intercourse was recognized as a normal, common phenomenon, much of the guilt attending it would be relieved. It is the guilt, rather than the fantasizing itself, that may be harmful to the relationship.

EROTIC DREAMS. Although there is considerable research about sexual fantasies, research about erotic dreams is almost nonexistent. Almost all of the men and two-thirds of the women in Kinsey's (1953) study reported having had overtly sexual dreams. Like fantasies, dreams do not usually go far beyond an individual's experience. But while fantasies tend to be logical and related to ordinary reality, the images of dreams are frequently very intense. Individuals may awaken in the night to find their bodies moving as if they were making love. Both men and women may experience nocturnal orgasms.

MASTURBATION. **Masturbation** is stroking, rubbing, caressing, or otherwise stimulating the genitals to give sexual pleasure. Individuals may masturbate during particular periods of their lives or throughout their entire lives. Kinsey (1953) reported that 92 percent of the men and 58 percent of the women he interviewed said that they had masturbated. Today both the incidence and frequency of masturbation appear to have increased slightly. Male African Americans are less accepting of masturbation than whites (Cortese, 1989; Wilson, 1986). Among college women, masturbation becomes increasingly accepted as a healthy sexual activity as they progress in their education; this is especially true if they have studied sexuality. As women continue through college, greater numbers practice masturbation (Davidson and Darling, 1988). Although there is no comparable evidence for college males, based on Kinsey data (1984), it is likely that the overwhelming majority have masturbated.

Masturbation is one way in which people learn about their bodies, what pleases them sexually, how their bodies respond, and what their natural sexual rhythms are.

Masturbation is an intrinsically and seriously disordered act.

Vatican Declaration Concerning Sexual Questions, 1976

Don't knock masturbation, it's having sex with someone I deeply love.

Woody Allen

Remember this →

Pioneer sex therapists William Masters and Virginia Johnson (1970) instructed their clients to masturbate as a means of overcoming specific sexual problems and discovering their sexual potential. Estimates of success range from 20 to 82 percent (Wakefield, 1987). The success rates of masturbation exercises for **preorgasmic** women (those who have not experienced orgasm) are unclear, however.

Although the frequency of masturbation often decreases significantly when a sexual partner is available, masturbation is not necessarily a substitute for intercourse. Studies of married men and women suggest that both continue to masturbate (Petersen et al., 1983; Tavris and Sadd, 1977). The majority of wives who masturbate do so when their husbands are away. In one study, 70 percent of the women did not tell their husbands about masturbating (Grosskopf, 1983).

Husbands tend to masturbate more frequently than wives; 43 percent of the husbands versus 22 percent of the wives in a *Playboy* study masturbated more than once a week (Petersen et al., 1983). Husbands' motives, however, were different from wives'. Husbands tended to masturbate as a supplement to intercourse rather than as substitute for it. Among elderly married men, about 50 percent masturbated regularly (Weizman and Hart, 1987).

We don't know the effect of masturbation on marriage, although guilt about it may be a negative factor. The fact that most husbands and wives do not tell each other about masturbation suggests that for whatever reason—guilt, embarrassment, or shame—they are not communicating about an important aspect of their sexuality.

Interpersonal Sexuality

Interpersonal sexuality is more complex than autoerotic sexuality because it involves two people with different scripts, moods, desires, cycles, and feelings who have to synchronize their sexuality with each other. This is true of heterosexual, gay, lesbian, and bisexual couples.

Sexual interactions may or may not include intercourse. Virginity does not necessarily make a person asexual. A man or woman may engage in numerous noncoital activities, such as pleasuring, kissing, petting, oral sex, and so on. As anyone who has ever engaged in any of these activities knows, they may be extremely erotic. Penetration is not the test of sexuality.

ORAL SEX. In recent years, oral sex has become a part of our sexual scripts (Gagnon, 1986). Psychologist Lilian Rubin (1990) reports young women today express pleasure about oral sex, in contrast to twenty years ago; a minority of middle-aged women, who earlier believed oral sex was "dirty" or immoral, continue to feel some ambivalence (Rubin, 1990). **Cunnilingus** refers to the erotic stimulation of a woman's vulva by her partner's mouth and tongue. (*Cunnilingus* is derived from the Latin *cunnus* [vulva] and *lingere* [to lick]. **Fellatio** refers to the oral stimulation of a man's penis by his partner's sucking and licking. (*Fellatio* is from the Latin *fellare* [to suck].) Cunnilingus and fellatio may be performed singly or mutually. Between 60 and 95 percent of the men and women in various studies report that they have engaged in oral sex (Delamater and MacCorquodale, 1979; Petersen et al., 1983).

Among girls of junior-high-school age, more have given or received oral sex than have engaged in sexual intercourse; among boys, more have had sexual intercourse than have given or received oral sex. For both sexes, fellatio is less common than either sexual intercourse or cunnilingus (Newcomer and Udry, 1985). A study (Moffatt, 1989) of university students of both sexes found that oral sex was regarded as an egalitarian, mutual practice. Students felt less guilty about it than sexual inter-

And not yet cloy thy lips with loathed
  satiety,
But rather famish them amid their plenty,
Making them red and pale with fresh
  variety;
Ten kisses short as one, one long as twenty:
A Summer's day will seem an hour but
  short
Being wasted in such time-beguiling sport.

William Shakespeare

course because oral sex was not "going all the way." Another study (Herold and Way, 1983) of female undergraduates found that 61 percent had engaged in oral sex. The best predictors of whether these women engaged in oral sex were if they felt guilt about it, had experienced sexual intercourse, and were committed in their dating relationships. Some women feel that fellatio is more intimate than sexual intercourse, whereas others feel that it is less intimate. The overwhelming majority of men enjoy giving oral sex to their partners (Petersen et al., 1983).

Participants often express concern about whether they give oral sex "correctly" and whether their partners enjoy it. Both men and women occasionally complain about their partners' genital hygiene. For women, they key issue is whether to swallow the ejaculate; men are generally in favor of it, whereas women differ considerably and are concerned about the aesthetics of it (Moffatt, 1989).

Unless the possibility of HIV infection is completely ruled out, fellatio should be practiced only with a condom, because the virus that causes AIDS is carried in semen and may infect a person through cuts or sores in the mouth. (HIV does not infect through ingestion [swallowing].)

SEXUAL INTERCOURSE. **Sexual intercourse** is penile/vaginal penetration and stimulation. Although reproduction traditionally was the only legitimate aim of sexual inter-

PERSPECTIVE

The Myth of Sexual Addiction

Are you a sex addict? As you read descriptions of sexual addiction, you may begin to think that you are. But don't believe everything you read.

"The moment comes for every addict," wrote psychologist Patrick Carnes (1983), who developed and marketed the idea of sexual addiction, "when the consequences are so great or the pain so bad that the addict admits life is out of control because of his or her sexual behavior." Money is spent on pornography, affairs threaten a marriage, masturbation replaces jogging, fantasies interrupt studying. . . . Sex, sex, sex is on the addict's mind. And he or she has no choice but to engage in these activities.

Sex addicts' lives are filled with guilt or remorse. They cannot make a commitment; instead, they move from one affair to another. They make promises to themselves, to their partners, and to God to stop, but they cannot. Like all addicts, they are powerless before their addiction (Carnes, 1983; Martin, 1989). Their addiction is rooted in deep-seated feelings of worthlessness, despair, anxiety, and loneliness. These feelings are temporarily allayed by the "high" obtained from sexual arousal or orgasm. Sex addicts, writes Carnes, go through a four-step cycle.

1. *Preoccupation* with sex, an obsessive search for sexual stimulation. Everything passes through a sexual filter. Sex becomes an intoxication, a high.
2. *Ritualization,* or special routines that lead to sex. The ritual may include body oils and massage, cruising, watching, candles next to the bed, champagne.
3. *Compulsive sexual behavior,* such as masturbation, bondage, extramarital affairs, incest, or exhibitionism.
4. *Despair,* the addicts' realization that they are helpless to change their sexual addiction. Guilt, feelings of isolation, or suicidal tendencies may be present.

There are several levels of sexual addiction, categorized according to behavior. The first level of behaviors includes excessive masturbation, numerous heterosexual relationships, interest in pornography, relations with prostitutes, and homosexuality. The second level includes exhibitionism, voyeurism, and obscene phone calls. The third level includes child molestation, incest, and rape. The addict moves from one level to the next in search of excitement and satisfaction.

Sexual addiction is viewed in the same light as alcoholism and drug addiction; it is an activity over which the addict has no control. And like alcoholism, Carnes suggests recovery through a version of Alcoholics Anonymous's Twelve Step Program. The first step is for the addict to admit that he or she is helpless to end the addiction. Subsequent steps include turning to a Higher Power for assistance, listing all moral shortcomings, asking forgiveness from those who have been harmed and making amends to them, and finding a spiritual path to wholeness.

After reading this description of sexual addiction, do you feel a little uneasy? Do some of the signs of sexual addiction seem to apply directly to you? Are you wondering, "Am I a sex addict?" Don't worry; you're probably normal. The reason you might think you're suffering from

course (and continues to be so for the Catholic Church and some traditionalist groups), for most people reproduction is usually not their primary motive for having sexual intercourse. (In fact, at any single time, the majority of people probably fervently hope that pregnancy does not occur.) Instead, sexual intercourse is a complex interaction. As with many other types of activities, the anticipation of reward triggers a pattern of behavior. The reward may not necessarily be orgasm, however, because the meanings of sexual intercourse vary considerably at different times for different people. There are many motivations for sexual intercourse; sexual pleasure is only one. These motivations include showing love, having children, giving and receiving pleasure, gaining power, ending an argument, demonstrating commitment, seeking revenge, proving masculinity or femininity, or degrading someone (including yourself). One man said (in Hite, 1981), "Even more important than orgasm is being able to wrap your arms and legs and whatever else around another human being. It makes you feel less alone, more alive. There's nothing like it."

In contemporary American sexual practices, sexual intercourse is regarded as "real sex," whereas other sexual practices, such as fondling, petting, partner masturbation,

PERSPECTIVE

sexual addiction is that its definition taps into many of the underlying anxieties and uncertainties we feel about sexuality in our culture. The problem lies not in you but in the concept of sexual addiction.

Although the sexual addiction model has found some adherents among clinical psychologists, they are clearly a minority. There are a few people, it is true, who are compulsive in their sexual behaviors, but compulsion is not addiction. The influence of the "sexual addict" model is not due to its impact on therapy, psychology, and social work. Its influence is due mainly to its popularity with the media, where talkshow hosts such as Geraldo Rivera interview "sex addicts" and advice columnists such as Ann Landers caution their readers about the signs of sexual addiction. The popularity of an idea is no guarantee of its validity, however.

The sex addiction model has been rejected by a number of sex researchers as nothing more than pop psychology. These researchers suggest that the idea of sexual addiction is really repressive morality in a new guise. It is a conservative reaction to sexual diversity, eroticism, and sex outside of monogamous relationships. It makes masturbation a sign of addiction, just as in early times masturbation was viewed as a sign of moral degeneracy. According to the sexual addiction model, sex is healthy if it takes place within a relationship; outside a relationship it is pathological (Levine and Troiden, 1988).

The critiques of the sexual addiction model by sex researchers have undermined its credibility (Barth and Kinder, 1987; Coleman, 1986; Levine and Troiden, 1988). First, the researchers point out, addiction requires physiological dependence on a chemical substance arising from habitual use. Sex is not a substance. Nor is there physiological distress, such as diarrhea, convulsions, or delirium, from withdrawal. Second, research fails to convincingly document sexual addiction as a clinical condition. There is virtually no empirical evidence to support the sexual addiction model. What little evidence there is comes from small clinical samples in which there are no comparable control groups. Indeed, the case studies Carnes describes in his book are not even real. "The stories used in this book," Carnes (1983) writes, "are fictionalized composites." As a result, one study calls the literature on sexual addiction "purely conjecture" (Barth and Kinder, 1987). Third, there is no sexual hierarchy. To suggest masturbation leads to pornography, pornography to exhibitionism, and exhibitionism to rape borders on the irresponsible. Fourth, the sexual addiction model is highly moralistic. The committed, monogamous, heterosexual relationship is the model against which all other behaviors are measured. Nonprocreative sex, such as masturbation is viewed as symptomatic. Gay and lesbian sex is also considered symptomatic. Fifth, the characteristics of the addictive process—preoccupation, ritualization, compulsive sexual behavior—are subjective and value laden. Levine and Troiden (1988) note: "Each of these characteristics could just as well describe the intense passion of courtship or the sexual routines of conventional couples." Nor is there evidence to support the notion that a person goes through three levels of behavior in search of greater excitement. "Carnes' notion of levels of addiction is a classic instance of moral judgment parading as scientific fact" (Levine and Troiden, 1988).

If your sexual activities are harming others or if you fear that you may harm yourself, you are well advised to consult a therapist. The chances are, however, that your sexuality and your unique expression of it is as normal as anyone else's.

and oral sex are not the "real thing" (Hite, 1976; Moffatt, 1989) Sexual success is equated with orgasm, frequency, techniques, variety, and emotional mastery of the sexual experience (Moffatt, 1989). The emphasis on sexual intercourse, however, limits the playfulness and diversity of eroticism. As Hite (1976) observed:

There is no reason why physical intimacy with men should always consist of "foreplay" followed by intercourse and male orgasm; and there is no reason why intercourse must always be part of heterosexual sex. Sex is intimate physical contact for pleasure, to share pleasure with another person (not just alone). You can have sex to orgasm, or not to orgasm, genital sex, or just physical intimacy—whatever seems right to you. There is never any reason to think the "goal" must be intercourse and to try to make what you feel fit into that context.

Sexual intercourse without a condom is unsafe sex unless the possibility of HIV infection has been absolutely ruled out. To prevent the transmission of HIV and other sexually transmitted diseases (as well as to prevent pregnancy), men and women should engage in sexual intercourse only if they use a condom.

"THIS IS INTIMACY? A CLOSE RELATIONSHIP WITH GOOD COMMUNICATION IS INTIMACY? I THOUGHT INTIMACY WAS SOMETHING PHYSICAL."

ANAL INTERCOURSE. In anal intercourse the male inserts his erect penis into his part-ner's anus. Both heterosexuals and gay men participate in this activity. For hetero-sexual couples who engage in it, anal intercourse is generally an experiment or occa-sional activity rather than a common mode of sexual expression. A 1987 *Redbook* survey of the magazine's female readers found that 43 percent of its respondents had tried anal intercourse, but only 12 percent reported enjoying it (Rubenstein and Tavris, 1987). For many gay men, anal intercourse is an important mode of sexual interaction.

Because of AIDS, however, anal intercourse among both gay men and heterosexu-als is a potentially dangerous form of sexual interaction. It is the most prevalent mode of sexually transmitting HIV because the delicate membranes lining the anus are easily torn, providing a path of entry for HIV carried in the semen. If a couple practices anal intercourse, they should engage in it *only* if both are certain that they are free from HIV *and* if they use a condom.

❖ SEXUALITY AND AGING

Our bodies and sexuality develop and change from birth through old age. During puberty we develop secondary sex characteristics and become fertile. These changes are essential for the expression of adult sexuality, which is characterized by autoerot-ic and interpersonal sexual behaviors. It is not until middle age that additional important body changes affecting sexuality occur.

Sexuality and Middle Age

Men and women view aging differently. As men approach their fifties, they fear the loss of their sexual capacity but not their attractiveness; in contrast, women fear the

Sex contains all, bodies, souls,
Meanings, proofs, purities, delicacies,
    results, promulgations,
Songs, commands, health, pride, the
    seminal milk
All hopes, benefactions, bestowals, all
    loves, beauties, delights of the earth,
These are contain'd in sex as parts of itself
    and justifications of itself.

Walt Whitman (1819–1892)

loss of their attractiveness but generally not their sexuality. As both age, purely psychological sitmuli, such as fantasies, become less effective for arousal. Physical stimulation remains effective, however.

Among American women, sexual responsiveness continues to grow from adolescence until it reaches its peak in the late thirties or early forties; it is usually maintained at more or less the same level into the sixties and beyond. Men's physical responsiveness is greatest in late adolescence or early adulthood; beginning in men's twenties, responsiveness begins to slow imperceptibly. Changes in male sexual responsiveness become apparent only when men are in their forties and fifties. As a man ages, achieving erection requires more stimulation and time and the erection may not be as firm.

Around the age of fifty, the average American woman begins **menopause,** which is marked by the cessation of the menstrual cycle. Menopause is not a sudden event. Usually, for several years preceding menopause, the menstrual cycle becomes increasingly irregular. Although menopause ends fertility, it does not end interest in sexual activities. The decrease in estrogen, however, may cause thinness and dryness in the vagina that makes intercourse painful. The use of vaginal lubricants will remedy much of the problem. A review of the literature on the effects of hormone replacement therapy (HRT) on sexual functioning indicates that estrogen therapy leads to gynecological improvement and thus improves the context for unimpaired sexual activity (Walling, Andersen, and Johnson, 1990). There is no male equivalent to menopause. Male fertility slowly declines, but men in their eighties are often fertile.

Most studies on aging and sexuality indicate a decline in sexual desire or interest as people age. But a recent longitudinal study (Hällstrom and Samuelsson, 1990), in which almost 700 middle-aged women were interviewed twice, at a six year interval, suggests that sexual desire tends to be more stable than originally believed. Almost two-thirds of the women studied experienced no significant change in their levels of desire after six years. Twenty-seven percent experienced a decline, while 10 percent experienced an increase. What is most notable about this study is that it shows the impact of marital satisfaction and mental health on sexual desire. Desire is not related to increasing age alone. Not surprisingly, many of the women whose desire decreased over six years felt that their marriages lacked intimacy, had spouses who were alcoholic, and were themselves depressed. Such an unhappy combination is a sure antidote to desire. Those whose desire increased had initially experienced weaker desire, had troubled marriages, and had been depressed. Six years later, as their marriages improved and their mental health improved, their desire increased, moving them closer to the average.

Because of physical changes, noted Herant Katchadourian (1987), "Middle-aged couples may be misled into thinking that this change heralds a sexual decline as an accompaniment to aging." Katchadourian continued:

Sexual partners who have been together for a long time have the benefits of trust and affection. In the younger years of marriage, sex tends to be a battleground where scores are settled and peace is made, but if a couple has stuck together until middle age, sex should become a demilitarized zone. . . . They continue to enjoy the physical pleasures of sex but do not stop there . . . the sensual quality of the person, rather than the body as such, becomes the main course.

Sexuality and the Aged

The sexuality of the aged tends to be invisible in our culture. According to Georgia Barrow (1989), there are several reasons for this. First, we associate sexuality with the

Both researchers and the general public tend to ignore the emotional and sensual qualities of the relationships of the aged.

young, assuming that sexual attraction exists only between those with youthful bodies. Interest in sex is considered normal and virile in twenty-five-year-old men, but in seventy-five-year-old men it is considered lechery (Corby and Zarit, 1983). Second, we associate the idea of romance and love with the young; many of us find it difficult to believe that the aged can fall in love or love intensely. Yet a fifty-seven-year-old woman said of a seventy-two-year-old man she had recently met (quoted in Barrow, 1989):

It was as if I were 17 and had never been on a date. I had never turned anybody on in my life, so far as I knew. Now, all of a sudden, it was Christmas. Believe it or not, we fell in love.

Third, we continue to associate sex with procreation, measuring a woman's femininity by her childbearing and mother role and a man's masculinity by the children he sires. Finally, the aged generally do not have as strong sexual desires as the young and they are not expressed as openly.

Sexuality is one of the least understood aspects of life in old age. Many older people continue to adhere to the standards of activity or physical attraction they held when they were young. Sexual behavior is defined by researchers and the general population alike as masturbation, sexual intercourse, or orgasm. These definitions have "overshadowed the emotional, sensual, and relationship qualities that give meaning, beyond release, to sexual expression. . . . What has been ignored are the walking hand-in-hand or arm-in-arm; the caring for one another; the touching and holding, with or without intercourse" (Weg, 1983b). A study of 200 men and women between eighty and one hundred years of age confirms the most common form of erotic activity as touching and caressing without intercourse. Masturbation was the next most frequent, followed by sexual intercourse (Bretschneider and McCoy, 1988). About half of elderly married men report masturbating regularly (Weiztman and Hart, 1987). Although masturbation may be the only significant genital outlet for an older man or woman, society disapproves of it (Pratt and Schmall, 1989).

The greatest determinants of an aged individual's sexual activity are health and the availability of a partner. A major study of older people found only 7 percent of those who were single or widowed to be sexually active, in contrast to 54 percent of those living with a partner (Verwoerdt et al., 1969). Frequency of sexual intercourse for the latter group, with an average age of seventy years, ranged from three times a week to once every two months. Those who described their sexual feelings as having been weak or moderate in their youth stated that they were without sexual feelings. Those who do not have partners may turn to masturbation as an alternative (Pratt and Schmall, 1989).

Physiologically, men are less responsive than women. The decreasing frequency of intercourse and the increasing time required to attain an erection produce anxieties in many older men about erectile dysfunctions (impotence), anxieties that may very well lead to dysfunctions. When the natural slowing down of sexual responses is interpreted as the beginning of sexual dysfunctioning, this self-diagnosis triggers a spiral of fear and even greater difficulty in having or maintaining an erection. One study (Weitzman and Hart, 1987) found that about 31 percent of elderly male respondents were unable to have an erection.

Women, who are sexually capable throughout their lives, have different concerns. They face greater social constraints than men (Robinson, 1983). Women are confronted with an unfavorable sex ratio (twenty-nine males for every one hundred females over sixty-five years), a greater likelihood of widowhood, norms against marrying (let alone cohabitating with) younger men, less probability of remarriage, the double standard of aging, and inhibiting gender roles. Grieving over the death of a partner, isolation, and depression also affect their sexuality (Rice, 1989).

After age seventy-five, a significant decrease in sexual activity takes place. This seems to be related to health problems, such as heart disease, arthritis, and diabetes. Often older people indicate that they continue to feel sexual desires; they simply lack the ability to express them because of their health (Verwoerdt et al., 1969). In a study (White, 1982) of men and women in nursing homes, whose ages averaged eighty-two years, 91 percent reported no sexual activity immediately prior to their interviews. Seventeen percent of these men and women, however, expressed a desire for sexual activity. Unfortunately, most nursing homes makes no provision for the sexuality of the aged. Instead, they actively discourage sexual expression—not only sexual intercourse but also masturbation—or try to sublimate their clients' erotic interests into crafts or television. Such manipulations, however, do little to satisfy the erotic needs of the elderly.

For some of the very old, noted Erik Erikson (1986), "memories seem to evoke an immediate, sensual reinvolvement in their earliest adulthood commitments to intimacy." Erikson related the story of one elderly woman, who vibrantly recalled meeting her husband:

I was crazy about him. We went out together for three months, but he never touched me. Finally I told him, "Something better happen tonight or else." I wouldn't explain any more. So he kissed me that night and he kissed me until the day he died.

"Reminiscing about the sensuality of early love," Erikson (1986) wrote, "enables her to view with life-span perspective the unwelcome extent to which she now remains largely apart. Perhaps, in eliciting the feelings of an earlier time, it also helps fill this current void." Many older widows do not miss the sexual aspect of their lives, however, as much as they do the social aspects of their married lives. It is the companionship, the activity, the pleasure found in their partners that these older women most acutely miss (Malatesta, Chambless, Pollack, and Cantor, 1989).

❖ REFLECTIONS   *What are your perceptions of sexuality among the aged? Are you able to imagine an aged relative, such as a grandparent, as being romantic? Sexual? Why?*

❖ SEXUAL DYSFUNCTIONS

At various times, couples may experience sexual difficulties in their relationships. Often these problems are transitory, lasting anywhere from a few days to a few weeks or months. Such difficulties may occur because of fatigue, illness, stress, or situational problems. If such problems persist, however, they may result in **sexual dysfunctions**—that is, the inability to give and receive sexual satisfaction. Dysfunctions are extremely common in both marital and nonmarital relationships for short or long periods of time (Masters and Johnson, 1970). Heterosexuals, gay men, and lesbians alike may experience sexual problems.

Although some sexual dysfunctions are physical in origin, most are psychological (Kaplan, 1979). Some dysfunctions have immediate causes, others originate in conflict within the self, and still others are rooted in a particular sexual relationship. The possibility of a physical basis for a sexual dysfunction should be the first to be explored, however, especially if the male has prostate problems (Roen, 1974) or if there is chronic pain (Maruta and McHardy, 1983). Alcoholism may also be an important factor (Roehrich and Kinder, 1991; Schiavi, 1990).

The most common dysfunctions among men include **erectile dysfunction,** the inability to achieve or maintain an erection, and **premature ejaculation,** the inability to delay ejaculation after penetration. It is estimated that about 4 to 9 percent of males experience erectile dysfunctions and 36 to 38 percent experience premature ejaculation problems. **Delayed orgasm** (difficulty in ejaculating) is another common problem, experienced by as many as 3 to 8 percent of men (Spector and Carey, 1990).

The most common sexual dysfunction for women is **orgasmic dysfunction,** the inability to attain orgasm; between 5 to 10 percent of women in the general population are believed to experience this problem. **Arousal difficulties,** the inability to become erotically stimulated, and **dyspareunia,** painful intercourse, are also fairly common. Between 11 and 48 percent of the population, according to diverse studies, have arousal problems (Spector and Carey, 1990).

Both sexes may suffer from **hypoactive sexual desire** (formerly called **inhibited sexual desire**), inhibited or limited sexual desire, a common but only recently recognized problem (Kaplan, 1979). In the 1970s, women were more likely than men to complain about hypoactive desire, accounting for 70 percent of women seeking sex therapy. By the end of the 1970s, almost half the couples entering therapy complained of this problem. It was estimated that about 34 percent of women and 16 percent of men experienced hypoactive desire. It continues to be a major problem, but today more men than women complain that they lack desire (Spector and Carey, 1990).

Research and treatment of sexual dysfunctions have been directed toward resolving erection problems, premature ejaculation, and lack of orgasm. In these areas, successful treatment may reach 70 to 80 percent. Hypoactive sexual desire responds to treatment in only about 10 percent of the cases. Hypoactive sexual desire is related to other sexual dysfunctions insofar as it is rooted in anxiety. Usually, however, it stems from deeper, more intense sexual anxiety, greater hostility toward the partner, and more pervasive defenses than those found among people with erectile and orgasmic difficulties (Kaplan, 1979). Sometimes hypoactive desire is a means of coping with other sexual dysfunctions that precede it. Kolodny and his colleagues (1979) observed, "By developing a low interest in sexual activity, the person avoids the unpleasant consequences of sexual failure such as embarrassment, loss of self-esteem, and frustration."

More recently, therapists are discovering a deeper problem than hypoactive sexual desire—**sexual aversion**—in which individuals have an actual aversion or phobic response to sex and purposely avoid sex (DSM-III-R, 1987; Kaplan, 1987). The very idea of sex is repellent to these individuals. Often they avoid relationships in order to repress their sexual fears. Curiously, for many phobic individuals, the thought of sex is worse than the actual act, and once they begin a sexual activity they are able to overcome their aversion (Kaplan, 1987). Unfortunately, their sense of dread often returns and the thought of sex again strikes fear in them.

Individual Causes of Dysfunctions

Dysfunctions tend to be rooted in relationship interactions, but the causes may also be individual. Sometimes it is simple sexual ignorance that prevents partners from being fully sexual with each other. "Many couples do not know very much about sexuality and are too guilty and frightened to explore and experiment," writes Kaplan (1979).

PERFORMANCE ANXIETIES. Fear of failure is probably the most important immediate cause of erectile dysfunctions and, to a lesser extent, of orgasmic dysfunctions in women (Kaplan, 1979). If a man does not become erect, anxiety is a fairly common response. Some men experience their first erectile failure when a partner initiates or demands sexual intercourse. Women are permitted to say no, but many men have not learned that they too may say no to sex. Women suffer similar anxieties, but they tend to center around orgasmic abilities rather than the ability to have intercourse. If a woman is unable to experience orgasm, a cycle of fear may arise, preventing future orgasms. Often a man will insist that his partner have an orgasm, but the orgasm is not so much for her as it is for reassurance or proof of his sexual ability. Such demands often lead a woman to fake an orgasm. A related source of anxiety is an excessive need to please one's partner (Kaplan, 1979).

CONFLICTS WITHIN THE SELF. People often feel guilty about their sexual feelings. But guilt and emotional conflict do not usually eliminate a person's sexual drive; rather, they inhibit the drive and alienate a person from his or her sexuality. A person comes to see sexuality as something bad or "dirty," not something to be happily affirmed. Sexual expression is forced, Kaplan (1979) wrote, "to assume an infinite variety of distorted, inhibited, diverted, sublimated, alienated and variable forms to accommodate the conflict." Sometimes the conflicts result in less-than-satisfying sexual interaction, a lowering of pleasure, a fear of sexuality. These psychic conflicts are deeply rooted; often they are unconscious. Among gay men and lesbians, concerns about their sexual orientation may be an important cause of conflicts (George and Behrendt, 1987).

Relationship Causes of Dysfunctions

Rage, anger, disappointment, and hostility sometimes become a permanent part of marital interaction. Such factors ultimately affect the sexual relationship, for sex is like a barometer for the whole relationship. Kaplan (1979) suggested that marital discord affects our sexuality in six ways: (1) transferences, (2) lack of trust, (3) power struggles, (4) contractural disappointments, (5) sexual sabotage, and (6) lack of communication.

TRANSFERENCE. **Transference** refers to the redirection of feelings we have about someone else (usually parents or other important persons) toward our partners. For example, if we had an unhappy love affair in the past, we may transfer some of our feelings about our previous partner to our present one. If we believe we were deprived of our mother's attention, we may feel our partner is similarly depriving us.

LACK OF TRUST. Love, intimacy, and sexuality require trust. Without it, we are unwilling to expose ourselves, our feelings, or our sexuality. With trust we become transparent; it is no slight coincidence that we speak of standing naked before our partner both metaphorically and physically. We are at our most vulnerable when we are sexually intimate; we must trust that we have nothing to fear if we give ourselves sexually.

greatest causes of relationship decline

POWER STRUGGLES. Power struggles take place when domination is a central theme in a relationship. Sexuality becomes a tool in struggles for control. A man may force his wife to submit to him sexually or engage in sexual activities she does not like. She may humiliate him by forcing him to perform, by withholding sex, or by being nonresponsive or nonorgasmic. The results of such unconscious power struggles may be lessened desire, poor sexual interaction, erectile problems, or orgasmic dysfunction. Sexual responsiveness to the partner becomes tantamount to submission; sexual pleasure is forgotten.

CONTRACTUAL DISAPPOINTMENTS. Contractual disappointments stem from the unwritten marriage contracts between couples. These unwritten contracts are the usually unconscious assumptions and expectations about how each should act in the marriage. A man, for example, may assume that he and his wife will have children when they marry, but the woman may not want children. Because the two never discuss the issue, it does not become a source of discord until after marriage.

SEXUAL SABOTAGE. Partners may engage in sexual sabotage, for example, by asking for sex at the wrong time, putting pressure on each other, or frustrating or criticizing each other's sexual desires and fantasies. People most often do this unconsciously; to engage in sexual sabotage consciously would appear to be vicious. Although this lack of awareness may partly absolve a person, it makes solving the problem more difficult.

COMMUNICATION PROBLEMS. Finally, lack of communication is one of the most important factors underlying sexual dysfunctions. A person cannot be a sexual mind-reader; each partner must be told how the other feels about sex and about ways of being sexual. If neither knows how the other feels—especially if one or both partners fake responses—a great amount of harmful misinformation may be conveyed.

◆ No man is always able to have an erection, and no woman is always able to be orgasmic. Our sexuality does not always meet our expectations or those of our partner. Once we realize that important truth, we free ourselves from many of our anxieties, which are responsible for many sexual difficulties. When we do have sexual dysfunctions over a period of time, it is wise to check our health and health habits. Are we ill? What kind of medications are we taking? Are we drinking alcohol before we have sex? Are we fatigued? Discounting health problems, we should then look both at our own feelings about sex and at the state of our relationship. Most sexual difficulties take place within troubled relationships or arise from feelings of individual inadequacies. These can often be dealt with successfully. Then troubled or nonexistent sex can be transformed into satisfaction and fulfillment.

❖ SUMMARY

◆ Our sexuality depends more on learning than on biological drives. Sexual impulses are organized by our *sexual script,* shared conventions and signals that enable two persons to engage in sexual activity.
◆ Sexual scripts are learned at first from parents, peers, and the media. As a person becomes sexually experienced, his or her partners become extremely important as a source of learning.

◆ Traditional male sexual scripts include denial or nonexpression of feelings, emphasis on performance and being in charge, belief that men always want sex and that all physical contact leads to sex, and assumptions that sex equals intercourse and that sexual intercourse always leads to orgasm. Traditional female sexual scripts suggest that sex is both good and bad (depending on the context), sex is for men, men should know what women want, women shouldn't talk about sex, women should look like beautiful models, women are nurturers, and there is only one right way to experience an orgasm.

◆ Contemporary male/female sexual scripts are more egalitarian, consisting of beliefs that sex is a positive good, involves a mutual exhange, may be initiated by either sex, and so on.

◆ The sexual response cycle consists of three phases: *desire, excitement,* and *orgasm.* Desire represents the psychological component, and excitement and orgasm represent the physiological components.

◆ *Autoeroticism* is sexual activity that involves only the self. It includes sexual fantasies, erotic dreams, and masturbation.

◆ Sexual fantasies are probably the most universal of all sexual behaviors. They are normal aspects of our sexuality. Erotic fantasies serve several functions: (1) they take our generalized sexual drives and help define and direct them, (2) they allow us to plan or anticipate erotic situations, (3) they provide a pleasurable escape from routine, and (4) they provide clues about the unconscious.

◆ *Masturbation* is an important way to learn about sexuality. People masturbate by stroking, rubbing, caressing, or otherwise stimulating their genitals. Most men and the majority of women have masturbated. People continue to masturbate during marriage, although married men tend to masturbate to supplement their sexual activities whereas women tend to masturbate as a substitute for such activities.

◆ Erotic dreams are widely experienced. People may have orgasms during their dreams.

◆ Oral sex involves *cunnilingus, fellatio,* or mutual oral stimulation. Oral sex has become widely accepted. It is practiced by heterosexuals, gay men, and lesbians.

◆ *Sexual intercourse* is penile/vaginal penetration and stimulation. It is a complex interaction, involving more than erotic pleasure or reproduction. It is a form of communication that may express a host of feelings, including love, hate, need, and contempt.

◆ Anal intercourse is practiced by heterosexuals and gay men. From a health perspective it is dangerous, because it is primarily through anal intercourse that HIV is sexually transmitted.

◆ In middle age, women tend to reach their sexual peak, which is often maintained into their sixties; they also experience *menopause,* the cessation of menstruation. The sexual responsiveness of men declines somewhat, causing men to require greater stimulation and time to become aroused. There is no male equivalent to menopause.

◆ The sexuality of the aged tends to be invisible because we associate sexuality with youth and because the elderly themselves do not have desires as strong as they did in their youth. Men fear erectile dysfunctions, whereas women may be anxious about their physical attractiveness and face greater social constraints than men. The main determinants of sexual activity in old age are the availability of a partner and a person's state of health.

◆ *Sexual dysfunctions* are problems in giving and receiving erotic satisfaction. The most common male problems are *erectile dysfunction, premature ejaculation,* and *delayed orgasm.* The most common female problems are *orgasmic dysfunction, arousal difficulties,* and *dyspareunia* (painful intercourse). Both men and women are subject to *hypoactive (inhibited or limited) desire* and *sexual aversion.*

◆ Most sexual dysfunctions are psychological in origin, but physical or hormonal causes should not be discounted. There are a number of causes of sexual dysfunctions, including sexual ignorance, performance anxieties, and conflicts within the self. Relationship causes include transference, lack of trust, power struggles, contractual disappointments, sexual sabotage, and lack of communication.

Answers to Preview Questions

The answers to the preview questions at the beginning of the chapter are listed below. As you check your answers, whether you were correct or not, think about your reasons for each response. What were they? What was their source? How valid is the source? As you read the chapter, you will find the questions discussed in greater depth.

1.	F	6.	F
2.	F.	7.	T
3.	T	8.	T
4.	T	9.	F
5.	T	10.	T

❖ SUGGESTED READINGS

The most important scholarly journals devoted to human sexuality include *Journal of Sex Research, Archives of Sexual Behavior,* and *Journal of Psychology and Human Sexuality. Current Research Updates, Human Sexuality* is an interdisciplinary journal that abstracts relevant articles from 671 journals. *Journal of Homosexuality* explores gay and lesbian sexuality. *Family Planning Perspectives* publishes studies primarily relating to contraceptive use, abortion, and adolescent pregnancy. *Sexuality Today* is a weekly newsletter briefly describing news, events, and conferences of interest to those in the field.

Barbach, Lonnie. *For Yourself,* New York: 1982 (paperback). A guide for understanding women's sexuality; includes exercises.

Boston Women's Health Book Collective. *The New Our Bodies, Ourselves.* New York: Simon and Schuster, 1984 (paperback). A landmark self-help book on women's sexuality and health.

Brecher, Edward. *Love, Sex, and Aging.* Boston: Little, Brown, 1984. Discussion and survey of sexuality and love among those over sixty years of age.

Comfort, Alex. *The Joy of Sex: A Gourmet Guide to Lovemaking.* Updated edition. New York: Crown Publishers, 1986 (paperback). The classic "how-to-do-it" book with tasteful, erotic artwork; has ended up on many a coffee table.

Huxley, Aldous. *Brave New World.* New York: Perennial Library, 1969 (paperback). The classic anti-utopian novel, written over fifty years ago, which anticipated many of today's trends, including permissive sex and the new birth technologies.

Levine, Linda, and Lonnie Barbach. *The Intimate Male: Candid Discussions about Women, Sex, and Relationships.* New York: Signet Books, 1983 (paperback). An informative book that reveals men's attitudes and feelings about sex and relationships.

Moffatt, Michael. *Coming of Age in New Jersey: College and American Culture.* New Burnswick, N.J.: Rutgers University Press, 1989. An anthropological study of college students, including their sexuality.

Strong, Bryan, and Christine DeVault. *Understanding Our Sexuality,* 2d ed. St. Paul, Minn.: West Publishing Co., 1988. A comprehensive introduction to human sexuality.

Vance, Carole, ed. *Pleasure and Danger.* Boston: Routledge & Kegan Paul, 1984 (paperback). A thoughtful and challenging collection of feminist essays on major sexual issues confronting American women and society.

Suggested Films

Everything You Ever Wanted to Know about Sex (But Were Afraid to Ask) (1972). Woody Allen's episodic comedy about chastity, bestiality, sex research, and sperm.

Heavy Petting (1989). Satirical documentary about sexual mores in the 1950s and 1960s.

READINGS

THE SLUMBER PARTY

Marilyn Hiller. From "Saturday Night Live."

In this classic skit from the television series "Saturday Night Live," Gilda Radner, Laraine Newman, Jane Curtin, and Madeline Kahn portray twelve-year-olds discussing sex. Although it is comedy, it strikes us as true. Why? At age twelve, what were your beliefs concerning sex? How did you learn about sex? What did your parents tell you?

(A darkened living room, with single lantern-type light used for camping. Girls huddled around Madeline on the floor with pillows, blankets, etc. Assorted old pizza boxes, coke bottles, strewn around them.)

MADELINE: (enormously confidential) . . . so then, the man gets bare naked in bed with you and you both go to sleep which is why they call it sleeping together. Then you both wake up and the man says, "Why don't you slip into something more comfortable"—no, wait, maybe that comes before—it's not important—and then the man says . . . (light goes on at top of staircase)

MOTHER'S VOICE: Gilda, it's five A.M. When does the noise stop?

GILDA: We're just going to sleep, Mother.

MOTHER'S VOICE: What are you talking about at this hour?

GILDA: School!

MOTHER'S VOICE: Well, save it for the morning.
(Door slams. Lights out)

JANE: (to Madeline, as if nothing has happened) And then the man . . .

MADELINE: Anyway . . . (Brings girls closer, whispers something inaudible. We finally hear:) . . . then the man (whispers) in you and then you scream and then he screams and then it's all over.
(Moment of silence. The girls sit there shocked and horrified)

LARAINE: (making throwing-up sounds, pulling blanket up over her head) That's disgusting!

GILDA: You lie, Madeline.

MADELINE: Cross my heart and hope to die. My brother told me in my driveway.

GILDA: Your brother lies, Madeline.

MADELINE: No, sir.

JANE: Come on. Isn't he the one who said if you chew your nails and swallow them a hand will grow in your stomach?

MADELINE: Well, it's also true because I read it in this book.

JANE: What'd it say?

MADELINE: It said, "The first step in human reproduction is . . . the man (whispers)

LARAINE: (hysterical, coming out from under covers) It's disgusting!

(Laraine, Gilda and Jane all do fake throwing up)

MADELINE: It's true.

JANE: Well, I just know it can't be true because nothing that sickening is true.

MADELINE: Boogers are true.
(the girls consider this for a moment)

GILDA: Well, I mainly don't believe it because I heard from my sister about this girl who this guy jumped out from the bushes and forced to have a baby.

MADELINE: (smugly) How?

GILDA: I don't know. I think he just said, "Have a baby right now."

MADELINE: Oh, sure, Gilda. And you think that would work if I tried it on you?

GILDA: (scared) Hey, don't. O.K.?

MADELINE: Well, don't worry. It wouldn't because that's not how it's done. How it's done is . . . the man . . .

LARAINE: Don't say it again, O.K.? I just ate half a pizza, O.K.?

GILDA: (thoughtfully) So that's why people were born naked.

JANE: Yeah.

LARAINE: But how could you face the man after? Wouldn't you be so *embarrassed*?

JANE: I'd have to kill myself after. I mean, I get embarrassed when I think how people standing next to me can see inside my ear.

MADELINE: Well, that's why you should only do it after you're married. Because then you won't be so embarrassed in front of your husband after because you're in the same *family*.

LARAINE: Oh, well, I really want to get married now. *Not!*

MADELINE: But the worst thing is—our *parents* do it, you know?

GILDA: Come on!

MADELINE: Gilda, think: none of us would be here unless our parents did it *at least once*.

(Moment of silence. They all consider the horror of this)

JANE: (horrorized) My parents did it at least twice. I have a sister.

GILDA: (greater horror) And my parents did it at least three times. I have a sister *and* a brother.
(they all turn to give her a "you're dirty" look)

GILDA: But, like, I know they didn't do it because they *wanted* to. They did it because they *had* to. To have children.

MADELINE: (accusing) They could have adopted children.

GILDA: Yeah, but adopted children are a pain. You have to teach them how to look like you.

LARAINE: Well, my father would never do anything like that to my mother. He's too polite.

MADELINE: My father's polite and we have six kids.

LARAINE: He's obviously not as polite as you think. (they glare at each other)

JANE: I wonder whose idea this was.

MADELINE: (offhand) God's.

JANE: Oh, come on. God doesn't go around thinking up sickening things like this for people to do.

GILDA: Maybe God just wants you to do it so you'll appreciate how good the rest of your life is.

JANE: Maybe.

LARAINE: (to Madeline) How long does it take?

MADELINE: Stupid! That depends on how big the girl's stomach is and how fast she can digest.

GILDA: Oh.

JANE: Can you talk during it?

MADELINE: You have to hold your breath or else it doesn't work.
(various vomit sounding shrieks, screams, etc.)

JANE: Well, I'm just telling my husband I'm not going to do it. (to heaven) Tough beansies.

MADELINE: What if he says he'll get divorced from you if you didn't do it?
(the girls consider this)

JANE: I would never marry someone like that.

MADELINE: What if you did by accident? What if . . . (making up story) . . . you met him in a war and married him real fast because you felt sorry for him since he'd probably get killed only he didn't and then you were stuck with him?

GILDA: (moved by emergency) Look—let's make this pact right now that after we get married, if our husbands make us do it, we'll call each other on the phone every day and talk a lot to help keep our minds off it, like our mothers do.

JANE: Right.

MADELINE: Right.

LARAINE: Right, because it's *disgusting*.

continued on next page

(makes some throw-up sound. Ducks under covers)
(Laraine turns out flashlight)

JANE: Well, don't worry, we'll never have to keep this pact because I'll never do it.

GILDA: Me, neither.

MADELINE: Me, neither.
(there is a beat)

LARAINE: (quietly) I might.
(fade out)

WHEN IN DOUBT, SAY NO

Cynthia Heimel

What does the author mean when she says, "Sex with the wrong man for the wrong reasons is an act against ourselves and against the cosmos"? Are men also pressured to have sex when they don't want to? In what ways are the pressures different? How do you say no?

The man has blond hair, cropped in the latest Beatle do. His name may well have been Barry. Moments ago there had been five people goofing around in my room at the hippie commune, now there was just this guy and me. He came over and sat next to me on my bed, which was a mattress on the floor. He started playing with my hair, and I was suddenly struck mute. His other hand started playing with my breast. I turned away.

"What's the matter with you?" he demanded.

"Oh, nothing," I muttered tentatively.

"Don't you like me?" he demanded, his hand closing commandingly over my errant breast.

"I like you okay," I said in a tiny voice, "but I only met you a half hour ago.

"So what?" he asked in an infinitely patient, reasonable tone. "I can tell you're not one of those old-fashioned chicks full of sexual guilt and repression, are you?"

"Well, no."

"Okay, then. We're both grown-ups, we both want to do it, what's stopping us?"

"But I don't want to do it."

"What's the matter, you don't like me?"

"I like you."

"What's wrong with you then? You uptight?"

"Maybe a little."

"Look, Sandy, you're gonna have to get over these hang-ups. A guy like me needs a girl who doesn't make everything into a big deal, a girl who can *go with it*. Now come on, don't be so straight. Take your clothes off."

Reader, I took my clothes off, every goddamned stitch. I was too embarrassed not to. We had what might be called sex, but I just felt like a dead halibut. An orgasm? You're kidding. I didn't even know what an orgasm was.

This happened in 1967, when I was a teenage casualty of the sexual revolution. People have told me, and I'm sure they're right, that the sexual revolution was good stuff. The word "liberating" is often employed. But all it seemed to do for me was to remove a rather crucial option—saying no. Men, instead of pleading and begging, became self-righteous and glib. They guilt-tripped us into opening our legs.

This can't still be happening, 17 years later. Can it? I have heard disquieting rumors that it can, and is. That in dormitories all over the land the words "Whatsa matter? You uptight?" are ringing out in loud, clear tones. This will never do.

It is every woman's inalienable right to be hung up, uptight, and repressed. If we're not, if we say yes when we'd rather say no, if we cave in under psychological pressure, we fall prey to the dead-halibut syndrome. We have more sex and enjoy it not at all.

Everytime we say yes under pressure, we are doing perceptible and real damage to our admittedly resilient, but still tender, psyches. Each yes-under-pressure reduces self-esteem and plays havoc with our feelings of autonomy. And we get pretty irritated with ourselves if we go through with a sex act just because we were too wimpy, or too timid, or too ambivalent to say "Not on your life, Charlie," or "Shove it, Basil." We start thinking we are sorry excuses for women. We stop wanting to get out of bed in the morning.

And then we get mad. "How dare that creep manipulate me like that!" we rant to ourselves. "Why, he's nothing but a filthy, misbegotten, supremacist creep pig! In fact, all men are slimy, perverted warthogs, and any woman who has anything to do with them should have her head examined!"

All men are not slimy warthogs. Some men are silly giraffes, some woebegone puppies, some insecure frogs. But if one is not careful, those slimy warthogs can ruin it for all the others. Every yes-under-pressure we utter will increase our resentment of the male race threefold. And once resentment takes hold, it is relentless. We'll take it out on anyone who comes near us, even woebegone puppy-men who wouldn't hurt a flea. Before we know it, we could end up not having any sex at all.

Which would be sad, because we are all sex maniacs. Oh, yes we are. Sex is the greatest thing humankind ever devised. It puts a spring to the step and a smile on the lips.

Why, only this morning, I was chasing the man I live with around the apartment.

"No!" he shouted, "I have to go to work! I have to make breakfast! I am not a sex object!"

continued on next page

"Of course you're not a sex object, darling," I crooned, easing him into a corner and fondling his privates, "but don't you think maybe we could just do it for ten minutes? How above five?"

"Leave me alone, you wanton hussy," he whispered.

I ache for this man. Sometimes he just looks at me in a certain way, and I go weak at the knees and become a helpless puddle of desire. I beg, I plead, I cajole, I'd rather have sex with him than write.

But before I met him, I hadn't slept with anyone for seven months. Nobody inspired me. And if there's one thing I've learned, it's that you have to wait for it. Sex with the wrong man for the wrong reasons is an act against ourselves and against the cosmos.

Never again will I have sex just because I think I'm supposed to. I don't need the dull aching feelings of guilt, anger, depression, and stupidity. If any man has the unmitigated gall to tell me I'm uptight, I'll throw him out the window, or tell his mother on him. Men who do this sort of thing should never be encouraged, since they are inevitably lousy in bed anyway.

No, the only time I want to have sex is when I think I will drop dead with desire unless I get it. When the man inspires such fervor in me that I become shameless, crazed.

That's the way it's supposed to be.

CHAPTER 8

Sexuality
and Relationships

PREVIEW

To gain a sense of what you already know about the material covered in this chapter, answer "true" or "false" to the following statements. You will find the answers on page 241.

1. Although there is general toleration among college students of different sexual standards of morality, women who engage in casual sex experience disapproval. True or false?
2. Both men and women report feelings of obligation or pressure to engage in sexual intercourse. True or false?
3. Heterosexuals who have positive attitudes about sexuality are less accepting of gay men and lesbians than those who have negative attitudes. True or false?
4. A decline in the frequency of intercourse generally indicates problems in the marital relationship. True or false?
5. The American Psychiatric Association has rejected the idea that homosexuality is a form of mental disorder. True or false?
6. Latinos are generally less permissive about sex than African Americans or Anglos. True or false?
7. The most important factor determining whether a couple uses contraception is the frequency of intercourse. True or false?
8. Condoms are highly effective in protecting against sexually transmitted disease, including HIV. True or false?
9. College students rarely put themselves at risk for HIV. True or false?
10. The pro-life leadership believes that abortion should be outlawed in all cases *except* when the pregnant woman's life is threatened. True or false?

*The degree and kind of a person's sexuality
reaches up into the ultimate pinnacle of his
spirit.*

Friedrich Nietzsche

Is sex dirty? Only if it's done right.

Woody Allen

W̲E ARE SEXUAL FROM BIRTH TO DEATH. Our initial experiences are exploratory and
tentative, especially in adolescence and early adulthood. For most, the first
experience of intercourse is premarital, but for others this experience takes place
within marriage. Whatever the context, these are profound experiences, marking an
important personal and cultural transition from virgin to non-virgin status. One
never forgets losing his or her virginity. In this chapter we will explore some of the
meanings of our sexual experiences in premarital, marital, and extramarital contexts
and will also explore gay and lesbian sexuality. Finally, we will discuss contraception, abortion, and sexually transmitted diseases.

❖ PREMARITAL SEXUALITY

Increased Legitimacy of Sex Outside of Marriage

Over the last several decades, there has been a remarkable increase in the acceptance
of premarital sexual intercourse. We use the term *premarital* to refer to sexual activities between unmarried adolescents and young adults. When discussing the sexual
activities of unmarried middle-aged and older single adults (whether never married,
divorced, or widowed) we use the term *nonmarital* sexuality. While taking place outside of marriage, the sexual activities of unmarried older adults are not "premarital"
in the same sense as those of never-married adolescents and young adults.

For adolescents and young adults, the advent of effective birth control methods,
changing gender roles that permit females to be sexual, and delayed marriages have
played a major part in the rise of premarital sex. For middle-aged and older adults,
increasing divorce rates and longer life expectancy have created an enormous pool of
once-married men and women who engage in nonmarital sex. Only extramarital
sex—sex outside the marital relationship—continues to be consistently frowned
upon.

The increased legitimacy of sex outside of marriage has transformed both dating
and marriage. Sexual intercourse has become an acceptable part of the dating process for many couples, whereas only petting was acceptable before. Furthermore,
marriage has lost some of its power as the only legitimate setting for sexual intercourse (Furstenberg, 1980). One important result is that many people no longer feel
that they need to get married to express their sexuality in a relationship (Scanzoni,
Polonko, Teachman, and Thompson, 1989).

There appears to be a general expectation among students that they will engage in
sexual intercourse sometime during their college career (Komarovsky, 1985; Moffatt,
1989). One researcher (Moffatt, 1989) declared in his study of urban college students that "the value of premarital chastity was . . . almost as dead as the dodo."
Although college students expect sexual involvement to occur within an emotional
or loving relationship (Robinson et al, 1991), this emotional connection may be relatively transitory. Psychologist Lilian Rubin (1990) notes:

A one-night stand with a friend is acceptable; with a stranger it's looked upon askance,
although it's certainly not uncommon. The emotional connection that's supposed to be a pre-
requisite to a sexual one need not be a substantial or lasting one. Liking someone is enough to
justify spending a night or a weekend, even on the first meeting.

Whatever their beliefs about sexuality, most people seem to accept divergent
moral standards. When Mirra Komarovsky (1985) asked students, "Who, in your
opinion, is more on the defensive in this college—a virgin or a sexually experienced

student?" the common response was the former. Involuntary virgins may experience their virginity as an embarrassment. Said one female university student (quoted in Moffatt, 1989), "By the time I turned 20 I was growing anxious about my virginity. I was ready to get rid of it but nobody wanted the damn thing."

In the Komarovsky study, although acceptance of sexual activity was the norm, there were limits. If a woman had sexual intercourse, it was to take place in the context of a committed relationship. Women who "slept around" were morally censured. Reflecting the continuing double standard, men are not usually condemned as harshly as women for casual sex. Indeed, several studies (Jacoby and Williams, 1985; Williams and Jacoby, 1989) report that as dating or marital partners men prefer women whose sexual experience does not go beyond breast fondling.

Komarovsky found that virginity was acceptable if it reflected deeply held religious beliefs. If a person was a virgin for moral rather than religious reasons, it was assumed that he or she had psychological problems. Men and women who remained virgins generally developed groups of friends who shared their religious values. In a generally permissive atmosphere, these groups provided support and validation for those who chose to remain virgins.

Factors Leading to Premarital Sexual Involvement

What are the factors that lead men and women to have premarital intercourse? What influences the timing of sex in their relationship? Researcher Susan Sprecher (1989) identifies individual, relationship, and environmental factors affecting the decision to have premarital intercourse.

For human beings, the more powerful need is not for sex per se, but for relationship, intimacy and affirmation.

Rollo May

INDIVIDUAL FACTORS. There are a number of individual factors influencing the decision to have premarital intercourse. These include previous sexual experience, sexual attitudes, personality characteristics, and gender. The more premarital sexual experience a man or woman has had in the past, the more likely he or she is to engage in sexual activities in the present. Once the psychological barrier against premarital sex is broken, sex appears to become less taboo. This seems to be especially true if the earlier sexual experiences were rewarding in terms of pleasure and intimacy. Those with liberal sexual attitudes are more likely to engage in sexual activity than those with restrictive attitudes. In terms of personality characteristics, men and women who did not feel high levels of guilt about sexuality were more likely to engage in sex, as were those who valued erotic pleasure.

RELATIONSHIP FACTORS. Two of the most important factors determining sexual activity in a relationship are the level of intimacy in the relationship and the length of time the couple has been together. Even those who are less permissive in their sexual attitudes accept sexual involvement if the relationship is emotionally intimate and long-standing. Individuals who are less committed (or not committed) to a relationship are less likely to be sexually involved. The style of love discussed in Chapter 5 also seems to have an effect. Ludic lovers were more sexually permissive than agapic lovers. Some evidence also suggested that storgic and pragmatic lovers were less permissive. Finally, persons in equitable relationships, wherein power is shared equally, are more likely to be sexually involved than those in inequitable ones.

Your Moral Standards and Premarital Intercourse

As we move from adolescence to adulthood, we reevaluate our moral standards, moving from moral decision making based on authority to standards based on our own personal principles of right and wrong and caring and responsibility (Gilligan, 1982; Kohlberg, 1969). We become responsible for developing our own moral code, which includes sexual issues. Then we undertake the difficult task of linking our behavior to our morality (see Kupersmid and Wonderly, 1980).

Sociologist Ira Reiss (1967) has described four moral standards of premarital sexuality. The first is the *abstinence standard,* which was the official sexual ideology in American culture until the 1950s and early 1960s. This belief held that it is wrong for either men or women to engage in sexual intercourse before marriage regardless of the circumstances or their feelings for each other. The second is the *double standard,* which was widely practiced but rarely approved publicly and permitted men to engage in premarital intercourse. Women, however, were con-

sidered immoral if they had premarital intercourse. *Permissiveness with affection* represents a third standard. It describes sex between men and women who have an affectionate, stable, and loving relationship. This standard is widely held today (Sprecher et al., 1988). *Permissiveness without affection* is the fourth standard. It holds that people may have sexual relationships with each other even if there is no affection or commitment.

Do you believe premarital intercourse is morally acceptable? Why? If so, which of the moral standards most closely fits your standards for premarital sexual intercourse? Why do you hold these standards? Are these the same standards you held one year ago? Five years ago? If they have changed, how do you account for the change? What is the relationship between your moral standards and your sexual behaviors? Is your actual sexual behavior consistent with your moral standards? If your behavior is different from your moral standards, how do you account for the difference? How do you feel about the difference between the two? Are your moral standards the same as those of your current or most recent partner? Have you been in relationships in which you and your partner had different standards? How were the differences resolved? Are your standards similar to those of your friends?

Abstinence sows sand all over the ruddy limbs and flaming hair.

William Blake (1757–1827)

ENVIRONMENTAL FACTORS. In the most basic sense, the physical environment affects the opportunity for sex. Since sex is a private activity, the opportunity for it may be precluded by the presence of parents, friends, roommates, or children. The cultural environment also affects premarital sex. The values of one's parents or peers may encourage or discourage sexual involvement. A person's ethnic group also affects premarital involvement: generally, African Americans are more permissive than whites; Latinos are less permissive than Anglos. Furthermore, a person's subculture—such as the university or church environment, the divorced world, the gay and lesbian community—exerts an important influence on sexual decision making.

❖ MARITAL SEXUALITY

It is better to marry than to burn.

Corinthians 7:9

When people marry, they may discover that their sexual lives are very different than they were before marriage. Sex is now morally and socially sanctioned. It is in marriage that the great majority of heterosexual sexual activities take place. Yet if we were to judge by the media, little sex occurs within marriage. On television soaps, twenty-four times as much sex takes place between unmarried partners as between married ones. Furthermore, erotic activity is often linked with violence (Roberts, 1982). Sexual research is not much different from the media. There are literally hundreds of studies on adolescent sexuality, nonmarital sexuality, extramarital sexuality, gay and lesbian sexuality, and sexual variations. Almost no studies, however, exist on marital sexuality (P. MacCorquodale, 1989). Researchers probably know more about moon rocks than they do about marital sex.

Sexuality can be expressed in erotic playfulness.

Role of Sexuality

Marital sex tends to diminish in frequency the longer a couple is married. For newly married couples, the average rate of marital intercourse is about three times a week. As the partners get older, the frequency declines. In early middle age, a married couple makes love an average of one and a half to two times a week. After age fifty, the rate is about once a week or less. (These are *average* rates, individual couples may make love more or less often and still be in the normal range.) Sex also becomes more routine in marriage.

Sex is only one bond among many in marriage. It is a more important bond in cohabitation than in marriage because cohabitors don't have the security and future orientation of marriage to cement their relationship. Most married couples don't seem to feel that declining frequency is a major problem especially if they rate their overall relationship as good. Blumstein and Schwartz (1983) found that most married people attributed the decline to lack of time or physical energy or to "being accustomed" to each other. Also, other activities and interests engage them besides sex. But if the frequency of sex is low in cohabiting relationships, discord is likely.

Marriage has many pains but celibacy has no pleasures.

Samuel Johnson (1709–1784)

New Meanings to Sex

Sexuality within marriage is substantially different from premarital and nonmarital sex in at least three ways. First, sex in marriage is expected to be monogamous over a lifetime. Second, procreation is a legitimate goal. Third, sex takes place in the everyday world.

The vow of fidelity is an absurd commitment, but it is the heart of marriage.

Robert Capon

Remember this

Sexuality is a good gift from God and is a fundamental means of realizing life-in-community. This gift includes all that it means to be male and female and is not limited to coital behavior. All expressions of human sexuality affect the emergence of genuine personhood and should reflect a concern for personal integrity, relational fidelity and the equality of men and women.

United Methodist Church

A Frontier Guard

*The bamboo leaves rustle
On this cold, frosty night.
I am wearing seven layers of clothing
But they are not as warm, not as warm
As the body of my wife.*

Anonymous, 8th-Century Japanese

MONOGAMY. The most significant factor shaping marital sexuality is the expectation of **monogamy,** sexual exclusiveness. Before or after marriage, a person might have various sexual partners, but within marriage, all sexual interactions are expected to take place between spouses. This expectation of monogamy lasts a lifetime; a person marrying at age twenty commits himself or herself to forty to sixty years of sex with one person and no others. Within a monogamous relationship, each partner must decide how to handle fantasies, desires, and opportunities for extramarital sexuality. For example, do you tell your spouse that you have fantasies about other people? That you masturbate? Do you flirt with others? Do you have an extramarital relationship? If so, do you tell your spouse? How do you handle sexual conflicts or difficulties with your partner? How do you deal with sexual boredom or monotony?

SOCIALLY SANCTIONED REPRODUCTION. Sex also takes on a procreative aspect within marriage. Until recently, procreative sex within marriage was the only acceptable form of sex in Western culture. Now sex and reproduction can be separated by means of birth control. Although it is obviously possible to get pregnant before marriage, marriage is the only socially sanctioned setting in which to have children in our society. When a couple marry, they are confronted with the task of deciding whether or not to have children. It is one of the most crucial decisions they will make. Having children alters a person's life even more than marriage: marriages can be dissolved, but a person never stops being a parent.

If the couple decide to have a child, the nature of their sexual interactions may change from being simply an erotic activity to an intentionally reproductive act as well. Many parents who planned their children speak of the difference between sex as pleasure and sex as reproduction. One woman told the authors:

We wanted to have a child for a long time and when I quit taking birth control pills, we started making love to have a child. Each time we did it, we knew we might be conceiving. That made it really different from before when it just felt good or was fun. I can't explain why, just that it was really different knowing that we might be creating something.

CHANGED SEXUAL CONTEXT. The sexual context changes with marriage. Because married life takes place in a day-to-day living situation, sex must also be expressed in the day-to-day world. Before marriage, sex may have taken place only in romantic or seductive settings, at home when parents were away, or in the back seat of a car. These situations make sexual encounters highly charged with emotions ranging from intense love to anxiety and fear.

After marriage, sex must be arranged around working hours and at times when the children are at school or asleep. Sometimes one or the other partner may be tired, frustrated, or angry. The emotions associated with premarital sex may disappear. Some of the passion of romantic love eventually disappears as well, to be replaced with a love based on caring and commitment.

A primary task in marriage is to make sex meaningful in the everyday world. Sex in marriage is a powerful bond. Although we may tend to believe that good sex depends on good techniques, it really depends more on the quality of the marriage. One woman remarked to her husband, "What really turns me on is to see you doing housework." The husband, perplexed, asked why, because housework did not make him feel particularly sexy. "Because when I see you vacuuming, it gives me a warm feeling of love for you, which makes me want to make love with you." If the marriage is happy, the couple is more likely to have good sex; if it is unhappy, the unhappiness is likely to be reflected in the sexual relationship.

Sex therapists are turning increasingly to examining marital dynamics rather than the individual as the source of sexual problems (Kaplan, 1979). As Blumstein and Schwartz (1983) point out, "An unhappy sex life does not necessarily mean that a couple is sexually incompatible. Their sexual relationship may be undermined by other problems." It does not matter what the conflict is about—housework, children, money—it is likely to be carried over into the bedroom.

❖ EXTRAMARITAL SEXUALITY

Most people decry extramarital sexuality, but many engage in it. In fact, one researcher (Sponaugle, 1989) estimates that at least 52 million Americans have engaged in extramarital sex at least once during their marriages. Extramarital involvements assume many forms (see Thompson, 1983, and Sponaugle, 1990, for reviews of the research literature). These involvements may be (1) sexual but not emotional, (2) sexual and emotional, or (3) emotional but not sexual (Thompson, 1984). Very little research has been done on extramarital relationships in which both people are emotionally but not sexually involved. Thompson's study, however, found that of 378 married and cohabiting individuals, the three types of extrarelational involvement were about equally represented. Twenty-one percent had been in relationships that were primarily sexual, 19 percent in relationships that were sexual and emotional, and 18 percent in relationships that were emotional but not sexual. All told, 43 percent had been in some form of extramarital relationship.

Extrarelational experiences are not confined to married and cohabiting couples. Couples in exclusive dating relationships are also involved in sexual activities outside the relationship. As we saw earlier in our discussion of dating, a large percentage of persons in "exclusive" dating couples are involved in various erotic activities outside the relationship. It may very well be that those who engage in sex outside of their exclusive dating relationships are also more likely to engage in extramarital sex. Up to this point, however, research has not explored the possible relationship between the two.

Models of nonexclusive marital relationships may be grouped into several types: extramarital sexuality, nonsexual extramarital relationships, open marriage, sexually open marriage, swinging, and group marriage (Weiss, 1983).

Extramarital Sex in Exclusive Marital Relationships

In marriages that assume emotional and sexual exclusivity, mutuality and sharing are emphasized. Extramarital sexual relationships are assumed to be destructive of the marriage; close friendships with members of the other sex may also be judged to be threatening. The possibility of infecting one's husband or wife with a sexually transmitted disease (STD) must also be considered. As a result of these marital assumptions, extramarital relationships almost always take place without the knowledge or permission of the other partner. If the marital assumptions are violated, we have "guidelines" on how to handle the violation. According to David Weiss (1983): "These guidelines encourage the 'adulterer' to be secretive and discreet, suggest that guilt will be a consequence, and maintain that the spouse will react with feelings of jealousy and rejection if the [extramarital sex] is discovered."

If the extramarital relationship is discovered, a marital crisis probably ensues. Many married people feel that the spouse who is unfaithful has broken a basic trust. Sexual accessibility implies emotional accessibility. When a person learns that his or

Adultery in your heart is committed not only when you look with concupiscence [strong or excessive sexual desire] at a woman who is not your wife. The husband must not use his wife, her femininity, to fulfill his instinctive desire. Concupiscence. . . . diminishes the richness of the perennial attraction of persons for interpersonal communication. Through such a reduction, the other person becomes the mere object for satisfying a sexual need and it touches the dignity of the person.

Pope John Paul II

Why should we take advice on sex from the Pope? If he knows anything about it, he shouldn't.

George Bernard Shaw

her spouse is having an affair, the emotional commitment of that spouse is brought into question. How can you prove that you still have a commitment? You cannot. Commitment is assumed; it can never be proven. Furthermore, the extramarital relationship may imply to the partner (rightly or wrongly) that he or she is sexually inadequate or uninteresting.

Extramarital Sex in Nonexclusive Marital Relationships

There are several types of nonexclusive marriages (Weiss, 1983): (1) open marriage in which intimate but nonsexual friendships with others are encouraged, (2) sexually open marriages, (3) swinging, and (4) group marriage/multiple relationships. The marriage relationship is considered the primary relationship in both nonconsensual extramarital relationships (described previously) and in open marriages and swinging relationships. Only the group marriage/multiple relationships model rejects the primacy of the marital relationship. Group marriage is the equal sharing of partners, as in polygamy; it may consist of one man and two or more women, one woman and two or more men, or two or more couples.

SWINGING. Swinging (also called mate sharing or wife swapping) is a form of consensual extramarital sex in which couples engage in sexual activities with others in a social context clearly defined as recreational sex. Swinging is structured to prevent intimacy. Such social contexts include swinging parties or commercial club settings. Married couples swing together (Weiss, 1983). Forming an intimate relationship with an extramarital partner is prohibited.

No comittment →

It has been estimated that 2 percent of adult Americans have engaged in swinging (Weiss, 1983). Although swingers are popularly perceived to be deviant, radical, or psychologically troubled, they tend not to differ significantly from most Americans. They tend to be white, middle-class, politically conservative, and quite "normal" except for their swinging. They tend to be less religious than nonswingers (Jenks, 1985; Weiss, 1983). It is not known what impact the AIDS crisis has had on swinging, though anecdotal information suggests the epidemic has not affected it.

OPEN MARRIAGE. The partners in a sexually open marriage have mutually agreed that each may have openly acknowledged and independent sexual relationships with others. There has been little research on sexually open marriages. Blumstein and Schwartz (1983) found that 15 to 26 percent of the couples in their sample had "an understanding" that permitted extramarital relations in certain circumstances. The rules differ from couple to couple. Blumstein and Schwartz observe:

An open relationship does not mean that anything goes . . . . The most important rules provide emotional safeguards—for example, never seeing the same person twice, never giving out a phone number, never having sex in a couple's bed or with a mutual friend. Sex outside the relationship is potentially very disruptive. Traditional marriages have dealt with this by ruling out nonmonogamy. Couples who engage in open relationships formulate rules to guide their behavior, to make outside sex very predictable and orderly. These rules remind the partners that their relationship comes first and anything else must take second place.

An intriguing study (Rubin and Adams, 1986) attempted to measure the impact of sexually open marriages on marital stability. The researchers matched eighty-two couples in 1978 and were able to do a follow-up study of seventy-four couples five years later. It was found that there was no significant difference in marital stability related to whether the couple was sexually open or monogamous in their marriage.

Among those marriages that broke up, the reasons given were not related to extramarital sex. No appreciable differences were found in terms of marital happiness or jealousy.

Even though considerable numbers of Americans engage in extramarital sexual behavior, it does not appear that they reject the monogamous norm. Extramarital affairs will probably continue for the most part as secretive affairs.

Motivation in Extramarital Relationships

People who engage in extramarital affairs have a number of different motivations, and these affairs satisfy a number of different needs. John Gagnon (1977) described the appeal that extramarital affairs have for the people involved:

Most people find their extramarital relationships highly exciting, especially in the early stages. This is a result of psychological compression: the couple gets together; they are both very aroused (desire, guilt, expectation); they have only three hours to be together. . . . Another source of attraction is that the other person is always seen when he or she looks good and is on best behavior, never when feeling tired or grubby, or when taking care of children, or when cooking dinner. . . . Each time, all the minutes that the couple has together are special because they have been stolen from all these other relationships. The resulting combination of guilt and excitement has a heightening effect, which tends to explain why people may claim that extramarital sex and orgasms are more intense.

Most extramarital sex does not involve a love affair but is generally self-contained and more sexual than emotional (Gagnon, 1977). Affairs that are both emotional and sexual appear to detract most from the marital relationship, whereas affairs that are only sexual or only emotional seem to detract least (Thompson, 1984). More women than men have emotional affairs; almost twice as many men as women have affairs that are only sexual. About equal percentages of men and women are involved in affairs that are both sexual and emotional.

Studies have found little significant correlation between social background characteristics and extramarital sexuality (Thompson, 1983). Personal characteristics and the quality of the marriage appear to be more important, and of the two, personal characteristics—alienation, need for intimacy, emotional independence, and egalitarian sex roles—were stronger correlates of extramarital sex than the quality of the marriage (Thompson, 1984). Nevertheless, the lower the marital satisfaction and the lower the frequency and quality of marital intercourse, the greater the likelihood of extramarital sexual relationships. Most people become involved in extramarital sex because they feel that something is missing in their marriage. Whatever the state of their marital relationship, they have not judged it defective enough to consider divorce. Extramarital relationships are a compensation or substitute for these deficiencies. They help maintain the status quo by giving emotional satisfaction to the unhappy partner.

Research by Ira Reiss and his colleagues (1980) suggested that extramarital affairs appear to be related to two variables: unhappiness of the marriage, and premarital sexual permissiveness. Generally speaking, in happy marriages a partner is less likely to seek outside sexual relationships. If a person had premarital sex, he or she is more likely to have extramarital sex. Persons who break the social prohibition against premarital sex are less likely to be restrained by prohibitions against extramarital sex. Once the first prohibition is broken, the second holds less power.

Most men and women whose marriages break up after their involvement in an extramarital affair feel that the affair was an effect rather than a cause of marital

A cuckold is the husband of an unfaithful wife—a far nastier and more humiliating state. . . than being the wife of a philanderer, for which in fact no word exists.

Anne Fausto-Sterling, *Myths of Gender*

see person at their best
everything planned

problems. But if their spouse was also involved in such an affair, they identify the spouse's infidelity as a cause of marital problems (Spanier and Margolis, 1983).

❖ REFLECTIONS   *What impact do you believe secretive extramarital relationships have on a marriage? On a cohabiting relationship? What impact do open extramarital relationships have?*

❖ GAY AND LESBIAN RELATIONSHIPS

When you prevent me from doing anything I want to do, that is persecution; but when I prevent you from doing anything you want to do, that is law, order, and morals.

George Bernard Shaw

Between 3 and 10 percent of the American population is gay or lesbian (Marmor, 1980). In discussing gay men and lesbians, like many researchers, we generally do not use the terms *homosexual* and *homosexuality,* because they continue to convey negative or pathological connotations. Instead, we use **gay** or **gay male** to refer to men and **lesbian** to refer to women. Replacing the term *homosexual* is critical in expanding our understanding of gay men and lesbians. It helps us see gay men and lesbians as whole persons by underlining the fact that sexuality is not the only aspect of their lives: their lives also include love, commitment, desire, caring, work, children, religious devotion, passion, politics, loss, and hope. Sex is important, obviously, but it is not the only significant aspect of their lives, just as it is not the only significant aspect of the lives of heterosexuals.

Those with gay or lesbian orientations have been called sinful, sick, or perverse, reflecting traditional religious, medical, and psychoanalytic approaches. Contemporary thinking in sociology and psychology has rejected these older approaches as biased and unscientific. Instead, sociologists and psychologists have focused their work on how men and women come to identify themselves as gay or lesbian, how they interact among themselves, and what impact society has on them (Heyl, 1989). Researchers reject the idea that gay men and lesbians are inherently deviant or pathological. As noted sociologist Howard Becker (1963) pointed out, "deviant behavior is behavior that people so label." Deviance is created by social groups that make rules whose violation results in violators being labeled deviant and treated as outsiders. Gay and lesbian behavior, then, is deviant only insofar as it is called deviant.

Twenty years ago, the American Psychiatric Association rejected the idea that gay or lesbian orientations are pathological. Today, the majority of mental health professionals and researchers consider them to be legitimate sexual orientations (Cabai, 1988). In fact, the only psychological disorder today associated with being gay or lesbian is *ego-dystonic homosexuality,* which occurs when an individual has a persistent desire to switch from a gay or lesbian orientation to a heterosexual one because of the distress caused by their orientation (DSM-IV, 1991; Lief and Kaplan, 1986).

Gay and Lesbian Identities

THE FORMATION OF SEXUAL IDENTITY. How does one "become" gay, lesbian, bisexual—or even heterosexual, for that matter? A person's sexual orientation is very complex, depending on the interaction of numerous factors. These factors, which may be a combination of social and personal ones, lead to the unconscious formation or construction of a person's sexual identity. Two of the most important factors are (1) the gender of one's sexual partner and (2) whether a person labels himself or herself as heterosexual, gay, lesbian, or bisexual.

Sexual behaviors are not sufficient for identifying oneself as heterosexual, gay, lesbian, or bisexual. Various studies indicate that as many as 20 to 37 percent of

[handwritten margin note: self labeling *]*

YUK

American males, for example, have had orgasms with other males, but only 5 to 10 percent identify themselves as gay; among women, about 13 percent have had orgasms with other women, but only 1 to 3 percent identify themselves as lesbian (see DeCecco and Shively, 1983/1984; Fay et al., 1989; Kinsey, 1948, 1953; Marmor, 1980). The fact that these people's choice of sexual partners may contradict their sexual identity as heterosexual points out the complexity of sexual identity. Here is a crucial point regarding sexual orientation: a person needs to *feel* that he or she is gay or lesbian or heterosexual. Sexual identity is a subjective experience.

To make the question of sexual orientation even more complicated, sexual behaviors or feelings may change for some people, so that they redefine their sexual orientation. This plasticity in behavior or identity has led some researchers to believe that the concepts of heterosexual, gay, lesbian, and bisexual identities are meaningless. Instead, they argue, we are sexual beings, with more or less flexible erotic responses (see DeCecco and Shivley, 1983/1984).

There are over a million and a half gay or lesbian couples living together in the United States. Same-sex couples often adopt a "best-friend" relationship model rather than a traditional marriage model, so that there tends to be more sharing and equality than in many heterosexual relationships.

IDENTIFYING ONESELF AS GAY OR LESBIAN. Many researchers believe that a person's sexual interest or direction as heterosexual, gay, or lesbian is established by age four or five (Marmor, 1980). But identifying oneself as gay or lesbian takes considerable time and includes several phases, usually beginning in late childhood or early adolescence (Blumenfeld and Raymond, 1989; Troiden, 1988). Homoerotic feelings, that is, feelings of sexual attraction to members of the same sex, almost always precede gay or lesbian activity by several years (Bell et al., 1981). Various studies have indicated that the average gay male does not identify himself as gay until age nineteen to twenty-one (Troiden and Goode, 1980). The more heterosexual experiences during high school that a boy has beyond kissing, the longer it takes him to recognize that he is fundamentally gay. The significant factor is that he is less likely to enjoy his youthful heterosexual encounters (Bell et al., 1981).

The first phase in acquiring a gay or lesbian identity is marked by fear and suspicion that somehow one's desires are different. At first, the person finds it difficult to label these emotional and physical desires for the same sex. His or her initial reactions often include fear, confusion, or denial. Worse, adolescents fear their family's discovery of their homoerotic feelings. "Nowhere has the hostility to homosexuality been more frightening to large numbers of gay men and lesbians than in their own families, forcing them to feel like minority group members in their own homes" (Voeller, 1980). In the second phase, the person actually labels these feelings of attraction, love, and desire as gay. If the feelings recur often enough, a person is eventually forced to acknowledge that they are gay or lesbian feelings. The third phase includes the person's self-definition as gay. This may take considerable struggle, for it entails accepting a label that society generally calls deviant. Questions then arise about whether to tell parents or friends—whether to hide one's identity ("go into the closet") or make the identity known ("come out of the closet").

Some gay men or lesbians may go through two additional phases. One phase is to enter the gay subculture. A gay person may begin acquiring exclusively gay friends, going to gay bars and clubs, or joining gay activist groups. In the gay world, gay and lesbian identities incorporate a way of being in which sexual orientation is a major part of their identity as a person. As Michael Denneny (quoted in Altman, 1982) said: "I find my identity as a gay man as basic as any other identity I can lay claim to. Being gay is a more elemental aspect of who I am than my profession, my class, or my race."

Similarly, Pat Califia (quoted in Weeks, 1985) said: "Knowing I was a lesbian transformed the way I saw, heard, perceived the whole world. I became aware of a network of sensations and reactions that I had ignored all my life."

The final phase begins with a person's first gay or lesbian love affair. This marks the commitment to unifying sexuality and affection. Sex and love are no longer separated. Most gay men and lesbians have had such love affairs, despite the stereotypes of anonymous gay sex.

COMING OUT. Being gay or lesbian is increasingly associated with a total life-style and way of thinking (Conrad and Schneider, 1980). In making gay or lesbian orientation a life-style, **coming out** (publicly acknowledging one's gayness) has become especially important as an affirmation of one's sexuality (Richardson, 1984). Coming out is a major decision, because it may jeopardize many relationships, but it is also an important means of self-validation. By publicly acknowledging one's gay or lesbian orientation, a person begins to reject the stigma and condemnation associated with it (Friend, 1980). Generally, coming out occurs in stages, first involving family members, especially the mother and siblings and later the father. Coming out to the family often creates a crisis, but generally the family accepts the situation and gradually adjusts (Holtzen and Agresti, 1990). Misinformation about gay and lesbian sexuality, religious beliefs, and homophobia, however, often interfere with parental response, initially making adjustment difficult (Borhek, 1988; Cramer and Roach, 1987). After the family, friends may be told, and, in fewer cases, employers and co-workers.

Gay men and women are often "out" to varying degrees. Some may be out to no one, not even themselves. Some are out only to their lovers, others to close friends and lovers but not to their families, employers, associates, or fellow students. Others may be out to everyone. Because of fear of reprisal, dismissal, or public reaction, gay and lesbian school teachers, police officers, members of the military, politicians, and members of other such professions are rarely out to their employers, co-workers, or the public.

Gay and Lesbian Couples

In 1987, there were over 1.5 million gay or lesbian couples living together. Ninety-two thousand of these couples had children living with them (U.S.Bureau of the Census, 1987). The relationships of gay men and lesbians have been stereotyped as less committed than heterosexual couples because (1) gay men and lesbians cannot legally marry, (2) they may not appear to emphasize sexual exclusiveness, and (3) heterosexuals misperceive love between gay and lesbian couples as being somehow less "real" than love between heterosexuals. Numerous similarities exist between gay and heterosexual couples, according to Letitia Peplau (1981; 1988). Regardless of their sexual orientation, most people want a close, loving relationship with another person. For gay men, lesbians, and heterosexuals, intimate relationships provide love, satisfaction, and security. There is one important difference, however. Heterosexual couples tend to adopt a traditional marriage model, whereas gay couples tend to have a "best-friend" model. Peplau (1988) observes:

A friendship model promotes equality in love relationships. As children, we learn that the husband should be the "boss" at home, but friends "share and share alike." Same-sex friends often have similar interests, skills, and resources—in part because they are exposed to the same gender-role socialization in growing up. It is easier to share responsibilities in a relationship when both partners are equally skilled—or inept—at cooking, making money, disclosing feelings, or whatever.

With this model, tasks and chores are often shared, alternated, or done by the person who has more time. Usually, both members of the couple support themselves; rarely does one financially support the other (Peplau and Gordon, 1982).

Few gay and lesbian relationships are divided into the traditional heterosexual provider/homemaker roles. Among heterosexuals, these divisions are gender-linked as male or female. But in cases in which the couple consists of two men or two women, these traditional gender divisions make no sense. As one gay male remarked, "Whenever I am asked who is the husband and who is the wife, I say, 'We're just a couple of happily married husbands.'" Tasks are often divided pragmatically, according to considerations such as who likes cooking more (or dislikes it less) and work schedules (Marecek, Finn, and Cardell, 1988). Most gay couples are dual-worker couples; neither partner supports or depends on the other economically. Further, since gay and lesbian couples are the same sex, the economic discrepancies based on greater male earning power are absent. One partner does not necessarily have greater power than the other based on income. Although gay couples emphasize egalitarianism, if there are differences in power, they are attributed to personality; if there is an age difference, the older partner is usually more powerful (Harry, 1988).

For both gay men and lesbians, love serves an important function in solidifying their sexual identity and connecting their sexuality with affection. One major study (Bell and Weinberg, 1978) found that virtually every gay man and lesbian who was interviewed had experienced at least one long-term relationship. Almost all the respondents reported that the relationship was important and meaningful to them. One gay man said, "I got a feeling of being loved and having my love accepted. It was a great feeling—companionship and mutual dependence." A lesbian commented about her first relationship, "I got a deeper understanding of another person's capacity for feeling."

Because they confront societal hostility, gay men and lesbians fail to receive the general social support given heterosexuals in maintaining relationships. One rarely finds parents, for example, urging their gay or lesbian children to make a commitment to a stable same-sex relationship or, if the relationship is rocky, to stick it through.

The Gay Response to HIV and AIDS

Although HIV and AIDS strikes heterosexuals as well as gay men, gays experience not only the disease itself but also the stigma attached to it by the larger society. Because there is little support from the larger world for gay men infected with HIV and those with AIDS symptoms, the gay and lesbian communities have become major advocates and sources of support (Altman, 1986). They have been instrumental in the development of research foundations, education and counseling programs, and outreach programs for those infected with HIV or diagnosed with AIDS.

Because of the HIV/AIDS crisis, gay men have altered their sexual behavior patterns considerably. As a result of their efforts, their rate of HIV infection has diminished significantly. The greatest increases in HIV infection and AIDS rates are now found among heterosexuals who contract the virus sexually and users of intravenous (IV) drugs (and their infants). The changes in gay male behavior led the national AIDS commission to indicate that the main reservoir for the transmission of HIV is no longer gay men but IV-drug users.

The urban gay subculture once viewed their sexuality as a celebration of homoeroticism and self, a response to centuries of repression. But the HIV/AIDS crisis devastated the generation of gay baby boomers. "The only social activity was going to funerals," said one gay journalist (Salholz, 1990). The HIV/AIDS crisis led to reevaluation of the role of sexuality in gay culture. Sex became associated with death. Therapist Douglas Carl (1986) wrote, "The pressure on gay men to couple has increased dramatically; at the same time, young people who have never before considered death must deal with it on a daily basis." Fear and celibacy became a way of life. Now a younger generation of gay men are seeking to present a sex-positive message, uniting an affirmation of their sexuality as the deepest expression of self with a commitment to safe sex practices.

Homophobia

The response to gay men and lesbians has varied considerably in different cultures. Among seventy-six cultures studied by Ford and Beach (1972), almost two-thirds accepted certain forms of male-to-male sexuality. Our own society's hostility toward gay men and lesbians represents a minority viewpoint. Conventional fears, anxieties, and guilt about sexuality merge with stereotypes of gay men and lesbians to create **homophobia**, the fear or hatred of gay men and lesbians. Homophobia continues to be widespread in the United States. A recent Gallup poll found that only 47 percent of all adults believe that gay and lesbian relations between consenting adults should be legal.

IMPACT OF HOMOPHOBIA. It is well established that many of the problems facing gay men and lesbians result from the social and cultural contexts in which they live (Herek, 1984, 1986). As a result of homophobia, gay men and lesbians are discriminated against in employment, military service, housing, and parental rights. Gay men and lesbians face imprisonment for engaging in the same sexual activities (such as oral-genital sex) in which heterosexuals commonly engage (*Harvard Law Review*, 1990). There were over 7,000 hate incidents, including 62 murders, reported against gay men and lesbians in 1988. Almost one-fifth of the incidents occurred on college campuses. These included physical attacks on lesbian sorority members at UCLA and, at another campus, rallies in which protesters wore Ku Klux Klan-style robes and chanted "Queers, go home" (Pogatchnik, 1990). (Twenty-two states have hate-crime laws, but thirteen of them exclude gay-related incidents.) Medical and public health efforts against HIV (human immunodeficiency virus) infections and AIDS were inhibited at first because the disease was perceived as "the gay plague" and was considered "punishment" against gay men for their "unnatural" sexual practices (Altman, 1986). Indeed, because of HIV and AIDS homophobia has intensified in many quarters (Forstein, 1988).

Gay men and lesbians may experience rejection by family, friends, and peers. Such rejection may lead gay men and lesbians themselves to feel homophobic—against themselves, unable to accept their sexuality; against their partners; and against other gay men or lesbians (George and Behrendt, 1987; Sophie, 1987). If they internalize society's hostility, gay men and lesbians may become depressed and feel themselves to be perverted, evil, or sick (Warren, 1980).

Homophobia adversely affects heterosexuals as well. First, it creates aversive emotions in heterosexuals, such as fear and hatred, that affect their own psychological functioning and well-being. Second, it alienates them from their gay or lesbian family members, friends, neighbors, or coworkers. For fear of rejection, gay and lesbian children may hide their orientation from their family. Sometimes a family discovers that a member is gay only after he has been infected with HIV or develops AIDS

Morality is the custom of one's country and the current feeling of one's peers. Cannibalism is moral in a cannibal country.

Samuel Butler (1612-1680)

Dear Abby

In response to a homophobic reader who launched into a bitter tirade against gay men moving into a house across the street and then asked: "How can we improve the quality of the neighborhood?" Abigail van Buren replied: "You could move."

symptoms. Then the family must deal with both their own homophobia and the illness or death or dying of their son, brother, or father. Third, homophobia limits heterosexuals' range of feelings and behaviors, such as hugging or being emotionally intimate with same-sex friends, because of their fear that such intimacy may be gay or perceived as gay (Thompson, Grisanti, and Pleck, 1985). This may lead to exaggerated displays of masculinity or femininity.

SOURCES OF HOMOPHOBIA. Homophobia is derived from several sources (Marmor, 1980): (1) a deeply rooted insecurity about one's own sexuality and gender identity, (2) a strong fundamentalist religious orientation, and (3) ignorance about gay men and lesbians. In addition, homophobic individuals are less likely to have had personal contact with gays or lesbians, are more likely to be older and less well educated, and are more likely to express traditional, restrictive attitudes toward sex and to manifest more guilt about sex (Herek, 1984). Some research (Herek, 1986) suggests that the traditional heterosexual male gender role includes homophobia. Traditional male heterosexuals affirm their heterosexuality by strongly expressing whom they are *not* (that is, gay men).

> *Sin is whatever obscures the soul.*
>
> André Gide

Much homophobia finds justification in selected passages in the Judeo-Christian scriptures (Boswell, 1980; Bullough, 1976; see Edwards, 1989, for a critique of creationist homophobia). As historian John Boswell noted (1980), however, "Religious beliefs may cloak or incorporate intolerance. . . . Careful analysis can almost always differentiate between conscientious application of religious ethics and the use of religious precepts as justification for personal animosity or prejudice." Although both gay and lesbian sexuality were condemned in Leviticus ("Thou shalt not lie with mankind, as with womankind" [18:22]), the same book equally condemned lying and stealing ("Thou shalt not steal nor deal falsely, nor lie to one another" [19:11]). Yet neither liars nor thieves were later denounced—or burned—with the same moral vengeance as were gay men and lesbians. In the story of Sodom and Gommorah, according to the book of Ezekiel (16:49–50), Sodomites "were haughty and did abominable things." Within the Biblical context, the conventional meaning of the word *abominable* is idolotry or the worshipping of idols (Bullough, 1976).

> *Sin is geographical.*
>
> Bertrand Russell

In the Christian New Testament, there were no condemnations of gay and lesbian sexuality by Jesus of Nazareth. Paul of Tarsus condemned same-sex sexuality, but he also condemned usurers and the wealthy, who were never persecuted. In Biblical times, there was little persecution of men and women for sexual "abomination." Persecution did not occur until the Middle Ages, when gay men and lesbians were beaten, burned, hanged, and mutilated as apostates and witches (Boswell, 1980). (In fact, the derisive word *faggot* is a reference to the faggots used to kindle fires for burning heretics and witches.) By the nineteenth century, homophobia had become institutionalized in Christian churches and Jewish synagogues. This continued homophobia causes great pain to devout gay men and lesbians (Coleman, 1989; McNeil, 1988).

Gay and lesbian African Americans face a double issue. They must deal with their own self-acceptance as gays and lesbians in an African-American culture that tends to be nonaccepting of their orientation. They must also deal with being African-Americans in a gay and lesbian subculture that is overwhelmingly white (Loiacano, 1989). Latinos also face similar cultural and identity issues. Their difficulties are compounded, however, by the Catholic church's pervasive cultural influence, which continues to negate gay sexuality (Carballo-Dieguez, 1989).

Blacks face cultural persecution

Latinos face religious persecution

Something is happening to gay men, and we are suddenly no longer affiliated with the family. Where do they think we came from? The cabbage patch?

Larry Kramer

The Catholic Church says it's OK to be gay, as long as you don't practice homosexuality. I say it's OK to be Catholic as long as you don't practice Catholicism.

Bob Smith

ELIMINATING HOMOPHOBIA. What can be done to end homophobia? Education and positive social interactions appear to be important vehicles for change. Education can affect negative attitudes. Two researchers (Serdahely and Ziemba, 1984) studied the effect of including a unit on gays and lesbians in their human sexuality course. They found that students who, at the beginning of the course, scored above the class mean on homophobic attitudes had a significant decrease in their scores by the end.

Researcher Gregory Herek (1984) suggests that homophobia may be reduced by arranging positive interactions between heterosexuals and gay men and lesbians in settings of equal status, common goals, cooperation, and a moderate degree of intimacy. Such interactions may occur when family members or close friends disclose their gay or lesbian orientation. Other interactions should emphasize common group membership (such as religious, social, ethnic, or political groups) on a one-to-one basis.

Herek suggested that those holding negative attitudes based on biblical teachings be exposed to other biblical interpretations about gays and lesbians. Today many churches and synagogues are attempting to generate a moral force to overcome homophobia (Berliner, 1987). Methodists, Lutherans, and Presbyterians are currently reviewing their teachings. The Rev. Denis Moore (1990) wrote, "It is not whom one chooses as a love partner but that one chooses to be a loving human being that is of moral significance. Unloving heterosexuality is no virtue and loving homosexuality is no vice." In 1990, the Reformed branch of Judaism accepted gay men and lesbians as rabbis.

Finally, homophobia may be eliminated by focusing on changing institutions that legitimize and perpetuate prejudice and hostility towards gay men and lesbians (Plummer, 1981). These include such major institutions as churches, government, the military, courts and the law, and public schools and higher education. There is some improvement, as in the liberalization of some churches and synagogues just discussed, but progress is painfully slow. A few universities have recently permitted gay and lesbian couples to live in married student apartments and granted them benefits previously reserved for married students. Students on numerous campuses have protested the dismissal of gay men from ROTC units and subsequent government orders for them to repay their scholarships (Gross, 1990). In a few high schools, discussions of gay and lesbian sexuality, as well as issues surrounding homophobia, are now included in sex education classes.

❖ REFLECTIONS   *If you are heterosexual, do you feel comfortable among gay men and lesbians? If you are gay, do you feel comfortable around heterosexuals? Why?*

❖ SEXUAL ISSUES: CONTRACEPTION, ABORTION, AND SEXUALLY TRANSMITTED DISEASES

Most of us probably think of sexuality in terms of love, passionate embraces, and entwined bodies. Sex involves all of these, but what we so often forget (unless we are worried) is that sex is also a means of reproduction and a pathway to infection. Whether we like to think about it or not, many of us (or our partners) are vulnerable to unintended pregnancies and sexually transmitted diseases (STDs). And not thinking about unintended pregnancies and STDs does not prevent them. Indeed, avoidance may even contribute to the likelihood of their occurring. Unless we are sexually abstinent, it is necessary to think about unintended pregnancies and STDs and then take the necessary steps to prevent them. If a woman accidentally becomes pregnant, she must make the difficult decision either to give birth or to have an abortion.

PERSPECTIVE

Sexual Responsibility

Because we have so many sexual choices today, we need to understand what responsibilities our sexuality entails. Sexual responsibility includes the following:

DISCLOSURE OF INTENTIONS. Each person needs to reveal to the other whether a sexual involvement indicates love, commitment, recreation, and so on.

FREELY AND MUTUALLY AGREED-UPON SEXUAL ACTIVITIES. Each individual has the right to refuse any or all sexual activities without the need to justify his or her feelings. There can be no physical or emotional coercion.

USE OF MUTUALLY AGREED-UPON CONTRACEPTION IN SEXUAL INTERCOURSE IF PREGNANCY IS NOT INTENDED. Both persons in a sexual relationship are *equally* responsible for preventing an unintended pregnancy in a mutually agreed-upon manner.

USE OF SAFE SEX PRACTICES. Each person is responsible for practicing safe sex unless both have been monogamous with each other for at least five years. Safe sex practices (discussed in the Resource Center) guard against sexually transmitted diseases, especially HIV/AIDS. Such practices do not transmit semen, vaginal secretions, or blood during sexual activities.

DISCLOSURE OF INFECTION FROM OR EXPOSURE TO STDS. Each person must inform his or her partner about having or being exposed to an STD because of the serious health consequences, such as infertility or pelvic inflammatory disease, that may follow untreated infections. If you are infected, you must refrain from behaviors such as sexual intercourse, oral-genital sex, or anal intercourse, which may infect your partner. To help insure that STDs are not transmitted, use a condom.

ACCEPTANCE OF THE CONSEQUENCES OF YOUR SEXUAL BEHAVIOR. Each person needs to be aware of and accept the possible consequences of his or her sexual activities. These consequences can include emotional changes, pregnancy, and sexually transmitted diseases. Because sexual interactions often change the nature of a relationship, this means accepting responsibility for the emotional changes that may occur for both yourself and your partner. If an unintended pregnancy results, you must make a responsible decision and acknowledge or support the feelings of your partner.

Responsibility in many of these areas is facilitated when sex takes place within the context of an ongoing relationship. In that sense, sexual responsibility leads to a question of values. Is responsible sex possible outside an established relationship? Are *you* able to act sexually responsible? Sexual responsibility also leads to the question of the purpose of sex in your life. Is it for intimacy, erotic please, reproduction, or other purposes?

Using Contraception

A woman has about a 2 to 4 percent chance of becoming pregnant during intercourse without contraception. **Contraception** is the prevention of conception using any of a number of devices, techniques, or drugs. If intercourse occurs the day before ovulation, the chance of conception is 30 percent; if it occurs on the day of ovulation, there is a 50 percent chance of pregnancy. Over the period of a year, a couple that does not use contraception has a 90 percent chance of pregnancy. (See Resource Center for information on choosing a contraceptive method.)

The key to contraceptive effectiveness is diligent and consistent use. A diaphragm in the bathroom, a condom in the wallet, or pills in the dispenser are useless for preventing pregnancies. Your intentions may be good, but good intentions are not good contraceptives.

CONTRACEPTIVE USE. Because the possibility of pregnancy is so high for a sexually active couple, it seems reasonable that sexually active men and women would use contraception to avoid unintended pregnancy. In recent years, some increase in contraceptive use has been seen. One major study found that during their first

Read well [handwritten annotation]

intercourse, nearly two-thirds of the teenage girls surveyed used contraception (Forrest and Singh, 1990). As men and women age, they become more consistent contraceptive users. One national study found that only about 7 percent of the sexually active women did not use contraception during intercourse (Bachrach, 1984). Twice as many single women (whether never married, separated, or divorced) as married women did not use contraception.

Numerous studies have indicated that the most consistent users of contraception are men and women who explicitly communicate about contraception. Those at greatest risk are those in casual dating relationships and those who infrequently discuss contraception with their partners or others. A review of the literature on the interpersonal factors in contraceptive use concluded, "Individuals in stable, serious relationships of long duration who had frequent, predictable patterns of sexual activity were most likely to use contraception" (Milan and Kilmann, 1987).

Adolescents are especially vulnerable to unintended pregnancy because the younger a person is at first intercourse, the less likely he or she is to use contraception. African-American adolescents are especially vulnerable to unintended pregnancies as they are four times as likely as whites to have ever had sexual intercourse (Furstenberg, Morgan, Moore, and Peterson, 1987). Among adolescents, those whose parents discussed sexuality were more likely to use contraception (Baker, Thalberg, and Morrison, 1988). A study of 600 white, African-American, Latino, and Asian-American adolescents and young adults indicated that all groups had poor knowledge about contraception and STDs. Asian-Americans and Latinos had poorer knowledge than their white and African-American counterparts (Moore and Erickson, 1985). Another study (Scott, Shifman, Orr, and Owen, 1988) found that in a comparison between Latino and African-American inner-city adolescents, Latino boys had the greatest contraceptive knowledge, whereas Latino girls had the least. Adolescent African-American males had somewhat lower rates of condom use at first intercourse than whites. At most recent intercourse, however, African-Americans had higher rates of condom use (Pleck, 1989).

TAKING CHANCES. Most people know they are taking a chance when they don't use contraception. The more frequently a person engages in unprotected intercourse without a resultant pregnancy, however, the more likely he or she is to take chances again (Luker, 1975). A subtle psychology develops: somehow, apparently by will power, good vibes, or the gods' kindly intervention, the woman will not get pregnant. Eventually, the woman or couple will feel almost magically invulnerable to pregnancy. Each time they are lucky, their risk taking is reinforced.

The consequences of an unintended pregnancy—economic hardships, interruption of education, adoption, or abortion—may be overwhelming. Why, then, do people take chances in the first place? Part of the reason is faulty knowledge. People often underestimate how easy it is to get pregnant. Also, they may not know how to use a contraceptive method correctly, especially if they use the calendar (rhythm) method (which is not too reliable to begin with). Finally, Kristin Luker (1975) suggests that we can look at contraceptive use in terms of a cost/benefit analysis. She observes, "The decision to take a contraceptive risk is typically based on the *immediate* costs of contraception and the *anticipated* benefits of pregnancy." But the anticipated benefits usually prove illusory. "The potential benefits of pregnancy seldom become real; they vanish with the verdict of a positive pregnancy test or [are] later outweighed by the actual costs of the pregnancy." Some of the costs are acknowledging sexuality; planning, obtaining, and continuing contraception; and lack of spontaneity.

Many people conceptualize their dissatisfaction with life in terms of sexual problems, but their real difficulty lies in misunderstanding the role of sex in life. As a rule, they feel that the meaning of sex in life is fixed, when in fact it is constantly developing and changing—it is free. That simple insight, when integrated fully into the lifestyle of an individual, can liberate him from the chains of his pain.

Peter Koestenbaum, Existential Sexuality

Acknowledging Sexuality. On the surface, it may seem fairly simple to acknowledge that we are sexual beings, especially if we have conscious sexual desires and engage in sexual intercourse. Yet acknowledging our sexuality is not necessarily easy, for sexuality may be surrounded by feelings of guilt, conflict, and shame. The younger or less experienced we are, the more difficult it is to acknowledge our sexuality.

Planning Contraception. Planning contraception requires us to admit not only that we are sexual but also that we plan to be sexually active. Without such planning, men and women can pretend that their sexual intercourse "just happens" in a moment of passion, when they have been drinking, or when the moon is full—even though it happens frequently.

Developments in the past generation have shifted contraceptive responsibility from the man to the woman, requiring women to more consciously define themselves as sexual. To do so, they have had to abandon traditional, passive sexual roles. Many women are reluctant to plan contraceptive use because they fear they will be regarded as sexually aggressive or promiscuous.

Since it is women who get pregnant, men tend to be unaware of their responsibility or to downplay their role in conception and pregnancy. Males, especially adolescents, lack the awareness that supports contraceptive planning (Freeman, 1980). Yet males are more fertile than females. The average male is fertile twenty-four hours a day for fifty or more years. Females, in contrast, are fertile only a few days of the month for thirty-five years or so.

Obtaining Contraception. Difficulty in obtaining contraception may be a deterrent to using it. It is often embarrassing for sexually inexperienced persons. Buying condoms, foam, or sponges at the local drugstore is a public announcement that a person is sexual. Who knows if your mother, teacher, or minister might be down the aisle buying toothpaste (or contraceptives, for that matter) and might see you? Adolescent girls may be too embarrassed to undergo the pelvic examination necessary for obtaining birth control pills.

Continuing Contraception. Many people, especially women using pills, practice contraception consistently and effectively within a steady relationship but give up their contraceptive practices if the relationship breaks up. They define themselves as sexual only within the context of a relationship. When men or women begin a new relationship, they may not use contraception because the relationship has not yet become long term; they do not expect to have sexual intercourse or to have it often. They are willing to take chances.

Lack of Spontaneity. Using contraceptive devices such as condoms or a diaphragm may destroy the feeling of spontaneity in sex. For those who justify their sexual behavior with romantic impulsiveness, using these devices seems cold and mechanical. Others do not use them because it would mean untangling bodies and limbs, interrupting the passion of the moment.

Many men and women fantasize that even an "accidental" pregnancy might be beneficial. These anticipated benefits include (1) proving womanhood or manhood, (2) proving fertility, (3) defining a commitment, and (4) defining or redefining a person's relationship to his or her parents. Unfortunately, once a woman becomes pregnant, the anticipated benefits often fail to materialize.

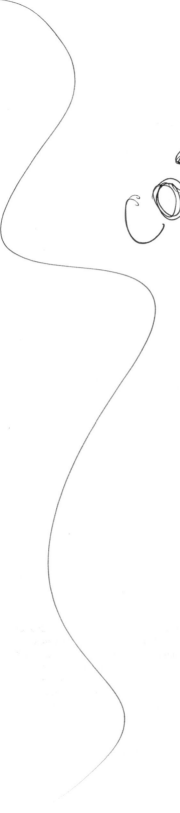

❖ REFLECTIONS   *For yourself, how would you weigh the benefits of pregnancy against its costs? Do you take chances?*

Volo comparare nonnulla tegumembra [Latin]. "I'd like to buy some condoms."

MEN AND CONTRACEPTION. Because women bear children and have most of the responsibility for raising them, they may have a greater interest than their partners in controlling their fertility. Nevertheless, it is unfair to assume, as people generally do in our society, that the total responsibility for contraception should be the woman's. Men may participate in contraception by using condoms, which are quite effective when used properly, especially in combination with a spermicide. (See the Resource Center for hints on how to use condoms properly.) Condoms have the additional advantage of being effective in helping prevent the spread of STDs, including HIV. They are also known as prophylatics because they protect against disease.

In addition to using a condom, there are other ways a man can help take contraceptive responsibility. These include the following:

◆ Explore ways of making love without intercourse.
◆ Help pay doctor or clinic bills and share the cost of pills or other contraceptive supplies.
◆ Check on supplies, help keep track of the menstrual cycle, and help his partner with supplies.
◆ In a long-term relationship, if no (or no more) children are wanted, he can have a vasectomy.

❖ REFLECTIONS   *Is it important to you (or your partner) for the male to be an active participant in the practice of contraception? Why?*

The Abortion Controversy

The abortion controversy involves deep moral choices and conflicting visions of society. It touches on our attitudes toward women's rights, the family, childbearing and children, and the nature of our society. What rights do women have over their bodies? What rights do blastocysts, embryos, and fetuses have? What is the importance of children and family in our lives? What does the legalization or criminalization of abortion say about the kind of society we envision? These questions have become very real as the Reagan/Bush Supreme Court may very well overturn the Roe vs. Wade decision that guaranteed a woman's right to abortion. If the decision is overturned, each state legislature will determine what abortion rights, if any, will be granted.

Those supporting the prohibition of abortion generally identify themselves as "pro-life." Those supporting a woman's right to choose for herself whether to have an abortion generally identify themselves as "pro-choice." But we must remember that such labels often confuse rather than clarify issues. They are used as moral symbols to gain support for or against legal abortion. Indeed, the advocates of both positions all too often seek to vilify the other as malevolent, elite, and conspiratorial, leaving little room for rational discourse (Vanderford, 1989). Many on both sides of the argument feel uncomfortable about the pro-life and pro-choice labels. "Pro-life is misleading because it begs the question of what really serves human life and welfare; pro-choice is no less misleading because it begs the question of whether freedom of choice ought to be made an ultimate moral value. . ." (Callahan and Callahan, 1984).

In 1985, there were about 1.6 million abortions, representing an abortion rate of 2.8 abortions per 100 women of childbearing age. The abortion rate was 2.3 per 100 women for whites and 5.6 per 100 for African-Americans (U.S. Bureau of the Census, 1990). Among adolescents, Latinos have a lower abortion rate than either Anglos or African-Americans (Aneshensel, Fielder, and Becerra, 1989). Seventeen percent of abortions were performed on married women and 83 percent were performed on unmarried women in 1985. Twenty-five percent of the women were fifteen to nineteen years old; 35 percent were twenty to twenty-four years old. About 1 percent each of women having abortions were below fifteen years and over forty years old (U.S. Bureau of the Census, 1990).

Most Americans occupy a middle position in the abortion debate. The majority believe women should have access to legal abortion when the fetus is defective or the pregnancy is the result of rape or incest. There is less support for abortion when the pregnancy is unintended, as is the case for most women seeking an abortion. The moral beliefs of those opposing abortion reinforce their desire to make it illegal. But those supporting the legal right to abortion frequently have more complex responses: they may have moral reservations about abortion but nevertheless support the right of others to decide (Scott, 1989). (For information on abortion methods and the effects of abortion on women and their partners, see the Resource Center.)

PRO-LIFE ARGUMENT. For those who oppose abortion, there is a basic principle from which their arguments follow: the moment an egg is fertilized, it becomes a human being with the full rights and dignity afforded other humans. A zygote is no less human than a fetus, and a fetus is no less human than a baby. Morally, aborting a zygote or embryo is the equivalent of killing a person.

In addition, pro-life advocates argue that abortion is the first step toward a euthanasia society, in which undesirable humans will be eliminated. If we allow the elimination of blastocysts or embryos, they argue, what is to stop the killing of the disabled, the elderly, or the merely inconvenient? Finally, pro-life advocates argue that there are thousands of couples who want to adopt children but are unable to do so because pregnant women abort rather than give birth.

Even though the majority of those opposing abortion would allow rape and incest (and sometimes a defective embryo or fetus) as exceptions, the pro-life leadership generally opposes any exception except to save the life of the pregnant woman. To abort the zygote of a rape or incest survivor, they reason, is still taking an innocent human life.

PRO-CHOICE ARGUMENT. Those who believe that abortion should continue to be legal present a number of arguments, including (1) a pregnant woman's right to choose, (2) the lack of 100-percent-effective contraception, and (3) the social and personal consequences of making abortion illegal. Furthermore, pro-choice advocates point out that over 90 percent of abortions are performed in the first trimester (three months) of pregnancy, well before the fetus is developed sufficiently to survive outside the womb.

First, for pro-choice men and women, the fundamental issue is *who* decides whether a woman will bear children: the woman or the state. Since women continue to bear the primary responsibility for rearing children, pro-choice advocates believe that women should not be forced to give birth to unwanted children. Becoming a mother alters a woman's role more profoundly than almost any other event in her life; it is more significant than marrying. When women have the choice of becoming mothers, they are able to decide the timing and direction of their lives.

Second, while pro-choice advocates support sex education and contraception to eliminate much of the need for abortion, they believe that abortion should continue to be available as birth control backup. Because no contraceptive is 100 percent effective, unintended pregnancies occur even among the most conscientious contraceptive users. For couples using oral contraception over a period of twenty-five years, because the pill has a 2 percent failure rate, there is a fifty-fifty chance that they will have an unintended pregnancy.

Third, if abortion is made illegal, large numbers of women nevertheless will have illegal abortions, substantially increasing the likelihood of dangerous complications, infections, and death. U.S. Surgeon-General Everett Koop (1989) determined that all available evidence suggests positive mental and physical health outcomes following legal abortion; there is no scientific evidence of negative health effects. Statistically speaking, legal abortion is significantly safer for women than childbirth.

WORLD VIEWS OF PRO-LIFE AND PRO-CHOICE ACTIVISTS. Sociologist Kristin Luker (1984) has examined female pro-life and pro-choice activists to understand how their abortion positions relate to some of their other values. Activists from the two sides have very little in common in terms of how they see the world. This is especially true for the issues of gender roles, sex, and parenthood. Activists' views on abortion are closely tied to these other issues.

First, gender roles are perceived radically differently. Pro-life activists tend to believe that men and women are inherently different. Men are rational and instrumental; women are emotional and expressive. Men are best suited to the world of work and power, whereas women exercise their feminine qualities as housewives, rearing children and caring for their husbands. Pro-choice activists, by contrast, believe that men and women are fundamentally similar and equal. They see women's family roles of mother and wife as potential barriers to independence and to full equality at home and in the workplace.

Second, the two sides disagree on the purpose of sexuality. Pro-life activists believe that the primary purpose of sex is reproduction. As a result, most are opposed to the use of contraception. One activist said (in Luker, 1984):

The frame of mind in which you know there might be conception in the midst of sex is quite different from that in which you know that there could not be conception. . . . I don't think that people who are constantly using physical, chemical means of contraception ever really experience the sex act in all of its beauty.

The pro-life activists belief in the reproductive purpose of sex leads them to oppose premarital sex because those involved in it are not seeking procreation. They are opposed to adolescent sex because teenagers are not prepared for parenthood. And the availability of contraception, they believe, merely encourages teenagers to be sexual.

Pro-choice supporters focus on the emotional and erotic qualities of sex: sex is an end in itself. To separate sex from reproduction, they encourage contraception. Almost without exception, however, they oppose the use of abortion as a routine method of birth control. As one pro-choice women explained (in Luker, 1984):

I take the idea of ending the life of a fetus very, very gravely. . . . That doesn't in any way diminish my conviction that a woman has a right to do it, but I become distressed when people regard pregnancy lightly and ignore the spiritual significance of a pregnancy.

Third, the two sides see parenthood quite differently, reflecting their views on gender roles and sexuality. Pro-life activists see motherhood as woman's natural role.

I disagree And I don't! (handwritten)

Since it is natural, it does not require careful planning or timing through contraceptive use. Further, since they believe that motherhood is a woman's most fulfilling role, pro-life activists cannot understand why a woman would want to postpone or avoid pregnancy in favor of work, a career, or school.

Similarly, pro-choice women cannot understand why others would want to rush into parenthood. They believe that parenthood needs to be deferred until the couple has established trust and intimacy. In addition, a couple needs to wait until they have the financial security and emotional resources to raise children in a caring, nurturing environment. In fact, they worry about how easy it is to become a parent, for many people don't know what it takes to be a good parent. Abortion, they believe, will enhance parenting in the long run by making it optional.

Preventing Sexually Transmitted Diseases (STDs)

STDS AND HIV/AIDS. "Do you have chlamydia, gonorrhea, herpes, syphilis, HIV, or any other sexually transmitted disease?" is hardly a question you want to ask someone on a first date. But it is a question to which you need to know the answer before you become sexually involved. Just because a person is nice is no guarantee that he or she does not have an STD. No one can tell by a person's looks, intelligence, or moral fervor whether he or she has contracted a sexually transmitted disease. And the costs are too great in this age of HIV/AIDS to become sexually involved with a person without knowing the answer to this question.

Americans are in the middle of the worst STD epidemic in our history. In 1989, more than 13 million Americans were infected by STDs. College students are as vulnerable as anyone else. Untreated chlamydia and gonorrhea have led to pelvic inflammatory disease (PID) in 1.7 million women annually, many of whom become sterile (Hilts, 1990). A 1989 survey of 17,000 college students, in fact, indicated that 0.2 percent of students were infected by HIV (Johnson, 1990). Overall, HIV has infected as many as 1.5 million Americans. By July 1990, 143,000 Americans had developed or died from AIDS. HIV and AIDS cases are increasing at a disproportionate rate for African Americans and Latinos; sexually transmitted cases among heterosexuals are increasing at a greater rate than among gay men (*Morbidity and Mortality Weekly Reports*, 1990). These figures indicate that virtually all adults in the United States will be related to, personally know, work with, or go to school with people who are infected with HIV or know others whose friends, relatives, or associates test HIV-positive.

AIDS is particularly devastating because it is both incurable and death-dealing. AIDS is an acronym for **acquired immune deficiency syndrome.** It is called

Acquired	because people are not born with it;
Immune	because the disease relates to the immune system;
Deficiency	because of the body's lack of immunity;
Syndrome	because the symptoms occur together as a group.

Although there is no vaccine to prevent or cure HIV infection (the **human immuno deficiency virus** that causes AIDS) or the subsequent AIDS symptoms, we have considerable knowledge about the nature of the virus and how to prevent its spread.

◆ *AIDS is caused by the human immunodeficiency virus (HIV), which attacks the body's immune system.* HIV is carried in the blood, semen, and vaginal secretions of infected persons. The virus may incubate up to five years or longer. At this time, it is believed that most who carry the virus will develop the symptoms that inevitably lead to AIDS.

YOU CAN'T LIVE ON HOPE.

NO SE PUEDE VIVIR DE ESPERANZAS.

Now, there's something real old, but still hot news;
It's been around since Lincoln, but out of view;
You'd stuff it in your wallet so your mom can't see;
It's called the condom, baby, and you better believe;
It ain't under the shelf now, it's on display;
With all this disease going around today;
You need peace of mind when you do the wild thing;
So, a condom, brother, don't forget to bring!
Now, if what I say sounds a little bit sleazy;
If using a condom makes you feel kind of queasy;
Don't take it too hard 'cause there's no doubt,
That modern diseases can take you out!
So, don't be ashamed, take one when you go dancin'
And use the condom for a little romancin',
'Cause bein' safe don't mean you're weak;
And you won't find yourself up the creek!
Protect yourself! Word! Protect yourself! Homeboy!
Protect yourself! My man, if I was you, I'd . . .
Protect yourself!

Fat Boys, "Protect Yourself"

The AIDS crises pits two basic human goals and needs against one another: seeking love and avoiding death.

Lynn Miller

Pneumonia & Skin cancer [handwritten annotation]

◆ *HIV is transmitted only in certain clearly defined circumstances: the exchange of blood (as by shared needles), sexual contact involving semen or vaginal secretions, or prenatally, from an infected woman to her fetus through the placenta.*

◆ *Heterosexuals, bisexuals, and gay men and lesbians are susceptible to the sexual transmission of HIV.* Currently four percent of AIDS cases are attributed to heterosexual transmission. The rate of heterosexual HIV transmission, however, is rising at three times the rate of gay transmission and almost twice the rate of transmission by intravenous needles. Among women, heterosexual contact accounts for almost 30 percent of AIDS cases.

◆ *There is a definable progression of HIV infection and a range of illnesses associated with it known as AIDS.* HIV attacks the immune system. Once the immune system is impaired, AIDS symptoms occur as opportunistic diseases that the body normally resists infect the individual. The most common opportunistic diseases are *Pneumocystis carinii* pneumonia and Kaposi's sarcoma, a skin cancer. It is an opportunistic disease rather than HIV that kills the person with AIDS.

◆ *The presence of HIV can be detected through antibody testing.* To date there are no widely available tests to detect the presence of HIV itself. The Western Blot and ELISA antibodies tests are *reasonably* accurate blood tests that show whether the body has developed antibodies in response to HIV. HIV antibodies develop between one and six months after infection. Antibody testing should take place at one- and six-month intervals. The Western Blot test is more accurate but also more expensive. If the antibody is present, the test will be positive. That means that the person has been infected with HIV and an active virus is present. The presence of HIV does not mean, however, that the person necessarily will develop AIDS symptoms in the near future. (Often the ELISA test is administered first and if the result is positive, the Western Blot is recommended as a follow up.)

◆ *All those with HIV (whether or not they have symptoms) are HIV carriers.* They may infect others through unsafe sexual activity or by sharing needles; if they are pregnant, they may infect the fetus.

The development of AIDS symptoms in HIV-positive individuals may be slowed by the use of AZT drug therapy. The earlier an HIV-positive person begins taking AZT, the more effective it is in retarding AIDS symptoms. Because early therapy is important, any person who believes that he or she may have been exposed to HIV should be tested—but no sooner than one month following the suspected exposure (to allow time for antibodies to appear). A sound nutritional regimen, in conjunction with the appropriate drug therapy, may help maintain health when HIV is diagnosed early. Once AIDS symptoms develop, *Pneumocystis carinii* pneumonia may also be treated with AZT.

PROTECTING YOURSELF AND OTHERS. Although some people have changed their behaviors to reduce the risk of STD and HIV infection, many continue to jeopardize their health and lives—as well as the health and lives of their partners' and loved ones—by failing to take adequate precautions. They worry about STDS and HIV but do not take the necessary steps—such as *always* using condoms—to prevent infections. One study of sexually active young adults found that 44 percent had not changed their behavior in any way to reduce the risk of HIV infection (Cochran, Keidan, and Kalechsteir, 1989). A recent study of female college students found that except for an increase in regular condom use—from 21 percent in 1986 to 41 percent in 1989—"public health campaigns have not had a substantial influence on the habits and behavior of these well-educated young adults" (DeBuono, Zinner, Daamen, and McCormack, 1990). Said one male university student from Illinois, who knew that heterosexuals are at risk for contracting HIV, "I just don't see AIDS as being much of a threat to heterosexuals, and I don't find a lot of pleasure in using a condom" (Johnson, 1990). Another study of college students found that they believe they can "identify" infected men and women (Maticka-Tyndale, 1991). An Ohio female student explained why she does not insist that her partner use a condom: "I have an attitude—it may be wrong—that any guy I would sleep with would not have AIDS" (Johnson, 1990).

However difficult it may be, the key to protecting ourselves and others is talking with our partners about STDs in an open, nonjudgmental way. To prevent the transmission of STDs, there are several things an individual needs to know about a partner before becoming sexually involved.

◆ *Does he or she have an STD?* The best way of finding out is by asking. If you feel nervous about broaching the subject, you can rehearse talking about it. Write out what you want to say, engage yourself in an imaginary dialogue, or role play with a friend. It may be sufficient to ask in a light-hearted manner, "Are you as healthy as you look?" Or, because many people are uncomfortable asking about STDs, you can open up the topic by revealing your anxiety: "This is a little difficult for me to talk about because I like you and I'm embarrassed, but I'd like to know whether you have herpes, or HIV, or something like that." And if you have an STD, you can say, "Look, I like you, but we can't make love right now because I have a chlamydial infection and I don't want you to get it."

Keep in mind that even a person who believes he or she doesn't have an STD may honestly not know. Women with chlamydia and gonorrhea, for example, are generally asymptomatic. Both men and women infected with HIV may be asymptomatic for years, although they are capable of spreading the infection through sexual contact. It pays to be cautious. Either refrain from sex or use a prophylactic—a condom or the recently developed women's condom..

◆ *Does he or she have multiple sex partners?* The more sex partners a person has, the more likely he or she is to contract an STD. A person who has multiple partners should be checked annually for STDs. A person is at higher risk for contracting HIV if he or she is ▬▬ sexually involved with a gay or bisexual male, an IV-drug user (or former user), a prostitute, or a hemophiliac (Hearst and Hulley, 1988).

Because of multiple partners, a person does not simply have sex with an individual but with that person's sexual history. And that history can be quite involved over a short period of time. Imagine, for example, that John and Mary have sexual intercourse with each other. Each of them has three sexual partners a year, and each of those partners had three a year, and each of those partners had three a year. Then take a paper and pencil and diagram how many individuals John and Mary are linked to sexually over a period of five years. Mathematically the equation is $3^5 \times 2$.

◆ *Does he or she have condoms?* If you don't know whether your partner has an STD, use a condom. Even if you don't discuss STDs, condoms are simple and easy to use without much discussion. Both men and women can carry them. (About 40 percent of condom sales are now to women.) A woman can take a condom from her purse and give it to her partner; if he doesn't want to use it, she can say, "No condom, no sex."

A latex condom is an excellent prophylactic against most STDs when properly used. It is not 100 percent effective in preventing STDs, however. A conservative estimate is that condoms are about 90 percent effective (Hearst and Hulley, 1988). Spermicides with nonoxynol-9 (or condoms treated with the spermicide) give additional protection against some STDs, possibly including HIV. (See Resource Center for more detailed information on STDs and HIV/AIDS.)

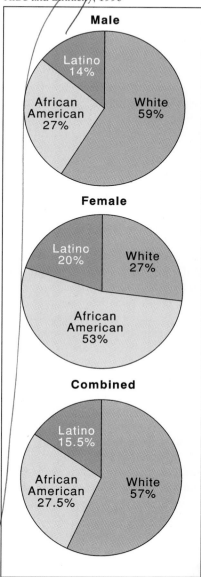

FIGURE 8.1

AIDS and Ethnicity, 1990

Male
Latino 14%
African American 27%
White 59%

Female
Latino 20%
White 27%
African American 53%

Combined
Latino 15.5%
African American 27.5%
White 57%

SOURCE: HIV/AIDS Surveillance Report, August, 1990

Safe Sex: Ten Top Obstacles (or Excuses)
The heat of the moment
Talking about safe sex
Putting on a condom
Buying a condom
Condom as unromantic
Partner not wanting to use condom
Anticipating partner's objection to condom
Difficulty in using condom
Rejection by partner
Loss of partner
Unavailability of condoms

❖ REFLECTIONS   *How do you deal with the issue of STDs in your relationships? Do you discuss the topic with a partner prior to becoming sexually involved? How
do you or would you bring up the topic of STDs? Have you ever contracted an STD? If so,
how did you feel about your partner? Yourself?*

❖ SUMMARY

◆ Premarital sexual intercourse is widely accepted. On college campuses, there is widespread acceptance of divergent
sexual standards. The sexual double standard continues,
however; women are condemned if they engage in sexual
intercourse outside a committed relationship, whereas men
are not.

◆ In sexual decision making, loving or liking is often the
most important factor determining first intercourse or intercourse with a new partner.

◆ Martial sexuality is generally expected to be *monogamous,*
sexually exclusive, takes place in a day-to-day context, and
includes reproduction as a socially sanctioned goal. Sex is
only one bond among many in marriage. Marital sex tends
to decline in frequency over time, but this does not generally signify marital deterioration.

◆ Extramarital sexual involvements assume three basic
forms: primarily sexual, primarily emotional, and emotional
and sexual. Women are increasingly engaging in extramarital affairs; male involvement has remained relatively high.
Most people have extramarital affairs because they feel that
something is lacking in their marriage. The two most important factors predicting extramarital involvement are whether
the marriage is happy and whether the individual was permissive about premarital sex.

◆ Approximately 3 to 10 percent of the population is gay or
lesbian. Large numbers of people have had both heterosexual
and same-sex experiences. Of these, some consider themselves gay or lesbian and others believe that they are bisexual, but the great majority consider themselves heterosexual.

◆ *Coming out,* identifying oneself as gay or lesbian, occurs
over considerable time, usually beginning in late childhood
or adolescence. The earliest phase begins with fear or suspicion that one's sexual desires are different or strange. In the
second phase the person labels these feelings as gay. The last
phase consists of defining oneself as gay or lesbian. Two
additional phases include entering the gay subculture and
having a long-term gay or lesbian relationship. As a result of
the AIDS crisis, gay men are changing their sexual behaviors
to diminish their risks.

◆ *Homophobia* refers to fear or hatred of gay men and lesbians. Many of the problems facing gay people, such as discrimination, are a result of homophobia. Homophobia may
be eliminated through education and positive interactions
between heterosexuals and gays and enlightening such
homophobic institutions as religion and the military.

◆ Many people knowingly risk pregnancy from unprotected intercourse. The "luckier" they are at risk taking, the
more likely they are to take chances again. They begin to
feel invulnerable. People also take risks because of faulty
knowledge: they don't understand how conception occurs
or how birth control methods work.

◆ People may weigh the costs of contraception against the
anticipated benefits of pregnancy. Some of the costs include
acknowledging sexuality; obtaining, planning and continuing contraception; and lack of spontaneity. "Benefits"
include proving manhood or womanhood, proving fertility,
defining a commitment, and defining a relationship to one's
parents.

◆ In the abortion controversy, pro-life advocates argue that
life begins at conception, that abortion leads to euthanasia,
and that many who want to adopt are unable to because
fewer babies are born as a result of abortion. Pro-choice advocates argue that women have the right to decide whether to
continue a pregnancy, that abortion is needed as a birth
control alternative because contraceptives are not 100 percent effective, and that if abortion is made illegal, women
will have unsafe illegal abortions.

◆ World views of pro-life and pro-choice activists differ
significantly along issues of gender roles, sex, and parenthood. Pro-life activists generally believe that men and
women are inherently different, that sex is for reproduction,
and that motherhood is woman's natural role. Pro-choice
activists believe that men and women are fundamentally
similar and equal, that sex is an end in itself, and that motherhood requires timing and preparation.

◆ Sexually transmitted diseases (STDs) are epidemic in the
United States. The key to protecting oneself against STDs is
discussing them with one's partner *before* engaging in sexual
activities. A person needs to know if the partner has an STD
and whether he or she has multiple sex partners. Condoms
should be used to substantially reduce the risk of STD transmission.

Answers to Preview Questions

The answers to the preview questions at the beginning of
the chapter are listed below. As you check your answers,
whether you were correct or not, think about your reasons
for each response. What were they? What was their source?
How valid is the source? As you read the chapter, you will
find the questions discussed in greater depth.

1. T	6. T
2. T	7. F
3. F	8. T
4. F	9. F
5. T	10. T

❖ SUGGESTED READINGS

Barbach, Lonnie. *For Each Other: Sharing Sexual Intimacy.* New York: Anchor/Doubleday, 1982 (paperback). A popular self-help book to assist women in dealing with the complexities of their sexual lives.

Blumstein, Philip, and Pepper Schwartz. *American Couples: Money, Work and Sex.* New York: McGraw-Hill, 1983 (paperback). An important sociological study of heterosexual and gay cohabiting and married couples.

Brown, Rita Mae. *Rubyfruit Jungle.* New York: Bantam, 1973 (paperback). The classic, brilliantly funny novel about growing up lesbian in the South.

Clark, Don. *The New Loving Someone Gay.* Berkeley, Calif.: Celestial Arts Press, 1987 (paperback). A sensitive exploration of what it means to be gay. Not only for gay men and lesbians but also for their heterosexual friends, families, and associates who need to explore their own feelings and confusions—and build new relationships based on a sympathetic understanding.

Gregor, Thomas. *Anxious Pleasures: The Sexual Lives of an Amazonian People.* Chicago: University of Chicago Press, 1985 (paperback). An exceptional look into the unique sexual world of the Mehinaku Indians of Brazil.

Leavitt, David. *The Lost Language of Cranes.* New York: Alfred Knopf, 1986 (paperback). The poignant story of a young gay man and his mother and father (who denies his own homoerotic feelings).

Luker, Kristin. *Abortion and the Politics of Motherhood.* Berkeley, Calif.: University of California Press, 1984 (paperback). A sociological study based on in-depth interviews that examines the divergent world views that separate pro-life and pro-choice activists from each other.

Pittman, Frank. *Private Lives: Infidelity and the Betrayal of Intimacy.* New York: W. W. Norton, 1989 (paperback). An intelligent, thoughtful look at extra-marital affairs.

Rubin, Lilian. *Erotic Wars.* New York: Farrar, Giroux, and Strauss, 1990 (paperback). A fine portrayal by a thoughtful therapist of the yearnings and misunderstandings between men and women.

Shilts, Randy. *And the Band Played On: People, Politics, and the AIDS Epidemic.* New York: St. Martin's Press, 1987. A compelling story of the medical, political, and human response to the AIDS crisis.

Tribe, Laurence. *Abortion: The Clash of Absolutes.* New York: W. W. Norton, 1990. A comprehensive, objective examination of the abortion controversy.

Zilbergeld, Bernie. *Male Sexuality.* New York: Bantam, 1979 (paperback). An exploration of the dangers of rigid male gender roles in being sexual.

Suggested Films

The Incredible Lightness of Being (1989). The award winning adaptation of Milan Kundera's novel of love, sex, and friendship against the backdrop of the fall of Prague in 1968.

Longtime Companion (1990). A moving film about love, friendship, and AIDS in one segment of the gay community.

Pillow Talk (1959). Classic Doris Day sex comedy depicting Rock Hudson's pursuit of the virginal Doris's virtue, providing a glimpse of pre–sexual revolution standards.

sex, lies, and videotape (1989). Subtle exploration of themes of honesty, communication, and sexuality.

She's Got to Have It (1988). Spike Lee's film about a young African-American woman and her relationships.

Women in Love (1970). Ken Russell's adaptation of D. H. Lawrence's novel depicting the conflict between love, passion, and death.

READINGS

❖
WAS IT GOOD FOR YOU?

Sara Jennifer Malcolm

In this article from Ms. magazine, a college sophomore reflects on female orgasm. While Masters and Johnson (1966) argued that females are "normally" orgasmic in intercourse, Shere Hite (1976) contended that most women need direct manual stimulation of the clitoris to be orgasmic, either before, during, or after intercourse. What view does the author take? How does she support her view? What is her evidence? What forms of pressure do women feel regarding the need to be orgasmic?

Over lunch with my mother, I finally mustered up the courage to talk about my problem. For more than six months, I'd been having a wonderful relationship—my first "real" sexual experience—and now my boyfriend and I were at an impasse. I knew my body was capable of orgasms during masturbation and foreplay, but I had never been able to reach a climax *during sexual*

continued on next page

intercourse. I was frustrated and worried. What were we doing wrong?

Mom put down her coffee. "Where did you get the idea that women always have orgasms during intercourse?" She explained that few of us are biologically constructed to allow for such an orgasm. Many women, herself included, grew up believing that orgasm inevitably results from male penetration, while in reality the majority of women can only experience clitoral orgasm, that is, orgasm as a result of direct or indirect clitoral stimulation. I was dumbfounded. She smiled, adding, "We're having the same discussion I went through with my friends fifteen years ago."

I told her that my friend Lisa insisted she's had orgasms during intercourse. "Well, Lisa might be one of the rare ones," Mom responded. "Or she might be lying, as so many women do for the same reason you feared admitting it. Each woman thinks it's her own private, secret failure."

It turned out Lisa *had* been lying. Not only to me but to her sexual partners as well. When I told her my newly acquired information, she too admitted to years of faking orgasm and hiding her feelings of inadequacy. A few days after our conversation, Lisa worked up the nerve to raise the subject with her mother who admitted she had never had one orgasm during sexual intercourse. It was the first time they had had such an honest discussion about sex. I've never seen a friend so relieved. "I feel as though a weight has been lifted," Lisa said.

She wasn't the only one. The first time my friend Emily had sex, she wanted to say to the guy, "Is that what everyone's been making such a fuss about?" My friend Janet told me that in her 10 brief sexual relationships, she had only had three orgasms in total—not one of them coming as a result of intercourse. Again I heard the syndrome of self-criticism and embarrassment. She felt it was her fault—*she* wasn't able to relax, she was afraid of "letting go." It was an empty feeling and one she avoided confronting.

Another close friend, Rebecca, said, "I know a lot of my friends have faked it and they say the guy can't tell the difference." Women can't blame men for not knowing the truth about female sexuality if we are not even honest with ourselves. One woman's lies hurts all of us and silence leads to confusion and stifled desire.

The media is perhaps the largest source of misinformation. According to most films, women reach a climax almost every time a man gets on top of them. The sight of women writhing in bliss and coming to screaming sweaty orgasms on the screen sets up a standard that we aspire to. It makes us all think: What do these women know that we don't?

Jacqueline Bisset whimpers with ecstasy in both an airplane lavatory (*Rich and Famous*) and a glass elevator (*Class*). I remember reading in one of those teen magazines that in *Endless Love*

Brooke Shields had to facially express an orgasm during intercourse with her boyfriend in front of the fire. After many unconvincing takes, the director finally resorted to pinching her toe until her exclamation of pain constituted an authentic picture.

Because our society puts so much emphasis on intercourse, I anticipated not just the emotional climax but the ultimate physical peak as well. It didn't happen. As long as most young women approach sex with grand expectations for orgasm during intercourse, we're heading for inevitable disappointment.

What's worse, the stakes keep getting higher. The *latest* goal is the *simultaneous* orgasm. Each time we jump a hurdle, yet another is placed in our path to sexual fulfillment. Each one of these standards has a built-in feature. For myself, I was wrestling with trying to please my boyfriend while also trying to articulate how he should go about pleasing me, while *also* trying to relax into being pleased. Once I became more at ease about all this—once I knew I was normal—the pressure was off. I enjoyed intercourse for what it gave me emotionally *and* physically, with no further unrealistic expectations. I realized that if I want sexual satisfaction, it's my responsibility to communicate what is and is not pleasurable.

Judging from my own and other young women's experiences, many men are under the impression that intercourse is as "good" for us as it is for them. I can't speak for them, but it does seem that men progress more directly toward a sexual peak while we, or at least I, tend to zigzag toward it.

For me, intercourse may not lead to ultimate sexual fulfillment, but I am now able to appreciate it for its own sensations and the power of its intimacy. I can accept that there are women who do experience vaginal orgasm without any clitoral stimulation, and others—such as my sister—who have experimented with different positions for more direct clitoral pressure during intercourse.

There seems to be a general consensus among women my age that finding the words (and the courage) to convey which sexual activities make us feel good is a task we're often tempted to avoid. We fear our being too aggressive and demanding will risk losing the romance and spontaneity. The deification of intercourse belittles the other aspects of lovemaking that are equally valid and often even more enjoyable. As Lonnie Barbach writes in *For Yourself: The Fulfillment of Female Sexuality* (Doubleday): "To make intercourse the goal of sex does a grave disservice to many enjoyable ways of touching."

It is ironic and distressing that something so universal as sex is a conversational taboo. Not only are we uncommunicative about it with our closest friends, but many of us don't talk openly with our partners. My friends and I have found that, in the long run, it is worth the struggle and the awkwardness. Once you have worked out with your partner what each of you specifically can do to make the other feel best, you'll find real sexual pleasure.

THE MEANING OF EXTRAMARITAL AFFAIRS

Maggie Scarf. Except from *Intimate Partners*

According to Maggie Scarf, when extramarital affairs occur, the deceived partner may be angrier at the third party than at his or her partner. Why? Do you believe this is true? What does the author believe an extramarital relationship signifies in terms of intimacy? Do you agree? Why?

We may, in this culture, have experienced a revolution in our sexual mores, but most spouses continue to feel intensely afflicted and distressed by a partner's violation of the boundaries around the marital relationship. This is true even in situations in which the deceived mate has himself been the deceiver at an earlier time in the relationship. One husband, who had had a long affair several years before he discovered that his wife was now extramaritally involved, described his own reactions in the following manner: "I felt furious, betrayed; I felt as if I couldn't *trust* her! I felt that there was someone else out there who knew all about me, and who had, for that reason, *triumphed!* He had—even though I didn't know who he was—*bested* me, taken away something that was mine, exclusively!"

This man was angrier at the unknown lover than he was at his wife. His experience was that of having been defeated in a contest with the other man involved in this three-person relationship—and his reaction was by no means atypical. For, as a study carried out by J. L. Francis demonstrates, males do tend to associate their jealous, angry feelings with the rival male in the emotional triangle. Females, on the other hand, tend to associate their feelings of jealousy with a more global, generalized sense of loss—the loss of the partner's attention, caring and concern.

The very existence of the affair has, plainly, transformed the couple's relationship from a two-person into a three-person system—and this triangle is affected by pressures emanating from the third person who has entered the marriage and become part of it. "The identity of the extramarital partner, the degree of emotional involvement, and the nature of the sexual practices are matters of major impact," reports sexual researcher Anthony P. Thompson.

"There is often," writes Thompson, "a tenacious interest in the disclosure of endless details and many spouses exert pressure to know everything. This process is stressful for both partners as queries and disclosures are likely to hit upon areas which are most sensitive and threatening for the married couple. . . ." Kissing and telling can be extremely painful to the betrayed mate,

who *needs to know,* and yet finds it hard to tolerate hearing about what actually did happen.

In the wake of the affair's revelation, the comparative status of the two marital partners inevitably changes. The partner who has been involved extramaritally is, to some degree, the one in the more powerful position. For while his spouse feels staggered, helplessly enraged, overwhelmed, and the like, he feels—amid whatever guilt feelings he may be experiencing—victorious and attractive.

His sense of self-esteem may have been enhanced by the relationship, making him feel more likable and confident, while his partner's self-concept will, as a result of the affair's revelation, inevitably be deflated and diminished. The faithful spouse is thus, because she feels hurt, one down and inadequate, at a power disadvantage in the relationship. This may, in fact, have been among the betrayer's motivations for having become involved in the affairs in the first place.

....

An affair may be thought of as an emotional distance regulator. The very existence of a third person in the marital system indicates that the couple is having trouble handling problems of separateness and closeness. According to clinical psychologist Betsy Stone, it is generally the case that in a marriage where one partner is having an outside relationship, the other partner has *also* been fantasizing about becoming involved extramaritally.

What that implies is that there are no real "innocent victims" and "vile offenders," but that who happens to go outside the marriage first has to do with matters of opportunity and timing. Both members of the couples are lusting in their hearts for—or at least dreaming of—other partners, because both are feeling profoundly alienated and disappointed.

An affair is, in this sense, not something that happens *to* somebody, it is something that happens *between two people.* And often it is the weaker spouse who acts first; he or she makes a strengthening move by getting into a coalition with the extramarital partner. Becoming involved in an outside relationship is, for this person, an adaptive maneuver—a way of dealing with the problems in the relationship. The affair itself is a symptom, the symptom of a global marital disturbance; it is not the disturbance itself.

The affair's very existence does, however, indicate that the intimacy in the couple's emotional system is out of balance. Someone is frightened about getting too close, or someone is overly frustrated—hungering for an intimacy that is lacking. Let me say, right away, that the word "intimacy" is not meant to imply candlelight, a table for two in a small bistro, a violinist playing gypsy melodies as the absorbed couple engages in mutually fascinating, intensely romantic conversation. What is meant

continued on next page

by "intimacy," in this context, is something different, closer to each person's ordinary reality. Intimacy is, as understood here, an individual's ability to talk about *what he really is,* and *to say what he wants and needs,* and *to be heard by the intimate partner.*

This involves, for instance, a person's being able to tell his mate about how rotten and defeated he happens to be feeling rather than having to pretend to be always masterful and adequate. Or, to take another example, it involves being able to make his sexual needs and friendship choices explicit, rather than remaining inarticulate about them—and then feeling exploited by and angry at the spouse.

If, however, the fear of getting too close (so close that the mate will see and condemn his weakness and failings) is the husband's problem, an affair provides a pseudosolution. For if he has another, secret partner, he is not as close to his wife as he feared he was becoming; she does not know something important about *who he really is.* The furtiveness, secrecy and time constraints upon the outside relationship, moreover, set certain external limits upon the degree of intimacy that can be achieved in the extramarital relationship.

When, on the other hand, it is the wife who is extramaritally involved, it is usually—though certainly not always—due to a *hunger* for emotional intimacy rather than a wish to avoid it. The wife is someone who, hopelessly outdistanced in her emotional pursuit, has given up the chase and gone outside the marriage to find what the husband will not give her—acceptance, validation of her worth, the willingness to listen to her talk about *who she is, as a person,* and learn about *what she needs and wants.*

For her, as for the emotional distancer, sexuality is not really the primary motivation for the affair. Just as he became involved in an outside relationship in order to avoid the demands of real intimacy, she has gotten into an affair in a desperate attempt to achieve feelings of closeness. With her lover she can, at least, get the physical sensations of touching, hugging; she can be *attended to.* And she can, at the same time, give up the endlessly frustrating pursuit of her endlessly frustrating partner.

When intimacy, in a marriage, is an impossibility—when talking about one's fears, needs, desires, sexual requests, etc., to the partner is out of the question—the unheard person begins feeling powerless, resigned, alienated. The extramarital affair develops as a way of finding a comforter and ally.

The failure of trust, closeness, mutual attentiveness to each other's needs and wishes, inevitably gives way to a desperate struggle between the partners—a struggle for power and control. What the spouses cannot get from each other, by a process of mutually satisfying collaboration and negotiation, each tries to *extract* from the other by means of manipulation and/or force. It is as if the lack of intimacy has created a vacuum at the center of the relationship—and the power struggle rushes in to fill it.

HINTS ON CONDOM USE

Bryan Strong and Christine DeVault

In this excerpt from their book, Understanding Our Sexuality, *the authors offer tips on correct condom use.*

◆   Use condoms every time you have sexual intercourse; this is the key to successful contraception and disease prevention.

◆   Use a spermicide with the condom. Foam and film are both easy to apply. Spermicide helps protect against pregnancy and STDs, including chlamydia, gonorrhea, herpes, and HIV.

◆   Do not put a condomless penis into the vagina! Even if the man has great "control," there is *always* the possbility of pre-ejaculatory leakage.

◆   Leave about a half-inch of space at the condom tip, and roll the condom all the way down to the base of the penis.

◆   *Soon* after the ejaculation, the penis should be withdrawn. Make sure someone holds the base of the condom firmly against the penis as it is withdrawn.

◆   After use, check the condom for possible torn spots. If you are not using a spermicide (you should be!) and you find a tear or hole, *immediately* insert foam or jelly into the vagina. This may reduce the chance of pregnancy. If torn condoms are a persistent problem, use a water-based luricant such as K-Y jelly or a spermicide to reduce friction.

◆   Do not reuse condoms.

◆   Keep condoms in a cool, dry and *convenient* place.

◆   To protect against HIV and other organisms, use a latex condom, *not* one made of animal tissue.

If you or your partner are uncomfortable with condom use, consider the following:

◆   Communication is crucial. It may seem "unromantic," but planning your contraception strategy *before* you are sexually entangled is essential. Giving or getting a disease or worrying about pregnancy is about as *unromantic* as you can get. Consider visiting a family planning clinic for counseling—together. Neither partner should be forced to use a form of birth control he or she is truly unhappy with. But the issue of protection must be dealt with—by both of you.

◆   Don't forget your sense of humor and playfulness. Condoms can actually provide lots of laughs, and laughter and sex go well together. Fancy condoms—colored, ribbed, glow-in-the-dark, etc.—are popular for their entertainment value.

Stand your ground. (This is mainly for women, as it is generally men who object to condoms.) Unless you want to be pregnant and are sure your partner is free of STDs, you need protection during sex. If he says no to condoms, you can say no to him. If he cares about you, he will work with you to find birth control and "safe sex" methods that suit you both.

Pregnancy and Childbirth

To gain a sense of what you already know about the material covered in this chapter, answer "true" or "false" to the following statements. You will find the answers on page 280.

1. Infertility is increasing among American couples of all age groups. True or false?
2. Miscarriage and stillbirth are considered major life events. True or false?
3. Untreated sexually transmitted disease is a primary cause of infertility in women. True or false?
4. There are approximately 15,000 births per year from artificial insemination. True or false?
5. Even a moderate amount of alcohol consumption affects the fetus. True or false?
6. A woman with an inactive genital herpes virus must deliver her baby by cesarean section. True or false?
7. The United States has one of the lowest rates of infant mortality of any industrialized nation. True or false?
8. One out of every ten births is by cesarean section. True or false?
9. Midwives generally have as good or better a safety record than physicians for normal births. True or false?
10. Breastfeeding generally provides better nutrition and protection for babies than infant formula. True or false?

In traditional sexual thought, sex was justified primarily, sometimes exclusively because it was necessary to the propagation of the species. Since one of the premises of the modern tradition in sexual thought has been that sex is a valuable end in itself, modern theorists, by way of reaction, have generally inclined to belittle the reproductive perspective on sexuality.

Paul Robinson, The Modernization of Sex

THE BIRTH OF A WANTED CHILD is considered by many parents to be the happiest event of their lives. Today, however, pain and controversy surround many aspects of this altogether natural process. As we struggle to balance the rights of the mother, the father, the fetus, and society itself in these matters, we find ourselves considering the quality of life as well as life's mere existence.

For most American women, pregnancy will be relatively comfortable and the outcome predictably joyful. Yet for increasing numbers of others, especially among the poor, the prospect of having children raises the spectres of drugs, disease, malnutrition, and familial chaos. Then there are those couples who have dreamed of and planned for families for years only to find that they are unable to conceive.

In this chapter we will view pregnancy and childbirth as both biological and social processes. In addition, we will consider infertility, reproductive technologies, adoption, and pregnancy loss. We will look at the emotional aspects of pregnancy and the challenges of the transition to parenthood.

❖ INFERTILITY

Infertility is generally defined as the inability to conceive a child after trying for a year or more. Until recently, the problem of infertility attracted little public attention. In the last few years, however, numerous couples, many of whom have deferred pregnancy because of career plans or later marriages, have discovered that they are unable to conceive or that the woman is unable to carry the pregnancy to live birth. Still, a recent study by the National Center for Health Statistics (Cimons, 1990) showed that overall, the fertility rate for American women is not declining. In 1988, 8.4 percent of women aged fifteen to forty-four years had an "impaired ability" to have children. This means that one out of twelve or thirteen American couples is involuntarily childless. The greatest increase in infertility is found among young couples in the twenty- to twenty-four-year-old bracket. Their infertility rate rose from 3.6 percent in 1965 to 10.6 in 1982. Infertility among young African-American couples has risen even more dramatically; it is almost twice that of white couples (Faludi, 1989). Every year well over a million American couples seek help for infertility.

Female Infertility

The leading cause of female infertility is blocked fallopian tubes, generally the result of **pelvic inflammatory disease (PID)**, an infection of the fallopian tubes or uterus that is usually sexually transmitted. It can be caused by gonococcus or chlamydia bacteria or several other organisms. About 1.7 million cases of PID were treated in 1986; doctors estimate that about half of the cases go untreated because PID is often symptomless, especially in the early stages (Hilts, 1990a). Generally, only the woman with PID seeks treatment, and the man from whom she contracted the bacteria that caused it may continue to pass it on (Hilts, 1990a). Surgery, including laser surgery, may restore fertility if the damage has not progressed too far. Septic abortions, abdominal surgery, and certain types of older IUDs can also lead to PID. (See Resource Center for information on prevention and treatment of sexually transmitted diseases.)

The second leading cause of infertility in women is **endometriosis**; it is sometimes called the "career woman's disease" because it is most prevalent in women aged thirty and over, many of whom have postponed childbirth. In this disease, uterine tissue grows outside the uterus, often appearing on the ovaries, in the fallopian

Leading causes of infertility
1) Blocked tubes (PID) causes this
2) Endometriosis

tubes (where it may also block the tubes), and in the abdominal cavity. In its most severe form it may cause painful menstruation and intercourse, but most women with endometriosis are unaware that they have it. Hormone therapy and sometimes surgery are used to treat endometriosis. Benign growths such as fibroids and polyps may also affect a woman's fertility. Surgery can restore fertility in many of these cases.

In addition to physical causes, there may be hormonal reasons for infertility. The pituitary gland may fail to produce sufficient hormones (follicle-stimulating hormone, or FSH, and luteinizing hormone, or LH) to stimulate ovulation, or it may release them at the wrong time. Hormonal deficiencies may be corrected by therapy with fertility drugs. Stress, which may be increased by the anxiety of trying to achieve a pregnancy, may also contribute to lowered fertility (Menning, 1988). Occasionally, immunological causes may be present, the most important of which is the production of sperm antibodies by the woman. For some unknown reason, the woman is allergic to her partner's sperm and her immune system produces antibodies to destroy them.

Other factors can cause infertility. Toxic chemicals or exposure to radiation threaten a woman's reproductive capacity. Smoking may reduce fertility in women (Baird and Wilcox, 1985). Increasing evidence indicates that the daughters of mothers who were prescribed diethylstilbestrol (DES) to increase their fertility have a significantly higher infertility rate, although studies remain somewhat contradictory (Berger and Goldstein, 1984). Nature also plays a part. Beginning around age thirty, women's fertility naturally begins to decline. By age thirty-five, about one-fourth of women are infertile (Carroll, 1990).

Male Infertility

The primary causes of male infertility are low sperm count, lack of sperm motility (ability to move spontaneously), or blocked passageways. Some studies show that men's sperm counts have dropped by as much as 50 percent over the last thirty years (Andrews, 1984; Faludi, 1989). As with women, environmental factors may contribute to men's infertility. Increasing evidence suggests that toxic substances— such as lead or chemicals found in some solvents and herbicides—are responsible for decreased sperm counts (Andrews, 1984). Smoking may produce reduced sperm counts or abnormal sperm (Evans, 1981). Prescription drugs such as cimetidine (Tagamet) (for ulcers), prednisone, or some medications for urinary tract infections have also been shown to affect the number of sperm that a man produces (Andrews, 1984). Large doses of marijuana cause decreased sperm counts and suppression of certain reproductive hormones. These effects are apparently reversed when marijuana smoking stops (Ehrenkranz and Hembree, 1986). Men are more at risk than women from environmental factors because they are constantly producing new sperm cells; for the same reason, men may also recover faster once the affecting factor has been removed (Menning, 1988).

Sons of mothers who took DES may have increased sperm abnormalities and fertility problems (Retik and Bauer, 1984). Too much heat may temporarily reduce a man's sperm count (the male half of a couple trying to conceive may want to stay out of the hot tub for a while). A fairly common problem is the presence of a varicose vein called a **varicocele** above the testicle. The varicocele may be surgically removed, but unless the man has a fairly good sperm count to begin with, his fertility may not improve.

Ancient man knew nothing of the sperm and the ovum. This knowledge belongs to the era of the microscope. For him the seminal fluid was the substance that grew into the child—drawing sustenance from the womb of the pregnant woman, absorbing the blood that issued periodically from the womb when there was no child there. The woman's body nurtured the seed, as the soil nurtured the grain of rice. But the seed was the man's seed and the child was the man's child. It was his ongoing spirit, his continuing life.

David Mace and Vera Mace, Marriage: East and West

Emotional Responses to Infertility

By the time a couple seek medical advice about their fertility problems, they may have already experienced a crisis in confronting the possibility of not being able to become biological parents. Many such couples feel they have lost control over a major area of their lives (Callan, 1987). A number of studies suggest that women generally are more intensely affected than men (Brand, 1989; McEwan, Costello, and Taylor, 1987; Raval et al., 1987). After seeking help, childless couples typically go through three phases, according to Miriam Mazor (1979) (also see Mazor and Simons, 1984):

The first phase revolves around the injury to the self implicit in the situation. Patients are pre-occupied with the infertility study and with formulating theories about why it is happening to them, what they have done wrong, why they are so defective and bad that they are denied something the rest of the world takes for granted. The second phase occurs when treatment is unsuccessful; it involves mourning the loss of the children the partner will never bear and an intense examination of what parenthood means to them as individuals, as a couple, and as members of families and of society. Finally, in the third phase, they must come to terms with the outcome of the study: they must make some kind of decision about their future, whether to pursue plans for adoption or for donor insemination or to adjust to childlessness and go on with life.

Infertility Treatment

Almost without exception, fertility problems are physical, not emotional, despite myths to the contrary that often prevent infertile couples from seeking medical treatment. The two most popular myths are that anxiety over becoming pregnant leads to infertility and that if an infertile couple adopts a child, the couple will then be able to conceive on their own (Kolata, 1979). Neither has any basis in medical fact, although it is true that some presumably infertile couples have conceived following an adoption. (This does not mean, however, that one should adopt a child to reme-dy infertility.) Approximately 10 percent of cases of infertility are unexplained. In some of these cases, fertility is restored for no discernable reason; in others, the infertility remains a mystery (Jones, 1989). About 60 percent of couples with serious infertility problems will eventually achieve a pregnancy (Lord, 1987). (See Porter and Christopher, 1984, for a review of infertility, coping patterns, and treatment.)

Artificial Insemination

When childlessness is the result of male infertility (or low fertility) or a genetically transmitted disorder carried by the male, couples may try **artificial insemination.** Single women who want children but who have not found an appropriate partner or who wish to avoid emotional entanglements have also made use of this technique, as have lesbian couples. The American Fertility Society estimates that there are about 30,000 births a year from artificial insemination (Kantrowitz and Kaplan, 1990).

During ovulation, semen is deposited by syringe near the cervical opening. The semen may come from the partner; if he has a low sperm count, several collections of semen may be taken and frozen, then collectively deposited in the woman's vagi-na, improving the odds of conception. If the partner had a vasectomy earlier, he may have had the semen frozen and stored in a sperm bank. If the man is sterile or has a genetically transferable disorder, **therapeutic donor insemination (TDI)** (also known as artificial insemination by donor [AID]) may be used. Anonymous donors—often medical students—are paid nominal amounts for their deposits of semen which may be used at once or frozen. Artificial insemination tends to produce males rather than females; in the general population, about 51 percent of the children born are male, but this figure reaches almost 60 percent when conception is achieved artificially. Artificial insemination has a success rate of about 60 percent for infertile couples.

Most doctors inseminate women at least twice during the preovulatory phase of their menstrual cycle; on the average, women who become pregnant have received inseminations over a period of two to four months (Curie-Cohen, 1979; Scott et al., 1990).

The practices of fertility clinics and sperm banks vary widely with respect to medical and genetic screening and limitations on the number of times a particular donor may be used. In a study by the Congressional Office of Technology Assessment in 1988, more than half the physicians surveyed said they did not screen donors for HIV. The commercial sperm banks surveyed did screen for HIV, however, as well as for most other sexually transmitted diseases (Gaines, 1990). There has been one reported case in the United States of a woman contracting HIV through donated semen (Chiasson, Stoneburner, and Joseph, 1990). The American Fertility Society (1990) has issued guidelines for screening semen donors for HIV. The Society has concluded that "under present circumstances the use of fresh semen for donor insemination is no longer warranted and that all frozen specimens should be quarantined for 180 days and the donor retested and found to be seronegative for HIV before the specimen is released." Although the viability of sperm is reduced by freezing, new techniques of cryopreservation minimize the deleterious effects (Shanis, Check, and Baker, 1989). Recent studies show that TDI with frozen semen can have a success rate comparable to that with fresh semen (Byrd et al., 1990; Scott et al., 1990).

GIFT and ZIFT

Another fertilization technique, **gamete intrafallopian transfer (GIFT)**, may be recommended for couples who have no known reason for their infertility. In this process, sperm and eggs are collected from the parents and deposited together in the fallopian tube. In 1988, 892 live GIFT babies were delivered, including 159 sets of twins, 34 sets of triplets, 3 sets of quadruplets, and 1 set of quintuplets (Perlman, 1990).

In **ZIFT (zygote intrafallopian transfer)**, eggs and sperm are united in a petri dish and then transferred to the fallopian tube to begin cell division. In 1988 there were 98 ZIFT babies, representing a success rate of about 20 percent (Perlman, 1990).

In Vitro Fertilization

In vitro fertilization (IVF) entails combining sperm and egg in a laboratory dish and subsequently implanting the blastocyst into the uterus of the mother or a surrogate. Sometimes the blastocyst is frozen and stored, to be implanted at a later date. The egg can come from the mother or from a donor. If it is a donor ovum, the donor may be artificially inseminated with the father's sperm and, the embryo removed from the donor and transplanted in the mother-to-be's uterus.

The first birth achieved through IVF occurred in 1978 in England. Successful pregnancies from this procedure have since come to term in the United States, Australia, the Netherlands, and several other countries. The number of IVF births is

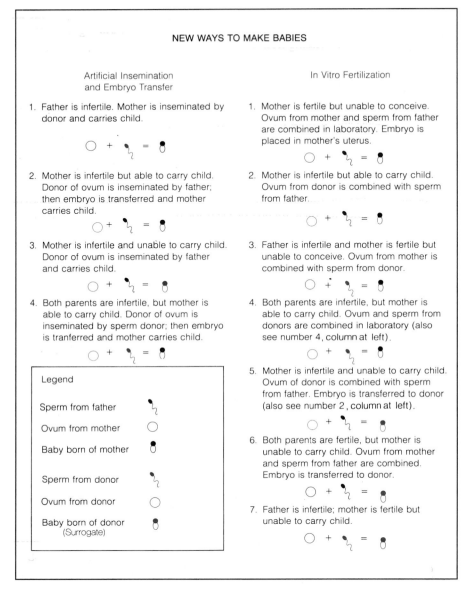

NEW WAYS TO MAKE BABIES

Artificial Insemination and Embryo Transfer

1. Father is infertile. Mother is inseminated by donor and carries child.

2. Mother is infertile but able to carry child. Donor of ovum is inseminated by father; then embryo is transferred and mother carries child.

3. Mother is infertile and unable to carry child. Donor of ovum is inseminated by father and carries child.

4. Both parents are infertile, but mother is able to carry child. Donor of ovum is inseminated by sperm donor; then embryo is tranferred and mother carries child.

Legend

Sperm from father

Ovum from mother

Baby born of mother

Sperm from donor

Ovum from donor

Baby born of donor (Surrogate)

In Vitro Fertilization

1. Mother is fertile but unable to conceive. Ovum from mother and sperm from father are combined in laboratory. Embryo is placed in mother's uterus.

2. Mother is infertile but able to carry child. Ovum from donor is combined with sperm from father.

3. Father is infertile and mother is fertile but unable to conceive. Ovum from mother is combined with sperm from donor.

4. Both parents are infertile, but mother is able to carry child. Ovum and sperm from donors are combined in laboratory (also see number 4, column at left).

5. Mother is infertile and unable to carry child. Ovum of donor is combined with sperm from father. Embryo is transferred to donor (also see number 2, column at left).

6. Both parents are fertile, but mother is unable to carry child. Ovum from mother and sperm from father are combined. Embryo is transferred to donor.

7. Father is infertile; mother is fertile but unable to carry child.

increasing every year. In 1988, 3,427 IVF babies were delivered in the United States. These procedures are all quite costly and must usually be repeated a number of times before viable pregnancy results. Varying success rates—from 12 to something over 20 percent—have been reported for IVF (Jones, 1989; Yulsman, 1990).

Surrogate Motherhood

The idea of one woman bearing a child for another is not new. In the Old Testament (Genesis 16:1–15), Abraham's wife Sarah, finding herself unable to conceive, arranged for her husband to impregnate her servant Hagar. These days the procedures are considerably more complex, and the issues are definitely cloudier.

For couples in which the woman cannot conceive, or can conceive (provide an ovum) but cannot carry a child because of uterine problems, **surrogate motherhood** may seem to be a blessing from heaven. To others it is a sexist practice, tantamount to baby-selling or "wombs for rent." Both Orthodox Judaism and Roman Catholicism flatly oppose it. Others object to surrogacy on the grounds that it has racist overtones: most couples who engage surrogate mothers are white and want a child who "looks like them." It might be cheaper and less troublesome ethically to adopt a child, especially a child from a foreign country or one with "special needs"; the adopted child, however, would most likely not be white (or Anglo). Undoubtedly a number of ethical and legal issues are raised. The most important of these, according to medical law expert Lori Andrews (1984), is "whether each feels the other side will keep its promises."

Some people question the motives of surrogate mothers. There have been cases of women having babies for their friends or even for their relatives. In 1991 a South Dakota woman became the first American "surrogate granny" when she was implanted with the fertilized ova of her daughter, who had been born without a uterus (Plummer and Nelson, 1991). Some women simply extend this kind of altruism to women they don't know. One surrogate mother sent the adoptive mother a poem (quoted in Kantrowitz et al., 1987): "Roses are red/Violets are blue/We're going to have a baby/Congratulations to you, too." A study of 125 surrogate candidates found their major motivations to be money (they are usually paid $10,000 to $25,000 or more), liking to be pregnant, and unreconciled birth traumas, such as abortion or relinquishing a child for adoption (Parker, 1983). In this country, several hundred (possibly as many as 500) children each year are born to surrogate mothers (Andrews, 1984; Woodward, 1987). A number of agencies now exist to match surrogates and couples, highlighting the commercial potential of surrogacy.

Well-publicized court battles involving surrogacy point to the need for some kind of regulation. In the celebrated "Baby M" case, after numerous legal twists and turns, the New Jersey Supreme Court ruled in 1988 that contracts involving surrogate motherhood in exchange for money were illegal. It also ruled that a woman could volunteer to become a surrogate as long as no money was paid and she was allowed to revoke her decision to give up the child. "We . . . restore the surrogate as mother of the child. She is not only the natural mother, but also the legal mother," the court wrote (cited in Hanley, 1988). The baby in question was allowed to remain in the custody of her biological father and his wife, a situation previously determined to be in the child's best interests. A lower court subsequently awarded the surrogate mother six hours a week of unsupervised visitation with the child.

In 1990, however, a California Superior Court judge denied a surrogate mother parental rights. In this case, the genetic mother (who had had a hysterectomy that did not remove her ovaries) and her husband contributed the egg and sperm for in vitro fertilization. The embryo was then transplanted in the uterus of the surrogate, who had contracted with the genetic parents to carry the fetus for $10,000. In delivering his ruling, the judge declared that the surrogate had served in the role of a foster parent. "I decline to split the child emotionally between two mothers," he said. He also urged the legislature to set guidelines that take the new medical technologies into consideration (Mydans, 1990).

Although many states have laws prohibiting women from taking payment in exchange for giving a child up for adoption, most have not as yet enacted legislation specifically relating to surrogacy. Exceptions are Nevada, which has legitimized surrogacy contracts involving payment, and Arkansas, which specifies that the couple who contract with the surrogate are the legal parents. Several other states have declared such contracts unenforceable, while at least one state is considering making surrogacy for pay a felony (Budiansky, 1988). Proposed legislation in other states would require all parties to undergo counseling and the surrogate and biological father to be screened for genetic and sexually transmitted diseases (Donovan, 1986). (See Andrews, 1984, for guidelines on choosing surrogacy.)

For some people involved in surrogacy, the outcome seems to be satisfying and joyful. One couple attended the delivery of their baby. The father wrote (Shapiro, 1987):

> Finally the baby's head emerged. Lynne [his wife] looked over at me, her eyes glowing. The nurses were also smiling. "One more push, Martha," the doctor said, "Here it comes . . . and it's . . . a baby girl."
>
> I couldn't tell if she was pretty or not. . . . Her mouth . . . was definitely familiar—exactly like one of my nieces.
>
> Lynne had moved to Martha's side and was holding her hand. Martha turned toward her and said, "Lynne, go see your baby."

Adoption

The mother that carries you in her heart is your true mother.

Heather Guffee

It is estimated that a little over 2 percent of the American population is adopted (Samuels, 1990). Adoption is the traditionally acceptable alternative to pregnancy for infertile couples. (See reading, "Fertility and Family," by Katherine Bouton.) In recent years, many Americans—married and single, childless or with children—have been choosing to adopt for other reasons as well. They may have concerns about overpopulation and the number of homeless children in the world. They may wish to provide families for older or disabled children. Although tens of thousands of parents and potential parents are currently waiting to adopt, there is a shortage of available healthy babies (especially healthy *white* babies) in this country. In 1970 the number of adoptions per year peaked at 175,000. Today the number has declined, owing to more effective birth control and an increase in the number of single mothers who choose to keep their children. The National Committee for Adoption estimates that there were over 60,000 adoptions by nonrelatives in 1986; precise figures are unavailable, as the federal government has not kept statistics on adoptions since 1975 (Gibbs, 1989).

For domestic adoptions arranged by agencies, the wait for a healthy infant or toddler averages one to five years (Kennedy, 1984). Because of this relatively long waiting period, many couples (and some single women) are arranging their own adoptions with birth mothers, using newspaper advertisements and the help of lawyers or agencies specializing in "open" or "cooperative" adoptions (Caplan, 1990; Gibbs, 1989; Lord, 1987). In **open adoption,** the birth mother has an active role in selecting her child's new parents. She may choose to continue to have some form of contact with her child or the adoptive parents—anything from receiving pictures and an update on the child's birthday to having some type of visitation as a family friend.

The costs of open adoption tend to run between $6,000 and $20,000 or more, depending on lawyer and agency fees and the birth mother's expenses (if the state allows these to be covered by the adoptive parents). Adoption laws vary widely from state to state; six states prohibit private adoption, whereas California and Texas have laws that are considered quite supportive of it (Gibbs, 1989; see Caplan, 1990, for an absorbing and well-researched account of open adoption).

Many adoption experts agree that some form of open adoption is usually in the best interests of both the child and the birth parents. One study of sixty-eight parents who had given up their infants in closed adoption revealed that fifty still

Don't tell

experienced the pain of loss ten to thirty-three years later, and fifty-six (82 percent) wished that they could reunite with their children when they reached adulthood (Sorosky, Baran, and Pannor, 1978). Adopted children have been disproportionately represented in mental health clinics. Some researchers suggest that this may be due to "genealogical bewilderment," a condition that may lead to learning disabilities and social dysfunction as a result of feeling cut off from one's roots (Theroux, 1990). Several states have now enacted laws allowing adoptees to get copies of their original birth certificates. Other states have set up voluntary registries to assist adoptees and biological parents who wish to meet each other.

Some professionals in the adoption field believe that it is not in the child's best interest to tell him or her of the adoption. Psychiatrist Dennis Donovan thinks that children should be given only the information they ask for (only if they ask) and no more. He believes that telling a child he or she was loved by the birth mother but was still given up blocks the child's ability to attach (cited in "At a Glance," 1990).

In addition to open adoptions, foreign adoptions are also increasingly favored. In 1987, more than 10,000 foreign-born children were admitted to the United States as immigrant orphans (Lewin, 1990). Over half of those adoptions were from Korea, the principal source of foreign children in recent years. During the last few years, however, foreign adoptions have declined somewhat because of the Korean government's efforts to phase out its foreign adoption program. Traditionally Koreans have been unwilling to adopt unrelated children because of the culture's strong emphasis on bloodlines, but as Korean attitudes change, more and more Korean orphans will stay in their birth country (Lewin, 1990). International adoption agencies are working to expand their programs in India, the Philippines, Colombia, and a number of other Asian and Latin American countries. For foreign adoptions, the waiting period is usually around a year, although it may be longer depending on the political climate of the country in question. The costs vary widely, depending on the number and kind of agencies involved and whether or not the parents travel to pick up their child.

Families with children from other cultures face challenges in addition to those faced by other adoptive families. There is usually little information about the birth parents and no opportunity for continued contact. Older children from foreign countries must deal with the loss of their birth parents and other significant people. They must also adjust to different customs, strange food, and a baffling new language. To combat a sense of rootlessness, many parents of foreign-born children endeavor to give them an understanding of their birth country and its culture. They often participate in supportive networks with other adoptive families.

Adoptive families face unique problems and stresses. They may struggle with the physical and emotional strains of infertility; they endure uncertainty and disappointment as they wait for their child; and they may have spent all their savings and then some in the process. Still, most adopting families report feeling greatly enriched by the experience (Brodzinsky and Huffman, 1988). One mother wrote (Sylviachild, 1984):

Adoption is another way of building families; for after our child is with us, the same issues of sleeping through the night, parent exhaustion, learning to parent, coping with the first fever, bad diaper rash, ear infections, enjoying, worrying, teaching and learning with our child, and all the other wonderful and frustrating parts of being a family occur whether we have adopted or given birth to our child.

Adopted children may feel uniquely loved. Suzanne Arms (1990) recounted, "When Joss was six, he was overheard explaining to a friend how special it was to be adopted. Apparently," she added, "he made a good case for it, because when his

Most adoptive families feel greatly enriched by the experience of adoption, as witnessed by this proud big brother and his new sister.

Life is full of unfamiliar, even unprecedented relationships, and adopted or not, part of life is adjusting, seeing that diversity is enriching, even when it's not all good.

Phyllis Theroux

friend got home, he told his mother he wanted to be adopted so he could be special too." (See the Resource Center for organizations to contact about adoptions.)

❖ REFLECTIONS   *Is the ability to create a child important to your sense of self-fulfillment? If you discovered that you were infertile, what do you think your responses would be?*

❖ REPRODUCTIVE TECHNOLOGY

During the last twenty years we have witnessed an explosion of scientific and technological developments in the area of reproduction. In the wake of this explosion, we are left with legal, moral, and ethical questions unlike any that humanity has had to face before. Many of these questions have no apparent answer but only beget more questions. In 1987 the Vatican addressed many of these issues in a doctrinal statement entitled "Instruction on Respect for Human Life in Its Origin and on the Dignity of Procreation: Replies to Certain Questions of the Day." It declared its moral opposition to a wide range of birth technologies, including embryo transfer, experiments with embryos, most forms of artificial insemination, and surrogate motherhood.

Combating Infertility

The concern with infertility that has swept the United States has created opportunities for scientific research and economic opportunism. The paramount value that many of us place on fertility—equating it with maturity, creativity, productivity, accomplishment, and the essence of our maleness or femaleness—has fueled the engine of reproductive technology. The techniques and technologies developed to achieve conception include fertility drugs, artificial insemination and the establishment of sperm banks, in vitro fertilization (including embryo freezing), surrogate motherhood, and embryo transplants.

Sex preselection techniques are also a subject of much interest, although consistently reliable methods for assuring the gender of one's choice do not yet exist. Research indicates that the odds may be swayed slightly (Glass and Ericsson, 1982; Hewitt, 1987; Whelan, 1986). In addition to the desire to bear children, the desire to bear *healthy* (perfect?) children has encouraged the development of new diagnostic technologies.

Diagnosing Abnormalities of the Fetus

Ultrasound examinations use high frequency sound waves to create a picture of the fetus *in utero.* The sound waves are transmitted through a quartz crystal; when they detect a change in the density, the sound waves bounce back to the crystal. The results are interpreted on a television-like screen; the picture is called a **sonogram.** Sonograms are used to determine fetal age and the location of the placenta; when used with amniocentesis, they help determine the fetus's position so that the needle may be inserted safely. Often, it is possible to determine the fetus's sex. More extensive ultrasound techniques can be used to gain further information if there is the possibility of a problem with the fetus's development. Although no problems in humans have been noted to result from ultrasound, high levels of ultrasound have created problems in animal fetuses.

Union between man and woman is a creative act and has something divine about it. . . . The object of love is a creative union with beauty on both the spiritual and physical levels.

Plato, The Symposium

If your parents didn't have any children, there's a good chance that you won't have any.

Clarence Day

In **amniocentesis**, amniotic fluid is withdrawn from the uterus with a long, thin needle inserted through the abdominal wall. The fluid is then examined for evidence of possible birth defects such as Down's syndrome, Tay-Sachs disease, spina bifida, and other conditions caused by chromosomal abnormalities. The sex of the fetus can also be determined. Eighty to 90 percent of amniocentesis tests are performed in cases of "advanced" maternal age, usually when the mother is over thirty-five. The test is performed at about sixteen weeks of gestation.

Alpha-feto protein (AFP) screening is a test (or series of tests) done on the mother's blood after sixteen weeks of gestation. It reveals neural tube defects such as anencephaly and spina bifida. It is much simpler than amniocentesis but sometimes yields false positive results (Samuels and Samuels, 1986). If the results are positive, other tests, such as amniocentesis or ultrasound, will be performed to confirm or negate the AFP screening findings.

Amniocentesis carries a slight risk (a 1/2 to 2 percent chance of fetal death, depending on how early in pregnancy the test is performed (Brandenburg et al., 1990; Hanson et al., 1990; McCormack et al., 1990). For approximately 95 percent of women who undergo prenatal testing, the results are negative. The results of amniocentesis and AFP screening can't be determined, however, until approximately twenty weeks of pregnancy; consequently, if the pregnancy is terminated through abortion at this stage, the process is likely to be physically and emotionally difficult.

A promising alternative to amniocentesis recently introduced in the United States is **chorionic villus sampling (CVS)**. This procedure involves removal through the abdomen (by needle) or through the cervix (by catheter) of tiny pieces of the membrane that encases the embryo; it can be performed between nine and eleven weeks of pregnancy. The relative safety of CVS is still under study. In 32,000 procedures, there was a 1.9 percent miscarriage rate (Kolata, 1987). Some of these miscarriages, however, would have occurred anyway. An advantage of CVS is that it can yield results sooner than amniocentesis (Kolker, 1989).

If a fetus is found to be defective, it may be carried to term, aborted, or, in rare but increasing instances, surgically treated while still in the womb (Kolata, 1990). Gene therapy, in which defective enzymes in the genes of embryos are replaced by normal ones, is considered a challenging frontier of reproductive medicine (Lyon, 1985).

During childbirth, mothers and infants are likely to be attached to various types of monitoring machines. Studies have shown that while fetal monitoring is helpful in high-risk cases, it is generally not helpful in normal (low-risk) situations. The 1988 National Commission to Prevent Infant Mortality stated that although "sophisticated technologies and great expense can save babies born at risk . . . , the lack of access to health care, the inability to pay for health care, poor nutrition, unsanitary living conditions, and unhealthy habits such as smoking, drinking and drug use all threatened unborn children" (cited in Armstrong and Feldman, 1990).

❖ BEING PREGNANT

Pregnancy Tests

Chemical tests designed to detect the presence of **human chorionic gonadotropin (HCG)**, a hormone secreted by the placenta, usually determine pregnancy approximately two weeks following a missed (or spotty) menstrual period. In the **agglutination test,** a drop of the woman's urine causes a test solution to coagulate if she is not pregnant; if she is pregnant, the solution will become smooth and milky in consis-

UNDERSTANDING YOURSELF

Ethics of Reproductive Technology

The desire to have healthy, happy, beautiful children is understandable, basic, and human. But in the face of today's reproductive technology, many of us may have to search our souls for the answers to a number of ethical questions. When faced with infertility, the possibility of birth defects, or the likelihood of a difficult labor, we need to weigh the possible benefits of a given technique against the costs and risks involved. What are your feelings about the following reproductive issues?

◆ *Fetal diagnosis:* If you (or your partner) were pregnant, would you choose to have ultrasound? Should ultrasound be used routinely in all pregnancies or only in selected cases, such as when the mother is over thirty-five or there is a suspected problem? When would you consider amniocentesis appropriate? Should all fetuses be electronically monitored during birth (entailing the attachment of electrodes to the infant's scalp *in utero*), or should this technique be reserved for problem births? Would you want your child to be routinely monitored in this way?

◆ *Cesarean section:* How would you determine that C-section was necessary for yourself or your partner? Should vaginal delivery be attempted first? What if it was a breech birth? What if you (or your partner) had had a previous C-section?

◆ *Artificial insemination and in vitro fertilization:* Should these techniques be available to anyone who wants them? Under what circumstances, if any, would you use these techniques? What are the rights of *all* the parties involved: parents, donors, physicians, child? What are the embryo's or fetus's rights? For example, does a frozen embryo have the "right to life" if its parents die before it is implanted in a surrogate?

◆ *Surrogate motherhood:* Should a woman be allowed to "carry" a pregnancy for a couple using father-donated sperm? Does it matter if profit is involved? Should a contract involving surrogate motherhood be legally binding? Whose rights should take precedence, those of the surrogate (who is the biological moth-

er) or of the couple (which includes the biological father)? What are the child's rights? Who decides? Can you think of a circumstance when you might wish to have the services of a surrogate mother? Could you be a surrogate or accept your partner being one?

◆ For all the preceding techniques, consider the following questions: Who is profiting (scientists, physicians, business people, donors, parents, children)? Who is bearing the greatest risks? How great are the costs—monetary and psychological—and who is paying them? What are the long-range goals of this technology? Are we "playing God?" How might this technology be abused? Are there certain techniques you think should be outlawed?

◆ *Abortion:* When do you think human life begins? Do we ever have the right to take human life? Under what conditions, if any, should abortion be permitted? Whenever the pregnant woman requests it? If there is a serious birth defect? If there is a minor birth defect (such as a shortened limb)? If the fetus is the "wrong" sex? If rape or incest led to the pregnancy? Under what conditions, if any, would you have an abortion or want your partner to have one? If you had an unmarried pregnant teenage daughter, would you encourage her to have one?

◆ *Tissue donation:* Is it appropriate to use the tissues or organs of human corpses for medical purposes? Is it appropriate to use aborted fetuses for tissue donation? For research?

◆ *Life and death:* Is prolonging the life of an infant always the most humane choice? What if it also prolongs suffering? Should life be prolonged whenever possible, at all costs? Who decides?

◆ *Fertility and fulfillment:* Do you think your reproductive values and feelings about your own fertility (or lack of it) are congruent with reality, given the world's population problems? For you, are there viable alternatives to conceiving or bearing a child? What are they? Would adoption be one alternative? Why?

For further discussion of these issues, see Corea, 1985; Lyon, 1985; Shelp, 1986; for a thoughtful discussion of reproductive technology from a feminist viewpoint, see Rowland, 1987; for a discussion of this topic with special reference to Canada, see Eichler, 1989.

tency. Home pregnancy tests to detect HCG may be purchased in most drugstores. The directions must be followed closely. Blood analysis can also be used to determine if a pregnancy exists. Although such tests diagnose pregnancy with better than 95 percent accuracy, no absolute certainty exists until a fetal heartbeat and movements can be detected or ultrasound is performed.

The first reliable physical sign of pregnancy can be distinguished about four weeks after a woman misses her period. By this times, changes in her cervix and pelvis are apparent during a pelvic examination. **Hegar's sign**—a softening of the uterus just above the cervix, which can be felt through the vagina—is particularly useful to the examiner. A slight purple hue colors the labia minora; the cervix also takes on a purple color rather than its usual pink.

The Pregnant Woman and Her Partner

A woman's feelings during pregnancy will vary dramatically according to who she is, how she feels about pregnancy and motherhood, whether the pregnancy was planned, whether she has a secure home situation, and many other factors. Her feelings may be ambivalent; they will probably change over the course of the pregnancy.

A woman's first pregnancy is especially important because it has traditionally symbolized her transition to maturity. Even as social norms change and it becomes more common and "acceptable" for women to defer childbirth until they've established a career or for them to choose not to have children, the significance of first pregnancy should not be underestimated. It is a major developmental milestone in the lives of mothers—and of fathers as well (Notman and Lester, 1988; Snarey et al., 1987; for male procreative consciousness, see Marsiglio, 1991).

A couple's relationship is likely to undergo changes during pregnancy. It can be a stressful time, especially if the pregnancy was unanticipated. Communication is especially important at this time, because each partner may have preconceived ideas about what the other is feeling. Both partners may have fears about the baby's well-being, the approaching birth, their ability to parent, and the ways in which the baby will interfere with their own relationship. All of these concerns are normal. Sharing them, perhaps in the setting of a prenatal group, can deepen and strengthen the relationship (Kitzinger, 1989). If the pregnant woman's partner is not supportive or if she does not have a partner, it is important that she find other sources of support—family, friends, women's groups—and that she not be reluctant to ask for help.

A pregnant woman's relationship with her own mother may also undergo changes. In a certain sense, becoming a mother makes a woman the equal of her own mother. She can now lay claim to being treated as an adult. Women who have depended on their mothers tend to become more independent and assertive as their pregnancy progresses. Women who have been distant, hostile, or alienated from their own mothers may begin to identify with their mothers' experience of pregnancy. Even women who have delayed childbearing until their thirties may be surprised to find their relationships with their mothers changing and becoming more "adult." Working through these changing relationships is a kind of "psychological gestation" that accompanies the physiological gestation of the fetus (Silver and Campbell, 1988).

The first **trimester** (three months) of pregnancy may be difficult physically for the expectant mother. She may experience nausea, fatigue, and painful swelling of the breasts. She may also have fears that she may miscarry or that the child will not be normal. Her sexuality may undergo changes, resulting in unfamiliar needs (for more, less, or differently expressed sexual love), which may in turn cause anxiety. Education about the birth process and her own body's functioning as well as support from partner, friends, relatives, and health-care professionals are the best antidotes to fear.

During the second trimester, most of the nausea and fatigue disappear, and the pregnant woman can feel the fetus move within her. Worries about miscarriage will probably begin to diminish, too, for the riskiest part of fetal development has passed. The pregnant woman may look and feel radiantly happy. She will very likely feel proud of her accomplishment and be delighted as her pregnancy begins to show. She may feel in harmony with life's natural rhythms. One mother wrote (in Jones, 1989):

A couple's relationship may change during pregnancy. Sharing feelings and maintaining emotional closeness are especially important at this time.

Since mother is not all there is to any woman, once she becomes a mother, how does a woman weave the mother into her adult self?

Andrea Eagan

Predicting the Date of Birth
Everyone wants to know when his or her baby's going to be born. It is fairly simple to figure out the date: add seven days to the first day of the last menstrual period. Then subtract three months and add one year. For example, if a woman's last menstrual period began on July 17, 1992, add seven days (July 24). Next subtract three months (April 24). Then add one year. This gives the expected date of birth as April 24, 1993. Few births actually occur on the date predicted, but 60 percent of babies are born within five days of the predicted time.

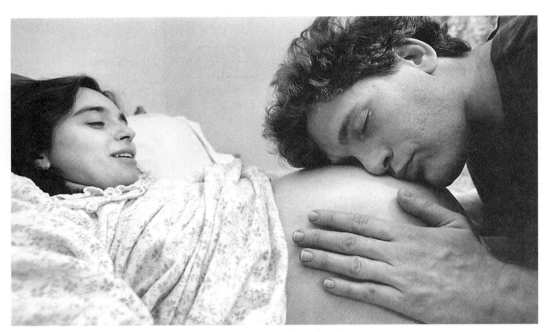

Expectant parents may feel that the fetus is already a member of the family.

I love my body when I'm pregnant. It seems round, full, complete somehow. I find that I am emotionally on an even keel throughout; no more premenstrual depression and upsets. I love the feeling that I am never alone, yet at the same time I am my own person. If I could always be five months pregnant, life would be bliss.

Some women, however, may be concerned about their increasing size. They may fear that they are becoming unattractive. A partner's attention and reassurance will ease these fears.

The third trimester may be the time of the greatest hardships in daily living. Water retention (**edema**) is a common problem during late pregnancy. Edema may cause swelling in the face, hands, ankles, and feet, but it can often be controlled by cutting down on salt and carbohydrates in the diet. If dietary changes do not help this condition, a pregnant woman should consult her physician. Her physical abilities are limited by her size. She may be forced by her employer to stop working (many public schools, for example, do not allow women to teach after their sixth month). A family dependent on the pregnant woman's income may suffer a severe financial crunch.

The woman and her partner may become increasingly concerned about the upcoming birth. Some women experience periods of depression in the month preceding their delivery; they may feel physically awkward and sexually unattractive. Many feel an exhilarating sense of excitement and anticipation marked by energetic bursts of industriousness. They feel that the fetus is a member of the family (Stanton, 1985). Both parents may begin talking to the fetus and "playing" with it by patting and rubbing the mother's belly.

The principal developmental tasks for the expectant mother may be summarized as follows (Valentine, 1982; also see Notman and Lester, 1988; Silver and Campbell, 1988; and Snarey et al., 1987):

Man is a rational animal, but only women can have babies.

Anonymous

Odds of Multiple Births
Twins: one out of every 90 births.
Triplets: one out of every 9,000 births.
Quadruplets: one out of every 500,000 births.

◆ Development of an emotional attachment to the fetus
◆ Differentiation of the self from the fetus
◆ Acceptance and resolution of the relationship with the woman's own mother
◆ Resolution of dependency issues (generally involving parents or husband/partner)
◆ And, increasingly, evaluation of practical/financial responsibilities

And for the expectant father:

◆ Acceptance of the pregnancy and attachment to the fetus
◆ Evaluation of practical/financial responsibilities
◆ Resolution of dependency issues (involving wife/partner)
◆ Acceptance and resolution of the relationship with the man's own father

Fetal Development

Fertilization usually occurs when the ovum is in the fallopian tube. The **zygote** (fertilized ovum) begins to develop at once. During the first week, as it makes its way toward the uterus, the zygote's cells will divide once or twice a day, creating a **blastocyst.** The blastocyst then implants itself in the uterine wall, which has spent the past three weeks preparing for its arrival. Within nine months, a single cell will become the 6,000 billion cells that constitute a human being (see Figure 9.2).

The blastocyst rapidly grows into an **embryo** (which will, in turn, become a **fetus** around the eighth week of development). During the third week of development, the first body segments and the brain begin to be formed. Heart, circulatory system, and digestive system develop in the fourth week. The fifth week sees the formation of arms and legs; the heart begins to pump blood. In the sixth week the eyes and ears form. At eight weeks the fetus is about the size of a thumb; its face and features begin to form, and its bones and internal organs develop. Arms, hands, fingers, legs, feet, toes, and eyes are almost fully developed at twelve weeks. At fifteen weeks, the fetus has a strong heartbeat, fair digestion, and active muscles. Most bones are developed by then, and the eyebrows appear. At this stage the fetus is covered with a fine, downy hair called **lanugo.**

Throughout its development, the fetus is nourished through the **placenta.** The placenta begins to develop from part of the blastocyst during the first week after fertilization. It grows larger as the fetus does, passing nutrients from the mother's bloodstream to the fetus, to which it is attached by the umbilical cord. The placenta serves as a biochemical barrier; it allows dissolved substances to pass to the fetus but blocks blood corpuscles and large molecules.

By five months, the fetus is ten to twelve inches long and weighs between one-half and one pound. The internal organs are well developed, although the lungs cannot function well outside the uterus. At six months, the fetus is eleven to fourteen inches long and weighs more than a pound. At seven months, it is thirteen to seventeen inches long, weighing about three pounds. At this point, most healthy fetuses are viable—that is, capable of surviving outside the womb (although some fetuses are viable at five or six months, they require specialized care to survive). The fetus spends the final two months of gestation growing rapidly. At term (nine months), it will be about twenty inches long and weigh about seven pounds. (Color photographs on pages 262–263 show embryonic and fetal development.)

Complications of Pregnancy

Usually, pregnancy proceeds without major complications. Good nutrition is one of the most important factors in having a complication-free pregnancy. However, some women experience minor to serious complications, which we discuss here.

What did you look like before you were conceived?

Zen Koan (Riddle)

Yes—the history of man for the nine months preceding his birth would, probably be far more interesting, and contain events of greater moment, than all the three score and ten that follow.

Samuel Coleridge

FIGURE 9.2

Embryo and Fetus Growth

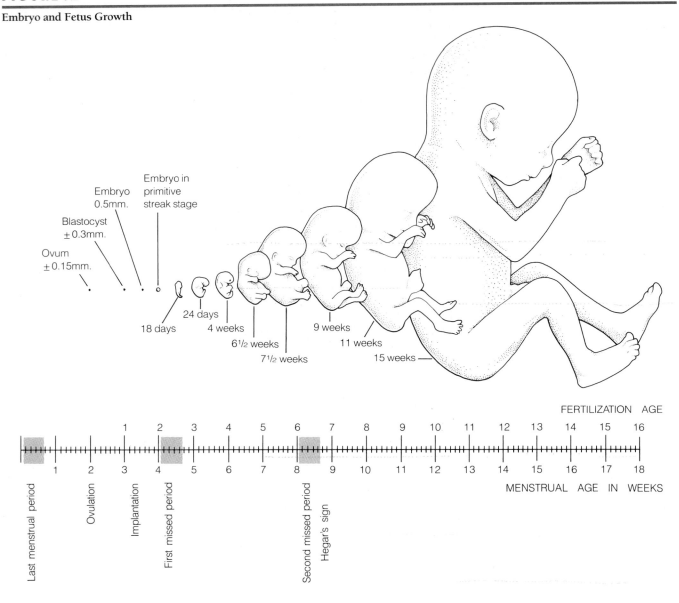

THE PLACENTA AND HARMFUL SUBSTANCES. Substances other than nutrients may reach the developing embryo or fetus through the placenta. Although few extensive studies have been done on the subject, toxic substances in the environment may affect the health of the fetus. Whatever a woman eats or drinks is eventually received by the embryo or fetus in some proportion. A fetus's blood-alcohol level, for example, is equal to that of the mother (Rosenthal, 1990).

Studies have linked chronic ingestion of alcohol during pregnancy to **fetal alcohol syndrome (FAS)**, which can include unusual facial characteristics, small head and body size, congenital heart defects, defective joints, poor mental capabilities, and abnormal behavior patterns. Lesser amounts of alcohol may result in **fetal alcohol effect (FAE),** the most common problem of which is growth retardation (Waterson and Murray-Lyon, 1990). The Centers for Disease Control estimate that more than 8,000 alcohol-affected babies are born every year in this country (2.7 babies out of every 1,000). Some studies place the figure much higher—as high as 50,000 alcohol-affected births per year (Getlin, 1989). The Centers for Disease Control also report that FAS is six times more common in African Americans than in whites and thirty times more common in Native Americans (Rosenthal, 1990). (Studies have also found that African-American and Latina women are more likely to abstain from alcohol than white women and that a woman's level of alcohol consumption rises with her education and income [Rosenthal, 1990].) Most experts counsel pregnant women to abstain entirely from alcohol because there is no safe dosage known at this time.

Mothers who regularly use opiates (heroin, morphine, codeine, and opium) are likely to have infants who are addicted at birth. Cocaine—especially in the smokeable "crack" form—can cause devastating birth defects (see "Crack Babies" in the Perspective section). A study in New York of drug-exposed infants revealed that the opiate-exposed babies showed more neurological damage than the cocaine-exposed babies and that those infants exposed to polydrug abuse (both opiates and cocaine) were worse off than those exposed to any single drug in terms of gestational age at birth, birthweight, and length of hospital stay (Kaye et al., 1989). A 1989 study in Rhode Island found that 35 (7.5 percent) out of the 465 women in labor who were studied had drug traces in their urine (Centers for Disease Control, 1990). (The urine samples were provided to the Department of Health without names to protect the women's anonymity, although various demographic data were supplied.)

Cigarette smoking affects the unborn child as well. Babies born to women who smoke during pregnancy are an average of one-fourth to one-half pound lighter at birth than babies born to nonsmokers. Smoking has been implicated in sudden infant death syndrome, respiratory disorders in children, and various adverse pregnancy outcomes, but there is controversy about the extent of damage done by tobacco and the mechanisms by which it occurs (Abel, 1984; Enkin, 1984).

Prescription drugs should be used only under strict medical supervision, as some may cause serious harm to the fetus. Isotretinoin (Acutane), a popular anti-acne drug, has been implicated in over 1,000 cases of severe birth defects over the past several years (Kolata, 1988). Vitamins, aspirin, and other over-the-counter drugs, as well as large quantities of caffeine-containing food and drink (coffee, tea, colas, chocolate) should be avoided or used only under medical supervision. Vitamin A in large doses can cause serious birth defects.

INFECTIOUS DISEASES. Infectious diseases can also damage the fetus. If a woman contracts German measles (rubella) during the first three months of her pregnancy, her child may be born with physical or mental disabilities. Immunization against rubella is available, but it must be done before the woman is pregnant; otherwise the injection is as harmful to the fetus as the disease itself. Sexually transmitted diseases may also damage the fetus. In 1988, the Centers for Disease Control recommended that *all* pregnant women be screened for hepatitis-B, a virus that can be passed to the infant at birth. If the mother tests positive, her child can be immunized immediately following birth (Moore, 1988). A woman with gonorrhea may expose her child to blindness from contact with the infected vagina; the baby will need immediate

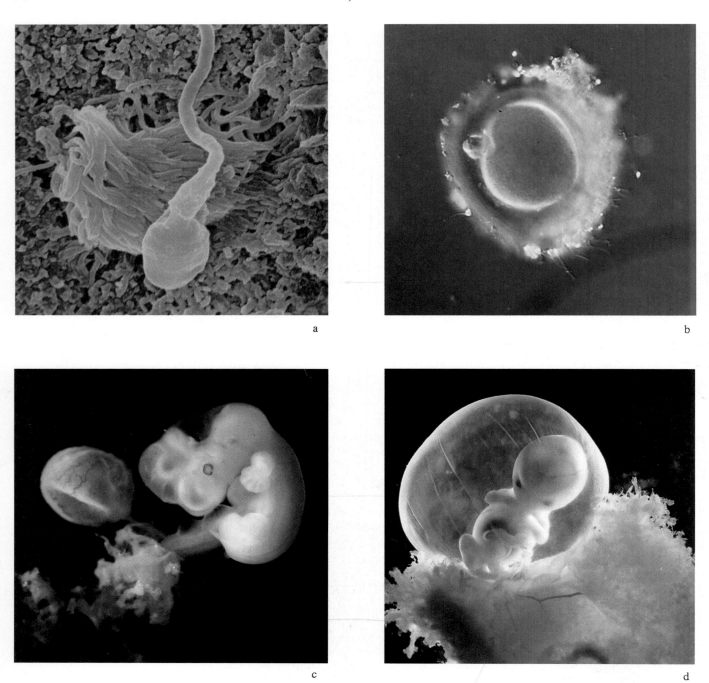

a

b

c

d

antibiotic treatment. A woman with HIV or AIDS has a 30 to 40 percent chance of passing the virus to the fetus via the placenta (Cowley, 1990; Fischl et al., 1987). The number of infants with HIV or AIDS is increasing as more women become infected with the virus either before or during pregnancy. In 1989 there were 547 newborns who were HIV-positive, a 38 percent increase over the previous year (Cowley, 1990). Nationwide, more than 1,600 children have AIDS, and three times that number are estimated to be infected with HIV ("AIDS and Children," 1989).

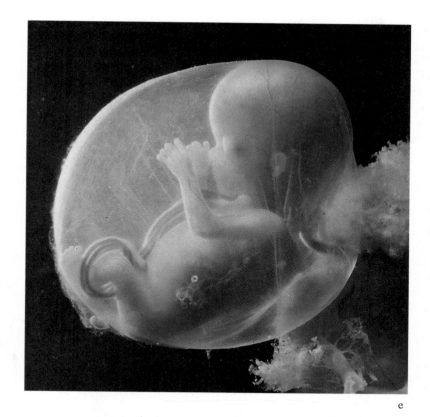

e

a. After ejaculation, several million sperm move through the cervical mucus toward the fallopian tubes; an ovum has descended into one of the tubes. En route to the ovum, millions of sperm are destroyed in the vagina, uterus, or fallopian tubes. Some go the wrong direction in the vagina and others swim into the wrong tube.

b. The ovum has divided for the first time following fertilization, the mother's and father's chromosomes have united. In subsequent cell divisions the genes will be identical. After about a week, the blastocyst will implant itself into the uterine lining.

c. The embryo is five weeks old and is two-fifths of an inch long. It floats in the embryonic sac. The major divisions of the brain can be seen as well as an eye, hands, arms, and a long tail.

d. The embryo is now seven weeks old and is almost an inch long. Its outer and inner organs are developing. It has eyes, a nose, mouth, lips, and tongue.

e. At twelve weeks, the fetus is over three inches long and weighs almost an ounce.

f. At sixteen weeks, the fetus is more than six inches long and weighs about seven ounces. All its organs have been formed. The time that follows is now one of simple growth.

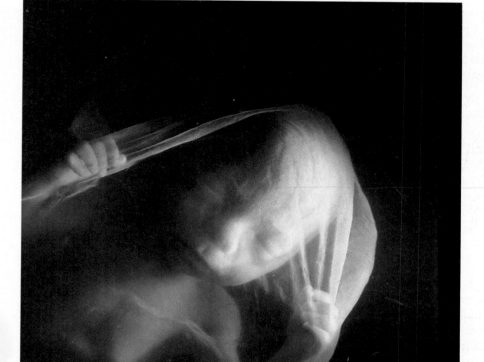

f

The increasingly widespread incidence of genital herpes may present some hazards for newborns. The herpes simplex virus may cause brain damage and is potentially life-threatening for these infants. Careful monitoring by a physician can determine whether or not a vaginal delivery should take place. Charles Prober (1987) and colleagues at the Stanford Medical School have extensively studied births to mothers with herpes. They found that a number of infants born to infected mothers had herpes antibodies in their blood; these infants did not contract herpes during vaginal delivery. Although the harmful potential of neonatal herpes should not be underestimated, if the appropriate procedures are followed by the infected mother and her physician or midwife, the chance of infection from genital lesions is minimal (Dr. Margaret Yonekura in "Neonatal Herpes . . . ," 1984). The Centers for Disease Control estimate the incidence of neonatal herpes to be 400 to 1,000 cases annually (Stone et al., 1989). An initial outbreak of herpes can be dangerous if the woman is pregnant; the virus may be passed through the placenta to the fetus. In rare cases, herpes-infected infants may be born to mothers who show no symptoms themselves. This indicates that undiagnosed intrauterine herpes infections may be passed to the fetus (Stone et al., 1989).

Once the baby is born, a mother who is experiencing a herpes outbreak should wash her hands often and carefully and not permit contact between her hands, contaminated objects, and the baby's mucous membranes (inside of eyes, mouth, nose, penis, vagina, and rectum). If the father is infected, he should do likewise until the lesions have subsided.

ECTOPIC PREGNANCY. In **ectopic pregnancy** (tubal pregnancy), the incidence of which has more than quadrupled in the last twenty years, the fertilized egg implants itself in the fallopian tube. Generally this occurs because the tube is obstructed, most often as a result of pelvic inflammatory disease (Hilts, 1990a). The pregnancy will never come to term. The embryo may spontaneously abort, or the embryo and placenta will continue to expand until they rupture the fallopian tube. **Salpingectomy** (removal of the tube) and abortion of the embryo or fetus may be necessary to save the mother's life.

TOXEMIA AND ECLAMPSIA. **Toxemia,** which may appear in the twentieth to twenty-fourth week of pregnancy, is characterized by high blood pressure and edema (fluid retention and swelling). It can generally be treated through nutritional means. If untreated, toxemia can develop into **preeclampsia** after the twenty-fourth week.

Preeclampsia is characterized by increasingly high blood pressure. These conditions are also known as **gestational edema-proteinuria-hypertension complex.** If untreated they can lead to **eclampsia,** maternal convulsions that pose a serious threat to mother and child. Eclampsia is not common; it is prevented by keeping the blood pressure down through diet, rest, and sometimes medication. It is important for a pregnant woman to have her blood pressure checked regularly.

LOW BIRTH WEIGHT. Prematurity or **low birth weight (LBW)** is a major complication in the third trimester of pregnancy, affecting about 7 percent of newborns yearly (over 260,000 in 1987) in the United States (U.S. Bureau of the Census, 1990). The most fundamental problem of prematurity is that many of the infant's vital organs are insufficiently developed. An LBW baby usually weighs less than 5.5 pounds at birth. Most premature infants will grow normally, but many will experi-

In July 1989 in a Florida court, Jennifer Clarise Johnson, 23, was convicted on drug delivery charges. What was unusual about Ms. Johnson's case was the method of delivery for which she was convicted: through the umbilical cord to her unborn child. Previously, Ms. Johnson had tried to enter a drug treatment program but was turned away because she was pregnant (Lewin, 1990). Increasingly, the criminal justice system is being used to deal with the problem of drug use by pregnant women. This approach has provoked a heated controversy between law enforcement officials and health and civil liberties groups. Prosecutors acknowledge that poor members of ethnic minorities are disproportionately arrested and prosecuted, and both sides agree that early treatment would be a better solution than punishment (Kolata, 1990). Treatment, however, is rarely available. Still, something must be done.

Since 1985, when crack cocaine hit the streets of many large cities, hundreds of thousands of drug-damaged children have been born each year. A national study by Ira Chasnoff (1988), president of the National Association for Perinatal Addiction Research and Education, revealed that at least 375,000 drug-affected babies are born annually in the United States. This figure represents about 11 percent of all births. Dr. Chasnoff believes the actual numbers may be much higher because drug screening is not routine in all hospitals, nor is it always reliable (Kantrowitz, 1990). Additional surveys indicate that the number of drug-affected newborns is increasing dramatically with each passing year (Dorris, 1990; Kantrowitz, 1990). The drug used by most pregnant women is cocaine—usually in the smokable crack form. Many women use other drugs as well.

The horror wrought by crack is unprecedented not only in the great number of people affected but also in the extent of the damage the drug can cause. Cocaine constricts the blood vessels, cutting off the fetus's oxygen supply. Addicted

Crack Babies

mothers have reported that "whenever they smoke crack during pregnancy, the fetus kicks madly, as though in protest of being strangled" (Hopkins, 1990). Studies have indicated that crack-affected babies have up to a 60 percent chance of dying in utero or during the first year (Hopkins, 1990). Those who survive may suffer a host of physical and emotional disabilities. Many are born prematurely (Cherukuri et al., 1988); in addition to the usual problems associated with low birth weight, they are likely to exhibit poor brain growth, intracranial lesions, or hydrocephaly. They may suffer from seizures, strokes, apnea (breathing stoppage), kidney problems, or crumbling cartilage. Because their mothers may use drugs intravenously or be sexually involved with men who do, these children are also at increased risk for contracting HIV (Chasnoff, 1988; Hoegerman et al., 1990).

Crack babies may be psychologically affected as well. Ira Chasnoff describes them as "hypersensitive" (quoted in Rist, 1990). They are easily overwhelmed, resist human contact, and often cry inconsolably for hours on end in the catlike wail characteristic of the neurologically damaged.

As the first generation of crack-affected children enters school, the public is being forced to recognize the extent of their devastation. In addition to the drug damage, many of them also suffer from the effects of abuse and neglect as a result of being raised in dysfunctional families (Chasnoff, 1988; Karan, 1989). They may

suffer a wide range of learning disabilities and "social disabilities" as well. Often they don't know to play—with others or even by themselves. They are often unresponsive and are characterized as "remorseless." They apparently lack "that essential empathy, that motivation toward cooperation, upon which a peaceful and harmonious classroom—and society—so depends" (Dorris, 1990).

It is clear that this country faces a problem of unprecedented gravity concerning the future of its children. The answers aren't at all clear. Some educators are hopeful that with early and intensive intervention, these children can be reached and brought into the mainstream. The Salvin School in Los Angeles is a public preschool program where crack-affected children really do learn some fundamental social skills in addition to standard preschool skills. The school also has a teacher/student ratio of three to eight, a psychologist, a social worker, a pediatrician, and a speech therapist on the staff and costs over $15,000 per student per year (Hopkins, 1990; Rist, 1990).

Many crack-affected children, abandoned by their mothers at birth, are being raised by other family members or in foster homes or have been adopted. These children and others, whose families have managed to wrest themselves from crack's stranglehold, may have a chance at normalcy given the appropriate educational and social support. How they will obtain that support remains to be seen. It will require a commitment from many segments of society—from elected officials to law enforcement personnel to social workers, physicians, teachers, and taxpayers. The issues are complex but must be faced.

Michael Dorris (1990) writes, "If we close our eyes we condemn children not yet even conceived to preordained existences of sorrow and deprivation, governed by prison, victimization and premature death."

ence disabilities. LBW infants are subject to various respiratory problems as well as infections. Feeding, too, is a problem because the infants may be too small to suck a breast or bottle, and their swallowing mechanisms may be too underdeveloped to permit them to drink. As premature infants get older, problems such as low intelligence, learning difficulties, poor hearing and vision, and physical awkwardness may become apparent.

Premature delivery is one of the greatest problems confronting obstetrics today. About half the cases are related to teenage pregnancy, smoking, poor nutrition, and poor health in the mother (Schneck et al, 1990); the causes of the other half are unknown. One study of LBW babies found a six-fold increase in the risk of low birthweight if the mother had financial problems during pregnancy (Binsacca et al., 1987). (A 1987 study of 1,382 women indicated that delaying childbearing until after age thirty-five does *not* increase the risk of delivering an LBW infant [Barkan and Bracken, 1987].)

Prenatal care is extremely important as a means of preventing prematurity (Rush et al., 1988). A third of all LBW births could be averted with adequate prenatal care (Scott, 1990b). For this reason, the federal government's reduction or elimination of supplemental assistance for pregnant women on welfare has created alarm among many health professionals. Marian Wright Edelman, president of the Children's Defense Fund, blames the government for a "lack of very basic supports" (quoted in "U.S. Assailed on Infant Mortality," 1987). We need to understand that if children's needs are not met today, we will all face the consequences of their deprivation tomorrow. The social and economic costs are bound to be very high.

❖ REFLECTIONS   *What concerns do (or will) you (and your partner) have about the prenatal health of a child you have conceived? (Think in terms of your own health, medical history, genetic background, drinking and smoking habits, exposure to disease, chemicals, and radiation, and so on.) If you have legitimate concerns, where can you get more information? In what practical ways can you deal with your concerns?*

❖ PREGNANCY LOSS

The loss of a child through miscarriage, stillbirth, or death during early infancy is often a devastating experience that has been largely ignored in our society. The statement, "You can always have another one," may be meant as consolation, but it is particularly chilling to the ears of a grieving mother. In the past few years, however, the medical community has begun to respond to the emotional needs of parents who have lost a pregnancy or an infant.

Spontaneous Abortion

Spontaneous abortion (miscarriage) is a powerful natural selective force toward bringing healthy babies into the world. About one out of four women is aware she has miscarried at least once (Beck, 1988). Studies indicate that at least 60 percent of all miscarriages are due to chromosomal abnormalities in the fetus (Adler, 1986). Furthermore, as many as three-fourths of all fertilized eggs do not mature into viable fetuses (Beck, 1988). A recent study found that 32 percent of implanting embryos miscarry (Wilcox et al., 1988). The first sign that a pregnant woman may miscarry is vaginal bleeding ("spotting"). If a woman's symptoms of pregnancy disappear and she develops pelvic cramps, she may be miscarrying; the fetus is usually expelled by uterine contractions. Most miscarriages occur between the sixth and eighth weeks of pregnancy (Welch and Herman, 1980). Evidence is increasing that certain occupations involving exposure to chemicals increase the likelihood of spontaneous abortions (Hemminki et al., 1983).

Infant Mortality

The U.S. infant mortality rate has halted its decreasing trend and seems to be stabilized at approximately 11 deaths per 1,000 births (U.S. Bureau of the Census, 1988). Nevertheless, among developed nations, our country ranks twenty-second for low infant mortality (Hilts, 1990b). (This means that twenty-one countries have *lower* infant mortality rates than the United States.) In some inner-city areas such as Detroit, Washington, D.C., and parts of Oakland (California), the infant mortality rate approaches that of nonindustrialized countries, with more than 20 deaths per 1,000 births (Petit, 1990). Approximately 40,000 American babies less than one year old die each year. Most of these infants are victims of the poverty that often results from racial or ethnic discrimination. Up to a third of these deaths could be prevented if mothers were given adequate health care (Scott, 1990a). The infant mortality rate for African Americans is almost twice that for whites. Native Americans are also at high risk; for example, about one out of every 67 Navajo infants dies each year (Wilkerson, 1987). Since 1981, the federal government has dramatically cut pregnancy and infant care programs such as WIC (Women, Infants, and Children) programs to fund its record-breaking military budget. Medicaid and Aid to Families with Dependent Children have also been cut, leaving many families without pre- or postnatal care. On the state level also, the current trend is to cut back on medical and health care for low-income people. In countries such as France, Sweden, and Japan, for example, all pregnant women are entitled to free prenatal care. Free health care and immunizations are also provided for infants and young children. Working Swedish mothers are guaranteed one year of paid maternal leave, and French families in need are paid regular government allowances (Scott, 1990a). Although the United States has the resources to support its mothers and children in similar ways, such programs are few and far between. We are one of the wealthiest countries in the world, but our families do not necessarily reap the benefits suggested by that wealth.

Although many infants die of poverty-related conditions, others die from **congenital** problems (conditions appearing at birth) or from infectious diseases, accidents, or other causes. Sometimes the causes of death are not apparent; in 1985, one out of every 378 infant deaths was attributed to **sudden infant death syndrome (SIDS)**, a particularly perplexing phenomenon wherein an apparently healthy infant dies suddenly while sleeping.

Coping with Loss

The depth of shock and grief felt by many who lose an infant before or during birth is sometimes difficult to understand for those who have not had a similar experience. What they may not realize is that most women form a deep attachment to their children even before birth. At first, the attachment may be a "fantasy image of [the] future child" (Friedman and Gradstein, 1982). During the course of the pregnancy, the mother forms an actual acquaintance with her infant through the physical sensations she feels within her. Thus the death of the fetus can also represent the death of a dream and of a hope for the future. This loss must be acknowledged and felt before psychological healing can take place (Panuthos and Romeo, 1984).

Women (and sometimes their partners) who must face the loss of a pregnancy or a young infant generally experience similar stages in their grieving process. The feelings that are experienced are influenced by many factors: supportiveness of the partner and other family members, reaction of social networks, life circumstances at the time of the loss, circumstances of the loss itself, whether other losses have been experienced, the prognosis for future childbearing, and the woman's unique personality (Friedman and Gradstein, 1982). Physical exhaustion and, in the case of miscarriage, hormone imbalance often compound the emotional stress of the grieving mother. The initial stage of grief is often one of shocked disbelief and numbness. This stage gives way to sadness, spells of crying, preoccupation with the loss, and perhaps loss of interest in the rest of the world. Emotional pain may be accompanied by physical sensations and symptoms, such as tightness in the chest or stomach, sleeplessness, and loss of appetite. It is not unusual for parents to feel guilty as if they had somehow caused the loss, although this is rarely the case. Anger (toward the physician, perhaps, or God) is also a common emotion. (In Chapter 13, death and the grieving process are discussed at greater length.)

Experiencing the pain of loss is part of the healing process. This process takes time—months, a year, perhaps more for some. Support groups or counseling are often helpful, especially if healing does not seem to be progressing—if, for example, depression and physical symptoms don't appear to be diminishing. (See Resource Center for support groups.) Keeping active is another way to deal with the pain of loss, as long as it isn't a way to avoid facing feelings. Projects, temporary or part-time work, or travel (for those who can afford it) can be ways of renewing energy and interest in life. Planning the next pregnancy may be curative, too, keeping in mind that the body and spirit need some time to heal. It is important to have a physician's input before proceeding with another pregnancy; specific considerations may need to be discussed, such as a genetic condition that may be passed to the child or a physiological problem of the mother. If future pregnancies are ruled out, the parents need to take stock of their priorities and consider other options that may be open to them, such as adoption. Counselors and support groups can be invaluable at this stage.

Dear Auntie will come with presents and will ask, "Where is our baby, sister?" And, Mother, you will tell her softly, "He is in the pupils of my eyes. He is in my bones and in my soul."

Rabindranath Tagore

❖ GIVING BIRTH

Labor and Delivery

Throughout a woman's pregnancy, she occasionally feels contractions of her uterus that are strong but usually not too painful. These are called **Braxton Hicks contractions.** They exercise the uterus, preparing it for labor. During labor these contractions also begin the **effacement** (thinning) and **dilation** (opening up) of the cervix. It is difficult to say exactly when labor starts, which helps explain the great differences reported in lengths of labor for different women. When the uterine contractions become regular, true labor begins. During these contractions, the lengthwise muscles of the uterus involuntarily pull open the circular muscles around the cervix. This process generally takes from two to thirty-six hours. Its duration depends on the size of the baby, the baby's position in the uterus, the size of the mother's pelvis, and the condition of the uterus. The length of labor tends to shorten after the first birth experience.

Labor can generally be divided into three stages (see Figure 9-3). The first stage is usually the longest, lasting from four to sixteen hours. An early sign of first-stage labor is the expulsion of a plug of slightly bloody mucus that has blocked the opening of the cervix during pregnancy. At the same time or later on, there is a second fluid discharge from the vagina. This discharge, referred to as the "breaking of the waters," is the **amniotic fluid,** which comes from the ruptured **amniotic membrane.** (Because the baby is subject to infection after the protective membrane breaks, the woman should receive medical attention soon thereafter, if she has not already.)

The contractions at the end of the first stage of labor, which is called **transition,** come more quickly and are much more intense. Many women report this as the most difficult part of labor. During the last part of first-stage labor, the baby's head enters the birth canal. This marks the shift from dilation of the cervical opening to expulsion of the infant. The cervix is now almost fully open, but the baby is not yet completely in position to be pushed out. Some women may feel despair, isolation, and anger at this point. Many appear to lose faith in those assisting in the birth. A woman may find that management of the contractions seems beyond her control; she may be afraid that something is wrong. At this time she needs the full support and understanding of her helpers. Transition is usually, though not always, brief (half an hour to one hour).

Second-stage labor begins when the baby's head moves into the birth canal and ends when the baby is born. During this time many women experience a great force in their bodies. Some women find this the most difficult part of labor. Others find that the contractions and bearing down bring a sense of euphoria. One father described his wife's second-stage labor (Jones, 1986):

When the urge to bear down swept through her, Jan felt as if she were one with all existence and connected with the vast primordial power that summons life forth from its watery depths.

The baby is usually born gradually. With each of the final few contractions, a new part of the infant emerges. The baby may even cry before he or she is completely born, especially if the mother did not have medication. Sheila Kitzinger (1985) described the moment of birth as a sexual event:

. . . The whole body slips out in a rush of warm flesh, a fountain of water, a peak of overwhelming surprise and the little body is against her skin, kicking against her thighs or swimming up over her belly. She reaches out to hold her baby, firm, solid, with bright, bright eyes. A peak sexual experience, the birth passion, becomes the welcoming of a new person into life.

The baby will still be attached to the **umbilical cord** connected to the mother, which is not cut until it stops pulsating. He or she will appear wet, often covered by a milky substance called **vernix.** The head may look oddly shaped at first, from the molding of the soft plates of bone during birth. This shape is temporary, and the baby's head usually achieves a normal appearance within twenty-four hours.

After the baby has been delivered, the uterus will continue to contract, expelling the placenta (afterbirth) and completing the third and final stage of labor. The doctor or midwife will examine the placenta to make sure that it is whole. If the pactitioner has any doubt that the entire placenta has been expelled, he or she may examine the uterus to make sure no parts of the placenta remain to cause adhesions or hemorrhage.

For a few days following labor (especially if it is a second or subsequent birth), the mother will probably feel strong contractions as the uterus begins to return to its pre-birth size and shape. This process, called **involution,** takes about six weeks. She will also have a bloody discharge called **lochia,** which continues for several weeks.

[Power] sounds in our bodies. Contractions creep up, seizing ever stronger until they make a mockery of all the work we have done on our own. Birth can silence our ego and, for the moment, we feel ourselves overcome by a larger life pounding through our own.

Penny Armstrong and Sheryl Feldman, A Wise Birth

FIGURE 9.3

Childbirth

During the last phase of pregnancy, the fetus usually settles in a head-down position. In the first stage of labor (a), Braxton Hicks contractions begin effacement and dilation of the cervix. When the cervix is fully dilated (b), the baby's head can enter the birth canal; usually the amniotic membrane has ruptured by this time. During second-stage labor (c), the baby moves through the birth canal and into the outside world. The soft bones of the head may be "molded" by pressure in the birth canal, resulting in a temporarily unusual appearance. The placenta (d), is expelled during third-stage labor.

Choices in Childbirth

HOSPITAL BIRTH. The impersonal, routine quality of hospital birth is increasingly being questioned. As Margaret Mead observed, hospital conditions have generally been designed not for the woman who is giving birth but "primarily to facilitate the ministrations of the obstetrician" (Mead, 1975). One woman described her initial feelings in the hospital (in Leifer, 1990):

When they put that tag around my wrist and put me into that hospital gown, I felt as if I had suddenly just become a number, a medical case. All of the excitement that I was feeling on the way over to the hospital began to fade away. It felt like I was waiting for an operation, not about to have my baby. I felt alone, totally alone, as if I had just become a body to be examined and not a real person.

Another woman was shocked at the impersonal treatment (in Leifer, 1990):

And then this resident gave me an internal [examination], and it was quite painful then. And I said: "Could you wait till the contraction is over?" And he said he had to do it now, and I was really upset because he didn't even say it nicely, he just said: "You'll have to get used to this, you'll have a lot of this before the baby comes."

Some hospitals are responding to the need for a family-centered childbirth. The father does not necessarily need to handcuff himself to the delivery table to be present during the birth. Indeed, fathers may often participate today. Nor do the mother and the infant always need to be separated immediately after birth. Hospitals may permit rooming-in (the baby stays with the mother rather than in the nursery) or a modified form of rooming-in. Regulations vary as to when the father and other family members and friends are allowed to visit. Some hospitals restrict visits to specific visiting hours, even if the mother and the child are in the same room.

But the norm is still all too often the impersonal birth. During one of the most profound experiences of her life, a woman may have her baby among strangers to whom birth is merely routine. She will probably be given a routine enema and have her pubic hair shaved, even though surgery is not anticipated. She and her unborn child will likely be wired to beeping machines. During delivery, she will probably be given an **episiotomy** (a surgical procedure enlarging the vaginal opening by cutting through the perineum toward the anus), whether or not it is actually needed. A recent study of a larger inner-city hospital revealed an episiotomy rate of 80 percent (Hetherington, 1990); yet one midwife who has assisted at over 1,200 births reported a rate of less than 1 percent (Armstrong and Feldman, 1990). Some form of anesthetic will be administered in most cases, as well as various hormones (to intensify the contractions and to shrink the uterus after delivery). The mother isn't the only recipient of the drugs, however; they go directly through the placenta to the baby, in whom they may reduce heart and respiration rates.

The baby is usually delivered on a table, against the force of gravity. He or she may be pulled from the womb with forceps. In most cultures, a woman gives birth while sitting in a birthing chair, kneeling or squatting. Until the present century, most American women used birthing chairs; the delivery table was instituted for the convenience of the physician. A few hospitals use a motorized birthing chair that can be raised, lowered, or tilted according to the physician's and the woman's needs.

Following birth, the baby is generally taken to a nursery and is diapered and clothed, his or her first lesson, observed Margaret Mead (1975), "in expecting cloth to intervene between one body and the next." If the baby has not been drugged, his

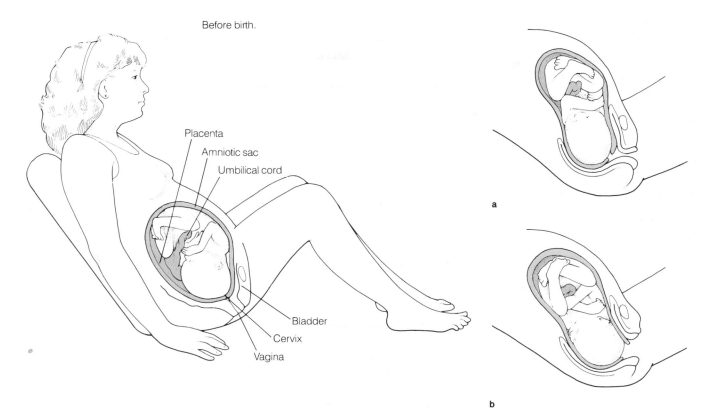

Before birth.

Placenta

Amniotic sac

Umbilical cord

Bladder

Cervix

Vagina

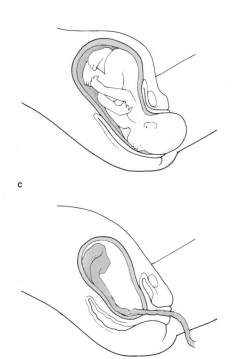

a

b

c

d

or her lips are ready for sucking, seeking the breast that is not there. If the infant is a boy, the foreskin of the penis may be cut off within the next day or two (see p. 276 for discussion of circumcision). During the next two or three days, the infant will be brought to the mother at scheduled intervals for feeding and visiting. In the last few years, some hospitals have tried to comply with mothers' wishes for "demand" feeding (when the baby feels hungry, as opposed to when the hospital wants to feed the child), but because most hospital maternity wards are busy places, they often find it difficult to meet the individual needs of many infants and mothers. If the mother is breastfeeding, a rigid hospital schedule can make it difficult for her to establish a feeding routine with her child.

Childbirth does not have to be this way. Increasingly, Americans are choosing alternatives of prepared childbirth, rooming-in, birthing centers, home births, and midwives. The chief of obstetrics at a major hospital observed, "It's a major upheaval in medicine, and the conflict has tended to polarize the consumer and the care giver. The basic problem is that we have changed obstetrics with the latest medical advances and not incorporated essentially humanistic considerations" (Trafford, 1980; see Pallow-Fleury, 1983, for questions to ask about a hospital's birth policies).

CESAREAN SECTION. **Cesarean section** (C-section) is the removal of the fetus by an incision in the mother's abdominal and uterine walls. The first reported cesarean section performed on a living woman occurred in the seventeenth century, when a butcher cut open his wife's uterus to save her and their child. In 1970, 5.5 percent of American births were done by cesarean section. Today cesarean births account for about 24 percent of all births; more than 900,000 women have C-sections each year (U.S. Bureau of the Census, 1990). This represents more than a 400 percent increase in twenty years.

Although there is a decreased mortality rate for infants born by C-section, the mothers' mortality rate is higher. As with all major surgeries, there are possible complications, and recovery can be slow and difficult.

Hoping to reduce the alarming increase in C-sections, the National Institutes of Health have issued the following guidelines:

◆ Because a woman has had a previous cesarean delivery does not mean that subsequent deliveries must be C-sections; whenever possible, women should be given the option of vaginal birth.

◆ Abnormal labor does not mean that a C-section is necessary. Sleep or medication may resolve the problems. Only after other measures have been tried should a physician perform a cesarean, unless the infant is clearly in danger.

◆ Breech babies (those who enter the birth canal buttocks or feet first) do not necessarily require C-sections. A physician's experience using his or her hands to deliver the baby vaginally is crucial.

If a woman does not want a C-section unless it is absolutely necessary, she should learn about her physician's attitude and record on cesareans. It is noteworthy that the greatest number of cesareans are performed in the socioeconomic group of women with the lowest medical risk (Hursh and Summey, 1984). In a study of 245,854 births, the C-section rate for middle- and upper-income women was 22.9 percent, whereas for lower-income women it was 3.2 percent (Gould et al., 1989). Therefore, it is assumed that cesareans are often performed for reasons other than medical risk. Some of the reasons offered include threat of malpractice (although such suits are apparently rare for vaginal deliveries), lack of physician training in vaginal births, and "economic incentives" for the hospital and the physician (Cohen and Estner, 1983). A 1987 international study by the U.S. Department of Health and Human Services urged the medical community to consider the appropriateness of the continued rise in C-sections (Notzon et al., 1987).

THE MEDICALIZATION OF CHILDBIRTH. In this century, American childbirth has moved from the home to the hospital. It has, for the most part, moved from the hands of female midwives to the hands (and instruments) of male doctors. Although only 5 to 10 percent of births actually require medical procedures, we seem to assume that childbirth is an inherently dangerous process. Of course, in high-risk cases, the advances of technology can and do save lives. But the questions remain: Why do women accept unnecessary, uncomfortable, demeaning, and even dangerous intervention in the birth process? Why do they tolerate a 24 percent cesarean rate, a 61 percent episiotomy rate, the almost universal administration of drugs, and the use of intrusive fetal monitoring—not to mention routine enemas and shaving of pubic hair? Why do they allow their infant boys to have their penises surgically altered? Why do they accept, often without question, the physician's opinion over their own gut feelings?

Penny Armstrong and Sheryl Feldman (1990) suggest that society's increasing dependence on technology has hampered women's ability to view birth as a natural process for which they are naturally equipped. Women have allowed themselves to be persuaded that technology can do the job better than they can on their own.

Society expects birth technology to deliver a "product"—a "perfect" baby—without understanding that nature has already equipped women to deliver that product without much outside interference in the physical process (although encouragement and emotional support are paramount). Sheila Kitzinger (1989) writes:

It is not advances in medicine but improved conditions, better food and general health which have made childbirth much safer for mothers and babies today than it was 100 years ago. The rate of stillbirths and deaths in the first week of life is directly related to a country's gross national product and to the position of the mother in the social class.

The idea that the pain of childbirth is to be avoided at all costs is a relatively new one. When Queen Victoria accepted ether during labor in 1853, she undoubtedly had little idea of the precedent she was setting. It was, in fact, the increasing use of anesthesia in the nineteenth century that brought childbirth into the hospital. While today's advocates of "natural" childbirth do not deny that there is pain involved, they do argue that it is a different pain from that of injury and that normally it is worth experiencing. This "pain with a purpose" is an intrinsic part of the birth process (Kitzinger, 1989). To obliterate it with drugs is to obliterate the mother's awareness and the baby's as well, depressing the child's breathing, heart rate, and general responsiveness in the process.

Another aspect of dependence on technology is that we get the feeling we are omnipotent and should be able to solve any problem. Thus if something goes wrong with a birth—if a child is stillborn or has a disability—we look around for something or someone to blame. We have become unwilling to accept that some aspects of life and death are beyond human control.

Prospective parents face a daunting array of decisions. The more informed they are, however, the better able they will be to decide what is right for them. (See Suggested Readings at end of chapter and the Resource Center for more information on childbirth.) According to Armstrong and Feldman (1990):

Teaching women that they have say—whether they consciously exercise it or not—is a major educational undertaking, one that requires breaking the hold obstetrical medicine has on the American imagination and helping women to rediscover their natural power at birth.

PREPARED CHILDBIRTH. **Prepared childbirth** (or natural childbirth) was popularized by Grantly Dick-Read (1972) in the first edition of his book *Childbirth Without Fear* in the 1930s. Dick-Read observed that fear causes muscles to tense, which in turn increases pain and stress in childbirth. He taught both partners about childbirth and gave them physical exercises to ease muscle tension. Encouraged by Dick-Read's ideas, women began to reject anesthetics during labor and delivery and were consequently able to take a more active role in childbirth as well as be more aware of the process.

In the 1950s, Fernand Lamaze (1956, 1970) developed a method of prepared childbirth based on knowledge of conditioned reflexes. Women learn to mentally separate the physical stimulus of uterine contractions from the conditioned response of pain. With the help of a partner, women use breathing and other exercises throughout labor and delivery. Although Lamaze did much to advance the cause of prepared childbirth, he has been criticized by other childbirth educators as too controlling or even "repressive" according to Armstrong and Feldman (1990). One does not give birth, they write, "by direction, as if it were a flight plan."

Prepared childbirth, then, is not so much a matter of controlling the birth process as of understanding it and having confidence in nature's plan. "One attends one's physiological voice," write Armstrong and Feldman (1990). "One credits the

. . . in the 19th century, the possibility of eliminating "pain and travail" created a new kind of prison for women—the prison of unconsciousness, of numbed sensations, or amnesia, and complete passivity.

Adrienne Rich, Of Woman Born

Women can give birth by the action of their own bodies, as animals do. Women can enjoy the process of birth and add to their dignity by being educated to follow the example set by instinctive animals.

Dr. Robert A. Bradley

information coming from one's body and one's psyche; one follows one's impulses." Michael Odent, who heads a remarkable maternity clinic in Pithiviers, France, believes strongly that laboring mothers should be allowed freedom to give birth in their own ways. In *Birth Reborn* (1984) he writes:

We encourage women in labor to give in to the experience, to lose control, to forget all they have learned—all the cultural images, all the behavioral patterns. The less a woman has learned about the "right" way to have a child, the easier it will be for her.

Clinical studies consistently show better birth outcomes for mothers who have had prepared childbirth classes (Conway, 1980). Prepared mothers (who usually attend classes with the father or other partner) handle pain more successfully, use less medication and anesthesia, express greater satisfaction with the childbirth process, and experience less postpartum depression than women undergoing routine hospital births (Hetherington, 1990).

BIRTHING ROOMS AND CENTERS. Birth (or maternity) centers, institutions of long standing in England and other European countries (see Odent, 1984), now are being developed in the United States. In 1990 there were 132 free-standing birth centers in this country (Armstrong and Feldman, 1990). Although they vary in size, organization, and orientation, birth centers share the view that childbirth is a normal, healthy process that can be assisted by skilled practitioners (midwives or physicians) in a homelike setting. The mother (or couple) has considerable autonomy in deciding the conditions of birth—lighting, sounds, visitors, delivery position, and so on. Some of these centers can provide some kinds of emergency care; all have procedures for transfer to a hospital if necessary.

An extensive survey of 11,814 births in birth centers in 1988 concluded that "birth centers offer a safe and acceptable alternative to hospital confinement for

selected pregnant women, particularly those who have previously had children, and that such care leads to relatively few cesarean sections" (Rooks et al., 1989). Another large study showed that free-standing birth centers are associated with "a low cesarean section rate, low neonatal mortality [or] no neonatal mortality" (Eakins, 1989). Some hospitals now have their own birthing centers (or rooms) that provide for labor and birth in a comfortable setting and allow the mother or couple considerable autonomy. Hospital practices vary widely, however; prospective parents should carefully determine their needs and thoroughly investigate their options.

HOME BIRTH. Home births have increased during the last two decades, although they still constitute a small fraction of total births, amounting to not quite 2 percent, according to available data. Home births tend to be safer than hospital births if they are supervised by midwives or physicians. This is, in part, the result of careful medical screening and planning that eliminate all but the lowest-risk pregnancies. A couple can create their own birth environment at home, and home births cost considerably less, usually at least one-third less, than hospital delivery. With the supervision of an experienced practitioner, a couple have little to worry about. But if a woman is at risk, she is wiser to give birth in a hospital where medical equipment is readily available.

MIDWIFERY. The United States has an increasing number of certified nurse-midwives who are trained not only as registered nurses but also in obstetrical techniques. They are well qualified for routine deliveries and minor medical emergencies. They also often operate as part of a total medical team that includes a backup physician, if needed. Their fees are generally considerably less than a doctor's. Nurse-midwives usually participate in both hospital and home births, although this may vary according to hospital policy, state law, and the midwives' preference. (Massachusetts, Alabama, South Dakota, and Wisconsin bar nurse-midwives—although not necessarily lay midwives—from attending home births ["Massachusetts Midwife . . . ," 1987].)

Lay midwifery, in which the midwives are not formally trained by the medical establishment but by other experienced midwives, has also increased in popularity in the past two decades. Many satisfactory births with lay midwives in attendance have been reported, but extensive, reliable information is not available, owing to the "underground" nature of lay midwifery, which is often practiced outside of (and without the support of) the regular practice of medicine. Many midwives belong to organized groups; a number of these groups use some form of self-certification to insure that high professional standards are maintained (Butter and Kay, 1990).

If a woman decides she wants to give birth with the aid of a midwife outside a hospital setting, she should have a thorough medical screening to make sure she or her infant will not be at risk during delivery. She should learn about the midwife's training and experience, what type of backup services the midwife has in the event of complications or emergencies, and how the midwife will handle a transfer to a hospital if it becomes necessary.

❖ REFLECTIONS *In having a baby, what factors are (or will be) important to you in choosing a birth method, setting, practitioner, and so on? If you are a man, how have you chosen (or will you choose) to be involved in the birth of your child? If you are a woman, what extent of participation in childbirth do (or will) you expect from your partner?*

The Question of Circumcision

In 1975, the American Academy of Pediatrics and the American College of Obstetricians and Gynecologists issued a statement declaring that there is "no absolute medical indication" for routine circumcision. This surgical operation, which involves slicing and removing the sleeve of skin (foreskin) that normally covers the glans penis, has been performed routinely on newborn boys in the United States since the 1930s (Romberg, 1985). Circumcision is often done without anesthesia. It is obviously painful; in some tribal societies it is performed to initiate boys into the harsh realities of manhood. It carries medical risks in 4 to 28 percent of the cases (Samuels and Samuels, 1986). The principal risks are excessive bleeding, infection, and faulty surgery. It can be life-threatening.

In spite of the fact that it is not a medical necessity, almost 60 percent of newborn boys were circumcised in 1985, according to the National Center for Health Statistics. Although this represents a substantial drop from an estimated 93 percent being circumcised in 1975, it still places the United States far ahead of other Western countries, which circumcise less than 1 percent of their newborn boys. The exception is Israel; in Judaism the ritual circumcision, the *bris,* is an important religious event. Circumcision has religious significance for Moslems as well (Bullough, 1976).

Besides religious reasons, the other reasons given by parents for circumcising their infants are "cleanliness" and "so he'll look like his dad." A circumcised penis is not necessarily any cleaner than an intact one. Infants do not require cleaning under their foreskins (Brody, 1985); adults do, but it is no more difficult to wash under one's foreskin than behind one's ears. If reasonable cleanliness is observed, an intact penis poses no more threat of disease to a man's sexual partner than a circumcised one would. As for "looking like dad," most parents can probably find ways to keep their son's self-esteem intact along with his foreskin. There is no evidence we know of to suggest that little boys are seriously traumatized if dad's penis doesn't look exactly like theirs. We know one dad (circumcised) who says to his sons (uncircumcised), "Boy, you guys are lucky. You should've seen what they did to me!"

❖ AFTER THE BIRTH

Breastfeeding

About three days after childbirth, **lactation**—the production of milk—begins. Before lactation, sometimes as early as the second trimester, a yellowish liquid called **colostrum** is secreted by the nipples. It is what nourishes the newborn infant before the mother's milk comes in. Colostrum is high in protein and contains antibodies that help protect a baby from infectious diseases. Hormonal changes during labor begin the changeover from colostrum to milk, but unless a mother nurses her child, her breasts will soon stop producing milk. If she chooses not to breastfeed, she is usually given an injection of estrogen soon after delivery to stop lactation. It is not certain, however, whether estrogen is actually effective; furthermore, it may cause an increased risk of blood clotting.

Breastfeeding has declined significantly over the last few years, dropping from 60% to 52% between 1984 and 1988. Nutritionists are alarmed. A mother's milk—if she is healthy and has a good diet—offers the best nutrition for the baby. In addition, her milk contains antibodies that will protect her child from infectious diseases. Finally, a breastfed baby is less likely to become constipated, contract skin diseases, or develop respiratory infections. Low birth-weight babies, similarly, do best with mother's milk rather than formula or mature milk from a donor, since "nature

---

And you shall circumcise the flesh of your foreskin: and it shall be a token of the covenant between Me and you.

Genesis (17:9-14)

It is not to diffuse you that you were born of your mother and father—it is to identify you,
It is not that you should be undecided, but that you should be decided.
Something long preparing and formless is arrived and formed in you,
You are thenceforth secure, whatever comes or goes.

Walt Whitman

adapts mother's milk to meet infant's needs" (Johnson and Goldfinger, 1981). A benefit to the mother is that hormonal changes, stimulated by breastfeeding, cause the uterus to contract and help ensure its return to a normal state. The American Academy of Pediatricians endorses total breastfeeding for a baby's first six months. Breastfeeding has psychological as well as physical benefits. Nursing provides a sense of emotional well-being for both mother and child through close physical contact. A woman may feel that breastfeeding affirms her body, giving her assurance that she is plentiful, capable of nourishing, able to sustain the life of another through her milk.

American mothers may worry about whether they will be able to breastfeed "properly." But what the distinguished physician Dr. Niles Newton wrote in 1955 still applies today:

Successful breast-feeding is the type of feeding that is practiced by the vast majority of mothers all over the world. It is a simple, easy process. When the baby is hungry, it is simply given a breast to suck. There is an abundance of milk, and the milk supply naturally adjusts itself to the child's growth and intake of other foods.

Many American women choose not to breastfeed. Their reasons include the inconvenience of not being able to leave the baby for more than a few hours at a time, tenderness of nipples (which generally passes within several days to two weeks), and inhibitions about nursing a baby, especially in public. If a woman works, bottle feeding may be her only practical alternative, as American companies rarely provide leaves, part-time employment, or nursing breaks for their female

All is beautiful
All is beautiful
All is beautiful, yes!
Now Mother Earth
And Father Sky
Join one another and meet
forever helpmates
  All is beautiful
  All is beautiful
  All is beautiful, yes!
Now the night of darkness
And the dawn of light
Join one another and meet
forever helpmates
  All is beautiful
  All is beautiful
  All is beautiful, yes!
Now the white corn
And the yellow corn
Join one another and meet
forever helpmates
  All is beautiful
  All is beautiful
  All is beautiful, yes!
Life that never ends
Happiness of all things
Join one another and meet
Forever helpmates
  All is beautiful
  All is beautiful
  All is beautiful, yes!

Navajo Night Chant

employees. Some women may have a physical condition that precludes breastfeeding. Some men feel jealous of the baby's intimate relationship with their partner. Others feel incompetent because they cannot contribute to nourishing their child.

Bottle feeding an infant does make it possible for the father and other caregivers to share in the nurturing process. Some mothers (and fathers) have discovered that maximum contact and closeness can be enjoyed when the infant is held against their naked breast while nursing from a bottle.

Making Adjustments

The time immediately following birth is a critical period for family adjustment. No amount of reading, classes, and expert advice can prepare expectant parents for the real thing. The three months or so following childbirth (the "fourth trimester") constitute the **postpartum period.** This time is one of physical stabilization and emotional adjustment. New mothers, who may well have lost most of their interest in sexual activity during the last weeks of pregnancy, will probably find themselves returning to prepregnancy levels of desire and coital frequency. Some women may have difficulty reestablishing their sexual lives because of fatigue, physiological problems such as continued vaginal bleeding, and worries about the infant (Reamy and White, 1987).

The postpartum period also may be a time of significant emotional upheaval. Even women who had easy and uneventful births may experience a period of "postpartum blues" characterized by alternating periods of crying, unpredictable mood changes, fatigue, irritability, and occasionally mild confusion or lapses of memory. A woman has irregular sleep patterns because of the needs of her newborn, the discomfort of childbirth, or the strangeness of the hospital environment. Some mothers may feel lonely, isolated from their familiar world. Many women blame themselves for their fluctuating moods. They may feel that they have lost control over their lives because of the dependency of their newborns. One woman commented (Boston Women's Book Health Collective, 1978):

We often feel guilty, because we think our own inadequacies are the cause of our unhappiness. We rarely question whether the roles we have are realizable. Because of social pressures surrounding motherhood, and the mystique of the maternal instinct . . . many women are unable to pinpoint their feelings of confusion and inadequacy or are unable to feel that it is legitimate to verbalize their hesitation and problems.

Biological, psychological, and social factors are all involved in postpartum depression. Biologically, during the first several days following delivery, there is an abrupt fall in certain hormone levels. The physiological stress accompanying labor, as well as dehydration, blood loss, and other physical factors, contribute to lowering the woman's stamina. Psychologically, conflicts about her ability to mother, ambiguous feelings toward or rejection of her own mother, and communication problems with the infant or partner may contribute to the new mother's feelings of depression and helplessness. Finally, the social setting into which the child is born is important, especially if the infant represents a financial or emotional burden for the family. Postpartum counseling prior to discharge from the hospital can help couples gain perspective on their situation so that they know what to expect and can evaluate their resources (Reamy and White, 1987).

Although the postpartum blues are felt by many women, they usually don't last more than a couple of weeks. Interestingly, men seem to get a form of postpartum blues as well. Dr. Martha Zaslow and her colleagues (1981) at the National Institute of Child Health observed, "It looks increasingly as if a number of the things we assumed about mothers and motherhood are really typical of parenthood." When infants arrive, many fathers do not feel prepared for their new parenting and financial responsibilities. Some men are overwhelmed by the changes that take place in their marital relationship. Fatherhood is a major transition for them, but their feelings are overlooked, because most people turn their attention to the new mother. (The transition to parenthood for mothers and fathers is discussed at greater length in Chapter 11.)

Perhaps the new father will be allowed (or expected) to have equal status with the mother as a nurturing parent and to take on an equal share of household and child-rearing duties. Then, not only will the mother be able to experience some relief from the physical drain of motherhood, but the father also may experience his family from within rather than as a burdened provider watching from the outside. Studies indicate that "parental similarities far outweigh differences, suggesting that beyond the biological advantage accorded the mother by virtue of her physiology, both parents are equally capable of caring for their young" (Belsky et al., 1984). Both traditional gender roles and our traditional work structure, which does not permit men the opportunity to be at home or to work part-time, stand in the way of fathers participating equally (or replacing mothers) as the primary nurturers. Nature does not prevent men from nurturing, but societal expectations and the social structure do.

The birth of a child is one of the most important events in many people's lives. It fills mothers and fathers alike with a deep sense of accomplishment. The experience itself is profound and totally involving. A father described his daughter's birth (in Armstrong and Feldman, 1990):

Toward the end, Kate had her arms around my neck. I was soothing her, stroking her, and holding her. I felt so close. I even whispered to her that I wanted to make love to her—It wasn't that I would have or meant to—it's just that I felt that bound up with her.

Colleen was born while Kate was hanging from my neck. . . . I looked down and saw Mimi's [the midwife's] hands appearing and then, it seemed like all at once, the baby was in them. I had tears streaming down my face. I was laughing and crying at the same time. . . . Mimi handed her to me with all the goop on her and I never even thought about it. She was so pink. She opened her eyes for the first time in her life right there in my arms. I thought she was the most beautiful thing I had ever seen. There was something about that, holding her just the way she was. . . . I never felt anything like that in my life.

❖ SUMMARY

◆ *Infertility* is defined as the inability to conceive a child after trying for a year or more. The primary causes of male infertility are low sperm count, blocked passageways, and lack of sperm motility. The primary causes of female infertility are blocked fallopian tubes (often the result of *pelvic inflammatory disease*), *endometriosis*, and hormal abnormalities.

◆ The explosion of technological developments in the reproductive field have led to new legal and ethical considerations. These technologies include *ultrasound, chorionic villus sampling, amniocentesis, fetal monitoring, artificial insemination, in vitro fertilization, embryo transfer*, and *surrogate motherhood*. Artificial insemination involves depositing sperm by syringe in a woman's vagina. It is successful about 60 percent of the time. In vitro fertilization (IVF) involves combining sperm and egg in the laboratory and implanting the resultant blastocyst in the uterus of the mother or surrogate.

◆ About 2 percent of the American population is adopted. *Open adoption*, in which the birth mother is actively involved in the process, is increasing, as are foreign adoptions.

◆ The first reliable test of pregnancy can be made two to four weeks after a woman misses her menstrual period. A chemical test called the *agglutination test* will determine the presence of *human chorionic gonadotropin* (HCG) in the urine. *Hegar's sign,* a softening of the uterus, can be detected by a trained examiner. Pregnancy is confirmed by the detection of fetal heartbeats and movements or examination by ultrasound.

◆ A woman's feelings will vary greatly during pregnancy, owing to a number of factors. It is important for her to be able to share her fears and to have support from her partner, friends, relatives, and health-care workers.

◆ *Fertilization* of the ovum by a sperm usually takes place in the fallopian tube. During the first week, the fertilized ovum *(zygote)* divides many times to form a *blastocyst,* which implants itself in the uterine wall. It becomes an *embryo,* then a *fetus,* which is nourished through the *placenta,* an organ that gathers nutrients from the mother's bloodstream and passes them to the fetus via the *umbilical cord.*

◆ Harmful substances—including cocaine, opiates, tobacco, alcohol, marijuana, barbiturates, and caffeine—may be passed to the embryo or fetus through the placenta. Infectious diseases, such as rubella, may damage the fetus. Sexually transmitted diseases may be passed to the infant through the placenta or through the birth canal during childbirth.

◆ *Ectopic pregnancies, spontaneous abortion, preeclampsia,* and *low birth weight* are the most important complications of pregnancy. Preeclampsia is characterized by increasingly high blood pressure after the twenty-fourth week of pregnancy. Premature or low-birth-weight (LBW) babies usually weigh less than 5.5 pounds at birth; often their vital organs are not sufficiently developed.

◆ About 15 percent of pregnancies end in *spontaneous abortion* (miscarriage), largely because of chromosomal abnormalities in the fetus. Infant mortality rates in the United States are high compared to those in other industrialized nations. Infants of poor families are at particularly high risk. Loss of pregnancy or death of a young infant is recognized as a serious life event; parents who suffer this loss need support during the grieving process.

◆ Throughout pregnancy a woman feels *Braxton Hicks contractions,* which exercise the uterus in preparation for labor. The Braxton Hicks contractions also begin the *effacement* (thinning) and *dilation* (opening up) of the cervix to permit delivery.

◆ Labor can be divided into three stages. First-stage labor begins when uterine contractions become regular. When the cervix has dilated approximately ten centimeters, the baby's head enters the birth canal; this is called *transition.* In second-stage labor, the baby emerges from the birth canal. In third-stage labor, the placenta (afterbirth) is expelled.

◆ *Cesarean section* is the removal of the fetus by an incision through the mother's abdomen into her uterus. A dramatic increase in C-sections in recent years has led to criticism that the procedure is used more often than necessary.

◆ *Prepared childbirth* encompasses a variety of methods that stress the importance of understanding the birth process and of relaxation and emotional support of the mother during childbirth.

◆ Hospital birth practices, which have been designed for the convenience of the hospital rather than that of the mother, child, and father have come under increasing criticism. Professionally staffed birthing centers and special birthing rooms in hospitals are providing attractive alternatives to impersonal hospital birth settings for normal births.

◆ Nurse-midwives and lay midwives are trained in obstetric techniques. Many women are now choosing midwives to deliver their babies because they want home births, cannot afford physicians, or prefer the attendance of a woman (most physicians are male, most midwives female).

◆ *Circumcision,* the surgical removal of the foreskin, has been performed routinely in this country for many years. There are no medical reasons for this painful and sometimes dangerous procedure, and the practice is being increasingly questioned. Circumcision holds religious meaning for Jews and Muslims.

◆ About 60 percent of American women breastfeed their children today. Mother's milk is more nutritious than formula or cow's milk and provides immunities to many diseases. Nursing offers emotional rewards to mother and infant.

◆ A critical adjustment period follows the birth of a child. The mother may experience feelings of depression (sometimes called "postpartum blues") that are a result of biological, psychological, and social factors. Participation of the father in nurturing the infant and performing household duties may help alleviate both the mother's and father's feelings of confusion and inadequacy.

Answers to Preview Questions

The answers to the preview questions at the beginning of the chapter are listed below. As you check your answers, whether you were correct or not, think about your reasons for each response. What were they? What was their source? How valid is the source? As you read the chapter, you will find the questions discussed in greater depth.

1.	F	6.	F
2.	T	7.	F
3.	T	8.	F
4.	F	9.	T
5.	T	10.	T

❖ SUGGESTED READINGS

For the most current research findings in obstetrics, see *Obstetrics and Gynecology, The New England Journal of Medicine,* and *JAMA: Journal of the American Medical Association.* For reports on the ethical aspects of biomedical issues, see *The Hastings Center Report.*

Arms, Suzanne. *Adoption: A Handful of Hope.* Berkeley, Calif.: Celestial Arts, 1990 (paperback). A compassionate look at a number of birthmothers and adoptive families and at the issues raised by adoption.

Armstrong, Penny, and Sheryl Feldman. *A Wise Birth.* New York: William Morrow and Company, 1990 (paperback). Written with intelligence and warmth, this thought-provoking book explores the effects of medical technology and technological thinking on modern childbirth.

Boone, Margaret S. *Capital Crime: Black Infant Mortality in America.* Newbury Park, Calif.: Sage Publications, 1989. A sobering look at the devastating effects of discrimination and poverty on African-American children.

Dorris, Michael. *The Broken Cord.* New York: Harper Perennial, 1990 (paperback). A moving account of the author's experience with his adopted son, affected by fetal alcohol syndrome.

Gilman, Lois. *The Adoption Resource Sourcebook.* New York: Harper and Row, 1987 (paperback). A comprehensive guide for those who are contemplating adoption.

Kitzinger, Sheila. *The Complete Book of Pregnancy and Childbirth.* New York: Knopf, 1989 (paperback). A comprehensive, sensitive, and down-to-earth manual for those who are contemplating pregnancy or those who want to understand more about its physiological and psychological aspects.

Menning, Barbara Eck. *Infertility: A Guide for the Childless Couple,* 2d ed. New York: Prentice-Hall Press, 1988 (paperback). Useful information for couples facing infertility.

Panuthos, Claudia, and Catherine Romeo. *Ended Beginnings: Healing Childbearing Losses.* New York: Warner Books, 1984 (paperback). A sensitive approach to healing the grief involved in miscarriages, stillbirths, and neonatal death.

Samuels, Mike, and Nancy Samuels. *The Well Pregnancy Book.* New York: Summit Books, 1986 (paperback). A thorough and practical guide through all phases of pregnancy. If you read just one book on pregnancy, it should probably be this one.

Spock, Benjamin, and Michael Rothenberg. *Dr. Spock's Baby and Child Care.* New York: Pocket Books, 1985 (paperback). Still the "baby bible."

Wertz, Richard, and Dorothy Wertz. *Lying-In: A History of Childbirth in America.* New York: The Free Press, 1977 (paperback). The transformation of childbirth from a family-centered event taking place in the home to an impersonal technological event taking place in the hospital.

READINGS

❖
FERTILITY AND FAMILY: AN OBSESSION WITH PREGNANCY

Katherine Bouton

Katherine Bouton, after delaying pregnancy until her thirties, found that she could not carry one to term. Although she and her husband were delighted with their adopted child, she still had an "overwhelming desire" for the experience of pregnancy and childbirth. To what lengths was she willing to go? What was the doctor's role in her decision-making process? What was the eventual outcome? Has Ms. Bouton resolved her feelings about infertility? In what ways?

When you absolutely cannot have children, it's called sterility. When it seems to be taking an awfully long time but you still hope, that's called infertility. . . . Infertility is worse.

I know because when I finally found out that I absolutely could not have children—without the benefit of miraculous technological intervention—it was a tremendous relief. I could get on with life.

Like most of my contemporaries I spent my twenties trying not to get pregnant. I took the Pill, I tried an IUD, I ended up with a diaphragm. I spent most of my thirties trying to do just the opposite. When I married at 32, my husband and I decided to have children right away since I was getting along in age. At least I thought so at the time. Now that I'm 39 I feel as if I have at least three or four childbearing years ahead of me. The fertility specialist I used to see, when I was still suffering from infertility, now restricts his practice to women between the ages of 40 and 45.

I only gradually realized that I was going to have trouble getting pregnant. Each step led so naturally to the next that I always thought I was on the verge of success. Charts and daily temperature readings led to mild fertility drugs, which led to stronger drugs, easy tests led to harder tests, and exploratory surgery led to major surgery. The last was supposed to do it—my blocked fallopian tubes were now relatively clear. In the meantime, my husband and I had submitted an application to adopt, and barely a year after my tubal surgery, we had a baby. No pregnancy, but a baby, which was what we were after anyway. He was perfect. We were deliriously happy. And if I *were* to get pregnant, it would be fine. We wanted more than one.

Our baby was seven months old when I found out I was pregnant. "I can't be pregnant," I protested. "I just had my period." I was wrong. They always say you can't be just a little bit preg-

continued on next page

nant, but that's what I was. My blood tests showed a very low hormonal level, which my astute gynecologist recognized as a sign of a misplaced (tubal) pregnancy, a condition known as an ectopic (from the Greek "out of place") pregnancy. He sent me for a sonogram, and before I knew it I was in the hospital undergoing surgery to extract the rogue embryo before it ruptured my fallopian tube. The surgery was a success, my tube was saved, my doctor was deservedly proud of himself. After a week in the hospital I went home to my baby. I'd had enough of pregnancy for a while.

The following December, when our son was 16 months old, I got pregnant again. Once again I had not missed my period, but I'd dreamed on three separate occasions that I was pregnant. I felt bloated and nauseated. Again, we hadn't been trying and again I didn't believe it could be possible. This time the numbers looked more encouraging. A blood test a few days later was less promising and a sonogram revealed another ectopic. Another surgery. Another heroic job by my gynecologist.

Paradoxically, these catastrophic pregnancies left me with an overwhelming desire to get pregnant again. I wanted to see a pregnancy through to term. What I had wanted before was a baby. Now I had a baby, a wonderful one, and what I wanted was the experience of pregnancy and childbirth.

Although my gynecologist thought there was still a chance for a normal pregnancy, I was wary of another ectopic and so was he. He suggested we apply to an in vitro fertilization program. I was an ideal candidate, having demonstrated my fertility twice in the past year.

In vitro fertilization is a grueling and expensive procedure, which I will not go into here. But it worked. I got pregnant on my very first try. For the third time in 15 months. My blood tests were terrific, soaring off the charts. The in vitro team hinted at the possibility of twins or even triplets. My own gynecologist, whose assistant was giving me the endless shots of hormones that are part of the in vitro program, was as pleased as if he'd done it himself.

Then, one afternoon, in the tenth week of this pregnancy, as I was crossing a busy street, holding my two-year-old by the hand, I doubled over with a pain in my abdomen. We made it to a taxi, and my child, who even at two was able to rise to an occasion, sat patiently by my side, although his preferred taxi mode was trying to climb out the window. I have never felt so sick, but I refused to believe it was anything but an acute attack of gas. Even my gynecologist refused to believe it, which was why he let me run the risk of rupture and hemorrhage overnight. First thing the next morning I had a sonogram, and within an hour I was once again being admitted for emergency surgery, to the total disbelief of everyone. How could this embryo, so carefully placed in my uterus, have made its way into my fallopian tube? The others had simply failed to make their way down. This one had apparently walked up.

I told my doctor that I wanted my tubes removed, and that my husband agreed. We couldn't go through this again. He demurred. It was so final, he said. I insisted. When I woke up, three hours later, they were gone. I have never felt so immensely relieved, or so sad.

It's been a year and a half since the last time I was pregnant. For the first time in 20 years I haven't thought, when my period was late or I felt some unexplained nausea, that I might be pregnant. In my twenties I would have feared that I was, in my thirties I'd have hoped. Now I figure that my body is simply being unreliable, in its own not very amusing way. Not that I've gotten over infertility. I'm still deeply angry and resentful about what I've gone through and what I never got a chance to go through.

But—and here's the really important part—I no longer suffer from infertility. I'm not simply failing to produce, I'm incapable of producing, and in my mind that means I've graduated from being infertile to being sterile. And it's a great improvement.

We're expecting a second child any day now, from the agency through which we adopted our first. We plan trips, without fearing that I might be pregnant. I can accept assignments and long-term projects with at least the normal minimal assurance that I won't be physically incapacitated in the middle of them. We're making the most of the life we have now, and have stopped worrying about the life we would have if only . . .

We're a family, which is what we were aiming for in the first place.

A NATIVE AMERICAN BIRTH STORY

Marcie Rendon. From *Birth Stories* (edited by Janet Isaacs Ashford).

Marcie Rendon, a Native American midwife, recalls the births of each of her three daughters. How does each birth situation reflect the prevailing attitudes of its time and place? Rendon asks if a Native American birth story is "any different than any woman's birth story." What do you think? What is the story of your birth?

A Native American birth story. Is it any different than any woman's birth story? Any mother, the world over, could come upon a woman in labor anyplace and recognize what was happening. And feel at one with, be supportive of, the woman in labor.

Ever since I can remember, I knew I wanted to have my babies at home. There was never a question in my mind whether I would have children or not. I just knew I would and that I wanted them born at home. I figured, women have given birth since time began, our bodies know what to do and how to do it.

There isn't a birth story. There are birth stories. Mine began with my asking, "Grandpa, tell me again, how were you born?"

"In the snow, girl, just dropped in the snow. My ma didn't know nothin. Raised in mission schools. Didn't know nothin. Just dropped in the snow. Till my grandma heard her cryin and came out and found us. Thought she had to go to the bathroom; went out and dropped me right in the snow. Raised in mission schools. Didn't know nothin.

"Now your ma, she was born the old way. In the fall, during wild rice season. Right there in ricing camp. Your grandma and me were ricing when your ma started to be born. Three old ladies helped her. They stuck sticks in the ground like crutches. Your grandma squatted, hanging on them under her arms. They had medicines for her. Right there. Knew what to do to help your ma be born. Yep, right there in ricing camp, your ma was born. The old way, no trouble. Me, I was dropped in the snow. Thought she had to go to the bathroom. Didn't know nothing. Raised in mission schools."

My birth. Born to an alcoholic mother. Suffering withdrawal along with her during the hospital stay. Nursing, etched in my being as a wordless memory. Remembering her story, laughing. "When I was nursing I had so much milk. My breasts were so big I'd take bets in the bar. I'd take bets that I could set a glass of beer on my tits and drink the foam off. Got a lot of free drinks that way." Laughter. Laughter that filled the whole room. Caught everyone up in it. My mother, dead in my eighteenth year, from alcohol.

Birth stories. My daughters, children of my grandfathers' and grandmothers' dreams. You were a reality long before my passion and your father's seeds conceived you on those winter and spring nights. Visions preceded flesh from my womb. And my generations shall be as one. Spirits healing my mother's madness, my father's sadness. As the daughters of my grandfathers' and grandmothers' dreams touch hands with wind and water, light and love. .

"Tell me Mom, how was I born?" asks my seven-year-old.

Conception. Christmas Eve. Warm glow as the spark of your being ignites. I remember standing at the window that night watching the lights glitter on the snow, knowing that night that you were started in me.

"Your daddy told me I was crazy because I wanted to have you at home. I asked all over, trying to find a midwife. Everyone told me there weren't any, that midwives were a hundred years ago. So I decided I'd have you at home alone. I kept saying, 'Women have given birth since time began; my body knows what to do.' And your daddy just kept telling me I was crazy. As it was, I didn't get any support to have you at home and we ended up in the hospital. They strapped me down and I had to physically fight the nurses, doctor and anesthesiologist not to be gassed or drugged. Your daddy just kept telling me to be good and cooperate. I had back labor and I just kept seeing the fear in his eyes and wishing it would go away. I just wanted to have you my way, with no interference. And you ended up being born by forceps because I wouldn't cooperate. All my energy went into fighting the nurses and doctors until my body just gave up and they pulled you out. But you were a beautiful little girl. When I first got to hold you and nurse you, you just smiled right at me. They didn't want me to nurse you. They kept giving me sugar water to give to you. They told me you'd dehydrate and have brain damage if I didn't give it to you. So I'd drink it myself or pour it down the toilet to keep them off my back. When we went home I was black and blue from where the straps had been, from fighting them so hard to have you the way I'd wanted to have you." My first daughter, Rachel Rainbeaux. My "One of Many Dreams." Rainbeaux. The one who fights for life with every ounce of muscle and energy in her little body.

"And me, Mommy, how was I born?" asks my five-year-old.

"You, my girl, were born in a midwife unit. Again, I wanted to have you at home, but couldn't find a midwife to come. So the midwife unit was a compromise to your dad, who was still too scared to do it alone at home.

"You were conceived in Denver. I remember standing outside after work, waiting for your daddy to pick me up. It was April and it started to rain snow. Huge, soaking wet snowflakes. At the same time I could feel my body ovulating. That night we made love and right afterwards my whole body started to shake. I told your daddy, 'I'm pregnant. You have to get me something to eat.' He thought I was being really silly. I said, 'No, for real, get me something to eat.' So he brought me a big bowl of corn-flakes. That's the night you were started.

"You were born in a hospital midwife unit. The whole birth was beautiful. Calm. Peaceful. Except I had back labor again, even though I'd made one of the nurse-midwives promise I wouldn't have back labor twice in a row. Only during transition did I lose it; the back labor got so bad I said, 'That's it. I quit, give me a cigarette. I'm done.' Everyone just laughed at me and ten minutes later you were born. Another beautiful girl who smiled right at me. I got to hold you right away. Hold you. Love you. Nurse you."

"And my foot, Mom. Tell me about my foot."

"You were born with a crooked foot. So they put a tiny little cast on it the day after you were born and then you had surgery on it when you were four months old."

Simone. My Starfire, with the warmth of a soft summer night, the flicker of eternity in her eyes. Rainy Day Woman—life giver—love flows out of your being and waters the souls of those you touch.

The next four years. Mothering. A divorce. Single parenting. Welfare. Apprenticing. Midwifing. Mothering.

"And the baby, Mom," the seven and five-year-old say. "Where was she born? You finally got to have one of us at home, didn't you?"

continued on next page

My baby, four months old and growing. My home birth. What will I tell her when she's old enough to ask?

"You, my baby girl, were born at home. On the living room floor. Twenty-four hours of the hardest work I ever hope to do. Twenty-four hours of excruciating back labor. You were conceived November 2, 1982. It was right after the full moon, but it was a really cold, dark, hard night. Your dad and I had been seeing each other off and on. That just happened to be one of the 'on' nights. But the thing I remember most was that for about a month before that, every night when I'd got to bed, I'd hear three knocks on the window. I'd say, 'Bendigan, come in,' like I was taught to say when the spirits are heard. Well, November 2 was the last night I heard the three knocks. Again I knew I was pregnant right away. It was so free this time, because I knew I could do whatever I wanted with the pregnancy and birth. I could have women around me to be supportive of me. I spotted a little blood in the third month, so in the seventh month we went up north to be doctored by a medicine man for a low placenta. The very first time he saw me, he said, 'Another girl, huh? Well, we'll keep prayin for a boy.' He also told me my delivery would be dangerous, to not have anyone around who would be afraid. Well babe, you were born in the heat of the hottest summer I remember. We spent all our money all summer going where it was cool—swimming, air-conditioned shopping malls, swimming, to friends' houses that had air-conditioning, and swimming again. Your birth. Like I said, long and hard. Twenty-four hours of excruciating back labor. I walked and squatted the whole time. Trying to dance you down into a more straight up and down position. We had a grandmother, a midwife and an apprentice here to help us. Three of the most beautiful women I've ever seen. At one point I got a contraction band around my uterus, looked like a rubber band being tightened around my belly. I got scared for you. I said, 'I want to go in.' I started praying the Serenity Prayer—God grant me the serenity to accept the things I cannot change (the band, the back labor, the pain), and the courage to change the things I can (my position). I walked from the dining room to the living room and squatted down by a chair. The band disappeared and I started pushing. Hard work. Three hours of pushing during which time I visualized the Viet Nam war. Telling myself, if my brother could live through that, I could live through pushing one baby out. Just before you were born I told them I was bleeding. They said no, there wasn't any blood. Your head was born, your shoulders stuck. As soon as you were completely born the blood gushed out. Your cord was too short to nurse you or even pick you up enough to tell if you were a girl or boy. But you were lying on my belly. The first thing you did was lift your head up, look at me and smile. Another beautiful girl. They had to call another midwife to help stop the bleeding and fix the tear. And you baby, you never missed a beat. Like a turtle, your little heart never even flickered a sign of distress. Born at home. I held you, nursed you, loved you. Another beautiful, beautiful girl."

Awanewquay. Quiet, calm, peaceful little woman. Awan. Fog Woman. Three knocks announcing your intention. Birth and death inseparable. Birth—the coming of the spirit to this world. Death—the going of the spirit to that world. Fog Woman. The cloud of mystery. With your sisters I felt strong, powerful. After they were born I felt, if I can do that, I can move mountains. Well, honey, with you I moved the mountain. With all humbleness, I moved the mountain.

A Native American birth story. It is the story of the generations. I gave birth because I was born a woman. The seeds of the future generations were carried in my womb. I remember conception because the female side of life is always fertile first. I gave birth three times as naturally as possible, given the situation, because as a woman my body and heart knew what to do. I nursed because my breasts filled with milk. I remember their names because that is how they will be recognized by their grandfathers and grandmothers who have gone on before. I am a mother because I was given three daughters to love. I am a midwife because women will continue to give birth. That is my story. Megwitch. I am Marcie Rendon, Awanewquay, of the Eagle Clan, Ojibwe.

PART FOUR

Development

Marriage as Process

To gain a sense of what you already know about the material covered in this chapter, answer "true" or "false" to the following statements below. You will find the answers on page 318.

1. More women than men tend to live with their parents. True or false?
2. Marriage more than parenthood radically affects a woman's life. True or false?
3. The advent of children generally increases a couple's marital satisfaction. True or false?
4. Grandparents tend to play an authoritative role in the lives of African Americans. True or false?
5. The elderly have one of the lowest poverty rates of any group in the United States. True or false?
6. The empty nest syndrome, characterized by maternal depression after the last child leaves home, is a major problem in American families. True or false?
7. Enduring marriages almost always have a high level of marital satisfaction. True or false?
8. Most elderly men and women see their children two or fewer times a year. True or false?
9. Widows generally remarry within two years. True or false?
10. Parenting roles change rather than end once children leave home. True or false?

*. . . if one advances confidently in the
direction of his dreams, and endeavors to
live the life which he has imagined, he will
meet with a success unexpected in his
common hours.*

Henry David Thoreau

M ARRIAGE IS A PROCESS IN WHICH PEOPLE INTERACT WITH EACH OTHER, create families, and give each other companionship and love. Marriage is not static; it is
always changing to meet new situations, new emotions, new commitments and
responsibilities. The marriage process may begin informally with cohabitation or formally with engagement. Marriage itself ends with divorce or with the death of a partner. We may begin marriage thinking we know how to act within it, but we find that
the reality of marriage requires us to be more flexible than we had anticipated. We
need flexibility to meet our needs, our partners' needs, and the needs of the marriage. We may have periods of great happiness and great sorrow within marriage.
We may find boredom, intensity, frustration, and fulfillment. Some of these may
occur because of our marriage; others may occur in spite of it. But, as we shall see,
marriage encompasses many possibilities.

❖ THE DEVELOPMENTAL PERSPECTIVE

The developmental framework, one of the most influential ways of looking at families, is an interdisciplinary approach that unites sociology and related disciplines
with child and human development (Duvall, 1988). It sees individual and family
development as interacting with each other.

The Individual Life Cycle

Our identity, our sense of who we are, is not fixed or frozen. It changes as we
mature. At different points in our lives, we are confronted with different developmental tasks. Our growth as human beings depends on the way we resolve these
problems. Erik Erikson (1963) describes the human life cycle as containing eight
developmental stages. At each stage we have an important developmental task to
accomplish, and each stage intimately involves the family. The way we deal with
these stages, which are summarized here, is strongly influenced by our families and
marriages. We cannot separate our identity from either.

INFANCY: TRUST VERSUS MISTRUST. In the first year of life, children are wholly dependent on their parenting figures for survival. It is then they learn to trust by having
their needs satisfied, by being loved, held, and caressed. Without loving care, the
infant may develop a mistrusting attitude toward others and toward life in general.

TODDLER: AUTONOMY VERSUS SHAME AND DOUBT. Between ages one and three, children learn to walk and talk; they begin toilet training. At this stage they need to
develop a sense of independence and mastery over their environment and themselves. Parents need to encourage independence and make toilet training a positive
rather than shameful experience.

EARLY CHILDHOOD: INITIATIVE VERSUS GUILT. Ages four to five are years of increasing
independence. The family must allow the child to develop initiative while at the
same time directing the child's energy. The child must not be made to feel guilty
about his or her desire to explore the world.

SCHOOL AGE: INDUSTRY VERSUS INFERIORITY. Between ages six and eleven, children
begin to learn that their activities pay off, that they can be creative. The family needs

peers can be very cruel.

to encourage the child's sense of accomplishment. Failing to do so may lead to feelings of inferiority in the child.

ADOLESCENCE: IDENTITY VERSUS ROLE DIFFUSION. The years of puberty between ages twelve and eighteen may be a time of turmoil, when adolescents try new roles as they make the transition to adulthood. To make a successful transition, they need to develop goals, a philosophy of life, a sense of self. The family needs to be supportive as the adolescent tentatively explores adulthood. If the adolescent fails to establish a firm identity, he or she is likely to drift without purpose.

YOUNG ADULTHOOD: INTIMACY VERSUS ISOLATION. These are the years when the adolescent leaves home and begins to establish intimate ties with other people through cohabitation, marriage, or other important intimate relationships. Without making other intimate connections, the young adult may be condemned to isolation and loneliness.

ADULTHOOD: GENERATIVITY VERSUS SELF-ABSORPTION. Now the individual establishes his or her own family and finds satisfaction in family relationships. It is a time of creativity. Work becomes important as a creative act, perhaps as important as family or an alternative to it. The failure to be productive may lead to self-centeredness and a "what's-in-it-for-me" attitude toward life.

production, making something of oneself

The young are slaves to dreams; the old servants of regrets. Only the middle aged have all their senses.

Hervy Allen

MATURITY: INTEGRITY VERSUS DESPAIR. In old age, the individual looks back on life to understand its meaning—to assess what has been accomplished and to gauge the meaning of his or her relationships. Those who can make a positive judgment have a feeling of wholeness about their lives. The alternative is despair.

when people become unhappy now they look back at how they acted

❖ **REFLECTIONS** *As you look at these stages, where are you in the life cycle? What is the psychological task that Erikson says you need to accomplish? Is it an important issue for you? How are you resolving it?*

The Family Life Cycle

Just as individuals have life cycles with specific stages, so do marriages and families. Within these stages each marriage and family has its own unique history (Aldous, 1978). The concept of the **family life cycle** uses a developmental framework to explain people's behavior in families. According to the developmental framework, families change over time in terms of both the people who are members of the family and the roles they play. At various stages in the family life cycle, the family has different developmental tasks to perform. Much of the behavior of family members can be explained in terms of the family's developmental stage. The key factor in such developmental studies is the presence of children. The family organizes itself around its childrearing responsibilities. A woman's role as wife is different when she is childless than when she has children. A man's role is different when he is the father of a one-year-old than when he is the father of a fifteen-year-old.

The family life-cycle approach gives us important insights into the complexities of family life. Not only is the family performing various tasks during its life cycle, but each family member takes on various developmental tasks during each stage of the life cycle. The task for families with adolescents is to give their children greater

The whole world is a comedy to those who think, a tragedy to those who feel.

Horace Walpole (1717–1797)

autonomy and independence. While the family is coping with this new developmental task, an adolescent daughter has her own individual task of trying to develop a satisfactory identity. Meanwhile, her older brother is struggling with intimacy issues, her younger sister is developing industry, her parents are dealing with issues of generativity, and her grandparents are confronting issues of integrity.

STAGES OF THE FAMILY LIFE CYCLE. One of the most widely used approaches divides the family life cycle into eight stages (Duvall and Miller, 1985). The eight-stage approach reflects the model life cycle. It does not encompass the family life cycle of single-parent or remarried families.

◆ *Stage I: Beginning Families.* During this stage, the married couple has no children. In the past this stage was relatively short, because children soon followed marriage. Today, however, it may last until a couple is in their late twenties or thirties. On the average, this stage is about two or three years. In the 1980s the average age for women to have their first child was twenty-five. Most studies on marital satisfaction agree that couples experience their greatest satisfaction in this stage (Glenn, 1991).

◆ *Stage II: Childbearing Families.* Because families tend to space their children about thirty months apart, the family is still considered to be forming. By this time the average family has two children. Although mothers are deeply involved in childbearing and childrearing, about half work outside the home. Stage II lasts around two and a half years. Marital satisfaction begins to lessen and continues to decline through the stage of families with schoolchildren (IV) or those with teenagers (V).

◆ *Stage III: Families with Preschool Children.* This family's oldest child is thirty months to six years. The parents, especially the mother, are still deeply involved in childrearing. This stage lasts about three and a half years.

◆ *Stage IV: Families with Schoolchildren.* This family's oldest child is between six and thirteen years old. With the children in school and more free time, the mother has more options available to her. By now, most women have reentered the job market. This stage lasts about seven years.

◆ *Stage V: Families with Adolescents.* In a family with adolescents, the oldest child is between thirteen and twenty years old. Marital satisfaction reaches its nadir. This stage lasts about seven years.

◆ *Stage VI: Families as Launching Centers.* By this time, the first child has been launched into the adult world. This stage lasts until the last child leaves home, a period averaging about eight years. Virtually all studies show that marital satisfaction begins to rise for most couples during this stage.

◆ *Stage VII: Families in the Middle Years.* This stage lasts from the time the last child has left home to retirement. It is commonly referred to as the "empty nest" stage. It is a distinct new phase in the family life cycle (Borland, 1982). Until this century most parents continued to have children until middle age, and the childrearing and launching periods were extended into old age. The empty nest period has increased from two to thirteen years in this century; it is one of the most dramatic changes that has occurred in the family life-cycle pattern (Glick, 1977a). More recently, however, because of deferred marriage and the high cost of housing, many adult children continue to live at home or return home after being away for a number of years. This "not-so-empty nest" phase, argue some scholars, constitutes a more recent variation in the middle-years stage (Glick, 1989; Mattessich and Hill, 1987). At this time, many families begin caretaking activities for elderly relatives, especially parents and parents-in-law.

◆ *Stage VIII: Aging Families.* The working members of the aging family have retired. Usually, the husband retires before the wife, since he tends to be older. If the wife works, the husband may remain alone at home until she also retires (Keith et al., 1981). Chronic illnesses begin to take their toll. Eventually, one of the spouses dies, usually the husband. The surviving spouse may live with other family members or be cared for by them.

FAMILY LIFE-CYCLE VARIATIONS. A major limitation of the family life-cycle approach is its tendency to focus on the intact nuclear family as "the family." Paul Glick, who coined the term "family life cycle" in 1947, has noted that there are a number of social changes affecting the traditional family life cycle (Glick, 1989). Deferred marriages, the rise of cohabitation, divorce, remarriage, single parenthood, and gay and lesbian families introduce notable variations in the life course of the family. As marriages are increasingly deferred, cohabitation rates have skyrocketed. It may be useful, Glick suggests, to include a cohabitational stage that recognizes the significance of living together in family development. In addition, the family life cycle of single adults is considerably different from that of their married counterparts. For childless adults who have never married, the families of orientation may become the central family focus. Single women, for example, may be intimately connected to their parents as caregivers; these women may be tied to children as aunts (Allen and Pickett; 1987; Allen, 1989).

Scholars are also recognizing the importance for ethnicity to family life cycles. The timing of the various stages, for example, is affected by ethnicity. African Americans are less likely to marry than whites; blacks who marry often do so at a later age. Single parenthood is more prevalent among African-American families than among white ones. In 1988, for example, 59 percent of black families were headed by single parents compared to 22 percent of white families (Rawlings, 1989). African Americans are also more likely than whites or Latinos to begin their family life cycle with unmarried single-parent families.

Of all these variations, researchers are increasingly focusing on two common alternatives to the traditional intact family life cycle: the single-parent and the stepfamily life cycles. Today, nearly one out of three families is a single-parent family, formed either through divorce or births to single women.

Most single-parent families are headed by divorced women, who usually divorce between stages II and IV, during the childbearing through school-age stages. About 72 percent of recently divorced women will remarry. If they remarry, the single-parent stage generally lasts between three and six years. If these divorced women do not remarry, they continue their single parenting until their adolescent children are launched (Mattessich and Hill, 1987).

The second type of single-parent family originates with unmarried mothers. Almost one out of every four births in this country is to an unmarried mother. Currently more than half of the children born to African Americans and 17 percent of those born to whites are born to unmarried mothers (U.S. Bureau of the Census, 1991). Some of the mothers are divorced but the majority have never been married. About a third are adolescents and another third are between ages twenty and twenty-four years. They usually have become pregnant unintentionally. Their family life cycle begins with a single-parent family as its first stage. In this stage, the young mother (especially if she is adolescent) and her child often live with the child's grandmother or cohabit with the child's father. The second stage may be marriage. After marriage, the family life cycle may follow more traditional patterns or diverge back into the single-parent pattern. Families that begin with single parenthood, however, are more likely to be unstable (Mattessich and Hill, 1987).

The number of marriages is greater in proportion to the ease and convenience of supporting a family. When families can be easily supported, more persons marry and earlier in life.

Benjamin Franklin

T A B L E 10.1   Individual and Marital Stages of Development

ITEM	STAGE 1 (18–21 YEARS)	STAGE 2 (22–28 YEARS)	STAGE 3 (29–31 YEARS)	STAGE 4 (32–39 YEARS)	STAGE 5 (40–42 YEARS)	STAGE 6 (43–59 YEARS)	STAGE 7 (60 YEARS AND OVER)
Individual stage	Developing roots	Provisional adulthood	Transition at age 30	Settling down	Mid-life transition	Middle adulthood	Older age
Individual task	Developing autonomy	Developing intimacy and occupational identification; getting into the adult world	Deciding about commitment to work and marriage	Deepening commitments; pursuing more long-range goals	Searching for "fit" between aspirations and environment	Restabilizing and reordering priorities	Dealing effectively with aging, illness, and death while retaining zest for life
Marital task	Shift from family of origin to new commitment	Provisional marital commitment	Commitment crisis; restlessness	Productivity: children, work, friends, and marriage	Summing up: success and failure are evaluated and future goals sought	Resolving conflicts and stabilizing the marriage for the long haul	Supporting and enhancing each other's struggle for productivity and fulfillment in face of the threats of aging
Marital conflict	Original family ties conflict with adaptation	Uncertainty about choice of marital partner; stress over parenthood	Doubts about choice come into sharp conflict; rates of growth may diverge if spouse has not success- fully negotiated stage 2 because of parental obligations	Husband and wife have different and conflicting ways of achieving productivity	Husband and wife perceive "success" differently; conflict between individual success and remaining in the marriage	Conflicting rates and directions of emotional growth; concerns about losing youthfulness may lead to depression and/or acting out	Conflicts are generated by rekindled fears of desertion, loneliness, and sexual failure
Intimacy	Fragile intimacy	Deepening but ambivalent intimacy	Increasing distance while partners make up their minds about each other	Marked increase in intimacy in "good" mar- riages; gradual distancing in "bad" marriages	Tenuous intimacy as fantasies about others increase	Intimacy is threatened by aging and by boredom vis-à-vis a secure and stable rela- tionship; departure of chil- dren may in- crease or decrease intimacy	Struggle to main- tain intimacy in the face of eventual separation; in most marriages this dimension achieves a stable plateau
Power	Testing of power	Establishment of patterns of conflict resolution	Sharp vying for power and dominance	Establishment of definite patterns of decision making and dominance	Power in outside world is tested vis-à-vis power in the marriage	Conflicts often increase when children leave, and security appears threatened	Survival fears stir up needs for control and dominance

continued on next page

T A B L E 10.1   Individual and Marital Stages of Development (*continued*)

ITEM	STAGE 1 (18–21 YEARS)	STAGE 2 (22–28 YEARS)	STAGE 3 (29–31 YEARS)	STAGE 4 (32–39 YEARS)	STAGE 5 (40–42 YEARS)	STAGE 6 (43–59 YEARS)	STAGE 7 (60 YEARS AND OVER)
Marital boundaries	Conflicts over in-laws	Friends and potential lovers; work versus family	Temporary disruptions including extramarital sex or reactive "fortress building"	Nuclear family closes boundaries	Disruption due to reevaluation; drive versus restabilization	Boundaries are usually fixed except in crises such as illness, death, job change, and sudden shift in role relationships	Loss of family and friends leads to closing in of boundaries; physical environment is crucial in maintaining ties with the outside world

From Levinson et al., 1974. Reprinted with permission from Berman, F., & Lief, H. Marital therapy from a psychiatric perspective: An overview, *American Journal of Psychiatry*, 132(6): 586, June 1975.

Stepfamilies are formed when either the husband or wife has children from a previous marriage or relationship. After single parenthood, the stepfamily generally forms during the school-age and adolescent family stages (Mattessich and Hill, 1987). The parents and stepparents, who are usually aged thirty years or older, have a double developmental task: they must simultaneously enter beginning marriage *and* childrearing stages.

❖ REFLECTIONS   *As you examine the different stages, find the stage in which your family of orientation or marriage is. What are the tasks it confronts? In what individual developmental tasks are the different members of your family engaged?*

❖ BEGINNING MARRIAGES

Cohabitation, Engagement, and Weddings

The first stage of the family life cycle may begin with engagement or cohabitation followed by a wedding, the ceremony that represents the beginning of a marriage.

Engagement is the culmination of the formal dating process. Today, in contrast to the past, engagement has greater significance as a ritual than as a binding commitment to be married. Engagement is losing its ritualistic meaning, however, as more couples start out in the less traditional "getting together" pattern or live together. These couples are less likely to become formally engaged. Instead, they announce that they "plan to get married." Because it lacks the formality of engagement, "planning" to get married is also less socially binding.

Engagement performs several functions:

◆ Engagement signifies a commitment to marriage and helps define the goal of the relationship as marriage.
◆ Engagement prepares couples for marriage by requiring them to think about the realities of everyday married life—money, friendships, religion, in-laws. They are expected to begin making serious plans about how they will live together as a married couple.

Courtship is as old as Adam and Eve, who got off to a fast start by being naked when they met.

Jack Smith

To speak frankly, I am not in favour of long engagements. They give people the opportunity of finding out each other's character before marriage, which I think is never advisable.

Oscar Wilde, The Importance of Being Earnest

Matrimony is a process by which a grocer acquires an account the florist had.

Francis Rodman

◆ Engagement is the beginning of kinship. The future marriage partner begins to be treated as a member of the family. He or she begins to become integrated into the family system.
◆ Engagement allows the prospective partners to strengthen themselves as a couple. The engaged pair begin to experience themselves as a social unit. They leave the youth or singles culture and prepare for the world of the married, a remarkably different world.

COHABITATION. The rise of cohabitation has led to its becoming an alternative beginning of the contemporary family life cycle (Glick, 1989; Surra, 1991). A quarter of the men and women who marry, for example, are living together at the time of their marriage; forty percent of couples who remarry live together prior to marriage (Coleman and Ganong, 1991; Glenn, 1991). They may have children.

Honor—a moral cousin of manners—requires your telling the truth about yourself before the wedding.

Miss Manners

Although cohabiting couples may be living together before marriage, their relationship is not legally recognized until the wedding. Nor is the relationship afforded the same social legitimacy. Relatives do not consider cohabitors, for example, as kin such as sons-in-law or daughters-in-law. At the same time, however, there is some evidence that cohabitation helps prepare a couple for marriage and weeds out incompatible couples (Glenn, 1991). It also performs some of the same functions as engagement, such as preparing the couple for some of the realities of marriage and helping them think of themselves in terms of being a couple as well as individuals.

Ceremonies are the outward expression of inner feeling.

Lao-tzu (d. 531 B.C.)

THE WEDDING. Weddings are ancient rituals that symbolize a couple's commitment to each other. The word *wedding* is derived from the Anglo-Saxon *wed,* meaning "pledge" (Chesser, 1980). The exchanging of rings dates back to ancient Egypt and symbolizes trust, unity, and timelessness, since a ring has no beginning and no end. It is a powerful symbol. (When singles meet for the first time, one of their first acts may be to glance at each other's fingers to see if there is a wedding ring.) To return a ring or take it off in anger is a symbolic act. Not wearing a ring may be a symbolic statement about a marriage. Another custom, carrying the bride over the threshold, was practiced in ancient Greece and Rome. It was a symbolic abduction growing out of the belief that a daughter would not willingly leave her father's house. The eating of cake is similarly ancient, representing the offerings made to household gods; the cake made the union sacred (Coulanges, 1960). The honeymoon tradition can be traced to a pagan custom for insuring fertility: each night after the marriage ceremony, the couple drank honey wine until the moon completed a full cycle. The honeymoon was literally a time of intoxication for the newly married man and woman.

Marriage often unites for life two people who scarcely know each other.

Honoré Balzac

Church weddings are medieval in origin, a result of the church expanding its power over secular matters. Before that time, marriage was a family affair in which the father "gave" his daughter away in marriage. The church usurped the family's power and declared marriage a sacrament. As a divine institution, marriage could not be dissolved.

Whether a first or second (or third) marriage, the central meaning of a wedding is that it symbolizes a profound life transition. Most significantly, the man and woman take on marital roles. For young men and women entering marriage the first time, marriage signifies a major step into adulthood. Some of the apprehension felt by those planning to marry may be related to their taking on these important new roles and responsibilities. Many will have a child in the first year of marriage. (Over 20 percent of all women are pregnant when they marry.) Therefore, the wedding must be considered a major rite of passage. Before a man and a woman exchange their marriage vows, they are single, and their primary responsibilities are to themselves.

Weddings are ceremonies that mark the transition from singlehood to marriage. They symbolize the entrance into society's major adult roles: husband/wife and (potentially) father/mother.

Their parents may have greater claims on them than they do on each other. But with the exchange of a few words, they are transformed. When they leave the wedding scene, they leave behind singlehood. They are now responsible to each other as fully as they are to themselves and more than they are to their parents.

❖ REFLECTIONS *Do you plan to have (or did have) an informal wedding? What will the wedding symbolize for you? What will it symbolize for your families of orientation? How will it assist the transition to marital roles?*

Establishing Marital Roles

The expectations that two people have about their own and each other's marital roles are based on gender roles and their own experience. There are four traditional assumptions about husband/wife responsibilities: (1) The husband is the head of the household, (2) the husband is responsible for supporting the family, (3) the wife is responsible for domestic work, and (4) the wife is responsible for childrearing.

The traditional assumptions about marital responsibilities do not necessarily reflect marital reality, however. For example, the husband traditionally may be regarded as head of the family, but power tends to be shared. With the rise of dual-earner families, there is no longer a single provider. Both men and women contribute to the financial support of the family; in fact, women earn more than men in about 20 percent of marriages (Atkinson and Boles, 1984). Although responsibility for domestic work still tends to reside with women, men are beginning to share housework. The mother is generally still responsible for childrearing, but fathers are beginning to participate more.

Although tradition has assigned many of these responsibilities along gender lines, they do not always fit the temperament and abilities of a particular husband and wife or the needs of the family.

Married in haste, we repent at leisure.

William Congreve (1670–1729)

. . . until two people, who are married, look into each other's eyes and make a solemn commitment to each other—that they will stop at nothing, that they will face any cost, any pain, any struggle, go out of their way so that they may learn and seek in order that they may make their marriage a continuously growing experience—until two people have done that they are not in my judgement married.

David Mace and Vera Mace

There are a number of marital tasks that newly married couples need to begin in order to build and strengthen their marriages. The failure to successfully complete these tasks may contribute to what researchers identify as the "duration of marriage effect," the tendency for marital satisfaction to decrease over time (see Perspective, pp. 302–303). These tasks are primarily adjustment tasks and include the following:

◆ *Establishing marital and family roles.* Discuss marital role expectations for self and partner; make appropriate adjustments to fit each other's needs and the needs of the marriage. Discuss childbearing issues; negotiate parental roles and responsibilities.

◆ *Providing emotional fulfillment and support for each other.* Learn how to give and receive love and affection, support the other emotionally and fulfill one's own identity as both an individual and a partner.

◆ *Adjusting personal habits.* Adjust to each other's personal ways by enjoying, accepting, tolerating, or changing personal habits, tastes, and preferences, such as differing sleep patterns, levels of personal and household cleanliness, musical tastes, and spending habits.

◆ *Negotiating gender roles.* Adjust gender roles and tasks to reflect individual personalities, skills, needs, interests, and equity.

◆ *Making sexual adjustments with each other.* Learn how to physically show affection and love, discover mutual pleasures and satisfactions, negotiate timing and activities, and decide on the use of birth control.

◆ *Establishing family/employment priorities.* Balance employment and family goals; recognize importance of unpaid household labor as work; negotiate childcare responsibilities; decide on whose employment, if either, receives priority. Divide household responsibilities equitably.

◆ *Developing communication skills.* Share intimate feelings and ideas with each other. Learn how to talk to each other about difficulties. Share moments of joy and pain. Establish communication rules, such as never threatening or walking out during a disagreement. Learn how to negotiate differences to enhance the marriage.

◆ *Managing budgetary and financial matters.* Establish mutually agreed-upon budget; make short-term and long-term financial goals, such as saving for vacations or home purchase. Establish rules for resolving money conflicts.

◆ *Establishing kin relationships.* Participate in extended family; manage boundaries between family of marriage and family of orientation.

◆ *Participating in larger community.* Make friends; meet neighbors. Become involved in community, school, church, or political activities.

As you can see, there are numerous tasks that a newly married couple must undertake as their marriage takes form. If the tasks are undertaken in a spirit of love and cooperation, they offer the potential for marital growth, richness, and connection. (Whitbourne and Ebmeyer, 1990). But if they are avoided or undertaken in a selfish or rigid manner, the result may be conflict and marital dissatisfaction.

IDENTITY BARGAINING. People carry around idealized pictures of marriage long before they meet their marriage partner. They have to adjust these preconceptions to the reality of their partner's personality and the circumstances of their marriage. The process of adjustment is called **identity bargaining** (Blumstein, 1975). The most important person in this process is the partner. Mirra Komarovsky (1987) pointed out that a spouse has a "vital stake" in getting his or her partner to fulfill certain obligations. "Hardly any aspect of marriage is exempt from mutual instruction and pressures to change," she wrote.

Identity bargaining is a three-step process:

◆ First, a person has to identify with the role he or she is performing. A man must *feel* that he is a husband and a woman must *feel* that she is a wife. The wedding ceremony acts as a catalyst for role change from the single state to the married state.

◆ Second, a person must be treated by the other as if he or she fulfills the role. The husband must treat his wife as a wife; the wife must treat her husband as a husband. The problem is that a couple rarely agrees on what actually constitutes the roles of husband and wife. This is especially true now as the traditional content of marital roles is changing.

◆ Third, the two people must negotiate changes in each other's roles. A woman may have learned that she is supposed to defer to her husband, but if he makes an unfair demand, how can she do this? A man may believe his wife is supposed to be receptive to him whenever he wishes to make love, but if she is not, how should he interpret her sexual needs? A woman may not like housework (who does?), but she may be expected to do it as part of her marital role. Does she then do all the housework or does she ask her husband to share responsibility with her? A man believes he is supposed to be strong, but sometimes he feels weak—does he reveal this to his wife? Eventually, these adjustments must be made. At first, however, there may be confusion; both partners may feel inadequate because they are not fulfilling their role expectations.

Although some may fear losing their identity in the give and take of identity bargaining, the opposite may be true: one's sense of identity may actually grow in the process of establishing a relationship. A major study by Whitbourne and Ebmeyer (1990) on marriage and identity concludes:

Couples can grow as individuals and as a pair through the operation of the identity processes. . . . The attempt that couples make to accommodate each other has its benefits as the alliance between them is strengthened and solidified. . . . The relationship between identity and intimacy is reciprocal. Perhaps the greatest impetus for growth of identity is through the unique and intense bond that the intimate relationship can offer.

In the process of forming a relationship, you discover yourself. An intimate relationship requires you to define who you are.

Establishing Boundaries

When young people marry, they often have strong ties to their parents. Until the wedding, their family of orientation has greater claim to their loyalties than their spouse-to-be. Once the ceremony is completed, however, the newlyweds must establish their own family independent of their families of orientation. The couple must negotiate a different relationship with their parents, siblings, and in-laws. Loyalties must shift from their families of orientation to their newly formed family. The families of orientation must accept and support these breaks (Minuchin, 1974). Indeed, opening themselves to outsiders who have become in-laws places no small stress on families (Carter and McGoldrick, 1989).

The new family must establish its own boundaries. The couple must decide how much interaction with their families is desirable and how much influence their families of orientation may have. There are often important ties to the parents that may prevent new families from achieving their needed independence. First is the tie of habit. Parents are used to being superordinate; children are used to being subordinate. The tie between mothers and daughters is especially strong; daughters often experience greater difficulty separating themselves from their mothers than do sons.

Marriage is that relation between men and women in which the independence is equal, the dependence mutual and the obligation reciprocal.

L. Anspacher

It is an easier thing to be a lover than a husband, for the same reason that it is more difficult to be witty everyday than now and then.

Honoré Balzac

When a young man marries, he divorces his mother.

Yiddish Proverb

T A B L E 10.2 Changing Marital Roles: Norms and Behaviors

DOMAIN	NORMS	CHANGE OCCURRED[1]	IMPLEMENTATION BY MAJORITY
1. Division of Labor			
Economic	acceptance of wives' and mothers' labor force participation	yes	yes
	acceptance of shared responsibility for provider role	low	no
Housework	acceptance of mutual and flexible participation in housework	yes	yes
	acceptance of shared responsibility for housework	low	no
Childcare	acceptance of mutual and flexible participation in childcare	yes	yes
	acceptance of shared responsibility for children	low	no
Total work	acceptance of equality in spouses' work load	yes	yes
2. Authority	acceptance of shared participation in all family decisions	yes	yes
	acceptance of shared authority	low	no
	acceptance of use of similar power tactics	?[3]	?
	rejection of use of physical force[2]	?	(yes)
3. Sexual relations	acceptance of same sexual standards for both sexes	yes	partially
	acceptance of right to equal sexual gratification	yes	yes
	acceptance of shared participation in sexual decisions	yes	no

DOMAIN	BEHAVIOR	CHANGE OCCURRED[1]	IMPLEMENTATION BY MAJORITY
1. Division of Labor			
Economic	wives' and mothers' labor force	yes	yes
	equal contribution of spouses to family income	some	no
Housework	mutual and flexible participation in housework	low	no
	equal time spent with housework	low	no
Childcare	mutual and flexible participation in childcare	some	no
	equal time spent with childcare	low	no
Total work	equal workload of spouses	low	no
2. Authority	shared participation in all family decisions	low	no
	use of similar power tactics by both partners	?	no
	use of physical force	?	(yes)
3. Sexual relations	equal participation in sexual activities	yes	partially
	equal sexual gratification	yes	partially
	shared participation in sexual decisions	some	no

[1]Change refers to evidence regarding increased acceptance/enactment of norms/behaviors characteristic of the sex-role transcendent model, implementation refers to the acceptance/enactment of such norms/behaviors by the majority (over 50%).

[2]Application of the majority rule is probably inappropriate here, but the majority of respondents reject use of physical force in marital relations.

[3]? indicates lack of clear empirical evidence.

SOURCE: From M. Szinovacz. "Changing Family Roles and Interactions." *The Marriage and Family Review.* 7(3/4), 1984.

These continuing ties may cause an adult child to feel conflicting loyalties toward parents and spouse (Cohler and Geyer, 1982). Much conflict occurs when a spouse feels an in-law is exerting too much influence on his or her partner—for example, a mother-in-law insisting that her son visit each Sunday and the son accepting despite the protests of his wife, or a father-in-law warning his son-in-law to establish himself in a career or risk losing his wife. If conflict occurs, husbands and wives need to put the needs of their spouses ahead of their parents.

Another tie to the family of orientation may be money. Newly married couples often have little money or credit with which to begin their families. They may turn to parents to borrow money, cosign loans, or obtain credit. But financial dependence keeps the new family tied to the family of orientation. The parents may try to exert undue influence on their children because it is their money, not their children's money, that is being spent. They may try to influence their children's purchases; they may refuse to loan money to buy something of which they disapprove.

The critical task is to form a family that is interdependent rather than totally independent or dependent. It is a delicate balancing act as parents and their adult children begin to make adjustments to the new marriage. We need to maintain bonds with our families of orientation and to participate in the extended family network, but we cannot let those bonds turn into chains.

> Some young men and women use marriage as a means of breaking away from overpossessive parents. But marriage which is considered by the participants as part of the strategy of emancipation from parents will bring with it tremendous psychological hazards. Despite their ostensible defiance, children who seek so drastic a means of establishing their independence have by no means done so efficiently. The complexities and subtleties of this parent-child battle reflect themselves in the marriage itself. In-law problems may thus be one phase of parent-child relational problems.
>
> *Jessie Bernard*

❖ YOUTHFUL MARRIAGES II → IV

Youthful marriages represent stages II through IV in the family life cycle: childbearing families (stage II), families with small children (stage III), and families with school-age children (stage IV).

> Any marriage, happy or unhappy, is infinitely more interesting and significant than any romance, however passionate.
>
> *W. H. Auden*

Impact of Children

Husband and wife both usually work until their first child is born; about half of all working women leave the workplace for at least a short period of time to attend to childrearing responsibilities after the birth of their first child. The husband continues his job or career. Although the first child makes him a father, fatherhood generally does not radically alter his relationship with his work. The woman's life, however,

Reprinted by permission of UFS, Inc.

changes dramatically with motherhood. If she continues her outside employment, she is usually responsible for arranging child care and juggling her employment responsibilities when her children are sick. And, if her story is like that of most employed mothers, she continues to have primary responsibility for the household and children. If she withdraws from the workplace, her contacts during most of the day are with her children and possibly other mothers. This relative isolation requires her to make considerable psychological adaptation in her transition to motherhood, leading in some cases to unhappiness or depression. Typical struggles in families with young children concern child-care responsibilities and parental roles. The woman's partner may not understand her unhappiness because he sees her fulfilling her roles as wife and mother. She herself may not fully understand the reasons for her feelings as she is performing her traditional roles. The partners may increasingly grow apart during this period. During the day they move in different worlds, the

The most dramatic change experienced by a married couple is the birth or adoption of their first child. As a result, mother/father roles are added to wife/husband roles.

world of the workplace and the world of the home; during the night they cannot relate easily because they do not understand each other's experiences.

Individual Changes

Around the time people are in their thirties, the marital situation changes substantially. The children have probably started school and the mother, who usually has the lioness's share of duties, now begins to have more freedom from childrearing responsibilities. She evaluates her past and decides on her future. The majority of women who left jobs to rear children return to the workplace by the time their children reach adolescence. By working, women generally increase their marital power.

Husbands in this period may find that their jobs have already peaked; they can no longer look forward to promotions. They may feel stalled and become depressed as they look into the future, which they see as nothing more than the past repeated for thirty more years. Their families may provide emotional satisfaction and fulfillment, however, as a counterbalance to workplace disappointments.

Seldom, or perhaps never, does a marriage develop into an individual relationship smoothly and without crises; there is no coming to consciousness without pain.

Carl Jung

❖ MIDDLE-AGED MARRIAGES   Ⅴ , Ⅵ

Middle-aged marriages generally represent stages V and VI in the family life cycle: families with adolescents (stage V) and families as launching centers (stage VI). Couples in these stages are usually in their forties and fifties.

Families with Adolescents

Adolescents require considerable family reorganization on the part of the parents: they stay up late, infringe upon their parents' privacy, and leave a trail of empty pizza cartons, popcorn, dirty clothes, and spilled soft drinks in their wake. As Carter and McGoldrick (1989) pointed out:

The best way to keep children at home is to make the home atmosphere pleasant—and let the air out of the tires.

Dorothy Parker

Families with adolescents must establish qualitatively different boundaries than families with younger children. . . . Parents can no longer maintain complete authority. Adolescents can and do open the family to a whole array of new values as they bring friends and new ideas into the family arena. Families that become derailed at this stage are frequently stuck at an earlier view of their children. They may try to control every aspect of their lives at a time when, developmentally, this is impossible to do successfully. Either the adolescent withdraws from the appropriate involvements for this developmental stage or the parents become increasingly frustrated with what they perceive as their own impotence.

Increased family conflict may occur as adolescents begin to assert their autonomy and independence (Troll, 1985). Conflicts over tidiness, study habits, communication, and lack of responsibility may emerge. Adolescents want rights and privileges but have difficulty accepting responsibility. Conflicts are often contained, however, by both parents and adolescents tacitly agreeing to avoid "flammable" topics such as how the teenager spends his or her time. Such tactics may be useful in maintaining family peace, but in the extreme they can backfire by increasing family distance and inauthenticity. Despite the growing pains accompanying adolescence, parental bonds generally remain strong (Gecas and Seff, 1991).

Examining Marital Satisfaction

Because marriage and the family have moved to the very center of people's lives as a source of personal satisfaction, we now evaluate them according to how well they fulfill emotional needs. Marital satisfaction influences not only how we feel about our marriages and our partners, but it also affects how we feel about ourselves. If we have a good marriage, we tend to feel happy and fulfilled (Glenn, 1991).

Considering the various elements that make up or affect a marriage—from identity bargaining to economic status—it should not be surprising that marital satisfaction ebbs and flows. The ebb, however, begins relatively early for many couples. Researchers have found significant declines in the average level of marital satisfaction beginning in the first year of marriage (McHale and Huston, 1985). In some cases the decline in marital satisfaction during the first stage of marriage may mean that we have chosen the wrong partner. In fact, those with low marital satisfaction during the beginning marriage stage are four to five times as likely to divorce as those with high satisfaction (Booth et al., 1986). Satisfaction generally continues to decline during the first ten years of marriage, perhaps longer (Glenn, 1989). Studies consistently indicate that marital satisfaction changes over the family life cycle, following a U-shaped or curvilinear curve (Glenn, 1991; Suitor, 1991). Satisfaction is highest during the initial stages then begins to decline but rises again in the later years. There seems to be little difference in marital satisfaction between first marriages and remarriages (Vemer et al., 1989).

It was once thought that those couples with average or higher marital satisfaction would have stable marriages whereas those with low satisfaction would have divorce-prone marriages. Although low marital satisfaction may make a marriage more likely to end in divorce, marital dissatisfaction alone cannot predict eventual divorce (Kitson and Morgan, 1991). Many unhappy marriages continue to endure in the face of misery and discord; sometimes they outlast much happier marriages. Unhappy marriages continue if there are too many barriers to divorce (such as a potential decline in the standard of living) and if the available alternatives seem less attractive than the current marriage. And happier marriages sometimes end in divorce if there are few barriers and better alternatives (Glenn, 1991; see Chapter 16 for a discussion of marital cohesiveness).

Decline in Marital Satisfaction: Who's to Blame—Children or Time?

Why does marital satisfaction tend to decline soon after marriage? Two explanations for changes in marital satisfaction have been given by researchers. The first explanation ascribes the changing patterns of satisfaction to the presence of children. The second points to the effects of time on marital satisfaction.

CHILDREN AND MARITAL SATISFACTION
Traditionally, researchers have attributed decline in marital satisfaction to the arrival of the first child: children take away from time a couple spends together, are a source of stress, and cost money. The decline reaches its lowest point when the oldest child enters adolescence (or school, according to some studies). When children begin leaving home, marital satisfaction begins to rise again.

It seems paradoxical that children cause marital satisfaction to decline. For many people, children are among the things they value most in their marriages. In fact, children may not be the monsters that some researchers believe them to be. First, attributing the decline to children creates a single-cause fallacy—that is, attributing a complex phenomenon to one factor when there are probably multiple causes. Second, the arrival of children at the same time that marital satisfaction declines may be coincidental, not causal. Other undetected factors may be at work. Although many societal factors make child-rearing a difficult and sometimes painful experience for some families, it is also important to note that children create parental roles and the family in its most traditional sense. The marital relationship may be less than fulfilling with children present, but many couples may make a trade-off for fulfillment in their parental roles. In times of marital crisis, parental roles may be the glue that holds the relationship together until the crisis passes. Many couples will endure intense situational conflict, not for the sake of the marriage but for the sake of the children.

Don't blame children [handwritten annotation]

Families as Launching Centers

Some couples may be happy or even grateful to see their children leave home, some experience difficulties with this exodus, and some continue to accommodate their adult children under the parental roof.

[handwritten margin notes: Dave | Pia / introverted | extroverted / messy | tidey / job | bills ─ everything! / house - Yard - garage / Children / maintenance / Job / School — this is me]

PERSPECTIVE

If the crisis can be resolved, the marriage may be even more solid than before. We need to balance marital satisfaction with family satisfaction.

THE DURATION OF MARRIAGE AND MARITAL SATISFACTION More recently, researchers have looked for factors besides children that might explain decline in marital satisfaction. The most persuasive alternative is the **duration-of-marriage effect.** The duration-of-marriage effect refers to the accumulation over time of various factors, such as unresolved conflicts, poor communication, grievances, role overload, heavy work schedules, and child-rearing responsibilities, that cause marital disenchantment.

The duration-of-marriage effect is most notable during the first stage of marriage rather than during the transition to parenthood that follows (White and Booth, 1985). This early decline may reflect the replacement of unrealistic expectations about marriage by more realistic ones, challenging us to be intimate and loving in the every day world. Since beginning marriage requires us to undertake numerous relational tasks, the transition from singlehood to marriage is a time filled with challenges. How we handle these challenges may set the tenor for our marriages for years to come. Those who handle them successfully have the tools with which to enhance their marriages; those who fail may see their marriages decline in satisfaction.

Social and Psychological Factors in Marital Satisfaction

Social factors are important ingredients in marital satisfaction. Income level, for example, is a significant factor. Blue-collar workers have less marital satisfaction than white-collar, managerial, and professional workers because their lower income creates financial distress (Feldman and Feldman, 1975). Unemployment and economic uncertainty as sources of stress and tension also directly affect marital satisfaction. If a couple has an insufficient income or is deeply in debt, how to allocate their resources—for rent, repairing the car, buying a CD player—becomes critical, sometimes involving conflict-filled decisions.

Psychological factors also affect marital satisfaction (Richard, Wakefield, and Lewak, 1990). Although it was once believed that marital satisfaction was dependent on a partner's fulfilling complementary needs and qualities (an introvert marrying an extrovert, for example), research has failed to substantiate this assertion. Instead, success seems to depend on partners being similar in their psychological makeup and personalities. Outgoing people are happier with outgoing partners; tidy people like tidy mates. Furthermore, a high self-concept (how a person perceives himself or herself) as well as how the spouse perceives the person also contributes to marital satisfaction.

A psychological perspective may help to explain why many middle-years marriages experience low levels of satisfaction. The middle stages of the family life cycle are also when adults enter midlife, a time characterized by psychological crises and reevaluation. The causes of decreased marital satisfaction may be the result of the adults' own psychological concerns and distress. Steinberg and Silverberg (1987) suggest, "It is reasonable to assume that these feelings may provoke disenchantment in the marital relationship, regardless of changes in the adolescent or parent-adolescent relationship."

Even though much of the literature points to declines in marital satisfaction, we must remember that not all marriages suffer a significant decline. For many marriages, the decline is small or rises in satisfaction after a relatively short period. Even for those whose marriages decrease significantly in satisfaction, the decline may be offset by other satisfactions, such as pleasure in parental roles or a sense of security. Studies consistently demonstrate, for example, that the psychological and physical health of married men and women tends to be better than that of individuals who are unmarried (Gove, Styles, and Hughes, 1990).

It is important to understand that marital satisfaction is not static. It fluctuates over time, battered by stress, enlarged by love. Husband and wife continuously maneuver through myriad tasks, roles, and activities—from scrubbing floors to kissing each other—to give their marriages form. Children, who bring us both delight and frustration, constrain our lives as a couple but challenge us as mothers and fathers and enrich our lives as a family. Trials and triumphs, laughter and tears, punctuate the daily life of marriage. If we are committed to each other and to our marriage, work together in a spirit of flexibility and cooperation, find time to be alone together, and communicate with each other, we lay the groundwork for our marriages being rich and meaningful.

As children are "launched" from the family (or ejected, as some parents wryly put it), the parental role becomes increasingly less important in daily life. The period following the child's exit is commonly known as the "empty nest" period. Most parents make the transition reasonably well (Anderson, 1988). In fact, marital satisfaction generally begins to rise for the first time since the first stage of

Better a Socrates dissatisfied than a pig satisfied.

John Stuart Mill

The proverbial minister, priest and rabbi were debating the point at which life begins. The priest said, "Life begins at the moment of conception, when the sperm invades the egg." The minister insisted that "Life begins at birth, with that first breath of God's air." But the rabbi, older and wiser, said "You're both too young to know this, but life doesn't really begin until the kids leave home and the dog dies."

Frank Pittman

After the kids
leave home,
*   some parents*
*   suffer*
*   from the*
*   empty-nest syndrome;*
Others—
*   change the locks!*

Anonymous

marriage (Glenn, 1991). For some parents, however, the empty nest is seen as the end of the family. Children have been the focal point of much family happiness and pain—and now they are gone.

Traditionally, it has been asserted that the departure of the last child from home leads to an **empty nest syndrome** among women, characterized by depression and identity crisis. The problem with the idea of the empty nest syndrome is that there is little evidence for it being widespread. Rather, it is a myth that reinforces the traditional view that women's primary identity is found in motherhood. Once deprived of their all-encompassing identity as mothers, the myth goes, women lose all sense of purpose. In reality, however, mothers may be more likely to complain that their adult children have *not* left home.

The couple must now recreate their family minus their children. Their parental roles become less important and less stressful on a day-to-day basis (Anderson, 1988). The husband and wife must rediscover themselves as man and woman. Some couples may divorce at this point if the children were the only reason the pair remained together.

THE NOT-SO-EMPTY NEST: ADULT CHILDREN AT HOME. Just how empty homes actually are after children reach eighteen is open to question. In fact, the majority of unmarried adult children do not leave home until they are more than twenty-four years old. Adult children may live at home while attending college or working; some may have returned following divorce. Most children, however, move away from home when they marry.

The number of adult children living at home has grown over the last few decades as young adults continue to delay marriage. Skyrocketing housing costs, which amount to between 60 and 90 percent of a young adult's income, have also kept them at home (Saluter, 1989). Today, about 70 percent of never-married men and women aged eighteen to twenty-four years live at home with their parents. Although stereotypes suggest that men are more independent than women, when it comes to leaving home, men apparently exhibit more dependent behavior. Broken down by gender, about 61 percent of young men and 48 percent of young women live with their parents. Almost a third of divorced men and women return home (Saluter, 1989). Researchers note that there are important financial and emotional reasons for this trend (Mancini and Bliezner, 1991). High unemployment, housing costs, and poor wages lead to adult children returning home. High divorce rates as well as personal problems push adult children back to the parental home for social support, childcare, as well as cooking and laundry service.

Young adults at home are such a common phenomenon that one of the leading family life-cycle scholars suggests a new family stage—adult children at home (Aldous, 1990). This new stage is not one that parents had anticipated. About 80 percent of the parents with children twenty-two and over had not expected the child to be living at home, according to one study (Clemens and Axelson, 1985). Almost half reported serious conflict with their children. For parents, the most frequently mentioned problems were the hours of their children's coming and going and their failure to clean and maintain the house. Most wanted their children to be "up, gone, and on their own."

Reevaluation

Middle-aged people find that they must reevaluate relations with their children, who have become independent adults, and must incorporate new family members as in-laws. Some must also begin considering how to assist their own parents, who are

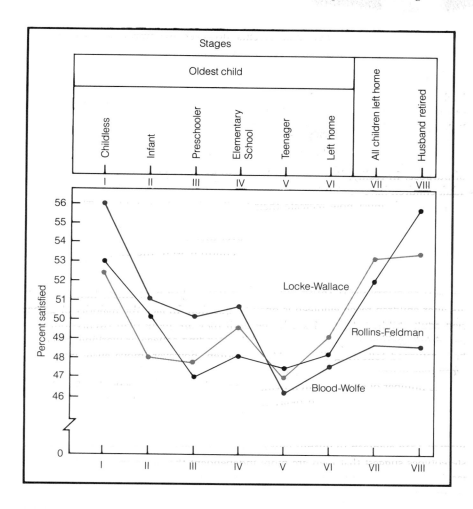

Stages

Oldest child

Childless | Infant | Preschooler | Elementary School | Teenager | Left home | All children left home | Husband retired

I | II | III | IV | V | VI | VII | VIII

Percent satisfied

Locke-Wallace

Rollins-Feldman

Blood-Wolfe

I | II | III | IV | V | VI | VII | VIII

FIGURE 10.1

This figure shows the average standard scores on marital satisfaction over eight stages of the family life cycle, as indicated by three separate studies. Note that all three record a sharp decline in marital satisfaction around the time of the birth of children and a sharp increase in marital satisfaction when children leave home.

Source: Boyd C. Rollins and Kenneth L. Cannon, "Marital Satisfaction over the Family Life Cycle," *Journal of Marriage and the Family*, May 1974.

becoming more dependent as they age. (See Mancini and Bliezner, 1991, for research review of aging parents and adult children.)

Couples in middle age tend to reexamine their aims and goals (Levinson, 1977; Rubin, 1976; Steinberg and Silverberg, 1987). On the average, husbands and wives have thirteen more years of marriage without children than they used to, and during this time their partnership may become more harmonious or more strained. The man may decide to stay at home more and not work as hard as before. The woman may commit herself more fully to her job or career or she may remain at home, enjoying her new child-free leisure. Because the woman has probably returned to the workplace, wages and salary earned during this period may represent the highest amount the couple will earn.

As people enter their fifties, they probably have advanced as far as they will ever advance in their work. They have accepted their own limits, but they also have an increased sense of their own mortality. Not only do they feel their bodies aging, but they begin to see people their own age dying. Some continue to live as if they were ageless—exercising, working hard, keeping up or even increasing the pace of their activities. Others become more reflective, retreating from the world. Some may turn outward, renewing their contacts with friends, relatives, and especially their children.

re-evaluation in middle age

When I was young, I was told: "You'll see when you're fifty." I am fifty and I haven't seen a thing.

Erik Satie

Anyone who fails to go along with life remains suspended stiff and rigid in mid-air. That is why so many people get wooden in their old age; they look back and cling to the past with a secret fear of death in their hearts. From the middle of life onward, only he remains virtually alive who is ready to die with life, for in the secret hour of life's midday the parabola is reversed, death is born. We grant goal and purpose to the ascent of life, why not to the descent?

Carl Jung

All the world's a stage
And all the men and women
*   merely players:*
They have their exits and their
*   entrances:*
And one man in his time plays
*   many parts,*
His acts being seven ages. At
*   first the infant,*
Mewling and puking in the
*   nurse's arms.*
Then the whining school-boy,
*   with his satchel*
And shining morning face,
*   creeping like snail*
Unwillingly to school. And
*   then the lover,*
Sighing like furnace, with a
*   woeful ballad*
Made to his mistress's eyebrow.
*   Then a soldier,*
Full of strange oaths, and
*   bearded like the pard,*
Jealous in honor, sudden and
*   quick in quarrel,*
Seeking the bubble reputation
Even in the cannon's mouth.
*   And then the justice,*
In fair round belly with good
*   capon lined,*
With eyes severe and beard of
*   formal cut,*
Full of wise saws and modern
*   instances;*
And so he plays his part. The
*   sixth age shifts*
Into lean and slippered
*   pantaloon,*
With spectacles on nose and
*   pouch on side,*
His youthful hose, well saved,
*   a world too wide*
For his shrunk shank; and his
*   big manly voice,*
Turning again toward childish
*   treble, pipes*
And whistles in his sound.
*   Last scene of all,*
That ends this strange eventful
*   history,*
Is second childishness and
*   mere oblivion,*
Sans teeth, sans eyes, sans
*   taste, sans everything.*

William Shakespeare, As You Like It

❖ LATER-LIFE MARRIAGES

Later-life marriages represent the last two stages (stages VII and VIII) of the family life cycle. A later-life marriage is one in which the children have been launched and the partners are middle-aged or older. During this period, the three most important factors affecting middle-aged and older couples are health, retirement, and widowhood (Brubaker, 1991). In addition, these women and men must often assume caretaking roles of their own aging parents or adjust to adult children who have returned home.

Later middle-aged men and women tend to enjoy good health, are firmly established in their work, and have their highest discretionary spending power, because their children are gone (Voydanoff, 1987). As they age, however, they tend to cut back on their work commitments for both personal and health reasons.

As they enter old age, men and women are better off than we have been accustomed to believe (Aldous, 1987). Beliefs that the elderly are neglected and isolated tend to reflect myth more than reality (Bengston and Robertson, 1985). A national study of the aged found that 41 percent of those with children see or talk with them daily, 21 percent twice a week, and 20 percent weekly. Over half have children within thirty minutes driving time (U.S. Bureau of the Census, 1988).

Beliefs that the elderly are a particularly poverty-stricken group are also misleading. Because of government programs benefiting the elderly, the poverty rate for the elderly declined during the 1980s while that of other groups substantially increased. The poverty rate for the general population in 1986 was 14.7 percent, but it was only 7 percent of those over sixty-five. We must not think, however, that all aged people are generally well off. The poverty rate for aged African Americans was 22.1 percent, and it was 17.3 percent for Latinos; these figures, however, were below the overall poverty rates for both groups (U.S. Bureau of the Census, 1990).

The health of the elderly also appears to be improving as they increase their longevity. Half of those between seventy-five and eighty-four years are free of health problems that require special care or limit their activities. Bernice Neugarten notes, "Even in the very oldest group, those above eighty-five, more than one-third report no limitation due to health" (Toufexis, 1988). Individuals between seventy-five and eighty gained four years in life expectancy between 1968 and 1980. More married couples are living into old age; there are fewer widows at younger ages.

The Intermittent Extended Family: Sharing and Caring

Although many later-life families contract in size as children are launched, pushed, or cajoled out of the nest, other families may expand as they come to the assistance of family members in need. Families are most likely to become an **intermittent extended family** during their later-life stage (Beck and Beck, 1989). Intermittent extended families are families that take in other relatives during a time of need. These families "share and care" when younger or older relatives are in need or crisis: they help daughters who are single mothers; a sick parent, aunt, or uncle; an unemployed cousin (see Chapter 13 for a discussion of family caregiving). When the crisis passes, the dependent adult leaves and the family resumes its usual structure.

Intermittent extended families tend to be linked to ethnicity. Using national population studies, researchers estimate that the families of almost two-thirds of African-American women and a third of white women were extended for at least some part of the time during their middle age. Latino women are more likely than non-Latino women to form extended households (Tienda and Angel, 1982). Asian families are also more likely to live at some time in extended families. There are two reasons for the prevalence of extended families among certain ethnic groups. First, extended families are by cultural tradition more significant to African-Americans, Latinos, and Asian-Americans than to whites. Second, ethnic families are more likely to be economically disadvantaged. They share households and pool resources as a practical way to overcome short-term difficulties. In addition, there is a higher rate of single parenthood among African Americans that makes mothers and their children economically vulnerable. These women often turn to their families of orientation for emotional and economic support until they are able to get on their own feet.

Parenting and Grandparenting

PARENTING. A few years ago, a Miami Beach couple reported their son missing (Treas and Bengston, 1987):

Joseph Horowitz still doesn't understand why his mother got so upset. He wasn't "missing" from their home in Miami Beach: he had just decided to go north for the winter. Etta Horowitz, however, called authorities. Social worker, Mike Weston finally located Joseph in Monticello, N.Y., where he was visiting friends. Etta, 102, and her husband, Solomon, 96, had feared harm had befallen their son Joseph, 75.

Parenting does not end when children grow up. Most elderly parents still feel themselves to be parents, but they are parents in different ways. Their parental role is considerably less important in their daily lives. They generally have some kind of regular contact with their adult children, usually by letters or phone calls; parents and adult children also visit each other fairly frequently and often celebrate holidays or birthdays together. One study (Aldous, 1987) found that middle-class parents typically assisted their children financially or provided services. Parents made loans, gave gifts, or paid bills for their children around six times a year; they also provided child care about the same number of times. They assisted in shopping, house care, and transportation and also helped in times of illness.

Yet parents do not necessarily assist their children equally. Joan Aldous (1987) noted, "Parents were most in touch with children who, although adults, were most in need of parental attentions." Parents tend to assist those whom they perceive to be in need, especially children who are single or divorced. Parents perceive their single children as being "needy" because they have not yet established themselves in occupational and family roles. These children may need financial assistance and may lack intimate ties; their parents may provide both until their children are more firmly established. Parents often assist divorced children, especially if grandchildren are involved, by providing financial and emotional support. They also provide child-care and housekeeping services. Parents generally provide the greatest assistance to their children who are single mothers.

In providing assistance to their children, the parents exercised considerable control over whom they would help and how involved they would become. Despite their continued parental concern, they tended to be maritally rather than parentally oriented. They valued their independence from their children. When one woman was asked how she would feel about an adult child coming back home to live, she exclaimed, "Oh, God, I wouldn't like it. I'm tired of waiting on people" (Aldous, 1987).

In Aldous's study, adult children generally reciprocated in terms of physical energy. They helped in household chores and yard work about six times a year; they also assisted to some extent with physical care during illness.

Love seems the swiftest, but it is the slowest of all growths. No man or woman really knows what perfect love is until they have been married a quarter of a century.

Mark Twain

Many a man that cudden't direct ye to th' drug store on th' corner whin he was thirty will get a respectful hearin' whin age has further impaired his mind.

Finley Peter Dunne, Old Age

Some elderly parents never cease being parents because they provide home care for children who are severely limited either physically or mentally. Many elderly parents, like middle-aged parents, are taking on parental roles again as divorced children return home for financial or emotional reasons. Although we don't know how elderly parents "parent," presumably they are less involved in traditional parenting roles. The presence of adult children in aging families does not seem to detract from marital quality as it does when children remain home in middle-aged families (Suitor and Pillemer, 1987). According to Aldous the major drawback was that husband/wife conflict increased if there was parent/child conflict.

GRANDPARENTING. The image of the lonely, frail grandmother in a rocking chair needs to be discarded, notes researcher Gregory Kennedy (1990). Grandparents are often not very old, nor are they very lonely. And they are certainly not absent in contemporary American family life. Grandparents are "a very present aspect of family life, not only for young children but young adults as well," writes Kennedy.

Grandparenting is expanding tremendously these days, creating new roles that relatively few Americans played a few generations back (Cherlin and Furstenberg, 1986). Three-quarters of older Americans are grandparents. The typical fifteen-year-old has more than a fifty-fifty chance of having three grandparents living. Of those Americans who are grandparents, 40 percent are also great-grandparents!

Grandparents play important emotional roles in American families; the majority appear to establish strong bonds with their grandchildren (Cherlin and Furstenberg, 1986; Kennedy, 1990). A recent study (Kennedy, 1990) found that almost half of the student respondents had at least one grandparent living in the same town; another fifth had a grandparent living within fifty miles. More than half of the students felt very close to at least one grandparent; a few identified their closest relationship as being with a stepgrandparent. Grandparents are important in helping achieve family cohesiveness by conveying family history, stories, and customs. They frequently act as a stabilizing force for their children and grandchildren when the families are divorcing and reforming as single-parent families or stepfamilies (Barranti, 1985).

Grandparents are often involved in the daily care of their grandchildren. About a fourth of preschoolers of employed mothers are cared for by their grandmothers for an average of twenty-seven hours per week (Presser, 1989). Furthermore, about 5 percent of all children live with their grandparents; of these, about one-third are cared for only by their grandparents. According to one study, 13 percent of African-American children, 5 percent of Latino children, and 3 percent of white children lived with their grandparents (Saluter, 1990). Kennedy (1990) found that African Americans more than whites expected grandparents to be authority figures, to provide childrearing assistance, and to assist with parent/child communication. He also found that students in single-parent families and stepfamilies expected grandparents to be more involved and influential than those in intact families.

Grandparenting tends to fall into three distinct styles, according to a national study of 510 grandparents by Andrew Cherlin and Frank Furstenberg (1986):

◆ *Companionate.* Most grandparents perceive their relationships with their grandchildren as companionate. The relationships are marked by affection, companionship, and play. Because these grandparents tend to live relatively close to their grandchildren, they can have regular interaction with them. Companionate grandparents do not perceive themselves as rule makers or enforcers; they rarely assume parent-like authority. Companionate grandparents accounted for 55 percent of the grandparents in the survey.

1. Avoid fried meats which angry up the blood.
2. If your stomach disputes you, lie down and pacify it with cool thoughts.
3. Keep the juices flowing by jangling around gently as you move.
4. Go very lightly on the vices, such as carrying on in society. The social ramble ain't restful.
5. Avoid running at all times.
6. Don't look back. Something might be gaining on you.

Satchel Paige

Lecture ———————→

◆ *Remote.* Remote grandparents are not intimately involved in their grandchildren's lives. Their remoteness, however, is due to geographical remoteness rather than emotional remoteness. Geographical distance prevents regular visits or interaction with their grandchildren that would bind the generations together more closely. About 29 percent of the grandparents were classified as remote.

◆ *Involved.* Involved grandparents are actively involved in what have come to be regarded as parenting activities: making and enforcing rules and disciplining children. Involved grandparents (most often grandmothers) tend to emerge in times of crisis, such as when the mother is an unmarried adolescent or enters the workforce following divorce. Some involved grandparents may become "over involved," however. They may cause confusion as the family tries to determine who is the real head of the family. Involved grandparents made up 16 percent of the grandparents in the study.

What determines the amount of interaction between grandparents and grandchildren? Cherlin and Furstenberg (1986) succinctly summed up the three most important factors: "distance, distance, and distance." Other factors include age, health, employment, personality, and other responsibilities (Troll, 1985). The middle generation is usually responsible for determining how much interaction takes place between grandparents and grandchildren. If rivalry rather than cooperation ensues, the middle generation may restrict grandparent/grandchildren interaction. But most families gain from such interactions (Barranti, 1985).

Single parenting and remarriage has made grandparenthood more painful and problematic for many grandparents. Stepfamilies have created stepgrandparents, who are often confused about their grandparenting role. Are they *really* grandparents? The grandparents whose son or daughter does not have custody often express concern about their future grandparenting role (Goetting, 1990). Although research indicates that children in stepfamilies tend to do better if they continue to have contact with both sets of grandparents, it is not uncommon for the parents of the non-custodial parent to lose contact with their grandchildren (Bray and Berger, 1990).

❖ REFLECTIONS   *Think about your grandparents. How many are alive? What kind of relationship do (or did) you have with them? What role do (or did) they play in your life and your family's life?*

Retirement and Widowhood

Retirement, like other life changes, has the potential for satisfactions and problems. In a time of relative prosperity for the elderly, retirement is an event to which older couples generally look forward. The key to marital satisfaction in these later years is continued good health (Brubaker, 1991).

RETIREMENT. There is a growing trend toward early retirement among financially secure men and women. Changing social mores have led many to value leisure more than increased buying power and other job benefits. In fact, today three-fourths of men and more than four-fifths of women choose to collect their social security checks before they reach sixty-five years (Dentzer, 1990). Two scholars (Treas and Bengston, 1987) note, "Together with greater prosperity, early retirement has probably reordered the preoccupations of later life toward greater concern with leisure activities—a development most compatible with the historic shift to companionate marriages." The bumper sticker "We're spending our children's inheritance" seen on campers and RVs captures this shift in sentiment.

We have not finished thinking, imagining, acting. It is still possible to know the world; we are unfinished men and women.

Carlos Fuentes

Marital Satisfaction

An important question in studying marital satisfaction is how to measure it (Fincham and Bradbury, 1987). One measure widely used is Graham Spanier's Dyadic Adjustment Scale which we have reprinted here. The Dyadic Adjustment Scale is an example of the type of questionnaire scholars use as they examine marital adjustment. What are the advantages of a questionnaire such as this? The disadvantages?

Answer the questions and then ask yourself if you think these questions can measure marital satisfaction. (Hint: You must first define what marital satisfaction is.) If you are currently involved in a relationship or marriage, you and your partner might be interested in answering the questions separately and comparing your answers. Do you have similar perceptions of your relationship? At the end of this course, answer the questions again without referring to your first set of answers. Then compare your responses. What do you infer from this comparison?

(For an exchange regarding the concept of adjustment, see Trost, 1985, and Spanier, 1985.)

	Always Agree	Almost Always Agree	Occasionally Disagree	Frequently Disagree	Almost Always Disagree	Always Disagree
1. Handling family finances	5	4	3	2	(1)	0
2. Matters of recreation	5	4	3	2	(1)	0
3. Religious matters	5	4	3	2	1	(0)
4. Demonstrations of affection	5	4	3	(2)	1	0
5. Friends	5	4	(3)	2	1	0
6. Sex relations	5	4	(3)	2	1	0
7. Conventionality (correct or proper behavior)	5	4	(3)	2	1	0
8. Philosophy of life	5	4	3	2	1	(0)
9. Ways of dealing with parents or in-laws	5	4	(3)	2	1	0
10. Aims, goals, and things believed important	5	4	3	2	1	(0)
11. Amount of time spent together	5	4	3	(2)	1	0
12. Making major decisions	5	4	3	2	(1)	0
13. Household tasks	5	4	3	2	1	(0)
14. Leisure time interests and activities	5	4	3	2	1	(0)
15. Career decisions	5	4	(3)	2	1	0

	All the Time	Most of the time	More Often Than Not	Occasionally	Rarely	Never
16. How often do you discuss or have you considered divorce, separation, or terminating your relationship?	0	1	2	(3)	4	5
17. How often do you or your mate leave after a fight?	0	1	2	3	4	(5)
18. In general, how often do you think that things between you and your partner are going well?	5	4	(3)	2	1	0
19. Do you confide in your mate?	5	4	(3)	2	1	0
20. Do you ever regret that you married (or live together)?	0	1	2	(3)	4	5
21. How often do you and your partner quarrel?	0	1	2	(3)	4	5
22. How often do you and your mate "get on each other's nerves"?	0	1	(2)	3	4	5

[handwritten: more so on mine]

	Every Day	Almost Every Day	Occasionally	Rarely	Never
23. Do you kiss your mate?	(4)	3	2	1	0

	All of Them	Most of Them	Some Them	Very Few of Them	None of Them
24. Do you and your mate engage in outside interests together?	4	3	2	1	(0)

How often would you say the following events occur between you and your mate?

	Never	Less Than Once a Month	Once or Twice a Month	Once or Twice a Week	Once a Day	More Often
25. Have a stimulating exchange of ideas	(0)	1	2	3	4	5
26. Laugh together	0	1	2	3	(4)	5
27. Calmly discuss something	0	1	2	3	(4)	5
28. Work together on a project	(0)	1	2	3	4	5

These are some things about which couples sometimes agree and sometimes disagree. Indicate if either item below caused differences of opinions or were problems in your relationship during the past few weeks (check yes or no).

Yes No

29. 0 (1) Being too tired for sex.
30. 0 (1) Not showing love.

31. The dots on the following line represent different degrees of happiness in your relationship. The middle point, "happy," represents the degree of happiness of most relationships. Please circle the dot that best describes the degree of happiness, all things considered, of your relationship.

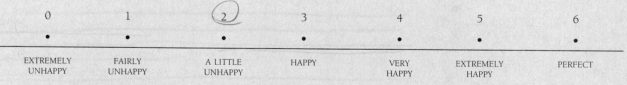

0	1	(2)	3	4	5	6
EXTREMELY UNHAPPY	FAIRLY UNHAPPY	A LITTLE UNHAPPY	HAPPY	VERY HAPPY	EXTREMELY HAPPY	PERFECT

32. Which of the following statements best describes how you feel about the future of your relationship?
 _5_ I want desperately for my relationship to succeed, and would go to almost any length to see that it does.
 _4_ I want very much for my relationship to succeed, and will do all I can to see that it does.
 (3) I want very much for my relationship to succeed, and will do my fair share to see that it does.
 _2_ It would be nice if my relationship succeeded, but I can't do much more than I am doing now to help it succeed.
 _1_ It would be nice if it succeeded, but I refuse to do any more than I am doing now to keep the relationship going.
 _0_ My relationship can never succeed, and there is no more than I can do to keep the relationship going.

When men reach their sixties, they usually retire from their jobs, losing a major activity through which they defined themselves. In spite of this, most men look favorably on retirement. Their role as husband becomes more important as they focus on leisure activities with their wives. In addition, many retirees are not really retired; many continue working part-time (Dentzer, 1990). Volunteer activities become more important. At home, the division of labor becomes somewhat more egalitarian; men participate in more household activities than they did when they were working (Rexroat and Shehan, 1987).

If the woman worked outside the home, she may experience some feelings of loss upon retirement, especially if she was involved in a career (Johnson and Price-Bonham, 1980). A woman who retires may not find herself facing the same identity issues as a man, however, because women often have had (or continue to have) important family roles as wife, homemaker, grandmother, and possibly mother.

If a woman has been a full-time homemaker, she probably experiences no abrupt role change in her sixties. There is no retirement for homemakers, however ironic that may be. Because "a woman's work is never done," homemakers may have the last laugh, for if they choose, they can perform their traditional role without any interruption throughout their entire lives.

The marital relationship generally continues along the same track following retirement: those who had vital, rewarding marriages will probably continue to have happy marriages, whereas those whose marriages were difficult will continue to have unsatisfying relationships (Brubaker, 1991). The retired couple experiences the highest degree of marital satisfaction since the first family stage, when they had no children (Johnson et al., 1986).

Although retirement affects marital interaction, changes in health are far more important over the long run. As long as both partners are healthy, the couple can continue their marital relationship unfettered. If one becomes ill or disabled, the other generally comes to his or her aid, providing care and nurturance. One study (Johnson, 1985) of elderly marriages in which a spouse was recuperating from hospitalization found high levels of marital adjustment; husbands and wives dealt positively with their caregiving demands. Ill spouses also receive help from other family members, including their adult children, siblings, and other relatives.

WIDOWHOOD. Marriages are finite; they do not last forever. Eventually, every marriage is broken by divorce or death. Despite high divorce rates, most marriages end with death, not divorce. "Until death do us part" is a fact for most married people.

In 1989, almost two-thirds of those between sixty-five and seventy-four years were married. Among those eighty-five years and older, however, only 4 percent were married; the remainder were widowed. Because of difference in longevity, most widowed persons are women. Among women from sixty-five to seventy-four, 51 percent lived with their husbands, but only 9 percent over age eighty-four lived with a spouse. In contrast, among men sixty-five to seventy-four years, 78 percent lived with their wives; among those over eight-four years, 48 percent lived with a spouse (Saluter, 1990). Because of the disproportionate sex ratio of women to men, one researcher estimated that fewer than 5 percent of women widowed over age fifty-five will remarry (Hiltz, 1978). If a woman is widowed at fifty-five and dies at seventy-five, she may have spent as much time as a widow as she spent raising children.

Widowhood is often associated with a significant decline in income, plunging the grieving spouse into financial crisis and hardship in the year or so following death. This is especially true for poorer families (Smith and Zick, 1986). For both men and women among the elderly, their financial situation is related to their feelings of well-being.

Recovering from the loss of a spouse is often difficult and prolonged (Kübler-Ross, 1982). (See Chapter 13 for discussion of death and the grieving process.) The woman may experience considerable disorientation and confusion from the loss of her role as a wife and companion. Having spent much of her life as part of a couple—having mutual friends, common interests, shared goals—the widow suddenly finds herself alone. Whatever the nature of her marriage, she experiences grief, anger, distress, and loneliness. Physical health appears to be tied closely to the emotional stress of widowhood. Widowed men and women experience more health problems over the fourteen months following their spouses' death than those with spouses. Over time, however, widows appear to regain much of their physical and emotional health (Brubaker, 1991).

Eventually widows adjust to the loss. Some like their new freedom. Others believe that they are too old to remarry; still others cannot imagine living with someone other than their former husband. (Those who had good marriages think of remarrying more often than those who had poor marriages.) A large number of elderly men and women live together without remarrying. For many widows, widowhood lasts the rest of their lives.

❖ MARRIAGE AND FAMILY TYPOLOGIES

Examining marriages and families in terms of the family life cycle is an important way of exploring the different tasks we must undertake at different times in our relationships. Another way of examining marriages and families is in terms of typologies. A **typology** is the systematic classification of types, that is, things sharing common traits or qualities. Researchers have developed several typologies of marriages, including motives for maintaining marriage (Weishaus and Field, 1988), marital quality (Brubaker, 1985), marital and family functioning (Olsen et al., 1983), and enduring marriages (Cuber and Haroff, 1974; Weishaus and Field, 1988). In this section, we will examine two of the most influential typologies: enduring marriages and family functioning.

Enduring Marriages

The search for marital satisfaction and happiness is continual for both married couples and researchers. But we may also look at marriage according to stability rather than satisfaction. What researchers find is what many of us already know: often little correlation exists between happy marriages and stable ones. Many unhappily married couples stay together; some happily married couples undergo a crisis and break up.

John Cuber and Peggy Haroff (1974) studied more than 400 married persons who had "normal" marriages. Subjects were upper middle class, ranging in age from thirty-five to fifty-five. Each person in the marriages under study considered himself or herself to be content, if not actually happy. Cuber and Haroff found several distinct types of marriages representing "different kinds of adjustment and different conceptions of marriage." These types of marriages were (1) conflict-habituated marriage, (2) devitalized marriage, (3) passive-congenial marriage, (4) vital marriage, and (5) total marriage.

Partners gave their own personal meaning to their marriage. In none of the types of marriage did there seem to be a cycle in which a marriage began blissfully and

The pursuit of happiness is a most ridiculous phrase: if you pursue happiness you'll never find it.

C. P. Snow

ended in disillusionment or disengagement. For example, many of the passive-congenial marriages (described briefly below) began that way and continued on the same level; neither partner experienced any particular disappointment with the habits of living that the couple had fashioned. Some couples may move from one style of marriage to another, but this occurs infrequently. Cuber and Haroff emphasized that relationships tend to continue their style over long periods of time without changing.

The Cuber and Haroff study is a descriptive study of marriages that stands in remarkable contrast to studies that look at marital satisfaction. Beneath the studies of happiness and satisfaction lie certain value judgments about how marriages ought to be. People with different values will judge marriages differently. Generally, these studies begin with the idea that marriages (*ought to* is the hidden term) provide companionship, shared activities, intimacy, and love. But Cuber and Haroff found that these characteristics are not necessary for partners to feel that their marriage is good. The five types of marriages in the study are described in the following sections.

CONFLICT-HABITUATED MARRIAGE. In this form of marriage, conflict, not harmony, is the most distinguishing characteristic. Couples fight and fight and fight; they need each other for sparring partners. They may bruise each other both physically and emotionally, but they do not believe such fighting is a reason for divorce. They sense that they probably could not get along with anyone else any better; fighting is acceptable behavior for them.

Few people outside the family group may know about the fighting, which is usually discreet, rarely taking place in front of others. Although a couple may engage in recriminations about the past or bitter personal attacks, their conflict usually takes the form of small quarrels: "You didn't put the cap on the toothpaste"; "Look at the dishes! You call *that* clean!" A few days after a fight, the couple may not even be able to remember what they fought about, but they fight continually. The channeling of conflict and the repression of hostility become a dominant force in their lives. Conflict and hostility make up a considerable portion of their interaction.

DEVITALIZED MARRIAGE. This type of marriage is most marked by the contrast between its earlier years and its present. At first, this kind of marriage was filled with vitality; the husband and wife were deeply in love with each other, spent considerable time together, and had a good sex life. They enjoyed each other and were closely identified with each other. Now whatever time they spend together is "duty time," whether it is entertaining, spending time with their children, or meeting their community responsibilities. Yet they get along well enough with each other that they do not contemplate divorce. Sometimes the wife may be unhappy if she does not have a career to compensate for the deficiencies of the relationship. Both partners sense a lack of alternatives or possibilities; both are unwilling to take the chance of finding a better partner, believe they have too much to lose if they fail. Psychological comfort is a key value for them.

PASSIVE-CONGENIAL MARRIAGE. This type of marriage varies little from the devitalized marriage except that the couple never had high emotions to begin with. Couples begin passive-congenial marriages with low expectations, which change little over the years. Partners do not gain their satisfaction from each other but from their outside relationships. The husband gains it from his work and his male companions, with whom he goes fishing, bowling, or to sports events. The wife achieves satisfaction from her children, her friends, and her job or career, if she has one.

The greatest happiness you can have is knowing that you do not necessarily require happiness.

William Saroyan

Marriage must continually vanquish the monster that devours everything, the monster of habit.

Honoré Balzac

80% of marriage are there

Based on convenience

Considerable role segregation exists in these marriages. Each partner has his or her proper sphere of activities, duties, and responsibilities. Some people drift into passive-congenial relationships. Expected to marry, not wanting to be lonely, they choose a partner without feeling deep involvement. Others pick this relationship because it fits their career needs and gives them considerable independence. Devoting themselves to their careers rather than to each other, they are freed from having to adjust to their spouse's needs. Cuber and Haroff point out that "the passive-congenial marriage is thus a mood as well as a mode."

VITAL MARRIAGE. In this type of marriage, the partners' lives are closely intertwined through matters that are important to both of them. Being together brings mutual excitement, satisfaction, and pleasure. One man said of his wife, "The things we do together aren't fun intrinsically—the ecstasy comes from being *together in the doing.*"

Outwardly, the lives of those engaged in vital marriages seem like most other marriages. Partners in vital marriages belong to groups, entertain, and care for their children just like everybody else, but privately they experience a strong, positive psychological bonding. Conflict is not central to their relationship. When conflict does occur, it is about matters that are important to both rather than trivial problems. Both partners are willing to compromise and to sacrifice for the sake of each other and their relationship. This type of marriage and the total marriage described next conform more closely to the marriage ideals of our culture.

TOTAL MARRIAGE. The total marriage is similar to the vital marriage, except that husband and wife participate in each other's lives more completely and on more levels. The husband and wife, for example, may work together on projects such as research or counseling, or they may be craftspeople who share the labor of making and selling their own products. Total marriages have few areas of tension because difficulties are resolved as they arise, preventing a slow simmering of hostility or a spillover into other areas. "When faced with differences, they can and do dispose of the difficulties without losing their feeling of unity or their sense of the vitality and centrality of their relationship. This is the mainspring" (Cuber and Haroff, 1974).

Cuber and Haroff view the first three types of marriages as *utilitarian* marriages. These marriages are based on convenience and lack of better alternatives. The last two are viewed as *intrinsic* marriages; the marital interactions are inherently rewarding. The researchers estimate that about 80 percent of American marriages are utilitarian, 15 percent are vital, and 5 percent are total. What these five types of marriages have in common is that they are all enduring. They do not represent degrees of marital happiness and satisfaction.

Family Functioning: The Circumplex Model

The Circumplex Model of family systems is one of the most important models to examine how families function (Olson et al., 1983). Based on systems theory (see Chapter 3), the Circumplex Model divides marriages and families into three types: balanced, mid-range, and extreme.

COHESION, ADAPTABILITY, AND COMMUNICATION. According to the Circumplex Model, there are three important components of family dynamics: cohesion, adaptability and communication. Cohesion and adaptability are central dimensions to family functioning. Communication facilitates or discourages cohesion and adapt-

The critical period in matrimony is breakfast time.

A.P. Herbert

> 15% — intrinsic — inherently rewarding

> 5%

this is from the 50% that make it.

FIGURE 10.2

Relationship of Satisfaction Scales, Stages of Family Life Cycles, and Dimensions of the Circumplex Model.

Family members' responses relating to satisfaction with marital and family relationships and quality of life are viewed across the family life cycle. Family response to stress is a significant factor in measuring family strength.

Source: (top and bottom) David Olson et al., *Families.* Copyright © 1983 by Sage Publications, Inc.

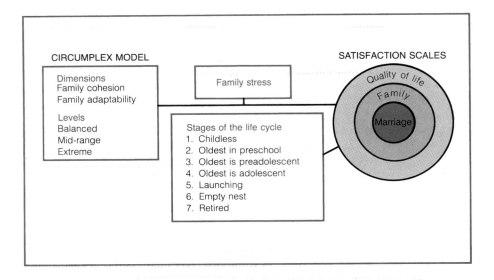

FIGURE 10.3

The Circumplex Model of Marital and Family Systems.

Balanced families, those with moderate levels of cohesion and adaptability, are seen as having the greatest marital and family strengths across the family life cycle.

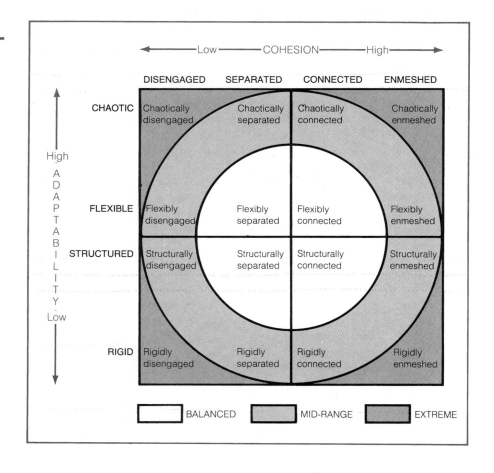

ability. Positive communication enables family members to understand, empathize with and support each other. Negative communication, such as criticism, blaming, and yelling, detract from family members' ability to be cohesive and adaptable.

Cohesion refers to the emotional bonding family members have with each other. It is measured by degrees of emotional bonding, time spent together, decision making patterns, interests, friends, and recreation. **Adaptability** is the ability of the family system to adjust its rules, power structure, and relationship patterns in response to change. These changes include developmental changes (such as children becoming adolescents), structural changes (the wife becoming employed), or stress (a family member becoming chronically ill). Adaptability includes degrees of family control and discipline, styles of negotiation, and family rules and roles.

FAMILY FUNCTIONING: BALANCED, MID-RANGE, AND EXTREME. Cohesion and adaptability are not "all or nothing" measures. Instead, their levels vary from high to low. Levels of cohesion, for example, may be disengaged (very low), separated (low to moderate), connected (moderate to high), or enmeshed (very high). Levels of adaptability may be rigid (very low), structured (low to moderate), flexible (moderate to high) or chaotic (very high).

There are four levels of cohesion and four levels of adaptability. Putting these levels together creates sixteen possible combinations, as you can see in Figure 10.3. These combinations can be reduced to three global types of families: balanced, midrange, and extreme. Balanced families fall into the central cells of cohesion and adaptability. Mid-range families fall into an extreme cell on one dimension and into a central cell on another dimension. Extreme families fall into extreme cells on both cohesion and adaptability dimensions.

Families vary in their levels of cohesion and adaptability throughout the family life cycle. Family cohesion appears to be highest among families in the early stages of the family life cycle, lower during adolescent and launching stages, and higher again during the empty nest and retirement stages. Families experience the lowest levels of cohesion during the adolescent and launching stages because children are attempting to differentiate themselves from their families. Family adaptability follows patterns similar to cohesiveness: during adolescent and launching stages, families appeared to be least adaptable.

According to the Circumplex Model, families function best when cohesion and adaptability are balanced rather than extreme. Depending on the family stage, between 50 to 60 percent of families are balanced, 25 to 40 percent are mid-range, and about 12 to 18 percent are extreme (Olson et al., 1983).

◆ REFLECTIONS *Examine your family of orientation or marriage using the Circumplex Model and the accompanying diagram. Is your family balanced, mid-range, or extreme? Why? What could you do to improve cohesion, adaptability and communication in your family?*

❖ SUMMARY

◆ The eight developmental stages of the life cycle described by Erik Erickson include (1) infancy: trust versus mistrust, (2) toddler: autonomy versus shame and doubt, (3) early childhood: initiative versus guilt, (4) school age: industry versus inferiority, (5) adolescence: identity versus role diffu-

sion, (6) young adulthood: intimacy versus isolation, (7) adulthood: generativity versus self-absorption, and (8) maturity: integrity versus despair.
◆ The *family life cycle* examines developmentally how families change over time in terms of both the people who are members of the family and the roles they play. The family life cycle consists of eight stages: beginning families, childbearing

families, families with preschool children, families with schoolchildren, families with teenagers, families as launching centers, families in the middle years, and aging families.

◆ Variations on the traditional life cycle include ethnic, single-parent, and stepfamily variations.

◆ Engagement is the culmination of the formal dating pattern. It prepares the couple for marriage by involving them in discussions about the realities of everyday life, it involves family members with the couple, and it strengthens the couple as a social unit. Cohabitation performs many of the same functions as engagement.

◆ A wedding is an ancient ritual that symbolizes a couple's commitment to each other. It marks a major transition in life as the man and woman take on marital roles.

◆ Marriage involves many powerful traditional role expectations, including assumptions that the husband is head of the household and is expected to support the family and that the wife is responsible for housework and childrearing.

◆ Marital tasks include establishing marital and family roles, providing emotional support for each other, adjusting personal habits, negotiating gender roles, making sexual adjustments, establishing family/employment priorities, developing communication skills, managing budgetary and financial matters, establishing kin relationships, and participating in the larger community.

◆ Couples undergo *identity bargaining* in adjusting to marital roles. This is a three-step process: a person must identify with the role, the person must be treated by the other as if he or she fulfills that role, and both people must negotiate changes in each other's roles.

◆ A critical task in early marriage is to establish boundaries separating the newly formed family from the couple's family of orientation. Ties to the families of orientation may include habits of subordination and economic dependency.

◆ In youthful marriages, about half of all working women leave the work force to attend to childrearing responsibilities.

◆ In middle-aged marriages, women may question their role as mother; men often feel disappointment with their work. Families must deal with issues of independence of their adolescent children. Most women do not suffer from the *empty nest syndrome*—that is, depression over the end of their active mother role. In fact, for many families, there is no empty nest because of the increasing presence of adult children in the home. As children leave home, parents reevaluate their relationship with each other and their life goals.

◆ In later-life marriages, no children are present. The most important factors affecting this life-cycle stage are health, retirement, and widowhood. As a group, the aged have the lowest poverty level of any group; they have good health through the early years of old age and regular contact with their children. Many, especially ethnic families, have *inter-mittent extended families,* in which aging parents, adult children, or other relatives periodically live with them during time of need.

◆ Parenting roles continue through old age. Elderly parents provide financial and emotional support to their children; they often take active roles in childcare and housekeeping for their daughters who are single parents. Divorced children and those with physical or mental limitations may continue living at home.

◆ Grandparenting is an important role for the middle aged and aged; it provides them with a sense of continuity. Grandparents often provide extensive childcare for grandchildren. Approximately 5 percent of American children live with their grandparents. Grandparenting can be divided into three styles: companionate, remote, and involved.

◆ Marriage and family *typologies* sytematically categorize families according to types, that is, shared traits and characteristics. Two of the most important typologies are the enduring marriage typology and the circumplex model of family functioning. *Enduring marriages* can be divided into five basic types: conflict-habituated, devitalized, passive-congenial, vital, and total. The fact that a marriage endures does not necessarily mean that it is a happy one, although couples in enduring marriages usually describe their marriages as satisfactory.

◆ The *Circumplex Model* argues that the most important dimensions of family functioning are *cohesion, adaptability,* and *communication* (which facilitates cohesiveness and adaptability). Depending on their degree of cohesion and adaptability, families are divided into three basic types: balanced, mid-range, and extreme. The most functional families are balanced.

Answers to Preview Questions

The answers to the preview questions at the beginning of the chapter are listed below. As you check your answers, whether you were correct or not, think about your reasons for each response. What were they? What was their source? How valid is the source? As you read the chapter, you will find the questions discussed in greater depth.

1.	F	6.	F
2.	F	7.	F
3.	F	8.	F
4.	T	9.	F
5.	T	10.	T

❖ SUGGESTED READINGS

Allen, Katherine. *Single Women/Family Ties.* Newbury Park, Calif.: Sage Publications, 1989. An exploration of the family roles that single women play as adult children, aunts, and siblings.

Brubaker, Timothy, ed. *Family Relationships in Later Life.* Newbury Park, Calif.: Sage Publications, 1990 (paperback). A collection of scholarly articles reviewing major themes in aging families.

Carter, Betty, and Monica McGoldrick, eds. *The Changing Family Life Cycle,* 2d ed. Boston: Allyn and Bacon, 1989. A fine collection of essays on the family life cycle from a family-therapy perspective.

Cherlin, Andrew, and Frank Furstenberg, Jr. *The New American Grandparent.* New York: Basic Books, 1986. The first major study that examines the significance and styles of grandparenting in contemporary America.

Leonard, Robin, and Elias Stephen. *Family Law Dictionary: Marriage, Divorce, Children, and Living Together.* Berkeley, Calif.: Nolo Press, 1988 (paperback). A useful source on the legal aspects of marriage and cohabitation.

Levinson, Daniel. *The Seasons of a Man's Life.* New York: Ballantine Books, 1977 (paperback). The groundbreaking study of the developmental tasks confronting men through their life cycle.

Markides, Kyiados, and Charles Mindel. *Aging and Ethnicity.* Newbury Park, Calif.: Sage Publications, 1987 (paperback). A good introduction to aging among African Americans, Latinos, Asian Americans, and other ethnic groups.

Walsh, Froma, ed. *Normal Family Processes.* New York: Guilford Press, 1982. An outstanding collection of essays on aspects of the family life cycle.

Washington, Mary Helen, ed. *Memory of Kin: Stories about Family by Black Writers.* New York: Anchor, 1991 (paperback). A compelling collection of short stories and poems by African-American writers, ranging from Langston Hughes to Alice Walker.

Whitbourne, Susan, and Joyce Ebmeyer. *Identity and Intimacy in Marriage: A Study of Couples.* New York: Springer-Verlag, 1990 (paperback). An outstanding book describing how the individual identities of two people interact to create a relationship. Scholarly but readable.

Suggested Films

Fanny and Alexander (1983). Academy-award winning film directed by Ingmar Bergman; an opulent, turn-of-the-century family saga seen through the eyes of a young brother and sister.

Mr. and Mrs. Bridge (1990). The story of the painfully respectable middle-western, middle-aged, middle-class Bridge family (played by Paul Newman and Joanne Woodward), "monsters of moderation," who are neither consciously happy nor unhappy.

On Golden Pond (1981). An elderly couple, played by Henry Fonda and Katharine Hepburn, return to their lakefront summer home where their daughter (Jane Fonda) reconciles with her curmudgeon father.

The Trip to Bountiful (1985). Geraldine Page portrays a widow determined to return to her home in Bountiful, Texas, one last time.

READINGS

TWO IN A BLANKET

John Fire/Lame Deer. Excerpt from *Lame Deer, Seeker of Visions.*

Wedding ceremonies not only unite families, they also affirm group identity. The wedding ceremony described in this excerpt helps affirm the couple's ethnic identity as Native Americans rather than their tribal identity as Navajos. If you are unmarried, and plan to marry at some time, what identities or values will your wedding affirm? If you are now married or have been married, what did your ceremony affirm?

More and more often, young Indian couples who have been married in the white man's way only, in a church, or just in the marriage bureau where they took out a license, feel that something is missing. They don't feel properly wedded until I join them together in the old, Indian way, with a blanket around them, their hands grasping the sacred pipe, their wrists bound together with a strip of red cloth. My ceremonies are very simple, with no trimmings. You have seen me do this in South Dakota and, once, in your own place where I married that beautiful young Navajo couple. Your place is good for that, because you have my buffalo skull from the sun dance, and also because there's always some sweet grass and *kinnickinnick* in your home, you got everything I need.

During such a ceremony, when I want the spirit to affect me, I wear no fancy outfit. I take my shirt off. I want my arms to be bare. I want to get that smoke around me, be touched by it. A ceremony like this is like a dream. I can sense things that I don't notice otherwise. During that rite, when I touched the young couple, I felt a good fortune and it made me glad. On the other side, I had two sad handshakes there from the right. Those people could fall sick, or even be dead in a year or two. I don't even know them, but their handshake told me of a misfortune. I sense this only when the pipe—the stem and the bowl—are

continued on next page

joined together, ready for the smoke. The moment I open up the pipe, disconnect it, these feelings of good or bad things to come disappear.

I put a red blanket over this Navajo boy and girl, let them take hold of the peace pipe, tied their hands together with a cloth, sang the old prayers over them. Now this is what I told them: "We are here in the big white man's city. You are supposed to stand on the earth, your mother, but you are in an apartment way up on the eighth floor. I will ask this of you, while I am doing my work, I want you to pretend that you are at home. Forget this old city, remember that there's a hill, a spot of earth you feel drawn to which made you feel the presence of the spirits. Pretend that you are standing there on top of the world. A city is not the right place for an Indian ceremony, but our thinking will make it right. Forget about the traffic, the big noise outside, concentrate, hold onto this pipe; that way our ceremony will be good, and from the four corners of the world, from the sky above and from the earth beneath, the blessing of the Great Spirit will be with us.

"The same way, the Indian people who are here with us remember where you are from. Remember your parents at home, remember your grandfathers, remember the hard times you had, and the good times, too. Remember it always. I give you a looking glass, a very small-size looking glass. Now, what do you see? You see an Indian face in there. All the joy and suffering of all of us, the things we did, the things that were done to us, it can be seen in your faces. So before anything else, know what you are—an Indian fighting to survive in a rugged, tough world.

"But you and her alone, the spirit is with you as you stand there under this blanket, and the Great Spirit will give you a little gift, a new life, and only when you get this gift will my ceremony be complete. It's a nest you are building, and I pray to the Great Spirit to help you. And now we are all going to smoke the pipe. *He-hechetu.*"

❖

MARITAL TASKS: BREAKING PARENTAL TIES

Jean Marzollo

One of the most important tasks a newly-married couple (especially a young couple) must perform is to establish their own family separate from the family of their parents. Why is forming a separate family unit sometimes a problem? Do men and women experience this problem differently? Why? What can be done to overcome conflicting demands between the spouse and his or her parents?

Ellen holds the set of calligraphy pens tightly on her lap and eyes the sleet hitting the windshield. "Please slow down," she says tensely.

"I'm not speeding," Tom answers, equally on edge. They are driving home from Ellen's mother's house, where they have been to a disastrous birthday party for Ellen. Although they've been married only six months, they don't feel like newlyweds.

"I really do like the pens," says Ellen, who has recently taken up calligraphy.

"I felt so stupid when you were opening them," Tom replies. "Your mother and father gave you so many presents, and they know I can't afford to give you much. I told you I didn't want to go there. Why couldn't we have gone out to dinner alone?"

"You know how Mother is," Ellen says. "She lives for our visits. And she loves birthdays. It would have hurt her terribly if we hadn't shown up."

"Well, I hate having to play second fiddle. I mean—for Pete's sake, your mother gave you a carload of expensive things and I gave you three felt-tipped calligraphy pens."

"No one cared. Why did you have to ruin the whole party with your sulking?"

Ellen begins to cry. She feels sorry for herself, it's her birthday after all—and sorry for her mother, who only wanted the evening to be festive. Ellen has always been her mother's pride and joy, and she feels it would be selfish not to visit as often as possible. She wonders why Tom can't understand.

Julie often feels just as Ellen does.

Julie's father, retired and recently widowed, lives alone in a town in Florida. She lives an hour away with her husband Wayne and their two-year-old son, Wayne Jr. Every day after Wayne leaves for work, Julie puts Wayne Jr. into his car seat and drives the forty miles to her father's house. There, her father and the baby watch TV while Julie cleans the house, weeds the garden, shops at the local supermarket and cooks a hearty, nutritious lunch with enough leftovers for her dad's dinner.

Often, Julie returns home too exhausted to shop and cook again, so when her husband comes home, she frequently suggests going to McDonald's. Wayne doesn't mind a burger and fries once in a while, but he misses Julie's cooking. He's beginning to feel angry that Julie cooks every day for her father and rarely for him. Their dinner hour, once a special time, is now hurried and harried.

Wayne's afraid to tell Julie what's really on his mind because he knows how much Julie loves her father and he's ashamed of feeling jealous of a lonely old man. He's afraid, too, that if he complains, Julie will suggest that her father move in with them. Wayne wants to avoid that because whenever Julie's dad is around, Wayne feels left out.

For her part, Julie's not happy about devoting more time and energy to her father than to her husband, but she believes that her dad really needs her. She's sure that if she stopped seeing her father so often, there would be a hole in his life that no one else could fill.

Ellen and Julie are having trouble with their marriages because they are too close to their parents. To complicate matters, neither woman realizes that the parents are the problem—both believe that the fault lies with their husbands.

A great many young wives find themselves similarly torn between their husbands and their parents. Even though they're married, they haven't yet left the nest. According to Dr. Bruce M. Forester, assistant professor of psychiatry at Columbia University and a psychiatrist in private practice in New York City, "Overinvolvement with parents causes the most trouble in early marriage—more than sex or any other issue."

If you sense such a conflict in your marriage, keep these questions in mind:

◆ Who has the most control over your actions—you, your parents or your husband?
◆ Whom do you care most about pleasing—yourself, your parents or your husband?
◆ Who depends on you most—your parents or your husband?

If your most frequent answer is "my parents," you do indeed have a problem. Being so involved with Mom and Dad endangers your marriage because it creates an imbalance; your life is weighted too heavily in your parents' favor. The solution isn't to shift all the weight over to your husband; instead, you need to put yourself in charge. You are the core of your own life, and you're now establishing the most intimate bond you'll every experience—the one with your mate. That bond requires most of your attention right now because you're laying the foundation for a lifetime partnership. To be successful, you must let go of your parents.

Dr. Sonya Rhodes, a New York City family therapist and co-author of *Surviving Family Life . . .* , has written about stages in family development. She says you can be shackled to your parents by some very powerful bonds.

If you need your parents' money, for example, you may feel emotionally indebted to an excessive degree. Or if your parents are very attached to you and have centered their lives around you, you may feel extremely guilty about going your own way. You may fear that you will make your parents angry, sad—even sick—if you "abandon" them.

The first step, according to Forester, is to talk to your husband. How is he feeling—left out? Jealous? Hurt? Talk about your own feelings, which might include guilt, fear and confusion.

Once you've established that you do have a problem, "The next step is to draw up a plan together," says Forester. "You must work out a strategy that will gradually loosen the parental tie, but in a very tactful way."

If you're lucky enough to be able to talk directly to your parents, do so. For example, Julie might say to her father, "I love you very much, but I feel that visiting you every day is hurting my marriage. You're in good health and sociable. Maybe it's time you went out and met more people. Seeing less of each other will be better for both of us. From now on, I'll just come once a week."

Forester suggests that if you don't feel you can be blunt without causing tremendous hurt, you can back off more subtly.

For example, says Forester, if Julie couldn't speak frankly to her father, she might try withdrawing gradually. "In the first week, Julie can say, 'Look, Dad, I won't be able to come this Thursday.' And she can continue to cancel once a week for a few weeks. Then she can start canceling twice a week, always giving advance notice. Finally she can say, 'You know, it'd be great if you started seeing friends more often. I care about you and I want you to have companionship.' This way, everyone knows what's going on but no one needs to feel hurt or rejected."

Remember too that although making the break is very tough for both you and your parents, this crisis can bring you and your husband closer. It can reinforce your mutual commitment and strengthen your confidence in your ability to weather future crises together. Breaking away from your parents is almost guaranteed to be very hard, but the eventual rewards for everyone involved are immeasurable.

It isn't only wives who have trouble breaking away from Mom and Dad. Husbands can be overinvolved with parents too.

Gwen and Mark, for example, have been married a year. They don't have children yet, but Gwen feels they're already a family of three: Gwen, Mark, and Mark's mother. Mark's mother, a widow, is in the habit of dropping by a couple of times a week with homemade goodies. Naturally, she likes to chat awhile.

Mark doesn't mind his mother's frequent visits, but Gwen does. She has asked Mark to explain to his mother that the two of them, who both work, need more time alone. Lately, she hears herself nagging, and that frightens her. Mark feels torn between his mother and his wife. He wishes Gwen would understand his mother's good intentions and be nicer to her.

If you, like Gwen, are married to a man who's tied to his parents, you will have to tread carefully.

◆ Approach him gently. Be honest with your husband about the problems, but talk to him in a way that shows how much you care. Dr. Bruce M. Forester recommends saying something like, "I know you love your parents very much, and I love them too, but I think we're spending too much time with them. I'd like to be alone with you more often. How can we work this out?"
◆ Avoid, at all costs, hurling accusations at your husband or his parents. "If you scold, you're acting like a mother," Dr. Forester says. "If his real mother is apt to yell at him too, he'll feel that everyone is treating him like a kid."

continued on next page

◆ If you resent visiting his parents often, Dr. Penelope Russianoff suggests your husband go alone occasionally. "You can say, 'I have a feeling your parents might enjoy being alone with you sometimes. Why don't I visit some friends while you go to your folks' this Sunday?' Afterward you can tell him what a great time you had," Russianoff adds. "He may feel more inclined to join you next time.

◆ You can't change his relationship with his parents overnight. It helps if you can see that his parents are probably well-meaning; they're not deliberately trying to interfere.

❖

AT GRANDMA'S TABLE

Anne McCarroll

Grandparents have a special role in the lives of their grandchildren. What did this woman learn at "grandma's table"? What have you learned at your "grandma's table"?

The happiest times of my childhood were not family outings, vacations, parties or recess. The happiest times were the hours spent around the kitchen table of my grandmother's house on Highland Avenue in Dayton, Ohio.

It was there the aunts, uncles and cousins gathered and talked for hours. They didn't all live there, of course, but they dropped in at their pleasure, sure of a warm welcome and something good to eat no matter the time of day.

No one ever, as I recall, played a game at that table. They talked and laughed. To me, it was more enjoyable than Monopoly, checkers or gin rummy. They didn't need to play games to be interested or entertained. Each came equipped with an active mind and a lively sense of humor.

There are families whose time together is ever structured around an activity—a game of Monopoly, tennis, sailing or cards—and I've sometimes felt sorry for them. There's a danger they'll miss the real fun—the talking, the sharing of thoughts and ideas, hopes and concerns, the funny things that happen, the characters they meet, the ironies of life.

At my grandmother's table there would be talk over dinner—and as people lingered over dessert. Then we would move to the living room—or, on warm summer evenings, to the backyard—for more conversation. Late in the evening, everyone would return to the table for another piece of pie, a dish of ice cream, a glass of milk.

Recently, reading Russell Baker's biography, *Growing Up,* I found that he, too, cherishes memories of kitchen table talk.

"I loved the sense of family warmth," Baker writes, "that radiated through long kitchen nights of talk. . . . I was receiving an education in the world and how to think about it. What I

absorbed most deeply was not information but attitudes, ways of looking at the world that were to stay with me for many years."

I understand that because I still draw on deposits made in my memory during the hours around that table. No one preached or pontificated—as so many adults in the presence of children are apt to do. And yet, I learned so much about life.

I knew how each of my aunts and uncles felt about their jobs, their friends, religion, the state of the world, the man in the White House. And I knew their hopes and dreams.

There was not, around the table, a need to impress, a need to seem more than one was. They spoke of their failures as openly as their successes, of a mistake in judgment, a poor decision, a thoughtless remark or an embarrassing moment. I learned from their honesty, their openness, empathy and insights.

And they knew what I thought, what I felt—for we children entered into conversations. Our opinions were considered, our ideas respected.

The people around the table were different from one another. (Grammy did not turn out a uniform product.) It was not sameness that bound them together, but genuine caring for one another—and a shared sense of humor.

They knew they were not alike—talked about it, laughed about it. I suppose it was there that I learned not to tolerate differences—but to enjoy them.

I think this is why, although many people go through life always seeking their own kind, I've always preferred to know a variety of people—of different ages and interests. And I still enjoy the company of people older than I am as well as my peers.

It was at that kitchen table that I realized there is no one right way to live, to think, to be. Grammy imposed no family norm to which one must conform to be accepted, to be loved.

My children never sat at Grammy's table. She was gone before they were born. But their lives are infinitely richer for all that I learned there.

And the joy that I've found in my own family was influenced enormously by the joy I found in the family of my childhood.

Families who find pleasure in conversation may stay closer, I think, than those in which the focus is on activities. One can play tennis or golf or bridge or backgammon with anyone who has learned the game. A golf or bridge partner is easily replaced. There is an ample supply of tennis partners—one needn't leave the neighborhood to find one. It is the conversations that are special—that make one's family unique and irreplaceable.

I want to know, when my cousin visits, how his life is going, not if his backhand has improved. (I can talk backhands with the neighbors.) I want to know which dreams have come true, which have been replaced by new ones.

But that's because of the hours at Grammy's table—where everyone cared more about what you were and what you thought—than what you did or where you went.

READINGS

An acquaintance said recently, "My grandmother had a beautiful carved oak credenza; it was the most important piece of furniture in her house."

Grammy had some carved oak pieces, too. I never thought them important.

But her kitchen table—that was important.

CHAPTER 11

Parents and Children

PREVIEW

To gain a sense of what you already know about the material covered in this chapter, answer "true" or "false" to the following statements. You will find the answers on page 353.

1. Egalitarian marriages usually remain so after the birth of the first child. True or false?
2. Specific strategies may be developed to cope with parental stress. True or false?
3. A maternal instinct has been proved to exist in humans. True or false?
4. Playing with dolls can help both girls and boys to become good parents. True or false?
5. The great majority of married men say that they get greater satisfaction from the husband-father role than from their work. True or false?
6. Most studies show that regular day care by nonfamily members is detrimental to intellectual development. True or false?
7. A link between television violence and aggressive behavior in children has not been scientifically proved. True or false?
8. Many parents follow the advice of "experts" even though it conflicts with their own opinions, ideas, or beliefs. True or false?
9. Among siblings, the order of birth and spacing between births influence the development of each child. True or false?
10. Fathers and other male relatives are far more likely than day-care workers to sexually abuse children. True or false?

Aunt Tillie: Do you like children?
Uncle Gus: I do if they're properly cooked.

W.C. Fields

❖ SHOULD WE OR SHOULDN'T WE? CHOOSING TO HAVE CHILDREN

PARENTHOOD MAY NOW BE CONSIDERED A MATTER OF CHOICE owing to widespread use of birth control. If men and women want to have children, they can decide when to have them. As a result, America's birthrate has fallen to an average of two children per marriage, the number deemed ideal by 56 percent of the people interviewed in a 1985 Gallup poll. A little more than twenty-five years ago, 37 percent of those interviewed wanted a large family of four or more children. Today only 11 percent want so large a family. Approximately 2 percent want no children at all, according to the 1985 poll, but that number is expected to increase (see Nock, 1987).

In some areas, "reproductive decision-making" workshops and classes are being offered to help women order their priorities about career, life-style, and childrearing. One study found that 42 percent of the women who attended such a workshop were able to make a clear reproductive choice at the program's conclusion (Daniluk and Herman, 1984).

Child-Free Marriage

In recent articles and discussions of marriages in which there are no children, the term *childless* is often replaced by **child-free.** This change in terminology reflects a shift of values in our culture. Couples who do not choose to have children need no longer be viewed as lacking something hitherto considered essential for personal fulfillment. Indeed, the use of the suffix "free" suggests liberation from the bonds of a potentially oppressive condition (see Callan, 1985). Women who choose to be child-free are generally well educated and career oriented. One woman expressed her feelings as follows (in Boston Women's Health Book Collective, 1978a).

When I see someone who's dragging along a child who's screaming and I'm on a date with a man who's saying "You're not a whole woman if you can't have my baby," then I say, "Why don't you go over to that child and listen to the screaming for a few minutes?" The reality is that there's a lot of noise. There's a lot of mess. And it's not just for a few days. It's for years.

Even when there is less familiar and societal pressure to reproduce, the decision to remain without children is not always easily made. Although the partners in some child-free marriages have never felt that they wanted to have children, for most the decision seems to have been gradual. J.E. Veevers (1980) identified four stages of this decision process:

1. The couple decides to postpone children for a definite time period (until he gets his degree, until she gets her promotion, and so on).
2. When the time period expires, they decide to postpone children indefinitely (until they "feel like it").
3. They increasingly appreciate the positive advantages of being child-free (as opposed to the disadvantages of being childless).
4. The decision is made final, generally by the sterilization of one or both partners.

Studies of child-free marriages show nine basic categories of reasons given by those who have chosen this alternative (Houseknecht, 1987). The categories in descending order of importance are as follows:

◆ Freedom from child-care responsibility and greater opportunity for self-fulfillment
◆ More satisfactory marital relationship

◆ Wife's career considerations
◆ Monetary advantages
◆ Concern about population growth
◆ General dislike of children
◆ Early socialization experiences and doubts about parenting ability
◆ Concern about physical aspects of childbirth
◆ Concern for children in present world conditions

Couples usually have some idea that they will or will not have children before they marry. If the intent isn't clear from the start or if one partner's mind changes, the couple may have serious problems ahead. A New York banker, aged forty-four, whose wife had been continuing to postpone childbirth, complained in frustration, "What these intelligent women owe the world is not just what they do or who they are—they owe the world a legacy to pass on" (in Francke, 1980).

Many studies of child-free marriages indicate a higher degree of marital adjustment or satisfaction than is found among couples with children. In one study, child-free women reported more frequent exchange of stimulating ideas with their husbands, more shared projects and outside interests, and greater agreement on household tasks and career decisions (Houseknecht, 1982). These findings are not particularly surprising if we consider the great amount of time and energy that childrearing entails. It has also been observed that divorce is more probable in child-free marriages, perhaps because, unlike some other unhappily married couples, the child-free couples do not stay together "for the sake of the children" (Glenn and McLanahan, 1982; see Houseknecht, 1987, for a review of the current literature on voluntary childlessness. See also the reading, "On Not Having Kids," by John Hubner).

Deferred Parenthood

A report from the National Center for Health Statistics (1982) indicated that a "baby boomlet" was in progress in the early 1980s. Births to women in their thirties more than doubled between 1970 and 1979 and continued to increase in the 1980s. In 1989 the U.S. Bureau of the Census reported a "bumper crop" of four million babies (to women of all ages). This increase in births is attributed to the fact that women in their thirties (themselves products of the post-World War II baby boom) have postponed childbirth. Although most women still begin their families while in their twenties, demographers predict that the trend toward later parenthood will continue to grow, especially in middle- and upper-income groups (Price, 1982; Whitehead, 1990).

The average age at marriage has increased slowly and steadily since 1960. More career and life-style options are available to single women than in the past. Marriage and reproduction are no longer economic or social necessities. People may take longer to search out the "right" mate (even if it takes more than one marriage to do it), and they may wait for the right time to have children. Increasingly effective birth control (including safe, legal abortion) has also been a significant factor in the planned deferral of parenthood.

Besides giving parents a chance to complete education, build careers, and firmly establish their own relationship, delaying parenthood can also be advantageous for other reasons. Maternity and medical expenses, food, furniture and equipment, clothes, toys, baby-sitters, lessons, and summer camp are costly. In 1989 the annual cost of raising a child ranged from $4,100 to $9,770, depending on the family's income level, age of the child, and region of residence (Lino, 1990). (These costs are based on two-parent, two-child families; with three or more children, the cost per child declines.) To raise a child through age seventeen runs from $81,810 to $160,080 in current, non-inflated dollars. Obviously, parents who have had a chance to establish themselves financially will be bet-

Am I Parent Material?

These questions are designed to stimulate ideas that you may not have thought about. There are no right answers and no grades—your answers are right for you and may help you decide for yourself whether or not you want to be a parent. Because we all change, your answers to some of these questions may change two, five, even ten years from now. You *do* have a choice. Check out what you know and give it some thought. Then do what seems right for you.

Does Having and Raising a Child Fit the Life-Style I Want?

1. What do I want out of life for myself? What do I think is important?
2. Could I handle a child and a job at the same time? Would I have time and energy for both?
3. Would I be ready to give up the freedom to do what I want to do, when I want to do it?
4. Would I be willing to cut back my social life and spend more time at home? Would I miss my free time and privacy?
5. Can I afford to support a child? Do I know how much it takes to raise a child?
6. Do I want to raise a child in the neighborhood where I live now? Would I be willing and able to move?
7. How would a child affect *my* growth and development?
8. Would a child change my educational plans? Do I have the energy to go to school and raise a child at the same time?
9. Am I willing to give a great part of my life—*at least eighteen years*—to being responsible for a child? And am I prepared to spend a large portion of my life being concerned about my child's well-being?

What's In It for Me?

1. Do I like doing things with children? Do I enjoy activities that children can do?
2. Would I want a child to be "like me"?
3. Would I try to pass on to my child my ideas and values? What if my child's ideas turn out to be different from mine?
4. Would I want my child to achieve things that I wish I had but didn't?
5. Would I expect my child to keep me from being lonely in my old age? Do I do that for my parents? Do my parents do that for my grandparents?
6. Do I want a boy or a girl child? What if I don't get what I want?

7. Would having a child show others how mature I am?
8. Will I prove I am a man or a woman by having a child?
9. Do I expect my child to make my life happy?

Raising a Child: What's There to Know?

✓1. Do I like children? When I'm around children for a while, what do I think or feel about having one around all the time?
✓2. Do I enjoy teaching others?
✓3. Is it easy for me to tell other people what I want, or need, or what I expect of them? *my children yes*
✓✓4. Do I want to give a child the love he or she needs? Is loving easy for me?
✓ ✓✓5. Am I patient enough to deal with the noise and the confusion and twenty-four-hour-a-day responsibility? What kind of time and space do I need for myself?
6. What do I do when I get angry or upset? Would I take things out on a child if I lost my temper? *NO*
7. What does discipline mean to me? What does freedom, or setting limits, or giving space mean? What is being too strict or not strict enough? Would I want a perfect child?
8. How do I get along with my parents? What will I do to avoid the mistakes my parents made? *We learn from our past!*
9. How would I take care of my child's health and safety? How do I take care of my own?
10. What if I have a child and find out I made a wrong decision?

Have My Partner and I Really Talked about Becoming Parents?

1. Does my partner want to have a child? Have we talked about our reasons?
2. Could we give a child a good home? Is our relationship a happy and strong one?
3. Are we both ready to give our time and energy to raising a child?
4. Could we share our love with a child without jealousy?
5. What would happen if we separated after having a child, or if one of us should die?
6. Do my partner and I understand each other's feelings about religion, work, family, child raising, future goals? Do we feel pretty much the same way? Will children fit into these feelings, hopes, and plans?
7. Suppose one of us wants a child and the other doesn't? Who decides?
8. Which of these questions do we need to *really* discuss before making a decision?

ter able to bear the economic burdens of childrearing. Ann Goetting's (1986) review of parental satisfaction research revealed that "those who postpone parenthood until other components of their lives—especially their careers—are solidified" express enhanced degrees of satisfaction. Older parents may also be more emotionally mature and thus more capable of dealing with parenting stresses (although age isn't necessarily indicative of emotional maturity). In addition, as Jane Price (1982) wrote, "Combating the aging process is something of a national preoccupation. . . . In our society, the power of children to revitalize and refresh is part of the host of forces encouraging men and women to become parents much later than they did in the past."

❖ REFLECTIONS   *If you don't have children: Do you want children? When? How many? What factors do you need to take into consideration when contemplating a family for yourself? Does your partner (if you have one) agree with you about having children?*

❖ BECOMING A PARENT

A man and woman who become parents enter a new phase of their lives. More than marriage, parenthood signifies adulthood—the final, irreversible end of youthful roles. A person can become an ex-spouse but never an ex-parent. The irrevocable nature of parenthood may make the first-time parent doubtful and apprehensive, especially during the pregnancy. Yet people have few ways of preparing for parenting. Parenthood has to be learned experientially (although ideas can modify practices). A person may receive assistance from more experienced parents, but each new parent has to learn on his or her own. (See Goetting, 1986, and Umberson, 1989, for reviews of the literature on parental satisfaction.)

Transition: Parental Stress

The abrupt transition from a nonparent to a parent role may create considerable stress. Parents take on parental roles literally overnight, and the job goes on without relief around the clock. Many parents express concern about their ability to meet all the responsibilities of childrearing (see Klinman and Vukelich, 1985).

Many of the stresses felt by new parents closely reflect gender roles (Scott and Alwin, 1989; see Cowan and Cowan, 1988, for a study of changes in male and female roles after birth). Overall, mothers seem to experience greater stress than fathers (Harriman, 1983). Although a couple may have an egalitarian marriage before the birth of the first child, the marriage usually becomes more traditional once a child is born. The wife may give up her job to rear the child. Because her husband is usually away at work during the day, the housework becomes her full responsibility. Her world narrows, focusing increasingly on the demands of motherhood. If the mother must continue to work in addition to the father, or if the woman is single, she will have a dual role as both homemaker *and* provider. She will also probably have the responsibility for finding adequate child care, and it will probably be she who stays home with the child when he or she is sick.

A study by Jacqueline Ventura (1987) found multiple role demands to be the greatest source of stress for mothers. Thirty-five percent of mothers were concerned about juggling a job, parenting, housekeeping, and "taking care of husband." (A "small number of fathers also described the struggle to finish take-home work or household tasks and help with child care.") A study by Judith Myers-Walls (1984) found that mothers' adjustment to fulfilling multiple roles was made easier if they used the following coping strategies:

Having a family is like having a bowling alley installed in your head.

Martin Mull

— Women give up careers

Warning! The Surgeon General has determined that trying to be a good parent can be hazardous to your health.

Art Dworken

Coping Strategies

(1) holding a positive view of the situation, (2) developing a "salient" role (deciding which role should dominate when conflict arose), (3) compartmentalizing roles, and (4) compromising standards (of household cleanliness, for example). Abner Boles and Harriet Curtis-Boles (1986) suggest that African-American families' flexibility and egalitarianism may stand them in good stead during this transition to parenthood: "Black families have repeatedly demonstrated an ability to cross the boundaries of gender-linked sex roles and perform roles as needed to insure the effective functioning of the family."

There are various other sources of parental stress. Sixty-four percent of fathers in Ventura's study described severe stress associated with their work. A number of mothers and fathers were concerned about not having enough money. Other sources of stress involve infant health and care, infant crying, interactions with the spouse (including sexual relations), interactions with other family members and friends, and general anxiety and depression (Harriman, 1983; McKim, 1987; Ventura, 1987; Wilkie and Ames, 1986).

Although the first year of childrearing is bound to be stressful, the couple experience less stress if they (1) have already developed a strong relationship, (2) are open in their communication, (3) have agreed on family planning, and (4) originally had a strong desire for the child (Russell, 1974). Psychiatrist and researcher Jerry M. Lewis and colleagues (Lewis, Owen, and Cox, 1989) stress the importance of "marital competence" in the "successful incorporation of the child into the family." Another important factor in maintaining marital quality during this time is the father's emotional and physical support (Tietjen and Bradley, 1985). Jay Belsky (1986) writes, "The more help that husbands can be induced, encouraged, or coerced to give around the home, the less dissatisfied the wife is likely to be with the union."

Ventura (1987) suggests that families can be assisted by improved health care and support in three areas: (1) *Support:* During the prenatal period, parents need help locating community resources, such as La Leche League and child-care assistance, so that they can "restore their energy" during the postpartum period. Fathers need to be encouraged in their nurturing role. Employers need to restructure schedules, develop child-care programs, and institute parental leave policies. (2) *Coordination of care:* Parents need good communication and support from practitioners following the birth. They need "concrete explanations and demonstrations." Health practitioners, child-care providers, and community professionals need to coordinate their communication with each other. (3) *Anticipatory care and problem solving:* Teaching about development, childhood illnesses, and safety should be an ongoing part of clinic and child-care services. (For discussion of the transition to parenthood, also see Belsky, 1985a, 1985b, and 1985c; and Grossman et al., 1987. For a discussion of African-American couples and transition to parenthood, see Boles and Curtis-Boles, 1986.)

❖ REFLECTIONS   *If you have children: Did you plan to have them? What considerations led you to have them? What adjustments have you had to make? How did your relationship with your partner change?*

Parents and the Disabled Child

The advent of disability in a family, whether through birth, illness, or accident, is a tremendous stress on the family unit, especially at first. Parents may be overwhelmed with feelings of guilt, uncertainties about their parenting abilities, and fears about the future. Mothers especially feel the effects of this stress, because they are generally responsible for the child's day-to-day care. Siblings of disabled children also experience added stress. Some studies have indicated that the marital relationship may suffer in families with a disabled child, although it is only the already shaky marriages that are seriously threatened (Harris, 1984). Another study showed couples' marital adjustment to be unaffected (Collins, 1986). Healthy marriages may actually be enhanced through the experience of rearing a "special" child (Belsky et al., 1984). (The impact of disability and chronic illness on the family is discussed in greater detail in Chapter 13.)

Schneider (1983) developed a model describing stages of grief that is applicable to all life circumstances involving significant loss, including the loss of health or ability in a child. The six stages of this model are as follows:

1. Initial awareness, often accompanied by guilt and panic. If the loss event occurs at birth, the mother is especially tired and vulnerable at this stage.
2. Strategies to overcome loss, characterized by the ambiguity of holding on and letting go simultaneously.
3. Awareness of the extent and complications of loss. Much energy is consumed in dealing with this phase, often resulting in poor physical health. The griever experiences resentment, cynicism, and anger.
4. Completions: healing, acceptance of loss, resolution. This may be a lengthy process.
5. Resolution and reformations, bringing an enhanced sense of personal power.
6. Transcending loss, being free of its power to bind and limit. New energy and growth are now possible.

All parents at times find themselves torn between wanting independence for their children and wanting to protect them from pain. Parents of disabled children probably feel this conflict even more acutely than others. One of the main challenges that these parents face is assessing their child's ability to be independent and helping him or her to gain self-sufficiency. The National Information Center for Children and Youth with Handicaps (NICHY, 1990) suggests that this poses the greatest challenge to parents of girls, who are doubly stereotyped—both as "helpless, dependent" people with a disability and as "passive, dependent" females. NICHY suggests that parents help their children become independent by first of all looking within themselves to see what their own biases and expectations are. There may be changes that the parents or siblings can make in the way in which they treat the disabled child, such as letting him or her do things with less help. "The single, most important thing parents can do," according to NICHY, "is to expect [the child] to *aspire*." Parents can also help by being involved in the child's education and knowledgeable about the child's rights and opportunities.

Children are subject to numerous disabling afflictions and conditions—Down's syndrome, autism, cerebral palsy, cystic fibrosis, blindness, physical abnormalities, growth disorders, and injuries, to name just a few. Some of these disabilities are physical, some developmental, some both. Despite the prevalence of such conditions, we tend to shy away from anyone who is not "normal." Families of disabled children report that not only strangers but also friends, neighbors, family members, and even medical and service personnel treat them and their children insensitively. Such reactions serve to remind parents that their children are not valued by society. The parents may hold themselves responsible for the child's behavior or condition. In a study of families with disabled children, almost 40 percent reported that their children were not receiving needed educational, medical, or other services (Collins, 1986). This kind of treatment not only deprives the disabled and their families of much needed support and acceptance, but it also deprives the rest of society of valuable relationships and interactions. Families with disabled members need to fight social isolation by reaching out to their friends for assistance, forming networks with similar families, and learning to use existing community resources (see Resource Center at the end of the text).

*Cleaning and scrubbing can wait till
    tomorrow.
For babies grow up we've learned to our
    sorrow.
So quiet down cobwebs, dust go to sleep.
I'm rocking my baby and babies don't keep.*

Anonymous

Motherhood

Many women see their destiny as motherhood. Given the choice of becoming mothers or not (made possible through birth control), most women would probably choose to become mothers at some point in their lives, and they would make this choice for very positive reasons (see Cook et al., 1982; Gallup and Newport, 1990; Genevie and Margolies, 1987). But many women make no conscious choice; they become mothers without weighing their decision or considering its effect on their own lives and the lives of their children and partners. The consequences of a nonreflective decision—bitterness, frustration, anger, or depression—may be great. Yet it is also possible that a woman's nonreflective decision will turn out to be "right" and that she will experience unique personal fulfillment as a result.

Although researchers are unable to find any instinctual motivation for having children among humans (which does not necessarily mean that such motivation does not exist), they recognize many social motives impelling women to become mothers. When a woman becomes a mother, she may feel that her identity as an adult is confirmed. Having a child of her own proves her womanliness because from her earliest years she has been trained to assume the role of mother. She has changed dolls' diapers and pretended to feed them, practicing infant care. She played house while her brother built forts. The stories a girl has heard, the games she has played, the textbooks she has read, the religion she has been taught, the television she has watched—all have socialized her for the mother role. As Jessie Bernard (1982) wrote, "An inbred desire is no less potent than an instinctive one. The pain and anguish resulting from deprivation of an acquired desire for children are as real as the pain and anguish resulting from an instinctive one." Whatever the reason, most women choose motherhood.

And most, though not all, would choose it again. Interviews with 2,000 mothers found that eight out of ten would have children if they had the chance to do it again

Most mothers find fulfillment (as well as fatigue and frustration) in their motherhood roles. The overwhelming majority would choose to become mothers again if given the choice.

(Genevie and Margolies, 1987). Still, there remains an ambivalence that many mothers face. Liz Koch (1987) writes:

We fear we will lose ourselves if we stay with our infants. We resist surrendering even to our new-borns for fear of being swallowed up. We hear and accept both the conflicting advice that bonding with our babies is vital, and the opposite undermining message that to be a good mother, we must get away as soon and as often as possible. We hear that if we mother our own babies full time, we will have nothing to offer society, our husbands, ourselves, even our children. We fear isolation, lack of self-esteem, feelings of entrapment, of emotional and financial dependency. We fear that we will be left behind—empty arms, empty home, empty women, when our children grow away. . . . The reality is that in many ways contemporary America does not honor Mothering.

Koch observes that the "job" of mother is not valued because it is associated with "menial tasks of housekeeper, cook, laundrymaid" and so on. She writes:

If instead we looked at our mothering in and of itself, we could begin to separate the house from our role as mother. . . . It is also a way to educate our partners about the importance of caring for young children. . . . If we separate out and redefine our role as mother, it can become meaningful work, with intellectual, creative, and physical dimensions. . . . It becomes important to keep the creative juices flowing, like in any other profession, by meeting with colleagues, i.e. other mothers, and reading relevant material which can be assimilated by what feels right in our hearts.

Whether a mother is employed outside the home or works at home "full-time," her role deserves to be valued by society. Koch says of the "special state" of motherhood:

Being mothers is truly immersing ourselves in a special state, a moment to moment state of being. It is difficult to look at our day and measure success quantitatively. The day is successful when we have shared moments, built special threads of communication, looked deeply into our children's eyes and felt our hearts open. . . . It is important that we see our job as vitally important to our own growth, to our community, to society, and to world peace. Building family ties, helping healthy, loved children grow to maturity is a worthwhile pursuit. . . . The transmission of values is a significant reason to raise our own children. We are there to answer their questions and to show children, through our example, what is truly important to us.

Fatherhood

When we speak of "mothering" a child, everyone knows what we mean: nurturing, caring for, feeding, diapering, soothing, loving. Mothers generally "mother" their children almost every day of the year for at least eighteen consecutive years. The meaning of "fathering" is quite different. "Fathering" a child need take no more than a few minutes if we understand the term in its traditional sense—that is, impregnating the child's mother. Nurturant behavior by a father toward his child has not typically been referred to as "fathering." ("Mothering" doesn't seem appropriate either in this context.) The verb "to parent" has been coined to fill the need for a word that adequately describes the child-tending behaviors of both mothers and fathers (see Verzaro-Lawrence, 1981).

As we have seen, the father's traditional roles of provider and protector are instrumental; they satisfy the family's economic and physical needs. The mother's role in this traditional model is expressive; she gives emotional and psychological support for her family. However, the lines between these roles are becoming increasingly blurred because of economic pressures and new societal expectations.

From a developmental viewpoint, the father's importance to the family derives not only from his role as a representative of society, connecting his family and his culture, but also from his role as a developer of self-control and autonomy in his children. Research indicates that although mothers are inclined to view both sons and daughters as "simply children" and to apply similar standards to both sexes, fathers tend to be differently

It is so still in the house.
There is a calm in the house;
The snowstorm wails out there,
And the dogs are rolled up with snouts
*   under the tail.*
My little boy is sleeping on the ledge,
On his back he lies, breathing through his
*   open mouth.*
His little stomach is bulging round—
Is it strange if I start to cry with joy?

Eskimo mother's song

The family today emphasizes the expressive (emotional) qualities of all its members, including the father, much more than in the past.

involved with their male and female children. This may place a daughter at a disadvantage, since she has less opportunity to develop instrumental attitudes and behaviors. It may also be disadvantageous to a son, as it can limit the development of his own expressive patterns and interests (Gilbert et al., 1982). In contrast to this research, Kyle Pruett's study (1987) of "primary nurturing fathers" (fathers who provide the main day-to-day care) showed that these men treated their girl and boy children essentially equally.

In 1971, Rebelsky and Hanks found that fathers interacted an average of 37.7 seconds per day with their infant children (those between two weeks and three months of age). A more recent study found fathers averaging eight minutes per day with their children on weekdays and fourteen minutes per day on weekends (contrasted with homemaker mothers thirty and thirty-six minutes, respectively) (Fischman, 1986). In other studies, half the preschool children questioned said that they preferred television to daddy, and one child in ten said that the person that the child feared most was his or her father (none of them named mother as most feared) (Pogrebin, 1982a). Although fathers today are participating increasingly in pregnancy and birth processes, it is not clear that this involvement predisposes the father to greater participation with his children later on.

It appears that the family today emphasizes the expressive qualities of all its members, including the father, much more than in the past (Lamb, 1986). The "emergent" perspective described by Robert Fein (1980) views men as psychologically capable of participating in virtually all parenting behaviors (except gestation and lactation). Further, such participation is beneficial to the development and well-being of both children and adults. The implicit contradiction between the terms "real man" and "good father" needs to be resolved if boys are to develop into fathers who feel their "manhood enlarged and not depleted by active, caring fatherhood" (Pogrebin, 1982a). We see this contradiction epitomized by parents' fear of allowing boys to play with dolls. When a child plays with a doll, he or she is modeling the familiar parent/child relationship. By discouraging boys from "playing house," we create "an aversion to the very activities that make a man a good father" (Pogrebin, 1982a).

In support of this emergent view of fatherhood, Dr. Benjamin Spock (1968, 1976) has made a number of changes in his *Baby and Child Care* (otherwise known as the "Baby Bible"). On the subject of father participation in childrearing, the original version (1945) said:

A man can be a warm father and a real man at the same time . . . . Of course I don't mean that the father has to give as many bottles or change just as many diapers as the mother. But it's fine for him to do these things occasionally. He might make the formula on Sunday.

The revised edition (Spock and Rothenberg, 1985) advises *all* fathers to take on at least half of the child management duties and participate in the housework:

When a father does his share as a matter of course . . . it does much more than simply lighten his wife's work load and give her companionship. . . . It shows that he believes this work is crucial for the welfare of the family, that it calls for judgment and skill, and that it's his responsibility as much as it is hers. . . . This is what sons and daughters need to see in action if they are to grow up without sexist attitudes.

Research into father care of infants has revealed one dramatic finding: If a man is involved in the physical care of his own or someone else's child younger than three years, the probability that he will later be involved in the abuse of any child is greatly reduced (Parker and Parker, 1984 and 1986).

In his intensive study, Kyle Pruett (1987) found that "fatherhood is changing, with fastball speed, especially compared with the languid pace of social evolution." He concluded that fathers must be encouraged to develop the nurturing quality in themselves in

Don't be the man you think you should be, be the father you wish you'd had.

Letty Cottin Pogrebin

We learn from experience. A man never wakes up his second baby just to see it smile.

Grace Williams

order to experience the "unimagined rewards" of parenthood. James A. Levine, a former vice-president of the Bank Street College of Education who now leads fatherhood seminars at major corporations, says that the new father is a man who "attempts to make childrearing an important part of his life" (quoted in Lawson, 1990). Levine lists several trends that are indicative of the father's changing role: more men are attending the births of their children and taking time off from work afterward; more men are taking children to day care or to the doctor; more men are enrolled in parenting classes; diaper-changing tables are appearing in the men's rooms of airports and train stations; and fathers with babies are becoming highly visible in advertising (Lawson, 1990). "The truth is leaking out," Pruett writes, "through the real lives of men and their children that the uninvited, uninvolved, unwelcomed, inept father is moving toward obsolescence." (See the reading "Sharing the Baby" by Joanne Kates. See also Lamb, 1986, for a collection of essays on fatherhood in today's society.)

❖ REFLECTIONS   *How should childrearing tasks be delegated between spouses (or partners)? Are there any particular tasks that you believe either men or women should not do? How are tasks delegated in your household? Who should be responsible for children if they are ill? Who should be responsible for making baby-sitting or child-care arrangements?*

❖ OTHER IMPORTANT CHILD SOCIALIZERS

Child Care

Supplementary child care is a crucial issue for today's parents of young children. The number of dual-worker and single-parent families has doubled in the past decade; such families are now the rule rather than the exception. Many parents must look outside their homes for assistance in childrearing. About two million children currently receive formal, licensed day care, and another five million attend nursery schools. Uncounted millions are cared for by relatives or baby-sitters, and perhaps five million children under the age of ten have no one at all to look after them (Watson, 1984b). (See Chapter 12 for a discussion of the role of day care in maternal employment.) Day-care homes and centers, nursery schools, and preschools can relieve parents of some of their childrearing tasks and also furnish them with some valuable time of their own. Dr. Nathan Talbot (1976), professor of pediatrics at Harvard University, wrote:

With three provisos, these out-of-home experiences can so enrich a father's or mother's life that s/he is better able to serve the needs of the children than s/he would be if s/he stayed home all the time. The first proviso is that the children are well cared for. . . . The second is that at least one parent continues to be readily available to the children for a minimum of one or two hours most days. The third is that a parent . . . remain the person responsible for the upbringing of the children. . . . Supplementary child care can solidify rather than disrupt the family and can improve rather than hurt the children's chances for happy and developmentally rich lives.

What does group care have to offer children? Studies of infants and young children in group-care situations have shown that their development is stimulated or enhanced by enriched child-care environments (Belsky, 1991; Kutner, 1988). Emotional security and patterns of attachment to parents do not seem to be significantly altered by quality group-care experiences. Other studies have indicated that the overall effect of day care on intellectual development is neither beneficial nor adverse. Furthermore, in the case of disadvantaged families, high-quality child care has great positive effect (Belsky et al., 1984).

Dr. Burton White, director of Boston's Center for Parent Education, however, sees the trend toward increasing use of day care as a "disaster": "Both parents don't have to work—they both *want* to work to maintain a house and lifestyle. They are putting their desires above the welfare of the baby" (cited in Watson, 1984b). This assessment may apply to families in which one parent has a substantial income, but for many dual-earner families and most single-parent families, child care is a necessity, not a luxury. As Jay Belsky and colleagues (1984) point out, "Since it is unlikely that mothers will return in large numbers to the role of full-time homemakers, and that day care will go away, . . . the critical issue [in day care] is the condition of care."

National concern periodically is focused on day care by revelations of sexual abuse of children by their caregivers. Although these revelations have brought providers of child care under close public scrutiny and have alerted parents to potential dangers, they have also produced a backlash within the child-care profession. Some caregivers are now reluctant to have physical contact with the children; male child-care workers feel especially constrained and may find their jobs at risk (Chaze, 1984). A national study (Finkelhor, 1988), however, found that children have a far greater likelihood of being sexually abused by a father, step-father, or other relative than by a day-care worker. In 1985 the U.S. Department of Health and Human Services announced new day-care guidelines, calling for training of staff in the prevention and detection of child abuse, thorough checks on prospective employees, and allowance of parental visits at any time. But critics believe that the government should go farther in establishing standards for day care itself. Senator Paula Hawkins (quoted in Collins, 1985) stated, "They really have to consider the quality of the care, and not just the quality of the care-givers." Government funding and assistance for day-care programs remain small to nonexistent.

What can parents do to insure quality care for their children? In addition to the obvious requirements of cleanliness, comfort, good food, a safe environment, and an attentive, trained staff, parents should look for the following (from Watson, 1984b):

◆ *A stable staff.* Children are more secure when they know who is caring for them. Ideally, the staff should be trained in child development or psychology.
◆ *Small groups.* Infants especially need close attention and stimulation. Older preschoolers can function in groups of four to eight children per adult, depending on the children's ages.
◆ *Appropriate attention.* Children need attention appropriate to their developmental stage.
◆ *Appropriate activities.* Activities should be appropriate to the children's developmental stage, reflecting their needs to learn about themselves and their environment.
◆ *Parental involvement.* Parents should be welcomed and their involvement with the child-care program encouraged. (For more information, see Resource Center.)

As with a number of critical services in our society, those who most need supplementary child care are those who can least afford it. Child care done properly is a costly business (even though child-care work remains a relatively low-paying, low-status job). The United States is one of the few industrialized nations that does not have a comprehensive national day-care policy. In fact, beginning in 1981, the federal government dramatically cut federal contributions to day care; many state governments followed suit. Nathan Talbot (1976) observed that "we are shortchanging ourselves and the future of our nation by failing to invest in our children as our best and most critically important asset. . . . Child care is worthy of a position close to the top in our national hierarchy of priorities."

Television

In most American households the television is on at least seven hours each day. Starting around age four, most Americans watch an average of four hours of TV or more each

A body at rest tends to remain at rest.

Newton's First Law of Motion

day. The average American child, by the time he or she reaches eighteen, will have spent at least sixteen thousand hours watching television. No other activity except sleep occupies more time for children and adolescents (Brown, 1990; Singer, 1983). An average viewing week of thirty hours includes about four hundred commercials and provides a kaleidoscopic mix of Kix, Trix, Gummi Bears, Pound Puppies, jaded yuppies, Superman, Superboy, Super Mario Brothers, Classic Coke, practical jokes, violent crimes, cheap wine, fancy cars, fast food, Fred Flintstone, Freddy Krueger, and Peg Bundy. Thirty hours of watching television is thirty hours *not* spent interacting with family members, playing outside, playing creatively, reading, fantasizing, doing homework, exploring, or even napping. Besides limiting children's time for such pursuits, television has also been implicated in a number of individual, familial, and societal disorders.

Researchers have documented a variety of physiological effects produced by television, including altered brain-wave (trancelike) states and hyperactivity, impaired eye movements, and impaired hand and body use. Low levels of microwave radiation are emitted by color sets. Although the manufacturers assure us that we are in no danger, we are also cautioned not to sit too close "just in case." Television has also been observed to have deleterious effects on learning and perception, nutrition, life-style, and family and social relationships (Fabes, Wilson, and Christopher, 1989; Moody, 1980). Not all research supports the assertion that TV is detrimental to family life, however. Some studies have shown that positive feelings result when families share their viewing experience (Kubey and Csikszentmihalyi, 1990).

Much parent/child conflict revolves around eating habits. And anyone watching television, especially children's television, cannot help but be aware of the amount of junk-food advertising (for sweetened breakfast cereals, candy, sodas) directed toward children. One expert testified before Congress that "an advertisement to a child has the quality of an order, not a suggestion." Thus, responsible parents are put in the position of having to defend good nutrition against the incessant bombardment of commercials. Advertisers

To be able to fill leisure intelligently is the last product of civilization.

Bertrand Russell

Television provides role models for children. What kind of message do you believe this African-American child is receiving from her cartoon heroine?

count on the child's ability to influence parents' buying—where both children's and adults' products are concerned.

Because of the constant pressure to buy and the necessity of regulating their children's viewing habits, some parents choose not to have a television. Once the television is gone, it is often not missed. It may be missed more by adults who use it for their own entertainment and as a baby-sitter for their children. Children are peer oriented and have their friends to play with. The use of television as a baby-sitter underscores a dilemma for many parents: they disapprove of what their children see, but they also want to have the time to themselves that may be obtained by letting their children watch television.

Children learn about the world from watching television. Although some valuable and thought-provoking information may be gained from it (especially if the viewer is an economically or culturally "disadvantaged" child), much of television programming promotes or condones racist, sexist, agist, homophobic and other negative stereotypes. Images of women have improved in recent years, but depictions of the family still tend to be stereotypical or romanticized. Middle-class families are likely to be portrayed as "superpeople" who deal effectively with any problem, whereas working-class families (especially fathers) are more likely to be shown as inept (Fabes, Wilson, and Christopher, 1989). Researchers have expressed concern that the idealization of middle-class life presents unrealistic goals and may lead impressionable viewers to question the adequacy of their own lives.

Much television programming also promotes violence and fear (Fabes, Wilson, and Christopher, 1989). The cumulative effect of television, according to a report by the Annenberg School of Communications, is the creation of the "mean world syndrome," the belief that crime and violence are much more pervasive in the world than they actually are (Pogatchnik, 1990). A report issued by the National Institute of Mental Health stated that "overwhelming" evidence indicates that "excessive" violence on television causes aggressive behavior in children (Tooth, 1985). This conclusion was based on the results of approximately 2,500 separate studies conducted since the early 1970s. Besides encouraging aggressive behavior, television also has the effect of desensitizing viewers to observed violent acts. Children may learn to see violence as an acceptable means of problem solving and to show no moral outrage at acts of destructive aggression.

Kate Moody (1980) suggests the following criteria for helping parents to evaluate what their children watch:

1. What kind of distinction is made between reality and make-believe? If there is a transition between the two, is it clearly signaled to children?
2. Is the program geared to the child's level of understanding?
3. How are problems solved? By using others? By hitting? Revenge? Money? Magic? Cooperation?
4. What role models are offered? Are sex or race stereotypes reinforced?
5. What is the pace of the program? What special effects are used? What is the noise/confusion level?
6. How is humor used? Does a laugh track tell the child what is to be considered funny?
7. How is the world portrayed? As a dangerous and fearsome place?
8. What kind of commercials are associated with the program? Junk food? Fast cars? Personal hygiene products?
9. What is the child's response to the program? Is he or she aggressive, cooperative, excitable, calm? What kinds of play follow viewing?
10. Is the program good enough to be worth the parent's time?

. . . TV causes . . . serious and pervasive violence in normal . . . youngsters who watch TV attentively and regularly. What results from this psychic abuse is the impoverishment of personality and the trivialization of life.

Herb Kohl

We are drowning our youngsters in violence, cynicism and sadism piped into the living room and even the nursery. The grandchildren of kids who used to weep because the Little Match Girl froze to death now feel cheated if she isn't slugged, raped, and thrown into a Bessemer converter.

Jenkin Lloyd Jones

❖ CHILD DEVELOPMENT AND SOCIALIZATION

Who Is the Child? Theories of Socialization

Twentieth-century attitudes about children have been influenced by several theories of socialization.

THE PSYCHOANALYTIC MODEL. The modern heir to the ancient doctrine of inherent evil is the "impulse-taming" Freudian school of thought. Sigmund Freud's (1856-1939) contribution to the understanding of the human psyche is profound. His emphasis on the importance of unconscious mental processes and on the stages of psychosexual development has greatly influenced modern psychology. Freud's **psychoanalytic model** of child development holds that beneath the surface of each individual's consciousness is the repressed unconscious—a storm of contradictory impulses, controlled only by the individual's gradual internalization of societal restraints. It is the parents who are mainly responsible for the child's development. Between the ages of four and six, the child identifies with the parent who is of the same sex. Not becoming like that parent is a failure to reach maturity: the rebel is described as "infantile." The scientific thought of Freud"s time was greatly influenced by Charles Darwin's theories on evolution. As Jerome Kagan (1984) has pointed out, Freud viewed evolution as an apt metaphor for human behavior and constructed his theories in accordance with the scientific thought of his day.

STAGES OF COGNITIVE DEVELOPMENT. Beginning in the 1920s, the work of Jean Piaget continued to make use of the evolutionary model. Piaget observed that **cognitive development** occurs in discrete stages through which all infants and children pass. Based on the development of the brain and the nervous system, these stages occur at about the same time in the development of all children (unless they are mentally impaired). The stages can be seen as building blocks, each of which must be completed before the next one can be put into place. In Piaget's view, children develop their cognitive abilities through interaction with the world and adaptation to their surroundings. Children adapt by *assimilating* (making new information compatible with their world understanding) and *accommodating* (adjusting their cognitive framework to incorporate new experiences) (Dworetsky, 1990).

SOCIAL MOLDING. Theories of **social molding** view social experiences as the principal source of human variation. In this way of thinking, human nature is formed by culture, society, and the family. True, the infant or young child embodies a host of impulses, but these are given shape and direction through interactions. Children are first socialized through parental direction of their behavior. Parents teach children what is good, what is bad, what to eat, what not to eat, what to keep, what to share, how to talk, what to feel, what to think. Parents influence their children by *modeling* (serving as examples for their children) and by *defining* (establishing expectations for them) (Cohen, 1987).

Erik Erikson's work emphasizes parental and societal responsibilities in children's development. Each of Erikson's life-cycle stages (see Chapter 10) is centered around a specific emotional concern based on individual biological pressures and external sociocultural expectations and actions. (See Peterson and Rollins [1987] for a detailed critique of social molding theory.)

DEVELOPMENTAL INTERACTION. Parents do not simply give birth to children and then "bring them up." According to **developmental interaction** theory, the growth and devel-

> *. . . we have attributed the influence to [the mother] as if she was a sorceress. She's a good witch if the child turns out fine and a bad witch if he doesn't.*
>
> Jerome Kagan

> *The chief cause of human error is to be found in the prejudices picked up in childhood.*
>
> René Descartes

Children begin by loving their parents; after a time, they judge them; rarely, if ever, do they forgive them.

Oscar Wilde

opment of children takes place within a complex and changing family system. Not only are children socialized by their parents but they are also socializers in their own right. When an infant cries to be picked up and held, to have a diaper changed, or to be burped, or when she or he smiles when being played with, fed, or cuddled, the parents are being socialized. The child is creating strong bonds with the parents. Although the infant's actions are not at first consciously directed toward reinforcing parental behavior, they nevertheless have that effect. In this sense, children can be viewed as participants in creating their own environment and in contributing to their further development (see Peterson and Rollins, 1987).

In the developmental interaction model of family growth, social and psychological development are seen as lifelong processes, with each family member having a role in the development of the others. Siblings influence one another according to their particular needs and personalities. Also, according to Alfred Adler (1976) and others, sibling influence (or the lack of it, in the case of only children) is important in subtle yet powerful ways as the result of birth order and spacing (the number of years between sibling births) (also see Belsky et al., 1984). A study at Colorado State University, for example, found that a firstborn's self-esteem suffers if a sibling is born two or more years later but is not affected if the sibling is born less than two years later (Goleman, 1985). Furthermore, if the firstborn child is already five or six years old, the birth of a second sibling does not have the same impact. Another study, examining Mexican-American and Anglo children's perceptions of roles within their families, found that birth order and gender were important in both groups in determining roles. (The only ethnic differences found concerned the roles of last-born Mexican-American children. The researchers suggest that these children have a greater tendency than Anglo children to "stay out of the other family members' way" [Jaramillo and Zapata, 1987].) A study of African-American and white families indicated that race has no impact on the dynamics of birth order (Steelman and Powell, 1985).

In terms of the eight developmental stages of a human life cycle described by Erikson, parents are generally at the seventh stage (generativity) during their children's growing years, and the children are probably anywhere from the first stage (trust) to the fifth (identity) or sixth (intimacy). The parents' need to establish their generativity is at least partly met by the child's need to be cared for and taught. The parents' approach to child-rearing will inevitably be modified by the child's inherent nature.

The models we have described leave out something very crucial about human personality. Each person knows that his or her basic motives are not simply the result of biological drives nor is everything he or she does just the result of socialization. Something more human about human beings exists than these models acknowledge. This is the "I" within each person; it may be what philosophers have called the soul or it may be something else, but it has an existence of its own that resists biological and environmental pressures. Erik Erikson (1968) wrote:

What the "I" reflects on when it sees or contemplates the body, the personality, and the roles to which it is attached for life—not knowing where it was before or will be after—are the various selves which make up our composite Self. One should really be decisive and say that the "I" is all-conscious, and that we are truly conscious only insofar as we can say "I" and mean it. . . . to ignore the conscious "I" . . . means to delete the core of human self-awareness.

Psychosexual Development in the Family Context

Within the context of our overall growth, and perhaps central to it, our sexual selves develop. Within the family we learn how we "should" feel about our bodies, whether we

100010 *(handwritten)*

should be ashamed, embarrassed, proud, or indifferent. Some families are comfortable with nudity in a variety of situations: swimming, bathing, sunbathing, dressing or undressing. Others are comfortable with partial nudity from time to time: when sharing the bathroom, changing clothes, and so on. Still others are more modest and carefully guard their privacy. Most researchers and therapists would allow that all these styles can be compatible with the development of sexually well-adjusted children as long as some basic needs are met:

1. The child's body (and nudity) is accepted and respected.
2. The child is not punished or humiliated for seeing the parent naked, going to the toilet, or making love.
3. The child's needs for privacy are respected.

Families also vary in the amount and type of physical contact in which they participate. Some families hug and kiss, give back rubs, sit and lean on each other, and generally maintain a high degree of physical closeness. Some parents extend this closeness into their sleeping habits, allowing their infants and small children in their beds each night. (In many cultures, this is the rule rather than the exception.) Other families limit their contact to hugs and tickles. Variations of this kind are normal. Concerning children's needs for physical contact, we can make the following generalizations:

1. All children (and adults) need a certain amount of freely given physical affection from those they love. Although there is no prescription for the right amount or form of such expression, its quantity and quality both affect children's emotional well-being and the emotional and sexual health of the adults they will become (see Kagan, 1976).

2. Children should be told, in a nonthreatening way, what kind of touching by adults is "good" and what is "bad." They need to feel that they are in charge of their own bodies, that parts of their bodies are private property, and that no adult has the right to touch them with sexual intent. It is not necessary to frighten a child by going into great detail about the kinds of things that might happen. A better strategy is to instill a sense of self-worth and confidence in children so that they will not allow themselves to be victimized (Pogrebin, 1983). We also should learn to listen to children and to trust them. They need to know that if they are sexually abused, it is not their fault. They need to feel that they can tell about it and still be worthy of love. (See Strong and DeVault, 1988, for detailed information on psychosexual development throughout life.)

Conscience is the inner voice which warns us that someone may be looking.

H.L. Mencken

} *Self confidence (handwritten)*

Ethnicity and Child Socialization

A person's ethnicity is not necessarily fixed and unchanging. Researchers generally agree that ethnicity has both objective and subjective components. The objective component refers to one's ancestry, cultural heritage and, to varying degrees, physical appearance. The subjective component refers to whether one **feels** he or she is a member of a certain ethnic group, such as African American, Latino, Asian American, Native American, and so on. If both parents are from the same ethnic group, the child will probably identify as a member of that group. But if he or she has parents from different ethnic groups, ethnic identification becomes more complex. In such cases, one may identify with both groups, only one, or according to the situation—Latino when with Latino relatives and friends or Anglo when with Anglo friends and relatives. However we choose to identify ourselves, our families are the key to the transmission of ethnic identification.

Ethnicity (handwritten)
objective - physical (handwritten)
Subjective - emotional (handwritten)

A child's ethnic background affects how he or she is socialized. Latinos and Asian Americans, for example, stress the authority of the father in the family. In both groups, parents command considerable respect from their children, even when the children become adults. Older siblings, especially brothers, have authority over younger siblings

America's children are becoming increasingly ethnically diverse. By the year 2000, half of America's children will be from non-white or non-Anglo ethnic groups. In California, these children already represent the majority.

and are expected to set a good example (Becerra, 1988; Tran, 1988; Wong, 1988). Asian Americans tend to discourage aggression in children and for discipline rely on censure and shame rather than physical force.

Groups with minority status in the United States may be different from each other in some ways, but they also have much in common. For one thing, they emphasize education as the means for their children to achieve success. For another, they are often dual-worker families, so the children may have considerable exposure to television while the parents are away from home. This may be viewed as a mixed blessing: on the one hand, TV may help children who need to acquire English language skills; on the other, it can promote fear, violence, and negative stereotypes of women and minority status groups. It can discourage creativity and encourage passivity. Former world light heavyweight champion Jose Torres (1991) counsels young Latinos: "Instead of watching TV, read and write. Words are the symbols of reality, and a well-read person, skilled at decoding those symbols, is better able to comprehend and think about the real world."

Some American children are raised with a strong sense of ethnic identification, whereas others are not. Identification with a particular group gives a sense of pride, security, and belonging. At the same time, it can also give a sense of separateness from the mainstream society. Often, however, that sense of separateness is imposed by the greater society. Discrimination and prejudice shape the lives of many American children. According to Margaret Beale Spencer (1985), a minority status child's "acquisition of a healthy psyche requires an intervention between societally communicated cultural assumptions and the minority child's healthy psychological development." Nonminority status children generally do not experience this lack of congruence between society's values and healthy psychological development. Parents of ethnic minority children may try to prepare their children for the harsh realities of life beyond the family and immediate community (Peterson, 1985). One researcher (Richardson, 1981) wrote about African Americans:

PERSPECTIVE

Raising Children to Be Prejudice-Free

The world in which our grandparents grew up was simpler than our own in many ways. Towns and neighborhoods stayed the same from year to year, and customs didn't change much either. People passed their prejudices on to their children, who often accepted them without question, because they had little or no experience to teach them otherwise. George Simpson and Milton Yinger (1985) explain: "If asked why he dislikes a member of a minority group, [the child] will recite the reasons taught him by his culture, by the adults around him—always assuming, of course, that they are strictly his own reasons and that they are the true reasons."

In today's fast-changing world, we cannot afford to cling complacently to the narrow-mindedness and prejudices of the past. Technological advances in communication and transportation are quickly shrinking the distances between us and other peoples of the world. At home we are becoming more diverse ethnically and linguistically. By the year 2020, it is expected that one out of every three people in the United States will be from what we now call a "minority" group (Sobol, 1990). Timothy Bergen comments: "The future will be in a culturally pluralistic nation and a rapidly shrinking world" (quoted in Fuller, 1989/1990). We must learn to live together with respect and tolerance for our ethnic, cultural, and personal differences (see Matiella, 1991).

The following guidelines are suggested to help parents foster an appreciation of cultural differences in their children.

◆ Explore your family's heritage with your children. Look at old photos and talk to grandparents and other older family members. Find out about the hopes and dreams they had and the obstacles they overcame. Learn more about your cultural background through the art, music, and literature.

◆ Examine your own attitudes and knowledge about other ethnic groups. Expand your understanding of other cultures and encourage your child's interest in new cultural experiences. Possible resources include libraries, museums, language classes, travel agents, festivals, dances, concerts, music tapes, cookbooks, ethnic markets, and restaurants. Be sure that you have an up-to-date world map or globe for reference. Consider finding pen pals in other countries or helping to support a foreign child in need through an agency (such as PLAN International) that encourages correspondence between participants. Think about hosting a visiting high school or university student—for a school term or just for dinner.

◆ Whenever possible, take the opportunity to celebrate diversity and contradict stereotypes. Help children develop critical thinking so that they can recognize stereotyping—for example, in TV shows that always portray "the Native American in full headdress, the black man as the villain and Hispanics with lots of children" (Wardle, 1989/1990). Get children books, posters, videos, puzzles, and dolls that honor cultural and ethnic diversity.

◆ It's important to be open to questions about race and ethnicity so that children don't get the idea that these are taboo subjects. If you don't know an answer, do some research, or talk to your child's teacher or a librarian. If your son or daughter has a conflict with someone from another ethnic group, guide the child to deal with personal issues and not to blame the other person's culture or ethnic group. If you hear children using stereotyped or derogatory terms, inter-vene. Let them know it's not right to put others down or tease them about their differences. And watch your own language! Call ethnic groups by the names they prefer rather than common usage terms or slang that may be offensive.

◆ Select child-care groups and schools with ethnically diverse staffs and children. Support your children's friendships with others of diverse backgrounds. Make sure that schools teach positively about diversity and that events such as holiday programs don't enforce stereotypes. For example, Native Americans should be portrayed as a diverse people with unique ways of life, legends, philosophy, and contributions and not represented merely as "guests" of the Pilgrims on Thanksgiving. In addition, schools need to be sensitive to religious differences when planning such programs. With imagination, these events can be conducted so that they include presentations from diverse cultural groups and can be both entertaining and educational for all.

◆ Take action. Don't ignore bigotry when it happens. If someone makes a racist remark, say, "Please don't talk that way around me or my children." When your children see you standing up for your beliefs, they will learn to do the same. Encourage your child to respond to put downs or aggressive teasing with a stock response such as, "Don't call me that. It's not fair" ("Talking to Children. . . .," 1989/1990).

◆ It all starts with self-esteem. If we let children know that they are valued, they are more likely to find value in others. If they are sensitive to others' feelings, they are less likely to form prejudices.

Although these guidelines have been formulated with ethnic and cultural differences in mind, many of them can be applied to or adapted for learning to appreciate and accept people with other kinds of differences—such as those who have disabilities or who are gay or lesbian. (For a more complete discussion of children and cultural diversity, see Matiella, 1991.)

Black mothers know that their children will ultimately experience racism. They believe that racism experiences can be devastating and destructive if the child has not been prepared to recognize or develop techniques and strategies for coping with these experiences. The mothers also know that black children will ultimately have to know they are black and understand what a black identity means in a racist society.

Suggestions for raising children to be free of prejudice are given in this chapter's Perspective. (The relationship between ethnicity and family strength is discussed in Chapter 18.)

❖ GAY AND LESBIAN PARENTING

There may be as many as 1.5 million lesbian mothers rearing their children in the United States (Hoeffer, 1981). The number of gay fathers is estimated to be one to three million (Bozett, 1987b). Most of these parents are or have been married. Heterosexual fears about gay and lesbian parents center around parenting abilities, fear of sexual abuse, and worry that the children will become gay or lesbian.

Lesbian Mothers

While their sexual orientation is different from heterosexual single mothers, lesbian mothers share many similarities with them. One study of lesbian and heterosexual single mothers (Kirkpatrick et al., 1981) found that their life-styles, childrearing practices, and general demographic data were strikingly similar. One of the few areas in which lesbian and heterosexual mothers differed from each other was in cohabitation, according to another study (Lewin and Lyons, 1982). Most heterosexual mothers felt no need for secrecy if they were living with a man. But many lesbian mothers felt increased vulnerability to hostility from outsiders if they were cohabiting. In particular, they feared the responses from neighbors, their children's playmates, and their own parents. As a result, lesbian mothers may feel forced to exclude their partners from school or other social activities involving their children. Lesbians also fear losing their children in custody disputes. This fear is well-founded, as only about 15 percent of lesbian mothers win custody of their children. This is an improvement, however, over the situation in 1970, when less that 1 percent gained custody (Goldstein, 1986).

When children learn that their mothers are lesbians, according to one study of families with formerly married lesbian mothers, they are initially shocked (Lewis, 1980). At first, they tend to deny any pain or anger. Generally they have more difficulty in accepting their mother's lesbian identity than their parents' divorce or separation because there is no community of support. It is much easier to talk with others about their parents divorcing than about their mother being a lesbian. In Karen Lewis's study (1980), children between nine and twelve years of age felt a deep need to keep their mother's lesbian identity a secret. As a result, these children felt a sense of isolation; they were unable to talk over their feelings with their friends. Both children and older adolescents worried that they might become gay or lesbian or that others might think they were gay or lesbian. The boys tended to become angry at their mother's partner, blaming her for their mother's sexual orientation. But whatever the children's response, all expressed a desire to accept their mothers. "Problems between the mother and children," observed Lewis, "seemed secondary to the children's respect for the difficult step she had taken." Therapist Saralie Bisnovitch Pennington (1987) wrote, "I cannot emphasize enough that children fare best in homes where the mothers are secure in both their lesbian identity and their parental role, and where they have a strong support system that includes other lesbian mothers."

Some lesbians, especially those in committed relationships, are choosing to create families through artificial insemination. To date, there are no reliable data on the number of such births, but anecdotal information indicates that it is in the thousands. There are many questions raised when a lesbian couple contemplates having a baby in this way: Who will be the birth mother? What will the relationship of the other mother be? Will the donor be known or unknown? If known, will the child have a relationship with him? Will the child have a relationship with the donor's partner? Which, if any, of the child's grandparents will have a relationship with him or her? Will there be a legal contract between the parenting parties? There are few precedents to learn from or role models to follow in these cases (see Pies, 1987). Another issue that such couples have to face is that the nonbiological parent has no legal tie to the child. Furthermore, society may not recognize her as a "real" parent, since children are expected to have only one *real* mother and one *real* father. (For a personal account involving many of these issues, see the reading by a lesbian mother at the end of this chapter.)

Gay Fathers

The reasons gay men marry are generally the same reasons heterosexuals marry (Bozett, 1987b). These might be genuine love or companionship; pressure from family, friends, or girlfriend; an attempt to "cure homosexuality"; or lack of awareness that one is gay. Most marriages of gay men appear to start off satisfactorily. Over time, however, the sexual relationship declines and the man begins to participate in clandestine same-sex liaisons. Once they have children, most gay men tend to stay married (Ross, 1972, 1978). For those whose wives accept their sexual orientation, the marriage may be fairly stable. But for most it is likely to be characterized by deceit, shame, and increasing anger. If such marriages do end in divorce, however, it is not necessarily a direct result of the homosexuality; it seems that gay men's marriages "like most other marriages, deteriorate for a variety of reasons" (Bozett, 1987b).

Lesbian families created through artificial insemination are a unique family form. Are such families single-parent families, stepfamilies, or a new family form? One of the mothers in this photograph discusses the challenges faced by their family in the reading on pages 356–357.

Studies of gay fathers indicate that "being gay is compatible with effective parenting" (Bozett, 1987c; Harris and Turner, 1986). Furthermore, it appears that gays who disclose their orientation to their children and who have a stable gay relationship tend to provide better-quality parenting than those who remain married and keep their gayness hidden. Married gay fathers may spend much of their free time seeking out sexual partners; they may also be workaholics who spend much of their time away from home (Miller, 1979). One study of gay fathers (Turner, Scadden, and Harris, 1985) concluded that (1) most gay fathers have positive relationships with their children, (2) the father's sexual orientation is relatively unimportant to the relationship, and (3) gay fathers endeavor to create stable home environments for their children. Another study (Harris and Turner, 1985/1986) found that there were no significant differences in the parenting of gays, lesbians, and heterosexuals except that the nongay parents apparently tried harder to provide "opposite sex" role models. Although the research on children of gay fathers is fairly limited at this time, it seems to indicate that the children's responses are similar to those of children of lesbian parents. Their primary concerns, especially at first, are about what others may think. They are embarrassed if their fathers are blatantly gay, and they worry that others will think they are too. Nevertheless, even though "children may not understand why their fathers are gay, and some may strongly disapprove, the child-father bond is maintained" (Bozett, 1987).

Fears about Gay and Lesbian Parenting

Heterosexual fears about the parenting abilities of lesbians and gays are unwarranted. Fears of the sexual abuse of children by gay parents or their partners are completely unsubstantiated. A review of the literature on the children of gay men and lesbians found that there were virtually no documented cases of sexual abuse by gay parents or their lovers; such exploitation appears to be committed disproportionately by heterosexuals (Cramer, 1986).

Fears about gay parents rejecting children of the other sex also seem unfounded. Such fears reflect the popular misconception that being gay or lesbian is a rejection of members of the other sex. Many gay and lesbian parents go out of their way to make sure that their children have role models of both sexes. Many also say that they hope their children will develop heterosexual identities in order to be spared the pain of growing up gay in a homophobic society. One study (Green, 1978) of thirty-seven children of lesbians found that all developed heterosexual identities. Another study (Hoeffer, 1981) of the children of lesbians and single heterosexual mothers found a lack of notable differences between the children. Both groups of children preferred toys associated with traditional gender roles. Peers rather than parents seem to have the greatest influence on a child's gender-role behavior (Green et al., 1986; Hoeffer, 1981).

As Brenda Maddox (1982) observed, "Gay people, once they are parents, are no more theoretical than straight parents. They have produced the children. They love them."

❖ STYLES AND STRATEGIES OF CHILDREARING

A parent's approach to training, teaching, nurturing, and helping a child will vary according to cultural influences, the parent's personality, the parent's basic attitude toward children and childrearing, and the role model that the parent presents to the child.

Authoritarian, Permissive, and Authoritative Parents

The three basic styles of childrearing may be termed *authoritarian, permissive*, and *authoritative* (Baumrind, 1971, 1983).

Know!

__Authoritarian__ parents typically require absolute obedience. The parents' maintaining control is of first importance. "Because I said so," is a typical response to a child's questioning of parental authority, and physical force may be used to assure obedience. Working-class families tend to be more authoritarian than middle-class families. Diana Baumrind found that children of authoritarian parents tend to be less cheerful than other children and correspondingly more moody, passively hostile, and vulnerable to stress (see Belsky et al., 1984).

__Permissive__ attitudes are more popular in middle-class families than in working-class families. The child's freedom of expression and autonomy are valued. Permissive parents rely on reasoning and explanations. Yet permissive parents may find themselves resorting to manipulation and justification. The child is free from external restraints but not from internal ones. The child is supposedly free because he or she conforms "willingly," but such freedom is not authentic. This form of socialization creates a bind: "Do what we tell you to do because *you* want to do it." Two psychologists commented on internalized control as a means of socialization as follows (Sluzki and Eliseo, 1971):

"If you do not obey, we shall be angry with you, but if you obey only because we are telling you, we shall also be angry, because you should be independent." (That is, *want* to do whatever one *should* do of one's own will.) This injunction creates an untenable situation, because it demands that an external source be confused with an internal one.

Baumrind (1983) found that although children of permissive parents are generally cheerful, they exhibit low levels of self-reliance and self-control.

Parents with __authoritative__ attitudes toward childrearing rely on positive reinforcement and infrequent use of punishment. They direct the child in a manner that shows awareness of his or her feelings and capabilities. Parents encourage the development of the child's autonomy within reasonable limits and foster an atmosphere of give and take in parent/child communications. Parental support is a crucial ingredient in child socialization. It is positively related to cognitive development, self-control, self-esteem, moral behavior, conformity to adult standards, and academic achievement (Gecas and Seff, 1991). Control is exercised in conjunction with support by authoritative parents. Children raised by authoritative parents tend to approach novel or stressful situations with curiosity and show high levels of self-reliance, self-control, cheerfulness, and friendliness (Baumrind, 1983). The childrearing strategies discussed later in this chapter may be used by parents who take an authoritative approach to childrearing.

❖ REFLECTIONS   *In your family of orientation, what childrearing attitudes (authoritarian, permissive, or authoritative) predominated? Do you think these attitudes influenced your own development? How?*

How to Raise Your Child: The Needs of Parents and Children

About 150 years ago, Americans began turning to books to learn how to act and live rather than turning to each other. They began to lose confidence in their own abilities to make appropriate judgments. The vacuum that formed when traditional ways broke down under the impact of industrialization was filled by the so-called "expert." The old values and ways had been handed down from parents to child in an unending cycle; men and women had learned how to be mothers and fathers from their own parents. But with increasing mobility, the continuity of generations ceased. A woman's mother was often not physically present to help her with her first child. New mothers were not able to turn to their more experienced kin for help. Instead, they enlisted the aid of new authorities— the experts who through education and training supposedly knew what to do. If your

Because it's good for you. Reason given to make child eat food it does not want.

Miss Manners

constantly taking jabs

The secret of dealing successfully with a child is not to be its parent.

Mell Lazarus

be supportive allow them to be creative autonomy.

The perniciousness of so much of the advice from experts that pervades the media is that it undermines the confidence of parents in their own abilities and values, overemphasizes the significance of specific child-rearing techniques, and grossly misrepresents the contribution the expert in psychiatry or education can make to the conduct of ordinary family life.

Rita Kramer

baby was colicky, for example, the experts recommended a drop of laudanum in the baby's bottle. (The laudanum would put the baby to sleep, but it would also make him or her a heroin addict by the end of a year.)

Contemporary parents may still follow experts' advice even if it conflicts with their own beliefs. Yet if an expert's advice counters their own understanding, parents should carefully examine that advice as well as their own beliefs. All parents should take an expert's advice with at least a grain of salt. It is the parents' responsibility to raise their children, not the expert's.

CHILDREN'S DEVELOPMENTAL NEEDS. Although the relative effects of physiology and environment of human development are much debated by today's experts, it is clear that both nature and nurture play important roles. Jerome Kagan (1984) has presented a strong case for the role of biology in early development. He holds that the growth of the central nervous system in infants and young children ensures that such motor and cognitive abilities as walking, talking, using symbols, and becoming self-aware will occur "as long as children are growing in any reasonably varied environment where minimal nutritional needs are met and [they] can exercise emerging abilities." Furthermore, according to Kagan, children are biologically equipped for understanding the meaning of right and wrong by the age of two; but although biology may be responsible for the development of conscience, social factors can encourage its decline.

In addition to physiological maturation, important factors affecting early development are (1) the acquisition of knowledge, (2) the formation of attachments (especially maternal), and (3) individual temperamental differences (such as inhibited/restrained/watchful or uninhibited/energetic/spontaneous) (Kagan, 1984). Development in later childhood can also be profoundly affected by social forces.

Parents often want to know what they can do to raise healthy children. Are there specific parental behaviors or amounts of behaviors (say, twelve hugs a day?) that all children need to grow up healthy? Apart from saying that basic physical needs must be met (adequate food, shelter, clothing, and so on) along with some basic psychological ones, experts cannot give us detailed instructions. Jerome Kagan (1976) wrote:

Children do not require any specific actions from adults to develop optimally. There is no good evidence that children must have a certain amount or schedule of cuddling, kissing, spanking, holding, or deprivation of privileges in order to become gratified and productive adults. The child does have some psychologic needs, but there is no fixed list of parental behaviors that can be counted on to fill those requirements. The psychological needs of children vary with age and the context of their growth.

According to Kagan, in our society a child needs to:

1. Feel valued by parents and a few special adults (such as a teacher, aunt, or grandparent).
2. Develop autonomy in attitudes and behaviors.
3. Develop and perfect talents that are desirable in society.
4. Develop successfully in a sexual context and be able to love and be loved.

Kagan also observed that because our values tend to derive from our profit-oriented economic system, crowded urban conditions, and competitive institutions, in general they tend to emphasize self-interest, competitiveness, and narcissism. More humanistic values would foster intimacy, cooperation, and altruism.

Children have more strength, resiliency, and resourcefulness than people may ordinarily think. They can adapt to and overcome many difficult situations. Parents do not have to be overly concerned that their every action will overwhelmingly influence their

We can expect a conscience of every child. We don't have to build it in. All we have to do is arrange the environment so they don't lose it.

Jerome Kagan

As we grow up, we need to get different strokes from different folks in different settings to become sentient, capable, competent, and compassionate human beings.

Urie Bronfenbrenner

child's life. A mother can lose her temper and scream at her child and the child will most likely survive, especially if the mother later apologizes and shares her feelings with the child. A father can turn his child away with a grunt because he is too tired to listen and the child will not necessarily grow up neurotic, especially if the father spends some "special time" with the child later on. (Also see Bronfenbrenner, 1985, for a discussion of children's needs in modern society.)

SELF-ESTEEM. High self-esteem, what Erik Erikson called "an optimal sense of identity," is essential for growth in relationships, creativity, and productivity in the world at large. Low self-esteem is a disability that afflicts children (and the adults they grow up to be) with feelings of powerlessness, poor ability to cope, low tolerance for differences and difficulties, inability to accept responsibility, and impaired emotional responsiveness. Self-esteem has been shown to be more significant than intelligence in predicting scholastic performance.

A recent study of 3,000 children found that adolescent girls had lower self-images, lower expectations from life, and less self-confidence than boys (Daley, 1991). At age nine, most of the girls felt positive and confident, but by the time they entered high school, only 29 percent said they felt "happy" the way they were. The boys also lost some sense of self-worth, but not nearly as much as the girls. Ethnicity was an important factor in this study. African-American girls reported a much higher rate of self-confidence in high school than did white or Latina girls. Two reasons were suggested for this discrepancy: first, African-American girls often have strong female role models at home and in their communities; African-American women are more likely than others to have a full-time job and run a household. Second, many African-American parents specifically teach their children that "there is nothing wrong with them, only with the way the world treats them" (Daley, 1991). According to professor Carol Gilligan, this survey "makes it impossible to say that what happens to girls is simply a matter of hormones. . . . [It] raises all kinds of issues about cultural contributions, and it raises questions about the role of the schools, both in the drop of self-esteem and in the potential for intervention" (quoted in Daley, 1991).

Clemes and Bean (1983) describe four conditions necessary for developing and maintaining high self-esteem. (As you read the following, think about how families, schools, and other institutions could increase children's self-esteem.) The first condition is a sense of connectedness, of being an important part of a family, class, team, or other group and of being connected ("in touch") with our bodies. The second condition is a sense of uniqueness, a feeling that our specialness and differentness are supported and approved by others. Third is a sense of power, the belief that we have the capability to influence others, solve problems, complete tasks, make our own decisions, and satisfy our needs. Children develop a sense of power through sharing duties and responsibilities in the home and having clear limits and rules set for them. The fourth condition for the development of self-esteem is a sense of models. Human, philosophical, and operational models (mental constructs and images derived from experience) help us establish meaningful values and goals and clarify our own standards.

A study of 655 adolescents suggested that family support is "crucial for the development and maintenance of self-esteem among high-school-aged adolescents" (Hoelter and Harper, 1987; also see Gecas and Seff, 1991). Parents can foster high self-esteem in their children by (1) having high self-esteem themselves, (2) accepting their children as they are, (3) enforcing clearly defined limits, and (4) respecting individuality within the limits that have been set.

It's also important to single out the child's behavior—not the whole child—for comment (Kutner, 1988). Children (and adults as well) can benefit from specific information

We are born princes and the civilizing process makes us frogs.

Eric Berne

#1 problem poor self-esteem

The Meaning of Being Me

Who am I? Who am I?
Growing up isn't easy, no matter what
*   you think.*
No. No. It's hard. It's hard.
It's standing on the brink
*   of a mountain that*
*   you're afraid of.*
*   Sometimes I ask you who I am, but you*
*   don't tell me.*
*   Sometimes I ask myself who I am . . . .*
Still a kid?
Soon a grown-up person. (Will it be better
*   then?*
Can you tell me that . . . can I believe it?)
I hear a certain song and I get
*   tears in my eyes . . .*
I see a person and I get so angry—and he
*   never even said a word . . .*
It's hard growing up . . . it's so hard.
*   Why must it be so hard . . .*
The littlest rough spot and there I
*   go—crying,*
angry . . . up to my room to break
*   down—to kick—to have bad*
*   dreams—*
I hurt you, and you, and you, sometimes
*   –but I hurt me more times.*
I don't want to hurt you and I don't want to
*   hurt me—*
But it hurts so much not to know
*   how to answer,*
Who am I?

Susan, age 11. From Carole Klein, The Myth of the Happy Child

about how well they've performed a task. "You did a lousy job" not only makes us feel bad, but it also gives us no useful information about what would constitute a good job. Furthermore, "acknowledging your own needs and accepting them," according to Clemes and Bean, "can help you have patience and compassion for [children's] efforts to realize high self-esteem." (See Demo et al., 1987, for a discussion of self-esteem and the reciprocal character of parent/adolescent socialization.)

PARENTS' NEEDS. Although some parents' needs are met by their children, parents have other needs as well. Important needs of parents during the childrearing years are personal developmental needs (such as social contacts, privacy, and outside interests) and the need to maintain marital satisfaction. Yet so much is expected of parents that they often neglect these needs. Parents may feel a deep sense of guilt if their child is not happy or has some defect, an unpleasant personality, or even a runny nose. The burden is especially heavy for mothers, because their success is often measured by how perfect their children are. Children have their own independent personalities, however, and many forces affect a child's development and behavior. Nevertheless, as Philip Slater (1971) wrote, "Deep in their hearts most middle-class Spock-taught mothers believed that if they did their job well enough, all their children would be creative, intelligent, kind, generous, happy, brave, spontaneous, and good—each, of course in his or her own special way."

Accepting our limitations as parents (and as human beings) and accepting our lives as they are (even if they haven't turned out exactly as planned) can help us cope with the many stresses of childrearing in an already stressful world. Contemporary parents need to guard against the "burnout syndrome" of emotional and physical overload. Parents' careers and children's school activities, organized sports, scouts, and music, art, or dance lessons compete for the parents' energy and rob them of the unstructured (and energizing) time that should be spent with others, with their children, or simply alone. Learning to prioritize activities—deciding which are essential and which can be eliminated or postponed—is a valuable parenting skill.

Childrearing Strategies

One of the most challenging aspects of childrearing is knowing how to change, stop, encourage, or otherwise influence children's behavior. We can request, reason, explain, command, cajole, compromise, yell and scream, or threaten with physical punishment or the suspension of privileges; or we can just get down on our knees and beg. Some of these approaches may be appropriate at certain times; others clearly are never appropriate. Some may prove effective some of the time, some may never work very well, and no technique will work every time.

The techniques of childrearing currently taught or endorsed by educators, psychologists, and others involved with child development are included in programs such as Parent Effectiveness, Assertive Discipline, Positive Discipline, and numerous others. Although these approaches differ somewhat in their emphasis, they share most of the tenets that follow. (Also see Chapter 18 for a discussion of the traits of psychologically healthy families.)

RESPECT. Mutual respect between children and parents must be fostered in order for growth and change to occur. One important way to teach respect is by modeling—treating the child and others respectfully. Child psychologist Rudolph Dreikurs stressed the importance of treating children with kindness *and* firmness simultaneously. Counselor

Jane Nelsen (1987) writes, "Kindness is important in order to show respect for the child. Firmness is important in order to show respect for ourselves and the situation."

CONSISTENCY AND CLARITY. Consistency is crucial in childrearing. Without it, children become hopelessly confused and parents become hopelessly frustrated. Patience and teamwork (a united front) on the parents' part help insure consistency. Because consistency means following through with what we say, parents should beware of making promises or threats they won't be able to keep. Clarity is important for the same reason. A child needs to know the rules and the consequences for breaking them. This eliminates the possibilities of the child being unjustly disciplined or wiggling out through loopholes. ("But, Mom, I didn't know you meant not to walk on *this* clean carpet with my muddy shoes!")

LOGICAL CONSEQUENCES. One of the most effective ways we learn is by experiencing the logical consequences of our actions. Some of these consequences occur naturally—we forget our umbrella, we get wet. Sometimes parents need to devise consequences that are appropriate to their child's misbehavior. Dreikurs and Soltz (1964) distinguished between logical consequences and punishment. The "Three R's" of logical consequences dictate that the solution must be Related to the problem behavior, Respectful (no humiliation), and Reasonable (designed to teach, not to induce suffering). (See Nelsen, 1987, for specific examples of the application of natural or logical consequences.)

OPEN COMMUNICATION. The lines of communication between parents and children must be kept open. Numerous techniques exist for fostering communication. Among these are *active listening* and the use of *I-messages,* important components of Thomas Gordon's (1978) Parent Effectiveness program. In active listening, the parent verbally feeds back the child's communications in order to understand the child and help him or her understand the nature of the problem. I-messages are important because they impart facts without placing blame and are less likely to promote rebellion in children than are you-messages. (Communication techniques are discussed in greater detail in Chapter 14.)

Family meetings are another important way in which families can communicate. Regular weekly meetings provide an opportunity for being together and a forum for airing gripes, solving problems, and planning activities. Decisions are best reached by consensus rather than majority vote, as majority rule can lead to a "tyranny of the majority" in which the minority is consistently oppressed. If consensus can't be reached, the problem can be put on the next meeting's agenda, allowing time for family members to come up with alternative solutions (Nelson, 1987).

NO PHYSICAL PUNISHMENT. The American Psychological Association notes that "physical violence imprinted at an early age, and the modeling of violent behavior by punishing adults, induces habitual violence in children" (cited in Haferd, 1986). The American Medical Association also opposes physical punishment of children. While such punishment may "work" in the short run by stopping undesirable behavior, its long-range results—anger, resentment, fear, hatred—are appalling (Dodson, 1987). Besides, it often makes parents feel confused, miserable, and degraded, right along with their kids.

More effective types of discipline use some form of behavior modification. Rewards (hugs, stickers, special activities) are given for good behavior and privileges are taken away when misbehavior is involved. Good behavior can be kept track of on a simple chart listing one or several of the desired behaviors. Undesirable behavior may be met with the revocation of TV privileges or the curtailment of other activities. *Time-outs—*

Parents are the bones on which children sharpen their teeth.

Peter Ustinov

The chief tools of proper child rearing are example and nagging.

Miss Manners

Behavior modification

It takes eighteen years of constant work to get one into presentable shape so that a college will take him or her off your hands for the winter season, and it can easily take another 10 years of coaching and reviewing before someone will consent to take the child on permanently.

Miss Manners

Child rearing is the only task in the world where your goal is to make your own job obsolete.

Miss Manners

sending the child to his or her room or to a "boring" place for a short time or until the misbehavior stops—are useful for particularly disruptive behavior. They also give the parent an opportunity to cool off (Dodson, 1987; also see Canter and Canter, 1985).

❖ REFLECTIONS   *What childrearing strategies or techniques did your parents use? Which might (or do) you find useful in raising your own child?*

Although no childrearing technique is guaranteed to be 100 percent successful all the time, it is important for families to keep seeking ways to improve their communication and satisfaction. It is also important for parents to develop and maintain confidence in their own parenting skills, their common sense, and especially their love for their children.

SUMMARY

◆ Parenthood may now be considered a matter of choice owing to effective methods of birth control. *Child-free marriage* and *deferred parenthood* are alternatives that are growing in popularity.

◆ Parental roles are acquired virtually overnight and can create considerable stress. The main sources of stress for women involve traditional gender roles and multiple role demands (parent, spouse, provider). Other sources of stress for mothers and fathers are associated with work, not having enough money, worries about infant care and health, and interactions with spouse, family, and friends.

◆ Many women find considerable satisfaction and fulfillment in motherhood. Although there is no concrete evidence of a biological maternal drive, it is clear that socialization for motherhood does exist.

◆ The role of the father in his children's development is currently being reexamined. The traditional instrumental roles are being supplemented, and perhaps supplanted, by expressive ones.

◆ Supplementary child care outside the home is a necessity for many families. The development and maintenance of quality day-care programs should be a national priority.

◆ Television has recently been implicated in a number of individual, familial, and societal disorders. Commercials generally encourage poor nutritional habits and generate conflict between parent and child. Violence on television has been demonstrated to cause aggressive behavior in children. Families are often portrayed in a stereotypical or romanticized manner, and women and members of minority status groups may be presented negatively.

◆ Theories of child socialization include Freud's *psychoanalytic model,* Piaget's *stages of cognitive development,* and the *social molding* theory used by Erikson. In the *developmental interaction* theory of the family, family members are viewed as being interdependent in their growth, which continues

throughout their lives. Birth order and space between births are important. Each of us also has an "I"—a sense of self—that resists biological and environmental pressures.

◆ Psychosexual development begins in infancy. Infants and children learn from their parents how they should feel about themselves as sexual beings.

◆ Ethnicity profoundly influences the way children are socialized. Identification with a group gives a sense of pride and belonging. Minority status parents may try to give their children special skills for dealing with prejudice and discrimination.

◆ Lesbian mothers share many similarities with heterosexual mothers. Most gay fathers are married. Studies indicate that children of both lesbians and gay men fare best when the parents are secure in their sexual orientation and are open about it with their children. Although the children of gay and lesbian parents may have difficulty accepting their parents' gayness at first, they generally maintain close relationships with their parents and develop the same sexual orientations and gender roles as children of heterosexuals.

◆ Basic attitudes toward childrearing can be classified as *authoritarian, permissive,* and *authoritative.*

◆ Expert advice is often relied on by today's parents. It needs to be tempered by parents' confidence in their own parenting abilities and in their children's strength and resourcefulness.

◆ Children's basic psychological needs are to (1) feel valued by parents and a few special adults, (2) develop autonomy, (3) develop and perfect talents that are desirable in society, and (4) be successful at loving and being loved.

◆ High self-esteem is essential for growth in relationships, creativity, and productivity. Adolescent girls, especially nonblacks, are likely to be low in self-esteem. Parents can foster high self-esteem in their children by encouraging development of a sense of connectedness, uniqueness, power, and models.

◆ Contemporary strategies for childrearing include the elements of mutual respect, consistency and clarity, logical consequences, open communication, and behavior modification in place of physical punishment.

❖ SUGGESTED READINGS

Blume, Judy. *Letters to Judy: What Your Kids Wish They Could Tell You*. New York: Putnam's, 1986 (paperback). Judy Blume, one of the most popular writers of realistic juvenile fiction (her books are among the most banned in America) received thousands of letters from adolescents who didn't feel that their parents would listen to their problems. This book is a cross-section of these letters.

Brazelton, T. Berry. *On Becoming a Family: The Growth of Attachment*. New York: Delacorte, 1981 (paperback). A valuable (and readable) book on the development of bonds between infants and their parents.

Buscaglia, Leo F. *The Disabled and Their Parents*. New York: Holt, Rinehart and Winston, 1983. Compassionate advice that emphasizes seeing the person first and the disability second.

Coles, Robert. *The Spiritual Life of Children*. Boston: Houghton Mifflin, 1990. Interviews by a leading educator and child psychologist with children throughout the world. Reveals their concern about ultimate truths and their search for meaning in life.

Genevie, Lou, and Eva Margolies. *The Motherhood Report: How Women Feel about Being Mothers*. New York: Macmillan, 1987. Two thousand American mothers tell how they feel about mothering.

Greenfeld, Josh. *A Child Called Noah*. New York: Holt, Rinehart, 1972 (paperback). *A Place for Noah*. New York: Holt, Rinehart, 1978 (paperback). *A Client Called Noah*. New York: Holt, Rinehart, 1987. Three books chronicling in a highly readable manner the life of the author's brain-damaged son and his family. Demonstrates the strength of family love in the face of tragedy.

Hopson, Darlene, and Derek Hopson. *Different and Wonderful: Raising Black Children a Race-Conscious Society*. New York: Prentice-Hall, 1990. A childrearing guide for African-American families that addresses the issues of ethnicity and racism.

Kotlowitz, Alex. *There Are No Children Here*. New York: Doubleday, 1991. The compassionate, startling account of two boys growing up in the Chicago projects. One mother says, "There are no children here. They've seen too much to be children."

McAdoo, Harriette, and John McAdoo, eds. *Black Children: Social, Educational, and Parental Environments*. Newbury Park, Calif.: Sage Publications, 1985 (paperback). A valuable collection of essays that dispels many of the myths and stereotypes surrounding black children and families.

Nelson, Jane. *Positive Discipline*. New York: Ballantine Books, 1987 (paperback). Based on the psychology of Alfred Adler and Rudolph Dreikurs, this is a practical, positive guide for both parents and teachers.

Phinney, Jean, and Mary Jane Rotheram, eds. *Children's Ethnic Socialization: Pluralism and Development*. Newbury Park, Calif.: Sage Publications, 1987 (paperback). The role of ethnicity in child development.

Pogrebin, Letty Cottin. *Growing Up Free*. New York: McGraw-Hill, 1980 (paperback). Thoughtful advice on raising children without gender-role stereotypes.

Pruett, Kyle. *The Nurturing Father: Journey Toward the Complete Man*. New York: Warner Books, 1987 (paperback). A well-researched and insightful in-depth study of several young families in which the father is the primary nurturing parent.

Schulenberg, Joy. *Gay Parenting: A Complete Guide for Gay Men and Lesbians with Children*. New York: Anchor Books, 1987 (paperback). A useful guide to dealing with the special problems faced by lesbian and gay parents in raising their children.

Stern, Daniel. *Diary of a Baby*. New York: Basic Books, 1990. Dr. Stern, a psychiatrist and father, reveals the "mindscape" of Joey, a composite baby, at important stages of development from six weeks to four years of age. Engaging and original.

Suggested Films

The Color Purple (1985). Whoopi Goldberg stars as Celie, a young, Southern black woman who endures and overcomes a variety of hardships with the help of some unique friends and family members. Based on Alice Walker's Pulitzer Prize-winning book.

My Life as a Dog (1987). A Swedish film about growing up that is both touching and hilarious.

Parenthood (1989). The comedy.

Radio Days (1987). Woody Allen's tender and comic look at Jewish family life and growing up in New York.

Stand by Me (1986). An affectionate memoir of American boyhood in the 1950s. Based on a story by Steven King.

Answers to Preview Questions

The answers to the preview questions at the beginning of the chapter are listed below. As you check your answers, whether you were correct or not, think about your reasons for each response. What were they? What was their source? How valid is the source? As you read the chapter, you will find the questions discussed in greater depth.

1. F   6. F
2. T   7. F
3. F   8. T
4. T   9. T
5. T   10. T

ON NOT HAVING KIDS

Jon Hubner

As you read this essay, think about what it has to say about soci-ety's response to childless people. What are the author's reasons for not wanting to have children? What is your response to those reasons? Do you think a person's decision not to have children needs to be justified to others?

Before we left Boston for San Jose last fall, we had dinner with two couples we've known for years. We used to spend hours with them, discussing the pros and cons of starting a family. Within a few months, both couples had children. We thought it was going to be a bittersweet goodbye dinner, but they ganged up on us about having children as soon as we got our coats off. They kept telling us we didn't know what we were missing. We suggested they were missing a lot, too. That, they didn't like. "Well, people are having children later these days," one proud mother said. "There's still time. It's a matter of maturity. When you're ready, you'll know it."

That, I didn't like. Why should maturity be equated with hav-ing children? Before I could react, they hit us rapid-fire with a series of questions that probed like a scalpel. One new father, a psychiatrist, wondered if we might be just a bit narcissistic. His wife, a clinical psychologist, asked if we were perennial adoles-cents, afraid of the responsibility that comes with parenthood. She suggested that our relationship was too fragile for the strains of raising kids. They were as obnoxious as est graduates. We had two choices: laugh it off or tell them off.

"You want the truth?" I said. "Our sex life is so kinky, we'll never reproduce."

Nobody laughed. It was as if I'd committed heresy, joking about the hallowed act of creation. After a pause, the conversa-tion shifted to a safer topic: California.

Ann and I are not narcissistic. Our relationship has endured worse strains than the "terrible twos." It's not that we do not like children, either. We have loved several. We have friends here who have a wonderful 2-year-old daughter, so I catch glimpses of what I'm missing. The point is, I've chosen to miss it. We do not have children because we do not want any. If we did, we would have them.

I have no deep biological urge to reproduce myself. The world will get along fine without my kids, just as it will get along fine without me when I'm gone. I lack the drive to love, to nurture, and to shape another human being. Babies don't fascinate me. I'm like Queen Victoria: I like kids after they've left what she called the "frog stage."

I worry about money like most of us do, but if we had kids, I'd *really* worry about money. I don't want to spend money on Gerber's and Pampers and life insurance. I don't want to save for a college education. I'd rather save so I can go back to Morocco. I don't want to spend nights babysitting. I want to go to country bars. I don't want to spend Saturdays taking 5-year-olds to Great America. I want to go to Reno. If this sounds hedonistic, perhaps it is. But it is not self-destructive. Aristotle, a really nifty definition-maker, said that to be happy is to be always learning something. My job does that for me. I've chosen not to learn about the things a child could teach me.

I'm not convinced I would love my child simply because he or she was mine. Plenty of parents do not like their kids. You've seen them. We have a great friend who is a successful novelist. She has reached her 60s, has no children, and has no regrets. "It's a real longshot to produce a child that you would choose as a friend," she says. "Think about your family: Your child could turn out to be like any one of them. How many of them do you like enough to want to spend the next 18 years with?"

I suspect that in many cases, it is the parents' fault if they don't like their children. We had friends we stopped seeing because they have a kid who is a monster. The terror I'll call Joey is out of control the second his feet hit the floor. He is the product of what I call child idolatry: the child as center of the universe. The little creep controls every situation. Joey's parents are little more than serfs, the loyal subjects of a 4-year-old despot. "No Joey, daddy can't read you a story now, daddy is busy talking . . . Joey, don't shout at daddy . . . Please don't shout, Joey . . . Joey, don't cry . . . Oh, all right Joey! Get the damn book."

I think that if I had a child, I would spend most of the day worrying about him. Jeffrey is the closest I've come to being a father; he and his mother moved in next door to us when he was 2. He was so beautiful, his hands and cute little legs emerging from his favorite Levi cutoffs so delicate, that I wanted to pick him up and hug him and never let go. Every time he laughed, 1,000 volts shot up my spine. I'd think, do that again Jeffrey and I'll give you my house. If your best friend is the person you most enjoy being with, then that's what Jeffrey was to me. I liked the things he said and the way he said them. I liked watching *Sesame Street* with him. I liked the way he conned me into stop-ping for ice cream cones.

When Jeffrey was 6, they discovered he had cancer. His doc-tors told me he had a 50-50 chance to live six months. They wouldn't even give odds on a year. I took long walks, hunting the catharsis, trying to cry. Once I screamed and kicked a tree, but it was self-conscious and didn't help. Jeffrey was going to die.

He went through radiation and chemotherapy. When he lost his hair, his mother bought him a Dodger hat. He went back to school and never took the hat off. Any kid who tried to take it off was in for a fight. I refused to let myself hope, even when the cancer mysteriously went into remission.

Jeffrey survived! It is the one miracle I've seen. The cancer gradually disappeared; the doctors can't explain it. Jeffrey is 13 now, and he's still my man. But I never, ever, want to go through anything like that again.

Sometimes I think about moving into middle age, and then old age, without children. It is frightening. Loneliness is the enemy. For three years, we lived in New Hampshire, surrounded by retired couples. They wouldn't have had much to do besides read the *Boston Herald American* and bowl candlepins if it weren't for their children. Their families were scattered all over the country, so they didn't see their children or grandchildren often, but their families gave them a lot to think about. A letter or phone call was a major event. Still, with children or without, life for the elderly in this country is pretty bleak. We isolate old people. Those I've known spend far too much time alone. I'm hoping that if I make it to my 70s, there will be old-folks communes by then that will let me in.

As resolved as I am to not having children, I will always wonder what I have missed. The other day, I was walking around Vasona Park. I noticed a man who apparently had arrived late for a picnic. He was walking up a slight hill when his kids saw him. They jumped away from the picnic table and went running down the hill. The father scooped one up and swung him 'round and 'round while the other child danced about, waiting for an opening. Finally, the kid charged in and grabbed his father's leg. They wrestled for a while, and then walked hand-in-hand up to the picnic table.

As I watched, I wondered if the love that father has for his children is more profound than any love I've known. I'll always wonder about that.

❖

SHARING THE BABY

Joanne Kates

In this family, both parents are equally responsible for caring for their baby. What kinds of problems did this unexpectedly raise with the mother? What did the father gain from his involvement with his daughter that he might not have received if he had continued his career fulltime? Is such fulltime fathering possible for most men? Why?

Thirteen months ago Leon was not interested in babies. They didn't speak the language, and he was sure that if he touched one it would cry.

But I refused to play Mom to his traditional Dad. The deal I had spent years fighting for—and won—was that each of us would take equal responsibility for our baby, which meant equal career sacrifices. Mara was born in August 1985. Leon had quit his job in July to get ready to be a full-time father for her first

year. We knew that his career standing as a labor economist was good enough that he would have no trouble getting a new job when the time came. That was not the big risk. The risk was more personal: Would he like being a full-time parent? Without the validation he so frequently got in his work life, would he be able to believe in himself? He was not going to turn into an isolated drudge, because I would be working part time and therefore be with him and Mara most days. He wasn't going to lose his manhood because it was not solely vested in success. And yet the question remained. If he was not to be his usual hard-driving, overachieving man in a hurry, who would Leon be? Would it be enough for him? And for me? Our friends and families looked on with mixed emotions: they admired his guts, they envied his escape, however temporary, from the rat race, and yet it worried them to see a successful man become a professional diaper-changer.

When Mara was a week old, on a sunny summer day, Leon and I stood in our driveway saying goodbye to visiting friends. He held the baby in one hand; the other hand was in his pocket. He was a model of nonchalance. He learned to take care of a baby the same way he learned public speaking, the same way a horse takes a fence: you see the challenge, you fear it and then you meet it. He had quickly found out that what taking care of Mara asked of him, he delighted to give: tenderness, a gentle touch, hugs by the dozen. She rewarded him by lying around looking beatific and Buddha-like. And he began to believe in himself as a nurturer.

When Mara was 3 months old she got a cold. She woke frequently at night, crying because she couldn't breathe. The first time she awoke so miserable, Leon cried from sorrow and pity, his identification with her was so complete. It was a new definition of intimacy.

When Mara was 5 months old, we fought the war of the baby authorities. Leon wanted to feed her solid food for the first time. She was still being breast fed and I was not ready for a change. I cited Dr. Spock; he cited Penelope Leach. But the issue was not when to introduce baby to real food. The issue was *turf*. I clung to my exclusive connection. I, the staunch feminist who never wanted biology to determine destiny, was enjoying the responsibility of being Mara's sole source of nourishment. She had been fed by my body since she was smaller than a kernel of corn—for 14 months at that point. I got her to that smiling robust moment and I was possessive. It was a physical want; it underlay all our words of negotiation.

Leon wanted her that way too, and the only way he could have the satisfaction of feeding her was by starting her on solid food. I bought time with creative procrastination: after we get back from skiing . . . after we find the right baby cereal. . . . Just before she turned 6 months old, I gave in.

continued on next page

I am sometimes jealous of how much Leon dotes on Mara. When he calls her by pet names previously spoken only to me, when he ignores me and pays attention to her, I am sometimes sad at being displaced. Their tie is blood, and mine with Leon is based only on volition. Ours can be broken; theirs cannot. Although their love delights me, there are times when she looks up at him adoringly and I am jealous. That is the price I pay for sharing her equally with him. Women who do all the parenting, or who share it with paid helpers, have a special power that I have relinquished. It is the power of being everything to a child. I am not Mara's everything. She cares as much for Leon as for me. This is most difficult when I walk up the stairs to my study to write, and leave the two of them playing in the living room. He blows me a kiss. She doesn't even look up.

When she was 8 months old, a grinning little imp in overalls, we had an adventure. She and I flew across the Atlantic together without Leon. It would have been fun but for the timing: it was a peak moment for terrorism in Europe, and Leon lost sleep for fear of something happening to us. He feared most for Mara, because she seemed so vulnerable. It came as a shock to him that he could not, try as he might, guarantee her a safe world. That journey stood for him as a symbol of what he could not do for her, and yet wanted so badly: he wanted to shield her from pain, to make sure she would grow up safe, healthy and happy. It was a painful lesson.

Summer came. We made our annual migration to the lake, where we live on an island and our main mode of transit is a canoe. We have neither electricity, telephone nor running water there. It was not designed with babies in mind. Mara was 11 months old, a competent crawler and indefatigable investigator of the world below the two-foot level. All summer he put socks and shoes on her and I took them off. He put a sweater on her. I took it off. I would set her down in the dirt to play. He would pick her up. I accused him of overprotecting her. He called me cavalier. When you throw the old roles into the mixer and turn it on, more changes result than the ones you negotiated. We had a full-scale role reversal on our hands, Leon the nervous mother, me the laissez-faire father. It was understandable why each of us was overplaying our roles somewhat, since they were so new to us and we had so few models to follow.

The week after Mara's first birthday an old friend of Leon's tracked us down in the woods. He wanted to offer Leon a senior government job, the kind only a fool refuses. It was a high-pressure job in another city, a dream job for a man on the fast track. Two years ago Leon would have tried hard to persuade me to move West for this. He sat me down after Mara was in bed, laughed ruefully and said, "Guess what I just turned down." His year with Mara has made Leon unfit for worka-holism, because he's unwilling to settle for being no more than the bestower of a good-night kiss at the end of her day. I have been similarly altered by this child. So we have a new deal now:

Leon will do consulting three days a week; I will write three days a week. The rest of the time is for Mara. Look for us at the zoo: it's less crowded on weekdays.

A LESBIAN FAMILY

Jennifer Meyer

What are the unique problems of a lesbian family? What kind of kin relationships does this family have?

Every time I try to write in my sons' baby books, I get stuck on the page with the family tree. It presents such precise, unflexible categories: Mother, Father, Grandmother, Grandfather, and so on. I can't even begin to mold my family's make-up into such a shape.

I started with myself and Kate, our sons' primary parents. Then Toby's donor, and Jesse's donor, and Jesse's donor's girl-friend (who has been involved since the beginning). There's my mother, and Kate's mother, and Tobias' (the donor's) father and stepmother (who are involved actively as grandparents). But what about all of the boys' 'Aunties'—our friends who have spe-cial relationships with the kids? And the kids' godparents? What about our friends who used the same donor we used for our first son? Technically, their son is related to ours. And what about Judith and her kids, with whom we spend every holiday and share every important event?

As I attempted to add everyone I considered part of my "fami-ly" to my family tree, the page became a web of criss-crossed lines.

In these days of blended families, I don't think we're so unique with all our interconnections. In fact, in many ways, I feel we are very ordinary. We live in a nice but modest house on a quiet street. There's a swingset and a golden retriever in the back yard and the front yard's full of tricycles. I work and Kate stays home with the kids. All we're missing is the picket fence. Our more radical friends might say we've bought into the middle-class nuclear family model.

But every day, I'm reminded of our difference. Even the most innocent questions in line at the supermarket can put me on the spot. "Your baby's hair is beautiful! Is your husband dark?" "Are you still nursing him?" "Did you give birth to him at home?"

When my first son was born, I promised myself that I would never be ashamed of who we were as a family. That I would counter the shame society would try to force on us with a fierce pride. I wanted that pride to seep into my son's veins and nour-ish him, strengthen him for the battles he would inevitably have to fight.

When my son was three, he reminded me of that promise with his own openness. While traveling, we'd stopped for lunch in a small town in Washington state—not one I felt particularly at home in. When the waitress approached our booth, Toby stood up in his seat and announced, "My name is Toby and these are my two moms: Mama J. and Mama Kate." Kate and I both shrank two inches in our seats and acquired an immediate fascination with our menus.

"Maybe she didn't hear him," I thought as the waitress smiled benevolently at him. When I recovered, I looked again at Toby's face—beaming with self-confidence. And I realized that I had betrayed him. I had taught him to love who we were without teaching myself. And I vowed again to never hide.

Luckily, we live in a place where that is possible. Santa Cruz is relatively open and accepting—not exactly Utopia, but not the Bible Belt either. We don't *have* to hide from anybody. The children's pediatrician can never remember which of us gave birth to which child, but has always been very respectful of our situation. Toby's teachers are careful to say "parents" instead of "mom and dad" and to recognize all kinds of family units when discussing families. And the kids in Toby's class think Toby is incredibly lucky and special to have two moms. I'm grateful to live in such a place and don't think I'd be willing to live anywhere else where oppression is more overt.

Yet the little daily dilemmas are trying. Even though I've promised myself to never lie about our situation, there's always the question of how much to say, what to imply, and what to leave alone. If the waitress asks which of us is Toby's mom, what do we say? What's more harmful to Toby—watching the waitress' reaction if we say, "We both are," or having his relationship with Kate denied?

It's never easy, but I have developed a kind of "technique" for dealing with inquiring strangers like this. I answer directly and truthfully with a confidence that leaves no room for further questions or raised eyebrows. Then I withdraw, either by leaving or by ending the conversation. By the time what I've said has sunk in, I'm usually out of sight. Whatever their reaction might be, they can deal with it alone. Whether it's shock or curiosity, I'm not interested in it.

The hardest thing about being an alternative family is that society has no place for us. There's no checkbox for us when I fill out forms: Married? Single? Divorced? Separated? And on forms for the children, one of us has to put our name in the Father slot. When we were looking for a house to rent, it took almost a year because, even though I had an excellent job, we were viewed as an unwed mother and an unemployed student. And we were denied student housing because we weren't married (even though we were told heterosexuals didn't need to show a marriage license). We can't get family insurance or file joint taxes, and we can't even be legal guardian of each other's children! Because we don't fit into any of society's pigeonholes, we simply do not exist.

These are not issues I look at every day, and yet I live with them. They sit like rotten fruit in the back of the refrigerator. Even on the best days, when our donor's parents have come for a visit bearing presents for the children and I feel blessed for the family we've created, I still live with the knowledge that these people who visit two or three times a year have more legal right to my baby than I do.

"Don't you have contracts and wills and things?" a friend asked me incredulously when I mentioned this. It doesn't matter. They can all be contested. Donor contracts have never been tested in the courts. And since Kate and I can't adopt each other's birth children without giving up custody ourselves, if something happened to one of us, the other would have to fight for custody. Our children's destiny would depend on the personal biases and opinions of the judge in court that day.

Thinking about the obstacles we're up against, it's hard not to feel hopeless. It's all so big and out of my control. Recently, I suspected that my son had been turned down from a private school because of my lesbianism. The rage and powerlessness I felt tore me apart. Really for the first time, I realized what our alternative family could be up against in this society.

All my life I've been battling societal oppression and it's never fazed me, but this time they'd gotten to my child. And with the anger projected outward, there was also anger I projected inward. "How many other things are my children going to be excluded from because of the choices I've made for my life? How could I expect my children to suffer the oppression our lifestyle brings? How could I be so selfish? Maybe I was wrong to have children after all. . . ." The internalized oppression is even more insidious than the rest, and sometimes harder to resist.

To keep my sanity, to hang onto a sense of strength in my life, I keep my struggles limited to what I can handle. I know that by myself, I can't change society or its laws. But I can affect the people around me, the people I deal with every day. This is the way I choose to be politically active.

So as much as possible, I make myself visible. To other mothers in the park, checkers at the supermarket, to all those who ask, I say, yes, I am a lesbian and these are my children. To companies who write offering life insurance to me and my spouse, I respond, asking if they consider my lesbian lover my spouse. To salesmen who ask for the lady of the house, I say, here we are. By expecting, even *demanding*, recognition of my lover and children as a family unit, at least I'm making others aware of our existence. And perhaps one day there will be a place for us on the school forms: Mother #1 and Mother #2.

Will not be tested on this chapter read for fun!

Marriage, Work, and Economics

To gain a sense of what you already know about the material covered in this chapter, answer "true" or "false" to the following statements. You will find the answers on page 393.

1. In contrast to single-worker families, dual-career families tend to divide household work almost evenly. True or false?
2. Although the number of poor increased significantly during the last decade, the percentage of the population receiving welfare benefits declined. True or false?
3. It is generally agreed by economists that welfare encourages poverty. True or false?
4. Families make up about 25 percent of the homeless. True or false?
5. Women currently make 90 cents for every dollar that men earn. True or false?
6. Family well-being is a national priority. True or false?
7. The majority of female welfare recipients are on welfare as a result of a change in their marital or family status. True or false?
8. The majority of families are dual-earner families. True or false?
9. Women tend to interrupt their work careers for family reasons over thirty times as often as men. True or false?
10. Married women tend to earn more and have higher status jobs than single women. True or false?

HERE ARE THREE BRIEF EXCHANGES OVERHEARD AT A PARTY. Identify what is wrong with each of them.

◆ Exchange number one: "Do you work?" the man asks. "No, I'm a mother," the woman replies.
◆ Exchange number two: "What do you do?" the first woman inquires politely as she is introduced to another woman. "Nothing. I'm a housewife," the second responds. "Oh, that's nice," the first replies, losing interest.
◆ Exchange number three: "What do you do?" the man asks. "I'm a doctor," the woman responds as she picks up her child, who is impatiently tugging at her. "And I'm an architect," her husband says while nursing their second child with a bottle.

In the first exchange, the woman ignores that as a mother she works. In the second exchange, both women ignore the fact that as a homemaker, the second woman works. They also devalue such unpaid work in comparison to paid work. In the third exchange, the woman identifies herself as a physician without acknowledging that she is also a mother. Her husband makes the same mistake as he identifies himself as an architect without also noting that he is a father participating in the care of his infant. As husband and wife, father and mother, both the architect and physician are unpaid family workers making important—but generally unrecognized—contributions to the family's economy.

These examples point to a curious fact: when we think of work, we tend to recognize only paid work. Family work, such as caregiving activities or household duties, is not regarded as "real" work. Because it is unpaid, family work is ignored as being somehow inferior to paid work, regardless of how difficult, time-consuming, creative, rewarding, and important it is for our lives and future as human beings. This is not surprising, for in the United States employment takes precedence over family.

The role of work in families requires many of us to rethink the meaning of family. We ordinarily think of families in terms of relationships and feelings—the family as an emotional unit. But families are also economic units bound together by emotional ties (Ross, Mirowsky, and Goldsteen, 1991). Paid work and unpaid family work as well as the economy itself profoundly affect the way we live as families. Our most intimate relationships vary according to how husbands and wives participate in paid work and family responsibilities (Voydanoff, 1987).

There are two types of work in which families participate: family work and paid work. Family work is the work we perform in the home without pay: it includes housekeeping, household maintenance, and caring for children, the ill, and the aged. Women do the overwhelming majority of family work. Paid work is the work we do for salary or wages. Traditionally men have been responsible for paid work, but currently the vast majority of women—whether single or married, with children or without—are employed. Women either support themselves or make significant contributions to family income.

Our paid work helps shape the quality of family life: it affects time, roles, incomes, spending, leisure, even individual identities. Within our families, the time we have for each other, for fun, for our children, and even for sex is the time that is not taken up by paid work. The main characteristic of our paid work in relation to the family is its inflexibility. Work regulates the family. And for most families, as in the past, a woman's work molds itself to *her* family, whereas a man's family molds itself to *his* work (Degler, 1980; Ross, Mirowsky, and Goldsteen, 1991). We must constantly balance work roles and family roles.

❖ WORKPLACE/FAMILY LINKAGES

Outside of sleeping, probably the single activity to which the majority of employed men and women devote the most time is their jobs. And we know from our own experiences that our work or studies affect our personal relationships. Work/family conflict, especially relating to work schedules and demands and to children at home, is often a painful source of stress (Menaghan and Parcel, 1991). To date, however, most research has been devoted to descriptions of home life or work life, not to how the two interact with each other. Only recently have scholars begun to look at how our jobs affect our family life, causing moodiness, fatigue, irritability, and so on (Small and Riley, 1990; see review by Bronfenbrenner and Crouter, 1982).

Work Spillover

Common sense (in addition to our own fatigue) suggests that **work spillover**, the effect of work on other aspects of our lives, is important in family life. Work spillover affects individuals and families by absorbing their time and energy and impinging on their psychological states. It links our homelife to our workplace (Piotrkowski, 1979; Small and Riley, 1990). Work is as much a part of marriage as love. What happens at work—frustration or worry, a rude customer, an unreasonable boss—affects our moods, making us irritable or depressed. We take these moods home with us, affecting the emotional quality of our relationships.

Work spillover especially affects women. While for men excessive work time is the major cause of conflict between work and family, for married women it is fatigue and irritability. Joseph Pleck and his colleagues (1980) noted:

The greater family responsibilities for women may be the reason for higher reports that the physical and psychological consequences of work caused family problems. Fatigue and irritability brought home from work often makes performing family tasks more difficult. . . . Husbands generally spend longer hours on the job but perform fewer household tasks. Having the opportunity to rest after work may help make fatigue and irritability less of a problem for husbands.

As a result of work spillover, an employed woman's leisure is rarely spontaneous: it is fitted in or planned around her household work and paid work (Firestone and Shelton, 1988). The stress a husband experiences at his work can also diminish his wife's emotional health (Dooley and Catalano, 1991).

Role Strain: Role Overload and Inter-Role Conflict

For families in which both partners are employed, work-related problems are more severe for parents than for nonparents. Being a working parent means performing three roles simultaneously: worker, parent, and spouse (Voydanoff and Donnelly, 1989). Because the time, energy, and commitment needed to carry out these roles are interdependent, individuals may experience difficulties such as depression, fatigue, and irritability (Gruelzow et al., 1991; Voydanoff and Donnelly, 1989; Menaghan and Parcel, 1991). Such difficulties are referred to as **role strain**. Role-strain is the most pressing problem for working families (Hansen, 1991).

Two types of role strain are especially likely to occur among working parents: **role overload** and **inter-role conflict** (interference). Overload occurs when the total prescribed activities for one or more roles are greater than an individual can comfortably or adequately handle. In role overload—what might be called the "too-

Work is the refuge of people who have nothing better to do.

Oscar Wilde

If you don't want to work you have to work to earn enough money so that you won't have to work.

Ogden Nash

The family is very much alive as a work unit in which all members participate in tasks from house repairs to laundry, gardening and doing dishes. As homemakers, women are the primary workers in such family work. Since family work is unpaid (except sometimes for children's allowances for doing chores), it generally goes unrecognized.

many-hats" syndrome—a person can easily feel overwhelmed with the multiple responsibilities of parent/spouse/worker: she or he must care for children, be intimate with a spouse, work twelve hours a day, shop, clean house, take children to school, and so on. Inter-role conflict exists when responsibilities from the parent/spouse/worker roles conflict. In inter-role conflict, the expectations of the parent/spouse/worker roles may be contradictory or may require an individual to do two things at the same time. In this "too-many-balls-to-juggle" syndrome, for example, a parent may be expected to be in two places at once, such as at the job *and* at home caring for a sick child. Individuals high in self-esteem, however, seem to feel less inter-role conflict than those with low self-esteem (Mertensmeyer and Coleman, 1987). Women with high self-esteem, for example, accept lower housekeeping standards as realistic adjustments to their multiple roles rather than as signs of inadequacy.

Married women employed full-time often prefer working fewer hours as a means of reducing role strain (Moen and Dempster-McLain, 1987). Not surprisingly, because they have less role strain, single women (including those who are divorced) are often more advanced in their careers than married women (Houseknecht et al., 1987). They are more likely to be employed full-time and have higher occupational status and incomes. They are also more highly represented in the professions and hold higher academic positions.

❖ REFLECTIONS   *Much of the work/family linkage may also apply to the college environment. If you think of your student role as a work role and the college as the workplace, what types of work spillover do you experience in your personal or family life? If you are a homemaker or are employed (or both), what kinds of role strains do you experience?*

❖ EMPLOYMENT AND THE FAMILY LIFE CYCLE

Throughout the life cycle, families try to balance work needs and family needs, which change as we go through different stages of the family life cycle. Families may follow several patterns in combining family and employment responsibilities. The three main patterns are described in the following sections:

The Traditional-Simultaneous Work/Family Life-Cycle Model

The **traditional-simultaneous work/family life cycle** characterizes families in which the husband is regarded as the major economic provider with little responsibility for caregiving and household tasks. The wife, even if she is employed, continues to be primarily responsible for family work.

STAGES IN THE TRADITIONAL WORK/FAMILY MODEL.   Work and family life intersect the traditional-simultaneous work/family life cycle in five stages (for a more detailed discussion of the family life cycle, see Chapter 10).

1. Establishment/Novitiate
2. New Parents/Early Career
3. School-Age Family/Middle Career
4. Postparental Family/Late Career
5. Aging Family/Post Exit

Stages 1 through 4, in which paid work affects family life most significantly, are briefly described below.

If you make money your god, it will plague you like the devil.

Henry Fielding (1707–1754)

Money is a good thing to have. It frees you from doing things you dislike. Since I dislike doing nearly everything, money is handy.

Groucho Marx

ESTABLISHMENT/NOVITIATE STAGE. In the *establishment/novitiate stage,* men and women begin to establish their families and begin their paid work. Role sharing may be especially high during this stage for both men and women. Men are not expected to marry, for example, until they are able to support a family. (Women do not have this work-related constraint on *when* to marry.) Women may experience role conflict if they believe that they must subordinate their work or career needs to their husbands' advancement needs. During this stage and the next, families are the most likely to be poor, as responsibilities and expenses tend to outrun income (Voydanoff, 1991).

NEW PARENTS/EARLY CAREER STAGE. In the *new parents/early career stage,* role overload becomes an acute problem. As men and women are developing their career or work skills, they tend to emphasize their work roles: this brings with it long hours, fatigue, the need for additional education, work-related socializing, networking, and work brought home. At the same time, as they have children, their roles as parents become especially demanding (as well as rewarding): there are babies to diaper, noses to wipe, children to play with, grandparents to visit, lullabies to sing, doctors to see, child care to find, and so on. Role strain is greatest at this stage for employed women.

A number of factors determine whether women leave or remain in the work force at this stage (Huber and Spitze, 1983; Menaghan and Parcel, 1991; Spitze, 1991). These factors include (1) how much their income is needed, (2) the meaning and importance they attach to mother roles versus work roles, (3) whether they accept traditional or nontraditional gender roles, and (4) the degree of work spillover they experience.

It is not enough to be busy . . . the question is: what are we busy about?

Henry David Thoreau

SCHOOL-AGE FAMILY/MIDDLE CAREER STAGE. Inter-role conflict becomes high as work and parent roles conflict with each other in the *school-age family/middle career stage:* parent meetings versus business meetings, sick children versus work obligations, Little League versus overtime. Parental roles are more likely than spousal roles to contribute to role overload and inter-role conflict. In part, this may be because some harried husbands and wives neglect or "forget" their spousal roles altogether when attempting to cope with their parenting and work obligations. The estimated total work week for an employed woman with two children varies from seventy-one to eighty-three hours (Ferber and Birnbaum, 1980). Not surprisingly, it is during this stage that couples report the most notable decline in marital satisfaction.

POSTPARENTAL FAMILY/LATE CAREER STAGE. Many parents experience a paradox as they enter the *postparental family/late career stage.* Although they have more time to develop their parent/child relationships because they are now firmly established in their employment, they may find that their children have grown up and gone. At this time, husbands and wives reestablish their spousal relationship, which may have been languishing in neglect. Too often they discover the difficulty of renewing marital ties because they have grown apart emotionally and have developed separate interests. In addition, many middle-aged women who also planned to establish careers after their children left home find themselves responsible for the care of aged parents.

Alternative Work/Family Life-Cycle Approaches

The burdens and strains of combining paid work and family work have led many women who are both wives and mothers to modify the traditional pattern. The two

To reduce the wife's role overload ("too many hats") and inter-role conflict ("too many balls to juggle"), the husband may increase his participation in household work and child care. Most husbands, however, view their increased role as "helping" rather than sharing responsibilities.

alternative patterns are *sequential work/family role staging* and *symmetrical work/family role allocation.*

SEQUENTIAL WORK/FAMILY ROLE STAGING. The sequential work/family role-staging pattern is probably the most common for dual-earner marriages. This pattern reflects the adjustments women try to make in balancing work and family demands. Many of women's choices about employment and careers are based on their plans for a family and whether and when they will want to work (Burroughs et al., 1984). The key event is first pregnancy. Prior to pregnancy, most married women are employed. When they become pregnant, however, they begin leaving their jobs and careers to prepare for the transition to birth and parenthood. By the last month of pregnancy, 80 percent have left the work force. Within a year, slightly more than half of these women have returned to employment. Most women who leave their paid work do so because of impending birth. Those who return to employment are strongly motivated by economic considerations or need.

There are four common forms of sequential work/family patterns:

◆ *Conventional,* in which a woman quits her job after marriage or the birth of her first child and does not return.
◆ *Early interrupted,* in which a woman stops working early in her career in order to have children and resumes working later.
◆ *Later interrupted,* in which a woman first establishes her career, quits to have children (usually in her thirties), and then returns.
◆ *Unstable,* in which a woman goes back and forth between full-time paid employment and homemaking, usually according to economic need.

A major decision for a woman who chooses sequential work/family staging is at what stage in her life to have children. Should she have them early or defer them until later? As with most things in life, there are pros and cons. Early parenthood allows women to have children with others in their age group; they are able to share feelings and common problems with their peers. It also enables them to defer or formulate career decisions. At the same time, however, if they have children early, they may increase economic pressures on their beginning families. They also have greater difficulty in reestablishing their careers.

Women who defer parenthood until they reach their middle career stage often are able to reduce the role strain and economic pressures that accompany the new parent/early career stage of the traditional pattern. Such women, however, may not easily find other new mothers of the same age with whom to share their experiences. As older mothers, they may find it difficult to rear children. And some may decide that they do not want children because motherhood would interfere with their careers.

SYMMETRICAL WORK/FAMILY ROLE ALLOCATION. Families that try to reduce role overload and inter-role conflict may reallocate traditional family roles. Since both husband and wife are employed, both share in family work. Equity and fairness are thought to be more important than gender in dividing responsibilities and tasks. Women undertake some traditional male responsibilities, such as outside employment, car maintenance and hauling trash. Men do some traditional female tasks, such as cooking, shopping, cleaning, and child care. Although such families tend to be more egalitarian, men rarely share family responsibilities fifty-fifty (but they often think they do).

What distinguishes symmetrical families from traditional families is the extent of the responsibilities husbands and wives undertake. In traditional families, wives may *help* contribute to family income through their employment and men may *help* with the caregiving and household duties. But neither goes beyond "helping"; neither is responsible for these tasks. In symmetrical families, husbands are *responsible* for certain aspects of family work, and wives are *responsible* for contributing to family income.

Although symmetrical arrangements encourage gender equality, they are often resisted by men, who tend to be more committed to work roles than family roles. Such arrangements also require more commitment to work roles by women. Although married partners may consciously believe that such shifts are desirable, on an unconscious level they may resist such changes because of deeply held beliefs about the "proper" roles of husbands and wives. Both men and women may have difficulty in relinquishing beliefs that the traditional provider role is necessarily the most important male family role. They may be unable to envision gifts of love and time as equally (or more) important as paychecks.

❖ REFLECTIONS   *Which work/family pattern will you adopt (or have you adopted)? What would its benefits be for you? Its drawbacks? Which pattern did your family of orientation adopt? What were its benefits for your parents? Its drawbacks? Does their experience influence your choice of patterns?*

❖ THE FAMILY'S DIVISION OF LABOR

The Traditional Division of Labor: The Complementary Model

In the traditional division of labor in the family, work roles are complementary: the husband is expected to work outside the home for wages; the wife is expected to

I owe, I owe,
It's off to work I go.

Anonymous

Work expands so as to fill the time available for its completion.

Northcote Parkinson

remain at home caring for children and maintaining the household. (We discussed the childrearing aspect of family work in the previous chapter.) In what Berardo and colleagues (1987) refer to as "a residue of tradition," women—whether or not they are employed outside the home—remain primarily responsible for household tasks. The division of family roles along stereotypical gender lines is more characteristic of white families than African-American families. African-American women, for example, are less likely than white women to be exclusively responsible for household tasks (Broman, 1988; Maret and Finlay, 1984; Taylor et al., 1991).

MEN'S FAMILY WORK. Men's work traditionally takes place outside the home, where men fulfill their primary economic role as provider. The husband's role as provider is probably the male's most fundamental role in marriage (Menaghan and Parcel, 1991; Rubin, 1983). The basic equation is that if the male is a good provider, he is a good husband and a good father. This core concept seems to endure despite trends toward more egalitarian and androgynous gender roles.

Men are traditionally expected to contribute to family work by providing household maintenance. Such maintenance consists primarily of repairs, light construction, mowing the lawn, and other activities that are consistent with instrumental male norms. Men often contribute to housework and child care, although their contribution may not be notable in terms of the total amount of work to be done. Most studies find that women do twice as much family work as men (Spitze, 1991). Men tend to see their role in housekeeping or child care as "helping" their partner, not as assuming equal responsibility for such work. The more husbands define themselves as the provider, regardless of whether their wives are employed, the fewer household tasks husbands perform (Perry-Jenkins, 1988).

WOMEN'S FAMILY WORK. Women's family work is considerably more diverse than men's. Women's work permeates every aspect of the family. It ranges from housekeeping to child care, kin-keeping to organizing recreation, socializing children to caring for aged parents and in-laws, cooking to managing the family finances, to name but a few of the tasks. Ironically, family work is often invisible to the women who do most of it (DeVault, 1987). As Thompson and Walker (1991) observe, "Family work is unseen and unacknowledged because it is private, unpaid, commonplace, done by women, and mingled with love and leisure."

Although most women do paid work, contributing about 30 percent to the family's income, neither women nor their partners regard employment as a woman's fundamental role. Women are not duty-bound to provide; they are duty-bound to perform household tasks (Thompson and Walker, 1991). Even the law assumes that the wife is responsible for domestic work and childrearing (Weitzman, 1981). No matter what kind of work the woman does outside the home or how nontraditional she and her husband may consider themselves to be, there is seldom much equality when it comes to housework.

The greatest determinant of the amount of time a woman spends on housework is her employment status. Women spend less time on housework if they are employed (Berardo et al., 1987). Men may help their partners with washing dishes, vacuuming, or doing the laundry, but as long as they "help," household responsibility continues to fall on women.

The Homemaker Role

A woman's work may consist of unpaid family work as homemaker and paid work outside the home as employee or professional. Her work as homemaker has been

One man eats very little and is always full. But another man constantly eats and is always hungry. Why is that?

Zen riddle

traditionally considered to be her primary role. Because this work is performed by women and is unpaid, however, it has been denigrated as "women's work"—inconsequential and unproductive.

Women's work contribution to the family has not always been devalued. The role of homemaker or housewife was a nineteenth-century invention, created when industrialization removed many of women's productive tasks from the home and placed them in the factory (Degler, 1980). Even then, although women made fewer things at home, they nevertheless continued their service and childrearing roles: cooking, cleaning, sewing, raising children, and nurturing the family. With the rise of a money economy in which only paid work was recognized as real work, women's work in the home went unrecognized as necessary and important labor (Andre, 1981; Bernard, 1982). (If homemakers today were paid the going rate for their work, they would earn over $50,000 annually.) Even when women work for wages, their contribution to the family income is often underrated (Bird and Bird, 1985).

Sociologist Ann Oakley (1985) described four aspects of the homemakers' role:

◆ Exclusive allocation to women, rather than to adults of both sexes
◆ Association with economic dependence
◆ Status as nonwork, or its opposition to "real," economically productive work that is paid
◆ Primacy to women—that is, its priority over other roles

Although women's attitudes toward homemaking often reflect class differences, few women find the work itself satisfying. As Komarovsky (1987) wrote, "The esteem [homemakers] attach to their roles does not . . . ensure their contentment in it." Both working-class and middle-class women tend to feel tied down by their duties as wives and mothers.

Homemaking consists primarily of household work and, if children are present, childbearing tasks. It includes the following characteristics (Hochschild, 1989; Oakley, 1985):

1. Housework tends to isolate a woman at home. She cleans alone, cooks alone, launders alone, cares for children alone. Loneliness is a common complaint.
2. Housework is unstructured, monotonous, and repetitive. A homemaker never feels that her work is done. There is always more dust, more dishes, more dirty laundry.
3. The full-time homemaker role is restricted. For a woman who is not also employed outside the home, homemaking (which may also include childrearing) is essentially her only role. By contrast, a man's role is dual—employed worker and husband/father. If the man finds one role to be unsatisfactory, he may feel satisfaction in the other. It is much more difficult for a woman to separate the satisfaction she may get from being a mother from the dissatisfaction of household work.
4. Housework is autonomous. This is one of the most well-liked aspects of the homemaker role. Being her own boss allows a woman to direct a large part of her own life. In contrast to employment, this is a definite plus.
5. Homemakers work long days and nights. This is especially true for employed mothers. For employed women, there is a "second shift" of work that awaits them at home, requiring anywhere from fifty to one hundred or more hours a week.
6. Homemaking can involve childrearing. For many homemakers, this is their most important and rewarding work. They enjoy the interactions with their infants and children. Although they can also feel overwhelmed and exhausted by the demands of childrearing, relatively few would choose not to have children.
7. Homemaking often involves role strain, especially for employed mothers as they try to perform their various obligations as parent/spouse/worker.

I hate to be called a homemaker; I prefer "domestic goddess."

Roseanne Barr

Many women find satisfaction in the homemaker role, even in housework. Young women, for example, may find increasing pleasure as they experience a sense of mastery over cooking, entertaining, or rearing happy children.

If homemakers have formed a network among other women—friends, neighbors, relatives—they may share many of their responsibilities. They discuss ideas and feelings and give each other support. They may share tasks as well as problems.

❖ REFLECTIONS   *List the different tasks comprising family work in your family. What family work is given to women? To men? On what basis is family work divided? Is it equitable?*

❖ WOMEN IN THE LABOR FORCE

Women have always worked outside the home. Single women have traditionally been members of the work force since the early nineteenth century. And there have always been large numbers of working mothers, especially among African Americans and many other poor ethnic groups (Broman, 1988; Jones, 1985). What has changed significantly is the emergence since the 1960s of a predominant family form in which both husbands and wives/mothers work outside the home (Piotrkowski et al., 1987). Until the last decade, nonemployed wives and mothers were viewed as the norm. Recent research indicates that women's employment tends to have positive rather than negative effects on marriage. (See Spitze, 1991, for a review of the literature on women's employment and family relations; also see Menaghan and Parcel, 1991).

Why Women Enter the Labor Force

Economic necessity is a driving force for many women in the labor force. Among women in the work force in 1989, 26 percent were single, 15.6 percent were divorced or widowed, and 20 percent had husbands whose income was less than $15,000 (U.S. Bureau of the Census, 1990). Many married women and mothers entered the labor force or increased their working hours to compensate for their husband's loss in earning power (Menaghan and Parcel, 1991).

There are psychological reasons for employment as well. Employment may raise a woman's self-esteem and sense of control. Employed women are less depressed and anxious than nonemployed homemakers; they are also physically healthier (Gecas and Seff, 1989; Ross, Mirowsky, and Goldsteen, 1991). A thirty-one-year-old worker, the mother of five children, told how she felt about working in a factory (quoted in Rubin, 1976):

I really love going to work. I guess it's because it gets me away from home. It's not that I don't love my home; I do. But you get awfully tired of just keeping house. . . .

You know, when I was home, I was getting in real trouble. I had that old housewife's syndrome, where you either crawl in bed after the kids go to school or sit and watch TV by the hour. I was just dying of boredom.

There are two reasons that employment improves women's emotional and physical well-being (Ross, Mirowsky, and Goldsteen, 1991). First, employment decreases economic hardship, alleviating stress and concern not only for the woman herself but for other family members as well. For a single parent, her earnings may constitute her entire family's income. Second, an employed woman receives greater

Women constitute half the world's population, perform nearly two-thirds of its work hours, receive one-tenth of the world's income, and own less than one-hundredth of the world's property.

United Nations Report, 1985

Ah, the little troubles, Mr. Oliver, they ruin a woman's life. It's the devil, I do believe, as sends us the toothache and the east wind and tax on beer. As for your grand sorrows . . . it's almost a pleasure to grieve, all hung in weeds, like a weeping willow. But the price of eggs, Mr. Oliver, the price of eggs.

George Santayana, The Last Puritan

Doonesbury

BY GARRY TRUDEAU

Doonesbury; copyright 1987 Universal Press Syndicate. Reprinted with permission. All rights reserved.

domestic support from her partner. The more a woman earns in contrast to her partner, the more likely he is to share housework and child care.

Participation in the Labor Force

In 1988, 59 million women and 67 million men were employed; women made up 47 percent of the work force (U.S. Bureau of the Census, 1990). Between 1970 and 1988, the number of married women in the labor force almost doubled. The numbers of employed women between twenty-four and thirty-four years of age (the ages during which they are most likely to bear children) rose from 39 percent to 64 percent. In 39 percent of dual-worker families, however, both husband and wife preferred that the woman not work (Ross, Mirowsky, and Goldsteen, 1991).

Almost 4 million of the employed women are single mothers; more than a quarter have preschool children (U.S. Bureau of the Census, 1990). More than half of all mothers with young children are currently in the work force. Among mothers with preschool children, one out of six works full-time in shift work—that is, during afternoons, evenings, nights, or early morning; one out of five works part-time in shift work (Presser, 1986).

Women's Employment Patterns

The employment of women has generally followed a pattern that reflects their family and child-care responsibilities. Because of these demands, women must consider the number of hours they can work and what time of day to work. When family demands increase, wives, not husbands, tend to cut back on their job time (Berk, 1985; Pleck, 1985). As a result of family considerations, women's employment rates follow an M-shaped curve. Women's entry into the job market rises from age sixteen to twenty-four; at age twenty-five, their participation drops as they begin engaging in homemaking and child-care activities. Then, after thirty-five, the rates go up again, falling toward zero as women near retirement. This M-shaped pattern, may be changing, however, as more than half of the mothers with small children are employed. Nevertheless, women face considerable barriers in their access to well-paying status jobs (Bergen, 1991).

You can say this about ready-mixes—the next generation isn't going to have any trouble making pies exactly like mother used to make.

Earl Wilson

Because of family responsibilities, women tend to interrupt their job and career lives considerably more than men. Employment interruptions have an important impact on wages: the more or longer the interruptions, the lower the wages. A study by the Bureau of the Census ("Work Interruptions and Earnings," 1985) found that one-fourth of the men but three-fourths of the women had employment interruptions lasting six months or longer. Sixty-seven percent of women's work interruptions were for family reasons; only 2 percent of men's employment interruptions were for family reasons. Similar differences are found when comparing women who have been married (with children) to women who have never been married (without children). Among women age twenty-one to twenty-nine years, 21 percent of the never-married women have had work interruptions but 81 percent of the married women have had work interruptions.

Researchers have found that a woman's decision to remain in the work force or to withdraw from it during her childbearing and early childbearing years is critical for her later work-force activities (Rexroad, 1985). If a woman chooses to work at home caring for her children, she is less likely to be employed later. If she later returns to the work force, she will probably earn substantially less than women who have remained in the work force (Rexroad, 1985; Velsor and O'Rand, 1984).

❖ DUAL-EARNER MARRIAGES

Even though half of all married women held jobs in 1991, the great majority of these women were employed in low-paying, low-status jobs—secretaries, clerks, nurses, factory workers, and the like. Rising prices and declining wages pushed most of them into the job market. Employed mothers generally do not seek personal fulfillment in their work as much as they do additional family income. Their families remain their top priorities.

Dual-career families are a subcategory of dual-earner families. They differ from other dual-earner families insofar as both husband and wife have high achievement orientations, greater emphasis on gender equality, and a stronger desire to exercise their capabilities (Berardo et al., 1987). Unfortunately, they may find it difficult to achieve both their professional and family goals (Kilpatrick, 1982). Often they have to compromise one goal to achieve the other, because the work world generally is not structured to meet the family needs of its employees. As one study pointed out (Berardo et al., 1987):

The traditional "male" model of career involvement makes it extremely difficult for both spouses to pursue careers to the fullest extent possible, since men's success in careers has generally been made possible by their wives' assuming total responsibility for the family life, thus allowing them to experience the rewards of family life but exempting them from this competing set of responsibilities.

Division of Household Labor

Whether or not women are employed seems to have little impact on the division of household work. Studies suggest that employed women do twice as much housework as men (Benin and Agostinelli, 1988; Spitze, 1986). Men tend to shop rather than mop floors, clean toilets, iron, or wash dirty diapers. If the homemaker is employed thirty hours or more a week, she spends about five hours a day on housework instead of the eight hours that full-time homemakers spend. The husband's contribution to household work does not significantly increase if his spouse is

A man's work is from sun to sun, But woman's work is never done.

Folk saying

UNDERSTANDING YOURSELF

The Division of Labor: A Marriage Contract

How do you expect to divide household and employment responsibilities in marriage? More often than not, couples live together or marry without ever discussing basic issues about the division of labor in the home. Some think that things will "just work out." Others believe that they have an understanding, although they may discover later that they do not. Still others expect to follow the traditional division of labor. Often, however, one person's expectations conflict with the other's.

The following questions cover important areas of understanding for a marriage contract. These issues should be worked out before marriage. Although marriage contracts dividing responsibilities are not legally binding, they make explicit the assumptions that couples have about their relationships.

Answer these questions for yourself. If you are involved in a relationship, live with someone, or are married, answer them with your partner. Consider putting your answers down in writing.

◆ Which has the highest priority for you: marriage or your job? What will you do if one comes into conflict with the other? How will you resolve the conflict? What will you do if your job requires you to work sixty hours a week? Would you consider that such hours conflict with your marriage goals and responsibilities? What would your partner think? Do you believe that a man who works sixty hours a week shows care for his family? Why? What about a woman who works sixty hours a week?

◆ Whose job or career is considered the most important—yours or your partner's? Why? What would happen if both you and your partner were employed and you were offered the "perfect" job five hundred miles apart from your partner? How would the issue be decided? What effect do you think this would have on your marriage or relationship?

◆ How will household responsibilities be divided? Will one person be entirely, primarily, equally, secondarily, or not at all responsible for housework? How will this be decided? Does it matter whether a person is employed full-time as a clerk or a lawyer in deciding the amount of housework he or she should do? Who will take out the trash? Vacuum the floors? Clean the bathroom? How will it be decided who does these tasks?

◆ If you are both employed and then have a child, how will the birth of a child affect your employment? Will one person quit his or her job or career to care for the child? Who will that be? Why? If both of you are employed and a child is sick, who will remain home to are for the child? How will that be decided?

employed. A study of employed wives, for example, found that 39 percent had sole responsibility for child care (compared with 56 percent of nonemployed wives); 42 percent of employed wives were solely responsible for housework (compared with 57 percent of nonemployed wives); and 34 percent of employed wives were solely responsible for washing dishes (compared with 49 percent of nonemployed wives) (Maret and Finlay, 1984). A study of African-American families found that women were twice as likely as men to feel overworked (Broman, 1988). Men, moreover, tend to perceive that they do more housework than they actually do (Condron and Bode, 1982).

Various factors seem to affect men's participation in housework. Men tend to contribute more to household tasks when they have the fewest time demands from their jobs—that is, early in their employment careers and after retirement (Rexroat and Shehan, 1987). Gender-role orientation also seems to affect sharing in household tasks. In one study (Bird et al., 1984), men who believed in egalitarian roles accepted more responsibility for child care, meal preparation, and cleaning. Husbands' sharing of household work was also related to their wives being employed, especially if their wives were career-oriented. As wives' income rose, they reported more participation by husbands in household tasks; increased income and job status motivate women to secure their husbands' sharing of tasks. Another study found that the more expressive and mastery-oriented the wife, the more assistance she obtained from her husband (Nyquist et al., 1985). Men who were relatively expressive helped their wives more than men who were relatively aggressive, dominant, and emotionally "tough." Husbands in one study (Benin and Agostinelli, 1988) felt most satisfied in the division of household labor if tasks were divided equally, espe-

Cleaning . . . should be done from the top down—starting with the ceiling, which is ridiculous. Gravity takes care of that. If there were any dirt on the ceiling, it would fall off and land on the floor. The same goes for walls. Dirt falls right off them and lands on the floor. And you shouldn't fool around with the dirt on the floor, because it will get all over the walls and ceiling.

P. J. O'Rourke

cially if their total time spent on chores was small. Women appeared to be more satisfied if their husbands shared traditional women's chores rather than limiting their participation to traditional male tasks (such as mowing the lawn). But even men who contribute many hours to household labor do traditional male tasks (Blair and Lichter, 1991). Children appear to be less sex-segregated with their household work than their parents (Simons and Whitbeck, 1991). African Americans are less likely to divide household tasks along gender lines than whites (Maret and Finley, 1984).

Husbands and wives generally agree that if both work outside the home, household tasks should be divided equally (Huber and Spitze, 1983). Few couples do so, however. Some wives prefer the traditional division of labor or believe that higher-earning husbands should have fewer household responsibilities. In fact, most studies find that the majority of husbands and wives believe their family's division of labor is fair (Spitze, 1991). Studies increasingly show the importance of satisfaciton with the division of labor and marital satisfaction (Suitor, 1991).

Childrearing Responsibilities

Men increasingly believe that they should be more involved fathers than men have been in the past (Pleck, 1985). Yet the shift in attitudes has not greatly altered men's behavior. A recent study (Darling-Fisher and Tiedje, 1990) found that the father's time involved in child care is greatest when the mother is employed full time (fathers responsible for 30 percent of the care compared to mothers' 60 percent), less when she is employed part-time (fathers 25 percent versus 75 percent for mothers), and least when she is a full-time homemaker (fathers 20 percent versus 80 percent for mothers).

A review of studies (Lamb, 1987) on parental involvement in two-parent families concluded the following:

◆ Mothers spend from three to five hours of active involvement for every hour fathers spend, depending on whether the women are employed.
◆ Mothers' involvement is oriented toward practical daily activities, such as feeding, bathing, and dressing. Fathers' time is generally spent in play.
◆ Mothers are almost entirely responsible for child care: planning, organizing, scheduling, supervising, and delegating.
◆ Women are the primary caretakers; men are secondary.

Marital Power

An important consequence of women working is a shift in the decision-making patterns in a marriage. Although decision-making power in a family is not based solely on economic resources (personalities, for instance, also play a part), economics is a major factor. A number of studies suggest that employed wives exert greater power in the home than nonemployed wives (Ferber, 1982; Ybarra, 1982, but see Sexton and Perlman, 1989). Marital decision-making power is greater among women who are employed full-time than among those who are employed part time. Wives have the greatest power when they are employed in prestigious work, are committed to it, and have greater income than their husbands.

Some researchers are puzzled about why many employed wives, if they do have more power, do not demand greater participation in household work on the part of their husbands. Joseph Pleck (1985) suggests several reasons for women's apparent reluctance to insist on their husbands' equal participation in housework. These include:

Money is a source of power that supports male dominance in the family. . . . Money belongs to him who earns it, not to her who spends it, since he who earns it may withhold it.

Reuben Hill and Howard Becker

◆ Cultural norms that housework is the woman's responsibility
◆ Fears that demands for increased participation will lead to conflict
◆ Belief that husbands are not competent

Glenna Spitze (1991) believes that the division of housework will become an issue in relationships as women begin to react to the lack of equity. This may lead to increased divorce as "more women come to believe that a husband who divides labor equitably is a truly possible alternative."

Marital Satisfaction

How does employment affect marital satisfaction? Traditionally, this question was asked only of wives, not husbands; and even then, it was rarely asked of African-American wives, who had a significantly higher employment rate. In the past, married women's employment, especially maternal employment, was viewed as a problem. It was seen as taking way from a woman's time, energy, and commitment for her children and family. In contrast, *nonemployment* or *unemployment* was seen as the problem for men. But it is possible that the husband's work may *increase* marital and family problems by preventing him from adequately fulfilling his role as a husband or father: he may be too tired, too busy, or never there. It is also possible that a mother *not* being employed may affect the family adversely: her income may be needed to move the family out of poverty, and she may feel depressed from lack of stimulation (Menaghan and Parcel, 1991).

How does a woman's employment affect marital satisfaction? There does not seem to be any straightforward answer when comparing dual-earner and single-earner families (Piotrkowski et al., 1987). In part, this may be because there are trade-offs: a woman's income allows a family a higher standard of living, which compensates for the lack of status a man may feel for not being the "sole" provider. While men may adjust (or have already adjusted) to giving up their sole-provider

What shall it profit a man, if he shall gain the whole world, and lose his own soul?

Mark 8:36

TABLE 12.1 Percent of Family Members Reporting Work-Related Conflict

GROUP	NO CONFLICT	LITTLE CONFLICT	MODERATE CONFLICT	SEVERE CONFLICT
All family members*	24	41	24	10
Employed husbands with employed wives	27	42	21	11
No children	35	37	20	7
Preschool children	23	41	23	13
School-age children	20	47	21	12
Employed wives with employed husbands	23	39	28	10
No children	37	34	19	11
Preschool children	12	40	36	12
School-age children	16	44	31	9
Employed women in one-parent families	17	58	14	11
Preschool children	19	56	9	16
School-age children	26	60	18	7

*Total sample size is 1,064; percentages based on weighted sample.

NOTE: Figures may not add up due to rounding.

SOURCE: Joseph H. Pleck, Graham L. Staines, and Linda Lang, "Conflicts between work and family life," *Monthly Labor Review* 103(3):29–32, U.S. Department of Labor, Bureau of Labor Statistics, 1980.

ideal, women find current arrangements less than satisfactory. After all, women are bringing home additional income but are still expected to do the overwhelming majority of household work. Role strain is a constant factor for women, and in general, women make greater adjustments than men in dual-earner marriages. Wives are more likely to feel satisfied if their husbands do their share of household work. Wives who believe that their husbands do not do their share tend to be more critical. What appears to be important is not the number of hours that a husband puts in, but whether his wife believes he is doing his fair share of family work. The issue, then, is one of equity (Gaesser and Whitbourne, 1985; Benin and Nienstadt, 1985; Pleck, 1985; Thompson and Walker, 1991).

Studies of the effect of women's employment on the likelihood of divorce are not conclusive, but they do suggest a relationship (Spitze, 1991; White, 1991). Many studies suggest that employed women are more likely to divorce. Employed women are less likely to conform to traditional gender roles, which potentially causes tension and conflict in the marriage. They are also more likely to be economically independent and do not have to tolerate unsatisfactory marriages for economic reasons. Other studies suggest that the only significant factor in employment is the number of hours the wife works. Hours worked may be important because full-time work for both partners makes it more difficult for spouses to share time together. Numerous hours may also contribute to role overload on the part of the wife (Greenstein, 1990; South and Spitze, 1986; Spitze and South, 1985).

African-American women, however, are not more likely to divorce if they are employed. This may be because of their historically high employment levels and their husbands' traditional acceptance of such employment (Taylor et al., 1991).

Overall, despite an increased divorce rate, in recent years the overall effect of wives' employment on marital satisfaction has shifted from a negative impact to no impact or even a positive impact. If there are negative effects, they generally result from specific aspects of a woman's job, such as long hours or work stress (Spitze, 1991).

Coping with Dual-Earner Marriages

Dual-earner marriages are here to stay. They are particularly stressful today because society has not pursued ways to alleviate the work/family conflict. The three greatest social needs in dual-earner marriages are (1) redefining gender roles to eliminate role overload for women, (2) providing adequate child-care facilities for working parents, and (3) restructuring the workplace to recognize the special needs of parents and families (see Boken and Viveros-Long, 1981; Regan and Roland, 1985).

Coping strategies include reorganizing the family system and reevaluating household expectations. Husbands may do more housework. Children may take on more household tasks than before (Coggle and Tasker, 1982). Household standards—such as a meticulously clean house, complicated meal preparation, and washing dishes after every meal—may be changed. Careful allocation of time and flexibility assist in coping. Home economist Kathryn Walker (1982) suggested that the best way to organize is to ask fundamental life questions: "One begins any such process by asking: What do I want to get out of home life? Until we determine what is important and identify values and goals, we cannot really plan time." Dual-earner couples often hire outside help, especially for child care, which is usually a major expense for most couples. One of the partners may reduce his or her hours of employment. Or both partners may work different shifts to facilitate child care (but this usually reduces marital satisfaction as a result) (White and Keith, 1990).

T A B L E 12.2 Percent of Family Members Reporting Common Types of Work—Family Conflicts

GROUP	EXCESSIVE WORK TIME	SCHEDULE INCOMPATIBILITY	FATIGUE AND IRRITABILITY
All family members*	50	28	15
Employed husbands with employed wives	63	22	11
Employed wives with employed husbands	39	39	27
Employed women in one-parent families	10	50	15

*Total sample size is 372; percentages based on weighted sample of those experiencing moderate or severe conflict.

NOTE: Figures may not add up due to rounding.

SOURCE: Joseph H. Pleck, Graham L. Staines, and Linda Lang, "Conflicts between work and family life," *Monthly Labor Review* 103(3):29–32, U.S. Department of Labor, Bureau of Labor Statistics, 1980.

The goal for most dual-earner families is to manage their family relationships and their paid work to achieve a reasonable balance that allows their families to thrive rather than merely survive. Achieving such balance will continue to be a struggle until society and the workplace adapt to the needs of dual-earner marriages and families. (For a literature and resource review on balancing work and family, see Hansen, 1991.)

❖ REFLECTIONS *The chances are very good that if you cohabit or marry, you will be in a dual-earner relationship. How will you balance your employment and relationship or family needs?*

❖ FAMILY ISSUES IN THE WORKPLACE

Discrimination against Women

Because of the significant impact that women's earnings have on family well-being (whether a woman is a major contributor to a dual-earner family or the sole provider in single-parent family) women's issues are also important family issues.

ECONOMIC DISCRIMINATION. The effects of economic discrimination can be devastating for women. In 1989, women in the United States made 70 cents for every dollar that men earned (Pear, 1990). (In Sweden, women make 90 cents for every dollar made by men.) Because of the great difference in women's and men's wages, many women are condemned to poverty and are forced to accept welfare and its accompanying stigma. Wage differentials are especially important to single women. Women head 89 percent of all single-parent families and generally have to support these families. Thirty-six percent of female single-parent families live beneath the poverty level, compared with 13 percent for single-parent families headed by men (Weinberg, 1985).

Employment and pay discrimination is prohibited by Title VII of the 1964 Civil Rights Act. This law did not end the pay discrepancy between men and women,

There is a simple way to define a woman's job. Whatever the duties are—and they vary from place to place and from time to time—a woman's job is anything that pays less than a man will accept for comparable work.

Caroline Bird

however. Much of the earnings gap is the result of occupational differences, gender segregation, and women's tendency to interrupt their employment for family reasons and to take jobs that do not interfere extensively with their family life (Beller, 1984). Earnings are about 30 to 50 percent higher in traditionally male occupations, such as truck driver or corporate executive, than in predominantly female or integrated occupations, such as secretary or school teacher (Beller, 1982). The more an occupation is dominated by women, the less it pays.

In recent years, the idea of *comparable worth* has been proposed as a means of closing the gap between men's and women's wages. Many believe that jobs held mostly by women pay less than jobs held mostly by men because they are seen as "women's work" and are consequently devalued. Supporters of comparable worth argue that secretaries, nurses, and clerks should earn as much as truck drivers, mechanics, and construction workers according to measurements of the inherent worth of such jobs in terms of experience, knowledge and skills, mental demands, accountability, and working conditions. Opponents to comparable worth, however, argue that occupational wage differentials are the result of social norms, market forces, and women's own choices of putting family ahead of work. They argue that "inherent worth" is a subjective judgment and that wages should be set by the marketplace.

SEXUAL HARASSMENT. Sexuality exists in the workplace: individuals are attracted to each other, become romantically involved, engage in sexual humor, and reveal aspects of their sexual lives to each other (Gutek, 1985; Gutek et al., 1980). Sexuality becomes a problem, however, when it is used to harass another person. Women are particularly vulnerable to sexual harassment. Harassment may occur on several different levels. A woman may discover that a job, continued employment, advancement, or other benefits are dependent on being sexually available to her employer. Harassment can also come from a fellow employee who makes unwelcomed sexual advances, innuendoes, and suggestions. In fact, harassment by co-workers is more frequent than harassment by employers. Sexual harassment, like rape, is often impelled by power motives, not sexual ones. Harassment is used to dominate or humiliate another person.

Sexual harassment can have a variety of consequences. One study of workers who reported being sexually harassed (Gutek, 1985) found that 9.1 percent of the women and 1 percent of the men quit their jobs because of harassment. Almost 7 percent of the women and 2 percent of the men thought that they had been dismissed from their jobs as part of the harassment.

Economic Status of Ethnic Families

Inequality is as dear to the American heart as liberty itself.

William Dean Howells

OCCUPATIONAL STRATIFICATION AMONG MEN. It is generally accepted by labor economists that the relative success of native-born whites in contrast to African-Americans and Latinos is due to whites' having greater access to quality education and job training and the political leverage to protect their social and economic advantages. In addition, members of some ethnic groups lack proficiency in standard English, a critical skill, which prohibits them from employment in high-paying jobs (Bean and Tienda, 1987). Occupational differences exist along ethnic lines, which, in turn, affect the economic well-being of families (Billingsley, 1988; Malveaux, 1988). Although almost one-third of African Americans work in middle-class or professional occupations, the remainder are typically employed in declining industries or the lowest-paying jobs. Among African-American men, for example, the majority are employed in manufacturing and service jobs. Technological changes and foreign competition, especially in the automobile, steel, and industrial machines industries, have decimated American manufacturing, where African Americans once were employed in well-paying jobs. The economic basis of the male African American worker has been dramatically undercut, causing black unemployment rates to almost double, from 9 percent in 1950 to 17 percent in 1990. After the 1950s, African Americans have experienced unemployment rates twice as high or more as that of whites (Billingsley, 1988).

Occupational stratification also has an important effect on the potential earnings of Latinos. About 17 percent of native-born Latinos are in professional or managerial jobs, in contrast to 29 percent of Anglos. This number drops to 6 percent if the Latinos were foreign-born. With the notable exception of Cuban Americans, Latinos tend to be concentrated in blue-collar or service work. Among immigrants, farm laborers account for 12 percent of the employed (Bean and Tienda, 1987).

OCCUPATIONAL STRATIFICATION AMONG WOMEN. Employed women tend to be concentrated in relatively low-paying clerical and service occupations. At first glance, there do not appear to be major differences in the job distribution between white and African-American women, but African-American women tend to be employed in the lower-paying levels of these low-paying jobs. Writes Julianne Malveaux (1988): "In addition to being employed in jobs that are 'typically female,' Black women are also employed in jobs that are 'typically' or disproportionately Black female." For example, 41 percent of African-American women in the service industry work as chambermaids, welfare service aides, cleaners, and nurse's aides (three or four times their number overrepresented). Among the forty-eight types of clerical occupations, African-Americans are four times overrepresented in six categories: file clerks, typists, teacher aides, keypunch operators, calculating machine operators, and social welfare clerical assistants. These are among the lowest-paying clerical jobs (Malveaux, 1988).

The experience of Latinas is similar in many ways. Cuban-American and Puerto Rican women both have traditionally worked in large numbers; only in the last two decades have Mexican-American women significantly increased their rates of employment. Puerto Ricans and Mexican Americans tend to be concentrated in the lower-paying jobs. Mexican immigrant women enter agricultural jobs in large numbers. All are important in the low-paying service industries.

The overall result is that African-American, Mexican-American, and Puerto Rican families have lower incomes than whites/Anglos. Cuban-Americans do well economically because of the influx of upper- and middle-class refugees who fled the Castro regime in the early 1960s. Native-born Asian Americans usually have higher median incomes than non-Asians.

The lack of affirmative action and job training programs forces many ethnic group members into unemployment, underemployment, poverty, or welfare. Others turn to the military. Said one high school counselor (Harris, 1991), "The kids whose parents have set aside money for school, they're going on to school. But the other kids, they figure they can get training and skills and a chance for college in the military." As a result, in 1990, 38 percent of the Army was composed of minority-status group members, of which 29 percent were African Americans; 7 percent of the officers were from ethnic groups.

Lack of Adequate Child Care

As mothers enter the work force in ever-increasing numbers, high-quality, affordable child care has become even more important. Currently there are 29 million children under age fifteen years whose mothers are employed (U.S. Bureau of the Census, 1990). By 1995, researchers estimate that two-thirds of all preschool children and three-quarters of all school-age children will have mothers in the work force (Hofferth and Phillips, 1987).

INADEQUATE CHILD-CARE OPTIONS. For about 70 percent of employed mothers with children five to fourteen years, school attendance is their primary day-care solution. Women with preschool children, however, do not have that option; in-home care by a relative is their most important resource. As more mothers with preschool children become employed, families are struggling to find suitable child-care arrangements. This may involve constantly switching arrangements, depending on who or what is available and the age of the child or children (Floge, 1985). Relatives, especially fathers and grandparents, are important in caring for their family's children, tending to the needs of almost 40 percent of the children. About 14 percent of the children are cared for by their fathers, 18 percent by their grandparents, and 8 percent by other relatives, such as older brothers and sisters or aunts. The younger the child, the more likely he or she is to be cared for by the grandmother (Presser, 1989). Twenty-four percent of children are cared for in family day-care homes, 14 percent in day-care centers, and 7 percent in preschools (U.S. Bureau of the Census, 1990). Women often use three or four different arrangements—the child's father, relatives living in or outside the household, day-care, or a combination of these—before a child reaches school age. For African-American and Latina single mothers, living in an extended family in which they are likely to have other adults to care for their children is an especially important factor allowing them to find jobs (Rexroat, 1990; Tienda and Glass, 1985).

Frustration is one of the most common experiences in finding or maintaining day-care. Changing family situations, such as unemployed fathers finding work or grandparents becoming ill or over-burdened, may lead to these relatives being unable to care for the children. Family day-care homes and child-care centers often close because of low wages or lack of funding. Furthermore, day-care expenses, which run an average of $50 weekly, may prove to be too expensive for many families (U.S. Bureau of the Census, 1990). In fact, the high cost of child care is a major force keeping mothers on welfare from working (Joesch, 1991).

As the incidence of day-care inside the child's home by relatives or baby-sitters continues to decrease, over half the children of employed parents are cared for outside their own homes, mostly in family day-care settings. This shift from parent-care at home to day-care outside the home may have profound effects on how children are socialized (see Chapter 11). It certainly disturbs many parents, who wonder whether they are, in fact, good parents. Many parents express concern about their children being cared for outside their own family environment. Concerns about their children's development tends to negatively affect parental well-being and their feelings about work (Greenberger and O'Neil, 1990).

Those parents who accept the home-as-haven belief—that the home provides love and nurturing—prefer placing their children in family day-care homes. They believe that a home-like atmosphere is more likely to exist in family day-care than in preschool or children's centers, where greater emphasis is placed on education (Rapp and Lloyd, 1989). But we know relatively little about family day-care: it is the most widely used and least researched form of American child care (Goelman, Shapiro, and Pence, 1990).

IMPACT OF CHILD CARE ON EMPLOYMENT OPPORTUNITIES. For women, lack of child care or inadequate child care is one of the major barriers to equal employment opportunity (U.S. Commission on Civil Rights, 1981). Many women who want to work are unable to find adequate child care or afford it. This is especially true for young, unmarried, and poor mothers. Although child-care expenses amount to 22 percent of a poor person's weekly income and 10 percent of a single parent's, government tax credits for child care do little to help those in the most need (U.S. Bureau of the Census, 1990). In 1988, about half of the benefits went to the wealthiest third of families, while the poorest third received only 3 percent (Samuelson, 1988).

In a survey of working women, 29 percent of the clerical, service, factory, and plant workers cited child care as a major problem. Among professional, managerial, and technical workers, the figure rose to 36 percent (cited in U.S. Commission on Civil Rights, 1981). Almost 6 percent of employed mothers using child care reported time lost by themselves or their husbands because of difficulties with child-care arrangements (U.S. Bureau of the Census, 1987). It is estimated that only 2,500 out of the 44,000 largest corporations in the country offer any kind of day-care for their employees (Bowen, 1988).

Childrearing responsibilities make it more difficult for women to compete equally with men in the workplaces. One unemployed mother explained (U.S. Commission on Civil Rights, 1981):

You got children to take care of. And a man does not have that hanging around his neck. You have to be a superwoman in order to get the same job that the man would very easily fall into because he doesn't have to worry about the children going to the doctor; he doesn't have to worry about the children getting sick.

In a report issued by the U.S. House of Representatives' Select Committee on Children, Youth, and Families (1985), the committee found that more than 25 percent of unemployed parents said they would work if they could find child care. The committee also reported that in nearly 25 percent of all households with young children, one or more adults had to give up work, was unable to take a job, or had to discontinued education or training because of lack of child care.

IMPACT ON EDUCATIONAL OPPORTUNITIES. Child care is an important consideration for students with children. At the University of Michigan, 20 to 25 percent of such students would seek more employment or education if child-care services were available. Forty percent of colleges and universities—approximately 1,000—provide day-care facilities for students, and waiting lists are long. One student testified before the Select Committee (1985) about her child-care difficulties:

For a year I had to drive 40 miles a day to take my infant son to a Title XX [child care for low- and moderate-income families] licensed child-care provider. Several times I was nearly forced to terminate my schooling because I had no infant care. I have often missed exams and have had to take incomplete grades because of a sick child.

For some, child care determines the pace of their academic career; for others, it determines whether additional education can be pursued.

The U.S. Commission on Civil Rights (1981) concluded that the lack of child care or inadequate child care has the following consequences:

◆ Prevents women from taking paid jobs
◆ Keeps women in part-time jobs, most often with low pay and little career mobility
◆ Keeps women in jobs for which they are overqualified and prevents them from seeking or taking job promotions or the training necessary for advancement

◆ Conflicts sometimes with women's ability to perform their work
◆ Restricts women from participating in education programs

In 1990, the federal government passed its first child-care funding legislation, providing a block grant of $4 billion to the states for child-care subsidies over the next five years (De Witt, 1991). Even though the funds are meager compared to child-care needs, the legislation is an important milestone. For the first time in American history, the federal government has recognized the importance of child care for contemporary families.

CHILDREN'S SELF-CARE. Almost 5 percent of children between ages five and fourteen years care for themselves after school while their parents are at their jobs. Because of the lack of adequate after-school programs or prohibitive costs, children's **self-care** has quickly become a major form of child care (Koblinsky and Todd, 1989). Self-care has increased 40 percent since the early 1980s (U.S. Bureau of the Census, 1990). It is a rapidly growing phenomenon, largely the result of inadequate or costly child care and the increasing numbers of married and single mothers who work outside the home (Cole and Rodman, 1987). Self-care exists in families of all socio-economic classes. One study (Vandell and Corasaniti, 1985) of over 300 children in a well-to-do suburb near Dallas found that 23 percent cared for themselves after school.

The popular image of self-care arrangements is negative; such children are known pejoratively as "latchkey children." Research on self-care arrangements has been sketchy and often contradictory. Some studies find no differences in levels of achievement, fear, and self-esteem between children in day-care and self-care arrangements. Other studies do find such differences. Some children are frightened, others get into mischief, and still others enjoy their independence. These differences may result from the child's own readiness to care for himself or herself, the family's readiness, and community's suitability (Cole and Rodman, 1987). Rather than rejecting self-care altogether, researchers suggest that it may be appropriate for some children and not for others. Children who are mature physically, emotionally, and mentally, whose families are able to maintain contact, and who live in safe neighborhoods, for example, may have no problems in self-care. But if children are immature or live in unsafe neighborhoods, they may find themselves overwhelmed by anxiety and fear. Each child is an individual case. Parents need to evaluate whether self-care is appropriate for their children (see Cole and Rodman [1987] for suggested guidelines). Because of the rise in self-care, educators are developing programs to teach children and their parents such self-care skills as basic safety, time management, and other self-reliance skills (see Koblinsky and Todd, 1989, for research review).

Inflexible Work Environment

The chief value of money lies in the fact that one lives in a world in which it is overestimated.

H.L. Mencken

The workplace has failed to recognize that the family has radically altered during the last fifty years. Most businesses are run as if every worker were male with a full-time wife at home to attend to his and his children's needs. But the reality is that women make up a significant part of the work force, and *they* don't have wives at home. Allowances are not made in the American workplace for flexibility in work schedules, day-care, emergency time off to look after sick children, and so on. Many parents would reduce their work schedules to minimize work/family conflict (Moen and Dempster-McClain, 1987). Unfortunately, many don't have that option.

Carol Mertensmeyer and Marilyn Coleman (1987) note that our society provides little evidence that it esteems parenting. This seems to be especially true in the workplace, where corporate needs are placed high above family needs. Mertensmeyer and Coleman continue:

Family policymakers should encourage employers to be more responsive in providing parents with alternatives that alleviate forced choices that are incongruent with parents' values. For example, corporate-sponsored child care may offset the conflict a mother feels because she is not at home with her child. Flextime and paid maternal and paternal leaves are additional benefits that employers could provide employees. These benefits would help parents fulfill self and family expectations and would give parents evidence that our nation views parenting as a valuable role.

A model corporation would provide family-oriented policies that would benefit both its employees and itself, such as flexible work schedules, job-sharing alternatives, extended maternity and/or paternity leaves and benefits, and child-care programs or subsidies (Bowen, 1988; Raabe and Gessner, 1988). Such policies would increase employee satisfaction, morale, and commitment; they are not especially widespread, however (Orthner and Pittman, 1986).

In 1990, after decades of argument, Congress finally passed the Family and Medical Leave Act, which required employers to provide eighteen weeks of *unpaid* leave for mothers or fathers following birth or adoption or for the care of seriously ill children. Although most European countries provide *paid* leave, the President vetoed the legislation as unwarranted governmental intrusion into employment practices. (For a Senate voting model on parental leave, see Monroe and Garland, 1991; for a refutation of family leave policies based on the Connecticut experience, see Trzcinski and Finn-Stevenson, 1991.)

❖ REFLECTIONS   *Of the family economic issues discussed previously, have any affected you or your family? How? How were they handled?*

❖ POVERTY AND UNEMPLOYMENT

Although poverty and unemployment may appear to be only economic issues, they are not. The family and economy are intimately connected to each other. And economic inequality directly affects the well-being of America's disadvantaged families. Poverty drives families into homelessness. Poverty is consistently associated with marital and family stress, increased divorce rates, low birth weight and infant deaths, poor health, depression, lowered life-expectancy, and feelings of hopelessness and despair. Catherine Ross and her colleagues (Ross, Mirowsky, and Goldsteen, 1991) suggests the connection:

It is in the household that the larger social and economic order impinges on individuals, exposing them to varying degrees of hardship, frustration, and struggle. The struggle to pay the bills and to feed and clothe the family on an inadequate budget takes its toll in feeling run-down, tired, and having no energy, feeling that everything is an effort, that the future is hopeless, that you can't shake the blues, that nagging worries make for restless sleep, and that there isn't much to enjoy in life.

Poverty

DEMOGRAPHICS. Poverty has been increasing since 1981, primarily as a result of sharp swings in employment, an increase in single-parent families, and government cutbacks in assistance to low-income families. In 1989, more than 31.5 million Americans—over 12.8 percent of the population—lived in poverty, the lowest figure since 1980 but still higher than any time during the 1970s (Pear, 1990). If we include those who live in near-poverty (earning $14,000 or less for a family of four),

Therefore I tell you, do not be anxious about your life, what you shall eat or what you shall drink, nor about your body, what you shall put on. Is not life more than food, and the body more than clothing? Look at the birds of the air; they neither sow nor reap nor gather into barns, and yet your Heavenly Father feeds them. Are you not of more value than they? And which of you by being anxious can add one cubit to his span of life? And why are you anxious about clothing? Consider the lilies of the field. how they grow; they neither toil nor spin; yet I tell you, even Solomon in all his glory was not arrayed like one of these.

Matthew 6:25–29

PERSPECTIVE

"I don't know how I could express hunger," a mother said. "It was not to the point where I'd pass out. The children always ate. Maybe I didn't. Maybe not for two or three nights. Maybe some juice during the day, but that's not eating." The woman had lost her job because of a difficult pregnancy; welfare benefits arrived too late to prevent eviction. For a while she stayed with relatives, but then she was shunted from one welfare hotel to another; finally, after over a year of living in welfare hotels in New York City, she was moved to a city-renovated apartment. She was lucky, for there are few such apartments available, and the waiting period for low-income public housing is about eighteen years (Kozol, 1988; Roberts, 1988).

Others are not as lucky. They sleep in parks, on steps, in abandoned buildings. They are society's outcasts. A middle-aged, homeless artist, who used to sleep beneath the outstretched arms of Jesus at the front of St. Patrick's Cathedral in New York, moved to the south side of the cathedral "because the Fifth Avenue Association says I'm bad for the tourists." He now occupies a "cardboard condominium." "It's not bad," he says. "With your body heat you won't freeze to death, even if you cut a couple of holes to breathe" (Hevesi, 1986). One researcher (Rivlin, 1990) described homelessness:

Picture a day when you cannot be certain where you will sleep, how you will clean

Hungry and Homeless in America

yourself, how you will find food, how you will hang on to your belongings. . . , how you will be safe, how you will dress properly to get to work (for many homeless persons do, indeed, work), and for some, how you will fill up the long hours of a day and do so in a place that will not tolerate your presence. Ordinary activities become major struggles: finding places to wash hair or clothing, locating toilets when needed, surfaces on which to raise swollen feet, or finding food, places to keep warm in cold weather and to escape the rain, snow or summer heat.

On any given night, 735,000 Americans are homeless; between 1.3 and 2 million Americans were homeless at least one night during 1987. At least 100,000 were children, according to a major study by the National Academy of Science (1988). Probably more than 3 million

Americans go hungry at least occasionally (Marin, 1987).

The face of hunger and homelessness has changed since the 1970s. Then the homeless were most often single individuals who were drug addicts, alcoholics, or mentally ill persons forced into the streets with the closing of many mental health facilities. Today, however, more than 25 percent of the homeless are families; they represent the fastest-growing sector of the homeless (Kozol, 1988). Most homeless families consist of single mothers with two or three children, most of whom are preschoolers (Bassuk et al., 1986). In some metropolitan areas, as many as three-fourths of the homeless are single mothers (Axelson and Dail, 1988). The families became homeless when the mother lost a job, separated or divorced, became physically disabled or ill, was unable to get welfare, was cut from welfare or had benefits reduced, or was unable to make ends meet on a fixed income. Without the ability to pay their rent or mortgages, they were unable to find housing or were forced to leave their homes. For many, it is a downward spiral.

About half the mothers heading homeless families are between the ages of seventeen and twenty-five years; they are equally distributed between whites and African Americans; about 7 percent are Latinas or Asians. Only 10 percent are currently married. More than half are high school graduates and one-fifth have

The rich get richer and the poor get poorer

Miguel de Cervante 1547–1616

the numbers increase to almost one out of every five American families. Although we tend to think of poverty as primarily an urban phenomenon, over 9 million poor live in America's rural areas. In some Iowa counties, poverty rates approach 30 percent. It is particularly ironical that hunger is a common problem in America's farming heartland (Davidson, 1990).

Poverty levels differ according to certain characteristics. In 1988, a time of economic prosperity, the percentage of those living in poverty was 10 percent for whites, 33 percent for African Americans, 28 percent for Latinos, 12 percent for Asians, and 25 percent for Native Americans (U.S. Bureau of the Census, 1990). By family type, 19 percent of two-parent families with children are poor compared to 55 percent of single-parent families (U.S. Bureau of the Census, 1990). The

PERSPECTIVE

had some college. The majority of women became homeless because they fled a relationship rather than because of eviction or job loss. Frequently, a violent incident was the precipitating cause of their homelessness, as they escaped with their children. Homeless mothers report a lack of ongoing family, social, and emotional support. The overwhelming majority say their children are the most important source of support. Twenty-five percent of homeless mothers suffer severe depression or substance abuse, but it is not clear whether these are reactions to homelessness or causes of it (Axelson and Dail, 1988).

As a makeshift response to housing needs, some cities provide emergency shelters, usually barrack-style warehouses or single-occupancy hostels. Many shelters permit only women and children, requiring husbands and fathers in intact families to separate. Unless time limits are imposed, emergency shelters tend to become permanent residences. The shelters, however, are generally located in dangerous neighborhoods inhabited by transients, drug abusers, petty criminals, and prostitutes.

Shelters are often frightening environments for families. A twelve-year-old girl paints a desperate picture of life in a residential hotel (quoted in Edelman, 1989):

I don't like the hotel because there is always a lot of trouble there. I don't go down into the street because there is no place to play. . . . The streets are dangerous, with all kinds of sick people who are on drugs or crazy. My mother is afraid to let me go downstairs. Only this Saturday, my friend, the security guard at the hotel, Mr. Santiago, was killed on my floor. The blood is still on the walls and on the floor.

Under such conditions, children suffer developmental delays, severe depression and anxiety, and learning difficulties. They also suffer from malnutrition. One study (Bassuk and Rubin, 1987) found that as many as half of the school-age children in their sample were in need of psychiatric evaluation; they displayed symptoms of depression, including suicide attempts. Although most of the mothers are intensely concerned about their children's well-being and future, the women feel helpless to prevent the same misfortunes from befalling their own children (Axelson and Dail, 1988).

How did this crisis in hunger and homelessness originate? The two major factors were the lack of adequate income and lack of affordable housing (Edelman and Mihaly, 1989). First, poverty increased dramatically in the early and mid-1980s, tapered off, and then substantially increased again in 1991 with a new recession. Second, a housing crisis was slowly growing. While housing prices skyrocketed, low-income rentals decreased at the rate of 125,000 apartments a year (Whitman, 1987). Today there are more than twice as many poor households as there is affordable housing. The monthly AFDC housing allowance pays less than half the actual cost of rent. As Axelson and Dail (1988) note:

The underlying causes show every indication of persisting, and the dimensions of the problems are increasing as they become more tightly interwoven into issues of unemployment, housing scarcity, domestic violence and abuse, and cutbacks in a wide range of social services.

We like to find moral fault in the individual, attributing homelessness to character defects or drugs, rather than seeking solutions. A commitment to ending homelessness would include the following: (1) the development of low-cost housing and housing subsidy programs, (2) establishment of child-care programs that will allow homeless single mothers to work, (3) provision of mental health support to deal with psychological problems, and (4) initiation of job training and education programs to develop employable skills. As homeless families continue to live and sleep in the streets, in abandoned cars, and in rat-infested shelters, we are confronted with a basic question: Is this the best America can do for its most vulnerable families?

1990/1991 recession, coupled with cuts in public assistance, drove the poverty level up, especially among African Americans and Latinos.

SPELLS OF POVERTY. Few people choose to live on welfare. Most are forced into it by circumstances. And because circumstances change, the majority of welfare recipients tend to be in poverty for spells of time rather than permanently (Bane and Ellwood, 1986). About a quarter of the American population, in fact, requires welfare assistance at one time or another during their lives because of changes in families caused by divorce, unemployment, illness, disability or death (Duncan et al., 1984). About half of our children are vulnerable to poverty spells at least once during their childhood (Duncan and Rodgers, 1988). Many families receiving welfare are in the early

The stoical scheme of supplying our wants by lopping off our desires is like cutting off our feet when we want shoes.

Jonathan Swift (1667–1745)

Homeless families represent about a quarter of all the homeless population and are the fastest-growing segment of that population. Homeless children suffer depression, anxiety, and malnutrition. What would your life have been like if you had been raised without a home?

We hold the moral obligation of providing for old age, helpless infancy, and poverty far superior to that of supplying the wants of courtly extravagance.

Thomas Paine

stages of recovery from an economic crisis caused by the death, separation, divorce, or disability of the family's major wage earner. Many who accept government assistance return to self-sufficiency within a year or two. Only about 2 percent of the population depend heavily on welfare for more than seven out of ten years. Most of the children in these families do not receive welfare after they leave home.

There are two major factors related to the beginning and ending of spells of poverty: changes in income and changes in family composition. Thirty-eight percent of poverty spells begin with a decline in earnings of the head of the household, such as a job loss or a cut in work hours. Other causes include a decline in earnings of other family members (11 percent), the transition to single parenting (11 percent), the birth of a child to a single mother (9 percent), and the move of a youth to his or her own household (15 percent). One study of AFDC recipients found that most women required assistance as a result of changes in their family situation—45 percent after separation or divorce, 30 percent after becoming unmarried mothers. One-third of the women left the program within a year, half at the end of two years, and two-thirds within four years. About a third left the program because their income had increased, another third when they remarried or reconciled with their mate, and 14 percent when their children left home or grew up.

Poverty spells are shorter if they begin with a decline in income than if they begin with transition to single parenthood or the birth of a child to a single mother. Half of poverty spells end with an increase in the earnings of the head of household and 23 percent with an increase in earnings to other family members. Fifteen percent end when the family receives public assistance, and 10 percent end when a single mother marries.

Being rich is not just another way of being poor. . . . Your needs expand with your income and the world eventually takes away what it gives.

John Updike

INCOME AND WEALTH. There are vast disparities in income and wealth between white, African American, Latino, and other ethnic groups. In fact, in 1990 the U.S. Census Bureau reported that over the last two decades there has been a "growing inequality of income distribution" (Pear, 1990). In 1989, for example, the median income for whites was $30,406, which was almost 60 percent greater than the

$18,083 of African-Americans (Pear, 1990). During the 1980s, the income disparity grew enormously, with the wealthiest 20 percent receiving a substantially higher share at the expense of the middle class and poor. Between 1979 and 1989, for example, the most affluent 5 percent of American families increased their median income from $120,253 to $148,438, while the income of the poorest 20 percent of families decreased from $9,990 to $9,431. At the same time, changes in the federal tax burden decreased the share of income that the wealthiest paid in taxes and increased the share paid by the poorest. Between 1980 and 1990, the percentage of income paid by the poorest 20 percent increased by 16.1 percent while the share paid by the wealthiest 5 percent decreased by 9.5 percent ("Shifting the Burden," 1990).

The disparity in wealth was even greater than income. (Wealth is a person's net worth, which represents decades of differences in income, investment, and the inheritance of property.) This disparity grew significantly during the 1980s (Pear, 1991). The net worth of whites is ten times that of African Americans and eight times that of Latinos. The median net worth for whites was $43,280, for African Americans, $4,170, and for Latinos, $5,520.

THE PLIGHT OF YOUNG FAMILIES. Families headed by men and women younger than thirty years are experiencing "a frightening cycle of plummeting earnings and family incomes, declining marriage rates, rising out-of-wedlock birth rates, increasing numbers of single-parent families, and skyrocketing poverty rates," wrote Marian Wright Edelman (1988). The findings of a study on young families (Johnson, Sum, and Weill, 1988) bear out Edelman's statements. Consider the following:

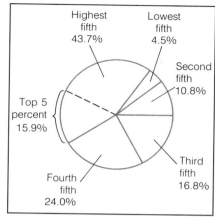

FIGURE 12.1

Money Income of Families, 1989

The distribution of family income is subject to great inequalities in the United States. The wealthiest 20 percent of families receive over 9 times as much income as the poorest 20 percent of families. The wealthiest 5 percent receive 13 times as much income as the poorest 20 percent.

Source: U.S. Bureau of the Census. *Statistical Abstract of the United States, 1990.* Washington, D.C.: Government Printing Office, 1990.

FIGURE 12.2

Individuals and Children Below Poverty Level, 1989

Source: U.S. Bureau of the Census. *Statistical Abstract of the United States, 1990.* Washington, D.C.: Government Printing Office, 1990.

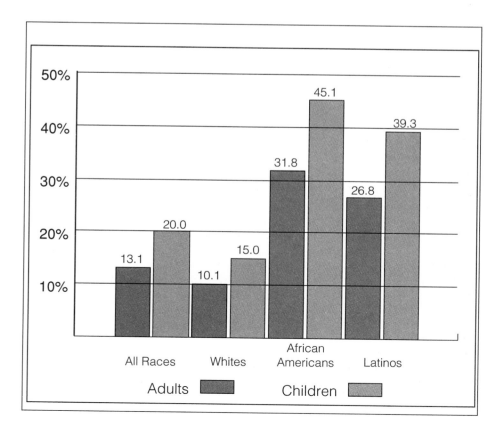

A Puerto Rican who didn't speak English came to the United States. He went along the streets of New York and came upon an expensive house. He went up to it and asked the butler in Spanish, "Who does this house belong to?"

The butler replied, "What did you say?"

The Puerto Rican misunderstood the butler, thinking he had said "Juan José."

The Puerto Rican went on and saw a beautiful car. He asked the man standing next to it, "Whose car is this?"

"What did you say?" asked the man.

"Dios mío!" exclaimed the Puerto Rican. "It belongs to Juan José."

Then he saw a prosperous clothing store. "Who owns this store?" asked the Puerto Rican.

"What did you say," was the reply.

Again the Puerto Rican thought the man had said Juan José.

The Puerto Rican saw a group of people surrounding two men fighting. "Who is fighting?" he asked.

"What did you say," replied the man.

"Juan José is fighting," the Puerto Rican said to himself.

Shortly afterward he came upon a funeral procession. "Whose funeral is this?" he asked.

"What did you say," a mourner asked.

"Oh, Juan José had died," the Puerto Rican murmured to himself.

Then the Puerto Rican saw a friend and said to him in Spanish, "Juan José has died. He was the richest man in all the United States. He wanted everything and would even fight to get it. And now he is dead. Poor Juan José that he didn't know better."

Puerto Rican folktale. (Originally West African Ananse [spider] tale brought to the Americas by enslaved blacks and modified over time to changed conditions.)

◆ The median income of families with young children fell 26 percent between 1973 and 1986. As a result, the poverty rate for young families soared from 12 percent to 22 percent. At the same time, the percentage of children living in poverty in young families rose from 21 to 35 percent.

◆ Young African-American and Latino families have suffered especially severe income losses. The median income of the heads of young African-American families has plummeted by half; for Latinos, the loss is one-third. Even among young African-American college graduates who head families, their median earnings have dropped 31 percent.

◆ Home ownership is beyond the reach of most young families. In 1973, it took one-fifth of a young family's median income to carry a mortgage; in 1986, it required 51 percent.

THE WORKING POOR. Since 1979, the largest increase in the numbers of poor has been among the working poor, because of low wages, occupational segregation, and the dramatic rise in single-parent families (Ellwood, 1988). Over 16 million poor men and women are "working poor." Although they work or are looking for work, they can not earn enough to raise themselves out of poverty. Almost 4 million worked full-time but remained poor (Chilman, 1991). A man or woman working full-time at minimum wage earns only 78 percent of the poverty-line income for a family of three. Almost half of two-parent working poor families had at least one adult working full-time. Four out of five poor, two-parent families are poor because of problems in the economic structure—low wages, job insecurity, or lack of available jobs. (See Chilman, 1991, for literature review.)

WOMEN, CHILDREN, AND POVERTY. The **feminization of poverty** is a painful fact. It has resulted primarily from high rates of divorce and increasing numbers of unmarried women with children (Hill, 1985). When women with children divorce, their income falls dramatically. In 1986, the median income of single-parent working women was $13,600 (U.S. Bureau of the Census, 1988).

Almost 40 percent of all children are poor; their poverty rate is the highest of any group. Like their parents, they move in and out of spells of poverty, depending on major changes in family structure, employment status of family members, or the disability status of the family head (Duncan and Rodgers, 1988). These variables, such as employment status, affect ethnic groups differently, accounting for differences in poverty rates. African Americans, for example, have significantly higher unemployment rates and numbers of never-married single mothers than other groups. As a result, their childhood poverty rates are markedly higher. Half of all African-American children under six years are poor; 40 percent of Latino children are poor, and 16 percent of white/Anglo children are poor (Pear, 1990). Being poor puts the most ordinary needs—from health care to housing—out of reach, jeopardizes the children's schooling, and undermines their sense of self (Edelman, 1989).

THE UNDERCLASS. In the last ten years, the underclass and homeless have become deeply disturbing features of American life, destroying cherished images of wealth and economic mobility. (For information about homelessness, see "Perspective," pages 382–383.) We must go back to the Great Depression of the 1930s when, in the words of President Franklin Delano Roosevelt, "one third of the nation was ill-fed, ill-clad, and ill-housed" to find greater despair. One commentator (DeParle, 1991) observed why many find the underclass and homeless so disturbing:

They suggest a second, separate America, a nation within a nation whose health, welfare, and social mobility evoke the Third World. Indeed visitors startled by rows of homeless lying in Grand Central Terminal in New York strain for analogies and produce the word "Calcutta."

It is not clear exactly what the underclass is (Auletta, 1982; Wilson 1989). It comprises not simply the poor, who have always existed in great numbers in America. The underclass is primarily a phenomenon of decaying cities, where poor African Americans and Latinos are overrepresented. The underclass feel excluded from society; indeed, it is often rejected by a society that neither understands nor empathizes with its plight (Appelbome, 1991). It is not a culture of poverty, however; the underclass's behaviors, actions, and problems are often a response to lack of opportunity, urban neglect, and inadequate housing and schooling.

The true test of civilization is a decent provision for the poor.

Samuel Johnson

With the flight of manufacturing, few job opportunities exist in the inner cities; the jobs that do exist are usually service jobs that fail to pay their workers sufficient wages to allow them to rise above poverty. Schools are substandard. Without adequate medical care, the infant death rate approaches that of Third World countries. HIV infection and AIDS are epidemic. The housing projects are infested with crime and drug abuse, turning them into kingdoms of despair. Gunfire punctuates the night. A woman addicted to crack explained, "I feel like I'm a different person when I'm not here. I feel good. I feel I don't need drugs. But being in here, you just feel like you're drowning. It's like being in jail. I hate the projects. I hate this rat hole" (DePerle, 1991).

Within the inner city, its residents struggle to maintain their dignity against surging hopelessness. They live day to day, fighting the forces that threaten to engulf them. A mother waiting for her child to return home from school said: "Mostly, you try to keep them away from the drugs and violence, but it's hard. I tell my oldest boy I don't want him hanging out with the boys who are getting in trouble, and he says, 'Aw, mama, ain't nobody else for me to be with'" (DePerle, 1991).

PUBLIC ASSISTANCE PROGRAMS. What is welfare? Welfare's most basic meaning refers to health, happiness, and well-being; the word itself is derived from the Old English *wel faren,* "to fare well." Over the last generation, however, driven by conservative beliefs, welfare has taken on a bad name. We no longer wish our poor *wel faren.* The war on poverty in the 1960s became the war on welfare in the 1980s. Instead of viewing poverty as a structural feature of our economy—caused by the shift from an industrial to service economy, the lack of opportunity, and discrimination—we blame the victim. Poverty is viewed as the result of individual character flaws—or even worse, as something inherently racial (Katz, 1990; Piven and Cloward, 1972).

American "means-tested" programs do indeed debilitate and demoralize. It is not receiving benefits that is damaging but rather the benefits are so low as to ensure physical misery and an outcast social status.

Fred Block

While poverty has increased, welfare benefits have not. In fact, the value of welfare benefits has decreased by over one-third since 1970, and fewer and fewer poor families are eligible for assistance (Kozol, 1988). The budget cutting of the 1990s is making a bad situation worse. Like many other states, for example, California cut the number of recipients of its Special Supplemental Food Program for Women, Infants and Children (WIC) program. One pregnant single parent with two children, a one-year-old and two-year-old, said (Mydans 1990): "It's going to be hard. The program helps a whole, whole lot. Sometimes you don't have the money to buy milk." To make up for the cuts, she will have to share some of the food she and her one-year-old receive from the program with her two-year-old, who is no longer eligible because of his age. And the high cot of child care keeps many AFDC mothers from working (Joesch, 1991).

In 1988, 6.1 percent of the population received public assistance; 3.8 million families, more than 11 million people, received AFDC (Aid to Families with Dependent Children) benefits, averaging $379 a month for a family with two children (U.S. Bureau of the Census, 1990). Seventy percent of single-parent families headed by women received government assistance, most often Medicaid or school lunches. Almost 40 percent of the poor, however, receive no assistance.

Despite the fact that 13 percent of the population currently lives in poverty, the number of people receiving government assistance has decreased from 6.5 percent of the population to 6.2 percent (U.S. Bureau of the Census, 1988). The number of people receiving foods stamps declined from 22 million in 1980 to 19.1 million in 1986 (U.S. Bureau of the Census, 1988). (And one does not live high on food stamps. The average food-stamp recipient receives 48 cents per meal per person; the highest amount received is 70 cents [Press, 1985]).

Unemployment

Unemployment is a structural part of the American economy; it is there in good times and bad times. In the best of times, there has been a 4 percent unemployment rate. In 1991, as many as 7 percent were officially unemployed, though the actual numbers were probably substantially higher. During the 1990/1991 recession, only one-third of unemployed men and women received unemployment benefits. Despite high unemployment, the proportion of those receiving unemployment insurance did not increase significantly, because the federal government and states gutted their unemployment insurance systems rather than raise taxes (Rosenbaum, 1990). In 1990, 2.3 million jobless men and women used up their unemployment benefits.

The human cost of these cutbacks is high. A common public policy assumption is that unemployment is primarily an economic problem. Yet joblessness also seriously affects health and the family's well-being (Liem and Rayman, 1982; Riegle, 1982). Two psychologists have called for "radically reshaping our sense of unemployment as not simply a problem in economics but as a factor in human and social welfare" (Liem and Rayman, 1982). (The psychological dimension of unemployment is discussed in Chapter 13.) The night before her unemployed husband left the state to take a temporary one-week job at one-fourth his former wage, for example, a woman let out her frustration, her eyes blazing with anger: "I'm holding down the fort. I'm paying his child support. I'm keeping things together. I'm pregnant. I'm tired, and I can't do it all" (Holmes, 1991). Her husband had been unemployed more than twenty-six weeks, the maximum period allowed for benefits by forty-eight states. Seventy-five percent of the unemployed had not found work four weeks after their benefits expired; ten weeks later, 60 percent were still unemployed (Holmes, 1991). Although in 1991 Congress provided for the extension of unemployment benefits to those who had already used theirs up, the President refused to release the funds.

The types of families hardest hit by unemployment are single-parent families headed by women, African-American and Latino families, and young families. African-American, Latino, and female-headed single-parent families tend to remain unemployed longer than other types of families. Because of discrimination and the resultant poverty, they may not have important education and employment skills. Young families with preschool children often lack the seniority, experience, and skills to quickly regain employment. "Since the parents of preschoolers are also the ones most likely to lose their jobs," observed Moen (1983), "the largest toll in an economic downturn is paid by families in the early years of childbearing and child-rearing."

Related to unemployment is underemployment. **Underemployment** has been defined in several different ways: inability to work as many hours as one would like,

When, in a city of 100,000, only one man is unemployed, that is his personal trouble, and for its relief we properly look to the character of the man, his skills, and his immediate opportunities. But when in a nation of 50 million employees, 15 million men are unemployed, that is an issue, and we may not hope to find its solution within the range of opportunities open to any one individual. The very structure of opportunities has collapsed. Both the correct statement of the problem and the range of possible solutions require us to consider the economic and political institutions of the society, and not merely the personal situation and character of a scatter of individuals.

C. Wright Mills, *The Sociological Imagination*

Prosperity doth best discover vice; but adversity doth best discover virtue.

Francis Bacon (1561–1626)

employment at lower pay than in previous work, or working in a job below one's qualifications. Underemployment particularly affects the working poor, workers whose plants have closed, and rural Americans. (About half of rural Americans are underemployed [Zvonkovic et al., 1988].) The underemployed include men and women who work part-time making pizza deliveries while they would like to work full-time; a $5-an-hour day laborer who made $15 an hour as a foundry worker prior to the steel plant's closing; a college graduate forced to work as a sales clerk because there are no managerial jobs available. Underemployment dramatically affects a family's income and raises stress levels. As many as 10 to 15 percent of employed persons may be underemployed; a quarter of all part-time workers desire full-time work (U.S. Bureau of Labor Statistics, 1988).

❖ REFLECTIONS   *Do you believe welfare helps or hinders families? Have you, your family, or friends received welfare assistance? If so, what were some of its effects?*

❖ FAMILY POLICY

As we examine America's priorities, it is clear that we have an implicit family policy that directs our national goals. Although it has never been articulated, it is very powerful in determining government and corporate policies. The policy is very simple: Families are not a national priority. And its corollary is equally simple: Neither are women and children.

Rising Interest and Obstacles

Over the years, a confusing combination of laws affecting families has been passed by state and federal governments. These laws include policies relating to family planning, abortion, sex education, foster care, maternal and child health, child support, AFDC, food stamps, and Medicare (Zimmerman and Owens, 1989). The issues underlying some of these laws, such as abortion, are controversial; others, such as child support, are not. But none of the family support programs that require substantial monies, such as AFDC and WIC, are adequately funded.

Since the late 1970s, interest has been rising in systematic, family-oriented legislation. A systematic approach to family policy may be defined as a set of objectives concerning family well-being and specific measures initiated by government to achieve them (Aldous and Dumon, 1991). Interest has been increasing for several reasons (Aldous and Dumon, 1991; Wisensale and Allison, 1989): (1) there has been a major increase in female-headed families because of the rise in divorce rates and births to single mothers; (2) women, especially mothers, have entered the labor force in unprecedented numbers; (3) problems confronting families, ranging from poverty to abuse, homelessness to inadequate child care, are increasingly viewed as social rather than individual problems; and (4) "the family" as symbol has become an ideological battlefield for liberals and conservatives.

With these various changes, why have we failed to develop supportive family policies? There are several reasons. First, there is strong political opposition based on different views of American families. Conservatives believe that the traditional family is the basis of society (Aldous and Dumon, 1991). Conservatives often oppose policies supporting families that do not conform to the ideal of the traditional two-parent family in which the father is the breadwinner and the mother is a housewife. This mythical, problem-free family of the past, where father knew best and mother baked cookies, is a powerful symbol. It stands at the center of resistance to legisla-

Money is a terrible master but an excellent servant.

P. T. Barnum

Money talks.

Folk saying

*Money doesn't talk
It swears.*

Bob Dylan

The stealth bomber is aptly named, for like a thief it steals from our nation's families, schools, and cities. Each stealth bomber represents fifty elementary schools, a thousand day-care centers, or 30,000 full four-year scholarships to a university.

Floyd Zimmerman

tion that assists single-parent and dual-earner families. Conservatives believe that AFDC benefits assisting single parents encourage unmarried women to bear children. According to conservatives, welfare benefits undermine the individual's desire to work. Furthermore, conservatives assert that welfare leads to family breakup. To end poverty, conservatives urge the elimination of welfare programs such as AFDC, food stamps, and housing subsidies. They believe that many of the poor are simply unwilling to work and that eliminating welfare would force them to work in order to survive. Private charities and local governments would care for the "truly needy" (Murray, 1984).

Liberals, in contrast, believe that America can be best served by recognizing the existence of diverse family forms. Many of America's families are vulnerable to poverty because of changes in the economy and family structures, especially the rise of divorce and single-parent families. Studies indicate that government welfare policies have had little to do with the rise of divorce, single-parent families, and births to single mothers. Instead, these are the result of broader social and economic changes (Aldous and Dumon, 1991; Danzinger and Plotknick, 1986). In contemporary society, most families become poor as a result of these larger changes. Welfare programs enable people to escape poverty rather than lure them into it. Liberals urge social policies to encourage self-sufficiency and to provide a decent standard of living for the poor. According to liberal thinkers, AFDC benefits provide a decent standard of living for the poor. According to liberal thinkers, AFDC benefits provide protection for poor families until they get on their feet again (Cherlin, 1988; Ellwood, 1988). Indeed, welfare benefits help stabilize families, as those states with the most generous welfare benefits also have the lowest divorce rates (Zimmerman, 1991).

Second, there are philosophical differences about the role of government in the family (Wisensale, 1990; Zimmerman, 1988). According to conservative thinking, the state is an intruder in the family. The family is the last bastion of privacy, and it should remain inviolable. "A man's home is his castle," is the conservative credo. For liberals and feminists, in contrast, the state is an enabler. It can protect women and children from abuse, assist families in rising above poverty through welfare benefits and training programs, provide publicly funded child care, and encourage corporations to be responsive to families through legislation and taxes. Most Americans, however, fall in the middle in their thinking.

Third, there is the question of the cost. In a conservative social climate burdened by enormous deficits from decades of unrestrained military spending, there is little political will to raise the necessary taxes to fund family programs. Instead, politicians "talk" family—but as we all know, talk is cheap. Until America makes a commitment to its families, our nation's families will continue to struggle and endure in a climate of neglect.

Elements of Family Policy

Let us assume, however, that the day has arrived when we have come to agree on the importance of our families. Imagine that family health and well-being have become a national priority. Here are some of the policies that might be instituted by government and business in the areas of education, health care, work, and social services (see Edelman, 1989; Macchiarola and Gartner, 1989; for suggestions on how to influence family legislation see Monroe, 1991; for discussion of think tanks involved in family policy, see Wisensale, 1991).

We spend more than $1 million a minute on the arms race in a world where 40,000 children in the developing countries die— not every month but every day.

Javier Perez de Cuellar, Secretary General, United Nations

The law, in its majestic equality, forbids the rich as well as the poor to sleep under bridges, to beg in the streets, and to steal bread.

Anatole France (1844–1924)

The question is not whether or not government will intervene. It will. The question is will it intervene for enhancement and prevention or respond to breakdown, problems, and deviance.

Alfred Kahn and Sheila Kamerman

HEALTH CARE

1. Guaranteed adequate medical care for every citizen, with a national health-care policy such as the kind that exists in Canada.
2. Prenatal and infant care for all mothers; adequate nutrition, immunizations, and "well baby" clinics to monitor infant health.
3. Medical and physical care of the aged and the disabled, including support for family caregivers.
4. Education for young people about sexuality and pregnancy prevention; implementation of comprehensive and realistic programs that address the economic and social realities of youth.
5. Education for all Americans about the realities of STDs, HIV, and AIDS. Guaranteed access to treatment.
6. Drug and alcohol rehabilitation programs available to all who want them.

SOCIAL WELFARE

1. Tax credits or income maintenance programs for families.
2. Child allowances to ensure a basic standard of living.
3. Child care for working or disabled parents; temporary respite child care when parents are ill or unable to care for their children; training of neighborhood day-care providers.
4. Advocacy for children, the aged, the disabled, and others who may not be able to speak up for themselves.
5. Attention given to problems of the homeless, such as food, shelter, medical and psychiatric care.
6. Regulation of children's television to promote literacy, good nutrition, humane values, and critical thinking.

EDUCATION

1. Implementation of preschool programs such as Head Start wherever needed.
2. Stress on the teaching of basic skills; use of innovative programs to reach *all* students, including out reach programs for adult literacy.
3. Work exposure for students who wish to work through programs such as Job Corps.
4. Guarantees that *all* Americans receive the benefits of education through the implementation of bilingual and multicultural programs, special education for the developmentally disabled, and adult education.

WORKPLACE

1. Paid parental leave for pregnancy and sick children; paid personal days for child and family responsibilities.
2. Flexible work schedules for parents whenever possible; job-sharing alternatives.
3. Increased minimum wage so that workers can support their families.
4. Policies to ensure fair employment for all, regardless of race, ethnicity, gender, sexual preference, or disability.
5. Pay equity between men and women for same or comparable jobs; affirmative action programs for women and ethnic groups.
6. Corporate child-care programs or subsidies for families.
7. Individual and family counseling services; provision of flexible benefit programs.

I was hungry—and a new committee was formed to study the causes of hunger.
I was sick—and legislators met again with new ideas for Medicare.
I was cold—and fuel bills were raised for more money to study the situation.
I was not safe in my home—and lawyers began to debate the reasons behind crime and what con be done about it.
I was lonely—and friends went into their churches to pray for me, and closed the door.
I am still hungry, sick, and lonely.

Anonymous, The Congressional Record

A modern nation's honor is not the honor of a warrior; it is the honor of a father providing for his children, it is the honor of a mother providing for her children .

E. L. Doctorow

The Christian ethic is incompatible with a primary or exclusive focus on maximization of profit. . . . Decisions must be judged in light of what they do for the poor, what they do to the poor, and what they enable the poor to do for themselves. The fundamental moral criterion for all economic decisions, policies, and institutions is this: They must be at the service of all people, especially the poor.

National Conference of Catholic Bishops, Pastoral Letter, 1986

At the 1990 United Nations World Summit on Children the United States refused to sign The Declaration on the Rights of Children because the Declaration prohibits the execution of children under age 18 and does not prohibit abortion The only other countries besides the United States that refused to sign the Declaration on the Rights of Children were Iraq, Iran, Libya, Cambodia, and China. We are not in good company. We need to do better for our families and children. They are our national strength, our treasure, and our future.

❖ SUMMARY

◆ Families may be examined as economic units bound together by emotional ties. Families are involved in two types of work: paid work at the workplace and unpaid work in the household.

◆ *Workplace/family linkages* are the ways in which employment affects family life. *Work spillover* is the effect that employment has on time, energy, and psychological functioning of workers and their families at home. *Role strain* refers to the difficulties that individuals have in carrying out multiple roles. Two types of role strain are *role overload*, which occurs when total prescribed activities for one or more roles are greater than an individual can handle, and *inter-role conflict*, which occurs when roles conflict with each other.

◆ Families must balance family/work needs throughout the family life cycle. The three basic work/family models are (1) the traditional/simultaneous work/family life cycle, (2) sequential work/family role staging, and (3) symmetrical work/family role allocation.

◆ The five stages of the traditional-simultaneous work/family model are (1) establishment/novitiate, (2) new parents/early career, (3) school-age family/middle career, (4) postparental family/late career, and (5) aging family/post exit. Major problems in this model are related to role strain. In the sequential pattern, women alternate work and mother roles rather than combine them. In the symmetrical pattern, men assume greater household and childrearing responsibilities.

◆ The traditional division of labor in the family follows a complementary pattern: the husband works outside the home for wages and the wife works inside the home without wages. Men's participation in household work is traditionally limited to repairs, construction, and yard work. Women's primary responsibility for household work and childrearing is part of the traditional marriage contract.

◆ Four aspects of the homemaker role are (1) its exclusive allocation to women, (2) its association with economic dependence, (3) its status as nonwork, and its (4) priority over other roles for women. Status accorded to homemakers depends on class. Working-class families accord homemakers greater status than do middle-class families.

◆ Characteristics of housework are that it (1) isolates the person at home, (2) is unstructured, monotonous, and repetitive, (3) is often a restricted, full-time role, (4) is autonomous, (5) is "never done," (6) may involve childrearing, and (7) often involves role strain.

◆ In 1988, 59 million women were employed, making up 47 percent of the work force. Women enter the work force for economic reasons and to raise their self-esteem. Employed women tend to have better physical and emotional health than nonemployed women. Women's employment tends to follow an M-shaped pattern; their labor-force participation is interrupted for family reasons over thirty times as often as it is for men.

◆ More than half of all women are in dual-earner marriages. Such women are more independent than nonemployed women and have increased power in decision making. Husbands generally do not significantly increase their share of household duties when their wives are employed. Employed mothers remain primarily responsible for childrearing. Women's employment has little or a slightly positive impact on marital satisfaction; there does seem to be a slightly greater likelihood of divorce.

◆ Family issues in the workplace include economic discrimination against women; sexual harrassment; occupational stratification for members of ethnic groups, especially women, placing them in lowest levels; lack of adequate child care; and an inflexible work environment.

◆ Almost 13 percent of the population of the United States live in poverty. Ten percent of whites, 33 percent of African Americans, 28 percent of Latinos, 12 percent of Asian Americans, and 25 percent of Native Americans are poor. The majority of poor people are women and children. Forty percent of all children are poor, representing the highest poverty rate of any group. There are significant differences between whites and members of ethnic groups in terms of income and wealth. The disparity increased dramatically during the 1980s.

◆ As many as 25 percent of Americans go through *spells of poverty,* during which time they need welfare assistance. Poverty spells generally occur because of divorce, the birth of a child to an unmarried mother, unemployment, illness, disability, or death of the head of household.. Young families are particularly vulnerable to poverty. The *underclass* are urban poor, disproportionately African American and Latino, who have little economic or social opportunity and are stigmatized by the larger society.

◆ Although most welfare recipients receive public assistance for less than two years, welfare is stigmatized. Welfare benefits have been cut, and fewer people receive welfare today increasing proverty.

◆ Unemployment most frequently affects female-headed single-parent families, African-American, and Latino families, and young families. Unemployment increased during the 1990/1991 recession. Unemployment insurance, however, inadequately protects workers. *Underemployment* particularly affects the working poor, workers whose plants have closed, and rural Americans.

◆ *Family policy* is a set of objectives concerning family well-being and the specific government measures designed to achieve those objectives. Family policy has been controversial because of conflicting viewpoints between conservatives and liberals about how best to help families, philosophical differences about the role of government, and the costs involved in its implementation. Family policy would contain provisions affecting health care, social welfare, education, and the workplace.

Answers to Preview Questions

The answers to the preview questions at the beginning of the chapter are listed below. As you check your answers, whether you were correct or not, think about your reasons for each response. What were they? What was their source? How valid is the source? As you read the chapter, you will find the questions discussed in greater depth.

1. F	6. F
2. T	7. T
3. F	8. T
4. T	9. T
5. F	10. F

❖ SUGGESTED READINGS

A useful journal for exploring economic aspects of the family is *Lifestyles: Family and Economic Issues.* Another useful periodical is *Family Economic Review,* published by the federal government. *The COFO Family Policy Report,* published by the Consortium of Family Organizations, is a newsletter oriented toward family policy and legislation.

Auletta, Ken. *The Underclass.* New York: Random House, 1982 (paperback). A well-written, balanced, and compassionate examination of the issues, problems, and people. This book continues to be relevant ten years after it was first published.

Baldwin, J., ed. *Whole Earth Ecolog.* New York: Crown Publishers, 1990 (paperback). The family is a consuming unit, and its habits—from its use of disposable diapers to its recycling (or lack of recycling) of products—have a significant impact on the environment. This special edition of the *Whole Earth Catalog* suggests products and ideas that may contribute to preserving our environment, ranging from energy-efficient lightbulbs to cohousing.

Bowen, Gary, and Dennis Orthner, eds. *The Organization Family: Work and Family Linkages in the U.S. Military.* New York: Praeger, 1989. An examination of the stresses and strains of military families.

Brazelton, T. Berry. *Working and Caring.* Reading, Mass.: Addison-Wesley, 1985 (paperback). A sensitive discussion of how professional, blue-collar, and single-parent families can deal with the dilemmas of work and childrearing; much useful advice.

Davidson, Osha Gray. *Broken Heartland: The Rise of America's Rural Ghetto.* New York: Free Press, 1990. A discussion of how America's agricultural heartland has become increasingly impoverished.

Hochschild, Arlie, with Anne Machung. *The Second Shift: Working Parents and the Revolution at Home.* New York: Viking, 1989 (paperback). Employed women work a first shift in the workplace and put in a second shift at home. An important, readable study of how dual-worker families cope.

Jones, Jacqueline. *Labor of Love, Labor of Sorrow: Black Women, Work, and the Family from Slavery to the Present.* New York: Vintage Books, 1985 (paperback). An outstanding study of African-American women and the forces that shaped their work and family lives.

Katz, Michael B. *The Undeserving Poor: From War on Poverty to War on Welfare.* New York: Pantheon Books, 1990 (paperback). Changing attitudes and policies toward the poor from the Johnson years to the Reagan era.

Komarovsky, Mirra. *Blue-Collar Marriage,* 2d ed. New Haven, Conn.: Yale University Press, 1987. The classic study of working-class families.

Kozol, Jonathan. *Rachel and Her Children: Homeless Families in America.* New York: Crown Publishers, 1988. A moving description of life among the homeless by one of America's leading journalists.

Rhodes, Richard. *Farm: A Year in the Life of an American Farmer.* New York: Simon and Schuster, 1989 (paperback). A compelling description of life and work on a Midwestern family farm.

Strasser, Susan. *Never Done: A History of American Housework.* New York: Pantheon Books, 1982 (paperback). A "sweeping" history of housework that puts dusting, vacuuming, and ironing into perspective. A must for dishpan hands.

Voydanoff, Patricia. *Work and Family Life.* Beverly Hills, Calif.: Sage Publications, 1987. A concise overview of current research on work, economics, and the family.

Wilson, Julius William, ed. *The Ghetto Underclass: Social Science Perspectives.* Newbury Park, Calif.: Sage Publications, 1989 (paperback). A collection of essays examining diverse aspects of ghetto life.

Wilson, Sarah Jane. *Women, the Family, and the Economy,* 2d ed. Toronto: McGraw-Hill Ryerson, 1986. A discussion of

women, employment, and gender roles in Canada. Contains
excellent bibliography.

Zavella, Patricia. *Women's Work and Chicano Families*. Ithaca, N.Y.:
Cornell University Press, 1987 (paperback). A well-written
anthropological study of Latina cannery workers and their
family lives.

Suggested Films

Do the Right Thing (1989). Spike Lee's controversial film on racism,
illustrating, among other things, its economic dimensions.

The Grapes of Wrath (1940). The classic film of a family fleeing the
Dust Bowl for California during the Depression.

Modern Times (1936). Charlie Chaplin's satire on social ills and
technological dehumanization. One of the greatest films of all
times.

Roger and Me (1989). The hotly-disputed documentary about a GM
plant closing, its corporate president (who refuses to be
interviewed), and the effects of the closing on the town and its
families.

Salt of the Earth (1953). Based on a true story—striking Latino
miners in New Mexico led to a victory by their wives and
families.

Sidewalk Stories (1989). A bittersweet story of a homeless man
taking on a child.

READINGS

WOMEN'S WORK AND CHICANO FAMILIES

Patricia Zavella. Excerpt from *Women's Work
and Chicano Families.*

*Patricia Zavella finds that the Latinas she interviewed experi-
enced few conflicts over role expectations in early marriage. The
greatest conflicts occurred when mothers went to work. Why do
you think this was the case? Why did the women in this study
seek employment? How do their experiences compare with those
of non-Latinas?*

The early years of marriage were times of mutual adjustment to
the traditional notions of family stressed during their socialization. My informants were sometimes overzealous in their
attempts to fulfill the image of a good wife. By the time she was
twenty-two, María López, who was reared in South Texas and
married at fifteen, had five children.

I was the one! I don't know why I was like that. I had all the little
kids, and I used to keep the house spotless—I'd mop in the mornings and in the evenings. I'd start dinner an hour early, so everything
would be ready when Victor came home. He'd just walk in and go
straight to the table, and I'd serve him. Everything would still be
steaming hot. And we'd all sit down and eat. Then he'd watch TV or
whatever, and I'd clean the kids' faces, change their clothes, and put
them to bed. Then I'd wash the dishes. I was busy working all day
long, and I didn't have to! Victor would tell me, "María, don't work
so hard. You don't have to do so much." But I felt that I had to.

María would customarily lay out her husband's clothes with
the rationale: "He expected to be waited on hand and foot by the
woman. He felt that women are there to serve the man. And
that's the way I was raised too. My mother did everything for my

father." Many women related similar incidents of catering to
their spouses or keeping spotless homes with little help from the
men. Women expected and even welcomed their child-care
responsibilities. María was defensive about this: "I don't think
that we should take turns taking care of the kids when they're
sick. I feel like that's my responsibility. *I'm* responsible for them
24 hours a day. And if they're sick I couldn't let him take care of
them. No, do you think he's going to worry about them all day
long?" In accordance with this traditional outlook, husbands
reciprocated by providing for their families. Women expected
marriage to be this way. As Connie remarked, "That's the way
it's always been."

María's beliefs about the traditional division of labor are illustrated in a classic argument she had with her brother-in-law,
who was reared in South Texas.

The other day Ray began talking about how women's work is easier
than men's work: "Women just sit around the house and watch TV."

So I asked, "Ray, what time do you get up to go to work?"
He said, "At 7:30."
I said, "I see, you go to work at 8:00."
He nodded
"And what time does Linda get up?"
"6:30."
"So when you get up she is already working, making tortillas,
making breakfast, coffee, and making your lunch. And then after
you've gone she has to wash the dishes and take care of the kids,
and wash and iron, and make something to eat for her and the kids.
Then you get out at five o'clock, and already by four o'clock you are
getting ready to come home. You know that you don't work very
hard that last hour.

"But for the woman, that is when her work has just begun. She has
to make dinner and have it ready so that when you get home, she
can serve you right away. And then after dinner you go watch TV or
whatever. She still has to wash the dishes, get the kids ready for bed,
make sure they're clean and covered. And you've already been relax-
ing for two hours. So the woman puts in more hours than you do."

READINGS

María has made an effective argument, pointing out the wife's work contribution. She did not want to claim that women's work was more important, however, just equal. So when her brother-in-law responded that men have more responsibilities, she agreed: "A man has the responsibility to bring in the money *para hacer los pagos* [to make the payments]. And he has to make sure that he has a job. A woman doesn't have the responsibility. If she works, fine; if not, it's all right. So, yes the man has more responsibility, but he doesn't work harder than the woman." María was pleased that she had won the argument. . . .

Few of the conflicts that arose in the early years of marriage were over role expectations. Husbands and wives expected that women would not have to work. Although some women worked during the first few years of marriage, almost all quit after their children were born. These early patterns of behavior would later become a source of adjustment or conflict when the wife went to work and could no longer meet her family members' needs in the manner in which they had grown accustomed.

The first years of married life usually were the hardest economically. Most informants had difficulties establishing a home, bringing up children who were born in quick succession, and handling the husband's unstable work histories. The women's husbands worked in low-paying, unskilled jobs—in construction, packing sheds, farm work, canneries, or other factories. These were the lean years of stretching the paycheck to make ends meet. Rosa's husband also worked in the cannery part-time, and his other job was that of a part-time clerk. She described how they managed: "When your husband doesn't have a steady job, you do things. Like we used to have a freezer and we used to make pretty good money in the summer time. I'd stock my freezer with all the essentials; then in the winter time we'd just skimp by on unemployment." Blanca Ramírez related a similar situation:

When we got married, we lived in a tiny house; we paid $25 rent. I was pregnant with my first son and was sick because I had a difficult pregnancy. And we didn't have a washing machine, we didn't have a car, and we had to go real far to wash clothes. And since we didn't have money for the dryer, we had to bring the clothes home to dry. And my poor husband didn't have a job. He could only work one or two days out of the week. He was getting unemployment, $39 a week, and we just couldn't make it.

Not being able to "make it" came from the hardship of low wages when work was available and even more when men were laid off. These years created pressures for the wife to help out. Some tried taking in ironing or doing babysitting for others at home, with the children around. But the meager income did not suffice, so the only alternative was to look for a job.

Virtually all of the women originally sought work for economic reasons. The actual decision was made after careful deliberation with husbands, although in several instances women had to argue their cases. Some men viewed working wives as a symbol of their own shortcomings as providers. Others worried about the effects on the children or household. In exchange for husbands' support, women agreed to certain restrictions. Lupe succinctly gave the reason for beginning her job search: "I did it for my family. We needed the money. Why else?" Yet as Lupe recalled, her husband "at first never wanted me to work," so she made some concessions. "He put pretty strict conditions for me to get a job. He wouldn't allow me to work nights or take the kids out of the house [for child care]."

For some of my informants, the decision to seek a paid job was also an assertion of their independence. Despite the dire situation of Blanca's family, her husband opposed the suggestion of her working: "He told me that he wanted a woman for his home and not to go to work. But I went anyway to help him, even though he didn't want me to." After long days spent looking for a job, Blanca recalled her husband's advice: "He said, 'Don't go back, you're not going to find a job anyway.'" Blanca shrugged: *"Tú sabes que en este mundo, uno tiene que cuidarse a sí mismo"* (You know that in this world one has to take care of oneself). Luz Gálvez also went against her husband's wishes: "At first he did mind, when the kids were small. We used to have a lot of arguments. But I went anyway." Rosa was able to persuade her husband to support her entrance into the labor market: "My husband didn't want me to work, period. But I convinced him."

Theoretically, taking a job against the husband's wishes could have jeopardized the marriage. However, several factors mitigated the husbands' opposition. Given the precariousness of their situations, the husbands could not legitimately argue against their wives going to work. Consequently, their protests may have masked their unstated desire to have wives enter the labor force. Indeed Victor López wanted María to work (while she was pregnant with their sixth child), with the idea that it would be a temporary solution until he found a job. But he said he did not like the idea and grumbled about it.

Married women with children had conflicting demands once they decided to get jobs. Working mothers had to find time to care for their families, yet spend long hours away from home. Recall the independent views expressed by Gloria Gonzales—"Women *should* work outside the home, see what they can do for themselves." Yet when asked why she had entered the labor force, she replied, "It was for my kids' benefit that I got a job and not for any thing else. My family comes first." Her husband's opposition and her children's needs at home prevented her from seeking a full-time job. By evoking traditional family ideology—"my family comes first"—she could rationalize her seemingly nontraditional actions and minimize her own independence. This would be necessary only for women who believed men should support families.

continued on next page

THE SECOND SHIFT

Arlie Hochschild. Excerpt from *The Second Shift*.

According to sociologist Arlie Hochschild, employed women perform a "second shift" of work at home as they perform their traditional spousal, parental, and household duties. What is the effect of this "second shift" on Nancy and Evan? On women in dual-worker families? On men?

Between 8:05 A.M. and 6:05 P.M., both Nancy and Evan are away from home, working a "first shift" at full-time jobs. The rest of the time they deal with the varied tasks of the second shift: shopping, cooking, paying bills; taking care of the car, the garden, and yard; keeping harmony with Evan's mother, who drops over quite a bit, "concerned" about Joey, with neighbors, their voluble baby-sitter, and each other. And Nancy's talk reflects a series of second-shift thoughts: "We're out of barbecue sauce. . . . Joey needs a Halloween costume. . . . The car needs a wash. . . ." and so on. She reflects a certain "second-shift sensibility," a continual attunement to the task of striking and restriking the right emotional balance between child, spouse, home, and outside job.

When I first met the Holts, Nancy was absorbing far more of the second shift than Evan. She said she was doing 80 percent of the housework and 90 percent of the childcare. Evan said she did 60 percent of the housework, 70 percent of the childcare. Joey said, "I vacuum the rug, and fold the dinner napkins," finally concluding, "Mom and I do it all." A neighbor agreed with Joey. Clearly, between Nancy and Evan, there was a "leisure gap": Evan had more than Nancy. I asked both of them, in separate interviews, to explain to me how they had dealt with housework and childcare since their marriage began.

One evening in the fifth year of their marriage, Nancy told me, when Joey was two months old and almost four years before I met the Holts, she first seriously raised the issue with Evan. "I told him: 'Look, Evan, it's not working. I do the housework, I take the major care of Joey, *and* I work a full-time job. I get pissed. This is *your* house too. Joey is *your* child too. It's not all *my* job to care for them.' When I cooled down I put to him, "Look, how about this: I'll cook Mondays, Wednesdays, and Fridays. You cook Tuesdays, Thursdays, and Saturdays. And we'll share or go out Sundays.'"

According to Nancy, Evan said he didn't like "rigid schedules." He said he didn't necessarily agree with her standards of housekeeping, and didn't like that standard "imposed" on him, especially if she was "sluffing off" tasks on him, which from time to time he felt she was. But he went along with the idea in principle. Nancy said the first week of the new plan went as follows. On Monday, she cooked. For Tuesday, Evan planned a meal that required shopping for a few ingredients, but on his way

home he forgot to shop for them. He came home, saw nothing he could use in the refrigerator or in the cupboard, and suggested to Nancy that they go out for Chinese food. On Wednesday, Nancy cooked. On Thursday morning Nancy reminded Evan, "Tonight it's your turn." That night Evan fixed hamburgers and french fries and Nancy was quick to praise him. On Friday, Nancy cooked. On Saturday, Evan forgot again.

As this pattern continued, Nancy's reminders became sharper. The sharper they became, the more actively Evan forgot—perhaps anticipating even sharper reprimands if he resisted more directly. This cycle of passive refusal followed by disappointment and anger gradually tightened, and before long the struggle had spread to the task of doing the laundry. Nancy said it was only fair that Evan share the laundry. He agreed in principle, but anxious that Evan would not share, Nancy wanted a clear, explicit agreement. "You ought to wash and fold every other load," she had told him. Evan experienced this "plan" as a yoke around his neck. On many weekdays, at this point, a huge pile of laundry sat like a disheveled guest on the living-room couch.

In her frustration, Nancy began to make subtle emotional jabs at Evan. "I don't know *what's* for dinner," she would say with a sigh. Or "I can't cook now, I've got to deal with this pile of laundry." She tensed at the slightest criticism about household disorder; if Evan wouldn't do the housework, he had absolutely *no* right to criticize how she did it. She would burst out angrily at Evan. She recalled telling him: "After work *my* feet are just as tired as *your* feet. I'm just as wound up as you are. I come home. I cook dinner. I wash and I clean. Here we are, planning a second child, and I can't cope with the one we have."

About two years after I first began visiting the Holts, I began to see their problem in a certain light: as a conflict between their two gender ideologies. Nancy wanted to be the sort of woman who was needed and appreciated both at home and at work—like Lacey, she told me, on the television show "Cagney and Lacey." She wanted Evan to appreciate her for being a caring social worker, a committed wife, and a wonderful mother. But she cared just as much that she be able to appreciate *Evan* for what *he* contributed at home, not just for how he supported the family. She would feel proud to explain to women friends that she was married to one of these rare "new men."

A gender ideology is often rooted in early experiences and fueled by motives formed early on, and such motives can often be traced to some cautionary tale in early life. So it was for Nancy. Nancy described her mother:

My mom was wonderful, a real aristocrat, but she was also terribly depressed being a housewife. My dad treated her like a doormat. She didn't have any self-confidence. And growing up, I can remember her being really depressed. I grew up bound and determined not to be like her and not to marry a man like my father. As long as Evan doesn't do the housework, I feel it means he's going to be like

READINGS

my father—coming home, putting his feet up, and hollering at my mom to serve him. That's my biggest fear. I've had *bad* dreams about that.

Nancy thought that women friends her age, also in traditional marriages, had come to similarly bad ends. She described a high school friend: "Martha barely made it through City College. She had no interest in learning anything. She spent nine years trailing around behind her husband [a salesman]. It's a miserable marriage. She hand washes all his shirts. The high point of her life was when she was eighteen and the two of us were running around Miami Beach in a Mustang convertible. She's gained seventy pounds and she hates her life." To Nancy, Martha was a younger version of her mother, depressed, lacking in self-esteem, a cautionary tale whose moral was "if you want to be happy, develop a career and get your husband to share at home." Asking Evan to help again and again felt like "hard work" but it was essential to establishing her role as a career woman.

For his own reasons, Evan imagined things very differently. He loved Nancy and if Nancy loved being a social worker, he was happy and proud to support her in it. He knew that because she took her caseload so seriously, it was draining work. But at the same time, he did not see why, just because she chose this demanding career, *he* had to change *his own* life. Why should her personal decision to work outside the home require him to do more inside it? Nancy earned about two-thirds as much as Evan, and her salary was a big help, but as Nancy confided, "If push came to shove, we could do without it." Nancy was a social worker because she loved it. Doing daily chores at home was thankless work, and certainly not something Evan needed her to appreciate about him. Equality in the second shift meant a loss in his standard of living, and despite all the high-flown talk, he felt he hadn't *really* bargained for it. He was happy to help Nancy at home if she needed help; that was fine. That was only decent. But it was too sticky a matter "committing" himself to sharing.

Two other beliefs probably fueled his resistance as well. The first was his suspicion that if he shared the second shift with Nancy, she would "dominate him." Nancy would ask him to do this, ask him to do that. It felt to Evan as if Nancy had won so many small victories that he had to draw the line somewhere. Nancy had a declarative personality; and as Nancy said, "Evan's mother sat me down and told me once that I was too forceful, that Evan needed to take more authority." Both Nancy and Evan agreed that Evan's sense of career and self was in fact shakier than Nancy's. He had been unemployed. She never had. He had had some bouts of drinking in the past. Drinking was foreign to her. Evan thought that sharing housework would upset a certain balance of power that felt culturally "right." He held the purse strings and made the major decisions about large purchases (like their house) because he "knew more about finances" and because he'd chipped in more inheritance than she when they married. His job difficulties had lowered his self-respect, and now as a couple they had achieved some ineffable "balance"— tilted in his favor, she thought—which, if corrected to equalize the burden of chores, would result in his giving in "too much." A certain driving anxiety behind Nancy's strategy of actively renegotiating roles had made Evan see agreement as "giving in." When he wasn't feeling good about work, he dreaded the idea of being under his wife's thumb at home.

Underneath these feelings, Evan perhaps also feared that Nancy was avoiding taking care of *him*. His own mother, a mild-mannered alcoholic, had by imperceptible steps phased herself out of a mother's role, leaving him very much on his own. Perhaps a personal motive to prevent that happening in his marriage—a guess on my part, and unarticulated on his—underlay his strategy of passive resistance. And he wasn't altogether wrong to fear this. Meanwhile, he felt he was "offering" Nancy the chance to stay home, or cut back her hours, and that she was refusing his "gift," while Nancy felt that, given her feelings about work, this offer was hardly a gift.

PART FIVE

Interiors

The Family and Health: Social and Psychological Perspectives

To gain a sense of what you already know about the material covered in this chapter, answer "true" or "false" to the following statements below. You will find the answers on page 433.

1. Health is the absence of illness or disease. True or false?
2. Happily married men and women tend to be healthier than unmarried individuals. True or false?
3. Economic recessions are associated with rises in family violence and alcoholism. True or false?
4. In contrast to women, men provide an insubstantial amount of caregiving for aged parents and in-laws. True or false?
5. Disabilities or chronic illnesses are not necessarily viewed negatively by families experiencing them. True or false?
6. Overall drug use is continuing to rise. True or false?
7. A beer is equal in alcohol content to a rum and Coke. True or false?
8. Feeling guilty is a normal part of the process of grieving. True or false?
9. Getting married is considered a stressful event in people's lives. True or false?
10. The families of drug addicts are often characterized by a lack of control over their feelings. True or false?

*Health and good estate of body are above
all good.*

Ecclesiastes 30:15

*Life is not merely living but living in
health.*

Martial (A.D. 40–104)

W̲HEN A PARENT BRINGS YOU SOUP as you lie sick in bed, when stress at work
leaves you too tired to play with your children or enjoy your partner, when
your spouse urges you to stop drinking, when a chronically ill child or aging parent
requires constant attention, or when a family member dies—we are reminded that
families consist of individuals with bodies. Our physical and emotional health are
critical elements of family life. Until very recently, researchers ignored this aspect of
family life. But during the last fifteen years, research has burgeoned on the relationship between families and health.

In this chapter we will focus on the social and psychological dimensions of families and health, for, as William Doherty and Thomas Campbell (1988) observe, "The
family affects the individual's health and the individual's health affects the family."
To understand the interactions between the two, we will first examine how marriage
may encourage mental and physical health among men and women. We will explore
the health care crisis and the various crises and stresses that affect our health and
well-being as families, such as economic distress. Then we will examine family caregiving for the disabled, the chronically ill, and the elderly. Next we will explore
death and grieving. Finally, we will look at alcohol and substance abuse, which may
insidiously destroy individuals and families.

❖ MARRIAGE, HEALTH, AND WELL-BEING

Health is a state of physical and mental well-being, not solely the absence of disease.
Physical well-being consists of feeling fit and able; for the disabled or chronically ill,
it refers to the ability to function within their limits. **Emotional well-being** refers to
feelings of happiness, hope, energy, and the zest for life (Ross, Mirowsky, and Goldsteen, 1991). Such positive definitions of health and well-being focus on the physical
and emotional quality of life rather than on illness and disease. Positive definitions
empower individuals to strive for wellness rather than passively accept sickness.

Marriage is good for your health, at least if you are happily married. As a whole,
married men and women tend to be healthier and happier than their unmarried
peers; they live longer, are less depressed, and have a higher general sense of well-
being. An important study found that those who reported themselves to be very
happily married had better emotional health than unmarried men and women.
Those who were "pretty happy" in their marriages reported about the same levels of
emotional well-being as those who were unmarried. Those who were unhappily
married were *more* emotionally distressed than unmarried men and women (Gove,
Hughes, and Style, 1983).

Researchers do not know at this time, however, how long-term heterosexual, gay,
or lesbian cohabitation affects health. Most likely, long-term cohabitation produces
many of the same positive health effects as does marriage. But because cohabiting
relationships do not receive the same level of societal support as marriage, the effects
may not be as strong.

There are two hypotheses as to why married individuals tend to be healthier than
unmarried men and women: the *self-selecting hypothesis* and the *enabling hypothesis*.
According to the self-selection hypothesis, married people tend to be healthier than
single individuals because they are healthier to begin with rather than because of any
benefits that marriage itself confers (Turner and Gartrell, 1978; Verbrugge, 1979).
Advocates of self-selection argue that healthy people select other healthy people to
marry, whereas unhealthy people are unable to find mates because they are undesirable. Close analysis of data fails to confirm this hypothesis.

Most researchers suggest that marriage *enables* people to be healthy (Gove, Style, and Hughes, 1990). How is it that marriage encourages health and well-being? There are appear to be three contributing factors (Ross, Mirowsky, and Goldsteen, 1991): (1) living with a partner, (2) social support, and (3) economic well-being.

LIVING WITH A PARTNER. Initially, researchers believed that the major health difference between married and single men and women resulted from the presence of another person, whether it was a roommate, friend, or spouse. More recently, it has been shown that not just anyone will do. It is the person's marital partner who is critical to his or her health—a spouse who will sustain the other in time of need, make chicken soup when the partner is sick, and dance with him or her when happy. Many of these same benefits may accrue to cohabiting partners as well, though there is no research available.

SOCIAL SUPPORT. Only a spouse is committed and involved enough to provide sufficient social support to improve a partner's health. Social support consists of both instrumental and emotional elements. Instrumental support includes such things as cooking for the other, doing favors, and providing economic security. But as far as health and well-being are concerned, emotional support—the sense of being loved and cared about, esteemed and valued—appears to be more important. When spouses are not supportive, are authoritarian, divide labor unfairly, or are degrading or demeaning, their partners are often demoralized, depressed, or unhappy.

A partner's social support improves physical health in several ways (Ross, Mirowsky, and Goldsteen, 1991). Social support (1) increases psychological well-being, (2) encourages and reinforces protective health behaviors, (3) provides secondary prevention, and (4) assists recovery. First, a partner who listens and cares helps reduce depression, anxiety, and other psychological problems. With improve-

Health is the state of physical and emotional well-being. Happily married individuals tend to be healthier than single men and women.

ment of a person's emotional well-being, his or her physical health and survival ability increase dramatically.

Second, a partner encourages and reinforces protective health behaviors. Compared to their unmarried peers, husbands and wives have better diets and are less likely to smoke, drink heavily, drive too fast, or take risks that increase the likelihood of accidents or injuries. Because women generally have healthier life-styles than men, when they marry, men's health behaviors and survival improve more significantly than women's (Ross, Mirowsky, and Goldsteen, 1991; Umberson, 1987).

Third, a partner provides secondary prevention by helping to identify or treat an illness or disease early. A woman expresses concern about her partner's continuing cough and fever and insists that he see a physician, who diagnoses viral pneumonia, a potential killer; a man notices a discoloration on his wife's back, which turns out to be a treatable skin cancer. Another makes a sneezing, wheezing partner rest instead of going to work or school, thereby speeding recovery and building resistance to other infections.

Finally, social support aids a partner's recovery. The love and care of a partner, his or her gestures of intimacy, small acts of thoughtfulness, a familiar hand soothing a feverish forehead or softly caressing the face—all assist in the psychological recovery following an illness. It is well-documented, for example, that intimacy encourages emotional recovery following a heart attack. A husband's high level of support and caring significantly reduces the depression and anxiety that a woman experiences as she lives with breast cancer.

ECONOMIC WELL-BEING. Married men and women have higher household incomes than unmarried people: an average of $33,500 for married couples compared to $28,600 for single men and $21,500 for single women. With higher incomes and economics of scale, married men and women are more likely to visit physicians and have health insurance. They are also less likely to experience high levels of stress occasioned by the daily grind of poverty. Poverty is associated with decreased life expectancy, higher infant mortality, and higher rates of infectious diseases, disability, and mortality. The poor are more likely to get sick; if they do get sick, they are less likely to survive. Because of the close tie between race or ethnicity and income, African Americans and Latinos are especially vulnerable to higher disease and mortality rates.

❖ THE HEALTH CARE CRISIS

Imagine that you are riding your bicycle to class. You are late, so you are pedaling especially fast, but you hit a rock, causing you to flip off your bicycle. You spin through the air and tumble against the concrete curb. You hear a crunching sound. You get up; you are dizzy and nauseous and your shoulder is in intense pain. You may have suffered a concussion and you think your shoulder might be broken. Across the street is a private hospital called Mount Profit which will take care of you immediately; ten miles away is the county hospital which will examine you in its emergency room, though you will probably have to wait two to six hours while the more serious gunshot and accident victims are treated. Which hospital will you choose? (Hint: it probably depends on whether you have medical insurance.)

America's health care system is a strange paradox. Health costs account for 12 percent of the United States' gross national product. We spend $2354 per capita on health care, four times as much as Germany and eight times as much as Canada. But despite our vast outlay of money and our ever-expanding medical technology, our infant death rate is among the higheset in the industrialized world. The health status of many of our African-American communities is that of third-world countries; a young black male in Detroit has a shorter life expectancy than his counterpart in Bangladesh. Almost half the poor are frozen out of the medical system, and the uninsured middle-class are petrified of losing their homes to medical bills. We are in crisis. And it is getting worse.

Health insurance has become one of the prime determinants of an individual's or family's access to medical care. The spiraling costs of medical care—up to thousands of dollars a day for hospital care—have made visits to the doctor or hospital out of the reach of most Americans without medical insurance. And yet, 33 million Americans—13 percent of the population—are uninsured. The figure rises to 22 percent for those between 16 and 24 years of age. Eighteen percent of whites, 30 percent of African Americans, and 41 percent of Latinos are uninsured (Friedman, 1991; Lewin, 1991).

Most insured people are covered either through their employment, through Medicare if they are very poor (only 40 percent of the poor are covered) or through Medicaid if they are elderly. Health insurance is closely tied to the workplace, through an employer's benefit program, usually a group insurance plan. An employee pays part or all of the insurance through his or her employer; the amount may be nominal or run into thousands of dollars per year. Because of the increasing insurance costs, employers are trying to curtail their coverage. Furthermore, employee group plans are usually not extended to part-time or temporary workers. Millions in low-paying service, retail, or agricultural jobs receive no benefits. And employees who lose their jobs often lose their coverage as well.

The connection of insurance benefits with employment may affect work decisions. A 1990 poll found that 15 percent of its respondents or their family members had changed jobs or remained on the same job because of health insurance benefits (Lewin, 1991). "Job lock" decribes the fear of changing jobs because of benefits loss. One woman, for example, wanted to go part-time to be with her young daughters but couldn't because she was once treated for breast cancer and would not be able to get insurance elsewhere. "The one thing I can't do now is quit because I have insurance here and I'm uninsurable if I leave," she said (Lewin, 1991).

It is often prohibitively expensive to purchase individual health insurance, costing thousands or even tens of thousands of dollars in yearly premiums. Often the insurance, despite its costs, exempts certain health categories if the individual has had any problems in the area. Other times the insurance company will exclude an individual altogether.

The effects of the insurance crisis are three-fold. First, it forces the uninsured to live in constant dread of a major medical expense that can destroy their savings or force them to sell their home. Second, it leads to deteriorating health, since the uninsured do not seek timely medical attention. For the uninsured, health problems require a triage approach. In one family, for example, the oldest child needs a tooth filled, the mother has abdominal pain that requires ultrasound, and the father has a sprained ankle he keeps on ice, hoping to avoid the cost of an X-ray. They put off treatment as long as possible. Finally, they decide to seek treatment for one member. On what basis? The basis of pain. The member with the most pressing pain—the father, in this case—sees a doctor. Yet the mother's abdominal pain may indicate a life-threatening tumor. The third effect of the insurance crisis is its impact on the ability of our public hospitals to function. Because so many Americans are uninsured, they turn to inexpensive or free public hospitals for medical treatment. As a result of budget cutbacks and growing numbers of uninsured, waits in public hospitals for nonemergency visits are routinely three to six months. Physicians and nurses are over-burdened by the numbers of patients. Over the last ten years, patient visits have increased between 70 to 100 percent while funding and staff have been dramatically cut because of conservative spending priorities and budget deficits.

As the medical insurance crisis continues, the most attractive alternative to the current job-linked or welfare-linked system appears to be that modeled by the Canadian "universal insurance system," which insures all its citizens and provides them with the choice of their own private physician (Erkholm, 1991). Because it is administered through one nonprofit agency instead of numerous for-profit insurance companies, it reduces net costs by approximately 20 percent. This cost reduction allows the government to cover at no greater expense individuals and families that would not ordinarily be insured in the U.S. system. Naturally, insurance companies fight such reform tooth and nail.

❖ STRESS AND THE FAMILY

Life involves constant change to which both the individual and the family must adjust (Bell et al., 1980). Change brings **stress**—psychological or emotional distress or disruption. It does not matter whether the change is for the better or the worse; stress is produced in either case. **Family stress** may be defined as "an upset in the steady state of the family" (Boss, 1987). Since all families undergo periods of stress, the ability to cope successfully is seen as an important factor in measuring family health.

Family Stress and Coping

Families constantly face stress, tension resulting from real or perceived demands that require the family system to adjust or adapt its behavior. (See Chapter 3 for discussion of family systems.) When a family is under stress, its members may experience **distress,** psychological and physical tension, such as intense upset, mood changes, headaches, and muscular tension. While both individuals and families must adapt to stressful events, they must also maintain their equilibrium. They must keep their identities intact. As a result, individuals and families are involved in a delicate balancing act to adapt to changing situations while maintaining their integrity. They respond to stress in many different ways. How we cope with stressful demands determines whether or not we experience a crisis.

VARIABLES AFFECTING FAMILY'S RESPONSE TO STRESSORS. There are six variables involved in a family's response to stress:

◆ *Stressor:* a life event, such as birth, departure of a family member, illness, or unemployment, that affects that family at a certain point in time and produces change in the family system.
◆ *Family hardship:* difficulties specifically associated with the stressor, such as loss of income in the case of unemployment.
◆ *Strains:* the tensions lingering from previous stressors or the tensions inherent in family roles, such as being a parent or spouse. Strains include the emotional scars from bitter or unresolved fights or the fatigue of parenting.
◆ *Resources:* the material, psychological, or social assets that can be used by the family to influence others or to cope with stress, such as money, emotional support, or friends.

Don't trouble trouble till trouble troubles you.

Traditional African-American proverb

Marriage, no less than life in general, is just one damned thing after another.

Frank Pittman

T A B L E 13.1 The Stages of the Family Life Cycle: Stress Points

FAMILY LIFE CYCLE STAGE	EMOTIONAL PROCESS OF TRANSITION: KEY PRINCIPLES	SECOND ORDER CHANGES IN FAMILY STATUS REQUIRED TO PROCEED DEVELOPMENTALLY
1. Between families: the unattached young adult	Accepting parent-offspring separation	a. Differentiation of self in relation to family of origin b. Development of intimate peer relationships c. Establishment of self in work
2. The joining of families through marriage: the newly married couple	Commitment to new system	a. Formation of marital system b. Realignment of relationships with extended family and friends to include spouse
3. The family with young children	Accepting new members into the system	a. Adjusting marital system to make space for child(ren) b. Taking on parenting roles c. Realignment of relationships with extended family to include parenting and grandparenting roles
4. The family with adolescents	Increasing flexibility of family boundaries to include children's independence	a. Shifting of parent/child relationships to permit adolescent to move in and out of system b. Refocus on mid-life marital and career issues c. Beginning shift toward concerns for older generation
5. Launching children and moving on	Accepting a multitude of exits from and entries into the family system	a. Renegotiation of marital system as a dyad b. Development of adult to adult relationships between grown children and their parents c. Realignment of relationships to include in-laws and grandchildren d. Dealing with disabilities and death of parents (grandparents)
6. The family in later life	Accepting the shifting of generational roles	a. Maintaining own and/or couple functioning and interests in face of physiological decline, exploration of new familial and social role options b. Support for a more central role for middle generation c. Making room in the system for the wisdom and experience of the elderly; supporting the older generation without overfunctioning for them d. Dealing with loss of spouse, siblings and other peers and preparation for own death. Life review and integration.

SOURCE: E. A. Carter and M. McGoldrick (eds.). *The Family Life Cycle: A Framework for Family Therapy* (New York: Gardner), 1980. Reprinted by permission.

◆ *Meaning:* how the family defines the event, such as perceiving it as a stressful but manageable problem or as "the end of the world."
◆ *Coping:* the process of using the resources the family has at its disposal. The family that copes well experiences much less stress than the family that copes poorly.

Families that are unable to cope find themselves moving from a state of stress into crisis (Boss, 1987). In crisis, the family system becomes immobilized and the family can no longer perform its functions.

STRESSORS. Stressors are the provoking event in family stress, so we will examine them in some detail. Stressors may be: (1) normative or nonnormative, (2) external or internal, (3) short-term or long-term, and (4) with norms or normless.

Normative and Nonnormative Stressors. Certain events are common in all families across the life cycle—birth, marriage, retirement, death of elderly members, and so on. These normative stressors are typical. (See Table 13.1 for stress points in the family life cycle.) Other family stressors are nonnormative or atypical for all families, such as accidental death, conflict over family roles, sudden loss of income, caring for a disabled or elderly family member. Although still stressful, normative stressors can be anticipated and some of their consequences alleviated.

External and Internal Stressors. In dealing with stress, it is important whether the stressor originates from inside or outside the family. External stressors can foster family unity if they are not so constant or overwhelming that they destroy the family. Natural disasters such as floods and hurricanes encourage family cooperation. Families tend to meet these kinds of events head on. Wars and persecution have similar effects.

But internal stressors can break the family apart. Severe illness, role strain, alcoholism, unemployment, extramarital affairs, or unexpected death may destroy the same family that heroically withstood a natural disaster or persecution. The family may search for a scapegoat, fight among themselves as to whom to blame, or take sides.

Short-term and Long-term Stressors. A short-term stressor, such as a broken leg or temporary unemployment, creates stress for a limited time. Such stress can be extremely painful, but the family may return to its normal pattern of interactions once the short-term stressor is eliminated. Long-term stressors, however, are generally more disruptive and require considerable family adjustment. A broken leg soon mends and the family may return to its usual mode of operation, but an amputated limb requires permanent change in the way the family works, such as other family members performing some of the responsibilities of the disabled member.

Stressors with and without Norms. Society often provides us with norms or guidelines that assist us in coping with stressors. If we give birth to a child under typical circumstances, our society validates us and provides us with guidelines as to how to feel and behave as the parents of a newborn, easing some of the stress associated with becoming a parent. Because we have fewer (or no) norms assisting us in the transition to parenthood if we are adoptive parents or gay or lesbian parents, however, we may experience a more stressful transition. Society is supportive of "normal" parenthood but often negative or hostile toward nonnormative parenthood.

THE DOUBLE ABC-X MODEL OF FAMILY STRESS. The most widely used model to explain family stress is the double ABC-X model (Olsen and McCubbin, 1983). A key concept in this model is the idea of **stressor pile up.** According to the double ABC-X model, during stress or crisis the family responds not only to a current stressor but also to family hardships and strains. Stressors, family hardships, and strains combine to create stressor pile up. Stressor pile up magnifies the impact of the stressor event, transforming a relatively minor stressor, such as going on a family vacation, into a catastrophic event. The stress of planning, packing, and leaving on a trip may bring other simmering problems to the surface. These problems may include lack of communication ("I thought *you* made the reservations"), inequitable distribution of power ("*you* always decide where we're going"), financial difficulties ("we can't afford this trip"), parental role issues ("why don't you ever help with the kids?") (Olsen and McCubbin, 1983; Patterson and McCubbin, 1983).

In the double ABC-X model:

Aa represents stressor pile up (the combination of the current stressor, family hardship, and strain),

*When sorrows come, they come not single spies,
But in battalions.*

William Shakespeare, Hamlet

B represents the family's coping resources,

C represents the family's *perception* of the stressor pile up, and

X represents the outcome of the situation, which includes the coping strategies that the family brings into play as well as any disruption that may occur if the family fails to cope adequately.

There are many kinds of resources (the "B factor") that a family or an individual can draw upon. These assets may be material, psychological, emotional or social. They include money, time, health, intelligence, information, job skills, relationships with others, and support from social networks. Lack of economic resources is a significant component in stress and crisis. For the poor, everyday life is stressful as they try to make ends meet. While a crisis such as illness or unemployment may be difficult but manageable for the middle-class family with savings and health insurance, for a poor family such a crisis can be overwhelming.

The mere possession of resources is no guarantee that they will be used, however. The double ABC-X model of family stress views the actual use of resources (coping)

One woe doth tread upon another's heel, So fast they follow.

William Shakespeare, Hamlet

FIGURE 13.1   The Double ABC-X Model

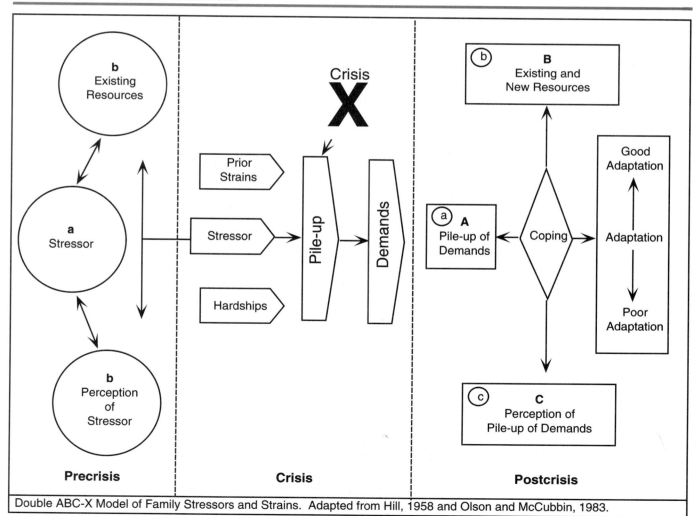

Double ABC-X Model of Family Stressors and Strains. Adapted from Hill, 1958 and Olson and McCubbin, 1983.

What's the worst that can happen? The storm picks up our house and plants it in a better neighborhood.

Roseanne Barr

as both a process among the B, C, and X factors and an outcome (part of X). How the family views a particular stressful event (the "C factor") is a significant variable in determining the eventual outcome. Viewing a stressful event as a crisis may very well lead to a crisis, as will utterly ignoring a situation that requires attention.

Recent research (McCubbin and McCubbin, 1987, 1989) suggests that strong families are much more successful in adapting to stress than weak families. Strong families tend to work together to resolve problems, are more democratic in their problem solving, delegate responsibilities, have considerable respect and affection for each other, and share values. These factors encourage family cohesion and support during times of stress. (See Chapter 18 for a discussion of coping mechanisms in strong families.) Weak families, however, tend to blame each other in stressful situations, are unwilling to ask for assistance or help from family members, are hesitant to shift or share burdens, and are reluctant to compromise. As a result, they have less flexibility and fewer family resources to deal effectively with stress and are more likely to have unfavorable outcomes.

❖ REFLECTIONS   *Using the double ABC-X model, examine a recent family stress or crisis. What were the stressor, the strain, the family hardship that combined to form the stressor pile up? What were your family's resources? Its coping behaviors? Was the crisis successfully or unsuccessfully resolved? Why?*

Economic Distress

Economic distress refers to those aspects of economic life that are potential stressors for individuals and families (Voydanoff, 1991). Major economic stressors include unemployment, poverty, and economic strain (such as financial concerns and worry, adjustments to changes in income, and feelings of economic insecurity).

IMPACT ON MARRIAGES AND FAMILIES.   In times of hardship, economic strain increases and the rates of infant mortality, alcoholism, family abuse, homicide, suicide, and admissions to psychiatric institutions and prisons also sharply increase (Liem and Rayman, 1982). Patricia Voydanoff (1991), one of the leading researchers in family/economy interactions, notes:

A minimum level of income and employment stability is necessary for family stability and cohesion. Without it many are unable to form families through marriage and others find themselves subject to separation and divorce. In addition, those experiencing unemployment or income loss make other adjustments in family composition such as postponing childbearing, moving in with relatives, and having relatives or boarders join the household.

Further, economic strain is related to lower levels of marital satisfaction as a result of financial conflict, the husband's psychological instability, and marital tensions.

Unemployment is a major stressor for individuals, with consequences spilling over into their families (Voydanoff, 1991). The families of the unemployed experience considerably more stress than those of the employed (see Gnezda, 1984, for a review of the effects of unemployment on family functioning). The most extensive work on the effects of unemployment has been done in the Boston area. Reports by Leim and colleagues (cited in Gnezda, 1984) indicate that in the first few months of unemployment, mood and behavior changes cause stress and strain in family relations. As families adapt to unemployment, family roles and routines change. The family spends more time together, but wives often complain of their husband's "getting in the way" and not contributing to household tasks. Wives may assume a

TABLE 13.2 Stress: How Much Can Affect Your Health?

Change, both good and bad, can create stress and stress, and if sufficiently severe, can lead to illness. Drs. Thomas Holmes and Minoru Masuda, psychiatrists at the University of Washington in Seattle, have developed the Social Readjustment Rating Scale. In their study, they gave a point value to stressful events. The psychiatrists discovered that in 79 percent of the persons studied, major illness followed the accumulation of stress-related changes totaling over 300 points in one year. Examine the scale that follows. Notice how most directly or indirectly relate to marriage and family. What stresses have you experienced in the past six months? What stresses do you expect to experience in the next six months?

LIFE EVENT	PAST 6 MOS.	VALUE	FUTURE 6 MOS.	LIFE EVENT	PAST 6 MOS.	VALUE	FUTURE 6 MOS.
Death of spouse	☐	100	☐	Outstanding personal achievement	☐	28	☐
Divorce	☐	73	☐	Wife beginning or ceasing work outside the home	☐	26	☐
Marital separation from mate	☐	65	☐	Beginning or ceasing formal schooling	☐	26	☐
Detention in jail or other institution	☐	63	☐	Major change in living conditions (e.g., building a new home, remodeling, deterioration of home or neighborhood)	☐	25	☐
Death of a close family member	☐	63	☐				
Major personal injury or illness	☐	53	☐	Revision of personal habits (dress, manners, association, etc.)	☐	24	☐
Marriage	☐	50	☐	Troubles with the boss	☐	23	☐
Being fired at work	☐	47	☐	Major change in working hours or conditions	☐	20	☐
Marital reconciliation with mate	☐	45	☐	Change in residence	☐	20	☐
Retirement from work	☐	45	☐	Changing to a new school	☐	20	☐
Major change in the health or behavior of a family member	☐	44	☐	Major change in usual type and/or amount of recreation	☐	19	☐
Pregnancy	☐	40	☐	Major change in church activities (e.g., a lot more or a lot less than usual)	☐	19	☐
Sexual difficulties	☐	39	☐				
Gaining a new family member (e.g., through birth, adoption, oldster moving in, etc.)	☐	39	☐	Major change in social activities (e.g., clubs, dancing, movies, visiting, etc.)	☐	18	☐
Major business readjustment (e.g., merger, reorganization, bankruptcy, etc.)	☐	39	☐	Taking out a mortgage or loan for a lesser purchase (e.g., for a car, TV, freezer, etc.)	☐	17	☐
Major change in financial state (e.g., a lot worse off or a lot better off than usual)	☐	38	☐				
Death of a close friend	☐	37	☐	Major change in sleeping habits (a lot more or a lot less sleep, or change in part of day when asleep)	☐	16	☐
Changing to a different line of work	☐	36	☐				
Major change in the number of arguments with spouse (e.g., either a lot more or a lot less than usual regarding childrearing, personal habits, etc.)	☐	35	☐	Major change in number of family get-togethers (e.g., a lot more or less than usual)	☐	15	☐
Taking out a mortgage or loan for a major purchase (e.g., for a home, business, etc.)	☐	31	☐	Major change in eating habits (a lot more or a lot less food intake, or very different meal hours or surroundings)	☐	15	☐
Foreclosure on a mortgage or loan	☐	30	☐	Vacation	☐	13	☐
Major change in responsibilities at work (e.g., promotion, demotion, lateral transfer)	☐	29	☐	Christmas	☐	12	☐
Son or daughter leaving home (e.g., marriage, attending college, etc.)	☐	29	☐	Minor violations of the law (e.g., traffic tickets, jaywalking, disturbing the peace, etc.)	☐	11	☐
In-law troubles	☐	29	☐				

Thomas Holmes and Minoru Masudu. *Social Readjustment Rating Scale.*

SOURCE: Reprinted with permission from the *Journal of Psychosomatic Research*, Vol. 11, pp. 213–218, T. H. Holmes, M.D.; The Social Readjustment Rating Scale © 1967, Pergamon Press Ltd.

greater role in family finances by seeking employment if they are not already employed. After the first few months of unemployment, wives of the unemployed begin to feel emotional strain, depression, anxiety, and sensitiveness in marital interactions. The children of the unemployed are more likely to avoid social interactions and tend to be more distrustful; they report more problems at home than children in families with employed fathers. Families seem to achieve stable patterns around new roles and responsibilities after six or seven months. If unemployment persists beyond a year, the family becomes highly vulnerable to marital separation and divorce; family violence may begin or increase at this time.

COPING WITH ECONOMIC DISTRESS. Economic distress does not necessarily lead to family disruption. (See Resource Center for economic coping resources.) In the face of unemployment, some families experience increased cohesion (Gnezda, 1984). Families with serious problems may disintegrate. Individuals and families use a number of coping resources and behaviors to deal with economic distress (Voydanoff, 1991). Coping resources include an individual's psychological disposition, such as optimism, a strong sense of self-esteem, and a feeling of mastery. Family coping resources include a family system that encourages adaptation and cohesion in the face of problems and flexible family roles that encourage problem solving. In addition, social networks of friends and family may provide important support, such as financial assistance, understanding, and a willingness to listen.

There are several important coping behaviors that assist families in economic distress. These include:

◆ *Defining the meaning of the problem.* Unemployment means not only joblessness. It can also mean diminished self-esteem if the person feels the job loss was his or her fault. If a worker is unemployed because of layoffs or plant closings, the individual and family need to define the unemployment in terms of market failure, not personal failure.

◆ *Problem solving.* An unemployed person needs to attack the problem by beginning the search for another job; dealing with the consequences of unemployment, such as by seeking unemployment insurance and cutting expenses; or improving the situation, such as by changing occupations or seeking job training or more schooling. Spouses and adolescents can assist by increasing their paid work effort. Studies suggest that about a fifth of spouses or other family members find employment after a plant closing.

◆ *Managing emotions.* Individuals and families need to understand that stress may create roller-coaster emotions, anger, self-pity, and depression. They need to talk with each other about their feelings; they need to support and encourage each other. They need to seek out individual or family counseling services to cope with problems before they get out of hand.

❖ FAMILY CAREGIVING

Caregiving for the Chronically Ill and Disabled

We have all experienced illness and accidents that have laid us low for a few days or longer. Illnesses and accidents affect us not only bodily but also psychologically. When we are sick or incapacitated, we are more prone to depression and mood swings. Illnesses are also stressful because they affect daily living patterns. A bout of the flu, for example, may put a student out of commission during finals week. A sprained ankle constrains mobility; a cold affects not only a sick child but also the parent who must stay home from work or school. Minor illnesses temporarily disrupt the structures of our lives and families.

Acute illnesses, such as appendicitis, require hospitalization but are of relatively short duration. Chronic illnesses, such as cystic fibrosis, diabetes, heart disease, arthritis, cerebral palsy, and asthma, never go away. A chronically ill person may be better sometimes, worse other times, but he or she remains ill. Similarly, physical limitations (such as impaired speech or movement, deafness, and blindness) and developmental impairments (such as Down's syndrome or autism) are lifelong. The care of those who are chronically ill, physically limited, or developmentally impaired is usually given at home by the family. Thus, the life course of the chronically ill or disabled, their caregivers, and their families is radically affected.

In many cases, the family must shape itself around the needs, limits, and potential of the ill or disabled family member. The magnitude of the problem for families can be imagined once we realize that as many as 2.4 million children under age seventeen have some degree of chronic activity limitation (Fitzgerald, 1987). (This represents over 5 percent of all American children.) In addition to these children, disabled, chronically ill, and aged adults must be cared for by their families. A conservative estimate would place between 6 and 10 percent of all American families caring for disabled, chronically ill, or aging family members.

FAMILY OUTCOMES.   Most studies suggest that chronic illnesses have negative effects on the family. Family disruption and decreased marital satisfaction, for example, are common consequences (Hafstorm and Schram, 1984). Other studies find positive or inconsequential effects (Master et al., 1983; Shapiro, 1983). Mark Peyrot and his colleagues (1988), found that the ultimate outcome of chronic illness is not necessarily bad. They found that after a period of disruption, some families resolved the crisis in a positive manner. Such families perceive the crisis as manageable and find the personal and social resources to create a favorable outcome. Several persons reported increased cohesiveness because they were compelled to spend more time with their families. Said one diabetic (Peyrot et al., 1988):

I'm closer to my family than I was. Prior to this [onset of diabetes] I was working eighty hours a week. I spend more hours at home than I did. For the first ten years my daughter never knew me because I was never at home.

Other families find hidden strengths and make their priorities more clear. Another respondent said (Peyrot et al., 1988), "The traumatic experiences that we've been through pulled us closer together, made our marriage stronger. It's pointed out the more important things."

Rosalyn Darling (1987) reported similar experiences in her examination of the consequences of disability on the family. Parents experienced sorrow over their children's disability and also a genuine love and joy for them. Many families thought themselves to be stronger as a result of dealing with a family member's disability (Darling and Darling, 1982). A sister explained her bond with a developmentally disabled brother:

It's not easy being green.

Kermit the Frog

My experiences with Steve have been . . . the most positive experiences in my life. . . . We are very close, and my relationship with Steve is very important to me. . . . If Steven could be normal, . . . I don't know what choice I'd make. . . . I think we'd be losing something very special. . . . It's pulled our whole family together.

Children infected with HIV have many special needs. In addition to possible health problems, they may face stigmatization at day-care centers, schools, and even from friends and family members. Their mothers may be too ill to care for them or may have died. Here, a woman and her foster daughters, who are HIV positive, share a special moment.

SOURCES OF STRESS. Families with chronically ill or disabled members are subject to various types of stresses, depending on the nature and severity of the illness or disability and whether the chronically ill or disabled person is a child, spouse or aged parent. While the care of the chronically ill or disabled child or spouse is regarded as an unpredictable stress, care of aging parents is considered a normative or predictable family stress (E. Brody, 1985; Matthews and Rosner, 1988). The general stresses experienced by families caring for ill or disabled members include the following (Darling, 1987; Patterson and McCubbin, 1983; Yura, 1987):

◆ *Strained family relationships,* including resentment by the caregiver or other family members; competition for time between the ill or disabled person, the caregiver, and family members; overt or covert rejection of the ill or disabled family member; and coalitions between the ill or disabled person and the primary caregiver that leave other family members out. Overprotection may be especially prominent in families with disabled children.

◆ *Modifications in family activities and goals,* such as reduced leisure, travel, or vacation time; change in personal or work goals (especially by the primary caregiver); and concern over having additional children if the illness or disability is genetic.

◆ *Increased tasks and time commitments,* such as the provision of special diets, daily therapy, or treatment; appointments and transportation to medical facilities; and possible need for constant attendance.

◆ *Increased financial costs* resulting from medication, therapy, medical consultation and treatment, special equipment needs, and so on. Babysitting is the largest single out-of-pocket expense for families with physically disabled children.

◆ *Special housing requirements,* such as a close proximity to medical facilities, optimal climate conditions, and special housing features (such as wheelchair ramps).

◆ *Social isolation,* resulting from the reactions of friends and relatives, individual or family embarrassment, limited mobility, fear of exposure to infections or conditions that might exacerbate the illness, inability to predict behavior, or lack of available time for social interactions.

◆ *Medical concerns,* such as the individual's willingness or ability to follow prescribed treatment, obtain competent medical care, or minimize pain and discomfort; and uncertainty of the medical prognosis.

◆ *Grieving* over disabilities and limitations, restricted life opportunities, and, for some, anticipation of early or painful death.

COPING STRATEGIES. Families who use dysfunctional coping techniques experience the most difficulty in handling chronic illnesses (Patterson and McCubbin, 1983). These dysfunctional techniques include coalitions of the ill person and the primary caretaker excluding other family members, denial of the problem, withdrawal from social involvements, inability (or refusal) to find outside help, or hostility—blaming the chronically ill person or other family members for the condition.

Functional coping techniques include "normalizing" the chronically ill or disabled person's life, aggressively seeking proper services, and working for societal changes that would be more supportive of the ill or disabled. Additional techniques include maintaining attitudes of optimism, faith, and courage and seeking social support in the community for the ill or disabled family member (Patterson and McCubbin, 1983; see Shapiro and Tittle, 1990, for discussion of adaptation patterns among Latinos). Hamilton McCubbin and his colleagues (1979) found three important successful coping patterns for families with chronically ill children. These patterns also may be applied to families with older chronically ill or disabled members:

◆ *Maintaining family integration, cooperation, and an optimistic definition of the situation.* Such families emphasize doing things together as a family, strengthening family relationships, and developing an overall optimistic attitude toward life, especially with the ill or disabled family member.

◆ *Maintaining social support, self-esteem, and psychological stability.* Spouses and parents maintain their own sense of well-being by being actively involved in outside social relationships and activities that enhance their self-esteem. They develop techniques for handling psychological tensions and strains, such as taking breaks from the situation, seeking counseling, and finding additional help.

◆ *Understanding the medical situation through communication with similar families and medical consultations.* Such families develop relationships with families that have similar problems; they share information and provide support for each other. They try to understand and master necessary medical information. They feel competent in operating home medical equipment. (See Resource Center for sources of support for the disabled and their families.)

❖ REFLECTIONS *Does your family, extended family, or the family of friends have a disabled or chronically ill member? What coping strategies are used? Are they effective or ineffective? How does the family perceive the impact of the disability or illness?*

Caregiving for the Aged

Although most elderly men and women are healthy and live independently, almost 85 percent of the 25.5 million elderly have at least one chronic illness. About 2 million elders need assistance with such daily living activities as bathing, dressing, eating, shopping, and managing money (Blieszner and Alley, 1990). At least 5 million American men and women care for an aged parent.

Even though elder care is often done with love, it can be the source of profound stress (Gelman et al., 1985):

There is a welter of conflicts, anxiety about their parents' needs colliding with the needs of their own families, the guilty longing for freedom rubbing up against the guilty conviction that they are not doing enough. For some, the ironic role reversal in becoming a parent to the parent is unsettling at a deep psychic level. The sudden or growing helplessness of people who were the authority figures in a child's life can be overwhelming.

Most elder care is provided by women, generally daughters or daughters-in-law (Mancini and Blieszner, 1991). Men, however, provide a substantial proportion of care for their aging parents or parents-in-law (Brubaker, 1991). Elder caregiving seems to affect husbands and wives differently. Women report greater distress and depression from caregiving than do men (Fitting et al., 1986). In part, this may be because men approach their daily caregiving activities in a more detached, instrumental way. Another factor may be that women frequently are not only mothers but also workers; an infirm parent can sometimes be an overwhelming responsibility to an already burdened woman. Fortunately, most adult children in a given family participate in parental caregiving in some fashion, whether it involves doing routine caregiving, providing backup, or giving limited or occasional care (Mancini and Blieszner, 1991).

Caregivers often experience conflicting feelings about caring for an elderly relative. The caregiver/parent relationship is strongly influenced by the history of the earlier parent/child relationship. The history of these interactions either facilitates or hinders caregiving (Horowitz and Shindelman, 1983). Women are initially more involved emotionally but tend to become more stoic and detached when a few years

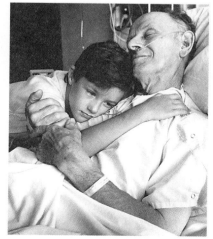

Illnesses and disabilities may bring out hidden strength in a family.

have passed; their responses become similar to male responses (Zarit, Todd, and Zarit, 1986). Many caregivers receive satisfaction from the affection they give to and receive from a beloved parent or relative; they often receive satisfaction from the very act of nurturing. These positive feelings help balance the negative aspects involved with primary caregiving (Sheehan and Nuttall, 1988; Walker, Shin, and Bird, 1990). The conflicts experienced by primary caregivers include the following (Springer and Brubaker, 1984):

◆ Earlier unresolved antagonisms and conflicts.
◆ The caregiver's inability to accept the relative's increasing dependence.
◆ Conflicting loyalties between spousal or childrearing responsibilities and caring for the elderly relative.
◆ Resentment toward the older relative for disrupting family routines and patterns.
◆ Resentment by the primary caregiver for lack of involvement by other family members.
◆ Anger or hostility toward an elderly relative who tries to manipulate others.
◆ Conflicts over money or inheritance.

Affection certainly eases the burdens, but it does not necessarily decrease the strains of caregiving that relatives experience (Sheehan and Nuttall, 1988). Elders are especially vulnerable to abuse by their children, (see Chapter 15). Caregiver education and training programs, self-help groups, caregiver services, and family therapy provide assistance in dealing with the problems encountered by caregivers. Of these, family therapy appears to be the most effective for dealing with the emotional aspects of caregiving (Sheehan and Nuttall, 1988). In addition, elders receiving Medicaid may be eligible for respite care and homemaker/housework assistance. (See Resource Center for elder-care referral services and organizations; also see Blieszner and Alley, 1990, for an overview of elder-care resources.)

Because elder care involves complex emotions raised by issues of dependency, adult children and their parents often postpone discussions until a crisis occurs. A recent study (Hansson et al., 1990) tried to identify the normative patterns of adult children's involvement in elder care. The researchers made three points: First, a threshold needed to be crossed at which time it became clear that the aging parent needed assistance. The threshold usually involved a health crisis, a gradual awareness of the risks associated with the parents' aging, or the death or illness of the spouse. One woman wrote (Levin, 1987):

The need for more involvement in our parents' care dawned slowly as they retired, became widowed, took ill. Initially we were sympathetic but took little direct action. Our participation increased when we began to see our parents having trouble managing not only their immediate financial affairs, but also *their* responsibilities towards their own very old parents and aging siblings.

Second, the developing pattern of involvement was conservative and followed an orderly procession. Adult children began monitoring their parents' health and logistical needs more closely. Third, children began to intervene in task-oriented areas, such as home maintenance, transportation, and dealing with the bureaucracy. The children's general goal was to help their parents maintain their independence as long as possible. Only after they had exhausted other alternatives were they likely to bring the parent to live with them or to place him or her in a retirement or convalescent home.

The best way for adult children to deal with elder care is to plan ahead with their siblings and with their aging parents, if they are willing. The major tasks include

(Levin, 1987): (1) planning for legal and financial incapacities; (2) managing income and expenses; (3) arranging for long-term care; (4) assessing capabilities of the whole family unit; (5) dividing responsibilities among parents, siblings, adult children, friends, and neighbors; and (6) determining community back-up services, such as meals-on-wheels programs, visiting nurses, and housekeeping services.

❖ REFLECTIONS   *As your parents become dependent, will you become the primary caregiver? Why? Are you, your parents, or other close relatives involved in caregiving activities with an aging relative? If so, what effect has that had on you, your family, or your relative's family?*

❖ DEATH AND DYING IN AMERICA

Everyone who reads this (not to mention those who wrote it!) will die. And even though on a cognitive level we know that death comes to us all, when we actually confront death or dying, we are likely to be surprised, shocked, or at a loss about what to do.

Attitudes toward Death

The nature and extent of our feelings and fears about death have to do with who we are—our age, sex, personality, spiritual beliefs, and so on. Our feelings also have to do with the person who has died—whether he or she was young or old, whether or not the death was expected, and what our relationship was.

CULTURAL CONTEXT. Our cultural context is important in determining our response to death. Although Americans today seem somewhat more willing to talk and act realistically about death than they were a decade or two ago, as a society we remain quite ambivalent about the subject. Our responses to death and dying fall into three categories: denial, exploitation, and romanticization (Rando, 1987).

Denial. Although the existence of death is not specifically denied, there are practices in our culture that make it hard to view death as the real part of life it actually is. The removal of old or dying people from the home to the hospital has encouraged the belief that death is unnatural, frightening, or even disgusting. In a way, we treat death like sex: we try to shield children from it, and we use euphemisms when we speak of it ("Aunt Helen passed away," "Fluffy was put to sleep").

Exploitation. At the opposite extreme of denial is the exploitation of death. Therese Rando (1987) writes:

While there has been a decline in the average individual's personal contact with death and dying, due to sociological changes and advances in technology, there has been an increase in exposure to violence and death through television, movies, and the print media. . . . Acts of murder, war, violence, terrorism, abuse, rape, crime, natural disasters, and so forth are exploited and sensationalized in the name of the public's right to know. Financial gains for the media and its sponsors are the obvious results.

The effects can be damaging. We may become overwhelmed by images of death and suffer from "annihilation anxiety." We may overcompensate and become aggressive or may withdraw and become desensitized to human pain. We may end up denying the realities of death altogether.

No man is an island, entire of itself; every man is a piece of the continent, a part of the main; if a clod be washed away by the sea, Europe is the less, as well as if a promontory were, as well as if a manor of thy friends or of thine own were. Any man's death diminishes me, because I am involved in mankind. And therefore never send to know for whom the bells tolls. It tolls for thee.

John Donne

I'm not afraid to die. I just don't want to be there when it happens.

Woody Allen

Death be not proud, though some have called thee
Mighty and dreadful, for thou art not so.
For those whom thou thinks't thou dost overthrow,
Die not, poor death, nor yet canst thou kill me.

John Donne, Holy Sonnets IX

We don't know life: how can we know death?

Confucius (551–479 B.C.)

HIV, AIDS and the Family

In contemporary America, those who are terminally ill are often stigmatized because they are dying. People feel uncomfortable in their presence and often avoid them. It is as if being with a dying person forces us to confront our own mortality and triggers irrational fears of somehow "catching" the death (De Spelder and Strickland, 1990). Those with HIV or AIDS suffer a double stigmatization: first, they are presumably dying; and second, they are presumably members of one of two highly stigmatized groups—gay men or IV-drug users. They are not AIDS victims or sufferers, but people *living* with AIDS.

Families are affected by HIV and AIDS in numerous ways. The following are real-life examples of how HIV and AIDS affect families and other intimate relationships (Macklin, 1988, 1989; Shilts, 1987):

◆ Parents reject their gay son because of his sexual orientation and reconcile with him only as he is dying.
◆ A grandmother whose daughter has died from AIDS now cares for her two orphaned HIV-positive grandchildren.
◆ A young executive who experimented with IV drugs five years earlier discovers he is HIV positive after he infects his wife, who in turn infects their two children neonatally; in three years, the entire family is dead.
◆ A mother discovers she is HIV-positive only after the birth of her infected son. She worries about who will care for her children if she dies.
◆ A woman's husband has AIDS and she fears that she is infected although she repeatedly tests HIV-negative.
◆ A married woman finds a notice in her lover's desk informing him that he is HIV-positive but is afraid of confronting him because she was snooping; she is afraid to talk with her husband because he believes she is monogamous.

The family system is disrupted when the family learns that one of its members has HIV or AIDS (Carter, 1989; Cates et al., 1990). The family may unite to support its infected member, or old issues may resurrect, renewing conflict between family members, especially if members focus on how the HIV was transmitted. HIV and AIDS not only transform the life of the infected individual but also the lives of those emotionally involved with him or her: lovers (past and present), partners or spouses, children, parents, brothers and sisters, friends, and caregivers. Furthermore, when people test HIV-positive or have AIDS, their partners may have been unaware of their drug use or sexual activities outside of their primary relationship. Both the infected and uninfected partners may have to confront a variety of issues (Carter, 1989). A wife may be unaware of her husband's bisexual orientation and his extramarital involvement with other men or women. She must deal simultaneously with his infection, his sexual orientation, and his extramarital involvement.

Problems Experienced by People with AIDS and Their Families

The problems that both the person with HIV or AIDS and his or her family and friends may experience include social stigma and isolation, fear of contagion, fear of infection, fear of abandonment, guilt, anger, grief, and economic hardship (Macklin, 1988). (For a discussion of children's understanding of AIDS from a developmental perspective, see Schvaneveldt, Lindauer, and Young, 1990).

SOCIAL STIGMA AND ISOLATION Unlike other terminally ill individuals, most of those with HIV or AIDS must deal with personal and societal hostility because of their sexual orientation or drug use. (Even those who are infected through blood transfusions, heterosexual intercourse, or prenatal exposure suffer stigmatization.) Some view AIDS as divine retribution for violating religious teachings against homosexuality; others believe that those with AIDS deserve the affliction because of their gay or drug activities. Some people with HIV or AIDS are fired from their jobs, evicted from their apartments, rejected by their lovers, or refused admission to school. Some families support their child through the illness but do not tell others that their son or daughter has AIDS (Cleveland et al., 1988).

FEAR OF CONTAGION Almost everyone who has a family member with HIV or AIDS experiences some fear of becoming infected themselves, even when they know there is no rational basis for the fear. Partners may hesitate to share the same bed, relatives may be reluctant to visit or dine together, or grandparents may be fearful of babysitting for an infected child. Relationships are often severely tested. Many relatives and friends feel unable to talk openly about their anxieties.

FEAR OF INFECTION Anxieties are high among members of high-risk groups. They may be reluctant to become involved in relationships for fear of trans-

PERSPECTIVE

mitting the virus or becoming infected themselves. They may fear being tested lest they discover that they are infected. If they are tested, they fear learning the results. And if they are HIV-positive, they wonder how long they have before AIDS symptoms occur.

FEAR OF ABANDONMENT Many with HIV or AIDS face rejection by their families not only because of their infection but also because of their sexual orientation. For many gay men, their families learn that they are gay at the same time they learn that they have AIDS. Some families are unable to cope with the needs of their dying child or sibling and consequently pull away. Others, however, stand by with increased resolve and love (Cleveland et al., 1988).

GUILT The person with HIV or AIDS may feel guilty for being gay or an IV-drug user. He or she may feel somehow "deserving" of the infection because of "immorality," "stupidity," or lack of awareness. Families that once rejected a dying family member because he was gay may feel guilt over their earlier rejection. Or they may feel guilty because they are unable to accept or care for their ill member.

ANGER Guilt and anger may alternate. At one time a person feels angry for being infected; at other times he or she may feel guilty about it. He or she may feel angry at family, friends, associates, and society for not being more supportive. Family members may feel angry at the person with HIV or AIDS for "getting" infected because of sexual orientation or drug behavior.

GRIEF There is no cure for HIV or AIDS. Also, researchers increasingly believe that most people infected with HIV will develop AIDS. Those with HIV and AIDS and their family and friends feel grief for the impending loss of health, potential, and life. The grief is compounded for partners, because some may be infected themselves. Because those with AIDS tend to be young adults, the feelings of grief and loss tend to be more intense. (In New York City, AIDS is the leading cause of death among men aged twenty-one to twenty-four years.)

ECONOMIC HARDSHIP AIDS is a costly disease. Medical and hospital expenses may run between $50,000 and $100,000. The loss of earning power, the cost of treatment, and the lack of adequate financial assistance spell financial ruin for many individuals and families. Those without health insurance face even greater hardships.

One consequence of these costs and the increasing lack of sufficient numbers of treatment facilities is a movement toward home care of persons with AIDS. More and more programs are experimenting with ways of assisting individuals to remain in their homes with the combined care of family, partners and professional caregivers. Hospice care—whose goal is to maximize the quality of life for the terminally ill—is also becoming a major alternative for persons in the last stages of AIDS (Magno, 1991).

Supporting Friends and Relatives with AIDS

If you have a friend or relative with HIV or AIDS, you can provide needed support without fear of contracting the infection yourself. Some things that you can do to show your caring are described below (Martelli et al., 1987; Moffat et al., 1987):

◆ Show your caring by visiting and keeping in contact.

◆ Touch your friend or relative; touch communicates love, warmth, and hope. Don't hesitate or be afraid to touch, despite whatever apprehension you might at first have.

◆ Call before visiting to make sure that your friend or relative feels like having a visitor at a particular time.

◆ Offer to talk about HIV or AIDS and its prognosis if the other person wants to express his or her feelings about them. Find HIV or AIDS support groups for your friend or relative.

◆ Take your friend or relative out to dinner, a movie, the park or beach, or a favorite spot if his or her health permits.

◆ Offer to shop or do household chores, banking, pet care, or other tasks. Provide transportation when needed.

◆ Organize your own support group to assist or be on call for your friend or relative. In this manner, you can create a network for sharing tasks and feelings.

◆ Be available. Encourage your friend or relative to reach out when he or she needs help.

In coping with AIDS, we must attempt to reduce the stigma and discrimination associated with it, work against homophobia, recognize the impact of the illness on the family, and encourage social, health, and economic programs that support persons with AIDS. For those with AIDS, we must focus on enhancing the quality of life, remembering that they are *living* with AIDS. We are all living until we die.

Romanticism. Sometimes our images of death are glamorized and glorified. Although some deaths are in fact peaceful and "beautiful," many are not. Those who have been led to expect a beautiful death (their own or another's) may be shocked and feel betrayed to discover the messy, frustrating, or ugly aspects of dying.

FEAR OF DEATH AND DYING. There are a number of fears and anxieties that many of us share regarding the dying process and death itself. When we think about dying, we may worry about being unable to care for ourselves and becoming a burden on those we love. We may worry about pain or physical impairment. We may fear isolation, loneliness, and separation from people who are dear to us. The finality of death is often fearsome; it implies the loss of relationships, the abandonment of goals, and an end to pleasure. For some, contemplating the possibilities of an unknown afterlife or the idea of eternal nothingness may be frightening. Others may be concerned about how their bodies will look after death and what will happen to them. One of the greatest fears aroused by the thought of death is the fear of losing control: the world will go on, but we will no longer have any effect on what happens in it.

Thanatologists (those who study death and dying) tell us that a certain amount of fear of death is a good thing (Rando, 1987). It certainly helps keep us alive. A certain amount of denial is healthy, too, for it prevents us from dwelling morbidly on the subject of death. What we need to develop is a realistic, honest view of death as part of life. Acknowledging that death exists can enrich our lives greatly. It can show us the importance of getting on with the "business of living," ordering our priorities, and appreciating what is around us. "The immediacy of death," writes Rando, "will lead to honesty with yourself, leading to the recognition that you have no choice but to be resigned to death and to focus all your energies on the creative reconstruction of the only existence you have."

The Process of Dying

Unless death comes very quickly and unexpectedly, the person who is dying will undergo a number of emotional changes in addition to physical ones. These changes are often referred to as "stages," although they do not necessarily happen in a particular order. Indeed, some of them may not be experienced at all, or a person may return again and again to a particular part of the process.

STAGES OF DYING. The stages of dying, discussed below, are similar to the stages of adaptation to other stressful situations (Leming and Dickinson, 1985; also see Kübler-Ross, 1969, 1982).

◆ *Anticipation.* At some time prior to our death, we begin to prepare for it by thinking about it, feeling anxious, or being actively involved in the dying processes of others. We may begin to mobilize our personal resources.
◆ *Onset of Stressful Event.* When we become acutely ill or are forcefully reminded of our mortality in some way, we begin to face the reality that death is actually approaching. We may use denial to shield ourselves from the implications of what is happening, but sooner or later we will probably acknowledge our death.
◆ *Disorganization.* Face to face with our life's ending, we may simply fall apart. Our symptoms may worsen (perhaps temporarily), and we may become quite emotional and find ourselves unable to think rationally. These are signs that our adaptation is progressing. This is the beginning of grieving, a process that can restore us to psychological wholeness.

◆ *Organization*. Disorganization is followed by organization, a return to more normal functioning and planning. At this point we look around and try to figure out what we need to do and who can help us. During this phase and the next, we may make our actual preparations for death.

◆ *Resolution*. Ideally, when we have found our own way through this uncertain and often painful process, we will feel a sense of mastery and achievement. If we have the energy and the support of others, we may feel a sense of exhilaration. If we have not already done so, we may plan for the future by dealing with property issues, wills, insurance, and so on. We may put renewed energy into relationships, "mend fences," or spend more time sharing memories with loved ones. We may put our spiritual house in order, and we may plan our funeral and burial or cremation.

NEEDS OF THE DYING. Robert Kavanaugh (1972) wrote:

No matter how we measure [one's] worth, a dying human being deserves more than efficient care from strangers, more than machines and antiseptic hands, more than a mouthful of pills, arms full of tubes and a rump full of needles. . . . More than furtive eyes, reluctant hugs, medical jargon, ritual sacraments or tired Bible quotes, more than all the phony promises for a tomorrow that will never come.

Aside from basic physical care and perhaps relief from pain, what a dying person needs can be summed up very succinctly: *to be treated as a human being.* Our society's own ambivalence and fear of death is all too often evident in the attitudes and actions of its doctors, nurses, and other medical personnel. In response to the impersonality that has generally characterized death and dying in the hospital setting, the hospice movement has gained momentum in the last two decades. A **hospice** may be an actual place where terminally ill people can be cared for with respect for their dignity. But it is also much more than that. It is a medical program that emphasizes both patient care (including management of pain and symptoms) *and* family support. The hospice provides education, grief counseling, financial counseling, and various types of practical assistance for home care of the dying person. It may also provide in-patient care in a noninstitutional setting. (The reading "The Last Days of Mary Ball" at the end of the chapter shows how a hospice can support a family in which someone is dying. See the Resource Center for information on locating a hospice program.)

Bereavement

Bereavement is our response to the death of a loved one. It includes the customs and rituals that we practice within our culture or subculture. It also includes the emotional responses and expressions of feeling that we call the grieving process.

MOURNING RITUALS. Our culture, religion, and personal beliefs all influence the type of rituals we participate in after someone dies. By prescribing a specific set of formalized behaviors, bereavement rituals can give us security and comfort; we don't have to think "What do I do now?" Social rituals such as funerals and wakes give us the opportunity to share our sorrow, to console and be consoled. A funeral also clearly marks the end of a life. Because we must face up to the fact that an important person in our life is gone, we can begin to move ahead to our "new" life. Religious rituals affirm a spiritual relationship for those who believe in them; for those who don't, they may be a source of tension or embarrassment.

*your hair is falling out, and
you are not so beautiful;
your eyes have dark shadows
your body is bloated; arms covered
with bruises and needlemarks;
legs swollen and useless . . .
your body and spirit
are weakened with toxic chemicals
urine smells like antibiotics,
even the sweat
that bathes your whole body
in the early hours of morning
reeks of dicloxacillin and
methotrexate.*

*you are nauseous all the time
i am afraid to move on the bed
for fear of waking you to moan
and lean over the edge
vomiting into the bag*

*i curl up fetally
withdraw into my dreams
with a frightened back to you . . .
and i'm scared
and i'm hiding
but i love you so much;
this truth does not change . . .
years ago,
when i met you, as we were falling in love,
your beauty attracted me:
long golden-brown hair
clear and peaceful green eyes
high cheekbones and long smooth
muscles
but you know—and this is true—
i fell in love with your soul
the real essence of you
and this cannot grow less beautiful . . .
sometimes these days
even your soul is cloudy
i still recognize you*

*we may be frightened
be hiding our sorrow
it may take a little longer
to acknowledge the truth,
but i would not want to be anywhere
else
i am here with you
you can grow less beautiful to the world
you are safe
i will always love you.*

Christine Longaker

Mourning rituals, such as funerals, help us in the healing process by recognizing the significance of a person in our lives and the reality of his or her death.

Every shut eye ain't sleep and every good-bye ain't gone.

Traditional African-American proverb

Once again I wasn't. Then I was. Now I ain't again.

Epitaph of Arthur C. Hormans

Happy is he who dies before his children.

Yoruba proverb

The believer, not the belief, brings peace.

Robert Kavanaugh

For some Americans, rituals having to do with the dead consist basically of a funeral service followed by burial, entombment, or cremation. For others, there are important practices to be observed long after the burial (or cremation). Under Jewish law, for example, there are three successive periods of mourning. The first of these, *shiva,* is a seven-day period during which the immediate family undergoes certain austerities, such as refraining from haircutting, shaving, and using cosmetics; going to work; or engaging in sexual relations. During the second period, *shloshim,* the prohibitions become less strict, and the final period, *avelut,* applies only if one's mother or father has died. During this eleven-month period, sons are to say *kaddish* (a form of prayer) for the parent daily. When the year of mourning is over, it is forbidden to continue practices that demonstrate grief (Kearl, 1989).

Among Latinos, *el Dia de los Muertos* (the Day of the Dead), an ancient ritual with Indian and Catholic roots that is observed on November first, is making a comeback (Garcia, 1990). In Mexico and other Latin American countries, the dead are honored with prayers, gifts of food, and a night-long graveside vigil; in the United States parades and special exhibits not only commemorate the dead but also celebrate the cultural heritage of the participants. At home, altars may be set up with pictures of those who have died, religious figures or pictures, candles, orange marigolds (the Aztec flower of death), offerings of the honored one's favorite food or drink, and perhaps cartoons or darkly humorous verses that "laugh in the face of death."

GRIEF AS A HEALING PROCESS. Like dying, grieving is a process. Thanatologists have variously described the stages of the grieving process (Kavanaugh, 1972; Kübler-Ross, 1982; Tallmer, 1987). There are also certain emotions or psychological states that may commonly be expected. Among these are shock, denial, depression, anger, loneliness, and feelings of relief. Guilt is also usually experienced as part of the grieving process (Tallmer, 1987). If we felt resentment or anger toward the dead person, we feel guilty when he or she dies, as if we somehow caused the death. If we are spared and another dies—in an accident, for example—we feel guilty for surviving. And if the deceased was a burden to us while alive, we feel compelled to shoulder a load of guilt now that the burden has been lifted.

One model looks at grieving as a four-stage process (Bowlby, 1980; Tallmer, 1987). (Remember that these stages, like those of dying, are not rigidly fixed; they may be experienced in varying sequences, simultaneously, or repeatedly.)

◆ *Numbness.* At the first news of death, we may feel stunned. Our actions may have a mechanical, robotlike quality. We may return to this stage periodically throughout mourning.

◆ *Separation Anxiety.* In this phase we "search" for our "lost" loved one. This stage is characterized by crying, outbursts of anger, pining, and calling out for the person who has died.

◆ *Despair.* Depression may set in when we realize that the person for whom we are mourning really is not going to come back. Behavior may become erratic and disorganized. Apathy may set in.

◆ *Acquisition of New Roles.* As depression diminishes, the grieving person finds that old roles and ways of relating are being replaced by new ones. At this point we may "internalize" the person we loved, making him or her "part of our inner life" (Viorst, 1986). We may even take on aspects of the person who has died. Consider the woman "who took up gardening after her brother, a passionate gardener, had died" or the "rather dull woman who acquired a gift for repartee after her husband, the witty one, had died" (Lily Pincus, cited in Viorst, 1986).

For some, most of the grieving process will be over in a matter of weeks or months. For others, it will occupy a year or two or maybe more. The first year will undoubtedly be the most difficult as holidays, birthdays, and anniversaries are experienced without the loved person. Grieving may occur sporadically for years to come, touched off by memories evoked by a particular date or by a special piece of music or a beautiful view that can no longer be shared. Healing, which is the goal of grieving, does not appear suddenly as the reward for all our suffering. Rather, it comes little by little as we work through grief (and around it and over it and under it and back through again), until we look at ourselves one day and find we are whole.

CONSOLING THE BEREAVED. When a friend or relative is bereaved, we may feel awkward or embarrassed. We may want to avoid the family of the person who has died because we "just don't know what to say."

That's okay. We really don't have to say much, except "I'm so sorry" and, perhaps, "How can I help?" Here are some suggestions for helping someone who is grieving.

◆ Listen, listen, listen. This may be the most helpful thing you can do.
◆ Express your own sadness about the death and your caring for the bereaved person, but don't say "I know how you feel" unless you really do—that is, unless you've experienced a similar loss.
◆ Talk about the person who has died. Recall special qualities he or she possessed and the good times you may have experienced. If the bereaved person begins to speak of the one who has died, don't change the subject.
◆ Give practical support: help with household tasks, do shopping or other errands, cook a meal, help with child care.
◆ If there are children, involve them in remembering. Support their grieving process (it will be different than an adult's).
◆ Don't: avoid the bereaved person because *you* are uncomfortable, worry about mentioning the dead person, or attempt to point out the "bright side."

All goes onward and outward,
Nothing collapses
And to die is different from
What anyone supposes
And luckier.

Walt Whitman

Flesh is merely a lesson.
We learn it
& pass on.

Erica Jong

yes ☺

The bridge between the known and the unknown is always love.

Stephen Levine

Thus shall you think of all this fleeting world: a star at dawn, a bubble in a stream, a flash of lightning in a summer cloud, a flickering lamp, a phantom, and a dream.

Diamond Sutra

I don't drink.

TABLE 13.3 The Signs of Alcoholism

YES	NO	QUESTIONS
____	____	1. Do you occasionally drink heavily after a disappointment, a quarrel, or when the boss gives you a hard time?
____	____	2. When you have trouble or feel under pressure, do you always drink more heavily than usual?
____	____	3. Have you noticed that you are able to handle more liquor than you did when you were first drinking?
____	____	4. Did you ever wake up on the "morning after" and discover that you could not remember part of the evening before, even though your friends tell you that you did not "pass out"?
____	____	5. When drinking with other people, do you try to have a few extra drinks when others will not know it?
____	____	6. Are there certain occasions when you feel uncomfortable if alcohol is not available?
____	____	7. Have you recently noticed that when you begin drinking you are in more of a hurry to get the first drink than you used to be?
____	____	8. Do you sometimes feel a little guilty about your drinking?
____	____	9. Are you secretly irritated when your family or friends discuss your drinking?
____	____	10. Have you recently noticed an increase in the frequency of your memory "blackouts"?
____	____	11. Do you often find that you wish to continue drinking after your friends say they have had enough?
____	____	12. Do you usually have a reason for the occasions when you drink heavily?
____	____	13. When you are sober, do you often regret things you have done or said while drinking?
____	____	14. Have you tried switching brands or following different plans for controlling your drinking?

On the whole I'd rather be in Philadelphia.

Epitaph suggested by W.C. Fields

Being able to share one's grief with others is a crucial part of healing. By "just" being around and "just" listening, we can be a positive part of the process.

❖ REFLECTIONS   *What experiences have you had with death and dying? How is the subject of death handled in your family? Have you made a will? Why or why not?*

❖ ALCOHOL, DRUG ABUSE, AND FAMILIES

America is currently facing a drug crisis in which the alcoholic or addict and his or her family are reciprocally involved. Dysfunctional families, in fact, often contribute to the development of alcoholism and drug addiction. As Robert Lewis (1989) noted:

Not only do dysfunctional families often produce addictive behavior in their members, but these addictions, in turn, then may affect the qualify of life, negatively impacting the behavior of family members and devitalizing and fracturing family relationships. The most demoraliz-

T A B L E 13.3 The Signs of Alcoholism

YES	NO	QUESTIONS
____	____	15. Have you often failed to keep the promises you have made to yourself about controlling or cutting down on your drinking?
____	____	16. Have you ever tried to control your drinking by making a change in jobs, or moving to a new location?
____	____	17. Do you try to avoid family or close friends while you are drinking?
____	____	18. Are you having an increasing number of financial and work problems?
____	____	19. Do more people seem to be treating you unfairly without good reason?
____	____	20. Do you eat very little or irregularly when you are drinking?
____	____	21. Do you sometimes have the "shakes" in the morning and find that it helps to have a little drink?
____	____	22. Have you recently noticed that you cannot drink as much as you once did?
____	____	23. Do you sometimes stay drunk for several days at a time?
____	____	24. Do you sometimes feel very depressed and wonder whether life is worth living?
____	____	25. Sometimes after periods of drinking, do you see or hear things that aren't there?
____	____	26. Do you get terribly frightened after you have been drinking heavily?

If you have answered "yes" to any of these questions, you have some of the symptoms that may indicate alcoholism.

Questions 1–8 relate to the early stages of alcoholism.
Questions 9–21 relate to the middle stage.
Questions 22–26 mark the beginning of the final stage.

Signs of Alcoholism is published by the National Council on Alcoholism

ing aspect of this reciprocity . . . is that addictions are often passed from one generation to later generations, unless there is successful intervention.

For example, authoritarian parents in a dysfunctional family may belittle and humiliate their children, shaming them into obedience. The children, however, may internalize this shame and develop a deep sense of inferiority. Lowered self-esteem may lead to addictive behaviors. The addiction becomes a defense against shame, a means of masking feelings of powerlessness and self-contempt, a way of medicating against the pain.

Over the past decade, family systems intervention has become one of the most important means of treating substance abuse. Family "love bonds" are utilized to work *for* the abuser rather than *against* the abuser; strong family feelings are focused on breaking the abuse rather than denying it or sustaining it.

Alcohol Abuse and Families

Alcohol is a drug. Many people, however, do no think of alcohol as a drug; instead, it is regarded as "a drink," a beer, a glass of wine, a rum and Coke. Yet, like certain illegal drugs such as marijuana and cocaine, alcohol alters an individual's mood and perceptions. The altered state produced by alcohol is a "high"; its more extreme manifestation is drunkeness. Because alcohol is a culturally accepted drug, the current antidrug climate largely excludes alcohol from national concern.

Consider the following statistics (Lord et al., 1987; Taylor, 1988; U.S. Bureau of the Census, 1990):

◆ Over 10 million men, women, *and* children are alcoholics. Nearly 18 million adults are problem drinkers.
◆ Between 1977 and 1987, more than 1 million Americans died from alcohol-related problems or accidents. The economic costs have exceeded a billion dollars.
◆ Alcohol-related death is the leading cause of death for persons between the ages of sixteen and twenty-four. Alcoholism is the fourth-ranked cause of death in the country. Alcohol is a factor in nearly half of America's murders, suicides, and accidental deaths. Drunk drivers are responsible for half of all driving fatalities.
◆ Twenty-four percent of the families responding to a recent Gallup poll reported family problems related to alcohol, twice the level reported ten years earlier (Gallup, 1987). Seven million children live in alcoholic families. An additional 21 million are adult children of alcoholics (Lord et al., 1987).
◆ Alcohol abuse by prospective mothers (and fathers) can cause serious fetal damage, resulting in fetal alcohol syndrome, low birth weight, and other impairments (see Chapter 9 for discussion of birth complications).

These are not abstract facts about alcohol. They affect millions of American families. Alcohol abuse undermines families, relationships, and hopes. Yet the popularly perceived image of the alcoholic as a "bum in the gutter" prevails because families tend to deny their alcoholism. (See Table 13.3 for signs of alcoholism.)

The abuse of alcohol can be seen as a symptom of a disorder that is both physical *and* emotional. Health professionals view alcoholism as a disease rather than a personal shortcoming. The American Medical Association (Lord et al., 1987) defines alcoholism as follows:

Alcoholism is an illness characterized by preoccupation with alcohol and loss of control over its consumption such as to lead usually to intoxication if drinking is begun, by chronicity, by progression, and by tendency toward relapse.

Although physiological and genetic factors may predispose a person to alcoholism (Blakeslee, 1984), it appears that problem drinking, like ordinary drinking, is a learned behavior. Most people in the United States learn to drink during adolescence; most adolescents have their first drink at home but do most of their drinking away from home, with their friends. The drinking behavior that children observe at home will greatly influence their own behavior. Many alcoholics have at least one alcoholic parent. Others drink as a means of coping with stress, anxiety, or low self-esteem.

Even though we drink substantially less distilled liquor than in the past, we still consume vast quantities of beer and increasing amounts of wine. Although the percentage of alcohol in beer and wine is lower than that in distilled liquor, drinkers often don't take into account the fact that distilled liquor is generally served diluted in mixed drinks. A five-ounce glass of wine contains as much alcohol as a standard highball; a can of beer is equal in alcohol content to a rum and Coke.

The heaviest drinkers are men between eighteen and twenty-five years. Adults drink 40.1 gallons of alcoholic drinks per capita; this includes 34.4 gallons of beer, 3.5 gallons of wine, and 2.4 gallons of distilled spirits, such as whiskey and vodka

(U.S. Bureau of the Census, 1991). Because this is the average rate for *all* Americans of drinking age, when you adjust for the nondrinkers and very light drinkers, you can see that the annual rate of consumption for drinkers is much higher. In fact, 10 percent of the nation's drinkers consume over half its alcohol (Lord et al., 1987).

Drinkers who are not alcoholics may also pose a danger to themselves and society. The social and economic costs of alcohol abuse are enormous. One of the heaviest costs in the devastation caused by drunk driving. Drivers in the eighteen to twenty-year-old age group are twice as likely as other drivers to be involved in alcohol-related accidents; 50 percent of all drivers killed in automobile accidents had been drinking (Givens, 1985; U.S. Bureau of the Census, 1991).

ALCOHOLISM AND THE FAMILY. Alcoholism is sometimes called a "family disease" because it involves all members of the family in a "complex interactional system" (Krimmel, 1973). (See Table 13.4 for "Children of Alcoholics Screening Test.") The principle of homeostasis—the tendency toward stability in a system—operates in alcoholic families, maintaining established behavior patterns and strengthening resistance to change. Many alcoholic families do not progress through the normal family life-cycle stages but remain in an unhealthy (yet stable) cycling between "sober and intoxicated interactional states" (Steinglass, 1983). Krimmel (1973) described the "pathological complementary relationship" between an alcoholic husband and his wife on the morning after a drinking bout:

[The] wife responds to her husband's plea of physical illness, shame, guilt or remorse with either sympathy and forgiveness or anger and punishment. . . . If the wife is forgiving the husband has learned that forgiveness for being drunk can be obtained, provided he is appropriately remorseful and very sick. If she punishes him. . . . his guilt and shame are relieved. . . . In either case, the pattern cannot be understood except in terms of the total sequence, as if it were designed to produce forgiveness or punishment or comfortable emotional distance. . . . The spouse may derive considerable gratification from the opportunity to be the forgiver or the punisher.

TREATMENT. In one sense alcoholism is not curable. Alcoholics must stay sober to stay well. For most alcoholics this means no more drinking, ever. Although recovery is possible, a major stumbling block exists to motivating the alcoholic to pursue it. *Denial* is used by the alcoholic and his or her family and friends. "I can quit any time," says the alcoholic, or "It's not my drinking that's the problem, it's . . . (anything else)." The spouse, parent, or lover colludes in maintaining the alcoholism by denying it: "Jane is not *really* like this. She's a wonderful person when she's sober." People often deny the fact of alcoholism because of the social stigma attached to the term *alcoholic*.

Treatment for alcoholism is generally not considered possible until the alcoholic makes the conscious choice to become well. Many must first "hit bottom" before they are willing to admit that they are alcoholics. But because families are often organized around protecting the alcoholic from the consequences of his or her alcoholism, the alcoholic is able to deny his or her alcoholism. Although adolescent alcoholics also deny their problems, research indicates that they are likely to perceive their need for help if they experience serious physiological consequences of their drinking, experience serious personal problems, or have another substance abuser in the family (Lorch and Dukes, 1989).

An educated public and an enlightened approach by professionals are essential to achieve progress in freeing millions from the destructive grip of alcoholism. Family

Alcoholism isn't a spectator sport. Eventually the whole family gets to play.

Joyce Rebeta-Burditt

T A B L E 13.4 Children of Alcoholics Screening Test (CAST)

CAST can be used to identify latency age, adolescent, and grown-up children of alcoholics.

Please check (✔) the answer below that best describes your feelings, behavior, and experiences related to a parent's alcohol use. Take your time and be as accurate as possible. Answer all 30 questions by checking either "yes" or "no."

Sex: Male _____   Female _____   Age: _____   *I was early teen*

YES	NO	QUESTIONS
✓	___	1. Have you ever thought that one of your parents had a drinking problem?
✓	___	2. Have you ever lost sleep because of a parent's drinking?
✓	___	3. Did you ever encourage one of your parents to quit drinking?
✓	___	4. Did you ever feel alone, scared, nervous, angry, or frustrated because a parent was not able to stop drinking?
✓	___	5. Did you ever argue or fight with a parent when he or she was drinking?
✓	___	6. Did you ever threaten to run away from home because of a parent's drinking?
✓	___	7. Has a parent ever yelled at or hit you or other family members when drinking?
✓	___	8. Have you ever heard your parents fight when one of them was drunk?
✓	___	9. Did you ever protect another family member from a parent who was drinking?
✓	___	10. Did you ever feel like hiding or emptying a parent's bottle of liquor? *I did*
✓	___	11. Do many of your thoughts revolve around a problem-drinking parent or difficulties that arise because of his or her drinking?
✓	___	12. Did you ever wish that a parent would stop drinking?
___	✓	13. Did you ever feel responsible for and guilty about a parent's drinking?
✓	___	14. Did you ever fear that your parents would get divorced due to alcohol misuse?
✓	___	15. Have you ever withdrawn from and avoided outside activities and friends because of embarrassment and shame over a parent's drinking problem?

---

support is very important; the best results seem to be obtained when the whole family is treated (Nace et al., 1982). Indeed, for many families it is imperative that the family be treated as a unit, because its structure and stability may be organized around the alcoholism (Steinglass, 1983). Self-help groups such as Alcoholics Anonymous and Al-Anon (for the families of alcoholics) have had good success rates. Organizations such as Adult Children of Alcoholics offer self-help for children of alcoholic families. (See Resource Center for more information.)

Drug Abuse and Families

Although alcohol is the most commonly used and misused mind-altering substance in the United States, a number of other drugs have achieved popularity among many Americans.

DRUGS AND DRUG USE. There are many kinds of *psychoactive* ("mind-affecting") drugs and many reasons for using them. After alcohol, the most commonly used psychoactive drugs include marijuana, hallucinogens (such as LSD, mescaline, and psilocybin),

We are never deceived: we deceive ourselves.

Johann Goethe

T A B L E 13.4 Children of Alcoholics Screening Test (CAST)

YES	NO	QUESTIONS
	✓	16. Did you ever feel caught in the middle of an argument or fight between a problem-drinking parent and your other parent?
	✓	17. Did you ever feel that you made a parent drink alcohol?
✓		18. Have you ever felt that a problem-drinking parent did not really love you?
✓		19. Did you ever resent a parent's drinking?
✓		20. Have you ever worried about a parent's health because of his or her alcohol use?
	✓	21. Have you ever been blamed for a parent's drinking?
✓		22. Did you ever think your father was an alcoholic? *my father visited taverns several times a week.*
✓		23. Did you ever wish your home could be more like the homes of your friends who did not have a parent with a drinking problem?
✓		24. Did a parent ever make promises to you that he or she did not keep because of drinking?
✓		25. Did you ever think your mother was an alcoholic? *She was an alcoholic*
✓		26. Did you ever wish that you could talk to someone who could understand and help the alcohol-related problems in your family?
✓		27. Did you ever fight with your brothers and sisters about a parent's drinking?
	✓	28. Did you ever stay away from home to avoid the drinking parent or your other parent's reaction to the drinking?
✓		29. Have you ever felt sick, cried, or had a "knot" in your stomach after worrying about a parent's drinking? *Saw a doctor for treatment of "nervous stomach"*
✓		30. Did you ever take over any chores and duties at home that were usually done by a parent before he or she developed a drinking problem? *Cooking & Cleaning*

25 TOTAL NUMBER OF "YES" ANSWERS

Score of 6 or more means that more than likely this child is a child of an alcoholic parent.

cocaine (and "crack," its smokable form), phencyclidine (PCP), *narcotics* ("sleep-inducing" drugs, principally heroin; also other opiates such as morphine and codeine), and inhalants (such as toluene in spray paints and nitrous oxide, or "laughing gas"). *Psychotherapeutic* ("mind-healing") drugs such as antidepressants, stimulants, and sedatives are widely used; among the most commonly abused drugs in this group are amphetamines ("speed") and the sedative-hypnotics such as methaqualone (Quaaludes), barbituates (such as secobarbital [Seconal] or "reds"), and diazepam (Valium). Drug use is prevalent in virtually all socioeconomic, sociocultural, and age groups (beginning with preteens). What varies is the drug of choice and the usage pattern.

Overall drug use seems to be declining since the peak years of the late 1970s. In fact, many experts suggest that America is in the midst of its third temperance movement (Kolata, 1991). Only the use of heroin and crack continues to maintain a steady level. These drugs continue to ravage Americans, especially poor Americans. There are numerous consequences, including the birth of "crack babies" (discussed in Chapter 9) and the spread of HIV to drug users, their sexual partners, and their children. Users of intravenously administered (IV) drugs represent the fastest grow-

Cigarettes kill more people each year than AIDS, heroin, crack, cocaine, alcohol, car accidents, fire, and murder combined.

Iris Shannon

Children of Alcoholics

Alcoholism affects not only the parents in an alcoholic family; it also affects the children, both while they are living at home and for years afterwards. Approximately 7 million children younger than eighteen are children of alcoholics (COA) who are living at home. Twenty-one million are the adult children of alcoholics (ACOA) (Lord et al., 1987). Because of family denial, many children of alcoholics may not be aware of the existence of alcoholism in their families. The Children of Alcoholics Screening Test (CAST) in Table 13.4 has been used to help identify preadolescent, adolescent, and adult children of alcoholics.

Children Living in Alcoholic Families

Alcoholic families tend to have rigid rules that affect everyone in the family (Wegscheider, 1989). The impact can be especially devastating to children. The arguments and tensions filling alcoholic homes are often more upsetting than the actual drinking. Children sometimes fear for their own safety, as alcoholism is often a part of child abuse and incest (see Chapter 15). Children of alcoholics learn three important rules: "Don't talk. Don't trust. Don't feel."

In order to survive family chaos, children take on certain roles. According to Sharon Wegscheider (1989), the four roles are hero, scapegoat, mascot, and lost child. The hero, who is usually the oldest child, becomes the family caretaker, the parent surrogate who runs the family. He or she is often a high achiever in school and sports. The scapegoat is the problem child, whose problems and troubles draw attention away from the alcoholism. The mascot is carefree and minimizes the alcoholism by clowning and joking around. The lost child withdraws in order to isolate himself or herself from the family turmoil. These roles, however, only superficially resolve the children's emotional problems in dealing with their family's alcoholism. Sooner or later, as adults, they may have to confront the painful consequences.

In attempting to cope, children may develop obsessive or rigid personalities; they frequently have poor self-images. They often feel guilty for not being able to "save" Mommy or Daddy from drinking. A twenty-one-year-old daughter recalled (Desmond, 1987): "When we were kids and our parents were drunk, it was our problem. Somehow it seems that we should be super people and make our family healthy."

Adult Children of Alcoholics

The consequences of family alcoholism may follow children long after they leave their families. One out of four children of alcoholics becomes an alcoholic, in contrast to one out of ten adults in the general population. According to Janet Woititz (1983), adult children of alcoholics may display some or all of the following traits to varying degrees. They:

◆ Must guess what normal behavior is.
◆ Find it difficult to complete a project.
◆ Lie even when it would be easy to tell the truth.
◆ Judge themselves harshly.
◆ Have difficulty having fun.
◆ Take themselves very seriously.
◆ Have difficulty in intimate relationships.
◆ Overreact to changes beyond their control.
◆ Seek affirmation and approval constantly.
◆ Feel different from others.
◆ Act excessively responsible or irresponsible.
◆ Are extremely loyal, even if the loyalty is undeserved.
◆ Lock themselves into courses of action without considering the consequences.

Because COAs grew up in dysfunctional families, they did not have healthy adult role models. As a consequence, they are likely to repeat many of the same patterns as their parents. Since they were used to caring for their parents, they choose partners who also need their care. They are willing to marry alcoholics or other troubled individuals because they have learned to tolerate unacceptable behavior. Unacceptable behavior may indeed seem quite normal.

ing segment of HIV infection and AIDS cases. The vast majority of those infected through IV drug use are the inner-city poor. As national drug use declines, warns Mitchell Rosenthal, the chairperson of the New York State Advisory Council on Drug Abuse, "the danger is that we will have a shrinking political interest in the problem, and the most vulnerable and high-risk populations will not get the kind of services they need" (quoted in Kolata, 1991).

Within the family, parents, adolescents, or both may be drug users. Adolescents (or adults, for that matter) may use drugs to resolve conflicts, escape stressful situations, express defiance of authority, or elicit sympathy. Emerging research suggests

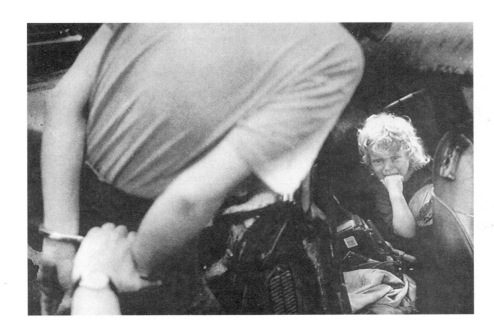

Drugs destroy not only individuals, but families as well.

that survivors of sexual abuse are significantly more likely to abuse drugs and alcohol as a form of self-medication and as a way to escape family problems (Harrison, Hoffman, and Edwall, 1989). Drug use may also be a symptom of serious disturbance and a threat to health or life. Teenage drug use is of particular concern to many families.

THE FAMILY'S ROLE IN DRUG ABUSE. Researchers are increasingly recognizing the role of the family in beginning, continuing, stopping, and preventing drug use by its members (Needle et al., 1983; Sorenson and Bernal, 1987; Textor, 1987). Some researchers (Stanton, 1979) believe that parents with marital problems use their adolescent's drug abuse as a means of avoiding their own problems. These families often deny the drug abuse and sometimes encourage it by providing money. In order to solicit care and attention from their parents, abusers engage in antisocial or self-destructive behavior. If the addict improves, however, the family suffers a crisis of its own: members become depressed, parents threaten divorce, siblings act out. Family members may sabotage the treatment of addicted members. These crises dissipate as soon as the drug user returns to his or her addiction. These families "need" their drug-abusing member to maintain their cohesiveness. The center of the problem is the family. In such cases, drug abuse is merely a symptom of family pathology.

The Addict. Drug abuse often begins as an adolescent problem; it may be tied to normal adolescent experimentation (Textor, 1987). Adolescents must deal with issues of family loyalty, separation and identity, and new ways of relating with their parents. Future addicts fail at most of these tasks. Early in life they may be identified as problem children; they are viewed as weak, immature, and needing help. Because they are limited in their development, they do not have sufficient coping skills; they are nonassertive and feel that they have little control over their lives. They often fail at school, are unable to find suitable work, and refuse to accept social responsibilities. They develop negative self-images. As Martin Textor (1987) observed:

Future drug addicts are usually alienated from their peers and socially isolated. They lack real relationships, experience few romantic episodes, and expect rejection by others. Therefore, they often use drugs as a means of coping with the absence of intimacy and as a source of relief from loneliness, despair, and frustration.

Drug abusers remain intimately involved with their families. They rarely achieve real independence. Because they feel trapped, addicts may attempt to rebel against their parents or punish them for not allowing them to be free of their emotional bondage.

Family life is usually dull, shallow, and without emotion (Textor, 1987). Family members feel alienated, lonely, and unaccepted. They feel anxious, depressed, guilty, and enraged. Communication is poor: it involves unclear messages, vague information-giving, lack of direct talk, avoidance of eye contact. There is little direct expression of positive or negative emotions, because family members are intensely concerned about controlling feelings.

Such families defend against their emptiness and anger "by heavy alcohol consumption, self-medication, or overeating, all which serve as anesthetics, tranquilizers, antidepressants" (Textor, 1987). Only by "getting high" can the addict experience and express strong emotions. The parents not only rationalize their own misuse of legal drugs, such as alcohol or tranquilizers, but often deny their child's substance abuse. If they do recognize the child's abuse, neither they nor the addict accepts responsibility for the abuse. They blame each other or outside influences. The parents may excuse the addict because his or her dependency absolves them from responsibility.

The parents usually have a poor marital relationship, experience emotional distance, lack intimacy, and are dissatisfied with their sex life. They have a vital stake in maintaining their child's addiction as a means of avoiding their own problems. Their child's addiction is their way of "solving" their marital problems. In order to change the addict, the family must change. Because of family involvement, drug-abuse programs often involve intensive family therapy.

❖ SUMMARY

◆ *Health* is a state of physical and mental well-being, not solely the absence of disease. *Physical well-being* consists of feeling fit and able. *Emotional well-being* consists of feelings of happiness, hope, energy, and zest for life.

◆ Happily married people tend to have better health than unmarried individuals. Marriage encourages health and well-being through (1) living with a partner, (2) social support, and (3) economic well-being. Social support improves physical health by (1) increasing psychological well-being, (2) encouraging and reinforcing protective health behaviors, (3) providing secondary prevention, and (4) aiding recovery.

◆ America is undergoing a severe health care crisis. Because of the high cost of medical care, the possession of health insurance has become a prime determinant of access to such care. Today, 13 percent of Americans do not possess health insurance; among African Americans and Latinos the percentage is significantly higher. Most health insurance is

linked to employment. Unemployed, part-time, and low-paid workers in service industries are usually not covered. Only 40 percent of the poor are covered. The most promising insurance reform may follow the Canadian model of universal health insurance coverage.

◆ *Stress,* psychological distress or disruption, occurs as a result of change. Both families and individuals attempt to maintain equilibrium in the face of stress. *Family stress* is "an upset of the steady state of the family." *Stress pileup*—prior strains and hardships converging with new stressors—is important in determining stress outcome. *Normative stress,* such as death of elderly members, is predictable and common to all families. *Nonnormative stress,* such as drug abuse, is neither predictable nor common to all families.

◆ The *double ABC-X* model is the most widely used model describing stress. **Aa** represents *stressor pile up,* the combination of stressors, family hardships and strains, **B** represents family coping resources, **C** represents perception of the stressor pile up, and **X** represents outcome.

◆ *Economic distress* refers to aspects of a family's economic life that may cause stress, including unemployment, poverty, and economic strain. Unemployment causes family roles to change; families spend more time together, but wives complain that husbands don't participate in housework. After about six months, a stable family pattern emerges. If unemployment continues beyond a year, families are vulnerable to divorce. Coping resources include family members' psychological disposition, an adaptive family system, and flexible family roles. Coping behaviors consist of defining the problem in a positive manner, problem solving, and managing emotions.

◆ Disabilities and chronic illnesses create many forms of stress, including strained family relationships, modifications in family activities and goals, increased tasks and time commitments, increased financial costs, special housing requirements, social isolation, medical concerns, and grieving. Functional coping patterns include maintaining family integration, social support, self-esteem, and psychological stability, as well as understanding the medical situation.

◆ Family caregiving activities often begin in middle-aged marriages when an aged parent becomes infirm or dependent. Caregivers tend to be women. Although they often experience stress, caregivers may also feel positively about helping a beloved parent or relative.

◆ Cultural influences on our perception of death cause us to respond with denial, exploitation, and romanticization. *Thanatologists,* people who study death and dying, tell us that the stages of dying are likely to include anticipation, onset of a stressful event, disorganization, organization, and resolution. Apart from physical care and relief from pain, the most important need of a dying person is to be treated as a human being. *Hospices* care for terminally ill individuals, emphasizing both patient care and family support.

◆ *Bereavement* is the response to the death of a loved one, including customs and rituals and the grieving process (emotional responses and expressions of feeling). Mourning rituals include the funeral service and burial or cremation. For Jews, there are three successive periods of mourning—*shiva, shloshim,* and *avelut;* among Latinos, *el Dia de los Muertos* (the Day of the Dead) is celebrated on November first. The grieving process may include numbness, separation anxiety, despair, and the acquisition of new roles.

◆ Alcoholism is primarily a learned behavior; it often begins as a means of coping with stress, anxiety, and low self-esteem. Alcoholism is regarded as a disease over which the alcoholic has no control. Family members unconsciously may help maintain the alcoholic's drinking. Alcoholism can be cured only if the alcoholic stops drinking permanently.

◆ Overall drug use is declining in this country. The family is often deeply implicated in sustaining drug abuse and addiction. Family members often use the abuser as a scapegoat to avoid dealing with their own problems, especially marital problems.

Answers to Preview Questions

The answers to the preview questions at the beginning of the chapter are listed below. As you check your answers, whether you were correct or not, think about your reasons for each response. What were they? What was their source? How valid is the source? As you read the chapter, you will find the questions discussed in greater depth.

1.	F	6.	F
2.	T	7.	T
3.	T	8.	T
4.	F	9.	T
5.	T	10.	T

❖ SUGGESTED READINGS

Useful journals for topics covered in this chapter include *American Journal of Public Health, Caregiving* (newsletter published by the National Council on Aging), *Death Studies, JAMA: Journal of the American Medical Association, Journal of Health and Social Behavior, New England Journal of Medicine,* and *Omega: Journal of Death and Dying.*

Biegel, David, Esther Sales, and Richard Shulz. *Family Caregiving in Chronic Illness.* Newbury Park, Calif.: Sage Publications, 1991. An examination of caregiving research and strategies related to care of family members living with Alzheimer's disease, mental illness, cancer, or other chronic health problems.

Boss, Pauline. *Family Stress Management.* Newbury Park, Calif.: Sage Publications, 1988 (paperback). How to recognize and manage situations and events that cause family stress.

Chilman, Catherine, et al., eds. *Chronic Illness and Disability.* Newbury Park, Calif.: Sage Publications, 1988 (paperback). Various illnesses and disabilities among family members, including the aged, and their impact on the family.

Doherty, William, and Thomas Campbell. *Families and Health.* Newbury Park, Calif.: Sage Publications, 1988 (paperback). The family's role in promoting health and its response and adaptation to illness.

Eldston, Ted, ed. *The AIDS Caregiver's Handbook.* New York: St. Martins Press, 1988 (paperback). A handbook covering the scientific, medical, nutritional, psychosocial, and spiritual aspects of AIDS; very useful for family and friends of persons with AIDS.

Larson, David, ed. *Mayo Clinic Family Health Book.* New York: Morrow Publishing Company, 1991. A comprehensive "everything-you-ever-wanted-to-know-about-your-health-but-were-afraid-to-ask"–type reference book. Covers the human life cycle, environmental hazards, medical emergencies, health behaviors and disorders, medical problems and treatment options, and organizational aspects of medicine (such as living wills, birth options, and so on).

Levine, Stephen. *Who Dies?* Garden City, N.Y.: Anchor Books, 1982 (paperback). Practical and spiritual insights for living and dying.

Macklin, Eleanor, ed. *AIDS and Families.* New York: Harrington Press, 1989. A comprehensive examination of AIDS education, risk, therapy, and social policy in relation to families.

Roth, Philip. *Patrimony.* New York: Simon and Schuster, 1991 (paperback). The autobiographical story by one of America's finest novelists about the world we enter when our parents begin to die.

Siegel, Bernie, *Love, Medicine & Miracles.* New York: Harper and Row, 1987 (paperback). A best-selling book in which a surgeon stresses the importance of an individual's mind and emotions in recovering from illness.

Silverman, Phyllis, *Widow to Widow.* New York: Springer Publishing Co., 1986. One of the leading researchers on widowhood discusses the emotional processes of bereavement and grief.

Sorenson, James, and Guillermo Bernal. *A Family Like Yours: Breaking the Pattern of Drug Abuse.* San Francisco, Calif.: Harper and Row, 1987 (paperback) A book for families with alcohol or other drug abuse problems that explains how drug abuse affects the family and ways to stop it.

Viorst, Judith. *Necessary Losses.* New York: Fawcett Gold Medal Books, 1987 (paperback). A wise and witty analysis of the stages of our lives and the "loves, illusions, dependencies and impossible expectations" that we must give up, including those surrounding death.

Wegscheider, Sharon. *Another Chance: Hope and Health for the Alcoholic Family,* 2d ed. Palo Alto, Calif.: Science and Behavior Books, 1989. An outstanding, easy-to-read approach to alcoholism in the family using a systems approach.

White, Evelyn, ed. *The Black Women's Health Book: Speaking for Ourselves.* Seattle, Wash.: Seal Press, 1990 (paperback) . Addresses the unique health problems faced by black women—such as high rates of infant deaths, AIDS, and murder; poverty and inadequate access to health institutions; and sickle cell anemia—as well as more general problems. Contributors include Alice Walker, Angela Davis, and Faye Wattleton.

Woititz, Janet. *Adult Children of Alcoholics.* Deerfield, Fla.: Health Communications, Inc., 1983 (paperback). The best-selling guide to the dilemmas that adult children of alcoholics face, written by a leader in the movement.

Suggested Films

Forbidden Games (1951). During World War II, a young Parisian girl is orphaned and is taken in by a peasant family. She develops a close friendship with the family's son and together they try to understand death. Intensely moving, sad, and comic.

My Left Foot (1989). Witty, brilliant story of the life of disabled artist Christy Brown. Oscar-winning performance by Daniel Day-Lewis.

Ordinary People (1980). A family disintegrates following its eldest son's death. The story is told from the point of view of his guilt-ridden younger brother. Winner of numerous Academy Awards.

Rain Main (1989). Dustin Hoffman portrays an autistic man in a fine comedy/drama.

I Never Sang for my Father (1977; also PBS American Playhouse, 1988). A middle-aged widower is faced with caring for his hard, unloving eighty-year-old father although he'd rather remarry and move elsewhere.

READINGS

DEPRESSION AMONG WOMEN

Daniel Goleman

Women are twice as likely to experience depression as men. A task force of the American Psychological Association suggests that women's high depression rate in part may be the result of social factors. What are these factors? How might they affect psychological well-being? What remedies would you suggest?

The rate of depression among women is twice that of men, and the higher incidence is mainly related to being female in the contemporary world, [according to] an expert panel of the American Psychological Association.

In a report, the association's Task Force on Women and Depression rebutted earlier work that had suggested that a higher reported rate of depression among women could be attributed to their being more inclined to admit emotional distress or to use mental health services.

The report, based on a review of recent studies, said the factors placing women at greater risk for depression included physical and sexual abuse, poverty, bias that persisted in forms like lower wages than those paid to men, unhappy marriages, hormonal changes over the menstrual cycle and childbirth, and a tendency to focus on depressed feelings rather than taking steps to master them. The report noted, for example, that women were more likely than men to be poor and to be single parents.

Psychotherapists should look for such underlying factors and take them into account in treating depression in women, the report urged.

READINGS

More than seven million American women have a diagnosable depression, and most of them go untreated, the report said. The report said one in four women would experience clinical depression some time in life, as against one in eight men.

"The majority of women with depression go untreated either because the depression is undetected or misdiagnosed," said Dr. Bonnie Strickland, a psychologist at the University of Massachusetts who formed the panel when she was president of the association in 1987.

Dr. Ellen McGrath, a psychologist in Brooklyn Heights who was chairwoman of the working group, said, "Women are truly more depressed than men, primarily due to their experience of being female in our contemporary culture."

Dr. Strickland added, "After working on our task force report, I'm amazed more women aren't depressed, just given their economics and general second-class citizen status."

The report cited violence against women as a major factor making them especially prone to depression. The report said 37 percent of women had suffered significant physical or sexual abuse by the age of 21.

"Abuse is a strong predictor of later depression," Dr. McGrath said. "It leads to the tough kind of depression, where you just don't know why you feel so bad."

Unhappy marriages lead to depression in women more often than in men, the panel's report said. "An unhappy or tension-filled marriage makes women three times more likely to get depressed than it does men in similar relationships," Dr. McGrath said.

Women's reproductive problems are another cause of depression. "Four of 10 women on birth control pills have some symptoms of depression," Dr. Strickland said. "And 10 percent of women have serious postpartum depression."

Women may inadvertently worsen their own depression, the report said. "Men usually distract themselves from depressed feelings, while women tend to dwell on those feelings," Dr. Strickland said.

"But at least in the short term, distracting yourself is better than brooding and ruminating. There are gender styles in how men and women handle those feelings, and the male approach, in this case, helps cut short the depression.

Women may intensify depression by getting together with other women to talk over their feelings, Dr. McGrath said. "If a woman is very depressed, it's not that helpful to talk over those feelings with another woman, because they can become partners in depression for each other," she said. "It's as though the depression were contagious."

Instead, Dr. McGrath said the panel concluded that a more effective approach was for a depressed woman to take some positive step, even if a small symbolic one, toward changing the circumstances that were leading to the depression.

"It might be insisting on talking to your boss who's been ignoring you," Dr. McGrath said. "You still have to process the feelings of depression or you'll stay vulnerable to them all over again later on. But it's a matter of timing. It's better to do that after you're out of the pit of depression. But that's the reverse order of the usual approach that has been taken with depressed women."

"Depression is three times higher among professional women than others," Dr. McGrath said. "The income and status don't buffer you from the pressures of role overload. Many professional women are working mothers, and there can be marital discord around a woman's professional power."

Several approaches to psychotherapy for depression are particularly well suited to women's problems, the report concluded.

One is "interpersonal therapy," a treatment typically limited to three months that uses the relationship between patient and therapist to examine the other major relationships in the patient's life.

"For women, relationships are a major source of feelings about oneself, while for men achievements are a more important source of self-esteem," Dr. McGrath said. "If a woman's relationships aren't working, it can trigger a depression."

In another approach recommended for depressed women, cognitive-behavioral therapy, patients learn to recognize and correct distorted, self-defeating thoughts that lead them to feel depressed.

The third recommended approach is feminist therapy, which takes into account issues of powerlessness and women's need for egalitarian relationships. "Feminist therapy gives you an analysis that makes sense of the social causes of your depression," Dr. McGrath said.

The report said that antidepressants were effective and necessary in treating certain kinds of depression, and noted that 70 percent of antidepressant prescriptions were given to women, but often without proper diagnosis or monitoring.

For less severe depressions, the report noted, interpersonal and cognitive-behavioral therapies had about the same success rate. But the dropout rate for patients using antidepressants is as high as two-thirds, and the report raised the question of "a danger that antidepressants may encourage dependency, passivity and victim psychology in women, which could reinforce depression over time."

The good news, said Dr. Strickland, is that "depression, if treated, begins to lift in three to four months for more than 80

continued on next page

percent of women, whether they are in therapy or getting medication."

❖

THE LAST DAYS OF MARY BALL

Judy Sklar Rasminsky

As you read this article, think about the needs of the dying and their families. What are the physical and psychological needs of Mary Ball? What are her family's needs? How does the hospice team help them?

It was in May 1978 that 30-year-old Mary Ball, a vivacious practical nurse, learned she was probably going to die. That month she had undergone four operations: the diagnosis was widespread cancer. Unprepared, panic-stricken, Mary became deeply depressed. The fact that her mother had died of cancer when Mary was 16 magnified her dread. Then one day her mother-in-law yelled at her, "You're not trying!" Mary realized that she wanted to make the most of her remaining time with her 32-year-old husband, Karl, and their two children.

Through 17 months of chemotherapy, she and Karl leaned on each other. Their hopes soared when Mary regained enough weight and strength to return to work. Then in 1980, there was more surgery, followed by more chemotherapy. The prognosis was not good. This is the story of Mary Ball's dying—and of how a remarkable program helped to ease her last four months with grace and dignity.

November 12, 1980. In bed in their trim little house in rural Northford, Conn., Mary and Karl cling together, crying. Earlier that day they have learned from Mary's doctor, Bruce Lundberg, that cancer has spread throughout her bones. No treatment will make her well. Dr. Lundberg has suggested a different kind of help—the Connecticut Hospice, a Branford-based team that, since 1974, has cared for more than 1,800 dying patients and their families.

November 13, 1980. A hospice nurse telephones to ask if she can visit that night. Mary and Karl say no. Mary has just had radiation treatment for her pain, and she is tired. Besides, they are uncertain, apprehensive. What are they getting into? They must know more before they involve the children, Karl, Jr., 15, and Matthew, 6.

November 17, 1980. The hospice nurse calls again. The Balls take the outstretched hand. Home-care nurse Florence Larson arrives. Forthright, lively and gray-haired, she has been a nurse for over 30 years. She tells them that the hospice team can assist with pain management, nursing care, household help, money problems, counseling for the children: "We will support you in whatever *you* want to do to make Mary's life as happy and normal as possible."

Mary would like to remain with her family as long as she can. Winter is the slack time for a painting contractor, and Karl will stay home to care for her. Florence says she will visit regularly. The hospice team will be available day or night, seven days a week.

Mary has one urgent question: Can her pain be controlled? Dr. Lundberg has suggested morphine, but she is scared of it. Florence gently explains that morphine is an excellent painkiller and the correct dose "won't bomb you out."

"Who will pay for all these services?" Karl asks. "Your insurance," Florence answers. "But you'll never see a bill. We'll handle the paper work."

When Florence leaves 90 minutes later, the Balls feel as if a weight has been lifted from their shoulders. But they do not want counseling for the children. "I want to deal with them in my own way," says Karl. Leery of interference in their lives, they ask Florence to come just once every two weeks.

November 24, 1980. Mary visits Dr. Lundberg. Her pain persists, and having mulled over Florence's explanation, she is willing to try morphine. Dr. Lundberg prescribes a dose to be taken orally every four hours.

November 27, 1980. Karl's brother and sister-in-law are at the house for Thanksgiving Day. Suddenly, Mary's pain becomes unbearable. Anxious not to spoil the holiday, she takes more morphine and huddles on the sofa in the den trying to hide her agony. Karl telephones Florence. She calls Dr. Lundberg, who doubles the dose of liquid morphine and prescribes a booster shot. Florence picks up the medicine at the hospice in-patient building. About an hour after Karl's call she is giving Mary a shot of morphine. A half-hour later, Mary's torment over, Florence leaves and the party goes on.

December 11, 1980. Dr. Lundberg and Mary discuss the prospect of more chemotherapy. They conclude that the risks outweigh the potential benefits at this stage. To Florence Mary says, "I don't want to feel sick. I want to use the time I have left to enjoy and be part of my family." Florence says, "I think that's up to you and your doctor, and I support you in that decision."

Christmas 1980. Mary makes three shopping trips to buy the family's presents. She tires easily, so Karl pushes her up and down the store aisles in a wheelchair that Florence has ordered. She attends a church pageant Matt is in and supervises the trimming of their tree. In good spirits, Mary refuses a visit from Florence.

December 31, 1980. Mary is constipated. Florences comes to her aid. Natural fruit juices finally do the trick. "Florence is my security blanket," says Mary. "It's a relief just to hear her voice." Florence always seems to have time for a chat, a cup of coffee, a back rub for Mary.

January 2, 1981. Unable to keep her liquid morphine down, Mary needs a booster shot. Noreen Peccini, another member of

continued on next page

the hospice home-care team, teaches Karl to give the injections to relieve him of the helplessness he hates. "Five years ago I couldn't even show him an I.V. bottle," grins Mary. "Now he does everything."

January 22, 1981. Mary is in greater pain, and Dr. Lundberg increases her morphine. She is eating less and sleeping more, but she is awake when the boys come home from school. Reserved and self-sufficient like his father, Karl, Jr., says little when he comes in to see her. Matt, ebullient and gregarious like his mother, hops into bed for a cuddle. Karl, Jr., still brings home top marks and plays football after school; Matt still asks Mary's permission to have friends over and she still reminds him to change his clothes. "We just take one day at a time," Karl says. "I answer the kids' questions and try to tell them things at the right time. I told Karl, Jr., that his mother might have to go into the hospice in-patient facility and he is aware of the eventuality and that is enough."

January 28, 1981. At 6:30 P.M., Florence receives a call from a terrified Karl: Mary's face is puffed up like a balloon. When Florence arrives at seven, Mary is so scared she has vomited. Florence establishes that the swelling isn't life-threatening. While she is alone with Florence, Mary's eyes fill with tears. "I am getting so discouraged," she says. "Sometimes I hate to tell Karl how much I hurt, because he goes crazy—not that crying is crazy—wishing he could do more for me." Florence sits with her a long time, talking quietly.

January 29, 1981. Hospice physician Will Norton visits to check on Mary's swelling. He notices her bed sores and orders a hospital bed with an automatic inflating and deflating mattress to relieve the pressure on her back. The bed, delivered the next day, makes Mary "at least 100 percent more comfortable."

February 10, 1981. Mary wakes up disoriented. For a moment she doesn't even recognize Karl. After he moves her about in the bed and gives her some apple juice, she is herself again. But she is no longer able to walk to the bathroom alone, and Karl wakes every three hours to give her her morphine and turn her in bed.

February 28, 1981. Mary's pain is increasing, her breathing is shallow, her pulse rapid. At times she is confused. "I'm taking a turn for the worse," she tells Karl.

March 2, 1981. Mary *is* worse. Her dying is down to a matter of days. She is relieved and ready, but suddenly desperately afraid of becoming a burden. Should she go to the in-patient facility? Florence consults with Karl, who assures Mary he can handle the situation. To take some of the pressure off Karl during the day, Florence arranges for eight-hour-a-day help.

Evening. Mary perks up when Charles Rodriguez, their minister, comes in. "You know, Charles, I'm dying," she says. "And I'm not frightened." Karl is immensely comforted to hear this.

March 3, 1981. On behalf of the children of the church, a boy presents Mary with a card and a dozen roses. As Karl arranges the flowers in the kitchen, Matt asks for one. Later he gives his

mother the rose and a card. On it he has drawn himself with arms spread wide, the way he did when he was very small, saying, "I love you, Mom, this much."

March 5, 1981. Mary's pain is excruciating. Karl calls the hospice for the go-ahead to give Mary a shot of morphine. Later Florence offers to stop by, but Karl says, "Gee, Florence, I don't think you need to. Everything is fine." Florence doesn't insist. "Mary is dying, and they're handling it," she says.

March 8, 1981. Mary has a 105-degree fever and is often delirious. Her family—sister, brother, father, aunt—come to say good-by.

March 9, 1981. Karl is worried that the children might be frightened by their mother's dying at home. He considers moving Mary to the hospice building. Yet he believes she still wishes to stay at home. Mary is in a dreamlike state, unresponsive; but, while Karl is talking with hospice nurse Ruth Mulhern, she becomes alert. The time has come for her to go into the hospice, she says. She thanks Karl for all he has done for her and tells him she loves him.

That afternoon, Florence helps to settle Mary into her new surroundings—a cheerful, plant-filled room at the hospice building.

March 10, 1981. Evening. Mary is in a dream world, but when Florence touches her she responds, "Florence, I'm so glad to see you." It is so like Mary to be thinking positively. Then she drifts away, and as Florence and Mary's aunt stand at her bedside, she quietly stops breathing.

Karl is walking out of his front door when the phone rings. The boys are already on the way to the car to go to the hospice. He calls them back and sits them down on the living room couch. As he puts an arm around each, he tells them that their mother has just died. Crying, he says, "Except for her love, you two are the greatest gift your mother ever gave me."

March 13, 1981. At Mary's wake, flowers overflow the room. Karl, Jr., stands beside his father. When Florence approaches, the shy, quiet boy, who never reaches out to people, embraces her.

March 14, 1981. The church is packed for Mary's funeral. At the close of the service, the congregation sings her favorite hymn, "All Things Bright and Beautiful," in celebration of her life.

March 24, 1981. Florence visits Karl. The boys have gone back to school. He is preparing to return to work. Karl's father, who came from Florida for Mary's funeral, will stay as long as he is needed. Florence tells Karl the hospice has volunteers trained to help families with their grieving. He declines more help, but thanks her for everything. "Without your assistance we couldn't have lived Mary's last months the way we wanted to," he says.

Back at the hospice, Florence has a sense of completion. She

continued on next page

shrugs off her colleagues' praise. "We're here to guide, not take over," she says. "From the day I walked in, I was amazed at the way Mary and Karl related to each other and to me. They never drained me; they gave. I always left there a little wiser."

❖

RULES IN ALCOHOLIC FAMILIES

Sharon Wegscheider. Excerpt from *Another Chance.*

According to family systems theory, all families are governed by rules. The rules of alcoholic families, however, are dysfunctional; they serve to maintain the status quo of alcoholism. What are the rules of alcoholic families, according to Wegscheider? Are there other rules that you can think of?

Let us now look at what goes on in an alcoholic family in the light of . . . system principles. . . . As you will recall, we described a system as "(1) made up of component parts that are (2) linked together in a particular way (3) to accomplish a common purpose."

We have only to consider the very first of those elements, the components, to realize that the alcoholic family is in for trouble. One member is hooked on an outside force and cannot move freely to maintain the system's balance. Because of that fact, he sends first ripples, then tidal waves of disturbance through the family system. Other members must adjust to this situation, and in time they become so damaged by the pressure and the postures they must assume to withstand it that they, too, start sending out waves of disturbance.

From this perspective, the alcoholic appears to be a very powerful person. And yet, [is he not] trapped and helpless, tossed on the ever stormier sea of his addiction? Here lies the paradox: *as the alcoholic gradually loses power over his own life and behavior, he wields more and more power over those of the people close to him.* Though he is increasingly dependent on them for support—emotional, social, and financial—he plays the dictator to get it. He controls what they say, what they do, what they think, even what they feel. The control is so constant, all-pervasive, and often subtle that they may not even be aware of it.

. . . the person who holds the power makes the rules. He literally designs the system, and he designs it in his own image. The problem is that in a dysfunctional family the most powerful person in terms of rule-making is also the most dysfunctional. In an alcoholic family that person is, of course, the Dependent. It should not surprise us, then, that the family takes on a group identity which mirrors that of the alcoholic, and soon everyone is displaying the psychological symptoms of his disease.

Predictably, alcoholic families are governed by rules that are inhuman, rigid, and designed to keep the system closed—unhealthy rules. They grow out of the alcoholic's personal goals, which are to maintain his access to alcohol, avoid pain, protect his defenses, and finally deny that any of these goals exists. Here are a few of the rules that I encounter again and again in my work with these families:

Rule: The Dependent's use of alcohol is the most important thing in the family's life. For example, he is obsessed with maintaining his supply, and the rest of the family is just as obsessed with cutting it off. While he hides bottles, they search for them. While he stockpiles, they pour liquor down the drain. Like two football teams, their goals lie in opposite directions, but they are all playing the same game. They all plan their days around the Dependent's drinking hours—he to be sure that nothing interferes, they to frustrate his plans, or to arrange to be home in order to meet his demands, or to arrange *not* be be home in order to avoid his fury or possible embarrassment in front of their friends. The Dependent's use of alcohol is the overriding family concern around which everything else revolves.

Rule: Alcohol is not the cause of the family's problems. At first, the drinker and his family deny that he is abusing alcohol. Later they deny that he is dependent on it. Finally, when dependency is glaringly evident, they insist that it is only a complicating factor, not the root of whatever difficulties have led them to seek help.

Rule: Someone or something else caused the alcoholic's dependency; he is not responsible. Here the Dependent's increasing tendency to project his guilt and to blame someone else for his situation gets crystallized into a rule and imposed on the rest of the family. The scapegoat may be his wife or a child in trouble or a job he does not like—anything. Curiously, the scapegoat often goes along with the delusion and is overwhelmed with guilt and feelings of worthlessness.

Rule: The status quo must be maintained at all cost. It is easier to understand the extremely rigid way an alcoholic family responds to change by [thinking of the family as a] mobile. If the largest [piece] were to become snagged on some outside object, the string with which it is attached would pull taut and the supporting sticks would become rigid. Something similar happens when one family member gets snagged on a chemical. What's more, he is afraid to get unsnagged, for he feels that without it he cannot survive. So as rule-maker he makes sure that the sticks and strings of the family system stay rigid enough to protect him from change.

Rule: Everyone in the family must be an "enabler." When you ask members of an alcoholic family how they feel about the Dependent's drinking, they are of course quick to say that they would do anything to get him to stop. But all the while they are unconsciously helping him to continue—"enabling" him. . . . One person in the family plays the role of chief Enabler, but according to this unwritten rule, everyone else must do his part, too, to protect the Dependent and his dependency. They alibi for him, cover up, take over his responsibilities, accept his rules and quirks docilely rather than rock the boat. These actions may be defended on the grounds of love or loyalty or family honor, but their effect is to preserve the status quo.

Rule: No one may discuss what is really going on in the family, either with one another or with outsiders. This is exactly the sort of rule we would expect in a system as unhealthy and closed as an alcoholic family. Feeling threatened, the rule-maker tries to avoid, first, letting people outside know about family affairs—specifically, the degree of his dependency and the magnitude of its impact on his wife and children—and second, letting family members have access to new information and advice from outside that might undermine their willingness to enable.

Rule: No one may say what he is really feeling. This is a standard rule in severely dysfunctional families. The rule-maker is in so much emotional pain himself that he simply cannot handle the painful feelings of his family, which make his own even sharper. So he requires that everyone's true feelings be hidden. As a result, communication among family members is severely hampered. What there is tends to be rigid, distorted, and incomplete, the messages bearing little resemblance to the real facts and feelings that exist.

Eventually as his disease advances, the alcoholic completely represses his own feelings and . . . unconsciously puts in their place false emotions that are less painful. These are the feelings that seem on the surface to prompt his actions. But to those who know him well, his performance is not quite convincing. They may respond as though they took his behavior at face value, but at some level they sense a second, subliminal message coming from the real self that he has repressed.

They are thus confronted with contradictory messages coming from different parts of the Dependent. One they hear with their rational minds, the other with intuition. They feel confused because the two messages are saying such totally different things:

"If these kids would show a little responsibility about money, I wouldn't have to be so hard on them." (I'm worried that I'm going to lose my job because I've called in sick so many Monday mornings).

"If you were more affectionate, I wouldn't stay out late at night." (I know I'm not satisfying you—I don't know what's happened to me lately.)

"Why should I go to church? That new minister is only interested in money." (I'm no damned good. I can't face the minister, or the congregation either.)

Most often the false emotion expressed in his behavior is the opposite of the true emotion that lies underneath. Aggressiveness masks fear; blaming masks guilt; control masks helplessness. But, ironically, his behavior evokes the same painful feelings in family members that the Dependent is feeling underneath. In the table . . . we can see the dynamics of contagion by which family members gradually come to manifest the psychological symptoms of alcoholism.

DEPENDENT'S TRUE FEELING	→	DEPENDENT'S BEHAVIOR	→	FAMILY MEMBERS' FEELINGS
Guilt, self-hatred		Self-righteousness, blaming		Guilt, self-hatred
Fear		Aggressiveness, anger		Fear
Helplessness		Controlling (of others)		Helplessness
Hurt		Abusiveness		Hurt
Loneliness, rejection		Rejecting		Loneliness, rejection
Low self-worth		Grandiosity, criticalness		Low self-worth

Communication and Conflict Resolution

P R E V I E W

To gain a sense of what you already know about the material covered in this chapter, answer "true" or "false" to the following statements. You will find the answers on page 464.

1. Touching is one of the most significant means of communication. True or false?
2. Always being pleasant and cheerful is the best way to avoid conflict and sustain intimacy. True or false?
3. Studies suggest that those couples with the highest marital satisfaction tend to disclose more than those who are unsatisfied. True or false?
4. Overall, men and women tend to touch about the same amount. True or false?
5. Conflict and intimacy go hand in hand in intimate relationships. True or false?
6. Good communication is primarily the ability to offer excellent advice to your partner to help him or her change. True or false?
7. Physical coercion is the method men use most frequently when disagreement arises between them and their partners. True or false?
8. The party with the least interest in continuing a relationship generally has the most power in it. True or false?
9. If you and your partner disagree about something, you should agree in order to avoid conflict. True or false?
10. Wives tend to give more negative messages than husbands. True or false?

*Whenever a feeling is voiced with truth and
frankness . . . a mysterious and
far-reaching influence is exerted. At first it
acts on those who are inwardly receptive.
But the circle grows larger and larger. . . .
The effect is but the reflection of something
that emanates from one's own heart.*

I Ching

Ｉ NTIMACY AND COMMUNICATION ARE INEXTRICABLY CONNECTED. When we speak of
communication, we mean more than just the ability to discuss problems and
resolve conflicts. We mean communication for its own sake: the pleasure of being in
each other's company, the excitement of conversation, the exchange of touches and
smiles, the loving silences. Through communication we disclose who we are, and
from this self-disclosure intimacy grows.

One of the most common complaints of married partners, especially unhappy
partners, is "We don't communicate." But it is impossible *not* to communicate—a
cold look may communicate anger as effectively as a fierce outburst of words. What
these unhappy partners mean by not communicating is that their communication
drives them apart rather than brings them together, feeds conflict rather than
resolves it. Communication patterns are strongly associated with marital satisfaction
(Noller and Fitzpatrick, 1991).

In this chapter we explore how communication brings people together: how to
develop communication skills, how to self-disclose, how to give feedback and affirm
your partner. We also discuss the relationship between conflict and intimacy,
exploring the types of conflict and the role of power in marital relationships. We
look at common conflicts about sex and money. Finally, we explore some ways of
resolving conflicts.

❖ COMMUNICATION PATTERNS IN MARRIAGE

There has been an explosion of research on marital communication in the last
decade. Researchers are finding significant correlations between the nature of marital
communication and satisfaction, as well as differences in male/female communication patterns in marriage.

Research Methodology

The expansion in research has been fueled by the development of video recording
technologies that allow researchers to examine interactions in great detail. Many of
these interactions have been recorded in natural settings, such as the home, supermarket, and child-care centers. The interactions are later microcoded (categorized
according to the various details).

Most of the studies involve convenience samples—that is, groups of easily accessible partners, such as those attending marital enrichment weekends, assertiveness
training workshops, and so on. Respondents tend to be heterosexual, white, middle-
class men and women (Noller and Fitzpatrick, 1991). There are almost no studies of
cohabitors, gay and lesbian couples, or African Americans, Latinos, Asian Americans,
and other ethnic groups. It is likely, however, that many of the findings can be
extended to these groups.

Communication Patterns and Satisfaction

Researchers have found a number of patterns that distinguish the communication
patterns in satisfied marriages in contrast to dissatisfied marriages (Hendrick, 1981;
Noller and Fitzpatrick, 1991; Schaap, Buunk, and Kerkstra, 1988). Couples in satisfied marriages tend to have the following characteristics.

◆ *Willingness to accept conflict but to engage in conflict in nondestructive ways.*

◆ *Less frequent conflict and less time spent in conflict.* Both groups, however, experience conflicts about the same topics, especially about communication, sex, and personality characteristics.

◆ *The ability to disclose or reveal private thoughts and feelings, especially positive ones, to one's partner.* Dissatisfied spouses tend to disclose mostly negative thoughts to their partners.

◆ *Expression by both partners of more or less equal levels of affective disclosures,* such as tenderness, words of love, touch.

◆ *More time spent talking, discussing personal topics, and expressing feelings in positive ways.* One study (Kirchler, 1989) found that satisfied couples spend more time together (seven hours per day) in contrast to five hours per day with distressed couples.

The ability to accurately **encode** *(send) verbal and nonverbal messages and accurately* **decode** *(understand) such messages from their spouses.* This is especially important for husbands. Unhappy partners may actually decode the messages of strangers more accurately than those from their partners.

Husband/Wife Differences in Marital Communication

For some time, researchers have been aware of gender differences in general communication patterns. More recently, they have discovered specific gender differences in marital communication (Noller and Fitzpatrick, 1991; Thompson and Walker, 1989).

First, wives send clearer messages to their husbands than their husbands send to them. Wives tend to be more sensitive and responsive to their husbands' messages, both during conversation *and* during conflict. They are more likely to reply to either positive messages ("You look great") or negative messages ("You look awful") than are their husbands, who may not reply at all.

Second, husbands more than wives tend to give neutral messages, such as, "It doesn't matter to me." Wives give more positive or negative messages. Because women tend to smile or laugh when they send messages, however, they send fewer clearly neutral messages. Husband's neutral responses make it more difficult for wives to decode what their partners really are trying to say. If a wife asks her husband if they should go to dinner or see a movie and he gives a neutral response, such as, "Whatever," does he *really* not care, or is he pretending he doesn't to avoid possible conflict?

Third, although communication differences in arguments between husbands and wives are usually small, they nevertheless follow a typical pattern. Wives tend to set the emotional tone of an argument. They escalate conflict with negative verbal and nonverbal messages ("Don't give me *that!*") or deescalate arguments by setting an atmosphere of agreement ("I understand your feelings"). Husbands' inputs are less important in setting the climate for resolving or escalating conflicts. Wives tend to use emotional appeals and threats more than husbands, who tend to reason, seek conciliation, and try to postpone or end an argument. A wife is more likely to say, "Don't you love me?" while a husband is more likely to say, "Be reasonable."

Studies suggest that poor communication skills precede the outset of marital problems (Markman, 1981; Markman et al., 1987). The material that follows will assist you in understanding and developing good communication skills.

❖ REFLECTIONS *Do you find husband/wife differences in communication tend to hold true in your intimate relationships? If so, how? Are there other differences?*

Married couples who love each other, tell each other a thousand things without talking.

Chinese proverb

A little sincerity is a dangerous thing, and a great deal of it is absolutely fatal.

Oscar Wilde

When in doubt, tell the truth.

Mark Twain

wives are clear

husband neutral

It is human nature to think wisely and act foolishly.

Anatole France (1844–1924)

❖ NONVERBAL COMMUNICATION

There is no such thing as not communicating. Even when you are not talking, you are communicating by your silence (an awkward silence, a hostile silence, a tender silence). You are communicating by the way you position your body and tilt your head, through your facial expressions, your physical distance from another person, and so on. Look around you. How are the people in your presence communicating nonverbally?

Much of our communication of feeling is nonverbal. We radiate our moods: a happy mood invites companionship; a solemn mood pushes people away. Joy infects; depression distances—all without a word being said. Nonverbal expressions of love are particularly effective—a gentle touch, a loving glance, or a flower.

One of the problems with nonverbal communication, however, is the imprecision of its messages. Is a person frowning or squinting? Does the smile indicate friendliness or nervousness? A person may be in reflective silence, but we may interpret the silence as disapproval or distance.

Functions of Nonverbal Communication

An important study of nonverbal communication and marital interaction found that nonverbal communication has three important functions in marriage (Noller, 1984): (1) conveying interpersonal attitudes, (2) expressing emotion, and (3) handling the ongoing interaction.

CONVEYING INTERPERSONAL ATTITUDES. Nonverbal messages are used to convey attitudes. Gregory Bateson described nonverbal communication as revealing "the nuances and intricacies of how two people are getting along" (quoted in Noller, 1984). Holding hands can suggest intimacy; sitting on opposite sides of the couch can suggest distance. Not looking at each other in conversation can suggest awkwardness or a lack of intimacy.

EXPRESSING EMOTIONS. Our emotional states are expressed through our bodies. A depressed person walks slowly, a happy person walks with a spring. Smiles, frowns, furrowed brows, tight jaws, tapping fingers—all express emotion. Expressing emotion is important because it lets our partner know how we are feeling so that he or she can respond appropriately. It also allows our partner to share our feeling, to laugh or weep with us.

HANDLING THE ONGOING INTERACTION. Nonverbal communications help us handle the ongoing interaction by indicating interest and attention. An intent look indicates our interest in the conversation; a yawn indicates boredom. Posture and eye contact are especially important. Are we leaning toward the person with interest or slumping back, thinking about something else? Do we look at the person who is talking or are we distracted, glancing at other people as they walk by, watching the clock?

Relationship between Verbal and Nonverbal Communication

The messages that we send and receive contain a verbal and a nonverbal component. The verbal part expresses the basic content of the message, whereas the nonverbal part expresses what is known as the *relationship* or *command* part of the message. The relationship part of the message tells the attitude of the speaker (friendly, neutral, hostile) and indicates how the words are to be interpreted (as a joke, request, or command). The full content of any message has to be understood according to both the verbal and nonverbal parts.

For a message to be most effective, both the verbal and nonverbal components must be in agreement. If you are angry and say, "I am angry," and your facial expression and voice both show anger, the message is clear. But if you say, "I am angry," in a neutral tone of voice and smile, your message is ambiguous. If you say, "I'm not angry," but clench your teeth and use an angry voice, your message is also unclear.

Eye Contact and Touching

Two of the most important forms of nonverbal communication are eye contact and touch.

EYE CONTACT. Much can be discovered about a relationship by watching how people look at each other. Making eye contact with another person, if only for a split second longer than usual, is a signal of interest. If the look is returned twice, it is an invitation to be approached. When you can't take your eyes off another person, you probably have a strong attraction to him or her. In fact, you can easily distinguish people in love by their prolonged looking into each other's eyes. In addition to eye contact, dilated pupils may be an indication of sexual interest (or poor lighting).

Research suggests that the amount of eye contact between a couple in conversation can distinguish between those who have high levels of conflict and those who don't. Those with the greatest degree of agreement have the greatest eye contact with each other (Beier and Sternberg, 1977). Those in conflict tend to avoid eye contact (unless it is a daggerlike stare).

Sociologist Georg Simmel (1950) described interactions based on mutual glances or eye contact. For him, eye contact was "the purest and most direct reciprocity that exists anywhere." He wrote:

Words must be supported by one's entire conduct. If words and conduct are not in accord and not consistent, they will have no effect.

I Ching

The union and interaction of individuals is based upon mutual glances. This is perhaps the purest and most direct reciprocity that exists anywhere. . . . So tenacious and subtle is this union that it can only be maintained by the shortest and straightest line between the eyes, and the smallest deviation from it, the slightest glance aside, completely destroys the unique character of this union.

Georg Simmel

Touch and eye contact are important forms of communication even during disagreements for they demonstrate continued caring.

So tenacious and subtle is this union that it can only be maintained by the shortest and straightest of line between the eyes . . . the slightest deviation from it, the slightest glance aside, completely destroys the unique character of this union.

TOUCHING. It is difficult to overestimate the significance of touch. Touch is a life-giving force for infants. If they are not touched, they may fail to thrive and may even die (Montagu, 1986). We hold hands with small children and those we love. When we are moved by someone or something, we speak of being "touched." Gathering in a circle for the "laying on of hands" has a spiritual significance that may go beyond our eveyday "worldly" experience.

As with eye contact, touching is a form of communication. The amount of contact from almost imperceptible touches to "hanging all over" each other, helps differentiate lovers from strangers. How and where a person is touched can suggest friendship, intimacy, love, or sexual interest.

Growing research on touch indicates that it often signals intimacy, immediacy, and emotional closeness (Thayer, 1986). In fact, touch may very well be the closest form of nonverbal communication. One researcher (Thayer, 1986) wrote: "If intimacy is proximity, then nothing comes closer than touch, the most intimate knowledge of another." And touching seems to go "hand in hand" with self-disclosure. Those who touch seem to self-disclose more; in fact, touch seems to be an important factor in prompting others to talk more about themselves (Heslin and Alper, 1983; Norton, 1983).

Despite stereotypes of women touching and men avoiding touch, studies suggest that there are no consistent differences between the sexes in the amount of overall touching (Andersen et al., 1987). Men do not seem to initiate touch with women any more than women do with men. Women are markedly unenthusiastic about receiving touches from strangers, however, and express greater concern about being touched. For women, there is greater touch avoidance unless there is a relational context with the man (Heslin and Alper, 1983). However, in situations with sexual overtones, men, regardless of their marital status initiate more touching than women (Blumstein and Schwartz, 1983).

❖ REFLECTIONS   *As you examine your own nonverbal communication, think about instances in which you and another person have had significant eye contact. What did the eye contact mean? Think about how you and your partner touch. What are the different kinds of touching you do? The kinds your partner does? What are the different meanings you ascribe to touch given and touch received?*

DEVELOPING COMMUNICATION SKILLS

Why People Don't Communicate

We can learn to communicate, but it is not always easy. Male gender roles, for example, work against the idea of expressing feelings. The traditional male gender role calls for men to be strong and silent, to ride off into the sunset alone. If men talk, they talk about things—cars, politics, sports, work, money—but not about feelings. Also, people may have personal reasons for not expressing their feelings. They may have strong feelings of inadequacy: "If you *really* knew what I was like, you wouldn't like me." They may feel ashamed of or guilty about their feelings: "Sometimes I feel attracted to other people, and it makes me feel guilty because I *should* only be

PERSPECTIVE

Ten Rules for Avoiding Intimacy

Communication

If you want to avoid intimacy, here are ten rules that have proved effective in nationwide testing with lovers, husbands and wives, parents and children. Follow these guidelines and you'll never have an intimate relationship.

1. Don't talk. This is the basic rule for avoiding intimacy. If you follow this one rule, you will never have to worry about being intimate again. Sometimes, however, you may be forced to talk. But don't talk about anything meaningful. Talk about the weather, baseball, class, the stock market—anything but feelings.

2. Never show your feelings. Showing your feelings is almost as bad as talking, because feelings are ways of communicating. If you cry or show anger, sadness, or joy, you are giving yourself away. You might as well talk, and if you talk you could become intimate. So the best thing to do is remain expressionless (which, we admit, is a form of communication, but at least it is giving the message that you don't want to be intimate).

3. Always be pleasant. Always smile, always be friendly, especially if something's bothering you. You'll be surprised at how effective hiding negative feelings from your partner is in preventing intimacy. It may even fool your partner into believing that everything's okay in your relationship.

4. Always win. If you can't be pleasant, try this one. Never compromise, never admit that your partner's point of view may be as good as yours. If you start compromising, that's an admission that you care about your partner's feelings, which is a dangerous step toward intimacy.

5. Always keep busy. Keeping busy at school or work will take you away from your partner, and you won't have to be intimate. Your partner may never figure out that you're using work to avoid inti-

macy. Because our culture values hard work, he or she will feel unjustified in complaining. Incidentally, devoting yourself to your work will nevertheless give your partner the message that he or she is not as important as your work. You can make your partner feel unimportant in your life without even talking!

6. Always be right. There is nothing worse than being wrong, because it is an indication that you are human. If you admit you're wrong, you might have to admit your partner's right, and that will make him or her as good as you. If he or she is as good as you, then you might have to consider your partner, and before you know it, you will be intimate!

7. Never argue. If you can't always be right, don't argue at all. If you argue, you might discover that you and your partner are different. If you're different, you may have to talk about the differences so that you can make adjustments. And if you begin making adjustments, you may have to tell your partner who you *really* are, what you *really* feel. Naturally, these revelations may lead to intimacy.

8. Make your partner guess what you want. Never tell your partner what you want. That way, when your partner tries to guess and is wrong (as he or she often will be), you can tell your partner that he

or she doesn't really understand or love you. If your partner did love you, he or she would know what you want without asking. Not only will this prevent intimacy but it will drive your partner crazy as well.

9. Always look out for number one. Remember, you are number one. All relationships exist to fulfill *your* needs, no one else's. Whatever you feel like doing is just fine. You're okay—your partner's not okay. If your partner can't satisfy your needs, he or she is narcissistic; after all, you are the one making all the sacrifices in the relationship.

10. Keep the television on. Keep the television turned on at all times, during dinner, while you're reading, when you're in bed, and while you're talking (especially if you're talking about something important). This rule may seem petty compared with the others, but it is good preventive action. Watching television keeps you and your partner from talking to each other. Best of all, it will keep you both from even noticing that you don't communicate. If you're cornered and have to talk, you can both be distracted by a commercial, a seduction scene, or the sound of gunfire. And when you actually think about it, wouldn't you rather be watching "The Simpsons" or "A Different World" anyway?

We want to caution students that this list is not complete. Everyone knows additional ways for avoiding intimacy. These may be your own inventions or techniques that you have learned from your boyfriend or girlfriend, friends, or parents. To round out this compilation, list additional rules for avoiding intimacy on a separate sheet of paper. The person with the best list wins—and never has to be intimate again.

attracted to you." They may feel vulnerable: "If I told you my *real* feelings, you might hurt me." They may be frightened of their feelings: "If I expressed my anger, it would destroy you." Finally, people may not communicate because they are fearful that their real feelings and desires will create conflict: "If I told you how I felt, you would get angry" (also see Cole and Cole, 1985).

Obstacles to Self-Awareness

Before we can communicate with others, we must first know how we ourselves feel. Yet we often place obstacles in the way. First, we suppress "unacceptable" feelings, especially feelings such as anger, hurt, and jealousy. After a while, we don't even consciously experience them. Second, we deny our feelings. If we are feeling hurt and our partner looks at our pained expression and asks us what we're feeling, we may reply, "Nothing." We may actually feel nothing because we have anesthetized our feelings. Third, we displace our feelings. Instead of recognizing that we are jealous, we may accuse our partner of being jealous; instead of feeling hurt, we may say our partner is hurt.

Becoming aware of ourselves requires us to become aware of our feelings. Perhaps the first step toward this self-awareness is realizing that feelings are simply emotional states—they are neither good nor bad in themselves. As feelings, however, they need to be *felt,* whether they are warm or cold, pleasurable or painful. They do not necessarily need to be acted out or expressed. It is the acting out that holds the potential for problems or hurt.

Feelings as Guides for Actions

Feelings are valuable guides for actions. If we feel irritated at a partner, the irritation is a signal that something is wrong and we can work toward change. But if we suppress or deny our feeling, perhaps because we are fearful of conflict, we do not have the impetus for change. The cause remains and the irritation increases until it is blown out of proportion; a minor annoyance becomes a major source of anger. If we are bothered by our partner leaving dirty dishes scattered around the house, we can say so and he or she has the option to change. But if we suppress or deny our irritation, the piles of dirty dishes may grow to towering heights, green mold may invade the house, and we may feel alienated from our partner without giving him or her the opportunity to change. Finally, when we become aware of our feeling, it may have grown to such intensity that we fly into a rage when we see one dirty plate, crash the dish to the floor, slam the door, and walk out.

Self-Disclosure

Through communication we reveal ourselves to others. This is called **self-disclosure.** We live much of our lives playing roles—as student, worker, husband, wife, son, or daughter. We live and act these roles conventionally. They do not necessarily reflect our deepest selves. If we pretend that we are only these roles and ignore our deepest selves, we have taken the path toward loneliness, isolation, and despair. We may reach a point at which we no longer know who we are. Almost 150 years ago Nathaniel Hawthorne cautioned, "No man, for any considerable period, can wear one face to himself, and another to the multitude, without finally getting bewildered as to which may be true." In the process of revealing ourselves to others, we discover who we are. In the process of our sharing, others share themselves with us. Self-disclosure is reciprocal.

Words are given to man to enable him to conceal his true feelings.

Voltaire (1694–1778)

She generally gave herself very good advice (though she seldom followed it).

Lewis Carroll

KEEPING CLOSED. If I do not disclose myself, I receive no feedback from my partner. Our relationship remains closed. We are isolated, untouched by each other. If I do not disclose myself, neither will my partner. My silence obliges him or her to remain silent. If I do not disclose myself, I will remain ignorant of myself, for my partner will not speak to me truthfully. My partner will tell me only what he or she believes I want to hear. But my partner does not truly know who I am, because I am afraid to reveal myself.

Men are less likely than women to disclose intimate things about themselves. Having been taught to be strong, they are more reluctant to express feelings of weakness or tenderness. Women find it easier to disclose their feelings, perhaps because from earliest childhood they are encouraged to express them (see Notarius and Johnson, 1982). These differences can drive wedges between men and women. One sex does not understand the other. One man complained of his wife: "Yakketty-yakkers, that's what girls are. Well, I don't know; guys talk too. But, you know, there's a difference, isn't there? Guys talk about things and girls talk about feelings" (Rubin, 1976). The differences may plague a marriage until neither partner knows what the other wants; sometimes partners don't even know what they want for themselves. In one woman's words (quoted in Rubin, 1976):

I'm not sure what I want. I keep talking to him about communication, and he says, "Okay, so we're talking; now what do you want?" And I don't know what to say then, but I know it's not what I mean. I sometimes get worried because I think maybe I want too much. He's a good husband; he works hard; he takes care of me and the kids. He could go out and find another woman who would be very happy to have a man like that, and who wouldn't be all the time complaining at him because he doesn't feel things and get close.

What is missing is the intimacy that comes from self-disclosure. People live together, or are married, but they feel lonely. There is no contact. And the loneliest loneliness is to feel alone with someone with whom we want to feel close.

HOW MUCH OPENNESS? Can too much openness and honesty be injurious to a relationship? How much should intimates reveal to each other? Some studies suggest that less marital satisfaction results if partners have too little or too much disclosure; a happy medium offers security, stability, and safety. But a review of studies on the relationship between communication and marital satisfaction finds that a linear model of communication is more closely related to marital satisfaction than the too-little/too-much curvilinear model (Boland and Follingstad, 1987). In the linear model of communication, the greater the self-disclosure, the greater the marital satisfaction, provided that the couple is highly committed to the relationship and willing to take the risks of high levels of intimacy. Two researchers who tried to test the two approaches empirically found evidence to support only the linear model (Jorgensen and Gaudy, 1980). They cautioned, nevertheless, that couples unskilled or not used to high levels of self-disclosure might need to understand its significance before embarking on such a highly charged undertaking. Furthermore, more recent studies suggest that high levels of negativity are related to marital distress (Noller and Fitzpatrick, 1991). It is not clear whether the negativity reflects the marital distress or causes it. Most likely, the two interact and compound each other's effects.

Giving Feedback

Self-disclosure is reciprocal. If we self-disclose, we expect our partner to self-disclose as well. As we self-disclose, we build trust; as we withhold self-disclosure, we erode

If we had no faults, we should not take so much pleasure in noting them in others.

François de La Rochefoucauld

If you don't risk anything, you risk even more.

Erica Jong

There is no greater lie than a truth misunderstood.

William James

A monk asked: "How does one get emancipated?" The master said: "Who has ever put you in bondage?"

D.T. Suzuki (1870–1966), Zen Flesh, Zen Bones

I hope you have not been leading a double life, pretending to be wicked and being really good all the time. That would be hypocrisy.

Oscar Wilde

A sound marriage is not based on complete frankness; it is based on sensible reticence.

Morris L. Ernst

Styles of Miscommunication

Virginia Satir noted in *Peoplemaking* (1988), her classic work on family communication, that people use four styles of miscommunication: placating, blaming, computing, and distracting.

Placaters. Placaters are always agreeable. They are passive, speak in an ingratiating manner, and act helpless. If a partner wants to make love when a placater does not, the placater will not refuse because that might cause a scene. No one knows what placaters really want or feel—and they themselves often do not know.

Blamers. Blamers act superior. Their bodies are tense, they are often angry, and they gesture by pointing. Inside, they feel weak and want to hide this from everyone (including themselves). If a blamer runs short of money, the partner is the one who spent it; if a child is conceived by accident, the partner should have used contraception. The blamer does not listen and always tries to escape responsibility.

Computers. Computers are very correct and reasonable. They show only printouts, not feelings (which they consider dangerous). "If one takes careful note of my increasing heartbeat," a computer may tonelessly say, "one must be forced to come to the conclusion that I'm angry." The partner interfacing does not change expression and replies, "That's interesting."

Distractors. Distractors act frenetic and seldom say anything relevant. They flit about in word and deed. Inside, they feel lonely and out of place. In difficult situations, distractors light cigarettes and talk about school, politics, business, anything to avoid discussing relevant feelings. If a partner wants to discuss something serious, a distractor changes the subject.

As you look at these styles of miscommunication, do you find that any of these styles characterize your communication patterns? Your partner's style? Your parents', siblings', or children's? What happens if you and your partner have similar styles? Different styles? Are some styles complementary while others are not? What do you imagine a relationship would be like, for example, if both persons were placaters? If one were a placater and the other a blamer? If one were a blamer and the other a computer?

Me!

But I do trust Dave.

To say what we think to our superiors would be inexpedient; to say what we think to our equals would be ill-mannered; to say what we think to our inferiors is unkind. Good manners occupy the terrain between fear and pity.

Quentin Crisp

Excuses are always mixed with lies.

Arabic proverb

trust. To withhold ourselves is to imply that we don't trust the other person, and if we don't, he or she will not trust us.

A critical element in communication is feedback. If someone self-discloses to us, we need to respond to his or her self-disclosure. This response is called **feedback.** The purpose of feedback is to provide constructive information to increase another's self-awareness of the consequences of his or her behavior toward you.

If your partner discloses to you his or her doubts about your relationship, you can respond in a number of ways. Among these are remaining silent, venting anger, expressing indifference, or giving helpful feedback. Of these responses, feedback is the most constructive and the most likely to encourage change. (See the reading by Judith Viorst, "How to Fight Fair.")

First, you can remain silent. Silence, however, is generally a negative response, perhaps as powerful as saying outright that you do not want your partner to self-disclose this type of information. Second, you can respond angrily, which may convey the message to your partner that self-disclosing will lead to arguments rather than understanding and possible change. Third, you can remain indifferent, responding neither negatively nor positively to your partner's self-disclosure. Fourth, you can acknowledge your partner's feelings as valid (rather than right or wrong) and disclose how you feel in response to his or her statement. This acknowledgment and response is constructive feedback. It may or may not remove your partner's doubts, but it opens up the possibility for change, whereas silence, anger, and indifference do not.

Reprinted with special permission of North America Syndicate, Inc.

Some guidelines (developed by David Johnston for the Minnesota Peer Program) will help you engage in dialogue and feedback with your partner:

1. *Focus on "I" statements.* An "I" statement is a statement about *your* feelings: "I feel annoyed when you leave your dirty dishes on the living-room floor." "You" statements tell another person how *he* or *she* is, feels, or thinks: "You are such a slob. You're always leaving your dirty dishes on the living-room floor." "You" statements are often blaming or accusatory. Because "I" messages don't carry blame, the recipient is less likely to be defensive or resentful.

2. *Focus on behavior rather than on the person.* If you focus on a person's behavior rather than on the person, you are more likely to secure change. A person can change behaviors but not himself or herself. If you want your partner to wash his or her dirty dishes, say, "I would like you to wash your dirty dishes; it bothers me when I see them gathering mold on the living-room floor." This statement focuses on behavior that can be changed. If you say, "You are such a slob; you never clean up after yourself," then you are attacking the person, and he or she is likely to respond defensively. "I am not a slob. Talk about slobs, how about when you left your clothes lying in the bathroom for a week?"

3. *Focus feedback on observations rather than on inferences or judgments.* Focus your feedback on what you actually observe rather than what you think the behavior means. "There is a towering pile of your dishes in the living room" is an observation. "You don't really care about how I feel because you are always leaving your dirty dishes around the house" is an inference that a partner's dirty dishes indicate a lack of regard. The inference moves the discussion from the dishes to the partner's caring. The question "What kind of person would leave dirty dishes for me to clean up?" implies a judgment: only a morally depraved person would leave dirty dishes around.

A half truth is a whole lie.

Yiddish proverb

It is a luxury to be understood.

Ralph Waldo Emerson (1803–1892)

4. *Focus feedback on observations based on a more-or-less continuum.* Behaviors fall on a continuum. Your partner doesn't *always* do a particular thing. When you say that he or she does something sometimes or even most of the time, you are actually measuring behavior. If you say that your partner always does something, you are distorting reality. For example, there were probably times (however rare) when your partner picked up the dirty dishes. "Last week I picked up your dirty dishes three times" is a measured statement. "I *always* pick up your dirty dishes" is an exaggeration that will probably provoke a hostile response.

5. *Focus feedback on sharing ideas or offering alternatives rather than giving advice.* No one likes being told what to do. Unsolicited advice often produces anger or resentment because advice implies that you know more about what a person needs to do than the other person does. Advice implies a lack of freedom or respect. By sharing ideas and offering alternatives, however, you give the other person the freedom to decide based on his or her own perceptions and goals. "You need to put away your dishes immediately after you are done with them" is advice. "Having to step around your dirty dishes bothers me. What are the alternatives other than my watching my step? Maybe you could put them away after you finish eating, clean them up before I get home, or eat in the kitchen? What do you think?" is offering alternatives.

6. *Focus feedback according to its value for the recipient.* If your partner says something that upsets you, your initial response may be to lash back. A cathartic response may make you feel better for the time being, but it may not be useful for your partner. For example, your partner admits lying to you. You can respond with rage and accusations, or you can express your hurt and try to find out why he or she didn't tell you the truth.

7. *Focus feedback on the amount the recipient can process.* Don't overload your partner with your response. Your partner's disclosure may touch deep, pent-up feelings in you, but he or she may not be able to comprehend all that you say. If you respond to your partner's revelation of doubts with a listing of all the doubts you have ever experienced about yourself, your relationship, and relationships in general, you may overwhelm your partner.

8. *Focus feedback at the appropriate time and place.* When you discuss anything of importance, choose an appropriate time and place. Choose a time when you are not likely to be interrupted. Turn the television off and take the phone off the hook. Also, choose a time that is relatively stress free. Talking about something of great importance just before an exam or a business meeting is likely to sabotage any attempt at communication. Finally, choose a place that will provide privacy; don't start an important conversation if you are worried about people overhearing or interrupting you. A dormitory lounge during the soaps, Grand Central Station, a kitchen filled with kids, or a car full of friends are inappropriate places.

Mutual Affirmation

Good communication in an intimate relationship includes three elements: (1) mutual acceptance, (2) liking each other, and (3) expressing liking in both words and actions. Mutual acceptance consists of people accepting each other as they are, not as they would like each other to be. People are who they are, and they are not likely to change in fundamental ways without a tremendous amount of effort, as well as a considerable passage of time. The belief that an insensitive partner will somehow magically become sensitive after marriage, for example, is an invitation to disappointment and divorce.

If you accept people as they are, you can like them for their unique qualities. Liking someone is somewhat different from being romantically in love. It is not rare for people to dislike those whom they romantically love.

Mutual affirmation entails people telling their partners that they like them for who they are, that they appreciate the little things as well as the big things that they do. Think about how often you say to your partner, your parents, or your children, "I like you" or "I love you," "I appreciate your doing the dishes," "I like your smile." Affirmations are often most frequent during dating or the early stages of marriage or living together. As you get to know a person better, you may begin noting things that annoy you or are different from you. Acceptance turns into negation and criticism: "You're selfish," "Why don't you clean up after yourself," "Stop bugging me," "You talk too much."

If you have a lot of negatives in your interactions, don't feel too badly. Many of our negations are habitual. When we were children, our parents were probably often negating: "Don't leave the door open," "Don't leave your clothes piled in the bathroom," "Don't chew with your mouth open." How often did they affirm? Once you become aware that negations are often automatic, you can change them. Because negative communication is a learned behavior, you can unlearn it. One way is to consciously make the decision to affirm what you like; too often we take the good for granted and feel compelled to point out only the bad.

❖ REFLECTIONS   *To get a sense of how much you affirm or negate someone, keep track of your affirmations and negations. On a sheet of paper, label one column affirmations and the other column negations. Each time you make an affirmation of that person, give yourself a plus; each time you make a negation, give yourself a minus. At the end of the day, compare the numbers of pluses and minuses. How do you think he or she feels?*

❖ CONFLICT AND INTIMACY: TYPES OF CONFLICT

Conflict between people who love each other seems to be a mystery. The coexistence of conflict and love has puzzled human beings for centuries. An ancient Sanskrit poem reflected this dichotomy:

In the old days we both agreed
That I was you and you were me.
But now what has happened
That makes you, you
And me, me?

We expect love to unify us, but sometimes it doesn't. Two people do not become one when they love each other, although at first they may have this feeling. Their love may not be an illusion, but their sense of ultimate oneness is. In reality, they retain their individual identities, needs, wants, and pasts while loving each other— and it is a paradox that the more intimate two people become, the more likely they may be to experience conflict. But it is not conflict itself that is dangerous to intimate relationships; it is the manner in which the conflict is handled. Conflict is natural in intimate relationships. If this is understood, the meaning of conflict changes, and it will not necessarily represent a crisis in the relationship. David and Vera Mace (1979), prominent marriage counselors, observed that on the day of marriage, people have three kinds of raw material with which to work:

First, there are the things you have in common, the things you both like. Second are the things in which you are different, but the differences are complementary. . . . Third, unfortunately, are the differences between us which are not at all complementary, and cause us to meet head-on with a big bang. In every relationship between two people, there is a great deal

Kindness in words creates confidence. Kindness in thinking creates profoundness. Kindness in giving creates love.

Lao-Tze

Pass no judgement, and you will not be judged; do not condemn, and you will not be condemned; acquit, and you will be acquitted; give and gifts will be given to you . . . for whatever measure you deal out to others will be dealt to you in return.

Luke 6:37–38

All intimacies are based on differences.

Henry James (1843–1910)

A number of porcupines huddled together for warmth on a cold day in winter; but because they began to prick each other with their quills, they were obliged to disperse. However, the cold drove them together again, when just the same thing happened. At last, after many turns of huddling and dispersing, they discovered that they would be best off by remaining at a little distance from each other.

Arthur Schoepenhauer

The greatest thing in family life is to take a hint when a hint is intended—and not to take a hint when a hint isn't intended.

Robert Frost (1874–1963)

of those kinds of differences. So when we move closer together to each other, those differences become disagreements.

The presence of conflict within a marriage or family does not necessarily indicate that love is going or gone. It may mean just the opposite.

Basic versus Nonbasic Conflicts

If conflict unites marriages, what tears marriages apart? Paradoxically, it is also conflict. Two types of conflict—basic and nonbasic—affect the stability of a relationship. Basic conflicts challenge the fundamental assumptions or rules of a relationship, whereas nonbasic conflicts do not.

BASIC CONFLICTS. Basic conflicts revolve around carrying out marital roles and the functions of marriage and the family, such as providing companionship, working, and rearing children. It is assumed, for example, that a husband and wife will have sexual relations with each other. But if one partner converts to a religious sect that forbids sexual interaction, a basic conflict is likely to occur because the other spouse considers sexual interaction part of the marital premise. No room for compromise exists in such a matter. If one partner cannot convince the other to change his or her belief, the conflict is likely to destroy the relationship. Similarly, despite recent changes in family roles, it is still expected that the man will work to provide for the family. If he decides to quit work altogether and not function as a provider in any way, he is challenging a basic assumption of marriage. His partner is likely to feel that his behavior is unfair. Conflict ensues. If he does not return to work, she is likely to leave him.

NONBASIC CONFLICTS. Nonbasic conflicts do not strike at the heart of a relationship. The husband wants to change jobs and move to a different city, but the wife may not want to move. This may be a major conflict, but it is not a basic one. The husband is not unilaterally rejecting his role as a provider. If a couple disagree about the frequency of sex, the conflict is serious but not basic, because both agree on the desirability of sex in the relationship. In both of these cases, resolution is possible.

Situational versus Personality Conflicts

Some conflicts occur because of a situation and others occur because of the personality of one (or both) of the partners.

SITUATIONAL CONFLICTS. Situational conflicts occur when at least one partner needs to make changes in a relationship. Such conflicts are also known as *realistic* conflicts. They are based on specific demands, like putting the cap on the toothpaste, dividing housework fifty-fifty, sharing child-care responsibilities, and so on. Conflict arises when one person tries to change the situation about the toothpaste cap, housework, or child care.

PERSONALITY CONFLICTS. Personality conflicts arise not because of situations that need to be changed but because of personality, such as needs to vent aggression or to dominate. Such conflicts are essentially unrealistic. They are not directed toward

We are always willing to fancy ourselves within a little of happiness and when, with repeated efforts we cannot reach it, persuade ourselves that it is intercepted by an ill-paired mate since, if we could find any other obstacle, it would be our own fault that it was not removed.

Samuel Johnson

There is perhaps no phenomenon which contains so much destructive feeling as moral indignation, which permits envy or hate to be acted out under the guise of virtue.

Erich Fromm

Where he makes a jest, a problem lies. . . . Sometimes the jest brings the solution of the problem to light as well.

Sigmund Freud, Wit and Its Relation to the Unconscious

Lady Astor: If you were my husband, Winston, I'd put poison in your tea. Winston Churchill: If I were your husband, Nancy, I'd drink it.

making changes in the relationship but simply toward releasing pent-up tensions. Often this takes the form of violence: slapping, hitting, pushing, and shoving. Whereas situational conflicts can be resolved through compromise, bargaining, or mediation, personality conflicts often require a therapeutic approach. Such personality conflicts may pit a compulsive-type individual against a free spirit or a fastidious personality against a sloppy one.

Power Conflicts

The politics of family life—who has the power, who makes the decisions, who does what—can be every bit as complex and explosive as politics at the national level. Power is the ability or potential ability to influence another person or group (Scanzoni, 1979). Most of the time we are not aware of the power aspects of our relationships. One reason for this is that we tend to believe that intimate relationships are based on love alone. Another reason is that the exercise of power is often subtle. When we think of power, we tend to think of coercion or force; as we shall see, marital power takes many forms. A final reason is that power is not constantly exercised. It comes into play only when an issue is important to both people and they have conflicting goals.

CHANGING SOURCES OF MARITAL POWER. Traditionally, husbands have held ultimate authority over their wives. In Christianity, the subordination of wives to their husbands has its basis in the New Testament. Paul (Colossians 3: 18–19) stated:

Wives, submit yourselves unto your husbands, as unto the Lord. For the husband is the head of the wife, even as Christ is the head of the Church: and he is the savior of the body. Therefore, as the Church is subject unto Christ, so let the wives be to their own husbands in everything.

Such teachings reflected the dominant themes of ancient Greece and Rome. Western society continued to support wifely subordination to husbands. English common law stated: "The husband and wife are as one and that one is the husband." A woman assumed her husband's identity, taking his last name on marriage and living in his house.

The courts have institutionalized these power relationships. The law, for example, supports the traditional division of labor in most states, making the husband legally responsible for supporting the family and the wife legally responsible for maintaining the house and rearing the children. She is legally required to follow her husband if he moves; if she does not, she is considered to have deserted him. But if she moves and her husband refuses to move with her, she is also considered to have deserted him (Weitzman, 1981).

Absolute control of the family by the husband has substantially declined since the 1920s, however, and an egalitarian standard for sharing power in families has taken much of its place (Sennett, 1980). The wife who works has especially gained more power in the family. She has greater influence in deciding family size and how money is to be spent. Her status has risen to that of "junior partner"; relatively few women achieve absolute equality with their husbands in power, resources, and authority (Scanzoni, 1979). With the commitment to egalitarian relationships, however, men exercise their power differently and more subtly. Tension may exist between ideology and reality. Sociologist William Goode (1963) observed, "One partial resolution of the . . . tension is to be found in the frequent assertion from families of professional men that they should not make demands which would interfere with his work: he takes preference as a *professional,* not as a family head or as a male."

The formal and legal structure of marriage makes the male dominant, but the reality of marriage may be quite different. Sociologist Jessie Bernard (1982) made an important distinction between authority and power in marriage. Authority is based in law, but power is based in personality. A strong, dominant woman is likely to exercise power over a weak, passive man simply by the force of her personality and temperament. Bernard wrote:

Power, or the ability to coerce or to veto, is widely distributed in both sexes, among women as well as among men. And whatever the theoretical or conceptual picture may have been, the actual day-to-day relationships between husbands and wives have been determined by the men and women themselves. . . . Thus, keeping women in their place has been a universal problem, in spite of the fact that almost without exception institutional patterns give men positions of authority over them.

If we want to see how power really works in marriage, we must look beneath the stereotypes. Women have considerable power in marriage, although they often feel that they have less than they actually do. They may fail to recognize their power because cultural norms theoretically put power in the hands of their husbands, and the women look at norms rather than their own behavior. A woman may decide to work, even against her husband's wishes, and she may determine how to discipline the children. Yet she may feel that her husband holds the power in the relationship because he is supposed to be dominant. Similarly, husbands often believe that they have more power in a relationship than they actually do, because they see only traditional norms and expectations.

BASES OF MARITAL POWER. Power is not a simple phenomenon. It is generally agreed among researchers that family power is a dynamic, multidimensional process (Szino-vacz, 1987). Generally speaking, no single individual is *always* the most powerful person in every aspect of the family. Nor is power necessarily *always* based on gender, age, or relationship. Power often shifts from person to person, depending on the issue. According to J. P. French and Bertram Raven (1959), there are six bases of marital power: (1) *coercive power,* based on the fear that the partner will punish the other; (2) *reward power,* based on the belief that the other person will do something in return for agreement; (3) *expert power,* based on the belief that the other has greater knowledge; (4) *legitimate power,* based on acceptance of roles giving the other person the right to demand compliance; (5) *referent power,* based on identifying with the partner and receiving satisfaction by acting similarly; and (6) *informational power,* based on the partner's persuasive explanation.

Raven and his colleagues (1975) studied 746 men and women in Los Angeles to see how common these various sources of power were. Coercion and reward were not particularly significant. Wives described the source of their husbands' power as expert (37 percent), referent (36 percent), and legitimate (18 percent). Husbands described the source of their partners' power as referent (48 percent), legitimate (22 percent), and expert (21 percent). Women tended to attribute the source of their husbands' power to expertness and identification. In contrast, men tended to attribute referent power to their wives.

The basis of power varied according to the domain. Decisions to visit a friend or relative tended to be based on legitimate (43 percent) or referent (27 percent) power. Cleaning or repairing something in the house tended to be based on legitimate (35 percent) or expert (28 percent) power. Significantly, the basis of a spouse's

Power corrupts and absolute power corrupts absolutely.

Lord Acton (1834–1902)

Habit is the enemy of truth. Lies deny truth but habit ignores it.

Floyd Zimmerman

Hatred does not cease by hatred at any time. Hatred ceases by love. This is an unalterable law.

Siddartha Gautama, the Buddha (c. 563–483 B.C.)

[handwritten: So person thinks he can make demands because of higher pay]

The return of understanding after estrangement: Everything must be treated with tenderness at the beginning so that the return may lead to understanding.

I Ching

A word is not a sparrow. Once it flies, you can't catch it.

Russian proverb

power also varied according to marital satisfaction. Among highly satisfied couples, 49 percent attributed their spouses' power to referent power and 2 percent to coercion. Among those couples who were not satisfied at all, only 21 percent said their spouses' power was referent, whereas 42 percent believed their spouses' power lay in coercion (see also Bell et al., 1981).

RELATIVE LOVE AND NEED THEORY. Another way of looking at the sources of marital power is through the **relative love and need theory,** which explains power in terms of the individual's involvement and needs in the relationship. Each partner brings certain resources, feelings, and needs to a relationship. Each may be seen as exchanging love, companionship, money, help, and status with the other. What each gives and receives, however, may not be equal. One partner may be gaining more from the relationship than the other. The person gaining the most from the relationship is the one who is most dependent. Constantina Safilios-Rothschild (1970) observed:

> The relative degree to which the one spouse loves and needs the other may be the most crucial variable in explaining the total power structure. The spouse who has relatively less feeling for the other may be the one in the best position to control and manipulate all the 'resources' that he has in his command in order to effectively influence the outcome of decisions.

Love is a major power resource in a relationship. Those who love equally are likely to share power equally (Safilios-Rothschild, 1976). Such couples are likely to make decisions according to referent, expert, and legitimate power.

PRINCIPLE OF LEAST INTEREST. Akin to relative love and need as a way of looking at power is the **principle of least interest.** Sociologist Willard Waller (Waller and Hill, 1951) coined this term to describe the curious (and often unpleasant) situation in which the partner with the least interest in continuing a relationship has the most power in it. At its most extreme form, it is the stuff of melodrama. "I will do anything you want, Charles," Laura says pleadingly, throwing herself at his feet. "Just don't leave me." "Anything, Laura?" he replies with a leer. "Then give me the deed to your mother's house." Quarreling couples may unconsciously use the principle of least interest to their advantage. The less-involved partner may threaten to leave as leverage in an argument: "All right, if you don't do it my way, I'm going." The threat may be extremely powerful in coercing a dependent partner, while it may have little effect if it comes *from* the dependent partner, because he or she has too much to lose to be persuasive. The less-involved partner can easily call the bluff.

RETHINKING FAMILY POWER. Even though women have considerable power in marriages and families, it would be a serious mistake to overlook the inequalities between husbands and wives. As feminist scholars have pointed out, major aspects of contemporary marriage, such as the continued female responsibility for housework, inequities in sexual gratification (sex is often over when the male has *his* orgasm), the extent of violence against wives, and the sexual exploitation of children, point to important areas where women are clearly subordinate to men.

Feminist scholars suggest several areas that require further consideration (Szinovacz, 1987). First, they believe that too much emphasis has been placed on the marital relationship as the unit of analysis. Instead, they believe that researchers should explore the influence of the larger society on power in marriage—specifically, the relationship between the social structure and women's position in marriage.

All happy families are happy in the same way. Each unhappy family is unhappy in its own way.

Leo Tolstoy, Anna Karenina

For a marriage to be peaceful the husband should be deaf and the wife blind.

Spanish proverb

The awareness of sameness is friendship; the awareness of difference is love.

W.H. Auden

When a thing is funny, search it for a hidden truth.

George Bernard Shaw

In 11 - 14 months relationships that are not secure begin to crumble

Researchers could examine, for example, the relationship of women's socioeconomic disadvantages, such as lower pay and fewer economic opportunities than men, to female power in marriage.

Second, these scholars argue that many of the decisions that researchers study are trivial or insignificant in measuring "real" family power. Researchers cannot conclude that marriages are becoming more egalitarian on the basis of joint-decision making about such things as where a couple goes for vacation, whether to buy a new car or appliance, or which movie to see. The critical decisions that measure power are such issues as how housework is to be divided, who stays home with the children, and whose job or career takes precedence.

Some scholars suggest we shift the focus from marital power to family power. Researcher Marion Kranichfeld (1987) calls for a rethinking of power in a family context. Even if women's marital power may not be equal to men's, a different picture of women in families may emerge if we examine power within the entire family structure, including power in relation to children. The family power literature has traditionally focused on marriage and marital decision making. Kranichfeld, however, feels that such a focus narrows our perception of women's power. Marriage is not family, she argues, and it is in the larger family matrix that women exert considerable power. Their power may not be the same as male power, which tends to be primarily economic, political, or religious. But if power is defined as the ability to intentionally change the behavior of others, "women in fact have a great deal of power, of a very fundamental and pervasive nature so pervasive, in fact, that it is easily overlooked," according to Kranichfeld (1987). She further observes:

> Women's power is rooted in their role as nurturers and kinkeepers, and flows out of their capacity to support and direct the growth of others around them through their life course. Women's power may have low visibility from a nonfamily perspective, but women are the lynchpins of family cohesion and socialization.

> From a family perspective, women exercise power through much of their adult lives. As nurturers, they bear and rear children, instruct them in values, and help form their personalities. In addition they may care for their own aging and dependent parents. As kinkeepers, they maintain family cohesion by planning get-togethers with the extended family and writing or calling faraway relatives.

POWER VERSUS INTIMACY. The problem with power imbalances or the blatant use of power is the negative effect on intimacy. As Ronald Sampson (1966) observed in his study of the psychology of power, "To the extent that power is the prevailing force in a relationship—whether between husband and wife or parent and child, between friends or between colleagues—to that extent love is diminished." If partners are not equal, self-disclosure may be inhibited, especially if the powerful person believes his or her power will be lessened by sharing feelings (Glazer-Malbin, 1975). Genuine intimacy appears to require equality in power relationships. Decision making in the happiest marriages seems to be based not on coercion or tit for tat but on caring, mutuality, and respect for the other person. Women who feel vulnerable to their mates may withhold feelings or pretend to feel what they do not. Unequal power in marriage may encourage power politics. Each partner may struggle with the other to keep or gain power.

It is not easy to change unequal power relationships after they become embedded in the overall structure of a relationship, yet they can be changed. Talking, understanding, and negotiating are the best approaches. Still, in attempting changes, a person may risk estrangement or the breakup of a relationship. He or she must

---

"When I want to look at the world I see it the way you do. Then when I want to see it I look at the way I know and I perceive in a different way."
"Do things look consistently the same every time you see them?"
"Things don't change. You change your way of looking, that's all."

Carlos Castañeda, A Separate Reality

Marriage is one long conversation, chequered by disputes.

Robert Louis Stevenson

We are all inclined to judge ourselves by our ideals; others by their acts.

Harold Nicholson

It is possible for a man to wholly disappear and be merged in his manners.

Henry David Thoreau

weigh the possible gains against the possible losses in deciding whether change is worth the risk.

❖ CONFLICT RESOLUTION

Dealing with Anger

Love can be angry . . . with a kind of anger in which there is no gall, like the dove's and not the raven's.

Augustine of Hippo

Anger causes a man to be far from the truth.

Hasidic saying

Epitaph on His Wife

*Here lies my wife; here let her lie!
Now she's at rest.
And so am I.*

John Dryden (1631–1700)

Differences can lead to anger, and anger transforms differences into fights, creating tension, division, distrust, and fear. Most people have learned to handle anger by either venting or suppressing it. David and Vera Mace (1980) suggest that most couples go though a love-anger cycle. When a couple comes close to each other, they may experience conflict and they recoil in horror, angry at each other because just at the moment they were feeling close, their intimacy was destroyed. Each backs off; gradually they move closer again until another fight erupts, driving them away from each other. After a while, each learns to make a compromise between closeness and distance to avoid conflict. They learn what they can reveal about themselves and what they cannot. Because closeness brings conflict, they stop being close, and their relationship becomes empty and meaningless.

Another way of dealing with anger is suppressing it. Suppressed anger is dangerous because it is always there, simmering beneath the surface. Ultimately, it leads to resentment, that brooding, low-level hostility that poisons both the individual and the relationship.

Anger can be dealt with in a third way: recognizing it as a symptom of something that needs to be changed. If we see anger as a symptom, we realize that what is important is not venting or suppressing the anger but finding its source and eliminating it. David and Vera Mace (1980) wrote:

When your disagreements become conflict, the only thing to do is to take anger out of it, because when you are angry you cannot resolve a conflict. You cannot really hear the other person because you are just waiting to fire your shot. You cannot be understanding; you cannot be empathetic when you are angry. So you have to take the anger out, and then when you have taken the anger out, you are back again with a disagreement. The disagreement is still there, and it can cause another disagreement and more anger unless you clear it up. The way to take the anger out of disagreements is through negotiation.

Conflict Resolution and Marital Satisfaction

The family is a court of justice which never shuts down for day or night.

Malcolm de Chazal

If you are afraid of loneliness, don't marry.

Anton Chekhov (1860–1904)

The way in which a couple deals with conflict resolution both reflects and perhaps contributes to their marital happiness (Boland and Follingstad, 1987). Happy couples tend to act in positive ways to resolve conflicts, such as changing behaviors (putting the cap on the toothpaste rather than denying responsibility) and presenting reasonable alternatives (purchasing toothpaste in a dispenser). Unhappy or distressed couples, in contrast, use more negative strategies in attempting to resolve conflicts (if the cap off the toothpaste bothers you, then *you* put it on). A study of happily and unhappily married couples found distinctive communication traits as these couples tried to resolve their conflicts (Ting-Toomey, 1983). The communication behaviors of happily married couples displayed the following traits:

◆ *Summarizing.* Each person summarized what the other said. "Let me see if I can repeat the different points you were making."

◆ *Paraphrasing.* Each put what the other said into his or her own words. "What you are saying is that you feel badly when I don't acknowledge your feelings."

Ninety-nine lies may save you, but the hundredth will give you away.

West African proverb

◆ *Validation.* Each affirmed the other's feelings. "I can understand how you feel."
◆ *Clarification.* Each asked for further information to make sure that he or she understood what the other was saying. "Can you explain what you mean a little bit more to make sure that I understand you?"

In contrast, unhappily married couples displayed the following reciprocal patterns:

◆ *Confrontation.* Each member of the couple confronted. "You're wrong!" "Not me, buddy. It's you who's wrong."
◆ *Confrontation and defensiveness.* One confronted while the other defended himself or herself. "You're wrong!" "I only did what I was supposed to do."
◆ *Complaining and defensiveness.* One complained while the other was defensive. "I work so hard each day to come home to this!" "This is the best I can do with no help."

Fighting about Sex and Money

Even if, as the Russian writer Leo Tolstoy suggested, every unhappy family is unhappy in its own way, marital conflicts still tend to center around certain issues, especially communication, children, sex, money, personality differences, how to spend leisure, in-laws, infidelity, housekeeping, and physical abuse. In this section, we focus on two areas: sex and money. Then we discuss general ways of resolving conflicts.

FIGHTING ABOUT SEX. Fighting and sex can be intertwined in several different ways (Strong and DeVault, 1988). A couple can have a specific disagreement about sex that leads to a fight. One person wants to have sexual intercourse and the other does not, so they fight. A couple can have an indirect fight about sex. The woman does not have an orgasm, and after intercourse her partner rolls over and starts to snore. She lies in bed feeling angry and frustrated. In the morning she begins to fight with her partner because he never does his share of the housework. The housework issues obscures why she is really angry. Sex can also be used as a scapegoat for non-sexual problems. A man is angry that his wife calls him a lousy provider. He takes it out on her sexually by calling her a lousy lover. They fight about their lovemaking rather than the issue of his provider role. A couple can fight about the wrong sexual issue. A woman may berate her partner for being too quick in sex, but what she is really frustrated about is that he is not interested in oral sex with her. She, however, feels ambivalent about oral sex ("Maybe I smell bad"), so she cannot confront her partner with the real issue. Finally, a fight can be a cover-up. If a man feels sexually inadequate and does not want to have sex as often as his partner, he may pick a fight and make his partner so angry that the last thing she would want to do is to have sex with him.

In power struggles, sexuality can be used as a weapon, but this is generally a destructive tactic (Szinovacz, 1987). A classic strategy for the weaker person in a relationship is to withhold something that the more powerful one wants. In male/female struggles, this is often sex. By withholding sex, a woman gains a certain degree of power (Kaplan, 1979). Men also use sex in its most violent form: they use rape (including date rape and marital rape) to overpower and subordinate women. In rape, aggressive motivations displace sexual ones.

It is hard to tell during a fight if there are deeper causes than the one about which a couple is currently fighting. Are you and your partner fighting because you want sex now and your partner doesn't? Or are there deeper reasons involving power,

If I speak in the tongues of men and of angels, but have not love, I am as a noisy gong or a clanging cymbal.

I Corinthians 13:1

Keep thy eyes wide open before marriage, and half shut afterwards.

Benjamin Franklin (1706–1790), Poor Richard's Almanac

Those who warp the truth must inevitably be warped and corrupted themselves.

Arthur Miller

Nothing is so firmly believed as that which is least known.

Francis Jeffrey (1773–1850)

control, fear, or inadequacy? If you repeatedly fight about sexual issues without getting anywhere, the ostensible cause may not be the real one. If fighting does not clear the air and make intimacy possible again, you should look for other reasons for the fights. It may be useful to talk with your partner about why the fights do not seem to accomplish anything. Step back and look at the circumstances of the fight, what patterns occur, and how each of you feels before, during, and after a fight.

MONEY CONFLICTS. An old Yiddish proverb addresses the problem of managing money quite well: "Husband and wife are of the same flesh but they have different purses." Money is a major source of marital conflict. Intimates differ about spending money probably as much as or more than any other single issue.

Why People Fight about Money. Couples disagree or fight over money for a number of reasons. One of the most important reasons is power. Earning wages has traditionally given men power in families. A woman's work in the home has not been rewarded by wages. As a result, full-time homemakers have been placed in the position of having to depend on their husbands for money. In such an arrangement, if there are disagreements, the women is at a disadvantage. If she is deferred to, the old cliché, "I make the money but she spends it," has a bitter ring to it. As women increasingly participate in the work force, however, power relations within families are shifting. Studies indicate that women's influence in financial and other decisions increases if they are employed outside the home.

Another major source of conflict is allocation of the family's income. Not only does this involve decisions about who makes the decision, but it also includes setting priorities. Is it more important to pay a past-due bill or to buy a new television set to replace the broken one? Is a dishwasher a necessity or a luxury? Should money be put aside for long-range goals, or should immediate needs (perhaps those your partner calls "whims") be satisfied? Setting financial priorities plays on each person's values and temperament; it is affected by basic aspects of an individual's personality. A miser probably cannot be happily married to a spendthrift. Yet we know so little of our partner's attitudes toward money before marriage that a miser might very well marry a spendthrift.

Dating relationships are a poor indicator of how a couple will deal with money matters in marriage. Dating has clearly defined rules about money: either the man pays, both pay separately, or each pays alternatively. In dating situations, each partner is financially independent of the other. Money is not pooled as it usually is in marriage, and power issues do not necessarily enter spending decisions, since each person has his or her own money. Differences can be smoothed out fairly easily. Both individuals are financially independent before marriage but financially interdependent after marriage. Even cohabitation may not be an accurate guide to how a couple would deal with money in marriage as cohabitors generally do not pool all (or even part) of their income. It is the working out of financial interdependence in marriage that is often so difficult.

Talking about Money. Talking about money matters is difficult. People are very secretive about money. It is considered poor taste to ask people how much money they make. Children often do not know how much money is earned in their family; sometimes spouses don't know either. One woman recently remarked that it is easier to talk with a partner about sexual issues than money matters: "Money is the last taboo," she said. But, as with sex, our society is obsessed with money.

We find it difficult to talk about money for several reasons. First of all, we don't want to appear to be unromantic or selfish. If a couple is about to marry, a discussion of attitudes toward money may lead to disagreements, shattering the illusion of unity or selflessness. Second, gender roles make it difficult for women to express their feelings about money, since they are traditionally supposed to defer to men in financial matters. Third, because men tend to make more money than women, women feel their right to disagree about financial matters is limited. This is especially true if the woman is a homemaker and does not make a financial contribution, devaluing her child care and housework contributions.

Resolving Conflicts

There are a number of ways to end conflicts. You can give in, but unless you believe that the conflict ended fairly, you are likely to feel resentful. You can try to impose your will through the use of power, force, or the threat of force. But using power to end conflict leaves your partner with the bitter taste of injustice. Finally, you can end the conflict through negotiation. In negotiations, both partners sit down and work out their differences until they can come to a mutually acceptable agreement.

Conflicts can be solved through negotiation in three major ways: (1) agreement as a gift, (2) bargaining, and (3) coexistence.

Be to her virtues very kind,
Be to her faults a little blind.

Matthew Prior (1664–1721)

AGREEMENT AS A GIFT. If you and your partner disagree on an issue, you can freely agree with your partner as a gift. If you want to go to the Caribbean for a vacation and your partner wants to go backpacking in Alaska, you can freely agree to go to Alaska. An agreement as a gift is different from giving in. When you give in, you do something you don't want to do. When you agree without coercion or threats, the agreement is a gift of love. As in all exchanges of gifts, there will be reciprocation. Your partner will be more likely to give you a gift of agreement. This gift of agreement is based on referent power, discussed earlier.

Always forgive your enemies—nothing annoys them so much.

Oscar Wilde

BARGAINING. Bargaining means making compromises. But bargaining in relationships is different from bargaining in the marketplace or in politics. In relationships you don't want to get the best deal for yourself but the most equitable deal for both of you. At all points during the bargaining process, you need to keep in mind what is best for the relationship as well as for yourself and trust your partner to do the same. In a marriage, both partners need to win. The purpose of conflict in a marriage is to solidify the relationship, not make one partner the winner and the other the loser. To achieve your end by exercising coercive power or withholding love, affection, or sex is a destructive form of bargaining. If you get what you want, how will that affect your partner and the relationship? Will your partner feel you are being unfair and become resentful? A solution has to be fair to both, or it won't enhance the relationship.

Without forgiveness life is governed by . . . an endless cycle of resentment and retaliation.

Robert Assagioli

COEXISTENCE. Sometimes differences can't be resolved but they can be lived with. If a relationship is sound, differences can be absorbed without undermining the basic ties. All too often we regard a difference as a threat rather than as the unique expression of two personalities. Rather than being driven mad by the cap left off the toothpaste, perhaps we can learn to live with it.

❖ SUMMARY

◆ Research in marital communication has focused on convenience samples of white, middle-class couples. Important developments in research include video recording technology and microcoding of responses.

◆ Research indicates that happily married couples (1) are willing to engage in conflict in nondestructive ways, (2) have less frequent conflict and spend less time in conflict, (3) disclose private thoughts and feelings to partners, (4) express equal levels of affective disclosure, (5) spend more time together, and (6) accurately encode and decode messages.

◆ There are gender differences in marital communication. Wives send clearer messages; husbands tend to give neutral messages whereas wives tend to give more positive or negative messages; and wives tend to set the emotional tone and escalate arguments more than husbands.

◆ Communication includes both *verbal* and *nonverbal communication*. The functions of nonverbal communication are to convey interpersonal attitudes, express emotion, and handle the ongoing interaction. For communication to be unambiguous, verbal and nonverbal messages must agree. Silence can be a particularly destructive form of nonverbal communication.

◆ Barriers to communication are the traditional male gender role (because it discourages the expression of emotion), personal reasons such as feelings of inadequacy, and the fear of conflict.

◆ To express yourself, you need to be aware of your own feelings. We prevent *self-awareness* through *suppressing*, *denial*, and *displacement*. A first step toward self-awareness is realizing that our feelings are neither good nor bad but simply emotional states.

◆ *Self-disclosure* is the revelation of yourself to another. Without self-disclosure, a relationship remains closed. Men are less likely to self-disclose than women.

◆ According to some researchers, both low and high levels of self-disclosure are related to low marital satisfaction (curvilinear model). Other researchers maintain that a high level of self-disclosure is related to a high level of marital satisfaction, although it entails greater risks (linear model).

◆ *Feedback* is a constructive response to another's self-disclosure. Giving constructive feedback includes (1) focusing on "I" statements, (2) focusing on behavior rather than the person, (3) focusing feedback on observations rather than on inferences or judgments, (4) focusing feedback on the observed incidence of behavior, (5) focusing feedback on sharing ideas or offering alternatives rather than giving advice, (6) focusing feedback according to its value to the recipient, (7) focusing feedback on the

amount the recipient can process, and (8) focusing feedback at an appropriate time and place.

◆ *Mutual affirmation* includes mutual acceptance, mutual liking, and expressing liking in words and actions.

◆ Conflict is natural in intimate relationships. Types of conflict include *basic* versus *nonbasic* conflicts and *situational* versus *personality* conflicts. Basic conflicts may threaten the foundation of a marriage because they challenge fundamental roles; nonbasic conflicts do not threaten basic assumptions and may be negotiable. Situational conflicts are realistic conflicts based on specific issues; personality conflicts are unrealistic conflicts based on the need of the partner or partners to release pent-up feelings or on their fundamental personality differences.

◆ *Power* is the ability or potential ability to influence another person or group. Traditionally, legal as well as de facto power rested in the hands of the husband. Recently, wives have been gaining more actual power in relationships, although the power distribution still remains unequal.

◆ The six bases of marital power are *coercive, reward, expert, legitimate, referent,* and *informational*. These bases of power shift in different domains. Other theories of power include the *relative love and need theory*, and the *principle of least interest*.

◆ People usually handle anger in relationships by suppressing or venting it. Anger, however, makes negotiation difficult. When anger arises, it is useful to think of it as a signal that change is necessary.

◆ Major sources of conflict include sex and money. Conflicts about sex can be specific disagreements about sex, indirect disagreements in which a partner feels frustrated or angry and takes it out in sexual ways, arguments that are ostensibly about sex but that are really about nonsexual issues, or disagreements about the wrong sexual issue. Money conflicts occur because of power issues, disagreements over the allocation of resources, or differences in values.

◆ *Conflict resolution* may be achieved through negotiation in three ways: *agreement as a freely given gift, bargaining,* or *coexistence*.

Answers to Preview Questions

The answers to the preview questions at the beginning of the chapter are listed below. As you check your answers, whether you were correct or not, think about your reasons for each response. What were they? What was their source? How valid is the source? As you read the chapter, you will find the questions discussed in greater depth.

1. T   3. T
2. F   4. T

5. T	8. T
6. F	9. F
7. F	10. T

❖ SUGGESTED READINGS

Journal of Communication publishes studies on various aspects of communication, and *Journal of Nonverbal Behavior* explores nonverbal aspects of communication.

Gottman, John et al. *A Couple's Guide to Communication.* Champaign, Il.: Research Press, 1976 (paperback). A book that focuses on couples as the communication unit.

Montagu, Ashley. *Touching: The Human Significance of the Skin,* 3rd ed. New York: Harper and Row, 1986 (paperback). The classic study by a distinguished anthropologist on the significance of touch in human relationships.

Noller, Patricia. *Nonverbal Communication and Marital Interaction.* Oxford: Pergamon Press, 1984 (paperback). A scholarly examination of the role of nonverbal communication in marriage.

Satir, Virginia. *The New Peoplemaking,* rev. ed. Palo Alto, Calif.: Science and Behavior Books, 1988 (paperback). One of the most influential (and easy to read) books of the last twenty-five years on communication and family relationships.

Scanzoni, John. *Sexual Bargaining,* 2d ed. Englewood Cliffs, N. J.: Prentice-Hall, 1980 (paperback). A fine sociological study of power in intimate relationships.

Strayhorn, Joseph. *Talking It Out: A Guide to Effective Communication and Problem Solving.* Champaign, Ill.: Research Press, 1976 (paperback). A valuable study that provides exercises for improving your communication.

Tannen, Deborah. *You Just Don't Understand: Women and Men in Conversation.* New York: William Morrow and Company, 1990. A best-selling, intelligent, and lively discussion of how females use communication to achieve intimacy and males use communication to achieve independence and status.

Suggested Films

Two for the Road (1967). Albert Finney and Audrey Hepburn portray a bickering couple who reminisce about their twelve years of marriage.

sex, lies, and videotape (1989). Deceptions and self-deceptions in a conventional "happy" marriage are brought to light when an old friend, a drifter, reappears—with his video camera.

Who's Afraid of Virginia Woolf? (1966). Adapted from Edward Albee's play, *the* classic example of terrible communication and lack of conflict-resolution skills, starring Richard Burton and Elizabeth Taylor. (The Burton/Taylor couple was originally written as a gay couple.)

READINGS

INTIMACY AND INDEPENDENCE

Deborah Tannen. Excerpt from *You Just Don't Understand*

The author argues that the differences in the way men and women communicate are rooted in intimacy and independence needs. How do these different needs manifest themselves in the way men and women communicate with each other? Do you agree with the author's argument? Why? Can you think of ways in which men express intimacy needs and women independence needs?

Intimacy is key in a world of connection where individuals negotiate complex networks of friendship, minimize differences, try to reach consensus, and avoid the appearance of superiority, which would highlight differences. In a world of status, *independence* is key, because a primary means of establishing status is to tell others what to do, and taking orders is a marker of low status. Though all humans need both intimacy and independence, women tend to focus on the first and men on the second. It is as if their lifeblood ran in different directions.

These differences can give women and men differing views of the same situation, as they did in the case of a couple I will call Linda and Josh. When Josh's old high-school chum called him at work and announced he'd be in town on business the following month, Josh invited him to stay for the weekend. That evening he informed Linda that they were going to have a houseguest, and that he and his chum would go out together the first night to shoot the breeze like old times. Linda was upset. She was going to be away on business the week before, and the Friday night when Josh would be out with his chum would be her first night home. But what upset her the most was that Josh had made these plans on his own and informed her of them, rather than discussing them with her before extending the invitation.

Linda would never make plans, for a weekend or an evening, without first checking with Josh. She can't understand why he doesn't show her the same courtesy and consideration that she

continued on next page

shows him. But when she protests, Josh says, "I can't say to my friend, 'I have to ask my wife for permission'!"

To Josh, checking with his wife means seeking permission, which implies that he is not independent, not free to act on his own. It would make him feel like a child or an underling. To Linda, checking with her husband has nothing to do with permission. She assumes that spouses discuss their plans with each other because their lives are intertwined, so the actions of one have consequences for the other. Not only does Linda not mind telling someone, "I have to check with Josh"; quite the contrary—she likes it. It makes her feel good to know and show that she is involved with someone, that her life is bound up with someone else's.

Linda and Josh both felt more upset by this incident, and others like it, than seemed warranted, because it cut to the core of their primary concerns. Linda was hurt because she sensed a failure of closeness in their relationship: He didn't care about her as much as she cared about him. And he was hurt because he felt she was trying to control him and limit his freedom.

A similar conflict exists between Louise and Howie, another couple, about spending money. Louise would never buy anything costing more than a hundred dollars without discussing it with Howie, but he goes out and buys whatever he wants and feels they can afford, like a table saw or a new power mower. Louise is disturbed, not because she disapproves of the purchases, but because she feels he is acting as if she were not in the picture.

Many women feel it is natural to consult with their partners at every turn, while many men automatically make more decisions without consulting their partners. This may reflect a broad difference in conceptions of decision making. Women expect decisions to be discussed first and made by consensus. They appreciate the discussion itself as evidence of involvement and communication. But many men feel oppressed by lengthy discussions about what they see as minor decisions, and they feel hemmed in if they can't just act without talking first. When women try to initiate a freewheeling discussion by asking, "What do you think?" men often think they are being asked to decide.

Communication is a continual balancing act, juggling the conflicting needs for intimacy and independence. To survive in the world, we have to act in concert with others, but to survive as ourselves, rather than simply as cogs in a wheel, we have to act alone. In some ways, all people are the same: We all eat and sleep and drink and laugh and cough, and often we eat, and laugh at, the same things. But in some ways, each person is different, and individuals' differing wants and preferences may conflict with each other. Offered the same menu, people make different choices. And if there is cake for dessert, there is a chance one person may get a larger piece than another—and an even greater chance that one will *think* the other's piece is larger, whether it is or not.

HOW TO FIGHT FAIR

Judith Viorst

In this reading, Judith Viorst suggests fifteen ways to keep your fights fair. By fighting fairly, couples can use their inevitable conflicts to solidify rather than destroy their relationships. As you read her fighting rules, ask yourself which ones you tend to follow and which ones you tend to ignore. Do you use different rules when you fight with different people, such as friends, dates, partners, siblings, parents or children? Why? What other rules can you add to her list?

I was not fighting fair when I accused Milton of refusing to buy a new car because he was saving the money for the teenaged nymph he was doubtless planning to marry the minute I died an untimely death after the engine of our miserable blue station wagon stalled (yet again) in the middle of a highly trafficked intersection.

Wally was not fighting fair when he blamed his tension and subsequent defeat in the Shadybrook Tennis Club tennis finals on Annabel's not wanting to make love that morning.

And Shari was not fighting fair when she told Mike, who had promised to show up at three and showed up at four, that he was unconsciously perceiving her as the feared and hated mother of his childhood and making her pay for his mother's rejection of him.

No fair!

Now you may want to raise the question of whether it's possible in a marriage to feel furious, hurt, humiliated and/or betrayed and still have sufficient self-restraint to hit above the belt, to fight fair. And you may want to ask another, far more fundamental question: Can two normal people be married and never fight?

I'll start with that second question, to which I have a simple answer: Certainly not.

For the first thing we need to concede is that marriage is a difficult living arrangement and that, as William Dean Howells once wrote, ". . . the silken texture of the marriage tie bears a daily strain of wrong and insult to which no other human relation can be subjected without lesion."

And the next thing we need to concede is that, much as we deeply love and respect our spouses, there will be times when we deeply hate and despise them.

And the third thing we need to concede is that, rational and civilized though we may be, not all our marital differences can be resolved by simply sitting down and *talking* about them. Sooner or later, some feelings we feel and points we need to make will have to be communicated more . . . vigorously.

continued on next page

That vigorous form of communication is what most people mean when they use the word "fight."

Actually, I have become considerably less of a marital fighter in recent years—I just don't enjoy a good fight the way I used to. And although I still firmly believe that it is sometimes absolutely essential to have a fight, I am now more inclined to ask myself before I launch an attack—or before I respond to one—"Is this fight necessary?"

By that I mean: Will this fight resolve a current problem or prevent a future problem or provide a badly needed emotional outlet? Or will we both just wind up feeling bruised? And some-times—not always, but sometimes—having decided a fight can't do anything but hurt, I am able to persuade myself not to fight.

But what is a wife who decides not to fight to do with her feel-ings of anger? Linda offers one ingenious solution. When her husband Phil called from Albany and said that he was tied up and couldn't make the party that he'd practically sworn on his life he was going to make, Linda was apoplectic, but she also knew that she couldn't change his mind. "Hang on, Phil," she told him. "Let me take this in the kitchen." And she put down the phone and ran from the second floor, screaming at the top of her lungs all the way down the stairs: "Miserable, rotten, no-good son of a . . ." and a few other words I'd just as soon not mention. After that, she said, she was able to lift the receiver and ask, with relative calm, "So tell me, Phil, what time *should* I expect you?"

Now there is no point in not having a fight if what we have instead is a cold war (no talking except for basic queries like, "Would you consider it a vicious attack on your masculinity if I asked you to pass the butter?"), or if we translate our repressed rage into bleeding ulcers or headaches, or if we engage in some major marriage-threatening activity like taking a lover or hiring a divorce lawyer. But if we have to fight, and if we want to pre-serve—not massacre—our marriage, what are the limits we need to set to keep the fight we're fighting clean and constructive? Here, from some fighters I've talked with, are several suggestions.

1. *Avoid paranoid overstatements.* (See Milton and Judy's fight.)
2. *Accept responsibility for your own failures.* (See Wally and Annabel's fight.)
3. *Do not practice psychiatry without a license.* (See Shari and Mike's fight.)
4. *Don't wait too long.* We need to consider the story of the genie in the bottle who, during his first thousand years of incarceration, thinks, "Whoever lets me out will get three wishes," and who, during his second thousand years of incarceration, thinks, "Who-ever lets me out I'm gonna kill." Many of us, like that genie, seem to get meaner and more dangerous the longer our grievances are bottled up.
5. *Know what you want.* My friend Nina says that her idea of a clean fight is the delivery of the following crystal-clear message:

"I'm upset; here's why I am; here's what I want"—though it may take some time to figure out what she wants. Recently, for instance, while fighting with her husband yet again about work-ing late at the office night after night, it suddenly struck her that she didn't actually want him to say too hell with the work and miss his deadline, that all she really wanted was for him to say, "I miss you. I miss the baby. I feel terrible about not being home. And you're such a fabulous person for being able to han-dle everything while I'm gone."

She got it.

6. *Figure out what you're really, really fighting about.* There are many battles about, say, his forgetting to make hotel reservations for the car trip out West, or his failing to fuss over you when you get sick, that blow up into something utterly out of propor-tion and nasty because what you're really fighting about, and what's getting you so upset, is the thought that he wouldn't have been (a) so negligent or (b) so uncompassionate IF HE LOVED YOU.

But wait a minute. You may be able to avoid hurling a lot of unpleasant accusations at him if you can recognize that what you are really, *really* fighting about, as is often the case, is differ-ences in style, not lack of love. You may need to recognize, for instance, that although, while you were growing up, your daddy always made hotel reservations and got a million brochures and planned every step of a family trip in advance, some people like to improvise when they travel—that improvisation isn't the same as negligence. You may also need to recognize that although, while you were growing up, a sick person got ten glasses of orange juice and tons of attention and permission to fool around with Mommy's jewelry box, your husband's family was stoic about sickness—that not fussing doesn't have to mean not car-ing. And once you figure out that the real, real fight has nothing to do with IF HE LOVED YOU, you are more likely to have a clean and constructive fight.

7. *Stick to the point.* If you are having a fight about the way he is handling the children, I promise you that it will not advance your argument if you also note that he is overdrawn at the bank, talks with his mouth full and frequently leaves you the car with no gas in the tank.

8. *Stick to the present.* A sense of history is a wonderful thing. Total recall is certainly impressive. Memory and the long, long view surely contribute to the richness of life. But reaching back in time for crimes committed in, say, 1967, when you're fighting about a crime committed, say, yesterday, contributes—and I speak from experience—only trouble.

For several years, when fighting with my husband, I displayed my capacity for total recall, providing him with what I rather smugly liked to call "a sense of perspective." I would, for instance, point out to him that not only had he forgotten to pick up my blouse at the cleaners' that afternoon, but that he had also

continued on next page

failed in his stop-at-the-cleaners' assignments on the following 14 occasions. I would then list the dates and the garments he hadn't picked up, starting with the beige chiffon dress that—because of his carelessness—I wasn't able to wear to our engagement party.

After a couple of decades of this, however, it began to dawn on me that never once did Milton reply to my historical references with a "Hey, thanks for pointing out this destructive pattern of mine; I sure do appreciate it." Instead he replied with, "Bookkeeper! Scorekeeper!" and other far less charming epithets, and the fighting would deteriorate from there. I now follow—and strongly recommend—the statute of limitations my friends Hank and Gail have established: "No matter how perfectly something proves your point, you can't dredge it up if it's more than six months old."

9. *Never, never attack an Achilles' heel.* If your husband has confessed to you that his cruel high-school classmates nicknamed him "The Hairy Ape," and if, in adulthood, he still has fears about being furrier than most, you can—when you are furious—call him every name in the book, but you can't call him that one. I have a friend who (excuse the mixed metaphor) locates her Achilles' heel in "my fat butt, which I always worry about and which my husband has always assured me he loves." She says that if, in the course of a fight, he told her that he'd never liked her butt, she might never forgive him.

Two Achilles' heels that are mentioned so often that they must be universal are sexual performance and parents. It seems that it is tricky enough, in life's mellowest moments, to discuss sexual dissatisfactions with a mate; but to scream in the heat of battle, as Louise confessed she once did, that "At least my first husband knew where to put it," is a rotten idea. And so is calling your mother-in-law an "old bat," even though her own son—your husband—has used those very words on many occasions. For some reason, we all seem to feel that although we're allowed to criticize our parents, it's dirty pool for our spouses to be doing it.

10. *Don't overstate your injuries.* Don't claim—either directly or indirectly—that he is giving you migraines or destroying you psychologically unless he is. Oh, I know that it is sometimes tempting to score a few points by pressing your fingers to your temples and saying, in the middle of a fight, "Quick, get me my pills, the pain is blinding," or "Maybe I ought to go into psychoanalysis." It is also sometimes tempting to burst into tears—particularly of the "you're so brutal you even make strong women weep," muffled-sob variety. But don't. For overstating your injuries is not just dirty fighting; it is, sooner than you can imagine, ineffective. If you want him to believe that he's gone *too* far

when he's gone too far, you've got to try to maintain your credibility.

11. *Don't overstate your threats.* Many people, in the course of a fight, make threats they don't mean, like, "If you don't slow down, I'm getting out and walking," or "If you don't shut up, I'm moving to a hotel," or even "If you don't stop seeing her, I'm getting a divorce." The trouble with these threats is that there is always the risk of being called on them and either actually having to, say, get out and walk or losing a lot of face. Like overstatements of injury, these threats—if not followed through—are subject to the "boy who cried wolf" syndrome. Even worse, I know two women whose "if you don't stop seeing her" ultimatums converted painful marital fights into fierce and fatal power struggles, ending in divorces that neither couple, I am convinced, actually wanted.

12. *Don't just talk—listen.* You needn't go along with a word he says, but shut up long enough to let him say it. And pay attention. For as a lawyer friend likes to point out to her spouse in the midst of a fight: "You can disagree with what I say as long as you can repeat my views to my satisfaction."

13. *Give respect to feelings as well as to facts.* You are not allowed to say, when your husband tells you that he is feeling ignored or put down, "That's absurd. You shouldn't feel that way." You may argue that perhaps he is overreacting or misinterpreting, but you have to acknowledge that he feels what he feels.

14. *There needn't be one winner and one loser.* You both could agree to compromise. You both could agree to try harder. You each could understand the other's point of view. You also could lose without treating it as a defeat. You also could win (this really takes class!) without treating it as a victory.

15. *When you're finished fighting, do not continue sniping.* This includes doing take-backs like "I said I'd go but I didn't say I'd enjoy it," or staring bitterly out a window because, as you explain when asked what's wrong, "I guess my wounds don't heal as quickly as yours do." Nor, after a fight, is it useful to murmur things like "Why is it always my fault?" or "Why am I the one who makes all the concessions?" or—as in the fight between Milton and me—"Now that you've agreed to buy a new car, I only hope I survive until it gets here."

Though of course we are bound to slip, we at least should try to follow these tips. Let's face it: All is *not* fair in love and war. Clean and constructive fighting is better than down and dirty fighting, that's for sure. And fighting by the rules could help us live happily—although scrappily—ever after.

Family Violence and Sexual Abuse

P R E V I E W

To gain a sense of what you already know about the material covered in this chapter, answer "true" or "false" to the following statements. You will find the answers on page 498.

1. Intimate relationships of any kind increase the likelihood of violence. True or false?
2. Rape by an acquaintance, date, or partner is less likely than rape by a stranger. True or false?
3. Male aggression is generally considered to be a desirable trait in our society. True or false?
4. Studies of family violence have helped strengthen policies for dealing with domestic offenders. True or false?
5. Physically abused children are often perceived by their parents as "different" from other children. True or false?
6. Sibling violence is the most widespread form of family violence. True or false?
7. Relatively few missing children have been kidnapped by strangers. True or false?
8. In some cultures, circumcision might be considered abusive. True or false?
9. Sexual abuse by a family member is more likely to indicate a character disorder of the offender than a dysfunction of the family itself. True or false?
10. Brother/sister incest is generally harmless. True or false?

Despite fears to the contrary, it is not a stranger but a so-called loved one who is most likely to assault, rape, or murder us.

Russell and R. Emerson Dobash

You can always kill a relative with a gun that isn't loaded.

Mark Twain

IT IS AN UNHAPPY FACT that intimacy or relatedness in any form can increase the likelihood of violence or sexual abuse. Although this may seem odd at first, think about whom our society "permits" us to shove, hit, or kick. It is not a stranger, fellow student, co-worker, or employer, for if we assaulted any of them, we would run great risk of being arrested. It is with our intimates that we are allowed to do such things. Dating, loving, or being related seems to give us permission to be violent when we are angry. Those nearest and dearest are also those most likely to be slapped, punched, kicked, bitten, burned, stabbed, and shot (Gelles and Cornell, 1990; Gelles and Straus, 1988). For some boyfriends, husbands, or parents, intimacy seems to confer a right to be physically or sexually abusive. Only war zones and urban riot scenes are more dangerous places than families.

If this seems to be an exaggeration, consider the following points:

- ◆ Every thirty seconds, a woman is beaten by her boyfriend or husband.
- ◆ Thirty to 40 percent of college students in various studies report violence in dating relationships.
- ◆ At least a million American children are physically abused by their parents each year.
- ◆ Almost a million parents are physically assaulted by their adolescent or youthful children every year.
- ◆ As many as 27 percent of American women and 16 percent of men have been the victims of childhood sexual abuse, much of it in their own families.

Until the 1970s, Americans believed that when they locked their homes at night, they locked violence out; sadly, they also locked violence in (Walker, 1986). There is a note of hope, however. Due to the diligence of certain social scientists, physicians, mental health professionals, and concerned activists, family violence and sexual abuse are now matters of national concern. But even though these problems have been identified, there is much to be done toward reducing or eliminating them.

Researchers have not been in complete agreement about what constitutes violence. For the purposes of this book, we use Richard Gelles and Claire Pedrick Cornell's (1990) definition of **violence:** "an act carried out with the intention or perceived intention of causing physical pain or injury to another person." There are other prevalent forms of abuse, of course, such as neglect and emotional abuse, but the focus of this chapter is *physical* violence and sexual abuse. Violence may be seen as a continuum, with "normal" abuse (such as spanking) at one end and abusive violence (acts with high potential for causing injury) at the other extreme. We must look at the continuum as a whole to be concerned with "families who shoot and stab each other as well as those who spank and shove, . . . [as] one cannot be understood without considering the other" (Straus, Gelles and Steinmetz, 1980). (For a review of literature on domestic violence and sexual abuse of children, see Gelles and Conte, 1991.)

❖ MODELS OF FAMILY VIOLENCE

To better understand violence within the family, we must look at its place in the larger sociocultural environment (for the sociocultural roots, see Gil, 1986; Levine, 1986). Aggression is a trait that our society labels as generally desirable, especially for males. Getting ahead at work, asserting ourselves in relationships, and winning at sports are all culturally approved actions. But does aggression necessarily lead to violence? All families have their ups and downs, and all family members at times experience anger toward one another. How do we explain that violence erupts more frequently and with more severe consequences in some families than in others? The principal models used in understanding family violence are discussed in the following sections.

THE PSYCHIATRIC MODEL. The psychiatric model finds the source of family violence within the personality of the abuser. It assumes that he or she is violent as a result of mental or emotional illness, psychopathology, or perhaps alcohol or drug misuse. Although research indicates that fewer than 10 percent of family violence cases are attributable to psychiatric causes, the idea that people are violent *because* they are crazy or drunk is widely held (Gelles and Cornell, 1990; Steele, 1980). Gelles and Cornell (1990) suggest that this model is compelling because "if we can persist in believing that violence and abuse are the products of aberrations or sickness, and, therefore, believe ourselves to be well, then our acts cannot be hurtful or abusive."

THE ECOLOGICAL MODEL. The ecological perspective looks at the child's development within the family environment and the family's development within the community. Psychologist James Garbarino (1977, 1982) has suggested that cultural support for physical force against children combines with lack of family support in the community to increase the risk of intrafamily violence. Under this model, a child who doesn't "match" well with the parents (such as child with emotional or developmental disabilities) and a family that is under stress (from, for example, unemployment or poor health) and that has little community support (such as child care or medical care) is at increased risk for child abuse.

THE PATRIARCHY MODEL. The patriarchy (male-dominance) model of family violence draws its conclusions from a historical perspective. It holds that most social systems have traditionally placed women in a subordinate position to men, thus condoning or supporting the institution of male violence (Dobash and Dobash, 1979; Martin, 1981). There is no doubt that violence against women and children, and indeed violence in general, has had an integral place in most societies throughout history. Taken alone, however, this theory does not adequately explain the variations in degrees of violence among families in the same society. *Co-dependant*↖

> *Men are but children of a larger growth.*
>
> *John Dryden*

physical & mental violence

SOCIAL SITUATIONAL AND SOCIAL LEARNING MODELS. The social models are related to the ecological and patriarchy models in that they view the sources of violence as originating in the social structure. The social situational model views family violence as arising from two main factors: structural stress (such as low income or illness) and cultural norms (such as the "spare the rod and spoil the child" ethic) (Gelles and Cornell, 1990). In this model, groups with few resources, such as the poor, are seen to be at greater risk for family violence than those who are well-off. The social learning model holds that people learn to be violent from society at large and from their families. Although it is true that many perpetrators of family violence were themselves abused as children, it is also true that many victims of childhood violence do *not* become violent parents. These theories do not account for this discrepancy.

> *By our readiness to allow arms to be purchased at will and fired at whim, we have created an atmosphere in which violence and hatred have become popular pastimes.*
>
> *Martin Luther King, Jr.*

RESOURCE MODEL. William Goode's (1971) resource theory can be applied to family violence. This model assumes that social systems are based on force or the threat of force. A person acquires power by mustering personal, social, and economic resources. Thus, according to Goode, the person with the most resources is the least likely to resort to overt force. Gelles and Cornell (1990) explain, "A husband who wants to be the dominant person in the family but has little education, has a job low in prestige and income, and lacks interpersonal skills may chose to use violence to maintain the dominant position."

AN EXCHANGE/SOCIAL CONTROL MODEL. Gelles and Cornell (1990) posit a two-part theory of family violence. The first part, exchange theory, holds that in our interactions we constantly weigh the perceived rewards against the costs. When Gelles and Cornell say "people hit and abuse family members because they can," they are applying exchange theory. The expectation is that "people will only use violence toward family members when the costs of being violent do not outweigh the rewards." (The possible rewards of violence might be getting one's own way, exerting superiority, working off anger or stress, or exacting revenge. Costs could include being hit back, being arrested, being jailed, losing social status, or dissolving the family.)

Social control raises the costs of violent behavior through such means as arrest, imprisonment, loss of status, or loss of income. Three characteristics of families that may reduce social control—and thus make violence more likely—are the following:

1. *Inequality.* Men are stronger than women and often have more economic power and social status. Adults are more powerful than children.
2. *The Private Nature of the Family.* People are reluctant to look outside the family for help, and outsiders (the police or neighbors, for example) may hesitate to intervene in private matters. The likelihood of family violence goes down as the number of nearby friends and relatives increases (Gelles and Cornell, 1990; Nye, 1976).
3. *"Real Man" Image.* In some American subcultures, aggressive male behavior brings approval. The violent man in these groups may actually gain status among his peers for asserting his "authority."

The exchange/social control model is useful for looking at treatment and prevention strategies for family violence, which we will discuss later on in this chapter.

❖ BATTERED WOMEN

No one knows for certain how many battered women there are in the United States, but government figures indicate that battering is one of the most common and underreported crimes in the country. Here are some figures concerning violence against women in the United States (Gelles and Cornell, 1990; Gelles and Straus, 1988):

◆ About one woman in twenty-two is the victim of abusive violence each year.
◆ About half of battered women are beaten at least three times a year.
◆ One-third of murdered women were killed by their husbands or lovers.
◆ In a national survey, about one in four wives and one in three husbands said that slapping a partner was "at least somewhat necessary, normal, or good."

Battering, as used in the literature of family violence, is a catchall term that includes, but is not limited to, slapping, punching, knocking down, choking, kicking, hitting with objects, threatening with weapons, stabbing, and shooting. The use of physical force against women is certainly not a new phenomenon. It may be thought of as a time-honored tradition in our culture. The commonly used term *rule of thumb* derives from the legally sanctioned (until the nineteenth century) practice

The Mythology of Family Violence and Sexual Abuse

The understanding of family violence is often obscured by the different mythologies surrounding such violence. Below are twelve popular myths about family violence and sexual abuse in our society. Some of these myths may apply to some cases, but as generalizations they are not accurate. Many of these myths are accepted by the victims of family violence, as well as by the perpetrators themselves. As you look at the following myths, which ones do you believe (or have you believed)? What was the basis or source of your beliefs? If you no longer believe a particular myth, what changed your mind?

◆ Family violence is extremely rare.
◆ Family violence is restricted to families with low levels of education and low socioeconomic status.
◆ Most family violence is caused by alcohol or drug abuse.
◆ Violent spouses or parents have psychopathic personalities.
◆ Violent families are not loving families.
◆ Battered women cause their own battering because they are masochistic or crazy.
◆ A battered woman can always leave home.
◆ Most child sexual abuse is perpetrated by strangers.
◆ Sexual abuse in families is a fairly rare occurrence.
◆ Abused children will grow up to abuse their own children.
◆ The police give adequate protection to battered women.
◆ Most of society does not condone domestic violence.

These myths function to hide the extent of physical and sexual abuse that actually takes place inside a painfully large number of American families. Belief in these myths makes it possible to avoid some of the unhappy realities.

of "disciplining" one's wife with a switch or rod—provided it was no wider than the disciplinarian's thumb (a good example of the basis for the patriarchy model).

In recent years the subject of wife battering has gained public notoriety. It remains, however, subordinate in the public mind to the physical and sexual abuse of children. In part, this may be because historically and culturally, women are considered "appropriate" victims of domestic violence (Gelles and Cornell, 1990). Many expect, understand, and accept the idea that women sometimes need to be "put in their place" by men. Such misogynistic ideas provide the cultural basis for the physical and sexual abuse of women.

Battered Women and Battering Men

Battering occurs at all levels of society. It occurs most frequently among those under thirty years of age (Straus, Gelles, and Steinmetz, 1980), and it is apparently twice as prevalent among black couples as among white couples. It should be noted, however, that the rate of violence against black women by their partners appears to have dropped considerably in recent years. A 1985 survey showed a 43 percent decrease in such abuse since 1975 (Hampton, Gelles, and Harrop, 1989). (Possible reasons for this decline will be discussed later on.) Although no social class is immune to it, most studies find that marital violence is more likely to occur in low-income, low-status families (Gelles and Cornell, 1990; see Hampton, 1991 for a collection of essays on African-American family violence).

CHARACTERISTICS OF BATTERED WOMEN. Although early studies of battering relationships seemed to indicate a cluster of personality characteristics constituting a typical battered woman, more recent studies have not borne out this viewpoint. Factors such as self-esteem or childhood experiences of violence do not appear to be necessarily associated with a woman's being in an assaultive relationship (Hotaling and Sugarman, 1990). There are two characteristics, however, that do appear to be highly

[handwritten note in margin: 1/3 believe slapp is normal or good]

2 factors

correlated with wife assault: low socioeconomic status and a high degree of marital conflict. A number of studies have found that wife abuse is both more common and more severe in families of lower socioeconomic status (Gelles and Straus, 1988; Hotaling and Sugarman, 1986, 1990). Marital conflict—and the apparent inability to resolve it through negotiation and compromise—is also a factor in many battering relationships. Hotaling and Sugarman (1990) found that conflicts in these marriages often were associated with a difference in expectations about the division of labor in the family, frequent drinking by the husband, and the wife's having attained a higher educational level than the husband. These researchers concluded that it is not useful to focus "primarily on the victim in the assessment of risk to wife assault."

CHARACTERISTICS OF BATTERERS. A man who systematically inflicts violence on his wife or lover especially has some or all of the following traits (Edelson et al., 1985; Gelles and Cornell, 1990; Goldstein and Rosenbaum, 1985; Margolin, Sibner, and Gleberman, 1988; Walker, 1979, 1984).

◆ He believes the common myths about battering.
◆ He believes in the traditional home, family, and gender-role stereotypes.
◆ He has low self-esteem and may use violence as a means of demonstrating power or adequacy.
◆ He may be sadistic, pathologically jealous, or passive-aggressive.
◆ He may have a "Dr. Jekyll and Mr. Hyde" personality, being capable at times of great charm.
◆ He may use sex as an act of aggression.
◆ He believes in the moral rightness of his violent behavior (even though he may "accidentally" go too far).

Leonore Walker (1984) believes that a man's battering is not the result of his interactions with his partner or any kind of provocative personality traits of the partner. She wrote:

The best prediction of future violence was a history of past violent behavior. This included witnessing, receiving, and committing violent acts in [the] childhood home; violent acts toward pets, inanimate objects, or other people; previous criminal record; longer time in the military service; and previous expression of violent behavior toward women. If these items are added to a history of temper tantrums, insecurity, need to keep the environment stable, easily threatened by minor upsets, jealousy, possessiveness, and the ability to be charming, manipulative, and seductive to get what he wants, and hostile, nasty and mean when he doesn't succeed—then the risk for battering becomes very high. If alcohol abuse problems are included, the pattern becomes classic.

Sociologist Norman Denzin (1984) defined the violence of batterers as "the attempt to regain, through the use of emotional and physical force, something that has been lost." (Here we see resource theory at work.) Denzin wrote:

The goal of the violent act eludes the man of violence. He is drawn over and over again into the cycle of violence. He can never succeed in establishing his dominance and will over the will of the other. In this sense his violent actions are doomed to failure, yet his very failure destroys the relationship with the one he wishes to control.

BATTERED HUSBANDS. There have been speculations about the prevalence of battered husbands. We have, after all, the cartoon image of Blondie chasing Dagwood with a rolling pin. (We don't see Dagwood chasing Blondie with a gun or knife, however, which is a much more realistic depiction of family violence.) Although it is undoubtedly true that some men are injured in attacks by wives or lovers, "husband batter-ing" is probably a misleading term. The overwhelming majority of victims of adult family violence are women; men are rarely the victims of battery (Berk, Newton, and Berk, 1983). In one study (Saunders, 1986) investigating "husband abuse," the over-whelming majority of women reported that they acted in self-defense; they did not initiate the violence. Their actions did not cause noticeable injury. Indeed, a woman may attempt to inflict damage on a man in self-defense or retaliation, but most women have no hope of prevailing in hand-to-hand combat with a man. A woman may be severely injured simply trying to defend herself. As Gelles and Cornell (1990) observed, although there may be similar rates in hitting, "when injury is con-sidered, marital violence is primarily a problem of victimized women." While male violence dramatically overshadows female violence, female violence does exist. Suzanne Steinmetz (1987) suggests that some scholars "deemphasize the importance of women's use of violence." As such, there is a "conspiracy of silence [which] fails to recognize that family violence is *never* inconsequential."

The Cycle of Violence

Lenore Walker's (1979) research has revealed a three-phase battering cycle. The duration of each phase may vary, but the cycle goes on . . . and on.

◆ Phase One: *Tension Building*. Tension is in the air. She tries to do her job well, to be conciliatory. Minor battering incidents may occur. She denies her own rising anger. Tension continues to build.
◆ Phase Two: *The Explosion*. He loses control. Sometimes she will precipitate the incident to "get it over with." He generally sets out to "teach her a lesson" and goes on from there. This is the shortest phase, usually lasting several hours but sometimes continuing for two or three days or longer.
◆ Phase Three: *"In Love" Again*. Tension has now been released and the batterer is contrite, begs forgiveness, and sincerely promises never to do it again. She chooses to believe him and forgives him. This "symbiotic bonding" (interdependence) makes intervention, help, or change unlikely during this phase.

Often the battered woman is surprised by what has touched off the battering inci-dent. It may have been something outside the home—at the husband's job, for example. He may have come home drunk or he may have been drinking steadily at home. Alcohol is implicated in many battering incidents, possibly the majority. Results of studies of alcohol and battering vary widely; alcohol problems were reported for assaultive husbands in between 35 and 93 percent of cases, depending on the study (Leonard and Jacob, 1988; see Edelson et al., 1985, for a review of con-flicting studies about battering and alcohol use.) In a battering relationship, the woman may not only suffer physical damage but also may be seriously harmed emo-tionally by a constant sense of danger and the expectation of violence that weaves a "web of terror" about her (Edelson et al., 1985).

Marital Rape

Marital rape represents a form of battering. Studies have reported that at least one-third of battered women have also been sexually assaulted by their partners (Finkel-hor and Yllo, 1983; O'Reilly, 1983). According to David Finkelhor and Kersti Yllo (1985), "a marriage license is [considered] a license to rape." Although far too many husbands apparently agree with this statement, most states—beginning in the late

When we want to read of the deeds that are done for love, whither do we turn? To the murder column.

George Bernard Shaw

1970s—have enacted legislation to make at least some forms of marital rape illegal. As of 1990, forty-two states and the District of Columbia had enacted marital rape laws that prohibit husbands from forcing wives to engage in sex without their consent. In twenty-six of those states, husbands may be exempted from charges in some cases—for example, if they rape their wives by force but without imposing additional violence, such as threatening with a weapon, or if the woman is asleep, drugged, or ill (Russell, 1990). (When California adopted its marital rape law, state senator Bob Wilson protested, "If you can't rape your wife, who can you rape?" [O'Reilly, 1983].)

In Kentucky, Missouri, New Mexico, North Carolina, Oklahoma, South Carolina, South Dakota, and Utah, husbands can be prosecuted for marital rape only if they are living apart from their wives or if divorce proceedings have been started (Russell, 1990). And even though marital rape is now considered a crime in most states, there still remains the problem of enforcing the law. Many people discount rape in marriage as a "marital tiff" that has little to do with "real" rape (Finkelhor and Yllo, 1985). Many victims themselves have difficulty acknowledging that their husbands' sexual violence is indeed rape. And all too often, judges seem more in sympathy with the perpetrator than with the victim, especially if he is very intelligent, successful, and well-educated (Faidley, 1989). There is also the "notion that the male breadwinner should be the beneficiary of some special immunity because of his family's dependence on him" (Russell, 1990). Diana Russell goes on to say:

> On the basis of such an argument, it follows that it would be a violation of the principle of equity to incarcerate men who beat up and/or rape women who are *not* their wives. Specifically, it would not be fair to the wives and children of employed stranger rapists, acquaintance rapists, date rapists, lover rapists, authority figure rapists, or rapists who rape their friends. Why should these families have to endure the loss of their breadwinners if the families of husbands of rapists are spared this hardship?

Because these kinds of attitudes are so entrenched in the American psyche, marital rape remains mostly unpublicized and underreported.

In Russell's landmark study (1982, rev. 1990) on marital rape, 930 randomly selected women in San Francisco were interviewed. Eighty-seven out of the 644 who had ever been married (about 13 percent) had been raped by their husbands. Russell found that force was used in 84 percent of the rapes and the threat of force in 9 percent. (The remaining victims were asleep, intoxicated, or surprised and not able to resist.) Thirty-one percent of the wives reported their rapes as isolated events that occurred only once. But another 31 percent reported that they had been raped more than twenty times. Other studies of wives who had been raped by their husbands (cited in Russell, 1984) reported that between 59 to 87 percent were raped multiple times.

Marital rape victims experience betrayal, anger, humiliation, and guilt. Following their rapes, many wives feel intense anger toward their husbands. One woman said, "So, he says, 'You're my wife and you're gonna. . . I just laid there thinking 'I hate him, I hate him so much.' " Another expressed her humiliation and sense of "dirtiness" by taking a shower: "I tried to wash it away, but you can't. I felt like a sexual garbage can" (Finkelhor and Yllo, 1985). Some feel guilt and blame themselves for not being better wives. And some develop negative self-images and view their lack of sexual desire as a reflection of their own inadequacies rather than as a consequence of abuse.

Dating Violence and Rape

In the last decade or so, researchers have become increasingly aware that violence and sexual assault can take place in all forms of intimate relationships. Violence between intimates is not restricted to family members. Even casual or dating relationships can be marred by violence or rape. (See *Family Relations* 40:1 [Jan. 1991] for a collection of articles on courtship aggression.)

DATING VIOLENCE. There is an alarming incidence of physical violence in dating relationships. Evidence suggests that it approaches the level of marital violence (Lane and Gwartney-Gibbs, 1985). Recent studies indicate that both men and women engage in violent behavior in dating relationships (Makepeace, 1987). One sample of 325 college students indicated that 40 percent of the women and 30 percent of the men had inflicted or received violence in their dating relationships (Lane and Gwartney-Gibbs, 1985). Another study suggested that 30 percent of the women and 25 percent of the men were the recipients of dating violence (McKinney, 1986). Even though both sexes may be involved in dating violence, greater injury is almost always inflicted on women, and unlike men, they are also sexually assaulted (Makepeace, 1986; Sugarman and Hotaling, 1989).

Violence is not usually an isolated, one-time event. One study showed that the mean number of incidents for those involved in violent dating relationships was 9.6 (Roscoe and Benaske, 1985). Although it may seem logical to assume that dating violence leads to marital violence, little actual research has been done in this area. It does appear, however, that the issues involved in dating violence are different than those generally involved in spousal violence. While marital violence may erupt over domestic issues such as housekeeping and childrearing (Hotaling and Sugarman, 1990; Walker, 1984), dating violence is far more likely to be precipitated by jealousy or rejection (Lloyd and Emery, 1990; Makepeace, 1989). One woman recounted the following incident (Lloyd and Emery, 1990):

I was waiting for him to pick me up in front of school. I was befriended by some guys and we struck up a conversation. When my boyfriend picked me up he didn't say anything. When we got home, physical violence occurred for the first time in our relationship. I had no idea it was coming. He caught me on the jaw, and hit me up against the wall. I couldn't cry or scream or anything—all I could do was look at him. He picked me up and threw me against the wall and then started yelling and screaming at me that he didn't want me talking to other guys. . . .

Lloyd and Emery found the other themes of dating violence involved the man's use of alcohol or drugs, "unpredictable" reasons, and intense anger.

Although many women will leave a dating relationship after one violent incident, others will stay through repeated episodes. Women with "modern" gender-role attitudes are more likely to leave than those with traditional attitudes (Flynn, 1990). Women who leave violent partners cite the following factors in making the decision to break up: a series of broken promises that the man will end the violence, an improved self-image ("I deserve better"), escalation of the violence, and physical and emotional help from family and friends (Lloyd and Emery, 1990). Apparently, counselors, physicians, and law enforcement agencies are not widely used in these situations (Pirog-Good and Stets, 1989; see Lloyd, 1991, for implications for intervention in courtship violence.)

ACQUAINTANCE RAPE. Although the majority of rapes *reported* to the police are stranger rapes, rapists may be acquaintances, dates, husbands, fathers, or other family members, as well as strangers. As many as half or more of all rapes involve someone whom the victim knows or with whom she is acquainted (Russell, 1984). Because many people accept the myth that rapes are committed by strangers, many

jealousy & rejection

acquaintance rape victims do not perceive themselves as having been raped since the rapist is a date, boyfriend, or cohabitor (Finkelhor and Yllo, 1980; Russell, 1984). Nor do the men who sexually assault their dates, friends, or partners perceive themselves as rapists, because they, too, believe that rapists are strangers. These men also believe that as the woman's date, boyfriend or partner, they have the "right" to have sex with her. They may believe that women are sexually passive and that when they say "no," they really mean "yes" or "make me" (Lewin, 1985). In one study, 22.5 percent of the males surveyed thought that "forced sex" was acceptable under certain conditions. These men interpreted a woman asking a man out, going to his apartment, or allowing him to pay for the date as signs that she wanted sex, and they thought that rape could be justified if she refused (Muehlenhard, 1989).

One study (Koss, 1989) on sexual aggression in college (in which thirty-two schools and 6,159 students participated) indicated the following:

◆ Almost 54 percent of the women surveyed had been sexually victimized in some way.
◆ Fifteen percent of the women had been raped, and 12 percent had experienced attempted rape; almost 90 percent knew their assailants.
◆ Forty-seven percent of the rapes were by first dates, casual dates, or romantic acquaintances.
◆ Twenty-five percent of the men had perpetrated sexual aggression. Three percent had attempted rape and 4 percent had actually raped.
◆ Almost three-quarters of the raped women did not identify their experiences as rapes.

Acquaintance rape is difficult for many women to recognize since it does not meet stereotypical images of rape. As one rape crisis advocate (Sherman, 1985) noted, "Women are hesitant to think that someone they met in an English class or at a fraternity party might assault them. We tend to visualize rapists as wearing stocking masks and jumping out at a woman from dark alleys."

Why Women Stay in Violent Relationships

Violence in relationships generally develops a continuing pattern of abuse over time. We know from systems theory that all relationships have some degree of mutual dependence, and battering relationships are certainly no different. Women stay in or return to violent situations for many reasons. Some common ones are the following:

◆ *Economic dependence.* Even if a woman is financially secure, she may not perceive herself as being able to cope with economic matters.
◆ *Religious pressure.* She may feel that the teachings of her religion require her to keep the family together at all costs, to submit to her husband's will, and to try harder.
◆ *"The children need a father."* She may sincerely believe that even a father who beats the mother is better than no father at all. If the abusing husband also assaults the children, this may be the factor that motivates the woman to seek help (but not always).
◆ *Fear of being alone.* She may have no meaningful relationships outside her marriage. Her husband may have systematically cut off her ties to other family members, friends, and potential support sources. She has nowhere to go and no way to get any real perspective on her situation.
◆ *Belief in the American dream.* This woman has accepted without question the "cult of domesticity and beliefs of family harmony and bliss" (Dobash and Dobash, 1979).

Battering leaves women unsafe in their own homes.

Even though her existence belies this myth, she continues to believe that it is how it should (and can) be.

◆ *Pity.* She puts her husband's needs ahead of her own.

◆ *Guilt and shame.* She feels that it is her own fault if her marriage isn't working and that if she left, everyone would know she is a failure, or her husband might kill himself.

◆ *Duty and responsibility.* She feels she must keep her marriage vows "till death us do part."

◆ *Fear for her life.* She believes she may be killed if she tries to escape.

◆ *Love.* She loves him; he loves her. On her husband's death, one elderly woman (a university professor) spoke of her fifty-three years in a battering relationship (Walker, 1979): "We did everything together. . . . I loved him; you know, even when he was brutal and mean. . . . I'm sorry he's dead, although there were days when I wished he would die. . . . He was my best friend. . . . He beat me right up to the end. . . . It was a good life and I really do miss him."

Leonore Walker (1979) theorizes that women stay in battering relationships as a result of "learned helplessness." According to Walker, women who are repeatedly battered develop much lower self-concepts than women in nonbattering relationships. They begin to feel that they cannot control the battering or the events that surround them. Through a process of behavioral reinforcement, they learn to become helpless. As Walker noted, "Women are systematically taught that their personal wants, survival, and anatomy do not depend on effective and creative responses to life situations, but rather on their physical beauty to men. They learn that they have no direct control over the circumstances of their lives." If violence is used against them, women may even become desensitized to the accompanying pain and fear. The more it happens, the more helpless they feel and the less they are able to see alternative possibilities.

There are other reasons why women remain in or return to these relationships. They may have limited education or job skills and hence be economically dependent. Or they may think that they can stop the husband's violence. Lee Bowker (1983) reported that women used a variety of strategies to stop their husbands' abusiveness. These ranged from passive defense techniques (covering their bodies with

Remember this
learned helplessness -
ex children cannot change
their environment.
ex. an employer taking
advantage of you.

arms or hands) to seeking informal help (friends) or formal help (counseling through a social service agency). The particular strategy was not important in stopping the violence, however. What made the crucial difference appeared to be the woman's determination that the violence *must* cease.

Gelles and Straus (1979) found that women who left abusive marriages were often those who had received the most severe abuse. They also found that the age of the children in the family was significant. The older the children, the more likely they were to be involved in the parents' disputes. Many women left after their teenage children had been injured while trying to protect them.

Alternatives: Police Intervention, Shelters, and Abuser Programs

Professionals who deal with domestic violence have long debated the relative merits of *compassion versus control* as intervention strategies (Mederer and Gelles, 1989; Rosenfeld and Newberger, 1977). Although more understanding of the dynamics of abusive relationships and the deterrence process is clearly needed, we can see that both approaches have their place. Controlling measures (which raise the "costs" of violent behavior), such as arrest, prosecution, and imprisonment, and compassionate measures, such as shelters, education, counseling, and support groups, have been shown to be successful to varying degrees under varying conditions. Used together, these interventions may be quite effective. Mederer and Gelles (1989) suggest that control measures may be used to "motivate violent offenders to participate in treatment programs."

BATTERED WOMEN AND THE LAW. As a result of family violence studies and feminist pressure, there has been a movement toward an implementation of stricter policies for dealing with domestic offenders. In Minneapolis, a study (Sherman and Berk, 1984) determined that arrest was the most effective deterrent to repeated abuse; arrests in domestic violence cases there have tripled. If an officer believes that violence has occurred within four hours before the police arrived on the scene, he or she may make a *presumptive arrest* even if the battered spouse does not wish to press charges. The Minneapolis researchers discovered that arrest was almost twice as effective as counseling or ordering the assailant off the property in preventing a recurrent assault against a woman. Researcher Lawrence Sherman (1984) suggested that arrest is a powerful deterrent because generally "the power balance is distorted in favor of the one who has the bigger muscles. When they call the police, women involve the police muscles and even up the power balance."

A more recent study, however, questioned the accuracy of the Minneapolis study's conclusions. A replicated study in Omaha indicated that although arrest did not increase the level of later violence to the woman, neither did it reduce the amount of violence (Dunford, Huizinga, and Elliot, 1989). The study did find reduced levels of violence, however, if the assailant was not present when the police arrived and an arrest warrant was issued. Thus it appears that the *threat* of arrest (which lowers one's social status) may be a better deterrent than actual arrest (Gelles and Cornell, 1990; Mederer and Cornell, 1989). Today, nearly a third of the largest police forces in the nation are instructed to arrest the assailants, although the jury is still out as to whether mandatory arrest is actually effective.

There is a general perception that domestic disputes are the most dangerous form of police work, but this assumption has been challenged. Desmond Ellis (1987) suggests that instead of being a leading cause of police deaths, domestic disturbances accounted nationally for only 5.4 percent of police fatalities over a ten-year period.

Deaths associated with traffic pursuits and stops, in contrast, accounted for over 12 percent of police fatalities.

BATTERED WOMEN'S SHELTERS. At the point when a woman finds that she can leave an abusive relationship, even temporarily, she may have any of a number of serious needs. If she is fleeing an attack, she may need immediate medical attention and physical protection. She will need accommodation for herself and possibly her children. She will certainly need access to support, counseling, and various types of assistance—money, food stamps, or other basic survival items for herself and her children. She will need to deal with informed, compassionate professionals such as police, doctors, and social workers.

In the late 1970s, the shelter movement developed to meet the needs of many battered women. The shelter movement has grown slowly, hampered by lack of funding and mixed reaction from the public. There are an estimated 1,000 shelters throughout the United States, a vast improvement over the estimated *five or six* shelters in existence in 1976 (Gelles and Cornell, 1990). Besides offering immediate safe shelter (the locations of safe houses are usually known only to the residents and shelter workers), these refuges let battered women realize that they are not alone in their misery and help them form supportive networks with one another. They also provide many other services for battered women who call, such as information, advice, or referrals. Walker's (1979) research indicated that about 50 percent of women who stay longer than a week in shelters will not return to their battering relationships. She further noted that

the percentage rises dramatically if the safe house remains open to those women who return home and then want to come back to the refuge. . . The back and forth process may occur as often as five times before the battered woman is able to leave home permanently.

Those women who seem to benefit most from shelter stays are those who have decided to "take charge of their lives," according to one study (Berk, Newton, and Berk, 1986). Hampton, Gelles, and Harrop (1989) suggest that the dramatic drop in wife abuse among African Americans may be the result of black women's "increased status" coupled with their apparent willingness to make use of shelters and other programs.

ABUSER PROGRAMS. Programs for battering men appear to be helpful in some cases, but not all. Psychotherapy, group discussion, stress management, or communication skills classes may be available through mental health agencies, women's crisis programs, or various self-help groups. One study (Gondolf, 1988) looked at fifty-one men in a program for batterers and fifty-four men who had contacted the program but did not participate. The researchers found that the participants and nonparticipants had very different views on how to stop their violence. The participants felt that the social aspects of the program—friendship and group interaction—were useful. Nonparticipants "appeared more transient, resistant to help, and more evasive." Most men in both groups seemed to rely more on "willful self-restraint to stop their violence rather than on personal and social change." Gondolf suggests that anger control is not any more successful than any other technique for stopping violence and that it "may in fact divert abusers from developing more substantial stopping strategies." The extent to which attending such groups actually changes abusing men's violent behavior is difficult to measure (Gelles and Conte, 1991). Gondolf's studies of men who have completed voluntary programs (1987, 1988) showed that

In the United States we spend more money on shelters for dogs and cats than for human beings. If we have effective animal rescue shelters for abused dogs, cats, and bunny rabbits we should be able to spare something for people as well.

Murray Straus et al.

two-thirds to three-quarters of these men were subsequently nonviolent. Gondolf also confirmed the conclusion of a number of studies of women who are successful in stopping abuse: battered women play a crucial role in stopping the violence against them. Women's insistence on their partners' getting help (the "woman factor") apparently can influence men to "learn more or try harder" to change.

❖ REFLECTIONS   *In your family (including your extended family), has there been spousal violence? If so, what are the factors involved in causing it? Sustaining it? If your family has not been involved in spousal violence, what factors have protected it from violence?*

❖ VIOLENCE AGAINST CHILDREN

The history of children is not a particularly happy one. At various times and places, children have been abandoned to die of exposure in deserts, in forests, and on mountainsides or have simply been murdered at birth if they were deemed too sickly, ugly, of the wrong sex, or just impractical. Male children have been subjected to castration to make them fit for guarding harems or singing soprano in church choirs. (Of course, we are more "civilized" today. Imagine, however, taking a baby boy, tying him down, and cutting off his foreskin, causing him excruciating pain and

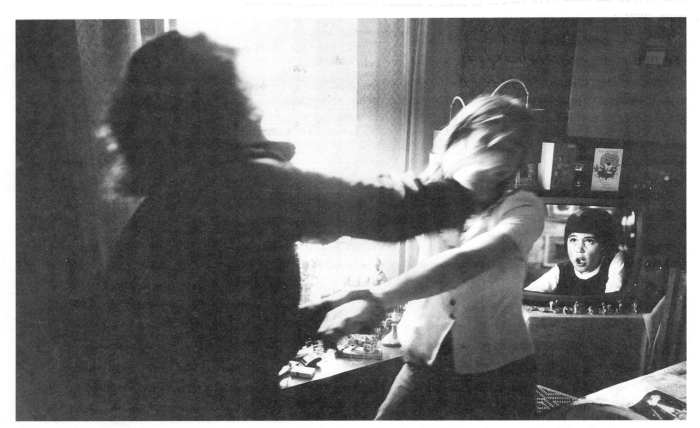

Children are the least protected members of our society. Much physical abuse is camouflaged as disciplining or the parent "losing" his or her temper.

possibly putting his life at risk. The practice of circumcision is routine in contemporary America [but not in Europe]. Still, there is no compelling medical reason for circumcision, only tradition [Kempe and Helfer, 1980].) These practices (and many others) have all been socially condoned in their time. In the societies in which they existed, they would not be recognized as abusive. In our society, some degree of physical force against children, such as spanking, is generally accepted as "normal." Most childrearing experts currently suggest that parents use alternative disciplinary measures.

Child abuse was not recognized as a serious problem in this country until the 1960s, with the work of C. H. Kempe and his colleagues, who coined the term *battered-baby syndrome*. It is now known that *at least* a million American children are physically abused by their parents each year (Gelles and Cornell, 1990); undoubtedly many cases go unnoticed or unreported. Parental violence is among the five leading causes of death for children between the ages of one and eighteen. In 1988, 1,225 children's deaths were directly attributable to their parents (Mitchell, 1989).

Families at Risk

Research suggests that there are three sets of factors that put families at risk for child abuse and neglect: parental characteristics, child characteristics, and the family ecosystem—that is, the family system's interaction with the larger environment (Burgess and Youngblood, 1987; Vasta, 1982). The characteristics described in the next sections are likely to be present in abusive families (Straus, Gelles, and Steinmetz, 1980; Turner and Avison, 1985).

PARENTAL CHARACTERISTICS. Some or all of the following characteristics are likely to be present in parents who abuse their children:

◆ The abusing father was physically punished by his parents, and his father physically abused his mother.
◆ The parents believe in corporal discipline of children and wives.
◆ The marital relationship itself may not be valued by the parents. There may be interspousal violence.
◆ The parents believe that the father should be the dominant authority figure.
◆ The parents are low in self-esteem.
◆ The parents have unrealistic expectations for the child.
◆ There is persistent role reversal in which the parents use the child to gratify their own needs, rather than vice versa.
◆ The parents appear unconcerned about the seriousness of a child's injury, responding with "Oh, well, accidents happen."

CHILD CHARACTERISTICS. Who are the battered children? Are they any different from other children? Surprisingly, the answer is often yes; they are different in some way or at least are perceived by their parents to be so. Brandt Steele (1980) noted that children who are abused are often labeled by their parents as "unsatisfactory." Unsatisfactory may include any of the following:

◆ A "normal" child who is the product of a difficult or unplanned pregnancy, is of the "wrong" sex, or is born outside of marriage.
◆ An "abnormal" child—premature or of low birth weight, possibly with congenital defects or illness.
◆ A "difficult" child—fussy, hyperactive, and so on.

America has sometimes been described as child-centered; however, any unbiased observer of child life in this nation will find that many millions of children are living and growing up under circumstances of severe social and economic deprivation. . . . Many of these children lack adequate nutrition, medical and dental care, and educational and vocational opportunities . . . . However high the prevalence of physical abuse of individual children within their families and homes may be, the abuse inflicted upon children collectively by society as a whole is far larger in scope and far more serious in its consequences.

David Gil, *Violence against Children*

Parents are the last people on earth who ought to have children.

Samuel Butler

Do not withhold correction from the child: For if you beat him with the rod, he will not die. Beat him with the rod and deliver him from hell.

Proverbs 23

PERSPECTIVE

The Epidemic of Missing Children: Myth or Reality?

In the morning, as they eat their cereal, children in homes throughout America look at milk cartons with photographs of "missing children." The faces stare from the cartons as if warning the children that they, too, may become missing if they are not careful. The photographs on milk cartons, grocery bags, billboards, and television give us the impression, observed pediatrician Benjamin Spock, that "children are being abducted all the time and that this child might be next" (Kilzer, 1985).

To protect their children, parents fingerprint them in massive identification programs. They buy books warning against strangers and have dentists implant computer identification chips in their children's teeth. Schools also often stress the threat posed by strangers.

A 1990 study commissioned by the Justice Department (Finkelhor, Hotaling, and Sedlak, 1990) has helped to put the missing children "problem" into perspective. Based on interviews conducted from July 1988 to January 1989, the researchers estimated that around 1,369,000 children are missing at some time during a given year in the United States.

Of this number, about 350,000 are abducted by a family member as a result of a custody dispute between parents. The researchers found that most of these children were back home within two days. All but 10 percent were home within a month. In 83 percent of the cases, the parent from whom the child was taken knew where the child was. Other major categories of missing children (in terms of numbers of children affected) include runaways (about 450,700 annually) and "thrownaways"—children who are forced by their parents to leave home (about 127,000). Another large category includes children who are lost, injured, or unable to return home for some other reason. This category, consisting of about 438,000 children annually, also includes a large number of "misplaced" children—those who forget or misunderstand where they are supposed to be. Most of these children return home within a day, but the fact that they are included in many estimates of missing children obscures the number that are actually missing.

A very small percentage of missing children are abducted by strangers. The researchers estimated the number to be between 200 and 300 annually. An additional 3,200 to 4,400 are "lured away," often in conjunction with a sexual assault; they are not kidnapped, however. In another study, based on data collected from six different sources, including the National Center for Missing and Exploited Children and various police records, Hotaling and Finkelhor (1990) estimated that between 52 and 158 children are murdered yearly in stranger abductions. In contrast, 1,100 children die yearly from parental abuse or neglect. (The United States leads the world in homicides for one to four year olds, most of whom are killed by a family member.)

Steele also notes that all too often a child's perceived difficulties are a *result* of abuse and neglect rather than a cause.

There was an old woman who lived in a shoe,
She had so many children she didn't know what to do.
She gave them some broth without any bread,
And whipped them all soundly and sent them to bed.

Mother Goose rhyme

FAMILY ECOSYSTEM. As discussed earlier in this chapter, the community and the family's relation to it may be relevant to the existence of domestic violence (Garbarino, 1977). The following characteristics may be found in families that experience child abuse:

◆ The family experiences unemployment.
◆ The family is socially isolated, with few or no close contacts with relatives, friends, and groups.
◆ The family has a low level of income, which creates economic stress.
◆ The family lives in an unsafe neighborhood, which is characterized by higher-than-average levels of violence.
◆ The home is crowded, hazardous, dirty, or unhealthy.
◆ The family is a single-parent family in which the mother works and is consequently overstressed and overburdened.
◆ There are family health problems.

PERSPECTIVE

About 2,000 children are victims of suicide every year and about 7,000 die in auto accidents.

Contrary to media claims, there is no upsurge in stranger abductions or in murders related to these abductions. Furthermore there is far greater risk to teenagers than to young children. Hotaling and Finkelhor (1990) write, "Runaways or children who are considered to be possible runaways are not regarded with the same solicitude as kidnap victims. Still, the data suggest that if the public is concerned about abducted and murdered children, it will have to broaden its concern to include the adolescent, who appears to be the child at highest risk."

If the epidemic of missing children is a myth, the public reaction to it is not. The myth has touched a very profound fear. In part, this fear may reflect anxieties about changing patterns of parenting and childrearing. With increasing numbers of mothers working, more children are being placed in child care than ever before. One psychologist suggests that "not being home may be tapping into hidden guilt" (Kilzer and Griego, 1985). For some, this fear may reflect anxieties concerning minorities and may touch on

xenophobia, as many stories involve specific ethnic groups or foreigners. One man recalled hearing of Mexicans abducting blonde, blue-eyed children to sell to childless couples. "They were also abducted and shipped to Africa or to Arabian harems; there were those who were forced into prostitution by Mafia pimps" (Schneider, 1987).

Whatever the source, the myth of missing children has severe consequences. First of all, it instills fear in children. Psychologist Lee Salk warns, "We are terrifying our children to the point where they are going to be afraid to talk to strangers" (Kantrowitz, 1986). Such fear makes it difficult to instill a basic sense of trust; it makes children anxious toward people they don't know and fearful of new situations. It makes them suspicious of foreigners and people who are different from themselves. Second, it affects our parenting style. It makes us afraid to let our children out of our sight. It creates anxiety in us when we are not at home or they are gone. Finally, it allows us to continue to believe that all families are happy and nurturing. It makes it easier to deny that families can be abusive, violent, or incestuous. Sexual abuse, a far more common problem than kidnapping, is much less often dis-

cussed by parents with their children. In one study, Finkelhor (1984) found that 84 percent of parents had discussed kidnapping, but only 29 percent had talked about sexual abuse with their children.

Children need to be taught to keep themselves safe at home and at the homes of friends, neighbors, and relatives as well as on the street. But it is not necessary to terrify them in the process. If they are allowed to develop their own good judgment skills and have high self-esteem, they will feel secure, competent, and in control of their own bodies and have the tools to help them stay out of risky situations. Parents need to look at where the most plausible dangers lie. They need to acknowledge the violence and sexual abuse within families that lead children to become runaways and suicides. Or they might become involved in promoting motor-vehicle safety (see Resource Center for information on Mothers Against Drunk Driving). As Hotaling and Finkelhor (1990) write, "Children being killed by strangers who abduct them are terrible and properly feared tragedies, but they are a small portion of children who die in tragic and preventable circumstances."

The likelihood of child abuse increases with family size. Parents of two children have a 50 percent higher abuse rate than do parents of a single child. The rate of abuse peaks at five children and declines thereafter. The overall child-abuse rate by mothers has been found to be 75 percent higher than that by fathers (Straus, Gelles, and Steinmetz, 1980). The responsibilities and tensions of mothering and the enforced closeness of mother and child may lead to situations in which women are likely to abuse their children. But, as David Finkelhor (1983) and others have pointed out, if we "calculate [child] vulnerability to abuse as a function of the amount of time spent in contact with a potential abuser, . . . we. . . . see that men and fathers are more likely to abuse."

Single parents—both mothers and fathers—are at especially high risk of abusing their children (Gelles, 1989). According to Gelles, "the high rate of abusive violence among single mothers appears to be a function of the poverty that characterizes mother-only families." He states that programs must be developed that are "aimed at ameliorating the devastating consequences of poverty among single parents. . . ." Single fathers, who show a higher abuse rate than single mothers, "need more than economic support to avoid using abusive violence toward their children."

There is no crime of which one cannot imagine oneself to be the author.

Johann Goethe

Intervention

The goals of intervention in domestic violence are principally to protect the victims and assist and strengthen their families. In dealing with child abuse, professionals and government agencies may be called on to provide medical care, counseling, and services such as day-care, child-care education, telephone crisis lines, and temporary foster care. Many of these services are costly, and many of those who require them cannot afford to pay. Since 1981, government support for such services has been drastically reduced by federal budget cuts. Our system does not currently provide the human and financial resources necessary to deal with these socially destructive problems.

The first step in treating child abuse is locating the children who are threatened. With heightened public awareness in recent years and mandatory reporting of suspected child abuse required of certain professionals (such as teachers, doctors, and counselors) in all fifty states, identifying these children is much easier now than it was two decades ago. Reported incidents of child abuse have increased greatly during this time, but the actual number of incidents appears to have decreased. This is good news as far as it goes. Still, there are unacceptably high levels of violence against children and not nearly enough resources to assist them. Child welfare workers are notoriously overburdened with cases, and adequate foster placement is often difficult to find (Gelles and Cornell, 1990).

Much intervention in child abuse appears to be equivalent to putting a Band-Aid on a huge malignant tumor. One survey of a number of treatment programs concluded that they were "in general . . . not very successful" (Daro and Cohn, 1988). Programs that stress education and early intervention may offer more hope. One such program, in which home visits were made by nurses to high-risk first-time mothers (teenagers, unmarried women, and women of low socioeconomic status) showed encouraging results. Those who were visited had fewer verified incidents of child abuse during their child's first two years. These mothers were also observed to punish their children less often and to provide "more appropriate play materials." Also, their children were seen less for accidents or poisoning than those in the comparison group (Olds, Henderson, Chamberlin, and Tatelbaum, 1986).

An innovative program called Project 12-Ways takes an "ecobehavioral" approach, working with both parents and the larger family ecosystem. Project 12-Ways teaches stress reduction and offers training in self-control, job-finding skills money management, and problem-solving skills. Parents are given social support, provided with counseling on how to find and use leisure time, and referred to alcohol or drug abuse programs. The program gives both parent and child basic skills training and provides education in home safety and cleanliness. Compared to foster placement, which was evaluated as being effective in reducing recurring incidences of child abuse in between 40 and 70 percent of cases, Project 12-Ways was found to be effective in 80 to 90 percent of the cases studied (Lutzer and Rice, 1984, 1986). Self-help groups such as Parents Anonymous offer nonjudgmental support and prove to be effective for parents committed to changing their behavior. (See Resource Center for information on Parents Anonymous.)

We have too many high-sounding words, and too few actions that correspond with them.

Abigail Adams (1744–1818)

A society which is mobilized to keep child molesters, kidnappers, and Satanists away from innocent children is not necessarily prepared to protect children from ignorance, poverty, and ill health.

Joel Best

❖ REFLECTIONS *If you were (or are) a parent, would you consider it violent to spank your child with an open hand on the buttocks if the child was disobedient? To slap your child across the face? Is it acceptable to spank your small child to teach him or her not to cross a busy street? To spank because you are angry?*

❖ THE HIDDEN VICTIMS OF FAMILY VIOLENCE

Most studies of family violence have focused on violence between spouses and parental violence toward children. There is, however, considerable violence between siblings, teenage children and their parents, and adult children and their aging parents. These are the "hidden victims" of family violence (Gelles and Cornell, 1990).

Sibling Violence

Violence between siblings is by far the most common form of family violence (Straus, Gelles, and Steinmetz, 1980). Most of this type of sibling interaction is simply taken for granted by our culture—"You know how kids are!" Straus and his associates, in a survey that included 733 families with two or more children, found that 82 percent of the children had used some sort of violence against a sibling in the preceding year. The National Association of Child Abuse estimated that 29 million siblings physically harm each other annually (Tiede, 1983). Straus and his colleagues reported these additional findings:

◆ The rate of sibling violence goes down with the increasing age of the child.
◆ Boys of all ages are more violent than girls. The highest rates of sibling violence occur in families with only male children.
◆ Violence between children often reflects what they see their parents doing to each other and to the children themselves.

The full scope and implications of sibling violence have not been rigorously explored. However, Straus, Gelles, and Steinmetz concluded that

conflicts and disputes between children in a family are an inevitable part of life. . . . But the use of physical force as a tactic for resolving their conflicts is by no means inevitable. . . . Human beings learn to be violent. It is possible to provide children with an environment in which nonviolent methods of solving conflicts can be learned. . . . If violence, like charity, begins at home, so does nonviolence.

Teenage Violence toward Parents

Most of us find it difficult to imagine children attacking their parents, because it so profoundly violates our image of parent/child relations. Parents possess the authority and power in the family hierarchy. Furthermore, there is greater social disapproval of a child striking a parent than of a parent striking a child; it is the parent who has the "right" to hit. Finally, parents rarely discuss such incidents because they are ashamed of their own victimization; they fear that others will blame them for the children's violent behavior (Gelles and Cornell, 1990).

Although we know fairly little about adolescent violence against parents, scattered studies indicate that it is almost as prevalent as spousal violence (Gelles and Cornell, 1990; Straus, 1980; Straus, Gelles, and Steinmetz, 1980). Gelles and Cornell suggest that 2.5 million parents are struck annually by their adolescent children. They report that about 900,000 parents are kicked, punched, bitten, beaten up, or have a gun or knife used on them by their teenage children each year.

The majority of youthful children who attack parents are between the ages of thirteen and twenty-four. Sons are slightly more likely to be abusive than daughters, and the rate of severe male violence tends to increase with age while that of females decreases. Boys apparently take advantage of their increasing size and the cultural expectation of male aggression. Girls, in contrast, may become less violent because society views female aggression more negatively. Most researchers believe that mothers are the primary targets of violence and abuse because they may lack physical strength or social resources and because women are "acceptable" targets for abuse (Gelles and Cornell, 1990).

Abuse of the Elderly

Of all the forms of hidden family violence, only the abuse of elderly parents by their grown children (or in some cases, grandchildren) has received considerable public attention. It is estimated that approximately 500,000 elderly are physically abused annually. An additional 2 million are thought to be emotionally abused or neglected. Much abuse of the elderly goes unnoticed, unrecognized, and unreported. Old people generally don't get out much and are often confined to bed or a wheelchair. Many do not report their mistreatment out of fear of institutionalization or other reprisal. Although some research indicates that the abused in many cases were, in fact, abusing parents, more knowledge must be gained before we can draw firm conclusions about the causes of elder abuse (Gelles and Cornell, 1990).

The most likely victims of elder abuse are the very elderly—in the majority of cases women—who are suffering from physical or mental impairments. Their advanced age renders them dependent on their caregivers for many if not all of their daily needs. It may be their dependency that increases their likelihood of being abused. Other research indicates that many abusers are financially dependent on their elderly parents; they may resort to violence out of feelings of powerlessness. Earlier research on elder abuse suggested that most abusers were the middle-aged daughters of the abused, but more recent studies show that sons are somewhat more likely to abuse (Pillemer, 1985).

While researchers are sorting out the whys and wherefores of elder abuse, battered old people have a number of crying needs. Pillemer and Suitor (1988) recommend the following services for elders and their caregiving families:

◆ Housing services, including temporary respite care to give caregivers a break and permanent housing such as rest homes, group housing, and nursing homes.
◆ Health services, including home health care, adult day-care centers, and occupational, physical, and speech therapy.
◆ Housekeeping services, including shopping and meal preparation.
◆ Support services, such as visitor programs and recreation.
◆ Guardianship and financial management.

❖ REDUCING FAMILY VIOLENCE

In every child who is born, under no matter what circumstances, and of no matter what parents, the potentiality of the human race is born again.

James Agee

Based on the foregoing evidence, you may by now have concluded that the American family is well on its way to extinction as we bash, thrash, cut, shoot, and otherwise wipe ourselves out of existence. Statistically, the safest family homes are those with one or no children in which the husband and wife experience little life stress and in which decisions are made democratically (Straus, Gelles, and Steinmetz, 1980). By this definition, most of us probably do not live in homes that are particularly safe. What can we do to protect ourselves (and our posterity) from ourselves?

Prevention strategies usually take one of two paths: eliminating social stress or strengthening families (Swift, 1986). Family-violence experts make the following general recommendations (Straus, Gelles, and Steinmetz, 1980):

◆ Reduce societal sources of stress, such as poverty, racism and inequality, unemployment, and inadequate health care.

◆ Eliminate sexism. Furnish adequate day-care. Promote educational and employment opportunities equally for men and women. Promote sex education and family planning to prevent unplanned and unwanted pregnancies.

◆ End social isolation. Explore means of establishing supportive networks that include relatives, friends, and community.

◆ Break the family cycle of violence. Eliminate corporal punishment and promote education about disciplinary alternatives. Support parent education classes to deal with inevitable parent/child conflict.

◆ Eliminate cultural norms that legitimize and glorify violence. Legislate gun control, eliminate capital punishment, and reduce media violence.

A . . . society which promotes the ownership of firearms, women and children; which makes homes men's castles; and which sanctions societal and interpersonal violence in the forms of wars, athletic contests, and mass media fiction (and news) should not be surprised to find violence in its homes.

Norman Denzin

❖ SEXUAL ABUSE IN FAMILIES

The incest taboo, nearly universal in human societies, prohibits sexual activities between closely related individuals. There are only a few exceptions, and these concern brother/sister marriages in the royal families of ancient Egypt, Peru, and Hawaii. **Incest** is generally defined as sexual intercourse between persons too closely related to legally marry (usually interpreted to mean father/daughter, mother/son, or brother/sister). Sexual abuse or sexual victimization in families may include incest, but it can also involve family members such as uncles, grandparents, and stepparents. Sexual activities including but not limited to intercourse are considered abusive when an adult or adolescent engages in them with a child or younger adolescent. It does not matter if the younger person is perceived by the older one as freely participating in the activity. A minor child cannot give **informed consent**, so the activity is considered self-serving for the adult or older adolescent.

Until the late 1960s, it was generally assumed that sexual abuse in families was a rare phenomenon. When such abuse became reportable under child abuse laws, however, the various protective care agencies were shocked and alarmed by the large numbers of cases that surfaced. At the same time, psychiatrists became increasingly aware of childhood sexual abuse among their clients (Rosenfeld, 1977). A recent national survey found that 27 percent of the women and 16 percent of the men surveyed had experienced sexual abuse as children (Finkelhor et al., 1990). Child sexual victimization can be divided into two categories: sexual activities between family members (intrafamilial abuse) or those activities between nonfamily members (extrafamilial abuse). The trend in current research is to look at child sexual abuse in general (Finkelhor, 1984). In doing so, researchers have found that intrafamilial and extrafamilial sexual abuse share many common elements. Because there are so many variables—such as the age and sex of the victims and perpetrators, their relationship, the type of acts involved, and whether there was force—one cannot automatically say that abuse within the family is more harmful than extrafamilial abuse.

Forms of Intrafamilial Sexual Abuse

It is not clear what type of sexual victimization is the most frequent (Peters et al., 1986; Russell, 1986). Some researchers believe that father/daughter (including stepfather/daughter) abuse is the most common; others think that brother/sister abuse is most common. Still other researchers believe that incest committed by uncles is the most common (Russell, 1986). Mother/son sexual relations are considered to be rare (or are underreported).

[handwritten margin note: most serious form of incest is between father-daughter step-father-daughter]

Lot went out of Zo'ar, and dwelled in the hills with his two daughters, for he was afraid to dwell in Zo'ar. So he dwelled in a cave with his two daughters. Then the first-born said to the other, "Our father is old, and there is not a man on earth to come into us in the manner of men. Let us make our father drink wine and we will lie with him that we may have offspring through our father." So they made their father drink wine that night and his older daughter went in and lay with her father. He did not know when she lay down or when she arose. And then on the next day, the older daughter said to the younger one, "Behold, I lay last night with our father. Let us make him drink wine again tonight, then you go in and lie with him that we may have children by our father." So they gave their father wine that night, and the younger daughter slept with him. He did not know when she lay down or when she arose. Thus both Lot's daughters became great with child by their father.

Genesis 19:30–36

FATHER/DAUGHTER ABUSE. There is general agreement that the most traumatic form of sexual victimization is father/daughter abuse, including that committed by stepfathers. One study (Russell, 1986) indicated that 54 percent of the girls sexually abused by their fathers were extremely upset. In contrast, 25 percent who were abused by other family members reported the same degree of upset. Over twice as many abused daughters reported serious long-term consequences. Some factors contributing to the severity of father/daughter sexual relations include the following:

◆ Fathers were more likely to have engaged in penile/vaginal penetration than other relatives (18 percent versus 6 percent).
◆ Fathers sexually abused their daughters more frequently than other perpetrators abused their victims (38 percent of the fathers sexually abused their daughters eleven or more times, compared to a 12 percent abuse rate for other abusing relatives).
◆ Fathers were more likely to use force or violence than others (although the numbers for both fathers and others were extremely low).

In the past, many have discounted the seriousness of sexual abuse by a stepfather, because incest is generally defined legally as sexual activity between two biologically related persons. The emotional consequences are just as serious, however. Sexual abuse by a stepfather still represents a violation of the basic parent/child relationship. As Judith Herman (1981) noted, psychologically it does not matter if the father and child are related by blood. "What matters is the relationship that exists by virtue of the adult's parental power and the child's dependency." In fact, sexual abuse committed by stepfathers often is greater in severity. Forty-one percent of the abusing stepfathers in Russell's study (1986) abused their daughters more than twenty times. Only 17 percent of biological fathers abused their daughters that frequently. In 47 percent of the cases involving stepfathers, the abuse continued for a year or more. In contrast, 28 percent of incest committed by biological fathers continued that long.

BROTHER/SISTER SEXUAL VICTIMIZATION. There are contrasting views concerning the consequences of brother/sister incest. Researchers generally have expressed little interest in it. Most have tended to view it as harmless sex play or sexual exploration between mutually involved siblings. The research, however, has generally failed to distinguish between exploitative and nonexploitative brother/sister sexual activity. Russell (1986) suggests that the idea that brother/sister incest is usually harmless and mutual may be a myth. In her study, the average age difference between the brother (age 17.9 years) and sister (10.7 years) is so great that the siblings can hardly be considered peers. The age difference represents a significant power difference. Furthermore, not all brother/sister sexual activity is "consenting"; considerable physical force may be involved. Russell wrote:

So strong is the myth of mutuality that many victims themselves internalize the discounting of their experiences, particularly if their brothers did not use force, if they themselves did not forcefully resist the abuse at the time, if they still continued to care about their brothers, or if they did not consider it abuse when it occurred. And sisters are even more likely than daughters to be seen as responsible for their own abuse.

Russell discovered that 2 percent of the women in her random sample had at least one sexually abusive experience with a brother.

UNCLE/NIECE VICTIMIZATION. Both Alfred Kinsey (1953) and Diane Russell (1986) found the most common form of intrafamilial sexual abuse to involve uncles and nieces. Russell reported that almost 5 percent of the women in her study had been molested by their uncles, slightly more than the percentage abused by their fathers. The level of severity of the abuse was generally less in terms of the type of sexual acts and the use of force. Although such abuse does not take place within the nuclear family, many victims found it quite upsetting. A quarter of the respondents indicated long-term emotional effects (Russell, 1986).

The Abusers and the Abused

Despite the high rates of intrafamily sexual victimization, when we think of **pedophilia**—sexual attraction to or sexual use of children—we tend to think in terms of strangers. But like so many of our images of deviant individuals, our image of sex offenders is more imagination than reality (see Finkelhor, 1984, for public perceptions concerning pedophilia). In the majority of instances, the sexual abuser is known to the victim: he is a father, brother, uncle, neighbor, friend, or acquaintance. Russell (1984) found that in extrafamilial sexual abuse, 41 percent of the perpetrators were intimately connected to the victim (friend, family friend, and so on), and 42 percent were acquaintances. Another common misconception is that most sexual abusers are gay men; instead, most are heterosexual men. Even males who sexually abuse boys are not necessarily gay, note researchers (Groth and Gray, 1982). The child's age more than sex appears to be important for most male pedophiles.

The most dangerous stereotype, however, is that the offender is responding to the sexual advances of a precocious child. In this stereotype, "the offender himself is the victim of a provocative and seductive child, for here the victim is blamed for being abused, and the actual offender is not held fully responsible for his behavior" (Groth and Birnbaum, 1978; Groth, 1980). The Biblical story of Lot (see marginalia on facing page) gives religious sanction to this myth. Other misconceptions include that the sexual abuser is an old man, someone who is insane or developmentally disabled, an alcoholic or drug addict, or a sexually frustrated or oversexed individual.

CHILDREN AT RISK. Not all children are equally at risk for sexual abuse. Although any child can be sexually abused, some groups of children are more likely to be victimized than others. A review (Finkelhor and Baron, 1986) of the literature indicates that those children at higher risk for sexual abuse are the following:

◆ Female children
◆ Preadolescent children
◆ Children with absent or unavailable parents
◆ Children whose relationships with parents are poor
◆ Children whose parents are in conflict
◆ Children who live with a stepfather

The majority of sexually abused children are girls (Finkelhor, 1984), but boys are also victims. The ratio of girls to boys appears to be between 2.5 and 4 to 1 (Finkelhor and Baron, 1986). We have only recently recognized the sexual abuse of boys; this neglect has been part of the more general neglect of all sexual victimization of males (Russell, 1984). Finkelhor (1979) speculates that males tend to underreport sexual abuse because they experience greater shame; they feel that their masculinity has been undermined. Boys tend to be blamed more than girls for their victimization, especially if they did not forcibly resist: "A real boy would never let someone do *that* without fighting back" (Rogers and Terry, 1984).

This drawing was made by an adolescent who was impregnated by her father. According to psychologists, it expresses her inability to deal with body images, especially genitalia, and her rejection of her body's violation.

Most sexually abused children are between eight and twelve years of age when the abuse first takes place. Children between ten and twelve years appear to be the most vulnerable, while those under ages six and seven seem to be less vulnerable (Finkelhor and Baron, 1986). Children who have poor relationships with their parents (especially mothers) or whose parents are absent or unavailable and have high levels of marital conflict appear to be at higher risk. A child in such a family may be less well supervised and, as a result, more vulnerable to manipulation and exploitation by an adult. In this type of family, the child may be unhappy, deprived, or emotionally needy; the child may be more responsive to the offers of friendship, time, and material rewards promised by the abuser.

Finally, children with stepfathers are at greater risk for sexual abuse. Russell (1986) found that only 2.3 percent of the daughters studied were sexually abused by their biological fathers. In contrast, 17 percent were abused by their stepfathers. The higher risk may result from the incest taboos not being as strong in step-relationships and because stepfathers have not built up inhibitions resulting from parent/child bonding beginning from infancy. As a result, stepfathers may be more likely to view the child sexually. In addition, stepparents may also bring into the family step-relatives—their own parents, siblings, or children—who may feel no incest-related prohibition about becoming sexually involved with stepchildren.

THE FAMILY CLIMATE. Although traditionally we have viewed the sexual abuse of children as the result of some kind of character disorder or personality type, it now appears that it is a symptom of severe family dysfunction. To explain the dynamics of such behavior, researchers generally use a family systems model (discussed in Chapter 3). In this model, each family member has different needs and plays different roles.

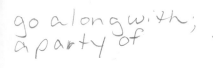

The role of mothers in their daughters' abuse has been much debated (Finkelhor, 1979; Herman, 1981). It has been suggested that some mothers may unconsciously "collude" in their husband's exploitive acts (Justice and Justice, 1979). These women have sexually withdrawn from their husbands and may talk themselves out of suspicions about their husbands' behavior. But it is important not to blame the victims' mothers for the abuse, as it would misdirect the responsibility from the offender. To blame mothers for the exploitation of their daughters, Russell (1986) points out, assumes that "daughters must be chaperoned in their own homes to be safe." The role of mothers in *protecting* their daughters (and sons) from sexual aggression is well-substantiated, however (Gelles and Conte, 1991).

Justice and Justice (1979) noted several factors that appeared to be prevalent in homes where father/daughter incest occurs. It should be noted that these characteristics need not be present for abuse to occur; they are *not* causes of sexual abuse.

◆ The father is under severe stress (from job or family changes, moving, and so on). He may increase his drinking.
◆ Sex ceases between the father and the mother.
◆ The mother leaves her husband and daughter alone (for example, by working nights or being sick).
◆ The daughter is hungry for affection.
◆ The family's sexual climate is either very lax or very repressive.

Effects of Sexual Victimization

There are numerous well-documented consequences of child sexual abuse that hold true for both intrafamilial and extrafamilial abuse (see Browne and Finkelhor, 1986, for a review of the literature). These include both initial and long-term consequences.

INITIAL EFFECTS OF SEXUAL ABUSE. The initial consequences, those occurring within the first two years, include those in the following list. The proportion of victimized children who experience these disturbances ranges from a quarter to almost two-thirds, depending on the study. To date, however, the empirical literature remains sketchy (Browne and Finkelhor, 1986).

◆ *Emotional disturbances,* including fear, anger and hostility, guilt and shame.
◆ *Physical consequences,* including difficulty in sleeping, changes in eating patterns, and pregnancy.
◆ *Sexual disturbances,* including significantly higher rates of open masturbation, sexual preoccupation, and exposure of the genitals.
◆ *Social disturbances,* including difficulties at school, truancy, running away from home, and early marriages by abused adolescents.

LONG-TERM EFFECTS OF SEXUAL ABUSE. Although there can be some healing of the initial effects, child sexual abuse may leave lasting scars on the adult survivor. These adults often have significantly higher incidences of psychological, physical, and sexual problems than the general population. These problems include the following (Browne and Finkelhor, 1986):

◆ *Depression,* the most frequently reported symptom of adults sexually abused as children.
◆ *Self-destructive tendencies,* including suicide attempts and thoughts of suicide.
◆ *Somatic disturbances and dissociation,* including anxiety and nervousness, eating disorders (anorexia and bulimia), feelings of "spaciness," out-of-body experiences, and feelings that things are "unreal."
◆ *Negative self-concept,* including feelings of low-self esteem, isolation, and alienation.
◆ *Interpersonal relationship difficulties,* including difficulties in relating to both sexes, parental conflict, problems in responding to their own children, and difficulty in trusting others.
◆ *Revictimization,* in which women abused as children are more vulnerable to rape and marital violence.
◆ *Sexual problems,* in which survivors find it difficult to relax and enjoy sexual activities, or avoid sex and experience hypoactive (inhibited) sexual desire and lack of orgasm.

A MODEL OF SEXUAL ABUSE TRAUMA. As we have seen, there are numerous initial and long-term consequences of childhood sexual abuse. Together, these consequences create a traumatic dynamic that affects the child's ability to deal with the world. Finkelhor and Browne (1986) suggest a model of sexual abuse that contains four components: traumatic sexualization, betrayal, powerlessness, and stigmatization. When these factors converge as a result of sexual abuse, they affect the child's cognitive and emotional orientation to the world. They create trauma by distorting a child's self-concept, world view, and affective abilities. These consequences affect abuse survivors not only as children but also as adults.

Traumatic Sexualization. Traumatic sexualization refers to the process in which the sexually abused child's sexuality developed inappropriately and becomes interpersonally dysfunctional. Finkelhor and Browne note:

It occurs through the exchange of affection, attention, privileges, and gifts for sexual behavior, so that the child learns sexual behavior as a strategy for manipulating others to get his or her other developmentally appropriate needs met. It occurs when certain parts of the child's anatomy are fetishized and given distorted importance and meaning. It occurs through the misconceptions and confusions about sexual behavior and morality that are transmitted to the child from the offender. And it occurs when very frightening memories and events become associated in the child's mind with sexual activity.

Sexually traumatized children learn inappropriate sexual behaviors (such as manipulating an adult's genitals for affection), are confused about their sexuality, and inappropriately associate certain emotions—such as loving and caring—with sexual activities.

As adults, sexual issues may become especially important. Survivors may suffer flashbacks, sexual dysfunctions, and negative feelings about their bodies. They may also be confused about sexual norms and standards. A fairly common confusion is the belief that sex may be traded for affection. Some women label themselves as "promiscuous," but this label may be more a result of their negative self-image than their actual behavior. There seems to be a history of childhood sexual abuse among many prostitutes.

Betrayal. Children feel betrayed when they discover that someone on whom they have been dependent has manipulated, used, or harmed them. Children may also feel betrayed by other family members, especially mothers, for not protecting them from abuse.

As adults, survivors may experience depression as a manifestation, in part, of extended grief over the loss of trusted figures. Some may find it difficult to trust others. Other survivors may feel a deep need to regain a sense of trust and become extremely dependent. Distrust may manifest itself in hostility and anger. In adolescents, antisocial or delinquent behavior may be a means of protecting themselves from further betrayal. Anger may express a need for revenge or retaliation. Other times, distrust may manifest itself in social isolation and avoidance of intimate relationships.

Powerlessness. Children experience a basic kind of powerlessness when their bodies and personal space are invaded against their will. A child's powerlessness is reinforced as the abuse is repeated.

In adulthood, powerlessness may be experienced as fear or anxiety; a person feels unable to control events. Adult survivors often believe that they have impaired coping abilities. This feeling of ineffectiveness may be related to the high incidence of depression and despair among survivors. Powerlessness may also be related to increased vulnerability or revictimization by rape or marital violence; survivors feel unable to prevent subsequent victimization. Other survivors, however, may attempt to cope with their earlier powerlessness by an excessive need to control or dominate others.

Stigmatization. Stigmatization refers to ideas of badness, guilt, and shame about sexual abuse that are transmitted to abused children and then internalized by them. Stigmatization is communicated in numerous ways. The abuser conveys it by blaming the child or, through his secrecy, communicates a sense of shame. If the abuser

Abuse leaves children feeling broken and alone.

pressures the child for secrecy, the child may also internalize feelings of shame and guilt. Children's prior knowledge that their family or community consider such activities deviant may contribute to their feelings of stigmatization.

As adults, survivors may feel extreme guilt or shame about having been sexually abused. They may have low self-esteem because they feel that the abuse had made them "spoiled merchandise." They also feel different from others, because they mistakenly believe that they alone have been abused.

Treatment Programs

There is a growing trend toward dealing with child sexual abuse, especially father/daughter incest, through therapy programs working in conjunction with the judicial system rather than breaking up the family by removing the child or the offender (Nadelson and Sauzier, 1986). Because the offender is often also the breadwinner, incarcerating him may greatly increase the family's emotional distress. The district attorney's office may work with clinicians in evaluating the existing threat to the child and deciding whether to prosecute or refer the offender to therapy (or both). The goal is not simply to punish the offender but to try to assist the victim and the family in coming to terms with the abuse.

Many of these clinical programs work on several levels at once: they treat the individual, the father/daughter relationship, the mother/daughter relationship, and the family as a whole. They work on developing self-esteem and improving the family and marital relationships. If appropriate, they refer individuals to alcohol- or drug-abuse treatment programs.

A crucial ingredient to many treatment programs is individual and family attendance at self-help group meetings. These self-help groups are composed of incest survivors, offenders, mothers, and other family members. Self-help groups such as Parents United and Daughters and Sons United assist the offender in acknowledging his responsibility and in understanding the impact of the incest on all involved. "No matter the extenuating circumstances . . . , his action betrayed his child and wife and their reliance on him as father and husband," wrote Henry Giarretto (1976), director of one of the most longstanding treatment programs. (See Resource Center for information on treatment program for sexual abuse.)

❖ REFLECTIONS   *Have you or anyone you know been sexually abused? If so, how was the abuse ended? What were the consequences for the survivors? For the family? Are there still issues that need to be resolved?*

❖ PREVENTING SEXUAL ABUSE

The idea of preventing sexual abuse is relatively new. Prevention programs began about a decade ago, a few years after programs were started to identify and help child or adult survivors of sexual abuse. Such prevention programs have been hindered, however, by three factors (Finkelhor, 1986a, 1986b):

◆ Sexual abuse is complicated by different concepts of appropriate sexual behavior and partners, which are not easily understood by children.
◆ Sexual abuse, especially incest, is a difficult and scary topic for adults to discuss with children. Children who are frightened by their parents, however, may be less able to resist abuse than those who are given strategies of resistance.
◆ Sex education is controversial. Even where it is taught, instruction often does not go beyond physiology and reproduction. The topic of incest is especially opposed.

We are healthy only to the degree that our ideas are humane.

Kurt Vonnegut, Jr.

In confronting these problems, child abuse prevention (CAP) programs have been very creative. These programs typically aim at three audiences: children, parents, and professionals, especially teachers. CAP programs aimed at children include plays, puppet shows, filmstrips, videotapes, books, and comic books to teach children that they have rights. Children have the right to control their own bodies and genitals and to feel "safe," and they have the right not to be touched in ways that feel confusing or wrong. The CAP programs stress that the child is not at fault when such abuse does occur. They also try to give children possible courses of action if someone tries to sexually abuse them. In particular, children are advised to tell someone they trust (and to keep telling until they are believed).

Other programs focus on educating parents who, it is hoped, will in turn educate their children. These programs aim at helping parents discover abuse or abusers by identifying warning signs. The programs assume that the participants are not abusers or potential abusers. Parents seem reluctant, however, to deal with sexual abuse issues with their children, according to David Finkelhor (1986a). First, many do not feel that their children are at risk. Second, parents are fearful of unnecessarily frightening their children. Third, parents feel uncomfortable about talking with their children about sex in general, much less such tabooed subjects as incest. In addition, parents may not believe their own children or may feel uncomfortable confronting a suspected abuser, who may be a partner, uncle, friend, or neighbor.

Child abuse prevention programs have also directed attention to professionals, especially teachers, physicians, mental health professionals, and police officers. Because of their close contact with children and their role in teaching children about the world, teachers are especially important. Professionals are encouraged to be watchful for signs of sexual abuse and to investigate children's reports of such abuse. A number of schools have instituted programs to educate students and their parents as well.

❖ SUMMARY

◆ Any form of intimacy or relatedness increases the likelihood of violence or abuse. The mythology of family violence, however, obscures many of its real features. *Violence* is defined as "an act carried out with the intention or perceived intention of causing physical pain or injury to another person."

◆ The principal models used to study sources of family violence are: the *psychiatric model,* which finds the source of violence within the personality of the abuser; the *ecological model,* which looks at both the child's development in the family context and the family's development within the community; the *patriarchy model,* which finds violence to be inherent in male-dominated societies; the *social learning model,* in which violence is seen as a behavior learned within the family and larger society; the *social-situational model,* which views family violence as arising from a combination of structural stress and cultural norms; the *resource model,* which assumes that force is used to compensate for the lack of personal, social, and economic resources; and the *exchange/social control model,* which holds that people weigh the costs versus the rewards in all their actions and that they

will use violence if the social controls (costs) are not strong enough. Three factors that may reduce social control are inequality of power in the family, the private nature of the family, and the "real man" image.

◆ *Battering* is the use of physical force against another person; it includes slapping, punching, knocking down, choking, kicking, hitting with objects, threatening with weapons, stabbing, and shooting. Wife battering is one of the most common and most underreported crimes in the United States.

◆ Although there does not appear to be a "typical" battered woman, there are two characteristics that correlate highly with wife assault: low socioeconomic status and a high degree of marital conflict.

◆ A man who batters probably has some or all of the following characteristics: low self-esteem, belief in common myths about battering, traditional beliefs about the family, pathological personality characteristics, use of sex as aggression, and a belief in the moral rightness of his aggression.

◆ The three-phase *cycle of violence* in battering relationships includes (1) the tension-building phase, (2) the explosive phase, and (3) the resolution (love) phase.

◆ Marital rape is a form of battering. Many people, including victims themselves, have difficulty acknowledging that forced sex in marriage is rape, just as it is outside of marriage.

◆ The prevalence of violence and sexual assault in dating relationships is alarming. Violence is often precipitated by jealousy or rejection. Acquaintance rape may not be recognized by either the assailant or the victim, because they think that rape is done by strangers.

◆ Women may stay in or return to battering relationships for a number of reasons, including economic dependency, religious pressure or beliefs, the perceived children's need for a father, pity, guilt, a sense of duty, fear, and love. They may also be paralyzed by "learned helplessness." Women may leave violent relationships when the level of violence increases or their children become threatened. Women may also try to stop their husbands' violence. The most important factor in stopping abuse appears to be the woman's own determination that it must stop.

◆ The issue of compassion versus control is significant in domestic violence intervention. Arrest, prosecution, and imprisonment are examples of control; shelters and support groups (including abuser programs) are examples of compassionate intervention.

◆ At least a million children are physically abused by their parents each year. Many abuse cases are unreported. Parental violence is one of the five leading causes of childhood death.

◆ Families at risk for child abuse often have specific parental, child, and family ecosystem characteristics. Parental characteristics include a physically abused father, belief in corporal punishment, a devalued marital relationship and interspousal violence, low self-esteem, father dominance, unrealistic expectation for the child, parent/child role reversal, and lack of parental concern about the child's injury. Child characteristics include a "normal" child who is the product of a difficult or unplanned pregnancy, is the wrong sex, or is born outside of marriage; an "abnormal" child with physical or medical problems; or a "difficult" child. The family ecosystem includes the general social and economic environment in which the family lives; characteristics in families at risk include such conditions as poverty, unemployment, unsafe neighborhoods, and social isolation.

◆ Mandatory reporting of suspected child abuse may be helping to decrease the number of abused children. However, social workers are still overburdened, and services such as foster care are in short supply. Early intervention and education may be successful in reducing abuse, but there is a shortage of government funds for these and other programs to assist the victims of family violence.

◆ The hidden victims of family violence include siblings (who have the highest rate of violent interaction), parents assaulted by their adolescent or youthful children, and elders assaulted by their middle-aged children.

◆ Some recommendations for reducing violence include: (1) reducing sources of societal stress, such as racism and poverty; (2) eliminating sexism; (3) establishing supportive networks; (4) breaking the family cycle of violence; and (5) eliminating the legitimization and glorification of violence.

◆ *Incest* is defined as "sexual intercourse between persons too closely related to marry." Sexual victimization of children may include incest, but it can also involve other family members and other sexual activities. Child sexual victimization can be extrafamiliar or intrafamiliar.

◆ The most serious form of child sexual abuse is probably father/daughter (or stepfather/daughter) incest. Stepfathers abuse their daughters at significantly higher rates than do biological fathers. Brother/sister incest is often serious if it is exploitative or abusive.

◆ *Pedophilia* is sexual attraction to or sexual use of children. Most sexual abusers are known to their victims. Children at risk for sexual abuse include females, preadolescents, children with absent or unavailable parents, children with poor parental relationships, children with parents in conflict, and children living with a stepfather.

◆ A family systems model is useful for understanding child sexual abuse. Characteristics of homes in which such abuse occurs may include a father under severe stress, cessation of sexual relations between the father and mother, a father and daughter left alone regularly, an affection-deprived daughter, and a sexual climate that is either very lax or very repressive.

◆ There are both initial and long-term effects of child sexual abuse. The initial effects include emotional disturbances, physical consequences, and sexual and social disturbances. The long-term effects include depression, self-destructive tendencies, somatic disturbances and dissociation, negative self-concept, interpersonal relationship difficulties, revictimization, and sexual difficulties.

◆ The survivors of sexual abuse frequently suffer from sexual abuse trauma, characterized by traumatic sexualization, stigmatization, betrayal, and powerlessness.

◆ Offenders are increasingly being sent into treatment programs in an attempt to assist the incest survivor and family in coping with the crisis that incest creates. Self-help groups are important for many survivors of sexual abuse.

Answers to Preview Questions

The answers to the preview questions at the beginning of the chapter are listed below. As you check your answers, whether you were correct or not, think about your reasons for each response. What were they? What was their source?

How valid is the source? As you read the chapter, you will find the questions discussed in greater depth.

1. T	6. T
2. F	7. T
3. T	8. T
4. T	9. F
5. T	10. F

❖ SUGGESTED READINGS

Bass, Ellen, and Louise Thornton. *I Never Told Anyone: Writings by Women Survivors of Child Sexual Abuse.* New York: Harper Colophon Books, 1983 (paperback). A moving collection of poems, stories, and first-person accounts of child sexual abuse.

Freeman, Lory. *My Body is Mine.* Seattle, Wash.: Parenting Press, 1982. An illustrated booklet for children on the differences between "good" touching and "bad" touching. Also available in Spanish as *Mi Cuerpo Es Mio.*

Gelles, Richard, and Murray A. Straus. *Intimate Violence.* New York: Simon and Schuster, 1988. A readable overview of family violence based on the research of two leading authorities in the field.

Gordon, Linda. *Heroes of Their Own Lives: The Politics and History of Family Violence, 1880–1960.* New York: Viking, 1988. An important historical study of family violence, power, and gender roles.

Greven, Philip. *Spare the Child.* New York: Alfred A. Knopf (1990). A scholarly and impassioned study of the physical punishment of children in America and its roots in the Protestant ethic.

Hampton, Robert, ed. *Black Family Violence: Current Research and Theory.* N.Y.: Lexington Books, 1991. A comprehensive, multidisciplinary collection of essays.

Kempe, C. Henry, and Ruth Kempe. *The Common Secret: Sexual Abuse of Children and Adolescents.* New York: W. H. Freeman, 1984. An excellent, immensely readable book aimed at both professionals and the public; includes information on evaluating children and treating offenders.

NiCarthy, Ginny. *Getting Free: A Handbook for Women in Abusive Relationships.* Seattle, Wash.: The Seal Press, 1986 (paperback). Practical and sympathetic discussion of abuse to help battered women make decisions, get assistance, and survive.

Pirog-Good, Maureen, and Jan Stets, eds. *Violence in Dating Relationships: Emerging Social Issues.* N.Y.: Praeger, 1989. Scholarly collection of essays on physical violence and rape in dating.

Rhodes, Richard. *A Hole in the World: An American Boyhood.* New York: Simon and Schuster, 1990. A powerful personal account of abuse and survival by a noted author.

Russell, Diana E. H. *Rape in Marriage,* rev. ed. Bloomington, Ind.: Indiana University Press, 1990. A superbly researched, clear, and sobering view of sexual violence against women by their husbands and lovers.

Russell, Diana E. H. *The Secret Trauma: Incest in the Lives of Girls and Women.* New York: Basic Books, 1986. An important, comprehensive study of incest.

White, Evelyn C. *Chain Chain Change.* Seattle, Wash.: The Seal Press, 1985 (paperback). Directed toward the African-American woman who wants to understand the role of violence and emotional abuse in her life. Discusses stereotypes and cultural assumptions and offers practical information about getting help.

Zambrano, Myrna M. *Mejor Sola Que Mal Acompañada.* Seattle, Wash.: The Seal Press, 1985 (paperback). Assistance for Latino women in escaping abuse. Written in Spanish.

Suggested Films

The Burning Bed (1985) Farrah Fawcett as a desperate wife who sets her husband afire after years of abuse. Based on Faith McNulty's book.

The 400 Blows (French, 1959) A young boy, emotionally and physically abused by his parents, searches for meaning in his life. Directed by François Truffaut; one of the great films of the twentieth century.

King Lear (PBS Great Performances, 1986) Sir Lawrence Olivier, the greatest Shakespearean actor of the 20th Century portrays King Lear, the archetypical abused elder.

READINGS

THE DEADLY RAGE OF A BATTERED WIFE

Janet Bukovinsky

Although the story of Dorothy Rapp may seem particularly chilling as an account of subjugation and terror, it is in some sense a "classic" *case in which many elements of the battered woman syndrome may be recognized. How do you feel about the jury's verdict in the case? In the decade since Dorothy Rapp killed her husband law enforcement policies have changed in many states. Do you think arrest or the threat of arrest would have kept Bill Rapp from battering his wife?*

Bill Rapp spent a lot of time in the toolshed. He was meticulous about rearranging the tools hanging on the walls and about

READINGS

sharpening his log-splitting wedges and the chain saws he used to cut firewood. He worked as a welder in a Paterson, N. J., foundry.

Back in 1953, he'd moved his wife and baby from Colorado, where he was stationed as a staff sergeant in the Air Force, to New Jersey. They bought a red house in a nice residential neighborhood in Fair Lawn.

On March 26, 1981, Bill and Dorothy Rapp were sitting in their living room in front of the fireplace. Dorothy, a soft-faced woman whose mouth seemed to melt away at its corners, had a cold. She was bundled up in a flannel nightgown and her yellow terrycloth robe. The night was chilly, and their house had no central heating system. The Rapps burned wood to keep warm.

Bill was an alcoholic. He had already put away most of his nightly quart of vodka after dinner. He started picking on Dorothy that night, as usual, berating her because she hadn't brought in another load of wood chips for the fire.

He was drunk. There were plenty of wood chips in the house. Dorothy knew what was coming.

He threw her a punch that landed, hard, in her face, and he started pummeling her. Dorothy steeled herself to the familiar rhythm of his blows, yelling at him to stop, fighting back half-heartedly. When he did, she went into their bedroom and lay down in the dark on their double bed.

She was 48. Her life had been this way for 30 years, since she married Bill in Aurora, Col., when she was 18 and he 19. They had rented a little trailer there, and Dorothy soon became pregnant.

Bill's reaction to the news was an awful omen of things to come. It was the first time he beat her. He picked her up and threw her 36 feet—the length of the trailer. She slid on her side into the bedroom.

Bill Rapp's fury as he hurled his 110-pound wife across the trailer shocked her, but it was a kind of excruciating homecoming for Dorothy. At that point, Bill hadn't done anything to his wife that her father hadn't done to her mother.

"That's the way men are," counseled her mother the next day. "You married him for better or worse, until death do you part."

Dorothy returned to the trailer, and her life became one long bout of flinching and screaming.

He followed her into the bedroom, turned on the light and proceeded to drag her from the bed. "You didn't bring in enough wood chips," he screamed. "Go get more." Dorothy didn't argue.

When he threatened her life, as he had with a machete two weeks earlier, she would try to talk him out of his rage.

But tonight she sensed that the path of least resistance was the safest. She put on her slippers and went out into the darkness to fetch more wood chips. Then she went upstairs, where her 25-year-old son, James, was watching television.

He had heard the screams. They were nothing new to him. When the screams grew so agonized that James knew his mother needed help, he'd intervene, grappling with his father.

Tonight, he grimly advised Dorothy to stay out of Bill's way. The two of them heard the back door slam. Bill must have gone outside to his toolshed. She went downstairs, lay back down in their bed and dozed.

Bill was rarely sober now, except at work, and when he was drunk he seemed to prefer beating her to almost any other activity, including sex.

Dorothy spent most of her time in the house. She knew how to drive, but Bill took the car to work. She'd walk to the store or watch soap operas and crochet afghans, which she sold.

On that day in March, nearly one year ago, Dorothy woke for the second time that evening. Bill had come back and was pounding on the back of her head—a favorite spot for abusive men's fists, since hair covers the bruises. He was punching her stomach and back, breaking several of her ribs, she was later to learn.

Dorothy curled her body into a ball, trying to make herself as small as possible. Bill grabbed a handful of her hair and tore it out. His inexplicable wrath was worse than usual.

When he came at her with the machete two weeks earlier, she'd run in terror to a neighbor's house to call the police, who had responded innumerable times to domestic argument calls at the Rapp resident. Bill met them out front, subdued and charming. Just a squabble, he told them.

Dorothy was standing on the sidewalk sobbing. "He's going to kill me!" she screamed. "Can't you just take him down [to the station] and talk to him?" The policed advised her to leave and did so themselves.

When Bill ceased his latest round of beating, Dorothy lay, still curled up, with her back to him. She could see him in the mirror.

He took his hunting rifle from under the bed. It was a .30–.30 lever-action Winchester, a relatively lightweight gun and a legal hunting weapon. Dorothy heard a click as Bill pulled down the lever and inserted one bullet. He rested the gun against the wall near the top of the bed, on "his" side. "Your name is on that bullet," he used to tell her when he threatened her with the gun. "Don't you move or breathe until I come back," he seethed. "You're really going to get it." Then he went outside again.

Dorothy soon got out of bed. She picked up the rifle. She walked outside to the small porch. Bill was on his way back to the house. Dorothy couldn't see him well because a shelf on the porch obstructed her view. She stuck the barrel of the rifle through a space in the porch railing, aimed "in front of the sound of his voice" and touched the trigger.

The bullet with Dorothy Rapp's name on it struck Bill Rapp as he was walking toward his house with a chain-saw sharpener in his hand. It entered the front of his body, traveled on a downward path and exited under his left arm. His heart exploded.

continued on next page

Still holding the Winchester, Dorothy went into their bedroom and called the police. "Send somebody, an ambulance. I just shot my husband."

James came downstairs. "What was that?" he asked.

"I just shot Daddy."

At the trial of Dorothy Rapp last November, the prosecution charged that she had committed premeditated manslaughter—that, as a battered wife, she had reason enough to hate Bill and want to blow him away. Her attorney, Frank Lucianna, characterized her as the archetypal battered wife, paralyzed by fear and guilt. . . .

No socioeconomic group is immune. Connie Francis was a battered wife; so was Doris Day. The 1974 Nobel Peace Prize winner, the late Eisaku Sato, was publicly accused by his wife of abusing her prior to his nomination for the award.

The FBI believes that only one in 10 instances of marital abuse is reported. When the police respond to domestic violence calls, they simply aren't much help.

"Many police officers do not treat assault by a man upon his wife or female companion as a criminal act requiring arrest," said Clyde Allen, chairperson of the N. J. Advisory Committee to the U. S. Commission on Civil Rights.

Dorothy Rapp had found no ally in the police. "There were many times that the police discouraged me," she said. "I wanted to press charges, but they said I shouldn't do that, that I'd be wasting the court's time."

The police never saw Bill Rapp beating his wife. In New Jersey, acts classified as offenses, such as disorderly person charges (most applicable to wife-beating cases) must be witnessed by an officer for an arrest to be made.

At Dorothy Rapp's trial, Frank Lucianna suggested to the jury that the police had been such frequent visitors to the Rapp residence that they had simply stopped filing reports. He was determined to prove that Dorothy had acted in self-defense—that she had fired the shot to prevent Bill from killing her that night.

The fact that Dorothy was so completely subjugated by her husband was also important to her defense, in proving that she didn't have the strength to leave him. Julia Blackman Doron, a professor of psychology at Barnard College and an expert on battered wives, testified. She described Dorothy as a "psychologically cornered" woman, so entrenched in the morass of her marriage that she didn't know how to begin escaping her husband. Bill discouraged her from establishing contact with the outside world. She hadn't worked for years and had no close friends. She was, said Doron, a prisoner in her own home.

The man who beats his wife is often, according to Dr. Arnold Hutschnecker, "a frail boy who did not give his ambition attainable goals in a world of reality. He had no conscious awareness of what it meant to feel secure, to be a man with self-confidence and self-esteem." Hutschnecker, Richard Nixon's former physician, was describing Lee Harvey Oswald, a chronic wife-beater.

The advice that Dorothy received from her mother in 1952, when Bill first beat her, was cited by Lucianna as part of the syndrome that kept her bound to Bill. Her mother viewed divorce as a failure of the most "womanly" role—keeping one's family together.

Had Dorothy been able to look beyond her mother's limited perspective, she might have been able to divorce Bill, though it's difficult to say whether a judge's decree and a piece of paper would have been enough of a deterrent when the urge to beat her washed over him.

Dorothy Rapp was found innocent of manslaughter on November 18. It was the first time that the battered-wife defense was successfully used in a murder trial in New Jersey. The jury of seven men and five women deliberated for less than two hours.

BREAKING THE SILENCE

Meredith Maran

As you read the following factual account of incest, note to what extent the family members resemble the corresponding profiles in the text of the chapter. What reasons does each person give for his or her role in the incest? What is the therapist's role in helping the family to heal?

Jim's shoulders slump as his oldest daughter speaks. "My dad has been molesting me for about 10 years," Rachel begins calmly. "I knew it was wrong because he always said it was our little secret, that he'd go to jail if I told anyone. I loved my dad more than I loved anyone, and I kept thinking about how much my little sisters needed him—but I was afraid that he'd start doing it to them. So I made a deal with him: I wouldn't tell if he promised not to touch my sisters. He swore I was the only one, so I learned to cope. I learned to separate my self from my body—it was just my body lying there on that bed; my dad would never do those things to the real me. At first, I'd be upset for weeks every time he molested me. Near the end I'd gotten to where he'd finish and I'd get up and forget about it within an hour or two."

Sandy's [Rachel's mother] eyes are shut. Rachel glares again at Jim and continues.

"Then one day I heard Lisa crying in her room. I felt like my heart was on fire—I just knew what was wrong. She didn't want to say anything because he'd told her she was the only one. Finally she admitted that Dad had been handling her. When Sarah got home, Lisa and I talked to her. That's when we found out that he'd been molesting all three of us since we were babies.

"Mom wanted to call the police right away. But we told her we'd deny everything if she did. We didn't want to lose our dad, we didn't want our family to fall apart. We just wanted him to stop molesting us."

When Sandy confronted him, Jim cried and swore that it would never happen again, confiding for the first time that he'd been molested by his uncle for several years early in his childhood. Succumbing to the pleas of the man she'd loved for 20 years and the daughters she lived her life for, Sandy agreed to keep Jim's crime a secret. The next day, she installed deadbolts on each girl's bedroom door and ordered them to lock themselves in at night. And she swore to her husband that she'd have him arrested if he ever again attempted to have sex with their daughters.

"That next year was terrible for all of us," Sandy remembers. "I was losing my love for Jim, and I was terrified that he'd molest again. I kept asking the girls over and over if he was trying anything, and they kept promising me that everything was fine. I wanted to believe them so I shut out the little voice inside that told me something was wrong. I'd loved that man since I was 15 years old. I'd struggled so long to build the kind of family I thought we had—and I couldn't stand the thought of breaking it up, let alone telling the world that my husband was a child molester!

"Besides, Jim was our breadwinner. My income barely covered the groceries. So I prayed and prayed that somehow things would work out."

Sandy Rand's desperate decision not to report her husband's crime is one many wives of incest perpetrators make. Fear of devastating legal consequences, public humiliation and loss of income has made incest a painfully guarded secret for untold numbers of victims. But keeping sexual abuse a family secret only allows the abuse to continue. Without treatment, both the perpetrators and the victims may pass their behavior from generation to generation.

Sandy learned this lesson the hard way: Exactly one year after she'd agreed not to report the incest in her family, 12-year-old Sarah came to her in tears. Jim had been begging her for the "special backrubs" that his older daughters now refused to give him.

"When Sandy confronted me the first time," Jim says now, "I knew I was in trouble, that I'd have to convince her to keep it in the family. But when she came to me about Sarah, I knew that I'd go to jail, that I'd never be with my wife and daughters again. Mostly I felt . . . relief. I'd been trying for so long to get Sandy to kick me out—seeing other women, picking fights—because I knew I'd never be able to stop as long as I lived with my daughters. As I watched her dial that phone, all that I could think was, 'It's finally over.'"

The first call Sandy made was to Parents United. The counselor she spoke to explained that if Sandy gave Jim's name, PU would be legally obligated to report him to the police. Things would go better, the counselor said, if Jim turned himself in with the help of a lawyer who worked with PU on such cases. Rachel, Lisa, and Sarah didn't want to go to the meeting with the lawyer, but Sandy insisted. "Even after everything that had happened to them, the girls still didn't want Jim to go to jail. I hoped the lawyer would convince them that we were doing the right thing."

It was in the lawyer's office that the history of Jim's sexual abuse of his daughters was told in its entirety for the first time. He admitted everything: How he'd begun fondling Rachel when she was 4; how he'd developed an elaborate system of household chores that always left one daughter available to him; how he'd recently begun begging Rachel to let him penetrate her. He told how frightened he'd become when Sarah had had her first asthma attack while he was molesting her. Hearing his three-hour confession, Jim's victims began to feel the rage they'd been swallowing for so many years.

"Something snapped inside me," Rachel remembers. "Before that, there was no wrong to him. He was my best friend, my wonderful dad. I believed him when he said he molested me because I was so pretty and he loved me so much. But as I was listening to the whole story, I was filled with hate. This man we all worshiped had been hurting us horribly all our lives. We told Mom to go ahead and send him to jail. At that moment, I hoped he'd never get out." She glances at Jim, whose reddened eyes meet hers. "Sometimes I still think he should spend his life in there."

Because Jim pleaded guilty, there was no trial. . . . He was sentenced to one year in Elmwood County Jail. His confession, clean police record, and willingness to undergo therapy qualified him for the county Child Sexual Abuse Treatment Program. Jim was placed on work furlough on the condition that he attend weekly counseling sessions and donate weekend labor to Parents United.

"My first night at Elmwood," Jim says, "was when it really hit me. If any other man had done those things to my daughters, I would have taken him apart. But that monster was me." His voice quavers; he swallows hard. "I would have given my life to make up to my daughters for what I'd done." When he was offered an early release after six months, his daughters protested unanimously; they wanted their father to finish his sentence. Jim passed up the release and spent the full year in jail.

Jim's removal from their home provided no respite for his wife and daughters. The girls turned their anger on Sandy, accusing her of not protecting them, of not having sex with Jim often enough, of not loving and understanding them as their father had done. "They called me names I'd never heard from

continued on next page

their mouths before," Sandy says, looking down at Sarah. "They wouldn't obey me, they wouldn't listen or talk to me. They refused to go to counseling. Because of the molest, they'd been made wards of the court and I knew if they kept up their acting out I would lose them forever. So I did what I had to do to save what was left of our family."

What Sandy did was write a letter to the judge asking him to order her daughters into individual and family therapy. "At first we fought it, 'cause we were forced to go," Lisa remembers. "But then we realized that we couldn't keep our feelings inside forever. Plus, with our dad gone, we needed help dealing with Mom. It was like a war at our house."

Rachel adds quickly, "We still don't get along that well with her. It'll never be like it was with Dad. But at least now Theresa's [the therapist] taught us to communicate."

"I still love my wife deeply," Jim says, his eyes on Sandy. "But I know I've lost her. And my daughters . . . last week when we had our first session with the whole family, they told me they still love me but they hate me, too. I don't blame then one bit. I took the love they were giving me truthfully, I turned it around and abused them as women instead of protecting them as daughters. I knew I had a problem, but I blamed it on everyone else: my uncle who molested me, Sandy, my boss . . . Now I can only blame myself. None of this would have happened if I'd gotten help before it was too late."

"It *is* too late," Sandy says quickly. "I still love this man. But my girls come first with me, and my girls want this marriage to end. So 20 years is dissolved. I've lost more than my husband because of sexual abuse. I lost my father years ago when he abused Rachel. I lost all my friends—they were mostly people Jim and I worked with and I didn't want them to know what we were going through. I lost my job because I fell apart emotionally. The worst thing I lost was my self-esteem: as a wife, a mother, a woman.

"Right now the only thing that gives me hope is the changes I see in myself and in my daughters. We're all independent now. I just graduated from a nursing program, so I'll never rely financially on anyone again. Rachel's got herself a good job so she can take care of herself, and she's engaged to a fine young man. Lisa—she's always been so quiet—speaks up more now. Sarah's learning not to blame herself for things that have been done to her. In a way, my daughters and I have grown up together through this tragedy. I've learned along with them how I was raised to be a victim, like my mother was before me. I know my daughters won't raise *their* daughters that way! And we've all learned to say no—a word that as females we were taught never to say."

Rachel jerks her head angrily. "You make it sound so easy, Mom. What about the other things we learned?" She turns to me. "Like not to trust anyone, ever. Like growing up believing that you pay for love with sex. Like having to lie to everyone all

your life. I'm *still* lying, trying to explain why I won't let Dad walk me down the aisle on my wedding day. And Lisa's still two grades behind because she was afraid to come home to do her homework. And Sarah's still got her asthma. As long as my sisters and I are suffering because of what he did, I'll *never* forgive him."

"It hurts deep down to face up to what I've done to you," Jim says. He is sobbing now. "I'm so sorry . . ."

Rachel didn't let him finish. "You should feel sorry—I don't accept your apology. You can sit there and talk about facing up to it. Well, we face up to it whether we want to or not! Do you know that Lisa just lost her babysitting job because the parents found out she was molested? Do you know that Sarah still wakes up screaming almost every night? Do you know that none of us has a single friend who knows the truth about us! You just make me feel guilty with all your damn apologies, and I don't want to hear them anymore."

Sarah begins to wheeze. Sandy sits her up; Lisa digs through Sarah's book bag and pulls out a bronchial inhaler. As Sarah's panting slows, Lisa stares straight at me for a long moment.

"You said you wanted to know our story," she says. "Well, now you see how it is for us. And I want you to write it all down. I want every kid who's being molested right now to know that they shouldn't keep it a secret, that they deserve help and they can get help. And I want every man out there to know what it does to children to be sexually abused."

Tears run down her cheeks. "If we can keep this from happening to just one girl or one boy, maybe all this pain will be worth it."

❖

ACQUAINTANCE RAPE

Daniel Goleman

What is acquaintance rape? How does it differ from rape by a stranger? According to this article, why is acquaintance rape so prevalent? What is the influence of the double standard? What can be done to prevent acquaintance rape?

Researchers tying to understand the relative frequency of rape between acquaintances are focusing their attention on the radical differences in how men and women interpret each other's interest in a sexual encounter.

Surveys have found that as many as one in four women report that a man they were dating persisted in trying to force sex on them despite their pleading, crying, fighting him off or screaming. In one survey of women on 32 college campuses, 15 percent had experienced at least one rape, and 89 percent of the time it was by men the women knew. Half the rapes occurred during a date.

READINGS

By better understanding what leads to such rapes, researchers hope to be able to offer guidelines to women and men that will help to lower the risk of their occurrence.

Some research points to the pernicious effects of the sexual double standard that holds, as one psychologist put it, "that nice women don't say yes, and real men don't listen to no." Other studies focus on what makes certain men more likely to force themselves on an unwilling woman, or if there are factors that make a woman more likely to become the victim.

While rape between strangers has long been the subject of scientific study, largely because of the accessibility of convicted rapists, the research on rape among acquaintances has been slower to develop.

"Most acquaintance rapes are never reported, let alone prosecuted, and few men admit to having forced sex on a woman," said Dr. Andrea Parrot, a psychologist at Cornell University. "It makes it difficult to study."

Despite the high proportion of women who have experienced forced sex, very few men admit to having been involved in such acts. In one survey of 1,152 male college students, just 17 admitted to using physical force to have sexual intercourse with a woman when she did not want to.

There is wide agreement among researchers that many men and women involved in instances of forced sex do not realize that, legally, the encounter usually meets the legal definition of rape. Re-searchers say this, along with factors such as shame, account for the vast underreporting of such incidents.

"When men are asked if there is any likelihood they would force a woman to have sex against her will if they could get away with it, about half say they would," said Dr. Neil Malamuth, a psychologist at the University of California at Los Angeles. "But if you ask them if they would rape a woman if they knew they could get away with it, only about 15 percent say they would."

Those who change their answers do not seem to realize that there is no difference between rape and forcing a woman to have sex against her will, Dr. Malamuth said. The difference is in the words used to describe the same act. Many women, too, share the confusion, and so may not realize that they have been raped.

Specific definitions vary from state to state, but researchers consider a sexual encounter to be rape if a man forces a woman to have sex against her will or without her consent. The woman need not explicitly protest; women who fear for their lives or safety during a rape often seem to comply. But the researchers say it can be considered rape if the woman does not explicitly consent.

Some women are unable to consent because, for instance, they have passed out while drunk. A sexual encounter may also be considered rape if force or the threat of force is used, Dr. Parrot said.

Some of the newest research on forced sex points to the influence of the sexual double standard.

"The double standard labels women who are free about having sex as loose, but sees sexually active men as studs," said Dr. Charlene Muehlenhard who, with Marcia McCoy, presented data this month at the annual meeting of the American Psychological Association in New Orleans.

Like many people, the researchers had assumed that the double standard had eroded as the status of women changed. But from the data accumulating on rape among acquaintances, little seems to have changed.

One result, Dr. Muehlenhard said is that women who do not want to appear to be loose offer "token protest, in which the woman says no, but means yes."

In a survey of 610 women published last year, Dr. Muehlenhard found that more than a third had, at least once put up such token resistance when they actually wanted to have sex. Women who believed their dates hold to the double standard were most likely to use the tactic of a false protest, presumably not to seem "loose."

The trouble is, Dr. Muehlenhard says, that men tend to see all such protests as token resistance, a no that really means yes. Indeed, she says, the scenario where a forceful man continues a sexual advance despite a woman's protest, until she melts in compliance, is commonly depicted in films and books.

"This sexual script sends men the message that they should not believe women's refusals," Dr. Muehlenhard said. "This can lead to rape in some instances. Men can easily forget that most often no means no. If a man wants to avoid rape, he should believe what a woman tells him."

The double standard also creates pressures on men to force themselves on women, Dr. Muehlenhard said. "The problem is that we give men the message that if you're not sexually active, there's something wrong with you," she said. "At the same time, we tell women they will seem loose if they give in too readily."

In another study, to be published in *The Journal of Sex Research,* 63 percent of men said they had sex when they did not want to, Dr. Muehlenhard found. "Sometimes it was because a woman made sexual advances and the man felt he would look bad to her—seem shy, afraid or gay—if he didn't go along," she said. "Some were instances of peer pressure from other men, such as at a party where others are having sex."

To be sure, factors other than the double standard are at work in rapes of acquaintances. This month in *The Journal of Sex Research,* Dr. Malamuth reported on a series of recent studies intended to identify attributes that make some men more likely than others to force sex on a woman.

Dr. Malamuth used a combination of questionnaires about attitudes toward sex. He also observed the reactions of men to stories depicting sexual incidents. While the men read the stories, a sensor detected the degree of their sexual arousal.

continued on next page

The men who were most likely to become aroused by a story in which a woman was forced to have sex despite protests tended to share other attitudes. One of these was the idea that dominance itself was a motive for sex; they agreed with statements like "I enjoy the conquest." Another is hostility toward women, as expressed in sentiments like "women irritate me a great deal more than they are aware of."

A third, not surprisingly, is an acceptance of sexual violence. For instance, they might agree with the statement, "Sometimes the only way a man can get a cold woman turned on is to use force."

Differences between men and women in how they perceive a romantic encounter also contribute to rapes of acquaintances, according to research by Dr. R. Lance Shotland, a psychologist at Pennsylvania State University. In a study published last year in *The Social Psychology Quarterly*, Dr. Shotland and Jane Craig, a research associate, found that men tended to interpret a woman's actions on a date, even such innocuous acts as speaking in a low voice or smiling, as indicating that she was interested in sex. Women, however, tended to see the same behaviors as simply being "friendly."

Other research has shown that men, particularly younger ones, tend to have difficulty discriminating between what women do that is merely friendly, and what indicates sexual interest. A woman drinking, coming to a man's apartment or wearing "sexy" clothes, for instance, all tended to be seen by men as indicators that the woman was interested in sex, while women did not agree, Dr. Muehlenhard found in a 1985 study.

In a 1979 California study, 43 percent of men of high school and college age said that by the fifth date it was "acceptable" for a man to force sex on a woman, and 39 percent of the men said it was acceptable if the man had "spent a lot of money on her."

Assumptions like these about the acceptability of sex are at play in gang rape, a rare event that occurs disproportionately on college campuses, where most cases go unreported, according to Dr. Chris O'Sullivan, a psychologist at Bucknell University. In a study this year of 23 incidents of gang rape, she found that the men involved seem to think that what they were doing was "O.K.," most often because they regarded the woman as promiscuous.

In virtually all the incidents, the raped woman was known by one or more of the men. Most of the rapes involved fraternities, or football or basketball teams.

The women who are raped by these groups are, in the men's eyes, distinguished from the women they date in terms of respectability. One man involved in a gang rape by football teammates, told Dr. O'Sullivan that the woman "had not, in fact, been raped because she had dated two of them previously," and had hurt the men's feeling by indiscriminately having sex with each of them.

Women who socialize with the men on an equal footing, on the other hand, are unlikely to be victims of group rape, Dr. O'Sullivan said, both because of their "respectability" and because they understand the mores of the men's groups. Thus, women who date fraternity members learn not to go upstairs to a bathroom in the fraternity house unless another woman accompanies them, and that getting drunk at a party is taken as a signal of availability.

As a gang rape proceeds, according to other research, as each successive man takes his turn, the woman is increasingly seen as "a whore" who deserves to be raped.

In research published in 1983, Dr. Shotland and Dr. Lynne Goodstein found that even when a woman protests that she does not want to have sex, both men and women tended to fault the woman if she did not resist at the beginning of the encounter.

Research by Dr. Muehlenhard on effective tactics to avoid date rape shows that the woman should make clear early in the encounter that she is not interested in having sex. Other effective approaches were physical resistance, screaming and claiming to have a venereal disease. But the single most powerful tactic of all was the statement, "This is rape and I'm calling the cops."

Changes

Coming Apart: Separation and Divorce

To gain a sense of what you already know about the material covered in this chapter, answer "true" or "false" to the following statements. You will find the answers on page 529.

1. Half of all current American marriages end in divorce within seven years. True or false? T

2. African Americans living in the South have a greater likelihood of divorcing than those living in the West. True or false? F

3. A child born today has about a fifty-fifty chance of living in a single-parent family or stepfamily before he or she reaches age eighteen. True or false? T

4. The critical emotional event in a marital breakdown is the separation rather than the divorce. True or false? T

5. Anglos have a higher divorce rate than Latinos. True or false? F

6. Divorce is an important element of the contemporary American marriage system because it reinforces the significance of emotional fulfillment in marriage. True or false? T

7. The higher an individual's employment status, income, and level of education, the greater the likelihood of divorce. True or false? F

8. Social scientists increasingly consider divorce to be part of the normal family life cycle. True or false? T

9. Those whose parents are divorced have a significantly greater likelihood of themselves divorcing. True or false? T

10. Marital conflict in an intact two-parent family is more harmful to children than living in a tranquil single-parent family or stepfamily. True or false? T

12:30

*Experience is the name everyone gives to
their mistakes.*

Oscar Wilde

*Love, the quest; marriage, the conquest;
divorce, the inquest.*

Helen Rowland

*A man should not marry a woman with the
mental reservation that, after all, he can
divorce her.*

Talmud: Yebamoth

Americans' feelings about marriage and divorce seem strangely paradoxical. Consider the following (Coleman and Ganong, 1991; White, 1991):

◆ *Americans like marriage:* They have one of the highest marriage rates in the industrialized world.
◆ *Americans don't like marriage:* They have one of the highest divorce rates in the world.
◆ *Americans like marriage:* They have one of the highest remarriage rates in the world.

What sense can we make from the fact that we are one of the most marrying, divorcing, and remarrying nations in the world? What does our high divorce rate actually tell us about how we feel about marriage?

Scholars suggest that divorce does not represent a devaluation of marriage but, oddly enough, an idealization of it. We would not divorce if we did not have so much hope about marriage fulfilling our various needs (Furstenberg and Spanier, 1987). In fact, divorce may very well be a critical part of our contemporary marriage system, which emphasizes emotional fulfillment and satisfaction. Frank Furstenberg and Graham Spanier (1987) note:

Divorce can be seen as an intrinsic part of a cultural system that values individual discretion and emotional gratification. Divorce is a social invention for promoting these cultural ideals. Ironically, the more divorce is used, the more exacting the standards become for those who marry. . . . Divorce . . . serves not so much as an escape hatch from married life but as a recycling mechanism permitting individuals a second (and sometimes third and fourth chance) to upgrade their marital situation.

Our high divorce rate also tells us that we may no longer believe in the permanence of marriage. Norval Glenn (1991) suggests that there is a "decline in the ideal of marital permanence and . . . in the expectation that marriages will last until one of the spouses dies." Instead, marriages disintegrate when love goes or a potentially better partner comes along. Divorce is a persistent fact of American marital and family life and one of the most important forces affecting and changing American lives today (Furstenberg and Cherlin, 1991).

Before 1974 "until death do us part" reflected reality. Then a surge in divorce rates occurred in the mid-1960s that did not level off until the 1990s. In 1974, a watershed in American history was reached when more marriages ended by divorce than by death. Today between 50 to 60 percent of all new marriages are likely to end in divorce (Martin and Bumpass, 1989).

Not only does divorce end marriages and break up families, it also creates new forms from the old ones. It creates remarriages (which are very different from first marriages). It gives birth to single-parent families and stepfamilies. Today about one out of every five American families is a single-parent family; more than half of all children will become stepchildren by the year 2000 (Glick, 1989). (In contrast, only 13 percent of Canadian families are "lone-parent" families [Statistics Canada, 1990].) And about half of current marriages include at least one spouse who is remarried (Bumpass, Sweet, and Martin, 1990). Within the singles subculture is an immense pool of divorced men and women (most of whom are on their way to remarriage). But divorce does not create these new forms easily. It gives birth to them in pain and travail.

Research traditionally looked on divorce from a deviance perspective (Coleman and Ganong, 1991). It was assumed that normal, healthy individuals married and remained married. Those who divorced were considered abnormal, immature, narcissistic, or unhealthy in some manner. Social scientists, however, are increasingly viewing divorce as one path in the normal family life cycle. Those who divorce are not necessarily different from those who remain married. If we begin to regard divorce in this light, social scientists reason, part of the pain accompanying divorce may be diminished, as those involved will no longer regard themselves as "abnormal" (Raschke, 1987).

Social scientists express their greatest concern about the effects of divorce on children (Aldous, 1987; Wallerstein and Blakeslee, 1989). But even in studies of the children of divorce, the research may be distorted by traditional assumptions about divorce being deviant (Amato, 1991). For example, problems that children experience may be attributed to divorce rather than to other causes, such as personality traits or parental abuse. Although some effects are caused by the disruption of the family itself, others may be linked to the new social environment—most notably poverty and parental stress—into which children are thrust (McLanahan and Booth, 1991; Raschke, 1987).

In this chapter we look at marital separation, the changes an individual undergoes when he or she separates, no-fault divorce, custody, and the impact of divorce on children. In the next chapter we will examine how people put their lives back together after divorce and how, in doing so, they create new family structures.

> It's one thing marrying the wrong person for the wrong reasons: it's another sticking it out with them.
>
> Philip Roth, Letting Go

> Divorces are made in heaven.
>
> Oscar Wilde

❖ MARITAL SEPARATION

One of the most notable changes in recent divorce research is the recognition that divorce is not a single act but a process (Kitson and Morgan, 1991). The crucial event in a marital breakdown is the act of separation. Divorce is a legal consequence that follows the emotional fact of separation (Melichar and Chiriboga, 1988).

Although separation generally precedes divorce, not all separations lead to divorce. As many as one couple out of every six that remains married is likely to have separated for at least two days (Kitson, 1985). The majority of separated women are between fifteen and forty-five years old; a greater proportion of African Americans than whites are separated. A high proportion of women who are poor (and even more who are poor and have children) are separated (Norton and Moorman, 1987).

One study found that of those who separated, 40 percent reconciled at least once; 18 percent reconciled twice or more (Bumpass, Martin, and Sweet, 1991). Unfortunately, we don't know much about marital separation. We don't know, for example, which separations are likely to lead to reconciliations, divorce, or long-term separation (Morgan, 1988; South and Spitz, 1986). Those who reconcile may have separated in order to dramatize their complaints, create emotional distance, or dissipate their anger (Kitson, 1985). Almost all who reconciled did so within a year; 45 percent reconciled within a month. Of those who reconciled, about two-fifths were together at the time they were interviewed (Bumpass et al., 1991).

Uncoupling: The Process of Separation

The trends in divorce are fairly clear, but the causes are not. Sociologists can describe societal, demographic, and family factors that appear to be associated with divorce (see "Perspective"). Unfortunately, such variables tell us only about groups rather than individuals. Similarly, divorced men and women can tell us what they *believe* were the causes of their divorces. But human beings do not always know the

> Marriage is the chief cause of divorce.
>
> Groucho Marx

[handwritten margin note: Not all Separations lead to divorce]

Don't leave in a huff. Leave in a minute and a huff. If you can't leave in a minute and a huff, leave in a taxi.

Groucho Marx

. . .rather bear those ills we have Than fly to others we know not of.

William Shakespeare

As for infidelity, which has been blamed for so many divorces, that doesn't seem to be the real issue. It might be closer to the truth to say that people divorce not because one or both partners have been unfaithful, but because they are faithful—not to each other, but to themselves.

Anatole Broyard

Because divorce has become part of contemporary marital norms, it is part of the normal life cycle for many marriages.

reasons for their own actions. They can deceive themselves, blame others, or remain ignorant of the causes (Burns, 1984). Sometimes marital complaints are culled from long-term marital problems as a justification for the split-up. Gay Kitson and Marvin Sussman (1982) observed that the study of marital complaints as causes of divorce is merely the study of people's perceptions: "It is perhaps an impossibility to determine what 'really' broke up the marriage." Robert Weiss (1975) used the term "account" to describe the individual's personal perception of the breakup. These accounts focus on a few dramatic events or factors in the marriage. Because accounts are personal perceptions, each spouse's account is often very different; what is important to one partner may not be important to the other. Sometimes the accounts of ex-spouses seem to describe entirely different marriages.

People do not suddenly separate or divorce. Instead, they gradually move apart through a set of fairly predictable stages. Sociologist Diane Vaughan (1986) calls this process "uncoupling." The process appears to be the same for married or unmarried couples and for gay, lesbian, and heterosexual relationships. The length of time together does not seem to affect the process. Uncoupling begins," Vaughan observes, "as a quiet, unilateral process." Usually one person, the initiator, is unhappy or dissatisfied but keeps such feelings to himself or herself. The initiator often ponders fundamental questions about his or her identity: "Who am I? Who am I in this relationship? What do I want out of my life? Can I find it in this relationship?" The dissatisfied partner may attempt to make changes in the relationship, but these are often unsuccessful, as he or she may not really know what the problem is.

Because the dissatisfied partner is unable to find satisfaction within the relationship, he or she begins turning elsewhere. This is not a malicious or intentional turning away; it is done to find self-validation without leaving the relationship. In doing so, however, the dissatisfied partner "creates a small territory independent of the coupled identity." This creates a division within the relationship. Gradually, the dissatisfied partner voices more and more complaints, which make the relationship and partner increasingly undesirable. The initiator begins thinking about alternatives to the relationship and comparing the costs and benefits of these alternatives. Meanwhile, both the initiator and his or her partner try to cover up the seriousness of the dissatisfaction, submerging it in the little problems of everyday living.

Marital Cohesiveness

Whatever the demographic or personal reasons we may find for divorce, the ultimate reasons may escape us. Another way to understand divorce, however, is to examine marital cohesiveness, the factors that help maintain a marriage. According to George Levinger (1979), people remain married because of (1) sources of attraction, (2) barriers against leaving, and (3) sources of alternate attraction. In this model, *attraction* refers to positive forces that keep people in a relationship, *barriers* are restraining forces that keep people from leaving a relationship, and *alternative attractions* are other persons, relationships, or activities that compete with the marital relationship. The importance of each factor changes during people's lives (White and Booth, 1991).

Although Levinger's model is not romantic, it may be realistic. For those who have been ambivalent about ending a long-term relationship, these three factors may seem all too familiar.

Attractions

Attractions include caring for one's partner, the desire for companionship, sexual pleasure, and other affectionate aspects of the relationship. They also included a good standard of living (such as home ownership or family income), similar social values, and educational and occupational status. It is not uncommon for people to stay together because they love their house more than each other.

Barriers

Barriers to breaking up include feelings of obligation, moral proscriptions, and external pressures. One of the strongest restraints is a couple's (especially the mother's) deep sense of love for and moral obligation to their dependent children (Levinger, 1979). One study, for example, has shown that women with children are significantly less liberal toward divorce than women without children (Jorgensen and Johnson, 1980). The presence of children, however, has little effect on men's attitudes toward divorce. The couple may also feel an obligation to the marriage itself, even if they have ceased loving each other. They may also believe that they are morally obliged by their religion not to divorce. Finally, they may feel external pressures not to divorce. (What will our parents say? What will our friends say?) Family and community pressures have been powerful constraints on divorce in the past, but such constraints have weakened in recent years. (For the significance of commitment, see Sabatelli and Cecil-Pigo, 1985; Swenson and Trahaug, 1985; also see Heaton and Albrecht, 1991).

Alternatives

The alternatives to marriage may include singlehood and greater independence and self-direction, especially for women who may have felt their potential curtailed in marriage. Also, a person may find (or believe that he or she may find) greater happiness with another partner.

Because of the ease with which divorce may be obtained, we are living in a marriage system in which everyone is permanently available as a spouse and is continually comparing his or her current marriage with other potential marriages or with singlehood. As a result, they may not fully commit (Glenn, 1991). If a person's present marital relationship appears strikingly less favorable than the alternatives and if the barriers to leaving the marriage do not cancel out the value of the alternatives, then the marriage is more likely to dissolve. Richard Udry (1981) found that marriages in which many marriage alternatives were available to both spouses had high divorce rates. What is striking, moreover, is that marital alternatives are a better predictor of divorce than marital satisfaction. People often stay in unhappy marriages if they believe that they do not have good alternatives. They may also leave relatively satisfactory marriages if they think that their alternatives are better. In a society in which everyone is available, whether married or not, people may tend to see the grass as being greener on the other side of the fence. If the fence (barrier) is not too high, people may abandon their familiar turf for the greener pastures on the other side. Unfortunately, that grass on the other side may prove to be only Astroturf.

Levels of attraction, like barriers and alternatives, change over the course of an individual's life (White and Booth, 1991). This may account for the greater likelihood of divorce occurring in the first years of marriage instead of in longer-lasting marriages. Two researchers note (White and Booth, 1991), "Because barriers are few and alternatives high, people in short marriages get divorced even when their marriages are not very unhappy." Rather than accept an unfulfilling marriage, men and women in their youth are more likely to divorce, as they may be childless, not own a house, and feel that they could do much better than their current spouse. Things change as the marriage continues and the partners grow older. In long marriages, there are more barriers, such as children or home ownership, and fewer alternatives, such as a dearth of attractive, unattached potential partners. The level of marital unhappiness needs to be much higher to lead to divorce in such marriages.

This model of marital cohesiveness may be useful for examining the cohesiveness of your own relationship. Take two sheets of paper; entitle one "Myself" and the other "My Partner." Divide each sheet into three columns. Label the first column "Attractions," the second one "Barriers," and the third one "Alternatives." Then list the various attractions, barriers, and alternatives in your current relationship (or a previous one if you are no longer in a relationship) for both you and your partner. Based on the attractions, barriers, and alternatives for both you and your partner, how cohesive do you think your relationship is? For you, which element is the most important for maintaining your relationship? For your partner? Are there things you can do (or not do) to make it more cohesive?

Things You Told Me

I am a lousy housekeeper
I don't wash the dishes often enough
When I do wash the dishes, I run the water
*   too much*
When I clean up, I do it in the wrong order
The mustard is on the wrong shelf in the
*   refrigerator*
I arrange our refrigerator wrong
My inconsiderate children step on the
*   papers you have left neatly stacked on*
*   the living room floor*
I raise my children wrong
My little boy doesn't wash his dish
He washes his dish wrong
We make too much noise
I cut wrapping paper wrong
I massage you wrong
I touch wrong
I kiss wrong
I make love wrong
I am too sexual
My hugs are too sexual
I lay with my arm across the wrong part of
*   your body (which hurts your stomach or*
*   makes you itch)*
I pull your hair when I embrace you
I take too long to come
Or sometimes (and this is worse) I don't
*   come at all*
I sleep too close
I don't sleep close enough
I express my feelings wrong
I handle your anger wrong
I communicate wrong
I don't always like the things you like and I
*   say so—this is wrong*
I share my enthusiasm wrong
I'm wrong to be upset by your disrespect
for me
I buy you the wrong presents
I take the wrong routes when I drive from
*   one place to another*
I drive too slow
I am too hesitant when I drive
I shift too late or too early
I drive in the wrong gear
I don't pass the slow cars when I should
I drive in the wrong lane
I ask too much of you
I relate to people wrong
I forget things because I pay attention
*   wrong*
I don't always understand what you are
*   trying to say because I listen wrong*
I'm illogical
I complain too much
I have bad manners
I'm inconsiderate

(continued on next page)

Eventually the initiator decides that he or she can no longer go on. There are several strategies for ending the relationship. One way is simply to tell the partner that the relationship is over. Another way is to consciously or unconsciously break a fundamental rule in the relationship, such as by having an extramarital affair.

Uncoupling does not end when the end of a relationship is announced, or even when the couple physically separate. Acknowledging that the relationship cannot be saved represents the beginning of the last stage of uncoupling. Vaughan (1986) wrote:

> Partners begin to put the relationship behind them. They acknowledge that the relationship is unsaveable. Through the process of mourning they, too, eventually arrive at an account that explains this unexpected denouement. "Getting over" a relationship does not mean relinquishing that part of our life that we shared with another, but rather coming to some conclusion that allows us to accept and understand its altered significance. Once we develop such an account, we can incorporate it into our lives and go on.

Separation Distress

Our married self becomes part of our deepest self. Therefore, when people separate or divorce, many feel as if they have "lost an arm or a leg." This analogy, as well as the traditional marriage rite in which a man and a woman are pronounced "one," reveals an important truth of marriage: the constant association of both partners makes each almost a physical part of the other. This dynamic is true even if two people are locked in conflict; they, too, are attached to each other (Masheter, 1991).

Marital roles, however, end with separation and divorce: the man is no longer a husband and the woman is no longer a wife. If these former partners are also parents, their parental roles alter as well. In most cases, a woman becomes *more* a mother and a man becomes *less* a father. A woman's parent role becomes more significant and all-encompassing while a man's becomes less so. An important task for those who separate is to create new identities that reflect their new status (or nonstatus, as some feel).

Most newly separated people do not know what to expect. There are no divorce ceremonies or rituals to mark this major turning point. Yet people need to understand divorce to alleviate some of its pain and burden. Except for the death of a spouse, divorce is the greatest stress-producing event in life (Holmes and Rahe, 1967). The changes that take place during separation are crucial, because at this point a person's emotions are rawest and most profound. Men and women react differently during this period, although both are more depressed than their married or divorced counterparts. Men have a generally lower sense of well-being than women, yet women undergo greater emotional upheaval (Gove et al., 1990; Raschke, 1987).

Researchers have considerable knowledge about the negative consequences accompanying marital separation, some of which we will discuss in the sections that follow. In looking at this negative impact, however, we need to keep in mind Helen Raschke's (1987) caution: "The psychological and emotional consequences of separation and divorce have been more distorted than any of the other consequences as a result of the deviance perspective." The negative aspects of separation are balanced sooner or later, notes Raschke, by positive aspects, such as the possibility of finding a more compatible partner, constructing a better (or different) life, developing new dimensions of the self, enhancing self-esteem, and marrying a better parent for one's children. These positive consequences may follow or be intertwined with separation distress. In the pain of separation, we may forget that a new self will eventually emerge.

Almost everyone suffers separation distress when a marriage breaks up. The distress is real but, fortunately, not everlasting (although it may seem so). It is situational and is modified by numerous external factors. About the only men and women who do not experience distress are those whose marriages were riddled by high levels of conflict. In these cases, one or both partners may view the separation with relief (Raschke, 1987).

During separation distress, almost all attention is centered on the missing partner, and is accompanied by apprehensiveness, anxiety, fear, and often panic. "What am I going to do?" "What is he or she doing?" "I need him . . . I need her . . . I hate him . . . I love him . . . I hate her . . . I love her. . . ." Sometimes, however, the immediate effect of separation is not distress but euphoria. This usually results from feeling that the former spouse is not necessary, that one can get along better without him or her, that the old fights and the spouse's criticism are gone forever, and that life will now be full of possibilities and excitement. That feeling is soon gone. Almost everyone falls back into separation anxiety (Weiss, 1975).

FACTORS AFFECTING DISTRESS. Separation distress affects people in a variety of ways. An unexpected separation is probably most painful for the partner who is left. Other factors affecting distress include the length of time married, who takes the initiative in leaving, whether someone new is found, the quality of the postmarital relationship, and personal resources.

How much warning! Did they know it was coming.

Length of Time Married. Separations that take place during the first two years of marriage are less difficult for the husband and wife to weather. Those couples who separate after two years find separation more difficult, since it seems to take about two years for people to become emotionally and socially integrated into marriage and their marital roles (Weiss, 1975). After that point, additional years of marriage seem to make little difference. Generally, a person married for two years will suffer distress over the loss of marital roles as much as one married ten years.

The Leaver and the Left. Considerable research has focused on finding out whether being the initiator makes a difference in separation distress (Buehler, 1987). It appears that the initiator has a greater sense of personal control over his or her life (Petit and Bloom, 1984). Noninitiators feel powerless, because they are unable to prevent the leaving. All they can do is stand by and watch their lives disintegrate. Initiators frequently feel a strong sense of guilt about hurting their partners and may worry about their own capacity to make emotional commitment (Weiss, 1975). Noninitiators often have a more difficult time accepting the divorce, experience more loneliness, and miss their former spouse more than they are missed (Spanier and Thompson, 1983, 1984). Who leaves whom does not seem to make much difference in the length or intensity of separation distress, but it does affect the character of the distress.

Finding Someone New. A new relationship reduces much of the distress caused by separation and almost entirely prevents the loneliness caused by emotional isolation. It also reinforces a person's sense of self-worth. But it does not entirely eliminate separation distress. It does not end the disruption of intimate personal relations with the former partner, children, friends, and relatives (Weiss, 1975). If the newly separated person was involved extramaritally with someone prior to the separation, the involvement may have provided needed emotional support and intimacy as the marriage unraveled. Such an extramarital relationship rarely ends in marriage; following divorce, however, the nature of the affair may change.

Quality of the Postmarital Relationship. After separation, husbands and wives may treat each other in ways that range from friendly consideration and care to outright hostility and warfare. Civilized divorces are certainly to be desired, especially if children are involved, but they are not easy to achieve. It usually takes considerable time for emotions to cool and wounds to heal. It may also require substantial effort and insight for the ex-partners to get beyond blame, hurt, and anger. If former partners do achieve friendly relations, they may feel reassured that the years they spent together were not meaningless. For some people, however, the quality of their former marriage may have been so poor that it isn't worth the effort to maintain contact.

Resources. The more resources a person has, the better he or she may handle the separation crisis. These resources may be emotional as well as social and financial. Too often people blame themselves for not adjusting well to a marital breakup; they feel depressed and are angry with themselves for feeling depressed. People who are more resilient and have greater energy and imagination tend to do better than others. Those who have a tendency to withdraw, whose self-confidence is usually low, and who panic or get depressed easily have a harder time recovering. A person who becomes socially isolated following a breakup tends to be susceptible to an emotional or health breakdown (Pilisuk, 1982).

For a newly separated person, the old social world breaks up and must be recreated separate from the former partner (Milardo, 1987). Parents become an important resource for their divorcing adult children (Johnson, 1988). They provide economic assistance and emotional support; they are also important for their grandchildren in easing the divorce transition. Relatives of the former spouse often become unavailable, distant, or hostile. One study found that 70 percent of in-laws disapproved of the former spouse (Spanier and Thompson, 1987). Friends may splinter, some remaining friendly to both partners, others being friends only with one or championing one over the other. But the emotional support of friends often proves to be stronger than that of family (Spanier and Thompson, 1987). Friends thus become especially important in overcoming the isolation and loneliness that generally accompanies a separation. One woman, as she planned to leave her husband, made a determined effort to establish a network of friends to help cushion the shock. Eventually the distress wanes and life returns to a more stable pattern. The ups and downs associated with the separation disappear.

LONELINESS. As the separation continues, separation distress slowly gives way to loneliness. Eventually, loneliness becomes the most prominent feature of the broken relationship. Old friends can sometimes help provide stability for a person experiencing a marital breakup, but those who give comfort need to be able to tolerate the other person's loneliness. One man told the authors that he counts as true friends only those who listened to him being miserable day after day. However, separated people often consider themselves a burden and will turn away from old friends who seem happy and content. In fact, married friends are generally supportive during the first two months, but then their contacts with the separated person rapidly decline, perhaps in part because they related to the person as part of a couple rather than as an individual in his or her own right (Hetherington et al., 1977).

Hope in reality is the worst of all evils, because it prolongs the torments of man.

Friedrich Nietzsche

Divorce Song

*I thought you were good.
I thought you were like silver. But you are lead.
Now look at me on the mountain top
As I walk through the sun.
I am sunlight.*

Tsimshian traditional song

One must first have chaos in oneself to give birth to a dancing star.

Friedrich Nietzsche

Beginning group therapy with other recently divorced people may help. Within such a group, separated or divorced people discover that their loneliness is not unusual and that they are not going crazy; on the contrary, their response is quite normal under the circumstances.

ESTABLISHING A POSTDIVORCE IDENTITY. A person goes through two distinct phases in establishing a new identity following marital separation: transition and recovery (Weiss, 1975). The *transition period* begins with the separation and is characterized by separation distress and then loneliness. In this period's later stages, most people begin functioning in an orderly way again, although they still may experience bouts of upset and turmoil. The transition period generally ends within the first year. During this time, individuals have already begun making decisions that provide the framework for new selves. They have entered the role of single parent or non-custodial parent, have found a new place to live, have made important career and financial decisions, and have begun; to date. Their new lives are taking shape.

The *recovery period* usually begins in the second year and lasts between one and three years. By this time the separated or divorced individual has already created a reasonably stable pattern of life. The marriage is becoming more of a distant memory, and the former spouse does not arouse the intense passions he or she once did. Mood swings are not as extreme and depressed periods are fewer. Yet the individual still has self-doubts that lie just beneath the surface. A sudden reversal, a bad time with the kids, doubts about a romantic involvement can suddenly destroy a divorced person's confidence. By the end of the recovery period, the distress has passed. Those who have a strong sense of well-being are more likely to remarry within a few years (Spanier and Furstenberg, 1982).

It takes some people longer than others to recover, because each person experiences the process in his or her own way. But most are surprised by how long the recovery takes—they forget that they are undergoing a major discontinuity in their lives. Weiss (1975) estimates that it takes between two and four years after the initial separation for a divorced person to establish a new identity, to feel strong and confident. It is probably closer to four years for most. By anyone's reckoning, that is a long time, especially because it is a time marked by mood swings, uncertainty, and questioning.

Dating Again

A first date after years of marriage and subsequent months of singlehood evokes some of the same emotions felt by inexperienced adolescents. Separated or divorced men and women who are beginning to date again may be excited, nervous, worry about how they look, and wonder whether or not it is okay to hold hands, kiss, or make love. They may feel that dating is incongruous with their former selves or be annoyed with themselves for feeling excited and awkward. Furthermore, they have little idea of the norms of postmarital dating (Spanier and Thompson, 1987).

For many divorced men and women, the greatest problem is how to meet other unmarried people. They believe that marriage has put them "out of circulation" and many are not sure how to get back in. Because of the marriage squeeze, separated and divorced women in their thirties or older are at a particular disadvantage: considerably fewer men are available than women. The problem of meeting others is most acute for single mothers who are full-time parents in the home, since they lack opportunities to meet potential partners. Divorced men, having fewer child-care

To free oneself is nothing; it's being free that is hard.

André Gide

Excuses

Are you leaving because you are hungry? Aha! Is your stomach your master?

Are you leaving me to cover yourself? Have I not a blanket on my bed?

Are you leaving me because you are thirsty?
Then take my breast, it flows over for you.

Traditional African poem

Sometimes I wonder if men and women really suit each other. Perhaps they should live next door and just visit now and then.

Katharine Hepburn

PERSPECTIVE

Factors Affecting the Likelihood of Divorce

Almost everyone who marries today knows that he or she has a fifty-fifty chance of divorcing later. The uncertainty of marital success dogs many of us. For some people it creates an underlying sense of fear as they make their commitments; for others, it makes them hesitant to make a commitment for fear of failure. But if we can be aware of some of the factors associated with divorce, we can overcome the disadvantages associated with them. Such knowledge empowers us to have successful marriages.

It may be difficult to discover the underlying reasons for any individual divorce, but researchers have found various factors related to divorce. Some are societal, others are demographic, and still others are related to the nature of marriage or family itself. We will review some of those factors related to increased divorce probability in this Perspective (see White, 1991, for a literature review).

Societal Factors

The divorce rate in our society has shifted from less than 10 percent at the beginning of the twentieth century to between 50 and 60 percent as we approach the twenty-first century. Such a dramatic change points to the need for societal rather than individual explanations.

Changed Nature Of The Family. The shift from an agricultural society to an industrial one undermined many of the family's traditional functions (as discussed in Chapter 2). Schools, the media, and peers are now important sources of child socialization and child care. Hospitals and nursing homes manage birth and care for the sick and aged. Because the family pays cash for goods and services rather than producing or providing them itself, its members are no longer interdependent.

As a result of losing many of its social and economic underpinnings, the family is no longer a necessity. It is now simply one of many choices we have: we may choose singlehood, cohabitation, marriage—or divorce. And if we choose to divorce, we enter the cycle of choices again—singlehood, cohabitation, or marriage and possibly divorce for a second time. A second divorce leads to our entering the cycle for a third time, and so on.

Social Integration. Social integration, the degree of interaction between individuals and the larger community, is emerging as an important factor related to the incidence of divorce. The social integration approach regards such factors as urban residence, church membership, and population change as being especially important (Breault and Kposowa, 1987; Glenn and Shelton, 1985; Glenn and Supancic, 1984).

In this country, the rates of divorce increase from east to west. The highest rate is found in California, where two divorces currently occur for every three marriages. The greater likelihood for divorce in the West and Southwest may be caused by the higher rates of residential mobility and lower levels of social integration with extended families, ethnic neighborhoods, and church groups (Glenn and Supancic, 1984; Glenn and Shelton, 1985). Among African Americans, the lowest divorce rate is found among those born and raised in the South; African Americans born and raised in the North and West have the highest divorce rates. One study found that urban residence was the highest correlate of divorce (Breault and Kposowa, 1987). Those who live in urban areas, where the divorce rate is higher than in rural areas, for example, are less likely to be subject to the community's social or moral pressures. They are more independent and have greater freedom of personal choice.

Demographic Factors

Socioeconomic Status. Socioeconomic status is probably the most important correlate of divorce. Overall, the higher the socioeconomic status—comprised of employment status, income, and education, which tend to be interrelated—the lower the likelihood of divorce. Since the 1960s, however, the divorce rate of groups with higher socioeconomic status is approaching that of lower socioeconomic groups (Raschke, 1987).

Employment Status. Among whites, a higher divorce rate is more characteristic of low-status occupations, such as factory worker, than of higher-status occupations, such as executive (Greenstein, 1985; Martin and Bumpass, 1989). Unemployment, which contributes to marital stress, is also related to increased divorce rates.

Studies conflict as to whether employed wives are more likely than nonemployed wives to divorce; overall, though, the findings seem to suggest that female employment contributes to the likelihood of divorce since the wife is less dependent (White, 1991). Wives' employment may lead to conflict about the traditional division of household labor, child-care stress, and other work spillover problems that, in turn, create marital distress.

Income. The higher the family income, the lower the divorce rate for both whites and African Americans. Interestingly, the higher a woman's individual income, the greater the chances of divorce, perhaps because such women are not economically dependent on their husbands or because conflict over inequitable work/family roles increases marital tension.

Educational Level. The higher the educational level for whites, the lower the divorce rate. Divorce rates among African Americans are not as strongly affected by educational levels. Men and women with only a high-school education are more likely to divorce than those with a college education (Glick, 1984b).

Ethnicity. African Americans are more likely than whites to divorce. The relation between ethnicity and divorce is not surprising because of the strong correlation between socioeconomic status and divorce; the lower the socioeconomic class, the more likely a person is to divorce. As income levels for African Americans increase, in fact, divorce rates decrease; they become similar to those of whites (Raschke, 1987). Combined data from several national surveys taken between 1973 and 1980 indicate that 22.2 percent of white males and 37.2 percent of African-American males who have ever been married have divorced; the corresponding figure for white females is 23.5 percent and for African-American females is 42.2 percent (Glenn and Supancic, 1984). Current census data suggests that the same difference continues in the 1990s (U.S. Bureau of the Census, 1991).

Among Latino groups there are different divorce rates. Mexican Americans and Cubans have lower divorce rates than Anglos; the divorce rate among Puerto Ricans, however, approaches that of African Americans (Frisbie, 1986). If we examine marital disruption rates (which includes marital separation as well as divorce), Mexican Americans and Cuban Americans have disruption rates more or less the same as Anglos (Bean and Tienda,

1987; Vega, 1991). Among Puerto Ricans, the rates of marital disruption are the highest of any ethnic group in the United States. These recent findings stand in contrast to the old belief that Latino families are more stable than Anglo families (Vega, 1991).

Religion. The frequency with which people attend religious services (not necessarily the depth of their beliefs) tends to lower the divorce rate (Glenn and Supancic, 1984). Among white males, the rate of divorce for those who never attend religious services is three times as high as for those who attend two or three times a month. The lowest divorce rate is for Jews, followed by Catholics and then Protestants.

Because the Roman Catholic Church prohibits divorce, more Catholics than Protestants are separated (Raschke, 1987). For the same reason, a significant number of Catholic marriages are annulled; in 1983, for example, 74,139 Catholic marriages were annulled on the grounds of psychological immaturity (Neuman, 1985). (Pope John Paul II has cautioned bishops against using "psychiatric examinations" as the basis of annulment [Armstrong, 1987].)

Life Course Factors

Intergenerational Transmission. Both African Americans and whites have a slightly increased likelihood of divorce if their family of origin was disrupted by divorce or desertion (Raschke, 1987). One study (Glenn and Kramer, 1987), however, found a statistically significant relationship for daughters of divorced white parents; they may be more prone to divorce because they tend to marry at an early age. Another study (Amato, 1988) comparing adults from divorced and intact families found that both groups held similar attitudes toward marriage. All in all, coming from a divorced family appears to have relatively little effect on adult childrens divorcing.

Age at Time of Marriage. Adolescent marriages are more likely to end in divorce than marriages that take place when people are in their twenties or older. This is true for both whites and African Americans. Younger partners are less likely to be emotionally mature; they are often pressured into marriage because of pregnancy, which is also correlated with a higher divorce rate. After age twenty-six for men and age twenty-three for women, however, age at marriage seems to make little difference (Glenn and Supancic, 1984).

Premarital Pregnancy and Childbirth. Premarital pregnancy by itself does not significantly increase the likelihood of divorce. But if the pregnant woman is adolescent, drops out of high school, and faces economic problems following marriage, the divorce rate increases dramatically. If a women gives birth prior to marriage, the likelihood for divorce in a subsequent marriage increases, especially in the early years. This negative effect on marriage is stronger for whites than African Americans (White, 1991).

Remarriage. The divorce rate among those who remarried in the 1980s is so far about 25 percent higher than it is for those who entered first marriages (White, 1991). It is not clear why there is a higher divorce rate in remarriages. Some researchers suggest that the cause may lie in a "kinds-of-people" explanation. The probability factors associated with the kinds of people who divorced in first marriages—low levels of education, unwillingness to settle for unsatisfactory marriages, and membership in certain ethnic groups—are present in subsequent marriages, increasing the likelihood of divorce (Martin and Bumpass, 1989). Others argue that the dynamics of second marriages, especially the presence of stepchildren, increase the chances of

remember that

continued on next page

PERSPECTIVE

divorce (White and Booth, 1985). Step-family research, however, does not provide much support for this hypothesis (see Coleman and Ganong, 1991).

FAMILY PROCESSES

Marital Happiness. Although it seems reasonable that there would be a strong link between marital happiness (or, rather, the lack of happiness) and divorce, this is true only during the earliest years of marriage. Those who have low marital-happiness scores in the first years of marriage are four to five times more likely to divorce within three years than those with high marital happiness (Booth et al., 1986). The relationship between low marital happiness and divorce decreases in later stages of marriage, however (White and Booth, 1991). In fact, alternatives to one's marriage and barriers to divorce appear to influence divorce decisions more strongly than marital happiness, as discussed in "Understanding Yourself."

Children. It is not clear what relation, if any, children have to the likelihood of divorce (Raschke, 1987). Children were once considered a deterrent to divorce—"staying together for the sake of the children"—but 60 percent of all divorces now take place among couples who have children. The birth of the first child reduces the chance of divorce to almost nil in the year following birth; this preventive effect does not hold true for subsequent births (White, 1991). One of the most significant recent findings, however, indicates that parents of sons are less likely to divorce than parents of daughters. The researchers suggest that fathers participate more in the parenting of sons than daughters, thereby creating greater involvement for the men (Morgan, Lye, and Condran, 1988).

In some instances, children may be related to higher divorce rates. Premaritally conceived children and physically or mentally limited children are associated with divorce. Children in general contribute to marital dissatisfaction and possibly divorce, according to one researcher (Raschke, 1987): "It could be expected that normal children at least contribute to strains in an already troubled marriage, given the consistent findings that children, especially in adolescent years, lower marital satisfaction." At the same time, however, women without children have considerably higher divorce rates than women with children.

Marital Problems. If you ask divorced people to give the reasons for their divorce, they are not likely to say "I blame the changing nature of the family" or "It was demographics." They are more apt to respond "She was on my case all the time" or "He just didn't understand me." Or, if they are charitable, "It wasn't right for us."

Personal characteristics leading to conflicts are obviously very important factors in the dissolution of relationships.

Studies of divorced men and women cite such problems as alcoholism, drug abuse, marital infidelity, sexual incompatibility, and conflicts about gender roles as leading to their divorces. Kitson and Sussman (1982) found that the four most common reasons given were, in descending order of frequency, personality problems, home life, authoritarianism, and differing values. Extramarital affairs ranked seventh. Complaints associated with gender roles accounted for 35 percent of the men's responses and 41 percent of women's responses. But because the studies included only divorced respondents, it is difficult to tell whether the presence of these factors can predict divorce. We know from studying enduring marriages that marriages often continue in the face of such problems.

❖ REFLECTIONS *As you look at the various factors involved in divorce, which factors reflect your life? If you are married or involved with someone, which factors reflect your partner's life? What impact do you think these factors might have on whether you might divorce? Why? If you are divorced, which of these factors were present? What influence did they have?*

The problem of a satisfactory marriage remains incapable of purely private solutions.

C. Wright Mills

responsibilities and more income than divorced women, tend to have more active social lives.

Dating fulfills several important functions for separated and divorced people. First, it is a statement to both the former spouse and the world at large that the individual is available to become someone else's partner (Vaughan, 1986). Second, dating is an opportunity to enhance one's self-esteem (Spanier and Thompson, 1987). Free from the stress of an unhappy marriage, dating may lead people to discover, for example, that they are more interesting and charming than either they or (especially) their former spouses had imagined. Third, dating initiates individuals into the singles subculture where they can experiment with the freedom about which they may have fantasized when they were married. Interestingly, Spanier and Thompson (1987) found no relationship between dating experience and well-being following separation.

Several features of dating following separation and divorce differ from premarital dating. First, dating does not seem to be a leisurely matter. Divorced people "are too pressed for time, too desperately in search of the 'right' person to waste time on a first date that might not go well" (Hunt and Hunt, 1977). Second, dating may be less spontaneous if the divorced woman or man has primary responsibility for children. The parent must make arrangements about child care; he or she may wish not to involve the children in dating. Third, finances may be strained; divorced mothers may have income only from low-paying or part-time jobs or AFDC benefits while having many child-care expenses. In some cases a father's finances may be strained by paying alimony or child support. Finally, separated and divorced men and women often have a changed sexual ethic based on the simple fact that there are few (if any) divorced virgins (Spanier and Thompson, 1987).

Sexual activity is an important component in the lives of separated and divorced men and women. Engaging in sexual relations for the first time following separation assists people in accepting their newly acquired single status. Because sexual fidelity is usually an important element in marriage, becoming sexually active with someone other than one's spouse is a dramatic symbol that the old marriage vows are no longer valid (Spanier and Thompson, 1987). Men initially tend to enjoy their sexual freedom following divorce, but women generally do not find it as meaningful. For men, sexual experience following separation is linked with their well-being. Sex seems to reassure men and bolster their self-confidence. Sexual activity is not as strongly connected to women's well-being (Spanier and Thompson, 1987). After a while, sex becomes a secondary consideration in dating as people look for a deeper, more intimate relationship (Kohen et al., 1979).

❖ DIVORCE CONSEQUENCES

Most divorces are not contested; between 85 and 90 percent are settled out of court through negotiations between spouses or their lawyers. But divorce, whether it is amicable or not, is a complex legal process, involving highly charged feelings about custody, property, and children (who are sometimes treated by angry partners as property to be fought over).

No-Fault Divorce

Since 1970, beginning with California's Family Law Act, forty-eight states have adopted no-fault divorce (while still providing for "legal grounds" divorce when applicable). (See Resource Center for breakdown of divorce laws by state.)

BASIC ASPECTS OF NO-FAULT DIVORCE. No-fault divorce has changed four basic aspects of divorce (Weitzman and Dixon, 1980; Weiztman, 1985), described below. Although no-fault has had no effect on divorce rates, it has decreased the time involved in the legal process (Kitson and Morgan, 1991).

1. No-fault divorce has eliminated the idea of fault-based grounds. Under no-fault divorce, no one is accused of desertion, cruelty, adultery, impotence, crime, insanity,

or the host of other melodramatic acts or omissions. Neither party is found guilty of anything; rather, the marriage is declared unworkable and is dissolved. Husband and wife must agree that they have irreconcilable differences (which they need not describe) and that they believe it is impossible for their marriage to survive the differences.

2. No-fault divorce eliminates the adversary process. The stress and strain of the courtroom are eliminated under the new procedure. There is little research, however, to document whether no-fault divorce has been successful in lowering the distress level or conflict among divorcing couples (Kitson and Morgan, 1991).

3. The bases for no-fault divorce settlements are equity, equality, and need rather than fault or gender. "Virtue" is no longer financially rewarded, nor is it assumed that women need to be supported by men. Community property is to be divided equally, reflecting the belief that marriage is a partnership with each partner contributing equally, if differently. The criteria for child custody are based on a sex-neutral standard of the "best interests of the child" rather than a preference for the mother.

4. No-fault divorce laws are intended to promote gender equality by redefining the responsibilities of husbands and wives. The husband is no longer considered head of the household but is an equal partner with his wife. The husband is no longer solely responsible for support, nor the wife for the care of the children. The limitations placed on alimony assume that a woman will work.

UNANTICIPATED CONSEQUENCES OF NO-FAULT DIVORCE. When California passed the first no-fault divorce law, reformers were optimistic about its results. No-fault has been successful in eliminating much of the sham and acrimony that resulted from traditional divorce law. However, sociologist Lenore Weitzman argued in her landmark work, *The Divorce Revolution* (1985), that no-fault divorce's gender-neutral rules, designed to treat men and women equally, have placed older homemakers and mothers of young children at a disadvantage: *poverty!*

> Since a woman's ability to support herself is likely to be impaired during marriage, especially if she is a full-time homemaker and mother, she may not be "equal" to her former husband at the point of divorce. Rules that treat her as if she is equal simply serve to deprive her of the financial support she needs.

Husbands typically enhance their earning capacity during marriage. In contrast, wives typically decrease their earning capacity because they either quit or limit their participation in the work force to fulfill family roles. This withdrawal from full participation limits their earning capacity when they reenter the work force. Divorced homemakers have out-dated experience, few skills, and no seniority. Furthermore, they continue to have the major responsibility and burden of childrearing.

Probably the most damaging unintended consequence of the no-fault divorce laws is that they systematically impoverish divorced women and their children. When women divorce, they are often left in great economic hardship. A single mother's income is about 67 percent of her predivorce income, while the income of a divorced man is about 90 percent of his predivorce income (Duncan and Hoffman, 1985). Because over half of the children born today will live in a single-parent family at some point during their childhood, through no-fault divorce rules "we are sentencing a significant proportion of the next generation of American children to periods of financial hardship" (Weitzman, 1985).

Economic Consequences

One of the most striking differences between two-parent and single-parent families is poverty. One out of every two single mothers lives below the poverty level, whereas only one out of ten two-parent families is poor (McLanahan and Booth, 1991). The overwhelming majority of single mothers have become poor as a result of their marital disruption. They became poor because of (1) the low-earning capacity of the mother, (2) lack of child support, and (3) inadequate welfare benefits (discussed in Chapter 12).

EMPLOYMENT. Separation and divorce dramatically change many mothers' employment patterns. If a mother was not employed prior to separation, she is likely to seek a job following her split-up. The reason is simple: If she and her children relied on alimony and child support alone, they would soon find themselves on the street. One study found that the proportion of mothers employed 1,000 hours or more a year increased from 51 percent to 73 percent following divorce (Duncan and Hoffman, 1985). Most employed single mothers are still on the verge of financial disaster, however. On the average, they earn only a third as much as married fathers. This is partly because women tend to earn less than men and partly because they work fewer hours, primarily because of child-care responsibilities (Garfinkel and McLanahan, 1986). The general problems of women's lower earnings capacity and lack of adequate child care are particularly severe for single mothers. Sex discrimination in employment and lack of societal support for child care condemn millions of single-mother families to poverty.

ALIMONY AND CHILD SUPPORT. Alimony and child support payments do little to alleviate the financial struggles of single-parent families. Most women and children experience dramatic downward mobility following divorce. For many women, their source of income changes from primarily joint wages earned during marriage to their own wages, private transfers (child support payments, alimony, and help from relatives), and welfare. Private transfers account for 35 percent of the annual income for lower-income women, 55 percent for middle-income women, and 73 percent for upper-income women. Welfare and food stamps account for 60 percent of the income of lower-income women, 37 percent of middle-income women, and 26 percent of upper-income women. ("Lower-," "middle-," and "upper" income classifications denote the woman's economic status prior to divorce.)

In 1989 less than 14 percent of divorcing women received alimony. Child support was awarded to 67 percent of white women, 33.7 percent of African-American women, and 40.9 percent of Latina women. About 58 percent of single mothers were awarded child support, but only 50 percent received full payment, 26 percent received partial payment, and 24 percent received none (U.S. Bureau of the Census, 1990). Federal law provides that by 1994, all child support payments will be automatically withheld from parental paychecks (Hinds, 1989). But even when fathers pay support, the amount is generally low. It generally depends more on the father's circumstances than the needs of the mother and children (Teachman, 1991). Alimony and child support payments make up only about 10 percent ($1,246) of the income of white single mothers and 3.5 percent ($322) of the income of African-American single mothers (McLanahan and Booth, 1991). Studies indicate that fathers are generally able to pay about twice the amount they currently pay (Garfinkel and Oellerich, 1989). Although some argue that divorced and remarried fathers cannot pay additional support without pushing themselves and their new families into poverty, evidence indicates that this is not true in the majority of cases (Duncan and Hoffman, 1985).

When the legal system treats men and women equally at the point of divorce, it ignores very real economic inequalities between men and women in our society, inequalities that marriage itself creates.

Lenore Weitzman, The Divorce Revolution

While there is general approval, at least in principal, of child support, alimony is more controversial. In the past, alimony represented the continuation of the husband's responsibility to support his wife. Today, however, the objectives of alimony are not clear (Oster, 1987). Currently, laws suggest that alimony should be awarded on the basis of need to those women who would otherwise be indigent. At the same time, there is a strong countermovement in which alimony represents the return of a woman's "investment" in marriage (Oster, 1987; Weitzman, 1985). Weitzman argues that a woman's homemaking and child-care activities must be considered important contributions to her husband's present and future earnings. If divorce rules don't give a wife a share of her husband's enhanced earning capacity, then the "investment" she made in her spouse's future earnings is discounted. According to Weitzman, alimony and child support awards should be made to divorced women in recognition of the wife's primary child-care responsibilities and her contribution to her husband's work or career. Such awards will help raise divorced women and children above the level of poverty to which they have been cast as a result of no-fault divorce's specious equality. A recent landmark court decision, in fact, upheld the "investment" doctrine by ruling that a woman who supported her husband during his medical education was entitled to a portion of his potential lifetime earnings as a physician (Oster, 1987).

❖ CHILDREN AND DIVORCE

When I can no longer bear to think of the victims of broken homes, I begin to think of the victims of intact ones.

Peter DeVries

A traditional nuclear family, merely because it is intact, does not necessarily offer an advantage to children over a single-parent family or stepfamily. A traditional family racked with spousal violence, sexual or physical abuse of children, alcoholism, neglect, severe conflict, or psychopathology creates a destructive environment that is likely to inhibit children's healthy development. As Anne Goetting (1981) observed in her review of the research literature on divorce, marital conflict in a two-parent family is more harmful to children than living in a tranquil single-parent family or stepfamily. One study (Hess and Camara, 1979) comparing the behavior of children from traditional nuclear and divorced families found that relationships among family members were more important influences on behavior than marital status. Children living in happy two-parent families appear to be the best adjusted and those from conflict-ridden two-parent families appear to be the worst adjusted. Children from single-parent families are in the middle. The key to children's adjustment following divorce is a lack of conflict between divorced parents (Kline, Johnston, and Tschann, 1991).

Telling children that their parents are separating is one of the most difficult and unhappy events in life. Whether or not the parents are relieved about the separation, they often feel extremely guilty about their children. Children are generally aware of parental discord and are upset by the separation, although their distress may not be apparent. However, parental separation and divorce may not be equally disturbing for all children. Several studies (Kurdek et al., 1981; Kurdek and Siesky, 1980) suggest that divorce is not necessarily perceived by children as an overly distressing experience. Other studies found that about 25 percent of children of divorced parents were extremely depressed five years following the divorce (Wallerstein and Blakeslee, 1989). A recent study utilized a **meta-analysis** approach (combining statistical data from previous studies and reanalyzing it) of earlier divorce studies on the impact of parental divorce of the well-being of their children in adulthood (Amato and Keith, 1991) and found very little difference in the well-being of children from divorced families and intact families.

The Three Stages of Divorce for Children

Growing numbers of studies have appeared on the impact of divorce on children, but these studies frequently contradict one another. Part of the problem is a failure to recognize divorce as a process for children as opposed to a single event. Divorce is a series of events and changes in life circumstances. Many studies focus on only one part of the process and identify that part with divorce itself. Yet at different points in the process, children are confronted with different tasks and adopt different coping strategies. Furthermore, the diversity of children's responses to divorce is the result, in part, of differences in temperament, sex, age, and past experiences (Hetherington, Cox, and Cox, 1979).

Children experience divorce as a three-stage process, according to Wallerstein and Kelly (1980b). Studying sixty California families during a five-year period, these researchers found that for children divorce consisted of initial, transition, and restabilized stages.

◆ *Initial Stage.* The initial stage, following the decision to separate, was extremely stressful; conflict escalated and unhappiness was endemic. The children's aggressive responses were magnified by the parents' inability to cope because of the crisis in their own lives.

◆ *Transition Stage.* The transition stage began about a year after the separation, when the extreme emotional responses of the children had diminished or disappeared. The period was characterized by restructuring of the family and by economic and social changes: living with only one parent and visiting the other, moving, making new friends and losing old ones, financial stress, and so on. The transition period lasted between two and three years for half the families in the study.

◆ *Restabilization Stage.* Finally came the restabilized stage, which the families had reached by the end of five years. Economic and social changes had been incorporated into daily living. The postdivorce family, usually a single-parent or stepfamily, had been formed.

Children's Responses to Divorce

Younger and older children respond differently to divorce, mainly in the way in which they express—or do not express—their feelings.

YOUNGER CHILDREN. Younger children react to the initial news of a parental breakup in many different ways. Feelings range from guilt to anger and from sorrow to relief, often vacillating among all of these. The most significant factor affecting children's responses to the separation is their age. Preadolescent children, who seem to experience a deep sadness and anxiety about the future, are usually the most upset. Some may regress to immature behavior, wetting their beds or becoming excessively possessive. Most children, regardless of their age, are angry because of the separation. Very young children tend to have more temper tantrums. In one three-year study of forty-eight preschoolers, the play patterns regressed both cognitively and socially shortly after divorce (Hetherington et al., 1979). A year following the divorce, the children showed high rates of dependency, acting out, seeking help, and behaving noncompliantly. Slightly older children become aggressive in their play, games, and fantasies— for example, pretending to hit one of their parents.

Children of school age may blame one parent and direct their anger toward him or her, believing the other one innocent. But even here the reactions are varied. If the father moves out of the house, the children may blame the mother for making

Why is happiness such a precious thing? What have we done with our lives so that everywhere we turn, no matter how hard we try not to, we cause other people sorrow?

William Styron

3 stage process for children

him go or they may be angry at him for abandoning them, regardless of reality. Younger schoolchildren who blame their mother often mix anger with placating behavior, fearing she will leave them. Preschool children often blame themselves, feeling that they drove their parents apart by being naughty or messy. They beg their parents to stay, promising to be better. It is heartbreaking to hear a child say, "Mommy, tell Daddy I'll be good. Tell him to come back. I'll be good. He won't be mad at me any more."

Problems seem to be compounded when there are children of various ages. The parents must deal with a range of responses that can be almost overwhelming. One woman (quoted in Hunt and Hunt, 1977) said:

My fourteen-year-old son was mortified and went to elaborate lengths to keep anyone from knowing. My twelve-year-old daughter had seen it coming; she cried a lot, but in the main she seemed vastly relieved. The eight-year-old blamed herself for all our quarrels and threw up regularly for weeks. The seven-year-old told his father, "We'll get it all fixed up so you can come back, Dad," but he had tantrums, played with matches in his room, and stole money from my purse.

When parents separate, children want to know with whom they are going to live. Feeling strong bonds with the parent who left, they want to know when they can see him or her. If they have brothers or sisters, they want to know if they will remain with their siblings. They especially want to know what will happen to them if the parent they are living with dies. Will they go to their grandparents, their other parent, an aunt or uncle, or a foster home? These are practical questions, and children have a right to answers. They need to know what lies ahead for them amidst the turmoil of a family split-up so that they can prepare for the changes ahead. Some parents report that their children seemed to do better psychologically than they themselves did prior to a split-up. Children often have more strength and inner resources than parents realize. Yet in a study in which 560 divorced parents were asked to assess the impact of their divorce on their children two years after it had occurred, the majority felt that their children had been affected negatively (Fulton, 1979).

The outcome of separation for children, Weiss (1975) observed, depends on several factors related to the children's age. Young children need a competent and loving parent to take care of them; they tend to do poorly when a parenting adult becomes enmeshed in constant turmoil, depression, and worry. With older, preadolescent children, the presence of brothers and sisters help, because the children have others to play with and rely on in addition to the single parent. If they have good friends or do well in school, this contributes to their self-esteem. Regardless of the child's age, it is important that the absent parent continue to play a role in his or her life. The children need to know that they have not been abandoned and that the absent parent still cares (Wallerstein and Kelly, 1980b). They need continuity and security even if the old parental relationship has radically changed.

The financial effect of divorce appears to have some impact on a child's later adjustment. Economic stress is particularly acute in divorced families. One study of twenty-five seven- to thirteen-year-olds found that all who were maladjusted came from families that had experienced a 50 percent drop in income (De Simone-Luis et al., 1979). Another study found limited financial resources an important variable in determining stress among children of divorce (Hodges et al., 1979).

ADOLESCENTS. Family life before separation seems to affect how adolescents respond to their parent's divorce. In one study, 76 percent of the adolescents reported that there had been conflict in the marriage before separation (McLoughlin and Whitfield, 1984). Sixty percent of the conflict was verbal, but 38 percent was both verbal and physical. In spite of the reported conflict, almost half of these adolescents were surprised that their parents had split up. They had come to view conflict as a normal part of marital life.

Adolescents also find parental separation traumatic. About half the adolescents studied felt relieved that their parents had separated; the other half were troubled. Those who were glad came from homes that had considerable conflict; after the divorce, they tended to believe that their parents' divorce was a good idea. Only about 40 percent of the adolescents continued contact with the noncustodial parent; of these, 68 percent saw the parent once a month or more. The 60 percent who did not see their noncustodial parent usually chose not to do so. This was especially true of daughters whose fathers had been involved in an extramarital relationship (McLoughlin and Whitfield, 1984).

Adolescents tend to protect themselves from the conflict preceding separation by distancing themselves. Although they usually experience immense turmoil within, they may outwardly appear cool and detached. Unlike younger children, they rarely blame themselves. Rather, they are likely to be angry with both parents, blaming them for upsetting their lives. Adolescents may be particularly bothered by their parents' beginning to date again. Some are shocked to realize that their parents are sexual beings, especially when they see a separated parent kiss someone or bring someone home for the night. The situation may add greater confusion to the adolescents' emerging sexual life. Some may take the attitude that if their mother or father sleeps with a date, why can't they? Others may condemn their parents for acting "immorally."

HELPING CHILDREN ADJUST. Helen Raschke's (1987) review of the literature of children's adjustment after divorce found that the following factors were important:

◆ Prior to separation, open discussion with the children of the forthcoming separation and divorce and problems associated with them.
◆ The child's continued involvement with the noncustodial parent, including frequent visits and unrestricted access.
◆ Lack of hostility between the divorced parents.
◆ Good emotional and psychological adjustment to the divorce on the part of the custodial parent.
◆ Good parenting skills and the maintenance of an orderly and stable living situation for the children.

Children as Pawns

Continued involvement with the children by both parents is important for the children's adjustment. The greatest danger is that children may be used as pawns by their parents after a divorce. The recently divorced often suffer from a lack of self-esteem and a sense of failure. One means of dealing with the feelings caused by divorce is to blame the other person. To prevent further hurt or to get revenge, divorced parents may try to control each other through their children. Myron Harris (1972) wrote:

The need to find oneself loved and reassured as to being adequate or exceptional as a parent becomes particularly strong when all else is taken away. Thus, the opportunity for utilizing other individuals in this security-pursuing endeavor beckons most strongly—in fact, more strongly to the unconscious parts of ourselves than to the conscious, for the former are desperate, painfully needful, crying, and often panicked, while the latter have managed somehow

When Jason and the Argonauts returned from their search for the Golden Fleece, he had taken a new wife. His wife Medea was enraged with grief, anger, and jealousy. A sorceress, she wove a golden cloth which she gave to Jason's bride. When she wore it, it turned to flames and burned her to death. Then Medea killed her two children to take revenge upon the unfaithful Jason and fled the palace in a chariot pulled by dragons.

Greek myth

to be more reasonable and socially restrained. It is obvious that the presence of children makes them an easily available commodity for use.

Harris suggested that divorced parents who use their children may employ one or more of the following tactics:

1. *Alienating children's affection.* Because one parent feels deprived of the former spouse's affection, he or she may try to deprive the other parent of the children's affection. If, say, the wife had an affair during the time of the split up, the husband may try to have the wife declared an unfit mother as revenge. She may be a wholly competent, trustworthy mother, but in his rage the husband does not see that. He is so wounded that he wants to hurt his wife as he has been hurt. The children, of course, are torn by divided loyalties.

2. *Using children to maintain bonds.* Children are sometimes used to continue the attachment between divorced spouses. On the pretext of asking for advice or assistance, a man may call his former spouse. "What shall I do about Sonia being sick all the time? Do you think it's serious? Do you think I should send her to summer school?" Although such questions may be legitimate, they can be used to hold on to an ex-spouse, keeping him or her tied to the intimate workings of the family. Some may hope that if they hold on long enough, there will be a reconciliation. Here again the child is being manipulated.

3. *Demanding total allegiance.* Each parent may demand the children's total allegiance. The mother may attack the father in front of the children or denigrate him in his absence; the father may similarly attack the mother, telling the children that she is a bad person and parent. Harris described one case in which each divorced partner attempted to turn the children against the other:

> The effort to force them into the position of hostages, held in emotional bondage to the parent with whom they were spending time, was so persisting and unrelenting that the children were forced to alternately deny love to the opposing parent and avow loyalty only to the parent with whom they were currently spending time.

The children in this case were four and five years old. It is not difficult to imagine their stress and confusion.

4. *Holding children hostage.* Children may be used directly as hostages for money, emotional support, or services. In one divorce agreement, the woman spelled out rigid visitation privileges, and whenever her former husband was late with support payments, was late in picking up the child, or had to cancel a visit, she would refuse to allow him to see the child next time.

Types of Custody

Of all the issues surrounding separation and divorce, custody issues are generating the "greatest attention and controversy" among researchers (Kitson and Morgan, 1991). When the court awards custody to one parent, the decision is generally based on one of two standards: the best interests of the child or the least detrimental of the available alternatives (Musetto, 1981). In practice, however, custody of the children is usually awarded to the mother. Three reasons can be given for this: (1) women usually prefer custody and men do not, (2) custody to the mother is traditional, and (3) the law reflects a bias that assumes women are naturally better able to care for children.

The major types of custody are sole, joint, and split. In **sole custody**, the child lives with one parent, who has sole responsibility for physically raising the child and making all decisions regarding his or her upbringing. There are two forms of **joint custody**: legal and physical. In joint legal custody, the children live primarily with one parent, but both share jointly in decisions about their children's education, religious training, and general upbringing. In joint physical custody, the children live with both parents, dividing time more or less equally between the two households. Under **split custody,** the children are divided between the two parents, the mother usually taking the girls and the father the boys. About 5 percent of children from divorced families are shared in split custody arrangements (Spanier and Furstenberg, 1987).

Sole custody has been the prevailing practice in the United States; about 70 percent of all custody is sole custody. Since women have traditionally been responsible for childrearing, sole custody by mothers has seemed the closest approximation to the traditional family, especially if the father is given free access (Awad and Parry, 1980). Furthermore, many men have not had the day-to-day responsibilities of childrearing and do not feel (or are not perceived to be) competent in that role.

In recent years, increasing numbers of fathers have been gaining custody of their children following divorce (Pearson et al., 1982). Thirteen percent of single families were headed by men in 1990. A child's adjustment to the father as a single parent, according to one study, appears to depend on how well the father parents (Santrock and Warsack, 1979). Although parenting has been primarily the mother's task, increasing numbers of men may have joint or sole custody of their children as new parenting roles evolve.

SOLE CUSTODY. Sole custody does not mean that the noncustodial parent is prohibited from seeing his or her children. Wallerstein and Kelly (1980b) believe that if one parent is prohibited from sharing important aspects of the children's lives, he or she will withdraw from the children in frustration and grief. Children experience such withdrawal as a rejection and suffer as a result. Generally, it is considered in the best interests of the child for him or her to have easy access to the noncustodial parent. If it is the father, his relationship with his child often changes in a positive manner as a result of the divorce, since he has increased opportunity to interact with his child in a conflict-free atmosphere (Friedman, 1980). The relationship between the visiting parent and child may change in unexpected ways. One study showed that the changes for better or worse in the relationship were related to the difficulties and psychological conflicts arising from visitation and divorce, the father's ability to deal with the limitations of his visiting relationship, and the age and sex of the child (Wallerstein and Kelly, 1980a).

JOINT CUSTODY. Joint custody, in which both parents continue to share legal rights and responsibilities as parents, is becoming increasingly widespread. Thirty-three states now have joint custody laws (Freed and Walker, 1988). Wallerstein and Kelly (1980b) argue that such arrangements may work out for the best interests of the child. Joint custody does not necessarily mean that the child's time is evenly divided between the parents but that "two committed parents, in two separate homes [care] for their youngsters in a postdivorce atmosphere of civilized, respectful exchange."

A number of advantages accrue to joint custody. First, it allows both parents to continue their parenting roles. Second, it avoids a sudden termination of a child's relationship with one of his or her parents. Joint custody fathers tend to be more

"Best interests of the child." . . .It makes me want to laugh, to see it stated so baldly, as if it were a simple thing. It is almost all there is to being a good parent: best interests of the child, assessed incessantly, in everything from toilet training to religious education. But it is simple only when the issue at hand is putting fingers in a fire or going barefoot in the snow. The rest of the time it means separating what is good for the child from what is good for you. In that sense, it feels as if you are doing the impossible.

Anna Quindlen

[handwritten margin notes:]
parents, this is today, their right

2 standards
- best interest of child
- least detrimental

- childs inner resources

- Today there are many forms. Custodial parent is assigned but the non-custodial is very active in childs life.

involved with their children, spending time with them and sharing responsibility and decision making (Bowman and Ahrons, 1985). Third, by dividing the labor, it lessens many of the burdens of constant child care experienced by most single parents. Joint custody, however, requires considerable energy from the parents in working out both the logistics of the arrangement and their feelings about each other (see "Binuclear Families" in Chapter 17). Many parents with joint custody find it difficult, but they nevertheless feel that it is satisfactory. The children do not always like joint custody as much as the parents do. About a third of the children in one study valued the arrangement because it gave them access to both parents, but they felt overburdened by the demands of two households (Steinman, 1981).

Inevitably, there are benefits and drawbacks to any custody arrangement. Joint custody should be available as an alternative but not automatically awarded. Sometimes, although it may be in the best interests of the parents for each of them to continue parenting roles, it may not necessarily be in the best interests of the child. Derdeyn and Scott (1984) noted, "There is a marked disparity between the power of the joint custody movement and the sufficiency of evidence that joint custody can accomplish what we expect of it." For parents who *choose* joint custody, it appears to be satisfactory. But when joint custody is mandated by the courts over the opposition of one or both parents, it may be problematic at best. Joint custody may force two parents to interact ("cooperate" is too benign a word) in instances in which they would rather never see each other again, and the resulting conflict and ill-will may end up being detrimental to the children.

CUSTODY DISPUTES AND CHILD STEALING. The "best-interests" and "least detrimental alternative" standards by which parents are awarded custody are vague. This may encourage custody fights because it makes the outcome of custody hearings uncertain and increases hostility; any derogatory evidence or suspicions, ranging from dirty faces to child abuse, may be considered relevant (Mnookin, 1975). As a result, child custody disputes are fairly common in the courts. As many as one-third of all postdivorce legal cases involve children (Emery and Wyer, 1987).

As discussed in Chapter 15, about 350,000 children are abducted each year by family members in child custody disputes. Most are returned in two days to a week, and generally the parent from whom the child was taken knows the child's whereabouts (Hotaling, Finkelhor, and Sedlack, 1990; Finkelhor, Hotaling, and Sedlak, 1991). According to researcher David Finkelhor, the number of family abductions could be reduced significantly. Under the present system, courts don't respond to people's needs and fears in bitter custody disputes. "For many people, going into court for custody is too risky, too expensive, and too time-consuming," Finkelhor notes (quoted in Barden, 1990), "so they grab the child." Finkelhor suggests that much child stealing could be prevented by the court assigning a mediator to whom the distressed parents could turn in times of crisis. Mediation would ease parental anxiety and offer an alternative to legal proceedings, which tend to inflame the situation.

◆ There is no denying that separation or divorce is filled with pain for everyone involved—husband, wife, and children. But it is not only an end, it is also a beginning of a new life for each person. This new life includes new relationships and possibilities, new families with unique relationships: the single-parent family and the stepfamily. We will explore these family forms in the next chapter.

❖ SUMMARY

◆ *Divorce* is an integral part of the contemporary American marriage system, which values individualism and emotional gratification. Divorce serves as a recycling mechanism, giving people a chance to improve their marital situation by marrying again. Researchers are increasingly viewing divorce as a normal part of the family life cycle rather than as a form of deviance.

◆ Divorce creates the single-parent family, remarriage, the stepfamily, and the singles subculture. The divorce rate increased significantly in the 1960s but leveled off in the early 1990s. About half of all current marriages end in divorce.

◆ *Uncoupling* is the process by which couples drift apart in predictable stages. Initially, uncoupling is unilateral; the initiator begins to turn elsewhere for satisfactions, creating an identity independent of the couple. The initiator voices more complaints and begins to think of alternatives. Eventually the initiator ends the relationship. Uncoupling ends when both partners acknowledge that the relationship cannot be saved.

◆ In establishing a new identity, newly separated people go through transition and recovery. Transition begins with the separation and is characterized by *separation distress,* a condition of general stress, anxiety, and anger. Separation distress is usually followed by loneliness. Separation distress is affected by (1) whether the person had any forewarning, (2) length of time married, (3) who took the initiative in leaving, (4) whether someone new is found, and (5) available resources. The more personal, social and financial resources a person has at the time of separation, the easier the separation generally will be. Women generally experience dramatic downward mobility.

◆ Dating again is important for separated or divorced people. Their greatest social problem is meeting other unmarried people. Dating is a formal statement of the end of a marriage; it also permits individuals to enhance their self-esteem.

◆ *No-fault divorce* has revolutionized divorce by eliminating fault-finding and the adversarial process and by treating husbands and wives as equals. The most damaging unintended consequence of no-fault divorce is the growing poverty of divorced women with children.

◆ The economic consequences of divorce include impoverishment of women, changed female employment patterns, and very limited child support and alimony.

◆ Children in the divorce process go through three stages: (1) the initial stage, lasting about a year, when turmoil is greatest; (2) the transition stage, lasting up to several years, in which adjustments are being made to new family arrangements, living and economic conditions, friends, and social environment; and (3) the restabilized stage, when the changes have been integrated into the children's lives.

◆ A very significant factor affecting the responses of children to divorce is their age. Young children tend to act out and blame themselves, whereas adolescents tend to remain aloof and angry at both parents for disrupting their lives. Adolescents may be bothered by their parent's dating again.

◆ The outcome of divorce for children depends on several factors, including their own inner resources, contact with the noncustodial parent, economic stability, and, for younger children especially, a nurturing, competent parent.

◆ Divorced parents may use their children against each other. Such parents may attempt to (1) deprive the other parent of the children's affection, (2) use the children to maintain bonds with the divorced spouse, (3) demand the children's total allegiance, and (4) use the children directly as hostages for money, emotional support, or services.

◆ The major types of custody are *sole, joint,* and *split.* Custody is generally based on one of two standards: the best interests of the child or the least detrimental of the available alternatives. Custody is generally awarded to the mother. Recently, however, more fathers have been gaining custody; the child's adjustment to living with the father depends on the father's parenting capabilities, not his gender. Joint custody has become more popular because men are becoming increasingly involved in parenting.

◆ As a result of custody disputes, as many as 350,000 children are stolen from custodial parents each year. Most are returned home within a week. Court-assigned mediation would help ease parental anxiety and present alternatives to custody-related abductions.

Answers to Preview Questions

The answers to the preview questions at the beginning of the chapter are listed below. As you check your answers, whether you were correct or not, think about your reasons for each response. What were they? What was their source? How valid is the source? As you read the chapter, you will find the questions discussed in greater depth.

1. T	6. T
2. F	7. F
3. T	8. T
4. T	9. F
5. T	10. T

❖ SUGGESTED READINGS

Ahrons, Constance, and Roy Rodgers. *Divorced Families: A Multidisciplinary Developmental View.* New York: W.W. Norton, 1987. A family life-cycle approach to understanding the developmental issues involving divorce and remarriage.

Arendell, Terry. *Mothers and Divorce: Legal, Economic, and Social Dilemmas.* Berkeley, Calif.: University of California Press, 1987. A well-written examination of the lives of sixty divorced women that looks at the legal, economic, and social consequences of divorce.

Furstenberg, Frank, and Andrew Cherlin. *Divided Families.* Cambridge, Mass.: Harvard University Press, 1991. A concise overview of marital disintegration, economic consequences of divorce, and children's adjustment.

Price, Sharon J., and Patrick McKenry. *Divorce.* Beverly Hills, Calif.: Sage Publications, 1988 (paperback). A concise survey of current knowledge on separation and divorce.

Spanier, Graham, and Linda Thompson. *Parting: The Aftermath of Separation and Divorce,* rev. ed. Newbury Park, Calif.: Sage Publications, 1987 (paperback). The process of separation and divorce, including drifting apart, distress, friends and relatives, dating and sexuality, and well-being.

Triere, Lynette. *Learning to Leave: A Woman's Guide.* New York: Warner Books, 1983 (paperback). Sometimes it's better to leave for the right reasons than to stay for the wrong ones.
This book helps women sort out their feelings; men may also find it useful.

Vaughan, Diane. *Uncoupling: Turning Points in Intimate Relationships.* New York: Oxford University Press, 1986 (paperback). A sociological examination of the process by which couples become ex-couples.

Wallerstein, Judith, and Sandra Blakeslee. *Second Chances: Men, Women, and Children a Decade after Divorce.* New York: Ticknor & Fields, 1989 (paperback). A best-selling book documenting the impact of divorce on families by one of the leading psychologists in the field.

Weiss, Robert. *Marital Separation.* New York: Basic Books, 1975 (paperback). An outstanding (and readable) study of the emotional and psychological process of separation. A must for anyone undergoing separation or divorce.

Weitzman, Lenore. *The Divorce Revolution.* New York: Free Press, 1985. An exploration of the unintended (and disastrous) economic effects of no-fault divorce laws on women.

Suggested Films

Kramer vs. Kramer (1979). Father parents his son after his wife leaves. Stars Dustin Hoffman and Meryl Streep, who fight a bitter custody battle.

An Unmarried Woman (1978). This Paul Mazursky film stars Jill Clayburgh as a single woman who struggles—and succeeds—in coping after her husband leaves her.

READINGS

CHILDREN OF DIVORCE: TEN YEARS AFTER

Judith Wallerstein

Judith Wallerstein's work with the children of divorce has been extremely influential. In this ten-year clinical follow-up of children who were six to eight years old at the time of their parents' divorce, Wallerstein finds that as the children enter young adulthood, about half continue to be affected by the divorce. What are these effects? Do you think the problems are caused by divorce? What other causes might there be? How does not having a comparable control group of non-divorced children affect her findings? Do you believe the feelings expressed by these young adults are significantly different from young adults whose parents were not divorced? If your parents were divorced, do you believe you were similarly affected. (For a critique of the concept of "children of divorce," see Amato, 1991.)

ATTITUDES AND FEELINGS TOWARD PAST AND PRESENT

In their unhappiness, their loneliness, their sense of neediness and deprivation, the youngsters now 16 to 18 years old suffered more than the other age groups in the study. The divorce was regarded as the central experience in their lives by over half of these young people, who spoke longingly of their lives in the intact, predivorce family. Some volunteered that their difficulties had escalated through the years, indicating that they had been more protected from parental quarrels when they were younger. An overwhelming majority, boys and girls alike, spoke wistfully of their longing for an ideal intact family. These feelings were unrelated to their judgment of the wisdom of their parents' decision to divorce. The majority, in fact, regarded their parents as incompatible, the divorce as irreversible, and the relationship between the parents as beyond repair. Nevertheless, they often explained a change in one parent's mood as a reflection of a major change in the other parent's life, as if it were self-evident that strong, invisible ties between the divorced parents had lasted over the years or as if their view of their parents, as a couple, had endured. Tom told us, "Mom's been bitchy since Dad's new wife had a baby."

Their sense of powerlessness in the face of the major event in their lives was striking. This was conveyed along with a sad, somewhat stoic acceptance of their experience. Alice said:

I don't know if divorce is ever a good thing, but if it is going to happen, it is going to happen. If one person wants out, he wants out. It can't be changed. I get depressed when I think about it. I get sad and angry when I think about what happened to me.

The recurring theme was loss of the father, even though there seemed to be almost no link between the father for whom they yearned and the actual father, to whom access was entirely open and who in many instances lived nearby. When asked if she had gained anything from the divorce, Olga said emphatically, "Absolutely no." Asked what she had lost, the girl responded, "My father. Being close to my dad. I wish it were different, but it is not going to change. It is too late." Olga's father lived nearby and she saw him monthly. He paid little attention to her at these meetings, preferring his son.

Larry's father also lived close by. The boy and his mother had asked the father to take Larry into his home, but the father had refused. Larry told us:

Life has been worse for me than for other kids because I was a divorced kid. Most of my friends had two parents and those kids got the things that they wanted. Not having a dad is tough for me. I wanted to live with him but he would not take me. He never told me why.

Karl, who lived with his mother and stepfather and two older sisters, said, "I needed a father, not because I like him more, but because there was no one in the home like me. That's my true feeling." We were interested that Karl did not include his stepfather in his perspective of someone who would be like him within the home.

Perhaps one clue to the distress expressed by so many youngsters was their sense of the unavailability of the working mother. It was not unusual for the youngster to equate the mother's unavailability with uninterest or rejection. Chuck said that his mother did not care for him. She was busy working all the time. "She does not pay any attention to me. I want her to be a mom with an interest in what I am doing with my life, not just a machine that shells out money." It would appear that the longing for the father may reflect not only feelings about the father, but also the feeling so many of these young people had of being rejected by a busy, working mother who was not available to them, and the overall sense that so many shared of not having been provided with the close support that they wished for and needed from their family during their childhood and adolescent years. It is possible that, in the same way that the youngest group of children at the ten-year mark were preoccupied with the idealized family of their fantasies, these youngsters were preoccupied with the lost father as the symbolic equation of the divorce. Their preoccupation with the father, unrelated to the actual quality of their father-child relationships, repeats their responses of ten years earlier.

Finally, although resentment was surely implicit in many of the statements of these young people, overt expression of anger toward parents, especially toward fathers, was uncommon. One of the distinguishing characteristics of this entire group, particularly the boys, was the muting of anger. This psychological stance parallels the limited acting out among these young people. Speaking of his father, who refused to support his college career unless the boy came to live with him and the new stepmother, even though the tension in the remarriage was very high, Andy said:

He won't change. He won't allow anything else to come into his mind. I just learn to accept it. Sometimes I feel sorry for him. He really needs a wife. He and his new wife just don't get along.

Sometimes the need to avoid anger pushed youngsters into far-fetched apologies for their parents. Kelly told us how angry her mother had been when Kelly asked to live with her father. She had been ostracized by her mother; she was even asked to eat at a separate table following her request. Kelly confided, "I can't really blame my mom completely. She stayed up all night to take care of me when I was one year old."

ATTITUDES TOWARD THE FUTURE

Most of these young people believe in romantic love. With few exceptions, they expect to fall in love, marry, and have children of their own. Like most of the other young people in this study, their values are conservative. They do not regard the divorced family as a new social norm. They consider divorce a solution that reflects marital failure, one that should be used only as a last resort when there are children. They agree on divorce when there is physical violence in the family. They believe, on balance, that divorce helps parents, not children. Their values include fidelity and life-long commitment. It is painful for them to acknowledge what many of them know, that one of their parents had been unfaithful during the marriage. Anger at a parent whom they know to have been promiscuous can be very bitter. Describing her father's many affairs, Betty said tartly,

Some day he won't be able to cultivate all those 21-year-old girls and life will catch up with him. He is going to be an old man and he will be punished.

Close to two thirds of these young people were apprehensive about the possibility of disruption in their own future marriages. Girls were especially fearful that their marriages would not endure. A recurrent theme was a sense of vulnerability and fear of being hurt by romantic relationships. Talking about the future, Brenda said,

It is hard to make a commitment. All the work and all the trust that is involved. I don't want to get married and do what my mom did. I

continued on next page

don't know if marriage will last or not. How can you be sure that marriage will last? I hate to think of what will happen. I am afraid. I am afraid of being hurt. That's why I am a loner.

One half of the boys and girls were fearful of being betrayed, not only in their future, but in their present relationships as well. Of all the age groups, these youngsters were most worried about repeating their parents' relationship patterns and mistakes. Nancy said, "I always find myself attracted to guys who treat you bad." Maureen said, "A problem I have is not being able to show my feelings. I am afraid that they might get stepped on. Once in a relationship, I feel that I will be afraid of losing it if I get attached." Teresa said, "There is a lonely, shaky part of me. I am afraid of what happened to my parents happening to me."

A repeated fear among the boys, somewhat different from the fear of betrayal that the girls emphasized, was their fear of being unloved. Zachary said, "The divorce made me cautious of my relationships. Whenever I meet a girl, I have the unconscious feeling that when she gets to know me she will not love me."

A substantial minority of these young people, however, felt that they were but little influenced by their parents' failures and were relatively confident about the future. Several sought role models elsewhere in order to build their expectations on a solid ground. Barbara told us that she had selected her grandparents and their long-lasting marriage as the model for her future plans.

I look at my grandparents who have been married 40 years. I don't look at divorce. It does not cross my mind. I don't think, if I got married, I would get a divorce. I don't worry about losing relationships.

Several young people told of their pleasure with the intact families of their boyfriends or girlfriends and their reassurance in finding examples of stable, happy marriages. Susan told us,

My boyfriend has a family and I love his family. His parents have been married a long time. They are Irish. The kids all live at home. It is fun to be around them. I am always over there.

INDEPENDENCE

The forthcoming move toward independence created a great deal of anxiety in these young people. Although many . . . spoke proudly of their independence as a positive outcome of their parents' divorce, their behavior was often discrepant with their pronouncements. Mary told us: "Nobody helped me. Just my own determination and my friends." She had learned from a soccer accident that, "If you want to play, you play in pain." Diana said, "The outcome of the divorce was that to survive I had to be independent." Others told us how they had learned to solve problems on their own. Yet, although most of them were employed at least part-time and taking responsibility for themselves to a high degree, few spoke of *wanting* to establish themselves independently, and only three of these young people had left home to live on their own. Several of the youngsters who spoke bravely of their independence had suffered intensely during their freshman year at college and sought to return home.

A dream of Katherine's, which occurred during her freshman year at an out-of-town college, reveals some of the difficulties faced by these young people who were attempting to establish independence at a time when their own insecurities and need for parenting dominated their thoughts. Katherine told us,

I had a dream at mid-term. In real life, I told a friend that the first thing I would do when I would get home was that I would hug my dad, and that would be proof that he loved me, and that I loved him. In the dream, I came home and my dad wasn't there. The person who met me said, "Haven't you forgotten that your dad is dead?"

Katherine said that what disturbed her most was not that her dad was dead, but that there was no one to hug her, and she had worried so much about getting home for a hug.

It appears that independent behavior, and the pride young people feel in it, can mask an intense hunger for further nurturance and powerful feelings of not being sufficiently nurtured to make it on one's own without "playing in pain."

CHAPTER 17

New Lives, New Families

PREVIEW

To gain a sense of what you already know about the material covered in this chapter, answer "true" or "false" to the following statements. You will find the answers on page 557.

1. Researchers are increasingly viewing stepfamilies as normal families. True or false?
2. Divorce does not end families. True or false?
3. Shared parenting tends to be the strongest tie holding former spouses together. True or false?
4. Second marriages are significantly happier than first marriages. True or false?
5. Welfare payments place the majority of single-parent families above the poverty level. True or false?
6. Children tend to have greater power in single-parent families than in traditional nuclear families. True or false?
7. Few former spouses with children have cooperative relationships with each other. True or false?
8. Stepmothers generally experience less stress in stepfamilies than stepfathers because stepmothers are able to fulfill themselves by nurturing their stepchildren. True or false?
9. Researchers are increasingly finding that remarried families and intact nuclear families are similar to each other in many important ways. True or false?
10. People who remarry and those who marry for the first time tend to have similar expectations. True or false?

THE 1990S MARK THE DEFINITIVE SHIFT from a traditional marriage and family system to a pluralistic one. The traditional family system, based on life-time marriage and the intact nuclear family as its norm, is giving way to a pluralistic one created by divorce, remarriage, and births to single women. This new pluralistic family system consists of three major types of families: (1) intact nuclear families, (2) single-parent families, and (3) stepfamilies. The dominance of the new system is attested to by the following facts (Bumpass, Sweet, and Martin, 1990; Coleman and Ganong, 1991; Demo and Acock, 1991; Gongla and Thompson, 1987):

◆ The chances are more than two out of three that an individual will divorce, remarry, or live in a single-parent family or stepfamily as a child or parent sometime during his or her life.
◆ Remarriage is as common as first marriage. Half of all recent marriages involve at least one previously married partner.
◆ Over one-fifth of all families are currently single-parent families. Single-parent families are growing faster in number than any other family form. Approximately half of all children born in the 1990s will live in single-parent families sometime during their childhoods.
◆ Over 2.3 million households have stepchildren living with them; the number of noncustodial stepfamilies without children living with them is significantly higher. One-sixth of all children, almost 10 million, are currently members of stepfamilies. Over a third of all children can expect to live in a stepfamily at sometime during their childhood.

Because of this shift to a pluralistic family system, researchers are beginning to reevaluate single-parent families and stepfamilies and to view them as typical rather than deviant family forms (Coleman and Ganong, 1991; Pasley and Ihinger-Tallman, 1987). It is useful to see these families as different structures pursuing the same goals as traditional nuclear families: the provision of intimacy, economic cooperation, the socialization of children, and the assignment of social roles and status.

If we shift our perspective from structure to functions, the important question is no longer whether a particular family form is deviant. (If prevalence of a family form determines deviance, logic tells us that the traditional nuclear family may soon become deviant.) The important question becomes whether a specific family—regardless of whether it is a traditional, single-parent, or stepfamily—succeeds in performing its functions (Ahrons and Rodgers, 1987; Gongla and Thompson, 1987). In a practical sense, as long as a family is fulfilling its functions, it is a *normal* family. As Bert Adams (1985) observes, ". . . whether we see today's changes as problems or solutions depends to a great extent on what we value most."

The dramatic rise in single-parent families and stepfamilies over the last twenty years is the result of shifting social values and trends rather than individual shortcoming or pathologies. Single-parent families and stepfamilies have become a natural part of the contemporary American marriage system. As such, they are not problems in themselves. Instead, to a great extent, many of their problems lie in the stigma attached to them and their lack of support by the larger society (Ahrons and Rodgers, 1987; Gongla and Thompson, 1987). If we are going to strengthen these families, note Constance Ahrons and Roy Rodgers (1987), "we must unambiguously acknowledge and support them as normal, prevalent family types that have resulted from major societal trends and changes."

❖ REFLECTIONS   *What effect does it have on your views of single-parent and stepfamilies to think of them as "normal" families? As "abnormal" or "deviant" families?.*

Do you believe single-parent families and stepfamilies should be considered "normal" or "deviant" families? Why?

❖ THE BINUCLEAR FAMILY

One of the most unique, complex, and ambiguous relationships in contemporary America is what some researchers are beginning to call the binuclear family (Ahrons and Rodgers, 1987). The binuclear family is a postdivorce family system with children. It is the original nuclear family divided in two. The binuclear family consists of *two* nuclear families—the maternal nuclear family headed by the mother (the ex-wife) and the paternal one headed by the father (the ex-husband). Both single-parent families and stepfamilies are forms of binuclear families.

Divorce ends a marriage but not a family. It dissolves the husband/wife relationship but not the father/mother, mother/child, or father/child relationship. The family reorganizes itself into a binuclear family. In this new family, ex-husbands and ex-wives may continue to relate to each other and to their children, although in substantially altered ways. The significance of the maternal and paternal components of the binuclear family varies. In families with joint physical custody, the maternal and paternal families may be equally important to their children. In single-parent families headed by women, the paternal family component may be minimal.

Complexity of the Binuclear Family

The binuclear family system may be the most complex in America today. Consider the family history of two children, Paige and Daniel Brickman. (See Figure 17.1 for a diagram of their binuclear family.)

The binuclear family is the post-divorce family consisting of two nuclear families, the nuclear family that includes the mother (or ex-wife) and that which includes the father (or ex-husband). The creation of the bi-nuclear family presents both rewards and challenges for its members.

When Paige was six and Daniel eight, their parents separated and divorced. The children continued to live with their mother, Sophia, in a single-parent household while spending weekends and holidays with their father, David. After a year, David began living with Jane, a single mother, who had a five-year-old daughter, Lisa.

Three years after the divorce, Sophia married John, who had joint physical custody of his two daughters, Sally and Mary, aged seven and nine. Paige and Daniel continued living with their mother while their stepfather's children lived with them every other week. After two years of marriage, Sophia and John had a son, Joshua. About the same time, David and Jane split up; they continued to maintain close ties because of the bonds formed between David and Lisa. A year later, David married Julie, who had physical custody of two children, Sally and Gabriel; the next year, they had a son, David, Jr. Lisa visits every few weeks.

Although Paige and Daniel's binuclear family is not at all unusual, don't be surprised if it's hard to figure out who's related to whom. As Ahrons and Rodgers (1987) point out, "The variations in family structure that result from remarriage in binuclear families almost defy categorization." Ten years after their parents divorced, Paige's and Daniel's family consists of the following family members: two biological parents, two stepparents, three stepsisters, one stepbrother, and two half brothers. In addition, they had a "cohabiting" stepmother and stepsister with whom they continued to have close ties. Their extended family includes two sets of biological grandparents and stepgrandparents, and a large array of biological and step aunts, uncles, and cousins. Paige and Daniel continue to have two households to which they belong as children.

Subsystems in the Binuclear Family

To clarify the different relationships, researchers divided the binuclear family into five subsystems (Ahrons and Rodgers, 1987):

◆ Former spouse subsystem
◆ Remarried couple subsystem
◆ Parent/child subsystem
◆ Sibling subsystems: step- and half-siblings
◆ Mother/stepmother—father/stepfather subsystems

FORMER SPOUSE SUBSYSTEM. Although divorce severs the husband/wife relationship, the mother/father relationship endures as former spouses continue their parenting responsibilities. While the degree of involvement for the noncustodial parent varies, children generally benefit from the continued involvement of both parents. The former spouses, however, must deal with a number of issues. These include the following:

◆ Anger and hostility toward each other as a result of their previous marriage and separation.
◆ Conflict regarding child custody, parenting styles, values, and aspirations concerning their children.
◆ Shifting roles and relationships between former spouses when one or both remarry.
◆ The ability to incorporate others as stepparents, stepsiblings, and stepgrandparents into the family system when one or both former spouses remarry.

As long as former spouses are able to separate parenting from personal issues involving each other, they may form effective coparenting relationships. Ahrons and Wallisch (1987) indicated that about half of the former spouses in their study are able to work well with each other; another quarter interact, but with substantial conflict. About a quarter are unable to coparent because of the high degree of conflict.

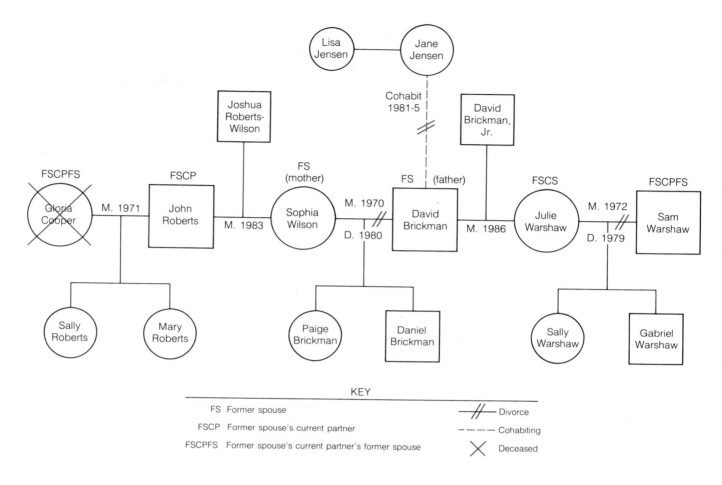

KEY

FS	Former spouse	——#——— Divorce	
FSCP	Former spouse's current partner	————— Cohabiting	
FSCPFS	Former spouse's current partner's former spouse	✕ Deceased	

REMARRIED COUPLE SUBSYSTEM. Remarried couples are generally unprepared for the complexities of remarried life. If they have physical custody of children from the first marriage, they must provide access between the children and the noncustodial parents. Both custodial and noncustodial parents must facilitate the exchange of children, money, decision-making power, and time. This may often be difficult. Typical marital issues such as power and intimacy may become magnified, as they frequently involve not only the remarried couple but the former spouse as well. Because of custody arrangements, for example, the former spouse may exercise veto power over the remarried couple's plan to take a family vacation because it conflicts with visitation.

PARENT-CHILD SUBSYSTEMS. Remarriage is probably more difficult for children than parents. While parents are caught in the excitement of romance, their children may be reacting with anxiety and distress. Their parents are making choices that affect the children but over which the children themselves have little or no control. Furthermore, remarriage destroys the children's fantasies that their parents will reunite.

FIGURE 17.1

Diagram of Binuclear Family

The binuclear family consists of five subsytems: former spouse, remarried couple, parent/child, sibling (biological, step, and half), and mother-stepmother/father-stepfather subsystems. Identify these subsystems in the diagram above.

Children may not want the stepparent to function as a parent for various reasons. The children may feel, for example, that the stepparent is usurping the role of the absent biological parent. Or they may resent the stepparent's intrusion into their restructured single-parent family.

Both the biological parent and stepparent must make adjustments. Former single parents, for example, must adjust to the presence of a second parent in decision-making and childrearing practices. Stepparents, however, have the greatest adjustment to make. Because remarried families tend to model themselves after traditional nuclear families, stepparents often expect that the stepparent role will be similar to the parent role. Stepfathers who have their own children may feel conflict because they are "more" a father to their stepchildren than to their biological ones. Stepmothers, however, seem to experience greater stress than stepfathers. The stress may result from stepmothers' relatively high degree of involvement in child-care and nurturing activities, which are not adequately acknowledged or appreciated by stepchildren.

Following remarriage, the level of contact between children and nonresidential parents changes significantly. The average level of weekly contact for a single father is double that of a remarried father. If both parents remarry, the level of contact drops 300 percent (Furstenberg and Nord, 1982).

SIBLING SUBSYSTEMS: STEPSIBLINGS AND HALF-SIBLINGS. When parents remarry, their children may acquire "instant" brothers or sisters who may differ considerably in age and temperament. The sibling relationships may be especially complex in binuclear families. Consider Paige and Daniel's stepsibling and half-sibling relationships. In their mother's family the two children had to adjust to a half-brother and two stepsisters who lived with them half-time. In their father's family, they adjusted to a "cohabiting" sibling who was "like" a sister. When their father remarried, they gained two stepsiblings and a little later a half-brother. To make matters more complex, biological relationships do not guarantee emotional closeness. Paige feels closest, for example, to her "cohabitant sibling" Lisa and her stepsister Sally, neither of whom lived with her. Daniel, however, feels closest to Mary, his stepsister, and Joshua, his half-brother.

All things being equal, stepsiblings are predisposed to bond with each other because family norms require affection between family members (Pasley, 1987). Bonding will occur most rapidly when siblings are of similar age and sex, have similar experiences and values, are interdependent, and perceive greater rewards than costs in their relationships.

Stepsiblings and siblings contend with each other for parental affection, toys, attention, physical space, and dominance. Sharing a parent with a new stepparent is often difficult enough, but to share the parent with a stepsibling can be overwhelming. Visiting biological children compete with stepchildren who are living with the visiting children's biological parent.

MOTHER/STEPMOTHER—FATHER/STEPFATHER SUBSYSTEMS. The relationship between new spouses and former spouses often influences the remarried family. The former spouse can be an intruder in the new marriage, a source of conflict between the remarried couple. Other times the former spouse is a handy scapegoat for displacing problems. Much of the current spouse/former spouse interaction depends on how the ex-spouses themselves feel about each other. Ahrons and Rodgers (1987) found that about half of current spouses felt somewhat detached from the former spouse; they felt as if they were "acquaintances." About a quarter liked the former spouse, and the remaining quarter reported feeling competitive or jealous.

PERSPECTIVE

Strengthening Binuclear Families

Because binuclear families are becoming a family norm, it is important for us to strengthen rather than stigmatize them. We can do much as individuals and as a society to assist these families. Some of the strategies that those involved in binuclear families can use are described in the following paragraphs.

Divorce Mediation and Therapy

Divorce mediation and therapy strive to minimize the pain and acrimony involved in divorce, as the quality of coparenting relationships is significantly affected by the emotional terms on which husbands and wives divorce (Ahrons and Rodgers, 1987). No-fault divorce eliminates some of the blaming that accompanies divorce, but property, support, custody, and visitation issues are often characterized by bitter conflict and recriminations. Mediation encourages divorcing spouses to try to resolve their differences through negotiation and compromise with the help of a trained mediator.

Divorce therapy helps individuals and families come to terms with the end of their marriages. In particular, divorce therapy assists individuals in resolving their feelings of failure and their anger toward their former spouses. For children, divorce therapy aids in the avoidance of self-blame and assists the transition to single-parent families or stepfamilies.

Normalizing Binuclear Families

Cultural stereotypes depict single-parent families, stepfamilies, and stepchildren as deviant or abnormal (Coleman and Ganong, 1987). Such stereotypes are unrealistic and damaging, however; they distort the actual picture of these families. We need to recognize that there is noth-

ing deviant or pathological about single-parent families or stepfamilies. Binuclear families have become normal families in the contemporary American family system. Stepfamilies, indeed, may not be especially different from traditional nuclear families. Children and parents, face similar issues in all types of families. Parents and stepparents alike, for example, are likely to experience difficulties with favoritism, discipline, and child care (Ihinger-Tallman and Pasley, 1987).

Use of Therapy in Managing Binuclear Family Dynamics

Individuals and families need to recognize that they undergo immense stress as they move from nuclear families to single-parent families or stepfamilies. Rather than waiting until problems become uncontrollable, individuals and families should seek assistance while the problems still remain manageable. Ihinger-Tallman and Pasley (1987) suggest that families use therapeutic interventions to explore the following issues:

◆ Grief resolution following the end of the first marriage
◆ Creation of an environment that will assist custodial and noncustodial parents

in dealing with coparenting issues
◆ Right of parents to consider their needs as being as important as those of their children
◆ Development of problem-solving and negotiation skills
◆ Exploration of alternative roles, rules, and rituals in both single-parent families and stepfamilies
◆ Identification of stepparent behaviors that enhance the relationship between stepparent and stepchild
◆ Consolidation of parental and step-parental authority

Societal Recognition

Societal institutions need to recognize both the normality and widespread existence of binuclear families. Most social institutions, such as schools, religious groups, health-care organizations, and government agencies, ignore the needs of these families. Instead, they are geared toward serving traditional nuclear families. Schools, for example, often fail to inform noncustodial parents of parent/teacher meetings. Or they may schedule such meetings for times when working single-parents are unable to attend. Teachers sometimes assume that simply because a child is a member of a single-parent family or stepfamily, he or she will have emotional problems or learning difficulties.

The challenge before us as individuals and as a society is to recognize that binuclear families are normal families. It is our responsibility to strengthen these families in every way we can.

❖ REFLECTIONS *Are you involved in a binuclear family? If so, in what role? Which subsystems are functional or dysfunctional in your binuclear family? How do you imagine conflict within the former spouse subsystem would affect children in a binuclear family?*

❖ SINGLE PARENTING

Single-parent families are the fastest growing family form in the United States. No other family type has increased in number as rapidly. Between 1960 and 1989, the percentage of single-parent families almost tripled, from 9 percent to 24 percent. During the last few years, however, the rate of increase has slowed, especially for African-American families (Saluter, 1990). As many as 64 percent of white children and 89 percent of African-American children born in 1980 will spend part of their childhood in a single-parent family (Hofferth, 1985). The single-parent family, more than the dual-worker family or stepfamily, is a radical departure from the traditional nuclear family. Both the dual-worker family and the stepfamily are two-parent families; the single-parent family is not.

In previous generations, the life pattern most women experienced was (1) marriage, (2) motherhood, and (3) widowhood. Single-parent families existed in the past, but they were formed by widowhood rather than divorce or births to unmarried women; significant numbers were headed by men. But a new marriage and family pattern has taken root. Its greatest impact has been on women and their children. The life pattern many women now experience is (1) marriage, (2) motherhood, (3) divorce, (4) single parenting, (5) remarriage, and (6) widowhood. Divorce is a key factor creating today's single-parent family. For those who are not married at the time of their child's birth, the pattern may be (1) motherhood, (2) single parenting, (3) marriage, and (4) widowhood.

Single parenting is difficult, but for many single parents the problems are manageable in comparison to the misery and hopelessness of unhappy or abusive marriages. Although most studies emphasize the stress of single parenting, some studies view it as building strength and confidence in many women. Miller (1982) observed:

A significant number of the single women studied have solved many extraordinary problems in the face of formidable obstacles. Their single parenthood has led to personal growth for many. In adulthood they have made major revisions in their roles in life and in their self- and object-representations. Many have become contributors to their community, and their children are often a source of strength rather than difficulty.

Characteristics of Single-Parent Families

Single-parent families share a number of characteristics, including the following: (1) creation by divorce or births to unmarried women, (2) usually female-headed households, (3) significance of ethnicity, (4) poverty, (5) diversity, and (6) transitional character.

CREATION BY DIVORCE OR BIRTHS TO UNMARRIED WOMEN. Single-parent families tend to be created by marital separation, divorce, or births to unmarried women rather than by widowhood. In fact, in less than twenty years, births to unmarried women have increased fourfold: from 7 percent in 1970 to 29 percent in 1988 of all births (Rawlings, 1989).

In contrast to single parenting by widows, parenting by divorced or unmarried mothers receives less social support. A divorced mother usually receives less assistance from her own kin and considerably less (or none) from her former partner's relatives. Widowed mothers, however, often receive social support from their husband's relatives. Our culture is still ambivalent about divorce and considers single-parent families deviant. (See Leslie and Grady, 1985.)

FEMALE-HEADED HOUSEHOLDS. Eighty-seven percent of single-parent families are headed by women. This has important economic ramifications because of sex discrimination in wages and job opportunities as discussed in Chapter 12.

SIGNIFICANCE OF ETHNICITY. Ethnicity is an important demographic factor in single-parent families (Saluter, 1990). In 1989, among white children, 19 percent lived in single-parent families; among African Americans, 55 percent lived in such families; among Latinos, 31 percent lived in single-parent families. Four times as many whites lived in two-parent families as in single-parent families; in African-American families, about a third more children lived in single-parent families than in two-parent families (Saluter, 1990). White single mothers were more likely to be divorced than their African-American or Latino counterparts, who were likely to be unmarried at the time of the birth or widowed. Of single parents, fifty percent of white mothers, 24 percent of African-American mothers and 30 percent of the Latino mothers were divorced (Johnson, 1980). African-American and Latino families are more likely to live below the poverty level, both as single-parent and two-parent families.

POVERTY. Married women usually experience a sharp drop in their income when they separate or divorce (as discussed in Chapter 16). Among unmarried single mothers, poverty and motherhood go hand in hand. Because they are women, because they are often young, and because they are frequently from ethnic minorities, they have few financial resources. Single mothers are under constant economic stress trying to make ends meet (McLanahan and Booth, 1991). They work at low wages or endure welfare or both. They are unable to plan because of their constant financial uncertainty. They move more frequently than two-parent families as economic and living situations change, uprooting themselves and their children. They accept material support from kin, but at the price of receiving unsolicited "free advice," especially from their mothers.

DIVERSITY OF LIVING ARRANGEMENTS. There are many different kinds of single-parent households. Single-parent families show great flexibility in managing child care and housing with limited resources. In doing so, they rely on a variety of household arrangements. Only about 56 percent of single-parent households consist of just a single parent and his or her children (Payton, 1982). Forty-four percent of single parents head other types of family structures. Some rent out rooms. A third live in modified extended families consisting of their own children and another adult who is a relative, a boarder, or a cohabitant. Many adolescent and young African-American mothers live with their own mothers in a three-generation setting.

TRANSITIONAL FORM. Single parenting is usually a transitional state. A single mother has strong motivation to marry or remarry because of cultural expectations, economic stress, role overload, and a need for emotional security and intimacy. For many, however, especially single women in their thirties and forties, single parenting has become a more intentional and less transitional life-style (Gongla and Thompson, 1987). Some older women choose unmarried single parenting because they have not found a suitable partner and are concerned about declining fertility. Others choose single parenting because they do not want their lives and careers encumbered by the compromises necessary in marriage. And still others choose it because they don't want a husband or because they are lesbian.

Children in a Single-Parent Family

More than 60 percent of people who divorce have children living at home. One study indicated that children remain in single-parent homes an average of about 6 years for whites and 7.5 years for African Americans (Hofferth, 1985). Of children born in 1980 who will live in a single-parent family, white children can expect to spend about 31 percent of their childhood in single-parent families, African-American children about 59 percent.

STABILITY AND LONELINESS. After a divorce, the single parent is usually glad to have the children with him or her (Weiss, 1979). Everything else seems to have fallen apart, but as long as divorced parents have their children, they retain their parental function. Their children's need for them reassures them of their own importance. The mother's success as a parent becomes even more important to counteract the feelings of low self-esteem that result from divorce. Feeling depressed, the mother knows she must bounce back for the children. Yet after a short period, she comes to realize that her children do not fill the void left by her divorce. The children are a chore as well as a pleasure, and she may resent being constantly tied down by their needs. Thus minor incidents with the children—a child's refusal to eat or a temper tantrum—may get blown out of proportion.

A major disappointment for many new single parents is the discovery that they are still lonely. It seems almost paradoxical. How can a person be lonely amid all the noise and bustle that accompany children? However, children do not ordinarily function as attachment figures; they can never be potential partners. The attempt to make them so is harmful to parent and child. Yet children remain the central figures in the lives of single parents. This situation leads to a second paradox: although children do not completely fulfill a person, they rank higher in most single mothers' priorities than anything else (Weiss, 1975).

CHANGED FAMILY STRUCTURE. A single-parent family is not the same as a two-parent family with one parent temporarily absent (Weiss, 1976, 1979). The permanent absence of one parent dramatically changes the way in which the parenting adult relates to the children. Generally, the mother becomes closer and more responsive to her children. Her authority role changes, too. A greater distinction between parents and children exists in two-parent homes. Rules are developed by both mothers and fathers. Parents generally have an implicit understanding to back each other up in childrearing matters and to enforce mutually agreed-on rules. In the single-parent family no other partner is available to help maintain such agreements; as a result, the children may find themselves in a much more egalitarian situation. Consequently, they have more power to negotiate rules. They can badger a single parent into getting their way about staying up late, watching television, or going out. They can be more stubborn, cry more often and louder, whine, pout, and throw temper tantrums. Any parent who has tried to get children to do something they do not want to do knows how soon he or she can be worn down. So single parents are more willing to compromise: "Okay, you can have a *small* box of Cocoa Puffs. Put that large one back and promise you won't fuss like this anymore." In this way, children acquire considerable decision-making power in single-parent homes. They gain it through default—the single parent finds it too difficult to argue with them all the time.

Children in single-parent homes may also learn more responsibility. They may learn to help with kitchen chores, to clean up their messes, or to be more considerate. In the single-parent setting, the children are encouraged to recognize the work their mother does and the importance of cooperation. One woman related how her husband had always washed the dishes when they were still living together. At that time it had been difficult to get the children to help around the house, particularly with the dishes. Now, she said, the children always do the dishes—and they do the vacuuming and keep their own rooms straightened up, too (also see Greif, 1985).

LONG-TERM CONSEQUENCES. Throughout the 1970s, most research examining the impact of single-parent families on children was positive. These studies focused on the strengths of single-parent families, celebrating the ingenuity and energy of single mothers. In part, this was a reaction to the earlier pathological view of single parenting. While single parents continue to demonstrate love and creativity in the face of adversity, more recent research on their children has not been as optimistic as it once was. A review (McLanahan and Booth, 1991) of the relevant studies found that young children from mother-only families tended not to do as well academically as those from two-parent families. In adolescence and young adulthood, children from single-parent families had fewer years of education and were more likely to drop out of high school. They had lower earnings and were more likely to be poor. They were more likely to marry young, have children early (whether married or single), and divorce. These conclusions are consistent for whites, African Americans, Latinos, and Asian Americans.

It is not entirely clear whether these results are due to the nature of the family structure or to the debilitating effects of poverty. The reviewers note that socioeconomic status accounts for some, but not all, of the effects. Some of the effects are attributed to family structure. But Harriet Pipes McAdoo (1988) traces the cause to poverty. She notes that African-American families are able to meet their children's needs in a variety of structures. "The major problem arising from female-headed families is poverty," she wrote. "The impoverishment of Black families has been more detrimental than the actual structural arrangement."

The single parent family is the fastest growing family form in the United States. Eighty-seven percent are headed by women. Over half of all African-American children live in single-parent families.

❖ NONCUSTODIAL PARENTS

Researchers know very little about noncustodial or nonresidential fathers (Depner and Bray, 1990). They know even less about noncustodial mothers, who account for about 13 percent of noncustodial parents (Christensen, Dahl, and Rettig, 1990). What we do know about men, however, tells us that they often suffer grievously from the disruption or disappearance of their father role following divorce. They feel depressed, anxious, guilt-ridden; they feel a lack of self-esteem (Arditti, 1990). The change in status from full-time father to noncustodial parent leaves fathers bewildered about how they are to act: there are no norms for an involved noncustodial parent. This lack of norms makes it especially difficult if the relationship between the former spouses is bitter. Without adequate norms, fathers may become "Disneyland Dads," interacting with their children during weekends, taking them to movies, out for pizza; or they may become "Disappearing Dads," absenting themselves from any contact at all with their children. For many concerned noncustodial fathers, the question is simple but painful: "How can I be a father if I'm not a father anymore?"

Many fathers are not successful in being noncustodial fathers and abandon the role altogether. Children tend to have little contact with the nonresidential parent. A national survey of children ages eleven to sixteen years with divorced parents found that less than half had seen their father in the previous year (Furstenberg, Morgan, and Allison, 1986). In a study by Frank Furstenberg and Christine Nord (1982), only 16 percent of the children saw their nonresident father as much as once a week; almost 40 percent of the children had had no contact with their father in five years or even knew where he was living.

The reduced contact between nonresidential fathers and children seems to weaken the bonds of affection. One study of college students found that children in single-mother families tend to feel less close to their fathers than those in two-parent families. Seventeen percent of the students from single-mother families reported feeling close to their fathers, in contrast to 38 percent of those from two-parent families (White, Brinkerhoff, and Booth, 1985). Many years later, when the divorced fathers are middle-aged or elderly, they continue to have less contact with their adult children than married fathers. Divorced fathers are less likely to consider their children as sources of support in times of need (Cooney and Uhlenberg, 1990). Furstenberg and Nord (1982) concluded that "marital dissolution involves either a complete cessation of contact between the nonresidential parent and child or a relationship that is tantamount to a ritual form of parenthood."

❖ REFLECTIONS   *If you are or have been a member of a single-parent family, what were its strengths and weaknesses? What do you know of the strengths and weaknesses of friends and relatives in single-parent families?*

❖ REMARRIAGE

Marriage is made in Heaven, but second marriages are arranged by people.

Yiddish proverb

Samuel Johnson described remarriage as "the triumph of hope over experience." And Americans are a hopeful people. About half of all divorced women remarry within seven years of separation. Among those who remarry between twenty-four and thirty-four years of age, the time between divorce and remarriage is about three years (Bumpass, Sweet, and Martin, 1990).

For the younger age groups, this quickness to remarry is somewhat paradoxical. Many newly divorced men and women express great wariness about marrying again.

Yet at the same time they are actively searching for mates. Women often view their divorced time as important for their development as individuals, whereas men, who often complain that they were pressured into marriage before they were ready, become restless as "born-again bachelors" (Furstenberg, 1980).

Remarriage Rates

Over half of all marriages in the United States are marriages in which at least one partner has been previously married (Bumpass, Sweet, and Martin, 1990). Remarriage is more or less standard for divorced persons, but the rates have been declining, especially for African Americans and women under age twenty-five years. In addition to age and ethnicity, the presence of children may also affect remarriage.

AGE. A man's or woman's age at the time of separation is the greatest individual factor affecting remarriage. As with the "marriage market" in first marriages, as a person ages, the number of potential partners declines; at the same time one's own "marketability" decreases with increasing age. For women, the highest remarriage rate takes place in their twenties; it declines by a quarter in their thirties and by two-thirds in their forties. As we saw in Chapter 4, the double standard of aging affects women more negatively than men.

Remarriage rates for younger women have been declining. Their remarriage rates, in fact, have dropped by almost half since 1965. The decrease may be related to women choosing to cohabit rather than remarry.

ETHNICITY. Ethnicity also affects remarriage rates. About 55 percent of white women and 42 percent of African-American women remarry. Latinos are less likely to

1. Bride 2. Groom 3. Groom's daughter from first marriage 4. Bride's mother 5. Bride's mother's current lover 6. Bride's sperm donor father 7.&8. Sperm donor's parents who sued for visitation rights to bride 9. Bride's mother's lover at time of bride's birth 10. Groom's mother 11. Groom's mother's boyfriend 12. Groom's father 13. Groom's stepmother 14. Groom's father's third wife 15. Groom's grandfather 16. Groom's grandfather's lover 17. Groom's first wife

remarry than either whites or African Americans. The remarriage rates have been declining for African Americans, although first-marriage rates have also been declining.

PRESENCE OF CHILDREN. Although children from earlier marriages traditionally have been thought to decrease the likelihood of remarriage, the evidence is mixed. A review of the literature found that the presence of children decreases the rate of marriage by about one-quarter (Bumpass, Sweet, and Martin, 1990). The effects are most marked when a woman has three or more children. Most of the research, however, is ten to fifteen years old, and the increased prevalence of single-parent families and stepfamilies may have decreased some of the negative impact of children.

Courtship

The norms governing courtship prior to first marriage are fairly well defined. As courtship progresses, individuals spend more time together; at the same time, family and friends limit their time and energy demands because "they're in love." Courtship norms for second marriages, however, are not especially clear (Rodgers and Conrad, 1986). For example, when is it acceptable for formerly married (and presumably sexually experienced) men and women to become sexually involved? What type of commitment validates "premarital" sex among postmarital men and women? How long should courtship last before a commitment to marriage is made? Without clear norms, courtship following divorce can be plagued by uncertainty about what to expect.

One clear difference, however, appears to be in terms of cohabitation. Although 15 to 25 percent of people marrying for the first time may be living together at the time of marriage, 40 percent of those remarrying are cohabiting (Coleman and Ganong, 1991). This larger percentage may reflect the desire to test their compatibility in a "trial marriage" to prevent later marital regrets (Buunk and van Driel, 1989).

If neither partner has children, courtship for remarriage may resemble courtship before the first marriage, with one major exception: the memory of the earlier marriage exists as a model for the second marriage. It may trigger old fears, regrets, habits of relating, wounds, or doubts. At the same time, having experienced the day-to-day living of marriage, the partners have more realistic expectations. Their courtship may be complicated if one or both are noncustodial parents. In that event, visiting children present an additional element.

Courtship differs considerably from that preceding a first marriage if one or both members in the dating relationship is a custodial parent. Single parents are not often a part of the singles world, because such participation requires leisure and money, which single parents generally lack. Children rapidly consume both of these resources.

Although single parents may wish to find a new partner, their children usually remain the central figures in their lives. This creates a number of new problems. First, the single parent's decision to go out at night may lead to guilt feelings about the children. If a single mother works and her children are in day care, should she go out in the evening or stay at home with them? Second, a single parent must look at a potential partner as a potential parent as well. A person may be a good companion and confidant and be fun to be with, but if he or she does not want to assume parental responsibilities, the relationship will often stagnate or be broken off. Too, a single parent's new companion may be interested in assuming parental responsibilities, but the children may regard him or her as an intruder and try to sabotage the new relationship.

A single parent may also have to decide whether to permit a lover to spend the night when the children are in the home. This is often an important symbolic act. For one thing, it brings the children into the parent's new relationship. If the couple have no commitment, the parent may fear the consequences of the children's emotional involvement with the lover; if they break up, the children may be adversely affected. Single parents are often hesitant to expose their children again to the distress of separation; the memory of the initial parental separation and divorce is often still painful. For another thing, having a lover spend the night reveals to the children that their parent is a sexual being. This may make some single parents feel uncomfortable and may also make the parent vulnerable to moral judgment by his or her children. Single parents are often fearful that their children will lose respect for them under such circumstances. Sometimes children do judge their parents harshly, especially their mothers. Parents are often deeply disturbed at being condemned by children who do not understand their need for love, companionship, and sexual intimacy. Finally, having someone sleep over may trigger the resentment and anger that the children feel toward their parents for splitting up. They may view the lover as a parental replacement and feel deeply threatened.

Characteristics of Remarriage

Remarriage is considerably different from first marriage in a number of ways. First, the new partners get to know each other during a time of significant changes in life relationships, confusion, guilt, stress, and mixed feelings about the past (Keshet, 1980). They have great hope that they will not repeat past mistakes, but there is usually some fear that the hurts of the previous marriage will recur (McGoldrick and Carter, 1989). The past is still part of the present. A Talmudic scholar once commented, "When a divorced man marries a divorced woman, four go to bed."

Remarriages occur later than first marriages. People are at different stages in their life cycles and may have different goals (Furstenberg, 1980). A woman who already has had children may enter a second marriage with strong career goals. In her first marriage, raising children may have been more important (see Teachman and Heckert, 1985).

Divorced people have different expectations of their new marriages. In a study of second marriages in Pennsylvania, Furstenberg (1980) discovered that three-fourths of the couples had a different conception of love than couples in their first marriages. Two-thirds thought they were less likely to stay in an unhappy marriage; they had already survived one divorce and knew they could make it through another. Four out of five believed their ideas of marriage had changed. One woman said:

I think second marriages are less idealistic and a little more realistic. You realize that it's going to be tough sometimes but you also know that you have to work them out. You come into a second marriage with a whole new set of responsibilities. It's like coming into a ballgame with the bases loaded. You've got to come through with a hit. Likewise, there's too much riding on the relationship; you've got to make it work and you realize it more after you've been divorced before. You just have to keep working out the rules of the game.

Finally, the majority of remarriages create stepfamilies. Sixty percent of remarriages include a parent with physical custody of one or more children. Another 20 percent include a noncustodial parent (Weingarten, 1980). A single-parent family is generally a transition family leading to a stepfamily, which has its own unique structure, satisfactions, and problems.

Marital Satisfaction and Stability

According to various studies, remarried people are about as satisfied or happy in their second marriages as they were in their first marriage. As in first marriages, marital satisfaction appears to decline with the passage of time (Coleman and Ganong, 1991). Yet despite the fact that marital happiness and satisfaction are more or less the same in first and second marriages, remarried couples are more likely to divorce. How do we account for this paradox? Researchers have suggested several reasons for the higher divorce rate in remarriage. First, persons who remarry after divorce are more likely to use divorce as a way of resolving an unhappy marriage. Furstenberg and Spanier (1987) noted that they were continually struck by the willingness of remarried individuals to dissolve unhappy marriages: "Regardless of how unattractive they thought this eventuality, the great majority indicated that after having endured a first marriage to the breaking point they were unwilling to be miserable again simply for the sake of preserving the union."

Second, remarriage is an "incomplete institution" (Cherlin, 1978, 1981). Society has not evolved norms, customs, and traditions to guide couples in their second marriages. As Andrew Cherlin (1978) observed:

Problems are created by a complex family structure which cannot occur in first marriages. Because of the lack of social regulation, each family must devise its own solutions to these problems. The work of establishing rules increases the potential for conflict among family members, and the increased conflict, in turn, increases the likelihood of divorce.

There are no rules, for example, defining a stepfather's responsibility to a child: Is he a friend, a father, a sort of uncle, or what? Nor are there rules establishing the relationship between an individual's former spouse and his or her present partner: are they friends, acquaintances, rivals, or strangers? Remarriages don't receive the same family and kin support as do first marriages.

Third, remarriages are subject to stresses that are not present in first marriages. Perhaps the most important stress is stepparenting. Children can make the formation of the husband/wife relationship more difficult because they compete for their parents' love, energy, and attention. In such families, time together alone becomes a precious and all-to-rare commodity. Furthermore, although children have little influence in selecting their parent's new husband or wife, they have immense power in "deselecting" them. Children have "incredible power" in maintaining or destroying a marriage, observed Marilyn Ihinger-Tallman and Kay Pasley (1987):

Children can create divisiveness between spouses and siblings by acting in ways that accentuate differences between them. Children have the power to set parent against stepparent, siblings against parents, and stepsiblings against siblings.

❖ REFLECTIONS   *If you were seeking a marital partner, would you consider a previously-married person? Why?*

❖ THE STEPFAMILY

Remarriages that include children are very different from those that do not. The families that emerge from remarriage with children are known as stepfamilies, but they are also called *blended, reconstituted,* or *restructured families* by social scientists, names that emphasize their structural differences from other families. Satirist Art Buchwald,

UNDERSTANDING YOURSELF

Parental Images: Biological Parents versus Stepparents

We seem to hold various images or stereotypes of parenting adults, depending on whether they are biological parents or stepparents. Our images affect how we feel about families and stepparents (Coleman and Ganong, 1987). The following instrument (modeled after one devised by Ganong and Coleman [1983]) will help give you a sense of how you perceive parents and stepparents.

The instrument consists of nine dimensions of feelings presented in a bipolar fashion—that is, as opposites, such as "hateful/affectionate," "bad/good," and so on. You can respond to these feelings on a seven-point scale, with 1 representing the negative pole and 7 the positive pole. For example, if you were using this instrument to determine perceptions about aardvarks, you might feel that aardvarks are extremely affectionate, so you would give them a 7 on the hateful/affectionate dimension. But you might also feel that aardvarks are not very fair, so you would rank them 2 on the unfair/fair continuum.

To use this instrument, take four separate sheets of paper. On one sheet, write "Stepmother," on the second, "Stepfather," on the third, "Biological Mother," and on the fourth, "Biological Father." On each sheet, number 1 to 7 in a column, with each number representing a dimension. Number 1 would represent "hateful/affectionate," and so on. Then, using the seven-point scale on each sheet, score your general impressions about biological parents and stepparents.

The seven-point scale is as follows:

Negative						Positive
1	2	3	4	5	6	7

The dimensions are as follow:

1. Hateful/affectionate
2. Bad/good
3. Unfair/fair
4. Cruel/kind
5. Unloving/loving
6. Strict/not strict
7. Disagreeable/agreeable
8. Rude/friendly
9. Unlikeable/likeable

After you've completed these, compare your responses for stepmother, stepfather, biological mother, and biological father. Do you find differences? If so, how do you account for them?

---

however, calls them "tangled families." He may be close to the truth in some cases. Nevertheless, by the year 2000, there may be more stepfamilies in America than any other family form (Pill, 1990). If we care about families, we need to understand and support stepfamilies.

Stepfamilies: A Different Kind of Family

When we enter a stepfamily, many of us expect to recreate a family identical to an intact family. The intact nuclear family becomes the model against which we judge our successes and failures. But researchers believe that stepfamilies are significantly different from intact families (Coleman and Ganong, 1991; Pill, 1990). If we try to make our feelings and relationships in a stepfamily identical to those of an intact family, we are bound to fail. But if we recognize that the stepfamily works differently and provides different satisfactions and challenges, we can appreciate the richness it brings us and have a successful stepfamily.

STRUCTURAL DIFFERENCES. Six structural characteristics make the stepfamily different from the traditional first-marriage family (Visher and Visher, 1979). Each one is laden with potential difficulties.

1. In stepfamilies, almost all members have lost an important primary relationship. The children may mourn the loss of their parent or parents and the spouses the loss of their former mates. Anger and hostility may be displaced onto the new stepparent.
2. One biological parent lives outside the current family. He or she may either support or interfere with the new family. Power struggles may occur between the absent parent and the custodial parent, and there may be jealously between the absent parent and the stepparent.
3. The relationship between a parent and his or her children predates the relationship between the new partners. Children have often spent considerable time in a single-parent family structure. They have formed close and different bonds with their parent. A new husband or wife may seem to be an interloper in the children's special relationship with their parent. A new stepparent may find that he or she must compete with the children for their parent's attention. The stepparent may even be excluded from the parent-child system.
4. Stepparent roles are ill-defined. No one knows quite what he or she is supposed to do as a stepparent. Most stepparents try role after role until they find one that fits.
5. Many children in stepfamilies are also members of the noncustodial parent's household (as discussed earlier in "The Binuclear Family"). Each home may have differing rules and expectations. When conflict arises, children may try to play one household against the other. Furthermore, as Visher and Visher (1979) observed:

The lack of clear role definition, the conflict of loyalties that such children experience, the emotional reaction to the altered family pattern, and the loss of closeness with their parent who is now married to another person create inner turmoil and confused and unpredictable outward behavior in many children.

6. Children in stepfamilies have at least one extra pair of grandparents. Children get a new set of stepgrandparents, but the role these new grandparents are to play is usually not clear. A study by Spanier and Furstenberg (1980) found that grandparents were usually quick to accept their "instant" grandchildren.

Before we examine the stepfamily, we would do well to keep in mind that when Ganong and Coleman (1984) reviewed the empirical literature comparing stepfamilies to traditional nuclear families, they found no significant differences in relationships with stepfathers as compared to fathers, perceptions of parental happiness, degree of family conflict, and positive family relationships. Only the clinical literature tends to uphold the image of stepfamilies beset by conflict and traumas (Ganong and Coleman, 1986). One researcher (Chilman, 1986) pointed out:

Clinicians particularly tend to view this family form as traumatic because they see the selected group of troubled people who come for counseling. They do not see those who are making a relatively trouble-free adjustment to their marriage.

It may well be that stepfamilies are not very different from traditional nuclear families. We perceive them as being different because we use a "deficit model" in examining them (Coleman and Ganong, 1991). Thus we look for deficiencies and exaggerate problems or differences.

DIFFERENCES IN COHESION AND ADAPTABILITY. As we saw in Chapter 10, cohesion and adaptability are important dimensions of family behavior (Carter and McGoldrick, 1989; Olson et al., 1983). When examining stepfamilies, we need to understand the balance between emotional involvement and individual autonomy. Do healthy stepfamilies handle issues of cohesion and adaptability differently than members of healthy intact families? This is especially important if children are active members of a binuclear family. How do they manage being members of *two* nuclear families? Do stepfamilies have less cohesion than intact families? Do they have more adaptability?

According to Cynthia Pill (1990), healthy stepfamilies may differ from healthy intact families on both dimensions: Healthy stepfamilies are less cohesive and more adaptable than healthy intact families. Pill found that healthy stepfamilies demonstrated "remarkable capacity to allow for differences among family members and to permit looser, more flexible family relationships." Stepfamilies did not demand family unity at the price of individuality. Pill found that many healthy stepfamilies, for example, allowed their children to decide whether to come on the family vacation together or to spend time with their other birth parent. She also found that the closest emotional relationships generally were formed between biologically related family members. This meant that the stepparent was not necessarily as emotionally close as he or she might have been if the children were biologically related. Yet the stepparents noted this in a matter-of-fact manner, observing that it was understandable. Pill wrote:

While many stepparents wished that they might have been a part of the children's lives at an earlier stage, both because of the influence they would have had in the formation of the children's values and also because of the bonding that would have occurred, most were accepting of the limitations that entering children's lives later in their development brings.

Because stepfamilies had to continually adapt to the coming and going of family members, stepfamilies needed to be more adaptable than intact families: they needed to adjust expectations, define and redefine roles (such as redefining the father role to fit the stepfather), and create a meaningful definition of "family" for stepfamilies.

The overwhelming majority of stepfamilies felt they had become "family." When asked how they thought they had become a family, the family members replied that they had developed a sense of connectedness and a mutual feeling of caring and support among family members. Sharing major life events, such as birth or death, and living their mundane, everyday life together were the major factors giving them a sense of family identity and helping to solidify family feelings. Such experiences might include eating spaghetti together when wild noodles, dripping with tomato sauce, flapped against Mom's white dress. Or they might include common occurrences such as holding hands in prayer, dancing to favorite music, Dad's "stupid" but endearing jokes, or stories about dating disasters. Stepfamilies collect trivia, record odd events in the family's collective unconscious, recall revealing incidents, and weave these diverse strands together to create a family story or mythology. In creating family stories, stepfamilies begin to see themselves as uniquely different from all other families. And in doing so, stepfamilies become families in the deepest, most profound sense.

Problems of Women and Men in Stepfamilies

Most people go into stepfamily relationships expecting to recreate the traditional nuclear family found on "The Cosby Show" or "Family Ties"; they are full of love, hope, and energy. Perhaps the hardest adjustment they have to make is realizing that stepfamilies are different from traditional nuclear families—and that being different does not make stepfamilies inferior. A nuclear family is neither morally superior to the stepfamily nor a guarantor of happiness.

*Queen: No, be assur'd you shall not find
    me, daughter,
After the slander of most stepmothers,
Evil-ey'd unto you.*

*Imogen: Dissembling courtesy! How fine
    this tyrant
Can tickle where she wounds.*

Shakespeare, Cymbeline

WOMEN IN STEPFAMILIES. Stepmothers tend to experience more problematic family relationships than stepfathers (Santrock and Sitterle, 1987). To various degrees, women enter stepfamilies with certain feelings and hopes. Stepmothers generally expect to do the following (Visher and Visher, 1979):

◆ Make up to the children for the divorce.
◆ Create a happy, close-knit family and a new nuclear family.
◆ Keep everyone happy.
◆ Prove that they are not wicked stepmothers.
◆ Love their stepchild instantly and as much as their own biological children.
◆ Receive instant love from their stepchildren.

Needless to say, most women are disappointed. Expectations of total love, happiness, and the like would be unrealistic in any kind of family, traditional as well as stepfamily. The warmer a woman is to her stepchildren, the more hostile they may become to her because they feel she is trying to replace their "real" mother. If a stepmother tries to meet everyone's needs—especially her stepchildren's, which are often contradictory, excessive, and distancing—she is likely to exhaust herself emotionally and physically. It takes time for her and her children to become emotionally integrated as a family.

The greater problems full-time stepmothers experience may be due to the differences between families with stepfathers and those with stepmothers (Furstenberg and Nord, 1985). Bitter custody fights may leave the children emotionally troubled and hostile to stepmothers, whom they perceive as "forcibly" replacing their mothers. In other instances, children, especially adolescents, may move from their mother's home to their father's because their mother can no longer handle them. In either case, the stepmother may be required to parent children who have special needs or problems. Stepmothers may find these relationships especially difficult. Typically, stepmother/stepdaughter relationships are the most problematic (Clingempeel et al., 1984). Relationships become even more difficult when the stepmothers never intended to become full-time stepparents.

MEN IN STEPFAMILIES. Different stepfamily expectations are placed on men. Because men are generally less involved in childrearing, they usually have no "cruel stepparent" myths to counter. Nevertheless, men entering stepparenting roles may find certain areas particularly difficult at first (Visher and Visher, 1979). A critical factor in a man's stepparenting is whether he has children of his own. If he does, they are more likely to live with his ex-wife. In this case, the stepfather may experience guilt and confusion in his stepparenting, because he feels he should be parenting his own children. When his children visit, he may try to be "superdad," spending all his time with them and taking them to special places. His wife and stepchildren may feel excluded and angry.

A stepfather usually joins an already established single-parent family. He may find himself having to squeeze into it. The longer a single-parent family has been functioning, the more difficult it usually is to reorganize it; the children may resent his "interfering" with their relationship with their mother (Wallerstein and Kelly, 1980). His ways of handling the children may be different from his wife's, resulting in conflict.

Working out rules of family behavior is often the area in which a stepfamily encounters its first real difficulties. Although the mother usually wants help with discipline, she often feels protective if the stepfather's style is different from hers. To allow a stepparent to discipline a child requires trust from the biological parent and a willingness to let go. Disciplining often elicits a child's testing response: "You're not my real father. I don't have to do what you tell me." Disciplining establishes legitimacy because only a parent or parent-figure is expected to discipline in our culture. Disciplining, however, may be the first step toward family integration, because it establishes the stepparent's presence and authority in the family.

The new stepfather's expectations are important. Often, however, they are exceedingly unrealistic. "The usual situation," Visher and Visher (1979) noted, "is that he is blind to the complexity of the situation." He believes that "love will conquer all" and that the problems can be easily resolved—usually by his wife. The researchers continued:

Very often, as tension develops in the stepfamily, the husband looks to his wife to improve the situation. He considers that she is the one responsible for the daily functioning of the family and therefore it is her mismanagement that is causing the upset. Frequently, the wife has the same expectations of herself and tries harder and harder to cope with and alter the situation. The harder she tries the worse things get, and the relationship between the couple usually suffers. The expectation that the wife is responsible for the emotional relationships within the family is unrealistic, for no single person can unravel the complicated stepfamily situation.

Conflict in Stepfamilies

Achieving family solidarity in the stepfamily is a complex task. When a new parent enters the former single-parent family, the family system is thrown off balance. Where equilibrium once existed, there is now disequilibrium. A period of tension and conflict usually marks the entry of new people into the family system. Questions arise about them: Who are they? What are their rights and their limits? Rules change. The mother may have relied on television as a baby-sitter, for example, permitting the children unrestricted viewing in the afternoon. The new stepfather, however, may want to limit the children's afternoon viewing, creating tension. To the children, everything seemed fine until this stepfather came along. He has disrupted their old pattern. Chaos and confusion will be the norm until a new pattern is established, but it takes time for people to adjust to new roles, demands, limits, and rules.

Conflict takes place in all families—traditional nuclear families, single-parent families, and stepfamilies. If some family members do not like each other, they will bicker, argue, tease, and fight. Sometimes they have no better reason for disruptive behavior than that they are bored or frustrated and want to take it out on someone. These are fundamentally personal conflicts. Other conflicts are about definite issues: dating, use of the car, manners, television, friends. These can be between partners, between parents and children, or among the children themselves. There are certain types of stepfamily conflicts, however, whose frequency, intensity, or nature distinguish them from conflicts in traditional nuclear families. These conflicts are about favoritism, divided loyalties, and material goods and services.

FAVORITISM. Favoritism exists in families of first marriages as well as in stepfamilies. In stepfamilies, however, the favoritism often takes a very different form. Whereas a parent may favor a child in a biological family on the basis of age, sex, or personality, in stepfamilies favoritism tends to run along kinship lines. A child is favored by one or the other parent because he or she is the parent's biological child; or if a new child is born to the remarried couple, they may favor him or her as a child of their joint love. In American culture, where parents are expected to treat children equally, favoritism based on kinship seems particularly unfair.

DIVIDED LOYALTY. "How can you stand that lousy, low-down, sneaky, dirty mother [or father] of yours?" asks (or more accurately, demands) a hostile parent. It is one of the most painful questions children can confront, for it forces them to take sides for and against someone they love. One study (Lutz, 1983) found that about half of the adolescents studied confronted situations in which one divorced parent talked negatively about the other. Almost half of the adolescents felt themselves "caught in the middle." Three-quarters found such talk stressful.

Divided loyalties put children in no-win situations, forcing them not only to choose between parents but to reject new stepparents. Children feel disloyal to one parent for loving the other parent or stepparent. But divided loyalties, like favoritism, can exist in traditional nuclear families as well. This is especially true of conflict-ridden families in which warring parents seek their children as allies.

DISCIPLINE. Researchers generally agree that discipline issues are among the most important causes of conflict among remarried families (Ihinger-Tallman and Pasley, 1987; Knaub et al., 1984; Messinger, 1976). Discipline is especially difficult to deal with if the child is not the person's biological child. Disciplining a stepchild often gives rise to conflicting feelings within the stepparent. Stepparents may feel that they are overreacting to the child's behavior, that their feelings are out of control, and that they are being censured by the child's biological parent. Compensating for fears of unfairness, the stepparent may become overly tolerant.

The specific discipline problems vary from family to family, but a common problem is interference by the biological parent with the stepparent (Mills, 1984). The biological parent may feel resentful or overreact to the stepparent's disciplining if he or she has been reluctant to give the stepparent authority. As one biological mother who believed she had a good remarriage stated (quoted in Ihinger-Tallman and Pasley, 1987):

Sometimes I feel he is too harsh in disciplining, or he doesn't have the patience to explain why he is punishing and to carry through in a calm manner, which causes me to have to step into the matter (which I probably shouldn't do). . . . I do realize that it was probably hard for my husband to enter marriage and the responsibility of a family instantly . . . but this has remained a problem.

As a result of interference, the biological parent implies that the stepparent is wrong and undermines his or her status in the family. Over time, the stepparent may decrease his or her involvement in the family as a parent figure.

MONEY, GOODS, AND SERVICES. Problems of allocating money, goods, and services exist in all families, but they can be especially difficult in stepfamilies. In first marriages, husbands and wives form an economic unit in which one or both may produce income for the family; husband and wife are interdependent. Following divorce, the binuclear family consists of two economic units, the custodial family and the noncustodial family. Both must provide separate housing, which dramatically increases their basic expenses. Despite their separation, the two households may nevertheless continue to be extremely interdependent. The mother in the custodial single-parent family, for example, probably has reduced income. She may be employed but still dependent on child-support payments or AFDC. She may have to rely more extensively on child care, which may drain her resources dramatically. The father in the noncustodial family may make child-support payments or contribute to medical or school expenses, which depletes his income. Both households have to deal with financial instability. Custodial parents can't count on always receiving their child-support payments, which makes it difficult to undertake financial planning. The rate of noncompliance in making child-support payments increases over time. By the third year after divorce, noncompliance increases to 60 percent; by the fifth year, it is as high as 80 percent (Kressel, 1985).

When one or both of the former partners remarry, their financial situation may alter significantly. Upon remarriage, the mother receives less income from her former partner or welfare benefits. Instead, her new partner becomes an important contributor to family income. At this point, a major problem in stepfamilies arises. What responsibility does the stepfather have in supporting his stepchildren? Should he or the biological father provide financial support? Because there are no norms, each family must work out its own solution.

Stepfamilies typically have resolved the problem of distributing their economic resources by using a *one-pot* or *two-pot* pattern (Fishman, 1983). In the one-pot pattern, families pool their resources and distribute them according to need rather than biological relationship. It doesn't matter whether the child is a biological child or stepchild. One-pot families typically have relatively limited resources and consistently fail to receive child support from the noncustodial biological parent. By sharing their resources, one-pot families increase the likelihood of family cohesion.

In two-pot families, resources are distributed by biological relationship; need is secondary. These families tend to have a higher income and one or (usually) both parents have former spouses who regularly contribute to the support of their biological children. Expenses relating to children are generally handled separately; usually there are no shared checking or savings accounts. Two-pot families maintain strong bonds between members of the first family. For these families, a major problem is achieving cohesion in the stepfamily while maintaining separate checking accounts.

Just as economic resources need to be redistributed following divorce and remarriage, so do goods and services (not to mention affection). While a two-bedroom home or apartment may have provided plenty of space for a single-parent family with two children, a stepfamily with additional residing or visiting stepsiblings can experience instant overcrowding. Rooms, bicycles, and toys, for example, need to be shared; larger quarters may have to be found.

Time becomes a precious commodity for harried parents and stepparents in a stepfamily. When visiting stepchildren arrive, duties are doubled. Stepchildren compete with parents and other children for time and affection.

It may appear that remarried families are confronted with many difficulties, but traditional nuclear families also face financial, loyalty, and discipline problems. We need to put these problems in perspective. (After all, half of all current marriages end in divorce, which suggests that first marriages are not problem-free.) When all is said and done, the problems that remarried families face may not be any more overwhelming than those faced by traditional nuclear families (Ihinger-Tallman and Pasley, 1987).

❖ REFLECTIONS   *Think about the issues of favoritism, loyalty, discipline, and the distribution of resources. Do you experience them in your family of orientation? If so, how are they similar or different from stepfamily conflicts? If you are in a stepfamily, do you experience them in your current family? How are they similar or how do they differ between your original family and your current family? If you are a parent or stepparent, how are these issues played out in your current family?*

Stepfamily Strengths

Because we have traditionally viewed stepfamilies as deviant, we have often ignored their strengths. Instead, we have only seen their problems. Let us end this chapter, then, by focusing on the strengths of stepfamilies.

FAMILY FUNCTIONING. While traditional nuclear families may be structurally less complicated than stepfamilies, stepfamilies are nevertheless able to fulfill traditional family functions. A binuclear single-parent, custodial, or noncustodial family may provide more companionship, love, and security than the particular traditional nuclear family it replaces. If the traditional nuclear family was ravaged by conflict, violence, sexual abuse, or alcoholism, for example, the single-parent family or stepfamily that replaces it may be considerably better. There may not be as much emotional closeness as in first families, but second families generally experience less trauma and crisis (Ihinger-Tallman and Pasley, 1987).

New partners may have greater objectivity regarding old problems or relationships (Ihinger-Tallman and Pasley, 1987). First, new partners can accelerate emotional disengagement between former spouses. Such disengagement leads to the dampening of conflicts. Second, once an individual is involved in a new marriage, he or she may feel less of a need to hold onto bitterness and enmity (Furstenberg and Spanier, 1987). Third, new partners are sometimes able to intervene between former spouses to resolve longstanding disagreements, such as custody or child-care arrangements.

IMPACT ON CHILDREN. Stepfamilies potentially offer children a number of benefits that can compensate for the negative consequences of divorce.

◆ Children gain multiple role models from which to choose. Instead of having only one mother or father after whom to model themselves, children may have two mothers or fathers, the biological parents and the stepparents.
◆ Children gain greater flexibility. They may be introduced to new ideas, different values, alternative politics. For example, while biological parents may be unable to encourage certain interests, such as music or model airplanes, because they lack training or interest, a stepparent may play the piano or be a diehard modeler. In such cases, that stepparent can assist his or her stepchildren in pursuing their development. In addition, children often have alternative living arrangements that enlarge their perspectives.
◆ Stepparents may act as a sounding board for their children's concerns. They may be a source of support or information in areas in which the biological parents feel unknowledgeable or uncomfortable.
◆ Children may gain additional siblings, either as stepsiblings or half-siblings.
◆ Children gain an additional extended kin network, which may become as important and loving (or more) as their original kin network.
◆ Finally, children may gain parents who are happily married. Most research indicates that children are significantly better adjusted in happily remarried families than in conflict-ridden traditional nuclear families.

As we near the twenty-first century, it is clear that the American family is no longer what it was at the beginning of the twentieth century. The single-parent family or stepfamily, however, does not imply an end to the American family. Rather, these forms provide different paths that contemporary American families take as they strive to fulfill the hopes, needs, and desires of their members. And they are becoming as Amercian as Beaver Cleaver's family and apple pie.

❖ SUMMARY

◆ The *binuclear family* is a postdivorce family system with children. It consists of two nuclear families, the mother-headed family and the father-headed family, and children. Both single-parent families and stepfamilies are forms of binuclear families.

◆ The binuclear family consists of five subsystems: former spouse, remarried couple, parent/child, sibling, and mother/stepmother–father/stepfather subsystems.

◆ Single parenting is an increasingly significant family form in America. Single-parent families tend to be created by divorce or births to single women, are generally headed by women, are usually poor, involve a wide variety of household types, are predominantly African-American or Latino, and are usually a transitional stage.

◆ Relations between the parent and his or her children change after divorce: the single parent generally tends to be emotionally closer but to have less authority. Most single parents work; child care is a constant problem. Dating poses unique problems for single parents: they may feel guilty for going out, they must look at potential partners as potential parents, and they must deal with their children's judgments or hostility.

◆ Courtship for second marriage does not have clear norms. Individuals seem to take about as long in second marriage courtship as in first marriage courtship. If children are not involved from the earlier marriage, the only major difference between first and second marriage courtship is that the first marriage exists as a model. Courtship is complicated by the presence of children, for remarriage involves the formation of a stepfamily.

◆ Remarriage differs from first marriage in several ways: partners get to know each other in the midst of major changes, they remarry latter in life, they have different marital expectations, and their marriage often creates a stepfamily.

◆ Marital happiness appears to be about the same in first and second marriages. Remarried men are more likely to express greater marital satisfaction. Remarried couples are slightly more likely to divorce than couples in their first marriages. This may be accounted for either by their willingness to use divorce as a means of resolving an unhappy marriage or because remarriage is an "incomplete institution." Stresses accompanying stepfamily formation may also contribute.

◆ Traditionally scholars have viewed stepfamilies from a "deficit" perspective. As a result, they assumed that stepfamilies were very different from traditional nuclear families. More recently, scholars have begun to view stepfamilies as normal families; they have found few significant differences in levels of satisfaction and functioning between stepfamilies and traditional nuclear families. Only clinical research continues to find significant difficulties; such findings, however, may be attributed to the clinical method's traditional focus on pathology.

◆ The *stepfamily* differs from the original family because (1) almost all members have lost an important primary relationship, (2) one biological parent lives outside the current family, (3) the relationship between a parent and his or her children predates the new marital relationship, (4) stepparent roles are ill-defined, (5) often children are members of the noncustodial parent's household, and (6) children have at least one extra pair of grandparents.

◆ Stepmothers tend to experience greater stress in stepfamilies than stepfathers. In part this may be because their families are more likely to have been subject to custody disputes or have children with troubled family history.

◆ Stepfathers tend not to be as involved as stepmothers. They often experience difficulty in being integrated into the family.

◆ A key issue for stepfamilies is family solidarity—the feeling of oneness with the family. Healthy stepfamilies may have less cohesion but greater adaptability than intact families. Conflict in stepfamilies is often over favoritism, divided loyalty, discipline, and money, goods, and services.

◆ Stepfamily strengths may include improved family functioning, and reduced conflict between former spouses. Children may gain multiple role models, more flexibility, concerned stepparents, additional siblings, additional kin, and happily-married parents.

Answers to Preview Questions

The answers to the preview questions at the beginning of the chapter are listed below. As you check your answers, whether you were correct or not, think about your reasons for each response. What were they? What was their source? How valid is the source? As you read the chapter, you will find the questions discussed in greater depth

1. T	6. T
2. T	7. F
3. T	8. F
4. F	9. T
5. F	10. F

❖ SUGGESTED READINGS

Einstein, Elizabeth. *The Stepfamily: Living, Loving, and Learning.* New York: Macmillan, 1982. The author's experiences as both a stepchild and stepparent are interwoven with interviews with stepfamilies and therapists working with stepfamilies.

Furstenberg, Frank, Jr., and Graham Spanier. *Recycling the Family: Remarriage after Divorce,* rev. ed. Newbury Park, Calif.: Sage Publications, 1987 (paperback). An in-depth examination of how second marriages differ from first marriages.

Ihinger-Tallman, Marilyn, and Kay Pasley. *Remarriage.* Newbury Park, Calif.: Sage Publications, 1987 (paperback). A useful introduction to issues involved in remarriage, including an examination of the strengths of remarried families.

Rickel, Annette. *Teen Pregnancy and Parenting.* New York: Hemisphere Publishing Company, 1989. A succinct overview of current research and a description of a peer intervention program in Detroit.

Visher, Emily, and John Visher. *Stepfamilies: A Guide to Working with Stepparents and Stepchildren.* Secaucus, N. J.: Citadel Press, 1979 (paperback). One of the best (and most readable) books available examining the problems confronting parents, stepparents, stepchildren, and stepfamilies in creating a new family.

Visher, Emily, and John Visher. *Old Loyalties, New Ties: Therapeutic Strategies with Stepfamilies.* New York: Bruner/Mazel, 1987. An excellent guide for professionals working with stepfamilies.

Weiss, Robert. *Going It Alone.* New York: Basic Books, 1979. A well-written study of the lives of single mothers.

Suggested Films

Alice Doesn't Live Here Anymore (1975). A woman's search for herself after her husband dies leaving her and her child penniless.

Cinderella (1950). Walt Disney's portrayal of the mythical cruel stepmother is indelibly etched in our minds.

READINGS

FRIENDS THROUGH IT ALL

Elizabeth Stark

There is much to be said about retaining friendly, cooperative relationships between former spouses. According to this excerpt, what are the advantages? Are there disadvantages? Have you maintained friendly relationships with former dating or marital partners? Why?

. . . The common image most people have of divorced couples is warring partners fighting over finances and custody issues. This stereotype, perpetuated in jokes, movies and television, has been accepted by society as the norm. The prevailing attitude is that "there's something a little crazy if you still have a good relationship with your ex-spouse," says Eleanor Macklin, a psychologist at Syracuse University. Even the words we use to describe divorced spouses, "ex" and "former," lack the capacity to indicate any kind of surviving relationship, [Constance] Ahrons points out. . . .

Many psychologists, such as Constance Ahrons and Macklin, now view divorce as more of a transition than an ending and are focusing on how to help families adapt. It's estimated that at least one of every three children growing up today will have a stepparent before they reach the age of 18. With so many parents getting divorced and remarrying other parents, the traditional concept of family is no longer adequate, Ahrons says. She uses the term "binuclear family" to refer to the families created by divorce and remarriage.

Many people mistakenly hope to "reconstitute" the nuclear family when they remarry and end up excluding the nonresiden-tial parents, says Margaret Crosbie-Burnett, a psychologist at the University of Wisconsin-Madison. "In this culture we tend to think that a child has to choose one real mom or dad. Of course it doesn't work," she says. "Kids can easily accept two sets of parents." Crosbie-Burnett found in her study of 87 "stepfather" families—families in which the mother had remarried and had custody of the children from the first marriage—that those who maintained a friendly, or at least businesslike, relationship with their ex-spouses were much happier than those with hostile or unfriendly relationships.

Ahrons believes that it's perfectly healthy for divorced couples to have feelings of kinship and that they shouldn't be discouraged. She has been following 98 divorced couples for the past five years in her Binuclear Family Project, interviewing not only former wives and husbands but any new spouses or "spouse equivalents" as well at one year, three years and five years after divorce. All of the divorced couples had had children together, and the average duration of their marriages had been 10 years. To be included in the study both spouses had to live in Dane County, Wisconsin, and the noncustodial parent must have seen the children at least once in the past two months. Of the 98 pairs, 54 had maternal custody, 28 had joint custody and 16 had paternal or split custody—in which each parent has custody of different children.

Based on the frequency and quality of their interactions, couples were divided into . . . four groups. . . . Perfect Pals made up 12 percent of the sample. These couples enjoyed each other's company and tended to stay involved i each other's lives, phoning to share exciting news, for example. They were also very child-centered and tried to put their children's interests ahead of their own anger and frustration. Many had joint custody, and none were remarried or living with someone.

READINGS

Ahrons interviewed one couple who actually shared a duplex apartment so that their children could come and go freely between their homes. The only drawback, they admitted, was lack of privacy, and they suspected that if one took on a new spouse or live-in lover, the arrangement might become awkward.

The largest group was Cooperative Colleagues, who made up 38 percent of the couples. They were not as involved in each other's lives as Perfect Pals, but they managed to minimize potential conflicts, to have a moderate amount of interaction and to be mutually supportive of each other. Ahrons sees them as the most realistic positive role model for divorcing couples.

Angry Associates, who accounted for 25 percent, also had a moderate amount of interaction, but the interactions were fraught with conflict. This group was unable to untangle spousal and parental issues, thus setting the scene for fighting when they dealt with each other.

The archetypal feuding partners, Fiery Foes, made up 24 percent of the couples. They had as little interaction as possible, argued when they did interact and did not cooperate at all in parenting. Ahrons suspects that this group may be underrepresented in her study since some of her criteria for inclusion would have ruled out many of the most antagonistic couples.

One of the major characteristics distinguishing the four groups was how they handled anger. Even Perfect Pals still harbored some anger over the divorce, but it was not a major part of the relationship and they were able to talk it out when it erupted. One said the relationship was "like having a good friend that you can still be angry with." Cooperative Colleagues and Angry Associates had about the same amount of anger, but Cooperative Colleagues could separate the old spousal issues from parental ones, while Angry Associates could not. Fiery Foes' anger was so overwhelming that it prevented any civil interaction.

Time, apparently, did not heal the wounds of divorce for the most antagonistic. Ahrons found that Angry Associates and Fiery Foes were just as angry about the divorce three years later as they were one year later. And all couples became more distant over time; interaction and positive feelings decreased over five years. . . .

It's clear that a cooperative and friendly relationship between ex-spouses is beneficial to their children, but is it harmful to later marriages or romances? According to a study by Macklin and Carolyn Weston, a psychology doctoral candidate at Syracuse University, friendship between ex-spouses is not necessarily bad and can even be beneficial to a second marriage.

Macklin and Weston interviewed members of 60 stepfather families; none of the stepfathers had any of their own children living in the household. Based on an earlier study by psychologist W. Glenn Clingempeel at Temple University, Macklin and

Weston suspected that those with moderate contact would have the happiest marriages. But they found that the more contact a woman had with her former husband, the happier the new marriage, as long as both she and her new husband agreed about the nature and frequency of contact. . . .

Why did frequent contact make for happier second marriages? First of all, Macklin says, "It works both ways. A happier new marriage may allow more contact with the ex-spouse." But the main reason, she explains, is parenting. Regular contact between former spouses usually ensures that the father will be more financially supportive and involved in routine coparenting. And new husbands are usually happier when they do not end up shouldering the entire burden of raising their stepchildren.

Marion, one of the women Macklin and Weston interviewed, is a case in point. She was devastated when her husband left her for another woman. But she decided that she had to put it all behind her and two years later began living with David, to whom she is now married. Eight years after the divorce, she and her ex-husband, Jack, are now on very good terms. Jack comes over sometimes to watch television with his two teenage sons and David, goes to baseball games with them and even has keys to the house. Both Marion and David feel that it is very important for her sons to be actively involved with their father. They say that the boys get the best of both worlds, two fathers.

In Marion's case, continuing friendship with her former husband did not stop her from remarrying someone else. Are there situations in which lingering attachments prevent divorced men and women from replacing the former spouse? Ahrons found that Perfect Pals, those who interacted frequently, had never remarried. But she feels this was due to the couples' preoccupation with their children, not with each other. "These parents are so wrapped up in their children, they don't want to remarry for fear it will upset the balance." Another possibility, she says, is that outsiders see this tight-knit unit and are put off. For these couples, parenting issues are probably what draw them together. . . .

Although some people question the point of continuing a relationship if a couple has no desire to reconcile, Gary Ganahl points out that "if a couple has children there is no question that they are going to have a continuing relationship." Keeping the relationship supportive and friendly benefits the children and in many cases can make life happier for the divorced couple.

On the other hand, Ahrons says, there are some situations where friendship between ex-spouses is impossible. The main point, according to all these researchers and specialists, is that it is not necessarily harmful for ex-spouses to be friendly. "Right now there are no positive norms or messages from society about divorce," Ahrons says. "Most people don't want to give up their

continued on next page

total history, but there is very little sanction or support for their relationship to continue."

During the course of her interviews Ahrons discovered that "no one had asked most of these couples positive questions about their divorce before. They had never thought of the concept of a binuclear family." She would like to provide a positive role model for couples who want to remain friendly. She thinks if people reacted to divorce with the expectation that relationships don't necessarily have to end, "maybe more spouses would be encouraged to have amicable relationships."

The main thing for everyone—therapists, friends, family and couples—to keep in mind, Ganahl says, is that "relationships change, but rarely dissolve after divorce."

PART SEVEN

Strengths

Marriage and Family Strengths

PREVIEW

To gain a sense of what you already know about the material covered in this chapter, answer "true" or "false" to the following statements. You will find the answers on page 579.

1. Researchers generally agree on the basic components of healthy families. True or false?
2. Among psychologically healthy families, family emotional health remains constant over the family life cycle. True or false?
3. A common way of measuring family strength is to see how a family responds to crisis. True or false?
4. The happiness of a couple before marriage is a good indicator of their happiness after they have children. True or false?
5. Although having a perfect family is difficult, it is possible. True or false?
6. Good communication is recognized by the overwhelming majority of researchers as the most important quality for family strength. True or false?
7. Children need to be taught respect and responsibility by their families. True or false?
8. Taking time to play is crucial to family health. True or false?
9. Seeking outside help for problems is a sign of family health. True or false?
10. The strong kinship networks of the African-American family developed during the time of slavery. True or false?

A good marriage is that in which each appoints the other guardian of his individuality.

Rainer Maria Rilke (1875–1926)

I F WE DEFINE THE FAMILY AS SIMPLY A PEOPLE-PRODUCING FACTORY, we will call all families that produce offspring "successful." Yet we know that a family has other important functions. As you will recall from Chapter 1, the basic tasks of the family are (1) reproduction and socialization, (2) economic cooperation, (3) assignment of status and social roles, and (4) intimacy. How well a family is able to accomplish these tasks appears to depend on a number of characteristics and abilities. (See the reading "Of Course You Love Them—but Do You Enjoy Them?" by Anita Shreve.) In this chapter we discuss the particular characteristics that seem to make marriages and families strong. We explore how culture and ethnicity can contribute to family success, and we examine how the relationships with the extended family, with friends, and with fictive kin (friends who are like family) help sustain the family unit. Finally, we look at the ecology of the family—that is, how the family interacts with the community.

❖ MARITAL STRENGTHS

Marriage may be seen as a forum for negotiating the balance between the desire for intimacy and the need to maintain a separate identity. To negotiate this balance successfully, we need to develop what sociologist Nelson Foote (1955) called "interpersonal competence," the ability to share and develop an intimate, growing relationship with another.

Marital Strengths versus Family Strengths

Many of the traits of healthy marriages are also found in healthy families, discussed later in this chapter. Indeed, marital competence can be viewed as a necessary basis for family success (Epstein et al., 1982; Lewis et al., 1976). It might seem ideal if couples could perfect their interpersonal skills before the arrival of children. Child-free couples generally have more time for each other and substantially less psychological, economic, and physical stress. In reality, however, many of our marital skills probably develop alongside our family skills. Thus, as we improve communication with our spouses, for example, our communication with our children also improves.

There have been hundreds of studies on marital happiness and very few (and those only in the last decade or so) on *family* happiness. Still, an argument can be made that certain kinds of strengths accrue only to families with children. The relationships of couples with children generally have greater stability than those of childless couples, because the emotional cost of a breakup is much greater when children are present. Also, the relationships of parents to their children are rewarding in and of themselves and fulfill much of the need for intimacy. Sometimes the bonds between the individual parent and the children or between the children themselves can sustain a family during times of marital stress. Furthermore, the growing acceptance of singlehood and child-free marriages notwithstanding, society expects its adults to be parents and rewards the attainment of the parental role with approval and respect.

Essential Marital Strengths

Therapist-researcher David Mace (1980) cites the essential aspects of successful marriage as commitment, communication, and the creative use of conflict. Recent research indicates that the strongest predictor of marital success may be the effectiveness of communication experienced by the couple before marriage (Goleman, 1985). Numerous studies show that there is a strong correlation between a couple's communication patterns and marital satisfaction (Noller and Fitzpatrick, 1991). Classes and workshops are being developed in many communities to help teach these vital marital skills to couples before they commit themselves to marriage. Communication and conflict resolution were discussed in Chapter 14.

Mace defines commitment in terms of the relationship's potential for growth. He wrote, "There must be a commitment on the part of the couple to ongoing growth in their relationship. . . . There is tremendous potential for loving, for caring, for warmth, for understanding, for support, for affirmation; yet, in so many marriages of today it never gets developed." Commitment to any endeavor—and marriage is certainly no exception—requires the willingness and ability to *work*. In their study of strong families, Nick Stinnett and John DeFrain (1985) quoted one-half of a married couple:

You know the stereotypical story of the couple who have the lavish wedding, expensive rings, and exotic honeymoon and then settle down. The work is over. She gets dumpy and nags; he gets sloppy and never again brings flowers. We were like that until one day when we examined our life together and found it lacked something. Then we decided that the wedding, rings, and honeymoon marked the beginning, *not* the end. *We* had to renew the marriage all along.

Commitment to the sexual relationship within marriage appears to be an important aspect of marital strength (Stinnett and DeFrain, 1985). All the families in the Stinnett and DeFrain study recommended sexual fidelity. An extramarital relationship does not mean the end of a strong marriage, however. Sometimes an affair can be a "catalyst for growth" (Stinnett and DeFrain, 1985). A couple may not realize how far they have drifted apart, how much their communication has deteriorated, or how important the marital relationship is until the extramarital relationship brings things into clearer focus. When spouses who love each other have sexual liaisons outside their marriage, it is almost certainly a sign that their relationship is in trouble. Yet they can then take the painful lessons they've learned and use them to forge a stronger and better marriage.

Another aspect of commitment is sacrifice. Often people give up things—work demands, social activities, or material goods—for those they love without thinking twice about it. Sometimes difficult choices must be made. Within a committed relationship, there is give-and-take so that neither partner ends up in the "martyr" role (see Stinnett and DeFrain, 1985). When spouses give up something in order to be together, they nurture the marriage relationship, which in turn supports and strengthens the individual.

A study (Bell, Daly, and Gonzales, 1987) of 109 married women revealed key strategies perceived to maintain marital closeness. They included:

◆ Honesty
◆ Listening
◆ Openness
◆ Physical and verbal affection

A Marriage Ring

*The ring so worn as you behold
So thin, so pale, is yet of gold;
The passion such it was to prove;
Worn with life's cares, love yet was love.*

George Crabbe (1754–1832)

The great secret of successful marriage is to treat all disasters as incidents and none of the incidents as disasters.

Harold Nicholson

◆ Physical attractiveness
◆ Sensitivity
◆ Supportiveness

The study also showed that the participating women believed themselves to be "more responsible than their husbands for the maintenance of their marriages." Whether or not the women were more responsible could not be determined by the research. The researchers did point out, however, that "individuals within close relationships tend to perceive themselves as more responsible than their partners for its positive aspects."

We can look at marriage as a kind of task to be performed (albeit willingly and joyfully) or as a growing thing to be nurtured. Whatever metaphor we choose, we see that the relationship requires time, energy, patience, thoughtfulness, planning, and perhaps a little more patience in order to grow and prosper. Commitment to this success (and the sacrifices that commitment may entail) is an essential component in the formation of strong marriages and strong families as well. In studying marriage and family strengths, researchers use models of family functioning such as the circumplex model discussed in Chapter 10. By discovering the components of healthy families, they hope to show us how to strengthen our own.

❖ FAMILY STRENGTHS

Of course, it's not really possible to make a family happy and healthy by merely prescribing a dose of good communication or a shot of trust. Researchers do observe, however, that certain characteristics tend to exist in the families that they view as successful.

Family as Process

Our family is not yet so good as to be degenerating.

Kurt Ewald

As the saying goes, "nobody's perfect," and neither is any family. Perfection in families, as in most other aspects of life, exists as an ideal, not as a reality. Family quality can be seen as a continuum, with a few very healthy or unhealthy families at either end and the rest somewhere in between. Also, family quality varies over the family life cycle. Generally, families experience increased stress during the childbearing and teenager phases of the cycle. The overall cohesiveness of the family is severely tested at these times, and although families often emerge stronger, they may have experienced periods of distrust, disorder, and unhappiness.

Families also are idiosyncratic: each is different from all the others. Some may function optimally when the children are very young and not so well when they become teenagers, whereas the reverse may be true for other families. Some families may possess great strengths in certain areas and weaknesses in other. But all families constantly change and grow. The family is a process.

Communication

The role of communication in establishing family strength is paramount. Whatever their differences, all researchers seem to agree that good communication skills are the bedrock of family success. Through communication, the family fulfills its roles, especially as a socializer of children and provider of intimacy; through communication, other important qualities of family success are generated.

The aspects of healthy communication were discussed in Chapter 14. The communication and conflict–resolution skills discussed there apply not only to parents' relationships with each other but also to parent/child and child/child relationships. Among the most significant things a family can teach its children are the value of expressing their feelings effectively and the importance of truly listening to the expressions of others.

❖ R E F L E C T I O N S   *What can you do to facilitate the development of more effective communication in your family?*

Affirmation, Respect, and Trust

AFFIRMATION. For most of us, the phrase that we like best to hear in the world consists of three little words. "I love you" may be a short sentence, but it can go a long way toward soothing a hurt, drying a tear, restoring a crumbling sense of self-worth, and maintaining a feeling of satisfaction and well-being. Supporting others in our family—letting them know we're interested in their projects, problems, feelings, and opinions—and being supported and affirmed in return is essential to family health (Gecas and Seff, 1991).

RESPECT. Another way we show that we care about our family members, friends, and fellow human beings is by according them respect for their uniqueness and differences, even if we may not necessarily understand or agree with them. Healthy families encourage the development of individuality in their members, though it may lead to difficulties when the children's views begin to diverge widely from those of their parents—on such subjects, for example, as religion, premarital sex, consumerism, patriotism, and childrearing. Criticism, ridicule, and rejection undermine

Although family strengths may vary over the life cycle, researchers observe certain characteristics such as affirmation, respect and common spiritual ground in healthy families.

self-esteem and severely restrict individual growth. Families that hamper the expression of their children's attitudes and beliefs tend to send into society children who are unable to respect differences in others. In addition to exhibiting respect for others, a healthy family member also insists on being respected in return.

TRUST. The establishment of trust, you will recall, is a child's first developmental stage acording to Erik Erikson. Not only must an infant develop trust in his or her parents but a growing child must also continue to feel that other family members can be relied on absolutely. In turn, children learn to act in ways that make their parents trust them. Children in healthy families are allowed to earn trust as deemed appropriate by the parents. Children who know they are trusted are then able to develop self-confidence and a sense of responsibility for themselves and others.

It is not only children who need to "earn" the right to be called trustworthy; parents do, too. It's important for parents to be realistic in their promises to children and honest about their own mistakes and shortcomings. It's also important for children to see that their parents trust each other.

ROLE MODELING. Many researchers agree that parental role modeling is a crucial factor in the development of qualities that ensure personal psychological health and growth (Epstein et al., 1982; Lewis et al., 1976). A loving relationship between parents, observed a family program administrator, "seems to breed security in the children, and, in turn, fosters the ability to take risks, to reach out to others, to search for their own answers, become independent, and develop a good self-image" (quoted in Curran, 1983). The more children observe their elders in situations that demonstrate mutual trust, respect, and care, the more they are encouraged to incorporate these successful and satisfying behaviors into their own lives. In divorced families, a continued positive relationship between the parents (if possible) is crucially important to the developing child (Goldsmith, 1982).

❖ REFLECTIONS   *Do you feel loved and supported by your family? Do you feel trusted? How would you like to be treated differently? Do you let your family know that you love them, that you respect and trust them?*

Responsibility, Morality, and Spiritual Wellness

One of the family's principal socializing tasks is to teach the responsibility of the individual for his or her own actions. Fostering morality, a code of ethics for dealing with our fellow human beings, is also essential.

RESPONSIBILITY AND MORALITY. The acquisition of responsibility is rooted in self-respect and an appreciation of the interdependence of people. When we as children develop a sense of our own self-worth, we begin to understand how much difference our own acts can make in the lives of others; this feeling of "making a difference" aids the further growth of self-esteem.

Successful families realize the importance of delegating responsibility (participating in household chores, sharing in family decisions, and so on) and of developing responsible behavior (completing homework, remembering appointments, keeping our word, cleaning up our own mess). Sometimes children may have to accept more responsibility than they want, as when their dual worker or single parents rely on them for assistance. Although these situations may be detrimental for children in families already suffering severe economic (or other) hardships, in many families children have come to benefit from the added responsibility; they feel a sense of

The family you come from isn't as important as the family you're going to have.

Ring Lardner (1885–1933)

accomplishment and worthiness. Parental acknowledgment for a job well done goes a long way toward building responsibility.

Healthy families also know the importance of allowing children to make their own mistakes and face the consequences. These lessons can be very painful at times, but they are stepping stones to growth and success. Along with a sense of responsibility, healthy families help develop their children's ability to discriminate between right and wrong. This morality may be grounded in specific religious principles but need not be; it is, however, based on a firm conviction that the world and its people must be valued and respected. Harvard psychologists Robert Coles and Jerome Kagan believe that children are naturally equipped with a basic moral sense; parents need to recognize and nurture that sense from early on. Beside helping children resolve their moral dilemmas, healthy parents take care to be responsible for their own behavior. Parental hypocrisy sets the stage for disrespect, disappointment, and rebellion.

❖ R E F L E C T I O N S   *Do you consider yourself to be a responsible person? A moral person? How did you get that way? Have you had any noteworthy experiences with hypocrisy (yours or someone else's)? How did these experiences feel?*

SPIRITUAL WELLNESS. The families in Stinnett and DeFrain's study (1985) described the "spiritual dimension" in various ways: "faith in God, faith in humanity, ethical behavior, unity with all living things, concern for others, or religion." It's necessary to have a broad definition of spirituality because the experience is entirely subjective; it means different things to different people. Yet strong families share common spiritual ground. In these families, spiritual wellness is a "unifying force, a caring center within each person that promotes sharing, love, and compassion for others. It is a force that helps a person transcend self and become part of something larger" (Stinnett and DeFrain, 1985).

Spirituality gives meaning, purpose, and hope. In the case of formal religions, it provides a sense of community and support (Abbott, Berry, and Meredith, 1990). In times of adversity, families tap their spiritual resources to gain the strength that they need to sustain themselves. Stinnett and DeFrain (1985) suggest seven ways to help spirituality work in families:

1. Set aside time each day for meditation, prayer, or contemplation. Try to get outdoors to enjoy the beauty of nature.
2. Join (or help form) a discussion group to consider religious or philosophical issues.
3. Examine your own values. Try keeping a journal of your thoughts.
4. Help your children to clarify their values.
5. Identify three of your strengths. Work on developing them more fully. Identify three of your weaknesses. Decide how you can improve in these areas.
6. Have regular family devotionals. "Read . . . inspirational material, pray, sing, count your blessings, reaffirm your love and commitment to each other."
7. Volunteer time, energy, and money to a cause that helps others.

Spiritual wellness, it should be noted, is not necessarily the same as religiosity. Rigid religious doctrines "that promote traditional sex roles or negative approaches to family planning" have been found by some researchers to be "detrimental to family life" (Abbott, Berry, and Meredith, 1990; Brigman, 1984). "There is a gray area between moral refraction and spiritual reflection as people look for life's purpose," Robert Coles says. "Religion has no monopoly on spirituality" (quoted in Mehren, 1990; see Coles, 1990, for a study of spirituality in children's lives).

There are only two lasting bequests we can hope to give our children. One is roots; the other, wings.

Hodding Carter

Traditions and Family History

Prune Cake

Cream: 1 c. brown sugar
*   1/2 c. shortening*

Add: 1 egg
*   3/4 c. combined orange and prune*
*   juice*
*   a little grated orange rind*
*   1 tsp. soda*
*   1 tsp. cinnamon*
*   1/2 tsp. allspice*
*   salt*
*   2 c. flour*

Beat and add 1 c. prunes cut in pieces; add nuts if desired. Bake at 350 for 35 min. or until done. [Grandma Mimi's note at bottom follows.] "Found this old recipe. It's the one I used during the Depression—made and sold for profit."

We can only hold to the name of family when we actively celebrate ourselves, tell each other stories, and pass the sense of oneness on to our children—the way we pass on a taste for chestnut stuffing or cranberry relish with orange. It is the traditions that we constantly create that become the special glue to hold us together over time and distance.

Ellen Goodman

"Coming of age" rituals, such as bar mitzvahs and bat mitzvahs, give young people a sense of continuity and identity within their culture or ethnic group.

TRADITION AND RITUAL. Through tradition and ritual, families find a link to the past and consequently a hope for the future. Traditions, especially those rooted in our cultural background, help give us a sense of who we are as a family and as a community. We have such strong feelings about our holiday rituals that sometimes our families suffer particular stresses during holiday times if expectations of family unity are not met.

There are many varieties of traditions and rituals, from elaborate holiday celebrations to daily or weekly routines. Children's bedtime rituals with blankets, books, bears, or prayers give security and comfort, as do Sunday morning rituals that find the family together in church or in bed with the funny papers. Large and small rituals, if not passed down from preceding generations, can be freshly created and passed *forward*. Therapist Mary Whiteside (1989) advises that stepfamilies may benefit particularly from the creation of new rituals, which can "generate a feeling of closeness" and "provide fuel for weathering the more difficult times." She adds, "As these experiments . . . succeed enough to recur and to emerge as customs, the stepfamily unit begins to feel as if it has a life of its own."

FAMILY HISTORY. Strong families often have a strong sense of family history. Like family traditions, family memorabilia—scrapbooks, photos, letters, recipes, and mementos—are a satisfying link to the past. As discussed in Chapter 2, the family is strengthened by a sense of connection to its roots. When we recall such family tales as the one in which "Grandma was seventeen, and she lost her bloomers on the dance floor," we not only have a good laugh on Grandma but we also identify with her chagrin and her resourcefulness (she kicked them behind a sofa), and perhaps we add to the story an account of an embarrassing moment of our own. Family stories may also bring up recurring themes unique to our particular family's experience (Martin, Hagestad, and Didrick, 1988).

❖ R E F L E C T I O N S   *Make a list of your family traditions. Where did they come from? Which are your favorites? Your least favorites? Would you like to create any new ones? Make a list of your daily and weekly family rituals. Note your favorites. Are there others you'd like to incorporate into your family routine?*

Ethnicity and the Family

Ethnicity, writes Monica McGoldrick (1982), "is more than race, religion, and national or geographic origin. . . . It involves conscious and unconscious processes that fulfill a deep psychological need for identity and a sense of historical continuity. It is transmitted by an emotional language within the family and reinforced by the surrounding community."

In the "melting pot" of American society, ethnicity is a complicated and ever-changing phenomenon. Although some ethnic groups intermarry with and adapt rapidly to mainstream society, others, by choice or by pressure from without, have retained many of their traditions and values. In this sense, the United States can be seen more as a cauldron of very complex stew than as a homogenized melting pot.

An ethnic group may possess particular strengths that help its families to survive in a larger society that is often less than welcoming and sometimes overtly hostile. During slavery and in its aftermath, for example, amid racism and discrimination, African Americans needed to rely on their own families and community strengths. Strong kinship networks have been a major resource of black families during times of trouble (Chatters, Taylor, and Neighbors, 1989; McGoldrick, 1982); these kinship patterns have their roots in the family forms of West Africa (Allen, 1978; Guttman, 1976). Family values such as unconditional love for children, respect for self and others, and the "assumed natural goodness of the child" are other strengths of the African-American family (Nobles, 1988). Robert Taylor (1990) and his colleagues noted that a distinctive task of African-American parents is to attempt to prepare their children for the "realities of being black in America." (Also see Hill, 1972; Nobles, 1988; Staples, 1976.)

Urban anthropologist John Price (1981) studied the ways in which Native Americans in Los Angeles adjusted to an urbanized life. He found that although some traditional family patterns (such as multifamily residences) have declined, kinship networks remain "strong and supportive." Indians from over 100 different tribes have found ways to share their pride in their common heritage through Native American sports leagues and dance groups, powwows, and traditional crafts. Many also "commute" frequently to the home reservation to renew their family and cultural ties.

Families in every American ethnic group, whether newly arrived, long settled, or Native American, have a richness of tradition and insight to add to society. Even those whose ancestors came here one or two or three hundred years ago and who consider themselves "mongrels" of no specific pedigree are likely to preserve some ethnic flavor within their families—in their holiday celebrations, traditional recipes, names, verbal expressions, or ties to the old world. A significant challenge to today's society is to preserve and protect the uniqueness of all the ethnic groups of which it is composed while allowing the fulfillment of the promise of "liberty and justice for all."

❖ R E F L E C T I O N S   *Do you consider yourself part of a particular ethnic group? Are there special strengths you see within your group? Would you consider your group to be assimilated into American society? Accepted by American society? If you don't consider yourself part of a particular group, do you nevertheless preserve certain aspects of your ancestors' ethnicity? If so, what are they?*

Cuando cuentes cuentos, cuenta cuantos cuentos cuentas cuando cuentas cuentos. (When you tell stories count how many stories you tell when you tell stories.)

Spanish tongue twister

If you don't know your past You don't know your future.

Ziggy Marley

PERSPECTIVE

Tradition and Ritual in Modern American Life

If we think about all the rituals and holidays that we take for granted in our lives, we may be forced to conclude that humans are just naturally "party animals." Our lives are measured with life-cycle rituals, mainly surrounding birth, the transition to adulthood, marriage, and death. Our years are punctuated with holidays and celebrations, both religious and secular. Weddings and funerals have their own unique characteristics among different ethnic groups, as do "baby-welcoming" rituals such as baptism among Christians and *bris* (circumcision) among Jews. Many ethnic and cultural groups also celebrate the child's transition to adult status—with *bar* or *bat mitzvahs*, church confirmations, or "coming-out" parties. Other rituals, such as family reunions or tribal gatherings (powwows), may be associated with a particular holiday or convened when the family or community feels the need.

In addition to "traditional" holidays celebrated in the United States, such as Christmas, Passover, and Thanksgiving, holidays introduced by more recent immigrants enrich our culture. *Yuan Tan* (Chinese New Year), *Tet* (Vietnamese New Year), *Hana Matsuri* (the Japanese observance of the Buddha's birthday), *Ramadan* (the Islamic month of fasting), and *el Dia de los Muertos* (the Latino Day of the Dead) are just a few examples of holidays currently celebrated by American families. Among African Americans, Juneteenth, a celebration of emancipation, is being revived in many parts of the country.

Although many holidays commemorate historic events, their origins may well lie in ancient rites having to do with the movements of the sun and moon, the cycle of the seasons, or other natural events, such as the flooding of a river or the ripening of acorns. The impulses that brought our ancestors together to celebrate the beginnings of new life or give thanks for a successful harvest may have since taken on different meanings, but the observances often retain their ancient symbols—fertile bunnies and decorated eggs, for example, or displays of scarecrows along with harvested grains, fruits, and nuts.

Besides giving people a way of expressing their unity with nature, ritual celebrations also bring them together in a common purpose and strengthen their bonds to each other and to the community. Some ceremonies, such as marriage, formally (we might say "legally") create new relationships (in-laws) with attendant duties and privileges. Rituals, such as coming-of-age ceremonies, also strengthen the ties of the individual to the group. Some elements common to many diverse rituals are the use of food and drink; costumes; music and dance; ritual objects such as candles, flowers, and feathers; representations of people or deities; and special words (prayers, chants, incantations, blessings, vows).

A brief sampling of current holidays and rituals practiced in the United States follows. The holidays are listed in the order they occur through the year.

◆ **Yuan Tan** Chinese New Year begins on the first day of the lunar year, at the first new moon when the sun is in the constellation known to Westerners as Aquarius (typically between January 10 and February 19). It is celebrated for fourteen days, until the full moon, culminating in a nighttime parade accompanied by fireworks and featuring a huge, bejeweled dragon with a papier-maché head, a long, red, fabric body, and the legs of many humans underneath. The dragon represents fertility and prosperity.

◆ **Tet** The Vietnamese New Year, *Tet Nguyen Dan*, also coincides with the start of the lunar year, although the celebration begins days earlier. Traditionally, Vietnamese families make new clothes and many new purchases in preparation for the coming year. The father or grandfather lights candles on the ancestral altar, and symbolic objects and many kinds of foods are offered. At midnight on the first day of the year, the ancestral spirits are welcomed. This day is considered portentious, so families carefully monitor their words and actions to insure a year of harmony and good fortune.

◆ **Hana Matsuri** On April 8, Japanese Buddhists commemorate the birthday of

---

If you cannot get rid of the family skeleton, you may as well make it dance.

George Bernard Shaw

Play and Leisure Time

"Lack of time . . . might be the most pervasive enemy the healthy family has" (Curran, 1983). Stress management, role overload, and executive burnout are concepts that would have been considered strange fifty or so years ago, yet now they are major themes in everyday life. The fast pace and complex activities of our lives threaten a crucial resource—time. Without time, families lack the opportunity to nurture the basic qualities, like communication, that ensure their health and growth.

PERSPECTIVE

Siddhartha Gautama, the Buddha. Traditionally, images of the infant Buddha are bathed with hydrangea tea, and flowers and chanting are offered at Buddhist shrines and temples. *Hana Matsuri* is also known as the Flower Festival.

◆ **Pesach** The Feast of the Passover is a Jewish festival that begins after the first full moon of spring (Nisan 15 on the Hebrew calendar). It commemorates the flight of the Jews from Egypt under the leadership of Moses. *Pesach* has been celebrated for more than 3,000 years. Associated with Passover is the *Seder,* a family service and meal in remembrance of the ancestors' hardships. Traditional foods include matzohs (unleavened bread) and lamb (a holdover from the ancient sacrificial rite).

◆ **Juneteenth** The African-American holiday Juneteenth originated in Texas following the Civil War. Although the Emancipation Proclamation became law in January 1863, the last slaves were not freed until June 19, 1865, when Union troops rode into Galveston, Texas. Traditionally, Juneteenth (along with other Jubilee or Freedom Days) included such events as barbecues, baseball games, speeches, parades, concerts, and dances. As African Americans moved northward, the holidays moved with them, but during World War II such celebrations were considered unpatriotic as they emphasized a separate history from the white majority. Renewed interest in black history has sparked the revival of Juneteenth in communities across the United States.

◆ **Ramadan** The Islamic Fast of *Ramadan* begins with the new moon of the tenth lunar month and lasts until the next new moon. During *Ramadan,* the faithful fast daily between daybreak and dusk and spend as much time as possible in the mosque (place of worship) or at prayer. A mosque may be brilliantly lit to commemorate Mohammed's illumination on the Night of Power. The Koran (the Muslim holy book) is read in its entirety over the course of the month. On the twenty-ninth night the fast is broken, and the feast of *Eid Ui Fitr* begins. There are special foods, confections, and presents for the children.

◆ **Christmas** Although the exact date of Jesus's birth is not known, it has been celebrated by Christians since the fourth century on December 25—around the time of the winter solstice, the Roman holiday Saturnalia, and the Jewish Chanukah. Over time Christmas has taken on many quasi-religious and nonreligious aspects, including feasts, the exchange of gifts, decorations (such as evergreen trees and branches, which symbolize eternal life), and rituals. The tradition of visits by Santa Claus (St. Nicholas) was brought to the New World by early Dutch immigrants. The cartoonist Thomas Nast first gave Santa his sleigh and reindeer to take presents to soldiers in the Civil War. Music and pageantry are important to many people's Christmas celebrations, and a variety of traditions are practiced all over America by different ethnic and cultural groups.

◆ **La Quinceañera** On their fifteenth birthdays, young women of Latin American descent may be "introduced" into society in a ritual celebration known as the *quinceañera* (fifteenth-year celebration). A great deal of preparation usually goes into the event, which begins with a special Catholic mass involving the girl's family and godparents and proceeds to a dance and feast that is generally as lavish as the parents can afford. There may be both a dance band and a *mariachi* band; the guest of honor and her attendants, in their matching formal dresses, open the party with a specially choreographed waltz.

◆ **Powwows** Powwows—large gatherings of various Native American groups—involve demonstrations and contests of singing, dancing, and drumming. Powwows are secular in nature, unlike tribal religious ceremonies, which are usually carried out solemnly in private. Some performers at powwows are professionals who travel the "powwow circuit," keeping the traditions of their particular tribe alive. But anyone can participate, even small children, learning the steps their people have done for hundreds of years in dances portraying different animals, hunting techniques, or historical events. Traditional songs may be augmented with modern verses—to honor veterans of Korea and Vietnam, for example (Pareles, 1990). Powwows help keep Native American culture alive. A Mohawk singer expressed his feelings (quoted in Pareles, 1990): "I didn't learn anything about my culture when I was younger. But the more I find out, the more I've been seeing the logic of it and how beautiful and natural it was."

Without time, families lack the opportunity to simply *be*. Healthy families realize that they need to get away from work and responsibilities and simply enjoy one another and life in general. Quality time together need not be spent on lengthy or expensive vacations; a relaxed meal or a game in which everyone participates can serve the same purpose a lot more often.

The capacity to enjoy our family, with humor and playfulness and without strict scheduling, seems to come more easily to some than to others. Parents may have difficulty learning to leave a messy desk at work or a sticky kitchen floor at home in

Tradition and ritual are central to our lives. Among Catholics, a child's first communion is an important milestone.

order to relax with each other or with their children. They may feel a moral obligation to be a "good provider" or a "perfect housekeeper," which precludes their closing the door on disorder and going for a walk in the park. Yet time taken to play and relax with our loved ones pays off in ways that clean desks and shiny floors never can. When we are realistic, we see that the papers will never stop flowing onto the desk and the jam will never stop dripping onto the floor, but our children and our mates will not be as they are now ever again. If we don't take the time now to enjoy our families, we've lost an opportunity forever. Healthy families know this and give play and leisure time high priority.

❖ R E F L E C T I O N S   *Do you feel that your family has enough time for play and leisure? Can you give up anything to spend more time with your family? Can you reorder your priorities? Can they? Make a list of things you'd like to do with your family if you had the time. Take the time.*

Coping with Stress

Among the resources a healthy family possesses are the coping strategies that it brings into play during stressful times. These strategies can be seen as part of a "pool of resources" that the family has available to draw from when the going gets tough (Stinnett and DeFrain, 1985). (The effects of stress on the family were discussed in Chapter 13.)

Everything comes of itself at the appointed time. This is the meaning of heaven and earth.

I Ching

POSITIVE ATTITUDE. An optimistic outlook and a tendency to look on the bright side of things characterize strong families. This doesn't mean that they don't recognize and deal with their problems, but they choose to dwell on the positive rather than the negative. Stinnett and DeFrain (1985) quoted one of their respondents:

I don't recommend that you burn the house to learn the lesson, but we did stand on our front lawn one frosty fall morning and looked at the pile of ashes that had been our home. And then we all looked at each other and suddenly we were hugging and crying with joy because *we were OK.*

ADAPTABILITY. Strong families often need to bend in order to avoid breaking. Under stress, family members may be required to change their routines or plans or to take on unfamiliar roles. If families are inflexible in their standards, expectations, or behavior, they may find themselves on a collision course with crisis.

UNITED FRONT. Healthy families support each other so that no individual has to bear a burden all alone. Family members can help each other by lending emotional or physical support. They offer a cheery word or a shoulder to cry on. They wash the dishes, take the kids on an outing, share belongings, lend money, or assist in a thousand other big and little ways.

SPIRITUAL RESOURCES. Faith, prayer, and a sense of greater purpose provide strength, comfort, and hope to many in times of hardship. The spiritual dimension of healthy families was discussed earlier in this chapter.

COMMUNICATION. The importance of good communication cannot be overstated. Not only does communication help us get through stressful times, but it can also prevent many potentially stressful events from occurring. Chapter 14 deals exclusively with this vital quality of healthy families.

GETTING HELP. Healthy families are not problem-free; they may even have as many problems as unhealthy families. What distinguishes them from their less-successful counterparts is their willingness to face problems head on and to get help when it's needed. Problems—large and small—beset all of us. Sometimes we don't recognize small problems until they've grown too big to ignore, but healthy families recognize a problem when they see one and are able to take responsibility for it. They know that for many kinds of family problems, they need to look at the entire family system to find solutions. Healthy families accept problems as they come along and have developed techniques for dealing with the smaller ones; when the large problems—the true crises—occur, the healthy family knows where to turn for help.

Although some family resources (such as private counseling) can be costly, many low-cost or free services are available. Preventive programs such as parent education classes and marriage enrichment workshops are designed to keep strong families strong. Other resources include support groups that deal with specific problems such as alcoholism, physical disabilities, or loss and grief; family counseling programs; and other programs, workshops, and classes offered by schools, churches, hospitals, and community health agencies. (A guide to finding family resources is included in the Resource Center at the end of this book.)

❖ REFLECTIONS   *Does your family seek outside help for problems? Make a list of all the resources available to you that you might want to use sometime. Note the ones you've used in the past. The next time you have a family problem, take a look at your list.*

If you're afraid of the dark, remember the night rainbow. If you lose the key to your house, throw away the house. And if it's the last dance, you better dance backwards.

Cooper Edens

Experience is not what happens to a man; it is what a man does with what happens to him.

Aldous Huxley (1894–1963)

Family Strengths Inventory

The Family Strengths Inventory was developed by Nick Stinnett and John DeFrain to identify areas of strengths and weaknesses in families. Complete the inventory and then compute the score by adding the numbers you have circled. (You might also have other family members complete it independently to get a sense of their perceptions of your family.) The score will fall between 13 and 65.

   What does the score mean, according to the researchers? A score below 39 is below average. It indicates that there are areas in your family relationships that need improving. Look at the areas in which you scored low to help you target where you need work. Scores from 39 to 52 are average. Scores above 52 indicate strong families. Consider discussing the inventory results with your family.

Family Strengths Inventory

Circle on a five-point scale (with 1 representing the least degree and 5 representing the greatest degree) the degree to which your family possesses each one of the following.

Spending time together and doing things with each other

   (1)   2   3   4   5

Commitment to each other

   (1)   2   3   4   5

Good communication (talking with each other often, listening well, sharing feelings with each other)

   (1)   2   3   4   5

Dealing with crises in positive manner

   1   (2)   3   4   5

Expressing appreciation to each other

   (1)   2   3   4   5

Spiritual wellness

   (1)   2   3   4   5

Circle the degree of closeness of your relationship with your spouse on a five-point scale (with 1 representing the least degree and 5 representing the greatest degree).

   (1)   2   3   4   5

Circle the degree of closeness of your relationship with your children on a five-point scale (with 1 representing the least degree and 5 representing the greatest degree).

   1   2   3   4   (5)

Circle the degree of happiness of your relationship with your spouse on a five-point scale (with 1 representing the least degree and 5 representing the greatest degree).

   (1)   2   3   4   5

Circle the degree of happiness of your relationship with your children on a five-point scale (with 1 representing the least degree and 5 representing the greatest degree).

   1   2   3   4   (5)

Some people make us feel good about ourselves. That is, they make us feel self-confident, worthy, competent, and happy about ourselves. What is the degree to which your spouse makes you feel good about yourself? Indicate on the following five-point scale (with 1 representing the least degree and 5 representing the greatest degree).

   (1)   2   3   4   5

Indicate on the following five-point scale the degree to which you think you make your spouse feel good about himself/herself (with 1 representing the least degree and 5 representing the greatest degree).

   1   2   (3)   4   5

Indicate on the following five-point scale the degree to which you think you make your children feel good about themselves (with 1 representing the least degree and 5 representing the greatest degree).

   1   2   3   4   (5)

❖ KIN AND COMMUNITY

Intimacy Needs

Whether we are married or single, we need relationships in which we can be intimate. Neither couples nor individuals can function well in isolation. Robert Weiss

(1969) noted that people have needs that can be met only in relationships with other people. These needs can be summarized as follows:

1. *Nurturing others.* This need is filled through caring for a partner, children, or other intimates both physically and emotionally.
2. *Social integration.* We need to be actively involved in some form of community; if we are not, we feel isolated and bored. We meet this need through knowing others who share our interests and participating in community or school projects.
3. *Assistance.* We need to know that if something happens to us, there are people we can depend on for help. Without such relationships, we feel anxious and vulnerable.
4. *Intimacy.* We need people who will listen to us and care about us; if such people are not available, we feel emotionally isolated and lonely.
5. *Reassurance.* We need people to respect our skills as persons, workers, parents, and partners. Without such reassurance, we lose our self-esteem.

The Extended Family: Helping Kin

Few aspects of family life exist to which relatives (especially parents and siblings) do not make a contribution (Schneider, 1980).

Among African-American families, grandparents are often a valuable resource for child care and child socialization (Flaherty, Facteau, and Garver, 1990; Kennedy, 1990). Adult siblings are also important sources of help in times of need, especially among African Americans (Chatters, Taylor, and Neighbors, 1989). Another way the black extended family takes care of its members is through the process of "absorption" or "informal adoption." Adults who are ill or aged or children whose parents are unable to care for them are absorbed into the homes of relatives who have the resources to support them. Children incorporated into the family in this way are treated as equals to the children already in the household (Martin and Martin, 1978).

In many families parents loan money to their adult children at low or no interest. They may give or loan them the down payment for a home, for example. The obligations that these loans and gifts entail differ according to a person's age and marital status. If the children are young and single, parents may still expect to exercise considerable control over their children's behavior in return for their support. But if the children are older or—more important—married, there are fewer obligations.

Even when extended families are separated geographically, they continue to provide emotional support (Anderson, 1982). Contacts with kin are especially important in the lives of the aged. As we saw earlier, the elderly tend to have frequent contact with their kin. A recent national study found that almost two-thirds had seen a child within the previous week (U.S. Bureau of the Census, 1988).

Fictive Kin

In addition to kinship networks, many families have extensive networks of **fictive kin** (also called *pseudokin*). As discussed in Chapter 1, people in these relationships treat each other as family even though they are not related by blood. Both financial and emotional support may be given in these networks; there is usually the expectation of reciprocity, the understanding that favors will be returned.

An important component in Latino family life is *compadrazgo*. In this relationship, a child's godparents (*padrinos*), who sponsor the child at baptism, become "compan-

Grandparents and grandchildren provide love and meaning for each other.

The more hands that are offered, the lighter the burden.

Haitian proverb

Families today create their own relatives as needed.

Barbara Settles

ion parents" (Fitzpatrick, 1981). Also, witnesses at a marriage may become the *compadres* of the married couple. *Compadres* feel "a deep sense of obligation to each other for economic assistance, support, encouragement, and even personal correction" (Fitzpatrick, 1981).

Friendship

Families today find close friends, casual acquaintances, and temporary support within a complex and changing social network. Traditional sources of community support, such as church groups, are augmented by other sources. Parents meet one another and form friendships in groups that center around their children—parent-teacher groups, scouts, athletic groups. Peer support groups and self-help groups are available to fill a variety of short- or long-term needs; lasting friendships are often formed within such contexts. People may join political groups to work with others for change in society; they join hobby groups, crafts clubs, or dance classes in order to share their special interests with others. Some networks of support provide specific information or services for dealing with specific needs, whereas others provide more general help (Cooke et al., 1988). Social networks enrich our day-to-day lives and provide vital assistance in times of stress and crisis. One study of social support found that the sources most often mentioned were relatives (other than spouse or children), close friends, special groups, and co-workers (Cooke et al., 1988).

The Family in the Community

FAMILY ECOLOGY. Urie Bronfenbrenner (1979) has proposed that we look at the family in an "ecological environment." He suggests that we think of this environment in terms of a set of nested Russian dolls. The developing child is the tiny innermost doll, contained inside the various systems—such as home or school—that influence him or her. The interplay among the many systems profoundly affects the child in their midst. Furthermore, the influences of external factors—such as the flexibility of the parents' job schedules or the availability of good health care—also play a critical role.

SUPPORT FOR THE FAMILY. The well-being of the family depends not solely on its own resources, then, but also on the support it receives from the community in which it is embedded (Unger and Sussman, 1990). This community includes extended family, friends, schools, employers, health-care providers, and government agencies at local, state, and federal levels. As discussed in Chapter 12, the United States is far behind most industrialized nations in terms of the support it gives families in the areas of health, education, social welfare, and workplace policy. The need for creativity and energy in these areas is great and presents challenges and opportunities for those who wish to work with the families of today and tomorrow.

Despite the complexities of modern life, the families that love and shelter and teach us remain America's greatest national resource. They deserve to be nurtured, strengthened, and protected.

Raising children isn't an individual act. It is a social and communal enterprise, involving kin, neighbors, other parents, friends, and many other unrelated adults.

Barbara Dafoe Whitehead

If you have built castles in the air, your work need not be lost; that is where they should be. Now put the foundations under them.

Henry David Thoreau

Here is the test to find whether your mission on earth is finished: If you're alive, it isn't.

Richard Bach, Illusions

The family, in all its forms, is a resource that needs to be nurtured, strengthened, and protected.

❖ SUMMARY

◆ Marital success requires the development of *interpersonal competence*. Commitment (including sexual fidelity and the willingness to sacrifice), communication, and the creative use of conflict are essential aspects of success in marriage.

◆ The family should be seen as a process; family health may change over the course of the family life cycle.

◆ Healthy families (1) develop communication skills; (2) give affirmation, respect, and trust; (3) teach responsibility and morality; (4) promote spiritual wellness; (5) preserve tradition and family history; (6) share play and leisure time; and (7) cope with stress by having a positive attitude, being adaptable, presenting a united front, using spiritual resources and good communication, and getting help when needed.

◆ A sense of ethnicity or cultural heritage is an important source of strength for many American families. Often an ethnic group possesses particular strengths that help its families survive in an indifferent or unwelcoming larger society.

◆ We all have needs that can be met only in close relationships with others. These needs are to nurture others, to be socially integrated in some form of community, to have assistance we can rely on, to be intimate with others, and to be reassured about our skills. Kin, friends (including *fictive kin*), neighbors, and a variety of social networks all contribute to our well-being. They provide assistance and emotional support that give our families added strength.

◆ The family exists in the environment of community and is influenced directly and indirectly by many systems existing outside of itself. The well-being of the family depends not only on its own resources but also on the support of the larger community. For this reason, policies supportive of the family are crucial to its survival.

Answers to Preview Questions

The answers to the preview questions at the beginning of the chapter are listed below. As you check your answers, whether you were correct or not, think about your reasons for each response. What were they? What was their source? How valid is the source? As you read the chapter, you will find the questions discussed in greater depth.

1. T	6. T
2. F	7. T
3. T	8. T
4. F	9. T
5. F	10. F

❖ SUGGESTED READINGS

Beavers, Robert W., and Robert Hampson. *Successful Families.* New York: Norton Publishing Co., 1990. A systems approach to building successful families.

Curran, Dolores. *Traits of a Healthy Family.* New York: Ballantine Books, 1983 (paperback). A useful, nontechnical introduction to the elements that contribute to family strengths.

McCubbin, Hamilton I., et al. *Family Types and Strengths.* Edina, Minn.: Bellwether Press, 1988 (paperback). Examines family strengths, emerging family types, and recent developments in family stress therapy, coping, and support.

McGoldrick, Monica, et al., eds. *Ethnicity and Family Therapy*. New York: Guilford Press, 1987. Over twenty-five ethnic groups are examined in separate chapters. Each chapter includes a historical overview, cultural traits, and values. Treats ethnicity as an important aspect of psychological functioning.

National Symposium on Family Strengths. *Family Strengths*. University of Nebraska Press, 1979—. A valuable collection of papers by leading researchers into family strengths. Published periodically in conjunction with the symposium; as of 1992, six volumes have been published.

Redford, Dorothy. *Somerset Homecoming: Recovering a Lost Heritage.* Garden City, NY: Doubleday Publishing Co., 1988. The story of Somerset plantation and the reunion of 2,000 slave descendants from that plantation. The discovery of roots, community, and strength.

Stinnett, Nick, and John DeFrain. *Secrets of Strong Families.* Boston: Little, Brown, 1985 (paperback). A well-written book that examines how and why certain families are successful in providing a sense of well-being for themselves and their members.

❖ SUGGESTED FILMS

Avalon (1990). A Jewish immigrant family grows and changes with the times as this tender (and often funny) story explores the role of memory and tradition in the family.

The Great Wall (1988). The comic story of a middle-aged Chinese-American visiting China as a tourist in search of his roots.

It's a Wonderful Life (1946). James Stewart's classic film about a man who believes he has failed and tries to kill himself, only to learn how his life has made others' lives fuller.

Roots (1977). The monumental TV miniseries that brings alive the generations of an African-American family from its tribal life in Africa to slavery and freedom in America.

Sweet Fifteen (1988; PBS) A young Mexican-American girl celebrates her (fifteenth birthday) with a startling revelation about her father.

READINGS

OF COURSE YOU LOVE THEM— BUT DO YOU ENJOY THEM?

Anita Shreve

This article summarizes Dr. Robert Beavers' five basic components of family success. Think about your own family as you read the article. Do you see areas where the potential for enjoyment could be further developed?

Today, with both fathers and mothers in most families working outside the home, children grow up exposed to a large number of authority figures beyond the family—day-care instructors, teachers, baby sitters. Furthermore, contemporary society places great demands on its people to be decision makers and autonomous—to grow up. For these reasons, according to Dr. Robert Beavers, clinical professor of psychiatry at the University of Texas Health Center, in Dallas, and director of the Southwest Family Institute, parents would do well to invite children to be full participants and partners in family life. As for the question "How well does my family function?" Dr. Beavers suggests that the only question you have to ask yourself is: "Am I enjoying my family?" This, he says, is the acid test for a healthy family.

The ability to take pleasure in one's family, and in oneself as a member of that family, is, according to the family specialist, the most important goal worth striving for. If the answer to "Do I like living here?" is yes, parents should relax and not put their families under the microscope. "But if the answer is no," Dr. Beavers says, "ask yourself another question: 'What is the thing that would make me enjoy this family more?' You have to ask yourself that because you can't acquire something you can't first imagine."

To help parents get more enjoyment from their families—and in turn make their families healthier—Dr. Beavers outlines five fundamental components of—or steps toward—family success. When you pay attention to these five components of a healthy family, he believes, family enjoyment will develop as a natural consequence.

1. It Starts with the Marriage

A strong, intimate, sexual, happy marriage in which the parents are truly good friends sets the tone for a happy family life. Research indicates that parents of healthy families share power, have a good sexual relationship and are separate individuals despite strong emotional ties. Most important, they act as a team.

"You have to have an intimate friend," says Dr. Beavers, "someone you can trust and with whom you can talk about the kids. This is absolutely vital and it's just as important for single parents too. They need to find someone—perhaps an older woman who has already had her children—to talk with about raising a family."

As with family success, assessing whether or not you have a good marriage starts with a simple question: "Do I like living with this person?"

"If you're not enjoying your marriage," Dr. Beavers says, "try to identify what it is that you need. Try to complete the sentence "I want _____.' Once you actually imagine what it is you need, you can set about trying to get it."

Although a happy marriage is optimal, it is possible to achieve a good family life without one—but only if parents act as a team. "I've seen families in which the parents had a terrible marriage but ran a 'good business,' says Dr. Beavers. "They could agree on how to run the household even though they didn't have intimacy themselves."

Finally, the psychiatrist warns, it's important for a parent not to team up with a child against the other parent. Such divisiveness leads inevitably to jealousy, anger and a destruction of whole-family intimacy.

2. Learn to Enjoy Your Children

The scene is a familiar one. During a dinner party at the home of friends of his parents, two-and-a-half-year-old Bill alternately stands on the table, spills his milk, refuses to eat anything that is put in front of him and catapults his peas from his own plate into his hostess's lap with uncanny accuracy. The entire dinner is punctuated with apologies and exclamations of helplessness and dismay. With the possible exception of Billy, everyone is miserable. What has gone wrong?

According to Dr. Beavers, Billy's parents have made themselves martyrs by refusing to lay down basic rules of behavior that would make their own lives easier and would allow them to enjoy their son. "There have to be certain basic rules designed expressly for Mom and Dad's comfort and based on the parents' desire to enjoy themselves. After all, if you don't have rights of your own, you can't very well give them to someone else."

"Thou shalt enjoy thy children" is the first commandment of parenting. Assuming a long-suffering air of martyrdom while the children run wild won't allow parents to take pleasure in them. "In cases in which they haven't set limits, the parents alternate between being 'dutiful' and 'going bananas,'" says Dr. Beavers. "Family rules need to be clear, agreed on, and enforced to give parents and children a secure and pleasant home."

3. Lead but Don't Control

Setting basic rules for young children, however, does not mean the same thing as trying to control their thoughts and feelings or ruling like a dictator. Research indicates that although power in healthy families rests securely with the parents, they do not rule as authoritarians. Instead they provide easy leadership, listening to children's opinions and feelings with respect and trying to solve disputes by clarifying issues and negotiating compromises.

Dr. Beavers, who describes himself as a "parent emeritus" and says he has been "consulted" rather than obeyed since his children were small, explains: "Parents cannot—and therefore shouldn't try to—control the thoughts and feelings of their children. Accepting that eliminates two-thirds of the problem of parenting."

He gives the example of the child who has bad grades in school: A parent cannot force a child to want to make good grades, but he or she can say, "We're going to have two hours in which there will be no distractions." This allows the child to decide for himself to do better in school by using that time to study.

Dr. Beavers believes working together as parents in developing and maintaining family rules is quite different from attempting to control a child's goals. "Efforts at controlling a child's directions, successes, loves and hates are always frustrating to both parent and child," he points out.

The benefits of relaxed leadership are enormous, for it allows the members of the family to be intimate. Or, put another way, you can't have intimacy if one person has power and the other doesn't. This can be seen most easily in a marriage. If all the power in the marriage rests with the husband and the wife is never consulted, respected, or allowed to make decisions, there can be no real intimacy between them. The same is true with children. If the parent demands unwavering obedience from the child without every considering the child's perceptions, the relationship will lack intimacy.

4. Learn How to Negotiate

Over the years, Dr. Beavers has learned to identify a healthy family on the basis of two criteria: (1) Do the members of a family feel good? ("Does it feel good to be around the others and do they have an air of feeling good themselves?"); and (2) Do they know how to negotiate?

"Healthy families know how this is done," he says. "In fact, negotiation may be the single most important factor in developing healthy relationships. Conflict is ever-present. But if a family can dicker its way through these conflicts, it's probably in pretty good shape."

Negotiating starts with an ability to resolve one's own feelings. Each of us has mixed attitudes about many issues. But if we're able to resolve our ambivalence and then communicate clearly these re- solved feelings—at the same time allowing other family members to do this too—then there is a fairly sound basis for good negotiating.

continued on next page

An illustration of this is a typical family trying to decide what to do on a free Sunday afternoon. Dad wants to mow the lawn. Michael, who is eight years old, wants the family to go bike riding around the lake. Mom wants to go the lake too, and thinks that two-year-old Jennifer will enjoy riding in the baby seat on the back of her bike. But she's ambivalent because she knows if the lawn doesn't get done, it will be a whole week before Dad can return to it. Mom resolves her ambivalence this way: "I'm torn, but I think a family outing is what we all need right now. Therefore I'll lobby for that." The family begins to negotiate. Dad comes on strong for mowing the lawn. Michael is equally determined to go bike riding. Mom, her feelings resolved, states her position but sees a way to bargain. "Let's take a picnic to the lake, eat lunch, ride for half an hour and then come home. By that time, the grass will be dry and Dad can mow the lawn." After a little more discussion, everyone agrees.

Members of healthy families express their feelings—whether they be anger, sadness, love or fear—because the family ambiance is basically one of understanding and warmth. But the idea of totally honest and open communication in a family is a myth, admits Dr. Beavers. "Only when your child is three years old will he or she be completely open and clear—able to say 'I hate you Mommy' as easily as 'I love you.' Part of being in an intimate relationship is learning to keep certain things to oneself."

5. Learn to Let Go

The usual image of the happy, healthy family is one in which all the family members enjoy doing the same things together—like camping, gardening, or just reading the paper on a rainy Sunday afternoon. But members of healthy families have also learned to be separate individuals, each with an ability to think for himself and to make decisions for himself. The ability to *choose* how to be or how to feel is called *autonomy,* and it is the most treasured asset a parent can give to a child.

Let's take the example of a nine-year-old girl named Joanne who has just formed a friendship with a new girl in school. The new friend is of a racial background different from Joanne's, and although her parents know better, they can't help but express reservations and concern based on lingering prejudices with which they themselves grew up. Joanne's affection for the girl is quite real, however, and the two have discovered they like many of the same activities. Because Joanne's parents have fostered in her an ability to think for herself, she feels good about her newly found friendship. If Joanne's parents had denied her the ability to think for herself and accept responsibility for her actions, she might have acquiesced to their nameless fears and prejudices and given up the friend—or kept her but felt uncomfortable and guilty about doing so.

"Autonomy *must* be developed," says Dr. Beavers. "One must learn what one feels and thinks and must be able to make decisions and accept responsibility for these decisions. For a parent, the job is to render oneself unnecessary, to see the family as a dissolving unit, leaving the couple with the love ties with which they began but allowing the children to move on. Thus parents have given their children autonomy."

Although it may at first seem strange and uncomfortable to think of the ultimate goal of the family as that of dissolving, this process is necessary in order for the children to grow up to be adults. Parents first need to have a firm sense of their own identity to help the children develop theirs. (Remember that you can't give to someone else what you don't have yourself.) A parent is a person first—and if this is made clear, it allows the child to realize what a grownup can be—a separate individual with unique thoughts and feelings and perspectives. This process can then be facilitated by some of the parenting skills mentioned· earlier—setting basic rules, learning how to negotiate, inviting your children into the family as participants and encouraging the expression of feelings.

Being separate does not, however, mean being distant. According to Dr. Beavers, there is more autonomy in close-knit families than in distant ones. "In close-knit families the children feel the roots but know that those roots allow for some breathing space—allow them to say 'I choose.' To be close, you must first learn to be separate. You can't tolerate intimacy if you're not separate, because you fear you'll be swallowed up."

Although following these five steps may help you have a happier family life, it will be obvious to any parent that the steps are interrelated and complex and that family interaction cannot be easily divided into categories. Negotiating, for instance, is dependent on the individual family members' ability to develop autonomy; skill in negotiating with children may be directly related to how well the parents can negotiate and how happy their marriage is; establishing casual leadership probably will work only if everyone in the family already respects the basic family rules.

And certainly no one—especially Dr. Beavers—wants to see a family straining to conform to a rigid system of family life, especially if doing so doesn't make the members happy. In fact, the psychiatrist is the first to suggest that each couple try to find their own way of making a family. "Every marriage is like every new pregnancy," he says. "In the same way that there are infinite possibilities in the unborn, there are also infinite possibilities for a couple to create a family. When two people come together they hold between them the potential to make something unique—a way of being that has never been before. I like to think that instead of conforming to the way of making a healthy family, they will say, 'We can do it our way.'"

Resource
Center

REFERENCE GUIDES FOR STUDYING MARRIAGE AND THE FAMILY

The following reference guides are designed to assist the student in pursuing information or research in various aspects of marriage and the family.

Marriage and Family Studies

Representative subject headings in card catalogs and databases for marriage include:

- Betrothal
- Common law marriage
- Communication in marriage
- Courtship
- Deaf—Marriage
- Divorce
- Domestic relations
- Endogamy and exogamy
- Family
- Family life education
- Home
- Honeymoon
- Husbands
- Love
- Martial status
- Marriage counseling
- Married people
- Mate selection
- Matrimonial advertisements
- Matrimony
- Polyandry
- Polygamy
- Posthumous marriage
- Remarriage
- Sacraments
- Sex
- Sex in marriage
- Sexual ethics
- Teen-age marriage
- Weddings
- Wives

Representative subject headings for family include:

- Birth order
- Black families
- Brothers and sisters
- Children
- Clans and clan system
- Daughters-in-law
- Divorce
- Familial behavior in animals
- Family size
- Fathers
- Grandparents
- Households
- Jewish families
- Joint family
- Kinship
- Matriarchy
- Mothers
- Mothers-in-law

- ◆ Only child
- ◆ Parent and child
- ◆ Parenthood
- ◆ Parents
- ◆ Parents-in-law
- ◆ Polygamy
- ◆ Problem family

- ◆ Rural families
- ◆ Single-parent family
- ◆ Tribal and tribal system
- ◆ Twins
- ◆ Unmarried couples
- ◆ Widowers
- ◆ Widows

JOURNALS. The following periodicals are of major interest to researchers, teachers, and students of marriage and family.

Alan Booth's (ed.) *Contemporary Families: Looking Forward, Looking Back,* Minneapolis, Minn.: NCFR, 1991, is a decade review of research in the field.

American Journal of Family Therapy focuses on issues of particular interest to counselors and family therapists.

American Journal of Orthopsychiatry is a multidisciplinary journal focusing on human development and mental health.

Archives of Sexual Behavior is a major journal in sex research.

The Black Scholar frequently contains articles regarding family, gender roles, feminism, and so on, that are relevant to African Americans.

Canadian Journal of Sociology frequently contains articles about Canadian marriages and families. Volume 6, no. 3 (1981) is devoted to specific theoretical and empirical issues of Canadian families.

Family Law Quarterly reviews legal issues and the family.

Family Law Reporter is a weekly newsletter dealing with the legal aspects of family life, such as rights, violence, divorce, and abortion.

Family Planning Perspectives deals with birth control, sex education, and other aspects of family planning.

Family Process focuses on family psychotherapy, especially from a general systems approach.

Family Relations is a major journal emphasizing the implications of research on family counseling and services.

Hispanic Journal of Behavioral Science is a major journal addressing Latino issues, including the family.

Home Economics Research Journal is published bimonthly to encourage dialogue between home economists and scholars in related fields concerned with the well-being of the family and individuals.

Journal of Black Studies often includes articles relating to family issues.

Journal of Comparative Family Studies is dedicated to the cross-cultural study of marriage and the family.

Journal of Divorce focuses on divorce issues for counselors, therapists, lawyers, and family-life professionals.

Journal of Family History publishes historical articles; it focuses mostly on families in the United States, Canada, and Europe.

Journal of Family Issues is a multidisciplinary journal that alternates between general family issues and specific themes under a guest editor.

Journal of Family Violence is devoted to the emerging field of family violence.

Journal of the History of Sexuality is an interdisciplinary journal.

Journal of Home Economics focuses on general home economics themes and devotes a portion of each issue to a specific topic.

Journal of Marital and Family Therapy focuses on therapy issues, often from a family systems perspective.

Journal of Marriage and the Family is a multidisciplinary research journal devoted to the study of marriage and the family. It is the leading journal in the field. In 1990, it published its decade review of major trends in family research.

Journal of Personal and Social Relationships focuses on personal relationships from an interdisciplinary perspective.

Journal of Sex and Marital Therapy focuses on therapy issues.

Journal of Sex Research is an interdisciplinary journal that contains articles, commentary, and book reviews.

Marriage and Family Review contains current abstracts and review articles of scholarly interest.

Mediation Quarterly: Journal of the Academy of Family Mediators focuses on specific mediation topics in each issue.

Sage: A Scholarly Journal of Black Women devotes each issue to various aspects of women's lives, such as mother/daughter relations, health, and education.

Sex Roles: A Journal of Research is an interdisciplinary journal on research and theory regarding gender roles.

Signs: Journal of Women in Culture and Society is devoted to research, essays, reports, and commentaries about women.

Women and Society is a sociologically-oriented journal dealing with women's issues.

U.S. Bureau of the Census. *Current Population Reports,* Series P-20. Published several times annually; provides the latest demographic statistics on various aspects of marriage and the family.

BIBLIOGRAPHIES AND INDEXES. The most useful general bibliographies that index scholarly articles from the United States and Canada include *Sociological Abstracts* (published six times annually), *Psychological Abstracts* (published quarterly), *Social Science Index* (published quarterly), and *Social Sciences Citation Index.* Specific bibliographies on marriage and the family include *Inventory of Marriage and Family Literature* and *Sage Family Studies Abstracts.* Each issues of *Family Relations* contains a bibliography (compiled from Family Resources Database) and a review essay on a specific topic. Benjamin Schlesinger's *Canadian Family Studies: A Selected, Annotated Bibliography* (Chicago: CPL: Bibliographies, 1983) is useful for Canadian scholarship. W. Allen and colleagues' *Black American Families* (Westport, Conn.: Greenwood Press, 1986) and L. Davis's *The Black Family in the United States* (Westport, Conn.: Greenwood Press, 1986) are useful annotated bibliographies. Albert Camarillo's *Latinos in the United States* (Santa Barbara, Calif.: ABC-Clio, 1986) is a historical bibliography.

Robert Staples' "The Emerging Majority: Resources for Nonwhite Families in America," *Family Relations* 37:3 (July, 1988), is an excellent overview on ethnic families.

Reader's Guide to Periodical Literature contains subject and author indexes of more than 180 general publications (such as *Time, Newsweek,* and *Harper's*) in the United States. *The New York Times Index* is a guide to the contents of *The New York Times;* it includes brief summaries of articles. *Newspaper Index* lists the contents of *The New York Times, Los Angeles Times, Wall Street Journal,* and *Washington Post. Black Newspaper Index* indexes articles appearing in African-American newspapers. *HAPI: Hispanic American Periodical Index* indexes articles in Spanish and supplements index articles in English.

DATABASES. Many college, university, and public libraries have facilities for making computer searches on DIALOG and BRS information retrieval systems, which index U.S., Canadian, and many foreign language journals. These services will help you quickly compile bibliographies on virtually any topic in marriage and the family. You may request printouts of relevant bibliographic citations and journal abstracts. Check with your reference librarian about the available information retrieval services.

The most useful databases are PsycLit (based on *Psychological Abstracts*), Sociofile (based on *Sociological Abstracts*), Family Resources Database (based on *Inventory of Marriage and Family Literature*), Wilson Line (based on Social Sciences Index), and Cen-Data (which retrieves published and unpublished census data). Chicano Database (based on the *Hispanic American Periodical Index* and other sources) retrieves data on Mexican Americans in both English and Spanish. *Index Medicus* indexes medical publications.

Book Reviews

A book review is an article that describes and evaluates a book soon after its publication. Popular books may be published and reviewed almost simultaneously. More scholarly reviews may appear two or three years after publication.

To find a book review, you'll need the book's author, title, and date of publication. If you're not sure of this information, check the library catalog or ask at the reference desk for assistance. Some indexes list reviews under an author's name, while others may group them under the headings "Books" or "Book Reviews."

GENERAL BOOK REVIEW INDEXES

◆ *Book Review Digest* (1905–)
Lists and quotes form reviews in 95 popular journals from all disciplines.
◆ *Book Review Index* (1965–)
◆ *Combined Retrospective Index to Book Reviews in Scholarly Journals* (1886–1974)
Indexes over one million reviews in 459 journals in history, political science, and sociology.

GENERAL PERIODICAL INDEXES THAT INCLUDE BOOK REVIEWS

◆ *Arts and Humanities Citation Index*
◆ *General Science Index*
◆ *Humanities Index*
◆ *Magazine Index*
◆ *Readers' Guide to Periodical Literature*

◆ *Social Sciences Index*
◆ *Social Sciences Citation Index*

SPECIALIZED PERIODICAL INDEXES THAT INCLUDE BOOK REVIEWS

◆ *Alternative Press Index*
◆ *America: History and Life*
◆ *Chicano Periodical Index*
◆ *Education Index*
◆ *Guide to Reviews of Books from and about Hispanic America*
◆ *Hispanic American Periodical Index (HAPI)*
◆ *Historical Abstracts*
◆ *Index to Black Periodicals*
◆ *Index to Legal Periodicals*
◆ *Women Studies Abstracts*

Women's Studies

Representative subject headings used in catalogs and periodical indexes include:

◆ Abortion
◆ African-American women
◆ Education of women
◆ Feminism
◆ Lesbianism
◆ Matriarchy
◆ Mexican-American women
◆ Midwives
◆ Minority women
◆ Mothers
◆ Rape

◆ Sex roles
◆ Single women
◆ Women—Psychology
◆ Women—Crimes against
◆ Women—Employment
◆ Women, Jewish
◆ Women in Islam
◆ Women—Latin America
◆ Women scientists
◆ Women's rights
◆ Women's studies

Consult the *Library of Congress Subject Headings* to identify other headings.

ENCYCLOPEDIAS AND HANDBOOKS

◆ *American Women Writers: A Critical Reference Guide from Colonial Times to the Present.* 1979–1982. 4 vols.
◆ *Atlas of American Women.* 1987.
◆ *The Nature of Woman: An Encyclopedia and Guide to the Literature.* 1980. Short essays and quotations.
◆ *Women in the World: An International Atlas.* 1986.
◆ *Women's Action Almanac: A Complete Resource Guide.* 1979.

GUIDES TO THE LITERATURE

◆ *A Guide to Social Science Resources in Women's Studies.* 1978.
◆ *Introduction to Library Research in Women's Studies.* 1985.
◆ *Lesbianism: An Annotated Bibliography.* 1988.
◆ *Women in Popular Culture: A Reference Guide.* 1982.
◆ *Women of Color in the United States: A Guide to the Literature.* 1989.

INDEXES AND ABSTRACTS

◆ *Feminist Periodicals: A Current Listing of Contents.* 1981+.
◆ *Women Studies Abstracts.* 1972+.

Also check *Humanities Index, Alternative Press Index, Left Index, Psychological Abstracts, Social Sciences Index, Sociological Abstracts, Chicano Periodicals Index,* and *Index to Articles by and about Blacks.* Many of these indexes can be searched on computer or CD-Roms.

SELECTED BIBLIOGRAPHIES

◆ *Athena Meets Prometheus: Gender, Science and Technology: A Selected Bibliography.* 1988.
◆ *Black Women and Religion: A Bibliography.* 1980.
◆ *Feminism and Women's Issues.* 1989.
◆ *Jewish Women's Studies Guide.* 1982. Guide to courses with bibliographies.
◆ *Native American Women: A Contextual Bibliography.* 1983.
◆ *Older Women in 20th Century America: A Selected Annotated Bibliography.* 1982.
◆ *The Chicana: A Comprehensive Bibliographic Study.* 1975.
◆ *The State-by-State Guide to Women's Legal Rights.* 1987.
◆ *Violence against Women: An Annotated Bibliography.* 1981.
◆ *Women: A Bibliography of Bibliographies.* 1986.
◆ *Women and Feminism in American History: A Guide to Information Sources.* 1981.
◆ *Women of Color and Southern Women: A Bibliography of Social Science Research,* 1975–1988.
◆ *Women of South Asia: A Guide to Resources.* 1980.
◆ *Women's Studies: A Bibliography,* 1980–88.

BIOGRAPHICAL SOURCES

◆ *Index to Women of the World from Ancient to Modern Times: Biographies and Portraits.* 1970.
◆ *Notable American Women 1607–1950.* 3 vols. 1971.
◆ *Notable American Women: The Modern Period.* 1980.
◆ *Through a Woman's I: An Annotated Bibliography of American Women's Autobiographical Writings, 1946–1976.* 1983.

Ethnic Studies Periodicals

This list contains the titles of periodicals primarily concerned with the following American ethnic groups:

◆ African Americans
◆ Asian Americans
◆ Latinos
◆ Native Americans
◆ Ethnic studies in general

Although these periodicals contain much material that is useful to the ethnic studies student, remember that there are hundreds of other general and scholarly periodicals containing thousands of other articles on these ethnic groups.

Robert Staples' "The Emerging Majority: Resources for Nonwhite Families in America," *Family Relations* 37:3 (July 1988), is an excellent overview.

While browsing through the journals directly will lead you to many valuable articles, the following periodical indexes are useful:

◆ *Chicano Periodical Index*
◆ *HAPI: Hispanic American Periodicals Index*
◆ *Index to Periodical Articles by and about Blacks*
◆ *Sage Race Relations Abstracts*

Other more general indexes include the following:

◆ *Alternative Press Index*
◆ *America: History and Life*
◆ *American Statistics Index*
◆ *Education Index*
◆ *Left Index*
◆ *Public Affairs Information Service Bulletin*
◆ *Readers' Guide to Periodical Literature*
◆ *Sociological Abstracts*
◆ *Social Sciences Index*
◆ *Social Sciences Citation Index*
◆ *Women's Studies Abstracts*

AFRICAN AMERICANS

◆ *Black American Literature Forum*
◆ *Black Enterprise*
◆ *Black Law Journal*
◆ *The Black Nation*
◆ *Black Perspective in Music*
◆ *Black Scholar*
◆ *Burning Spear*
◆ *Callaloo: Journal of Afro-American and African Arts and Letters*
◆ *College Language Association (CLA) Journal: Afro-American, African and Caribbean Literature*
◆ *The Crisis*
◆ *Dollars & Sense*
◆ *Ebony*
◆ *Essence*
◆ *Freedomways*
◆ *Journal of Black Psychology*
◆ *Journal of Black Studies*
◆ *Journal of Negro Education*
◆ *Journal of Negro History*
◆ *Kokay I*
◆ *Living Blues*
◆ *Negro History Bulletin*
◆ *Obsidian II: Black Literature in Review*
◆ *Phylon, a Review of Race & Culture*
◆ *Review of Black Political Economy*
◆ *SAGE: A Scholarly Journal of Black Women*
◆ *Slavery & Abolition*
◆ *Southern Exposure*
◆ *Truth: Newsletter of the Association of Black Women Historians*
◆ *University of California, Los Angeles. Center for Afro-American Studies. CAAS Newsletter*
◆ *Western Journal of Black Studies*

ASIAN AMERICANS

◆ *Amerasia Journal*
◆ *Asiaweek: Journal for the Asian American Community*
◆ *East West*
◆ *East Wind*
◆ *Focus on Asian Studies*
◆ *Katipunan*
◆ *P/AAMHRC Research Review (Pacific/Asian American Mental Health Research Center)*
◆ *Pacific Citizen*
◆ *Pacific Ties*
◆ *Vietnam Forum*

LATINOS

- *Aztlan*
- *Bilingual Review, La Revista Bilingüe*
- *El Chicano*
- *Chicano Law Review*
- *Hispanic Journal of Behavioral Sciences*
- *Hispanic Link Weekly Report*
- *Imagine: International Chicano Poetry Journal*
- *Noticiero*
- *Nuestro*
- *Renato Rosaldo Lecture Series Monographs*
- *Revista Chicana-Requena*
- *Revista Mujeres*
- *El Tecolote*
- University of California, Los Angeles. Spanish Speaking Mental Health Research Center. *Research Bulletin.*

NATIVE AMERICANS

- *Akwesasne Notes*
- *American Indian Art Magazine*
- *American Indian Culture and Research Journal*
- *American Indian Law Review*
- *American Indian Libraries Newsletter*
- *American Indian Quarterly*
- *Daybreak Star*
- *Early American* (Newsletter of the California Indian Education Association)
- *Indian Affairs* (Newsletter of the Association on American Indian Affairs)
- *NCAI News* (National Congress of American Indians)
- *News from Native California*
- *Treaty Council News*
- *Wassaja* (national newspaper of Indian America)

GENERAL ETHNIC STUDIES

- *Ethnic Affairs*
- *Ethnic and Racial Studies*
- *Ethnic Forum*
- *Ethnic Groups*
- *Ethnic Reporter*
- *Explorations in Ethnic Studies*
- *Immigrants and Minorities*
- *Interracial Books for Children Bulletin*
- *Journal of American Ethnic History*
- *Journal of Ethnic Studies*
- *Race & Class*

African-American Studies

Representative subject headings used in catalogs and periodical indexes include:

- African Americans
- Black Muslims
- Black power
- Blacks
- Civil rights
- Discrimination
- Ethnic attitudes
- Minorities
- Negroes
- Race
- Racism
- Segregation

Consult the *Library of Congress Subject Headings* to identify other subject headings.

A decade review of scholarship on African-American families may be found in Robert Taylor, et al., "Black Families." In Alan Booth, ed., *Contemporary Families: Looking Forward, Looking Back.* Minneapolis, Minn.: NCFR, 1991.

SELECTED REFERENCE BOOKS

- *Dictionary of American Negro Biography.* 1982.
- *Encyclopedia of Black America.* 1981.
- *The Black American Reference Book.* 1976.
- *In Black and White.* 1980, 1985.
- *The Negro Almanac: A Reference Work on the Afro-American.* 1983.
- *Who's Who among Black Americans.* 1981
- *We the People: An Atlas of America's Ethnic Diversity.* 1988. See especially Chapter 10.

SELECTED BIBLIOGRAPHIES

- *Afro-American History: A Bibliography.* By Dwight LaVern Smith. Vol 1, 1974, and vol 2, 1981.
- *Black American Families: A Classified, Selectively Annotated Bibliography.* By W. Allen, et al. Westport, Conn.: Greenwood Press, 1986.
- *The Black Family in the United States: A Revised, Updated, Selectively Annotated Bibliography.* By L. Davis. Westport, Conn.: Greenwood Press, 1986.
- *Blacks in America: Bibliographical Essays.* 1971.
- *A Comprehensive Bibliography for the Study of American Minorities.* By Wayne Charles Miller. 1976.
- *Black Lesbians: An Annotated Bibliography.* 1981.
- *The Progress of Afro-American Women: A Selected Bibliography and Resource Guide.* By Janet L. Sims-Wood. 1980.
- *Resource Guide on Black Families in America.* By C.S. Howard. Washington, D.C.: Institute for Urban Affairs and Research, Howard University, 1980.

INDEXES AND ABSTRACTS

- *Alternative Press Index.* 1969— .
- *America: History and Life.* 1964— .
- *Biography Index.* 1946— .
- *Education Index.* 1929— .
- *Index to Periodical Articles by and about Blacks.* 1950— .
- *Index to Legal Periodicals.* 1926— .
- *Left Index.* 1982— .
- *Public Affairs Information Service Bulletin.* 1915— .
- *Readers Guide to Periodical Literature.* 1900— .
- *Sage Race Relations.* 1973— .
- *Social Sciences Index.* 1974— . See also the earlier title: *Social Sciences and Humanities Index,* 1965–1974; *International Index,* 1907–1965.
- *Women's Studies Abstracts.* 1972— .

SELECTED COMPUTER DATABASES

◆ *America: History and Life.* 1964— .
◆ *ERIC.* 1966— .
◆ *Magazine Index.* 1959–1970, 1973— .
◆ *National Newspaper Index.* 1979— .
◆ *P.A.I.S.* 1976— .
◆ *Social Scisearch.* 1972— .
◆ *Sociological Abstracts.* 1963— .

Latino Studies

Representative subject headings for this topic include:

◆ Agricultural laborers —United States
◆ American drama—Mexican-American authors
◆ Bilingualism
◆ Cuban Americans
◆ Education—Bilingual
◆ Ethnic attitudes
◆ Mexican-Americans
◆ Mexican-American literature
◆ Mexican-American women
◆ Mexicans in California
◆ Minorities
◆ Puerto Ricans
◆ Race discrimination

Consult the *Library of Congress Subject Headings* for other headings.

A decade review of scholarship on Latino families may be found in William Vega, "Hispanic Families." In Alan Booth, ed., *Contemporary Families: Looking Forward, Looking Back.* Minneapolis, Minn.: NCFR, 1991.

DICTIONARIES AND ENCYCLOPEDIAS

◆ *Dictionary of Mexican American History.* 1981.
◆ *Harvard Encyclopedia of American Ethnic Groups.* 1980.
◆ *El diccionario del español chicano* (Dictionary of Chicano Spanish). 1985.

HANDBOOKS, GUIDES AND DIRECTORIES

◆ *Bibliografia Chicana: A Guide to Information Sources.* 1975. Includes general references sources, Chicano periodicals, and newspapers.
◆ *Chicano Organizations Directory.* 1985.
◆ *Chicano Scholars and Writers: A Bio-bibliographical Directory.* 1979.
◆ *A Directory of Ethnic Publishers and Resource Organizations.* 1979. Includes bilingual publishers, Chicano Studies centers.
◆ *Hispanic Americans Information Directory.* 1990.
◆ *Hispanic Resource Directory.* 1988.
◆ *The Mexican Americans: A Critical Guide to Research Aids.* 1980. Extensive and annotated listing of sources and bibliographies.
◆ *Sourcebook of Hispanic Culture in the United States.* 1982. Short essays and bibliographies.
◆ *Who's Who: Chicano Office Holders.* 1977/78—.

BIBLIOGRAPHIES

◆ *Arte Chicano: A Comprehensive Annotated Bibliography of Chicano Art, 1965–1981.* 1985.
◆ *Bibliografia de Aztlan: An Annotated Chicano Bibliography.* 1971.
◆ *Bibliography of Mexican American History.* 1984.
◆ *The Chicana: A Comprehensive Bibliographic Study.* 1975.
◆ *Comprehensive Bibliography for the Study of American Minorities.* 1976. Essay and bibliography on all aspects of Mexican-American experience.
◆ *Literatura Chicana: Creative and Critical Writings through 1984.*
◆ *Mexican Americans.* 1973. Annotated bibliography. Includes arts, fiction, biographies, and film.
◆ *Mexican Americans: An Annotated Bibliography of Bibliographies.* 1984.
◆ *Reference Materials on Mexican Americans: An Annotated Bibliography.* 1976.
◆ *A Selected and Annotated Bibliography of Chicano Studies.* 1979.

SELECTED INDEXES AND ABSTRACTS

◆ *Alternative Press Index.* 1969— .
◆ *America: History and Life.* 1964— .
◆ *American Statistics Index.* 1973— .
◆ *Chicano Periodical Index.* 1967— .
◆ *Education Index.* 1929— .
◆ *HAPI: Hispanic American Periodicals Index.* 1970— .
◆ *Index to Legal Periodicals.* 1926— .
◆ *Left Index.* 1982— .
◆ *Psychological Abstracts.* 1927— .
◆ *Public Affairs Information Service Bulletin.* 1915— .
◆ *Readers Guide to Periodical Literature.* 1900— .
◆ *Sage Race Relations Abstracts.* 1973— .
◆ *Sociological Abstracts.* 1953— .
◆ *Social Sciences Index.* 1974— .
◆ *Social Sciences Citation Index.* 1966— .
◆ *Women's Studies Abstracts.* 1972— .

SELECTED COMPUTER DATABASES. *Chicano Database, ERIC* (education), *PsychInfo* (psychology), *Sociofile* (sociology), and GPO (U.S. government documents) may be searched on computer CDs.

Asian-American Studies

Subject headings for Asian American groups are complex and inconsistent. They may appear in any of these forms: **Asian Americans; Asians—United States; Asians in the United States**; or, for example: **Chinese Americans; Chinese—United States; Chinese in the United States.** For the most complete results, check all of these forms for the groups that interest you. Other representative subject headings used in catalogs and periodical indexes include:

- Chinese American women
- Chinese in California
- Chinese in New York City
- Discrimination
- Ethnic attitudes
- Filipino Americans

- Filipinos in San Francisco
- Japanese American art
- Japanese in Oregon
- Manzanar, Calif.
- Vietnamese Americans

Consult the *Library of Congress Subject Headings* to find other titles and subject headings.

SELECTED REFERENCE BOOKS

- *Dictionary of Asian American History.* 1986.
- *Harvard Encyclopedia of American Ethnic Groups.* 1980.
- *We the People: An Atlas of America's Ethnic Diversity.* 1988. See especially Chapter 12.

SELECTED BIBLIOGRAPHIES

- *Amerasia Journal.* Annual selected bibliography.
- *Asians in California.* By Sucheng Chan. 1986.
- *Asians in America: A Selected Annotated Bibliography.* 1983.
- *Pacific/Asian Americans.* By Indu Vohra-Sahu. 1983.
- *Minority Studies: A Selective Annotated Bibliography.* 1975.
- *Pacific/Asian Lesbian Book Collection.* By Alison Kim. 1987.
- *Selected Bibliography on the Asians in America.* By J. Lo Wong. Saratoga, Calif.: R and E Research Publishers, 1981.

SELECTED INDEXES AND ABSTRACTS

- *Alternative Press Index.* 1969— .
- *America: History and Life.* 1964— .
- *Biography Index.* 1946— .
- *Education Index.* 1929— .
- *Index to Legal Periodicals.* 1926— .
- *Left Index.* 1982— .
- *Public Affairs Information Service Bulletin.* 1915— .
- *Readers Guide to Periodical Literature.* 1900— .
- *Sage Race Relations.* 1973— .
- *Social Sciences Index.* 1974— . See also the earlier title: *Social Sciences and Humanities Index, 1965–1974; International Index, 1907–1965.*
- *Women's Studies Abstracts.* 1972— .

SELECTED COMPUTER DATABASES

- *America: History and Life.* 1964.
- *ERIC.* 1966— .
- *Magazine Index.* 1959–1970, 1973— .
- *National Newspaper Index.* 1979— .
- *P.A.I.S.* 1976— .
- *Social Scisearch.* 1972— .
- *Sociological Abstracts.* 1963— .

Native American Studies

Representative subjects headings used in catalogs and periodical indexes include:

- Civil rights
- Discrimination
- Ethnic attitudes
- Folk-lore, Indian
- Indians of North America

- Indians, treatment of
- Minorities
- Navaho Indians
- Race
- Race relations

Consult the *Library of Congress Subject Headings* to identify other subject headings. To find tribal names look in the subject catalog.

SELECTED REFERENCE BOOKS

- *Reference Encyclopedia of the American Indian.* vol. 1, 1986.
- *Great North American Indians: Profiles in Life and Leadership.* By Frederick J. Dockstader. 1977.
- *Guide to Research on North American Indians.* 1983.
- *Handbook of North American Indians.*

SELECTED BIBLIOGRAPHIES

- *A Bibliographical Guide to the History of Indian-White Relations in the United States.* 1977 and suppl. By Frances Paul Prucha. 1982.
- *Native American Periodicals and Newspapers.* 1828–1982.
- *Native American Women.* 1983.
- *The Urbanization of American Indians.* 1982.

SELECTED INDEXES AND ABSTRACTS

- *Abstracts in Anthropology.* 1970– .
- *Alternative Press Index.* 1969— .
- *America: History and Life.* 1964— .
- *Education Index.* 1929— .
- *Index to Legal Periodicals.* 1926— .
- *National Newspaper Index.*
- *Public Affairs Information Service Bulletin.* 1915— .
- *Readers Guide to Periodical Literature.* 1900— .
- *Social Sciences Index.* 1974— . See also the earlier title: *Social Sciences and Humanities Index, 1965–1974; International Index, 1907–1965.*
- *Sociological Abstracts.* 1953— .
- *Women's Studies Abstracts.* 1972— .

SELECTED COMPUTER DATABASES

- *America: History and Life.* 1964— .
- *ERIC.* 1966— .
- *Magazine Index.* 1959–1970, 1973— .
- *National Newspaper Index.* 1979— .
- *P.A.I.S.* 1976— .
- *Social Scisearch.* 1972— .
- *Sociological Abstracts.* 1963— .

SELF-HELP RESOURCE DIRECTORY

The information resources that follow include information centers and counseling centers, as well as support groups, prerecorded tape services, and crisis centers. Use them, share the questions that led you to call, and discover new information on numerous topics.

The directory is easy to use. Each resource is located under a general subject heading. You'll find a description of the service, its hours, and its location by city and state. To call a resource, follow the code found by its telephone number:

◆ LD—Long-distance. Many important resources must be dialed at your expense. Dial direct, if you can, and remember the difference in time.
◆ TF—Toll-free. Some organizations have toll-free numbers. The 800 prefix designates that convenience. Telephone these resources at no charge.

Need information on a topic that isn't included? Check your telephone directory for important local resources. If you can't find the information you need, check at the reference desk of your local public, college, or university library.

Adoption

ALMA Society
P.O. Box 154
Washington Bridge Station
New York, NY 10033
LD 212-581-1568

The Adoptees' Liberty Movement Association is a non-profit organization with chapters throughout the U.S. ALMA believes in the right of adult adoptees and the biological parents of adoptees to locate one another. It supports and assists biologically related people searching for each other. Call or write for membership information, newsletter, or chapter list.

International Concerns Committee for Children
911 Cypress Drive
Boulder, CO 80303
LD 303-494-8333
Monday–Friday   9 AM–4 PM

This organization provides information about ways to help homeless children, including foster parenting and adoption. It publishes the annual *Report on Foreign Adoption* (with frequent updates) containing current information on many aspects of adoption. It also maintains a listing service of children in urgent need of homes. In addition, it publishes a newsletter and provides information and counseling to adoptive families. Nominal cost for publications. Write or call for brochure. Leave a message and your call will be returned collect.

North American Council on Adoptable Children
1821 University Ave., Suite N-498
St. Paul, MN 55104
LD 612-644-3036
Monday–Friday   9 AM–5 PM

The council provides a wealth of information and support services to adoption agencies and parents. Call or write for publications.

Adoptive Families of America, Inc.
3333 Hwy. 100 North
Minneapolis, MN 55422
LD 612-535-4829

AFA is a private, nonprofit membership organization that provides problem-solving assistance and information to adoptive and prospective adoptive individuals and families. U.S. membership is $24 yearly and includes a subscription to *OURS Magazine*.

You can also contact the appropriate local government agency for adoption information. Check your telephone directory for your city or county's social services, family services, public welfare, child welfare, or social welfare department. Check the Yellow Pages under "Adoption."

AIDS and HIV

Good Samaritan Project Teen Hotline
Kansas City, MO
TF 800-234-TEEN (234-8336)
Monday–Saturday   4 PM–8 PM

Staffed by trained high school students, this hotline gives accurate information to teens and their parents.

San Francisco AIDS Foundation
25 Van Ness Ave.
San Francisco, CA 94103
TF 800-FOR-AIDS (800-367-2437)
LD (Tagalog) 415-864-5855 X 2087
LD (Spanish) 415-864-5855 X 2079
Monday–Friday   9 AM–9 P.M
Saturday and Sunday   11 AM–5 PM

The foundation promotes AIDS education and provides information and referrals to people with AIDS and their families. Support services provided in San Francisco area. Publications available.

National HIV and AIDS Information Service
TF 800-342-2437 (342-AIDS)
24 hours

The hotline can give you general information on HIV and AIDS and refer you to doctors, clinics, testing services, legal services, or counselors in your area. Spanish-speaking operators are available. Free brochures in a number of languages are available on request. For brochures in Spanish, call 800-344-SIDA; for others, call above number.

Alcohol and Drug Abuse

Al-Anon Family Groups
1372 Broadway
New York, NY 10018
TF 800-356-9996
Monday–Friday   8 AM–5 PM

Al-Anon is a worldwide fellowship for relatives and friends of alcoholics who "share their experience, strength and hope in order to solve their common problems and to help others do the same." There are over 25,000 Al-Anon groups, including 3,500 Alateen groups for teenagers. They publish numerous pamphlets, books, newsletters, and a magazine. Material is available in 24 languages as well as in Braille and on tape. Check your telephone directory for local listings or call above toll-free number for information.

Alcoholics Anonymous (AA)
P.O. Box 459, Grand Central Station
New York, NY 10163
LD 212-686-1100
Monday–Friday   9 AM–5 PM

AA is a voluntary worldwide fellowship of men and women who meet together to attain and maintain sobriety. There are no dues or fees for membership; the only requirement is a desire to stop drinking. There are over 87,000 groups and more than 1,790,000 members in 134 countries. Information on AA and chapter locations worldwide is available at the telephone number listed above. Check your telephone directory for local listings.

There are a growing number of alternative groups to AA. These groups emphasize personal responsibility and reject some of AA's views. SOS (Secular Organization for Sobriety), RR (Rational Recovery), and WFS (Women for Sobriety) are among the groups with increasing numbers of local chapters. Check your telephone directory or dial information.

Mothers Against Drunk Driving (MADD)
669 Airport Fwy., Suite 310
Hurst, TX 76053
LD 817-268-6233
FAX 817-268-6827

MADD's membership is made up of drunk-driving victims and concerned citizens. Its concerns are to speak on behalf of victims, to reform drunk-driving laws, and to educate the public. It assists victims with the legal process, conducts research, and sponsors workshops. Local chapters throughout the United States. Publications available. Write or call for program and membership information.

National Clearinghouse for Alcohol and Drug Information (NCADI)
P.O. Box 2345
Rockville,MD 20852
TF 800-729-6689
Monday–Friday   9AM–7 PM

NCADI provides a referral service, answering inquiries on alcohol- and drug-related subjects by telephone or mail. The clearinghouse also gathers and disseminates current information (including books, curriculum guides, directories, and posters) free of charge.

Phoenix House Foundation
164 W. 74th Street
New York, NY 10023
LD 212-595-5810
Monday–Friday   9AM–5 PM

Phoenix House is a multiservice drug abuse agency offering residential treatment in New York City and Southern California. It has numerous educational and treatment programs for youth and adults. Information and referrals are available on request.

Breastfeeding (SEE Infant Care)

Child Abuse

Clearinghouse on Child Abuse and Neglect Information
P.O. Box 1182
Washington, DC 20013
LD 703-821-2086
Monday–Friday   9 AM–5 PM

The clearinghouse provides information for professionals and concerned citizens interested in child maltreatment issues. A database of resources for professionals is available; the staff also performs searches for specific topics. Numerous publications, including bibliographies and research reviews, are available. Write or call for free catalog.

National Child Abuse Hotline
TF 800-422-4453
24 hours

Provides general information and referrals.

National Committee for Prevention of Child Abuse
332 S. Michigan Ave., Suite 950
Chicago, IL 60604-4357
LD 312-663-3520

NCPCA is a volunteer-based organization dedicated to reducing child abuse. It offers educational programs and materials and support and self-help groups for parents. There are numerous local chapters. Write or call for information and chapter list.

Parents Anonymous (PA)
7120 Franklin Ave.
Los Angeles, CA 90046
TF 800-421-0353
TF (California) 800-352-0386
Monday–Friday   9 AM–5 PM

Parents Anonymous has over 1,200 local chapters that provide support for parents who abuse or fear they may abuse their children. Parents Anonymous also publishes materials on child abuse; send SASE. Call toll-free number for information and crisis counseling.

Conflict Resolution

Children's Creative Response to Conflict (CCRC)
Box 271
Nyack, NY 10960
LD 914-358-4601
FAX 914-358-4924

CCRC's trained facilitators conduct workshops for students, teachers, and parents to learn cooperation and conflict-resolution skills. Teacher's handbook (in English or Spanish), newsletter, and other publications available. Write or call for brochure and list of local branches.

Consumer Services

Consumer Information Center
P.O. Box. 100
Pueblo, CO 81002
LD 719-948-3334

Numerous booklets on a variety of topics—careers, children, health, housing, money, and many others—are available. Booklets are free or in 50¢–$3.00 range. Write or call for catalog.

Consumer Product Safety Commission (CPSC)
5401 Westbard Ave.
Bethesda, MD 20207
LD 301-492-6580
Monday–Friday   9 AM–4:30 PM
TF (Automated machine) 800-638-2772
TTY for the deaf 800-492-8140

The CPSC is involved in the evaluation of the safety of products sold to the public. Commission staff members will answer questions and provide free printed materials on different aspects of consumer product safety, such as the safety of children's toys or household appliances. The commission does not answer questions from consumers on automobiles, cosmetics, drugs, prescriptions, warranties, advertising, repairs, or maintenance.

FDA Consumer Affairs Office
5600 Fishers Lane
Rockville, MD 20857
LD 301-443-5006
Monday–Friday   9 AM–5 PM

The Consumer Affairs offices provides information and referrals on food products, pharmaceutical drugs, and cosmetics.

Occupational Safety and Health Administration (OSHA)
200 Constitution Ave.
Washington, DC 20210
LD 202-523-8017
Monday–Friday   9 AM–5 PM

The OSHA Office of Information provides a referral service and basic information on job safety and the dangers posed by toxic substances in the workplace. There is no charge for pamphlets and booklets and a nominal charge for a catalog.

Disabled

Mainstream
1030 15th St., NW, Suite 1010
Washington, DC 20005
LD 202-898-1400 (Voice/TDD)
Monday–Friday   9 AM–5 PM

Mainstream provides information on affirmative action for the disabled and will make referrals to agencies or state offices. In Washington, D.C., and Dallas, Texas, Project LINK places workers with disabilities, free of charge. Workshops, publications, newsletter available. Write or call for information.

National Information Center for Children and Youth with Disabilities (NICHCY)
P.O. Box 1492
Washington, DC 20013
TF 800-999-5599
LD 703-893-6061
Monday–Friday   9 AM–5 PM

NICHCY is a national clearinghouse and referral source for parents of disabled children and professionals who work with them. Publications, including an informative newsletter and extensive resource list, provided free of charge.

Parents Helping Parents
535 Race St., Suite 220
San Jose, CA 95126
LD 408-288-5010

Parents Helping Parents is a support group for parents of children who are physically and/or mentally disabled. The group provides telephone counseling, and in-home visits if possible, information, and referrals to local agencies and support groups. Brochure available.

Drug Abuse (SEE Alcohol and Drug Abuse Prevention)

Environment

Conservation and Renewable Energy Inquiry and Referral Service (CAREIRS)
P.O. Box 8900
Silver Springs, MD 20907
TF 800-523-2929
TF (AK and HI) 800-233-3071

CAREIRS provides general and specific information on renewable energy technologies and energy conservation techniques for residential and commercial needs. CAREIRS offers more than 150 publications, fact sheets, bibliographies, and 500 computerized letter units free of charge.

Earthworks Press
1400 Shattuck Ave., Box 25
Berkeley, CA 94704
LD 415-841-5866

Earthworks publishes material for those concerned with protecting the environment. Check your local bookstore or write for such titles as *50 Simple Things You Can Do to Save the Earth* ($4.95), *30 Simple Energy Things You Can Do to Save the Earth* ($3.95), *The Recycler's Handbook* ($4.95), and *The Next Step: 50 More Things You Can Do to Save the Earth* ($5.95). Include $1.00 postage per book. Bulk rates available.

Family Planning

Planned Parenthood Federation of America
810 Seventh Ave.
New York, NY 10019
LD 212-541-7800

Most cities have a Planned Parenthood organization listed in the telephone directory. Planned Parenthood provides information, counseling, and medical services related to reproduction and sexual health to *anyone* who wants them. No one is denied because of age, social group, or inability to pay. Information can also be obtained through the national office, listed above.

Zero Population Growth
1400 16th St., NW, Suite 320
Washington, DC 20036
LD 202-332-2200
Monday–Friday   9 AM–5 PM

ZPG is a national, nonprofit membership organization that works to achieve a sustainable balance between the earth's population and its environment and resources. Teaching materials, numerous publications, and newsletter available. There is a charge for multiple copies.

Public Health Departments

Counties throughout the United States, regardless of size, have county health clinics that will provide low-cost family planning services. Some cities also have public health clinics. To locate them look up the city or county in the telephone directory, then check under headings such as:

Department of Health
Family Planning
Family Services
Health
Public Health Department
(City or County's name) Health (or Medical) Clinic

Fatherhood

The Fatherhood Project
c/o James Levine
330 7th Ave.
New York, NY 10001
LD 212-268-4846

"A national research, demonstration, and dissemination project designed to encourage wider options for male involvement in childrearing." Pamphlets available on various subjects related to families and work.

Gay and Lesbian Resources

National Federation of Parents FLAG
P.O. Box 27605
Washington, DC 27605
LD 202-638-4200

Parents FLAG (Parents and Friends of Lesbians and Gays) provides information and support for those who care about gay and lesbian individuals. Write or call for number of a parent contact in your area or check phone directory for regional offices. Publications available.

National Gay and Lesbian Task Force
1734 14th St. NW
Washington, DC 20009
LD 202-332-6483
Monday–Friday   9 AM–5 PM

The National Gay and Lesbian Task Force provides information and referrals on gay and lesbian issues and rights.

National Lesbian and Gay Lifeline
TF 800-LIFE-661 (800-543-3661)
6 PM–12 midnight

Counseling line provides support in various areas and referrals to groups such as gay and lesbian Alcoholics Anonymous.

Health Information

Alzheimer's Disease and Related Disorders Association
70 East Lake Street, Suite 600
Chicago, IL 60601
LD 312-853-3060

Supports family members of those affected by Alzheimer's disease and related disorders. Promotes research and education. Represents patients' continuing care needs to health-care agencies, government, business, and communities. Newsletter.

American Institute for Preventative Medicine
24450 Evergreen Rd., Suite 200
Southfield, MI 48075
LD 313-352-7666

For $2.00, the AIPM will send you a directory of toll-free numbers to call for advice and referrals on numerous health-related issues such as alcohol abuse or cancer.

Centers for Disease Control (CDC)
1600 Clifton Rd. NE
Atlanta, GA 30333
LD 404-639-3286
Monday–Friday   9 AM–5 PM

Inquiries from the public on topics such as preventative medicine, health education, immunization, and communicable diseases can be directed to the Office of Information at the CDC. The office will also answer questions on occupational safety and health issues, family planning, and public health problems such as lead-based paint and rodent control. Inquiries are answered directly or referred to an appropriate resource.

Family Caregivers of the Aging (see National Council on the Aging under "Seniors" heading)

Home Care Hotline
TF 800-847-8480
TF (NY) 800-422-4546

Sponsored by the National League of Nursing, the hotline provides information on the availability of home care resources and the location of accredited agencies.

Medicaid/Medicare
Department of Health and Human Services
Washington, DC
LD 202-245-7000
Monday–Friday   9 AM–5 PM

This consumer inquiry office answers questions on child health, social security, and all aspects of Medicaid and Medicare. The office also provides a referral service that includes listings of local welfare offices.

National Cancer Institute
9000 Rockville Pike, Rm. 340
Bethesda, MD 20892
TF 800-4-CANCER (422-6237)
HI 800-524-1234
Monday–Friday   9 AM–4:30 PM

Hotline counselors answer questions and give referrals to local doctors and support groups. For free brochures and other information, call or write.

National Health Information Center (NHIC)
P.O. Box 1133
Washington, DC 20013-1133
LD 301-565-4167
TF 800-336-4797 (referral database)

The NHIC is a central clearinghouse designed to refer consumers to health information resources. The clearinghouse has identified many groups and organizations that provide health information to the public. All health-related questions are welcomed, although the NHIC is unable to respond to questions requiring medical advice or diagnosis. A variety of publications is available.

TEL-MED
952 S. Mount Vernon
Colton, CA 92324
LD 714-825-6034
Monday–Friday   9 AM–5 PM

TEL-MED is a tape library of recorded medical messages. There are over 600 tapes, 3 to 7 minutes long, on different medical subjects. Titles include "Accidents in the Home," "Heart Attack," "Sleep," "Where Did I Come From, Mama?" and many others.

Infant Care

La Leche League International
P.O. Box 1209
Franklin Park, IL 60131-8209
LD 708-455-7730
LD 708-830-8087 (24 hour counseling hotline)

La Leche League provides advice and support for nursing mothers. Write for brochure or catalog of numerous publications. For local groups, check telephone directory or call the above number.

National Organization of Circumcision Information
Resource Centers (NOCIRC)
P.O. Box 2512
San Anselmo, CA 94979
LD 415-488-9883
Monday–Friday   9 AM–5 PM

NOCIRC is a nonprofit health resource center that provides medical and legal information of the subject of circumcision and female genital mutilation. It is against routine hospital circumcision of newborns. Pamphlets, newsletters, and referrals to physicians and lawyers are available. Send SASE with 2 oz. postage. Videotape for rent or purchase also available. Biannual international symposium.

Infertility

The American Fertility Society
2140 Eleventh Ave. South, Suite 200
Birmingham, AL 35205-2800
LD 205-933-8494
Monday–Friday   8:30 AM–4:30 PM

The American Fertility Society provides up-to-date information on all aspects of infertility, reproductive endocrinology, conception control, and reproductive biology. Booklets, pamphlets, selected reading list, resource lists, a medical journal, and postgraduate courses are available. Also available: ethical guidelines for new reproductive technologies, position paper on insurance for infertility services, and revised procedures for semen donation. Write or call for further information.

Resolve, Inc.
5 Water St.
Arlington, MA 02174
LD 617-643-2424
Monday–Friday   9 AM–4 PM

Resolve, a national nonprofit organization focusing on the problem of infertility, refers callers to chapters across the nation, provides fact sheets on male and female infertility, and publishes a newsletter and a directory of infertility resources. Phone counseling is also offered. There is a small charge for publications.

Marriage Enhancement

The Association for Couples in Marriage Enrichment
P.O. Box 10596
Winston-Salem, NC 26108
TF 800-634-8325
Monday–Friday   8:30 AM–5 PM

Established by David and Vera Mace, ACME is a nonprofit, nonsectarian organization that promotes activities to strengthen marriage. It offers weekend retreats, local chapter meetings, workshops, and conferences throughout the U.S. and Canada. Members may purchase books, tapes, and other materials at a discount. Write for brochures and resource list.

Worldwide Marriage Encounter
1908 E. Highland Ave., #A
San Bernardino, CA 92404
LD 714-881-3456
Monday–Friday   8:30 AM–5 PM

Although Marriage Encounter retreats are designed with Catholic couples in mind, spaces are also reserved for couples of other

faiths. Encounter weekends are offered in many parts of the country to enhance communication in marriage. A donation is asked but not required. Call or write for brochure and application.

Peace

Beyond War
222 High St.
Palo Alto, CA 94301-1097
LD 415-328-7756
FAX 415-328-7785

A nonprofit, nonpartisan educational foundation of volunteers in more than 40 states and 6 countries dedicated to "living in concert with the planet and with each other and contributing to the continuity of life."

The Friendship Force
Suite 575 South Tower
One CNN Center
Atlanta, GA 30303
LD 404-522-9490
FAX 404-688-6148

A nonprofit, nonpolitical organization designed to bring people of many countries together through international exchanges of "Citizen Ambassadors." There are over 100 chapters nationwide. Quarterly magazine is $5.00 per year.

Sane/Freeze: Campaign for Global Security
1819 H. St., NW, Suite 1000
Washington, DC 20006
LD 202-862-9740

Sane/Freeze seeks a comprehensive U.S.-Soviet nuclear test ban treaty, a bilateral halt to the nuclear arms race, deep reductions in nuclear weapons, and an end to U.S. military intervention abroad. Publications available.

20/20 Vision
695 Pleasant St., Suite 203
Amherst, MA 01002
TF 800-669-1782

For $20 a year, 20/20 Vision sends a monthly postcard with local and national military, environmental, and economic justice issues, including all information needed to write or call legislators. Local chapters are in more than 30 states.

Pregnancy (ALSO SEE Family Planning, Infant Care)

American College of Nurse-Midwives
1522 K St., NW, Suite 1000
Washington, DC 20005
LD 202-289-0171

Write or call the college for a directory of certified nurse-midwives in your area or to get information on accredited university-affiliated nurse-midwifery education programs.

Birthright
686 N. Broad St.
Woodbury, NJ 08096
TF 800-848-5683
Monday–Friday   9:30 AM–12:30 PM
                          7 PM–9 PM

Birthright is an assistance and counseling service for pregnant women. Services include telephone counseling in any aspect of pregnancy and referral to Birthright chapters and clinics throughout the U.S. and Canada. Birthright counsels against abortion and does not give out information concerning birth control.

National Abortion Rights Action League (NARAL)
1101 14th St., NW
Washington, DC 20005
LD 202-408-4600
Monday–Friday   9 AM–5:30 PM

A political organization concerned with family planning issues and dedicated to making abortion "safe, legal, and accessible" for all women. Affiliated with many state and local organizations. Newsletter and brochures available.

Teratogen Registry
TF 800-532-3749
Monday–Friday   9 AM–5 PM

When you're living for two, that means being twice as careful. Pregnant women and health-care professionals seeking the latest information about the effects of drugs and medications on unborn babies may use this free and confidential service. Pregnant women who have been exposed to suspected teratogens (substances harmful to the fetus) can also participate in a free follow-up program after birth.

Pregnancy Loss and Infant Death

Sudden Infant Death Syndrome Alliance
10500 Little Patuxent Pkwy., Suite 420
Columbia, MD 21044
TF 800-221-SIDS
LD 301-964-8000 (Maryland)

The National SIDS Alliance provides emotional support to families who have lost a child to sudden infant death syndrome. It has chapters throughout the U.S. and provides free crisis counseling, referrals, and information. It also supports research into SIDS. Free literature on request.

SHARE
St. Elizabeth's Hospital
211 South Third St.
Belleville, IL 62222

LD 618-234-2415
Monday–Friday   8 AM–4:30 PM

SHARE and its affiliate groups offer support for parents who have experienced miscarriage, stillbirth, or the death of a baby. They offer a manual on starting your own SHARE group, a national listing of groups and parent contacts, selected bibliography, resource manual on farewell rituals, children's books, and a newsletter. Check your local directory for groups, which may also be listed under "Sharing Parents," "Hoping and Sharing," "HAND," or a similar heading.

Rape

National Clearinghouse on Marital and Date Rape
2325 Oak
Berkeley, CA 94708
LD 415-548-1770
24 hours (message tape)

The clearinghouse provides information, referrals, seminars, and speakers covering numerous aspects of marital and date rape. There is a nominal charge for publications and consultation services. Calls returned collect.

Check your telephone directory for "Rape Crisis Center" or a similar listing to find the local crisis center nearest you; the service is available in almost all cities.

Runaways

National Runaway Switchboard
TF 800-621-3230

The National Runaway Switchboard provides toll-free telephone services for young people who have run away from home, those considering leaving home, and parents. The service helps young people define their problems, determines if an emergency exists, and refers callers to programs that provide free or low-cost help. Complete confidentiality is guaranteed. If the caller wants to reestablish communication with his or her family, a message can be taken for delivery within 24 hours.

Runaway and Homeless Youth Program
P.O. Box 1182
Washington, DC 20013

This program funds the preceding hotline and other services such as temporary shelters, counseling, and outreach programs. Write for brochure and other information.

Self-Help

National Self-Help Clearinghouse
25 W. 43rd St., Rm. 620

New York, NY 10036
LD 212-642-2944

The clearinghouse maintains a databank and referral service to provide information on thousands of self-help groups throughout the United States. They publish manuals and a newsletter on self-help. Write or call for information; send SASE if you want a list of local clearinghouse throughout the country.

The Consumer Information Center, part of the U.S. General Services Administration, offers numerous booklets on a variety of useful subjects. See "Consumer Services" section of Self-Help Resource Directory.

Seniors

Gray Panthers Project Fund
1424 16th St., NW, Suite 602
Washington, DC 20036
LD 202-387-3111
Monday–Friday   9 AM–5 PM

A multigenerational, intergenerational organization formed for education and advocacy, working to bring about an affordable, quality national health system protecting all ages. Works against all forms of discrimination to ensure economic justice. Promotes negotiation and other peaceful means of conflict resolution to replace war. Annual dues of $15.00 include quarterly newsletter.

National Council on the Aging
600 Maryland Ave., SW
Washington, DC 20024
LD 202-479-1200

Promotes the concerns of older Americans in many areas and develops methods and resources for meeting their needs. Consultations, speakers, meetings, programs, and many publications available. Family Caregivers of the Aging, part of the NCA, provides information and support for those caring for aging parents.

Sex Education and Sex Therapy

Sex Information and Education Council of the United States (SIECUS)
130 W. 42nd St., Suite 2500
New York, NY 10036
LD 212-819-9770

SIECUS is a nonprofit educational organization that promotes "healthy sexuality as an integral part of human life." It provides information or referrals to *anyone* who requests it. It maintains an extensive library and computer database. Publications include sex education guides for parents (in English and Spanish) and a comprehensive bimonthly journal, *SIECUS Report*. Memberships available.

American Association of Sex Educators, Counselors, and Therapists (AASECT)
435 N. Michigan Ave., Suite 1717
Chicago, IL 60611
LD 312-644-8557
FAX 312-644-0828
Monday–Friday   9 AM–5 PM

AASECT is a nonprofit educational association of physicians, counselors, social workers, educators, and so on. Its objectives are "to provide training and education in human sexuality and standards for sex education, counseling, and therapy programs." It publishes a newsletter and the *Journal of Sex Education and Therapy*.

Sexual Abuse

Parents United
P.O. Box 952
San Jose, CA 95108
LD 408-453-7616
TF 800-422-4453 (Crisis counseling)
Monday–Friday   9 AM–5 PM

Parents United and its related groups Daughters and Sons United and Adults Molested as Children United are self-help groups for all family members affected by incest and child sexual abuse. They provide referrals to treatment programs and self-help groups throughout the country. A number of informative publications are available, including a bimonthly newsletter. Write or call for literature list. The Giarretto Institute—at the above address and phone—is a separate nonprofit organization that provides treatment and therapist training.

Sexually Transmitted Diseases (ALSO SEE AIDS and HIV AND Health Information)

Herpes Resource Center
P.O. Box 13827
RTT Park, NC 27709
LD 919-361-8488
Monday–Friday   9 AM–7 PM

Provides referrals for people who are infected with herpes virus or who think that they may be. Confidential.

STD Hotline (American Social Health Association)
TF 800-227-8922
Monday–Friday   8 AM–11 PM

The STD Hotline provides information on all aspects of sexually transmitted diseases. It will describe symptoms but cannot provide diagnosis. It provides referrals for testing and further information. Confidentiality is maintained.

Single Parents

Parents Without Partners
8807 Colesville Rd.
Silver Springs, MD 20910
LD 301-588-9354
Monday–Friday   9 AM–5 PM

Parents Without Partners is a mutual support group for single parents and their children. It has numerous local groups with more than 115,000 members. It offers educational programs and literature, including *The Single Parent* magazine. It also offers low-cost recreation and member benefits such as insurance, credit card, auto club, discount travel, and scholarships for PWP children.

Single Mothers by Choice
P.O. Box 1642
New York, NY 10028
LD 212-988-0993

SMC is a national group that supports single mothers and single women who are considering motherhood. It offers workshops, support groups, a newsletter, a bibliography, and information about artificial insemination and adoption. Although based in New York City, it has members throughout the U.S. and Canada.

Suicide Prevention

The Samaritans
500 Commonwealth Ave.
Boston, MA 02215
LD 617-247-0220
24 hours

The Samaritans is a worldwide nonreligious organization of trained volunteers who talk with, and listen to, anyone who is suicidal, lonely, or depressed. The confidential service is dedicated to the prevention of suicide and the alleviation of loneliness and depression. Although the service is based in Massachusetts, staffers will help anyone in any area of the country. Brochures and pamphlets are available. Check your telephone directory white pages under "Suicide Prevention" for local listings.

Samariteen
LD 617-247-8050
3 PM–9 PM

Same as above but staffed by trained 16- to 19-year olds.

Surrogate Parenting

The Center for Surrogate Parenting, Inc.
8383 Wilshire Blvd., Suite 750
Beverly Hills, CA 90211

LD 213-655-1974 (collect accepted)
TF (CA only) 800-696-4664
Monday–Friday   9 AM–5 PM

The Center for Surrogate Parenting is a private organization that matches prospective parents and surrogates for a fee. Extensive screening is involved. Write or call for further information.

Terminal Illness

National Hospice Organization
1901 N. Moore St., Suite 901
Arlington, VA 22209
LD 703-243-5900
TF 800-658-8598 (Referrals only)
Monday–Friday   9 AM–5 PM

Hospices provide support and care for people in the final phase of terminal disease. There are over 1,700 hospice programs in the U.S., many of which are NHO members. The hospice "team" provides personalized care to minister to the physical, spiritual, and emotional needs of the patient and family. Call or write for literature and referral information.

Women

National Organization for Women (NOW)
1000 16th St., NW, Suite 700
Washington, DC 20036
LD 202-331-0066

NOW is an organization of women and men who support "full equality for women in truly equal partnership with men." NOW promotes social change through research, litigation, and political pressure. Newspaper and other publications available. Many cities have local chapters of NOW. Membership dues vary.

Work and Family

Families and Work Institute
330 7th Ave.
New York, NY 10001
LD 212-465-2044
FAX 212-465-8637

"A nonprofit research and planning organization committed to developing new approaches for balancing the changing needs of America's families with the continuing need for workplace productivity." The institute conducts research, disseminates information, and participates in planning and management training with businesses and organizations.

SEXUAL LIFE—TAKING CARE OF OUR BODIES*

❖ CHOOSING A METHOD OF BIRTH CONTROL

In order to be fully responsible in using birth control, a person must know the options available, how reliable these methods are, and the advantages and disadvantages (including possible side effects) of each method. Choosing the best form of birth control for yourself and your partner, especially if you have not been practicing contraception, is not easy. But knowing the facts about the methods gives you a solid basis from which to make decisions and more security once a decision is reached. If you need to choose a birth control method for yourself, remember that *the best method is the one you will use consistently.* When you are having intercourse, a condom left in a purse or wallet, a diaphragm in the bedside drawer, or a forgotten pill in its packet on the other side of town is not an effective means of birth control.

The following material is written in sufficient detail to serve as a reference guide for those who are seeking a birth control method or who have questions about their current method. Of course, a person with painful or unusual symptoms or with questions not dealt with here should seek professional advice from a physician or family planning clinic.

In the following text, where we discuss method effectiveness, *theoretical effectiveness* implies perfectly consistent and correct use; *user effectiveness* refers to *actual* use (and misuse) based on studies by health care organizations, medical practitioners, academic researchers, and pharmaceutical companies. User effectiveness is sometimes significantly lower than theoretical effectiveness because of factors that keep people from using a method properly or consistently. These factors may be inherent in the method or may be the result of a variety of influences on the user.

Hormonal Methods: The Pill and Implants

BIRTH CONTROL PILLS. "The pill" is actually a series of pills (20, 21, or 28 to a package) containing the synthetic hormones estrogen and progestin, which regulate egg production and the menstrual cycle. When taken for birth control they accomplish some or all of the following: inhibit ovulation, thicken cervical mucus (preventing sperm entry), inhibit implantation of the blastocyst, or promote early spontaneous abortion of the blastocyst. The pill produces basically the same chemical conditions that would exist in a woman's body if she were pregnant.

Oral contraceptives must be prescribed by a physician or family planning clinic. There are a number of brands available that contain varying amounts of hormones. Most commonly prescribed are the combination pills, which contain a fairly standard amount of

estrogen and differing doses of progestin according to the pill type. In the triphasic pill, the amount of progestin is altered during the cycle, purportedly to approximate the "normal" hormonal pattern. There is also a minipill containing progestin only, but it is generally prescribed only in cases where the woman should not take estrogen. It is considered slightly less effective than the combined pill, and it must be taken with precise and unfailing regularity to be effective.

With the 20- and 21-day pills, one pill is taken each day until they are all used. Two to five days later the woman should begin her menstrual flow. Commonly, it is quite light. (If the flow does not begin, the woman should start the next series of pills seven days after the end of the last series. If she repeatedly has no flow, she should talk to her health practitioner.) On the fifth day of her menstrual flow the woman should start the next series of pills.

The 28-day pills are taken continuously. Seven of the pills have no hormones. They are there simply to avoid breaks in the routine; some women prefer them because they find them easier to remember.

Along with the new contraceptive implants, the pill is considered the most effective birth control method available (except for sterilization) when used correctly. It is not effective when used carelessly. The pill must be taken every day, as close as possible to the same time each day. If one is missed, it should be taken as soon as the woman remembers and the next one taken on schedule. If two are missed, the method cannot be relied on and an additional form of contraception should be used for the rest of the cycle.

It should be remembered that the pill in no way protects against sexually transmitted diseases. Women on the pill should consider the additional use of a condom to reduce the risk of STDs.

Effectiveness. The pill is more than 99.5 percent effective theoretically. User effetiveness (the rate shown by actual studies) is between 95 and 98 percent.

Advantages. Pills are easy to take. They are dependable. No applications or interruptions are necessary before or during intercourse. Some women experience side effects that please them, such as more regular or reduced menstrual flow or enlarged breasts.

Possible Problems. There are many possible side effects, which may or may not bother the user, that can occur from taking the pill. Those most often reported are:

◆ change (usually decrease) in menstrual flow
◆ breast tenderness
◆ nausea or vomiting
◆ weight gain or loss

Some others are:

◆ spotty darkening of the skin
◆ nervousness, dizziness

---

* See Bryan Strong and Christine DeVault, *Understanding Our Sexuality* (2nd ed.), St. Paul, MN: West Publishing Co., 1988, for a more detailed discussion of birth control, sexually transmitted disease, and sexual health.

- loss of scalp hair
- change in appetite
- change (most commonly, decrease) in sex drive
- increase of body hair
- increase in vaginal discharge and yeast infections

These side effects can sometimes be eliminated by changing the prescription, but not always. Certain women react unfavorably to the pill because of existing health factors or extra sensitivity to female hormones. Women with heart or kidney diseases, asthma, high blood pressure, diabetes, epilepsy, gall bladder diseases, sickle-cell anemia, or those prone to migraine headaches or mental depression are usually considered poor candidates for the pill.

The pill also creates health risks, but to what extent is a matter of controversy. Women taking the pill stand a greater chance of problems with circulatory diseases, blood clotting, heart attack, and certain kinds of liver tumors. There is also an increased risk of contracting chlamydia. The health risks are low for the young (about half the number of risks encountered in childbirth), but they increase with age. The risk for smokers, women over 35, and those with certain other health disorders is about four times as great as childbirth. For women over 40 the risks are considered high. Current literature on the pill especially emphasizes the risks for women who smoke. Definite risks of cardiovascular complications and various forms of cancer exist due to the synergistic action of the ingredients of cigarettes and oral contraceptives.

A number of studies have linked pill use with certain types of cancer, but they have not been conclusive. The risk of some types of cancer, such as ovarian and endometrial, appears to be significantly *reduced* by pill use. On the other hand, a link between cervical cancer and long-term pill use has been suggested by several studies. Regular Pap smears are recommended as an excellent defense against cervical cancer, for pill users and nonusers alike.

Certain other factors may need to be taken into account in determining if oral contraception is appropriate. Young girls who have not matured physically may have their development slowed by early pill use. Nursing mothers cannot use pills containing estrogen because the hormone inhibits milk production. Some lactating women use the minipill successfully.

Millions of women (approximately 10 million in the U.S.) use the pill with moderate to high degrees of satisfaction. For many women, if personal health or family history does not contraindicate it, oral contraception is both effective and safe.

IMPLANTS. In December of 1990, the FDA approved a new contraceptive—thin, matchstick-sized capsules containing progestin that are implanted under a woman's skin. Over a period of up to five years, the hormone is slowly released. When the implants are removed, fertility is restored. A set of soft tubes is surgically implanted under the skin of the upper arm in a simple doctor's-office procedure with local anesthesia. Once implanted, the capsules are not visible but may be felt under the skin. The implants, under the tradename Norplant, are currently on the market in more than fourteen countries. The cost may run as high as several hundred dollars, but it is probably less expensive than a five-year supply of birth control pills.

Effectiveness. Although Norplant has not been observed or tested to the degree that other contraceptives have, initial reports indicate a failure rate one-tenth to one-twentieth that of the pill. It may be the most effective contraceptive ever marketed.

Advantages. Convenience is clearly a big advantage of the implant. Once the implant is in, there's nothing to remember, buy, do, or take care of.

Possible Problems. The chief side effect, experienced by about half of implant users, is a change in the pattern of menstrual bleeding, such as lengthened periods or spotting between periods. Norplant should not be used by women with acute liver disease, breast cancer, blood clots, or unexplained vaginal bleeding. Possible long-term negative effects are not known at this time.

Barrier Methods: Condom, Diaphragm, Cervical Cap, Sponge, and Women's Condom

Barrier methods are designed to keep sperm and egg from getting together. Barrier methods available to women are the diaphragm, the cervical cap, the contraceptive sponge (which also contains a sperm-killing chemical) and the women's condom. The barrier device used by men is the condom. The effectiveness of all barrier methods is increased by use with spermicides (sperm-killing chemicals).

CONDOMS. A condom is a thin sheath of rubber (or processed sheep's intestine) that fits over the erect penis and thus prevents semen from being transmitted. Condoms are available in a variety of sizes, shapes, and colors. Some are lubricated and some are treated with spermicides. They are easily obtainable from drug stores, and most kinds are relatively inexpensive. Condoms are the third most widely used form of birth control in the United States. In 1980, it was estimated that they were used by 40 million couples throughout the world.

Condoms not only provide effective contraception when properly used, they also guard against the transmission of a number of sexually transmitted diseases such as chlamydia, gonorrhea, genital herpes, and AIDS *if* they are made of latex rather than sheep's intestine. Due to increased publicity regarding the transmissibility of the AIDS virus (HIV), both heterosexuals and gay men are increasingly using latex condoms as prophylactic (disease-preventing) devices. Condom use does not guarantee *total* safety from STDs, however, as sexual partners may also transmit certain diseases by hand, mouth, and external genitalia other than the penis; also, condoms may occasionally tear or leak.

Today an estimated 40 percent of condoms are purchased by women, and condom advertising and packaging increasingly reflect this trend. Even if a women regularly uses another form of birth control, such as the pill or IUD, she may want to have the added protection provided by a condom, especially if it has been treated with spermicide (which provides further protection against disease organisms). Contraceptive aerosol foam and contraceptive film (a thin, translucent square of tissue that dissolves into a gel) are the most convenient spermicidal preparations to use with condoms.

Effectiveness. Condoms are 98 to 99 percent effective theoretically. User effectiveness is 90 percent. Failures sometimes occur from mishandling the condom, but they are usually the result of not putting it on until after some semen has leaked into the vagina, or simply not putting it on at all.

Advantages. Condoms are easy to obtain. They are easy for men and women to carry in a wallet or purse. They help protect against STDs, including herpes and HIV.

Possible Problems. The chief drawback to a condom is that it must be put on after the man has been aroused but before he enters his partner. This interruption is the major reason for users neglecting or "forgetting" to put them on. Some men complain that sensation is dulled, and (very rarely) cases of allergy to rubber are reported. Both problems can be remedied by the use of animal tissue condoms. These are thinner and conduct heat better. *Animal tissue condoms, however, should not be used for prophylaxis; viral STDs such as genital herpes and HIV may easily penetrate them.* The condom user must take care to hold the sheath at the base of his penis when he withdraws, in order to avoid leakage.

DIAPHRAGM. The diaphragm is a rubber cup with a flexible rim. It is placed in the vagina, blocking the cervix, to prevent sperm from entering the uterus and fallopian tubes. Different women require different sizes, and a woman may change sizes, especially after a pregnancy; the size must be determined by an experienced practitioner. Diaphragms are available by prescription from doctors and family planning clinics. Somewhat effective by itself, the diaphragm is highly effective when used with a spermicidal cream or jelly. (Creams and jellies are considered more effective than foam for use with a diaphragm.) Diaphragm users should be sure to use an adequate amount of spermicide and to follow their practitioner's instructions with care.

The diaphragm can be put in place up to two hours before intercourse. It should be left in place six to eight hours afterward. A woman should not dislodge it or douche before it is time to remove it. If intercourse is repeated within six hours, the diaphragm should be left in place but more chemical contraceptive should be inserted with an applicator. However, a diaphragm should not be left in place longer than 24 hours.

Diaphragms need to be replaced about once a year because the rubber deteriorates, losing elasticity and increasing the chance of splitting. Any change in the way the diaphragm feels, as well as any dramatic gain or loss of weight, calls for a visit to doctor or clinic to check the fit.

Effectiveness. When properly used, *with spermicide*, diaphragms are 98 percent effective. Numerous studies of diaphragm effectiveness have yielded varying results. Typical user effectiveness (actual statistical effectiveness) is in the 81 to 83 percent range. The lowest effectiveness ratings appear among young diaphragm users and inconsistent users.

Advantages. The diaphragm can be placed well before the time of intercourse. For most women, there are few health problems associated with its use. It helps protect against diseases of the cervix and PID.

Possible Problems. Some women dislike handling or placing diaphragms, or the mess or smell of the chemical contraceptives used with them. Some men complain of rubbing or other discomfort caused by the diaphragm. Occasionally a woman is allergic to rubber. Some women become more prone to urinary tract infections. As there is a small risk of toxic shock syndrome (TSS) associated with its use, a woman should not use a diaphragm under the following conditions:

◆ during menstruation or other bleeding
◆ following childbirth (for several months)
◆ during abnormal vaginal discharge
◆ if she has had TSS or if *Staphylococcus aureus* bacteria are present

She should also:

◆ never wear the diaphragm for more than 24 hours.
◆ learn to watch for the warning signs of TSS
   Fever (101° or higher)
   Diarrhea
   Vomiting
   Muscle aches
   Sunburnlike rash

CERVICAL CAP. The cervical cap is a small rubber barrier device that fits snugly over the cervix; it can be filled with spermicidal cream or jelly. Cervical caps come in different sizes and shapes; proper fit is extremely important, and not everyone can be fitted. Fitting must be done by a physician or at a health clinic.

Effectiveness. There is a limited amount of research data in this country regarding the cervical cap's effectiveness. Reported user effectiveness ranges from 73 to 92 percent.

Advantages. The cervical cap may be more comfortable and convenient than the diaphragm for some women. It does not interfere with the body physically or hormonally.

Possible Problems. Some users are bothered by an odor that develops from the interaction of the cap's rubber and either vaginal secretions or the spermicide. There is some concern that the cap may contribute to erosion of the cervix. If a woman's partner's penis touches the rim of the cap, it can become displaced during intercourse. Theoretically the same risk of TSS exists for the cervical cap as for the diaphragm. The precautions discussed in the section on diaphragms also apply.

CONTRACEPTIVE SPONGE. In 1983 the FDA approved the contraceptive sponge for over-the-counter sales. When inserted into the vagina, the polyurethane sponge blocks the opening of cervix and releases a spermicide. It must be left in place for at least six hours (or as long as 24 hours) following intercourse and then disposed of.

Effectiveness. The sponge has a theoretical effectiveness rate of about 87 to 90 percent. It has a user-effectiveness rate of about 83 percent. The lowest observed effectiveness rate is 72 percent. Higher failure rates seem to appear among women who have previously given birth.

Advantages. The sponge's advantages include convenience, safety, effectiveness, and possible prevention of some sexually transmitted diseases. It is easy to obtain.

Possible Problems. No long-term studies of the sponge's safety have been completed. It is recommended that the sponge *not* be used during menstruation because of the risk of toxic shock syndrome at that time. The precautions discussed in the section on diaphragms also apply to the contraceptive sponge. Some women report an unpleasant odor from the sponge; some report allergic reactions; others report inadvertently expelling the sponge during a bowel movement.

WOMEN'S CONDOM. The women's condom is a disposable, soft, loose-fitting polyurethane sheath with a diaphragm-like ring at each end. One ring is inside the sheath and is used to insert and anchor the condom next to the cervix. The larger outer ring remains outside the vagina and acts as a barrier, protecting the vulva and the base of the penis.

Because of the newness of this product, its effectiveness is not known at this time, although clinical tests have indicated that it is less likely to leak than men's latex condoms. In laboratory trials, the women's condom was not permeated by HIV or cytomegalovirus, indicating that it may be a promising alternative for both contraception and the control of STDs.

Spermicides

A spermicide is a substance that is toxic to sperm. The most commonly used spermicide in products sold in the United States is the chemical nonoxynol-9.

Spermicidal preparations are available in a variety of forms: foam, film, jelly, cream, tablets, and suppositories. Contraceptive sponges and some condoms are also treated with spermicides. Spermicidal preparations are considered most effective when used in combination with a barrier method.

A further benefit of spermicides is that they significantly reduce STD risk. Nonoxynol-9 has been demonstrated to have a toxic effect on a number of disease agents, including HIV. Of course, use of spermicides, although it lowers the risk of contracting an STD, does not entirely eliminate it.

CONTRACEPTIVE FOAM. Contraceptive foam is a chemical spermicide sold in aerosol containers. Methods of application vary with each brand, but usually foam is released deep in the vagina either directly from the container or with an applicator. It forms a barrier to the uterus and inactivates sperm in the vagina. It is most effective if inserted no more than half an hour before intercourse. Shaking the container before applying the foam increases its foaminess so that it spreads farther. The foam begins to go flat after about 30 minutes. It must be reapplied when intercourse is repeated.

Effectiveness. Foam has a theoretical effectiveness rate of 98.5 percent. User failure brings its effectiveness down to as low as 71 percent. User failures tend to come from not applying the foam every single time the couple has intercourse, from relying on foam inserted hours before intercourse, or from relying on foam placed hurriedly or not placed deep enough. If used properly and consistently, however, it is quite reliable. Used with a condom, it is highly effective.

Advantages. There are almost no medical problems associated with the use of foam. Foam helps provide protection against certain sexually transmitted diseases.

Possible Problems. Some women dislike applying foam. Some complain of messiness, leakage, odors, or stinging sensations. Occasionally, a woman or man may have an allergic reaction to it.

CONTRACEPTIVE FILM. Contraceptive film is a relatively new spermicidal preparation. It is sold in packets of small (2" square), translucent tissues. This thin tissue contains the spermicide nonoxynol-9; it dissolves into a sticky gel when inserted into the vagina. It should be inserted directly over the cervix, not less than five minutes or more than one-and-a-half hours before intercourse. It remains effective for two hours after insertion. Contraceptive film works effectively in conjunction with the condom.

Effectiveness. Extensive research has not been done on the effectiveness of film, due to its relative newness on the market. The highest effectiveness rates reported are from 82 to 90 percent. Of course, proper and consistent use with a condom highly increases the effectiveness.

Advantages. Film is easy to use for many women. It is easily obtained from a drugstore. It is easy to carry in a purse, wallet, or pocket.

Possible Problems. Some women may not like inserting the film into the vagina. Some women may be allergic to it. Increased vaginal discharge and temporary pain while urinating after using contraceptive film have been reported.

CREAMS AND JELLIES. These chemical spermicides come in tubes and are inserted with applicators or placed inside diaphragms or cervical caps. They can be bought without prescription at most drugstores. They work in a manner similar to foams but are considered less effective when used alone. Like foam, jellies and creams seem to provide some protection against venereal diseases. This factor makes their use with a diaphragm even more attractive.

SUPPOSITORIES AND TABLETS. These chemical spermicides are inserted into the vagina before intercourse. Body heat and fluids dissolve the ingredients, which will inactivate sperm in the vagina after ejaculation. They must be inserted early enough to dissolve completely before intercourse.

Effectiveness. Reports on these methods vary widely. It is suspected that the variations are connected with each user's technique of application. Directions for use that come with these contraceptives are not always clear. Jellies, creams, vaginal tablets, and suppositories should be used in conjunction with a barrier method for maximum effectiveness.

Advantages. The methods are simple and easily obtainable, with virtually no medical problems. They *help* protect against STDs, including chlamydia, trichomonas, gonorrhea, genital herpes, and HIV.

Possible Problems. Some people have allergic reactions to the spermicides. Some women dislike the messiness, smells, or necessity of touching their own genitalia. Others experience irritation or inflammation, especially if they use the method frequently. A few women lack the vaginal lubrication to dissolve the tablets in a reasonable amount of time. And a few women complain of having anxiety about the method's effectiveness during intercourse.

The IUD (Intrauterine Device)

The IUD is a tiny plastic or metal device that is inserted into the uterus through the cervical opening. The particular type of device determines how long it may be left in place—one year to indefinitely.

Although most IUDs have been withdrawn from the U.S. market because of the proliferation of lawsuits against their manufacturers in recent years, they are still considered a major birth control method. There clearly are some risks involved with the IUD, especially for certain women. Nevertheless, it remains the birth control method of about 70 million women throughout the world, including 40–45 million women in China.

Strictly speaking, the IUD is not a contraceptive. It is a birth control device that works principally by preventing the blastocyst from implanting in the uterine wall or by disrupting a blastocyst that has already implanted. The IUD may also serve to immobilize sperm and (in the case of progestin-bearing IUDs) induce thickened cervical mucus. IUDs must be inserted and removed by a trained practitioner.

Effectiveness. IUDS are 97 to 99 percent effective theoretically. User effectiveness is 90 to 96 percent.

Advantages. Once inserted, IUDs require little care. They don't interfere with spontaneity during intercourse.

Possible Problems. Insertion is often painful. Heavy cramping usually follows and sometimes persists. Menstrual flow usually increases. Up to one-third of users, especially women who have never been pregnant, expel the device within the first year. This usually happens during menstruation. The IUD can be reinserted, however, and many women retain it the second time.

The IUD is associated with increased risk of pelvic inflammatory disease (PID). Because of the risk of sterility induced by PID, many physicians recommend that women planning to have children use alternative methods. Women who have had PID or who have multiple sex partners should be aware that an IUD will place them at significantly greater risk of PID, STDs, and other infections.

The IUD cannot be inserted in some women due to unusual uterine shape or position. Until recently the IUD was considered difficult to insert and less effective for teenage girls. But newer, smaller IUDs have been found to provide good protection even for young teenagers.

Occasionally the device perforates the cervix. This usually happens at the time of insertion, if it happens at all. Removal sometimes requires surgery.

Sometimes pregnancy occurs and is complicated by the presence of the IUD. If the IUD is not removed, there is a 50 percent chance of spontaneous abortion; if it is removed, the chance is 25 percent. Furthermore, spontaneous abortions that occur when an IUD is left in place are likely to be septic (infection-bearing) and possibly life-threatening.

Fertility Awareness Methods

Fertility awareness methods of contraception require substantial education, training, and planning. They are based on a woman's knowledge of her body's reproductive cycle. These methods require high motivation and self-control; they are not for everyone.

Fertility awareness is also referred to as "natural family planning." Some people make the following distinction between the two. With fertility awareness, the couple may use an alternate method (such as diaphragm with jelly or condom with foam) during the fertile part of the woman's cycle. Natural family planning does not include the use of any contraceptive device and is thus considered more "natural"; it is approved by the Roman Catholic church.

Fertility awareness methods include the rhythm (calendar) method, the basal body temperature (BBT) method, the mucus (also called the Billings or ovulation) method, and the symptothermal method, which combines the latter two. These methods are not recommended for women who have irregular menstrual cycles, including postpartum and lactating mothers.

All women can benefit from learning to recognize their fertility signs. It is useful to know when the time of greatest likelihood of pregnancy occurs, both for women who wish to avoid pregnancy and for those who want to become pregnant.

BASAL BODY TEMPERATURE (BBT) METHOD. A woman's temperature tends to be slightly lower during menstruation and for about a week afterward. Just before ovulation it dips; then rises sharply (one-half to one whole degree) following ovulation. It stays high until just before the next menstruation period.

A woman practicing this method must record her temperature every morning upon waking for 6 to 12 months to have an accurate idea of her temperature pattern. When she is quite sure she recognizes the rise in temperature and can predict about when in her cycle it will happen, she can begin using the method. She will abstain from intercourse or use an alternate contraceptive method for three to four days before the expected risk and for four days after it has taken place. If she limits intercourse to only the "safe" time after her temperature has risen, the method is more effective. The method requires high motivation and control. For greater accuracy it may be combined with the mucus method described in the next section.

MUCUS METHOD (BILLINGS OR OVULATION METHOD). In many women, there is a noticeable change in the appearance and character of cervical mucus prior to ovulation. After menstruation, most women experience a moderate discharge of cloudy, yellowish or white mucus. Then, for a day or two, a clear, slippery mucus is secreted. Ovulation occurs immediately after the clear, slippery mucus secretions. The pre-ovulatory mucus is elastic in consistency, rather like raw egg white, and a drop can be stretched between two fingers into a thin strand (at least 6 cm.). This elasticity is called spinnbarkeit. Following ovulation, the amount of discharge decreases markedly. The four days before and the four days after these secretions are considered the unsafe days. An alternate contraceptive method may be used during this time. The method requires training and high motivation to be successful. Clinics are offered in some cities. (For more information, check with your local family planning or women's health clinic.) This method may be combined with the BBT method for greater effectiveness.

SYMPTO-THERMAL METHOD. When the BBT and mucus methods are used together, it is called the sympto-thermal method. Additional signs that may be useful in determining ovulation are midcycle pain in the lower abdomen on either side (mittelschmerz) and a very slight discharge of blood from the cervix ("spotting"). Women who wish to rely on fertility awareness methods of contraception should enroll in a class at a clinic. Learning to read one's own unique fertility signs is a complex process requiring one-to-one counseling and close monitoring.

CALENDAR METHOD. This method is based on calculating safe days based on the range of a woman's longest and shortest menstrual cycles. It is not practical or safe for women with irregular cycles. For women with regular cycles, the calendar method is reasonably effective because the period of time when an ovum is receptive to fertilization is only about 24 hours. As sperm generally live two to four days, the maximum period of time in which fertilization could be expected to occur may be calculated with the assistance of a calendar.

Ovulation generally occurs 14 (plus or minus two) days before a woman's menstrual period. Taking this into account, and charting her menstrual cycles for a minimum of eight months to determine the longest and shortest cycles, a woman can determine her expected fertile period.

During the fertile period, a woman must abstain from sexual intercourse or use an alternative method of contraception. A woman using this method must be meticulous in her calculations, keep her calendar up to date, and be able to maintain an awareness of what day it is. Statistically only about one-third of all women have cycles regular enough to satisfactorily employ this method.

EFFECTIVENESS OF FERTILITY AWARENESS METHODS. It is problematic to calculate the effectiveness of fertility awareness methods. With this type of contraception, in a sense, the user is the method; the method's success or failure rests largely on the woman's diligence. For those who have used fertility awareness with unfailing dedication, it has been demonstrated to be as much as 99 percent effective. Many studies, however, show fairly high failure rates. Some researchers believe that this is due to risk-taking during the fertile phase.

Additionally, there is always some difficulty in predicting ovulation with pinpoint accuracy; thus, there is a better chance of pregnancy as a result of intercourse prior to ovulation than as a result of intercourse following it. Furthermore, there is evidence that sperm may survive as long as five days. This suggests that unprotected intercourse any time prior to ovulation may be risky. All fertility awareness methods increase in effectiveness if intercourse is unprotected only during the safe period *following* ovulation.

Advantages. Fertility awareness (or natural family planning) methods are acceptable to most religious groups. They are free and pose no health risks. If a woman wishes to become pregnant, awareness of her own fertility cycles is very useful.

Possible Problems. These methods are not suitable for women with irregular menstrual cycles or couples who are not highly motivated to use them. Some couple who practice abstinence during fertile periods may begin to take risks out of frustration. These couples may benefit by exploring other forms of sexual expression; counseling can help.

Sterilization

Among married couples in the United States, sterilization (of one or both partners) is the most popular form of birth control. Approximately 27 percent of couples have chosen to be sterilized.

STERILIZATION FOR WOMEN. In 1984, the most recent year for which figures are available, about 64 percent of sterilizations were done on women. Most female sterilizations are tubal ligations, "tying the tubes." The two most common operations are laparoscopy and minilaparotomy. Less commonly performed types of sterilization for women are culpotomy, culdoscopy, and hysterectomy. Generally, this surgery is not reversible; only women who are completely certain that they want no (or no more) children should choose this method.

Sterilization for women is quite expensive. Surgeon, anesthesiologist, and hospital fees are substantial. The newer procedures in which the woman returns home on the same day have the advantage of being one-half to one-third as expensive as abdominal surgery, but still may cost hundreds or even thousands of dollars. Many health insurance policies will cover all or part of the cost of sterilization for both men and women. In some states, Medicaid pays for certain patients.

LAPAROSCOPY. Sterilization by laparoscopy usually requires a day or less in the hospital or clinic. General anesthesia is usually recommended. The woman's abdomen is inflated with gas to make the organs more visible. The surgeon inserts a rodlike instrument with a viewing lens (the laparoscope) through a small incision at the edge of the navel and locates the fallopian tubes (the ducts between the ovaries and the uterus). Through this incision or a second one, the surgeon inserts another instrument that closes the tubes. The tubes are usually closed by electrocauterization. Special small forceps that carry an electric current clamp the tubes and cauterize (burn) them. The tubes may also be closed off or blocked with tiny rings, clips, or plugs. There is a recovery period of several days to a week. During this time the women will experience some tenderness and some bleeding from the vagina. Rest is important.

MINILAPAROTOMY. Local or general anesthesia is used with minilaparotomy. A small incision is made in the lower abdomen, through which the fallopian tubes are brought into view. They are then tied off or sealed with electric current, clips, or rings. Recovery is the same as with laparoscopy.

CULPOTOMY AND CULDOSCOPY. In these operations, an incision is made at the back of the vagina. In culpotomy, the tubes are viewed through the incision and then tied or otherwise blocked, and cut. Culdoscopy is the same procedure but uses a viewing instrument called a culdoscope. The advantage of these procedures is that they leave no visible scars. They require more expertise on the part of the surgeon, however, and have higher complication rates than laparoscopy and minilaparotomy.

HYSTERECTOMY. Hysterectomy is not performed for sterilization except under special circumstances. Since it involves removal of the entire uterus, it is both riskier and more costly than other methods. It involves greater recovery time and, for some women, is potentially more difficult psychologically. It may be appropriate for women who have a uterine disease or other problem that is likely to require a future hysterectomy anyway.

Effectiveness of Sterilization for Women. Surgical contraception is essentially 100 percent effective. In *extremely* rare instances (less than ¼ of a percent), probably due to improperly done surgery, a tube may reopen or grow back together, allowing an egg to pass through.

Once sterilization is done, no other method of birth control will ever be necessary. (A woman who risks exposure to STDs, however, may wish to protect herself with a spermicide, condom, or women's condom.)

Sterilization does not reduce or change a woman's feminine characteristics. It is not the same as menopause and does not hasten the approach of menopause, as some people believe. A woman still has her menstrual periods until whatever age menopause naturally occurs for her. Her ovaries, uterus (except in the case of hysterectomy), and hormonal system have not been changed. The only difference is that sperm cannot now reach her eggs. (The eggs, which are released every month as before, are reabsorbed by the body.) Sexual enjoyment is not diminished. In fact, a high percentage of women report that they feel more relaxed during intercourse since anxiety about pregnancy has been eliminated. There do not seem to be any harmful side effects associated with female sterilization.

Sterilization should be considered irreversible. The most recently developed methods of ligation using clips, rings, or plugs may be more reversible than those employing electrocauterization, but the overall success rate for reversals is quite low; it is also very costly and not covered by most insurance plans. Only between 15 and 25 percent of women who seek to have their tubal ligations reversed succeed in conceiving.

The tubal ligation itself is a relatively safe procedure. With electrocauterization, there is a chance that other tissues in the abdomen may be damaged, especially if the surgeon is not highly skilled. These "bowel burns" may require further surgery but often heal on their own. Anesthesia complications are the most serious risk. The risk of death is quite low—four deaths per 100,000 operations. Infection is also a possibility; it may be treated with antibiotics.

STERILIZATION FOR MEN. A vasectomy is a minor surgical procedure that can be done in a doctor's office under local anethesia. It takes approximately half an hour. In this procedure, the physician makes a small incision (or two incisions) in the skin of the scrotum. Through the incision, each vas deferens (sperm-carrying tube) is lifted, cut, tied, and often cauterized with electricity. After a brief rest, the man is able to walk out of the office; complete recuperation takes only a few days.

A man may retain some viable sperm in his system for days or weeks following a vasectomy. He should use other birth control until his semen has been checked, about eight weeks following the operation.

Effectiveness. Vasectomies are 99.85 percent effective. In very rare cases, the ends of a vas deferens may rejoin; this is virtually impossible if the operation is correctly performed.

Advantages. No birth control method will ever be needed again, unless the man wishes to use a condom to prevent getting or spreading an STD. Sexual enjoyment will not be diminished; he will still have erections and orgasms and ejaculate semen. Vasectomy is relatively inexpensive as surgical procedures go.

Possible Problems. Compared to other birth control methods, the complication rates for vasectomy are very low. Most problems occur when proper antiseptic measures are not taken during the operation or when the man exercises too strenuously in the few days after it. Hematomas (bleeding under the skin) and granulomas (clumps of sperm) can be treated with ice packs and rest. Epididymitis (inflammation of the tiny tubes that connect the testicle and vas deferens) can be treated with heat and scrotal support.

One-half to two-thirds of men develop sperm antibodies following vasectomy. The body produces these antibodies in response to the presence of sperm that have been absorbed by body tissues. There is no physiological evidence that this poses any threat to health.

A few men, those who equate fertility with virility and potency, may experience psychological problems following vasectomy. However, according to the authors of *Contraceptive Technology* (Hatcher et al., 1986), "Most well-adjusted males will experience no adverse psychological changes following elective sterilization, if they understand what to expect . . . and are given an opportunity to express their fears and have their questions answered. . . ."

Among men who seek to have their vasectomies reversed, about 50 percent experience success. The cost is high and not covered by insurance in many cases. Vasectomy should be considered permanent.

Unreliable Methods of Contraception

COITUS INTERRUPTUS (WITHDRAWAL).   The oldest form of contraception known is coitus interruptus, which involves the withdrawal of the penis from the vagina prior to ejaculation. This method is widely used throughout the world today and can be considered somewhat successful for *some* people. Success may depend on technique, on combination with rhythm methods, or on physical characteristics of the partners (such as the tendency toward infertility in one or both partners).

A problem with this method is its riskiness. Secretions from the man's Cowper's glands, urethra, or prostate, which sometimes seep into the vagina before ejaculation, can carry thousands of healthy sperm. Also, the first few drops of ejaculate carry most of the sperm. If the man is slow to withdraw or allows any ejaculate to spill into (or near the opening of) the vagina, the woman may get pregnant. The highest observed effective rate using coitus interruptus is 84 percent. The actual user effectiveness rate is 77 percent. Although it is generally considered an unreliable method of birth control, coitus interruptus is certainly better than nothing.

DOUCHING.   To douche, a woman flushes the vagina with liquid. As a contraceptive method it is faulty because after the ejaculation, douching is already too late. By the time a woman can douche, the sperm may already be swimming through the cervix into the uterus. The douche liquid may even push the sperm into the cervix. Douching with any liquid, especially if done often, tends to upset the normal chemical balance in the vagina and may cause irritation or infection. There is also evidence that frequent douching can result in ectopic pregnancy.

LACTATION.   When a woman, after giving birth, breastfeeds her child, she may not begin to ovulate as long as she continues to nourish her child exclusively by breastfeeding. However, although some women do not ovulate while lactating, others do. Cycles may begin immediately after delivery or in a few months. The woman never knows when she will begin to be fertile. This is considered a method in some other countries, but the success ratings are extremely low.

MYTHICAL METHODS OF CONTRACEPTION.   There are many myths among young and old about contraception. The young hear many rumors. Some of the old, who should know better, still believe misconceptions hatched in "the old days" when contraceptive devices were not as easily obtained or as dependable as they are today. (The dependability of condoms, always the most easily purchased device, was greatly improved when the product came under the supervision of the Federal Trade Commission.) Today, when satisfactory methods are so easy to obtain, it is senseless for anyone to use risky ones.

Widely known methods that are *totally* useless include:

1. Standing up during or after intercourse (sperm have no problem swimming "upstream").
2. Taking a friend's pill the day of, or the day after, intercourse (doesn't work—may even be dangerous).
3. Only having intercourse occasionally (it is when, not how often, that makes a difference; once is enough if the woman is fertile at that time).
4. Using plastic wrap or plastic bags for condoms (too loose, undependable, and unsanitary).

❖ ABORTION

Most people, when they hear the word "abortion," think of a medical procedure or operation to end an unwanted pregnancy. But the word carries a wider range of meanings than most people realize.

Anytime a growing embryo or fetus is expelled from the uterus, an abortion has taken place. Such expulsion can happen naturally, or it can be made to happen in one of several ways. Many abortions happen spontaneously because the woman wears an IUD, because she suffers physical shock, because the fetus is not properly developed, or, more commonly, because physical conditions within the uterus break down and end the development of the embryo or fetus. Approximately one-third of all abortions reported in a year are spontaneous ("miscarriages"). Of the approximately 6 million pregnancies that occur in this country each year, more than half are unintentional. Of these, almost half are terminated by induced abortions.

Abortions can be induced in several ways. Surgical methods are most common, but the use of medications to induce abortion is also possible. Methods for early abortions (those performed in the first three months) differ from late abortions (those performed after the third month).

To facilitate the dilation of the cervix, many physicians insert a laminaria, a small stick of seaweed, into the cervical opening. The laminaria expands gradually, dilating the cervix gently in the process. It must be placed at least six hours prior to the abortion.

Surgical Methods of Abortion

Surgical methods include vacuum aspiration, dilation and curettage (D & C), dilation and evacuation (D & E), and hysterotomy, as well as several other methods.

VACUUM ASPIRATION (FIRST TRIMESTER METHOD). This method is performed under local anesthesia. The cervix is dilated with a series of graduated rods (laminaria may have been used to begin dilation). Then a small tube attached to a vacuum is inserted through the cervix. The uterus is gently vacuumed, removing the fetus, placenta, and endometrial tissue. The patient returns home the same day. She will experience cramping, bleeding, and, possibly, emotional reactions over the following days. Serious complications are unusual for a legal, properly performed abortion. Those problems that may arise are discussed in the section entitled "Adjustment Following Abortion."

DILATION AND CURETTAGE (D & C) (FIRST TRIMESTER METHOD). The cervix is dilated and the uterine wall scraped with a small spoon-shaped instrument (curette). Local or general anesthesia is given. It is generally considered less desirable than vacuum aspiration as it causes more bleeding, is more painful, and is sometimes less effective. Possible problems are discussed below.

DILATION AND EVACUATION (D & E) (SECOND TRIMESTER METHOD). This method is usually performed between the 13th and 20th week of pregnancy. Local or general anesthesia is used. The cervix is slowly dilated and the fetus removed by alternating curettage with the injection of a solution toxic to the fetus. Patients are usually given an intravenous solution of the hormone oxytochin to encourage contractions and limit blood loss. Because it is a second trimester procedure, a D & E is somewhat riskier and often more traumatic than a first trimester abortion.

HYSTEROTOMY (SECOND TRIMESTER METHOD). The fetus is removed through an incision made in the woman's abdomen. This is essentially a cesarean section—major surgery, requiring several days in the hospital. Its use is limited.

Other Methods of Abortion

Abortion can also be induced medically with injections or suppositories containing certain substances. These abortions are performed during the second trimester and generally require hospitalization. Prostaglandins, saline solutions, and urea are are common abortifacients. They are used singly or in varying combinations.

Many cells of the body contain prostaglandins. A prostaglandin is a type of fatty acid that is active in many kinds of body processes, including reproduction. Prostaglandins are injected into the amniotic sac or administered as vaginal suppositories to induce abortion. Some of the side effects associated with their use are gastrointestinal symptoms, cervical lacerations, and temperature elevation.

Saline solutions and solutions of urea are toxic to the fetus and can be injected amniotically. These solutions are relatively inexpensive; they are generally considered more effective when used in combination with prostaglandins.

Mifepristone, known popularly as RU-486, is an antiprogesterone steroid that acts as an abortifacient if taken orally or injected within the first six weeks of pregnancy. It is used in Europe and Asia but as of this writing is not available in the U.S. because FDA testing has been obstructed by anti-abortion groups.

Adjustment Following Abortion

Following an abortion, most women have some bleeding and cramps for about two weeks. Some women will have light menstrual-type bleeding as long as one to two weeks. The only cause for worry about bleeding is if it is heavier two days in a row than the heaviest day of normal menstrual flow. In order to protect herself against infection, a woman should not have sexual intercourse until she has had her follow-up visit. She should not use tampons for a week (sanitary napkins may be used instead) and should not douche for a week. Her usual period will begin about four to six weeks following the abortion. It is important to use contraception even if her period has not yet begun again since it is still possible to get pregnant. If her period does not begin within eight weeks of her abortion, she should call her clinic or physician.

Although many women feel a great sense of relief once an abortion is completed, many also experience a profound sense of loss. Some women are surprised at the intensity of their feelings. They need to understand that this grieving process is normal. Counseling can help.

Complication rates are low for legal abortions performed by qualified practitioners, especially for first trimester abortions. About 91 percent of abortions are performed before the 13th week of pregnancy; 99 percent are performed by 20 weeks, before the fetus is viable (able to survive outside the womb).

Properly done, first trimester abortions are statistically six times safer than childbirth. Later abortions are significantly more dangerous. The possible complications include infection and hemorrhage, often due to retained material in the uterus.

Men are often forgotten people in an abortion; attention is usually focused on the woman who is undergoing the agony of decision. If men are thought of, they are often regarded with hostility and blame. And yet they, like the women, may be undergoing their own private travail, experiencing guilt and anxiety, feeling ambiguous about the possibility of parenthood.

A common feeling men experience is powerlessness. They may try to remain cool and rational, believing that if they reveal their confused feelings they will be unable to give their partners emotional support. Since the drama is within the woman and her body, a man may feel he must not influence her decision.

There is the lure of fatherhood, all the same. A pregnancy forces the man to confront his own feelings about parenting. Parenthood for males, as for females, is a profound passage into adulthood. There is a mixture of pride and fear about being a potential father and a potential adult.

After the abortion, many men feel residual guilt, sadness, and remorse. It is not uncommon for some men to temporarily experience erectile or ejaculatory difficulties following an abortion. It is fairly common for couples to split up after an abortion: the stress, conflict, and guilt can be overwhelming. Many abortion clinics now provide counseling for men, as well as women, involved in abortion.

❖ SEXUALLY TRANSMITTED DISEASES (STDs)

Many people associate sexually transmitted disease (STD), also known as venereal disease (VD), with "loose" or "unclean" sexual behavior that they assume is practiced mostly by people in lower socioeconomic groups. They assume they will not become infected if they stay away from "those types." This view is dangerously wrong. Reports of infection come from all economic and education levels, and the total number rises each year. There are an estimated 13 million cases of STDs yearly (not including AIDS). Some clinics report that the incidence of STDs is highest among gay men, lowest among lesbian women, highest among both sexes between the ages of 20 and 24, and next highest among 15- to 20-year-olds. STDs are increasing dramatically among inner-city black and Latino populations and also, to some degree, among all groups of sexually active men and women.

VD and STD are general terms that refer to several different types of diseases closely associated with sexual contact. The most prevalent in the Untied States today are chlamydia, gonorrhea, genital warts, and genital herpes. Hepatitis B and syphilis are also increasingly widespread. Opportunistic infections associated with AIDS are a threat to everyone who does not practice "safe sex" or who uses intravenous drugs.

Chlamydia

Chlamydia is the most common venereal disease in America, affecting 4 to 5 million persons a year. The symptoms of chlamydia are similar to gonorrhea for both men and women. A man most often has a whitish discharge coming from his urethra; a woman is usually asymptomatic—that is, shows no symptoms. Chlamydia is a parasite, neither a virus nor a bacterium, which causes a variety of infections. Approximately 55 percent of the urinary tract infections seen in STD clinics are from chlamydia.

The risk of getting chlamydia from an infected partner is less than that of getting gonorrhea. The use of IUDs, however, is likely to increase the chance of getting chlamydia, gonorrhea, and/or PID (pelvic inflammatory disease). It is possible for a person to be infected with both gonorrhea and chlamydia; a treatment for gonorrhea will cure the gonorrhea but not the chlamydia.

Chlamydia is swiftly spreading in part because some physicians mistakenly diagnose it as gonorrhea and prescribe penicillin treatment. Most clinics and physicians do not have the facilities to test for chlamydia. Unfortunately, chlamydia does not respond to penicillin. Therefore, a man with a discharge should insist that a culture be taken to determine whether he is infected with chlamydia or gonorrhea or both. If he has chlamydia, the correct treatment for him and his partner is tetracycline. If the woman is pregnant, however, tetracycline must *not* be used; instead erythromycin should be used. Since there is a high incidence of persons suffering from both gonorrhea and chlamydia at the same time, tetracycline may become the treatment of choice for uncomplicated gonococcal infections.

Chlamydia is a serious disease, although traditionally it has not been treated as an important infection. For men, the serious consequences include sterility; for women, PID may be a consequence, possibly leading to hospitalization, tubal pregnancies, or sterility. Infected women who deliver may pass their infection on to their babies, causing serious eye infections and pneumonia.

Gonorrhea

This is an old disease, second only to the common cold in age and prevalence around the world. In the U.S., 1.8 million new cases are reported annually. In its early stage a man will usually notice a discharge of fluid from his penis two to seven days after sexual contact, a frequent desire to urinate, and a burning sensation when he does so. He will usually go to a doctor at this stage. If untreated, the male commonly suffers various complications, including inflammation of the testes, arthritis, skin infections, urinary disorders, and sterility.

Most women with gonorrhea are asymptomatic—that is, they show no symptoms. For this reason, if a man discovers that he has gonorrhea, it is imperative that he tell his partner so that she may be treated. Many cases in women go undetected until secondary symptoms of pain in the lower abdomen develop. This is the stage of pelvic inflammatory disease (PID). By this time the disease has moved into the fallopian tubes and glands surrounding the female organs. The result may be severe damage to tubes or ovaries, with resulting sterility.

The infection can usually be halted in men and women by penicillin or tetracycline. However, some strains of the gonococcus bacteria are resistant to the usual cures and are thus difficult to treat.

Genital Warts

About one million cases of genital warts are reported each year. Genital warts are caused by the human papilloma virus (HPV), a class of virus of which common skin warts are a member. Genital warts are usually small, ranging in size from a pencil point to a quarter inch in diameter; they may even be invisible to the naked eye. They may be white, gray, or pink and brown. They may be flat or round, smooth or bumpy; some look like tiny cauliflowers, others look like small fingers. In men, the warts are most commonly found on the penis; they may also be found in the anus. In women, they are usually found in the cervix, vagina, vulva, and anus.

Some venereal warts appear to be associated with cervical, vaginal, vulval, and penile cancers. It is not clear which strains of HPV are implicated in these cancers; some strains of flat venereal warts are the most likely culprits.

Detection of HPV in males can be done using a vinegar wash at a dermatologist's office. HPV can be detected in woman using a Pap test. External warts are easily removed by direct application of podophyllin. Internal warts can be removed through freezing or laser therapy. Once the warts are removed, the chances of developing cervical cancer diminish; it is not known what affect removal has on the incidence of other cancers of the lower genital tract.

Genital Herpes

A half million new cases of genital herpes are reported each year in the United States. No cure has been found for the disease, so it has spread rapidly and uncontrollably. Genital herpes is caused by a virus, generally herpes simplex type II (although 15 percent of genital herpes is caused by herpes simplex I, the virus responsible for oral and facial cold sores and fever blisters).

About 2 to 20 days after infection, blisters form on the penis or urethra in men and on the cervix, vagina, vulva, or anus in women. The sores are quite painful, and women may report pain during urination. Herpes sores may also appear around the mouth if a person has engaged in oral sex with someone who has an active case of herpes.

Once the disease is contracted, the carrier may experience repeated attacks. Although there is no cure, there are some treatments that reduce the pain and healing time of lesion outbreaks. These also reduce the chance of spreading the disease, which is most contagious during the prodromal (presymptom) stage that precedes blistering by about three days and during the blistering stage. Various ointments also help the lesions to heal quickly. The most effective of these on the market now is acyclovir (this is the generic name; brand names will be different). Acyclovir also mini-

mizes the pain for men but not for women. It is also available as an oral medication. It must be prescribed by a physician. Pregnant women with herpes need to be aware of possible risk to their newborn infants. Informed health practitioners can provide information regarding precautions and alternatives.

Syphilis

The incidence of syphilis is increasing among heterosexuals. It is caused by bacteria that are easy to identify with a blood test. It can be treated with penicillin or certain other antibiotics. The disease has four distinct stages that are alike for both women and men. The progression of the disease is not painful and is not easily noticed in its early stage by the person who has it. It is extremely important to arrest the disease in its early stage to avoid irreversible damage to body tissue.

EARLY STAGE.   A sore called a chancre (pronounced shanker) appears between ten days and three months after infection at the place of infection. This may be an internal site for a woman. It may look like a pimple, a blister, an ulcer, or a cold sore. It does not hurt. It will heal itself in one to ten weeks.

SECONDARY STAGE.   After the chancre heals, the disease spreads to other parts of the body. A rash breaks out (usually on the trunk of the body), but this rash is not painful or itchy. A person may also be bothered with low fever, sore throats, headaches, or other discomforts easily mistaken for ordinary ones. Sometimes lesions form in a mouth during this stage. If so, the mouth will be full of syphilis bacteria and the disease can be passed by kissing.

LATENT STAGE.   Beginning six months to two years after infection, the disease becomes latent. During this time the person does not infect others but still tests positive. This stage may continue indefinitely—even until death.

LATE STAGE.   The syphilis bacteria sometimes concentrate in certain parts of the body. Then the disease breaks loose. It may be in any part—liver, skin, heart, or central nervous system. Later lesions and ulcers appear. Tissue damage and several disabling diseases can develop. Direct damage, as well as that arising from complications, may prove fatal.

Hepatitis

Hepatitis is a disease of the liver, causing blood pigments that are normally destroyed by the liver to accumulate in the blood. It is one of the most prevalent sexually transmitted diseases among gay men. As a result of hepatitis, jaundice (the yellowing of eyes and skin) develops; other symptoms may include fatigue, nausea, and darkening of the urine. If left unchecked, hepatitis can disable the liver and cause death. Most people with hepatitis, however, recover in a few weeks without permanent damage if they seek treatment promptly.

Infectious hepatitis (Type A hepatitis) may be contracted in a number of ways, through unsanitary conditions, contaminated water or food, transfusion with contaminated blood, or feces. Persons engaging in anal/oral sex may contract infectious hepatitis from licking the anus. Immune serum globulin (ISG) injected before or after exposure may offer some protection against (or lessen the severity of) the infection.

Serum hepatitis (Type B hepatitis) is caused by the virus entering a person through a break in the skin or through mucous membranes and may be spread by infected needles and transfusions. It is also transmitted through saliva, blood, urine, semen, and vaginal secretions. There is some evidence that women may acquire serum hepatitis sexually; there is less evidence that heterosexual men acquire the infection sexually. Hepatitis B may be prevented through immunization.

❖ HIV AND AIDS

The AIDS virus (HIV—human immunodeficiency virus) affects people in a variety of ways. A few people have lived with an AIDS diagnosis for four or more years and continue to lead energetic and productive lives; others may die within a few days or weeks of their diagnosis. Some are sick throughout the course of disease, while others have periods of health alternating with periods of illness and disability.

AIDS is a very complex disease. Many of its symptoms resemble common signs of cold, the flu, and so on. The symptoms, however, are more severe and last over a significant period of time. But even if the symptoms are severe and long-lasting, they may be the result of illnesses other than AIDS. *AIDS cannot be self-diagnosed.* A person concerned with symptoms he or she thinks might be AIDS should arrange to be tested or consult a physician familiar with AIDS. (See the Self-Help Resource Directory for information about AIDS hotlines and referral services.)

When AIDS begins, a person may have several of the following symptoms. Remember, however, that these are also symptoms of other common and less serious infections.

◆ Persistent and unexplained fatigue
◆ Unexplained fever, shaking chills, or night sweats lasting several weeks or more
◆ Unexplained weight loss, usually more than 10 pounds.
◆ Unexplained swollen glands, usually in the neck, armpits, or groin, lasting more than two months
◆ Pinkish or purple blotches on or under the skin, inside the mouth, nose, eyelids, or rectum, which may initially resemble bruises but do not disappear
◆ Persistent diarrhea
◆ Persistent white spots or unusual blemishes about the mouth
◆ Persistent dry cough, especially if accompanied by shortness of breath, not caused by a common respiratory infection

AIDS Antibody Testing

There are no widely available tests for the presence of HIV. The AIDS antibody tests (ELISA and Western Blot), however, are simple and *reasonably* accurate blood tests that show whether the body has developed anitbodies in response to the AIDS virus.

Interpreting the results of the antibody test, however, is not straightforward. If the AIDS antibody is absent, the test will be *negative*. But a negative test can mean one of several things: (1) the person has not been infected with HIV, (2) the person has had contact with HIV but has not become infected (but is in danger of becoming infected with repeated exposure), or (3) the person has become infected within the previous two to eight weeks with HIV, but the body has not yet produced antibodies.

If the antibody is present, the test will be *positive*. If the test is positive, then the person has been infected with HIV and there is an *active* virus present. If the virus is present, the person is capable of transmitting it to others under certain conditions.

A person with a positive HIV diagnosis should consult right away with a physician experienced in treating HIV and AIDS. Early intervention is very important in maximizing the quality of health and life.

Transmission

HIV is not casually transmitted. Casual contact—such as playing, shaking hands, sharing food or glasses, sitting on toilet seats, even biting and spitting—is an unlikely means of passing the virus. Large numbers of people who have had casual contact with people with HIV or AIDS, such as friends, family members, co-workers, or fellow students, have not tested positive for HIV. Antibody tests of family members show no transmission through casual contact; only some husbands, wives, or lovers of those infected with HIV showed AIDS antibodies.

Nonsexually, HIV is transmitted through blood, primarily from the use of unsterilized needles by intravenous (IV) drug users. Previously, it was transmitted through infected donor blood; but since 1983 the nation's donor supply has been tested against AIDS.

Sexually, HIV is transmitted through semen and vaginal secretions. It is transmitted sexually to heterosexuals or homosexuals through various sexual practices—especially anal intercourse. (It is transmitted through anal intercourse because of the ease with which the delicate membranes of the rectum can be ruptured. The virus then enters the blood stream via infected semen.) Although gay men are the largest group that has been struck by the disease, it is not a gay disease but a viral disease. Its association with gay men is a result of their engaging in anal intercourse significantly more frequently than heterosexuals.

❖ SAFE SEX PRACTICES

In the age of AIDS, it is necessary for each of us to practice safe sex to prevent the spread of HIV (as well as other sexually transmitted diseases). Unless you know that both you and your partner are not carrying HIV, do not allow semen, vaginal secretions, or blood to come into contact with the penis, vagina, anus, or mouth. HIV has also been found in saliva, urine, and tears, but there is little or no risk of transmitting HIV through these fluids.

The following sexual practices are safe because there is no exchange of semen, vaginal secretions, or blood:

- Kissing
- Masturbation alone or with a partner
- Touching, hugging, caressing, massaging

The following sexual practices are *generally* safe because there is unlikely to be an exchange of semen, vaginal secretions, or blood:

- Vaginal intercourse with a latex condom or women's condom
- Oral sex with condom or latex barrier (dental dam)

The following sexual practices are *definitely unsafe* because there is an exchange of semen, vaginal secretions, or blood:

- Vaginal intercourse without a condom
- Anal intercourse with or without a condom
- Oral/anal sex

- Oral sex without a barrier
- Sharing objects inserted into the anus or vagina

(A federally funded study at UCLA has revealed dramatic differences in condom durability and effectiveness in impeding HIV. The top-ranked condom was Mentor, followed by Ramses Non-Lube, Ramses Sensitol, and Gold Circle Coin. [For a discussion of the study, see Parachini, 1988.])

In addition to the previously described sexual behaviors, individuals put themselves at higher risk if they engage in the following:

- Sex with gay or bisexual men
- Sex with multiple partners
- Sex with IV drug users
- Sex with prostitutes

The practice of safe sex calls for many of us to reevaluate the place of sexuality in our lives. We may have to change some of our sexual patterns. But whatever changes we must make will ultimately enhance our sexual activities by making them safe for ourselves and others.

FOR WOMEN

❖ BREAST SELF-EXAMINATION

Follow the steps in Figure R–1 to examine your breasts regularly once a month. This examination is best done after the menstrual period. If you find something you consider abnormal, contact your doctor for an examination. Most breast lumps are not serious, but all should come to the doctor's attention for an expert opinion after appropriate examination. You may have a condition that will require treatment or further study. If necessary, your doctor may recommend laboratory tests or X-rays as part of a more detailed examination. Follow your doctor's advice—your early recognition of a change in your breast and the doctor's thoughtful investigation will determine the safest course. Keep up this important health habit even during pregnancy and after menopause.

❖ MAINTAINING SEXUAL HEALTH

Vaginitis

There are a variety of urethral and vaginal infections that are considered venereal because they are aggravated or perpetuated by sexual contacts. Sometimes only one partner suffers from the discomfort, while the other seems to be resistant. Partner 2 acts as a carrier and continually reinfects partner 1. These diseases fall under the general category of vaginitis and include trichomoniasis,

candidiasis (yeast infection), and bacterial infections such as Gardnerella.

Here are some hints that may help a woman avoid vaginitis:

- Do not use vaginal deodorants, especially deodorant suppositories or tampons, because they upset the natural chemical balance within the vagina. Use douches rarely and then only for good reason, such as a diagnosed yeast infection. Despite what pharmaceutical companies advertise, the healthy vagina does not have an unpleasant odor. If the vagina does have an unpleasant odor, then something is wrong and you should check with a physician or health practitioner. (See Table R–1.)
- Regularly wash and rinse the vulva and anus. Be careful about using bubble baths or strongly perfumed soaps, since they may cause irritation.
- After a bowel movement, wipe the anus from the front to the back to prevent the spreading of germs from the anus to the vagina.
- Wear cotton underpants or underpants that have a cotton crotch, since nylon underpants and pantyhose keep heat and moisture in, encouraging bacterial growth.
- When lubricating the vagina, use only water-soluble lubricants. Vaseline is not water-soluble and tends to form a film on the walls of the vagina, which keeps heat and moisture in, encouraging infection.
- Have your male partner treated also. Vaginitis is often sexually transmitted. Be on the safe side and have your partner treated to prevent reinfection.

FIGURE R.1

Breast Self Examination

SOURCE: National Institutes of Health, *Breast Cancer: We're Making Progress Every Day*, NIH publication no. 83–2409, 1983 (a leaflet available from the National Cancer Institute).

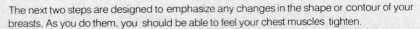

The next two steps are designed to emphasize any changes in the shape or contour of your breasts. As you do them, you should be able to feel your chest muscles tighten.

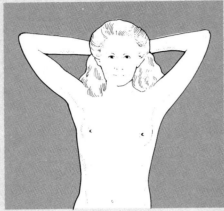

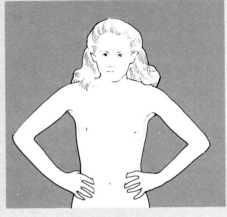

1. Stand before a mirror. Inspect both breasts for anything unusual, such as any discharge from the nipples or puckering, dimpling or scaling of the skin.

2. Watch closely in the mirror, clasp hands behind your head, and press hands forward.

3. Next, press hands firmly on hips and bow slightly toward the mirror as you pull your shoulders and elbows forward.

Some women do the next part of the exam in the shower. Fingers glide over soapy skin, making it easy to concentrate on the texture underneath.

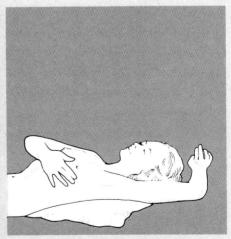

4. Raise your left arm. Use three or four fingers of your right hand to explore your left breast firmly, carefully, and thoroughly. Beginning at the outer edge, press the flat part of your fingers in small circles, moving the circles slowly around the breast. Gradually work toward the nipple. Be sure to cover the entire breast. Pay special

attention to the area between the breast and the armpit, including the armpit itself. Feel for any unusual lump or mass under the skin.

5. Gently squeeze the nipple and look for a discharge. Repeat the exam on your right breast.

6. Repeat steps 4 and 5 lying down. Lie flat on your back with your left arm over your head and a pillow or folded towel under your left shoulder. This positions flattens the breast and makes it easier to examine. Use the same circular motion described earlier. Repeat on your right breast.

Yeast Infection (Candidiasis)

If you suspect you have a *Candida* (yeast) infection, you may want to try treating it yourself:

◆ Plain yogurt applied to the vulva and vagina twice a day may eliminate symptoms. (The yogurt must contain live lactobacillus culture; this means pasteurized supermarket yogurt won't work. A trip to the health food store may be in order. Health stores may also stock homeopathic treatments for yeast.)

◆ Douching with a weak vinegar and water solution (two tablespoons vinegar to one quart of water) once every three days may also eliminate the symptoms.

◆ Nutrition can play a part. If you have recurring candidiasis, you might try increasing your intake of plain (health-food type) yogurt; you can also cut down on foods with high sugar or carbohydrate content.

◆ Stress can upset the vagina's chemical state, as can a change in the body's hormone levels. Pregnant women and women who use oral contraception are more susceptible to yeast infections, as are women who are taking antibiotics.

◆ Antifungal medicines such as clotrimazole (Gyne-Lotrimin) and miconazole (Monostat) are now available over the counter in cream or vaginal suppository form. If you have had a yeast infection before and recognize the symptoms, you may want to purchase one of these products. If you are not sure that you have a yeast infection, see your doctor or clinic.

◆ Since women with candidiasis may have trichomonas as well, they should be tested for both.

Symptoms often disappear in two or three days, but curing candidiasis usually requires one to four weeks of treatment.

Urinary Tract Infections (Cystitis)

Frequent painful urination often indicates the presence of a urinary tract infection.

PREVENTING CYSTITIS.   The following measures will lessen the likelihood of a cystitis attack:

◆ Urinate frequently. Holding back urine can weaken the muscles involved in urination; it can allow the buildup of concentrated, highly acidic urine.

◆ Urinate before intercourse and soon afterwards to flush bacteria from the urethra.

◆ Drink plenty of fluids (water is best), especially just prior to and just after intercourse.

◆ Eat a well-balanced diet and get plenty of rest, especially if your resistance is low.

◆ If you use a diaphragm and are troubled by cystitis, consider trying another form of contraception.

TREATING CYSTITIS.

◆ If you feel an attack coming on, drink copious amounts of water (at least sixteen glasses a day). It won't hurt you as long as

TABLE R–1	Vaginal Mucus and Secretions Chart				
COLOR	CONSISTENCY	ODOR	OTHER SYMPTOMS	POSSIBLE CAUSE	WHAT TO DO
clear	slightly rubbery; stretchy	normal	—	ovulation; sexual stimulation	nothing
milky	creamy	normal	—	preovulation	nothing
white	sticky, curdlike	normal	—	postovulation; the pill	nothing
brownish	watery and sticky	normal or slightly different	—	last days of period; spotting	nothing
white	thin, watery, creamy	normal to foul or fishy	itching	*Gardnerella* bacteria or nonspecific bacterial infection	see health practitioner
white	curdlike or flecks, slight amount of discharge	yeasty or foul	itching or intense itching	overgrowth of yeast cells, yeast infection	apply yogurt or vinegar solution; see health practitioner
yellow, yellow-green	smooth or frothy	usually foul	itchy; may have red dots on cervix	possible *Trichomonas* infection	see health practitioner
yellow yellow-green	thick, mucous	none to foul	pelvic cramping or pelvic pain	possible infection of fallopian tubes	see health practitioner *right away*

you urinate frequently! A pinch of baking soda in a glass of water can help neutralize the urine's acidity and ease the burning sensation. Avoid coffee, tea, colas, and alcohol, since they may irritate the urinary tract.

◆ Itchiness may be relieved by spraying or sponging water on the vulva and urethral opening. If urination is especially painful, try urinating while sitting in a few inches of warm water (in the bathtub or a large pan).

◆ If symptoms persist or in case of fever, consult your doctor or clinic. Sulfa drugs or other specific antibiotics will usually clear up the symptoms in several days. (A caution about using sulfa drugs: about 10–14 percent of African Americans have an inherited deficiency of a blood enzyme called glucose-6-phosphate-dehydrogenase (G6PD); sulfa drugs may cause a serious anemic disease in these people.)

❖ A GOOD DIET DURING PREGNANCY

The baby that you are carrying gets its food from you. You need to eat the right kinds of food to keep healthy and to help your baby grow. If you did not eat the rights kinds of foods before pregnancy, *NOW* is the time to begin good eating habits.

The chart in Table R–2 will help you select foods that provide the nutrients needed for good nutrition during pregnancy.

❖ PRACTICAL HINTS ON BREASTFEEDING

Some women start breastfeeding with perfect ease and hardly any discomfort. For others, it can be frustrating and sometimes painful,

TABLE R–2   Basic Foods You Need Each Day During Pregnancy

	UNDER 18 YEARS		OVER 18 YEARS		
	Before and During First Three Months of Pregnancy	Last Six Months of Pregnancy	Before and During First Three Months of Pregnancy	Last Six Months of Pregnancy	Counts as One Serving
Meat, fish, poultry, eggs, or alternates	2–3 servings	3 servings	2–3 servings	3 servings	2 to 3 ounces cooked lean meat, fish, or poultry without bone; 2 medium eggs, 4 tablespoons peanut butter; 1 cup cooked dried beans or peas; 1½ cups split pea or bean soup; 2 or 3 ounces cheddar-type cheese; ½ to ¾ cup cottage cheese; ¼ to ½ cup nuts or seeds.
Milk and milk products	3–4 cups	4–5 cups	3 cups	4 cups	1 cup (8 fluid ounces) of skim, whole, buttermilk, or diluted evaporated milk. The following foods provide as much calcium as a cup of whole milk: 1½ ounces cheddar-type cheese; 1 cup plain yogurt; 3 tablespoons regular nonfat dry milk; 6 tablespoons instant nonfat dry milk solids; 1½ cups cottage cheese; 1 cup custard or puddings made with milk; 1½ to 2 cups soup made or diluted with milk.
Fruits and vegetables (Vitamin C rich)	1 serving	1–2 servings	1 serving	1–2 servings	½ cup citrus juice or 1 medium orange; ½ grapefruit; ½ cantaloupe; ½ cup strawberries; ½ cup broccoli; ½ green pepper. You will need to eat 2 servings of foods that are fair sources of vitamin C. These foods include tomatoes, tomato juice, tangerines, tangerine juice, asparagus tips, raw cabbage, brussels sprouts, watermelon, and dark leafy greens.

This table continued on the next page.

but it need not be. Midwife Raven Lang tells us that the following method will lead to successful breastfeeding.

◆ When you first put the baby to your breast, limit her to one minute per breast. Try not to nurse again for a half hour to an hour. If the baby fusses, you can give her the end of your little finger (or a pacifier) to suck.

◆ The second hour, let her nurse two minutes at each breast; the third hour, three minutes; the fourth hour, four minutes and so on. Of course, your baby will not want to nurse every hour of the day and night. Thus the basic rule to follow is: increase your nursing time by only one minute per breast with each subsequent feeding, until you are nursing comfortably for as long a session as you and the baby both enjoy. Remember that for the first three days, the baby is getting colostrum only. By the time your true milk comes in on the third day, things should be going smoothly. Also, even a slow-nursing infant gets about four-fifths of her nourishment during the first five minutes.

◆ Lang says that although mothers are generally most effective when they care for their babies "by feel" rather than "by the book" (or in this case "by the clock"), the process of establishing breastfeeding is an exception to this "rule." Try it; you'll agree.

Most women find that a good nursing bra, one that provides good uplift and that opens easily for nursing, makes breastfeeding easier and more comfortable. Many wear such a bra day and night during the months they are nursing.

Rest and relax as much as possible during the months that you are breastfeeding, especially at the beginning. Your body is doing a tremendous amount of work and needs extra care.

TABLE R–2 (continued)

	UNDER 18 YEARS		OVER 18 YEARS		
	Before and During First Three Months of Pregnancy	Last Six Months of Pregnancy	Before and During First Three Months of Pregnancy	Last Six Months of Pregnancy	Counts as One Serving
Fruits and vegetables (Vitamin A rich)	1 serving	2 servings	1 serving	2 servings	½ cup deep yellow fruits and vegetables such as apricots, cantaloupe, carrots, pumpkins, sweet potatoes, winter squash, ½ to ¾ cup dark green leafy vegetables such as collard greens, mustard greens, chard, kale, turnip tops, spinach, broccoli, watercress. In addition to vitamin A, dark green leafy vegetables supply folacin, magnesium, and iron.
Other fruits and vegetables	2 servings	1 serving	2 servings	1 serving	½ cup of other fruits and vegetables such as green beans, wax beans, celery, corn, mushrooms, cauliflower, green peas, cucumbers, potatoes, lettuce, beets, pears, apples, bananas, pineapple, prunes, cherries, etc.
Breads and cereals (whole grain, enriched or restored)	4 servings	5–6 servings	4 servings	4–5 servings	1 slice bread; 1 muffin; 1 hamburger or hot dog roll, 4 to 5 saltine crackers; ½ to ¾ cup cooked cereals, rice, macaroni, noodles, spaghetti, and other pastas; ¾ cup (1 ounce) ready-to-eat cereal. Read labels and select whole grain or fortified breads and cereals. Avoid presweetened cereals.
Fats and sweets	These energy foods supply mostly calories. Eat them only in amounts to meet your energy needs after your nutritional requirements have been met.				

While nursing, find a position that is comfortable for you and your baby. A foot stool, a pillow, and a chair with arms are often helpful.

Touch the baby's cheek with the nipple to start. She will turn her head to grasp the nipple. (If you try to push her to the nipple with a finger touching her other cheek or chin, she will turn away from the nipple toward the finger.)

Allow her to grasp the entire darkly colored part of the breast in her mouth. She gets the milk by squeezing it from the nipple, not by actually sucking. Her grasp on your nipple may hurt for the first few seconds, but the pain should disappear once she is nursing in a good rhythm. When you want to remove her mouth from your breast, first break the suction by inserting your finger in the corner of her mouth. This will save sore nipples.

A small amount of milk may come out of your nipples between feedings. A small nursing pad or piece of sanitary napkin inserted in the bra over the nipple will absorb this milk, keeping the bra clean and preventing irritation of the nipple.

If your entire breast becomes sore, you may be able to relieve the painfulness simply by lifting and supporting the breast with one hand during nursing. Hot compresses between nursing sessions may further relieve soreness.

If you notice a spot of tenderness or redness on your breast or nipple that persists for more than two feedings, be sure to seek advice from your breastfeeding support group or physician promptly.

If you have difficulty beginning to breastfeed, don't give up! Ask friends, women's centers, clinics, or the local La Leche League chapter for help. Don't worry about not having enough milk; the more your baby nurses, the more you'll produce.

FOR MEN: TESTICULAR SELF-EXAM

Just as women practice breast self-examination each month, men should practice preventive medicine by doing testicular self-examination regularly. (See Figure R–2.)

The best time to discover any small lumps is right after a hot shower or bath, when the skin of the scrotum is most relaxed. Each testicle should be gently examined with the fingers of both hands, slowly and carefully. Learn what the collecting structure at the back of the testicle (the epididymis) feels like so that you won't mistake it for an abnormality. If you find any lump or growth, it most often will be on the front side of the testicle.

Any lumps or suspicious areas should be reported to your urologist promptly.

FIGURE R.2

Testicular Self Examination

Roll each testicle between the thumb and fingers; the testicles should feel smooth, except for the epididymis at the back of each. A hard lump, enlargement, or contour changes should be reported to your health care provider.

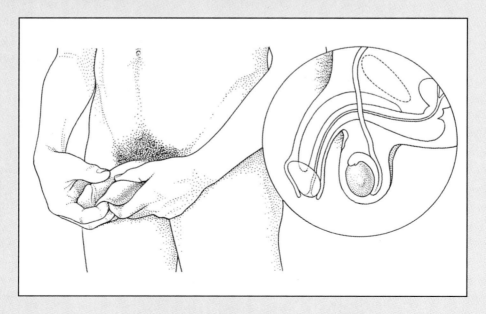

FAMILY MATTERS

❖ MARRIAGE LAWS BY STATE

STATE	AGE MARRIAGE CAN BE CONTRACTED WITHOUT PARENTAL CONSENT		AGE MARRIAGE CAN BE CONTRACTED WITH PARENTAL CONSENT		Maximum Period Between Exam & Issuance of License (Days)	COMMON-LAW MARRIAGE	
						May Be but Not Valid If Attempted After Date Shown	Contracted Recognized If Valid at Time & Place Where Contracted
	Male	Female	Male	Female			
Alabama	18	18	17	14	30	Yes	Yes
Alaska	18	18	16	16	30	1/1/64	Yes
Arizona	18	18	16	16	30	No	Yes
Arkansas	18	18	17	16	30	No	Yes
California	18	18	18	16	30	1895	Yes
Colorado	18	18	16	16	30	Yes	Yes
Connecticut	18	18	16	16	35	No	†
Delaware	18	18	18	16	30	No	Yes
Dist. of Columbia	18	18	16	16	30	Yes	Yes
Florida	18	18	18	16	30	1/1/68	Yes
Georgia	18	18	16	16	30	Yes	Yes
Hawaii	18	18	16	16	30	No	Yes
Idaho	18	18	16	16	—	Yes	Yes
Illinois	18	18	16	16	15	6/30/05	†
Indiana	18	18	17	17	30	1/1/58	†
Iowa	18	18	16	16	20	Yes	Yes
Kansas	18	18	18	18	30	Yes	Yes
Kentucky	18	18	none	none	15	No	Yes
Louisiana	18	18	18	16	10	No	†
Maine	18	18	16	16	60	†	†
Maryland	18	18	16	16	—	No	Yes
Massachusetts	18	18	18	18	30	No	Yes
Michigan	18	18	16	16	30	1/1/57	Yes
Minnesota	18	18	18	16	—	4/26/41	†
Mississippi	21	21	17	15	30	4/5/56	†
Missouri	18	18	15	15	15	3/3/21	†
Montana	18	18	18	18	20	Yes	Yes
Nebraska	19	19	17	17	30	Yes	Yes
Nevada	18	18	16	16	—	1923	Yes
New Hampshire	18	18	14	13	30	3/29/43	Yes
New Jersey	18	18	18	16	30	No	Yes
New Mexico	18	18	16	16	30	1/12/39	Yes
New York	18	18	16	14	30	No	Yes
North Carolina	18	18	16	16	30	4/29/33	Yes
North Dakota	18	18	16	16	30	No	Yes
Ohio	18	18	18	16	30	No	Yes
Oklahoma	18	18	16	16	30	Yes	Yes
Oregon	18	18	17	17	30	No	Yes

† Legal status unclear.

Table continued on the next page.

❖ MARRIAGE LAWS BY STATE   *continued*

	AGE MARRIAGE CAN BE CONTRACTED WITHOUT PARENTAL CONSENT		AGE MARRIAGE CAN BE CONTRACTED WITH PARENTAL CONSENT		Maximum Period Between Exam & Issuance of License (Days)	COMMON-LAW MARRIAGE	
						May Be Contracted but Not Valid If Attempted After Date Shown	Recognized If Valid at Time & Place Where Contracted
STATE	Male	Female	Male	Female			
Pennsylvania	18	18	16	16	30	Yes	Yes
Rhode Island	18	18	18	16	40	Yes	†
South Carolina	18	18	16	14	—	Yes	Yes
South Dakota	18	18	16	16	20	7/1/59	†
Tennessee	18	18	16	16	30	No	Yes
Texas	18	18	14	14	21	Yes	Yes
Utah	18	18	16	14	30	No	Yes
Vermont	18	18	16	16	30	No	†
Virginia	18	18	16	16	30	No	Yes
Washington	18	18	17	17	—	No	Yes
West Virginia	18	18	none	none	30	No	Yes
Wisconsin	18	18	16	16	20	1913	†
Wyoming	19	19	17	16	30	No	Yes

† Legal status unclear.

SOURCE: U.S. Department of Labor, Women's Bureau

❖ DIVORCE LAWS BY STATE

	"NO-FAULT" DIVORCE*		GROUNDS FOR ABSOLUTE DIVORCE						
STATE	Break-down	Separation	Cruelty	Desertion	Non-support	Alcohol/ Drugs	Felony	Impotency	Insanity
AL	X	2 yrs.	X	X	X	X	X	X	X
AK	X		X	X		X	X	X	X
AZ	X								
AR		3 yrs.	X	X	X	X	X	X	X
CA	X								X
CO	X								
CT	X	18 mos.	X	X	X	X	X		X
DE	X	6 mos.							
DC		6 mos–1 yr.							
FL	X								X
GA	X		X	X		X	X	X	X
HI	X	2 yrs.							
ID	X	5 yrs.	X	X	X	X	X		X
IL			X	X		X	X	X	
IN	X						X	X	X

* "No-fault" includes all proceedings where no proof for divorce is needed. Not called "no fault" in all states. Grounds in "no-fault" divorce may be "breakdown" (or "incompatibility") or separation.

This table continued on the next page.

❖ DIVORCE LAWS BY STATE *continued*

STATE	"NO-FAULT" DIVORCE* Break-down	Separation	GROUNDS FOR ABSOLUTE DIVORCE Cruelty	Desertion	Non-support	Alcohol/ Drugs	Felony	Impotency	Insanity
IA	X								
KS	X								
KY	X	1 yr.							
LA		1 yr.	X	X	X	X	X		
ME	X		X	X	X	X		X	X
MD		1–3 yrs.	X	X			X	X	X
MA	X	6 mos.–1 yr.	X	X	X	X	X	X	
MI	X								
MN	X								
MS	X		X	X		X	X	X	X
MO	X								
MT	X								
NB	X								
NV	X	1 yr.							X
NH	X	2 yrs.	X	X	X	X	X	X	
NJ		18 mos.	X	X		X	X		X
NM	X		X	X					
NY		1 yr.	X	X			X		
NC		1 yr.						X	X
ND	X		X	X	X	X	X	X	X
OH	X	2 yrs.	X	X		X	X	X	X
OK	X		X	X	X	X	X	X	X
OR	X								
PA	X	3 yrs.	X	X			X	X	X
RI	X	3 yrs.	X	X	X	X	X	X	
SC		1 yr.	X	X		X			
SD			X	X	X	X	X		
TN	X		X	X	X	X	X	X	
TX	X	3 yrs.	X	X			X		X
UT			X	X	X	X	X	X	X
VT		6 mos.	X	X	X		X		X
VA		6 mos–1 yr.	X	X			X		
WA	X								
WV	X	1 yr.	X	X		X	X		X
WI	X	1 yr.							X
WY	X	2 yrs.							X

* "No-fault" includes all proceedings where no proof for divorce is needed. Not called "no fault" in all states. Grounds in "no-fault" divorce may be "breakdown" (or "incompatibility") or separation.

SOURCE: U.S. Department of Labor, Women's Bureau (1982).

❖ GENETIC COUNSELING

About 2 to 4 percent of American children are born with birth defects. Each year, 1 to 2 million infants, children, and adults are hospitalized for treatment of birth defects. These birth defects involve abnormalities of body structure or function, which may be genetically caused, the result of environmental influence on the fetus, or both. About 20 percent are inherited; 20 percent are caused by environmental influences on the fetus (such as smoking, drinking, diet, drugs, or exposure to toxic chemicals); and the remainder result from heredity and the environment interacting with each other.

Hereditary defects result from the interaction of the mother's and father's genes. Not all genes have an equal effect. Some genes are dominant over other genes, which are called recessive. The odds that a child will inherit a particular trait and the degree to which that trait will appear depend on many interrelated factors. These include: (1) whether the trait is dominant or recessive, (2) the degree to which either parent has the trait, (3) the child's sex, and (4) the overall genetic makeup of the parents.

Individuals with hereditary defects are at significant risk in passing their disorder on to their children. Others are healthy themselves but carry a recessive abnormal gene; if they mate with another carrier of the same abnormal gene, there is a 25 percent risk in each pregnancy of having a child with that particular birth defect. (Each of us probably carries two to eight abnormal recessive genes.) Finally, there are some female carriers of sex-linked recessive traits who themselves are healthy but will pass the abnormal gene to half their children. Theoretically, half their sons will inherit the defect (such as hemophilia), while half their daughters will be carriers.

While any couple may have a child with a birth defect or hereditary disease, some individuals or couples are at high risk. Some can be identified during routine medical examination. Women over 35 years, persons with congenital defects or hereditary diseases, and women who have had multiple miscarriages are all at higher risk than the rest of the population. Others can be identified by a careful review of their family medical history. Each person should obtain a family medical history from his or her parents and keep it as part of his or her permanent records.

Factors and risks that indicate the need for genetic counseling include those shown in Table R–3.

In genetic counseling, persons or couples who are at high risk are interviewed to determine whether they are potential carriers of birth defects to their unborn children. Blood tests or other tests may be performed. After the diagnosis is made, the meaning of the disorder, its prognosis, and its treatment are explained. Finally the genetic cause of the disorder is determined, along with an estimate of the risks of passing on a birth defect. If the disorder can be detected prenatally, the risks and benefits of amniocentesis and

TABLE R–3

FACTOR	RISK TO CHILD
Maternal age 35 years or older	Chromosomal anomaly
Previous child with chromosomal abnormality	Chromosomal anomaly
Adult with congenital abnormality	Occurrence in child
Previous child with congenital abnormality	Occurrence in child
Previous child with autosomal recessive gene (such as cystic fibrosis) or sex-linked conditions such as hemophilia	Recurrence
Family history of autosomal recessive gene or sex-linked condition	Occurrence in child
Adult with known hereditary syndrome	Occurrence in child
Ashkenazi Jew	Tay-Sachs disease
African heritage	Sickle cell anemia
Mediterranean ethnic group	Thalassemia
Infertility or multiple miscarriages	Chromosomal abnormality
Parent taking teratogen	Child with multiple congenital abnormalities
Family history of diabetes mellitus	Child with congential malformation; diabetes mellitus
Deafness	Deafness
Psychosis	Psychosis

other techniques are explained; the couple's feelings about abortion are discussed so that they can make an informed and appropriate (for them) decision in the event that the fetus is affected by the condition. Genetic counseling may be time-consuming, but for those at risk, it can improve the chances of giving birth to healthy children.

❖ CHOOSING DAY CARE

Day care refers to any formal arrangement in which someone who is not a child's parent takes care of that child during the day. Traditionally, a child spent time with a parent—usually the mother—during the day. Now, this is not always possible.

Some families depend on day care to make life livable. Single-parent families as well as families with both parents working usually need to find some sort of day care for their children. If the children are school-aged, especially in the upper grades, the parent may ask a friend, neighbor, or relative to watch the child until after work. This arrangement might be quite informal. Sometimes such convenience is impossible. Then a parent must make formal arrangements. The varieties of child-care possibilities are unending, but day-care arrangements usually fall into one of the general categories listed here.

Neighborhood Childcare Cooperatives

Cooperatives work under the principle that each person involved will watch other peoples' children for a certain amount of time in exchange for someone else watching theirs. Each cooperative has its own rules. Generally, neighborhood cooperatives are only suitable for people who work part-time or for people who have definite periods of time available and a suitable home to offer the group. An advantage is that cooperatives may take very young children, even infants. It depends on the group. There usually is no exchange of money.

Freelance or Licensed Babysitters

People who like to babysit in their homes can often be found. They may sit for one or many children. They charge. Some states require sitters, especially those who take in more than one child, to be licensed. Sitters also may take very young children and infants. It depends on the sitter. Cost depends on the sitter's rates.

Day-Care Centers

These are organizations that provide day care, usually from 7:30 or 8 AM to 6 PM, for a fee, at a particular site. They are often located in churches or community centers. Most require children to be toilet trained before joining. The age of the oldest children allowed varies. Generally, day-care centers tend to serve either the two- to six-year-old age group or the five-to-nine age group. Costs vary and always go up with inflation and more respectable salaries for the staff. Cur-

rently, monthly costs start at about $500 per child for full-time care. Some centers are partial cooperatives, requiring parental participation in some way. Some have scholarship funds. Most are acceptable institutions to the government, which may provide day-care assistance to some low-income families.

The demand for day care today is greater than the spaces available. The best sources usually fill their lists for fall by June or midsummer. It is wise to check the possibilities well before your personal needs arise. Nothing is as informative as a visit to the day-care facility or home.

Here is a checklist of questions to help you judge each place:

◆ What is the ratio of adults to children?
◆ How large are the grounds?
◆ What kinds of toys, games, or playground equipment are provided?
◆ What activities, if any, are led (music, dance, art)?
◆ Do the children have nap time? Is it required?
◆ Does the caregiver have pets?
◆ Does the facility meet your standards of cleanliness?
◆ Is it run cooperatively?
◆ Will parents be asked to provide snacks or participate in work weekends? If so, how often?
◆ What food is served?
◆ Do the sitter, staff, or members of the cooperative seem generally to hold your values?
◆ Do you trust the judgment of the adult(s) running the show?
◆ When do half days end/start?
◆ Can the caregiver accommodate irregular hours (if you need to work an extra or different shift, can your child stay on short notice)?
◆ What does caregiver do when faced with medical emergencies?
◆ What funds might be available to children attending (city, county, state, federal, or other)?

❖ RIGHTS OF THE DISABLED*

Is Your Disability Covered?

In its section 504 regulation, HHS identified a "handicapped" person as anyone with a physical or mental disability that substantially impairs or restricts one or more of such major life activities as walking, seeing, hearing, speaking, working, or learning. A history of such disability, or the belief on the part of others that a person has such a disability, whether it is so or not, also is recognized as a "handicap by the regulation." Handicapping conditions include, but are not limited to:

◆ Alcoholism**
◆ AIDS (presumptive disability)
◆ Cancer
◆ Cerebral palsy

* U.S. Department of Health and Human Services.
** The U.S. Attorney General has ruled that alcoholism and drug addiction are physical or mental impairments that are "handicapping conditions" if they limit one or more of life's major activities.

- Deafness or hearing impairment
- Diabetes
- Drug addiction**
- Epilepsy
- Heart disease
- Mental or emotional illness
- Mental retardation
- Multiple sclerosis
- Muscular dystrophy
- Orthopedic, speech, or visual impairment
- Perceptual handicaps such as dyslexia, minimal brain dysfunction, and developmental aphasia.

What You Can Do

If you believe that your rights have been violated because of your disability or your child's disability by a business, hospital, physician, school, college, or any other institution receiving HHS assistance, write, giving details, to: Office for Civil Rights, Dept. of Health and Human Services, in your region.

** The U.S. Attorney General has ruled that alcoholism and drug addiction are physical or mental impairments that are "handicapping conditions" if they limit one or more of life's major activities.

MONEY MATTERS

❖ MANAGING YOUR MONEY

The Management Process

A plan for money management is important for everyone. However, no readymade plan fits every family, couple, or individual. Every household is different—not only in the number and characteristics of its members, but also in its values, needs, wants, and resources. Only you can decide how your money should be spent, taking into consideration your income, the number and ages of your household members, where you live and work, your preferences, your responsibilities, and your goals for the future. By following a money management plan, you can be confident that expenses will be met and savings will be available. A plan can let you know where you stand financially and prevent emergencies from causing a financial strain.

Remember three basic concepts when developing a personal money management plan:

- *Set realistic objectives.* Objectives set too high may lead to frustrations that could cause you to abandon your plan.
- *Be flexible.* Your plan will require adjustments to keep up with your changing life cycle and financial situation. Do not make a plan so tight that each new development requires an entirely new plan.
- *Be specific.* State your objectives concisely. If goals are vague, objectives may never be met, and you and other household members may have different ideas of what the end product will be.

* SOURCE: Joyce M. Pitts, *The Principles of Managing Your Finance,* U.S. Department of Agriculture, Agricultural Research Service (1986).

Evaluating Your Current Situation with a Net Worth Statement

The first step in developing a money management plan is to evaluate your current situation. An excellent way to do this is to prepare a *net worth statement.* Worksheet 1 can be used to add together your assets (what you own) and subtract from that the sum of your liabilities (what you owe). Space is provided for you to calculate your net worth statement now and again one year from now.

To determine the value of your *assets,* start with cash available. Include your checking and savings accounts, as well as your home bank. Now list all your investments, including bonds, mutual funds, life insurance cash values, and others. List additional assets using the current market value for your house, real estate, automobiles, jewelry, antiques, and other personal items.

To determine your *liabilities,* list the amount that you owe to all your creditors and lenders. Remember to include current bills, charge accounts, mortgage balance, and loans against your life insurance.

By subtracting liabilities from assets, you can determine your *net worth.* Look closely at your final net worth figure. Do you own more than you owe? Consider what you would like this figure to be a year from now. What do you need to do to achieve that goal?

Prepare a new net worth statement at the same time each year to reflect the changes in your finances. The market value of your assets (house, stock, or cars) may have declined or risen. You may have paid off one loan or gained another. A new net worth statement next year will help you decide if the money management plan you are developing now has helped put you ahead.

WORKSHEET 1: NET WORTH STATEMENT

ASSETS (WHAT YOU OWN)	FIRST YEAR	SECOND YEAR
Liquid		
Cash		
Bank		
Checking		
Savings		
Certificates		
Other		
Savings bonds		
Other bonds		
Corporate		
Municipal		
Utility		
Life insurance		
Mutual funds		
Other		
Other assets		
Retirement plans		
Private pension plan		
Profit-sharing plan		
Home		
Other real estate		
Car(s)		
Furniture		
Large appliances		
Antiques and art		
Jewelry		
Silverware		
Stamp or coin collection		
Debts others owe you		
Other		
Total Assets		

LIABILITIES (WHAT YOU OWE)	FIRST YEAR	SECOND YEAR
Current bills		
Charge accounts		
Credit cards		
Taxes		
Installments		
Mortgages		
Other		
Total Liabilities		

Net worth (Total assets minus total liabilities)

First Year: _____ – _____ = _____

Second Year: _____ – _____ = _____

Planning to Reach Your Goals

An important step in developing a money management plan is to set household and individual goals. Goals are wants, needs, and future objectives for your household and its members. Goals may be long-term, intermediate, or immediate.

Long-term goals are those you hope to reach in 10 to 20 years or perhaps even longer. Long-term goals are often considered first so that they can be incorporated into the plan from the start. They are guided by expected changes in your household's life cycle and must sometimes be adjusted for future expected income and price changes. Long-term goals include such things as paying off a mortgage, putting children through college, or providing for a comfortable retirement.

Intermediate goals are those to be reached within the next five years or so. These goals may reflect the changes that will occur due to your increased income or larger family. Intermediate goals might include such things as a down payment on a house, a new car, or increased life insurance.

Immediate goals are those to be reached within the next five years or so. These are basic needs that must be met even at the expense of some future goals. Immediate goals may include paying current bills, maintaining health insurance, and buying food and clothing.

Addressing goals in this order ensures savings for long-term and intermediate goals and prevents immediate goals from pushing future ones aside. If you income is low, you may be able to meet only immediate goals. But you still should make intermediate and long-term plans that could help you to get ahead in the future.

Decide Which Goals Are Most Important to You

Think carefully about your financial goals. Many of us would like to be financially secure, own a large home, drive a fancy car, educate ourselves or our children, take long vacations, and so on. Realistically, however, most of us cannot have it all. We must select and work toward those goals that are most important to us and the ones we will be able to obtain. The following process may help you work through your goal-selection decisions.

Set goals. Keep a listing of the goals that you and your family hope to achieve. Use Worksheet 2.

Rank goals. List your goals in their order of importance to you and your household.

Assign dollar values to goals. You will not be able to assign a dollar value to all goals now, but to most you will. For example, if you plan to buy a new car next year and you know the amount of the down payment, put this on your worksheet.

Reevaluate your goals. After developing your budget, take another look at Worksheet 2. You may need to drop, postpone, or revise some of your goals. Decide how much change you are willing and able to make. For example, are you willing to change jobs or give up other goals in order to achieve a goal that is more important to you? Think about the tradeoffs of saving for long-term and intermediate goals versus using income for current expenses. How much choice do you have? Can you, and do you want to, cut down

on some immediate goals (current expenses) to improve your chances of meeting your log-term goals? Refer to your goals often as you plan.

Common Goals Throughout the Life Cycle

Some goals are universal to all households, such as providing for sufficient food, comfortable shelter, and financial security. But most goals change as household members progress through the life cycle. When you are young and single, goals generally relate to your own personal development. When you are married and have children, your first priorities may switch from yourself to your children—establishing an education fund, for example. Different types of households use different ways to meet the same goal. For example, a retired couple may provide for their continued financial security during times of high inflation by cutting expenses. A young couple may seek higher paying employment instead.

Look over the following description of household types and determine which group your household resembles. Do you have goals similar to the ones stated for your group? Look at the goals for the other groups. They may help you anticipate future needs. This listing is not meant to be all-inclusive. However, it can be a starting point in determining your current and long-term goals and how those goals may change in years to come.

HOUSEHOLD TYPE 1: SINGLES. This household type consists of adults who have never married, or who are widowed or divorced. It includes persons from age 18 to 54 who are considered to be self-supporting, even though they may be living with relatives or friends and sharing some household expenses. Income for this group may not be high, particularly for the younger members. Important goals involve the individual's personal, educational, and financial development.

HOUSEHOLD TYPE 2: SINGLE PARENTS. Members of this household group may also have never married or are widowed or divorced. Unlike Type I household, they are parents living with dependent children. The critical financial goals for single parents often relate to the care of their children and themselves.

HOUSEHOLD TYPE 3: YOUNG COUPLES. This household type is often called the beginning family or the beginning marriage stage. It is a period of personal and financial adjustment for two persons. Ages of couples in this group typically range from about 18 to 34. There are no children and there are often two incomes. Important goals involve setting up a household and adjusting to each other's needs.

HOUSEHOLD TYPE 4: YOUNG FAMILIES. In this growing-family stage, parents are typically young—age 18 to 34—and have dependent children in the household. There may be two incomes. Critical goals include protecting the family income and rearing the children.

WORKSHEET 2: PROJECTING GOALS

LONG-TERM AND INTERMEDIATE

Goal	Cost of Goal	Number of Years before Needed	Amount Already Saved	Amount to Save Each Year	Amount to Save Each Month
1.					
2.					
3.					
4.					
5.					
6.					
7.					
8.					
9.					
10.					
Total					

IMMEDIATE

Goal	Cost of Goal	Number of Years before Needed	Amount Already Saved	Amount to Save Each Year	Amount to Save Each Month
1.					
2.					
3.					
4.					
5.					
6.					
7.					
8.					
9.					
10.					
Total					

HOUSEHOLD TYPE 5: MIDDLE FAMILIES. This household type is sometimes referred to the contracting family. Parents are typically 35 to 54 years old. Children are "leaving the nest" for college, careers, and marriage. Unique goals for this household include providing for children's college or vocational education, weddings, and the parents' eventual retirement.

HOUSEHOLD TYPE 6: MIDDLE COUPLES. This group consists of persons age 35 to 54 without children. This type of house-hold often contains two earners. Income is often quite high, making investment maximization and tax minimization important financial goals.

HOUSEHOLD TYPE 7: OLDER SINGLES. This group contains persons age 55 and older who may be retired. There is no spouse present in the household. The majority of older singles are females. The major financial goal is to provide adequate income and reserves that will last for the balance of the older single's lifetime.

HOUSEHOLD TYPE 8: OLDER COUPLES. This group consists of married couples ages 55 and over who also may be retired. Their major financial goal is maintenance of an adequate level of living for both persons for life.

The Budgeting Process

A budget is a plan for spending and saving. It requires you to estimate your available income for a particular period of time and decide how to allocate this income toward your expenses. A working budget can help you implement your money management plan. A well-planned budget does several things for you and your household. It can help you:

◆ Prevent impulse spending.
◆ Decide what you can or cannot afford.
◆ Know where your money goes.
◆ Increase savings.
◆ Decide how to protect against the financial consequences of unemployment, accidents, sickness, aging, and death.

A working budget need not be complicated or rigid. However, preparing one takes planning, and following one takes determination. You must do several things to budget successfully.

First, communicate with other members of your household, including older children. Consider each person's needs and wants so that all family members feel they are a part of the plan. Everyone may work harder to make the budget a success and be less

WORKSHEET 3: ESTIMATING YOUR INCOME

SOURCE	JANUARY	FEBRUARY	MARCH	APRIL	MAY	JUNE
Net salary:*						
Household member 1						
Household member 2						
Household member 3						
Household member 4						
Social Security payments						
Pension payments						
Annuity payments						
Veterans' benefits						
Assistance payments						
Unemployment compensation						
Allowances						
Alimony						
Child support						
Gifts						
Interest						
Dividends						
Rents from real estate						
Other						
Monthly Totals						

* Net salary is the amount that comes into the household for spending and saving after taxes, Social Security, and other deductions.

inclined to overspend if they realize the consequences. When families fail to communicate about money matters, it is unlikely that a budget will reflect a workable plan.

Second, be prepared to compromise. This is often difficult. Newlyweds, especially, may have problems. Each may have been living on an individual income and not be accustomed to sharing, or may have been in school and dependent on parents. If, for example, one wants to save for things and the other prefers buying on credit, the two will need to discuss the pros and cons of both methods and decide on a middle ground that each can accept. A plan cannot succeed unless there is a financial partnership.

Third, exercise willpower. Try not to indulge in unnecessary spending. Once your budget plan is made, opportunities to overspend will occur daily. Each household member needs to encour-

age the others to stick to the plan.

Fourth, develop a good recordkeeping system. At first, all members of the household may need to keep records of what they spend. This will show how well they are following the plan and will allow intermediate adjustments in the level of spending. Recordkeeping is especially important during the first year of a spending plan, when you are trying to find a budget that works best for you. Remember, a good budget is flexible, requires little clerical time, and most importantly, works for you.

Choosing a Budget Period

A budget may cover any convenient period of time—a month, three months, or year, for example. Make sure the period you use

JULY	AUGUST	SEPTEMBER	OCTOBER	NOVEMBER	DECEMBER	YEARLY TOTALS

is long enough to cover the bulk of household expenses and income. Remember, not all bills come due monthly and every household experiences some seasonal expenses. Most personal budgets are for 12 months. You can begin the 12-month period at any time during the year. If this is your first budget, you may want to set up a trial plan for a shorter time to see how it works.

After setting up your plan, subdivide it into more manageable operating periods. For a yearly budget, divide income and expenses by 12, 24, 26, or 52, depending on your pay schedule or when your bills come due. Most paychecks are received weekly or every two weeks. Although most bills come due once a month, not all are due at the same time in the month. Try using each paycheck to pay your daily expenses and expenses that will be due within the next week or two. This way you will be able to pay your bills on time. You may also want to allocate something from each paycheck toward large expenses that will be coming due soon.

Developing a Successful Budget

STEP 1: ESTIMATE YOUR INCOME.   Total the money you expect to receive during the budget period. Use Worksheet 3 as a guide in estimating your household income. Begin with regular income that you and your family receive—wages, salaries, income earned from a farm or other business, Social Security benefits, pension payments, alimony, child support, veterans' benefits, public assistance payments, unemployment compensation, allowances, and any other income. Include variable income, such as interest from bank accounts and investments, dividends from stock and insurance, rents from property you own, gifts, and money from any other sources.

If your earnings are irregular, it may be difficult to estimate your income. It is better to underestimate than overestimate income when setting up a budget. Some households have sufficient income, but its receipt does not coincide with the arrival of bills. For these households, planning is very important.

STEP 2: ESTIMATE YOUR EXPENSES.   After you have determined how much your income will be for the planning period, estimate your expenses. You may want to group expenses into one of three categories: fixed, flexible, or set-asides. Fixed expenses are payments that are basically the same amounts each month. Fixed regular expenses include such items as rent or mortgage payments, taxes, and credit installment payments. Fixed irregular expenses are large payments due once or twice a year, such as insurance premiums. Flexible expenses vary from one month to the next, such as amounts spent on food, clothing, utilities, and transportation. Set-asides are variable amounts of money accumulated for special purposes, such as for season expenses, savings and emergency funds, and intermediate and long-term goals.

Use old records, receipts, bills, and cancelled checks to estimate future expenses, if you are satisfied with what your dollars have done for you and your family in the past. If you are not satisfied, now is the time for change. Consider which expenses can be cut back and which expenses need to be increased. If you spent a large amount on entertainment, for example, your new budget may real-

locate some of this money to a savings account to contribute to some of your future goals.

If you do not have past records of spending, or if this is your first budget, the most accurate way to find out how much you will need to allow for each expense is to keep a record of your household spending. Carry a pocket notebook in which you jot down expenditures during a week or pay period and total the amounts at the end of each week. You may prefer to keep an account book in a convenient place at home and make entries in it. Kept faithfully for a month or two, the record can help you find out what you spend for categories such as food, housing, utilities, household operation, clothing, transportation, entertainment, and personal items. Use this record to estimate expenses in your plan for future spending. You also need to plan for new situations and changing conditions that increase or decrease expenses. For example, the cost of your utilities may go up.

Total your expenses for a year and divide to determine the amounts that you will have to allocate toward each expense during the budgeting period. Record your estimate for each budgetary expense in the space provided on Worksheet 4. Begin with the regular fixed expenses that you expect to have. Next, enter those fixed expenses that come due once or twice a year. Many households allocate a definite amount each budget period toward these expenses to spread out the cost.

One way to meet major expenses is to set aside money regularly before you start to spend. Keep your set-aside funds separate from other funds so you will not be tempted to spend them impulsively. If possible, put them in an account where they will earn interest. You may also plan at this point to set aside a certain amount toward the long-term and intermediate goals you listed on Worksheet 2. Saving could be almost as enjoyable as spending, once you accept the idea that saving money is not punishment but a systematic way of reaching your goals. You do without some things now in anticipation of buying what will give you greater satisfaction later.

You may want to clear up debts now by doubling up on your installment payments or putting aside an extra amount in your savings fund to be used for this purpose. Also, when you start to budget, consider designating a small amount of money for emergencies. Extras always come up at the most inopportune times. Every household experiences occasional minor crises too small to be covered by insurance but too large to be absorbed into the day-to-day budget. Examples may be a blown-out tire or an appliance that needs replacing. Decide how large a cushion you want for meeting emergencies. As your fund reaches the figure you have allowed for emergencies, you can start saving for something else. Now, record money allocated for occasional major expenses, future goals, savings, emergencies, and any other set-asides in the space provided for them on Worksheet 4.

After you have entered your fixed expenses and your set-asides, you are ready to consider your flexible expenses. Consider including here a personal allowance or "mad money" for each member of the household. A little spending money that does not have to be accounted for gives everyone a sense of freedom and takes some of the tedium out of budgeting.

WORKSHEET 4: EXPENSE ESTIMATE AND BUDGET BALANCING SHEET, FIXED EXPENSES (PREPARE FOR EACH MONTH)

MONTH

	Amount Estimated	Amount Spent	Difference
Rent			
Mortgage			
Installments:			
Credit card 1			
Credit card 2			
Credit card 3			
Automobile loan			
Personal loan			
Student loan			
Insurance:			
Life			
Health			
Property			
Automobile			
Disability			
Set-asides:			
Emergency fund			
Major expenses			
Goals			
Savings and investments			
Allowances			
Education:			
Tuition			
Books			
Transportation:			
Repairs			
Gas and oil			
Parking and tolls			
Bus and taxi			
Recreation			
Gifts			
Other			

TOTAL FIXED EXPENSES FOR MONTH

STEP 3: BALANCE. Now you are ready for the balancing act. Compare your total expected income with the total of your planned expenses for the budget period. If your planned budget equals your estimated future income, are you satisfied with this outcome? Have you left enough leeway for emergencies and errors? If your expenses add up to more than your income, look again at all parts of the plan. Where can you cut down? Where are you overspending? You may have to decide which things are most important to you and which ones can wait. You may be able to do some trimming on your flexible expenses.

Once you have cut back your flexible expenses, scan your fixed expenses. Maybe you can make some sizable reductions here, too. Rent is a big item in a budget. Some households may want to consider moving to a lower priced apartment or making different living arrangements. Others turn in a too-expensive car and seek less expensive transportation. Look back at Worksheet 2. You may need to reallocate some of this income to meet current expenses. Perhaps you may have to consider saving for some of your goals at a later date.

If you have cut back as much as you think you can or are willing to do and your plan still calls for more than you make, consider ways to increase your income. You may want to look for a better-paying job, or a part-time second job may be the answer. If only one spouse is employed, consider becoming a dual-earner family. The children may be able to earn their school lunch and extra spending money by doing odd jobs in your neighborhood, such as cutting grass or babysitting. Older children can work part-time on weekends to help out. Another possibility, especially for short-term problems, is to draw on savings. These are decisions each individual household has to make.

If your income exceeds your estimate of expenses—good! You may decide to satisfy more of your immediate wants or to increase the amount your family is setting aside for future goals.

Carrying Out Your Budget

After your plan is completed, put it to work. This is when your determination must really come into play. Can you and your family resist impulse spending?

BECOME A GOOD CONSUMER. A vital part of carrying out the budget is being a good consumer. Learn to get the most for your money, to recognize quality, to avoid waste, and to realize time costs as well as money costs in making consumer decisions.

KEEP ACCURATE RECORDS. Accurate financial records are necessary to keep track of your household's actual money inflow and outgo. A successful system requires cooperation from everyone in the household. Receipts can be kept and entered at the end of each budget period in a "Monthly Expense Record" (Worksheet 5). It is sometimes a good idea to write on the back of each receipt what the purchase was for, who made it, and the date. Decide which family member will be responsible for paying bills or making purchases and decide who will keep the record system up to date.

WORKSHEET 5: MONTHLY EXPENSE RECORD

MONTH:

YEAR:

DATE	EXPENSE ITEM	MORTGAGE/ RENT	HOUSEHOLD	UTILITIES	FOOD	CLOTHING	TRANSPORTATION	CHILD CARE	MEDICAL
TOTAL									

SAVINGS	DEBTS	INSURANCE	EDUCATION	PERSONAL CARE	RECREATION	GIFTS	BUSINESS RELATED	OTHER: TAXES, ALLOWANCES, LEGAL FEES

The household business recordkeeping system does not need to be complex. The simpler it is, the more likely it will be kept current. Store your records in one place—a set of folders in a file drawer or other fire-resistant box is a good place. You can assemble a folder for each of several categories including budget, food, clothing, housing, insurance, investments, taxes, health, transportation, and credit. Use these folders for filing insurance policies, receipts, warranties, cancelled checks, bank statements, purchase contracts, and other important papers. Many households also rent a safe deposit box at the bank for storing deeds, stock certificates, and other valuable items.

Evaluating Your Budget

The information on Worksheet 4 can help you determine whether your actual spending follows your plan. If your first plan did not work in all respects, do not be discouraged. A budget is not something you make once and never touch again. Keep revising until results satisfy you.

❖ DEALING WITH UNEMPLOYMENT*

STEP 1: TAKE TIME TO TALK.   Come right out and let your family know what's happened. Layoff? Plant closing? Depressed economy? Business down? Explain what happened. Break down the big words so that everyone understands. Especially the kids.

Fill in everyone at a family meeting or on a one-to-one basis. The important thing is don't leave anyone in the dark. If a family meeting seems out of the question, take time to talk when cleaning up after meals, cutting or raking the lawn, or taking trips to the store. Don't sugar-coat the facts or tell "fairytales." Living with less money will force your family to make hard changes. Yet let your kids know that even though there's less money, they can still count on a loving family—maybe more loving than ever.

STEP 2: TAKE TIME TO LISTEN.   Let everyone have a say about what these changes mean to him or her. Especially now, kids should be seen *and* heard.

Listen to words *and* actions. Is someone suddenly having a lot of crying spells, sleeping in late all the time, acting mean, drinking heavily, withdrawing, abusing drugs, complaining of stomach pains?

STEP 3: FIND OUT WHO'S HURTING.   Let everyone say what he or she is *really* feeling from time to time.

Just repeat whatever you hear, right when it's said. Then look for a nod to see if you heard it right. Is someone feeling helpless,

sad, unloved, confused, worried, frightened, angry, like a burden to the family?

Try not to say "You shouldn't feel that way" because someone may be in real pain. The best you can do is let your loved ones have their say and get it off their chest.

STEP 4: LET YOUR FEELINGS OUT, TOGETHER OR ALONE.   Give everyone in your family a space and time to let deep feelings out. Don't bottle them up or hide them from yourself. If you're not comfortable showing others how you feel or fear you may strike someone who's dear to you, consider getting out of the house for a run or a brisk walk; having a good cry, alone; hitting a cushion or pillow; going to your room, shutting the door, and screaming; or all of the above.

STEP 5: SOLVE PROBLEMS TOGETHER.   Every week, look at the changes taking place in your household and work out ways to deal with them. Working together as a team, your family can do more than survive. It can grow together and come through stronger.

Decide together things like: what we can't afford now; what things we can do for family fun that don't cost a lot of money; who will do what chores around the house; how we'll all get by with less. If your discussions break down, go back to Step 1.

If you have a lot of trouble going through these steps, professional help may be what you need. Call and make an appointment with the family service agency nearest you. Whether or not you have money to pay for the services, the agency will do its best to help your family. Remember, you're not alone.

❖ SOURCES OF HELP IN FINANCIAL CRISES

Aid to Families with Dependent Children (AFDC)

You may be entitled to AFDC if you have dependent children up to age 20 living with you who are your own or who are related to you. The program provides money and services to needy families with children until the families become self-supporting. The money for this program comes from federal, state, and county governments. The program is governed by federal and state laws but is administered through the county welfare department. Each state has different eligibility regulations, and they constantly change. Contact your local county welfare office to find out if your family qualifies.

Food Stamps

You may be eligible for food stamps that will help stretch your food dollar. Eligibility is based on the household's net monthly income and your assets. If you live in your own home, its value is not included in your assets. If you qualify for food stamps, your

* Source: WDIV/TV 4 A Post-Newsweek Station

allotment will be based on the number of people in your family, current or expected income, costs of shelter and dependent care, as well as other factors. These regulations are constantly changing, so check with your county welfare office.

Emergency Needs Program

Any person may apply for emergency help under the Emergency Needs programs administered by the Department of Social Services in some states. Emergency needs for food, clothing, rent, house payments, shelter, utility payments, taxes, security deposits, home repairs, appliances, furniture, transportation, and certain other necessities are considered under this program.

General Assistance (GA)

General Assistance Program is available in some states to those in need who do not qualify for other public aid. The program offers financial help and outpatient medical care. You can be working or receiving disability insurance or other compensation as long as you meet certain income requirements. Incomes of all your family members are considered when your eligibility is being determined.

Medical Assistance

Some states or counties have Medical Assistance programs to help needy persons pay for a variety of medical services.

Your eligibility for medical assistance is determined according to your particular situation and income. You may still be eligible if you own certain types of property. You may be allowed to have (1) a homestead; (2) household items; (3) any tangible personal item you use in earning money; and (4) one passenger car per family. However, you usually cannot claim exemptions for intangible property such as securities, bonds, or cash that's invested or deposited in a savings account if their value exceeds a specific (generally low) limit.

Unemployment Insurance

You will probably qualify for unemployment insurance, which is paid through a payroll tax by your employer, if you have been laid off or lost your job. Also, you may qualify if you are a veteran or a retiree. Unemployment benefits, however, usually do not last longer than six months to a year, depending on state and federal policies.

Mortgage Arrangements

If you are unable to make your mortgage payment because of unemployment, an extended strike, illness, or other circumstances beyond your control, you should contact your mortgage lender *immediately* to discuss your situation. It is best to talk in person with your lender if you can. You may be able to make special arrangements during the period that your income is reduced. If you cannot make such arrangements, you may be able to get other help as suggested below.

If you have an FHA-insured mortgage, ask your mortage lender to refer you to a HUD-approved home ownership counseling agency. The agency will discuss your problem with you and try to find solutions. If you have a VA mortgage or land contract, contact the VA Loan Service and Claims Section.

You may find that other bills are falling behind in addition to your mortgage payments. If so, credit counseling can help you.

Credit Counseling

If you are worried about past due bills, wage garnishment, repossessions, or mortgage foreclosure, help is available. Nonprofit family financial counseling services can help you work out your financial problems and help you get back on your feet with dignity and a minimum of confusion. They will assist you in working out a budget and a debt repayment schedule. Also, they provide professional counseling on money management, family budgeting, and wise use of credit. If needed, they will provide debt management services in which they negotiate with your creditors and forward your payments to them.

Counseling services are often free. For debt management services, fees are based on your ability to pay. No one is refused service because of inability to pay a fee. For referral to the office nearest you, call your local family services or consumer affairs offices.

Utility Assistance

You may qualify for help with your utility bills if you are having trouble paying them or are threatened with a shut-off. There are programs in many states that help those on a limited income to meet their utility payments. Also, assistance in weatherizing homes is available to keep utility costs down. To see if you are eligible for such assistance, contact your local department of social services.

The federal government offers a residential energy tax credit. If you have added insulation or certain other energy-conserving measures to your home since April 1977, you should apply for this credit on your federal income tax return.

Utility Shut-Offs (Gas, Electric, Telephone)

In most states, companies must allow you 14–21 days to pay your bills. If your bill is not paid within this period, you will receive a shut-off notice and ten additional days to pay or to register a complaint. If there is a valid medical emergency in your home, the companies may be prevented temporarily from shutting off your service. They may be able to shut off service only between the hours of 8 AM and 4 PM and not before a day when reconnection cannot be made. You have a right to challenge your bills if you think they are too high or incorrect. Ask for a hearing before the company's hearing examiner. If you are not satisfied with the examiner's decision, you can usually appeal it.

On any question or complaint you have about a utility bill, or if you cannot make full payment on any of your utilities, be sure to call the company's local office before your bill is due and ask for credit arrangements for partial payments. Approval of such a request usually depends on your payment history.

Legal Services

Persons with limited incomes can get legal counseling by contacting Legal Aid offices. Check in the Yellow Pages under "Attorneys."

CONSUMER INFORMATION

❖ SHOPPING FOR GOODS AND SERVICES

There are many criteria that you as a consumer can use to choose any product. The first step is to decide what your needs are. Is the purchase necessary at all? If the answer is "yes," you can form a clearer idea of your choice by listing your criteria before looking at the market.

For example, suppose you are choosing a blanket for your child's bed.

Necessary?	Yes, child complains of cold
Size?	Twin (single bed)
Long life?	Yes, she's young (10 to 15 years)
Color?	Anything but white
Dry-clean?	No
Warmth?	Very warm
Resale possibilities?	Not important

Equipped with these decisions, you can buy the quality you need and avoid features you do not need. Sometimes comparative shopping is not reasonable. If your car is sputtering, for example, immediate necessity has the strongest claim and you are likely to pull into the nearest gas station, not the cheapest. But for many purchases, especially the larger ones (rugs, appliances, automobiles, house paint), comparative shopping is worth the time and effort it requires. Telephoning two or three stores for price checks will usually give you an idea of high and low prices, and it only takes ten minutes.

Many people are unsure of the quality or special features of merchandise they are considering. Brand name advertising and store clerks' sales pitches are not necessarily reliable sources of information. In our example, how would you know what the warmest, longest-lasting, machine-washable blanket on the market might be? The publications of the Consumers Union and Consumers Research, Inc. are a good source of this type of information. These two nonprofit organizations for consumer protection and enlightenment test products at random and publish their findings. They are mostly testing for safety and efficiency. If you are basically interested in economy or style, your opinions may differ.

The *Consumer Reports Buying Guide* and *Consumers Research Annual Guide,* although they sometimes list brand names that have gone off the market during the year, have a wealth of information on a wide range of goods. You can receive a free copy of Consumer's Resource Handbook" by writing to: U.S. Consumer Information Center, Dept. 579L, Pueblo, CO 81009. (Also see Self-Help Resource Directory under "Consumer Services.")

Secondhand Goods

Many durable goods (as opposed to food or services) can be purchased secondhand and serve your need just as happily and more economically. A rake, a rug, a bicycle, a car would be some examples of this sort of purchase. Many people discard goods before they have worn out. If newness is not a major criterion, you can save many dollars by buying used items.

It is also wise to be cautious in making these purchases. Some people get carried away by the prospect of picking up something for almost nothing. Are you getting your money's worth? Many items—a rake or a bed frame, say—most people can judge themselves. But if the item requires repair or involves mechanical or electrical equipment, you can judge well only according to how much you know about that item. Do you want to spend six hours and several dollars repainting that chest of drawers? If you know nothing about cars, it is wise to consult or bring someone you trust with you to judge the car before you buy it. Buying secondhand goods you are unable to judge can be a way of throwing away money.

Newspaper want-ads, garage or tag sales, and secondhand stores are the most common sources for finding secondhand goods.

Buying Services

In the matter of buying services—insurance, gardening, hauling, plumbing—there is nothing like shopping around. Services are almost always competitive. There may be a going rate in the area for a particular service, but there is usually some company that hopes to get business by being cheaper. And for many services the price range varies widely. This may or may not reflect the quality of the service you will get. It is wise to ask lots of questions: Will repair-people make house calls? Will the garden clippings be hauled away? What does the insurance cover, exactly? Companies are used to getting these calls. You may run into some grouches, but most businesspeople will be happy to answer your questions. They are offering a service. You are paying. You have the right to know how your money will be spent.

Consumer Complaints

What do you do when you are tricked, gypped, or robbed? What do you do when the service is not provided or the item is no good?

The first step is to call or write the place of business. State the problem and state what you want (I want the item replaced. I want my money back. I expect you to do the work this week.) If you write, you should make sure that the letter has your address, it is dated, and you should make a copy of it to keep. Often the problem is unintentional. The storekeeper is happy to replace the item; the businessperson is happy to provide the service. if you cannot get prompt, courteous service from an employee, contact the manager. If the manager does not provide satisfaction, write directly to the president of the company or corporation, describing the problem. Letters to the president often produce quick action. Send a copy to the person with whom you were dealing.

You usually want to avoid calling in a third party. It always means time and trouble on your part. However, if you feel that you have been treated unfairly or that the provider does not respond to your complaint, you should tell the company that you intend to call in a consumer agency, and then do it.

Every state and most counties across the Untied States have a consumer affairs agency listed in the phone book under the name of the county you live in. This is the best place to start. Tell the person at the agency what sort of complaint you have. You will probably be referred to another number. There are many branches of consumer protection. These agencies usually carry weight with businesspeople. They are your "big stick." Often their interference will produce the results you want if you can prove your case. However, it may be months before this happens. Sometimes, though, they can do nothing (if the company has gone bankrupt, for instance). This possibility must be accepted.

❖ BUYING ON CREDIT

Credit buying is how most people purchase houses, automobiles, and other large consumer goods. This term also refers to some credit card buying. Buying on credit is always more expensive than purchasing with cash. Besides paying for the item, you are paying to use someone's money. This raises the price of the purchase considerably. Why does anyone do it, then? Why not wait until you have the cash to buy?

Buying on credit gives a person the advantage of using something he or she does not have the money to buy at the moment. If you buy a car on credit and your payments are $200 a month, you have the use of a car for about $6 a day for several years. And at the end of those years you own it.

How to Obtain Credit

Remember that credit is something like rented money. You want to rent it from the person who will charge you the least for borrowing. The lender wants to have some assurance that you will pay back the loan plus a little something for letting you use the money

in the first place. Some lenders can be quite mercenary about the "little something." This is why you want to know your options.

THE LENDER'S QUESTIONS. The lender will want to know how able or likely you are to pay back the debt:

◆ What your yearly income is
◆ How long you have worked at the same job
◆ How long you have lived where you live now
◆ What your normal expenses are per month
◆ How much will be available to pay a loan with
◆ What your past record for repaying loans shows (called a credit rating*)
◆ What assets (called collateral) you have that can cover the debt if you cannot repay. Assets include real estate (land, houses), savings accounts, stocks, cars, and other material goods

THE BORROWER'S RIGHTS. The 1968 Truth-in-Lending Act, which applies to loans of $25,000 or less from most regular institutions, requires the lender to tell the borrower exactly how much interest is being charged on the loan. Ask.

The 1975 Equal Credit Opportunity Act prohibits discrimination in lending on the basis of sex, age, or marital status. It is now illegal for lenders to demand that a person provide his or her spouse's name, salary, or job description when the person wants credit in his or her own name. A parent or spouse's co-signature cannot be required if the loan does not involve them. Alimony and child support payments must be considered regular income. Young couples do not need to divulge their methods of birth control or their intentions to bear children. And a lender cannot change the terms of credit because of a borrower's change in marital status, age, or job status.

The Equal Credit Opportunity Act was chiefly designed to end unfair practices against women. Banks and other lenders advise women to establish their own credit histories to avoid problems when borrowing. This can be done by obtaining credit cards in one's own name (Janet Doe not Mrs. John Doe) or by taking out and repaying a small loan.

Where to Get Money

The cheapest way to borrow money is from yourself (if you can).

SAVINGS. If you have a savings account, you can use it as collateral for a loan. You might be able to borrow up to 95 percent of the value of the account. If the loan is at 16 percent and your account makes 6 percent, the net interest on the loan is 10 percent.

LIFE INSURANCE. Certain life insurance policies have a pool of money—the cash value—from which you can borrow. It is your

---

* Paying your bills on time does not give you a good credit rating—you must prove you are capable of repaying *loans*.

money, so you cannot be turned down for the loan. If you do not or cannot repay, the debt is repaid from your insurance policy.

CREDIT UNIONS. Credit unions are cooperatives, so you must belong to use one. They are very attractive, however. The average interest on loans runs 2 to 3 percent less than commercial banks. If the cooperative has a good year, you will also get some money back at the end.

Other Sources of Credit

COMMERCIAL BANKS. Banks are the usual source for many business and personal loans, especially for cars and homes.

SALES FINANCE COMPANIES. These companies buy install-ment contracts, and their risks, from retail merchants. Most car loans that are not paid to commercial banks are paid to finance companies. About one-third of all personal loans also come from these finance companies.

CONSUMER FINANCE COMPANIES. These companies make small loans to consumers, usually at a very high interest rate. The loans are usually made for items other than the "biggies" (cars, homes, stereos)—for furniture, perhaps. The companies usually advertise their loan consolidation services on TV and radio—that is, paying several small loans with one bigger one.

Credit Cards

Credit cards issued by retail stores or national companies can be used in two ways. If you use your card only for purchases within your budget, you can always pay your credit card bill in full on time. Depending on the particular card, there may be no finance charge and no extra charges. You have used it like a check or like cash. It has the advantage of delaying cash payment, since it may take a month or more for a purchase to show on the bill. But you are not paying to borrow money, only for the item. Credit cards can also be used to buy items on credit—hence, the name. You can buy $200 speakers today, pay $20 plus finance charges for the next ten months, and use the speakers. Many credit card holders receive various "enhancements" along with their cards, such as travel and accident insurance, emergency cash, airline tickets, trav-el discounts, and bonus merchandise programs.

The pitfall of credit card buying is that these cards are easy to use but the finance charges are high, usually equivalent to 18 or 19 percent interest. Also, late charges are added if payments are not made within a certain number of days. Many people buy items on credit that are not worth the high price of the money they are using. Many people also overbuy without considering their income and so find themselves continually in debt. Only one-third of cred-it card users pay their bills before incurring finance charges (that is, interest).

Credit card charge accounts are also called "revolving charge plans." There is a top limit, but purchases are added as they are made without a new agreement being written. A credit card's top limit, however, is usually no more than several thousand dollars. Most large purchases must be financed differently.

If you need to make a purchase on credit, check with banks, saving and loan associations, finance companies, your credit union, your life insurance company, and possibly the company from which you are making the purchase to determine which one offers the lowest annual percentage rate (APR). Also compare the annual fees of credit cards. Some cards are available at no yearly charge.

❖ FAIR CREDIT REPORTING ACT*

If you have a charge account, a mortgage on your home, a life insurance policy, or if you have applied for a personal loan or a job, it is almost certain that somewhere there is a "file" that shows how promptly you pay your bills, whether you have been sued or arrested, or if you have filed for bankruptcy, and so on. Such a file may include your neighbors' and friends' views of your character, general reputation, or manner of living.

The companies that gather and sell such information to credi-tors, insurers, employers, and other businesses are called consumer reporting agencies, and the legal term for the report is a consumer report. If, in addition to credit information, the report includes interviews with a third person about your character, reputation, or manner of living, it is referred to as an investigative consumer report.

The Fair Credit Reporting Act became law on April 25, 1971. This act was passed by Congress to protect consumers against the circulation of inaccurate or obsolete information and to ensure that consumer reporting agencies adopt fair and equitable procedures for obtaining, maintaining, and giving out information about con-sumers. Under this law, you can take steps to protect yourself if you have been denied credit, insurance, or employment or if you believe you have had difficulties because of an inaccurate or an unfair consumer report.

You Have the Right:

1. To be told the name and address of the consumer reporting agency responsible for preparing a consumer report that was used to deny you credit, insurance, or employment or to increase the cost of credit or insurance.

2. To be told by a consumer reporting agency the nature, sub-stance, and sources (except investigative-type sources) of the infor-mation (except medical) collected about you.

3. To take anyone of your choice with you when you visit the consumer reporting agency to check on your file.

4. To obtain free of charge all information to which you are enti-tled if the request is made within 30 days after receipt of a notifica-

* Office of Consumer Affairs, Federal Deposit Insurance Corporation (1987).

tion that you have been denied credit, insurance, or employment because of information contained in a consumer report. Otherwise, the consumer reporting agency is permitted to charge a reasonable fee for giving you the information.

5. To be told who has received a consumer report on you within the preceding six months or within the preceding two years if the report was furnished for employment purposes.

6. To have incomplete or incorrect information reinvestigated unless the consumer reporting agency has reasonable grounds to believe that the dispute is frivolous or irrelevant. If the information is investigated and found to be inaccurate or if the information cannot be verified, you have the right to have such information removed from your file.

7. To have the consumer reporting agency notify those you name (at no cost to you), who have previously received the incorrect or incomplete information, that this information has been deleted from your file.

8. When a dispute between you and the reporting agency about information in your file cannot be resolved, you have the right to have your version of such dispute placed in the file and included in future consumer reports.

9. To request the reporting agency to send your version of the dispute to certain businesses without charge, if requested within 30 days of the adverse action.

10. To have a consumer report withheld from anyone who under the law does not have a legitimate business need for the information.

11. To sue a report agency for damages if the agency willfully or negligently violates the law; and, if you are successful, to collect attorney's fees and court costs.

12. Not to have adverse information reported after seven years. One major exception is bankruptcy, which may be reported for ten years.

13. To be notified by a business that it is seeking information about you that would constitute an investigative consumer report.

14. To request from the business that ordered an investigative consumer report more information about the nature and scope of the investigation.

15. To discover the nature and substance (but not the sources) of the information that was collected for an investigative consumer report.

The Fair Credit Reporting Act Does Not:

1. Require the consumer reporting agency to provide you with a copy of your file, although some agencies will voluntarily give you a copy.

2. Compel anyone to do business with an individual consumer.

3. Apply when you request commercial (as distinguished from consumer) credit or business insurance.

4. Authorize any federal agency to intervene on behalf of an individual consumer.

5. Require a consumer reporting agency to add new accounts to your file; however, some may do so for a fee.

How to Deal with Consumer Reporting Agencies

It you want to know what information a consumer reporting agency has collected about you, either arrange for a personal interview at the agency's office during normal business hours or call in advance for an interview by telephone. Some agencies will voluntarily make disclosure by mail. The consumer reporting agencies in your community can be located by consulting the Yellow Pages of your telephone book under such headings as "Credit" or "Credit Rating or Reporting Agencies."

If you decide to visit a consumer reporting agency to check on your file, the following check list may be of help. For instance, in checking your credit file, did you:

1. Learn the nature and substance of all the information in your file?

2. Find out the name of each of the businesses (or other sources) that supplied information on you to the reporting agency?

3. Learn the name of everyone who received reports on you within the past six months (or the last two years if the reports were for employment purposes)?

4. Request the agency to reinvestigate and correct or delete information that was found to be inaccurate, incomplete, or obsolete?

5. Follow up to determine the results of the reinvestigation?

6. Ask the agency, at no cost to you, to notify those you name who received reports within the past six months (two years if for employment purposes) that certain information was deleted?

7. Follow up to make sure that those named by you did, in fact, receive notices from the consumer reporting agency?

8. Demand that your version of the facts be placed in your file if the reinvestigation did not settle the dispute?

9. Ask the agency to send your statement of the dispute to those you name who received reports containing the disputed information within the past six months (two years if received for employment purposes)? A reasonable fee may be charged for this service if you have not incurred adverse action from a creditor within the last 30 days.

The federal agency that supervises consumer reporting agencies is the Federal Trade Commission (FTC). Questions or complaints concerning consumer reporting agencies should be directed to the Federal Trade Commission, Division of Credit Practices, Washington, D.C. 20580.

❖ BUYING A HOME*

What Can You Afford?

You've probably heard various ways to estimate what you can afford to spend on a home. These methods can be useful in arriving at approximate figures, but they overlook the variables that can affect your financial capability.

* Reprinted by permission from the CIRcular™ Consumer Information Report, "Steps to Buying a Home," copyright Bank of America NT&SA 1982, 1985.

Generally, the ideal monthly payments should equal about 25% of your gross monthly income, minus any outstanding debts. But you may be able to manage a monthly payment of up to 40 percent of your gross monthly income, depending on other factors. For example, you may be willing to cut back on other nonessential costs, or you may be at the start of a promising career.

To figure what you can spend on a home, you need to make two basic calculations: How much can you pay each month for the long-term expenses of owning a home? How much cash can you spend for the initial costs of buying a home?

MONTHLY HOUSING COSTS.   You can calculate how much you have to spend by preparing a personal financial statement that details total income and expenses. You'll also need this information when you apply for a loan. Begin preparing your statement by listing monthly income after taxes and other deductions. You should include your income and the income of anyone else participating in the purchase. Use an average figure if the income varies from month to month or year to year, and exclude any irregular income.

Next, estimate your average monthly expenses for all nonhousing items—food, clothing, savings, debts, and so on—and subtract them from your monthly net income. What's left is the maximum amount you can pay each month for all long-term home ownership costs.

Remember, in addition to loan payments, your monthly costs also include payments for taxes and assessments, insurance, maintenance, and utilities. Unless you're willing to stick to a very strict budget, you'll probably be more comfortable with a home loan payment that's less than the maximum amount you can afford. When you find a home in which you're interested, get estimates of monthly costs for the following:

Home Loan Payments. You'll probably take out a loan to pay a major part of the purchase price, so it's a good idea to shop for a loan before you look for a home. Talk to several lenders about your eligibility for a loan, the maximum amount you can reasonably expect, their current loan terms, and the monthly payments for different loan amounts, repayment periods, and interest rates.

Property Taxes. [Laws vary by state.] Improving the home can affect its tax valuation.

Property Insurance. The cost of insuring a home varies with the home's age, type of construction, and location. As a general estimate, the annual insurance premium is one-third of 1 percent of the home's price. For a more accurate figure, call several local insurance agents, describe the home, and ask what you must pay to insure it. Lenders usually require you to carry enough insurance to cover the amount of your loan, but you may consider getting more, based on the cost of replacing your home.

Repair and Utilities. These costs vary with the home's age, size, design, and condition.

Tax Considerations. At the present time, you can deduct your property taxes, the interest payments on your home, and the loan origination fee you pay your lender on your federal income tax returns. [State laws may vary.]

CASH NEEDED.   To calculate how much you have available to spend on a home, add up savings (other than an emergency reserve) and investments you might cash in. You'll need money for the following costs:

Professionals' Fees. You might hire professionals such as a housing inspector and an attorney during the home-buying process. Ask them for fee estimates first.

Closing Costs. These are fees for services, including those performed by the lender, escrow agent, and title company. Closing costs can range from several hundred to several thousand dollars. Federal law requires the lender to send you an estimate of the closing costs within three days after you've applied for the loan. Although local custom usually determines who—you or the seller—pays for what costs, you may be able to negotiate some of the fees. Include the results of any negotiations in your written purchase contract.

For a full explanation of various closing fees, read the booklet on settlement costs prepared by the U.S. Department of Housing and Urban Development (HUD). It's available free from lenders and HUD offices.

Down Payment. The usual down payment required by many lenders is 20 percent of the home's total cost. The actual amount depends on the type of loan, your lender's policy, and current economic conditions. Typically, for down payments of less than 20 percent, the lender will require that the buyer purchase private mortgage insurance (PMI). PMI protects the lender against loss if you don't pay as agreed.

It is possible to reduce or eliminate your need for down payment cash. For instance, you can:

◆ Apply for a Federal Housing Administration [or a] Veterans Administration loan, which require relatively low down payments. . . .
◆ Lease a home with an option to buy it at a later date for an agreed-upon price. Usually, some or all of the rent you pay is credited against the purchase price. The buyer may have to pay an added charge for this option.

Select an Area

The area you choose can greatly affect your pocketbook as well as your personal happiness. For instance, you should consider how far the home is from your job and what distance you're willing to commute each day. Drive around and note the neighborhoods that appeal to you. Ask city officials, real estate agents, local businesspeople, and your prospective neighbors about the following points:

PUBLIC SERVICES.   How close is the fire station? Where is the nearest hospital? Is reliable public transportation available? Are good schools nearby? And can your children safely and easily walk or take transportation to get to them?

PUBLIC SAFETY.   Get crime statistics from the local police. Ask for a report or map indicating the crime rates for various areas.

ZONING AND TAXES.   Contact the city or county planning department about plans for your area. Are there plans to widen the streets or add new buildings nearby? Ask the local tax assessor about assessments—charges for local public improvement such as paving, street lighting, and public transit. Have they been rising sharply, and are they likely to continue doing so? Find out about my local homeowner's tax exemptions or other tax credits you may be entitled to receive.

ENVIRONMENTAL CONDITIONS.   City of county planning officials can tell you about such problems as flooding, erosion, smog, fire hazards, and earthquake fault lines that are present in your area.

Look for Homes

Begin looking for houses that best meet your needs. Consider the following:

TYPE OF OWNERSHIP.   Do you want to live in a single- or multiple-family residence? Or are you interested in a condominium or a planned unit development (PUD)? With a condominium or PUD, you and the other owners share rights to some parts of the property, called common areas. Usually, you'll also have to pay homeowner's dues.

LENGTH OF USE.   Many people stay in their homes longer than they originally planned. Look ahead at least five years and try to anticipate changes—such as family size—that might affect your housing needs.

SPACE.   Measure your present home's rooms, storage areas, and work surfaces, noting which spaces are large enough and which aren't. Then look for houses that are designed to meet your needs.

WHERE TO LOOK.   Find out about homes for sale by reading newspaper ads and by consulting real estate agents recommended by your friends, other agents, or the local real estate board. Pick up buyers' guides from realty and builders' associations, lenders, and stores. And ask friends living in the area to watch for home sales.

Inspect the Home

Inspect thoroughly any home you're interested in buying. Read books on homes and consult knowledgeable friends to learn how to inspect a home and judge the quality of the workmanship, materials, and design.

PROFESSIONAL INSPECTORS.   It's generally a wise investment to hire a housing inspector to confirm your own judgment about the home. A housing inspector—unlike an appraiser, who judges the dollar value of a home—provides a detailed, written evaluation of the home's condition. Fees typically range from $100 to $200. Before hiring an inspector, make sure he or she is licensed and bonded. Find out whether the inspector's work is guaranteed and, if so, for how long.

You also should have a licensed pest control inspector check the home whether or not the lender requires such an inspection. The seller usually pays the cost.

WARRANTIES.   The seller may provide a home protection contract (home warranty). Or you can purchase one from a home protection company. A typical new-home warranty, whose term may range from one to ten years, covers the home's structure, its major systems (plumbing, heating, and electrical), and any appliances sold with the home. On an existing home, the warranty typically covers major systems and appliances for one year.

Make an Offer

Consider making your first offer for less than the asking price if you think the home is overpriced for the market or the circumstances are favorable—for example, if the seller seems eager to close the sale.

THE PURCHASE CONTRACT.   When you decide what price to offer, you draw up a contract stating the sale terms. You submit your offer to the seller, who either accepts it as is or makes changes and sends it back to you. The contract goes back and forth as many times as necessary to reach an agreement. You should sign the contract only when both of you are satisfied.

According to state law, no agreement for the sale of real estate can be enforced unless it's in writing. Look over the contract carefully—with your legal adviser if possible—to make sure it covers all the sale conditions you want included. Following are some points you may wish to cover:

◆ The conditions under which the contract may be canceled without penalty—for instance, if you can't get the financing you want or if the home doesn't pass professional inspection.
◆ The closing costs you'll pay and those the seller will pay.
◆ An itemized list describing furnishings, appliances, and other personal property the sale includes and excludes.
◆ The date on which you'll check the home's condition before the sale is final.
◆ The date you get possession of the home.

THE DEPOSIT. At the time you sign the contract, you'll be asked for a deposit, sometimes referred to as earnest money. The amount can range from hundreds to thousands of dollars, depending on what you're willing to give and what the seller is willing to accept. The deposit usually is applied to the down payment or to your share of the closing costs. If the sale falls through, the deposit either will be kept by the seller or returned to you, according to the terms of your purchase contract.

ESCROW. Once you and the seller have signed a purchase agreement, you're ready to begin escrow—a procedure in which your deposit and any other pertinent documents are placed in the keeping of a neutral third party called the escrow agent. You and the seller must agree on the agent, who may be from a title insurance company, an escrow company, or the lender's own escrow department.

Escrow can begin before or after you've arranged financing. You and the seller negotiate and sign a set of escrow instructions listing the conditions (including financing) that must be met before the sale is finalized. The escrow agent distributes the money and documents according to the escrow instructions.

COMPARE LOAN TERMS. Before you choose a loan, it's critical that you compare the following loan terms for similar types of loans:

Down Payment and Loan Fees. Those vary with the lender and type of loan.

Interest Rate. This is the cost of borrowing the money, usually a percentage of the loan amount. A small variation in the interest rate can add up to thousands of dollars in the total loan payment amount.

The lender is required to tell you the annual percentage rate (APR). This is the cost of the loan per year including interest and additional finance charges, such as loan origination and certain closing fees. The APR expresses these charges as a percentage.

Repayment Period. With a fixed-rate loan, the longer the repayment period, the higher the total cost of the loan; but a shorter repayment period generally means a larger monthly payment. With an adjustable rate loan, the total cost and the monthly payment are affected by interest rate changes as well as by the repayment period. If your loan rate isn't fixed, you'll want to know whether you can extend the repayment period to reduce any increase in your monthly payment.

Prepayment. A lender may reserve the right to charge a fee—called a prepayment premium—if you pay back all or part of your loan early. Your promissory note (loan contract) usually will contain a clause describing under what conditions you must pay this premium. If the promissory note isn't specific, ask what these conditions are.

OTHER FINANCING. Instead of—or in addition to—getting a new loan from a lender, you may be able to obtain financing in one of the following ways:

Assumptions. Federal law permits lenders to make most loans nonassumable. To find out whether you can assume (take over) the seller's loan, check with the seller's lender. If the loan is assumable, you may be able to pay the seller the difference between the amount still owed on the loan and the purchase price and take over payments where the seller left off.

You make payment either to the seller or directly to the seller's lender. In the latter case, you may have to pay any loan fees and provide whatever credit information the lender requires.

An assumption can be a good arrangement if you can take over the loan at a lower-than-current interest rate. Some lenders, however, may require you to assume the loan at the current rate.

You may need more financing to make up the difference between the purchase price and the amount assumed. The seller often may carry the loan—grant you credit—for a short time (usually three to five years). This way, depending on the amount and the credit terms, you could have a large balloon payment. If you're thinking about having the seller carry the loan, consider whether you'll be able to meet the credit terms and make any balloon payment when it comes due. You'll also need to determine whether refinancing will be available, and, if not, whether the seller will extend the financing agreement.

As an alternative to assuming the seller's loan, you might negotiate with the seller's lender to give you a loan for the difference between the purchase price of the home and the down payment. In many cases, you can obtain an interest rate that's between the rate on the seller's original loan and the current rate.

Buy Downs. With a buy-down arrangement, the seller pays the lending institution an amount to lower the interest rate on your loan. Usually, the term is for a specified period of time—typically one to five years. After that, you pay the rate the lender was charging at the time you took out the loan.

Equity Sharing. Consider arranging for other investors to pay part of the loan, the down payment, or closing costs in exchange for part of the equity in your home. Many real estate agents and some states and local government agencies offer this kind of financing arrangement—sometimes called a shared-appreciation program.

In addition to all these financing alternatives, the seller may offer a variety of other arrangements. When considering any type of loan, be sure to get professional legal, tax, and real estate advice.

Close the Deal

Closing—also called settlement or closing escrow—is the final step. Before the sale is finalized, you must deposit in escrow all of the down payment and your closing costs. At the close of escrow, the agent will give your deposit and loan funds to the seller and have the deed recorded. After the recording, you'll receive the deed by mail in about 30 days.

❖ FAIR DEBT COLLECTION*

If you use credit cards, owe money on a loan, or are paying off a home mortgage, you are a "debtor." Most Americans are.

You may never come in contact with a debt collector. But if you do, you should know that there is a law to make sure you are treated fairly. The Fair Debt Collection Practices Act was passed by Congress in 1977 to prohibit certain methods of debt collection. Of course, the law does not erase any legitimate debt you owe.

The following questions and answers may help you understand your rights under the Debt Collection Act.

What Debts are Covered?

Personal, family, and household debts are covered under the act. This includes money owed for the purchase of a car, for medical care, or for charge accounts.

Who Is a Debt Collector?

A debt collector is any person, other than the creditor, who regularly collects debts owed to others. Under a 1986 amendment to the Fair Debt Collection Practices Act, this includes attorneys who collect debts on a regular basis. The act does not apply to attorneys who handle debt collection matters only a few times a year.

How May a Debt Collector Contact You?

A debt collector may contact you in person or by mail, telephone, or telegram. However, a debt collector may not contact you at inconvenient or unusual times or places, such as before 8 AM or after 9 PM, unless you agree. A debt collector may not contact you at work if the debt collector has reason to know that your employer disapproves.

Can You Stop a Debt Collector from Contacting You?

You may stop a debt collector from contacting you by writing a letter to the collection agency telling it to stop. Once the agency receives your letter, it may not contact you again except to say that there will be no further contact or to notify you that some specific action will be taken, if the debt collector or the creditor intends to take such action.

May a Debt Collector Contact Any Other Person Concerning Your Debt?

If you have an attorney, the collector may not contact anyone but the attorney. If you do not have an attorney, a debt collector may contact other people, but only to find out where you live or work.

* SOURCE: Federal Trade Commission, "Facts for Consumers" (1986).

In most cases, the collector is not allowed to tell anyone other than you or your attorney that you owe money. Collectors are usually prohibited from contacting any person more than once.

What Is the Debt Collector Required to Tell You about the Debt?

Within five days after you are first contacted, the debt collector must send you a written notice telling you the amount of money you owe; the name of the creditor to whom you owe the money; and what to do if you believe you do not owe the money.

If You Believe You Do Not Owe the Money, May a Debt Collector Continue to Contact You?

The debt collector may not contact you if, within 30 days after you are first contacted, you send the collector a letter saying you do not owe the money. However, a debt collector can begin collection activities again if you are sent proof of the debt, such as a copy of the bill.

What Types of Debt Collection Practices Are Prohibited?

HARASSMENT. Debt collectors may not harass, oppress, or abuse any person. For example, debt collectors may not:

◆ Use threats of violence or harm to the person, property, or reputation.
◆ Publish a list of consumers who refuse to pay their debts (except to a credit bureau).
◆ Use obscene or profane language.
◆ Repeatedly use the telephone to annoy someone.
◆ Telephone people without identifying themselves.
◆ Advertise your debt.

FALSE STATEMENTS. Debt collectors may not use any false statements when collecting a debt. For example, debt collectors may not:

◆ Falsely imply that they are an attorney or government representative.
◆ Falsely imply that you have committed a crime.
◆ Falsely represent that they operate or work for a credit bureau.
◆ Misrepresent the amount of the debt.
◆ Indicate that papers being sent are legal forms when they are not.

Also, debt collectors may not say that:

◆ You will be arrested if you do not pay your debt.
◆ They will seize, garnish, attach, or sell your property or wages, unless the collection agency or the creditor intends to do so, and it is legal.
◆ Actions will be taken against you that legally may not be taken.

Debt collectors may not:

◆ Give false credit information about you to anyone.
◆ Send you anything that resembles an official document from a court or government agency.
◆ Use a false name.

UNFAIR PRACTICES. Debt collectors may not engage in unfair practices in attempting to collect a debt. For example, debt collectors may not:

◆ Collect any amount greater than your debt, unless allowed by law.
◆ Deposit a postdated check before the date on the check.
◆ Make you accept collect calls or pay for telegrams.
◆ Take or threaten to take your property unless this can be done legally.
◆ Contact you by postcard.

What Control Do You Have over Payment of Debts?

If you owe several debts, any payment you make must be applied to the debt you choose. A debt collector may not apply a payment to any debt you believe you do not owe.

What Can You Do If You Believe a Debt Collector Broke the Law?

You have the right to sue a debt collector in a state or federal court within one year from the date you believe the law was violated. If you win, you may recover money for the damage you suffered. Court costs and attorney's fees also can be recovered. A group of people may sue a debt collector and recover money for damages up to $500,000, or 1 percent of the collector's net worth, whichever is less.

Where Can You Report a Debt Collector for an Alleged Violation of the Law?

Report any problems with a debt collector to your state attorney general's office. Many states also have their own debt collection laws and your attorney general's office can help you to determine your rights.

If you have a question about your rights under the Fair Debt Collection Practices Act, the Federal Trade Commission may be able to assist you. While the FTC cannot intervene in individual disputes, information from consumers about their experiences is vital to the enforcement of the act. Contact your regional FTC office or the Washington, D.C., office: 6th & Pennsylvania Avenues, N.W., Washington, D.C. 20580, (202) 326-2222.

Glossary

A

AaBC-X model of family stress See *Double ABC-X model of family stress.*

aberration A departure from what is culturally defined as "normal" behavior.

abortion The termination of a pregnancy either through miscarriage (spontaneous abortion) or through human intervention (induced abortion).

abstinence Refraining from sexual intercourse, often on religious or moral grounds.

abuelo [fem. -a] [Spanish] Grandfather; grandmother.

abuelos [Spanish] Grandparents.

abuse Mistreatment; wrong, bad, injurious, or excessive use.

acculturation The process of adapting to the patterns or customs of a different, usually dominant, culture.

acquaintance rape Rape in which the assailant is personally known to the victim.

adaptability Ability to adjust relationships, roles, and rules to changing circumstances.

adolescence The psychological state occurring during puberty.

adoption The process by which an individual or couple legally become the parents of a child not biologically their own.

adultery Sexual intercourse between a married person and someone other than his or her spouse.

affiliate To take in or adopt as a member.

affiliated family A family in which non-related individuals are treated as family members.

affinity 1. Relationship by marriage. 2. A close relationship.

affirmative action Programs that attempt to place qualified members of minorities in government, corporate, and educational institutions from which they have been historically excluded because of their minority status.

afterbirth The placenta and fetal membranes expelled from the uterus during the third stage of labor.

afterplay Erotic activity, such as kissing, caressing, sex talk, and oral/genital contact, following coitus.

agape According to sociologist John Lee's styles of love, altruistic love.

agglutination test A urine analysis test used to determine the presence of human chorionic gonadotropin (HCG) secreted by the placenta, which is an indication of pregnancy.

AIDS Acquired Immune Deficiency Syndrome. A generally fatal infection caused by the human immunodeficiency virus (HIV), which suppresses the immune system. Transmitted primarily through semen and blood.

alcoholism An illness characterized by preoccupation with alcohol and loss of control over its consumption so as to usually lead to intoxication, repetition, progression, and a tendency for relapse.

alimony Court-ordered monetary support to a spouse or former spouse following separation or divorce.

alpha-feto protein (AFP) screening Test(s) of a pregnant woman's blood that can reveal neural tube defects in the fetus.

amniocentesis A process in which amniotic fluid is removed by syringe to determine possible birth defects.

amniotic fluid The fluid surrounding the developing embryo or fetus within the amniotic sac.

amniotic sac A fluid-filled membrane pouch enclosing the fetus.

ampulla The upper part of the vas deferens, which contracts during emission.

anal intercourse Penetration of the anus by the penis.

androgynous gender role A gender role concept emphasizing flexibility in combining instrumental and expressive traits in accordance with individual differences.

androgyny The state of having flexible gender roles combining instrumental and expressive traits in accordance with unique individual differences.

annulment The legal invalidation of a marriage as if the marriage never occurred.

anus The orifice for the elimination of fecal matter.

artificial insemination Introduction of semen into the vagina by artificial means, usually a syringe.

artificial insemination by donor (AID) Artificial insemination using semen from someone other than the woman's partner, usually because of sterility or high risk of birth defect; also known as *therapeutic donor insemination (TDI).*

Asian American Collective term relating to those of Asian descent, such as Chinese American, Japanese American, Korean American, or Cambodian American.

assimilation Process by which individuals or groups adopt another group's culture and lose their original identity.

asymptomatic   Not showing symptoms.

attachment   Close, enduring emotional bonds.

atypical sexual behavior   A sexual behavior that departs from the norm; a sexual variation.

authoritarian parenting   A parenting style characterized by the demand for absolute obedience.

authoritative parenting   A parenting style that recognizes the parent's legitimate power and also stresses the child's feelings, individuality, and need to develop autonomy.

autoeroticism   Self stimulation or erotic behavior involving only the self; usually refers to masturbation, but also includes erotic dreams and fantasies.

B

barrier method   Any of a number of contraceptive methods that place a physical barrier between sperm and egg, such as the condom, diaphragm, and cervical cap.

Bartholin's glands   Two small secretory glands on either side of the vaginal entrance.

basal body temperature (BBT) method   A contraceptive method based on variations of the woman's resting body temperature, which rises 24 to 72 hours before ovulation.

basic conflict   Pronounced disagreement about fundamental marital roles, tasks, and functions. Cf. *nonbasic conflict*.

battered woman   A woman who has been repeatedly and systematically subjected to battering by her spouse or partner.

battering   Violent acts, such as hitting, slapping, beating, stabbing, or shooting.

BBT method   *See basal body temperature.*

bereavement   The response to a loved one's death, including customs, rituals, and the grieving process.

Billings method   See *mucus method*.

binuclear family   A postdivorce family with children, consisting of two nuclear families, one headed by the mother, the other by the father.

bipolar gender roles   The idea that male and female gender roles are polar opposites, with males possessing exclusively instrumental traits and females possessing exclusively expressive traits.

birth canal   The vagina, through which the fetus exits at birth.

birth control   Devices, drugs, techniques or surgical procedures used to prevent conception or implantation or to terminate pregnancy.

birth rate   See *crude birth rate*.

bisexual   Sexual involvement with both sexes, usually sequentially rather than during the same time period.

blastocyst   An early stage of the fertilized egg, containing about 100 cells; the blastocyst implants itself into the uterine lining.

blended family   A family consisting of two adults and one or more children from an earlier marriage or relationship. Also known as a *reconstituted family* or *stepfamily*.

boundary   In systems theory, the emotional or physical separation between subsystems or roles required for adequate functioning.

Braxton Hicks contractions   Uterine contractions that occur periodically throughout pregnancy and also initiate effacement and dilation of the cervix at the beginning of labor.

breakthrough bleeding   Erratic bleeding, also called "spotting," which takes place at times other than the usual menstrual period.

breech presentation   A fetal position in which the baby enters the birth canal buttocks or feet first.

bride price   The goods, services, or money a family receives in exchange for giving their daughter in marriage.

bundling   A colonial Puritan courtship custom in which a couple slept together with a board separating them.

C

calendar method   A fertility awareness method based on calculating "safe" days according to the range of a woman's longest and shortest menstrual cycles; also known as the the *rhythm method*.

candidiasis   A yeast infection caused by the *Candida albicans* organism; also called *moniliasis* and *yeast infection*.

case study   The in-depth examination of an individual or small group in clinical treatment in order to gather data and formulate hypotheses. Also known as *clinical study*.

celibacy   Abstinence.

cervical cap   A thimble-shaped cap that fits snugly over the cervix to prevent conception.

cervix   The narrow, lower end of the uterus that opens into the vagina.

cesarean section   Surgical delivery of the child through an incision in the mother's abdominal and uterine walls.

chancre   A painless sore or ulcer that may be the first symptom of syphilis.

chastity   The state of being morally or sexually pure.

Chicano   [fem. -a] A Mexican-American.

child-free marriage   A marriage in which the partners have chosen not to have children.

child neglect   Failure to provide adequate or proper physical or emotional care for a child.

child snatching   The kidnapping of one's own children, usually by the non-custodial parent.

child support   Court-ordered financial support by the non-custodial parent to pay or assist in paying expenses incurred by the custodial parent in childrearing.

chlamydia   A common sexually transmitted disease affecting the urinary tract or other organs.

chorionic villus sampling   Surgical removal through the cervix of a tiny piece of embryonic membrane to be analyzed for genetic defects.

chromosomes   The genetic material in the cell nucleus guiding the cell's development and division.

cilia   Hairlike filaments in the fallopian tubes that propel the ovum toward the uterus.

circumcision   The surgical removal of the foreskin.

Circumplex Model   Model of family functioning in which cohesion, adaptability, and communication are the most important dimensions.

clinical study   The in-depth examination of an individual or small group in clinical treatment in order to gather data and formulate hypotheses. Also known as *case study*.

clitoral glans   See *glans clitoridis*.

clitoral hood   A fold of skin from the labia covering the clitoris.

clitoris   An erotically sensitive organ located at the upper end of the vulva above the urethral opening.

cognition   The mental processes, such as thought and reflection, that occur between the moment we receive a stimulus and the moment we respond to it.

cognitive development   A model of child development in which growth is viewed as the mastery of specific ways of perceiving, thinking, and doing that occur at discrete stages.

cognitive social learning   A theory emphasizing the learning of behavior from others through positive and negative reinforcement.

cohabitation   The sharing of living quarters by two heterosexual, gay, or lesbian individuals who are involved in an ongoing emotional and sexual relationship.

cohesion   Binding together.

cohort   A group of persons experiencing a specific event at the same time, such as a birth cohort consisting of persons born in the same year.

coitus   Sexual intercourse.

coitus interruptus   The withdrawal of the penis from the vagina immediately before ejaculation; considered ineffective as a contraceptive measure.

colostrum   A nutritionally rich fluid secreted by the breasts the first few days following childbirth.

comadre   [Spanish] The godmother of one's child (literally, co-mother).

compadrazgo   [Spanish] The Latino institution of godparentage (literally, co-parentage)..

compadre   [Spanish] The godfather of one's child (literally, co-father).

compadres   [Spanish] The godparents of one's child.

commuter marriage   A marriage in which couples who prefer living together live apart in pursuit of separate goals.

companionate family   A family characterized by shared decision-making, emotional expressiveness, and democratic childrearing.

companionate love   A form of love emphasizing intimacy and commitment.

companionate marriage   A marriage characterized by shared decision-making and emotional and sexual expressiveness.

comparable worth   An economic model arguing that occupations traditionally employing women are compensated at a lower rate than those traditonally employing men as a result of sex discriminatiom and that to overcome income differences between men and women, pay should be based on experience, knowledge and skills, mental demands, accountability, and working conditions, not on specific occupations per se.

complementary marriage model   A model in which male employment outside the home and female work within the home are viewed as separate but interdependent.

conception   The union of sperm and ovum; impregnation.

condom   A sheath made from latex rubber or animal intestine that fits over the erect penis to prevent the deposit of sperm in the vagina; used as a contraceptive device and also as prophylaxis against sexually transmitted diseases (latex condoms only).

conflict-habituated marriage   An enduring marriage marked by continuous conflict.

conflict theory   A theory examining how individuals, groups, or organizations with competing interests interact with each other or the social structure and how these interactions lead to change.

congenital   From birth.

conjugal   Of marriage.

conjugal extended family   Extended family formed through marriages.

conjugal family   Family consisting of husband, wife, and children. See also *nuclear family*.

consanguineous   Of the same ancestry.

consanguineous extended family   An extended family formed through blood ties.

contraception   Devices, techniques or drugs used to prevent conception.

contraceptive sponge   A barrier device containing a spermicide that is inserted into the vagina prior to intercourse.

contraction   Tightening of a muscle.

contraindication   A symptom, sign or condition that indicates that a particular drug or device should not be used.

conventionality   In marriage and family research, the tendency of subjects to give conventional or conformist responses.

coping   The process of utilizing resources in response to stress

corona   The rim at the base of the glans penis.

corpora cavernosa   Two cylindrical bodies in the penis which fill with blood to produce an erection.

corpus spongiosum   A spongy cylindrical body in the penis which contains the urethra and fills with blood to produce an erection.

courtship   The process by which a commitment to marriage is developed.

couvade   The psychological or ritualistic assumption of symptoms of pregnancy and childbirth by the male.

Cowper's glands   Two glands in the male which secrete a clear substance during sexual excitement.

crisis   A turning point; a crucial time, stage, or event. See also *predictable crisis* and *unpredictable crisis*.

crisis model   A theoretical construct for studying family strengths, based on the family's ability to function during times of high stress.

crude birth rate (CBR)   The number of births in a single year, divided by the mid-year population, and multiplied by 1000. See also *fertility* and *fertility rate*.

crude death rate (CDR)   The number of deaths in a single year, divided by the mid-year population, and multiplied by 1000. See also *fertility* and *fertility rate*.

culpotomy   A technique of female sterilization in which the fallopian tubes are cut through an incision at the back of the vagina.

culture of poverty   The view that the poor form a qualitatively different culture from the larger society and that their culture accounts for their poverty.

cunnilingus   Oral stimulation of the female genitals.

custodial   Having physical or legal custody of a child. Cf. *noncustodial*.

custody   The care of a child. See also *joint custody, sole custody,* and *split custody.*

cycle of violence   The recurring three-phase battering cycle of (1) tension building, (2) explosion, (3) reconciliation.

cystitis   A urinary tract infection usually affecting women.

D

dating   A process in which two individuals meet to engage in activities together; dating may be either exclusive or non-exclusive.

Day of the Dead   See *el Dia de los Muertos.*

D&C   Dilation and curettage.

D&E   Dilation and evacuation.

death rate   See *crude death rate.*

deferred parenthood   The intentional postponement of child-bearing until after certain goals have been fulfilled.

demographics   The demographic characteristics of a population, such as family size, marriage and divorce rates, and ethnic and racial composition.

demography   The study of population and population characteristics, such as family size, marriage and divorce rates, and ethnic and racial composition.

denial   The conscious or unconscious refusal to recognize painful acts, situations, or ways of being.

dependent variable   A variable that is observed or measured.

DES   Diethylstilbestrol.

desire   Erotic sensations or feelings which motivate a person to seek out or receive sexual experiences.

developmental interaction   A socialization theory stressing the reciprocal nature of parents' and children's growth; development is seen as a lifelong process.

developmental perspective   An approach which emphasizes the family's changing roles and relationships over time, beginning with marriage and ending when both spouses have died.

developmental task   Appropriate activities and responsibilities individuals learn at different stages in the life cycle.

deviant   Departing from social or cultural norms.

devitalized marriage   An enduring marriage characterized by a lack of intimacy in contrast to earlier years.

el Dia de los Muertos   [Spanish] The Day of the Dead, Latino and Latin American holiday with Indian and Catholic roots honoring the the dead, celebrated on November 1.

Diagnostic and Statistic Manual of Mental Disorders (DSM-IV)   A manual published by the American Psychiatric Association establishing categories of psychiatric disorders and listing criteria for diagnosing such disorders.

diaphragm   A flexible rubber cup placed in the vagina to block the passage of sperm, preventing conception.

diethylstilbestrol (DES)   A synthetic estrogen ($C_{18}H_{20}O_2$) designed to prevent miscarriage that is associated with various reproductive abnormalities in the adult children of women who have taken it.

dilation   Opening of the cervix.

dilation and curettage (D&C)   First trimester abortion technique in which the embryo is removed from the uterus with a sharp instrument (curette).

dilation and evacuation (D&E)   Second trimester abortion technique in which suction and forceps are used to remove the fetus.

disability   A physical or developmental limitation. Preferred usage over "handicap."

discrimination   The process of acting differently toward a person or group because the individual or group belongs to a minority.

displaced homemaker   A full-time homemaker who has lost economic support from her husband as a result of divorce or widowhood.

distress   Psychological and physical tension, such as intense upset, mood changes, headaches, and muscular tension.

division of labor   The interdependence of persons with specialized tasks and abilities. Within the family, labor is traditionally divided along gender lines. Increasing female employment is leading to pressure for a more egalitarian or equitable division of household labor. See also *complementary marriage model.*

divorce   The legal dissolution of marriage. Cf. *separation.*

domestic partners act   Law granting certain legal rights similar to those of married couples to committed cohabitants, whether heterosexual, gay, or lesbian.

double ABC-X model   Model describing stress, in which *Aa* represents stressor pile up, *B* represents family coping resources, *C* represents perception of stressor pile up, and *X* represents outcome.

double standard of aging   The devaluation of women in contrast to men in terms of attractiveness as they age.

douching   Introducing water or liquid into the vagina for medical, or hygienic, or contraceptive reasons.

Down's syndrome   A chromosomal error characterized by mental retardation.

dowry   The property a woman brings to her husband upon marriage. [Archaic] A man's gift to his bride. Cf. *bride price.*

DSM-IV   *See Diagnostic and Statistical Manual of Mental Disorders.*

dual-career family   A type of dual-earner family in which both husband and wife are committed to careers.

dual-earner family   A family in which both husband and wife are employed. Also known as dual-worker family.

dual-worker family   A dual-earner family.

duration of marriage effect   Accumulation over time of various factors, such as poor communication, unresolved conflict, and role overload, on marital satisfaction.

dyad   A two-member group; a couple.

Dyadic Adjustment Scale A survey instrument developed by Graham Spanier which measures relationship satisfaction.

dysfunction Impaired or inadequate functioning, as in sexual dysfunction.

dyspareunia Painful sexual intercourse.

E

eclampsia Life threatening condition of late pregnancy brought on by untreated high blood pressure.

ecological model of family violence Model that examines the child's development within the family context and the family's development within the community to assess the risk of violence.

economic adequacy The psychological perception that one has sufficient income and economic resources.

ectopic pregnancy A pregnancy in which the fertilized egg implants in a fallopian tube instead of the uterus.

edema Fluid retention and swelling.

effacement Thinning of the cervix during labor.

egalitarian gender roles Gender roles in which men and women are treated equally.

ego dystonic homosexuality A psychiatric disorder in which an individual has a persistent desire to switch from a gay or lesbian to a heterosexual orientation because of the distress his or her homosexuality causes.

ejaculate [noun] Semen.

ejaculation The expulsion of semen during orgasm.

embryo In human beings, the early development of life between about one week and two months after conception.

emission The first stage of male orgasm during which the semen moves into the urethra.

empty nest syndrome A crisis experienced by parents as a result of grown children leaving home.

endogamy Marriage within one's social group. See also *exogamy.*

endometriosis A condition in which endometrial tissue grows outside the uterus.

engagement A pledge to marry.

epididymis Structure within the testis where sperm mature and are stored prior to ejaculation.

episiotomy An incision from the vagina toward the anus made to prevent tearing during childbirth.

equity theory A theory emphasizing that social exchanges must be fair or equally beneficial over the long run.

erectile dysfunction Inability or difficulty in achieving erection.

erection An erect penis.

eros 1. From the Greek εροσ [love], the fusion of love and sexuality. 2. According to sociologist John Lee's styles of love, the passionate love of beauty.

erotic Pertaining to sexuality, sensuality or sexual sensations.

estrogen Any of a group of hormones produced primarily by the ovaries which are significant in controlling the menstrual cycle, maintaining the vaginal lining, and producing breast growth during puberty. Also present in smaller amounts in the male.

ethnic group A large group of people distinct from others because of cultural characteristics, such as language, religion, and customs, transmitted from one generation to another.

ethnic stratification The hierarchal ranking of groups in superior and inferior positions according to ethnicity.

ethnicity Ethnic affiliation or identity.

ethnocentrism The emotionally-charged belief that one's ethnic group, nation, or culture is superior to all others. See also *racism.*

exchange/social control model of family violence Model that views abuser as weighing costs versus rewards and using violence if social controls (costs) are not strong enough to discourage it.

exchange theory See *social exchange theory.*

excitement phase In the sexual response cycle, the second stage, denoting sexual arousal.

exogamy Marriage outside one's social group. See also *endogamy.*

expressive traits Supportive or emotional traits or characteristics.

extended family The family unit of the parent/child nuclear family and other kin, such as grandparents, uncles, aunts, and cousins. See also **conjugal extended family** and *consanguineous extended family.*

extramarital Outside or in addition to the marital relationship.

F

FAE See *fetal alcohol effect.*

fallopian tubes Two tubes that extend from the ovaries to the uterus. After ovulation, an ovum moves through a fallopian tube, where fertilization may take place.

la familia [Spanish] Family. In Latino culture, a pattern of social organization which emphasizes the family and strong feelings centering on the family. See also *familialism.*

familialism A pattern of social organization in which family and strong feelings for the family are important.

family A unit of two or more persons, of which one or more may be children, who are related by blood, marriage, or affiliation, and who cooperate economically and share a common dwelling place.

family ecosystem Family interactions and adaptations with the larger social environment, such as schools, neighborhoods, or the economy.

family hardship Difficulties specifically associated with a stressor. See *also stressor.*

family life cycle A developmental approach which emphasizes the family's changing roles and relationships over time, beginning with marriage and ending when both spouses have died.

family of marriage The family an individual forms by marrying. Also called **family of procreation.** Cf. *family of orientation.*

family migration The geographical movement of a family.

family of orientation The family in which a person is reared as a child. Cf. *family of marriage*

family of origin   See *family of orientation*.

family policy   A set of objectives concerning family well being and specific measures initiated by government to achieve them.

family power   Power exercised by individuals in their family roles as mother, father, child, or sibling.

family of procreation   See *family of marriage*.

family role   A social role within the family, such as husband or wife, father or mother. See also *kinship role*.

family rule   A family's patterned or characteristic response to events, situations, or persons. See also *family systems theory, meta-rule,* and *hierarchy of rules*.

family stress   An upset in the steady functioning of the family.

family systems theory   A theory holding that family structure is created by the pattern of interactions between its various parts and that individual actions are strongly influenced by the family context.

family tree   Diagramatic representation of family and ancestors.

family work   The unpaid work that is undertaken by family members to sustain the family, such as housework, laundry, and other chores.

fantasy   The realm of imagination.

FAS   See *fetal alcohol syndrome*.

fecundity   A person's maximum biological capacity to reproduce.

feedback   A process in which the factors that produce a result are themselves modified by the result.

fellatio   Oral stimulation of the male genitals.

feminism   1. The principle that women should have equal political, social, and economic rights with men 2. The social movement to obtain for women political, social, and economic equality with men.

feminization of poverty   The shift of poverty to females.

fertility   The ability to conceive; a person's actual reproductive performance.

fertility awareness methods   Contraceptive method based on predicting a woman's fertile period and either avoiding intercourse or using an additional method of contraception during that interval.

fertility rate   The number of live births per 1000 women aged 15–44 years. See *birth rate*.

fertilization   Union of the egg and sperm. Also known as conception.

fetal alcohol effect (FAE)   Growth retardation caused by the mother's chronic ingestion of alcohol during pregnancy.

fetal alcohol syndrome (FAS)   A syndrome that may be characterized by unusual facial characteristics, small head and body size, poor mental capacities and abnormal behavior patterns and is caused by the mother's chronic ingestion of alcohol during pregnancy.

fetus   The unborn young of a vertebrate; the human embryo becomes a fetus at about the eighth week.

fictive kin   Nonrelated individuals who are treated as if they were related; pseudokin.

field of eligibles   A group of individuals of the same general background and age who are potential marital partners.

filial crisis   Psychological conflict and stress experienced by adult children when aged parents become dependent on them.

fimbriae   Delicate, hairlike projections extending from the end of the fallopian tube toward the ovary.

flextime   Flexible work schedules determined by employee/employer agreement.

foreplay   Erotic activity prior to coitus, such as kissing, carressing, sex talk, and oral/genital contact; petting.

foreskin   The sleeve of skin covering the tip of the penis; prepuce.

G

gamete   A reproductive cell (sperm or ovum) that can unite with another gamete to form a zygote.

gamete intrafallopian transfer (GIFT)   Sperm and eggs collected from parents and deposited in fallopian tube for fertilization.

gay   Pertaining to same sex relationships, especially among males. Cf. *lesbian*.

gay male   A male sexually oriented toward other males.

gender   Biologically, the division into male and female; sex.

gender identity   The psychological sense of whether one is male or female.

gender role   The traits and behaviors based on biological gender assigned to males and females by a culture.

gender role attitudes   The beliefs people have of themselves and others regarding appropriate male and female personality traits and behaviors.

gender role behavior   The actual activities or behaviors in which males or females engage according to their gender roles.

gender role stereotype   A rigidly held and oversimplified belief that all males and females possess distinctive psychological and behavioral traits as a result of their gender.

gender schema   The cognitive organization of individuals, behaviors, traits, objects, and such by gender.

gender theory   A theory in which gender is viewed as the basis of hierarchal social relations and justifies greater power to males.

generation   1. The approximately 30-year period between the birth of one generation and the next. 2. A group of people born and living during the same general time period.

genital herpes   A sexually transmitted disease caused by the herpes simplex virus type II, similar to cold sores or fever blisters but appearing on the genitals.

genitals   The external sex or reproductive organs.

genital warts   Warts on the genitals caused by human papilloma virus (HPV), a sexually transmitted virus.

genogram   A diagram of the emotional relationships of a family through several generations.

gestational edema-proteinuria-hypertension complex   A condition of pregnancy characterized by high blood pressure, toxemia, or pre-eclampsia.

getting together   A courtship process in which men and women congregate ("get together") in groups to socialize or engage in common activities or projects. Cf. *dating*.

GIFT   See *gamete intrafallopian transfer*.

glans clitoridis   The visible, erotically sensitive tip of the clitoris. Also known as *clitoral glans*.

glans penis   The erotically sensitive tip of the penis.

gonad   An ovary or testis.

gonadotropin   A type of hormone secreted by the pituitary gland that affects the gonads.

gonorrhea   A sexually transmitted disease caused by the *Neisseria gonorrhoeae* bacterium that initially infects the urethra in males and the cervix in females, or the throat or anus in either sex, depending on the mode of sexual interaction.

Gräfenberg spot   An erotically sensitive area on the anterior wall of the vagina midway between the introitus and cervix.

grandparenting   Performing the functions of a grandparent.

grieving process   Emotional responses and expressions of feeling over the death of a loved one.

guilt   The state or feeling that one has done something wrong.

H

halo effect   The tendency to infer positive characteristics or traits based on a person's physical attractiveness.

handicap   See *disability*.

Hegar's sign   A softening of the uterus just above the cervix which may be an early indication of pregnancy.

hierarchy of rules   The ranking of rules in order of significance.

health   The state of physical and mental well-being.

hepatitis   A liver disease causing blood pigments to accumulate. Type B (serum) hepatitis may be sexually transmitted.

herpes simplex type II   See *genital herpes*.

heterogamy   Marriage between those with different social or personal characteristics. See also *homogamy*.

heterosexuality   Sexual orientation toward members of the other sex.

heterosociality   Close association with members of the other sex.

Hispanic   A person of Spanish or Latin American origin or background; may be of any race. See also *Latino*.

HIV   Human immunodeficiency virus.

HIV-positive   Infected with HIV.

homemaker   1. A person who manages the home. 2. A housewife.

homeostasis   A social group's tendency to maintain internal stability through coordinated responses to compensate for environmental changes.

homogamy   Marriage between those with similar social or personal characteristics. See also *heterogamy*.

homophobia   Fear or hatred of gay males or lesbians.

homosexuality   Sexual orientation toward members of the same sex. See also *gay male* and *lesbian*.

homosociality   The tendency to associate mostly with members of the same sex.

hormone   A chemical substance, secreted by the endocrine glands into the bloodstream, which organizes and regulates physical development.

hospice   A place or program caring for the terminally ill, emphasizing both patient care and family support.

housewife   1. A person who manages the home. 2. A homemaker.

HSD   See *hypoactive sexual desire*.

human chorionic gonadotropin (HCG)   A hormone secreted by the placenta.

human immunodeficiency virus (HIV)   The virus causing AIDS.

human papilloma virus (HPV)   The virus causing warts, including genital warts.

hymen   Thin membrane that may partially cover the vaginal opening prior to first intercourse.

hypoactive sexual desire (HSD)   Inactive or limited sexual desire. Formerly known as *inhibited sexual desire*.

hypothesis   An unproven theory or proposition tentatively accepted to explain a collection of facts. See *working hypothesis*.

hysterectomy   The surgical removal of the uterus or part of the uterus.

hysterotomy   A surgical method of abortion in which the fetus is removed through an abdominal incision.

I

identity   An individual's core sense of self.

identity bargaining   The process of role adjustment, involving identifying with a role, interacting with others in that role, and negotiating changes in the role.

illegitimate   Not based on law, right, or custom. Formerly, born outside of marriage.

incest   Sexual intercourse between individuals too closely related to marry, usually interpreted to mean father/daughter, mother/son, or brother/sister.

independent variable   A variable that may be changed.

induced abortion   The termination of a pregnancy through human intervention.

ie [pronounced *ee-eh*]   The basic family unit in traditional Japanese society consisting of past, present, and future members of the extended family and their households.

infertility   The inability to conceive after trying for a year or more.

inhibited sexual desire   See *hypoactive sexual desire*.

institution   An enduring social structure built around a significant and distinct cluster of social values. Institutions include the family, religion, education, and government.

intrafamilial sexual abuse   Sexual activities within the family or extended family involving an adult or adolescent and a younger child. See also *incest*.

instrument   In social science, a research tool or device, such as a questionnaire, used to gather data about behaviors, attitudes, beliefs, or other such dimensions of an individual, group, or society.

instrumental traits   Task-oriented traits or characteristics.

intermarriage   Marriage between people of different ethnic or racial groups.

intermittent extended family   A family in which adult children (or other relatives) periodically live with their aging parents.

interpersonal competence   The ability to develop and share an intimate, growing relationship.

inter-role conflict   Conflict experienced when the role expectations of two or more roles are contradictory or incompatible. Also known as role interference and role conflict. See *role strain*.

intrauterine device (IUD)   A device inserted into the uterus to prevent conception or implantation of the fertilized egg.

introitus   The vaginal opening.

in vitro fertilization   The fertilization of an egg outside the body; "test tube" fertilization.

ISD   Inhibited sexual desire. See *hypoactive sexual desire*.

I-statement   In communication, a statement beginning with "I" that describes the speaker's feelings, such as "I feel upset when I see last week's dishes in the sink."

IUD   See *intrauterine device*.

J

joint custody   Custody in which both parents are responsible for the care of the child. Joint custody takes two forms: *joint legal custody,* in which the child lives primarily with one parent but both parents jointly share in important decisions regarding the child's education, religious training, and general upbringing, and *joint physical custody* in which the child lives with both parents in separate households and spends more or less equal time with each parent. See *also sole custody* and *split custody*.

joint legal custody   See *joint custody*.

K

Kaposi's sarcoma   An opportunistic skin cancer associated with AIDS.

kin   Relatives.

kinship   Family relationship.

kinship system   The social organization of related persons conferring rights and obligations based on an individual's status.

kiss   Touching or caressing with the lips.

L

labia majora   Two folds of spongy flesh extending from the mons veneris along the midline between the legs and enclosing the clitoris, labia minora, and urethral and vaginal openings.

labia minora   Two folds of skin within the labia majora; their upper portion forms a single fold over the clitoris known as the clitoral hood.

labor   The physical efforts of childbirth.

lactation   The production of milk.

la familia   See under *familia*

Lamaze method   A childbirth method in which the mother uses exercises and breathing techniques to assist her labor.

laparoscopy   Tubal ligation technique using a laparoscope (viewing instrument) to locate the fallopian tubes, which are then closed or blocked.

latchkey children   See *self-care*.

Latino [fem. -a]   A person of Latin American origin or ancestry; may be of any race. See also *Hispanic,* and *Spanish-speaking*.

legitimacy   The state or quality of being sanctioned by custom, rights, or law.

lesbian   A female sexually oriented toward other females.

life course   A developmental perspective of individual change focusing on (1) *individual time,* an individual's own life span, (2) *social time,* social transition points, such as marriage, and (3) *historical time,* the times in which a person lives.

life cycle   The developmental stages, transitions, and tasks individuals undergo from birth to death.

lochia   A bloody vaginal discharge that appears for several weeks following childbirth.

lone-parent family   [Canadian usage] Single-parent family.

low birth weight (LBW)   Generally, weighing less than 5.5 pounds at birth, often as a result of prematurity.

ludis   According to sociologist John Lee's styles of love, playful love.

M

macho [Spanish] In traditional Latin American usage, masculine, strong, or daring. In popular U. S. usage, excessively or stereotypically masculine.

madrina   [Spanish] Godmother.

majority group   A social category composed of people holding superordinate status and power and having the ability to impose their will on less powerful minority groups. Cf. *minority group*.

mania   According to sociologist John Lee's styles of love, obsessive love.

marital disruption   Marital instability that includes marital separation as well as divorce.

marital exchange   The process by which individuals trade resources with each other to secure the best marital partner. Traditionally, men exchanged their higher status and greater economic resources for women's physical attractiveness, expressive qualities, and childbearing and housekeeping abilities.

marital power   The power exercised by individuals as husband and wife. Cf. *family power*.

marital rape   Forced sexual contact by a husband with his wife.

marriage   Socially recognized union between a man and woman in which economic cooperation and legitimate sexual interactions and reproduction may take place.

marriage contract   1. The legal and moral rights and responsibilities entailed by marriage. 2. An explicit contract delineating specific terms of marriage which, depending on the terms, may be legally binding. 3. A non-legally binding agreement between partners, covering such areas as conflict resolution, division of household labor, employment, and childrearing responsibilities.

marriage gradient   The tendency for men to marry younger women of lower socioeconomic status and for women to marry older men of higher socioeconomic status.

marriage market   An exchange process in which individuals bargain with each other using their resources in order to find the best available partner for marriage. See *marital exchange*.

marriage squeeze   The phenomenon in which there are greater numbers of marriageable women than marriageable men according to their age and status. See also *marriage gradient*.

masturbation   Manual or mechanical stimulation of the genitals by self or partner; a form of autoeroticism.

matriarchal   Pertaining to the mother as the head and ruler of a family. Cf. *patriarchal*.

matriarchic   Pertaining to female rule. Cf. *patriarchic*.

matriarchy   A form of social organization in which the mother or eldest female is recognized as the head of the family, kinship group, or tribe, and descent is traced through her. Cf. *patriarchy*.

matrilineal   Descent or kinship traced through the mother. Cf. *patrilineal*.

mean world syndrome   The belief, resulting from television viewing, that the world is more dangerous and violent than it is in actuality.

meatus   The urethral opening.

menarche   The first menstrual period, beginning in puberty.

menopause   Cessation of menses for at least one year as a result of aging.

menses   The monthly menstrual flow.

menstrual cycle   The hormonally induced female cycle which begins with the development of an ovum in the ovarian follicle and the menstrual flow and ends with the degeneration of the corpus luteum.

menstruation   The discharge of blood and built-up uterine lining through the vagina that occurs approximately every four weeks among nonpregnant women between puberty and menopause.

meta-analysis   The re-analysis of combined statistical data from previous studies.

meta-rule   An abstract, general, unarticulated rule at the apex of the hierarchy of rules upon which other rules are based.

Mexican American   A U.S. citizen of Mexican ancestry.

midwife   A person who attends and facilitates birth.

mifepristone   See *RU-486*.

minilaparotomy   A method of tubal ligation in which the fallopian tubes are viewed and tied off through a single small incision in the lower abdomen.

minipill   A form of oral contraceptive containing only progesterone.

minority group   A social category composed of people who differ from the majority, who are relatively powerless, and who are subject to unfair and unequal treatment by the majority. Cf. *majority group*.

miscarriage   A spontaneous abortion.

model   A person who demonstrates a behavior observed and imitated by others.

modeling   A process in which learning takes place by imitating others.

monogamy   1. The practice of having only one husband or wife at a time. 2. [colloq.] Sexual exclusiveness.

mons veneris   The mound of fatty tissue over the pubic bone of the female, covered with pubic hair following puberty.

morality   A set of social, cultural, or religious norms defining right and wrong.

morning-after pill   See *postcoital birth control*.

morning sickness   Nausea experienced by many women during the first trimester of pregnancy.

mucus method   A contraceptive method that relies on predicting a woman's fertile period by observing changes in the appearance and character of her cervical mucus; also called Billings or ovulation method.

myotonia   The process of increasing muscular tension.

N

natural childbirth   See *prepared childbirth*.

natural family planning   A fertility awareness method of birth control that relies solely on predicting a woman's fertile period and avoiding intercourse on those days.

negative reinforcement   The process by which an unpleasant stimulus following a response decreases the likelihood that the response will be repeated.

nocturnal orgasm   Nonvoluntary ejaculation or orgasm occurring during sleep; also known as "wet dream."

no-fault divorce   The dissolution of marriage because of irreconcilable differences for which neither party is held responsible.

nonbasic conflict   Pronounced disagreement about non-fundamental or situational issues. Cf. *basic conflict*.

non-custodial   Not having physical or legal custody of a child. Cf. *custodial*.

nonmarital sex   Sexual intercourse outside of marriage by older singles.

nonverbal communication   Communication of emotion by means other than words, such as touch, body movement, and facial expression.

norm   A shared model or expectation of how a group *should* act or behave.

normal   Conforming to group or cultural norms.

normative   Establishing a norm or standard.

nuclear family   The basic family building block, consisting of at least a mother and child. In popular usage, thought of as consisting of a mother, father, and at least one child, all of whom are biologically related to each other; used interchangeably with *traditional family*.

nursing   Breastfeeding.

O

obstetrician   A physician specializing in pregnancy and childbirth.

occupational stratification   The hierarchal ranking in occupations in superior and inferior positions.

opportunistic disease   An infection that is normally resisted by the healthy immune system, such as *Kaposi's sarcoma* and *pneumocystis carinii pneumonia* associated with AIDS.

oral contraception   Contraceptive taken orally; the pill.

oral-genital sex   The erotic stimulation of the genitals by the tongue or mouth; fellatio, cunnilingus, or mutual oral stimulation.

orgasm   The release of physical tensions after the build-up of sexual excitement; usually accompanied by ejaculation in physically mature males.

orgasmic dysfunction   Inability to have orgasm.

orgasmic phase   The phase of the sexual response cycle characterized by orgasm.

orgasmic platform   The swelling of the outermost one-third of the vagina caused by vasocongestion during sexual arousal.

os   The cervical opening.

ovaries   The female gonads which produce estrogen and progesterone and release ova.

ovulation method   See *mucus method*.

ovum   The egg produced by the ovary. [plural] Ova

P

Pacific Islander   Collective term referring to those of native Hawaiian, Filipino, Guamamian, Samoan or other Melanesian, Micronesian, or Polynesian descent.

padrino   [Spanish] Godfather.

Pap smear   Pap test.

Pap test   The sampling of cervical cells to diagnose cancer or a precancerous condition.

parenting   The rearing of children.

passing   [colloquial] Pretending to be heterosexual when actually gay or lesbian.

passionate love   Intense, impassioned love. Cf. *companionate love*.

passive-congenial marriage   An enduring marriage characterized by low expectations and low levels of satisfaction from the beginning.

patriarchal   Pertaining to the father as the head and ruler of a family. Cf. *matriarchal*.

patriarchic   Pertaining to male rule. Cf. *matriarchic*.

patriarchy   A form of social organization in which the father or eldest male is recognized as the head of the family, kinship group, or tribe, and descent is traced through him. Cf. *matriarchy*.

patriarchy model of family violence   Model in which violence is seen as inherent in male-dominated societies.

patrilineal   Descent or kinship traced through the father. Cf. *matrilineal*.

pedophilia   Adult sexual attraction to children; the adult's use of children for sexual purposes.

peer   A person of equal status, as in age, class, position, or rank.

pelvic inflammatory disease (PID)   An infection of the fallopian tubes, often caused by gonorrhea or chlamydia, that may spread to the ovaries and uterus; severe cases may result in sterility. Also known as *salpingitis*.

penis   The male sexual organ through which semen is ejaculated and urine is passed.

perineum   The small band of muscular tissue separating the anus and the genitals.

permissive   A parenting style stressing the child's autonomy and freedom of expression over the needs of the parents.

period   Menses.

permissiveness with affection   Sexual norm permitting nonmarital sexual activity for both men and women in an affectionate relationship.

permissiveness without affection   Sexual standard permitting nonmarital sexual activity without regard as to the nature of the relationship.

personality conflict   Conflict based on personality characteristics; such conflicts are unlikely to be resolved. Cf. *situational conflict*.

petting   Foreplay; sexual contact usually referring to the manual or oral stimulation of the genitals or breasts.

phallus   Penis.

physical abuse   Intentional violent mistreatment. See *violence*.

PID   See *pelvic inflammatory disease*.

placenta   The organ of exchange between the embryo or fetus and the pregnant female through which nutrients and waste pass; the placenta also serves as an endocrine gland producing large amounts of progesterone and estrogen to maintain pregnancy.

pleasuring   The giving and receiving of sensual pleasure through touch.

plural marriage   The practice of having more than one husband or wife at the same time; polygamy.

pneumocystis carinii pneumonia   An opportunistic pneumonia associated with AIDS.

polyandry   The practice of having more than one husband at the same time. See also *polygamy*; cf. *polygyny*.

polygamy   The practice of having more than one husband or wife at the same time; plural marriage. See also *polyandry, polygyny*, and *consanguineous extended family*.

polygyny   The practice of having more than one wife at the same time. See also *polygamy*; cf. *polyandry*.

positive reinforcement   The process by which a stimulus following a response has the effect of increasing the likelihood that the response will be repeated.

POSSLQ   Person of opposite sex sharing living quarters; from U. S. Census terminology.

postcoital birth control   Birth control that is administered after intercourse has taken place, but before a diagnosis of pregnancy is possible; usually involves the administering of high-estrogen oral contraceptives. Also called "morning-after birth control."

postmarital sex   Sexual intercourse among previously married individuals.

postpartum period   The period of time following childbirth, around three months.

power   The ability to exert one's will, influence, or control over others.

power conflict   Pronounced disagreements concerning dominance.

powwows   Native American intertribal social gatherings centering around drumming and traditional dances.

pragma   According to sociologist John Lee's styles of love, practical love.

predictable crisis   Within the individual or family life cycle, normal but critical events, such as birth or death. Cf. *unpredictable crisis.*

pre-eclampsia   Increasingly high blood pressure during late pregnancy. See also *gestational edema-proteinuria-hypertension complex.*

premarital sex   Sexual intercourse prior to marriage.

prenatal   Before birth.

prepared childbirth   Birth philosophy stressing education and minimal use of anesthetics or other drugs; natural childbirth.

prepuce   Foreskin.

principle of least interest   A theory of power in which the person less interested in sustaining a relationship has the greater power.

pro-choice movement   Social movement that adovocates women's right to choose abortion.

profamily movement   A social movement emphasizing conservative family values, such as traditional gender roles, authoritarian childrearing, premarital virginity, and opposition to abortion.

progesterone   A hormone produced by the ovaries.

prolactin   A hormone that stimulates the production of milk by the mammary glands.

pro-life movement   Social movement that advocates against abortion.

prophylactic   [adjective] Protecting against disease. [noun] Condom.

propinquity   Spacial nearness.

prostaglandin   A hormone controlling muscle contractions.

prostaglandin injection   Abortion technique in which a prostaglandin solution is injected into the uterus, causing delivery of an unviable fetus.

prostate gland   A gland at the base of a man's bladder which produces most of the seminal fluid in the ejaculate.

prototype   A model.

pseudokin   See *fictive kin.*

pseudomutuality   The maintenance of a relationship with the pretense that it is mutually fulfilling.

psychiatric model of family violence   Model that assumes the source of violence to be in personality of abuser.

psychoanalytic model   The Freudian model of child socialization, in which maturity is seen as the ability to gain control over one's unconscious impulses.

psychosexual   Pertaining to the psychological aspects of sexuality.

psychosexual development   The growth of the psychological aspects (such as attitudes and emotions) of sexuality that accompany physical growth.

puberty   The period in which the individual develops secondary sex characteristics and becomes capable of reproducing.

pubococcygeus muscle   The muscle that surrounds and supports the vagina.

PWA   Person with AIDS.

Q

quickening   The time of first movement of the fetus which may be felt by the pregnant woman.

R

race   A large group of people defined as distinct because of genetically-transmitted physical characteristics, especially facial structure and skin color.

racism   The practice of discrimination and subordination based on the belief that race determines character and abilities. Cf. *sexism.*

rape   Sexual act against a person's will or consent as defined by law; may or may not include penile penetration of the vagina. Also known as *sexual assault.* See also *acquaintance rape* and *marital rape.*

rape trauma syndrome   A group of symptoms experienced by a rape survivor, including fear, self-blame, anxiety, crying, sleeplessness, anger, or rage.

rating-and-dating   The process described by sociologist Willard Waller in which men and women rated potential dates on a scale of one to ten and tried to date the highest rated individuals.

reconstituted family   See *blended family* or *stepfamily.*

refractory period   Following orgasm, the period during which the penis cannot respond to additional stimulation.

reinforcement   A behavior that strengthens the action or response preceding it.

relative love and need theory   A theory of power in which the person gaining the most from a relationship is the most dependent.

relocation camps   During World War II, camps in which Japanese Americans and Japanese Canadians of all ages were imprisoned without cause by their respective governments.

remarriage   A marriage in which at least one partner has been previously married.

reproductive organs   External and internal structures involved in reproduction.

resource   Anything that can be called into use or used to advantage, such as love, money, or approval, to exert influence or power.

resource model of family violence   Model that views force as used to compensate for lack of of personal, social, and economic resources.

rhythm method   See *calendar method*.

Roe v. Wade   U. S. Supreme Court decision (1972) affirming a woman's constitutional right to abortion based on the right to privacy.

role   The pattern of behavior expected of a person in a group or culture as a result of his or her social status, such as husband or wife in a family.

role conflict   See *inter-role conflict*.

role interference   See *inter-role conflict*.

role making   The creation or modification of existing roles.

role modeling   A significant means by which children are taught attitudes and behavior by learning to imitate adults whom they admire; role models may be "positive" or "negative."

role overload   The experience of having more prescribed activities in one or more roles than can be comfortably or adequately performed. See *role strain*.

role playing   The changing of one's roles in response to the roles of others.

role strain   Difficulties, tensions, or contradictions experienced in performing a role. See also *inter-role conflict* and *role overload*.

role taking   The tendency to take on roles in different social situations and to modify behaviors accordingly.

roleless role   A role for which there are no clear guidelines for behavior, such as stepparent, widow, and ex-in-law roles.

romantic love   Intense, passionate love. Cf. *companionate love*.

RU–486   An antiprogesterone steroid (mifepristone) that acts as an abortifacient if taken within the first six weeks of pregnancy; also used as monthly birth control pill if taken shortly before an expected menstrual period.

rule of thumb   Prior to the 19th century, the legally sanctioned practice of disciplining one's wife with a rod, provided it was not wider than the husband's thumb.

S

safe sex   Sexual practices, including the use of latex condoms, intended to prevent the transmission of bodily fluids, especially semen, that may contain HIV.

saline injection   Abortion technique in which a saline solution is injected into the uterus to induce delivery of an unviable fetus.

salpingitis   Infection of the fallopian tube.   See *pelvic inflammatory disease*.

sample   A group randomly and systematically selected from a larger group.

scapegoating   The conscious or unconscious singling out and blaming of an individual or group.

script   A mental map, plan, or pattern of behavior. See also *role*.

scrotum   The pouch of skin holding the testes.

secondary sex characteristics   The physical characteristics other than external genitals that distinguish the sexes from each other, e.g. breasts and body hair.

self-care   Children under age fourteen caring for themselves at home without supervision by an adult or older adolescent.

self-disclosure   The revelation of intimate feelings to another.

self-esteem   Feelings about the value of the self; high self-esteem includes feeling unique, having a sense of power, and feeling connected to others.

semen   The fluid containing sperm which is ejaculated, produced mostly by the prostate gland. Also known as *ejaculate*.

seminal fluid   The fluid containing sperm; semen.

seminiferous tubules   Tiny sperm-producing tubes within the testes.

separation   The physical parting of two married persons. Cf. *divorce*.

separation distress   A psychological state following separation, characterized by depression, anxiety, intense loneliness, and feelings of loss.

sequential work/family role staging   A pattern combining employment and family work in dual-earner families in which women leave employment during pregnancy and while their children are young and return to it at a later time.

sex   1. Biologically, the division into male and female. 2. Sexual activities.

sex hormones   Hormones such as testosterone and estrogen which are responsible for the development of secondary sex characteristics and for activating sexual behavior.

sexism   1. The belief that biological differences between males and females provide legitimate bases for female subordination. 2. The economic and social domination of women by men. Cf. *racism*.

sex organs   Internal and external reproductive organs; commonly refers only to the the penis, vulva, and vagina.

sex ratio   The ratio of men to women in a group or society.

sexual assault   A legal term referring to rape. See also *acquaintance rape, marital rape,* and *rape*.

sexual behavior   Behavior that is characterized by conscious psychological/erotic arousal (such as desire) and that may also be accompanied by physiological arousal (such as erection or lubrication) or activity (such as masturbation or coitus).

sexual desire   The psychological component that motivates sexual behavior.

sexual disorder   Psychological impairment of the capacity for sexual arousal, such as hypoactive sexual desire.

sexual dysfunction   Impaired physiological response in excitement or orgasmic phase of the sexual response cycle, such as erectile or orgasmic difficulties.

sexual harassment   Deliberate or repeated unsolicited verbal comments, gestures, or physical contact that is sexual in nature and unwelcomed by the recipient.

sexual identity   The individual's sense of his or her sexual self.

sexual intercourse   Coitus; heterosexual penile/vaginal penetration.

sexuality   The state of being sexual, which encompasses the biological, social, and cultural aspects of sex.

sexually transmitted disease (STD)   An infection that can be transmitted through sexual activities, such as sexual intercourse, oral/genital sex, or anal sex.

sexual orientation   Sexual attraction and interactions directed toward members of the other or same sex. Usually dichotomized as heterosexuality/homosexuality, but may also include bisexuality.

sexual preference   See *sexual orientation*.

sexual stratification   The hierarchical ranking in superior and inferior positions according to gender.

sexual variation   A departure from the sexual norms; atypical sexual behavior.

sibling   A brother or sister.

SIDS   See *sudden infant death syndrome*.

single-parent family   A family with children, created by divorce or unmarried motherhood, in which only one parent is present.

situational conflict   Conflict arising as the result of specific acts, events, behaviors, or situations, which are amenable to resolution. Cf. *personality conflict*.

social exchange theory   A theory which emphasizes the process of mutual giving and receiving of rewards, such as love or sexual intimacy, in social relationships.

social integration   The degree of interaction between individuals and the larger community.

social molding   A child socialization theory that views human emotions as formed by the influences of culture, society, and the family.

social-situational model of family violence   Model in which violence is seen as arising from a combination of family stress and cultural norms.

social structure   A network of interconnected roles and statuses that give structure to interactions.

social support   Instrumental and emotional assistance, such as physical care and love.

socialization   The shaping of individual behavior to conform to social or cultural norms.

socialization agent   Individuals, groups, institutions, or media, such as parents, schools, or television, which socialize the child.

socioeconomic status (SES)   Social status ranking determined by a combination of occupational, educational, and income levels.

sole custody   Child custody arrangement in which only one parent has both legal and physical custody of the child. See also *joint custody* and *split custody*.

sonogram   The picture produced by ultrasonography.

Spanish-speaking   Pertaining to Hispanic origin or ancestry.

spells of poverty   The periodical movement in and out of poverty.

sperm   The male gamete produced by the testis.

spermatogenesis   The production of sperm.

spermicide   A substance toxic to sperm, used for contraception, usually with a barrier device; available in a variety of forms, such as jelly, cream, aerosol foam, film, and suppository tablets. Spermicide containing nonoxynol-9 provides some protection against certain STDs, including gonorrhea, chlamydia, and HIV.

spinnbarkeit   The elastic condition of cervical mucus just prior to ovulation.

split custody   Custody of two or more children in which custody is divided between the parents, the mother generally receiving the girls and the father receiving the boys.

spontaneous abortion   The natural but fatal explusion of the embryo or fetus; miscarriage.

spotting   See *breakthrough bleeding*.

status   The position an individual occupies within a group.

STD   Sexually transmitted disease.

stepfamily   A family consisting of two adults and one or more children from an earlier marriage or relationship. Also known as *blended family* or *reconstituted family*.

stereotype   A rigidly held, conventional view of individuals, groups, or ideas, that fails to allow for individual differences or critical judgement.

sterilization   Intervention (usually surgical) making a person incapable of reproducing.

stigmatization   The process of labeling and internalizing perceptions of self, other individuals, groups, behaviors, feelings, or ideas as deviant.

stimulus-value-role   A theory of romantic development: *stimulus* brings people together; *value* is the compatibility of basic values; *role* is role fit.

strain   Tension lingering from previous stressors or tensions inherent in family roles. See also *stressor*.

storge   According to sociologist John Lee's styles of love, companionate love.

stress   Psychological or emotional distress or disruption.

stressor   A stress-causing event.

stressor pileup   The occurrence of a number of stresses within a short period of time which strains family coping abilities.

structural functionalism   A sociological theory that examines how society is organized and maintained by examining the functions performed by its different structures. In marriage and family studies, structural functionalism examines the functions the family performs for society, the functions the individual performs for the family, and the functions the family performs for its members.

subsystem   A system that is part of a larger system, such as the parent/child system being a subsystem of the family system.

sudden infant death syndrome (SIDS)   The death of an apparently healthy infant during its sleep from unknown causes.

surrogate mother   A woman who bears a child for another woman (often for money) and relinquishes custody upon birth; the pregnancy usually results from artificial insemination, in vitro fertilization, or embryo transplant.

sweating   The secretion of a mucuslike liquid from the vaginal walls during the excitement phase of the sexual response cycle.

symbiotic personality   A personality characterized by excessive dependency and need for closeness.

symbolic interactionism   A theory which focuses on the subjective meanings of acts and how these meanings are communicated through interactions and roles to give shared meaning.

symmetrical work/family role allocation   The interface between family and employment in which family work is divided more equitably and females have greater commitment to work roles than in the traditional division of labor. Cf. *sequential work/family role staging* and *traditional-simultaneous/work family life cycle.*

syphilis   A sexually transmitted disease whose first symptom is a painless chancre on the genitals, anus, or mouth; caused by the *Treponema pallidum* bacterium. Life threatening if untreated.

T

TDI   See *therapeutic donor insemination.*

tenting   The expansion and elevation of the innermost two-thirds of the vagina during sexual excitement.

teratogenic   Capable of producing fetal defects.

testes   The two male gonads which produce testosterone and manufacture sperm. [singular] Testis. Also known as testicles.

testicles   See *testes.*

testosterone   A hormone secreted in males by the testes; also secreted in smaller amounts in females by the ovaries. Sometimes referred to as the "male hormone."

thanatology   The study of death and dying.

theoretical effectiveness   The maximum effectiveness of a drug, device or method if used consistently, correctly, and according to instructions.

therapeutic donor insemination (TDI)   Artificial insemination with donated semen, often used if the male is sterile or has a genetically transferable disorder.

tithingman   In colonial New England, a man appointed by the church to supervise his neighbors' morality and behavior.

total marriage   An enduring marriage characterized by a high degree of interdependence in most areas.

toxemia   A condition of pregnancy characterized by high blood pressure and edema. See also *gestational edema-proteinuria-hypertension complex.*

toxic shock syndrome (TSS)   A potentially fatal infection caused by the *Staphylococcus aureus* bacterium and characterized by high fever, vomiting, diarrhea, and rash; TSS has been associated with the use of superabsorbent tampons.

traditional family   In popular usage, an intact, married two-parent family with at least one child, which adheres to conservative family values; an idealized family. Popularly used interchangeably with *nuclear family.*

traditional-simultaneous work/family life cycle   The interface between family and employment in which the husband is regarded as the primary economic provider with little responsibility for family work and the wife, regardless of her employment status, is primarily responsible for family work. Cf. *sequential work/family role staging* and *symmetrical work/family role allocation.*

trait   A distinguishing personality characteristic or quality.

transactional pattern   Habitual patterns of interaction.

transition   1. Passing from one stage or phase to another. 2. The entrance of the fetus' head into the birth canal, marking the end of the first stage of labor.

traumatic sexualization   The process of developing inappropriate or dysfunctional sexual attitudes, behaviors, and feelings by a sexually-abused child.

traveling time   The time immediately following the Civil War when former slaves traveled throughout the South in search of relatives separated by sale.

trial marriage   Cohabitation with the purpose of determining marital compatibility.

tubal ligation   A surgical method of female sterilization in which the fallopian tubes are tied off or closed, usually by laparoscopy.

tubal pregnancy   See *ectopic pregnancy*

two-component theory of emotions   The theory, according to Stanley Schacter, that for a person to experience an emotion, both physiological arousal and an appropriate emotional explanation for the arousal must be present.

typology   Systematic categorization according to types.

U

ultrasonography   Technological method used to view the fetus in utero by reflecting high frequency sound waves off it; ultrasound.

ultrasound   See *ultrasonography.*

umbilical cord   A hollow cord which connects the circulation system of the embryo or fetus to the placenta.

underclass   The socioeconomic class marked by persistent poverty and poor employabilty.

underemployment   Working at a job below one's qualifications, inability to work as many hours as desired, or working for less pay than in previous employment.

unpredictable crisis   An unforseen crisis, such as terminal illness in a child. Cf. *predictable crisis.*

unrequited love   Love that is not returned.

urethra   In the male, the duct inside the penis, through which semen is ejaculated and urine expelled; in the female, the duct through which urine is expelled.

urethritis   An infection of the urethra.

user effectiveness   The actual effectiveness of a drug, device, or method based on statistical information.

uterus   A hollow, muscular organ within the pelvic cavity in which the fertilized egg develops into the fetus; the womb.

V

vacuum aspiration   First trimester abortion method in which the contents of the uterus are removed by suction.

vagina   The passage leading from the vulva to uterus that expands during intercourse to receive the erect penis or during childbirth to permit passage of the child; the birth canal.

vaginismus   The involuntary constriction of the vaginal muscles which prohibits penetration.

vaginitis   Vaginal infection, most commonly *Trichomonas vaginalis, candidiasis,* or *Gardnerella vaginalis,* which may be sexually transmitted. Men may also acquire these infections but often remain asymptomatic.

variable   A situation or behavior that may be changed or varied.

variation   Departure from social or cultural norms.

varicocele   A varicose vein above the testicle.

vas deferens   One of two ducts that carry sperm form the testes to the seminal vesicles. [plural] Vasa deferentia.

vasectomy   A surgical form of male sterilization in which the vas deferens is severed.

vasocongestion   The increased supply of blood, especially to the genitals during sexual excitation.

VD   See *sexually transmitted disease.*

venereal disease   See *sexually transmitted disease.*

venereal warts   Warts in the genital or anal area which may be sexually transmitted; caused by the human papilloma virus (HPV).

vernix   A milky substance often covering infants at birth.

viability   Ability to live and continue to grow outside the uterus.

violence   The use of physical force to hurt, injure, or kill.

virginity   The state of not having engaged in sexual intercourse.

vital marriage   An enduring marriage characterized by the partners' lives being closely intertwined in important matters.

vulva   The external female genitalia, including the mons veneris, labia majora and labia minora, clitoris, and the vaginal and urethral openings.

W

wedding   The act of marrying; a marriage ceremony or celebration.

well-being, emotional   The state of feeling happy, hopeful, energetic, and zestful.

well-being, physical   The state of feeling fit and able; for the disabled or chronically ill, includes the ability to function within limits.

withdrawal   See *coitus interruptus.*

wolf child   A child abandoned at an early age who is then reared alone among animals; feral child.

womb   Uterus.

work spillover   Effect that employment has on time, energy, and psychological functioning of workers and their families.

working hypothesis   An unproven theory or proposition used as the basis for further investigation. See *hypothesis.*

workplace/family linkages   Ways in which employment affects families.

Z

ZIFT   See *zygote intrafallopian transfer.*

zygote   The fertilized egg.

zygote intrafallopian transfer (ZIFT)   Eggs and sperm united in a petri dish and then transferred to the fallopian tube to begin cell division.

Bibliography

Abbott, Douglas A., Margaret Berry, and William H. Meredith. "Religious Belief and Practice: A Potential Asset in Helping Families." *Family Relations* 39 (October 1990): 443–44.

Abel, Ernest L. "Smoking and Pregnancy." *Journal of Psychoactive Drugs* 16:4 (October–December 1984): 327–338.

Adams, Bert. "The Family: Problems and Solutions." *Journal of Marriage and the Family* 47:3 (August 1985): 525–529.

Adler, Alfred. "Individual Psychology Therapy." In W.S. Sahakian, ed., *Psychotherapy and Counseling*. Chicago: Rand McNally, 1976.

Adler, Jerry, et al. "The Joy of Gardening." *Newsweek* (July 26, 1982).

Adler, Jerry. "Learning From the Loss." *Newsweek* (March 24, 1986): 66–67.

Adler, Nancy, Susan Hendrick, and Clyde Hendrick. "Male Sexual Preference and Attitudes toward Love and Sexuality." *Journal of Sex Education and Therapy* 12:2 (Fall–Winter 1989): 27–30.

Ahrons, Constance, and Roy Rodgers. *Divorced Families: A Multidisciplinary View*. New York: W. W. Norton, 1987.

Ahrons, Constance, and Lynn Wallisch. "The Relationship Between Former Spouses." In Daniel Perlman and Steve Duck, eds. *Intimate Relationships: Development, Dynamics, and Deterioration*. Newbury Park, Calif.: Sage Publications, 1987.

"AIDS and Children: A Family Disease." *World AIDS Magazine* (November 1989).

Ainsworth, Mary, et al. *Patterns of Attachment: A Psychological Study of the Strange Situation*. Hillsdale, New Jersey: Erlbaum, 1978.

Albert, Alexa,and Kris Bulcroft. "Pets, Families, and the Life Course." *Journal of Marriage and the Family* 50:2 (May 1988): 543–552.

Aldous, Joan. "American Families in the 1980s: Individualism Run Amok?" *Journal of Family Issues* 8:4 (December 1987): 422–425.

_____.*Family Careers: Developmental Change in Families*. New York: Wiley, 1978.

_____. "New Views on the Family Life of the Elderly and Near-Elderly." *Journal of Marriage and the Family* 49 (May 1987): 227–234.

_____. Perspectives on Family Change." *Journal of Marriage and the Family* 52:3 (August 1990): 571–583.

_____, ed. *Two Paychecks*. Beverly Hills, Calif.: Sage Publications, 1982.

Aldous, Joan, and Wilfried Dumon. "Family Policy in the 1980s: Controversy and Consensus." In Alan Booth, ed. *Contemporary Families: Looking Forward, Looking Back*. Minneapolis, Minn.: National Council on Family Relations, 1991.

Aldous, Joan, and David Klein. "Sentiment and Services: Models of Intergenerational Relationships in Midlife." *Journal of Marriage and the Family* 53:3 (August, 1991): 595–608.

Allen, Katherine. *Single Women/Family Ties*. Newbury Park, Calif.: Sage Publications, 1989.

Allen, Katherine, and Robert Pickett. "Forgotten Streams in the Family Life Course." *Journal of Marriage and the Family* 49:3 (August 1987): 517–528.

Allen, W. R. "The Search for Applicable Theories of Black Family Life." *Journal of Marriage and the Family* 40 (February 1978): 117–129.

Allen, W. R., et al. *Black American Families*. Westport, Conn.: Greenwood Press, 1986.

Allgeier, Elizabeth, and Naomi McCormick, eds. *Gender Roles and Sexual Behavior*. Palo Alto, Calif.: Mayfield, 1982.

Altman, Dennis. *AIDS in the Mind of America*. Garden City, N.Y.: Anchor/Doubleday, 1985.

_____. *The Homosexualization of America, The Americanization of the Homosexual*. New York: St. Martin's Press, 1982.

Alvirez, David, and Frank Bean. "The Mexican-American Family." In C. H. Mindel and R. W. Habenstein, eds. *Ethnic Families in America*. New York: Elsevier, 1976.

Alwin, Duane, et al. "Living Arrangements and Social Integration." *Journal of Marriage and the Family* 47:2 (May 1985): 319–334.

Amato, Paul. "Parental Divorce and Attitudes toward Marriage and Family Life." *Journal of Marriage and the Family* 50 (May, 1988): 453–461.

The American Fertility Society. "New Guidelines for the Use of Semen Donor Insemination: 1990." *Fertility and Sterility* 53:3 (suppl. 1) (March 1990): 1S–13S.

American Psychiatric Association on Nomenclature and Statistics. *Diagnostic and Statistical Manual,* 4th ed. Washington, D. C.: American Psychiatric Association, 1991.

Anderson, Carol. "The Community Connection: The Impact of Social Networks on Family and Individual Functioning." In Froma Walsh, ed. *Normal Family Processes*. New York: Guilford Press, 1982.

Anderson, Stephen. "Parental Stress and Coping During the Leaving Home Transition." *Family Relations* 37 (April 1988): 160–165.

Anderson, Stephen, and Paul Nuttall. "Parent Communications Training Across Three Stages of Childrearing." *Family Relations* 36:1 (January 1987): 40–44.

Andre, Rae. *The Homemakers: The Forgotten Workers*. Chicago: University of Chicago Press, 1981.

Andrews, Lori. *New Conceptions: A Consumer's Guide to the Newest Infertility Treatments*. New York: St. Martin's Press, 1984.

Aneshensel, C., and L. I. Pearlin. "Structural Contexts of Sex Differences in Stress." In R. C. Barnett, L. Biener, and G. K. Baruch, eds., *Gender and Stress*. New York: MacMillan, 1987.

Aneshensel, Carol, Eva Fielder, and Rosina Becerra. "Fertility and Fertility-Related Behavior among Mexican-American and Non-Hispanic White Females." Journal of Health and Social Behavior 30:1 (March 1989): 56–78.

Anson, Ofra. "Marital Status and Women's Health Revisited: The Importance of a Proximate Adult." *Journal of Marriage and the Family* 51 (February 1989): 185–194.

Antill, J. K. "Sex Role Complementarity versus Similarity in Married Couples." *Journal of Personality and Social Psychology* 45 (1983): 145–155.

Applebome, Peter. "Although Urban Blight Worsens, Most People Don't Feel Its Impact." *The New York Times,* January 26, 1991: 1, 12.

Archer, Sally. "Career and/or Family: The Identity Process for Adolescent Girls." *Youth and Society* 16:3 (1985): 289–314.

Arditti, Joyce. "Noncustodial Fathers: An Overview of Policy and Resources." *Family Relations* 39:4 (October 1990): 460–465.

Arehart-Treichel, Joan. "Pets: The Health Benefits." *Science News* 121 (March 27, 1982): 220–223.

Arendell, Terry. *Mothers and Divorce: Legal, Economic, and Social Dilemmas.* Berkeley, Calif.: University of California Press, 1987.

Aries, Philippe. *Centuries of Childhood.* New York: Vintage Books, 1962.

_____. "The Sentimental Revolution." *Wilson Quarterly* 6:4 (1982): 46–53.

Arms, Suzanne. *Adoption: A Handful of Hope.* Berkeley, Calif.: Celestial Arts, 1990.

Armstrong, George. "Pope Sets Forth Annulment Policy." *San Jose Mercury News.* February 14, 1987: 14D.

Armstrong, Penny and Sheryl Feldman. *A Wise Birth.* New York: William Morrow and Co., 1990.

Aron, Arthur, and Elaine Aron. "Love and Sexuality." In Kathleen McKinney and Susan Sprecher, eds., *Sexuality in Close Relationships.* Hillsdale, N.J.: Erlbaum, 1991.

Aron, Arthur, Elaine Aron, and Joselyn Allen. "Unrequited Love as Self Expansion." Paper presented at Iowa Conference on Personal Relationships, Iowa City, 1989.

Aron, Arthur, Elaine Aron, Meg Paris, Paula Tucker, and Geraldine Rodriguez. "Falling in Love: A Review of the Literature." Second Iowa Conference on Personal Relationships, Iowa City, May 12, 1989.

Aron, Arthur, D. G. Dutton, E. N. Aron, and A. Iverson. "Experiences of Falling in Love." *Journal of Social and Personal Relationships* 6(1989): 243–257.

Askham, J. "Identity and Stability Within the Marriage Relationship." *Journal of Marriage and the Family* 38 (1976): 535–547.

"At a Glance." *OURS: The Magazine of Adoptive Families* 23:6 (Nov.–Dec. 1990): 63.

Atkinson, Alice, and Diedre James. "The Transition between Active and Adult Parenting: An End and a Beginning." *Family Perspective* 25:1 (1991): 57–66.

Atkinson, Jean. "Gender Roles in Marriage and the Family." *Journal of Family Issues* 8:1 (March, 1987): 5–41.

Atkinson, Maxine, and Jacqueline Boles. "WASP (Wives as Senior Partners)." *Journal of Marriage and the Family* 46:3 (November 1984): 861–870.

Atkinson, Maxine, and Becky Glass. "Marital Age Heterogamy and Homogamy, 1900 to 1980." *Journal of Marriage and the Family* 47:3 (August 1985): 685–691.

Atwater, Lynn. "Long-Term Cohabitation Without a Legal Ceremony Is Equally Valid and Desirable." In Harold Feldman and Margaret Feldman, eds., *Current Controversies in Marriage and the Family.* Beverly Hills, Calif.: Sage Publications, 1985.

Auletta, Ken. *The Underclass.* New York: Random House, 1982.

Awad, George, and Ruth Parry. "Access Following Marital Separation." *Canadian Journal of Psychiatry* 25(5) (August 1980): 357–365.

Axelson, Leland, and Paula Dail. "The Changing Character of Homelessness in the United States." *Family Relations* 37:4 (October 1988): 463–469.

Axelson, Marta, and Jennifer Glass. "Household Structure and Labor Force Participation of Black, Hispanic, and White Mothers." *Demography* 22 (1985): 381–394.

Bachrach, Christine. "Contraceptive Practice Among American Women, 1973–1982." *Family Planning Perspectives* 16(6) (November/December, 1984): 253–258.

Bahr, Kathleen. "Student Responses to Genogram and Family Chronology." *Family Relations* 39 (July 1990): 243–249.

Bahr, Stephen. "The Economics of Family Life: An Overview." *Journal of Family Issues* 3:2 (June 1982a): 139–146.

_____. "Effects on Power and Division of Labor in the Family." In Lois Hoffman and Ivan Nye, eds., *Working Mothers.* San Francisco, Calif.: Jossey-Bass, 1974.

_____, ed. *Economics of the Family.* Lexington, Mass.: Lexington Books, 1980.

_____. "The Economics of Family Life." Special issue, *Journal of Family Issues* 3:2 (June 1982b).

Baird, Donna, D. and Allen J. Wilcox. "Cigarette Smoking Associated with Delayed Conception." *Journal of the American Medical Association* 253(20) (1985): 2979–2983.

_____. "Future Fertility after Prenatal Exposure to Cigarette Smoke." *Fertility and Sterility* 46:3 (September 1986): 368–372.

Baker, Sharon, Stanton Thalberg, and Diane Morrison. "Parents' Behavioral Norms as Predictors of Adolescent Sexual Activity and Contraceptive Use." *Adolescence* 23 (Summer 1988): 265–282.

Balswick, Judith. "Explaining Inexpressive Males: A Reply to L'Abate." *Family Relations* 29 (1980): 231–233.

Bane, Mary Jo, and David Ellwood. "Slipping Into and Out of Poverty: The Dynamic of Spells." *Journal of Human Resources* 21 (1986): 1–24.

Bane, Mary Jo, and Paul A. Jargowsky. "The Links Between Public Policy and Family Structure: What Matters and What Doesn't." In Andrew J. Cherlin, ed., *The Changing American Family and Public Policy.* Washington, D.C.: The Urban Institute Press, 1988.

Baptiste, David. "The Image of the Black Family Portrayed by Television." *Marriage and Family Review* 10:1 (April 1983): 41–63.

Barbach, Lonnie. *For Each Other: Sharing Sexual Intimacy.* Garden City, N.Y.: Doubleday, 1982.

Barden, J. C. "Many Parents in Divorces Abduct Their Own Children." *The New York Times,* May 6, 1990: 10.

Barkan, Susan, and Michael Bracken. "Delayed Childbearing: No Evidence for Increased Low Risk of Low Birth Weight and Preterm Delivery." *American Journal of Epidemiology* 125:1 (1987): 101–109.

Barkas, J. L. *Single in America.* New York: Atheneum, 1980.

Baron, Larry. "Sex Differences in Attitudes and Experiences of Romantic Love." *Dissertation Abstracts International* 43 (1983): 3722A.

Barranti, Crystal C. Ramirez. "The Grandparent/Grandchild Relationship: Family Resource in an Era of Voluntary Bonds." *Family Relations* 34:3 (July 1985): 343–352.

Barrow, Georgia. *Aging, Ageism, and Society.* St. Paul, Minn.: West, 1989.

Barth, Robert, and Bill Kinder. "The Mislabeling of Sexual Impulsivity." *Journal of Sex and Marital Therapy* 13:1 (Spring, 1987): 15–23.

Basow, Susan. *Gender Stereotypes: Traditions and Alternatives,* 2d ed. Monterey, Calif.: Brooks/Cole, 1986.

Bass, Ellen, and Louise Thornton, eds. *I Never Told Anyone: Stories and Poems by Survivors of Child Sexual Abuse.* New York: Harper & Row, 1983.

Bassuk, Ellen, et al. "Characteristics of Sheltered Homeless Families." *American Journal of Public Health* 76 (1986): 1097–1101.

Bassuk, Ellen, and Lenore Rubin. "Homeless Children: A Neglected Population." *American Journal of Orthopsychiatry* 57:2 (April 1987): 279–286.

Baumrind, Diana. "Current Patterns of Parental Authority." *Developmental Psychology Monographs* 4:1 (1971): 1–102.

_____. "Parental Disciplinary Patterns and Social Competence in Children." *Youth and Society* 9:3 (March 1978): 239–276.

Bean, Frank, and Marta Tienda. *The Hispanic Population of the United States.* New York: Russell Sage Foundation, 1987.

Beauvoir, Simone de. *The Coming of Age.* New York: Putnam's, 1972.

_____. *The Second Sex.* New York: Knopf, 1948 and 1952.

Beavers, Robert, W. "Healthy, Midrange, and Severely Dysfunctional Families." In Froma Walsh, ed., *Normal Family Processes.* New York: Guilford Press, 1982.

Beavers, Robert W., and Robert Hampson, *Successful Families.* New York: Norton Publishing Co., 1990.

Becerra, Rosina. "The Mexican American Family." In Charles Mindel, Robert Habenstein, and Roosevelt Wright, Jr., eds., *Ethnic Families in America: Patterns and Variations,* 3d ed. New York: Elsevier North Holland, Inc., 1988.

Beck, Melinda. "Miscarriages." *Newsweek* (August 15, 1988): 46–49.

Beck, Rubye, and Scott Beck. "The Incidence of Extended Households among Middle-Aged Black and White Women." *Journal of Family Issues* 10:2 (June 1989): 147–168.

Becker, Howard. *Outsiders.* New York: Free Press, 1963.

Beeghley, Leonard, and Sellers, Christine. "Adolescent and Sex: A Structural Theory of Premarital Sex in the United States." *Deviant Behavior* 7:4 (1986): 313–336.

Beier, Ernst, and Daniel Stenberg. "Marital Communication." *Journal of Communication* 27:3 (Summer 1977): 92–97.

Belcastro, Philip. "Sexual Behavior Differences between Black and White Students." *Journal of Sex Research* 21:1 (February 1985): 56–67.

Bell, Alan, and Martin Weinberg. *Homosexualities: A Study of Diversities among Men.* New York: Simon & Schuster, 1978.

Bell, Alan, et al. *Sexual Preference: Its Development in Men and Women.* Bloomington: Indiana University Press, 1981.

Bell, Colleen, et al. "Normative Stress and Young Families: Adaptation and Development." *Family Relations* 29:4 (1980): 453–458.

Bell, Robert, John Daly, and Christina Gonzales. "Affinity-Maintenance in Marriage and Marriage Satisfaction." *Journal of Marriage and the Family* 49:2 (May 1987): 445–455.

Bellah, Robert, et al. *Habits of the Heart.* Berkeley, Calif.: University of California Press, 1985.

Beller, Andrea. "Occupational Segregation and the Earnings Gap." In U.S. Commission on Civil Rights, *Comparable Worth: Issue for the 80's,* Vol. 1. Washington, D.C., 1984.

_____. "Occupational Segregation by Sex: Determinants and Changes." *Journal of Human Resources* 17 (Summer 1982): 371–392.

Belsky, Jay. "Patterns of Marital Change and Parent-Child Interaction." *Journal of Marriage and the Family* 53:2 (May 1991): 487–498.

_____. "Transition to Parenthood." *Medical Aspects of Human Sexuality* (20) (Sept. 1986): 56–59.

_____. "Exploring Individual Differences in Marital Change Across the Transition to Parenthood: The Role of Violated Expectations." *Journal of Marriage and the Family* 47:4 (November 1985c): 1037–1044.

_____. "Stability and Change in Marriage Across the Transition to Parenthood: A Second Study." *Journal of Marriage and the Family* 47:4 (November 1985b): 855–865.

_____. "The Work-Family Interface and Marital Change Across the Transition to Parenthood." *Journal of Family Issues* 6 (June 1985a): 205–220.

_____. "Infant Day Care, Child Development, and Family Policy." *Society* 27:5 (July–August 1990): 10–12.

_____, et al. *The Child in the Family.* Reading, Mass.: Addison-Wesley, 1984.

Bem, Sandra. "Androgyny vs. the Tight Little Lives of Fluffy Women and Chesty Men." *Psychology Today* 9:4 (September 1975): 58–59ff.

_____. "Bem Sex-Role Inventory: Professional Manual." Palo Alto, Calif.: Consulting Psychologists Press, 1981.

_____. "Gender Schema Theory: A Cognitive Account of Sex Typing." *Psychological Review* 88 (1981): 354–364.

_____. "Gender Schema Theory and Its Implications for Child Development: Raising Gender-Aschematic Children in a Gender Schematic Society." *Signs* 8:4 (Summer 1983): 598–616.

_____. "The Measurement of Psychological Androgyny." *Journal of Consulting and Clinical Psychology* 42 (1974): 155–162.

_____. "Sex Role Adaptability: One Consequence of Psychological Androgyny." *Journal of Personality and Social Psychology* 31:4 (1975): 634–643.

Bengston, Vern and Joan Roberston, eds. *Grandparenthood.* Beverly Hills, Calif.: Sage Publications, 1985.

Benin, Mary, and Agostinelli, Joan. "Husbands' and Wives' Satisfaction with the Division of Labor." *Journal of Marriage and the Family* 50:2 (May 1988): 349–361.

Benin, Mary, and Barbara Nienstedt. "Happiness, Job Satisfaction, and Life Cycle." *Journal of Marriage and the Family* 47:4 (November 1985): 975–984.

Berardo, Donna, et al. "A Residue of Tradition: Jobs, Careers, and Spouses' Time in Housework." *Journal of Marriage and the Family* 49 (May 1987): 381–390.

Berardo, Felix. "Trends and Directions in Family Research in the 1980s." In Alan Booth, ed., *Contemporary Families: Looking Forward, Looking Back.* Minneapolis: National Council on Family Relations, 1991.

Berardo, Felix, and Constance Sheehan. "Family Scholarship: A Reflection of the Changing Family?" *Journal of Family Issues* 5:4 (December 1984): 577–598.

Berger, Mark J., and Donald P. Goldstein. "Infertility Related to Exposure to DES in Utero: Reproductive Problems in the Female." In Miriam Mazor and Harriet Simons, eds., *Infertility: Medical, Emotional, and Social Considerations.* New York: Human Sciences Press, 1984.

Berk, Richard, P. Newton, and Sarah F. Berk. "What a Difference a Day Makes: An Empirical Study of the Impact of Shelters for Battered Women." *Journal of Marriage and the Family* 48 (August 1986): 481–490.

Berk, Sarah. *The Gender Factory: The Apportionment of Work in American Households.* New York: Plenum Press, 1985.

Berliner, Arthur. "Sex, Sin, and the Church: The Dilemma of Homosexuality." *Journal of Religion and Health* 26:7 (Summer 1987): 137–142.

Berman, William. "Continued Attachment After Legal Divorce." *Journal of Family Issues* 6:3 (September 1985): 375–392.

Bernard, Jessie. *The Future of Marriage,* 2d ed. New York: Columbia University Press, 1982.

Berscheid, Ellen. "Emotion." In H. H. Kelley et al., eds. *Close Relationships.* New York: Freeman, 1983

_____. "Interpersonal Attraction." In G. Lindzey and Elliot Aronson, eds. *Handbook of Social Psychology.* New York: Random House, 1985.

_____ "Some Comments on Love's Anatomy: Or, Whatever Happened to Old-fashioned Lust?" In Robert Sternberg and Michael Barnes, eds., *The Psychology of Love.* New Haven, Conn.: Yale University Press, 1988.

Berscheid, Ellen, and Elaine H. Walster. "A Little Bit About Love." In T. L. Huston, ed., *Foundations of Interpersonal Attraction.* New York: Academic Press, 1974.

_____. *Interpersonal Attraction*. Reading, Mass.: Addison-Wesley, 1978.

Berstein, Barton, and Sheila K. Collins. "Remarriage Counseling: Lawyer and Therapist's Help with the Second Time Around." *Family Relations* 34:3 (July 1985): 387–391.

Best, Joel. *Threatened Children: Rhetoric and Concern About Child-Victims*. Chicago: The University of Chicago Press, 1990.

Bielby, William, and James Baron. "Woman's Place Is With Other Women: Sex Segregation in the Workplace." Unpublished paper, National Research Council, Workshop on Job Segregation by Sex, 1982.

Billingsley, Andrew. *Black Families in White America*. Englewood Cliffs, N.J.: Prentice-Hall, 1968.

_____. "The Impact of Technology on Afro-American Families." *Family Relations* 37 (October 1988): 420–425.

Billy, John, Nancy Landale, William Grady, and Denise Zimmerle. "Effects of Sexual Activity on Adolescent Social and Psychological Development." *Social Psychology Quarterly* 51:3 (September 1988): 190–212.

Binion, Victoria. "Psychological Androgyny: A Black Female Perspective." *Sex Roles* 22: 7–8 (April 1990).

Binsacca, B. D., et al. "Factors Associated with Low Birthweight in an Inner-City Population." *American Journal of Public Health* 77:4 (Apr. 1987): 505–506.

Bird, Gerald, and Gloria Bird. "Determinants of Mobility in Two-Earner Families: Does the Wife's Income Count?" *Journal of Marriage and the Family* 47:3 (August 1985): 753–758.

_____. "Satisfaction in Family, Employment, and Community Roles." *Psychological Reports* 55:2 (October 1984): 675–678.

Blair, Sampson, and Daniel Lichter. "Measuring the Division of Household Labor: Gender Segregation and Housework among American Couples." *Journal of Family Issues* 12:1 (March 1991): 91–113.

Blakely, Mary Kay. "Surrogate Mothers: For Whom Are They Working?" *Ms.* (March 1987): 18, 20.

Blakeslee, Sandra. "Scientists Find Key Biological Causes of Alcoholism." *New York Times,* August 14, 1984:19ff.

Blassingame, John. *The Slave Community*. New York: Oxford Unversity Press, 1972.

Blieszner, Rosemary, and Janet Alley. "Family Caregiving for the Elderly: An Overview of Resources." *Family Relations* 39:1 (January 1990): 97–102.

Block, Jeanne. "Differential Premises Arising from Differential Socialization of the Sexes: Some Conjectures." *Child Development* 54 (1983): 1335–1354.

Bloom, Bernard, et al. "Sources of Marital Dissatisfaction Among Newly Separated Persons." *Journal of Family Issues* 6:3 (September 1985): 359–373.

Blumberg, Rae Lesser, ed. *Gender, Family, and the Economy*. Newbury Park, Calif: Sage Publications, 1990.

Blumenfeld, Warren, and Diane Raymond. *Looking at Gay and Lesbian Life*. Boston: Beacon Press, 1989.

Blumstein, Philip. "Identity Bargaining and Self-Conception." *Social Forces* 53:3 (1975): 476–485.

Blumstein, Philip, and Pepper Schwartz. *American Couples*. New York: McGraw-Hill, 1983.

Bobo, Lawrence. *General Social Survey: 1990*. Chicago: National Opinion Research Center, 1991.

Bodnar, John. *The Transplanted: A History of Immigrants in Urban America*. Bloomington: Indiana University Press, 1985.

Bohannan, Paul. *Divorce and After*. New York: Doubleday, 1971.

Boken, Halcyone. "Gender Equality in Work and Family." *Journal of Family Issues* 5:2 (June 1984): 254–272.

Boken, Halcyone, and Anamarie Viveros-Long. *Balancing Jobs and Family Life: Do Flexible Work Schedules Work?* Philadelphia: Temple University Press, 1981.

Boland, Joseph, and Diane Follingstad. "The Relationship Between Communication and Marital Satisfaction: A Review." *Journal of Sex and Marital Therapy* 13:4 (Winter 1987): 286–313.

Boles, Abner J., and Harriet Curtis-Boles. "Black Couples and the Transition to Parenthood." *The American Journal of Social Psychiatry* 6:1 (Winter 1986): 27–31.

Boone, Margaret S. *Capital Crime: Black Infant Mortality in America*. Newbury Park, Calif.: Sage Publications, 1989.

Booth, Alan. "Who Divorces and Why: A Review." *Journal of Family Issues* 6:3 (September 1985): 255–293.

_____, ed. *Contemporary Families: Looking Forward, Looking Back*. Minneapolis, Minn.: National Council on Family Relations, 1991.

Booth, Alan, and John Edwards. "Age at Marriage and Marital Instability." *Journal of Marriage and the Family* 47:2 (February 1985): 67–74.

Booth, Alan, David Johnson, Lynn White, and John Edwards. "Divorce and Marital Instability over the Life Course." *Journal of Family Issues* 7 (1986): 421–442.

Booth, Alan, et al. "Predicting Divorce and Permanent Separation." *Journal of Family Issues* 6:3 (September 1985): 331–346.

Borhek, Mary. "Helping Gay and Lesbian Adolescents and Their Families: A Mother's Perspective." *Journal of Adolescent Health Care* 9:2 (March 1988):123–128.

Borland, Dolores. "A Cohort Analysis Approach to the Empty-nest Syndrome Among Three Ethnic Groups of Women: A Theoretical Position." *Journal of Marriage and the Family* 44 (February 1982): 117–129.

Boss, Pauline. "Family Stress." In Marvin B. Sussman and Suzanne K. Steinmetz, eds., *Handbook of Marriage and the Family*. New York: Plenum Press, 1987.

Boston Women's Health Book Collective. *The New Our Bodies, Ourselves*. New York: Simon & Schuster, 1984.

_____. *Our Bodies, Ourselves*. Boston: Little, Brown, 1978a.

_____. *Ourselves and Our Children*. New York: Random House, 1978b.

Boswell, John. *Christianity, Social Tolerance, and Homosexuality*. Chicago: University of Chicago Press, 1980.

Botkin, B.A., ed. *Lay My Burden Down: A Folk History of Slavery*. Chicago: University of Chicago Press, 1945.

Bourne, Richard, and Eli Newberger, eds. *Critical Perspectives on Child Abuse*. Lexington, Mass.: Lexington Books, 1979.

Bowen, Gary. "Corporate Supports for the Family Lives of Employees: A Conceptual Model for Program Planning and Evaluation." *Family Relations* 37 (April 1988): 183–188.

Bowker, Lee. *Beating Wife Beating*. Lexington, Mass.: Lexington Books, 1983.

Bowlby, John. *Attachment and Loss*. Three volumes. New York: Basic Books, 1969, 1973, 1980.

Bowman, Madonna, and Constance Ahrons. "Impact of Legal Custody Status on Father's Parenting Post-divorce." *Journal of Marriage and the Family* 47:2 (May 1985) 481–485.

Bozett, Frederick W., ed. *Gay and Lesbian Parents*. New York: Praeger, 1987a.

_____. "Gay Fathers." In Frederick W. Bozett, ed., *Gay and Lesbian Parents*. New York: Praeger, 1987b.

_____. "Children of Gay Fathers." In Frederick W. Bozett, ed., *Gay and Lesbian Parents*. New York: Praeger, 1987c.

Bradford, William. *History of Plymouth Plantation*. Cambridge, Mass.: Harvard University Press, 1945.

Bradley, Buff, et al. *Single Living Your Own Way*. Reading, Mass.: Addison-Wesley, 1977.

Bradley, E. Jane, and R. C. L. Lindsay. "Methodological and Ethical Issues in Child Abuse Research." *Journal of Family Violence* 2:3 (1987): 239–255.

Brand, H. J. "The Influence of Sex Differences on the Acceptance of Infertility." *Journal of Reproductive and Infant Psychology* 7:2 (April–June 1989): 129–131.

Brandenburg, H., et al. "Fetal Loss Rate After Chorionic Villus Sampling and Subsequent Amniocentesis." *American Journal of Medical Genetics* 35:2 (February 1990): 178–180.

Bray, James, and Sandra Berger. "Noncustodial Father and Paternal Grandparent Relationship in Stepfamilies." *Family Relations* 39:4 (October 1990): 414–419.

Breault, K. D., and Augustine Kposowa. "Explaining Divorce in the United States: A Study of 3,111 Counties, 1980." *Journal of Marriage and the Family* 49:3 (August 1987): 549–558.

Brenner, Harvey. "Influence of the Social Environment on Psychopathology: The Historic Perspective." In James Barrett et al., eds. *Stress and Mental Disorder*. New York: Raven, 1979.

_____. *Mental Illness and the Economy*. Cambridge, Mass.: Harvard University Press, 1973.

Bretschneider, Judy, and Norma McCoy. "Sexual Interest and Behavior in Healthy 80- to 102-Year-Olds." *Archives of Sexual Behavior* 17:2 (April 1988): 109–128.

Brigman, K. M. "Churches Helping Families." *Family Perspectives* 18:2 (1984): 77–84.

Bristor, Martha Wingerd. "The Birth of a Handicapped Child—A Holistic Model for Grieving." *Family Relations* 33:1 (January 1984): 25–32.

Broderick, Carlfred, and James Smith. "The General Systems Approach to the Family." In Wesley Burr et al., eds., *Contemporary Theories About the Family: General Theories/Theoretical Orientations*. New York: Free Press, 1979.

Brody, Elaine. "Parent Care as a Normative Family Stress." *Gerontologist* 25 (1985): 19–29.

Brody, Jane. "Assessing the Question of Male Circumcision." *The New York Times*, August 14, 1985: 18.

Brodzinsky, David M., and Loreen Huffman. "Transition to Adoptive Parenthood." *Marriage and Family Review* 12:3–4 (1988): 267–286.

Brodzinsky, David M. and Marshall D. Schechter, eds. *The Psychology of Adoption*. New York: Oxford University Press, 1990.

Broman, Clifford. "Gender, Work-Family Roles, and Psychological Well-Being of Blacks." *Journal of Marriage and the Family* 53:2 (May 1991): 509–520.

_____. "Household Work and Family Life Satisfaction among Blacks." *Journal of Marriage and the Family* 50:3 (August, 1988): 743–748.

_____. "Satisfaction among Blacks: The Significance of Marriage and Parenthood." *Journal of Marriage and the Family* 50:1 (February 1988): 45–51.

Bronfenbrenner, Urie. *The Ecology of Human Development*. Cambridge, Mass.: Harvard University Press, 1979.

_____. "The Parent/Child Relationship and Our Changing Society." In L. Eugene Arnold, ed., *Parents, Children and Change*. Lexington, Mass.: Lexington Books, 1985.

Bronfenbrenner, Urie, and Ann Crouter. "Work and Family Through Time and Space." In Sheila Kamerman and C. D. Hayes, eds., *Families That Work: Children in a Changing World*. Washington, D.C.: National Academy Press, 1982.

Brown, Elizabeth, and William R. Hendee. "Adolescents and Their Music." *Journal of the American Medical Association* 262:12 (Sept. 22/29, 1989): 1659–1663.

Brown, Patricia Leigh. "Where to Put the TV Set?" *The New York Times*, October 4, 1990: B4.

Browne, Angela, and David Finkelhor. "Initial and Long-Term Effects: A Review of the Research." In David Finkelhor, ed., *Sourcebook on Child Sexual Abuse*. Beverly Hills, Calif.: Sage Publications, 1986.

Brownmiller, Susan. *Against Our Will: Men, Women, and Rape*. New York: Simon & Schuster, 1975.

_____. *Femininity*. New York: Fawcett Columbine, 1983.

Brubaker, Timothy. "Families in Later Life: A Burgeoning Research Area." In Alan Booth, ed. *Contemporary Families: Looking Forward, Looking Back*. Minneapolis, Minn.: National Council on Family Relations, 1991.

Bruce, Martha, and Philip Leaf. "Psychiatric Disorders and 15-Month Mortality in a Community Sample of Adults." *American Journal of Public Health* 79 (1989): 727–730.

Bryant, Lois, Marilyn Coleman, and Lawrence Ganong. "Race and Family Structure Stereotyping: Perceptions of Black and White Nuclear Families and Stepfamilies." *Journal of Black Psychology* 15 (1988): 1–16.

Bryant, Z. Lois, and Marilyn Coleman. "The Black Family as Portrayed in Introductory Marriage and Family Textbooks." *Family Relations*. 37:3 (July 1988): 255–259.

Buchta, Richard. "Attitudes of Adolescents and Parents of Adolescents Concerning Condom Advertisements on Television." *Journal of Adolescent Health Care* 10:3 (May 1989): 220–223.

Budiansky, Stephen. "The New Rules of Reproduction." *U.S. News and World Report* (April 18, 1988): 66–69.

Buehler, Cheryl. "Initiator Status and the Divorce Transition." *Family Relations* 36 (January 1987): 82–86.

Bullough, Vern. *Sexual Variance in Society and History*. New York: John Wiley & Sons, 1976.

Bumpass, Larry, Teresa Castro Martin, and James Sweet. "The Impact of Family Background and Early Marital Factors on Marital Disruption." *Journal of Family Issues* 12:1 (March 1991): 22–44.

Bumpass, Larry, and James A. Sweet. "Children's Experience in Single Parent Families: Implications of Cohabitation and Marital Transition." *Family Planning Perspectives* 21:6 (November–December 1989): 256–260.

_____. "Differentials in Marital Stability." *Sociological Review* 37 (1972): 754–766.

Bumpass, Larry, James Sweet, and Teresa Castro Martin. "Changing Patterns of Remarriage." *Journal of Marriage and the Family* 52:3 (August 1990): 747–756.

Burgess, Ann W., ed. *Rape and Sexual Assault II*. New York: Garland Press, 1988.

Burgess, Ernest. "The Family as a Unity of Interacting Personalities." *The Family* 7:1 (March 1926): 3–9. Reprinted in Jerold Heiss, ed., *Family Roles and Interaction*. Chicago: Rand McNally, 1968.

Burns, Ailsa. "Perceived Causes of Marriage Breakdown and Conditions of Life." *Journal of Marriage and the Family* 46:3 (August 1984): 551–562.

Burns, Scott. *The Household Economy*. New York: Harper & Row, 1972.

Burr, Wesley. *Theory Construction and the Sociology of the Family*. New York: John Wiley and Sons, 1973.

Burr, Wesley, et al. *Contemporary Theories About the Family*. 2 vols. New York: Free Press, 1979.

Burroughs, Louise, et al. "Careers, Contingencies, and Locus of Control Among White College Women." *Sex Roles* 11(3/4) (1984): 289–302.

Buss, D. M. "Toward a Psychology of Person-Environment (PE) Correlation." *Journal of Personality and Social Psychology* 47 (1984): 361–377.

Butter, I. H., and B. J. Kay. "Self Certification in Law Midwives Organizations—A Vehicle for Professional Autonomy." *Social Science & Medicine* 30:12 (1990): 1329–1339.

Buunk, Bram, and Barry van Driel. *Variant Lifestyles and Relationships*. Newbury Park, Calif.: Sage Publications, 1989.

Byrd, W., et al. "A Prospective Randomized Study of Pregnancy Rates Following Intrauterine and Intracervical Insemination Using Frozen Donor Sperm." *Fertility and Sterility* 53:3 (March 1990): 521–527.

Byrne, Donn and Karen Murnen. *"Maintaining Love Relationships."* In Robert Sternberg and Michael Barnes, eds., *The Psychology of Love.* New Haven, Conn.: Yale University Press, 1988.

Cabai, Robert. "Gay and Lesbian Couples: Lessons on Human Intimacy." *Psychiatric Annals* 18:1 (January 1988):21–25.

Cado, Suzana, and Harold Leitenberg. "Guilt Reactions to Sexual Fantasies during Intercourse." *Archives of Sexual Behavior* 19:1 (1990): 49–63.

Callahan, Sidney, and Daniel Callahan. "Abortion: Understanding the Differences." *Family Planning Perspectives* 16:5 (September/October 1984): 219–221.

Callan, Victor. "The Personal and Marital Adjustment of Mothers and of Voluntarily and Involuntarily Childless Wives." *Journal of Marriage and the Family* 49:4 (November 1987): 847–856.

_____. "Perceptions of Parents, the Voluntarily and Involuntarily Childless: A Multidimensional Scaling Analysis." *Journal of Marriage and the Family* 47:4 (November 1985): 1045–1050.

Camarillo, Albert. *Chicanos in a Changing Society: From Mexican Pueblos to American Barrios in Santa Barbara and Southern California.* Cambridge, Mass.: Harvard University Press, 1979.

_____. *Latinos in the United States.* Santa Barbara, Calif.: ABC-Clio, 1986.

_____. *Mexican-Americans in Urban Society: A Selected Bibliography.* Berkeley, Calif.: Floricanto Press, 1986.

Canter, Lee, and Marlene Canter. *Assertive Discipline for Parents.* Santa Monica, Calif.: Canter and Associates, 1985.

Caplan, Lincoln. *An Open Adoption.* New York: Farrar, Straus & Giroux, 1990.

Cappell, Charles and Robert B. Heiner. "The Intergenerational Transmission of Family Agression." *Journal of Family Violence* 5:2 (June 1990): 121–134.

Carballo-Dieguez, Alex. "Hispanic Culture, Gay Male Culture, and AIDS: Counseling Implications." *Journal of Counseling and Development* 68:1 (September–October 1989): 26–30.

Cargan, Leonard, and Matthew Melko. *Singles: Myths and Realities.* Beverly Hills, Calif.: Sage Publications, 1982.

Carl, Douglas. "Acquired Immune Deficiency Syndrome: A Preliminary Examination of the Effects on Gay Couples and Coupling." *Journal of Marital and Family Therapy* 12:3 (July 1986): 241–247.

Carnes, Patrick. *Out of the Shadows.* Minneapolis, Minn.: CompCare Publications, 1983.

Carroll, Jerry. "Tracing the Causes of Infertility." *San Francisco Chronicle* (March 5, 1990): B3*ff.*

Carroll, Jerry, et al., "Differences in Males and Females in Motives for Engaging in Sexual Intercourse." *Archives of Sexual Behavior* 14 (1985): 131–139.

Carson, David K. et al. "Family of Origin Characteristics and Current Family Relationships of Female Adult Incest Victims." *Journal of Family Violence* 5:2 (June 1990): 153–172.

Carter, D. Bruce, ed. *Current Conceptions of Sex Roles and Sex Typing.* New York: Praeger, 1987b.

_____. "Sex Role Research and the Future: New Directions for Research." In D. Bruce Carter, ed., *Current Conceptions of Sex Roles and Sex Typing.* New York: Praeger, 1987a.

_____. "Societal Implications of AIDS and HIV Infections, HIV Antibody Testing, Health Care, and AIDS Education." *Marriage and Family Review* 13:1–2 (1989): 129–188.

Carter, Betty, and Monica McGoldrick, eds. *The Changing Family Life Cycle,* 2d ed. Boston: Allyn and Bacon: 1989.

Cassell, Carol. *Swept Away.* New York: Simon and Schuster, 1984.

Cate, Jim, Linda Graham, Donna Boeglin, and Steven Tielker. "The Effect of AIDS on the Family System." *Families in Society* 71:4 (April 1990): 195–201.

Cazenave, N. A. "'A Woman's Place': The Attitudes of Middle Class Black Men." *Phylon: The Atlanta University Review of Race and Culture* 44 (1983): 13–32.

Centers for Disease Control. "Statewide Prevalence of Illicit Drug Use by Pregnant Women—Rhode Island." *Morbidity and Mortality Weekly Report* 39:14 (April 3, 1990): 225–227.

Chasnoff, Ira J. "Drug Use in Pregnancy: Parameters of Risk." *Pediatric Clinics of North America* 35:6 (December 1988): 1403–1412.

Chatters, Linda M., Robert Joseph Taylor, and Harold W. Neighbors. "Size of Informal Helper Network Mobilized during a Serious Personal Problem among Black Americans." *Journal of Marriage and the Family* 51 (August 1989): 667–676.

Chaze, William. "New, Nationwide Drive to Curb Child Abuse." *U.S. News and World Report* (October 1, 1984).

Cherlin, Andrew J. "The Changing American Family and Public Policy." In Andrew J. Cherlin, ed., *The Changing American Family and Public Policy.* Washington, D.C.: The Urban Institute Press, 1988.

_____. *Marriage, Divorce, and Remarriage.* Cambridge, Mass.: Harvard University Press, 1981.

_____. "Remarriage as Incomplete Institution." *American Journal of Sociology* 84 (1978): 634–650.

_____. *The Changing American Family and Public Policy.* Washington, D.C.: The Urban Institute Press, 1988.

Cherlin, Andrew, and Frank Furstenberg, Jr. *The New American Grandparent.* New York: Basic Books, 1986.

Chesser, Barbara Jo. "Analysis of Wedding Rituals: An Attempt to Make Weddings More Meaningful." *Family Relations* (April 1980).

Chiasson, M.A., R.L. Stoneburner and S.C. Joseph. "Human Immunodeficiency Virus Transmission Through Artificial Insemination." *Journal of Acquired Immune Deficiency Syndromes* 3:1 (1990): 69–72.

Chilman, Catherine. "Working Poor Families: Trends, Causes, Effects, and Suggested Policies." *Family Relations* 40:2 (April 1991): 191–198.

Chilman, Catherine, et al., eds. *Variant Family Forms.* Beverly Hills, Calif.: Sage Publications, 1988.

Christenen, Andrew. "Dysfunctional Interaction Patterns in Couples." In Patricia Noller and Mary Anne Fitzpatrick, eds., *Perspectives on Marital Interaction.* Philadelphia, Penn.: Multilingual Matters, 1988.

Christensen, Donna, Carla Dahl, and Kathryn Rettig. "Noncustodial Mothers and Child Support: Examining the Larger Context." *Family Relations* 39:4 (October 1990): 388–394.

Christopher, F., and R. Cate. "Factors Involved in Premarital Decision-making." *Journal of Sex Research* 20 (1984): 363–376.

Christopher, F. Scott, Richard A. Fabes, and Patricia M. Wilson. "Family Television Viewing: Implications for Family Life Education." *Family Relations* 38:2 (April 1989): 210–214.

Ciancannelli, Penelope, and Bettina Berch. "Gender and the GNP." In Myra Marx Ferree and Beth Hess, eds., *Analyzing Gender.* Newbury Park, Calif.: Sage Publications, 1987.

Cimons, Marlene. "American Infertility Rate Not Growing, Study Finds." *The New York Times,* December 7, 1990: A3.

Claes, Jacalyn A. and David M. Rosenthal. "Men Who Batter Women: A Study in Power." *Journal of Family Violence* 5:3 (September 1990): 215–224.

Clark-Nicolas, Patricia, and Bernadette Gray–Little. "Effect of Economic Resources on Marital Quality in Black Married Couples." *Journal of Marriage and the Family* 53:3 (August 1991): 645–656.

Cleek, Margaret, and T. Allan Pearson. "Perceived Causes of Divorce: An Analysis of Interrelationships." *Journal of Marriage and the Family* 47:2 (February 1985): 179–191.

Clemens, Audra, and Leland Axelson. "The Not-So-Empty-Nest: The Return of the Fledgling Adult." *Family Relations* 34 (April 1985): 259–264.

Clemes, Harris, and Reynold Bean. *How to Raise Children's Self-Esteem.* San Jose, Calif.: Enrich, 1983.

Cleveland, Peggy, et al. "If Your Child Has AIDS...: Responses of Parents with Homosexual Children." *Family Relations* 37:2 (April 1988): 150–153.

Clingempeel, W. Glenn, and Eulalee Brand. "Quasi-kin Relationships, Structural Complexity, and Marital Quality in Stepfamilies: A Replication, Extension, and Clinical Implications." *Family Relations* 34:3 (July 1985): 401–409.

Clingempeel, W. Glenn, et al. "Stepparent-Stepchild Relationships in Stepmother and Stepfather Families: A Multimethod Study." *Family Relations* 33 (1984): 465–473.

Cochran, Susan, Jasen Keidan and Ari Kalechstein. "Sexually Transmitted Diseases and Acquired Immunodeficiency Syndrome (AIDS): Changes in Risk Reduction Behaviors among Young Adults." *Sexually Transmitted Diseases* 16:1 (January–March 1989): 80–86.

Coggle, Frances, and Grace Tasker. "Children and Housework." *Family Relations* 31 (July 1982): 395–399.

Cohen, Nancy Weiner, and Lois J. Estner. "Silent Knife: Cesarean Section in the United States." *Society* 21:1(147) (November–December 1983): 95–111.

Cohen, Theodore. "Remaking Men: Men's Experiences Becoming and Being Husbands and Fathers and Their Implications for Reconceptualizing Men's Lives." *Journal of Family Issues* 8:1 (March, 1987): 57–77.

Cohler, Bertram, and Scott Geyer. "Psychological Autonomy and Interdependence within the Family." In Froma Walsh, ed., *Normal Family Processes.* New York: Guilford Press, 1982.

Cole, Charles, and Anna Cole. "Husbands and Wives Should Have an Equal Share in Making the Marriage Work." In Harold Feldman and Margaret Feldman, eds., *Current Controversies in Marriage and the Family.* Beverly Hills, Calif.: Sage Publications, 1985.

Cole, Cynthia, and Hyman Rodman. "Latchkey Children: A Review of Policy and Resources" *Family Relations.* 36 (January 1987): 101–105.

Coleman, Elizabeth. "Sexual Compulsion vs. Sexual Addiction: The Date Continues." *SIECUS Report* 14 (1986): 7–10.

Coleman, Marilyn, and Lawrence Ganong. "The Cultural Stereotyping of Stepfamilies." In Kay Pasley and Marilyn Ihinger-Tallman, eds. *Remarriage and Stepparenting: Current Research and Theory.* New York: Guilford Press, 1987.

_____. "Remarriage and Stepfamily Research in the 1980s: Increased Interest in an Old Form." In Alan Booth, ed. *Contemporary Families: Looking Forward, Looking Back.* Minneapolis: National Council on Family Relations, 1991.

Coleman, Peter. *Gay Christians: A Moral Dilemma.* Philadelphia: Trinity Press, 1989.

Coles, Robert. *The Spiritual Life of Children.* Boston: Houghton-Mifflin, 1990.

Collier, J., M. Z. Rosaldo, and S. Yanagisako. "Is There a Family? New Anthropological Views." In B. Thorne and M. Yalom, eds., *Rethinking the Family: Some Feminist Questions.* New York: Longman, 1982.

Collins, Glenn. "Insensitivity to the Disabled." *The New York Times,* August 11, 1986: 18.

_____. "U.S. Day-Care Guidelines Rekindle Controversy." *New York Times,* February 4, 1985:20.

Condit, Celeste. *Decoding Abortion Rhetoric.* Urbana, Ill: University of Chicago Press, 1990.

Condrad, Peter, and Joseph Schneider. *Deviance and Medicalization: From Badness to Sickness.* St. Louis, Mo.: C. V. Mosby, 1980.

Condron, John, and Jerry Bode. "Rashomon, Working Wives, and Family Division of Labor: Middletown, 1980." *Journal of Marriage and the Family* 44:2 (May 1982): 421–426.

Condry, J. and S. Condry. "The Development of Sex Differences: A Study of the Eye of the Beholder." *Child Development* 47:4 (1976): 812–819.

Conway, Colleen. "Psychophysical Preparations for Childbirth." In Leota McNall, ed. *Contemporary Obstetric and Gynecological Nursing.* St. Louis, Mo.: C. V. Mosby, 1980.

Cook, Alicia, et al. "Changes in Attitudes Toward Parenting Among College Women: 1972 and 1979 Samples." *Family Relations* 31 (January 1982): 109–113.

Cook, Mark, ed., *The Bases of Human Sexual Attraction.* New York: Academic Press, 1981.

Cooke, Betty D., et al. "Examining the Definition and Assessment of Social Support: A Resource for Individuals and Families." *Family Relations* 37 (April 1988): 211–216.

Cooney, Teresa, and Peter Uhlenberg. "The Role of Divorce in Men's Relation with Their Adult Children after Mid-life." *Journal of Marriage and the Family* 52:3 (August 1990): 677–688.

Corby, Nan, and Judy Zarit. "Old and Alone: The Unmarried in Later Life." In Ruth Weg, ed., *Sexuality in the Later Years: Roles and Behavior.* New York: Academic Press, 1983.

Corea, Gena. *The Mother Machine: Reproductive Technology from Artificial Insemination to Artificial Wombs.* New York: Harper and Row, 1985.

Cortese, Anthony. "Subcultural Differences in Human Sexuality: Race, Ethnicity, and Social Class." In Kathleen McKinney and Susan Sprecher, eds., *Human Sexuality: The Societal and Interpersonal Context.* Norwood, N.J.: Ablex Publishing Corporation, 1989.

Cosby, Bill. "The Regular Way." *Playboy* (December 1968): 288–289.

Coulanges, Fustel de. *The Ancient City.* 1867. Reprint. New York: Anchor Books, 1960.

Cowan, Carolyn P., and Philip A. Cowan. "Who Does What When Partners Become Parents: Implications for Men, Women, and Marriage." *Marriage and Family Review* 12:3–4 (1988): 105–131.

Cowan, Philip, and Carolyn Cowan. "Becoming a Family: Research and Intervention." In Irving Sigel and Gene Brody, eds., *Methods of Family Research: Biographies of Research Projects.* Hillsdale, N.J.: Lawrence Erlbaum Associates, Publishers, 1990.

Cramer, D. "Gay Parents and Their Children: A Review of Research and Practical Implications." *Journal of Counseling and Development* 64 (1986): 504–507.

Cramer, David, and Arthur Roach. "Coming Out to Mom and Dad: A Study of Gay Males and Their Relationships with Their Parents." *Journal of Homosexuality* 14:1–2 (1987): 77–88.

Crandell, Barbara, et al. "Follow-up of 2000 Second-Trimester Amniocenteses." *Obstetrics and Gynecology* 56 (November 1980): 625–628.

Croby, Nan, and Judy Zarit. "Old and Alone: The Unmarried in Later Life." In Ruth Weg, ed., *Sexuality in the Later Years: Roles and Behavior.* New York: Academic Press, 1983.

Crosby, John, ed. *Reply to Myth: Perspectives on Intimacy.* New York: John Wiley, 1985.

Cuber, John, and Peggy Haroff. *Sex and the Significant Americans,* rev. ed. Baltimore: Penguin Books, 1965, 1974.

Culp, R. E., et al. "A Comparison of Observed and Reported Adult-Infant Interactions: Effects of Perceived Sex." *Sex Roles* 9 (1983): 475–479.

Curie-Cohen, M., et al. "Current Practice of Artificial Insemination by Donor in the United States." *New England Journal of Medicine* 300:11 (March 15,1979): 585–590.

Curran, Dolores. *Traits of a Healthy Family.* New York: Ballantine Books, 1983.

Daley, Suzanne. "Girls' Self-Esteem Is Lost on Way to Adolescence, New Study Finds." *The New York Times,* January 9, 1991: B1.

Daniluk, Judith, and Al Herman. "Parenthood Decision-Making." *Family Relations* 33 (October 1984): 607–612.

Danzinger, Sheldon, and Robert Plotnick. "Poverty and Policy: Lessons of the Last Two Decades." *Social Services Review* 60 (1986): 34–51.

Darling, Carol, and Kenneth Davidson. "Enhancing Relationships: Understanding the Feminine Mystique of Orgasm." *Journal of Sex & Marital Therapy* 12:3 (Fall 1986): 186–196.

Darling, Rosalyn, and J. Darling. *Children Who Are Different: Meeting the Challenges of Birth Defects in Society.* St. Louis, Mo.: C. V. Mosby, 1982.

Darling, Rosalyn Benjamin. "The Economic and Psychosocial Consequences of Disability: Family-Society Relationships." *Marriage and Family Review* 11:1–2 (Fall–Winter, 1987): 45–61.

Darling-Fisher, Cynthia, and Linda Tiedje. "The Impact of Maternal Employment Characteristics on Fathers' Participation in Child Care." *Family Relations* 39:1 (January 1990): 20–26.

Daro, Deborah, and Anne Cohen. "Child Maltreatment Evaluations Efforts: What Have We Learned?" In Gerald Hotaling, David Finkelhor, John Kirkpatrick, and Murray Straus, eds., *Coping with Family Violence: Research and Perspectives.* Newbury Park, Calif.: Sage Publications, 1988.

Davidson, Kenneth, and Carol Darling. "The Stereotype of Single Women Revisted." *Health Care for Women International* 9:4 (October–December, 1988): 317–336.

———. "Changing Autoerotic Attitudes and Practices among College Females: A Two-Year Follow-up Study." *Adolescence* 23 (Winter, 1988): 773–792.

Davidson, Kenneth, and Linda Hoffman. "Sexual Fantasies and Sexual Satisfaction: An Empirical Investigation of Erotic Thought." *Journal of Sex Research* 22 (May 1986): 184–205.

Davidson, J. Kenneth, Carol Darling, and Colleen Conway-Welch. "The Role of the Gräfenberg Spot and Female Ejaculation in the Female Orgasmic Response: An Empirical Analysis." *Journal of Sex and Marital Therapy* 15 (Summer 1989): 102–120.

Davis, Keith. "Near and Dear: Friendship and Love Compared." *Psychology Today* 19:2 (February 1985): 22–30.

Davis, L. *The Black Family in the United States.* Westport, Conn.: Greenwood Press, 1986.

Davitz, J. R. *The Language of Emotion.* New York: Academic Press, 1969.

Dawson, Deborah. "Family Structure and Children's Health and Well-Being." *Journal of Marriage and the Family* 53:3 (August 1991): 574–584.

Dean, Gillian, and Douglas Gurak. "Marital Homogagy: The Second Time Around." *Journal of Marriage and the Family* 40:3 (August 1978): 559–570.

DeBuono, Barbara, Stephen Zinner, Maxim Daamen, and William McCormack. "Sexual Behavior in College Women in 1975, 1986, and 1989." *New England Journal of Medicine* 322:12 (March 22, 1990): 821–825.

DeCecco, John, ed. *Gay Relationships.* New York: Haworth Press, 1988.

DeCecco, John, and Michael Shively. "From Sexual Identity to Sexual Relationships: A Conceptual Shift." *Journal of Homosexuality* 9(2/3) (Winter 1983/Spring 1984): 1–26.

Degler, Carl. *At Odds.* New York: Oxford University Press, 1980.

Delamater, J. D., and P. MacCorquodale. *Premarital Sexuality: Attitudes, Relationships, Behavior.* Madison: University of Wisconsin Press, 1979.

DeMaris, Alfred. "The Dynamics of Generational Transfer in Courtship Violence: A Biracial Exploration." *Journal of Marriage and the Family* 52 (February 1990): 219–231.

DeMaris, Alfred, and Gerald Leslie. "Cohabitation with the Future Spouse: Its Influence Upon Marital Satisfaction and Communication." *Journal of Marriage and the Family* 46:1 (February 1984): 77–84.

D'Emilio, John, and Estelle Freedman. *Intimate Matters: A History of Sexuality in America.* New York: Harper and Row, 1988.

Demo, David, and Alan Acock. "The Impact of Divorce on Children." In Alan Booth, ed., *Contemporary Families: Looking Forward, Looking Back.* Minneapolis: National Council on Family Relations, 1991.

Demo, David H., et al. "Family Relations and Self-Esteem." *Journal of Marriage and the Family.* 49:4 (November 1987): 705–716.

Demos, Vasilikie. "Black Family Studies in the *Journal of Marriage and the Family* and the Issue of Distortion: A Trend Analysis." *Journal of Marriage and the Family* 52 (August, 1990): 603–612.

Dentzer, Susan. "Do the Elderly Want to Work?" *U. S. News & World Report,* May 14, 1990: 48–50.

Denzin, Norman. "Toward a Phenomenology of Domestic Family Violence." *American Journal of Sociology* 90(30) (1984): 483–513.

DeParle, Jason. "Suffering in the Cities Persists as U. S. Fights Other Battles." *The New York Times,* January 27, 1991: 1, 15.

Depner, Charlene, and James Bray. "Modes of Participation for Noncustodial Parents: The Challenge for Research, Policy, Practice, and Education." *Family Relations* 39:4 (October 1990): 378–381.

Derdeyn, A. and E. Scott. "Joint Custody: A Critical Analysis and Appraisal." *American Journal of Orthopsychiatry* 54 (April 1984): 199–209.

De Simone-Luis, Judith, et al. "Children of Separation and Divorce: Factors Influencing Adjustment." *Journal of Divorce* 3:1 (Fall 1979): 37–42.

Desmond, Edward. "Out in the Open." *Time.* November 30, 1987: 80–90.

DeSpelder, Lynne Ann, and Albert Strickland, 3d ed. *The Last Dance: Encountering Death and Dying.* Palo Alto, Calif.: Mayfield Publishing Co. 1990.

DeVault, Marjorie. "Doing Housework: Feeling and Family Life." In Naomi Gerstel and Harriet Gross, eds., *Families and Work.* Philadelphia: Temple University Press, 1987.

De Witt, Karen. "U. S. Plan on Child Care Is Reported to be Stalled." *The New York Times,* January 17, 1991: A12.

Dick-Read, Grantly. *Childbirth Without Fear.* 4th ed. New York: Harper & Row, 1972.

Dilworth-Anderson, Peggye, and Harriette Pipes McAdoo. "The Study of Ethnic Minority Families: Implications for Practioners and Policymakers." *Family Relations* 37 (July 1988): 265–267.

Dinnerstein, Leonard, and David Reimers. *Ethnic Americans: A History of Immigration.* 3d ed. New York: Harper and Row, 1988.

Dion, Karen. "Physical Attractiveness, Sex Roles, and Heterosexual Attraction." In Mark Cook, ed., *The Bases of Human Sexual Attraction.* New York: Academic Press, 1981.

Dion, Karen, et al. "What Is Beautiful Is Good." *Journal of Personality and Social Psychology* 24 (1972): 285–290.

Dobash, R. Emerson, and Russell Dobash. *Violence Against Wives: A Case Against the Patriarchy.* New York: Free Press, 1979.

Dodson, Fitzhugh. "How to Discipline Effectively." In Eileen Shiff, ed., *Experts Advise Parents.* New York: Dell Publishing Co., 1987.

Dodson, Jualynne. "Conceptualizations of Black Families." In Harriette Pipes McAdoo, ed., *Black Families,* 2d ed. Newbury Park, Calif.: Sage Publications, 1988.

Doherty, William, and Thomas Campbell. *Families and Health.* Newbury Park, Calif.: Sage Publications, 1988.

Donovan, P. "New Reproductive Technologies: Some Legal Dilemmas." *Family Planning Perspectives* 18 (1986): 57ff.

Dooley, Karen, and Ralph Catalano. "Stress Transmission: The Effects of Husbands' Job Stressors on the Emotional Health of Their Wives." *Journal of Marriage and the Family* 53:1 (February 1991): 165–177.

Dorr, Aimee, Peter Kovaric, and Catherine Doubleday. "Parent-Child Coviewing of Television." *Journal of Broadcasting and Electronic Media* 33:1 (Winter 1989): 35–51.

Dorris, Michael. *The Broken Cord.* New York: Harper and Row, 1989.

_____. "A Desperate Crack Legacy." *Newsweek* (June 25,1990): 8.

Dreikurs, Rudolph, and V. Soltz. *Children: The Challenge.* New York: Hawthorne Books, 1964.

Drugger, Karen. "Social Location and Gender-Role Attitudes: A Comparison of Black and White Women." *Gender & Society* 2:4 (December 1988): 425–448.

DSM-IV. See American Psychiatric Association on Nomenclature and Statistics.

Duck, Steve, and Daniel Perlman. *Understanding Personal Relationships: An Interdisciplinary Approach.* Beverly Hills, Calif.: Sage Publications, 1985.

Duncan, Greg, and Saul Hoffman. "A Reconsideration of the Economic Consequences of Divorce." *Demography* 22 (1985): 485–498.

Duncan, Greg, and Willard Rodgers. "Longitudinal Aspects of Childhood Poverty." *Journal of Marriage and the Family* 50:4 (November 1988): 1007–1022.

Duncan, Greg, et al. *Years of Poverty, Years of Plenty.* Ann Arbor: Survey Research Center, Institute for Social Research, University of Michigan, 1984.

Dunford, Franklyn, David Huizinga, and Delbert Elliott. "The Role of Arrest in Domestic Assault: The Omaha Police Experiment." *Criminology* 28:2 (1990): 183–206.

Dutton, Donald, and Arthur Aron. "Some Evidence for Heightened Sexual Attraction under Conditions of High Anxiety." *Journal of Personality and Social Psychology* 30:4 (October 1974): 510–517.

Duvall, Evelyn. "Family Development's First Forty Years." *Family Relations* 37:2 (April 1988): 127–134.

Duvall, Evelyn, and Brent Miller. *Marriage and Family Development,* 6th ed. New York: Harper and Row, 1985.

Dworetsky, John P. *Introduction to Child Development,* 4th ed. St. Paul, Minn.: West Publishing Company, 1990.

Eakins, P. S. "Free-Standing Birth Centers in California." *Journal of Reproductive Medicine* 34:12 (December 1989): 960–970.

Edelman, Marian Wright. "Children at Risk." *Proceedings of the Academy of Political Science* 37:2 (1989): 20–30.

_____. "Children at Risk." In Frank J. Macchiarola and Alan Gartner, eds., *Caring for America's Children.* New York: The Academy of Political Science, 1989.

_____. Forward to Clifford Johnson, Andrew Sum, and James Weill *Vanishing Dreams: The Growing Economic Plight of America's Young Families.* Washington, D.C.: Children's Defense Fund, 1988.

Edelman, Marian, and Lisa Mihaly. "Homeless Families and the Housing Crisis in the United States." *Children and Youth Services Review* 11:1 (1989): 91–108.

Edleson, Jeffrey, et al. "Men Who Batter Women." *Journal of Family Issues* 6:2 (June 1985): 229–247.

Edwards, G. R. "A Critique of Creationist Homophobia." *Journal of Homosexuality* 18:3–4 (1989): 95–118.

Ehrenkranz, Joel R., and Wylie C. Hembree. "Effects of Marijuana on Male Reproductive Function." *Psychiatric Annals* 16:4 (April 1986): 243–248.

Ehrenreich, Barbara. *The Hearts of Men.* Garden City, New York: Anchor/Doubleday, 1984.

Ehrenreich, Barbara, and Deirdre English. *For Her Own Good: 150 Years of the Experts' Advice to Women.* Garden City, N.Y.: Anchor, 1979.

Eichler, Margrit. *Families in Canada Today.* Toronto: Gage, 1983.

_____. "Reflections on Motherhood, Apple Pie, the New Reproductive Technologies and the Role of Sociologists in Society." *Society-Societé* 13:1 (February 1989): 1–5.

Elder, Glen H., Jr. *Children of the Great Depression.* Chicago: University of Chicago Press, 1974.

Elder, Glen, and Jeffrey Liker. "Hard Times in Women's Lives: Historical Influences Across Forty Years." *American Journal of Sociology* 88:2 (September 1982): 241–269.

Ellis, Albert. *Sex without Guilt.* Secaucus, N.J.: Lyle Stuart, 1958.

Ellis, Albert, "The Justification of Sex Without Love." In John Crosby, ed., *Reply to Myth: Perspectives on Intimacy.* New York: John Wiley, 1985.

Ellis, Desmond. "Policing Wife Abuse: The Contribution Made by 'Domestic Disturbance' Deaths and Injuries among Police Officers." *Journal of Family Violence* 4:2 (1987): 319–333.

Ellison, Christopher. "Family Ties, Friendships, and Subjective Well-Being among Black Americans." *Journal of Marriage and the Family* 52 (May 1990): 298–310.

Ellwood, David. *Poor Support: Poverty in the American Family.* New York: Basic Books, 1988.

Emery, Robert, and Melissa Wyer. "Child Custody Mediation and Litigation: An Experimental Evaluation of the Experience of Parents." *Journal of Consulting and Clinical Psychology* 55:2 (1987): 179–186.

Enkin, Murray W. "Smoking and Pregnancy: A New Look." *Birth Issues in Perinatal Care and Education* 11:4 (Winter 1984): 225–229.

Erikson, Erik. *Childhood and Society.* New York: Norton, 1963.

_____. *Identity, Youth and Crisis.* New York: Norton, 1968.

_____. *Vital Involvements in Old Age: The Experience of Old Age in Our Time.* Boston: W. W. Norton, 1986.

Erkut, Sumru. "Exploring Sex-Differences in Expectancy, Attribution, and Academic Achievement." *Sex Roles* 9:2 (1983): 217–231.

Etaugh, Claire, and Barbara Petroski. "Perceptions of Women: Effects of Employment Status and Marital Status." *Sex Roles* 12 (1985): 329–339.

Etaugh, Claire, and J. Malstrom. "The Effect of Marital Status on Person Perception." *Journal of Marriage and the Family* 4 (1981): 801–805.

Evans, H. L., et al. "Sperm Abnormalities and Cigarette Smoking." *Lancet* 1:8221 (March 21, 1981): 627–629.

Fabes, Richard, and Jeremiah Strouse. "Perceptions of Responsible and Irresponsible Models of Sexuality." *Journal of Sex Research* 23:1 (February, 1987): 70–84.

Fabes, Richard, Patricia Wilson, and F. Scott Christopher. "A Time to Reexamine the Role of Television in Family Life." *Family Relations* 38:3 (July 1989): 337–341.

Fagot, Beverly, and Mary Leinbach. "Socialization of Sex Roles within the Family." In D. Bruce Carter, ed. *Current Conceptions of Sex Roles and Sex Typing.* New York: Praeger, 1987.

Faidley, Joyce. "Judge Mirrors Spouse-Abuse Myths." *Los Angeles Times,* July 9, 1989.

Faludi, Susan. "Barren, the Burden." *West* (April 16, 1989): 14–23.

Farber, Bernard, Charles H. Mindel, and Bernard Lazerwitz. "The Jewish American Family." In Charles H. Mindel, Robert W. Habenstein, and Roosevelt Wright, Jr., eds., *Ethnic Families in America: Patterns and Variations,* 3d ed. New York: Elsevier, 1988.

Fay, Robert, Charles Turner, Albert Klassen, and John Gagnon. "Prevalence and Patterns of Same-Gender Sexual Contact among Men." *Science* 243:4889 (January 20 1989): 338–348.

Featherstone, Helen. *A Difference in the Family.* New York: Basic Books, 1980.

Fehr, Beverly. "Prototype Analysis of the Concepts of Love and Commitment." *Journal of Personality and Social Psychology* 55:4 (1988): 557–579.

Fein, Robert. "Research on Fathering." In Arlene Skolnick and Jerome Skolnick, eds., *The Family in Transition.* Boston: Little, Brown, 1980.

Feirstein, Bruce. "Real Men Don't Eat Quiche." New York: Pocket Books, 1982.

Feldman, Harold, and Margaret Feldman. "The Family Life Cycle: Some Suggestions for Recycling." *Journal of Marriage and the Family* 37 (May 1975): 277–284.

Feldman, Shirley, and Sharon Churnin. "The Transition from Expectancy to Parenthood." *Sex Roles* 11(1/2) (1984): 61–78.

Ferber, Marianne. "Labor Market Participation of Young Married Women: Causes and Effects." *Journal of Marriage and the Family* 44:2 (May 1982): 457–468.

Ferber, Marianne, and Bonnie Birnbaum. "Economics of the Family: Who Maximizes What?" *Family Economics Review* (Summer–Fall, 1980): 13–16.

Ferman, Lawrence. "After the Shutdown: The Social and Psychological Costs of Job Displacement." *Industrial and Labor Relations Report* 18:2 (1981): 22–26.

Ferree, Myra Marx. "Beyond Separate Spheres: Feminism and Family Research." In Alan Booth, ed., *Contemporary Families: Looking Forward, Looking Back.* Minneapolis, Minn.: National Council on Family Relations, 1991.

Figley, Charles, ed. *Treating Families Under Stress.* New York: Brunner/Mazel, 1989.

Figley, Charles, and Hamilton McCubbin, eds. *Stress and the Family,* 2 vols. New York: Brunner/Mazel, 1983.

Fincham, Frank, and Thomas Bradbury. "The Assessment of Marital Quality." *Journal of Marriage and the Family* 49:4 (November 1987): 797–810.

Finkelhor, David. *Child Sexual Abuse: New Theory and Research.* New York: Free Press, 1984.

_____. "Common Features of Family Abuse." In David Finkelhor et al., eds., *The Dark Side of Families.* Beverly Hills, Calif.: Sage Publications, 1983.

_____. "Prevention Approaches to Child Sexual Abuse." In Mary Lystad, ed., *Violence in the Home: Interdisciplinary Perspectives.* New York: Brunner/Mazel, 1986b.

_____. "Prevention: A Review of Programs and Research." In David Finkelhor, ed. *Sourcebook on Child Sexual Abuse.* Beverly Hills, Calif.: Sage Publications, 1986a.

_____. *Sexually Victimized Children.* New York: Free Press, 1979.

Finkelhor, David, and Larry Baron. "High Risk Children." In David Finkelhor ed., *Sourcebook on Child Sexual Abuse.* Beverly Hills, Calif.: Sage Publications, 1986.

Finkelhor, David, and Angela Browne. "Initial and Long-Term Effects: A Conceptual Framework." In David Finkelhor, ed., *Sourcebook on Child Sexual Abuse.* Beverly Hills, Calif.: Sage Publications, 1986.

Finkelhor, David, Gerald Hotaling, and Andrea Sedlak. "Abduction of Children by Family Members." *Journal of Marriage and the Family* 53:3 (August 1991): 805–817.

Finkelhor, David, Gerald Hotaling, and Andrea Sedlak. *Missing, Abducted, Runaway, and Throwaway Children in America.* Washington, D.C.: U.S. Department of Justice, 1990.

Finkelhor, David, and Karl Pillemer. "Elder Abuse: Its Relationship to Other Forms of Domestic Violence." In Gerald T. Hotaling et al., eds., *Family Abuse and Its Consequences.* Newbury Park, Calif.: Sage Publications, 1988.

Finkelhor, David, and Kerst Yllo. "Forced Sex in Marriage: A Preliminary Research Report." National Institute of Mental Health, 1980.

_____. *License to Rape: The Sexual Abuse of Wives.* New York: Holt, Rinehardt, 1985.

Finkelhor, David, et al. eds. *The Dark Side of Families.* Beverly Hills, Calif.: Sage Publications, 1983.

Finkelhor, David, et al. "Sexual Abuse in Day Care: A National Study." National Center on Child Abuse and Neglect, University of New Hampshire: Family Research Laboratory, 1988.

Finkelhor, David, et al. "Sexual Abuse in a National Survey of Adult Men and Women." *Child Abuse and Neglect* 14:1 (1990): 19–28.

Firestone, Juanita, and Beth Anne Shelton. "An Estimation of the Effects of Women's Work on Available Leisure Time." *Journal of Family Issues* 9:4 (December 1988): 478–495.

Fischer, David Hackett. *Old Age in America.* Boston: Little, Brown, 1978.

Fischl, Margaret, et al. "Evaluation of Heterosexual Partners, Children, and Household Contacts of Adults with AIDS." *JAMA: Journal of the American Medical Association* 257:5 (February 6, 1987): 640–647.

Fischman, Joshua. "The Children's Hours." *Psychology Today* (October 1986): 16ff.

Fisher, William, and Donn Byrne. "Social Background, Attitudes, and Sexual Attraction." In Mark Cook, ed., *The Bases of Human Sexual Attraction.* New York: Academic Press, 1981.

Fisher, William, et al. "Erotophobia-Erotophilia as a Dimension of Personality." *Journal of Sex Research* 25:1 (February, 1988): 123–151.

Fishman, Barbara. "The Economic Behavior of Stepfamilies." *Family Relations* 32 (1983): 359–356.

Fitting, Melinda, Peter Rabins, M. Jane Lucas, and James Eastham. "Caregivers for Demented Patients: A Comparison of Husbands and Wives." *Gerontologist* 26 (1986): 248–252.

Fitzpatrick, Joseph. "The Puerto Rican Family." In Charles Mindel and Robert Habenstein, eds., *Ethnic Families in America,* 2d ed. New York: Elsevier North Holland, 1981.

Fitzpatrick, Joseph, and Lourdes Parker. "Hispanic-Americans in the Eastern United States." *Annals of the American Academy of Political and Social Science* 454 (March 1981): 98–110.

Flaherty, Mary Jean, Lorna Facteau, and Patricia Garver. "Grandmother Functions in Multigenerational Families." In Robert Staples, ed., *The Black Family: Essays and Studies,* 4th ed. Belmont, Calif.: Wadsworth Publishing Company, 1990.

Floge, Liliane. "The Dynamics of Child-Care Use and Some Implications for Women's Employment." *Journal of Marriage and the Family* 47:1 (February 1985): 143–154.

Flynn, Clifton P. "Sex Roles and Women's Response to Courtship Violence." *Journal of Family Violence* 5:1 (Mar. 1990): 83–94.

Fogel, Daniel. *Junipero Serra, the Vatican, and Enslavement Theology.* San Francisco, Calif.: ISM Press, 1988.

Foote, Nelson, and Leonard Cottrell. *Identity and Interpersonal Competence.* Chicago: University of Chicago Press, 1955.

Forrest, J. D., and S. Singh. "The Sexual and Reproductive Behavior of American Women, 1982–1988." *Family Planning Perspectives* 22:5 (September–October 1990): 206–214.

Ford, Clellan, and Frank Beach. *Patterns of Sexual Behavior.* New York: Harper and Row, 1972.

Forsstrom-Cohen, Barbara, and Alan Rosenbaum. "The Effects of Parental Marital Violence on Young Adults." *Journal of Marriage and the Family* 47:2 (May 1985): 467–472.

Forste, Renata, and Tim Heaton. "Initiation of Sexual Activity among Female Adolescents." *Youth and Society* 19:3 (March 1988): 250–268.

Forstein, Marshall. "Homophobia: An Overview." *Psychiatric Annals* 18:1 (January 1988): 33–36.

Foucault, Michel. *The History of Sexuality.* New York: Pantheon Books, 1979.

Francke, Linda Bird, et al. "Childless By Choice." *Newsweek* (January 14, 1980): 96.

Fraser, Antonia. *The Weaker Vessel*. New York: Alfred Knopf, 1984.

Freed, Doris, and Timothy Walker. "Family Law in the Fifty States. " *Family Law Quarterly* 21 (1988): 417–573.

Freedman, Estelle, and Barrie Thorne. "Introduction to 'The Feminist Sexuality Debates.'" *Signs: Journal of Women in Culture and Society* 10:1 (1984): 102–105.

Freeman, Ellen. "Adolescent Contraceptive Use." *American Journal of Public Health* 70 (August 1980): 790–797.

French, J. P., and Bertram Raven. "The Bases of Social Power." In I. Cartwright, ed., *Studies in Social Power*. Ann Arbor: University of Michigan Press, 1959.

Freud, Sigmund. *New Introductory Lectures on Psychoanalysis*. New York: Doubleday, 1933.

Friday, Nancy. *Men in Love*. New York: Delacorte Press, 1980.

Friedan, Betty. *The Feminine Mystique*. New York: Norton, 1963.

_____. *The Second Wave*. New York: Norton, 1980.

Friedman, H., M. Rohrbaugh, and S. Krakauer. *Family Process* 27 (1988): 293–303.

Friedman, Henry. "The Father's Parenting Experience in Divorce." *American Journal of Psychiatry* 137(10) (October 1980): 1177–1182.

Friedman, Rochelle, and Bonnie Gradstein. *Surviving Pregnancy Loss*. Boston: Little, Brown and Company, 1982.

Friend, Richard. "GAYging: Adjustment and the Older Gay Male." *Alternative Lifestyles* 3:2 (May 1980): 231–248.

Frisbie, W. Parker. "Variation in Patterns of Marital Instability among Hispanics." *Journal of Marriage and the Family* 48 (February 1986): 99–106.

Fromm, Erich. *The Art of Loving*. New York: Perennial Library, 1974.

Fuller, Mary Lou. "Help Your Family Understand 'It's a Small, Small World.'" *PTA Today* (December 1989–January 1990): 9–10.

Fulton, Julie. "Parental Reports of Children's Post-Divorce Adjustment." *Journal of Social Issues* 35:4 (1979): 126–139.

Furstenberg, Frank, K., Jr. "The New Extended Family: The Experience of Parents and Children after Remarriage." In Kay Pasley and Marilyn, Ihinger-Tallman, eds., *Remarriage and Stepparenting: Current Research and Theory*. New York: Guilford Press, 1987.

_____. "Recycling the Family: Perspectives for a Neglected Family Form." *Marriage and Family Review* 2:3 (1979): 12–22.

_____. "Reflections on Remarriage." *Journal of Family Issues* 1:4 (1980): 443–453.

Furstenberg, Frank K., Jr. and Andrew Cherlin. *Divided Families*. Cambridge, Mass.: Harvard University Press, 1991.

Furstenberg, Frank K., Jr., Philip Morgan, and Paul Allison. "Paternal Participation and Children's Well-Being after Marital Disruption." *American Sociological Review* 52 (1986): 695–701.

Furstenberg, Frank K., Jr., and Christine Nord. "The Life Course of Children of Divorce: Marital Disruption and Parental Contact." Paper presented at the annual meeting of the Population Association of America, San Diego, April 29–May 1, 1982.

_____. "Parenting Apart: Patterns of Childrearing after Marital Disruption." *Journal of Marriage and the Family* 47:4 (November 1985): 893–904.

Furstenberg, Frank K., Jr., and Graham Spanier. *Recycling the Family: Remarriage after Divorce*, rev. ed. Newbury Park, Calif.: Sage Publications, 1987.

Furstenberg, Frank, Jr., Philip Morgan, Kristin Moore, and James Peterson. "Race Differences in the Timing of Adolescent Intercourse." *American Sociological Review* 52:4 (August 1987): 511–518.

Furstenberg, Frank, K., Jr., et al. "Sex Education and Sexual Experience among Adolescents." *American Journal of Public Health* 75:11 (November 1985): 1331–1332.

Gaesser, David, and Susan Whitbourne. "Work Identity and Marital Adjustment in Blue-Collar Men." *Journal of Marriage and the Family* 47:3 (August 1985): 747–751.

Gagnon, John. "Attitudes and Responses of Parents to Pre-Adolescent Masturbation." *Archives of Sexual Behavior* 14:5 (1985): 451–466.

_____. *Human Sexualities*. New York: Scott, Foresman, 1977.

_____. "Sexual Scripts: Permanence and Change." *Archives of Sexual Behavior* 15:2 (April, 1986): 97–120.

Gagnon, John, and William Simon. "The Sexual Scripting of Oral Genital Contacts." *Archives of Sexual Behavior* 16:1 (February 1987): 1–25.

Gaines, Judith. "A Scandal of Artificial Insemination." *The Good Health Magazine/The New York Times Magazine* (October 7, 1990): 23ff.

Galligan, Richard. "Innovative Techniques (in studying marriage and the family): Siren or Rose?" *Journal of Marriage and the Family* 44:4 (November 1982): 875–888.

Gallup, George H., Jr., "One-fourth Report Family Problems Related to Alcohol." *San Jose Mercury News,* April 26, 1987: 22A.

Gallup, George H., Jr., and Frank Newport. "Parenthood—A Nearly Universal Desire." *San Francisco Chronicle,* June 4, 1990: B3.

Ganong, Lawrence, and Marilyn Coleman. "A Comparison of Clinical and Empirical Literature on Children in Stepfamilies." *Journal of Marriage and the Family* 48 (May 1986): 309–318.

_____. "The Effects of Remarriage on Children: A Review of the Empirical Literature." *Family Relations* 33 (1984): 389–405.

_____. "Sex, Sex Roles, and Family Love." *Journal of Genetic Psychology* 148 (March, 1987): 45–52.

Ganong, Lawrence, Marilyn Coleman, and Dennis Mapes. "A Meta-Analytic Review of Family Structure Stereotypes." *Journal of Marriage and the Family* 52 (May 1990): 287–289.

_____. "Stepparent: A Pejorative Term?" *Psychological Reports* 53:3 (June 1983): 919–922.

Garbarino, James. *Children and Families in the Social Environment*. Hawthorne, N.Y.: Aldine de Gruyter, 1982.

_____. "The Human Ecology of Child Maltreatment." *Journal of Marriage and the Family* 39:4 (Nov. 1977): 721–735.

Garfinkel, Irwin, and Sara McLanahan. *Single Mothers and Their Children: A New American Dilemma*. Washington, D.C.: The Urban Institute Press, 1986.

Garfinkel, Irwin, and Donald Oellerich. "Noncustodial Fathers' Ability to Pay Child Support." *Demography* 26 (1989): 219–233.

Gecas, Viktor, and Monica Seff. "Families and Adolescents." In Alan Booth, ed., *Contemporary Families: Looking Forward, Looking Back*. Minneapolis, Minn.: National Council on Family Relations, 1991.

_____. "Social Class, Occupational Conditions, and Self-Esteem." *Sociological Perspectives* 32 (1989): 353–364.

Gelfand, Donald, and Charles Barresi, eds. *Ethnic Dimensions of Aging*. New York: Springer Publishing, 1987.

Gelles, Richard J. "Applying Research on Family Violence to Clinical Practice." *Journal of Marriage and the Family* 44 (February 1982): 9–20.

_____. "Child Abuse and Violence in Single-Parent Families: Parent Absence and Economic Deprivation." *American Journal of Orthopsychiatry* 59:4 (Oct. 1989): 492–501.

_____. "An Exchange/Social Control Theory." In David Finkelhor et al., eds. *The Dark Side of Families*. Beverly Hills, Calif.: Sage Publications, 1983.

_____. "Parental Child Snatching: A Preliminary Estimate of the National Incidence." *Journal of Marriage and the Family* 46:3 (August 1984): 735–739.

Gelles, Richard J., and Jon R. Conte. "Domestic Violence and Sexual Abuse of Children: A Review of Research in the Eighties." In Alan Booth, ed. *Contemporary Families: Looking Forward, Looking Back*. Minneapolis, MN: National Council on Family Relations, 1991.

Gelles, Richard J., and Claire Pedrick Cornell. *Intimate Violence in Families,* 2nd ed. Newbury Park, Calif.: Sage Publications, 1985, 1990.

Gelles, Richard J., and John W. Harrop. "The Nature and Consequences of the Psychological Abuse of Children: Evidence from the Second National Family Violence Survey." Paper presented at the Eighth National Conference on Child Abuse and Neglect, 1989.

Gelles, Richard J., and Murray A. Straus. *Intimate Violence.* New York: Simon and Schuster, 1988.

Gelman, David. "Who's Taking Care of Our Parents?" *Newsweek* (May 6, 1985): 61–70.

Genevie, Lou, and Eva Margolies. *The Motherhood Report: How Women Feel about Being Mothers.* New York: MacMillan, 1987.

Genovese, Eugene. *Roll, Jordan, Roll.* New York: Harper & Row, 1976.

George, Kenneth, and Andrew Behrendt. "Therapy for Male Couples Experiencing Relationship Problems and Sexual Problems." *Journal of Homosexuality* 14:1–2 (1987): 77–88.

Gerson, Kathleen. *Hard Choices: How Women Decide About Work, Career, and Motherhood.* Berkeley: University of California Press, 1985.

Gerstel, Naomi. "Divorce and Stigma." *Social Forces* 34 (1987): 172–186.

Gerstel, Naomi, and Harriet Gross. *Commuter Marriage: A Study of Work and Family.* New York: The Guilford Press, 1984.

_____. *Families and Work.* Philadelphia: Temple University Press, 1987.

Getlin, Josh. "Legacy of a Mother's Drinking." *Los Angeles Times,* July 24, 1989: V1ff.

Giarretto, Henry. "Humanistic Treatment of Father-Daughter Incest." In Ray Helfer and Henry C. Kempe, eds., *Child Abuse and Neglect: The Family and the Community.* Cambridge, Mass.: Ballinger, 1976.

Gibbs, Nancy. "The Baby Chase." *Time* (October 9, 1989): 86–89.

Gibson, Rose. "Blacks at Middle and Late Life: Resources and Coping." *Annals of the American Academy* 464 (November 1982): 79–90.

Gil, David. "Sociocultural Aspects of Domestic Violence." In Mary Lystad, ed., *Violence in the Home: Interdisciplinary Perspectives.* New York: Brunner/Mazel, 1986.

Gilbert, Lucia, et al. "Perceptions of Parental Role Responsibilities: Differences Between Mothers and Fathers." *Family Relations* 31 (April 1982): 261–269.

Gilligan, Carol. *In a Different Voice: Psychological Theory and Women's Development.* Cambridge, Mass.: Harvard University Press, 1982.

Gilman, Lois. *The Adoption Resource Book,* rev. ed. New York: Harper & Row, 1987.

Givens, Ron. "A New Prohibition." *Newsweek On Campus* (April 1985): 7–13.

Glass, Robert H., and Ronald J. Ericsson. *Getting Pregnant in the 1980s.* Berkeley: University of California Press, 1982.

Glazer-Malbin, Nona, ed. *Old Family/New Family.* New York: Van Nostrand, 1975.

Glenn, Norval. "Duration of Marriage, Family Composition, and Marital Happiness." *National Journal of Sociology* 3 (1989): 3–24.

_____. "Interreligious Marriage in the United States: Patterns and Recent Trends." *Journal of Marriage and the Family* 44:3 (August 1982): 555–566.

_____. "Quantitative Research on Marital Quality in the 1980s: A Critical Review." In Alan Booth, ed., *Contemporary Families: Looking Forward, Looking Back.* Minneapolis: National Council on Family Relations, 1991.

Glenn, Norval, and Kathryn Kramer. "The Marriages and Divorces of the Children of Divorce." *Journal of Marriage and the Family* 49 (November 1987): 811–825.

_____. "The Psychological Well-Being of Adult Children of Divorce." *Journal of Marriage and the Family* 47:4 (November 1985): 905–912.

Glenn, Norval, and Sara McLanahan. "Children and Marital Happiness: A Further Specification of the Relationship." *Journal of Marriage and the Family* 43:1 (February 1982): 63–72.

Glenn, Norval, and Beth Ann Shelton. "Regional Differences in Divorce in the United States." *Journal of Marriage and the Family* 47:3 (August 1985): 641–652.

Glenn, Norval, and Michael Supancic. "The Social and Demographic Correlates of Divorce and Separation in the United States: An Update and Reconsideration." *Journal of Marriage and the Family* 46 (August 1984): 563–575.

Glick, Paul. "American Household Structure in Transition." *Family Planning Perspectives* 16(5) (September/October 1984): 205–211.

_____. "The Family Life Cycle and Social Change." *Family Relations* 38:2 (April 1989): 123–129.

_____. "Fifty Years of Family Demography." *Journal of Marriage and the Family* 50 (November 1988): 861–873.

_____. "Remarried Families, Stepfamilies and Stepchildren: A Brief Demographic Analysis." *Family Relations* 38 (1989): 24–27.

_____. "Updating the Life Cycle of the Family." *Journal of Marriage and the Family* 39:1 (February 1977): 5–14.

Glick, Paul, and Sung Ling Lin. "Recent Changes in Divorce and Remarriage." *Journal of Marriage and the Family* 49:4 (November 1986): 737–747.

Glick, Paul, and Graham Spanier. "Married and Unmarried Cohabitation in the United States." *Journal of Marriage and the Family* 42:1 (February 1980): 19–30.

Gnezda, Therese. "The Effects of Unemployment on Family Functioning." Prepared statement presented to the Select Committee on Children, Youth and Families. House of Representatives, Hearings on the New Unemployed. Detroit, Michigan, March 4, 1984. 35–7140. Washington, D.C.: U.S. Government Printing Office, 1984.

Goelman, Hillel, Ellen Shapiro, and Alan Pence. "Family Environment and Family Day Care." *Family Relations* 39:1 (January 1990): 14–19.

Goetting, Ann. "Divorce Outcome Research." *Journal of Family Issues* 2:3 (September 1981): 20–25.

_____. "The Developmental Tasks of Siblingship over the Life Cycle." *Journal of Marriage and the Family* 48:4 (November 1986): 703–714.

_____. "Parental Satisfaction: A Review." *Journal of Family Issues* 7:1 (March 1986): 83–109.

_____. "Patterns of Support among In-Laws in the United States: A Review of Research." *Journal of Family Issues* 11:1 (March 1990): 67–90.

_____. "The Six Stages of Remarriage: Developmental Tasks of Remarriage After Divorce." *Family Relations* 31 (April 1982): 213–222.

Goldsmith, Jean. "The Postdivorce Family." In Froma Walsh, ed., *Normal Family Processes.* New York: Guilford Press, 1982.

Goldsmith, Marsha. "Possible Herpes Virus Role in Abortion Studied." *Journal of the American Medical Association* 251(23) (1984): 3067–3070.

Goldstein, David, and Alan Rosenbaum. "An Evaluation of the Self-Esteem of Maritally Violent Men." *Family Relations* 34:3 (July 1985): 425–428.

Goldstein, R. "The Gay Family." *Voices* 11:27 (1986): 21–24.

Goleman, Daniel. "How Viewers Grow Addicted to Television." *The New York Times,* October 16, 1990: C1, C8.

_____. "Marriage: Research Reveals Ingredients of Happiness." *New York Times,* April 16, 1985:19–20.

_____. "Spacing of Siblings Strongly Linked to Success in Life." *New York Times,* May 28, 1985:17–18.

Gondolf, Edward W., "The Effect of Batterer Counseling on Shelter Outcome." *Journal of Interpersonal Violence* 3:3 (September 1988): 275–289.

_____. "Evaluating Progress for Men who Batter." *Journal of Family Violence* 2 (1987): 95–108.

_____. "Who Are These Guys? Toward A Behavioral Typology of Batterers." *Violence and Victims* 3:3 (Fall 1989): 187–203.

Gongla, Patricia, and Edward Thompson, Jr. "Single-Parent Families." In Marvin Sussman and Suzanne Steinmetz, eds., *Handbook of Marriage and the Family*. New York: Plenum Press, 1987.

Goode, William. *The Family*, 2d ed. Englewood Cliffs, N.J.: Prentice-Hall, 1982.

_____. "Force and Violence in the Family." *Journal of Marriage and the Family* 33 (November 1971): 624–636.

_____. "The Theoretical Importance of Love." *American Sociological Review* 24 (February 1959): 38–47.

_____. *World Revolution and Family Patterns*. New York: Free Press, 1963.

Gordon, Michael. *The American Family: Past, Present, and Future*. New York: Random House, 1978.

Gordon, Sol. "What Kids Need to Know." *Psychology Today* (October 1986): 46*ff*.

Gordon, Thomas. *P.E.T. in Action*. New York: Bantam Books, 1979.

Gottman, J. M. *Marital Interactions: Experimental Investigations*. New York: Academic Press, 1979.

Gough, Kathleen. "Is the Family Universal: The Nayar Case." In Norman Bell and Ezra Vogel, eds., *A Modern Introduction to the Family*. New York: Free Press, 1968.

Gould, Jeffrey B., Becky Davey, and Randall S. Stafford. "Socioeconomic Differences in Rates of Cesarean Section." *New England Journal of Medicine* 321:4 (July 27, 1989): 233–239.

Gove, Walter, Michael Hughes, and Carolyn Style. "Does Marriage Have Positive Effects on the Psychological Well-Being of the Individual?" *Journal of Health and Social Behavior* 24 (1983): 122–131.

Gove, Walter, Carolyn Style, and Michael Hughes. "The Effect of Marriage on the Well-Being of Adults." *Journal of Family Issues* 11:1 (March 1990): 4–35.

Grauerholz, Elizabeth. "Balancing the Power in Dating Relationships." *Sex Roles* 17:9/10 (1987): 563–571.

Green, Richard. "Sexual Identity of 37 Children Raised by Homosexual or Transsexual Parents." *American Journal of Psychiatry* 135:6 (June 1978): 692–697.

_____. *The "Sissy-Boy Syndrome" and the Development of Homosexuality*. New Haven, Conn.: Yale University Press, 1987.

Green, Richard, et al. "Lesbian Mothers and Their Children: A Comparison with Solo Parent Heterosexual Mothers and Their Children." *Archives of Sexual Behavior* 15 (1986): 167–184.

Greenberg, Dan, and Marsha Jacobs, *How to Make Yourself Miserable*. New York: Random House, 1966.

Greenberger, Ellen, and Robin O'Neil. "Parents' Concerns about Their Child's Development: Implications for Father's and Mother's Well-being and Attitudes toward Work." *Journal of Marriage and the Family* 52 (August 1990): 621–635.

Greenstein, Theodore. "Marital Disruption and the Employment of Married Women." *Journal of Marriage and the Family* 52 (1990): 657–676.

_____. "Occupation and Divorce." *Journal of Family Issues* 6:3 (September 1985): 347–357.

Greer, Germaine. *Sex and Destiny*. New York: Harper & Row, 1984.

Greeson, Larry, and Rose Ann Williams. "Social Implications of Music Videos for Youth: An Anlaysis of the Content and Effects of MTV." *Youth and Society* 18:2 (December 1986):177–189.

Gregor, Thomas. *Anxious Pleasures: The Sexual Lives of an Amazonian People*. Chicago: University of Chicago Press, 1985.

Greif, Geoffrey. "Children and Housework in the Single Father Family." *Family Relations* 34:3 (July 1985): 353–357.

_____. "Single Fathers Rearing Children." *Journal of Marriage and the Family* 47:1 (February 1985): 185–191.

Griego, Diana, and Louis Kilzer. "The Truth About Missing Kids: Exaggerated Statistics Stir National Paranoia." *The Denver Post,* May 12, 1985: 1–A, 14–A.

Griswold Del Castillo, Richard. *La Familia: Chicano Families in the Urban Southwest, 1848 to the Present*. Notre Dame, Ind.: University of Notre Dame, 1984.

Gross, Jane. "ROTC Under Siege for Ousting Homosexuals." *The New York Times,* May 6, 1990: 12.

Grosskopf, D. *Sex and the Married Woman*. New York: Wallaby, 1983.

Grossman, Frances, William Pollack, Ellen Golding, and Nicolina Fedele. "Affiliation and Autonomy in the Transition to Parenthood." *Family Relations* 36:3 (July 1987): 263–269.

Grossman, Frances, et al. *Pregnancy, Birth and Parenthood: Adaptations of Mothers, Fathers, and Infants*. San Francisco: Jossey-Bass, 1980.

Groth, Nicholas. *Men Who Rape: The Psychology of the Offender*. New York: Plenum Press, 1980.

Groth, Nicholas, and H. Jean Birnbaum. "Adult Sexual Orientation and Attraction to Underage Persons." *Archives of Sexual Behavior* 7:3 (May 1978): 175–181.

Groth, Nicholas, and Thomas Gary. "Heterosexuality, Homosexuality, and Pedophilia: Sexual Offenses Against Children." In Anthony Scacco, ed., *Male Rape: A Casebook of Sexual Aggression.*" New York: AMS Press, 1982.

Grover, Kelly, et al. "Mate Selection Processes and Marital Satisfaction." *Family Relations* 34:3 (July, 1985): 383–386.

Gruson, Lindsey. "Groups Play Matchmaker to Preserve Judaism." *New York Times,* April 1, 1985.

Gubman, Gayle, and Richard Tessler. "The Impact of Mental Illness on Families." *Journal of Family Issues* 8:2 (June 1987): 226–245.

Guelzow, Maureen, et al. "Analysis of the Stress Process for Dual-Career Men and Women." *Journal of Marriage and the Family* 53:1 (February 1991): 151–164.

Guhl, Beverly. *Purrfect Parenting*. Tucson, Ariz: Fisher Books, 1987.

Guidubaldi, John. "The Status Report Extended: Further Elaborations on the American Family." *School Psychology Review* 9:4 (Fall 1980): 374–379.

Guillemin, Jeanne Harley, and Lynda Lytle Holmstrom. "The Business of Childbirth." *Society* 23:5(183) (July–Aug. 1986).

Gump, J. "Reality and Myth: Employment and Sex Role Ideology in Black Women." In F. Denmark and J. Sherman, eds., *The Psychology of Women*. New York: Psychological Dimensions, 1980.

Gutek, Barbara. *Sex and the Workplace*. San Francisco, Calif.: Jossey-Bass Publishers, 1985.

Gutek, Barbara, et al. "Sexuality and the Workplace." *Basic and Applied Social Psychology* 1:3 (1980): 255–265.

Guttman, Herbert. *The Black Family: From Slavery to Freedom*. New York: Pantheon, 1976.

Gwartney-Gibbs, Patricia. "The Institutionalization of Premarital Cohabitation: Estimates from Marriage License Applications." *Journal of Marriage and the Family* 48 (May 1986): 423–434.

Haferd, Laura. "Paddling Returns to Child Rearing." *San Jose Mercury News,* December 20, 1986: 12D.

Hafstrom, Jeanne, and Vicki Schram. "Chronic Illness in Couples: Selected Characteristics, Including Wife's Satisfaction with and Perception of Marital Relationships." *Family Relations* 33 (1984): 195–203.

Halleck, Seymour. "Sex and Power." *Medical Aspects of Human Sexuality* (October 1969): 8–24.

Hahlweg, Kurt, and Michael Goldstein, eds. *Understanding Major Mental Disorder: The Contribution of Family Interaction Research*. New York: Family Process Press, 1987.

Hållstrom, Tore, and Sverker Samuelsson. "Changes in Women's Sexual Desire in Middle Life: The Longitudinal Study of Women in Gothenburg [Sweden]." *Archives of Sexual Behavior* 19:3 (1990): 259–267.

Hampton, Robert L., Richard J. Gelles and John W. Harrop. "Is Violence in Black Families Increasing? A Comparison of 1975 and 1985 National Survey Rates." *Journal of Marriage and the Family* 51:4 (Nov. 1989): 969–980.

Handlin, Oscar. *Boston's Immigrants*. Revised and enlarged edition. Cambridge, Mass.: Belknap University Press, 1979.

Hanley, Robert. "Surrogate Deals for Mothers Held Illegal in New Jersey." *The New York Times,* February 4, 1988: 1ff.

Hansen, Gary. "Balancing Work and Family: A Literature and Resource Review." *Family Relations* 40:3 (July, 1991): 348–353.

_____. "Extradyadic Relations During Courtship." *Journal of Sex Research* 23:3 (August, 1987): 383–390.

Hanson, F. W., et al. "Ultrasonography–Guided Early Amniocentesis in Singleton Pregnancies." *American Journal of Obstetrics and Gynecology* 162:6 (June 1990): 1381–1383.

Hanson, Sandra, and Theodora Oooms. "The Economic Costs and Rewards of Two-Earner, Two-Parent Families." *Journal of Marriage and the Family* 53:3 (August, 1991): 622–644.

Hansson, Robert, et al. "Adult Children with Frail Elderly Parents: When to Intervene?" *Family Relations* 39:2 (April 1990): 153–158.

Haring-Hidore, Marilyn, et al. "Marital Status and Subjective Well-Being: A Research Synthesis." *Journal of Marriage and the Family* 47:4 (November 1985): 947–953.

Harriman, Lynda. "Marital Adjustment as Related to Personal and Marital Changes Accompanying Parenthood." *Family Relations* 35:2 (April 1986): 233–239.

_____. "Personal and Marital Changes Accompanying Parenthood." *Family Relations* 32 (July 1983): 387–394.

Harris, Kathleen, and S. Philip Morgan. "Fathers, Sons, and Daughters: Differential Paternal Involvement in Parenting." *Journal of Marriage and the Family* 53:3 (August, 1991).

Harris, M. B., and P. H. Turner. "Gay and Lesbian Parents." *Journal of Homosexuality* 12:12 (1985–1986): 101–113.

Harris, Myron. "Children as Hostages." In Stuart Irving, ed., *Children of Separation and Divorce*. New York: Grossman, 1972.

Harris, Sandra. "The Family and the Autistic Child." *Family Relations* 33:1 (January 1984): 67–77.

Harrison, Patricia, Norman Hoffman, and Glenace Edwall. "Differential Drug Use Patterns among Sexually Abused Adolescent Girls in Treatment for Chemical Dependency." *International Journal of the Addictions* 24:6 (June 1989): 499–514.

Harry, Joseph. "Decision Making and Age Differences among Gay Male Couples." In John DeCecco, ed., *Gay Relationships*. New York: Haworth Press, 1988.

_____. "Gay Male and Lesbian Relationships." In Eleanor Macklin and R. Ruben, eds., *Contemporary Families and Alternative Lifestyles: Handbook on Research and Theory*. Beverly Hills, Calif.: Sage Publications, 1983.

Hartup, W. and Z. Rubin, eds. *Relationships and Development*. Hillsdale, N. J.: Erlbaum, 1986.

Harvard Law Review editors. *Sexual Orientation and the Law*. Cambridge, Mass.: Harvard University Press, 1990.

Haskell, Molly. "2000–Year–Old Misunderstanding: Rape Fantasy." *Ms.* 5 (November 1976): 84–86ff.

Hatcher, Robert, et al. *Contraceptive Technology*. New York: Irvington Publishers, 1986.

Hatfield, Elaine. "Passionate and Companionate Love." In Robert Sternberg and Michael Barnes, eds., *The Psychology of Love*. New Haven, Conn.: Yale University Press, 1988.

Hatfield, Elaine, and Richard Hapson. "Passionate Love/Sexual Desire: Can the Same Paradigm Explain Both?" *Archives of Sexual Behavior* 16:3 (June 1987): 259–278.

Hatfield, Elaine, and Susan Sprecher. *Mirror, Mirror: The Importance of Looks in Everyday Life*. New York: State University of New York, 1986.

Hatfield, Elaine, and G. William Walster. *A New Look at Love*. Reading, Mass.: Addison-Wesley, 1981.

_____. *A New Look at Love*. Reading, Mass.: 1978.

Hayes, Robert M. "Homeless Children." In Frank J. Macchiarola and Alan Gartner, eds., *Caring for America's Children*. New York: The Academy of Political Science, 1989.

Hazan, Cindy, and Philip Shaver. "Romantic Love Conceptualized as an Attachment Process." *Journal of Personality and Social Psychology* 52 (1987)L 511–524.

Hearst, Norman, and Stephen Hulley. "Preventing the Heterosexual Spread of AIDS. Are We Giving Our Patients the Best Advice?" *JAMA* 259:16 (April 22/29 1988): 2428–2432.

Heaton, Tim, and Stan Albrecht. "Stable Unhappy Marriages." *Journal of Marriage and the Family* 53:3 (August 1991): 747–758.

Heaton, Tim B., and E. L. Pratt. "The Effects of Religious Homogamy on Marital Satisfaction and Stability." *Journal of Family Issues* 7:2 (June 1990): 191–207.

Heaton, Tim, et al. "The Timing of Divorce." *Journal of Marriage and the Family* 47:3 (August 1985): 631–639.

Heer, D. M. "The Prevalence of Black-White Marriage in the United States, 1960 and 1970." *Journal of Marriage and the Family* 36 (1974): 246–259.

Hefferan, Colleen. "New Methods for Studying Household Production." *Family Economics Review* 3 (1982a): 16–25.

Hefner, R., M. Rebecca, and B. Oleshansky. "Development of Sex-Role Transcendence." *Human Development* 18 (1975): 143–158.

Heilbrun, Alfred, Dawna Wydra, and Lisa Friedberg. "Parent Identification and Gender Schema Development." *Journal of Genetic Psychology* 150:3 (September 1989): 293–300.

Heilbrun, Carolyn. *Toward a Recognition of Androgyny*. New York: Norton, 1982.

Hemminki, Kari, et al. "Spontaneous Abortion in an Industrialized Community in Finland." *American Journal of Public Health* 73:1 (January 1983): 32–37.

Hendrick, Clyde, and Susan Hendrick. "Research on Love: Does It Measure Up?" *Journal of Personality and Social Psychology* 56:5 (May 1989): 784–794.

_____. "Lovers Wear Rose Colored Glasses." *Journal of Social and Personal Relationships* 5:2 (May 1988a): 161–183.

_____. "A Theory and Method of Love." *Journal of Personality and Social Psychology* 50 (1986): 392–402.

Hendrick, Clyde, et al. "Do Men and Women Love Differently?" *Journal of Personality and Social Psychology* 48 (1984): 177–195.

Hendrick, Susan. "Self-Disclosure and Marital Satisfaction." *Journal of Personality and Social Psychology* 40 (1981): 1150–1159.

Hendrick, Susan, and Clyde Hendrick. "Multidimensionality of Sexual Attitudes." *Journal of Sex Research* 23:4 (November 1987): 502–526.

Hendricks, Glenn, Bruce Downing, and Amos Deinard, eds. *The Hmong in Transition*. Staten Island, New York: Center for Migration Studies of New York, 1986.

Henton, June, et al. "Romance and Violence in Dating Relationships." *Journal of Family Issues* 4 (September, 1983): 467–482.

Herek, Gregory. "Beyond 'Homophobia': A Social Psychological Perspective on Attitudes Toward Lesbians and Gay Men." *Journal of Homosexuality* 10(1/2) (Fall 1984): 1–21.

———. "On Heterosexual Masculinity: Some Psychical Consequences of the Social Construction of Gender." *American Behavioral Scientist* 29:5 (May–June 1986): 563–567.

———. "The Social Psychology of Homophobia: Toward a Practical Theory." *Review of Law and Social Change* 14:4 (1986): 923–934.

Herman, Judith. *Father-Daughter Incest*. Cambridge, Mass.: Harvard University Press, 1981.

Herold, Edward, and Leslie Way. "Oral-Genital Sexual Behavior in a Sample of University Females." *Journal of Sex Research* 19:4 (November 1983): 327–338.

Hess, Robert, and Kathleen Camara. "Post-Divorce Relationships as Mediating Factors in the Consequences of Divorce for Children." *Journal of Social Issues* 35:4 (1979): 79–96.

Hetherington, E. Mavis. "Divorce: A Child's Perspective." *American Psychologist* 34(10) (October 1979): 851–858.

Hetherington, E. Mavis, M. Cox, and R. Cox. "Family Interactions and the Social, Emotional, and Cognitive Development of Children Following Divorce." In V. C. Vaugh and T. B. Brazelton, eds., *The Family: Setting Priorities*. New York: Science and Medicine Publishers, 1979.

Hetherington, E. Mavis, et al. "The Aftermath of Divorce." In J. J. Stevens, Jr., and M. Matthews, eds., *Mother-Child, Father-Child Relations*. Washington, D.C.: NAEYC, 1977.

———. "The Development of Children in Mother-headed Families." In David Reiss and Howard Hoffman, eds., *The American Family: Dying or Developing?* New York: Plenum Press, 1979.

Hetherington, S. E. "A Controlled Study of the Effect of Prepared Childbirth Classes on Obstetric Outcomes." *Birth* 17:2 (June 1990): 86–90.

Hevesi, Dennis. "Homeless in New York City: A Day on the Streets." *The New York Times,* November 17, 1986: 13.

———. "TV News: Children's Scary Window on New York." *The New York Times,* September 11, 1990: A21.

Hewitt, J. "Preconceptional Sex Selection." *British Journal of Hospital Medicine* 37:2 (February 1987): 149ff.

Heyl, Barbara. "Homosexuality: A Social Phenomenon." In Kathleen McKinney and Susan Sprecher, eds., *Human Sexuality: The Societal and Interpersonal Context*. Norwood, N.J.: Ablex Publishing Corporation, 1989.

Hill, Charles, Letitia Peplau, and Zick Rubin. "Breakups Before Marriage: The End of 103 Affairs." *Journal of Social Issues* 32 (1976): 147–168.

Hill, Martha. "The Changing Nature of Poverty." *Annals of the American Academy of Political Science* 479 (May 1985): 31–37.

Hill, Reuben. "Generic Features of Families Under Stress." *Social Casework* 49 (February/March 1958): 139–150.

———. "Whither Family Research in the 1980's: Continuities, Emergents, Constraints, and New Horizons." *Journal of Marriage and the Family* 43:2 (May 1981): 255–257.

Hill, Robert B. *The Strengths of Black Families*. New York: Emerson Hall Publishers, 1972.

Hilton, Jeanne, and Virgina Haldeman. "Gender Differences in the Performance of Household Tasks by Adults and Children in Single-Parent and Two-Parent, Two-Earner Families." *Journal of Family Issues* 12:1 (March 1991): 114–130.

Hilton, N. Zoe. "When Is an Assault Not an Assault? The Canadian Public's Attitudes Toward Wife and Stranger Assault." *Journal of Family Violence* 4:4 (Dec. 1989): 323–337.

Hilts, Philip. "Growing Concern over Pelvic Infection in Women." *The New York Times,* October 11, 1990a.

———. "Life Expectancy for Blacks in U. S. Shows Sharp Drop." *The New York Times,* November 29, 1990b: A1, B7.

Hiltz, Roxanne. "Widowhood: A Roleless Role." *Marriage and Family Review* 1(6) (November/December 1978).

Hinds, Michael. "Better Traps Being Built for Delinquent Parents." *The New York Times,* December 9, 1989:10.

Hite, Shere. *The Hite Report*. New York: Macmillan, 1976.

———. *The Hite Report on Male Sexuality*. New York: Knopf, 1981.

Hochschild, Arlie, with Anne Machung. *The Second Shift: Working Parents and the Revolution at Home*. New York: Viking Press, 1989.

Hodges, William, et al. "Divorce and the Preschool Child." *Journal of Divorce* 3:1 (Fall 1979): 55–67.

Hoeffer, B. "Children's Acquisition of Sex-Role Behavior in Lesbian-Mother Families." *American Journal of Orthopsychiatry* 51 (1981): 536–544.

Hoegerman, G., et al. Drug Exposed Neonates." *Western Journal of Medicine* 152:1 (May 1990): 559–.

Hoelter, Jon W. "Factoral Invariance and Self-Esteem—Reassessing Race and Sex Differences." *Social Forces* 61:3 (March 1983): 834–846.

Hoelter, Jon, and Lynn Harper. "Structural and Interpersonal Family Influences on Adolescent Self-Conception." *Journal of Marriage and the Family* 49 (February 1987): 129–139.

Hofferth, Sandra. "Updating Children's Life Course." *Journal of Marriage and the Family* 47:1 (9 February 1985): 93–115.

Hofferth, Sandra, and Deborah A. Phillips. "Child Care in the United States, 1970 to 1995." *Journal of Marriage and the Family* 49:3 (August, 1987): 559–572.

Holmes, Steven. "On the Edge of Despair When Jobless Benefits End." *The New York Times,* January 28, 1991: A11.

Holmes, T., and R. Rahe. "The Social Readjustment Rating Scale." *Journal of Psychosomatic Medicine* 11 (1967): 213–218.

Holtzen, D. W., and A. A. Agresti. "Parental Responses to Gay and Lesbian Children." *Journal of Social and Clinical Psychology* 9:3 (Fall 1990): 390–399.

Hopkins, Ellen. "Childhood's End." *Rolling Stone* (October 18, 1990): 66–72ff.

Horowitz, A., and L. Shindelman. "Reciprocity and Affection: Past Influences on Present Caregiving." *Journal of Gerontological Social Work* 5 (1983): 5–20.

Hort, Barbara, Beverly Fagot, and Mary Leinbach. "Are People's Notions of Maleness More Stereotypically Framed than Their Notions of Femaleness?" *Sex Roles* 23:3–4 (February 1990): 197–212.

Hotaling, Gerald T., and David Finkelhor. "Estimating the Number of Stranger-Abduction Homicides of Children: A Review of Available Evidence." *Journal of Criminal Justice* 18:5 (1990): 385–399.

Hotaling, Gerald, David Finkelhor, John Kirkpatrick, and Murray Straus, eds. *Coping with Family Violence: Research and Perspectives*. Newbury Park, Calif.: Sage Publications, 1988.

Hotaling, Gerald T., and David B. Sugarman. "A Risk Marker Analysis of Assaulted Wives." *Journal of Family Violence* 5:1 (March 1990): 1–14.

Hotaling, Gerald T., et al., eds. *Family Abuse and Its Consequences*. Newbury Park, Calif.: Sage Publications, 1988.

Houseknecht, Sharon K., "Childlessness and Marital Adjustment." In Jeffrey Rosenfeld, eds., *Relationships: The Marriage and Family Reader*. Glencoe, Ill.: Scott, Foresman, 1982.

———. "Voluntary Childlessness." In Marvin B. Sussman and Suzanne K. Steinmetz, eds., *Handbook of Marriage and the Family*. New York: Plenum Press, 1987.

Houseknecht, Sharon K., Suzanne Vaughan, and Ann Statham. "The Impact of Singlehood on the Career Patterns of Professional Women." *Journal of Marriage and the Family* 49:2 (May, 1987): 353–366.

Howard, Judith. "A Structural Approach to Interracial Patterns in Adolescent Judgments about Sexual Intimacy." *Sociological Perspectives* 31:1 (January 1988): 88–121.

Huang, Lucy. "The Chinese American Family." In Charles Mindel, Robert Habenstein, and Roosevelt Wright, Jr., eds. *Ethnic Families in America: Patterns and Variations,* 3d ed. New York: Elsevier North Holland, Inc., 1988.

Huber, Joan, and Glenna Spitze. *Sex Stratification: Children, Housework, and Jobs.* New York: Academic Press, 1983.

Hunt, Morton, and Beatrice Hunt. *The Divorce Experience.* New York: McGraw-Hill, 1977.

Hurst, Marsha, and Pamela S. Summey. "Childbirth and Social Class: The Case of Cesarean Delivery." *Social Science and Medicine* 18:8 (1984): 621–631.

Huston, Ted, et al. "From Courtship to Marriage: Mate Selection as an Interpersonal Process." In Steve Duck and Robin Gilmore, eds., *Personal Relationships 2: Developing Personal Relationships.* London: Academic Press, 1981.

Ihinger–Tallman, Marilyn. "Sibling and Stepsibling Bonding in Stepfamilies." In Kay Pasley and Marilyn Ihinger-Tallman, eds., *Remarriage and Stepparenting: Current Research and Theory.* New York: Guilford Press, 1987.

Ihinger–Tallman, Marilyn, and Kay Pasley. "Divorce and Remarriage in the American Family: A Historical Review." In Kay Pasley and Marilyn Ihinger–Tallman, eds. *Remarriage and Stepparenting: Current Research and Theory.* New York: Guilford Press, 1987.

_____. *Remarriage.* Newbury Park, Calif.: Sage Publications, 1987.

_____, eds. *Remarriage and Stepparenting: Current Research and Theory:* New York, Guilford Press, 1987.

Imber, Johnathan. "The Future of Abortion Politics." *Contemporary Sociology* 19:2 (March 1990): 176–181.

Indivik, Julie, and Mary Fitzpatrick. "'If You Could Read My Mind, Love...,': Understanding and Misunderstanding in the Marital Dyad." *Family Relations* 44:4 (November 1982): 43–51.

Irving, Howard, et al. "Shared Parenting: An Empirical Analysis Utilizing a Large Data Base." *Family Process* 23 (1984): 561–569.

Ishwaran, Karigonder. *Marriage and Divorce in Canada.* Toronto: Methuen, 1983.

_____, ed. *Canadian Families: Ethnic Variations.* Toronto: McGraw-Hill Ryerson, 1980.

Itard, Jean. *The Wild Boy of Aveyron.* Reprinted in Lucien Malson, ed., *Wolf Children and the Problem of Human Nature.* New York: Monthly Review Press, 1972.

Jacoby, Arthur, and John Williams. "Effects of Premarital Sexual Standards and Behavior on Dating and Marriage Desirability." *Journal of Marriage and the Family* 47:4 (November 1985): 1059–1065.

Jacques, Jeffrey, and Karen Chason. "Cohabitation: Its Impact on Marital Success." *Family Coordinator* 28:1 (1979): 35–39.

Jaramillo, Patricio, and Jesse Zapata. "Roles and Alliances within Mexican-American Families." *Journal of Marriage and the Family* 49:4 (November 1987): 727–736.

Jenista, Jerri Ann. "Adoption of Foreign-Born Children by U.S. Citizens in 1984 by Country of Origin" (table). *OURS* 20:4 (July/August 1987): 15.

Jenks, Richard. "Swinging: A Replication and Test of a Theory." *Journal of Sex Research* 21:2 (May 1985): 199–210.

Joe, Tom, and Douglas W. Nelson. "New Future for America's Children." In Frank J. Macchiarola and Alan Gartner, eds., *Caring for America's Children.* New York: The Academy of Political Science, 1989.

Joesch, Jutta. "The Effect of the Price of Child Care on AFDC Mothers' Paid Work Behavior." *Family Relations* 40:2 (April 1991): 161–166.

John, Robert. "The Native American Family." In Charles Mindel, Robert Habenstein, and Roosevelt Wright, Jr., eds., *Ethnic Families in America: Patterns and Variations,* 3d ed. New York: Elsevier North Holland, Inc., 1988.

Johnson, Beverly. "Single Parent Families." *Family Economics Review* (Summer–Fall, 1980): 22–27.

Johnson, Carolyn, and Sharon Price-Bonham. "Women and Retirement: A Study and Implications." *Family Relations* (July 1980): 381–385.

Johnson, Clifford, Andrew Sum, and James Weill. *Vanishing Dreams: The Growing Economic Plight of America's Young Families.* Washington, D.C.: Children's Defense Funds, 1988.

Johnson, Coleen. "The Impact of Illness on Later-Life Marriages." *Journal of Marriage and the Family* 47 (1985): 165–172.

_____. "Postdivorce Reorganization of Relationships between Divorcing Children and their Parents." *Journal of Marriage and the Family* 50 (February 1988): 221–23.

Johnson, David, Lynn White, John Edwards, and Alan Booth. "Dimensions of Marital Quality: Toward Methodological and Conceptual Refinement." *Journal of Family Issues* 7 (1986): 31–49.

Johnson, Dirk. "At Colleges, AIDS Alarms Muffle Older Dangers." *The New York Times,* March 8, 1990: B8.

Johnson, G. Timothy, and Stephen Goldfinger, eds. *The Harvard Medical School Health Letter Book.* Cambridge, Mass.: Harvard University Press, 1981.

Johnson, Leanor Boulin. "Perspectives on Black Family Empirical Research: 1965–1978." In Harriette Pipes McAdoo, ed., *Black Families.* Newbury Park, Calif.: Sage Publications, 1988.

Johnston, Thomas F. "Alaskan Native Social Adjustment and the Role of Eskimo and Indian Music." *Journal of Ethnic Studies* 3/4 (Winter 1976): 21–36.

Jones, Carl. "Sharing the Childbirth Miracle." *Nurturing News.* 8:2 (1985): 5, 15ff.

Jones, Jacqueline. *Labor of Love, Labor of Sorrow: Black Women, Work, and the Family from Slave to the Present.* New York: Basic Books, 1985.

Jones, Jennifer, and David Barlow. "Self-Reported Frequencies of Sexual Urges, Fantasies, and Masturbatory Fantasies in Heterosexual Males and Females." *Archives of Sexual Behavior* 19:3 (1990): 269–279.

Jones, Maggie. *A Child by Any Means.* London: Piatkus, 1989.

Jorgensen, Stephen, and Russell Adams. "Predicting Mexican–American Family Planning Intentions: An Application and Test of a Social Psychological Model." *Journal of Marriage and the Family* 50 (February, 1988): 107–119.

Jorgensen, Stephen R., and J. C. Gaudy. "Self-Disclosure and Satisfaction in Marriage: The Relation Examined." *Family Relations* 29:3 (1980): 281–287.

Jorgensen, Stephen R., and A. C. Johnson. "Correlates of Divorce Liberality." *Journal of Marriage and the Family* 42 (1980): 617–622.

Justice, Blair, and Rita Justice. *The Abusing Family,* rev. ed. New York: Insight Books, 1990.

_____. *The Broken Taboo: Incest.* New York: Human Sciences Press, 1979.

Kach, Julie, and Paul McGee. "Adjustment to Early Parenthood." *Journal of Family Issues* 3:3 (September 1982): 375–388.

Kagan, Jerome. *The Nature of the Child.* New York: Basic Books, 1984.

_____. "The Psychological Requirements for Human Development." In Nathan Talbot, ed., *Raising Children in Modern America.* Boston: Little, Brown, 1976.

Kain, Edward. *The Myth of Family Decline: Understanding Families in a World of Rapid Change.* Lexington, Mass.: Lexington Books, 1990.

Kalmuss, Debra. "The Intergenerational Transmission of Marital Aggression." *Journal of Marriage and the Family* 46:1 (February 1984): 11–20.

Kamerman, Sheila, and C. D. Hayes, eds. *Families That Work: Children in a Changing World*. Washington, D.C.: National Academy Press, 1982.

Kanter, Rosabeth. "Why Bosses Turn Bitchy." *Psychology Today* 9(12) (May 1976): 56–59.

Kantor, David, and William Lehr. *Inside Families*. San Francisco, Calif.: Jossey-Bass, 1975.

Kantrowitz, Barbara. "The Crack Children." *Newsweek* (February 12, 1990): 62–63.

_____. "Who Keeps 'Baby M'?" *Newsweek* (January 19, 1987): 44–49.

Kantrowitz, Barbara, and David A. Kaplan. "Not the Right Family." *Newsweek* (March 19, 1990): 50–51.

Kaplan, A. "Clarifying the Concept of Androgyny: Implications for Therapy." *Psychology of Women* 3 (1979): 223–230.

Kaplan, A., and J. P. Bean. "From Sex Stereotypes to Androgyny: Considerations of Societal and Individual Change." In A. Kaplan and J. P. Bean, eds., *Beyond Sex-Role Stereotypes*. Boston: Little, Brown, 1976.

_____, eds. *Beyond Sex-Role Stereotypes*. Boston: Little, Brown, 1979.

Kaplan, Helen Singer. *Disorders of Desire*. New York: Simon & Schuster, 1979.

_____. *Sexual Aversion, Sexual Phobias, and Panic Disorders*. New York: Brunner/Mazel, 1987.

Karan, L. D. "AIDS Prevention and Chemical Dependence Treatment Needs of Women and Their Children." *Journal of Psychoactive Drugs* 21:4 (October–December 1989): 395–399.

Katchadourian, Herant. *Midlife in Perspective*. San Francisco, Calif.: W. H. Freeman, 1987.

Katz, Alvin, and Reuben Hill. "Residential Propinquity and Marital Selection: A Review of Theory, Method and Fact." *Marriage and Family Living* 20 (February 1958): 27–35.

Katz, Michael B. *The Underserving Poor: From War on Poverty to War on Welfare*. New York: Pantheon Books, 1990.

Kavanaugh, Robert. *Facing Death*. Baltimore, Md.: Penguin Books, 1972.

Kaye, K., et al. "Birth Outcomes for Infants of Drug Abusing Mothers." *New York State Journal of Medicine* 144:7 (May 1989): 256–261.

Kearl, Michael C. *Endings: A Sociology of Death and Dying*. New York: Oxford University Press, 1989.

Keith, Pat, et al. "Older Men in Employed and Retired Families." *Alternative Lifestyles* 4:2 (May 1981): 228–241.

Kelley, Harold. "Love and Commitment." In Harold Kelley et al., eds., *Close Relationships*. San Francisco, Calif.: Freeman, 1983.

Kelley, Harold. H., et al., eds. *Close Relationships*. San Francisco, Calif.: Freeman, 1983.

Kelley, Robert, and Patricia Voydanoff. "Work/Family Role Strain Among Employed Parents." *Family Relations* 34:3 (July 1985): 367–374.

Kelly, Susan. "Changing Parent-Child Relationships: An Outcome of Mother Returning to College." *Family Relations* 31 (April 1982): 287–294.

Kempe, C. Henry, and Ray Helfer, eds. *The Battered Child*, rev. ed. Chicago: University of Chicago Press, 1980.

Kennedy, David. *Birth Control in America*. New Haven: Yale University Press, 1970.

Kennedy, Donald. "Why Adoptions Get Harder Every Year." *U.S. News and World Report* (September 20, 1982).

Kennedy, Gregory. "College Students' Expectations of Grandparent and Grandchild Role Behaviors." *Gerontologist* 30:1 (1990): 43–48.

Keshet, Jamie. "From Separation to Stepfamily." *Journal of Family Issues* 1:4 (December 1980): 517–532.

Kessler-Harris, Alice. *A History of Wage-Earning Women in America*. New York: Oxford University Press, 1982.

_____. *Women Have Always Worked: A Historical Overview*. New York: McGraw-Hill, 1981.

Kett, Joseph. *Rites of Passage: Adolescence in America, 1790 to the Present*. New York: Basic Books, 1977.

Kikumura, Akemi, and Harry Kitano. "The Japanese American Family." In Charles Mindel, Robert Habenstein, and Roosevelt Wright, Jr., eds. *Ethnic Families in America: Patterns and Variations*, 3d ed. New York: Elsevier North Holland, Inc., 1988.

Kilpatrick, Allie. "Job Change in Dual-Career Families: Danger or Opportunity?" *Family Relations* 31 (July 1982): 363–368.

Kilzer, Louis. "Kid Fingerprinting a Sham, Foes Claim." *The Denver Post*, May 13, 1985a: 1–A, 14–A.

_____. "Public Often Not Told Facts in Missing Children Cases." *The Denver Post*, September 22, 1985b: 1–A, 14–A.

Kilzer, Louis, and Diana Griego. "Missing-Child Reports Bring Out Best, Worst." *The Denver Post*, May 13, 1985: 1–A, 14–A.

Kingston, Paul, and Stephen Nock. "Consequences of the Family Work Day." *Journal of Marriage and the Family* 47:3 (August 1985): 619–629.

Kinsey, Alfred, et al. *Sexual Behavior in the Human Female*. Philadelphia: Saunders, 1953.

_____, et al. *Sexual Behavior in the Human Male*. Philadelphia: Saunders, 1948.

Kirchler, Erich. "Everyday Life Experiences at Home: An Interaction Diary Approach to Assess Marital Relationships." *Journal of Family Psychology* 2 (1989): 311–336.

Kirkpatrick, Martha, et al. "Lesbian Mothers and Their Children: A Comparative Study." *American Journal of Orthopsychiatry* 51:3 (July 1981): 545–551.

Kitson, Gay. "Marital Discord and Marital Separation: A County Survey." *Journal of Marriage and the Family* 47 (1985): 693–700.

Kitson, Gay, and Leslie Morgan. "Consequences of Divorce." In Alan Booth, ed., *Contemporary Families: Looking Forward, Looking Back*. Minneapolis, Minn.: National Council on Family Relations, 1991.

Kitson, Gay, and Marvin Sussman. "Marital Complaints, Demographic Characteristics, and Symptoms of Mental Distress in Divorce." *Journal of Marriage and the Family* 44:1 (1982): 87–101.

Kitzinger, Sheila. *The Complete Book of Pregnancy and Childbirth*. New York: Knopf, 1989.

_____. *Woman's Experience of Sex*. New York: Penguin Books, 1985.

Klatch, Rebecca. "Coalition and Conflict Among Women in the New Right." *Signs* 13:4 (Summer 1988): 671–694.

Klein, Carole. *How It Feels to Be a Child*. New York: Harper Colophon Books, 1977.

Klein, David, and William Smith. "Historical Trends in the Marriage and Family Textbook Literature." *Family Relations* 34 (April 1985): 21–219.

Klinman, Deborah, and Carol Vukelich. "Mothers and Fathers: Expectations for Infants." *Family Relations* 34:3 (July 1985): 305–313.

Klinman, Deborah, et al. *Fatherhood, USA: The First National Guide to Programs, Services and Resources for and about Fathers*. New York: Garland Publishing Co., 1984.

Knapp, Mark, et al. "Compliments: A Descriptive Taxonomy." *Journal of Communication* 34:4 (Autumn 1984): 12–31.

Knaub, P. K., et al. "Strengths of Remarriage." *Journal of Divorce* 7 (1984): 41–55.

Knox, David. *Choices in Relationships*. St. Paul, Minn.: West, 1985.

_____. "Conceptions of Love at Three Developmental Levels." *Family Coordinator* 19 (1970): 151–156.

Knox, David, and K. Wilson. "Dating Behaviors of University Students." *Family Relations* 30 (1981): 83–86.

Koblinsky, Sally, and Christine Todd. "Teaching Self-Care Skills to Latchkey Children: A Review of the Research." *Family Relations* 38:4 (October 1989): 431–435.

Kohen, J. A., et al., "Divorced Mothers: The Costs and Benefits of Female Family Control." In G. Kevinger and O. C. Moles, eds., *Separation and Divorce*. New York: Basic Books, 1979.

Kohlberg, Lawrence. "The Cognitive-Development Approach to Socialization." In A. Goslin, ed., *Handbook of Socialization Theory and Research*. Chicago: Rand McNally, 1969.

Kohn, M. L. "Social Class and Parental Values." *American Journal of Sociology* 64 (1959): 337–351.

Kolata, Gina. "Anti-Acne Drug Faulted in Birth Defects." *The New York Times,* April 22, 1988: 1*ff.*

_____. *The Baby Doctors.* New York: Delacorte Press, 1989.

_____. "Early Warnings and Latent Cures for Infertility." *Ms.* (May 1979): 86–89.

_____. "Experts Declare Temperance Is Back in Style in America." *The New York Times,* January 1, 1991: B3.

_____. "A Major Operation on a Fetus Works for the First Time." *The New York Times,* May 31, 1990: B1*ff.*

_____. "Racial Bias Seen in Prosecuting Pregnant Addicts." *The New York Times,* July 20, 1990: A10.

_____. "Tests of Fetuses Rise Sharply Amid Doubts." *The New York Times,* September 22, 1987: 19–20.

Kolker, A. "Advances in Prenatal Diagnosis: Social–Psychological and Policy Issues." *Interanational Journal of Technology Assessment in Health Care* 5:4 (1989): 601–617.

Kolodny, Robert, et al. *Textbook of Sexual Medicine.* Boston: Little, Brown, 1979.

Komarovsky, Mirra. *Blue-Collar Marriage,* 2d ed. New Haven, Conn.: Yale University Press, 1987.

_____. "The New Feminist Scholarship: Some Precursors and Polemics." *Journal of Marriage and the Family.* 50:3 (August, 1988): 585–594.

_____. *Women in College.* New York: Basic Books, 1985.

Koop, Everett. "The U.S. Surgeon General on the Health Effects of Abortion." *Population and Development Review* 15:1 (March 1989): 172–175.

Koss, Mary. "Hidden Rape: Sexual Aggression and Victimization in a National Sample of Students in Higher Education." In A. W. Burgess, ed., *Rape and Sexual Assault II.* New York: Garland Press, 1988.

Koss, Mary, et al. "The Scope of Rape: Incidence and Prevalence of Sexual Aggression and Victimization in a National Sample of Higher Education Students." *Journal of Consulting and Clinical Psychology* 55:2 (April 1987): 162–170.

Koss, Mary, Thomas Dinero, Cynthia Seibel, and Susan Cox. "Stranger and Acquaintance Rape: Are There Differences in the Victim's Experience?" *Psychology of Women Quarterly* 12:1 (March 1988): 1–24.

Kozol, Jonathan. *Rachel and Her Children: Homeless Families in America.* New York: Crown Publishers, 1988.

Krames, Lester, Rebecca England, and Gordon Flett. "The Role of Masculinity and Femininity in Depression and Social Satisfaction in Elderly Years." *Sex Roles* 19:11–12 (December 1988): 713–721.

Kranichfeld, Marion. "Rethinking Family Power." *Journal of Family Issues* 8:1 (March 1987): 42–56.

Kressel, Kenneth. *The Divorce Process: How Professionals and Couples Negotiate Settlement.* New York: Basic Books, 1985.

Krimmel, Herman. "The Alcoholic and His Family." In Peter Bourne and Ruth Fox, eds., *Alcoholism: Progress in Research and Treatment.* New York: Academic Press, 1973.

Kubey, Robert, and Mihaly Csikszentmihalyi. *Television and the Quality of Life: How Viewing Shapes Everyday Experience.* Hillsdale, N.J.: Lawrence Erlbaum Associates, 1990.

Kübler-Ross, Elisabeth. *AIDS: The Ultimate Challenge.* New York: Macmillan, 1987.

_____, *On Death and Dying.* New York: Macmillan, 1969.

_____. *Working it Through.* New York: Macmillan, 1982.

Kupersmid, Joel, and Donald Wonderly. "Moral Maturity and Behavior: Failure to Find a Link." *Journal of Youth and Adolescence* 9 (June 1980): 249–261.

Kurdek, Lawrence, and Albert Siesky. "Children's Perceptions of Their Parents' Divorce." *Journal of Divorce* 3:4 (Summer 1980): 339–378.

Kurdek, Lawrence and J. Patrick Smith. "Partner Homogamy in Married, Heterosexual, Cohabiting, Gay, and Lesbian Couples." *Journal of Sex Research* 23:2 (May 1987): 212–232.

Kurdek, Lawrence, et al. "Correlates of Children's Long-Term Adjustment to Their Parents' Divorce." *Developmental Psychology* 17(5) (September 1981): 565–579.

Kutner, Lawrence. "Children Need Help Forming Self-Image." *The New York Times,* February 25, 1988: 21ff.

_____. "Parent & Child." *The New York Times,* November 1, 1990: B8.

Kutscher, Austin H., Arthur C. Carr, and Lillian G. Kutscher, eds. *Principles of Thanatology.* New York: Columbia University Press, 1987.

LaBeff, Emily, et al. "Gender Differences in Self Advertisements for Dates." *Free Inquiry in Creative Sociology* 17:1 (May 1989): 45–50.

Ladas, Alice, et al. *The G Spot.* New York· Holt, Rinehart and Winston, 1982.

Laing, R.D. *The Politics of the Family and Other Essays.* New York: Random House, 1972.

Lainson, Suzanne. "Breast-Feeding: The Erotic Factor." *Ms.* 11(8) (February 1983): 66ff.

Lamaze, Fernand. *Painless Childbirth.* Chicago: H. Regnery, 1970; 1st ed., 1956.

Lamb, Michael. *The Father's Role: Cross–Cultural Perspectives.* Hillsdale, N.J.: Lawrence Erlbaum, 1986.

Lane, K. E., and P. A. Gwartney-Gibbs. "Violence in the Context of Dating and Sex." *Journal of Family Issues* 6 (1985): 45–59.

Lantz, Herman. "Family and Kin as Revealed in the Narratives of Ex–Slaves." *Social Science Quarterly* 60:4 (March 1980): 667–674.

Larkin, Ralph. *Suburban Youth in Cultural Crisis.* New York: Oxford University Press, 1979.

LaRossa, Ralph, and Maureen LaRossa. *Transition to Parenthood: How Infants Change Families.* Beverly Hills, Calif.: Sage, 1981.

LaRossa, Ralph, and Jane Wolf. "On Qualitative Family Research." *Journal of Marriage and the Family* 47:3 (August 1985): 531–541.

Lasch, Christopher. *Haven in a Heartless World.* New York: Basic Books, 1977.

Lauer, Robert, and Jeanette Lauer. "The Long-Term Relational Consequences of Problematic Family Backgrounds." *Family Relations* 40:3 (July 1991): 286–291.

Lavee, Yoav, and David Olson. "Family Types and Response to Stress." *Journal of Marriage and the Family* 53:3 (August 1991): 786–798.

Laviola, Marisa. "Effects of Older-Brother Younger-Sister Incest: A Review of Four Cases." *Journal of Family Violence* 4:3 (Sept. 1989): 259–274.

Lawson, Carol. "Fathers, Too, Are Seeking a Balance between Their Families and Careers." *The New York Times,* April 12, 1990: B1ff.

Leboyer, Frederic. *Birth Without Violence.* New York: Knopf, 1975.

Lederer, William, and Don Jackson. *Mirages of Marriage.* New York: Norton, 1968.

Lee, John A. "Love-Styles." In Robert Sternberg and Michael Barnes, eds., *The Psychology of Love.* New Haven, Conn.: Yale University Press, 1988.

_____. *The Color of Love.* Toronto, Canada: New Press, 1973.

Lee, Thomas, Jay Mancini, and Joseph Maxwell. "Contact Patterns and Motivations for Sibling Relations in Adulthood." *Journal of Marriage and the Family* 52 (May 1990): 431–440.

Leifer, Myra. *Psychological Effects of Motherhood: A Study of First Pregnancy.* New York: Praeger, 1990.

Leites, Edmund. "The Duty to Desire: Love, Friendship, and Sexuality in Some Puritan Theories of Marriage." *Journal of Social History* 15:3 (Spring 1982): 383–408.

Leming, Michael R., and George E. Dickinson. *Understanding Dying, Death, and Bereavement.* New York: Holt, Rinehart and Winston, 1985.

Leonard, Kenneth E., and Theodore Jacob. "Alcohol, Alcoholism, and Family Violence." In Vincent B. Van Hasselt et al., eds., *Handbook of Family Violence.* New York: Plenum Press, 1988.

Leslie, Leigh, and Katherine Grady. "Changes in Mothers' Social Networks and Social Support Following Divorce." *Journal of Marriage and the Family* 47:3 (August 1985): 663–673.

Lesnick-Oberstein, M., and L. Cohen. "Cognitive Style, Sensation Seeking, and Assortative Mating." *Journal of Personality and Social Psychology* 46 (1984): 112–117.

Lévi-Strauss, Claude. "The Family." In Harry Shapiro, ed., *Man, Culture, and Society.* New York: Oxford University Press, 1956.

Levine, David. "Sociocultural Causes of Family Violence." *Journal of Family Violence* 1:1 (1986): 3–12.

Levine, Linda, and Lonnie Barbach. *The Intimate Male.* New York: Signet Books, 1983.

Levine, Martin. "The Sociology of Male Homosexuality and Lesbianism: An Introductory (Annotated) Bibliography." *Journal of Sexuality* 5:3 (Spring 1990): 249–275.

Levine, Martin, and Richard Troiden. "The Myth of Sexual Compulsivity." *Journal of Sex Research* 25:3 (August 1988): 347–363.

Levinger, George. "Marital Cohesiveness and Dissolution: An Integrative Review." *Journal of Marriage and the Family* 27 (1965): 19–28.

———. "A Social Psychological Perspective on Marital Dissolution." In George Levinger and O. C. Moles, eds., *Divorce and Separation.* New York: Basic Books, 1979.

Levinger, George, and O. C. Moles, eds. *Divorce and Separation: Context, Causes, and Consequences.* New York: Basic Books, 1979.

Levinson, Daniel J. *The Seasons of a Man's Life.* New York: Ballantine Books, 1977.

Lewin, Bo. "Unmarried Cohabitation: A Marriage Form in a Changing Society." *Journal of Marriage and the Family* 44:3 (August 1982): 763–773.

Lewin, E., and T. A. Lyons. "Everything in Its Place: The Coexistence of Lesbianism and Motherhood." In W. Paul et al., eds., *Homosexuality: Social, Psychological, and Biological Issues.* Newbury Park, Calif.: Sage Publications, 1982.

Lewin, M. "Unwanted Intercourse: The Difficulty of Saying No." *Psychology of Women Quarterly* 9 (1985): 184–192.

Lewin, Tamar. "Drug Use During Pregnancy: New Issue before the Courts." *The New York Times,* February 5, 1990: A1, A12.

———. "South Korea Slows Export of Babies for Adoption." *The New York Times,* February 12, 1990.

Lewis, Jerry M., ed. *The Birth of the Family: An Empirical Inquiry.* New York: Brunner/Mazel, 1989.

Lewis, Jerry M., Margaret Tresch Owen, and Martha J. Cox. "Family of Origin." In Jerry M. Lewis, ed., *The Birth of the Family: An Empirical Inquiry.* New York: Brunner/Mazel, 1989.

Lewis, Jerry M., et al. *No Single Thread.* New York: Brunner/Mazel, 1976.

Lewis, Karen. "Children of Lesbians: Their Point of View." *Social Work* 25:3 (May 1980): 198–203.

Lewis, Robert. "The Family and Addictions: An Introduction." *Family Relations* 38:3 (July 1989): 254–257.

Libby, Roger. "Social Scripts for Sexual Relationships." In Sol Gordon and Roger Libby, eds. *Sexuality Today and Tomorrow.* North Scituate, Mass.: Duxbury Press, 1976.

Lieberson, Stanley, and Mary Waters. *From Many Strands: Ethnic and Racial Groups in Contemporary America.* New York: Russell Sage Foundation, 1988.

Lief, Harold, and Helen Singer Kaplan. "Ego-Dystonic Homosexuality." *Journal of Sex and Marital Therapy* 12:4 (Winter 1986): 259–266.

Liem, Ramsay, and J. Liem. "Social Support and Stress: Some General Issues and Their Application to the Problem of Unemployment." In L. Ferman and J. Gordus, eds., *Mental Health and the Economy.* Kalamazoo, Mich.: Upjohn Institute, 1979.

Liem, Ramsay, and Paula Rayman. "Health and Social Costs of Unemployment." *American Psychologist* 37(10) (October 1982): 1116–1123.

Lindsey, Karen. *Friends as Family.* Boston: Beacon Press, 1982.

Lingren, Herbert, et al. "Enhancing Marriage and Family Competencies Through Adult Life Development." In Nick Stinnet et al., eds., *Family Strengths 4: Positive Support Systems.* Lincoln: University of Nebraska Press, 1982.

Lino, Mark. "Expenditures on a Child by Husband-Wife Families." *Family Economics Review* 3:3 (1990): 2–12.

Litwack, Leon. *Been in the Storm So Long.* New York: Alfred A. Knopf, 1979.

Lloyd, Sally A. "Conflict Types and Strategies in Violent Marriages." *Journal of Family Violence* 5:4 (December 1990): 269–284.

———. "The Darkside of Courtship: Violence and Sexual Exploitation. *Family Relations* 40:1 (January 1991): 14–20.

Lloyd, Sally A., and Beth C. Emery. "The Dynamics of Courtship Violence." Paper presented at the Annual Meeting of The National Council on Family Relations, Seattle, November 1990.

Lockhart, Lettie. "A Reexamination of the Effects of Race and Social Class on the Incidence of Marital Violence: A Search for Reliable Differences." *Journal of Marriage and the Family* 49 (August, 1987): 603–610.

Loiacano, Darryl. "Sex Identity Issues Among Black Americans: Racism, Homophobia, and the Need for Validation." *Journal of Counseling and Development* 68:1 (September–October 1989): 21–25.

Lombardo, W. K. et al. "Fer Cryin' Out Loud—There is a Sex Difference." *Sex Roles* 9 (1983): 987–995.

London, Richard, James Wakefield, and Richard Lewak. "Similarity of Personality Variables as Predictors of Marital Satisfaction." *Personality and Individual Differences* 11:1 (1990): 39–43.

Lopata, Helena. *Occupation: Housewife.* New York: Oxford University Press, 1972.

———. *Women As Widows: Support Systems.* New York: Elsevier, 1979.

Lord, Lewis. "Desperately Seeking Baby." *U. S. News & World Report* (October 5, 1987):58–65.

Lord, Lewis, et al. "Coming to Grips with Alcoholism." *U. S. News & World Report* (November 30, 1987): 56–62.

Losh-Hesselbart, Susan. "Development of Gender Roles." In Marvin Sussman and Suzanne Steinmetz, eds., *Handbook of Marriage and the Family.* New York: Plenum Press, 1987.

Lowry, Dennis, and David Towles. "Prime Time TV Portrayals of Sex, Contraception, and Venereal Disease." *Journalism Quarterly* 66:2 (Summer 1989): 347–352.

———. "Soap Opera Portrayals of Sex, Contraception, and Venereal Disease." *Journal of Communication* 39:2 (Spring 1989): 76–83.

Luker, Kristin. *Abortion and the Politics of Motherhood.* Berkeley: University of California Press, 1984.

———. *Taking Chances.* Berkeley: University of California Press, 1975.

Lurie, Elinore. "Sex and Stage Differences in Perceptions of Marital and Family Relationships." *Journal of Marriage and the Family* 36:2 (May 1974): 260–269.

Lutz, Patricia. "The Stepfamily: An Adolescent Perspective." *Family Relations* 32:3 (July 1983): 367–375.

Lutzer, John, and James Rice. "Using Recidivism Data to Evaluate Project 12-Ways: An Ecobehavioral Approach to the Treatment and Prevention of Child Abuse and Neglect." *Journal of Family Violence* 2:4 (1986): 283–290.

Lutzer, John and James Rice. "Project 12-Ways: Measuring Outcome of a Large-scale In-Home Service for the Treatment and Prevention of Child Abuse and Neglect." *Child Abuse and Neglect International Journal* 8 (1984): 519–524.

Lyon, Jeff. *Playing God in the Nursery.* New York: W. W. Norton, 1985.

McAdoo, Harriette. "Changes in the Formation and Structure of Black Families: The Impact on Black Women." Center for Research on Women, Wellesley College. Working Paper No. 182. Wellesley, Mass.: 1988.

_____, ed. *Black Families,* 2d ed. Beverly Hills, Calif.: Sage Publications, 1988.

McAdoo, Harriette Pipes, and John McAdoo, eds. *Black Children: Social, Educational, and Parental Environments.* Beverly Hills, Calif: Sage, 1985.

McCormack, M. J., et al. "Patient's Attitudes Following Chorionic Villus Sampling." *Prenatal Diagnosis* 10:4 (April 1990): 253–255.

McCubbin, Hamilton I., "Integrating Coping Behavior in Family Stress Theory." *Journal of Marriage and the Family* 41:2 (May 1979): 237–244.

McCubbin, Hamilton I., Constance Joy, and Elizabeth Cauble. "Family Stress and Coping: A Decade Review." *Journal of Marriage and the Family* 42:4 (November 1980): 855–871.

McCubbin, Hamilton I., and Marilyn A. McCubbin. "Typologies of Resilient Families: Emerging Roles of Social Class and Ethnicity." *Family Relations* 37 (July 1988): 247–254.

McCubbin, Hamilton I., and Anne I. Thompson, eds. *Family Assessment Inventories for Research and Practice.* Madison: University of Wisconsin Press, 1987.

McCubbin, Marilyn A. "Family Stress, Resources, and Family Types: Chronic Illness in Children." *Family Relations* 37 (April 1988): 203–210.

McCubbin, Marilyn A., and Hamilton I. McCubbin. "Theoretical Orientations to Family Stress and Coping." In Charles Figley, ed., *Treating Families Under Stress.* New York: Brunner/Mazel, 1989.

_____. "Family Stress Theory and Assessment." In Hamilton I. McCubbin and Anne I. Thompson, eds., *Family Assessment Inventories for Research and Practice.* Madison: University of Wisconsin Press, 1987.

McEwan, K. L., C. G. Costello, and P. J. Taylor. "Adjustment to Infertility." *Journal of Abnormal Psychology* 96:2 (May 1987): 108–116.

McGoldrick, Monica. "Normal Families: An Ethnic Perspective." In Froma Walsh, ed., *Normal Family Processes.* New York: Guilford Press, 1982.

McGoldrick, Monica, and Randy Gerson. *Genograms in Family Assessment.* New York: Norton, 1985.

McGoldrick, Monica, John Pearce, and Joseph Giordano. *Ethnicity and Family Therapy.* New York: Guilford Press, 1988.

McHale, Susan, and Ted Huston. "The Effect of the Transition to Parenthood on the Marriage and Family Relationship: A Longitudinal Study." *Journal of Family Issues* 6:4 (December 1985): 409–433.

McKim, Margaret K. "Transition to What? New Parents' Problems in the First Year." *Family Relations* 36 (January 1987): 22–25.

McKinney, Kathleen. "Perceptions of Courtship Violence: Gender Difference and Involvement." *Free Inquiry in Creative Sociology* 14:1 (May 1986): 61–66.

McKinney, Kathleen, and Susan Sprecher, eds. *Human Sexuality: The Societal and Interpersonal Context.* Norwood, N.J.: Ablex, 1989.

_____. *Sexuality in Close Relationships.* Hillsdale, N.J.: Erlbaum, 1991.

McLanahan, Sara, and Karen Booth. "Mother-Only Families: Problems, Prospects, and Politics." In Alan Booth, ed., *Contemporary Families: Looking Forward, Looking Back.* Minneapolis: National Council on Family Relations, 1991.

McLanahan, Sara, et al. "Network Structure, Social Support, and Psychological Well-Being." *Journal of Marriage and the Family* 43 (August 1981): 601–612.

McLoughlin, David, and Richard Whitfield. "Adolescents and Their Experience of Parental Divorce." *Journal of Adolescence* 7 (1984): 155–170.

McNeely, R. L., and Barbe Fogarty. "Balancing Parenthood and Employment: Factors Affecting Company Receptiveness to Family-Related Innovations in the Workplace." *Family Relations* 37 (April 1988): 189–195.

McNeil, John. *The Church and the Homosexual.* Boston: Beacon Press, 1988.

MacCorquodale, Patricia. "Gender and Sexuality." In Kathleen McKinney, and Susan Sprecher, eds. *Human Sexuality: The Societal and Interpersonal Context.* Norwood, N.J.: Ablex, 1989.

MacCorquodale, Patricia, and John DeLameter. "Self-Image and Premarital Sexuality." *Journal of Marriage and the Family* (May 1979): 327–33.

Macchiarola, Frank J., and Alan Gartner, eds. *Caring for America's Children.* New York: The Academy of Political Science, 1989.

Maccoby, Eleanor, and Carol Jacklin. *The Psychology of Sex Differences.* Stanford, Calif.: Stanford University Press, 1974.

Mace, David, and Vera Mace. "Enriching Marriage." In Nick Stinnet et al., eds., *Family Strengths.* Lincoln: University of Nebraska Press, 1979.

_____. "Enriching Marriages: The Foundation Stone of Family Strength." In Nick Stinnet et al. *Family Strengths: Positive Models for Family Life.* Lincoln: University of Nebraska Press, 1980.

Macklin, Eleanor, ed. *AIDS and Families.* New York: Harrington Park Publishers, 1989.

_____. "AIDS: Implications for Families." *Family Relations* 37:2 (April 1988): 141–149.

_____. "Nonmarital Heterosexual Cohabitation." *Marriage and Family Review* 1 (March/April 1978): 1–12.

_____. "Nontraditional Family Forms." In Marvin Sussman and Suzanne Steinmetz, eds., *Handbook of Marriage and the Family.* New York: Plenum Press, 1987.

Macklin, Eleanor, and Roger Rubin, eds. *Contemporary Families and Alternative Lifestyles: Handbook on Research and Theory.* Beverly Hills, Calif.: Sage Publications, 1983.

Maddox, Brenda. "Homosexual Parents." *Psychology Today.* (February, 1982): 62–69.

Madsen, William. *Mexican-American Youth of South Texas,* 2d ed. New York: Holt, Rinehart, and Winston, 1973.

Magno, Josefina. "The Hospice Concept of Care: Facing the 1990s." *Death Studies* 14:2 (1990): 109–119.

Makepeace, James. "Courtship Violence Among College Students." *Family Relations* 30:1 (January 1981): 97–102.

_____. "Dating, Living Together, and Courtship Violence." In Maureen Pirog-Good, and Jan Stets, eds., *Violence in Dating Relationships: Emerging Social Issues.* New York: Praeger, 1989.

_____. "Gender Differences in Courtship Violence Victimization." *Family Relations* 35:3 (July 1986): 383–388.

_____. "Social Factor and Victim-Offender Differences in Courtship Violence." *Family Relations* 36 (1987): 87–91.

Malatesta, Victor, Dianne Chambless, Martha Pollack, and Alan Cantor. "Widowhood, Sexuality, and Aging: A Life Span Analysis." *Journal of Sex and Marital Therapy* 14:1 (Spring 1989): 49–62.

Maloney, Lawrence. "Behind Rise in Mixed Marriages." *U. S. News & World Report* (February 10,1986): 68–69.

Malson, Lucien. *Wolf Children and the Problem of Human Nature.* New York: Monthly Review Press, 1972.

Malveaux, Julianne. "The Economic Status of Black Families." In Harriette Pipes McAdoo, ed., *Black Families,* 2d ed. Newbury Park, Calif.: Sage Publications, 1988.

Mancini, Jay, and Rosemary Blieszner. "Aging Parents and Adult Children: Research Themes in Intergenerational Relations." In Alan Booth, ed. *Contemporary Families: Looking Forward, Looking Back.* Minneapolis: National Council on Family Relations, 1991.

—————. "Research on Aging Parents and Adult Children." *Journal of Marriage and the Family* 51 (May 1989): 275–290.

Marecek, Jeanne, Stephen Finn, and Moda Cardell. "Gender Roles in the Relationships of Lesbians and Gay Men." In John DeCecco, ed., *Gay Relationships.* New York: Haworth Press, 1988.

Maret, Elizabeth, and Barbara Finlay. "The Distribution of Household Labor Among Women in Dual–Earner Marriages." *Journal of Marriage and the Family* 46 (1984): 357–364.

Margolin, Gayla, Linda Gorin Sibner, and Lisa Gleberman. "Wife Battering." In Vincent B. Van Hasselt et al., eds., *Handbook of Family Violence.* New York: Plenum Press, 1988.

Margolin, Leslie. "Abuse and Neglect in Nonparental Child Care: A Risk Assessment." *Journal of Marriage and the Family* 53:3 (August 1991): 694–704.

Margolin, Leslie, and Lynn White. "The Continuing Role of Physical Attractiveness in Marriage." *Journal of Marriage and the Family* 49 (February 1987): 21–27.

Margolin, Malcolm. *The Ohlone Way.* Berkeley: Heyday Books, 1978.

Marin, Peter. "Helping and Hating the Homeless." *Harper's,* (January 1987): 39–49.

Markman, Howard. "Prediction of Marital Distress: A Five-Year Follow-up." *Journal of Consulting and Clinical Psychology* 49 (1981): 760–761.

Markman, Howard, S. W. Duncan, R. D. Storaasli, and P. W. Howes. "The Prediction and Prevention of Marital Distress: A Longitudinal Investigation." In Kurt Hahlweg and Michael Goldstein, eds., *Understanding Major Mental Disorders: The Contribution of Family Interaction Research.* New York: Family Process Press, 1987.

Marmor, Judd. "Homosexuality and the Issue of Mental Illness." In Judd Marmor, ed., *Homosexual Behavior.* New York: Basic Books, 1980.

Marmor, Judd, ed. *Homosexual Behavior.* New York: Basic Books, 1980.

Martelli, Leonard, et al. *When Someone You Know Has AIDS: A Book of Hope for Family and Friends.* New York: Crown, 1987.

Martin, Del. *Battered Wives.* San Francisco, Calif.: New Glide, 1981.

Martin, Don, and Maggie Martin. "Selected Attitudes toward Marriage and Family Life among College Students." *Family Relations* 33 (1984): 293–300.

Martin, Elmer P., and Joanne Mitchell Martin. *The Black Extended Family.* Chicago: University of Chicago Press, 1978.

Martin, Grant. "Relationship, Romance, and Sexual Addiction in Extramarital Affairs." *Journal of Psychology and Christianity* 8:4 (Winter 1989): 5–25.

Martin, Peter, Gunhild O. Hagestad, and Patricia Diedrick. "Family Stories: Events (temporarily) Remembered." *Journal of Marriage and the Family* 50 (May 1988): 533–541.

Maruta, Toshihiko, and Mary Jane McHardy. "Sexual Problems in Patients with Chronic Pain." *Medical Aspects of Human Sexuality* 17:2 (February 1983): 68J–68Uff.

Mason, Karen, and Yu-Hsia Lu. "Attitudes toward Women's Familial Roles: Changes in the United States, 1977–1985." *Gender & Society* 2:1 (March 1988): 39–57.

"Massachusetts Midwife Curb Upheld." *The New York Times,* May 25, 1987: 5.

Masters, John, et al. "The Role of the Family in Coping with Childhood Chronic Illness." In Thomas Burish and Laurence Bradley, eds., *Coping with Chronic Disease.* New York: Academic Press, 1983.

Masters, William, et al. *Masters and Johnson on Sex and Human Loving.* Boston: Little, Brown, 1986.

Masters, William, and Virginia Johnson. *Human Sexual Inadequacy.* Boston: Little, Brown, 1970.

Matiella, Ana Consuelo. *Positively Different: Creating a Bias-Free Environment for Children.* Santa Cruz, Calif.: Network Publications, 1991.

Mattessich, Paul, and Reuben Hill. "Life Cycle and Family Development." In Marvin Sussman and Suzanne Steinmetz, eds., *Handbook of Marriage and the Family.* New York: Plenum Press, 1987.

Matthews, Sarah, and Tana Rosner. "Shared Filial Responsibility: The Family as the Primary Caregiver." *Journal of Marriage and the Family* 50:1 (February 1988): 185–195.

Mays, Vickie, and Susan Cochran. "Acquired Immunodeficiency Syndrome and Black Americans: Special Psychosocial Issues." *Public Health Reports* 102:2 (March/April, 1987): 224–232.

Mazor, Miriam. "Barren Couples." *Psychology Today* 12:12 (May 1979): 101–108, 112.

Mazor, Miriam, and Harriet Simons, eds. *Infertility: Medical, Emotional and Social Considerations.* New York: Human Sciences Press, 1984.

Mead, Margaret. *Male and Female.* New York: William Morrow, 1975.

Meckel, Richard. "Childhood and the Historians: A Review Essay." *Journal of Family History* 9:4 (Winter 1984): 415–424.

Mederer, Helen J., and Richard J. Gelles. "Compassion or Control: Intervention in Cases of Wife Abuse." *Journal of Interpersonal Violence* 4:1 (March 1989): 25–43.

Medoff, Marshall. "Constituencies, Ideology, and the Demand for Abortion Legislation." *Public Choice* 60:2 (February 1989): 185–191.

Mehren, Elizabeth. "Suddenly, I Saw God Smiling." *The New York Times,* December 12, 1990: E1, E5.

Meiners, Jane, and Geraldine Olson. "Household, Paid and Unpaid Work Time of Farm Women." *Family Relations* 37:1 (January 1988): 407–411.

Melichor, Joseph, and David Chiriboga. "Significance of Time in Adjustment to Marital Separation." *American Journal of Orthopsyciatry* 58:2 (April 1988): 221–227.

Melito, Richard. "Adaptation in Family Systems: A Developmental Perspective." *Family Processes* 24 (1985): 89–100.

Menaghan, Elizabeth, and Toby Parcel. "Parental Employment and Family Life: Research in the 1980s." In Alan Booth, ed., *Contemporary Families: Looking Forward, Looking Back.* Minneapolis, Minn.: National Council on Family Relations, 1991.

Menning, Barbara Eck. *Infertility: A Guide for Childless Couples,* 2d ed. New York: Prentice Hall, 1988.

Meredith, William, and George Rowe. "Changes in Lao Hmong Marital Attitudes after Immigration to the United States." *Journal of Comparative Family Studies* 17:1 (Spring 1986): 117–126.

Mertensmeyer, Carol, and Marilyn Coleman. "Correlates of Inter-Role Conflict in Young Rurals and Urban Parents." *Family Relations* 36 (October 1987): 425–429.

Messinger, Lillian. "Remarriage between Divorced People with Children from Previous Marriages: A Proposal for Preparation for Remarriage." *Journal of Marriage and Family Counseling* 2 (1976): 193–200.

Miall, Cherlene E. "The Stigma of Adoptive Parent Status: Perceptions of Community Attitudes Toward Adoption and the Experience of Informal Self-Sanctioning." *Family Relations* 36 (January 1987): 34–39.

Milan, Richard, Jr., and Peter Kilmann. "Interpersonal Factors in Premarital Contraception." *Journal of Sex Research* 23:3 (August, 1987): 321–389.

Milardo, Robert. "Changes in Social Networks of Women and Men Following Divorce: A Review." *Journal of Family Issues* 8 (1987) 78–96.

Miller, B. "Gay Fathers and Their Children." *The Family Coordinator* 28 (1979): 544–552.

Miller, Brent. *Family Research Methods.* Beverly Hills, Calif.: Sage Publications, 1986.

Miller, Brent, Kelly McCoy, Terrance Olson, and Christopher Wallace. "Parental Discipline and Control Attempts in Relation to Adolescent Sexual Attitudes and Behavior." *Journal of Marriage and the Family* 48:3 (August 1986): 503–512.

Miller, Jean B. "Psychological Recovery in Low-Income Single Parents." *American Journal of Orthopsychiatry* 52:2 (April 1982): 346–352.

Miller, John. *The First Frontier,* 2d ed. New York: Dell, 1975.

Miller, Randi, and Michael Gordon. "The Decline of Formal Dating: A Study in Six Connecticut High Schools." *Marriage and Family Relationships* 10:1 (April 1986): 139–154.

Mills, David. "A Model for Stepparent Development." *Family Relations* 33 (1984): 365–372.

Min, Pyong Gap. "The Korean American Family." In Charles Mindel, Robert Habenstein, and Roosevelt Wright, eds., *Ethnic Families in America: Patterns and Variations,* 3d ed. New York: Elsevier North Holland, Inc., 1988.

Mindel, Charles H., Robert W. Habenstein, and Roosevelt Wright, Jr., eds. *Ethnic Families in America: Patterns and Variations,* 3d ed. New York: Elsevier North Holland, Inc., 1976, 1981, 1988.

Minuchin, Salvador. *Families and Family Therapy.* Cambridge, Mass.: Harvard University Press, 1974.

_____. *Family Therapy Techniques.* Cambridge, Mass.: Harvard University Press, 1981.

Mintz, Steven, and Susan Kellogg. *Domestic Revolutions: A Social History of American Family Life.* New York: Free Press, 1988.

Mirandé, Alfredo. *The Chicano Experience: An Alternative Perspective.* Notre Dame, Ind.: University of Notre Dame Press, 1985.

Mirowsky, John, and Catherine Ross. "Belief in Innate Sex Roles: Sex Stratification versus Interpersonal Influence in Marriage." *Journal of Marriage and the Family* 49:3 (August, 1987): 527–540.

Mnookin, R. J. "Child-Custody Adjudication: Judicial Functions in the Face of Indeterminacy." *Law and Contemporary Problems* 39 (1975): 226–292.

Moen, Phyllis. "Unemployment, Public Policy, and Families: Forecasts for the 1980s." *Journal of Marriage and the Family* (November 1983): 751–760.

Moen, Phyllis, and Donna Dempster-McClain. "Employed Parents: Role Strain, Work Time, and Preferences for Working Less." *Journal of Marriage and the Family* 49:3 (August 1987): 579–590.

Moffatt, Betty Clare, et al. *AIDS: A Self-Care Manual.* Los Angeles: IBS Press, 1987.

Moffatt, Michael. *Coming of Age in New Jersey: College and American Culture.* New Brunswick, N.J.: Rutgers University Press, 1989.

Mohr, James. *Abortion in America: Origins and Evolution of National Policy, 1800–1900.* New York: Oxford University Press, 1980.

Monahan, Thomas. "Are Interracial Marriages Really Less Stable?" *Social Forces* 48 (1970): 461–473.

Money, John. *Love and Lovesickness.* Baltimore: Johns Hopkins University Press, 1980.

Monroe, Pamela, and James Garland. "Parental Leave Legislation in the U. S. Senate: Toward a Model Roll-Call Voting." *Family Relations* 40:2 (April 1991): 208–218.

Montagu, Ashley. *Touching,* 3d ed. New York: Columbia University Press, 1986.

Moody, Kate. *Growing Up on Television.* New York: Times Books, 1980.

Moore, Denis. "Ministering to Everyone." *San Jose Mercury News,* July 21, 1990: 10E, 12E.

Moore, Dianne, and Pamela Erickson. "Age, Gender, and Ethnic Differences in Sexual and Contraceptive Knowledge, Attitudes, and Behaviors." *Family and Community Health* 8:3 (November 1985): 38–51.

Moore, Kristin, and Isabel Sawhill. "Implications of Women's Employment for Home and Family Life." In Juanita Kreps, ed., *Women and the American Economy.* Englewood Cliffs, N.J.: Prentice-Hall, 1976.

Moore, Lisa J. "Protecting Babies from Hepatitis-B." *U.S. News & World Report* (May 9, 1988): 85.

Morbidity and Mortality Weekly Reports. "Update: Acquired Immunodeficiency Syndrome—United States." 39:5 (February 9, 1990): 80–82.

Morgan, Carolyn, and Alexis Walker. "Predicting Sex Role Attitudes." *Social Psychology Quarterly* 46 (1983): 148–153.

Morgan, Edmund. *The Puritan Family.* New York: Harper & Row, 1966; 1st ed., 1944.

Morgan, Leslie. "Outcomes of Marital Separation: A Longitudinal Test of Predictors." *Journal of Marriage and the Family* 50 (May 1988): 493–498.

Morgan, S. Philip, Diane Lye, and Gretchen Condran. "Sons, Daughters, and the Risk of Marital Disruption." *American Journal of Sociology* 94 (1988): 110–129.

Morrison, Donna, and Daniel Lichter. "Family Migration and Female Employment: The Problem of Underemployment among Migrant Women." *Journal of Marriage and the Family* 50 (February 1988): 161–172.

Mosher, Donald. "Sex Guilt and Sex Myths in College Men and Women." *Journal of Sex Research* 15:3 (August 1979): 224–234.

Moss, Peter, et al. "Marital Relations During the Transition to Parenthood." *Journal of Reproductive and Infant Psychology* 4:1–2 (September 1986): 57–67.

Muehlenhard, Charlene. "Misinterpreted Dating Behaviors and the Risk of Date Rape." *Journal of Social and Clinical Psychology* 9:1 (1988): 20–37.

Mugford, Stephen, and Jim Lally. "Sex, Reported Happiness, and the Well-Being of Married Individuals." *Journal of Marriage and the Family* 43:4 (November 1981): 969–975.

Mullan, Bob. *The Mating Trade.* Boston: Routledge & Kegan Paul, 1984.

Murdock, George. *Social Structure.* New York: Free Press, 1965; 1st ed., 1949.

_____. "World Ethnographic Sample." *American Anthropologist* 59 (1957): 664–687.

Murray, Charles. *Losing Ground: American Social Policy, 1950–1980.* New York: Basic Books, 1984.

Murstein, Bernard. "A Clarification and Extension of the SVR Theory of Dyadic Pairing." *Journal of Marriage and the Family* 49 (1987): 929–933.

_____. *Who Will Marry Whom: Theories and Research in Marital Choice.* New York: Springer, 1976.

Musetto, Andrew. "Standards for Deciding Contested Child Custody." *Journal of Clinical Child Psychology* 10:1 (Spring 1981): 51–55.

Mydans, Seth. "U. S. Food Program Tightens Its Belt and Millions on Welfare Feel Pinch." *The New York Times,* June 2, 1990: 10.

_____. "Surrogate Loses Custody Bid in Case Defining Motherhood." *The New York Times,* October 23, 1990.

Myers-Walls, Judith, and Fred Piercy. "Mass Media and Prevention: Guidelines for Family Life Professionals." *Journal of Primary Prevention* 5:2 (Winter 1984): 124–136.

Nace, Edgar, et al. "Treatment Priorities in a Family-Oriented Alcoholism Program." *Journal of Marital and Family Therapy* (January 1982): 143–150.

Nadelson, Carol, and Maria Sauzier. "Intervention Programs for Individual Victims and Their Families." In Mary Lystad, ed., *Violence in the Home: Interdisciplinary Perspectives.* New York: Brunner/Mazel, 1986.

Napier, Augustus, and Carl Whitaker. *The Family Crucible.* New York: Harper & Row, 1978.

Nasaw, David. *Children of the City: At Work and Play.* New York: Basic Books, 1985.

National Academy of Sciences. *Homelessness, Health, and Human Needs.* Washington, D.C.: National Academy Press, 1988.

Needle, Richard, et al. "Drug Abuse: Adolescent Addictions and the Family." In Charles R. Figley and Hamilton McCubbin, eds., *Stress and the Family: Coping with Catastrophe.* Vol. 2. New York: Brunner/Mazel, 1983.

Nelsen, Jane. *Positive Discipline.* New York: Ballantine Books, 1987.

Nelson, Margaret, and Gordon Nelson. "Problems of Equity in the Reconstituted Family: a Social Exchange Analysis." *Family Relations* 31 (April 1982): 223–231.

"Neonatal Herpes Is Preventable." *USA Today* 112, February 1984:8–9.

Neuman, Judith. "Divorced Catholics." *San Jose Mercury News,* June 1, 1985: 1C.

Nevid, Jeffrey. "Sex Differences in Factors of Romantic Attraction." *Sex Roles* 11(5/6) (1984): 401–411.

Newcomb, Michael. "Cohabitation in America: An Assessment of Consequences." *Journal of Marriage and the Family* (August 1979): 597–603.

Newcomb, Michael, and Peter Bentler. "Assessment of Personality and Demographic Aspects of Cohabitation and Marital Success." *Journal of Personality Development* 4:1 (1980): 11–24.

Newcomer, Susan, and Richard Udry. "Oral Sex in an Adolescent Population." *Archives of Sexual Behavior* 14:1 (February 1985): 41–46.

Newton, Niles. *Maternal Emotions.* New York: Basic Books, 1955.

NiCarthy, Ginny. *Getting Free: A Handbook for Women in Abusive Relationships.* Seattle, Wash.: Seal Press, 1986.

NICHY (National Information Center for Children and Youth with Handicaps). *News Digest* 14 (October 1990): 1–12.

Noble, Elizabeth. *Having Your Baby by Donor Insemination.* Boston: Houghton Mifflin, 1987.

_____. "Prenatal Exercise." In Stanley E. Sagov et al., eds., *Home Birth: A Practitioner's Guide to Birth Outside the Hospital.* Rockville, Md.: Aspen, 1984.

Nobles, Wade W. "African-American Family Life: An Instrument of Culture." In Harriette Pipes McAdoo, ed., *Black Families,* 2d ed. Newbury Park, Calif.: Sage Publications, 1988.

Nock, Steven. "The Symbolic Meaning of Childbearing." *Journal of Family Issues* 8:4 (December, 1987): 373–393.

Noller, Patricia. *Nonverbal Communication and Marital Interaction.* Oxford, England: Pergamon Press, 1984.

Noller, Patricia, and Mary Anne Fitzpatrick. "Marital Communication." In Alan Booth, ed., *Contemporary Families: Looking Forward, Looking Back.* Minneapolis: National Council on Family Relations, 1991.

_____, eds. *Perspectives on Marital Interaction.* Philadelphia: Multilingual Matters, 1988.

Norton, Arthur J. "Family Life Cycle: 1980." *Journal of Marriage and the Family* 45 (1983): 267–275.

Norton, Arthur, and Jeanne Moorman. "Current Trends in American Marriage and Divorce." *Journal of Marriage and the Family* 49 (1987): 3–14.

Notarius, Clifford, and Jennifer Johnson. "Emotional Expression in Husbands and Wives." *Journal of Marriage and the Family* 44:2 (May 1982): 483–489.

Notman, Malkah T., and Eva P. Lester. "Pregnancy: Theoretical Considerations." *Psychoanalytic Inquiry* 8:2 (1988): 139–159.

Notzon, Francis C., Paul J. Placek, and Selma M. Taffel. "Comparisons of National Cesarean-Section Rates." *New England Journal of Medicine* 316:7 (February 12, 1987): 386–389.

Nye, F. Ivan. "Fifty Years of Family Research." *Journal of Marriage and the Family* 50 (May 1988): 305–316.

_____. *Role Structure and Analysis of the Family.* Beverly Hills, Calif.: Sage Publications, 1976.

Nye, F. Ivan, and Felix Berardo, eds. *Emerging Conceptual Frameworks in Family Analysis.* 2 vols. New York: Praeger, 1981.

Nyquist, Linda, et al. "Household Responsibilities in Middle–Class Couples: The Contribution of Demographic and Personality Variables." *Sex Roles* 12(1/2) (1985): 15–34.

Oakley, Ann. *Sex, Gender, and Society,* rev. ed. New York: Harper and Row, 1985.

Odent, Michel. *Birth Reborn.* New York: Pantheon, 1984.

O'Flaherty, Kathleen, and Laura Eells. "Courtship Behavior of the Remarried." *Journal of Marriage and the Family* 50 (May 1988): 499–506.

Olds, David L., Charles Henderson, Jr., Robert Chamberlin, and Robert Tatelbaum. "Preventing Child Abuse and Neglect: A Randomized Trial of Nurse Home Visitation." *Pediatrics* 78 (July 1986): 65–78.

Olson, David. "Insiders' and Outsiders' Views of Relationships: Research Studies." In George Levinger and H. Rausch, eds., *Close Relations.* Amherst, Mass.: University of Massachusetts Press, 1977.

Olson, David H., et al. *Families.* Beverly Hills, Calif.: Sage Publications, 1983.

O'Reilly, Jane. "Wife Beating: The Silent Crime." *Time* (September 5, 1983).

Orlofsky, Jacob, and Connie O'Heron. "Stereotypic and Nonstereotypic Sex Role Trait and Behavior Orientations: Implications for Personal Adjustment." *Journal of Personality and Social Psychology* 52 (May, 1987): 1034–1042.

Orthner, D. K., and J. F. Pittman. "Family Contributions to Work Commitment." *Journal of Marriage and the Family* 48 (1986): 573–581.

Ortiz, Vilma, and Rosemary Santana Cooney. "Sex Role Attitudes and Labor Force Participation among Young Hispanic Females and Non-Hispanic White Females." *Social Science Quarterly* 65:2 (June 1984): 392–400.

Oster, Sharon. "A Note on the Determinants of Alimony." *Journal of Marriage and the Family* 49 (February 1987): 81–86.

Otto, Luther. "America's Youth: A Changing Profile." *Family Relations* 37:4 (October 1988): 385–391.

Pallow-Fleury, Angie. "Your Hospital Birth: Questions to Ask." *Mothering* (Winter 1983): 83–85.

Panuthos, Claudia, and Catherine Romeo. *Ended Beginnings: Healing Childbearing Losses.* New York: Warner Books, 1984.

Papp, Peggy. *The Process of Change.* New York: Guilford Press, 1983.

Parachini, Allen. "Breast-Feeding: Once on the Rise, Is Slowing." *Los Angeles Times,* December 20, 1985.

_____. "Condom Study Finding Wide Differences Among Brands." *Los Angeles Times,* June 29, 1988: V1, 3.

Pareles, Jon. "Indians' Heritage Survives in Songs." *The New York Times,* December 4, 1990: B1ff.

Parker, Hilda, and Seymour Parker. "Cultural Rules, Rituals and Behavior Regulation." *American Anthropologist* 86:3 (1984): 584–600.

_____. "Father–Daughter Sexual Child Abuse: An Emerging Perspective." *American Journal of Orthopsychiatry* 56:4 (October 1986): 531–549.

Parker, Philip. "Motivation of Surrogate Mothers—Initial Findings." *American Journal of Psychiatry* 140:1 (1983): 117–118.

Parr, Jay. *Childhood and Family in Canadian History.* Toronto: McClelland and Steward, 1982.

Parrot, Andrea, and Michael Ellis. "Homosexuals Should Be Allowed to Marry and Adopt or Rear Children." In Harold Feldman and Margaret Feldman, eds., *Current Controversies in Marriage and the Family.* Beverly Hills, Calif.: Sage Publications, 1985.

Parsons, Jacqueline. "Sexual Socialization and Gender Roles in Childhood." In Elizabeth Allgeier and Naomi McCormick, eds. *Gender Roles and Sexual Behavior.* Palo Alto, Calif.: Mayfield, 1982.

_____, ed. *The Psychobiology of Sex Differences and Sex Roles.* Washington, D.C.: Hemisphere, 1980.

Parsons, Talcott. "Family Structure and the Socialization of the Child." In T. Parsons and R. F. Bales, eds., *Family Socialization and Interaction Process.* Glencoe, Ill.: Free Press, 1955.

Parsons, Talcott, and R. F. Bales. *Family Socialization and Interaction Processes.* Glencoe, Ill.: Free Press, 1955.

Pasley, Kay. "Family Boundary Ambiguity: Perceptions of Adult Stepfamily Family Members." In Kay Pasley and Marilyn Ihinger-Tallman, eds., *Remarriage and Stepparenting: Current Research and Theory.* New York: Guilford Press, 1987.

Pasley, Kay, and Marilyn Ihinger-Tallman, eds. *Remarriage and Stepparenting: Current Research and Theory.,* New York: Guilford Press, 1987.

Patterson, G. *Families: Applications of Social Learning to Family Life.* Champaign, Ill.: Research Press, 1971.

Patterson, Joan, and Hamilton McCubbin. "Chronic Illness: Family Stress and Coping." In Charles R. Figley and Hamilton McCubbin, eds., *Stress and the Family: Coping with Catastrophe,* Vol. Two. New York: Brunner/Mazel, 1983.

Paul, W., J. Weinrich, J. Gonsiorek, and M. Hotvedt, eds. *Homosexuality: Social, Psychological, and Biological Issues.* Newbury Park, Calif.: Sage Publications, 1982.

Paulson, David. "Hot Tubs and Reduced Sperm Counts." *Medical Aspects of Human Sexuality* 14 (September 1980): 121.

Paulson, Morris J., Robert H. Coombs, and John Landsverk. "Youth Who Physically Assault Their Parents." *Journal of Family Violence* 5:2 (June 1990): 121–134.

Payton, Isabelle. "Single-Parent Households: An Alternative Approach." *Family Economics Review* (Winter 1982): 11–16.

Pear, Robert. "Rich Got Richer in 80's; Others Held Even." *The New York Times,* January 11, 1991: A1, A11.

_____. "U. S. Reports Poverty Is Down but Inequality Is Up." *The New York Times,* September 27, 1990: A12.

_____. "What Causes the High U.S. Rate of Infant Deaths?" *The New York Times,* March 20, 1985: 19.

Pearson, Jessica, et al. "Legal Change and Child Custody Awards." *Journal of Family Issues* 3:3 (March 1982): 5–24.

Pedhazur, E. J., and T. J. Tetenbaum. "Bem's Sex Role Inventory: A Theoretical and Methodological Critique." *Journal of Personality and Social Psychology* 37 (1979): 996–1016.

Peirce, Kate. "Sex Role Stereotyping of Children: A Content Analysis of the Roles and Attributes of Child Characters." *Sociological Spectrum* 9:3 (Fall 1989): 321–328.

Peek, Charles, et al. "Teenage Violence Toward Parents: A Neglected Dimension in Family Violence." *Journal of Marriage and the Family* 47:4 (November 1985): 1051–1058.

Pennington, Saralie Bisnovich. "Children of Lesbian Mothers." In Frederick W. Bozett, ed., *Gay and Lesbian Parents.* New York: Praeger, 1987.

Peplau, Letitia. "Research on Homosexual Couples." In John DeCecco, ed., *Gay Relationships.* New York: Haworth Press, 1988.

_____. "What Homosexuals Want." *Psychology Today* 15:3 (March 1981): 28–38.

Peplau, Letitia, and Steven Gordon. "The Intimate Relationships of Lesbians and Gay Men." In Elizabeth Allgeier and Naomi McCormick, eds., *Gender Roles and Sexual Behavior.* Palo Alto, Calif.: Mayfield, 1982.

Peplau, Letitia, et al. "Sexual Intimacy in Dating Relationships." *Journal of Social Issues* 33:2 (Spring 1977): 86–109.

Perlman, Daniel, and Steve Duck, eds. *Intimate Relationships: Development, Dynamics, and Deterioration.* Beverly Hills, Calif.: Sage Publications, 1987.

Perlman, David. "Brave New Babies." *San Francisco Chronicle,* March 5, 1990: B3ff.

Perry-Jenkins, Maureen. "Future Directions for Research on Dual-Earner Families: A Young Professional's Perspective." *Family Relations* 37:2 (April 1988): 226–228.

Peters, Stefanie, et al. "Prevalence." In David Finkelhor, ed., *Sourcebook on Child Sexual Abuse.* Beverly Hills, Calif.: Sage Publications, 1986.

Petersen, Larry. "Interfaith Marriage and Religious Commitment among Catholics." *Journal of Marriage and the Family* 48 (November 1986): 725–735.

Peterson, Gary W., and Boyd C. Rollins. "Parent-Child Socialization." In Marvin B. Sussman and Suzanne K. Steinmetz, eds., *Handbook of Marriage and the Family.* New York: Plenum Press, 1987.

Peterson, James R., et al. "Playboy's Readers' Sex Survey." *Playboy* (March, 1983).

Peterson, Marie Ferguson. "Racial Socialization of Young Black Children." In Harriette Pipes McAdoo and John McAdoo, eds., *Black Children: Social, Educational, and Parental Environments.* Beverly Hills, Calif.: Sage Publications, 1985.

Petit, Charles. "New Study to Ask Why So Many Infants Die." *San Francisco Chronicle,* May 9, 1990: A3.

Petit, Ellen, and Bernard Bloom. "Whose Decision Was It? The Effect of Initiator Status on Adjustment to Marital Disruption." *Journal of Marriage and the Family* 46:3 (August 1984): 587–595.

Peyrot, Mark, et al. "Marital Adjustment to Adult Diabetes: Interpersonal Congruence and Spouse Satisfaction." *Journal of Marriage and the Family* 50 (May 1988): 363–376.

Pies, Cheri. "Considering Parenthood: Psychological Issues for Gay Men and Lesbians Choosing Alternative Fertilization." In Frederick W. Bozett, ed., *Gay and Lesbian Parents.* New York: Praeger, 1987.

Pilisuk, Marc. "The Delivery of Social Support: The Social Innoculation." *American Journal of Orthopsychiatry* 52:1 (January 1982): 20–31.

Pill, Cynthia. "Stepfamilies: Redefining the Family." *Family Relations* 39:2 (April 1990): 186–193.

Pillemer, Karl. "The Dangers of Dependency: New Findings on Domestic Violence Against the Elderly." *Social Problems* 33 (1985): 146–158.

Pillemer, Karl, and J. Jill Suitor. "Elder Abuse." In Vincent B. Van Hasselt et al., eds., *Handbook of Family Violence.* New York: Plenum Press, 1988.

Pink, Jo Ellen, and Karen Smith Wampler. "Problem Areas in Stepfamilies: Cohesion, Adaptability, and the Stepfather-Adolescent Relationship." *Family Relations* 34:3 (July 1985): 327–335.

Piotrkowski, Chaya. *Work and the Family System*. New York: Free Press, 1979.

_____, et al. "Families and Work." In Marvin Sussman and Suzanne Steinmetz, eds., *Handbook of Marriage and the Family*. New York: Plenum Press, 1987.

Pirog-Good, Maureen A., and Jan E. Stets, eds. *Violence in Dating Relationships: Emerging Social Issues*. New York: Praeger, 1989.

Pivan, Frances Fox, and Richard Cloward. *Regulating the Poor*. New York: Vintage Books, 1972.

Pleck, Joseph. *The Myth of Masculinity*. New York: Norton, 1981.

_____. *Working Wives/Working Husbands*. Beverly Hills, Calif.: Sage Publications, 1985.

_____, et al. "Conflicts Between Work and Family Life." *Monthly Labor Review* 103:3 (1980): 29–32. U.S. Department of Labor, Bureau of Labor Statistics.

Plummer, K., ed. *The Making of the Modern Homosexual*. Totowa, N.J.: Barnes and Noble, 1981.

Plummer, William, and Margaret Nelson. "A Mother's Priceless Gift." *People Weekly* (August 26, 1991).

Pogatchnik, Shawn. "Kids' TV Gets More Violent, Study Finds." *Los Angeles Times,* January 26, 1990: F1, F27.

_____. "7000 Hate Crimes on Gays Reported in 1989." *Los Angeles Times,* June 8, 1990: A2.

Pogrebin, Letty Cottin. "Are Men Discovering the Joys of Fatherhood?" *Ms.* (February 1982): 41–46.

_____. *Family Politics*. New York: McGraw-Hill, 1983.

_____. *Growing Up Free: Raising Your Child in the 1980s*. New York: McGraw-Hill, 1980.

Pollis, Carol. "An Assessment of the Impacts of Feminism on Sexual Science." *Journal of Sex Research* 25:1 (February, 1988): 85–105.

_____. "Value Judgments and World Views in Sexuality Education." *Family Relations* 34 (April 1985): 285–290.

Porter, Nancy L., and F. Scott Christopher. "Infertility: Towards An Awareness of a Need Among Family Life Practitioners." *Family Relations* 33 (April 1984): 309–315.

Postman, Neil. *Amusing Ourselves to Death*. New York: Penguin, 1986.

Poussaint, Alvin. "What Every Black Woman Should Know about Black Men." *Ebony* 37 (August, 1982): 36–40.

Pratt, Clara, and Vicki Schmall. "College Students' Attitudes toward Elderly Sexual Behavior: Implications for Family Life Education." *Family Relations* 38 (April 1989): 137–141.

Press, Robert. "Hunger in America." *Christian Science Monitor,* February 15, 1985: 18–19.

Presser, Harriet. "Some Economic Complexities of Child Care Provided by Grandmothers." *Journal of Marriage and the Family* 51:3 (August 1989): 581–591.

_____. "Shift Work Among American Women and Child Care." *Journal of Marriage and the Family* 48 (August 1986): 551–663.

Price, J. H., and P. A. Miller. "Sexual Fantasies of Black and White College Students." *Psychological Reports* 54 (1984): 1007–1014.

Price, Jane. "Who Waits to Have Children? And Why?" In Jeffrey Rosenfeld, ed., *Relationships: The Marriage and Family Reader*. Glenview, Ill.: Scott, Foresman, 1982.

Price, John. "North American Indian Families." In Charles Mindel and Robert Habenstein, eds. *Ethnic Families in America: Patterns and Variations,* 2d ed. New York: Elsevier North Holland, Inc., 1981.

Price-Bonham, S., and J. O. Balswick. "The Noninstitutions: Divorce, Desertion, and Remarriage." *Journal of Marriage and the Family* 42 (1980): 959–972.

Prober, Charles, et al. "Low Risk of Herpes Simplex Virus Infections in Neonates Exposed to the Virus at the Time of Vaginal Delivery to Mothers with Recurrent Genital Herpes Simplex Virus Infections." *New England Journal of Medicine* 316 (January 29, 1987): 129–138.

Pruett, Kyle. *The Nurturing Father: Journey Toward the Complete Man*. New York: Warner Books, 1987.

Puglisi, J. T., and D. W. Jackson. "Sex Role Identity and Self-Esteem in Adulthood." *Journal of Aging and Human Development* 12 (1981): 129–138.

Raabe, Phyllis, and John Gessner. "Employer Family-Supportive Policies: Diverse Variations on the Theme." *Family Relations* 37 (April 1988): 196–202.

Ralebipi, Matabole D. Rocky. "Family Resource Database: Single Parents and Child Care [Bibliography]." *Family Relations* 38 (October 1989): 474–475.

_____. "Family Resource Database: Fathers and Child Care [Bibliography]." *Family Relations* 38 (October 1989): 475–476.

Ramsey, Patricia G. *Teaching and Learning in a Diverse World: Multicultural Education for Young Children*. New York: Teachers College Press, 1987.

Rando, Therese A. "Death and Dying Are Not and Should Not Be Taboo Topics." In Austin H. Kutscher et al., eds., *Principles of Thanatology*. New York: Columbia University Press, 1987.

Rapp, Gail, and Sally Lloyd. "The Role of 'Home as Haven' Ideology in Child Care Use." *Family Relations* 38 (October 1989): 427–430.

Raschke, Helen. "Divorce." In Marvin Sussman and Suzanne Steinmetz, eds., *Handbook of Marriage and the Family*. New York: Plenum Press, 1987.

Raval, H., et al. "The Impact of Infertility on Emotions and the Marital and Sexual Relationship." *Journal of Reproductive and Infant Psychology* 5:4 (October–December 1987): 221–234.

Raven, Bertram, et al. "The Bases of Conjugal Power." In Ronald Cromwell and David Olson, eds. *Power in Families*. New York: Halstead Press, 1975.

Ravinder, Shashi. "Androgyny: Is It Really the Product of Educated Middle-Class Western Societies?" *Journal of Cross Cultural Psychology* 18:2 (June 1987): 208–220.

Rawlings, Steve. "Families Maintained by Female Householders, 1970–1979." Bureau of the Census. *Current Population Reports.* Special Studies, Series P23, No. 107. Washington, D.C.: U. S. Government Printing Office, 1980.

_____. "Household and Family Characteristics: March 1983." U. S. Bureau of the Census. *Current Population Reports.* Series P-20, No. 388. Washington, D.C.: U. S. Government Printing Office, 1984.

_____. "Studies in Marriage and the Family: Single Parents and Their Children." Bureau of the Census. *Current Population Reports.* Special Studies, Series P-23, No.162, Washington, D.C.: U. S. Government Printing Office, 1989.

Reamy, Kenneth, and Susan White. "Sexuality in the Puerperium: A Review." *Archives of Sexual Behavior* 16:2 (1987): 165–187.

Rebelsky, F., and C. Hanks. "Fathers' Verbal Interaction with Infants in the First Three Months of Life." *Child Development* 42 (1971): 63–68.

Reed, David, and Martin Weinberg. "Premarital Coitus: Developing and Established Sexual Scripts." *Social Psychology Quarterly* 47:2 (June 1984): 129–138.

Reedy, M., et al. "Age and Sex Differences in Satisfying Love Relationships across the Adult Life Span." *Human Development* 24 (1981): 52–86.

Regan, Mary, and Helen Roland. "Rearranging Family and Career Priorities: Professional Women and Men of the Eighties." *Journal of Marriage and the Family* 47:4 (November 1985): 985–992.

Regan, Riley. "Alcohol Problems and Family Violence." In Jerry Flanzer, ed. *The Many Faces of Family Violence*. Springfield, Ill.: Charles C. Thomas, 1982.

Reid, Pamela, and L. Comas-Diaz. "Gender and Ethnicity: Perspectives on Dual Status." *Sex Roles* 22:7–8 (April 1990): 397–408.

Reinhold, Robert. "State of the States, 1991: Rocky, Almost Everywhere." *The New York Times,* January 14, 1991: A12.

Reiss, David. "Commentary: The Social Construction of Reality—The Passion Within Us All." *Family Process* 24:2 (June 1985): 254–257.

_____. *The Family's Construction of Reality.* Cambridge, Mass.: Harvard Press, 1981.

Reiss, Ira. *Family Systems in America,* 3d ed. New York: Holt, Rinehart, and Winston, 1980.

_____. *The Social Context of Premarital Sexual Permissiveness.* New York: Irvington, 1967.

_____, et al. *Journey into Sexuality: An Exploratory Voyage.* Inglewood Cliffs, N.J.: Prentice–Hall, 1986.

_____."A Multivariate Model of the Determinants of Extramarital Sexual Permissiveness." *Journal of Marriage and the Family* 42 (May 1980): 395–411.

Resnick, Sandven. "Informal Adoption among Black Adolescent Mothers." *American Journal of Orthopsychiatry* 60 (April 1990): 210–224.

Retik, Alan B., and Stuart B. Bauer. "Infertility Related to DES Exposure in Utero: Reproductive Problems in the Male." In Miriam Mazor and Harriet Simons, eds., *Infertility: Medical, Emotional, and Social Considerations.* New York: Human Sciences Press, 1984.

Rettig, K. D., and M. M. Bubolz. "Interpersonal Resource Exchanges as Indicators of Quality of Marriage." *Journal of Marriage and the Family* 45 (1983): 497–510.

Rexroat, Cynthia. "Race and Marital Status Differences in the Labor Force Behavior of Female Family Heads: The Effect of Household Structure." *Journal of Marriage and the Family* 52:3 (August 1990): 591–601.

_____. "Women's Work Expectations and Labor-Market Experiences in Early and Middle Life-Cycle Stages. *Journal of Marriage and the Family* 47:1 (February 1985): 131–142.

Rexroat, Cynthia, and Constance Shehan. "The Family Life Cycle and Spouses Time in Housework." *Journal of Marriage and the Family* 49 (November 1987): 737–750.

Rice, Susan. "Sexuality and Intimacy for Aging Women: A Changing Perspective." *Journal of Women and Aging* 1:1–3 (1989): 245–264.

Rich, Adrienne. "Compulsory Heterosexuality and Lesbian Existence." In Ann Snitow et al., eds., *Powers of Desire: The Politics of Sexuality.* New York: Monthly Review Press, 1983.

_____. *Of Woman Born.* New York: Norton, 1976.

Richardson, B.B. "Racism and Child-Rearing: A Study of Black Mothers." *Dissertation Abstracts* 42(1) (1981): 125–A.

Richardson, Diana. "The Dilemma of Essentiality in Homosexual Theory." *Journal of Homosexuality* 9:2–3 (Winter 1983/Spring 1984): 79–90.

Riegle, Donald. "The Psychological and Social Effects of Unemployment." *American Psychologist* 37(10) (October 1982): 1113–1115.

Riffer, Roger, and Jeffrey Chin. "Dating Satisfaction among College Students." *International Journal of Sociology and Social Policy* 8:5 (1988): 29–36.

Riportella-Muller, Roberta. "Sexuality in the Elderly: A Review." In Kathleen McKinney and Susan Sprecher, eds., *Human Sexuality: The Societal and Interpersonal Context.* Norwood, N.J.: Ablex Publishing Corporation, 1989.

Rist, Marilee C. "Crack Babies in School." *The American School Board Journal* CLVXXVI (January 1990): 19–24.

Rivlin, Leanne. "The Significance of Home and Homelessness." *Marriage and Family Review* 15:1/2 (1990): 39–57.

Robbins, Tom. *Still Life with Woodpecker.* New York: Bantam, 1980.

Roberts, Elizabeth. "Television and Sexual Learning in Childhood." In National Institute of Mental Health, *Television and Behavior.* Washington, D.C.: Government Printing Office, 1982:209–223.

Roberts, Linda, and Lowell Krokoff. "A Time Series Analysis of Withdrawal, Hostility, and Displeasure in Satisfied and Dissatisfied Marriages." *Journal of Marriage and the Family* 52:1 (February 1990): 95–105.

Roberts, Sam. "The Hunger Beneath the Statistics." *The New York Times,* May 23, 1988: A13.

Robertson, Elizabeth, et al. "The Costs and Benefits of Social Support in Families." *Journal of Marriage and the Family* 53:2 (May 1991): 403–416.

Robinson, Paul. *The Modernization of Sex.* New York: Harper & Row, 1976.

Robinson, Pauline. "The Sociological Perspective." In Ruth Weg, ed., *Sexuality in the Later Years: Roles and Behavior.* New York: Academic Press, 1983.

Rodgers, Roy, and L. Conrad. "Courtship for Remarriage: Influences on Family Reorganization after Divorce." *Journal of Marriage and the Family* 48 (1986): 767–775.

Rodman, Hyman, and Cynthia Cole. "When School-Age Children Care for Themselves: Issues for Family Life Educators and Parents." *Family Relations* 36 (January 1987): 92–96.

Roen, Philip. *Male Sexual Health.* New York: William Morrow and Co., 1974.

Rollins, B. C., and K. L. Cannon. "Marital Satisfaction over the Family Life Cycle: A Reevaluation." *Journal of Marriage and the Family* 36 (May 1974): 271–282.

Rollins, B. C., and H. Feldman. "Marital Satisfaction over the Family Life Cycle." *Journal of Marriage and the Marriage and the Family* 32 (February 1970): 20–28.

Romberg, Rosemary. *Circumcision: The Painful Dilemma.* South Hadley, Mass.: Bergin and Garvey, 1985.

Rooks, J., et al. "Outcomes of Care in Birth Centers." *New England Journal of Medicine* 321 (1989): 1804–1811.

Roopnarine, Jaipaul, Nina Mounts, and Glendon Casto. "Mothers' Perceptions of Their Children's Supplemental Care Experience: Correlation with Spousal Relationship." *American Journal of Orthopsychiatry* 56:4 (October 1986): 581–588.

Roos, Patricia, and Lawrence Cohen. "Sex Roles and Social Support as Moderators of Life Stress Adjustment." *Journal of Personality and Social Psychology* 52:3 (March, 1987): 576–585.

Roscoe, Bruce, and Nancy Benaske. "Courtship Violence Experienced by Abused Wives: Similarities in Patterns of Abuse." *Family Relations* 34:3 (July 1985): 419–424.

Rosenbaum, David. "Jobless Aid Dries Up as Recession Looms." *San Francisco Chronicle,* December 3, 1990: 2.

Rosenblatt, Paul, and Roxanne Anderson. "Human Sexuality in Cross-Cultural Perspective." In Mark Cook, ed., *The Bases of Human Sexual Attraction.* New York: Academic Press, 1981.

Rosenfeld, Alvin. "Sexual Misuse and the Family." *Victimology: An International Journal* 2:2 (Summer 1977): 226–235.

Rosenfeld, Alvin, and Eli Newberger. "Compassion vs. Control: Conceptual and Practical Pitfalls in the Broadened Definition of Child Abuse." In Richard Bourne and Eli Newberger, eds., *Critical Perspectives on Child Abuse.* Lexington, Mass.: Lexington Books, 1979.

Rosenkrantz, D., et al. "Sex Role Stereotypes and Self Concepts in College Students." *Journal of Consulting and Clinical Psychology* 32 (1968): 287–295.

Rosenthal, Carolyn. "Kinkeeping in the Familial Division of Labor." *Journal of Marriage and the Family* 47:4 (November 1985): 965–947.

Rosenthal, Elisabeth. "When a Pregnant Woman Drinks." *The New York Times Magazine,* February 4, 1990: 30ff.

Rosenzweig, Julie, and Dennis Daily. "Dyadic Adjustment/Sexual Satisfaction in Women and Men as a Function of Psychological Sex Role Self-Perception." *Journal of Sex and Marital Therapy* 15: (Spring 1989): 42–56.

Ross, Catherine, John Mirowsky, and Karen Goldsteen. "The Impact of the Family on Health." In Alan Booth, ed., *Contemporary Families: Looking Forward, Looking Back*. Minneapolis: National Council on Family Relations, 1991.

Ross, H. L. "Modes of Adjustment of Married Homosexuals." *Social Problems* 18 (1978): 385–393.

_____. "Odd Couples: Homosexuals in Heterosexual Marriage." *Sexual Behavior* 2 (1972): 42–49.

Ross, L., et al. "Television Viewing and Adult Sex-Role Attitudes." *Sex Roles* 8 (1982): 589–592.

Rossi, Alice. "Transition to Parenthood." *Journal of Marriage and the Family* 30 (February 1968): 26–39.

Rowland, Robyn. "Technology and Motherhood: Reproductive Choice Reconsidered." *Signs: Journal of Women in Culture and Society* 12:3 (1987): 512–528.

Rubenstein, C. "Wellness Is All." *Psychology Today* (October 1982): 27–37.

Rubenstein, Carin, and Carol Tavris. "Special Survey Results: 26,000 Women Reveal the Secrets of Intimacy." *Redbook* 159 (September 1987): 147–149*ff*.

Rubin, A. M., and J. R. Adams. "Outcomes of Sexually Open Marriages." *Journal of Sex Research* 22 (1986): 311–319.

Rubin, Lillian. *Erotic Wars*. New York: Farrar, Straus, and Giroux, 1990.

_____. *Intimate Strangers*. New York: Harper & Row, 1983.

_____. *Worlds of Pain*. New York: Basic Books, 1976.

Rubin, Nora Jean. *How to Care for Your Parents: A Handbook for Adult Children*. Washington, D.C.: Storm King Press, 1987.

Rubin, Zick. Introduction to Robert Sternberg and Michael Barnes, eds., *The Psychology of Love*. New Haven, Conn.: Yale University Press, 1988.

_____. *Liking and Loving: An Invitation to Social Psychology*. New York: Holt, Rinehart, and Winston, 1973.

_____. "Loving and Leaving: Sex Differences in Romantic Attachments." *Sex Roles* 7 (1981): 821–835.

_____. "Self Disclosure in Dating Relationships: Sex Roles and the Ethic of Openness." *Journal of Marriage and the Family* 42 (1980): 305–317.

_____, et al. "The Eye of the Beholder: Parents' View of Sex of Newborn." *American Journal of Orthopsychiatry* 44 (Fall 1974): 512–519.

Runyan, William. "In Defense of the Case Study Method." *American Journal of Orthopsychiatry* 52:3 (July 1982): 440–446.

Rush, D., et al. "The National WIC Evaluation." *American Journal of Clinical Nutrition* 48:2 (Suppl.) (August 1988): 439–483.

Russell, C. "Transition to Parenthood." *Journal of Marriage and the Family* 36 (May 1974): 294–302.

Russell, Diana E. H. *Rape in Marriage*, rev. ed. Bloomington, Ind.: Indiana University Press, 1982, 1990.

_____. *The Secret Trauma: Incest in the Lives of Girls and Women*. New York: Basic Books, 1986.

_____. *Sexual Exploitation: Rape, Child Sexual Abuse, and Workplace Harassment*. Beverly Hills, Calif.: Sage Publications, 1984.

Sabatelli, Ronald, and Erin Cecil–Pigo. "Relational Interdependence and Commitment in Marriage." *Journal of Marriage and the Family* 47:4 (November 1985): 931–938.

Safilios-Rothschild, Constantina. "Family Sociology or Wives' Sociology? A Cross-Cultural Examination of Decisionmaking." *Journal of Marriage and the Family* 31 (May 1969): 290–301.

_____. *Love, Sex, and Sex Roles*. Englewood Cliffs, N.J.: Prentice-Hall, 1977.

_____. "A Macro- and Micro-Examination of Family Power and Love: An Exchange Model. *Journal of Marriage and the Family* 38 (1976): 355–362.

_____. "The Study of the Family Power Structure." *Journal of Marriage and the Family* 32 (November 1970): 539–543.

_____, ed. *Toward a Sociology of Women*. Lexington, Mass.: Xerox, 1972.

Salgado de Snyder, V. Nelly, Richard Cervantes, and Amado Padilla. "Gender and Ethnic Differences in Psychosocial Stress and Generalized Distress among Hispanics." *Sex Roles* 22:7–8 (April 1990): 441–453.

Salholz, Eloise. "The Future of Gay America." *Newsweek* (March 12, 1990): 20–25.

Saluter, Arlene. "Marital Status and Living Arrangements: March 1989." Bureau of the Census. *Current Population Reports.* "Population Characteristics." Series P-20, No. 445. Washington, D.C.: U. S. Government Printing Office, 1991.

_____. "Singleness in America." Bureau of the Census. *Current Population Reports.* "Special Studies." Series P-23, No. 162. Washington, D.C.: U. S. Government Printing Office, 1989.

Sampson, Ronald. *The Problem of Power*. New York: Pantheon Books, 1966.

Samuels, Michael, and Nancy Samuels. *The Well Pregnancy Book*. New York: Summit Books, 1986.

Samuels, Shirley. *Ideal Adoption: A Comprehensive Guide to Forming an Adoptive Family*. New York: Insight Books, 1990.

Samuelson, Robert. "Childcare Revisited." *Newsweek* (August 8, 1988): 53.

Sánchez-Ayéndez, Melba. "The Puerto Rican American Family." In Charles Mindel, Robert Habenstein, and Roosevelt Wright, Jr., eds., *Ethnic Families in America: Patterns and Variations,* 3d ed. New York: Elsevier North Holland, Inc., 1988.

Santrock, John. *Life-Span Development*. Dubuque, Iowa: William C. Brown. 1983.

Santrock, John, and Karen Sitterle. "Parent-Child Relationships in Stepmother Families." In Kay Pasley and Marilyn Ihinger-Tallman, eds., *Remarriage and Stepparenting: Current Research and Theory*. New York: Guilford Press, 1987.

Santrock, John, and Richard Warsack. "Father Custody and Social Development in Boys and Girls." *Journal of Social Issues* 35:4 (1979): 112–125.

Satir, Virginia. *Conjoint Family Therapy*. Palo Alto, Calif.: Science and Behavior Books, 1967.

_____. *The New Peoplemaking,* rev. ed. Mountain View, Calif.: Science and Behavior Books, 1988.

Saunders, Daniel. "When Battered Women Use Violence: Husband-Abuse or Self-Defense." *Victim and Violence* 1:1 (1986): 47–60.

Scales, Peter. "Sex in Politics and Policy." *Marriage and Family Review* 6:3–4 (Fall/Winter 1983): 47–59.

Scanzoni, John. "Reconsidering Family Policy: Status Quo or Force for Change?" *Journal of Family Issues* 3:3 (September 1982): 277–300.

_____. *Sexual Bargaining*. Englewood Cliffs, N.J.: Prentice-Hall, Inc., 1980, 2d ed.

_____. "Social Processes and Power in Families." In W. Burr et al., eds. *Contemporary Theories about the Family,* Vol. 1. New York: Free Press, 1979.

Scanzoni, John, Karen Polonko, Jay Teachman, and Linda Thompson. *The Sexual Bond: Rethinking Families and Close Relationships*. Newbury Park, Calif.: Sage Publications, 1989.

Schaap, Cas, Bram Buunk, and Ada Kerkstra. "Marital Conflict Resolutions." In Patricia Noller and Mary Anne Fitzpatrick, eds., *Perspectives on Marital Interaction*. Philadelphia: Multilingual Matters, 1988.

Schlesinger, Benjamin. *Canadian Family Studies: A Selected, Annotated Bibliography*. Chicago: CPL Bibliographies, 1983.

Schmitt, Bernard, and Robert Millard. "Construct Validity of the Bem Sex Role Inventory: Does the BSRI Distinguish between Gender-Schematic and Gender Aschematic Individuals?" *Sex Roles* 19:9–10 (November 1988): 581–588.

Schneck, M. E., et al. "Low-Income Adolescents and Their Infants: Dietary Findings and Health Outcomes." *Journal of the American Dietetic Association* 90:4 (April 1990): 555–558.

Schneider, David. *American Kinship: A Cultural Account,* 2d ed. Chicago: University of Chicago Press, 1980.

Schneider, Peter. "Lost Innocents: The Myth of Missing Children." *Harper's Magazine* (February, 1987): 47–53.

Schooler, Carmi, et al. "Work for the Household: Its Nature and Consequences for Husbands and Wives." *American Journal of Sociology* 90:1 (July 1984): 97–124.

_____. "Psychological Effects of Complex Environments During the Life Span: A Review and Theory." In Carmi Schooler and K. Warner Schaie, eds., *Cognitive Functioning and Social Structure over the Life Course.* Norwood, N.J.: Ablex, 1987.

Schooler, Carmi, and K. Warner Schaie, eds. *Cognitive Functioning and Social Structure over the Life Course.* Norwood, N.J.: Ablex, 1987.

Schumm, Walter. "Marriage and Parenthood Are Necessary for a Happy Life for Both Men and Women." In H. Feldman and M. Feldman, eds., *Current Controversies in Marriage and the Family.* Beverly Hills, Calif.: Sage, 1985.

_____, et al. "His and Her Marriage Revisited." *Journal of Family Issues* 6 (June 1985): 211–227.

Schvaneveldt, Jay. "The Interactional Framework in the Study of the Family." In F. Ivan Nye and Felix Berardo, eds., *Emerging Conceptual Frameworks in Family Analysis,* 2d ed. New York: Praeger, 1981.

Schvaneveldt, Jay, Shelley Lindauer, and Margaret Young. "Children's Understanding of AIDS: A Developmental Viewpoint." *Family Relations* 39:3 (July 1990): 330–335.

Schwebel, Andrew, Mark Fine, and Maureena Renner. "A Study of Perceptions of the Stepparent Role." *Journal of Family Issues* 23:1 (March 1991): 43–57.

Scott, Clarissa, Lydia Shifman, Lavenda Orr, and Roger Owen. "Hispanic and Black American Adolescents' Beliefs Relating to Sexuality and Contraception." *Adolescence* 23:91 (Fall 1988): 667–688.

Scott, David, and Bernard Wishy, eds. *America's Families: A Documentary History.* New York: Harper & Row, 1982.

Scott, Jacqueline. "Conflicting Beliefs about Abortion: Legal Approval and Moral Doubts." *Social Psychology Quarterly* 52:4 (December 1989): 319–328.

Scott, Jacqueline, and Duane F. Alwin. "Gender Differences in Parental Strain: Parental Role or Gender Role?" *Journal of Family Issues* 10:4 (December 1989): 482–503.

Scott, Jacqueline, and Howard Schuman. "Attitude Strength and Social Action in the Abortion Dispute." *American Sociological Review* 53:5 (October 1989): 785–793.

Scott, Janny. "Low Birth Weight's High Cost." *Los Angeles Times,* December 3, 1990b, A1.

_____. "Trying to Save the Babies." *Los Angeles Times,* December 24, 1990a: A1, 18ff.

Scott, Joan. "Gender: A Useful Category of Historical Analysis." *American Historical Review* 91 (1986): 1053–1075.

Scott, S. G., et al. "Therapeutic Donor Insemination with Frozen Semen." *Canadian Medical Association Journal* 143:4 (August 15, 1990): 273–278.

Scott-Jones, Diane, and Sherry Turner. "Sex Education, Contraceptive and Reproductive Knowledge, and Contraceptive Use among Black Adolescent Females." *Journal of Adolescent Research* 3:2 (Summer 1988): 171–187.

Sears, David. "College Sophomores in the Laboratory: Influences of Narrow Data Base on Social Psychology's View of Human Nature." *Journal of Personality and Social Psychology* 51 (August, 1986): 515–530.

Seidman, Steven. "Constructing Sex as a Domain of Pleasure and Self-Expression: Sexual Ideology in the Sixties." *Theory, Culture, and Society* 6:2 (May 1989): 293–315.

Select Committee on Children, Youth and Families, U.S. House of Representatives. *Families and Child Care: Improving the Options.* Report 98–1180. 98th Congress, 2nd Session. Washington, D.C.: U.S. Government Printing Office, 1985.

Sennett, Richard. *Authority.* New York: Knopf, 1980.

Serdahely, William, and Georgia Ziemba. "Changing Homophobic Attitudes through College Sexuality Education." *Journal of Homosexuality* 10:1–2 (Fall 1984): 148ff.

Settles, Barbara H. "A Perspective on Tomorrow's Families." In Marvin Sussman and Suzanne Steinmetz, eds., *Handbook of Marriage and the Family.* New York: Plenum Press, 1987.

Sexton, Christine, and Daniel Perlman. "Couples' Career Orientation, Gender Role Orientation, and Perceived Equity as Determinants of Marital Power." *Journal of Marriage and the Family* 51:4 (November 1989): 933–941.

Shanis, B. S., J. H. Check, and A. F. Baker. "Transmission of Sexually Transmitted Diseases by Donor Semen." *Archives of Andrology* 23:3 (1989): 249–257.

Shannon, Thomas. *Surrogate Motherhood.* New York: Crossroad Publishing Co., 1988.

Shapiro, David. "No Other Hope for Having a Child." *Newsweek* (January 19, 1987): 50–51.

Shapiro, Joanna. "Family Reactions and Coping Strategies in Response to the Physically Ill or Handicapped Child: A Review." *Social Science and Medicine* 17 (1983): 913–931.

Shapiro, Johanna, and Ken Tittle. "Maternal Adaptation to Child Disability in a Hispanic Population." *Family Relations* 39:2 (April 1990): 179–185.

Shaver, Phillip, et al. "Love as Attachment: The Integration of Three Behavioral Systems." In Robert Sternberg and Michael Barnes, eds. *The Psychology of Love.* New Haven, Conn.: Yale University Press, 1988.

Shaw, David. "Despite Advances, Stereotypes Still Used by Media." *Los Angeles Times,* December 12, 1990: A31.

Sheehan, Nancy, and Paul Nuttall. "Conflict, Emotion, and Personal Strain Among Family Caregivers." *Family Relations* 37:1 (January 1988): 92–98.

Shelp, Earl. *Born to Die?* New York: The Free Press, 1986.

Sherman, Beth. "Spanking: Experts Say No." *San Jose Mercury,* June 24, 1985.

Sherman, Lawrence, and Richard Berk, Jr. "The Special Deterrent Effects of Arrest for Domestic Violence." *American Sociological Review* 49 (1984): 261–272.

"Shifting the Burden." *Los Angeles Times,* April 16, 1990: A5.

Shilts, Randy. *And the Band Played On: Politics, People, and the AIDS Epidemic.* New York: St. Martins Press, 1987.

Shimkin, Demitri, Edith Shimkin, and Dennis Frate. *The Extended Family in Black Societies.* The Hague, Netherlands: Mouton Publishers, 1978.

Shostak, Arthur B. "Singlehood." In Marvin Sussman and Suzanne Steinmetz, eds., *Handbook of Marriage and the Family.* New York: Plenum Press, 1987.

_____. "Tomorrow's Family Reforms: Marriage Course, Marriage Test, Incorporated Families, and Sex Selection Mandate." *Journal of Marital and Family Therapy* 7:4 (October 1981): 521–528.

Sidorowicz, Laura, and G. Sparks Lunney. "Baby X Revisited." *Sex Roles* 6:1 (February 1980): 67–73.

Signorielli, Nancy. "Children, Television, and Gender Roles—Messages and Impact." *Journal of Broadcasting and Electronic Media* 33:3 (Summer 1989): 325–331.

_____. "Television and Conceptions about Sex Roles—Maintaining Conventionality and the Status Quo." *Sex Roles* 21:5–5 (September 1989): 341–350.

Silver, Donald, and B. Kay Campbell. "Failure of Psychological Gestation." *Psychoanalytic Inquiry* 8:2 (1988): 222–233.

Simmel, Georg. *The Sociology of Georg Simmel.* Edited by K. Wolff. New York: Free Press, 1950.

Simon, William, and John Gagnon. "Sexual Scripts." *Society* 221:1 (November–December 1984): 53–60.

Simpson, George Eaton, and J. Milton Yinger. *Racial and Cultural Minorities: An Analysis of Prejudice and Discrimination.* New York: Plenum Press, 1985.

Simpson, Jeffrey. "The Dissolution of Romantic Relationships: Factors Involved in Relationship Stability and Emotional Distress." *Journal of Personality and Social Psychology* 53:4 (1987): 683–694.

Simpson, Jeffrey, et al. "The Association between Romantic Love and Marriage: Kephart (1967) Twice Revisited." *Personality and Social Psychology Bulletin* 12 (1986): 363–372.

Singer, Dorothy, G. "A Time to Reexamine the Role of Television in Our Lives." *American Psychologist* 38 (1983): 815–816.

Singer, Peter, and Deane Wells. *Making Babies: The New Science and Ethics of Conception.* New York: Charles Scribner's Sons, 1985.

Sinnott, Jan. *Sex Roles and Aging: Theory and Research from a Systems Perspective.* New York: Karger, 1986.

Skolnick, Arlene, and Jerome Skolnick, eds. *Family in Transition.* Boston: Little, Brown, 1980.

Slater, Philip. *The Pursuit of Loneliness.* Boston: Beacon Press, 1971.

Sluzki, C. E., and V. Eliseo. "The Double Bind as a Universal Pathogenic Situation." *Family Process* 10 (1971): 397–410.

Small, Stephen, and Dave Riley. "Toward a Multidimensional Assessment of Work Spillover into Family Life." *Journal of Marriage and the Family* 52:1 (February 1990): 51–61.

Smelser, Neil, and Erik Erikson, eds. *Themes of Work and Love in Adulthood.* Cambridge, Mass.: Harvard University Press, 1980.

Smith, Daniel, and Michael Hindus. "Premarital Pregnancy in America: 1640–1971." *Journal of Interdisciplinary History* 4 (Spring 1975): 537–570.

Smith, E. J. "The Black Female Adolescent: A Review of the Educational, Career, and Psychological Literature." *Psychology of Women Quarterly* 6 (1982): 261–288.

Smith, Ken, and Cathleen Zick. "The Incidence of Poverty among the Recently Widowed: Mediating Factors in the Life Course." *Journal of Marriage and the Family* 48 (1986): 619–630.

Snarey, John, et al. "The Role of Parenting in Men's Psychosocial Development." *Developmental Psychology* 23:4 (July 1987): 593–603.

Sobol, Thomas. "Understanding Diversity." *Educational Leadership* 48:3 (November 1990): 27–30.

Sonenstein, F. L., J. H. Pleck, and L. C. Ku. "Sexual Activity, Condom Use, and AIDS Awareness among Adolescent Males." *Family Planning Perspectives* 21:4 (July/August 1989): 152–158.

Sontag, Susan. "The Double Standard of Aging." *Saturday Review* 55 (September 1972): 29–38.

Sophie, Joan. "Internalized Homophobia and Lesbian Identity." *Journal of Homosexuality* 18:3–4 (1989): 95–118.

_____. "Internalized Homophobia and Lesbian Identity." *Journal of Homosexuality* 14:1–2 (Fall/Winter 1987): 53–65.

Sorenson, James, and Guilermo Bernal. *A Family Like Yours: Breaking the Pattern of Drug Abuse.* San Francisco, Calif.: Harper and Row, 1987.

Sorosky, Arthur, Annette Baran, and Ruben Pannor. *The Adoption Triangle: The Effects of the Sealed Record on Adoptees, Birth Parents, and Adoptive Parents.* Garden City, N.Y.: Anchor Press, 1978.

South, Scott, and Glenna Spitze. "Determinants of Divorce over the Marital Life Course." *American Sociological Review* 47 (1986): 583–590.

Spanier, Graham B. "Improve, Refine, Recast, Expand, Clarify—But Don't Abandon." *Journal of Marriage and the Family* 47:4 (November 1985): 1073–1074.

_____. "Measuring Dyadic Adjustment." *Journal of Marriage and the Family* 38 (February 1976): 15–28.

Spanier, Graham B. and Frank Furstenberg, Jr. "Remarriage After Divorce: A Longitudinal Analysis of Well-being." *Journal of Marriage and the Family* 44:3 (August 1982): 709–720.

_____. "Remarriage and Reconstituted Families." In Marvin Sussman and Suzanne Steinmetz, eds. *Handbook of Marriage and the Family.* New York: Plenum Press, 1987.

Spanier, Graham B. and R. L. Margolis. "Marital Separation and Extramarital Sexual Behavior." *Journal of Sex Research* 19 (1983): 23–48.

Spanier, Graham B. and Linda Thompson. "A Confirmatory Analysis of the Dyadic Adjustment Scale." *Journal of Marriage and the Family* 44:3 (August 1982): 731–738.

_____. *Parting: The Aftermath of Separation and Divorce,* rev. ed. Beverly Hills, Calif.: Sage Publications, 1984, 1987.

_____. "Relief and Distress after Marital Separation." *Journal of Divorce* 7 (1983): 31–49.

Spanier, Graham B. et al. "Marital Trajectories of American Women: Variations in the Life Course." *Journal of Marriage and the Family* 47:4 (November 1985): 993–1003.

Spector, I. P., and Carey, M. P. "Incidence and Prevalence of the Sexual Dysfunctions—A Critical Review of the Empirical Literature." *Archives of Sexual Behavior* 19:4 (August 1990): 389–408.

Spence, Janet, and L. L. Sawin. "Images of Masculinity and Feminity." In V. O'Leary, et al., eds., *Sex, Gender, and Social Psychology.* Hillsdale, N.J.: Erlbaum, 1985.

Spence, Janet, et al. "Ratings of Self and Peers on Sex Role Attributes and the Relation to Self-Esteem and Conceptions of Masculinity and Femininity." *Journal of Personality and Social Psychology* 32 (1975): 29–39.

_____. "Sex Roles in Contemporary Society." In G. Lindzey and Elliot Aronson, eds., *Handbook of Social Psychology.* New York: Random House, 1985.

Spencer, Margaret Beale. "Racial Variations in Achievement Prediction." In Harriette Pipes McAdoo and John McAdoo, eds., *Black Children: Social, Educational, and Parental Environments.* Beverly Hills, Calif.: Sage Publications, 1985.

Spiegel, Lynn. *Installing the Television Set: Television and the Family Ideal in Postwar America.* Chicago: University of Chicago Press, 1991.

Spitze, Glenna. "The Division of Task Responsibility in U.S. Households: Longitudinal Adjustments to Change." *Social Forces* 64 (1986): 689–701.

_____. "Women's Employment and Family Relations: A Review." In Alan Booth, ed., *Contemporary Families: Looking Forward, Looking Back.* Minneapolis: National Council on Family Relations, 1991.

Spitze, Glenna, and Scott South. "Women's Employment, Time Expenditure, and Divorce." *Journal of Family Issues* 6:3 (September 1985): 307–329.

Spock, Benjamin. *Baby and Child Care.* New York: Pocket Books, 1945, 1965, and 1976.

Spock, Benjamin, and Michael Rothenberg. *Dr. Spock's Baby and Child Care.* New York: Pocket Books, 1985.

Sponaugle, G. C. "Attitudes Toward Extramarital Relations." In Kathleen McKinney and Susan Sprecher, eds., *Human Sexuality: The Societal and Interpersonal Context.* Norwood, N.J.: Ablex Publishing Corporation, 1989.

Sprecher, Susan. "Sex Differences in Bases of Power in Dating Relationships." *Sex Roles* 12(34) (1985): 449–462.

_____, et al. "Sexual Relationships." In Kathleen McKinney and Susan Sprecher, eds., *Human Sexuality: The Societal and Interpersonal Context.* Norwood, N.J.: Ablex Publishing Corporation, 1989.

_____. "A Revision of the Reiss Premarital Sexual Permissiveness Scale." *Journal of Marriage and the Family* 50:3 (August, 1988): 821–828.

Sprey, Jetse. "Current Theorizing on the Family: An Appraisal." *Journal of Marriage and the Family* 50 (November 1988): 875–890.

Springer, D., and D. Brubaker. *Family Caregivers and Dependent Elderly: Minimizing Stress and Maximizing Independence.* Beverly Hills, Calif.: Sage Publications, 1984.

Stanton, M. Colleen. "The Fetus: A Growing Member of the Family." *Family Relations* 34:3 (July 1985): 321–326.

Stanton, M. D. "Family Treatment Approaches to Drug Abuse Problems: A Review." *Family Processes* 18 (1979): 251–280.

Staples, Robert. "The Black American Family." In Charles Mindel, Robert Habenstein, and Roosevelt Wright, Jr., eds. *Ethnic Families in America: Patterns and Variations,* 3d ed. New York: Elsevier North Holland, Inc., 1988.

_____. "The Black American Family. In Charles Mindel and Robert Habenstein, eds. *Ethnic Families in America.* 1st ed. New York: Elsevier North Holland, 1976.

_____. "The Emerging Majority: Resources for Nonwhite Families in the United States." *Family Relations* 37:3 (July 1988): 348–354.

_____, ed. *The Black Family: Essays and Studies,* 3d ed. Belmont, Calif.: Wadsworth Publishing Co., 1988, 1991.

Staples, Robert, and A. Mirandé. "Racial and Cultural Variations among American Families: A Decennial Review of the Literature." *Journal of Marriage and the Family* 42 (1980): 887–922.

Statistics Canada. *Canada Yearbook.* Ottawa: Supply and Services, 1990.

Steck, L., D. Levitan, D. McLane, and H. H. Kelley. "Care, Need, and Conceptions of Love." *Journal of Personality and Social Psychology* 43 (1982): 481–491.

Steele, Brandt F. "Psychodynamic Factors in Child Abuse." In C. Henry Kempe and Ray Helfer, eds., *The Battered Child.* Chicago: University of Chicago Press, 1980.

Steelman, Lala Carr, and Brian Powell. "The Social and Academic Consequences of Birth Order: Real, Artifactual, or Both?" *Journal of Marriage and the Family* 47 (1985): 117–124.

Stein, Peter, ed. *Single.* Englewood Cliffs, N.J.: Prentice-Hall, 1976.

Stein, Peter, and Meryl Fingrud. "The Single Life Has More Potential for Happiness than Marriage and Parenthood for Both Men and Women." In Harold Feldman and Margaret Feldman, eds., *Current Controversies in Marriage and the Family.* Beverly Hills, Calif.: Sage Publications, 1985.

Steinberg, Laurence, and Susan Silverberg. "Marital Satisfaction in Middle Stages of Family Life Cycle." *Journal of Marriage and the Family* 49:4 (November 1987): 751–760.

Steinglass, Peter. "A Life History Model of the Alcoholic Family." In David Olson and Brent Miller, eds., *Family Studies Review Yearbook,* Vol. 1. Beverly Hills, Calif.: Sage, 1983.

_____, et al. *The Alcoholic Family.* New York: Basic Books, 1987.

Steinman, Susan. "The Experience of Children in a Joint-Custody Arrangement: A Report of a Study." *American Journal of Orthopsychiatry* 51:3 (July 1981): 403–414.

Steinmetz, Suzanne. "Family Violence." In Marvin Sussman and Suzanne Steinmetz, eds., *Handbook of Marriage and the Family.* New York: Plenum Press, 1987.

Stephen, Beverly. "How Today's Woman Plans Her Wedding." *San Francisco Chronicle,* April 19, 1982.

Stephen, Timothy. "Fixed-Sequence and Circular-Causal Models of Relationship Development: Divergent Views on the Role of Communication in Intimacy." *Journal of Marriage and the Family* 47:4 (November 1985): 955–963.

Stephen, Timothy, and Teresa Harrison. "A Longitudinal Comparison of Couples with Sex-Typical and Non-Sex-Typical Orientations to Intimacy." *Sex Roles* 12(1/2) (1985): 195–205.

Sternberg, Robert. "Triangulating Love." In Robert Sternberg and Michael Barnes, eds., *The Psychology of Love.* New Haven, Conn.: Yale University Press, 1988.

_____. *The Psychology of Love.* New Haven, Conn.: Yale University Press, 1988.

Sternberg, Robert, and Michael Barnes. "Real and Ideal Others in Romantic Relationships: Is Four a Crowd?" *Journal of Personality and Social Psychology* 49 (1985): 1589–1596.

Stets, Jan E., "Verbal and Physical Agression in Marriage." *Journal of Marriage and the Family* 52 (May 1990): 501–514.

Stets, Jan E., and Maureen A. Pirog-Good. "Patterns of Physical and Sexual Abuse for Men and Women in Dating Relationships: A Descriptive Analysis." *Journal of Family Violence* 4:1 (March 1989): 63–76.

Stets, Jan E., and Murray A. Straus. "The Marriage License as a Hitting License: A Comparison of Assaults in Dating, Cohabitating and Married Couples." *Journal of Family Violence* 4:2 (June 1989): 161–180.

Stevens, Gillian, and Robert Schoen. "Linguistic Intermarriage in the United States." *Journal of Marriage and the Family* 50:1 (February 1988): 267–280.

Stinnet, Nick. "In Search of Strong Families." In Nick Stinnet et al., eds., *Building Family Strengths.* Lincoln: University of Nebraska Press, 1979.

_____, et al., eds. *Building Family Strengths.* Lincoln: University of Nebraska Press, 1979.

Stinnett, Nick, and John DeFrain. *Secrets of Strong Families.* Boston: Little, Brown and Company, 1985.

Stockard, Janice. *Daughters of the Canton Delta: Marriage Patterns and Economic Strategies in South China, 1860–1930.* Stanford, Calif.: Stanford University Press, 1989.

Stone, Katherine M., et al. "National Surveillance for Neonatal Herpes Simplex Virus Infections." *Sexually Transmitted Diseases* 16:3 (July–September 1989): 152–160.

Strasser, Susan. *Never Done: A History of American Housework.* New York: Pantheon Books, 1982.

Straus, Murray. "Preventing Violence and Strengthening the Family." In Nick Stinnett, et al., eds. *Family Strengths* 4. Lincoln: University of Nebraska Press, 1980.

Straus, Murray, and Richard Gelles. "Societal Change and Change in Family Violence from 1975 to 1985 as Revealed by Two National Surveys." *Journal of Marriage and the Family* 48 (August 1986): 465–479.

Straus, Murray, Richard Gelles, and Suzanne Steinmetz. *Behind Closed Doors.* Garden City, N.Y.: Anchor Books, 1980.

Strong, Bryan, and Christine DeVault. "Inside America's New Families." *Family Life Educator* 1:3 (Spring 1983): 9–11.

_____. *Understanding Our Sexuality,* 2d ed. St. Paul, Minn.: West Publishing Co., 1988.

Strube, Michael J., and Linda Barbour. "Factors Related to the Decision to Leave an Abusive Relationship." *Journal of Marriage and the Family* 46:4 (November 1984): 837–844.

Sue, D. "Erotic Fantasies of College Students during Coitus." *Journal of Sex Research* 15 (1979): 299–305.

Sugarman, David B., and Gerald T. Hotaling. "Dating Violence: Prevalence, Context, and Risk Markers." In Maureen Pirog-Good and Jan Stets, eds. *Violence in Dating Relationships: Emerging Social Issues.* New York: Praeger, 1989.

Suitor, J. Jill. "Marital Quality and Satisfaction with Division of Household Labor." *Journal of Marriage and the Family* 53:1 (February 1991): 221–230.

Suitor, J. Jill, and Karl Pillemer. "The Presence of Adult Children: A Source of Stress for Elderly Couples' Marriages?" *Journal of Marriage and the Family* 49:4 (November 1987): 717–725.

Sullivan, Harry Stack. *The Collected Works of Harry Stack Sullivan.* New York: Norton, 1952.

Sunoff, Alvin. "A Conversation with Jerome Kagan." *U. S. News and World Report* (March 25, 1985): 63–64.

Surra, Catherine. "Research and Theory on Mate Selection and Premarital Relationship in the 1980s." In Alan Booth, ed., *Contemporary Families: Looking Forward, Looking Back.* Minneapolis: National Council on Family Relations, 1991.

Sussman, Marvin B., and Susan K. Steinmetz, eds. *Handbook of Marriage and the Family.* New York: Plenum Press, 1987.

Swensen, C. H., Jr. "The Behavior of Love." In H. A. Otto, ed., *Love Today: A New Exploration.* New York: Association Press, 1972.

Swenson, Clifford, and Geir Trahaug. "Commitment and the Long-Term Marriage Relationship." *Journal of Marriage and the Family* 47:4 (November 1985): 939–945.

Swift, Carolyn. "Preventing Family Violence: Family-Focused Programs." In Mary Lystad, ed. *Violence in the Home: Interdisciplinary Perspectives.* New York: Brunner/Mazel, 1986.

Sylviachild, Abby Joan. "Infertility and Adoption." In Janet Isaacs Ashford, ed., *Birth Stories.* Freedom, Calif.: Crossing Press, 1984.

Symons, Donald. *The Evolution of Human Sexuality.* New York: Oxford University Press, 1979.

Synder, M., and J. A. Simpson. "Orientation toward Romantic Relationships." In Daniel Perlman and Steve Duck, eds. *Intimate Relationships: Development, Dynamics, and Deterioration.* Beverly Hills, Calif.: Sage Publications, 1987.

Szapocznik, Jose, and Roberto Hernandez. "The Cuban American Family." In Charles Mindel, Robert Habenstein, and Roosevelt Wright, Jr., eds. *Ethnic Families in America: Patterns and Variations,* 3d ed. New York: Elsevier North Holland, Inc., 1988.

Szinovacz, Maximiliane. "Family Power." In Marvin Sussman and Suzanne Steinmetz, eds., *Handbook of Marriage and the Family.* New York: Plenum Press, 1987.

Talbot, Nathan, ed. *Raising Children in Modern America.* Boston: Little, Brown, 1976.

"Talking to Children about Prejudice." *PTA Today* (December 1989–January 1990): 7–8.

Tallmer, Margot. "Grief as a Normal Response to the Death of a Loved One." In Austin H. Kutscher, et al., eds., *Principles of Thanatology.* New York: Columbia University Press, 1987.

Tanfer, Koray. "Patterns of Premarital Cohabitation among Never-Married Women in the United States." *Journal of Marriage and the Family* 49 (August 1987): 683–697.

Tanke, E. D. "Dimensions of the Physical Attractiveness Stereotype: A Factor/Analytic Study." *Journal of Psychology* 110 (1982): 63–74.

Tavris, Carol, and Susan Sadd. *The Redbook Report on Female Sexuality.* New York: Dell, 1977.

Tavris, Carol, and Carole Wade. *The Longest War: Sex Differences in Perspective,* 2d ed. New York: Harcourt Brace Jovanovich, 1984.

Taylor, Ella. "From the Nelsons to the Huxtables: Genre and Family Imagery in American Network Television." *Qualitative Sociology* 12:1 (Spring 1989a); 13–28.

_____. *Prime-Time Families: Television Culture in Postwar America.* Berkeley, Calif.: University of California Press, 1989b.

Taylor, Patricia. "It's Time to Put Warnings on Alcohol." *The New York Times,* March 20, 1988: B2.

Taylor, Robert J. "Need for Support and Family Involvement among Black Americans." *Journal of Marriage and the Family* 52 (August 1990): 584–590.

_____. "Receipt of Support from Family among Black Americans." *Journal of Marriage and the Family* 48 (February 1986): 67.

Taylor, Robert J., Linda M. Chatters, M. Belinda Tucker, and Edith Lewis. "Developments in Research on Black Families." In Alan Booth, ed., *Contemporary Families: Looking Forward, Looking Back.* Minneapolis: National Council on Family Relations, 1991.

Teachman, Jay. "Receipt of Child Support in the United States." *Journal of Marriage and the Family* 53:3 (August 1991): 759–772.

Teachman, Jay, and Alex Heckert. "The Impact of Age and Children on Remarriage." *Journal of Family Issues* 6 (June 1985): 185–203.

Teachman, Jay D., and Karen A. Polonko. "Cohabitation and Marital Stability in the United States." *Social Forces* 69:1 (September 1990): 207–220.

_____. "Timing of the Transition to Parenthood: A Multidimensional Birth-interval Approach." *Journal of Marriage and the Family* 47:4 (November 1985): 867–879.

Teeser, Abraham, and Richard Reardon. "Perceptual and Cognitive Mechanisms in Human Sexual Attraction." In Mark Cook, ed., *The Bases of Human Sexual Attraction.* New York: Academic Press, 1981.

Tennov, Denise. *Love and Limerence: The Experience of Being in Love.* New York: Stein and Day, 1979.

Testa, Ronald, Bill Kinder, and Gail Ironson. "Heterosexual Bias in the Perception of Loving Relationships of Gay Males and Lesbians." *Journal of Sex Research* 23:2 (May 1987): 163–172.

Textor, Martin. "Family Therapy with Drug Addicts: An Integrated Approach." *American Journal of Orthopsychiatry* 57:4 (October 1987): 495–507.

Thayer, Leo O. *On Communication.* Norwood, N.J.: Ablex Publishing, 1987.

Theroux, Phyllis. "Tell Them I'm Carrying Their Baby." *The New York Times Book Review,* July 8, 1990: 7.

Thompson, Anthony. "Emotional and Sexual Components of Extramarital Relations." *Journal of Marriage and the Family* 46:1 (February 1984): 35–42.

_____. "Extramarital Sex: A Review of the Research Literature." *Journal of Sex Research* 19:1 (February 1983): 1–22.

Thompson, Edward, Christopher Grisanti, and Joseph Pleck. "Attitudes toward the Male Role and Their Correlates." *Sex Roles* 13:7–8 (October 1985): 413–427.

Thompson, Linda and Alexis Walker. "Gender in Families: Women and Men in Marriage, Work, and Parenthood." In Alan Booth, ed., *Contemporary Families: Looking Forward, Looking Back.* Minneapolis: National Council on Family Relations, 1991.

Thompson, Linda, et al. "Developmental Stage and Perceptions of Intergenerational Continuity." *Journal of Marriage and the Family* 47:4 (November 1985): 913–920.

Thomson, Keith. "Research on Human Embryos: Where to Draw the Line." *American Scientist* 73:2 (March–April 1985): 187–189.

Thorne, B., and M. Yalom, eds. *Rethinking the Family: Some Feminist Questions.* New York: Longman, 1982.

Thornton, Arland. "The Courtship Process and Adolescent Sexuality." *Journal of Family Issues* 11:3 (September 1990): 239–273.

_____. "Changing Attitudes toward Family Issues in the United States." *Journal of Marriage and the Family* 51:4 (November 1989): 873–893.

_____, et al. "Causes and Consequences of Sex-Role Attitudes and Attitude Change." *American Sociological Review* 48 (1983): 211–227.

Tienda, Marta, and Ronald Angel. "Headship and Household Composition among Blacks, Hispanics, and Other Whites." *Social Forces* 61 (1982): 508–531.

Tienda, Marta, and Jennifer Glass. "Household Structure and Labor Force Participation of Black, Hispanic, and White Mothers." *Demography* 22 (1985): 381–394.

Tietjen, Anne M., and Christine F. Bradley. "Social Support and Maternal Psychosocial Adjustment during the Transition to Parenthood." *Canadian Journal of Behavioural Science* 17:2 (April 1985): 109–121.

Ting-Toomey, Stella. "An Analysis of Verbal Communication Patterns in High and Low Marital Adjustment Groups." *Human Communications Research* 9:4 (Summer 1983): 306–319.

Tooth, Geoffrey. "Why Children's TV Turns Off So Many Parents." *U.S. News and World Report* (February 18, 1985): 65.

Torres, José. "A Letter to a Child Like Me." *Parade Magazine* (February 26, 1991): 8–9.

Torrey, Barbara. "Aspects of the Aged: Clues and Issues." *Population and Development Review* 14:3 (September 1988): 489–497.

Toufexis, Anastasia. "Older—but Coming on Strong." *Time* (February 22, 1988): 76–79.

Trafford, Abigail. "Medical Science Discovers the Baby." *U.S. News and World Report* (November 10, 1980): 59–62.

Tran, Than Van. "The Vietnamese American Family." In Charles H. Mindel, Robert W. Habenstein, and Roosevelt Wright, Jr., eds., *Ethnic Families in America: Patterns and Variations,* 3d ed. New York: Elsevier, 1988.

Treas, Judith, and Vern L. Bengtson. "The Demography of Mid- and Late-Life Transitions." *Annals of the American Academy* 464 (November 1982): 11–21.

_____. "The Family in Later Years." In Marvin Sussman and Suzanne Steinmetz, eds., *Handbook of Marriage and the Family.* New York: Plenum Press, 1987.

Tribe, Laurence. *Abortion: Clash of Absolutes.* New York: Norton, 1990.

Troiden, Richard. *Gay and Lesbian Identity: A Sociological Analysis.* New York: General Hall, 1988.

Troiden, Richard, and Erich Goode. "Variables Related to the Acquisition of a Gay Identity." *Journal of Homosexuality* 5 (Summer 1980): 383–392.

Troll, Lillian. "The Contingencies of Grandparenting." In Vern Bengston and Joan Roberston, eds., *Grandparenthood.* Beverly Hills, Calif.: Sage Publications, 1985a.

_____. *Early and Middle Adulthood,* 2d ed. Monterey, Calif.: Brooks/Cole Publishing Co., 1985b.

Trost, Jan. "Abandon Adjustment!" *Journal of Marriage and the Family* 47:4 (November 1985): 1072–1073.

True, Reiko Homma. "Psychotherapeutic Issues with Asian American Women." *Sex Roles* 22:7–8 (April 1990): 477–485.

Trzcinski, Eileen, and Matia Finn-Stevenson. "A Response to Arguments against Mandated Parental Leave: Findings from the Connecticut Survey of Parental Leave Policies." *Journal of Marriage and the Family* 53:2 (May 1991): 445–460.

Tucker, Sandra. "Adolescent Patterns of Communication about Sexually Related Topics." *Adolescence* 24:94 (Summer 1989): 269–278.

Turner, P. H., L. Scadden, and M. B. Harris. "Parenting in Gay and Lesbian Families." Paper presented at the first meeting of the Future of Parenting Symposium, Chicago, Ill., March, 1985.

Turner, R. "Rising Prevalence of Cohabitation in the United States May Have Partially Offset Decline in Marriage Rates." *Family Planning Perspectives* 22:2 (March–April 1990): 90–91.

Turner, R. Jay, and William R. Avison. "Assessing Risk Factors for Problem Parenting: The Significance of Social Support." *Journal of Marriage and the Family* 47:4 (November 1985): 881–892.

Turner, R. Jay, and J. W. Gartrell. "Social Factors and Psychiatric Outcome: Toward a Resolution of Interpretive Controversies." *American Sociological Review* 43 (1978): 1–23.

"U.S. Assailed on Infant Mortality." *The New York Times,* February 3, 1987: 18.

Udry, J. Richard. "Marriage Alternatives and Marital Disruption." *Journal of Marriage and the Family* 43 (November 1981): 889–897.

_____. *The Social Context of Marriage.* Philadelphia: Lippincott, 1974.

Ulrich, Patricia. "The Determinants of Depression in Two-Income Marriages." *Journal of Marriage and the Family* 50 (February 1988): 121–131.

Umberson, Debra. "Family Status and Health Behaviors: Social Control as a Dimension of Social Integration." *Journal of Health and Social Behavior* 28 (1987): 306–319.

_____. "Parenting and Well-Being: The Importance of Context." *Journal of Family Issues* 10:4 (December 1989): 427–439.

Umberson, Debra, and Walter R. Gove. "Parenthood and Psychological Well-Being: Theory, Measurement, and Stage in the Family Life Course." *Journal of Family Issues* 10:4 (December 1989): 440–462.

Unger, Donald G., and Marvin B. Sussman. "Introduction: A Community Perspective on Families." *Marriage and Family Review* 15:1/2 (1990).

Urwin, Charlene. "AIDS in Children: A Family Concern." *Family Relations* 37:2 (April 1988): 154–159.

U.S. Bureau of the Census. "Changes in American Family Life." *Special Studies.* Series P-23, No. 163. Washington, D.C.: U.S. Government Printing Office, 1989.

_____. "The Hispanic Population in the United States: March, 1990." *Current Population Reports.* Series P-20, No. 449. Washington, D.C.: U.S. Government Printing Office, 1991.

_____. "Marital Status and Living Arrangements: March, 1987." *Current Population Reports.* Series P-20. Washington, D.C.: U.S. Government Printing Office, 1988.

_____. "Marital and Living Arrangements: March, 1988." *Current Population Reports.* Series P-20. Washington, D.C.: U.S. Government Printing Office, 1989.

_____. "Marital and Living Arrangements: March, 1989." *Current Population Reports.* Series P-20. Washington, D.C.: U.S. Government Printing Office, 1990.

_____. "Marital and Living Arrangements: March, 1990." *Current Population Reports.* Series P-20. Washington, D.C.: U.S. Government Printing Office, 1991.

_____. *Statistical Abstract of the United States,* 109th ed. Washington, D.C., 1989.

_____. *Statistical Abstract of the United States,* 110th ed. Washington, D.C., 1990.

_____. *Statistical Abstract of the United States,* 111th ed. Washington, D.C.: U.S. Government Printing Office, 1991.

_____. "Studies in Marriage and the Family." *Special Studies.* Series P-23, No. 162. Washington, D.C.: U.S. Government Printing Office, 1989.

_____. "Who's Minding the Kids?" Washington, D.C.: U.S. Government Printing Office, 1987.

U.S. Bureau of Labor Statistics. "Employment and Earnings." Washington, D.C.: U.S. Government Printing Office, 1988.

U.S. Commission on Civil Rights. *Child Care and Equal Opportunity for Women.* Clearinghouse Publication No. 67, June 1981.

Urwin, Charlene. "AIDS in Children: A Family Concern." *Family Relations* 37:2 (April 1988): 154–159.

Valentine, Deborah. "The Experience of Pregnancy: A Developmental Process." *Family Relations* 31 (April 1982): 243–248.

Vance, Carole, ed. *Pleasure and Danger: Exploring Female Sexuality.* Boston: Routledge and Kegan Paul, 1984.

Vandell, Deborah, and Mary Anne Corasaniti. "After School Care: Choices and Outcome for Third Graders." Paper presented to Association for the Advancement of Science, May 27, 1985.

Vanderford, Marsha. "Vilification and Social Movements: A Case Study of Pro-Life and Pro-Choice Rhetoric." *Quarterly Journal of Speech* 75:2 (May 1989): 166–182.

Van Hasselt, Vincent B., et al., eds. *Handbook of Family Violence.* New York: Plenum Press, 1988.

Vann, Richard. "The Youth of Centuries of Childhood." *History and Theory* 21:2 (1982): 279–297.

Vasquez-Nuthall, E., I. Romero-Garcia, and B. De Leon. "Sex Roles and Perceptions of Femininity and Masculinity of Hispanic Women: A Review of the Literature." *Psychology of Women Quarterly* 11 (1987): 409–426.

Vaughan, Diane. *Uncoupling: Turning Points in Intimate Relationships.* New York: Oxford University Press, 1986.

Veevers, Jean. *Childless by Choice.* Toronto: Buttersworth, 1980.

_____. "Voluntary Childlessness." *Family Coordinator* 22 (April 1973): 199–206.

Vega, William. "Hispanic Families." In Alan Booth, ed., *Contemporary Families: Looking Forward, Looking Back.* Minneapolis: National Council on Family Relations, 1991.

Velsor, Ellen, and Angela O'Rand. "Family Life Cycle, Work Career Patterns, and Women's Wages at Midlife." *Journal of Marriage and the Family* 46:2 (May 1984): 365–373.

Vemer, Elizabeth, Marilyn Coleman, Lawrence Ganong, and Harris Cooper. "Marital Satisfaction in Remarriage: A Meta-analysis." *Journal of Marriage and the Family* 53:1 (August 1989): 713–726.

Ventura, Jacqueline N. "The Stresses of Parenthood Reexamined." *Family Relations,* 36 (January 1987): 26–29.

Vera, Hernan, et al. "Age Heterogamy in Marriage." *Journal of Marriage and the Family* 47:3 (August 1985): 553–566.

Verbrugge, Lois. "From Sneezes to Adieu: Stages of Health for American Men and Women." *Social Science and Medicine* 22 (1986): 1195–1212.

_____. "Marital Status and Health." *Journal of Marriage and the Family* 41 (May 1979): 267–285.

Verdery, E. Augustus. "Treatment of the Alcoholic by the Non-physician." In Peter Bourne and Ruth Fox, eds., *Alcoholism: Progress in Research and Treatment.* New York: Academic Press, 1973.

Verwoerdt, A., et al. "Sexual Behavior in Senescence." *Geriatrics* 24 (February 1969): 137–157.

Verzaro-Lawrence, Marce. "Shared Childrearing: A Challenging Alternative Lifestyle." *Alternative Lifestyles* 4:2 (May 1981): 205–217.

Viorst, Judith. *Necessary Losses.* New York: Fawcett Gold Medal, 1987.

Visher, E.B., and J. Visher. *Stepfamilies: A Guide to Working with Stepparents and Stepchildren.* New York: Brunner/Mazel, 1979.

Voeller, Bruce. "Society and the Gay Movement." In Judd Marmor, ed., *Homosexual Behavior.* New York: Basic Books, 1980.

Voydanoff, Patricia. "Economic Distress and Family Relations: A Review of the Eighties." In Alan Booth, ed., *Contemporary Families: Looking Forward, Looking Back.* Minneapolis: National Council on Family Relations, 1991.

_____. *Work and Family Life.* Newbury Park, Calif.: Sage Publications, 1987.

_____. "Work Role Characteristics, Family Structure Demands, and Work/Family Conflict." *Journal of Marriage and the Family* 50:3 (August 1988): 749–761.

Voydanoff, Patricia, and Brenda Donnelly. "Work and Family Roles and Psychological Distress." *Journal of Marriage and the Family* 51:4 (November 1989): 933–941.

Voydanoff, Patricia, and Linda Majka, eds. *Families and Economic Distress: Coping Strategies and Social Policy.* Beverly Hills, Calif.: Sage Publications, 1988.

Wakefield, Jerome. "The Semantics of Success: Do Masturbation Exercises Lead to Partner Orgasm?" *Journal of Sex and Marital Therapy* 13 (Spring 1987): 3–14.

Walker, Alexis J. "Reconceptualizing Family Stress." *Journal of Marriage and the Family* 47:4 (November 1985): 827–837.

_____, et al. "Feminist Programs for Families." *Family Relations* 37:1 (January 1988): 17–22.

Walker, Alexis J., Hwa-Yong Shin, and David Bird. "Perceptions of Relationship Change and Caregiver Satisfaction." *Family Relations* 39:2 (April 1990): 147–152.

Walker, Alexis J., and Linda Thompson. "Feminism and Family Studies." *Journal of Family Issues* 5:4 (December 1984): 545–570.

Walker, Kathryn. "At Home: Organizing Eases the Load." *U.S. News and World Report* (January 25, 1982).

Walker, Lenore. *The Battered Woman Syndrome.* New York: Harper Colophon, 1979.

_____. *The Battered Woman.* New York: Springer Publishing Co., 1984.

_____. "Psychological Causes of Family Violence." In Mary Lystad, ed., *Violence in the Home: Interdisciplinary Perspectives.* New York: Brunner/Mazel, 1986.

Waller, Willard. "The Rating and Dating Complex." *American Sociological Review* 2 (1937): 727–734.

Waller, Willard, and Reuben Hill. *The Family: A Dynamic Interpretation.* New York: Dryden Press, 1951.

Wallerstein, Judith. "Children of Divorce: Report of a Ten-Year Follow-Up of Early Latency-Age Children." *American Journal of Orthopsychiatry* 57:2 (April 1987): 199–211.

Wallerstein, Judith, and Joan Kelly. *Surviving the Breakup: How Children and Parents Cope with Divorce.* New York: Basic Books, 1980b.

_____. "Effects of Divorce on the Visiting Father-Child Relationship." *American Journal of Psychiatry* 137(12) (December 1980a): 1534–1539.

Wallerstein, Judith, and Sandra Blakeslee. *Second Chances: Men, Women, and Children a Decade After Divorce.* New York: Ticknor & Fields, 1989.

Walling, Mary, Barbara Andersen, and Susan Johnson. "Hormonal Replacement Therapy for Postmenopausal Women: A Review of Sexual Outcomes and Related Gynecologic Effects." *Archives of Sexual Behavior* 19:2 (1990): 119–127.

Walsh, Froma, ed. *Normal Family Processes.* New York: Guilford Press, 1982.

Walster, Elaine, and G. William Walster. *A New Look at Love.* Reading, Mass.: Addison-Wesley, 1978.

Wardle, Francis. "Helping Children Respect Differences." *PTA Today* (December 1989–January 1990): 5–6.

Warren, Carol. "Homosexuality and Stigma." In Judd Marmor, ed. *Homosexual Behavior.* New York: Basic Books, 1980.

Warren, Mary Anne. "The Abortion Struggle in America." *Bioethics* 3:43 (October 1989): 320–332.

Waterson, E. J., and I. M. Murray-Lyon. "Preventing Alcohol Related Birth Damage: A Review." *Social Science and Medicine* 30:3 (1990): 349–364.

Watkins, Susan Cotts, and Jane Menken. "Demographic Foundations of Family Change." *American Sociological Review* 52 (1987): 346–358.

Watson, Roy. "Premarital Cohabitation vs. Traditional Courtship: Their Effects on Subsequent Marital Adjustment." *Family Relations* 32:1 (January 1983): 139–147.

Watson, Russell. "A Hidden Epidemic." *Newsweek* (May 14, 1984a): 30–36.

_____. "What Price Day Care?" *Newsweek* (September 10, 1984b): 14–21.

Wedemeyer, Nancy, and Harold Grotevant. "Mapping the Family System: A Technique for Teaching Family Systems Theory Concepts." *Family Relations* 31 (April 1982): 185–193.

Weeks, M. O'Neal, and Bruce Gage. "A Comparison of the Marriage-Role Expectations of College Women Enrolled in a Functional Marriage Course in 1961, 1972, and 1978." *Sex Roles* 11(5/6) (1984): 377–388.

Weeks, Jeffrey. *Sexuality and Its Discontents.* London: Routledge & Kegan Paul, 1985.

Weg, Ruth. "Introduction: Beyond Intercourse and Orgasm." *Sexuality in the Later Years: Roles and Behavior.* New York: Academic Press, 1983b.

_____. "The Physiological Perspective." In Ruth Weg, ed. *Sexuality in the Later Years: Roles and Behavior.* New York: Academic Press, 1983c.

_____, ed. *Sexuality in the Later Years: Roles and Behavior.* New York: Academic Press, 1983a.

Wegscheider, Sharon. *Another Chance: Hope and Health for the Alcoholic Family,* 2d ed. Palo Alto, Calif.: Science and Behavior Books, 1989.

Weinberg, Daniel. "Measuring Poverty." *Family Economic Review* 2 (1985): 9–13.

Weinberg, Martin, and Colin Wilson. "Black Sexuality: A Test of Two Theories." *Journal of Sex Research* 25:2 (May 1988): 197–218.

Weiner, L., B. A. More, and P. Garrido. "FAS/FAE: Focusing Prevention on Women at Risk." *International Journal of the Addictions* 24:5 (May 1989): 385–395.

Weingarten, Helen. "Marital Status and Well-Being: A National Study Comparing First-Married, Currently Divorced and Remarried Adults." *Journal of Marriage and the Family* 47:3 (August 1985): 653–662.

_____. "Remarriage and Well-Being." *Journal of Family Issues* 1:4 (December 1980): 533–559.

Weishaus, Sylvia, and Dorothy Field. "A Half Century of Marriage: Continuity or Change?" *Journal of Marriage and the Family* 50:3 (August 1988): 763–774.

Weiss, David, and Joan Jurich. "Size of Community as a Predictor of Attitudes toward Extramarital Sexual Relations." *Journal of Marriage and the Family* 47:1 (February 1985): 173–178.

Weiss, David. "Open Marriage and Multilateral Relationships: The Emergence of Nonexclusive Models of the Marital Relationship." In Eleanor Macklin and Roger Rubin, eds., *Contemporary Families and Alternative Lifestyles.* Beverly Hills, Calif.: Sage Publications, 1983.

Weiss, Robert. "The Fund of Sociability." *Transactions* (July/August 1969): 36–43.

_____. *Going It Alone.* New York: Basic Books, 1979.

_____. *Marital Separation.* New York: Basic Books, 1975.

_____. "Men and the Family." *Family Processes* 24 (1985): 49–58.

_____. "The Study of Loneliness." In Peter Stein, ed. *Single Life.* New York: St. Martin's Press, 1981.

Weitzman, Lenore. *The Divorce Revolution: The Unexpected Social and Economic Consequences for Women and Children in America.* New York: The Free Press, 1985.

_____. *The Marriage Contract.* Englewood Cliffs, N.J.: Prentice-Hall, 1978.

_____. *The Marriage Contract: Spouses, Lovers, and the Law.* New York: Macmillan, 1981.

Weitzman, Lenore, and Ruth Dixon. "The Transformation of Legal Marriage through No-Fault Divorce." In Arlene Skolnick and Jerome Skolnick, eds., *Family in Transition.* Boston: Little, Brown, 1980.

Weizman, R., and J. Hart. "Sexual Behavior in Healthy Married Elderly Men." *Archives of Sexual Behavior* 16:1 (February 1987): 39–44.

Welch, Mary, and Dorothy Herman. "Why Miscarriage Is So Misunderstood." *Ms.* (February 1980): 14–22.

Wertz, Richard, and Dorothy Wertz. *Lying-In: A History of Childbirth in America.* New York: Harper & Row, 1978.

Whitbourne, Susan, and Joyce Ebmeyer. *Identity and Intimacy in Marriage: A Study of Couples.* New York: Springer-Verlag, 1990.

White, Charles. "Sexual Interest, Attitudes, Knowledge, and Sexual History in Relation to Sexual Behavior of the Institutionalized Aged." *Archives of Sexual Behavior* 11 (February 1982): 11–21.

White, Gregory. "Jealousy and Partner's Perceived Motives for Attraction to a Rival." *Social Psychology Quarterly* 44:1 (March 1981): 24–30.

_____. "Inducing Jealousy: A Power Perspective." Personality and Social Psychology Bulletin 6:2 (June 1980a): 222–227.

_____. "Physical Attractiveness and Courtship Progress." *Journal of Personality and Social Psychology* 39:4 (October 1980b): 660–668.

White, James. "Premarital Cohabitation and Marital Stability in Canada." *Journal of Marriage and the Family* 49 (August 1987): 641–647.

White, Joseph, and Thomas Parham. *The Psychology of Blacks: An African-American Perspective,* 2d ed. Englewood Cliffs, N.J.: Prentice-Hall, Inc., 1990.

White, Lynn. "Determinants of Divorce." In Alan Booth, ed., *Contemporary Families: Looking Forward, Looking Back.* Minneapolis: National Council on Family Relations, 1991.

White, Lynn, and Alan Booth. "Divorce over the Life Course: The Role of Marital Happiness." *Journal of Family Issues* 12:1 (March 1991): 5–22.

_____. "The Transition to Parenthood and Marital Quality." *Journal of Family Issues* 6 (1985): 435–449.

White, Lynn, David Brinkerhoff, and Alan Booth. "The Effect of Marital Disruption on Child's Attachment to Parents." *Journal of Family Issues* 6 (1985): 5–22.

White, Lynn, and Bruce Keith. "The Effect of Shift Work on the Quality and Stability of Marital Relations." *Journal of Marriage and the Family* 52:2 (May 1990): 453–462.

Whitehead, Barbara Dafoe. "How to Rebuild a 'Family-Friendly' Society." *Des Moines Sunday Register,* October 7, 1990: 3C.

Whiteside, Mary F. "Family Rituals as a Key to Kinship Connections in Remarried Families." Family Relations 38 (January 1989): 34–39.

Whitman, David. "The Coming of the 'Couch People.'" *U.S. News & World Report* (August 3, 1987): 19–21.

Wiehe, Vernon. *Sibling Abuse: The Hidden Physical, Emotional, and Sexual Trauma.* Lexington, Mass.: Lexington Books, 1990.

Wiehe, Vernon R. "Religious Influence on Parental Attitudes Toward the Use of Corporal Punishment." *Journal of Family Violence* 5:2 (June 1990): 173ff.

Wilcox, Allen, et al. "Incidents of Early Loss of Pregnancy." *New England Journal of Medicine* 319:4 (July 28, 1988): 189–194.

Wilcox, Clyde. "Political Action Committees and Abortion: A Longitudinal Analysis." *Women and Politics* 9:1 (1989): 1–19.

Wilkerson, Isabel. "Infant Mortality: Frightful Odds in Inner City." *The New York Times,* June 26, 1987: 1ff.

Wilkie, Colleen F., and Elinor D. Ames. "The Relationship of Infant Crying to Parental Stress in the Transition to Parenthood." *Journal of Marriage and the Family* 48:3 (August 1986): 545–550.

Wilkinson, Doris, Esther Ngan-Ling Chow, and Maxine Baca Zinn, eds. Special issue: "Transforming Social Knowledge: The Interlocking of

Race, Class, and Gender." *Gender & Society,* September 1992.

Williams, John, and Arthur Jacoby. "The Effects of Premarital Heterosexual and Homosexual Experience on Dating and Marriage Desirability." *Journal of Marriage and the Family* 51 (May 1989): 489–497.

Williams, Juanita. "Middle Age and Aging." In Juanita Williams, ed., *Women: Behavior in a Biosocial Context.* New York: Norton, 1977.

Wilson, Julius W., ed. *The Ghetto Underclass: Social Science Perspectives.* Newbury Park, Calif.: Sage Publications, 1989.

Wilson, Melvin N., Timothy Tolson, Ivora Hinton, and Michael Kiernan. "Flexibility and Sharing of Childcare Duties in Black Families." *Sex Roles* 22:7–8 (April 1990): 409–425.

Wilson, Pamela. "Black Culture and Sexuality." *Journal of Social Work and Human Sexuality* 4:3 (Spring 1986): 29–46.

Wilson, Sarah Jane. *Women, the Family, and the Economy,* 2d ed. Toronto: McGraw-Hill Ryerson, 1986.

Winch, Robert. *Mate Selection: A Study of Complementary Needs.* New York: Harper & Row, 1958.

Winn, Rhoda, and Niles Newton. "Sexuality and Aging: A Study of 106 Cultures." *Archives of Sexual Behavior* 11:4 (August 1982): 283–298.

Wise, P. H., and A. Meyer. "Poverty and Child Health." *Pediatric Clinics of North America* 35:6 (December 1988): 1169–1186.

Wisensale, Steven. "Approaches to Family Policy in State Government: A Report on Five States." *Family Relations* 39:2 (April 1990b): 136–140.

———. "The Family in the Think Tank." *Family Relations* 40:2 (April 1990a): 199–207.

Wisensale, Steven, and Michael Allison. "Family Leave Legislation: State and Federal Initiatives." *Family Relations* 38:2 (April 1989): 182–189.

Wishy, Bernard. *The Child and the Republic.* Philadelphia: Lippincott, 1968.

Woititz, Janet. *Adult Children of Alcoholics.* Deerfield, Fla: Health Communications, Inc., 1983.

Wolf, Rosalie S., and Karl A. Pillemer. "Intervention, Outcome, and Elder Abuse." In Gerald T. Hotaling et al., eds. *Coping with Family Violence.* Newbury Park, Calif.: Sage Publications, 1988.

Wolkind, Stephen, and Eva Zajicek, eds. *Pregnancy: A Psychological and Social Study.* New York: Grune and Stratton, 1981.

Wong, Morrison G. "The Chinese American Family." In Charles H. Mindel, Robert W. Habenstein, and Roosevelt Wright, Jr., eds., *Ethnic Families in America: Patterns and Variations,* 3d ed. New York: Elsevier, 1988.

Woodward, Kenneth. "New Rules for Making Love and Babies." *Newsweek* (March 23, 1987): 42–43.

"Work Interruptions and Earnings." *Family Economics Review* 2 (1985): 30–31.

Wyatt, Gail Elizabeth. "The Aftermath of Child Sexual Abuse of African American and White Women: The Victim's Experience." *Journal of Family Violence* 5:1 (March 1990): 61–81.

Wyatt, Gail, Stefanie Peters, and Donald Guthrie. "Kinsey Revisited II: Comparisons of the Sexual Socialization and Sexual Behavior of Black Women over 33 Years." *Archives of Sexual Behavior* 17:4 (August 1988): 289–332.

Wynn, Ruth, and Christine Fletcher. "Sex Role Development and Early Educational Experiences." In D. Bruce Carter, ed., *Current Conceptions of Sex Roles and Sex Typing.* New York: Praeger, 1987.

Ybarra, Lea. "When Wives Work: The Impact on the Chicano Family." *Journal of Marriage and the Family* (February 1982): 169–178.

Yogev, Sara, and Jane Brett. "Perceptions of the Division of Housework and Child Care and Marital Satisfaction." *Journal of Marriage and the Family* 47:3 (August 1985): 609–618.

Yulsman, Tom. "A Little Help for Creation." *The Good Health Magazine, The New York Times,* October 7, 1990: 22ff.

Yura, Michael. "Family Subsystem Functions and Disabled Children: Some Conceptual Issues." *Marriage and Family Review* 11:1–2 (1987): 135–151.

Zarit, Stephen, P. Todd, and J. Zarit. "Subjective Burden of Husbands and Wives as Caregivers: A Longitudinal Study." *Gerontologist* 26 (1986): 260–266.

Zaslow, Martha, et al. "Depressed Mood in New Fathers." Unpublished paper presented to the Society for Research in Child Development. Boston, April 1981.

Zavella, Patricia. *Women's Work and Chicano Families.* Ithaca, N.Y.: Cornell University Press, 1987.

Zilbergeld, Bernie. *Male Sexuality.* New York: Bantam Books, 1979.

Zimmerman, Shirley L. "State Level Public Policy Choices as Predictors of State Teen Birth Rates." *Family Relations* 37 (July 1988): 315–321.

———. "The Welfare State and Family Breakup: The Mythical Connection." *Family Relations* 40:2 (April 1991): 139–147.

———. *Understanding Family Policy: Theoretical Approaches.* Beverly Hills, Calif.: Sage, 1988.

Zimmerman, Shirley L., and Phyllis Owens. "Comparing the Family Policies of Three States: A Content Analysis." *Family Relations* 38:2 (April 1989): 190–195.

Zinn, Maxine Baca. "Family, Feminism, and Race." *Gender & Society* 4 (1990): 68–82.

Zvonkovic, Anisa, et al. "Making the Most of Job Loss: Individual and Marital Features of Job Loss." *Family Relations* 37:1 (January 1988): 56–61.

Index

ACKNOWLEDGMENTS

22 Excerpted from *NEWSWEEK* Special Edition: The American Family in the 21st Century. All rights reserved. Copyright © Winter/Spring 1990. Used with permission; **24** Marilyn Ihinger-Tallman, *The Journal of Family Issues,* 8(4), pp. 444–447. Copyright © 1991. Reprinted by permission of Sage Publications; **57** From "The Rise of David Levinsky," by Abraham Cahan, Copyright 1917 by Harper & Row, Publishers, Inc.; renewed 1945 by Abraham Cahan. Reprinted by permission of Harper & Row, Publishers, Inc.; **58** From "Beyond the American Dream: How Southeast Asian Refugees Define Success in Their Lives," by James M. Freeman and Usha Welaratna. Copyright © June 24, 1990. Used with permission; **83** "Selected Attitudes Toward Marriage and Family Life Among College Students," D. Martin and M. Martin, *Family Relations,* Volume 33:2, pp. 293-300. Copyrighted 1984 by the National Council on Family Relations, 1910 West County Road B, Suite 147, St. Paul, Minnesota 55113. Reprinted by permission; **87** Excerpted from "Black Families in White America," p. 201 by Andrew Billingsley. Copyright © 1968. Used with permission of Prentice Hall, a division of Simon & Schuster, Englewood Cliffs, N.J.; **117** Excerpted from the *Utne Reader,* by the *San Jose Mercury News,* April 28, 1991, C:1, 4, "The Decline of Men." Used with permission; **119** Excerpted from *Women and Self-Esteem,* by Linda Sanford and Mary Donovan. Copyright © 1984 by Linda Tschirhart Sanford. Used by permission of Doubleday, a division of Bantam Doubleday Dell Publishing Group, Inc.; **143** Excerpted from *Love the Way You Want It,* by Robert J. Sternberg. Copyright © 1991 by Robert J. Sternberg. Used with permission of Bantam Books, a division of Bantam Doubledday Dell Publishing Group, Inc; **145** Copyright 1984 by Leo F. Buscaglia, Inc.; **176** From *The Los Angeles Times,* Feb. 28, 1991, B1, 5. "Numbers Up, Status Down for the Family of One." Used with permission; **177** Copyright © 1986 by the New York Times Company. Reprinted by permission; **210** © Copyright National Broadcasting Company, Inc., 1976; **212** © Copyright Cyntiha Heimel, 1986; **241** Copyright © 1984, Sara Jennifer Malcolm, published in *Ms,* October, 1984; **243** From *Intimate Partners* by Maggie Scarf, Copyright 1987 by Maggie Scarf. Reprinted by permission of Random House, Inc.; **244** From "Understanding Our Sexuality," p. 413, ©West Publishing 1988, as adapted by the authors; **281** Copyright Katherine Bouton, 1987. Katherine Bouton is a freelance journalist; **319** Excerpted from "Lame Deer, Seeker of Visions," pp. 132-134. Used with permission; **320** "Succeeding in the Union" by Jean Marzollo. Copyright, 1985. Reprnted with permission from *The San Jose Mercury News;* **322** "The Warm Memories that Began at Grandma's Table," by Anne McCarroll, *The Christian Science Monitor,* December 25, 1985; **354** Reprinted by permission of *The San Jose Mercury News;* **355** Copyright © 1986 by The New York Times Company. Reprinted by permission; **356** ©Copyright Jennifer Meyer, *Matrix Newsmagazine;* **394** Reprinted from Patricia Zavella: *Women's Work & Chicano Families: Cannery Workers of the Santa Clara Valley.* Copyright ©1987 by Cornell University. Used by permission of the publisher, Cornell University Press; **396** Excerpted from "The Second Shift," by Arlie Hochschild and Ann Machung. Copyright © 1989 by Arlie Hochschild; pp. 37-41. Used with permission of Viking Penguin, a division of Penguin Books USA, Inc.; **434** Copyright © 1990 by the New York Times Company. Reprinted by permission; **436** Excerpted from "The Hospice Approach," as reprinted from the *Reader's Digest,* Vol. 119 (October 1981): 178-184. Used with permission of the author, Judy Sklar Rasminsky; **438** Reprinted by permission of the author and publisher, Sharon Wegscheider-Cruse, *Another Chance,* published by Science and Behavior Books, Inc. Palo Alto, CA USA; **465** Excerpted from "You Just Don't Understand," pp. 26-28. Used with permission; **466** Copyright © 1984 by Judith Viorst. Originally appeared in *Redbook;* **498** © Janet Bukovinsky/*New Jersey Monthly,* 1982; **500** Copyright 1984, Merideth Maran, excerpted from *West Magazine,* May 20, 1984; **502** From "When the Rapist Is Not a Stranger," copyright © 1989 by The New York Times Company. Reprinted by permission; **530** From "Children of Divorce: Report of a Ten-Year Follow-Up of Latency Age Children," by Judith Wallerstein, *American Journal of Orthopsychiatry,* Volume 57:2, pp. 204-207. Copyright ©1988 the American Orthopsychiatric Association, Inc. Reproduced by permission; **558** Reprinted with permission from *Psychology Today Magazine,* copyright © 1986 (PT Partners, L. P.); **580** Copyright © 1983 by Anita Shreve. All rights reserved. Reprinted by permission of the author.

PHOTO CREDITS

xxvi © Laurie DeVault; **6** *Sub-Urban Gothic,* 72" × 78", John Hannaford; **7** Courtesy Christine DeVault; **10** *The Wedding Lover's Quilt I,* 1986, 77 1/2" × 58"; Acrylic on canvas, tie-dyed, printed,